TEACHER'S EDITION

Houghton
Mifflin
Harcourt

collections

GRADE 12

Program Consultants:

Kylene Beers

Martha Hougen

Carol Jago

William L. McBride

Erik Palmer

Lydia Stack

HISTORY

Cover, Title Page Photo Credits: © Image Ideas/jupiterimages/Getty Images

Printed in the U.S.A.

ISBN 978-0-544-08716-3

2 3 4 5 6 7 8 9 10 0914 22 21 20 19 18 17 16 15 14 13

4500432006   A B C D E F G

Houghton
Mifflin
Harcourt

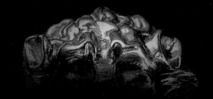

collections

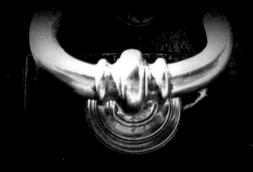

Teacher's Edition Table of Contents

Kylene Beers Nationally known lecturer and author on Reading and Literacy; 2011 recipient of the Conference on English Leadership Exemplary Leader Award; coauthor of *Notice and Note: Strategies for Close Reading*; former President of the National Council of Teachers of English. Dr. Beers is the nationally known author of *When Kids Can't Read: What Teachers Can Do* and coeditor of *Adolescent Literacy: Turning Promise into Practice*, as well as articles in the *Journal of Adolescent and Adult Literacy*. Former editor of *Voices from the Middle*, she is the 2001 recipient of NCTE's Richard W. Halley Award, given for outstanding contributions to middle-school literacy. She recently served as Senior Reading Researcher at the Comer School Development Program at Yale University as well as Senior Reading Advisor to Secondary Schools for the Reading and Writing Project at Teachers College.

Martha Hougen National consultant, presenter, researcher, and author. Areas of expertise include differentiating instruction for students with learning difficulties, including those with learning disabilities and dyslexia; and teacher and leader preparation improvement. Dr. Hougen has taught at the middle school through graduate levels. Recently her focus has been on working with teacher educators to enhance teacher and leader preparation to better meet the needs of all students. Currently she is working with the University of Florida at the Collaboration for Effective Educator Development, Accountability, and Reform Center (CEEDAR Center) to improve the achievement of students with disabilities by reforming teacher and leader licensure, evaluation, and preparation. She has led similar efforts in Texas with the Higher Education Collaborative and the College & Career Readiness Initiative Faculty Collaboratives. In addition to peer-reviewed articles, curricular documents, and presentations, Dr. Hougen has published two college textbooks: *The Fundamentals of Literacy Assessment and Instruction Pre-K–6* (2012) and *The Fundamentals of Literacy Assessment and Instruction 6–12* (2014).

Carol Jago Teacher of English with 32 years of experience at Santa Monica High School in California; author and nationally known lecturer; and Past President of the National Council of Teachers of English. Currently serves as Associate Director of the California Reading and Literature Project at UCLA. With expertise in standards assessment and secondary education, Ms. Jago is the author of numerous books on education, including *With Rigor for All* and *Papers, Papers, Papers*, and is active with the California Association of Teachers of English, editing its scholarly journal *California English* since 1996. Ms. Jago also served on the planning committee for the 2009 NAEP Framework and the 2011 NAEP Writing Framework.

William L. McBride Curriculum Specialist. Dr. McBride is a nationally known speaker, educator, and author who now trains teachers in instructional methodologies. He is coauthor of *What's Happening*, an innovative, high-interest text for middle-grade readers, and author of *If They Can Argue Well, They Can Write Well*. A former reading specialist, English teacher, and social studies teacher, he holds a master's degree in reading and a doctorate in curriculum and instruction from the University of North Carolina at Chapel Hill. Dr. McBride has contributed to the development of textbook series in language arts, social studies, science, and vocabulary. He is also known for his novel *Entertaining an Elephant*, which tells the story of a veteran teacher who becomes reinspired with both his profession and his life.

Erik Palmer Veteran teacher and education consultant based in Denver, Colorado. Author of *Well Spoken: Teaching Speaking to All Students* and *Digitally Speaking: How to Improve Student Presentations*. His areas of focus include improving oral communication, promoting technology in classroom presentations, and updating instruction through the use of digital tools. He holds a bachelor's degree from Oberlin College and a master's degree in curriculum and instruction from the University of Colorado.

Lydia Stack International ESL consultant. Director of the Screening and Assessment Center in the San Francisco Unified School District. Her areas of expertise are English language teaching strategies, ESL standards for students and teachers, and curriculum writing. Her teaching experience includes 25 years as an elementary and high school ESL teacher. She is past president of TESOL. Her awards include the James E. Alatis Award for Service to TESOL and the San Francisco STAR Teacher Award. Her publications include *On Our Way to English*; *Wordways*; *Games for Language Learning*; and *Visions: Language, Literature, Content*.

Additional thanks to the following Program Reviewers:

Rosemary Asquino
Sylvia B. Bennett
Yvonne Bradley
Leslie Brown
Haley Carroll
Caitlin Chalmers
Emily Colley-King
Stacy Collins
Denise DeBonis
Courtney Dickerson
Sarah Easley
Phyllis J. Everette
Peter J. Foy Sr.

Carol M. Gibby
Angie Gill
Mary K. Goff
Saira Haas
Lisa M. Janeway
Robert V. Kidd Jr.
Kim Lilley
John C. Lowe
Taryn Curtis MacGee
Meredith S. Maddox
Cynthia Martin
Kelli M. McDonough
Megan Pankiewicz

Linda Beck Pieplow
Molly Pieplow
Mary-Sarah Proctor
Jessica A. Stith
Peter Swartley
Pamela Thomas
Linda A. Tobias
Rachel Ukleja
Lauren Vint
Heather Lynn York
Leigh Ann Zerr

Blended classroom?   Flipped?   Traditional approach?

Collections offers maximum **flexibility** for planning instruction.

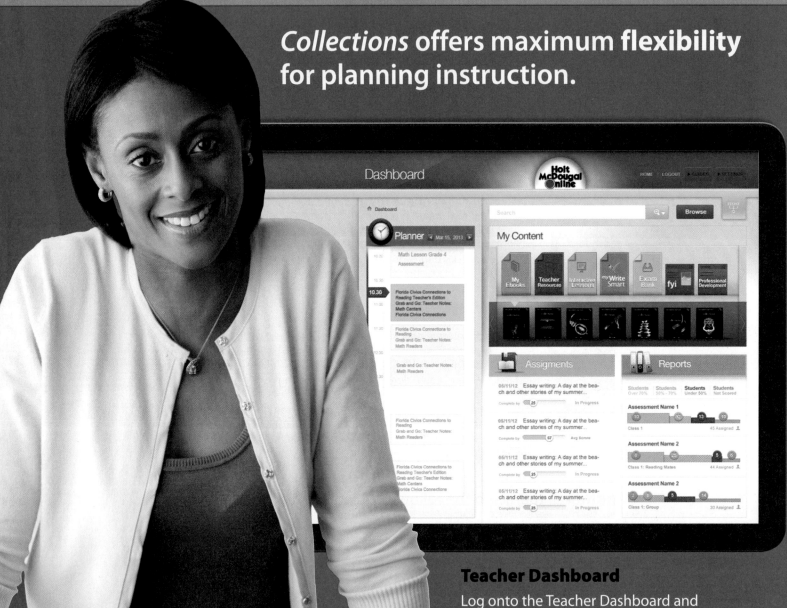

Teacher Dashboard

Log onto the Teacher Dashboard and *my*SmartPlanner. Use these **versatile** and fully **searchable** tools to **customize** lessons that engage students and achieve your instructional goals.

Text Complexity Rubrics

help you identify dimensions of complex text.

Text Complexity Rubric

A Quilt of a Country
Lexile: 1260L

Quantitative Measures	
	Levels of Meaning/Purpose
	more than one purpose; implied, easily identified from context
Qualitative Measures	**Structure**
	organization of main ideas and details complex but mostly explicit
	Language Conventionality and Clarity
	some unfamiliar, academic, or domain-specific words
	Knowledge Demands
	extensive knowledge of history required

COLLECTION 1 INSTRUCTIONAL OVERVIEW — PLAN

Collection 1 Lessons	Key Learning Objective	Performance Task	Vocabulary Strategy	Language and Style	Student Instructional Support	CLOSE READER Selection
ANCHOR TEXT Argument by Anna Quindlen "A Quilt of a Country," p. 000 — Lexile 1260	The student will be able to... analyze an author's claim and delineate and evaluate an argument	Writing Activity: Argument	Patterns of Word Changes	Noun Clauses	**Scaffolding for ELL Students:** Understand Cultural References **When Students Struggle:** Summarize (label not in TE)	Blog by Eboo Patel "Making the Future Better, Together" p. 000 — Lexile 0000
ANCHOR TEXT Short Story by Nadine Gordimer "Once Upon a Time," p. 000 — Lexile 1390	The student will be able to... analyze author's choices concerning the structure of a text and determine and make inferences about the theme of a work of fiction	Speaking Activity: Fairy Tale	Words from Latin	Prepositional Phrases	**Scaffolding for ELL Students:** Language: Dialect **When Students Struggle:** - Theme - Words from Latin **To Challenge Students:** Write from Author's Perspective	Short Story by Lisa Fugard "Night Calls" p. 000 — Lexile 0000
Essay by Kimberly M. Blaeser from "Rituals of Memory," p. 000 — Lexile 1390	The student will be able to... determine a central idea and analyze its development over the course of a text	Speaking Activity: Discussion	Denotations and Connotations		**Scaffolding for ELL Students:** Analyze Language **When Students Struggle:** Main Idea and Supporting Details	
Speech by Abraham Lincoln "The Gettysburg Address," p. 000 — Lexile 1170	The student will be able to... analyze an author's purpose and the use of rhetorical devices in a seminal U.S. document	Speaking Activity: Presentation	Multiple-Meaning Words	Parallel Structure	**Scaffolding for ELL Students:** Analyze Language **When Students Struggle:** Comprehension **To Challenge Students:** Tone and Structure	Speech by Bill Clinton "Oklahoma Bombing Memorial Address," p. 000 — Lexile 0000
Photo Essay "Views of the Wall," p. 000 — Poem by Alberto Ríos "The Vietnam Wall," p. 000	The student will be able to... analyze the representation of a subject in two separate mediums	Media Activity: Reflection			**Scaffolding for ELL Students:** Build Background **When Students Struggle:** Compare Text and Photos	

COLLECTION 1 DIGITAL OVERVIEW

mySmartPlanner | eBook | *myNotebook* | *my WriteSmart* | fyi

Collection 1 Lessons	Media	Teach and Practice		Assess	
Student Edition | eBook	Video Links	**Close Reading and Evidence Tracking**		**Performance Task**	Online Assessment
ANCHOR TEXT Argument by Anna Quindlen "A Quilt of a Country"	Audio "A Quilt of a Country"	**Close Read Screencasts** - Modeled Discussion 1 (lines 22-28) - Modeled Discussion 2 (lines 72-79) - Close Read application pdf (lines 00-000)	**Strategies for Annotation** - Delineate and Evaluate an Argument - Patterns of Word Change	Writing Activity: Argument	Selection Test
CLOSE READER Blog by Eboo Patel "Making the Future Better, Together"	Audio "Making the Future Better, Together"				
ANCHOR TEXT Short Story by Nadine Gordimer "Once Upon a Time"	Audio "Once Upon a Time"	**Close Read Screencasts** - Modeled Discussion 1 (lines 1-10) - Modeled Discussion 2 (lines 121-130) - Close Read application pdf (lines 000-000)	**Strategies for Annotation** - Analyze Author's Choices: Text Structure	Speaking Activity: Fairy Tale	Selection Test
CLOSE READER Short Story by Lisa Fugard "Night Calls"	Audio "Night Calls"				
Essay by Kimberly M. Blaeser from "Rituals of Memory"	Audio from "Rituals of Memory"		**Strategies for Annotation** - Determine Central Idea - Denotation and Connotation	Speaking Activity: Discussion	Selection Test
Speech by Abraham Lincoln "The Gettysburg Address"	Video HISTORY "The Gettysburg Address: A New Declaration of Independence" Audio "The Gettysburg Address"		**Strategies for Annotation** - Analyze Seminal U.S. Documents	Speaking Activity: Presentation	Selection Test
CLOSE READER Speech by Bill Clinton "Oklahoma Bombing Memorial Address"	Audio "Oklahoma Bombing Memorial Address"				
Photo Essay Views of the Wall — Poem by Alberto Ríos "The Vietnam Wall"	Video HISTORY "Remembering Fallen Friends" Audio "The Vietnam Wall"		**Strategies for Annotation** - Analyze Representations in Different Mediums	Media Activity: Reflection	Selection Test
Collection 1 Performance Tasks: A Preparing a Speech B Writing an Analytical Essay	fyi hmhfyi.com	**Interactive Lessons** A Writing Arguments A Giving a Presentation	B Writing Informative Texts B Using Textual Evidence	A Preparing a Speech B Writing an Analytical Essay	Collection Test

For Systematic Coverage of Writing and Speaking & Listening Standards	**Interactive Lessons** Writing as a Process Participating in Collaborative Discussions	**Lesson Assessments** Writing as a Process Participating in Collaborative Discussions

Print planning

pages show the integrated Table of Contents and all assets in the **Student Edition** and the **Close Reader.**

ENGAGEMENT

Digital natives? Media enthusiasts? Writers?

Collections engages learners with today's digital tools.

Voices and images

from **A&E®, bio.®,** and **HISTORY®** transport students to different times and places.

***my*Notebook**

stores students' annotations and notes for use in **Performance Tasks.**

Online Tools

allow students to annotate critical passages for discussion and writing, by using **highlighting, underlining,** and **notes.**

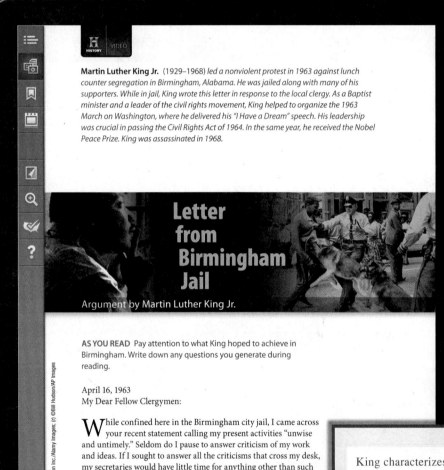

Martin Luther King Jr. (1929–1968) *led a nonviolent protest in 1963 against lunch counter segregation in Birmingham, Alabama. He was jailed along with many of his supporters. While in jail, King wrote this letter in response to the local clergy. As a Baptist minister and a leader of the civil rights movement, King helped to organize the 1963 March on Washington, where he delivered his "I Have a Dream" speech. His leadership was crucial in passing the Civil Rights Act of 1964. In the same year, he received the Nobel Peace Prize. King was assassinated in 1968.*

Letter from Birmingham Jail

Argument by Martin Luther King Jr.

AS YOU READ Pay attention to what King hoped to achieve in Birmingham. Write down any questions you generate during reading.

April 16, 1963
My Dear Fellow Clergymen:

While confined here in the Birmingham city jail, I came across your recent statement calling my present activities "unwise and untimely." Seldom do I pause to answer criticism of my work and ideas. If I sought to answer all the criticisms that cross my desk, my secretaries would have little time for anything other than such correspondence in the course of the day, and I would have no time for constructive work. But since I feel that you are men of genuine good will and that your criticisms are sincerely set forth, I want to try to answer your statement in what I hope will be patient and reasonable terms.

10   I think I should indicate why I am here in Birmingham, since you have been influenced by the view which argues against "outsiders coming in." I have the honor of serving as president of the Southern Christian Leadership Conference, an organization

Student Note ✕

King characterizes his critics as "men of good-will" to suggest that an understanding can be reached with them.

✓ Save to Notebook   Delete   Save

*my*Notebook

King characterizes his critics as "men of good-will" to suggest that an understanding can be reached with them.

Informational text

on **fyi** is linked to each collection topic and is **curated** and **updated** monthly.

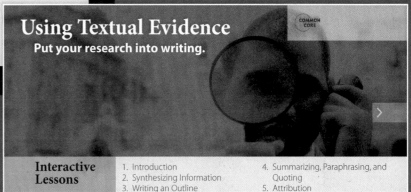

Available in Your eBook

Digital Collections

for **writing, speaking,** and **listening** provide opportunities for in-depth instruction and practice in key 21st-century skills.

Available in Your eBook

Media Lessons

prompt students to read **news reports, literary adaptations, ads,** and **websites** as complex texts.

PREPARATION

Collections prepares students for rigorous expectations.

Background *The Hmong (hmông) are an ethnic group from southern China, Laos, Vietnam, and Thailand. In the 1970s, war and conflict caused many of the Hmong people in Laos to flee to refugee camps in Thailand. Author* **Kao Kalia Yang** *(b. 1980) was born in one of these camps. She moved with her family, including her older sister Dawb, to Minnesota in 1987. Four other siblings were born in the United States, where all the Yang children received their educations.*

from
The Latehomecomer

Memoir by Kao Kalia Yang

SETTING A PURPOSE As you read, notice the challenges and the opportunities that life in a new country presents Kao Kalia Yang and her family. How does Yang react to her situation?

We had been in America for almost ten years. I was nearly fifteen, and Dawb had just gotten her driver's license. The children were growing up. We needed a new home—the apartment was too small. There was hardly room to breathe when the scent of jasmine rice and fish steamed with ginger mingled heavily with the scent of freshly baked pepperoni pizza—Dawb's favorite food. We had been looking for a new house for nearly six months.

It was in a poor neighborhood with houses that were
10   ready to collapse—wooden planks falli[ng]
away, sloping porches—and huge, old tr[ees]
realty sign in the front yard, a small pat[ch]
of the white house. It was one story, wit[h]
and a single wide window framed by bla[ck]
black door. There was a short driveway

(c) ©Houghton Mifflin Harcourt; (tr) ©Der Yang

Anchor Texts
drive each collection and have related selections in the **Close Reader.**

Close Reading Screencasts
provide **modeled conversations** about text at point of use in your **eBook.**

> I was feeling a strong push to reinvent myself. Without my realizing, by the time high school began, I had a feeling in the pit of my stomach that I had been on simmer for too long. I wanted to bubble over the top and douse the confusing fire that burned in my belly. Or else I wanted to turn the stove off. I wanted to sit cool on the burners of life, lid on, and steady. I was ready for change, but there was so little in my life that I could adjust. So life took a blurry seat.

These images give the impression the narrator is uncomfortable.

Background *A member of the Standing Rock Sioux,* **Susan Power** *was born in 1961 and grew up in Chicago. She spent her childhood listening to her mother tell stories about their American Indian heritage. These stories later served as inspiration for Power's writing. As a young girl, Power made frequent visits with her mother to local museums—trips that inspired her memoir "Museum Indians."*

Museum Indians

Memoir by Susan Power

Close Reader

allows students to apply standards and practice close reading strategies in a consumable **print** or **digital** format.

CLOSE READ
Notes

1. **READ ▷** As you read lines 1–16, begin to cite text evidence.

- Underline a metaphor in the first paragraph that describes the mother's braid.
- Underline a metaphor in the second paragraph that describes the mother's braid differently.
- In the margin, note the adjectives the narrator uses to describe the braid.

A snake coils in my mother's dresser drawer; it is thick and black, glossy as sequins. My mother cut her hair several years ago, before I was born, but she kept one heavy braid. It is the <u>three-foot snake</u> I lift from its nest and handle as if it were alive.

"Mom, why did you cut your hair?" I ask. I am a little girl lifting a <u>sleek black river</u> into the light that streams through the kitchen window. Mom turns to me.

"It gave me headaches. Now put that away and wash your hands for lunch."

10   "You won't cut *my* hair, will you?" I'm sure this is a whine.

"No, just a little trim now and then to even the ends."

I return the dark snake to its nest among my mother's slips, arranging it so that its thin tail hides beneath the wide mouth sheared

thick
black
glossy

SUCCESS

Independence?   Confidence?   Achievement?

Collections scaffolds assessment demands in the classroom.

Performance Tasks

create opportunities for students to respond **analytically** and **creatively** to complex texts.

*my*WriteSmart

provides a **collaborative** tool to revise and edit **Performance Tasks** with peers and teachers.

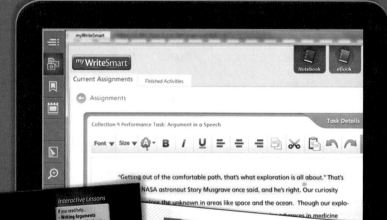

*my*WriteSmart

Notebook   eBook

Current Assignments   Finished Activities

Assignments

Collection 4 Performance Task: Argument in a Speech   Task Details

Font ▾ Size ▾ A ▾ B *I* U ☰ ☰ ☰ ⧉ ✂ 📋 ↶ ↷

"Getting out of the comfortable path, that's what exploration is all about." That's
NASA astronaut Story Musgrave once said, and he's right. Our curiosity
[...] the unknown in areas like space and the ocean. Though our explo-
[...] advances in medicine

Interactive Lessons
If you need help...
• Writing Arguments
• Using Textual Evidence

COLLECTION 1
PERFORMANCE TASK

Write an Argument

This collection focuses on how and why Europeans came to the Americas
and what happened as they settled in unfamiliar environments.
Relocating to the Americas dramatically changed settlers' lives. In turn,
the settlers changed the Americas through their interaction with its land
and its native populations. Look back at the anchor text, "Of Plymouth
Plantation," and at other texts you have read in this collection. Synthesize
your ideas about them by writing an argument. Your argument should
persuade readers to agree with your claim about how immigration
changed America, and how America changes those who come here.

COMMON CORE

W 1a–e Write arguments
to support claims in an
analysis of substantive
topics or texts, using valid
reasoning and relevant and
sufficient evidence.

W 9 Draw evidence from
literary or informational
texts to support analysis,
reflection, and research.

An effective argument

- identifies a central issue or question
- states a precise claim in response to the question
- develops the claim with valid reasons and relevant evidence, such as examples and quotations from the texts
- anticipates opposing claims and counters them with well-supported counterclaims
- establishes clear, logical connections among claims, counterclaims, reasons, and evidence
- includes an introduction, a logically structured body including transitions, and a conclusion
- maintains an appropriate tone based on its audience and context
- follows the conventions of written English

PLAN   *my*Notebook

Analyze the Text Think about the following questions as they
relate to the anchor text, "Of Plymouth Plantation":

- Why did European settlers come to the New World?
- When settlers came to explore and settle the Americas, how did it change their lives?
- What changes did these settlers bring to the Americas?

Choose one question to address in your argument. Then, select three
texts from this collection—including "Of Plymouth Plantation"—that
provide evidence for your position. These texts might present similar or
different views from each other.

ACADEMIC VOCABULARY
As you share your
ideas about the role
of immigration in
American society,
be sure to use
these words.

adapt
coherent
device
displace
dynamic

Collection Performance Task **103**

COLLECTION 6 TASK A
ARGUMENT

	Ideas and Evidence	Organization	Language
ADVANCED	• The introduction is memorable and persuasive; the claim clearly states a position on a substantive topic. • Valid reasons and relevant evidence from the texts convincingly support the writer's claim. • Counterclaims are anticipated and effectively addressed with counterarguments. • The concluding section effectively summarizes the claim.	• The reasons and textual evidence are organized consistently and logically throughout the argument. • Varied transitions logically connect reasons and textual evidence to the writer's claim.	• The writing reflects a formal style and an objective, or controlled, tone. • Sentence beginnings, lengths, and structures vary and have a rhythmic flow. • Spelling, capitalization, and punctuation are correct. • Grammar and usage are correct.
COMPETENT	• The introduction could do more to capture the reader's attention; the claim states a position on an issue. • Most reasons and evidence from the texts support the writer's claim, but they could be more convincing. • Counterclaims are anticipated, but the counterarguments need to be developed more. • The concluding section restates the claim.	• The organization of reasons and textual evidence is confusing in a few places. • A few more transitions are needed to connect reasons and textual evidence to the writer's claim.	• The style is informal in a few places, and the tone is defensive at times. • Sentence beginnings, lengths, and structures vary somewhat. • Several spelling and capitalization mistakes occur, and punctuation is inconsistent. • Some grammatical and usage errors are repeated in the argument.
	• The introduction is ordinary; the claim identifies an issue, but the writer's position is not clearly stated. • The reasons and evidence from the texts are not always logical or relevant. • Counterclaims are anticipated but not addressed logically. • The concluding section includes an incomplete summary of the claim.	• The organization of reasons and textual evidence is logical in some places, but it often doesn't follow a pattern. • Many more transitions are needed to connect reasons and textual evidence to the writer's position.	• The style becomes informal in many places, and the tone is often dismissive of other viewpoints. • Sentence structures barely vary, and some fragments or run-on sentences are present. • Spelling, capitalization, and punctuation are often incorrect but do not make reading the argument difficult. • Grammar and usage are incorrect in many places, but the writer's ideas are still clear.
	• The introduction is missing. • Significant supporting reasons and evidence from the texts are missing. • Counterclaims are neither anticipated nor addressed. • The concluding section is missing.	• An organizational strategy is not used; reasons and textual evidence are presented randomly. • Transitions are not used, making the argument difficult to understand.	• The style is inappropriate, and the tone is disrespectful. • Repetitive sentence structure, fragments, and run-on sentences make the writing monotonous and hard to follow. • Spelling and capitalization are often incorrect, and punctuation is missing. • Many grammatical and usage errors change the meaning of the writer's ideas.

604 Collection 6

Common Core Assessment

print and **online** resources provide instruction in three steps: **Analyze the Model, Practice the Task, and Perform the Task.**

STEP
2

PRACTICE THE TASK

Should a business have the right to ban teenagers?

You will read:
▶ A NEWSPAPER AD
  Munchy's Promise
▶ A BUSINESS ANALYSIS
  Munchy's Patrons in July–October
▶ A STUDENT BLOG
  Munchy's Bans Students!
▶ A NEWSPAPER EDITORIAL
  A Smart Idea Can Save a Business

You will write:
▶ AN ARGUMENTATIVE ESSAY
  Should a business have the right to ban teenagers?

Unit 1: Argumentative Essay **9**

Mr. Jones,
Here is the analysis of
July vs. October data.
Your Accountant,
Hector Ramirez, CPA

Munchy's Patrons in October
- minors
- adults

73%

Monthly Sales
- minors
- adults

September   October

...hart.
...wn in the graph?
...wo forms of data.

Unit 1: Argumentative Essay **11**

...ty studies on sleep deprivation have ...only thing that might improve. An ...ositively affect a student's mood ...says that when he was in school, ...nd were better rested. With ...hers and students would get along

...agers should take affirmative ...therwise adjust to the reality of ...em to research done in the 1990s, ...nd wake patterns in adolescents ...xperts talked, and California ...stened. She introduced House ..., the "ZZZ's to A's Act," to ...earlier than 8:30 A.M.

...ng again. It's 7:00 A.M. You say to ...nd I've got plenty of time to get ...e a huge difference in your mood

...ool should start later? If so, which data was the most

You use an effective transition to create cohesion and signal the introduction of another reason. Your language is formal and non-combative. You remain focused on your purpose.

You anticipated and addressed an opposing claim that is likely to occur to your audience. Your answer to the opposing claim is well-supported with valid evidence.

Smooth flow from beginning to end. Clear conclusion restates your claim. Your evidence is convincing. Excellent use of conventions of English. Good job!

Unit 1: Argumentative Essay **7**

Graphics

enhance instruction making **Common Core Assessment** unique and effective.

Common Core Enrichment App

provides instant feedback for **close reading practice** with appeal for today's students.

COLLECTION 1
Chasing Success

Collection Overviews

Each collection suggests different starting points, as well as overviews of digital resources and instructional topics for selections.

COLLECTION PERFORMANCE TASKS

Annotated Student Edition Table of Contents

Topical Organization

Each collection reflects an engaging topic that connects selections for discussion and analysis, so students can explore several dimensions of the topic.

COMMON CORE

COLLECTION **1**

Chasing Success

Close Reader

eBook *Explore It!*

 Video Links  eBook *Read On!* Novel list and additional selections Visit hmhfyi.com for current articles and informational texts.

Image Credits: ©Jonathan Griffith/Aurora Photos/Corbis

KEY LEARNING OBJECTIVES
Cite text evidence to support inferences.
Determine central ideas.
Analyze conflict in drama.
Analyze symbols in drama.
Analyze word choice.
Analyze structure of an argument.
Analyze drama interpretations.
Integrate and evaluate information.

Common Core State Standards

Each collection addresses a range of **Common Core State Standards,** ensuring coverage of the Reading Literature and Reading Informational Texts standards.

Close Reader

The **Close Reader** provides selections related to the collection topic for additional practice and application of close reading skills and annotation strategies.

COLLECTION 2
Gender Roles

Student Edition + Close Reader

In each collection, the collection topic is explored in both the **Student Edition** and **Close Reader** selections. This page shows how the two components are integrated.

COLLECTION PERFORMANCE TASKS

Annotated Student Edition Table of Contents

Anchor Texts

Complex and challenging, the anchor texts provide a cornerstone for exploring the collection topic, while also being integral to the Collection Performance Task. Close Reader selections relate to the Student Edition anchor texts.

Variety of Genres

Both the Student Edition and the Close Reader include a variety of genres of literary texts, informational texts, and media. The genre of each selection is clearly labeled.

COMMON CORE

COLLECTION 2
Gender Roles

Close Reader

KEY LEARNING OBJECTIVES

Support inferences and draw conclusions.
Determine central ideas.
Summarize text.
Analyze ideas and events.
Analyze narrator of a poem.
Analyze setting of a story.

Determine figurative meanings.
Analyze frame story.
Analyze counterarguments.
Analyze rhetorical devices.
Determine author's point of view.
Integrate and evaluate information.

Image Credits: ©Hill Street Studios/Blend Images/Corbis

eBook *Explore It!*

▶ Video Links HISTORY A+E

eBook *Read On!*
Novel list and additional selections

fyi Visit hmhfyi.com
for current articles and
informational texts.

Collection Performance Tasks

Collection Performance Tasks present a cumulative task for students. To develop writing or speaking products, students draw on their reading and analysis of the collection's selections, as well as additional research.

COLLECTION 3
Voices of Protest

Themes Across Time

Classic and contemporary selections illustrate how themes and topics transcend time and remain relevant to today's readers.

COLLECTION PERFORMANCE TASKS

Annotated Student Edition Table of Contents

COMMON CORE

COLLECTION **3**

Voices of Protest

Close Reader

Image Credits: ©Steve Schapiro/Corbis

KEY LEARNING OBJECTIVES
Cite text evidence to support inferences.
Analyze cause and effect.
Analyze word choice and tone.
Determine connotative meanings.
Analyze satire.

Integrate and evaluate information.
Delineate and evaluate an argument.
Analyze foundational documents.
Comprehend historical context.

eBook *Explore It!*

▶ Video Links **HISTORY** **A&E**

eBook *Read On!*
Novel list and additional selections

 Visit hmhfyi.com for current articles and informational texts.

eBook

The eBook, both Student Edition and Teacher's Edition, is the entryway to a full complement of digital resources.

COLLECTION **4**

Seeking Justice, Seeking Peace

Cultural Diversity

To enrich students' perspectives, both the Student Edition and the Close Reader include selections by writers from diverse cultures.

Image Credits: ©Rob Howard/Corbis

Annotated Student Edition Table of Contents

Compare Text and Media

Students compare and contrast selections and media, exploring elements such as structure and themes. By deepening understanding of texts and media, these comparisons enrich analysis and discussion.

COMMON CORE

COLLECTION **4**

Seeking Justice, Seeking Peace

Close Reader

DRAMA
from The Tragedy of Hamlet, Act I. Scenes 1–2   William Shakespeare

SPEECH
Nobel Peace Prize Acceptance Speech   Wangari Maathai

Image Credits: ©Rob Howard/Corbis

KEY LEARNING OBJECTIVES	Support inferences and draw conclusions. Determine central ideas. Analyze ideas and events. Analyze conflict in drama. Determine figurative meanings.	Analyze language in soliloquies. Analyze story structure. Analyze structure of an argument. Analyze irony. Analyze drama interpretations.

eBook *Explore It!*

▶ Video Links   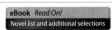 eBook *Read On!* Novel list and additional selections   **Visit hmhfyi.com** for current articles and informational texts.

Informational Texts

From feature articles to speeches to literary criticism, students read and analyze a variety of informational texts.

Digital Resources

A range of digital resources in the eBook complements and enriches students' reading, including video links to additional literary and informational texts.

COLLECTION 5
Taking Risks

Contemporary Selections

Selections by contemporary writers promote new insights into classic selections, enriching students' understanding of both classic and recent texts.

Annotated Student Edition Table of Contents

Complex Texts

With rich themes, distinctive language, stylistic elements, and high knowledge demands, complex texts challenge students to grow as readers and thinkers.

COMMON CORE

COLLECTION 5
Taking Risks

Close Reader

KEY LEARNING OBJECTIVES
Support inferences and draw conclusions.
Determine themes.
Summarize text.
Analyze setting of a story.

Analyze characteristics of an epic.
Analyze Old English poetry.
Determine author's purpose.
Delineate and evaluate an argument.

Image Credits: ©Christoph Jorda/Corbis

eBook *Explore It!*

▶ Video Links   **eBook** *Read On!*  Novel list and additional selections   **Visit hmhfyi.com** for current articles and informational texts.

Supplemental Video

▶ This icon indicates supplementary video that accompanies selections. Adding the images and voices that make selections come alive, these video assets are available at point of use in the eBook.

INTEGRATED PROGRAM CONTENTS

Acclaimed Writers

Selections by acclaimed writers expose students to the very best in literary and nonfiction texts.

Annotated Student Edition Table of Contents

Media Analysis

Lessons based on media provide opportunities for students to apply analysis and techniques of close reading to other kinds of texts.

Complex Texts

To enrich the analysis and discussion of each text, students compare and contrast selections, exploring how the writers' choices affect meaning.

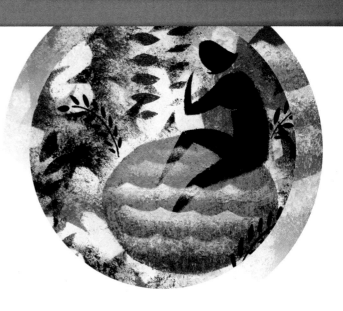

COMMON CORE

COLLECTION 6

Finding Ourselves in Nature

Close Reader

KEY LEARNING OBJECTIVES
Cite text evidence to support inferences.
Determine theme.
Determine figurative meanings.
Analyze structure.
Analyze frame story.

Analyze style.
Integrate and evaluate information.
Demonstrate knowledge of foundational works.
Comprehend cultural context in nonfiction.

Image Credits: ©Images.com/Corbis

eBook *Explore It!*

 Video Links **HISTORY** **A&E**

eBook *Read On!*
Novel list and additional selections

 Visit hmhfyi.com for current articles and informational texts.

fyi

The fyi website at hmhfyi.com provides additional contemporary informational texts to enhance each collection. Updated regularly, this site expands background knowledge and enhances discussion and research.

Student Resources

Information, Please

When students have questions, they can turn to Student Resources for answers. This section includes information about performance tasks, the nature of argument, vocabulary and spelling, and grammar, usage, and mechanics.

Word Knowledge

The Glossaries provide definitions for selection, academic, and domain-specific vocabulary, conveniently compiled in a single location.

Connecting to Your World

Every time you read something, view something, write to someone, or react to what you've read or seen, you're participating in a world of ideas. You do this every day, inside the classroom and out. These skills will serve you not only at home and at school, but eventually (if you can think that far ahead!), in your career.

The digital tools in this program will tap into the skills you already use and help you sharpen those skills for the future.

Start your exploration at my.hrw.com

Start with the Dashboard

Get one-stop access to the complete digital program for *Collections*, as well as management and assessment tools.

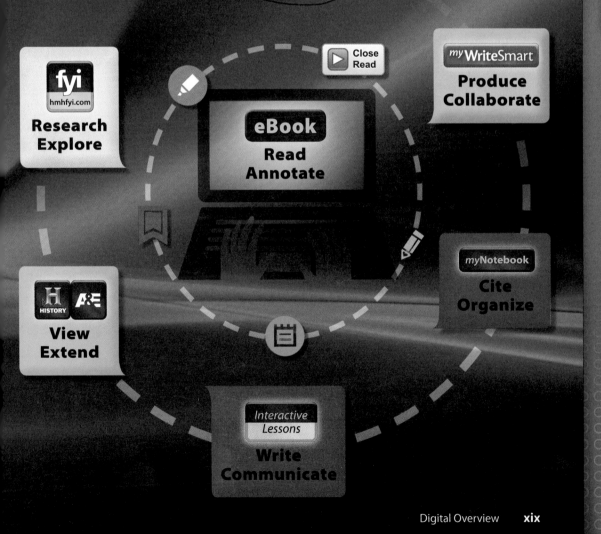

fyi hmhfyi.com
Research Explore

Close Read

my **WriteSmart**
Produce Collaborate

eBook
Read Annotate

*my*Notebook
Cite Organize

HISTORY **A&E**
View Extend

Interactive Lessons
Write Communicate

Writing and Speaking & Listening

Communication in today's world requires quite a variety of skills. To express yourself and win people over, you have to be able to write for print, for online media, and for spoken presentations. To collaborate, you have to work with people who might be sitting right next to you or at the other end of an Internet connection.

Comprehensive Standards Coverage

Twelve digital collections provide thorough coverage of all Writing and Speaking and Listening Common Core State Standards.

Available Only in Your eBook

Interactive Lessons

The interactive lessons in these collections will help you master the skills needed to become an expert communicator.

What Does a Strong Argument Look Like?

Read this argument and answer the questions about how the writer states and supports his position.

Tip

Pitching Perfect Pitch
by José Alvarez

Did you know that when you are listening to your favorite vocalist, you might be hearing a computer-generated pitch? Many record companies use pitch-correction software to ensure that their performers are pitch-perfect. While perfectionism is an admirable goal, there is a fine line between using technology to enhance music and using it to make performers into something they're not. Whether recording in the studio or playing a live performance, musicians should not use pitch-correction software. ●

Music production has become a digital experience. Producers use software to cut and paste pieces of music together, just like you cut and paste words together in your word-processing software. ○ When editing these different things together digitally, slight imperfections can occur where the pieces are joined. Enter the correction software. What began as a method to streamline the digital editing process has turned into an almost industry-wide standard of altering a musician"s work. "Think of it like plastic surgery," says a Grammy-winning recording engineer.

What is the writer's position, or **claim,** on the use of pitch-correction software?

☐ Musicians should learn to live with their imperfections.

☑ Musicians should never use the software.

☐ Musicians should use the software to enhance live performances only.

Writing Arguments
Master the art of proving your point.

COMMON CORE W 1, W 10

Interactive Lessons

1. Introduction
2. What Is a Claim?
3. Support: Reasons and Evidence
4. Building Effective Support
5. Creating a Coherent Argument
6. Persuasive Techniques
7. Formal Style
8. Concluding Your Argument

Student-Directed Lessons

Though primarily intended for individual student use, these interactive lessons also offer opportunities for whole-class and small-group instruction and practice.

Writing Informative Texts
Shed light on complex ideas and topics.

COMMON CORE W 2, W 10

Interactive Lessons

1. Introduction
2. Developing a Topic
3. Organizing Ideas
4. Introductions and Conclusions
5. Elaboration
6. Using Graphics and Multimedia
7. Precise Language and Vocabulary
8. Formal Style

Writing Narratives
A good storyteller can always capture an audience.

COMMON CORE W 3, W 10

Interactive Lessons

1. Introduction
2. Narrative Context
3. Point of View and Characters
4. Narrative Structure
5. Narrative Techniques
6. The Language of Narrative

DIGITAL
COLLECTIONS

Writing as a Process

Get from the first twinkle of an idea to a sparkling final draft.

COMMON CORE — W 4, W 5, W 10

Interactive Lessons	1. Introduction 2. Task, Purpose, and Audience 3. Planning and Drafting	4. Revising and Editing 5. Trying a New Approach

Teacher Support

Each collection in your teacher eBook includes

- support for English language learners and less-proficient writers
- instructional and management tips for every screen
- a rubric
- additional writing applications

Producing and Publishing with Technology

Learn how to write for an online audience.

COMMON CORE — W 6

Interactive Lessons	1. Introduction 2. Writing for the Internet	3. Interacting with Your Online Audience 4. Using Technology to Collaborate

Conducting Research

There's a world of information out there. How do you find it?

COMMON CORE — W 6, W 7, W 8

Interactive Lessons	1. Introduction 2. Starting Your Research 3. Types of Sources 4. Using the Library for Research	5. Conducting Field Research 6. Using the Internet for Research 7. Taking Notes 8. Refocusing Your Inquiry

Evaluating Sources
Approach all sources with a critical eye.

COMMON CORE W 8

Interactive Lessons

1. Introduction
2. Evaluating Sources for Usefulness
3. Evaluating Sources for Reliability

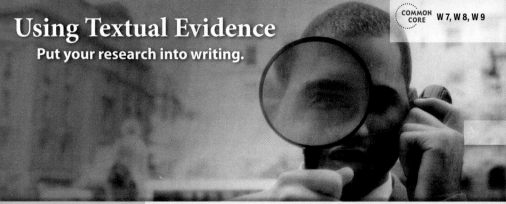

Using Textual Evidence
Put your research into writing.

COMMON CORE W 7, W 8, W 9

Interactive Lessons

1. Introduction
2. Synthesizing Information
3. Writing an Outline
4. Summarizing, Paraphrasing, and Quoting
5. Attribution

Participating in Collaborative Discussions

COMMON CORE SL 1

There's power in putting your heads together.

Interactive Lessons

1. Introduction
2. Preparing for Discussion
3. Establishing and Following Procedure
4. Speaking Constructively
5. Listening and Responding
6. Wrapping Up Your Discussion

Analyzing and Evaluating Presentations

COMMON CORE SL 2, SL 3, SL 6

Is there substance behind the style?

Interactive Lessons	**1.** Introduction	**4.** Tracing a Speaker's Argument
	2. Analyzing a Presentation	**5.** Rhetoric and Delivery
	3. Evaluating a Speaker's Reliability	**6.** Synthesizing Media Sources

Assessments in *my*WriteSmart

Test students' mastery of the standards covered in each digital collection by assigning the accompanying assessment in *my*WriteSmart.

Giving a Presentation

COMMON CORE SL 4, SL 6

Learn how to talk to a roomful of people.

Interactive Lessons	**1.** Introduction	**3.** The Content of Your Presentation
	2. Knowing Your Audience	**4.** Style in Presentation
		5. Delivering Your Presentation

Using Media in a Presentation

COMMON CORE SL 5

If a picture is worth a thousand words, just think what you can do with a video.

Interactive Lessons	**1.** Introduction	**3.** Using Presentation Software
	2. Types of Media: Audio, Video, and Images	**4.** Practicing Your Presentation

DIGITAL SPOTLIGHT

| eBook | *my*Notebook | **fyi** hmhfyi.com | *my* **Write**Smart |

Supporting
Close Reading,
Research, and Writing

Understanding complex texts is hard work, even for experienced readers. It often takes multiple close readings to understand and write about an author's choices and meanings. The dynamic digital tools in this program will give you opportunities to learn and practice this critical skill of close reading—and help you integrate the text evidence you find into your writing.

Integrated Digital Suite

The digital resources and tools in *Collections* are designed to support students in grappling with complex text and formulating interpretations from text evidence.

Learn How to Do a Close Read

An effective close read is all about the details; you have to examine the language and ideas a writer includes. See how it's done by accessing the **Close Read Screencasts** in your eBook. Hear modeled conversations about anchor texts.

Close Read Screencasts

For each anchor text, students can access modeled conversations in which readers analyze and annotate key passages.

of the birds, how they soared and glided overhead. He pointed out the slow, graceful sweep of their wings as they beat the air steadily, without fluttering. Soon Icarus was sure that he, too, could fly and, raising his arms up and down, skirted over the white sand and even out over the waves, letting his feet touch the snowy foam as the water thundered and broke over the sharp rocks. Daedalus watched him proudly but

Soon Icarus was sure that he, too, could fly and, raising his arms up and down, skirted over the white sand and even out over the waves, letting his feet touch the snowy foam as the water thundered and broke over the sharp rocks.

There might be a sense of danger here.

Daedalus watched him proudly but with misgivings. He called Icarus to his side and, putting his arm round the boy's shoulders, said, 'Icarus, my son, we are about to make our flight. No human being has ever traveled through the air before, and I want you to listen carefully to my instructions.

Annotate the Texts

Practice close reading by utilizing the powerful tools in your eBook. Mark up key ideas and ob[...] highlighters and sticky notes.

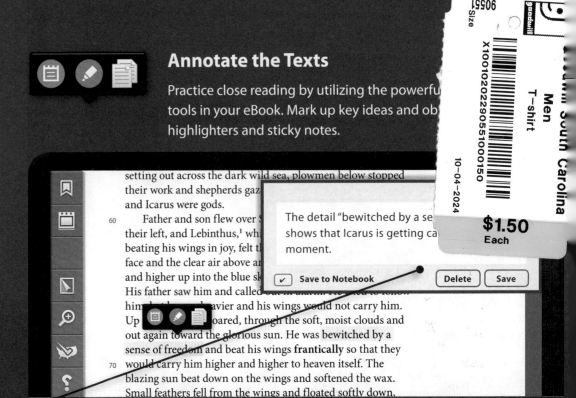

Digital Tools for Close Reading

Annotation tools allow students to note central ideas and details about an author's craft. Students can save their annotations to *my*Notebook, tagging them to particular performance tasks.

Collect Text Evidence

Save your annotations to your notebook. Gathering and organizing this text evidence will help you complete performance tasks and other writing assignments.

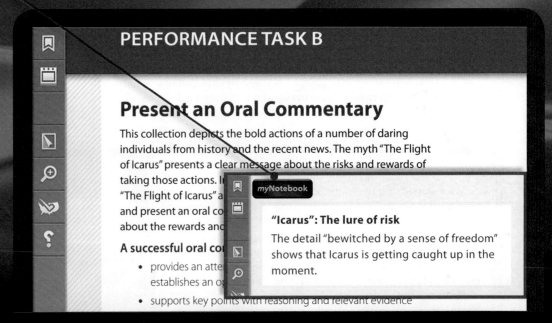

Find More Text Evidence on the Web

Tap into the *FYI* website for links to high-interest informational texts about collection topics. Capture text evidence from any Web source by including it in your notebook.

High-Interest Informational Text

Updated monthly, *FYI* features links to reputable sources of informational text.

Integrate Text Evidence into Your Writing

Use the evidence you've gathered to formulate interpretations, draw conclusions, and offer insights. Integrate the best of your text evidence into your writing.

Tools for Writing

Assign and manage performance tasks in *my*WriteSmart. Students can use the annotations they've gathered and tools for writing and collaboration to complete each task.

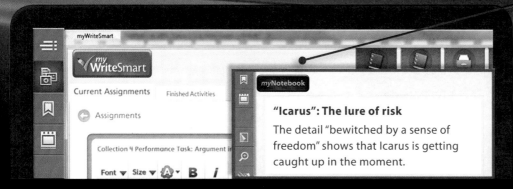

Correlation of *Collections*, Grade 12, to the English Language Arts Common Core State Standards

The grades 6–12 standards on the following pages define what students should understand and be able to do by the end of each grade. They correspond to the College and Career Readiness (CCR) anchor standards below by number. The CCR and grade-specific standards are necessary complements—the former providing broad standards, the latter providing additional specificity—that together define the skills and understandings that all students must demonstrate.

College and Career Readiness Anchor Standards for Reading

Common Core State Standards
KEY IDEAS AND DETAILS
1. Read closely to determine what the text says explicitly and to make logical inferences from it; cite specific textual evidence when writing or speaking to support conclusions drawn from the text.
2. Determine central ideas or themes of a text and analyze their development; summarize the key supporting details and ideas.
3. Analyze how and why individuals, events, and ideas develop and interact over the course of a text.
CRAFT AND STRUCTURE
4. Interpret words and phrases as they are used in a text, including determining technical, connotative, and figurative meanings, and analyze how specific word choices shape meaning or tone.
5. Analyze the structure of texts, including how specific sentences, paragraphs, and larger portions of the text (e.g., a section, chapter, scene, or stanza) relate to each other and the whole.
6. Assess how point of view or purpose shapes the content and style of a text.
INTEGRATION OF KNOWLEDGE AND IDEAS
7. Integrate and evaluate content presented in diverse formats and media, including visually and quantitatively, as well as in words.
8. Delineate and evaluate the argument and specific claims in a text, including the validity of the reasoning as well as the relevance and sufficiency of the evidence.
9. Analyze how two or more texts address similar themes or topics in order to build knowledge or to compare the approaches the authors take.
RANGE OF READING AND LEVEL OF COMPLEXITY
10. Read and comprehend complex literary and informational texts independently and proficiently.

Reading Standards for Literature, Grades 11–12 Students

Common Core State Standard	Student/Teacher's Edition

KEY IDEAS AND DETAILS

1. Cite strong and thorough textual evidence to support analysis of what the text says explicitly as well as inferences drawn from the text, including determining where the text leaves matters uncertain.

Student Edition
43, 44, 61, 90, 105, 106, 111, 220, 262, 283, 310, 332, 355, 377, 397, 426, 450, 515

Teacher's Edition
32, 34, 35, 37, 39, 43, 44, 61, 66a, 86, 87, 90, 93, 94, 95, 96, 97, 98, 101, 102, 104, 105, 106, 108a, 111, 220, 243, 245, 247, 253, 256, 262, 269, 283, 290, 291, 293, 294, 295, 307, 310, 332, 355, 371, 372, 377, 378a, 397, 410, 411, 412, 413, 414, 416, 417, 418, 420, 422, 423, 424, 426, 434, 440, 441, 446, 450, 515, 516a

2. Determine two or more themes or central ideas of a text and analyze their development over the course of the text, including how they interact and build on one another to produce a complex account; provide an objective summary of the text.

Student Edition
90, 355, 377, 426, 449, 450, 490, 514, 515

Teacher's Edition
59, 62a, 82, 83, 84, 85, 88, 90, 92a, 97, 106, 111, 257, 264, 268, 275, 289, 299, 304, 314, 317, 320, 333, 334, 335, 337, 338, 353, 355, 377, 398a, 418, 420, 423, 424, 426, 434, 435, 437, 438, 442, 443, 447, 448, 449, 450, 487, 490, 502, 503, 504, 505, 507, 509, 511, 512, 514, 515, 516b

3. Analyze the impact of the author's choices regarding how to develop and relate elements of a story or drama (e.g., where a story is set, how the action is ordered, how the characters are introduced and developed).

Student Edition
44, 60, 61, 85, 90, 105, 106, 262, 283, 332, 354, 355, 377, 425, 426, 449, 450, 515

Teacher's Edition
36, 39, 40, 41, 44, 46a, 48, 49, 50, 51, 52, 53, 54, 55, 56, 57, 58, 59, 60, 61, 62a, 79, 80, 81, 84, 85, 87, 88, 90, 92a, 93, 94, 96, 98, 99, 100, 101, 102, 103, 105, 106, 220a, 237, 238, 239, 240, 242, 243, 244, 245, 246, 248, 249, 251, 253, 254, 255, 256, 257, 258, 259, 260, 261, 262, 263, 265, 266, 267, 270, 271, 272, 273, 274, 276, 277, 278, 280, 283, 284, 285, 286, 287, 288, 289, 292, 296, 297, 298, 300, 303, 304, 305, 306, 308, 309, 311, 313, 314, 315, 316, 319, 320, 321, 322, 323, 324, 325, 326, 328, 329, 330, 332, 333, 336, 339, 340, 341, 342, 343, 346, 347, 348, 349, 350, 351, 352, 353, 354, 355, 356a, 360a, 372, 377, 410, 411, 412, 413, 414, 415, 417, 419, 420, 421, 422, 423, 424, 425, 426, 428a, 433, 435, 436, 437, 438, 439, 440, 441, 442, 443, 444, 445, 446, 449, 450, 452a, 506, 515

Common Core State Standard	Student/Teacher's Edition

CRAFT AND STRUCTURE

4. Determine the meaning of words and phrases as they are used in the text, including figurative and connotative meanings; analyze the impact of specific word choices on meaning and tone, including words with multiple meanings or language that is particularly fresh, engaging, or beautiful. (Include Shakespeare as well as other authors.)

Student Edition
43, 44, 111, 220, 262, 283, 310, 354, 355, 397, 425, 426, 450, 515

Teacher's Edition
32, 33, 35, 36, 38, 40, 41, 42, 43, 44, 46a, 109, 110, 111, 112a, 218, 219, 220, 220a, 240, 250, 252, 255, 262, 270, 279, 283, 286, 292, 294, 301, 302, 303, 305, 310, 315, 316, 318, 327, 328, 331, 334, 335, 347, 351, 354, 355, 373, 395, 396, 397, 398a, 398b, 410, 411, 416, 418, 419, 425, 426, 436, 439, 441, 445, 448, 450, 452a, 490a, 501, 503, 508, 515, 516a

5. Analyze how an author's choices concerning how to structure specific parts of a text (e.g., the choice of where to begin or end a story, the choice to provide a comedic or tragic resolution) contribute to its overall structure and meaning as well as its aesthetic impact.

Student Edition
85, 90, 332, 355, 376, 377, 489, 490, 514, 515

Teacher's Edition
78, 79, 82, 85, 90, 112a, 241, 245, 281, 332, 355, 370, 371, 372, 375, 376, 377, 378a, 444, 486, 487, 488, 489, 490, 490a, 502, 509, 510, 513, 514, 515, 516b

6. Analyze a case in which grasping point of view requires distinguishing what is directly stated in a text from what is really meant (e.g., satire, sarcasm, irony, or understatement).

Student Edition
209, 210, 310, 355, 376, 377, 397

Teacher's Edition
55, 200, 201, 202, 205, 206, 207, 208, 209, 210, 212a, 310, 337, 343, 344, 345, 346, 349, 355, 369, 371, 372, 373, 374, 376, 377, 397

INTEGRATION OF KNOWLEDGE AND IDEAS

7. Analyze multiple interpretations of a story, drama, or poem (e.g., recorded or live production of a play or recorded novel or poetry), evaluating how each version interprets the source text. (Include at least one play by Shakespeare and one play by an American dramatist.)

Student Edition
64, 66, 359, 360

Teacher's Edition
63, 64, 65, 66, 66b, 357, 358, 359, 360, 360a

8. (Not applicable to literature)

9. Demonstrate knowledge of eighteenth-, nineteenth- and early-twentieth-century foundational works of American literature, including how two or more texts from the same period treat similar themes or topics.

Student Edition
489, 490

Teacher's Edition
486, 487, 488, 489, 490

Common Core State Standard	Student/Teacher's Edition

RANGE OF READING AND LEVEL OF TEXT COMPLEXITY

10. By the end of grade 12, read and comprehend literature, including stories, dramas, and poems, at the high end of the grades 11–CCR text complexity band independently and proficiently.

Student Edition
43, 47–61, 77–90, 93–106, 235–355, 485–490, 514

Teacher's Edition
32, 34, 35, 37, 39, 43, 47–61, 77–90, 93–106, 235–355, 485–490, 514

Reading Standards for Informational Text, Grades 11–12 Students

Common Core State Standard	Student Edition and Teacher's Edition

KEY IDEAS AND DETAILS

1. Cite strong and thorough textual evidence to support analysis of what the text says explicitly as well as inferences drawn from the text, including determining where the text leaves matters uncertain.

Student Edition
16, 20, 28, 120, 127, 129, 130, 138, 166, 186, 195, 196, 367, 391, 392, 468, 469, 482, 498, 499

Teacher's Edition
6, 11, 13, 16, 19, 20, 20a, 25, 28, 120, 124, 127, 129, 130, 138, 140a, 153, 156, 157, 160, 166, 186, 186a, 190, 191, 193, 194, 195, 196, 367, 379, 380, 381, 382, 385, 386, 387, 388, 389, 390, 391, 392, 394a, 430, 454, 455, 456, 457, 458, 459, 460, 461, 462, 464, 465, 466, 467, 468, 469, 482, 493, 494, 496, 497, 498, 499, 500a

2. Determine two or more central ideas of a text and analyze their development over the course of the text, including how they interact and build on one another to provide a complex analysis; provide an objective summary of the text.

Student Edition
15, 16, 20, 127, 130, 137, 138, 175, 184, 366, 367, 392, 468, 469, 482, 499

Teacher's Edition
3, 4, 5, 9, 10, 14, 15, 16, 18a, 20, 20a, 30a, 123, 124, 125, 126, 127, 130, 132, 133, 134, 136, 137, 138, 140b, 175, 184, 361, 362, 363, 364, 365, 366, 367, 382, 384, 385, 386, 392, 453, 455, 456, 458, 460, 461, 462, 463, 464, 468, 469, 470a, 482, 492a, 494, 499

3. Analyze a complex set of ideas or sequence of events and explain how specific individuals, ideas, or events interact and develop over the course of the text.

Student Edition
129, 138, 175, 184, 195, 196, 210, 391, 392, 469, 482, 499

Teacher's Edition
128, 129, 138, 175, 180, 184, 187, 188, 190, 191, 192, 193, 194, 195, 196, 198a, 205, 210, 380, 381, 382, 384, 385, 386, 389, 390, 391, 392, 469, 482, 484a, 499

Common Core State Standard	Student Edition and Teacher's Edition

CRAFT AND STRUCTURE

4. Determine the meaning of words and phrases as they are used in a text, including figurative, connotative, and technical meanings; analyze how an author uses and refines the meaning of a key term or terms over the course of a text (e.g., how Madison defines *faction* in *Federalist* No. 10).

Student Edition
16, 127, 138, 165, 166, 175, 196, 210, 367, 481, 482, 499

Teacher's Edition
12, 13, 16, 115, 117, 118, 122a, 124, 127, 138, 140a, 152, 154, 155, 162, 163, 165, 166, 172, 175, 178, 181, 182, 193, 196, 210, 367, 368a, 382, 387, 432a, 454, 455, 457, 465, 479, 481, 482, 484a, 493, 494, 495, 499, 500a

5. Analyze and evaluate the effectiveness of the structure an author uses in his or her exposition or argument, including whether the structure makes points clear, convincing, and engaging.

Student Edition
16, 27, 28, 119, 120, 127, 166, 210, 366, 367, R16–R22

Teacher's Edition
16, 21, 22, 23, 24, 25, 26, 27, 28, 30a, 114, 115, 116, 117, 119, 120, 122a, 127, 153, 166, 210, 212a, 361, 362, 363, 364, 365, 366, 367, 368a, 381, 384, 389, 470a, R16–R22, R16, R19, R20

6. Determine an author's point of view or purpose in a text in which the rhetoric is particularly effective, analyzing how style and content contribute to the power, persuasiveness, or beauty of the text.

Student Edition
20, 28, 119, 120, 127, 137, 138, 166, 186, 196, 209, 210, 431, 432, 481, 482, 499, R16–R22

Teacher's Edition
20, 21, 23, 28, 113, 114, 115, 116, 117, 118, 119, 120, 123, 127, 130a, 131, 132, 133, 134, 135, 136, 137, 138, 156, 161, 163, 166, 168a, 178, 179, 186, 189, 192, 196, 198a, 200, 201, 202, 205, 206, 207, 208, 209, 210, 212a, 216a, 388, 394a, 430, 431, 432, 463, 477, 478, 479, 480, 481, 482, 495, 499, R16–R22

INTEGRATION OF KNOWLEDGE AND IDEAS

7. Integrate and evaluate multiple sources of information presented in different media or formats (e.g., visually, quantitatively) as well as in words in order to address a question or solve a problem.

Student Edition
15, 16, 130, 196, 216, 492

Teacher's Edition
3, 4, 5, 6, 7, 8, 9, 11, 15, 16, 18a, 119, 130, 130a, 196, 204, 213, 214, 215, 216, 216a, 491, 492, 492a

8. Delineate and evaluate the reasoning in seminal U.S. texts, including the application of constitutional principles and use of legal reasoning (e.g., in U.S. Supreme Court majority opinions and dissents) and the premises, purposes, and arguments in works of public advocacy (e.g., *The Federalist*, presidential addresses).

Student Edition
165, 166, 183, 184, 431, 432

Teacher's Edition
151, 152, 153, 154, 155, 157, 158, 159, 160, 161, 162, 164, 165, 166, 168a, 177, 178, 179, 180, 181, 182, 183, 184, 186a, 430, 431, 432, 432a

Common Core State Standard	Student Edition and Teacher's Edition
9. Analyze seventeenth-, eighteenth-, and nineteenth-century foundational U.S. documents of historical and literary significance (including The Declaration of Independence, the Preamble to the Constitution, the Bill of Rights, and Lincoln's Second Inaugural Address) for their themes, purposes, and rhetorical features.	**Student Edition** 166, 174, 175, 186 **Teacher's Edition** 166, 170, 171, 172, 173, 174, 175, 186

RANGE OF READING AND LEVEL OF TEXT COMPLEXITY

10. By the end of grade 12, read and comprehend literary nonfiction at the high end of the grades 11–CCR text complexity band independently and proficiently.	**Student Edition** 27, 119, 166, 209, 210, 361–367, 453–469, 498, 499 **Teacher's Edition** 21, 22, 27, 28, 114, 119, 166, 199, 200, 201, 203, 209, 210, 361–367, 453–469, 494, 495, 496, 498, 499

College and Career Readiness Anchor Standards for Writing

Common Core State Standards

TEXT TYPES AND PURPOSES

1. Write arguments to support claims in an analysis of substantive topics or texts, using valid reasoning and relevant and sufficient evidence.

2. Write informative/explanatory texts to examine and convey complex ideas and information clearly and accurately through the effective selection, organization, and analysis of content.

3. Write narratives to develop real or imagined experiences or events using effective technique, well-chosen details, and well-structured event sequences.

PRODUCTION AND DISTRIBUTION OF WRITING

4. Produce clear and coherent writing in which the development, organization, and style are appropriate to task, purpose, and audience.

5. Develop and strengthen writing as needed by planning, revising, editing, rewriting, or trying a new approach.

6. Use technology, including the Internet, to produce and publish writing and to interact and collaborate with others.

RESEARCH TO BUILD AND PRESENT KNOWLEDGE

7. Conduct short as well as more sustained research projects based on focused questions, demonstrating understanding of the subject under investigation.

Common Core State Standards
8. Gather relevant information from multiple print and digital sources, assess the credibility and accuracy of each source, and integrate the information while avoiding plagiarism.
9. Draw evidence from literary or informational texts to support analysis, reflection, and research.

RANGE OF WRITING

10. Write routinely over extended time frames (time for research, reflection, and revision) and shorter time frames (a single sitting or a day or two) for a range of tasks, purposes, and audiences.

Writing Standards, Grades 11–12 Students

Common Core State Standard	Student/Teacher's Edition	Digital Collection/Lesson
TEXT TYPES AND PURPOSES		
1. Write arguments to support claims in an analysis of substantive topics or texts, using valid reasoning and relevant and sufficient evidence.	**Student Edition** 138, 225–228, 332, 367, R2–R3 **Teacher's Edition** 138, 225–228, 332, 367, R2–R3	**Writing Arguments** • Introduction • What Is a Claim? • Support: Reasons and Evidence • Building Effective Support • Creating a Coherent Argument • Persuasive Techniques • Formal Style • Concluding Your Argument
a. Introduce precise, knowledgeable claim(s), establish the significance of the claim(s), distinguish the claim(s) from alternate or opposing claims, and create an organization that logically sequences claim(s), counterclaims, reasons, and evidence.	**Student Edition** R2–R3 **Teacher's Edition** R2–R3	**Writing Arguments** • What Is a Claim? • Creating a Coherent Argument
b. Develop claim(s) and counterclaims fairly and thoroughly, supplying the most relevant evidence for each while pointing out the strengths and limitations of both in a manner that anticipates the audience's knowledge level, concerns, values, and possible biases.	**Student Edition** R2–R3 **Teacher's Edition** R2–R3	**Writing Arguments** • Support: Reasons and Evidence • Building Effective Support

Common Core State Standard	Student/Teacher's Edition	Digital Collection/Lesson
c. Use words, phrases, and clauses as well as varied syntax to link the major sections of the text, create cohesion, and clarify the relationships between claim(s) and reasons, between reasons and evidence, and between claim(s) and counterclaims	**Student Edition** 28, R2–R3 **Teacher's Edition** 28, R2–R3	**Writing Arguments** • Creating a Coherent Argument
d. Establish and maintain a formal style and objective tone while attending to the norms and conventions of the discipline in which they are writing.	**Student Edition** R2–R3 **Teacher's Edition** R2–R3	**Writing Arguments** • Formal Style
e. Provide a concluding statement or section that follows from and supports the argument presented.	**Student Edition** R2–R3 **Teacher's Edition** R2–R3	**Writing Arguments** • Concluding Your Argument
2. Write informative/explanatory texts to examine and convey complex ideas, concepts, and information clearly and accurately through the effective selection, organization, and analysis of content.	**Student Edition** 71–74, 141–144, 426, 499, R4–R5, R8–R11 **Teacher's Edition** 71–74, 141–144, 426, 499, R4–R5, R8–R11	**Writing Informative Texts** • Introduction • Developing a Topic • Organizing Ideas • Introductions and Conclusions • Elaboration • Using Graphics and Multimedia • Precise Language and Vocabulary • Formal Style **Using Textual Evidence** • Writing an Outline
a. Introduce a topic; organize complex ideas, concepts, and information so that each new element builds on that which precedes it to create a unified whole; include formatting (e.g., headings), graphics (e.g., figures, tables), and multimedia when useful to aiding comprehension.	**Student Edition** R4–R5, R8–R11 **Teacher's Edition** R4–R5, R8–R11	**Writing Informative Texts** • Developing a Topic • Organizing Ideas • Introductions and Conclusions • Using Graphics and Multimedia
b. Develop the topic thoroughly by selecting the most significant and relevant facts, extended definitions, concrete details, quotations, or other information and examples appropriate to the audience's knowledge of the topic.	**Student Edition** 186, R4–R5, R8–R11 **Teacher's Edition** 186, R4–R5, R8–R11	**Writing Informative Texts** • Elaboration

Common Core State Standard	Student/Teacher's Edition	Digital Collection/Lesson
c. Use appropriate and varied transitions and syntax to link the major sections of the text, create cohesion, and clarify the relationships among complex ideas and concepts.	**Student Edition** R4–R5, R8–R11 **Teacher's Edition** R4–R5, R8–R11	**Writing Informative Texts** • Organizing Ideas
d. Use precise language, domain-specific vocabulary, and techniques such as metaphor, simile, and analogy to manage the complexity of the topic.	**Student Edition** R4–R5, R8–R11 **Teacher's Edition** R4–R5, R8–R11	**Writing Informative Texts** • Precise Language and Vocabulary
e. Establish and maintain a formal style and objective tone while attending to the norms and conventions of the discipline in which they are writing.	**Student Edition** R4–R5, R8–R11 **Teacher's Edition** R4–R5, R8–R11	**Writing Informative Texts** • Formal Style
f. Provide a concluding statement or section that follows from and supports the information or explanation presented (e.g., articulating implications or the significance of the topic).	**Student Edition** R4–R5, R8–R11 **Teacher's Edition** R4–R5, R8–R11	**Writing Informative Texts** • Introductions and Conclusions
3. Write narratives to develop real or imagined experiences or events using effective technique, well-chosen details, and well-structured event sequences.	**Student Edition** 398, 517–520, R6–R7 **Teacher's Edition** 398, 517–520, R6–R7	**Writing Narratives** • Introductions • Narrative Context • Point of View and Characters • Narrative Structure • Narrative Techniques • The Language of Narrative
a. Engage and orient the reader by setting out a problem, situation, or observation and its significance, establishing one or multiple point(s) of view, and introducing a narrator and/or characters; create a smooth progression of experiences or events.	**Student Edition** 16, 482, 517–520, R6–R7 **Teacher's Edition** 16, 482, 517–520, R6–R7	**Writing Narratives** • Narrative Context • Point of View and Characters • Narrative Structure
b. Use narrative techniques, such as dialogue, pacing, description, reflection, and multiple plot lines, to develop experiences, events, and/or characters.	**Student Edition** 517–520, R6–R7 **Teacher's Edition** 517–520, R6–R7	**Writing Narratives** • Narrative Structure • Narrative Techniques • The Language of Narrative

Common Core State Standard	Student/Teacher's Edition	Digital Collection/Lesson
c. Use a variety of techniques to sequence events so that they build on one another to create a coherent whole and build toward a particular tone and outcome (e.g., a sense of mystery, suspense, growth, or resolution).	**Student Edition** 517–520, R6–R7 **Teacher's Edition** 517–520, R6–R7	**Writing Narratives** • Narrative Structure
d. Use precise words and phrases, telling details, and sensory language to convey a vivid picture of the experiences, events, setting, and/or characters.	**Student Edition** 16, 44, 106, 397, 517–520, R6–R7 **Teacher's Edition** 16, 44, 106, 108a, 397, 398b, 517–520, R6–R7	**Writing Narratives** • The Language of Narrative
e. Provide a conclusion that follows from and reflects on what is experienced, observed, or resolved over the course of the narrative.	**Student Edition** 482, 517–520, R6–R7 **Teacher's Edition** 482, 517–520, R6–R7	**Writing Narratives** • Narrative Structure

PRODUCTION AND DISTRIBUTION OF WRITING

Common Core State Standard	Student/Teacher's Edition	Digital Collection/Lesson
4. Produce clear and coherent writing in which the development, organization, and style are appropriate to task, purpose, and audience. (Grade-specific expectations for writing types are defined in standards 1–3 above.)	**Student Edition** 20, 61, 64, 67–70, 71–74, 90, 106, 141–144, 145–148, 175, 210, 221–224, 225–228, 262, 399–402, 403–406, 471–474, 517–520 **Teacher's Edition** 20, 20a, 61, 64, 67–70, 71–74, 90, 106, 141–144, 145–148, 175, 210, 221–224, 225–228, 262, 399–402, 403–406, 471–474, 517–520	**Writing as a Process** • Task, Purpose, and Audience
5. Develop and strengthen writing as needed by planning, revising, editing, rewriting, or trying a new approach, focusing on addressing what is most significant for a specific purpose and audience. (Editing for conventions should demonstrate command of Language standards 1–3.)	**Student Edition** 67–70, 71–74, 141–144, 145–148, 221–224, 225–228, 399–402, 403–406, 471–474, 517–520 **Teacher's Edition** 67–70, 71–74, 141–144, 145–148, 221–224, 225–228, 399–402, 403–406, 471–474, 517–520	**Writing as a Process** • Introduction • Task, Purpose, and Audience • Planning and Drafting • Revising and Editing • Trying a New Approach

Common Core State Standard	Student/Teacher's Edition	Digital Collection/Lesson
6. Use technology, including the Internet, to produce, publish, and update individual or shared writing products in response to ongoing feedback, including new arguments or information.	**Student Edition** 67–70, 71–74, 141–144, 145–148, 221–224, 225–228, 399–402, 403–406, 471–474, 517–520 **Teacher's Edition** 67–70, 71–74, 141–144, 145–148, 221–224, 225–228, 399–402, 403–406, 471–474, 517–520	**Producing and Publishing with Technology** • Introduction • Writing for the Internet • Interacting with Your Online Audience • Using Technology to Collaborate

RESEARCH TO BUILD AND PRESENT KNOWLEDGE

Common Core State Standard	Student/Teacher's Edition	Digital Collection/Lesson
7. Conduct short as well as more sustained research projects to answer a question (including a self-generated question) or solve a problem; narrow or broaden the inquiry when appropriate; synthesize multiple sources on the subject, demonstrating understanding of the subject under investigation.	**Student Edition** 196, R8–R11 **Teacher's Edition** 196, R8–R11	**Conducting Research** • Introduction • Starting Your Research • Refocusing Your Inquiry **Using Textual Evidence** • Synthesizing Information
8. Gather relevant information from multiple authoritative print and digital sources, using advanced searches effectively; assess the strengths and limitations of each source in terms of the task, purpose, and audience; integrate information into the text selectively to maintain the flow of ideas, avoiding plagiarism and overreliance on any one source and following a standard format for citation.	**Student Edition** 196, R8–R11 **Teacher's Edition** 196, R8–R11	**Conducting Research** • Types of Sources • Using the Library for Research • Using the Internet for Research **Evaluating Sources** • Introduction • Evaluating Sources for Usefulness • Evaluating Sources for Reliability **Using Textual Evidence** • Summarizing, Paraphrasing, and Quoting • Attribution
9. Draw evidence from literary or informational texts to support analysis, reflection, and research.	**Student Edition** 71–74, 141–144, 184, 225–228, 471–474 **Teacher's Edition** 71–74, 141–144, 184, 225–228, 471–474	**Writing Informative Texts** • Elaboration **Conducting Research** • Taking Notes **Using Textual Evidence** • Introduction • Synthesizing Information • Summarizing, Paraphrasing, and Quoting
a. Apply *grades 11–12 Reading standards* to literature (e.g., "Demonstrate knowledge of eighteenth-, nineteenth- and early-twentieth-century foundational works of American literature, including how two or more texts from the same period treat similar themes or topics").	**Student Edition** 471–474, 490 **Teacher's Edition** 471–474, 490	

b. Apply *grades 11–12 Reading standards* to literary nonfiction (e.g., "Delineate and evaluate the reasoning in seminal U.S. texts, including the application of constitutional principles and use of legal reasoning [e.g., in U.S. Supreme Court Case majority opinions and dissents] and the premises, purposes, and arguments in works of public advocacy [e.g., *The Federalist*, presidential addresses]").

Student Edition
166, 471–474

Teacher's Edition
166, 471–474

RANGE OF WRITING

10. Write routinely over extended time frames (time for research, reflection, and revision) and shorter time frames (a single sitting or a day or two) for a range of tasks, purposes, and audiences.

Student Edition
67–70, 71–74, 141–144, 145–148, 220, 221–224, 225–228, 355, 399–402, 403–406, 471–474, 517–520

Teacher's Edition
67–70, 71–74, 106, 141–144, 145–148, 220, 221–224, 225–228, 355, 399–402, 403–406, 471–474, 517–520

Writing as a Process
• Task, Purpose, and Audience
Writing Arguments
Writing Informative Texts
Writing Narratives
Using Textual Evidence

College and Career Readiness Anchor Standards for Speaking and Listening

Common Core State Standards

COMPREHENSION AND COLLABORATION

1. Prepare for and participate effectively in a range of conversations and collaborations with diverse partners, building on others' ideas and expressing their own clearly and persuasively.

2. Integrate and evaluate information presented in diverse media and formats, including visually, quantitatively, and orally.

3. Evaluate a speaker's point of view, reasoning, and use of evidence and rhetoric.

Common Core State Standards

PRESENTATION OF KNOWLEDGE AND IDEAS

4. Present information, findings, and supporting evidence such that listeners can follow the line of reasoning and the organization, development, and style are appropriate to task, purpose, and audience.

5. Make strategic use of digital media and visual displays of data to express information and enhance understanding of presentations.

6. Adapt speech to a variety of contexts and communicative tasks, demonstrating command of formal English when indicated or appropriate.

Speaking and Listening Standards, Grades 11–12 Students

Common Core State Standard	Student/Teacher's Edition	Digital Collection/Lesson
COMPREHENSION AND COLLABORATION		
1. Initiate and participate effectively in a range of collaborative discussions (one-on-one, in groups, and teacher-led) with diverse partners on *grades 11–12 topics, texts, and issues*, building on others' ideas and expressing their own clearly and persuasively.	**Student Edition** 67–70, 106, 130, 145–148, 221–224, 283, 310, R12–R13, R14–R15 **Teacher's Edition** 66a, 67–70, 106, 130, 145–148, 221–224, 283, 310, R12–R13, R14–R15	**Participating in Collaborative Discussions** • Introduction • Preparing for Discussion • Establishing and Following Procedure • Speaking Constructively • Listening and Responding • Wrapping Up Your Discussion
a. Come to discussions prepared, having read and researched material under study; explicitly draw on that preparation by referring to evidence from texts and other research on the topic or issue to stimulate a thoughtful, well-reasoned exchange of ideas.	**Student Edition** 61, 67–70, 145–148, 186, 221–224, 377, 392, 450, 515, R12–R13, R14–R15 **Teacher's Edition** 61, 67–70, 145–148, 186, 221–224, 377, 392, 450, 515, R12–R13, R14–R15	**Participating in Collaborative Discussions** • Preparing for Discussion • Speaking Constructively
b. Work with peers to promote civil, democratic discussions and decision-making, set clear goals and deadlines, and establish individual roles as needed.	**Student Edition** 67–70, 145–148, 221–224, R12–R13, R14–R15 **Teacher's Edition** 67–70, 145–148, 221–224, R12–R13, R14–R15	**Participating in Collaborative Discussions** • Establishing and Following Procedure

Common Core State Standard	Student/Teacher's Edition	Digital Collection/Lesson
c. Propel conversations by posing and responding to questions that probe reasoning and evidence; ensure a hearing for a full range of positions on a topic or issue; clarify, verify, or challenge ideas and conclusions; and promote divergent and creative perspectives.	**Student Edition** 67–70, 145–148, 221–224, 432, R12–R13, R14–R15 **Teacher's Edition** 67–70, 140b, 145–148, 221–224, 432, R12–R13, R14–R15	**Participating in Collaborative Discussions** • Speaking Constructively • Listening and Responding
d. Respond thoughtfully to diverse perspectives; synthesize comments, claims, and evidence made on all sides of an issue; resolve contradictions when possible; and determine what additional information or research is required to deepen the investigation or complete the task.	**Student Edition** 67–70, 145–148, 221–224, R12–R13, R14–R15 **Teacher's Edition** 67–70, 145–148, 221–224, R12–R13, R14–R15	**Participating in Collaborative Discussions** • Listening and Responding • Wrapping Up Your Discussion
2. Integrate multiple sources of information presented in diverse formats and media (e.g., visually, quantitatively, orally) in order to make informed decisions and solve problems, evaluating the credibility and accuracy of each source and noting any discrepancies among the data.	**Student Edition** 130, 432 **Teacher's Edition** 130, 432	**Analyzing and Evaluating Presentations** • Introduction • Evaluating a Speaker's Reliability • Synthesizing Media Sources
3. Evaluate a speaker's point of view, reasoning, and use of evidence and rhetoric, assessing the stance, premises, links among ideas, word choice, points of emphasis, and tone used.	**Student Edition** 67–70, 138, 432, R14–R15 **Teacher's Edition** 67–70, 138, 432, R14–R15	**Analyzing and Evaluating Presentations** • Tracing a Speaker's Argument • Rhetoric and Delivery

PRESENTATION OF KNOWLEDGE AND IDEAS

4. Present information, findings, and supporting evidence, conveying a clear and distinct perspective, such that listeners can follow the line of reasoning, alternative or opposing perspectives are addressed, and the organization, development, substance, and style are appropriate to purpose, audience, and a range of formal and informal tasks.	**Student Edition** 138, 216, 221–224, 471–474, R14–R15 **Teacher's Edition** 66, 66b, 138, 216, 221–224, 471–474, R14–R15	**Giving a Presentation** • Introduction • Knowing Your Audience • The Content of Your Presentation • Style in Presentation
5. Make strategic use of digital media (e.g., textual, graphical, audio, visual, and interactive elements) in presentations to enhance understanding of findings, reasoning, and evidence and to add interest.	**Student Edition** 130, 196, 216, 360, 492 **Teacher's Edition** 130, 196, 216, 360, 492	**Using Media in a Presentation** • Introduction • Types of Media: Audio, Video, and Images • Using Presentation Software • Building and Practicing Your Presentation

Common Core State Standard	Student/Teacher's Edition	Digital Collection/Lesson
6. Adapt speech to a variety of contexts and tasks, demonstrating a command of formal English when indicated or appropriate. (See grades 11–12 Language standards 1 and 3 for specific expectations.)	**Student Edition** 64, 111, 120, 355 **Teacher's Edition** 64, 111, 120, 355	**Participating in Collaborative Discussions** • Speaking Constructively **Giving a Presentation** • Style in Presentation

College and Career Readiness Anchor Standards for Language

Common Core State Standards

CONVENTIONS OF STANDARD ENGLISH

1. Demonstrate command of the conventions of standard English grammar and usage when writing or speaking.

2. Demonstrate command of the conventions of standard English capitalization, punctuation, and spelling when writing.

KNOWLEDGE OF LANGUAGE

3. Apply knowledge of language to understand how language functions in different contexts, to make effective choices for meaning or style, and to comprehend more fully when reading or listening.

VOCABULARY ACQUISITION AND USE

4. Determine or clarify the meaning of unknown and multiple-meaning words and phrases by using context clues, analyzing meaningful word parts, and consulting general and specialized reference materials, as appropriate.

5. Demonstrate understanding of figurative language, word relationships, and nuances in word meanings.

6. Acquire and use accurately a range of general academic and domain-specific words and phrases sufficient for reading, writing, speaking, and listening at the college and career readiness level; demonstrate independence in gathering vocabulary knowledge when considering a word or phrase important to comprehension or expression.

Language Standards, Grades 11–12 Students

Common Core State Standard	Student/Teacher's Edition

CONVENTIONS OF STANDARD ENGLISH

1. Demonstrate command of the conventions of standard English grammar and usage when writing or speaking.

Student Edition
18, 30, 70, 74, 108, 122, 144, 198, 228, 402, 469, 474, 520, R23–R48

Teacher's Edition
18, 30, 70, 74, 108, 122, 130, 144, 198, 228, 402, 469, 474, 520, R23–R48, R31, R33, R35, R38, R42, R45, R47

a. Apply the understanding that usage is a matter of convention, can change over time, and is sometimes contested.

Student Edition
62, 91, R49, R51–52, R56

Teacher's Edition
48, 49, 62, 91, R49, R51–52, R56

b. Resolve issues of complex or contested usage, consulting references (e.g., *Merriam-Webster's Dictionary of English Usage, Garner's Modern American Usage*) as needed.

Student Edition
91, R49, R56, R57

Teacher's Edition
91, R49, R56, R57

2. Demonstrate command of the conventions of standard English capitalization, punctuation, and spelling when writing.

Student Edition
46, 74, 144, 228, 394, 402, 520, R23, R26–R28, R29

Teacher's Edition
46, 49, 74, 130, 144, 228, 394, 402, 520, R23, R26–R28, R29

a. Observe hyphenation conventions.

Student Edition
R23, R27

Teacher's Edition
R23, R27

b. Spell correctly.

Student Edition
74, 144, 228, 402, 520, R49, R57–R59, R60–R61

Teacher's Edition
74, 144, 228, 402, 520, R49, R57–R59, R60–R61

c. Correctly use punctuation, capitalization, and spelling in legible work.

Teacher's Edition
R7, R9, R16, R31, R51

Common Core State Standard	Student/Teacher's Edition

KNOWLEDGE OF LANGUAGE

3. Apply knowledge of language to understand how language functions in different contexts, to make effective choices for meaning or style, and to comprehend more fully when reading or listening.

Student Edition
62, 112, 168, 198, 428, 452, 484, 500

Teacher's Edition
48, 62, 112, 168, 198, 395, 396, 428, 452, 484, 500

---

a. Vary syntax for effect, consulting references (e.g., Tufte's *Artful Sentences*) for guidance as needed; apply an understanding of syntax to the study of complex texts when reading.

Student Edition
92, 140, 185, 212, 378, R2, R3

Teacher's Edition
92, 140, 185, 212, 370, 378, R2, R3

VOCABULARY ACQUISITION AND USE

4. Determine or clarify the meaning of unknown and multiple-meaning words and phrases based on *grades 11–12 reading and content*, choosing flexibly from a range of strategies.

Student Edition
17, 29, 45, 107, 167, 176, 121, 139, 211, 393, 427, 516, R49–R57

Teacher's Edition
17, 29, 45, 107, 167, 176, 121, 139, 211, 393, 427, 516, R49–R57

---

a. Use context (e.g., the overall meaning of a sentence, paragraph, or text; a word's position or function in a sentence) as a clue to the meaning of a word or phrase.

Student Edition
17, 121, 139, 211, 427, R23–R25, R49–R50

Teacher's Edition
17, 121, 139, 211, 427, R23–R25, R49–R50

---

b. Identify and correctly use patterns of word changes that indicate different meanings or parts of speech (e.g., *conceive, conception, conceivable*).

Student Edition
29, 167, R23, R31–R33, R33–R35, R36–R38, R49, R50–R51

Teacher's Edition
29, 167, R23, R31–R33, R33–R35, R36–R38, R49, R50–R51

---

c. Consult general and specialized reference materials (e.g., dictionaries, glossaries, thesauruses), both print and digital, to find the pronunciation of a word or determine or clarify its precise meaning, its part of speech, its etymology, or its standard usage.

Student Edition
45, 107, 176, 516, R49, R51–R52, R53–R54, R55, R56, R57

Teacher's Edition
45, 107, 176, 516, R49, R51–R52, R53–R54, R55, R56, R57

Common Core State Standard	Student/Teacher's Edition
d. Verify the preliminary determination of the meaning of a word or phrase (e.g., by checking the inferred meaning in context or in a dictionary).	**Student Edition** 107, 121, 211 **Teacher's Edition** 107, 121, 211
5. Demonstrate understanding of figurative language, word relationships, and nuances in word meanings.	**Student Edition** 111, 197, 210, 356, 397, 451, 481, 482, 516, R49–R50 **Teacher's Edition** 109, 110, 111, 112a, 130, 197, 210, 356, 397, 451, 479, 481, 482, 516, R49–R50
a. Interpret figures of speech (e.g., hyperbole, paradox) in context and analyze their role in the text.	**Student Edition** 111, 210, 356, 397, 481, 482 **Teacher's Edition** 111, 210, 356, 395, 396, 397, 398b, 481, 482, 516a
b. Analyze nuances in the meaning of words with similar denotations.	**Student Edition** 197, 451, 516 **Teacher's Edition** 197, 451, 516
6. Acquire and use accurately general academic and domain-specific words and phrases, sufficient for reading, writing, speaking, and listening at the college and career readiness level; demonstrate independence in gathering vocabulary knowledge when considering a word or phrase important to comprehension or expression.	**Student Edition** 2, 67, 71, 76, 141, 145, 150, 221, 225, 230, 368, 399, 403, 408, 470, 471, 476, 483, 517, R49, R55 **Teacher's Edition** 2, 67, 71, 76, 141, 145, 150, 221, 225, 230, 368, 399, 403, 408, 454, 455, 457, 470, 471, 476, 483, 517, R49, R55

Navigating Complex Texts

By Carol Jago

Reading complex literature and nonfiction doesn't need to be painful.

But to enjoy great poetry and prose you are going to have to do more than skim and scan. You will need to develop the habit of paying attention to the particular words on the page closely, systematically, even lovingly. Just because a text isn't easy doesn't mean there is something wrong with it or something wrong with you. Understanding complex text takes effort and focused attention. Do you sometimes wish writers would just say what they have to say more simply or with fewer words? I assure you that writers don't use long sentences and unfamiliar words to annoy their readers or make readers feel dumb. They employ complex syntax and rich language because they have complex ideas about complex issues that they want to communicate. Simple language and structures just aren't up to the task.

Excellent literature and nonfiction—the kind you will be reading over the course of the year—challenge readers in many ways. Sometimes the background of a story or the content of an essay is so unfamiliar that it can be difficult to understand why characters are behaving as they do or to follow the argument a writer is making. By persevering—reading like a detective and following clues in the text—you will find that your store of background knowledge grows. As a result, the next time you read about this subject, the text won't seem nearly as hard. Navigating a terrain you have been over once before never seems quite as rugged the second time through. The more you read, the better reader you become.

Good readers aren't scared off by challenging text. When the going gets rough, they know what to do. Let's take vocabulary, a common measure of text complexity, as an example. Learning new words is the business of a lifetime. Rather than shutting down when you meet a word you don't know, take a moment to think about the word. Is any part of the word familiar to you? Is there something in the context of the sentence or paragraph that can help you figure out its meaning? Is there someone or something that can provide you with a definition? When we read literature or nonfiction from a time period other than our own, the text is often full of words we don't know.

Each time you meet those words in succeeding readings you will be adding to your understanding of the word and its use. Your brain is a natural word-learning machine. The more you feed it complex text, the larger vocabulary you'll have and as a result, the easier navigating the next book will be.

Have you ever been reading a long, complicated sentence and discovered that by the time you reached the end you had forgotten the beginning? Unlike the sentences we speak or dash off in a note to a friend, complex text is often full of sentences that are not only lengthy but also constructed in intricate ways. Such sentences require readers to slow down and figure out how phrases relate to one another as well as who is doing what to whom. Remember, rereading isn't cheating. It is exactly what experienced readers know to do when they meet dense text on the page. On the pages that follow you will find stories and articles that challenge you at a sentence level. Don't be intimidated. By paying careful attention to how those sentences are constructed, you will see their meanings unfold before your eyes.

Another way text can be complex is in terms of the density of ideas. Sometimes a writer piles on so much information that you find even if your eyes continue to move down the page, your brain has stopped taking in anything. At times like this, turning to a peer and discussing particular lines or concepts can help you pay closer attention and begin to unpack the text. Sharing questions and ideas, exploring a difficult passage together, makes it possible to tease out the meaning of even the most difficult text.

> **"Your brain is a natural word-learning machine. The more you feed it complex text, the larger vocabulary you'll have."**

Poetry is by its nature particularly dense and for that reason poses particular challenges for casual readers. Don't ever assume that once through a poem is enough. Often, seemingly simple poems in terms of word choice and length—for example an Emily Dickinson, Mary Oliver, or W.H. Auden poem—express extremely complex feelings and insights. Poets also often make reference to mythological and Biblical allusions which contemporary readers are not always familiar with. Skipping over such references robs your reading of the richness the poet intended. Look up that bird. Check out the note on the page. Ask your teacher.

You will notice a range of complexity within each collection of readings. This spectrum reflects the range of texts that surround us: some easy, some hard, some seemingly easy but hard, some seemingly hard but easy. Navigating this sea of texts should stretch you as a reader and a thinker. How could it be otherwise when your journey is in the realms of gold? Please accept this invitation to an intellectual voyage I think you will enjoy.

Understanding the Common Core State Standards

What are the English Language Arts Common Core State Standards?

The Common Core State Standards for English Language Arts indicate what you should know and be able to do by the end of your grade level. These understandings and skills will help you be better prepared for future classes, college courses, and a career. For this reason, the standards for each strand in English Language Arts (such as reading informational text or writing) directly relate to the College and Career Readiness Anchor Standards for each strand. The Anchor Standards broadly outline the understandings and skills you should master by the end of high school so that you are well-prepared for college or for a career.

How do I learn the English Language Arts Common Core State Standards?

Your textbook is closely aligned to the English Language Arts Common Core State Standards. Every time you learn a concept or practice a skill, you are working on mastery of one of the standards. Each collection, each selection, and each performance task in your textbook connects to one or more of the standards for English Language Arts listed on the following pages.

The English Language Arts Common Core State Standards are divided into five strands: Reading Literature, Reading Informational Text, Writing, Speaking and Listening, and Language.

©svetikd/The Agency Collection/Getty Images

Strand	What It Means to You
Reading Literature (RL)	This strand concerns the literary texts you will read at this grade level: stories, drama, and poetry. The Common Core State Standards stress that you should read a range of texts of increasing complexity as you progress through high school.
Reading Informational Text (RI)	Informational text includes a broad range of literary nonfiction, including exposition, argument, and functional text, in such genres as personal essays, speeches, opinion pieces, memoirs, and historical and technical accounts. The Common Core State Standards stress that you will read a range of informational texts of increasing complexity as you progress from grade to grade.
Writing (W)	The Writing strand focuses on your generating three types of texts—arguments, informative or explanatory texts, and narratives—while using the writing process and technology to develop and share your writing. The Common Core State Standards also emphasize research and specify that you should write routinely for both short and extended time frames.
Speaking and Listening (SL)	The Common Core State Standards focus on comprehending information presented in a variety of media and formats, on participating in collaborative discussions, and on presenting knowledge and ideas clearly.
Language (L)	The standards in the Language strand address the conventions of standard English grammar, usage, and mechanics; knowledge of language; and vocabulary acquisition and use.

Common Core Code Decoder

The codes you find on the pages of your textbook identify the specific knowledge or skill for the standard addressed in the text.

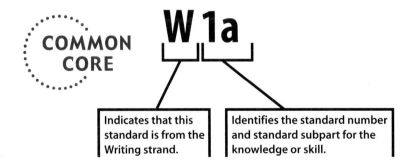

Indicates that this standard is from the Writing strand.	Identifies the standard number and standard subpart for the knowledge or skill.

English Language Arts
Common Core State Standards

Listed below are the English Language Arts Common Core State Standards that you are required to master by the end of grade 12. We have provided a summary of the concepts you will learn on your way to mastering each standard. The CCR anchor standards and high school grade-specific standards for each strand work together to define college and career readiness expectations—the former providing broad standards, the latter providing additional specificity.

College and Career Readiness Anchor Standards for Reading

Common Core State Standards

KEY IDEAS AND DETAILS

1. Read closely to determine what the text says explicitly and to make logical inferences from it; cite specific textual evidence when writing or speaking to support conclusions drawn from the text.

2. Determine central ideas or themes of a text and analyze their development; summarize the key supporting details and ideas.

3. Analyze how and why individuals, events, and ideas develop and interact over the course of a text.

CRAFT AND STRUCTURE

4. Interpret words and phrases as they are used in a text, including determining technical, connotative, and figurative meanings, and analyze how specific word choices shape meaning or tone.

5. Analyze the structure of texts, including how specific sentences, paragraphs, and larger portions of the text (e.g., a section, chapter, scene, or stanza) relate to each other and the whole.

6. Assess how point of view or purpose shapes the content and style of a text.

INTEGRATION OF KNOWLEDGE AND IDEAS

7. Integrate and evaluate content presented in diverse formats and media, including visually and quantitatively, as well as in words.

8. Delineate and evaluate the argument and specific claims in a text, including the validity of the reasoning as well as the relevance and sufficiency of the evidence.

9. Analyze how two or more texts address similar themes or topics in order to build knowledge or to compare the approaches the authors take.

RANGE OF READING AND LEVEL OF TEXT COMPLEXITY

10. Read and comprehend complex literary and informational texts independently and proficiently.

Reading Standards for Literature, Grades 11–12 Students

The College and Career Readiness Anchor Standards for Reading apply to both literature and informational text.

Common Core State Standards	What It Means to You
KEY IDEAS AND DETAILS	
1. Cite strong and thorough textual evidence to support analysis of what the text says explicitly as well as inferences drawn from the text, including determining where the text leaves matters uncertain.	You will use strong evidence from a text to support your analysis of its central ideas—both those that are stated directly and those that are suggested—and to show where the text leaves matters uncertain.
2. Determine two or more themes or central ideas of a text and analyze their development over the course of the text, including how they interact and build on one another to produce a complex account; provide an objective summary of the text.	You will analyze the development of at least two of a text's key ideas and themes by showing how they progress and interact throughout the text. You will also summarize the text as a whole without adding your own ideas or opinions.
3. Analyze the impact of the author's choices regarding how to develop and relate elements of a story or drama (e.g., where a story is set, how the action is ordered, how the characters are introduced and developed).	You will analyze the author's choices related to setting, plot structure, and characterization in a story or drama.
CRAFT AND STRUCTURE	
4. Determine the meaning of words and phrases as they are used in the text, including figurative and connotative meanings; analyze the impact of specific word choices on meaning and tone, including words with multiple meanings or language that is particularly fresh, engaging, or beautiful. (Include Shakespeare as well as other authors.)	You will analyze specific words and phrases in the text to determine both their figurative and connotative meanings, as well as how they contribute to the text's tone and meaning as a whole. You will also consider multiple-meaning words and vivid language.
5. Analyze how an author's choices concerning how to structure specific parts of a text (e.g., the choice of where to begin or end a story, the choice to provide a comedic or tragic resolution) contribute to its overall structure and meaning as well as its aesthetic impact.	You will analyze the ways in which the author has chosen to structure and order the text and determine how those choices shape the text's meaning and affect the reader.
6. Analyze a case in which grasping a point of view requires distinguishing what Is directly stated in a text from what is really meant (e.g., satire, sarcasm, irony, or understatement).	You will understand a point of view in which what is really meant is different from what is said or stated.

Common Core State Standards	What It Means to You
INTEGRATION OF KNOWLEDGE AND IDEAS	
7. Analyze multiple interpretations of a story, drama, or poem (e.g., recorded or live production of a play or recorded novel or poetry), evaluating how each version interprets the source text. (Include at least one play by Shakespeare and one play by an American dramatist.)	You will compare and contrast multiple interpretations of a story, drama, or poem, and analyze how each draws from and uses the source text.
8. (Not applicable to literature)	
9. Demonstrate knowledge of eighteenth-, nineteenth- and early-twentieth-century foundational works of American literature, including how two or more texts from the same period treat similar themes or topics.	You will analyze, compare, and contrast important eighteenth-, nineteenth-, and early-twentieth-century works of American literature.
RANGE OF READING AND LEVEL OF TEXT COMPLEXITY	
10. By the end of grade 12, read and comprehend literature, including stories, dramas, and poems, at the high end of the grades 11–CCR text complexity band independently and proficiently.	11. You will read and understand grade-level appropriate literary texts by the end of grade 12.

Reading Standards for Informational Text, Grades 11–12 Students

Common Core State Standards	What It Means to You
KEY IDEAS AND DETAILS	
1. Cite strong and thorough textual evidence to support analysis of what the text says explicitly as well as inferences drawn from the text, including determining where the text leaves matters uncertain.	You will use details and information from the text to support your analysis of its central ideas—both those that are stated directly and those that are suggested—and to show where the text leaves matters uncertain.
2. Determine two or more central ideas of a text and analyze their development over the course of the text, including how they interact and build on one another to provide a complex analysis; provide an objective summary of the text.	You will analyze the development of at least two of a text's key ideas by showing how they progress and interact throughout the text. You will also summarize the text as a whole without adding your own ideas or opinions.

Common Core State Standards	What It Means to You
3. Analyze a complex set of ideas or sequence of events and explain how specific individuals, ideas, or events interact and develop over the course of the text.	You will analyze the specific interactions among a set of ideas, individuals, or a sequence of events in a text.

CRAFT AND STRUCTURE

4. Determine the meaning of words and phrases as they are used in a text, including figurative, connotative, and technical meanings; analyze how an author uses and refines the meaning of a key term or terms over the course of a text (e.g., how Madison defines *faction* in *Federalist* No. 10).	You will analyze specific words and phrases in the text to determine their figurative, connotative, and technical meanings, as well as to uncover how an author uses them throughout a text.
5. Analyze and evaluate the effectiveness of the structure an author uses in his or her exposition or argument, including whether the structure makes points clear, convincing, and engaging.	You will examine a text's structure and evaluate whether it makes the author's claims clear, convincing, and interesting.
6. Determine an author's point of view or purpose in a text in which the rhetoric is particularly effective, analyzing how style and content contribute to the power, persuasiveness, or beauty of the text.	You will understand the author's purpose and perspective on a topic and analyze how the author uses language to affect the reader.

INTEGRATION OF KNOWLEDGE AND IDEAS

7. Integrate and evaluate multiple sources of information presented in different media or formats (e.g., visually, quantitatively) as well as in words in order to address a question or solve a problem.	You will integrate multiple and varied sources of information to address a question or solve a problem.
8. Delineate and evaluate the reasoning in seminal U.S. texts, including the application of constitutional principles and use of legal reasoning (e.g., in U.S. Supreme Court majority opinions and dissents) and the premises, purposes, and arguments in works of public advocacy (e.g., *The Federalist*, presidential addresses).	You will analyze the reasoning and underlying principles of important historical U.S. texts for their support of the principles of democracy.

Common Core State Standards	What It Means to You
9. Analyze seventeenth-, eighteenth-, and nineteenth-century foundational U.S. documents of historical and literary significance (including The Declaration of Independence, the Preamble to the Constitution, the Bill of Rights, and Lincoln's Second Inaugural Address) for their themes, purposes, and rhetorical features.	You will read and analyze important eighteenth-, nineteenth-, and early-twentieth-century documents pertaining to American history to determine their themes, purposes, and use of language.

RANGE OF READING AND LEVEL OF TEXT COMPLEXITY

10. By the end of grade 12, read and comprehend literary nonfiction in the grades 11–CCR text complexity band independently and proficiently.	You will demonstrate the ability to read and understand grade-level appropriate literary nonfiction texts by the end of grade 12.

College and Career Readiness Anchor Standards for Writing

Common Core State Standards

TEXT TYPES AND PURPOSES

1. Write arguments to support claims in an analysis of substantive topics or texts, using valid reasoning and relevant and sufficient evidence.

2. Write informative/explanatory texts to examine and convey complex ideas and information clearly and accurately through the effective selection, organization, and analysis of content.

3. Write narratives to develop real or imagined experiences or events using effective technique, well-chosen details, and well-structured event sequences.

PRODUCTION AND DISTRIBUTION OF WRITING

4. Produce clear and coherent writing in which the development, organization, and style are appropriate to task, purpose, and audience.

5. Develop and strengthen writing as needed by planning, revising, editing, rewriting, or trying a new approach.

6. Use technology, including the Internet, to produce and publish writing and to interact and collaborate with others.

RESEARCH TO BUILD AND PRESENT KNOWLEDGE

7. Conduct short as well as more sustained research projects based on focused questions, demonstrating understanding of the subject under investigation.

8. Gather relevant information from multiple print and digital sources, assess the credibility and accuracy of each source, and integrate the information while avoiding plagiarism.

Common Core State Standards

9. Draw evidence from literary or informational texts to support analysis, reflection, and research.

RANGE OF WRITING

10. Write routinely over extended time frames (time for research, reflection, and revision) and shorter time frames (a single sitting or a day or two) for a range of tasks, purposes, and audiences.

Writing Standards, Grades 11–12 Students

Common Core State Standards	What It Means to You

TEXT TYPES AND PURPOSES

1. Write arguments to support claims in an analysis of substantive topics or texts, using valid reasoning and relevant and sufficient evidence.	You will write and develop arguments with strong evidence and valid reasoning that include
a. Introduce precise, knowledgeable claim(s), establish the significance of the claim(s), distinguish the claim(s) from alternate or opposing claims, and create an organization that logically sequences claim(s), counterclaims, reasons, and evidence.	a. a clear organization of precise claims and counterclaims
b. Develop claim(s) and counterclaims fairly and thoroughly, supplying the most relevant evidence for each while pointing out the strengths and limitations of both in a manner that anticipates the audience's knowledge level, concerns, values, and possible biases.	b. relevant and unbiased support for claims that incorporates audience considerations
c. Use words, phrases, and clauses as well as varied syntax to link the major sections of the text, create cohesion, and clarify the relationships between claim(s) and reasons, between reasons and evidence, and between claim(s) and counterclaims.	c. use of transitional words, phrases, and clauses and varied sentence structures to link information and clarify relationships
d. Establish and maintain a formal style and objective tone while attending to the norms and conventions of the discipline in which they are writing.	d. a tone and style that is appropriate and that adheres to the conventions, or expectations, of the discipline
e. Provide a concluding statement or section that follows from and supports the argument presented.	e. a strong concluding statement or section that summarizes the evidence presented

Common Core State Standards	What It Means to You

TEXT TYPES AND PURPOSES

2. Write informative/explanatory texts to examine and convey complex ideas, concepts, and information clearly and accurately through the effective selection, organization, and analysis of content.

You will write clear, well-organized, and thoughtful informative and explanatory texts with

   a. Introduce a topic; organize complex ideas, concepts, and information so that each new element builds on that which precedes it to create a unified whole; include formatting (e.g., headings), graphics (e.g., figures, tables), and multimedia when useful to aiding comprehension.

   a. a clear introduction and an organization that builds on each successive idea, including formats, headings, graphic organizers (when appropriate), and multimedia

   b. Develop the topic thoroughly by selecting the most significant and relevant facts, extended definitions, concrete details, quotations, or other information and examples appropriate to the audience's knowledge of the topic.

   b. a sufficient variety of support and background information

   c. Use appropriate and varied transitions and syntax to link the major sections of the text, create cohesion, and clarify the relationships among complex ideas and concepts.

   c. appropriate and varied transitions and sentence structures

   d. Use precise language, domain-specific vocabulary, and techniques such as metaphor, simile, and analogy to manage the complexity of the topic.

   d. precise language, relevant vocabulary, and the use of comparisons to express complex ideas

   e. Establish and maintain a formal style and objective tone while attending to the norms and conventions of the discipline in which they are writing.

   e. an appropriate tone and style that adheres to the conventions, or expectations, of the discipline

   f. Provide a concluding statement or section that follows from and supports the information or explanation presented (e.g., articulating implications or the significance of the topic).

   f. a strong concluding statement or section that logically relates to the information presented in the text and that restates the importance or relevance of the topic

Common Core State Standards	What It Means to You

TEXT TYPES AND PURPOSES

3. Write narratives to develop real or imagined experiences or events using effective technique, well-chosen details, and well-structured event sequences.

You will write clear, well-structured, detailed narrative texts that

   a. Engage and orient the reader by setting out a problem, situation, or observation and its significance, establishing one or multiple point(s) of view, and introducing a narrator and/or characters; create a smooth progression of experiences or events.

   a. draw your readers in with a clear topic, well-developed point(s) of view, a well-developed narrator and characters, and an interesting progression of events or ideas

   b. Use narrative techniques, such as dialogue, pacing, description, reflection, and multiple plot lines, to develop experiences, events, and/or characters.

   b. use a range of literary techniques to develop and expand on events and/or characters

   c. Use a variety of techniques to sequence events so that they build on one another to create a coherent whole and build toward a particular tone and outcome (e.g., a sense of mystery, suspense, growth, or resolution).

   c. have a coherent sequence and structure that create the appropriate tone and ending for readers

   d. Use precise words and phrases, telling details, and sensory language to convey a vivid picture of the experiences, events, setting, and/or characters.

   d. use precise words, sensory details, and language in order to keep readers interested

   e. Provide a conclusion that follows from and reflects on what is experienced, observed, or resolved over the course of the narrative.

   e. have a strong and logical conclusion that reflects on the topic

PRODUCTION AND DISTRIBUTION OF WRITING

4. Produce clear and coherent writing in which the development, organization, and style are appropriate to task, purpose, and audience.

You will produce writing that is appropriate to the task, purpose, and audience for whom you are writing.

5. Develop and strengthen writing as needed by planning, revising, editing, rewriting, or trying a new approach, focusing on addressing what is most significant for a specific purpose and audience.

You will revise and refine your writing, using a variety of strategies, to address what is most important for your purpose and audience.

Common Core State Standards	What It Means to You
6. Use technology, including the Internet, to produce, publish, and update individual or shared writing products in response to ongoing feedback, including new arguments or information.	You will use technology to share your writing, provide links to other relevant information, and to update your information as needed.

RESEARCH TO BUILD AND PRESENT KNOWLEDGE

7. Conduct short as well as more sustained research projects to answer a question (including a self-generated question) or solve a problem; narrow or broaden the inquiry when appropriate; synthesize multiple sources on the subject, demonstrating understanding of the subject under investigation.	You will engage in short and more complex research tasks that include answering a question or solving a problem by using multiple sources. Your understanding of the subject will be evident in the product you develop.
8. Gather relevant information from multiple authoritative print and digital sources, using advanced searches effectively; assess the strengths and limitations of each source in terms of the task, purpose, and audience; integrate information into the text selectively to maintain the flow of ideas, avoiding plagiarism and overreliance on any one source and following a standard format for citation.	You will effectively conduct searches to gather information from a variety of print and digital sources and will evaluate each source in terms of the goal of your research. You will appropriately cite your sources of information and will follow a standard format for citation, such as the MLA or APA guidelines.

Common Core State Standards	What It Means to You

RESEARCH TO BUILD AND PRESENT KNOWLEDGE

9. Draw evidence from literary or informational texts to support analysis, reflection, and research.

   a. Apply *grades 11–12 Reading standards* to literature (e.g., "Demonstrate knowledge of eighteenth-, nineteenth- and early-twentieth-century foundational works of American literature, including how two or more texts from the same period treat similar themes or topics").

   b. Apply *grades 11–12 Reading standards* to literary nonfiction (e.g., "Delineate and evaluate the reasoning in seminal U.S. texts, including the application of constitutional principles and use of legal reasoning [e.g., in U.S. Supreme Court Case majority opinions and dissents] and the premises, purposes, and arguments in works of public advocacy [e.g., *The Federalist*, presidential addresses]")

You will paraphrase, summarize, quote, and cite primary and secondary sources, using both literary and informational texts, to support your analysis, reflection, and research, for purposes including

   a. written analysis of themes, author's choices, or point of view in American literature

   b. written analysis of central ideas, text structure, word choice, point of view, or reasoning in American literary nonfiction

RANGE OF WRITING

10. Write routinely over extended time frames (time for research, reflection, and revision) and shorter time frames (a single sitting or a day or two) for a range of tasks, purposes, and audiences.

You will write a variety of texts for different purposes and audiences over both short and extended periods of time.

College and Career Readiness Anchor Standards for Speaking and Listening

Common Core State Standards

COMPREHENSION AND COLLABORATION

1. Prepare for and participate effectively in a range of conversations and collaborations with diverse partners, building on others' ideas and expressing their own clearly and persuasively.

2. Integrate and evaluate information presented in diverse media and formats, including visually, quantitatively, and orally.

3. Evaluate a speaker's point of view, reasoning, and use of evidence and rhetoric.

Common Core State Standards

PRESENTATION OF KNOWLEDGE AND IDEAS

4. Present information, findings, and supporting evidence such that listeners can follow the line of reasoning and the organization, development, and style are appropriate to task, purpose, and audience.

5. Make strategic use of digital media and visual displays of data to express information and enhance understanding of presentations.

6. Adapt speech to a variety of contexts and communicative tasks, demonstrating command of formal English when indicated or appropriate.

Speaking and Listening Standards, Grades 11–12 Students

Common Core State Standards	What It Means to You

COMPREHENSION AND COLLABORATION

1. Initiate and participate effectively in a range of collaborative discussions (one-on-one, in groups, and teacher-led) with diverse partners on grades 11–12 topics, texts, and issues, building on others' ideas and expressing their own clearly and persuasively.	You will actively participate in a variety of discussions in which you
a. Come to discussions prepared, having read and researched material under study; explicitly draw on that preparation by referring to evidence from texts and other research on the topic or issue to stimulate a thoughtful, well-reasoned exchange of ideas.	a. have read any relevant material beforehand and have come to the discussion prepared with background research
b. Work with peers to promote civil, democratic discussions and decision-making, set clear goals and deadlines, and establish individual roles as needed.	b. work with others to establish goals, processes, and roles within the group in order to have reasonable discussions
c. Propel conversations by posing and responding to questions that probe reasoning and evidence; ensure a hearing for a full range of positions on a topic or issue; clarify, verify, or challenge ideas and conclusions; and promote divergent and creative perspectives.	c. ask and respond to questions, encourage a range of positions, and relate the current topic to other relevant information and perspectives
d. Respond thoughtfully to diverse perspectives; synthesize comments, claims, and evidence made on all sides of an issue; resolve contradictions when possible; and determine what additional information or research is required to deepen the investigation or complete the task.	d. respond to different perspectives, summarize points of agreement or disagreement when needed, help to resolve unclear points, and set out a plan for additional research as needed

Common Core State Standards	What It Means to You
2. Integrate multiple sources of information presented in diverse formats and media (e.g., visually, quantitatively, orally) in order to make informed decisions and solve problems, evaluating the credibility and accuracy of each source and noting any discrepancies among the data.	You will integrate multiple and varied sources of information, assessing the credibility and accuracy of each source to aid the group-discussion process.
3. Evaluate a speaker's point of view, reasoning, and use of evidence and rhetoric, assessing the stance, premises, links among ideas, word choice, points of emphasis, and tone used.	You will evaluate a speaker's argument and analyze the nature of the speaker's reasoning or evidence.

PRESENTATION OF KNOWLEDGE AND IDEAS

Common Core State Standards	What It Means to You
4. Present information, findings, and supporting evidence, conveying a clear and distinct perspective, such that listeners can follow the line of reasoning, alternative or opposing perspectives are addressed, and the organization, development, substance, and style are appropriate to purpose, audience, and a range of formal and informal tasks.	You will organize and present information, evidence, and your perspective to your listeners in a logical sequence and style that are appropriate to your task, purpose, and audience.
5. Make strategic use of digital media (e.g., textual, graphical, audio, visual, and interactive elements) in presentations to enhance understanding of findings, reasoning, and evidence and to add interest.	You will use digital media to enhance understanding and to add interest to your presentations.
6. Adapt speech to a variety of contexts and tasks, demonstrating a command of formal English when indicated or appropriate.	You will adapt the formality of your speech appropriately, depending on its context and purpose.

College and Career Readiness Anchor Standards for Language

Common Core State Standards

CONVENTIONS OF STANDARD ENGLISH

1. Demonstrate command of the conventions of standard English grammar and usage when writing or speaking.

2. Demonstrate command of the conventions of standard English capitalization, punctuation, and spelling when writing.

Common Core State Standards

KNOWLEDGE OF LANGUAGE

3. Apply knowledge of language to understand how language functions in different contexts, to make effective choices for meaning or style, and to comprehend more fully when reading or listening.

VOCABULARY ACQUISITION AND USE

4. Determine or clarify the meaning of unknown and multiple-meaning words and phrases by using context clues, analyzing meaningful word parts, and consulting general and specialized reference materials, as appropriate.

5. Demonstrate understanding of word relationships and nuances in word meanings.

6. Acquire and use accurately a range of general academic and domain-specific words and phrases sufficient for reading, writing, speaking, and listening at the college and career readiness level; demonstrate independence in gathering vocabulary knowledge when considering a word or phrase important to comprehension or expression.

Language Standards, Grades 11–12 Students

Common Core State Standards	What It Means to You
CONVENTIONS OF STANDARD ENGLISH	

1. Demonstrate command of the conventions of standard English grammar and usage when writing or speaking.
   a. Apply the understanding that usage is a matter of convention, can change over time, and is sometimes contested.
   b. Resolve issues of complex or contested usage, consulting references (e.g., *Merriam-Webster's Dictionary of English Usage, Garner's Modern American Usage*) as needed.
	You will correctly use the conventions of English grammar and usage, including
	   a. demonstrating that usage follows accepted standards and can change or be contested
	   b. using references to resolve disagreements or uncertainty about usage

2. Demonstrate command of the conventions of standard English capitalization, punctuation, and spelling when writing.
   a. Observe hyphenation conventions.
   b. Spell correctly.
	You will correctly use the conventions of standard English capitalization, punctuation, and spelling, including
	   a. hyphens
	   b. spelling

Common Core State Standards	What It Means to You

KNOWLEDGE OF LANGUAGE

3. Apply knowledge of language to understand how language functions in different contexts, to make effective choices for meaning or style, and to comprehend more fully when reading or listening.

   a. Vary syntax for effect, consulting references (e.g., Tufte's *Artful Sentences*) for guidance as needed; apply an understanding of syntax to the study of complex texts when reading.

You will apply your knowledge of language in different contexts to guide choices in your own writing and speaking by

   a. using appropriate references for guidance to vary your syntax and to understand syntax in complex texts

VOCABULARY ACQUISITION AND USE

4. Determine or clarify the meaning of unknown and multiple-meaning words and phrases based on grades 11–12 reading and content, choosing flexibly from a range of strategies.

   a. Use context (e.g., the overall meaning of a sentence, paragraph, or text; a word's position or function in a sentence) as a clue to the meaning of a word or phrase.

   b. Identify and correctly use patterns of word changes that indicate different meanings or parts of speech (e.g., *conceive, conception, conceivable*).

   c. Consult general and specialized reference materials (e.g., dictionaries, glossaries, thesauruses), both print and digital, to find the pronunciation of a word or determine or clarify its precise meaning, its part of speech, its etymology, or its standard usage.

   d. Verify the preliminary determination of the meaning of a word or phrase (e.g., by checking the inferred meaning in context or in a dictionary).

You will understand the meaning of grade-level appropriate words and phrases by

   a. using context clues

   b. applying various forms of words according to meaning or part of speech

   c. using reference materials to determine and clarify word meaning, part of speech, etymology, and standard usage

   d. inferring and verifying the meanings of words in context

Common Core State Standards	What It Means to You
VOCABULARY ACQUISITION AND USE	
5. Demonstrate understanding of figurative language, word relationships, and nuances in word meanings. a. Interpret figures of speech (e.g., hyperbole, paradox) in context and analyze their role in the text. b. Analyze nuances in the meaning of words with similar denotations.	You will understand figurative language, word relationships, and slight differences in word meanings by a. interpreting figures of speech in context b. analyzing slight differences in the meanings of similar words
6. Acquire and use accurately general academic and domain-specific words and phrases, sufficient for reading, writing, speaking, and listening at the college and career readiness level; demonstrate independence in gathering vocabulary knowledge when considering a word or phrase important to comprehension or expression.	You will develop and use a range of vocabulary at the college and career readiness level and will demonstrate that you can successfully acquire new vocabulary independently.

Image Credits: ©Jonathan Griffith/Aurora Photos/Corbis

Chasing Success

"If your success is not on your own terms, if it looks good to the world but does not feel good in your heart, it is not success at all."

—Anna Quindlen

CONNECTING WORD AND IMAGE

ASK STUDENTS to discuss how the collection opener image and the collection quotation work together to create a connection.

PERFORMANCE TASK PREVIEW

Point out to students that they will complete two performance tasks at the end of the collection. The performance tasks will require them to further analyze the selections in the collection and to synthesize ideas about these analyses. They will present their findings in a variety of products.

ACADEMIC VOCABULARY

View It!

Professional Development Podcast:

Academic Vocabulary

Students can acquire facility with the academic vocabulary words through frequent, repeated exposure as they analyze and discuss the selections in the collection. Academic vocabulary can be used in the following instructional contexts. This will enable students to incorporate the academic vocabulary words into their working vocabulary.

- Collaborative Discussion at the end of each selection
- Analyzing the Text questions for each selection
- Selection-level Performance Task
- Vocabulary instruction (for Critical Vocabulary and/or for Vocabulary Strategy)
- Language and Style
- End-of-collection Performance Task for all selections in the collection

ASK STUDENTS to review the Academic Vocabulary word list for this collection. You may wish to pronounce each word aloud, so students hear the correct pronunciation. Then, discuss the definitions and the related forms for each word. Remind students that they will encounter these five academic vocabulary words throughout the collection.

Chasing Success

Success may be sweet, but as this collection shows, it sometimes requires great sacrifice.

fyi
hmhfyi.com

COLLECTION

PERFORMANCE TASK Preview

At the end of this collection, you will have the opportunity to complete two tasks:

- Debate with classmates the merits of extending the school year to provide more time for learning, citing evidence from texts in the collection.

- Write an essay in which you compare and contrast the experiences of two characters or people from the texts, focusing on the sacrifices they make to succeed.

ACADEMIC VOCABULARY

Study the words and their definitions in the chart below. You will use these words as you discuss and write about the texts in this collection.

Word	Definition	Related Forms
accumulate (ə-kyoom´yə-lāt´) *v.*	to gather or pile up	accumulation, accumulative
appreciation (ə-prē´shē-ā´shən) *n.*	recognition of the quality, significance, or value of someone or something	appreciable, appreciate, appreciative
conform (kən-form´) *v.*	to be similar to or match something or someone; to act or be in accord or agreement	conformable, conformance, conformation, conformist, conformity
persistence (pər-sĭs´təns) *n.*	the act or quality of holding firmly to a purpose or task in spite of obstacles	persist, persistency, persistent
reinforce (rē´ĭn-fors) *v.*	to strengthen; to give more force to	reinforcement, reinforcer

2

USING COLLECTIONS YOUR WAY

Use the following information, along with the charts on the following pages, to help you decide how you want to introduce the collection. Based on your teaching style, your students' interests, or your instructional goals, you may want to structure this collection in various ways. You may choose different entry points each time you teach the collection.

"I emphasize informational texts."

This essay is a discussion of why some students are successful and others are not. **Malcolm Gladwell** approaches the subject by discussing various philosophies of education and relating those ideas to the practices and results of a particular school in the South Bronx.

Malcolm Gladwell (b. 1963) was born to an English father and a Jamaican mother. He grew up in rural Ontario, Canada. The author of several bestselling books, he is a staff writer for The New Yorker. Gladwell typically analyzes aspects of daily life, offering intriguing ideas about social phenomena and human behavior. "Marita's Bargain" is excerpted from Gladwell's third book, Outliers: The Story of Success, in which he explores the reasons why some people achieve success and others do not.

Marita's Bargain

Essay by Malcolm Gladwell

AS YOU READ Pay attention to details that describe KIPP students. Write down any questions you generate during reading.

In the mid-1990s, an experimental public school called the KIPP Academy opened on the fourth floor of Lou Gehrig Junior High School in New York City.[1] Lou Gehrig is in the seventh school district, otherwise known as the South Bronx, one of the poorest neighborhoods in New York City. It is a squat, gray 1960s-era building across the street from a bleak-looking group of high-rises. A few blocks over is Grand Concourse, the borough's main thoroughfare. These are not streets that you'd happily walk down, alone, after dark.

KIPP is a middle school. Classes are large: the fifth grade has two sections of thirty-five students each. There are no entrance exams or admissions requirements. Students are chosen by lottery, with any fourth grader living in the Bronx eligible to apply. Roughly half of the students are African American; the rest are Hispanic. Three-quarters of the children come from single-parent homes. Ninety percent qualify for "free or reduced lunch," which is to say that their families earn

[1] KIPP: "Knowledge Is Power Program," a national organization of charter schools.

Marita's Bargain   3

"I like to use a digital product as a starting point."

Michael Lewis delivered this speech at the Princeton graduation ceremonies in 2012. He discusses the role of accident and luck in the context of success. The point he tries to make to the graduating class is that people who are lucky "owe a debt" to the unlucky.

Michael Lewis (b. 1960) is the author of several bestselling books, including The Blind Side and Moneyball, both of which were made into successful movies. In his first book, Liar's Poker, he examines Wall Street practices based on his personal experiences as an investment banker. Lewis is a contributing editor for Vanity Fair and writes for The New York Times as well as other publications. A graduate of Princeton University, he returned to the school in 2012 during graduation weekend to deliver the baccalaureate address recorded in this video.

MEDIA ANALYSIS

Don't Eat Fortune's Cookie

Graduation Speech by Michael Lewis

AS YOU VIEW Pay attention to Lewis's ideas about success and rewards.

COLLABORATIVE DISCUSSION What ideas does Lewis express about success and how people are rewarded? With a partner, discuss how these ideas relate to students preparing to graduate from college.

Don't Eat Fortune's Cookie   19

"I rely heavily on novels and longer works."

Jamaica Kincaid's character, Annie John, muses about leaving Antigua to go to nursing school in England. Although Annie professes to be delighted that she is leaving, her inner dialogue reveals that she is nervous and will probably miss the island and her parents.

Jamaica Kincaid (b. 1949) was born Elaine Potter Richardson on the Caribbean island of Antigua in 1949. She left at seventeen to work in New York City. After a series of jobs, she became a writer for The New Yorker. In 1985, she published her first novel, Annie John, the last chapter of which is "A Walk to the Jetty." Like Kincaid herself, the protagonist is emotionally estranged from her mother at a young age. Kincaid revisits this theme often in her works. She also expresses her abhorrence of British colonial rule in Antigua, most notably in the nonfiction work A Small Place, which excited controversy for its deeply angry tone.

A Walk to the Jetty

from Annie John

Novel by Jamaica Kincaid

AS YOU READ Look for details that tell you how the narrator feels about the people and places in her life.

"My name is Annie John." These were the first words that came into my mind as I woke up on the morning of the last day I spent in Antigua, and they stayed there, lined up one behind the other, marching up and down, for I don't know how long. At noon on that day, a ship on which I was to be a passenger would sail to Barbados, and there I would board another ship, which would sail to England, where I would study to become a nurse. My name was the last thing I saw the night before, just as I was falling asleep; it was written in big black letters all over my trunk, sometimes followed by my address in Antigua, sometimes followed by my address as it would be in England. I did not want to go to England, I did not want to be a nurse, but I would have chosen going off to live in a cavern and keeping house for seven unruly men rather than go on with my life as it stood. I never wanted to lie in this bed again, my legs hanging out way past the foot of it, tossing and turning on my mattress, with its cotton stuffing all lumped just where it wasn't a good place to be lumped. I never wanted to lie in my bed again and hear Mr. Ephraim driving his sheep to pasture—a signal to my mother that she should get up to prepare my father's and my bath and breakfast. I never wanted to lie in my bed and

A Walk to the Jetty   31

mySmartPlanner | **eBook** | **myNotebook** | **my WriteSmart** | **fyi** hmhfyi.com

Collection 1 Lessons	Media	Teach and Practice
Student Edition | eBook	▶ Video Links HISTORY A&E	**Close Reading and Evidence Tracking**
ANCHOR TEXT — Essay by Malcolm Gladwell *"Marita's Bargain"*	🔊 **Audio** "Marita's Bargain"	**Close Read Screencasts** • Modeled Discussion 1 (lines 103–115) • Modeled Discussion 2 (lines 343–357) • Close Read application pdf (lines 387–394)	**Strategies for Annotation** • Support Inferences: Draw Conclusions • Analyze Word Choice • Determine Central Ideas • Context Clues
CLOSE READER — Book Excerpt by Paul Tough *Kewauna's Ambition*	🔊 **Audio** *Kewauna's Ambition*		
Graduation Speech by Michael Lewis *"Don't Eat Fortune's Cookie"*	🔊 **Audio** "Don't Eat Fortune's Cookie"		
CLOSE READER — Op-ed by Kay Bailey Hutchinson and Barbara Mikulski "A Right to Choose Single-Sex Education"	🔊 **Audio** "A Right to Choose Single-Sex Education"		
Science Article by Carol S. Dweck *"The Secret to Raising Smart Kids"*	🔊 **Audio** "The Secret to Raising Smart Kids"		**Strategies for Annotation** • Analyze Structure: Argument • Prefixes with Multiple Meanings
ANCHOR TEXT — Novel by Jamaica Kincaid *"A Walk to the Jetty"* from *Annie John*	🔊 **Audio** "A Walk to the Jetty" from *Annie John*	**Close Read Screencasts** • Modeled Discussion 1 (lines 13–22) • Modeled Discussion 2 (lines 304–313) • Close Read application pdf (lines 356–365)	**Strategies for Annotation** • Analyze Word Choice
CLOSE READER — Short Story by Penelope Lively *"Next Term, We'll Mash You"*	🔊 **Audio** "Next Term, We'll Mash You"		
Drama by Eugene O'Neill *ILE*	🔊 **Audio** *ILE*		**Strategies for Annotation** • Analyze Drama Elements: Character • Analyze Drama Elements: Conflict
Opera by Ezra Donner Media Versions of *ILE* Production Image Media Versions of *ILE*	🔊 **Audio** *ILE*		
Collection 1 Performance Tasks: **A** Debate an Issue **B** Write a Compare-Contrast Essay	**fyi** hmhfyi.com	**Interactive Lessons** **A** Writing an Argument **A** Participating in Collaborative Discussions	**B** Writing as a Process **B** Using Textual Evidence

	For Systematic Coverage of Writing and Speaking & Listening Standards	**Interactive Lessons** Writing as a Process Participating in Collaborative Discussions	**Lesson Assessments** Writing as a Process Participating in Collaborative Discussions

Assess		Extend	Reteach
Performance Task	**Online Assessment**	**Teacher eBook**	**Teacher eBook**
Writing Activity: Diary	Selection Test	**Integrate and Evaluate Information**	**Determine Central Ideas > Level Up Tutorial >** Main Idea and Supporting Details
Writing Activity: Review	Selection Test	**Making Inferences**	**Making Inferences > Level Up Tutorial >** Making Inferences
Writing Activity	Selection Test	**Summarize a Text > Interactive Whiteboard Lesson >** Evaluating an Argument	**Analyze Structure: Argument > Level Up Tutorial >** Analyzing Arguments
Writing Activity: Letter	Selection Test	**Analyze Story Elements: Setting> Interactive Whiteboard Lessons >** Role of Setting	**Analyze Word Choice: Tone> Level Up Tutorial >** Tone
Speaking Activity	Selection Test	**Analyze Theme > Interactive Whiteboard Lesson >** Analyze Theme	**Analyze Drama Elements: Symbol > Level Up Tutorial >** Symbols and Allegories
• Writing Activity: Critique • Media Activity: Set Design	Selection Test	**Cite Textual Evidence** **Participate in Collaborative Discussions > Interactive Lesson >** Participating in Collaborative Discussions **Present Information to Support a Viewpoint > Interactive Lesson >** Giving a Presentation	**Analyze Interpretations of Drama > Level Up Tutorial >** Elements of Drama
A Debate an Issue **B** Write a Compare-Contrast Essay	Collection Test		

Collection 1 Lessons	Key Learning Objective	Performance Task
ANCHOR TEXT **Essay by Malcolm Gladwell** **"Marita's Bargain," p. 3A** Lexile 1060L	**The student will be able to...** determine central ideas and integrate and evaluate information in an essay.	Writing Activity: Diary
Graduation Speech by Michael Lewis **"Don't Eat Fortune's Cookie," p. 19A**	**The student will be able to...** cite text evidence to support inferences.	Writing Activity: Review
Science Article by Carol S. Dweck Lexile 1400L **"The Secret to Raising Smart Kids," p. 21A**	**The student will be able to...** support inferences.	Writing Activity
ANCHOR TEXT Lexile 1290L **Novel by Jamaica Kincaid** **"A Walk to the Jetty" from *Annie John*, p. 31A**	**The student will be able to...** analyze the impact of an author's word choices and cite text evidence to support inferences.	Writing Activity: Letter
Drama by Eugene O'Neill ***ILE*, p. 47A**	**The student will be able to...** analyze elements of a drama, including conflict and symbolism.	Speaking Activity
Opera by Ezra Donner **Media Versions of *ILE*, p. 63A** **Production Image** **Media Versions of *ILE*, p. 65A**	**The student will be able to...** compare and analyze how a drama is interpreted in different mediums.	• Writing Activity: Critique • Media Activity: Set Design

Collection 1 Performance Tasks:
A Debate an Issue
B Write a Compare-Contrast Essay

Vocabulary Strategy	Language and Style	Student Instructional Support	CLOSE READER Selection
Context Clues	Subject-Verb Agreement	**Scaffolding for ELL Students:** • Vocabulary: Context Clues • Support Inferences **To Challenge Students:** Analyze a Theory **When Students Struggle:** • Central Ideas and Supporting Details • Cause and Effect	Book Excerpt by Paul Tough *Kewauna's Ambition*, p. 18b **Lexile 1220L**
		Scaffolding for ELL Students: Support Inferences	Op-ed by Kay Bailey Hutchinson and Barbara Mikulski "A Right to Choose Single-Sex Education," p. 20b **Lexile 1200L**
Prefixes with Multiple Meanings	Participles and Participial Phrases	**Scaffolding for ELL Students:** • Vocabulary: Multiple-Meaning Words • Comprehension: Structure of Argument **When Students Struggle:** • Compare and Contrast • Determine Information Validity **To Challenge Students:** Evaluate Sentence Structure	
Etymology	Dashes	**Scaffolding for ELL Students:** • Vocabulary: Figurative Language; Phrasal Verbs; Idioms; Multiple-Meaning Words • Language: Verb Tenses **When Students Struggle:** • Main Clause • Fluent Reading **To Challenge Students:** • Compare Points of View • Explore Nuances of Meaning	Short Story by Penelope Lively "Next Term, We'll Mash You," p. 46b **Lexile 780L**
	Dialect	**Scaffolding for ELL Students:** • Vocabulary: Context Clues; Idioms • Comprehension: Dialect • Language: Verb Usage **When Students Struggle:** • Set and Stage Directions • Compare and Contrast • Symbolic Meaning **To Challenge Students:** • Examine Arguments • Analyze Structure	
		Scaffolding for ELL Students: Analyze Interpretations of a Drama **When Students Struggle:** Compare and Contrast	

mySmartPlanner   Create lesson plans and access resources online.

ANCHOR TEXT   Marita's Bargain

Essay by Malcolm Gladwell

Why This Text?

Whether reading information in print or online, students need to be able to identify the most important ideas. This lesson analyzes how the details and other elements of this essay deliver the author's significant points about education.

Key Learning Objective: The student will be able to determine central ideas and integrate and evaluate information in an essay.

For additional practice:

Close Reader selection
"Kewauna's Ambition,"
Book Excerpt by Paul Tough

COMMON CORE   Common Core Standards

RI 1   Cite textual evidence to support analysis and inferences.

RI 2   Determine two or more central ideas of a text.

RI 4   Determine meaning of words and phrases as used in a text.

RI 5   Analyze and evaluate the structure an author uses in his or her exposition or argument.

RI 7   Integrate and evaluate multiple sources of information.

W 3a   Create a smooth progression of experiences or events.

W 3d   Use precise words and phrases.

L 1   Demonstrate command of the conventions of standard English grammar and usage.

L 4a   Use context as a clue to the meaning of a word or phrase.

▲ Text Complexity Rubric

Quantitative Measures	**Marita's Bargain** Lexile: 1060L
Qualitative Measures	**Levels of Meaning/Purpose** single topic
	Structure some sophisticated graphics, occasionally essential to understanding of the text
	Language Conventionality and Clarity straightforward sentence structure
	Knowledge Demands some specialized knowledge required
Reader/Task Considerations	Teacher determined Vary by individual reader and type of text

CLOSE READ

Malcolm Gladwell Have students read the information about the author. Explain to them that in his book *Outliers*, Gladwell questions the Horatio Alger myth—that a person can achieve success solely by virtue of ability and hard work. His case studies suggest another explanation for success, which is that "outliers," those who have risen above their peers in various fields, have had opportunities not necessarily afforded to others. They have also had the presence of mind and the talent to make the most of those advantages.

AS YOU READ Direct students to use the As You Read direction to focus their reading.

Determine Central Ideas   COMMON CORE RI 2

(LINES 1–17)

Tell students that the author of an essay includes only those details that will help accomplish his or her **purpose,** or reason for writing.

 CITE TEXT EVIDENCE Have students reread the first two paragraphs and explain why Gladwell includes this information. What idea about KIPP students does he want to convey? *(He provides the context to help readers understand the obstacles standing in the way of success for the "typical" KIPP student, such as a sometimes dangerous outside environment and limited family income.)*

Integrate and Evaluate Information   COMMON CORE RI 7

(LINES 9–17)

Explain that in his essay, Gladwell provides readers with specific factual information. He chooses different formats, or methods of presentation, to communicate these facts clearly and in a way that will make the most sense to his readers.

 ASK STUDENTS to reread the second paragraph of the essay, noting the statistics presented within the text. Why does Gladwell choose to write out this data rather than insert a table or chart? *(The statistics are fairly simple and can be stated clearly. Including numbers in the text encourages readers to pay closer attention to what they are reading. He may not have wanted to interrupt the flow of his essay with a graphic aid so close to the beginning.)*

Malcolm Gladwell *(b. 1963) was born to an English father and a Jamaican mother. He grew up in rural Ontario, Canada. The author of several bestselling books, he is a staff writer for* The New Yorker. *Gladwell typically analyzes aspects of daily life, offering intriguing ideas about social phenomena and human behavior. "Marita's Bargain" is excerpted from Gladwell's third book,* Outliers: The Story of Success, *in which he explores the reasons why some people achieve success and others do not.*

Marita's Bargain

Essay by Malcolm Gladwell

AS YOU READ Pay attention to details that describe KIPP students. Write down any questions you generate during reading.

 In the mid-1990s, an experimental public school called the KIPP Academy opened on the fourth floor of Lou Gehrig Junior High School in New York City.[1] Lou Gehrig is in the seventh school district, otherwise known as the South Bronx, one of the poorest neighborhoods in New York City. It is a squat, gray 1960s-era building across the street from a bleak-looking group of high-rises. A few blocks over is Grand Concourse, the borough's main thoroughfare. These are not streets that you'd happily walk down, alone, after dark.

10 KIPP is a middle school. Classes are large: the fifth grade has two sections of thirty-five students each. There are no entrance exams or admissions requirements. Students are chosen by lottery, with any fourth grader living in the Bronx eligible to apply. Roughly half of the students are African American; the rest are Hispanic. Three-quarters of the children come from single-parent homes. Ninety percent qualify for "free or reduced lunch," which is to say that their families earn

Image Credits: ©Edd Westmacott/Photoshot/Getty Images

---

[1] **KIPP:** "Knowledge Is Power Program," a national organization of charter schools.

Marita's Bargain   **3**

 Close Read Screencasts   ▶ *View It!*

Modeled Discussions

Have students click the *Close Read* icons in their eBooks to access two screencasts in which readers discuss and annotate the following key passages:

- explanation of the connection between Western agriculture and long summer vacations (lines 103–115)
- Marita's account of her demanding schedule (lines 343–357)

As a class, view and discuss at least one of these videos. Then have students pair up to do an independent close read of an additional passage—Gladwell's conclusion (lines 387–394).

TEACH

CLOSE READ

Determine Central Ideas COMMON CORE RI 2

(LINES 18–30)

Tell students that knowing Gladwell's perspective, or viewpoint, on his topic can help readers better understand the central ideas he wants to communicate. Remind students that words showing a judgment or opinion reveal perspective.

 CITE TEXT EVIDENCE Have students identify statements or phrases from this passage that reveal Gladwell's perspective on the KIPP Academy. *("it's clear that something is different," "hundreds of pennants from the colleges," "KIPP has become one of the most desirable public schools in New York City")*

Integrate and Evaluate Information COMMON CORE RI 7
(LINES 31–45)

Point out that in this passage, Gladwell again chooses to present statistics within the text.

 ASK STUDENTS to explain the two important numerical facts in this paragraph. How do these facts add to the picture that Gladwell is building of the KIPP Academy? *(Only 16 percent of South Bronx middle school students perform at or above their grade level in math; in the KIPP Academy, by eighth grade, 84 percent are performing at or above grade level in math. These numbers illustrate that KIPP Academy is a successful educational institution.)*

CRITICAL VOCABULARY

motley: Although the KIPP students share similar economic and social circumstances, they have varying levels of ability and diverse academic backgrounds.

ASK STUDENTS why the use of *motley* to describe these students is crucial to understanding Gladwell's point in this sentence. *(He wants readers to know that the students are not selected on the basis of their mathematical ability. Considering the students' motley backgrounds and abilities, the high rate of success in mathematics is even more amazing.)*

---

so little that the federal government chips in so the children can eat properly at lunchtime.

C 20 KIPP Academy seems like the kind of school in the kind of neighborhood with the kind of student that would make educators despair—except that the minute you enter the building, it's clear that something is different. The students walk quietly down the hallways in single file. In the classroom, they are taught to turn and address anyone talking to them in a protocol known as "SSLANT": smile, sit up, listen, ask questions, nod when being spoken to, and track with your eyes. On the walls of the school's corridors are hundreds of pennants from the colleges that KIPP graduates have gone on to attend. Last year, hundreds of families from across the Bronx entered the lottery for KIPP's two fifth-grade classes. It is no exaggeration to say that just over ten years into its existence, KIPP has become one of

30 the most desirable public schools in New York City.

D What KIPP is most famous for is mathematics. In the South Bronx, only about 16 percent of all middle school students are performing at or above their grade level in math. But at KIPP, by the end of fifth grade, many of the students call math their favorite subject. In seventh grade, KIPP students start *high school* algebra. By the end of eighth grade, 84 percent of the students are performing at or above their grade level, which is to say that this **motley** group of randomly chosen lower-income kids from dingy apartments in one of the country's worst neighborhoods—whose parents, in an

40 overwhelming number of cases, never set foot in a college—do as well in mathematics as the privileged eighth graders of America's wealthy suburbs. "Our kids' reading is on point," said David Levin, who founded KIPP with a fellow teacher, Michael Feinberg, in 1994. "They struggle a little bit with writing skills. But when they leave here, they rock in math."

There are now more than fifty KIPP schools across the United States, with more on the way. The KIPP program represents one of the most promising new educational philosophies in the United States. But its success is best understood not in terms of its curriculum, its

50 teachers, its resources, or some kind of institutional innovation. KIPP is, rather, an organization that has succeeded by taking the idea of cultural legacies seriously.

In the early nineteenth century, a group of reformers set out to establish a system of public education in the United States. What passed for public school at the time was a haphazard assortment of locally run one-room schoolhouses and overcrowded urban classrooms scattered around the country. In rural areas, schools closed in the spring and fall and ran all summer long, so that children could help out in the busy planting and harvesting seasons. In the city, many

60 schools mirrored the long and chaotic schedules of the children's working-class parents. The reformers wanted to make sure that all

motley
(mŏt´lē) *adj.* unusually varied or mixed.

4 Collection 1

SCAFFOLDING FOR ELL STUDENTS

Vocabulary: Context Clues Read aloud lines 1–45 while students follow along in the text. Have students assist you in a think-aloud, and work through context clues that clarify the meaning of unfamiliar terms. Say:

- (Lines 1-3) I can tell *KIPP* is an acronym, a word created by using the initial letters in a series of words, because it's all capital letters. How can I find out what it stands for? *(A footnote at the bottom of the page has an explanation for KIPP.)*

- I see that "Concourse" must be a "thoroughfare" (line 7), but I don't know what either word means. *(The sentences before and after are talking about streets; these must be words for "street.")*

4 Collection 1

> **"** Just over ten years into its existence, KIPP has become one of the most desirable public schools in New York City. **"**

children went to school and that public school was comprehensive, meaning that all children got enough schooling to learn how to read and write and do basic arithmetic and function as productive citizens.

But as the historian Kenneth Gold has pointed out, the early educational reformers were also tremendously concerned that children not get *too much* schooling. In 1871, for example, the US commissioner of education published a report by Edward Jarvis on the "Relation of Education to Insanity." Jarvis had studied 1,741 cases
70 of insanity and concluded that "over-study" was responsible for 205 of them. "Education lays the foundation of a large portion of the causes of mental disorder," Jarvis wrote. Similarly, the pioneer of public education in Massachusetts, Horace Mann, believed that working students too hard would create a "most pernicious influence upon character and habits. . . . Not infrequently is health itself destroyed by overstimulating the mind." In the education journals of the day, there were constant worries about overtaxing students or blunting their natural abilities through too much schoolwork.

The reformers, Gold writes:

80 strove for ways to reduce time spent studying, because long periods of respite could save the mind from injury. Hence the elimination of Saturday classes, the shortening of the school day, and the lengthening of vacation—all of which occurred over the course of the nineteenth century. Teachers were cautioned that "when [students] are required to study, their bodies should not be exhausted by long confinement, nor their minds bewildered by prolonged application." Rest also presented particular opportunities for strengthening **cognitive** and analytical skills. As one contributor to the *Massachusetts Teacher* suggested, "it is
90 when thus relieved from the state of tension belonging to actual study that boys and girls, as well as men and women, acquire the habit of thought and reflection, and of forming their own conclusions, independently of what they are taught and the authority of others."

cognitive
(kŏg′nĭ-tĭv) *adj.*
related to knowledge
or understanding.

Marita's Bargain **5**

APPLYING ACADEMIC VOCABULARY

reinforce	conform

As you discuss Gladwell's essay, incorporate these Collection 1 academic vocabulary words: *reinforce* and *conform*. Ask students to identify details in the essay that **reinforce** the idea that KIPP Academy is successfully educating its students. Then ask them to explain how the typical school year in effect today **conforms** to the 19th-century notion that students need intervals of rest.

Determine Central Ideas (LINES 65-94)

 COMMON CORE **RI 2**

Tell students that paragraphs, passages, and sections of a text all have main ideas. These main ideas contribute to the "bigger" central idea of the longer passage or the entire text. Explain that to find the main idea of any part of a work, readers must examine the details carefully to see what shared idea they develop.

E ASK STUDENTS to state the main idea of these two paragraphs. (*The 19th-century belief that students needed long periods of rest influenced the development of the American system of education.*)

Integrate and Evaluate Information (LINES 65–78)

 COMMON CORE **RI 7**

Point out the direct quotations that Gladwell includes in this part of the essay.

F ASK STUDENTS to explain how these quotations affect their understanding of the ideas in this part of the text. (*The use of direct quotations helps readers see firsthand how sincere early educators were about not "stressing" students. The quotations build understanding of the historical context of education in America.*)

> **CRITICAL VOCABULARY**
>
> **cognitive:** Educational reformers in the 19th century believed that breaks from school enabled students to develop their habits of reflection and independent thinking, thereby increasing their potential for retaining knowledge.
>
> **ASK STUDENTS** what kinds of activities could be done outside of school that would help strengthen cognitive skills while providing a break from the routine of classes. (*Reading, writing in a journal, participating in book clubs, and playing word or strategy games might help strengthen the ability to retain knowledge and increase understanding.*)

Support Inferences: Draw Conclusions

COMMON CORE RI 1

(LINES 95–115)

Remind students that they can draw conclusions, or make judgments, from the details in a text.

 ASK STUDENTS what conclusion Gladwell wants readers to draw about the Asian work ethic from the details in this passage. (*Asians view work as a part of their lives; they do not see it as something that they need a rest from.*)

Integrate and Evaluate Information (TABLE)

COMMON CORE RI 7

Explain that authors sometimes choose to present information quantitatively in a table, chart, or graph.

H **CITE TEXT EVIDENCE** Have students identify the disparities that this choice of a table format enables readers to see. (*They can see that the achievement gap between each class grows over the five-year period.*)

CRITICAL VOCABULARY

inviolate: According to Gladwell, the long summer vacation is so entrenched in the American culture that it will never be changed.

ASK STUDENTS to explain Gladwell's opinion as to whether summer vacation should remain inviolate. (*He feels that it is detrimental to many students' academic progress and therefore should be reconsidered or changed.*)

G This idea—that effort must be balanced by rest—could not be more different from Asian notions about study and work, of course. But then again, the Asian worldview was shaped by the rice paddy. In the Pearl River Delta, the rice farmer planted two and sometimes three crops a year.[2] The land was fallow only briefly. In fact, one of 100 the singular features of rice cultivation is that because of the nutrients carried by the water used in irrigation, the more a plot of land is cultivated, the more fertile it gets.

But in Western agriculture, the opposite is true. Unless a wheat- or cornfield is left fallow every few years, the soil becomes exhausted. Every winter, fields are empty. The hard labor of spring planting and fall harvesting is followed, like clockwork, by the slower pace of summer and winter. This is the logic the reformers applied to the cultivation of young minds. We formulate new ideas by analogy, working from what we know toward what we don't know, and what 110 the reformers knew were the rhythms of the agricultural seasons. A mind must be cultivated. But not too much, lest it be exhausted. And what was the remedy for the dangers of exhaustion? The long summer vacation—a peculiar and distinctive American legacy that has had profound consequences for the learning patterns of the students of the present day.

Summer vacation is a topic seldom mentioned in American educational debates. It is considered a permanent and **inviolate** feature of school life, like high school football or the senior prom. But take a look at the following sets of elementary school test-score results, and 120 see if your faith in the value of long summer holidays isn't profoundly shaken.

These numbers come from research led by the Johns Hopkins University sociologist Karl Alexander. Alexander tracked the progress of 650 first graders from the Baltimore public school system, looking at how they scored on a widely used math- and reading-skills exam called the California Achievement Test. These are reading scores for the first five years of elementary school, broken down by socioeconomic class—low, middle, and high.

inviolate
(ĭn-vī′ə-lĭt) *adj.* secure against change or violation.

H

Class	1st Grade	2nd Grade	3rd Grade	4th Grade	5th Grade
Low	329	375	397	433	461
Middle	348	388	425	467	497
High	361	418	460	506	534

Look at the first column. The students start in first grade with 130 meaningful, but not overwhelming, differences in their knowledge and

[2] **rice paddy . . . three crops a year:** The Pearl River Delta is an area in southeastern China where the Pearl River enters the South China Sea. It contains many rice paddies, flooded land used to grow rice.

Support Inferences: Draw Conclusions

COMMON CORE RI 1

Have students follow these steps for analysis of lines 95–115, using their eBook annotation tools:

- Highlight in yellow details that describe Asian agriculture.
- Highlight in blue features of Western agriculture. (*lines 104–108*)
- On a note, identify the differences between them. Use the notes to draw conclusions about the significance of the two different approaches to work.

In the Pearl River Delta, the rice farmer planted two and sometimes three crops a year. The land was fallow only briefly. In fact, one of the singular features of rice cultivation is that because of the nutrients carried by the water used in irrigation, the more a plot of land is cultivated, the more fertile it gets.

ability. The first graders from the wealthiest homes have a 32-point advantage over the first graders from the poorest homes—and by the way, first graders from poor homes in Baltimore are *really* poor. Now look at the fifth-grade column. By that point, four years later, the initially modest gap between rich and poor has more than doubled.

This "achievement gap" is a phenomenon that has been observed over and over again, and it typically provokes one of two responses. The first response is that disadvantaged kids simply don't have the same inherent ability to learn as children from more privileged 140 backgrounds. They're not as smart. The second, slightly more optimistic conclusion is that, in some way, our schools are failing poor children: we simply aren't doing a good enough job of teaching them the skills they need. But here's where Alexander's study gets interesting, because it turns out that neither of those explanations rings true.

The city of Baltimore didn't give its kids the California Achievement Test just at the end of every school year, in June. It gave them the test in September too, just after summer vacation ended. What Alexander realized is that the second set of test results allowed 150 him to do a slightly different analysis. If he looked at the difference between the score a student got at the beginning of the school year, in September, and the score he or she got the following June, he could measure—precisely—how much that student learned over the school year. And if he looked at the difference between a student's score in June and then in the following September, he could see how much that student learned over the course of the summer. In other words, he could figure out—at least in part—how much of the achievement gap is the result of things that happen during the school year, and how much it has to do with what happens during summer vacation.

160 Let's start with the school-year gains. This table shows how many points students' test scores rose from the time they started classes in September to the time they stopped in June. The "Total" column represents their cumulative classroom learning from all five years of elementary school.

Class	1st Grade	2nd Grade	3rd Grade	4th Grade	5th Grade	Total
Low	55	46	30	33	25	189
Middle	69	43	34	41	27	214
High	60	39	34	28	23	184

Here is a completely different story from the one suggested by the first table. The first set of test results made it look like lower-income kids were somehow failing in the classroom. But here we see plainly that isn't true. Look at the "Total" column. Over the course of five years of elementary school, poor kids "out-learn" the wealthiest kids

CLOSE READ

Integrate and Evaluate Information (TABLE)

COMMON CORE RI 7

Point out that tables often have titles that tell what the numbers refer to. However, Gladwell has chosen not to give titles to his tables. Instead, the text immediately before and after each table explains what is included and why it is significant.

CITE TEXT EVIDENCE Ask students what title they would give the table on this page to describe its contents, and point to the evidence that supports their title. *(Possible response: "Learning Gains During the School Year" because, according to the text, the table deals with gains between September and June.)*

TO CHALLENGE STUDENTS . . .

Analyze a Theory The theory about the relationship between agricultural rhythms and a society's ideas about work and vacation neatly explains the difference between educational approaches in Asia and the United States. Ask students, in small groups, to explore this idea in more depth by discussing these questions:

- Is the theory convincing? What further evidence could be used to support or prove the theory?
- Suppose Gladwell had decided to include a chart showing data to support the theory. What kind of chart would be most effective?
- Is this theory central to Gladwell's main argument? If not, what purpose does it serve in his essay?

Integrate and Evaluate Information (TABLE)

COMMON CORE RI 7

Remind students that the first table showed students in the low socioeconomic group lagging behind the other groups, while the second table showed these students keeping up. Point out that the third table helps explain the discrepancy between the other two. The "missing link" is data about what happens during summer vacation.

J ASK STUDENTS why Gladwell chooses to include all three tables instead of just presenting this one. *(Gladwell uses each table to help readers understand how Karl Alexander reached his conclusions, to dispel misconceptions about education, and to emphasize the importance of knowing this data and doing careful studies like Alexander's.)* Ask students how the use of tables in this part of the essay affects their perception of the credibility of Gladwell's information. Why? *(The tables add to the credibility of the information by presenting facts rather than opinions or interpretations. Readers can see the evidence for themselves.)*

---

170 189 points to 184 points. They lag behind the middle-class kids by only a modest amount, and, in fact, in one year, second grade, they learn more than the middle- or upper-class kids.

Next, let's see what happens if we look just at how reading scores change during summer vacation.

Class	After 1st	After 2nd	After 3rd	After 4th	Total
Low	−3.67	−1.70	2.74	2.89	0.26
Middle	−3.11	4.18	3.68	2.34	7.09
High	15.38	9.22	14.51	13.38	52.49

Do you see the difference? Look at the first column, which measures what happens over the summer after first grade. The wealthiest kids come back in September and their reading scores have jumped more than 15 points. The poorest kids come back from the holidays and their reading scores have *dropped* almost 4 points. Poor
180 kids may out-learn rich kids during the school year. But during the summer, they fall far behind.

Now take a look at the last column, which totals up all the summer gains from first grade to fifth grade. The reading scores of the poor kids go up by .26 points. *When it comes to reading skills, poor kids learn nothing when school is not in session.* The reading scores of the rich kids, by contrast, go up by a whopping 52.49 points. Virtually all of the advantage that wealthy students have over poor students is the result of differences in the way privileged kids learn while they are *not* in school. . . .

190 What Alexander's work suggests is that the way in which education has been discussed in the United States is backwards. An enormous amount of time is spent talking about reducing class size, rewriting curricula, buying every student a shiny new laptop, and increasing school funding—all of which assumes that there is something fundamentally wrong with the job schools are doing. But look back at the second table, which shows what happens between September and June. Schools *work*. The only problem with school, for the kids who aren't achieving, is that there isn't enough of it.

Alexander, in fact, has done a very simple calculation to
200 demonstrate what would happen if the children of Baltimore went to school year-round. The answer is that poor kids and wealthy kids would, by the end of elementary school, be doing math and reading at almost the same level.

Suddenly the causes of Asian math superiority become even more obvious. Students in Asian schools don't have long summer vacations. Why would they? Cultures that believe that the route to success lies in rising before dawn 360 days a year are scarcely going to give their children three straight months off in the summer. The school year

WHEN STUDENTS STRUGGLE . . .

Give students additional practice in identifying central ideas and supporting details by having them complete a chart similar to the one shown for lines 173–189. As needed, prompt students by providing the main idea or by working as a class to fill in supporting details first to arrive at the main idea (which is stated in a different way in lines 187-189).

After students have completed their charts, discuss the main idea of the passage and how it contributes to their understanding of what Gladwell is saying about the American system of education.

in the United States is, on average, 180 days long. The South Korean
210 school year is 220 days long. The Japanese school year is 243 days long.

One of the questions asked of test takers on a recent math test given to students around the world was how many of the algebra, calculus, and geometry questions covered subject matter that they had previously learned in class. For Japanese twelfth graders, the answer was 92 percent. That's the value of going to school 243 days a year. You have the time to learn everything that needs to be learned—and you have less time to unlearn it. For American twelfth graders, the comparable figure was 54 percent. For its poorest students, America doesn't have a school problem. It has a summer vacation problem, and 220 that's the problem the KIPP schools set out to solve. They decided to bring the lessons of the rice paddy to the American inner city.

Image Credits: ©Andrew Holbrooke/Corbis

"They start school at seven twenty-five," says David Levin of the students at the Bronx KIPP Academy. "They all do a course called thinking skills until seven fifty-five. They do ninety minutes of English, ninety minutes of math every day, except in fifth grade, where they do two hours of math a day. An hour of science, an hour of social science, an hour of music at least twice a week, and then you have an hour and fifteen minutes of orchestra on top of that. Everyone does orchestra. The day goes from seven twenty-five until five p.m. After 230 five, there are homework clubs, detention, sports teams. There are kids here from seven twenty-five until seven p.m. If you take an average

MAIN IDEA: *Long summer vacations have a negative impact on the academic progress of "poor" kids.*

SUPPORTING DETAILS:

Detail 1: *For "poor" kids, reading scores regress during the summer vacations that follow first and second grades.*

Detail 2: *The net result of all four summer vacations is that "poor" kids have improved their reading hardly at all.*

Detail 3: *During the same summer vacations, kids in the middle group improve their reading by a modest amount, and kids in the highest group improve a lot.*

CLOSE READ

Determine Central Ideas (LINES 211–221)

 COMMON CORE RI 2

Explain that some main ideas are stated directly in the text. Tell students to look especially at sentences near the beginning and end of a passage.

K CITE TEXT EVIDENCE Have students reread lines 211–221 and identify the sentence that expresses the most important point of this paragraph. (*"It [America] has a summer vacation problem...."*) Then ask students to identify the details that support this idea.

Integrate and Evaluate Information (PHOTOGRAPH)

 COMMON CORE RI 7

Tell students that photographs are another format that authors can use to convey information.

L ASK STUDENTS why this photograph is included in the essay. What effect is it meant to have on readers? (*This photograph enables readers to picture the inner city. This helps readers understand more clearly the environment in which the students at KIPP Academy live.*)

Determine Central Ideas (LINES 222–234)

 COMMON CORE RI 2

Remind students that in order to be a main idea, an idea must be supported by most or all of the details in a paragraph or passage.

M CITE TEXT EVIDENCE Have students find details in this passage that support the idea that taking advantage of an opportunity involves hard work. (*The school day goes from 7:25 in the morning to 5:00 at night, or sometimes later depending on what activities students are involved in. Students at KIPP spend 50 to 60 percent more time learning than students in other public schools.*)

CLOSE READ

Determine Central Ideas
COMMON CORE RI 2

(LINES 235–261)

Remind students that an author might combine several types of details to support and develop a central idea. The details could include facts, examples, anecdotes, statistics, and description.

(N) ASK STUDENTS what types of details Gladwell uses in these paragraphs to help readers understand how spending more time in school affects KIPP students and their education. *(He includes factual details about the schedule on Saturdays and during the summer. He illustrates how this extra time affects the students and teachers with an anecdote about what he observes in one classroom.)*

> **CRITICAL VOCABULARY**
>
> **counterintuitive**: The math teacher tells Gladwell that although students work more slowly through the material, they cover more, which is not what someone might expect.
>
> **ASK STUDENTS** to explain what the intuitive approach to covering more material would be. *(Intuitively, readers might think that covering material quickly would lead to covering more material.)* Then ask students why the KIPP's counterintuitive approach could actually be more effective. *(Because students learn concepts thoroughly the first time, they don't need as much time to review. Also, because of their depth of knowledge, they are more able to apply concepts to new material, thus decreasing the time it takes to understand it.)*

---

day, and you take out lunch and recess, our kids are spending fifty to sixty percent more time learning than the traditional public school student."

Levin was standing in the school's main hallway. It was lunchtime and the students were trooping by quietly in orderly lines, all of them in their KIPP Academy shirts. Levin stopped a girl whose shirttail was out. "Do me a favor, when you get a chance," he called out, miming a tucking-in movement. He continued: "Saturdays they come in nine to 240 one. In the summer, it's eight to two." By summer, Levin was referring to the fact that KIPP students do three extra weeks of school, in July. These are, after all, precisely the kind of lower-income kids who Alexander identified as losing ground over the long summer vacation, so KIPP's response is simply to not have a long summer vacation.

"The beginning is hard," he went on. "By the end of the day they're restless. Part of it is endurance, part of it is motivation. Part of it is incentives and rewards and fun stuff. Part of it is good old-fashioned discipline. You throw all of that into the stew. We talk a lot here about grit and self-control. The kids know what those words mean."

250 Levin walked down the hall to an eighth-grade math class and stood quietly in the back. A student named Aaron was at the front of the class, working his way through a problem from the page of thinking-skills exercises that all KIPP students are required to do each morning. The teacher, a ponytailed man in his thirties named Frank Corcoran, sat in a chair to the side, only occasionally jumping in to guide the discussion. It was the kind of scene repeated every day in American classrooms—with one difference. Aaron was up at the front, working on that single problem, for *twenty* minutes—methodically, carefully, with the participation of the class, working his way through 260 not just the answer but also the question of whether there was more than one way to get the answer. . . .

"What that extra time does is allow for a more relaxed atmosphere," Corcoran said, after the class was over. "I find that the problem with math education is the sink-or-swim approach. Everything is rapid fire, and the kids who get it first are the ones who are rewarded. So there comes to be a feeling that there are people who can do math and there are people who aren't math people. I think that extended amount of time gives you the chance as a teacher to explain things, and more time for the kids to sit and digest everything 270 that's going on—to review, to do things at a much slower pace. It seems **counterintuitive** but we do things at a slower pace and as a result we get through a lot more. There's a lot more retention, better understanding of the material. It lets me be a little bit more relaxed. We have time to have games. Kids can ask any questions they want, and if I'm explaining something, I don't feel pressed for time. I can go back over material and not feel time pressure." The extra time gave Corcoran the chance to make mathematics *meaningful*: to let his students see the clear relationship between effort and reward.

counterintuitive
(koun´tər-ĭn-tōō´ĭ-tĭv) *adj.* contrary to what one expects.

APPLYING ACADEMIC VOCABULARY

appreciation	persistence

As you discuss Gladwell's essay, incorporate the Collection 1 academic vocabulary words *appreciation* and *persistence*. Ask students to identify details that support the conclusion that students at KIPP Academy feel *appreciation* for the opportunity they have. Then ask them how KIPP students show the quality of *persistence*.

On the walls of the classroom were dozens of certificates from the
280 New York State Regents exam, testifying to first-class honors for
Corcoran's students. "We had a girl in this class," Corcoran said. "She
was a horrible math student in fifth grade. She cried every Saturday
when we did remedial stuff. Huge tears and tears." At the memory,
Corcoran got a little emotional himself. He looked down. "She just
e-mailed us a couple weeks ago. She's in college now. She's an
accounting major."

The story of the miracle school that transforms losers into winners
is, of course, all too familiar. It's the stuff of inspirational books and
sentimental Hollywood movies. But the reality of places like KIPP is
290 a good deal less glamorous than that. To get a sense of what 50 to 60
percent more learning time means, listen to the typical day in the life
of a KIPP student.

The student's name is Marita. She's an only child who lives in a
single-parent home. Her mother never went to college. The two of
them share a one-bedroom apartment in the Bronx. Marita used to go
to a parochial school down the street from her home, until her mother
heard of KIPP. "When I was in fourth grade, me and one of my other
friends, Tanya, we both applied to KIPP," Marita said. "I remember
Miss Owens. She interviewed me, and the way she was saying made it
300 sound so hard I thought I was going to prison. I almost started crying.

Marita's Bargain   **11**

CLOSE READ

Integrate and Evaluate

 COMMON CORE **RI 7**

(PHOTOGRAPH)

Remind students that photographs can sometimes
present new information as well as reinforce ideas.

Ⓞ ASK STUDENTS what feeling is conveyed by
this photograph and what idea it suggests. *(The
photograph shows a classroom with enthusiastic
students, similar to the math class described on
the previous page. It also shows that the students
apparently follow a strict dress code, and that the
teacher is dressed professionaly, wearing a tie. The
photograph brings out the idea that students will
embrace learning if the conditions are right.)*

Support Inferences

 COMMON CORE **RI 1**

(LINES 279–286)

Ⓟ CITE TEXT EVIDENCE Ask students what point
Gladwell is making about the teachers at KIPP
Academy in this paragraph. What details in the text
support this idea? *(Gladwell's point is that KIPP teachers
are invested in their students' success and that their
dedication pays off. Supporting details include the
"dozens of certificates . . . testifying to first-class honors
for Corcoran's students," the fact that Corcoran gets "a
little emotional" describing the hard-won success of
one particular student, and the fact that the student
is currently applying her math skills as an accounting
major in college.)*

Analyze Word Choice

 COMMON CORE RI 4

(LINES 305–325)

Point out that Gladwell chooses to include Marita's actual words in this passage.

Q **CITE TEXT EVIDENCE** Ask students to re-read lines 305 to 325 and then describe what **tone,** or attitude, Marita's words convey in this passage. Why does Gladwell want readers to hear this tone for themselves? *(Marita is matter-of-fact as she describes her daily routine, which includes waking up very early, rushing to get to school on time, and returning home from a full day at school to focus on homework, which can take anywhere from two hours to five hours. Marita shares the details of her routine without a hint of self-pity. Hearing Marita describe her situation in her own words enables readers to understand that, for her, working this hard is her way of achieving a desirable goal. She is grateful for this chance.)*

> **"**Our kids are spending fifty to sixty percent more time learning than the traditional public school student.**"**

And she was like, If you don't want to sign this, you don't have to sign this. But then my mom was right there, so I signed it."

With that, her life changed. (Keep in mind, while reading what follows, that Marita is twelve years old.)

"I wake up at five-forty-five a.m. to get a head start," she says. "I brush my teeth, shower. I get some breakfast at school, if I am running late. Usually get yelled at because I am taking too long. I meet my friends Diana and Steven at the bus stop, and we get the number one bus."

310 A 5:45 wakeup is fairly typical of KIPP students, especially given the long bus and subway commutes that many have to get to school. Levin, at one point, went into a seventh-grade music class with seventy kids in it and asked for a show of hands on when the students woke up. A handful said they woke up after six. Three quarters said they woke up before six. And almost half said they woke up before 5:30. One classmate of Marita's, a boy named José, said he sometimes wakes up at three or four a.m., finishes his homework from the night before, and then "goes back to sleep for a bit."

Marita went on:

320 I leave school at five p.m., and if I don't lollygag around, then I will get home around five-thirty. Then I say hi to my mom really quickly and start my homework. And if it's not a lot of homework that day, it will take me two to three hours, and I'll be done around nine p.m. Or if we have essays, then I will be done like ten p.m., or ten-thirty p.m.

Sometimes my mom makes me break for dinner. I tell her I want to go straight through, but she says I have to eat. So around eight, she makes me break for dinner for, like, a half hour, and then I get back to work. Then, usually after that, my mom wants to hear

330 about school, but I have to make it quick because I have to get in bed by eleven p.m. So I get all my stuff ready, and then I get into bed. I tell her all about the day and what happened, and by

Strategies for Annotation 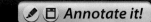 ✎ 🗐 *Annotate it!*

Analyze Word Choice

Have students use their eBook annotation tools to analyze lines 326–337, completing each of these steps:

- Highlight in yellow what Marita's mother wants her to do.
- Highlight in blue Marita's response to her mother's requests.
- Reread the highlighted text. Discuss in pairs the words and phrases that indicate Marita's attitude toward her nightly schedule.

> Sometimes my mom makes me break for dinner. I tell her I want to go straight through, but she says I have to eat. So around eight, she makes me break for dinner for, like, a half hour, and then I get back to work. Then, usually after that, my mom wants to hear

the time we are finished, she is on the brink of sleeping, so that's probably around eleven-fifteen. Then I go to sleep, and the next morning we do it all over again. We are in the same room. But it's a huge bedroom and you can split it into two, and we have beds on other sides. Me and my mom are very close.

She spoke in the matter-of-fact way of children who have no way of knowing how unusual their situation is. She had the hours of a 340 lawyer trying to make partner, or of a medical resident. All that was missing were the dark circles under her eyes and a steaming cup of coffee, except that she was too young for either.

"Sometimes I don't go to sleep when I'm supposed to," Marita continued. "I go to sleep at, like, twelve o'clock, and the next afternoon, it will hit me. And I will doze off in class. But then I have to wake up because I have to get the information. I remember I was in one class, and I was dozing off and the teacher saw me and said, 'Can I talk to you after class?' And he asked me, 'Why were you dozing off?' And I told him I went to sleep late. And he was, like, 'You need to go to 350 sleep earlier.'"

Marita's life is not the life of a typical twelve-year-old. Nor is it what we would necessarily wish for a twelve-year-old. Children, we like to believe, should have time to play and dream, and sleep. Marita has responsibilities. . . . Her community does not give her what she needs. So what does she have to do? Give up her evenings and weekends and friends—all the elements of her old world—and replace them with KIPP.

Here is Marita again, in a passage that is little short of heartbreaking:

360 Well, when we first started fifth grade, I used to have contact with one of the girls from my old school, and whenever I left school on Friday, I would go to her house and stay there until my mom would get home from work. So I would be at her house and I would be doing my homework. She would never have any homework. And she would say, "Oh, my God, you stay there late." Then she said she wanted to go to KIPP, but then she would say that KIPP is too hard and she didn't want to do it. And I would say, "Everyone says that KIPP is hard, but once you get the hang of it, it's not really that hard." She told me, "It's because you are 370 smart." And I said, "No, every one of us is smart." And she was so discouraged because we stayed until five and we had a lot of homework, and I told her that us having a lot of homework helps us do better in class. And she told me she didn't want to hear the whole speech. All my friends now are from KIPP.

CLOSE READ

Support Inferences

COMMON CORE RI 1, RI 4

(LINES 351–359)

In a nonfiction work, the author's feelings toward the subject are often revealed through the words and phrases he or she uses.

R CITE TEXT EVIDENCE Ask students what Gladwell's choice of words in this passage suggests about his view of Marita. Have them cite specific words and phrases from the text. *(He both admires and feels sorry for Marita. Words that reveal his attitude include "Children . . . should have time to play and dream, and sleep," "Marita has responsibilities," "Give up her evenings and weekends and friends," and "little short of heartbreaking.")*

SCAFFOLDING FOR ELL STUDENTS

Support Inferences Display these sentences from the essay:

- "The KIPP program represents one of the most promising new educational philosophies in the United States." (lines 47–48)
- "Aaron was up at the front, working on that single problem, for *twenty* minutes—methodically, carefully, with the participation of the class, working his way through. . . ." (lines 257–261)
- "Here is Marita again, in a passage that is little short of heartbreaking. . . ." (lines 358–359)

Ask volunteers to highlight words in each sentence that show an attitude or feeling. Elicit from students what those words reveal about Gladwell's view of his subject.

CLOSE READ

Determine Central Ideas RI 2

(LINES 387–394)

Point out that Gladwell repeats objections he has voiced earlier to the measures often proposed as ways to fix the American educational system.

S **ASK STUDENTS** how this repetition helps readers understand what Gladwell believes is important. *(By saying for a second time that smaller classes, more technology, and better facilities will not improve education, Gladwell makes clear his belief that it is more time in school and a different approach to education that is necessary.)*

> ### CRITICAL VOCABULARY
>
> **desultory:** Gladwell describes many public schools as lacking a plan for educating their students successfully.
>
> **ASK STUDENTS** to explain why Gladwell would not consider private or parochial schools to be desultory. *(He probably assumes they have a better philosophy of how to go about educating students and that they have thought about the best strategies for guiding their students to academic success. Also, they are not bound by the same rules and regulations and can forge their own paths.)*

COLLABORATIVE DISCUSSION Have students work independently to list the characteristics of KIPP students. Then have them meet in groups to share their lists and discuss the ways in which KIPP students differ from others in traditional public schools. Accept all reasonable responses.

ASK STUDENTS to share any questions they generated in the course of reading and discussing the selection.

Is this a lot to ask of a child? It is. But think of things from Marita's perspective. She has made a bargain with her school. She will get up at five-forty-five in the morning, go in on Saturdays, and do homework until eleven at night. In return, KIPP promises that it will take kids like her who are stuck in poverty and give them a chance to 380 get out. It will get 84 percent of them up to or above their grade level in mathematics. On the strength of that performance, 90 percent of KIPP students get scholarships to private or parochial high schools instead of having to attend their own **desultory** high schools in the Bronx. And on the strength of that high school experience, more than 80 percent of KIPP graduates will go on to college, in many cases being the first in their family to do so. . . .

Marita doesn't need a brand-new school with acres of playing fields and gleaming facilities. She doesn't need a laptop, a smaller class, a teacher with a PhD, or a bigger apartment. She doesn't need a higher 390 IQ or a mind as quick as Chris Langan's. All those things would be nice, of course. But they miss the point. Marita just needed a *chance*. And look at the chance she was given! Someone brought a little bit of the rice paddy to the South Bronx and explained to her the miracle of meaningful work.

desultory
(dĕs´əl-tôr´ē) *adj.*
lacking a fixed plan.

COLLABORATIVE DISCUSSION Are KIPP students different from other public school students? With a partner, discuss the qualities that KIPP students possess and how their circumstances distinguish them from other students. Cite evidence from the text to support your views.

WHEN STUDENTS STRUGGLE . . .

Reread lines 375–386 aloud to students. Point out that Gladwell develops a clear cause-and-effect relationship between the details in this paragraph. Explain that this cause-and-effect relationship helps convey the central idea of the last part of the essay. Have students work in pairs to complete a cause-and-effect chart with details from the paragraph. *(Cause: If Marita . . . gets up early, goes to school on Saturdays, and does her homework until late at night/Effect: Then . . . she will have a chance to improve her life by getting a scholarship to a better school and possibly going on to college.)* Use students' charts to guide them to an understanding of the point that Gladwell is making.

Determine Central Ideas

A **central idea** is an important idea or message that an author wants to convey. Although a central idea may be stated, more often readers must infer it from details in the text. Use these steps to identify the central ideas in "Marita's Bargain":

- Identify the **topic** of the work. The central ideas present insights or perspectives on this subject. Gladwell's broad topic is education; more specifically, he explores the impact of an experimental kind of public school on students.
- Analyze the **details** used to develop the discussion. Consider the kind of information these details present and how they reveal the author's view of the subject. For example, the facts, examples, and quotations about the rigorous schedule of KIPP Academy support Gladwell's opinion about this educational approach.
- Use subheadings, the title, and other **text features** as clues to help identify central ideas.
- Evaluate how the organization, or **structure,** of the work helps develop important ideas. For example, Gladwell devotes the last two sections of his essay to Marita's story, suggesting that he wants to convey a specific idea about the hard work that goes into achieving success.

Integrate and Evaluate Information

Information can be presented in a variety of formats and media, including maps, photographs, diagrams, charts, and video. **Quantitative formats,** which present numerical or statistical data, include tables and graphs, such as line graphs, bar graphs, and circle graphs. In "Marita's Bargain," Gladwell uses several **tables** to support his ideas. To analyze the information in a table, follow these steps:

- If the table has a title, read it to see what the table is about. Gladwell's tables do not have titles, but he introduces each one in the text immediately before it.
- Read the labels on the columns and rows, and make sure you understand what they mean. For example, the label "Class" in Gladwell's tables refers to the socioeconomic class of each group of students. The row labels divide the students into three groups: low, middle, and high.
- Scan the numbers to identify any obvious trends. Look across each row from left to right, and read each column from top to bottom. Do the numbers grow consistently larger or smaller? What might this mean?
- Read what the text says about the table. Gladwell follows each table with an explanation of the conclusions he draws from it. Then review the numbers in the table again to see if you agree with the author's interpretation.

TEACH

CLOSE READ

Determine Central Ideas

Tell students that although all the details in an essay such as this one relate to the same general topic, they may develop different central ideas. To find the central ideas in this essay, suggest that students take these steps:

- Identify and state the main idea of each major section of the essay.
- Ask: What "bigger" or broader ideas about education do the points from each section develop?

Integrate and Evaluate Information

Review the instructions with students, making sure that they understand the purpose of each type of format referred to. Then have them work in pairs to identify other places in the essay where Gladwell could have included a visual or quantitative aid. Ask them to explain their choices.

Strategies for Annotation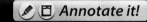

Determine Central Ideas

Divide the essay into five sections (lines 1–52; 53–115; 116–221; 222–286; 287–374). Assign each section to a group. Have groups use their eBook annotation tools to determine the central ideas of the essay, as follows:

- Highlight in pink significant details or observations that Gladwell makes in each major section of the essay.
- On a note, explain what the details reveal about his main idea in that part of the text.
- Have each group present Gladwell's central ideas about education from the major point of each section.

The story of the miracle school that transforms losers into winners is, of course, all too familiar. It's the stuff of inspirational books and sentimental Hollywood movies. But the reality of places like KIPP is a good deal less glamorous than that. To get a sense of what 50 to 60 percent more learning time means, listen to the typical day in the life of a KIPP student.

Analyzing the Text

Possible answers:

1. *He believes KIPP schools are providing students with the opportunity they need to make the most of their talent and succeed.*

2. *After reading section 2, readers understand that the public school schedule is based on ideas that no longer have relevance or validity. This information makes readers receptive to the idea that changes, such as modifying summer vacation, are necessary in the public school system.*

3. *The tables in section 3 present a number of different test results to support Gladwell's assertion that summer vacation is detrimental to students from lower-income homes. The tables are effective in the way they organize and present complicated data.*

4. *One reason that KIPP students are successful is the greater number of hours they spend in school. However, these students are also taught valuable lessons about self-discipline, respect for others, personal responsibility, and order through the school's code of behaviors and expectations. Another factor in their success is the fact that they want to be in the school. It is seen as a privilege to be a KIPP student.*

5. *His purpose is to show what life is really like for a student who attends the KIPP Academy. To accomplish this purpose, he includes Marita's own words describing her rigorous schedule and the kinds of sacrifices she has made.*

6. *The American school system needs to be changed in order to offer more students the opportunity to succeed. Changes in the system would enable more hard-working students to reap rewards from their sacrifice.*

7. *A bargain refers to an agreement made between two parties in which each fulfills responsibilities and gets something in return. It implies that the person making the agreement (the KIPP student) gets something advantageous out of it. Thus, the use of the word helps convey Gladwell's viewpoint that the hard-working students at KIPP Academy get the opportunity they need to make the most of their potential.*

8. *Students may say that this essay could be described as "political" because Gladwell is essentially advocating for changes that will improve the public school system. His message is that America is not doing enough for all of its students and needs to do more.*

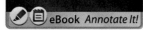 eBook *Annotate It!*

Analyzing the Text

Cite Text Evidence   Support your responses with evidence from the selection.

1. **Connect** This essay originally appeared in a book that explores whether success comes more from talent or opportunity. Based on the details in section 1 (lines 1–52), what does Gladwell believe about the success of students enrolled in the KIPP Academy?

2. **Analyze** Gladwell examines the history of the U.S. public school system in section 2 (lines 53–115) before he discusses summer vacation in section 3 (lines 116–221). How do the ideas and information in section 2 support his discussion in section 3?

3. **Evaluate** What is the function of the tables in section 3 (lines 116–221)? Are they effective in conveying Gladwell's central idea in this part of the essay? Explain why or why not.

4. **Cite Evidence** Is the success of the KIPP Academy based solely on the extended school day and year? Cite evidence from the essay to support your conclusion.

5. **Analyze** What is Gladwell's purpose in the last part of the essay? How does he achieve this purpose? Support your explanation with specific details from the text.

6. **Summarize** What are the central ideas of Gladwell's essay? Summarize these ideas in two or three sentences.

7. **Draw Conclusions** Why does Gladwell use the word "bargain" instead of "agreement" or "deal"? Explain how the connotation of this word helps to reinforce readers' understanding of Gladwell's perspective on the KIPP Academy.

8. **Synthesize** One critic suggested that "Marita's Bargain" and other essays in *Outliers* made it a more "political" book than his others. Does "Marita's Bargain" have a political message? Why or why not?

PERFORMANCE TASK

Writing Activity: Diary Gladwell describes how attending the KIPP Academy has affected Marita's relationships with her old friends who do not go to the school. Write a diary entry in which she reflects on the change in these friendships. Consider the following:

- Marita's feelings about the importance of succeeding in school
- the reaction of her old friends to the demands of the Kipp Academy
- the amount of free time Marita has outside of school
- Marita's relationship with her mother

Assign this performance task.

PERFORMANCE TASK

Writing Activity: Diary Have students reread the last section of the essay, starting on line 287. Suggest that they jot down details related to each of the bullet points in the Performance Task. Then remind them that a diary entry is written from the first-person point of view and reveals feelings as well as factual information.

Critical Vocabulary

motley   inviolate   desultory

cognitive   counterintuitive

Practice and Apply Complete each of the following sentence stems in a way that reflects the meaning of the Critical Vocabulary word.

1. Going to bed at a later hour to cure insomnia seems *counterintuitive* because . . .

2. The costumes worn by a harlequin or clown are described as *motley* because . . .

3. The town hall meeting was *desultory* because . . .

4. The trainer tested the player's *cognitive* skills after the concussion because . . .

5. The bank deposits were *inviolate* because . . .

Vocabulary Strategy: Context Clues

The context of an unfamiliar word—other words, sentences, and paragraphs around the word—often gives clues to its meaning. For example, the Critical Vocabulary word *motley* occurs in this context in the essay: "this motley group of randomly chosen lower-income kids from dingy apartments." The chart shows the kinds of context clues you could use to figure out the meaning of *motley* and other challenging words.

Synonym	A word or phrase before or after the unknown term has the same meaning. For example, the phrase "randomly chosen" suggests that *motley* means "varied" or "different from each other."
Example	The context may include examples that help illustrate a word's meaning. For example, Gladwell writes that summer vacation is an "inviolate feature of school life, like high school football or the senior prom." The examples that follow the signal word *like* suggest that *inviolate* means "secure against change."
Antonym	Sometimes a word that is the opposite of the unknown term appears in the context. This relationship is signaled by *but* or *unlike*. For example in this sentence, the word *organized* is the opposite of *desultory:* "Unlike her organized speech, his was desultory."
Restatement	Look for a restatement of a word's meaning before or after it. For example, "The house painter's efforts were desultory—rather hit or miss—making us wonder if the job would ever be completed."

Practice and Apply Find each of these words in the selection. Define it and explain the context clues that help you identify its meaning as it is used in the essay.

1. protocol

2. pernicious

3. respite

4. singular

Critical Vocabulary   **COMMON CORE** L 4a

Answers:

1. *people who suffer from insomnia need more sleep*

2. *they are in all different colors*

3. *the organizer did not create an agenda*

4. *the player's brain may have sustained damage*

5. *they were stored in a secure vault*

Vocabulary Strategy: Context Clues

Possible answers:

1. *a code of behavior; clues: "they are taught," "smile, sit up . . ."*

2. *damaging or harmful; clues: "Not infrequently is health itself destroyed by overstimulating the mind"*

3. *rest; clues: "the elimination of Saturday classes, the shortening of the school day, and the lengthening of vacation"*

4. *unique; clues: "the more a plot of land is cultivated, the more fertile it gets," "in Western agriculture, the opposite is true"*

Strategies for Annotation 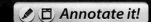 *Annotate it!*

Context Clues   **COMMON CORE** L 4a

Have students locate the sentences containing *protocol, pernicious, respite,* and *singular* in the essay. Encourage them to use their eBook annotation tools to complete these steps:

- Highlight each vocabulary word in green.
- Reread the surrounding sentences, looking for clues to the word's meaning. Underline any clues you find, such as examples, synonyms, or antonyms.
- Review your annotations and try to infer the word's meaning.

of mental disorder," Jarvis wrote. Similarly, the pioneer of public education in Massachusetts, Horace Mann, believed that working students too hard would create a "most pernicious influence upon character and habits. . . . Not infrequently is health itself destroyed by overstimulating the mind." In the education journals of the day, there

PRACTICE & APPLY

Language and Style: Subject-Verb Agreement

COMMON CORE L1

Have students work in pairs to find or write examples of sentences illustrating the various situations determining subject-verb agreement.

Possible answers:

Some of the stains had vanished.

There were two empty bottles in the sink.

The cellphone and its case have been misplaced.

Either the dog's sudden barks or his persistent growls are going to keep the cat away.

Then have pairs exchange their charts and work to assess the accuracy of each other's examples.

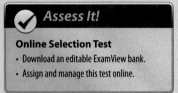

Assess It!

Online Selection Test
• Download an editable ExamView bank.
• Assign and manage this test online.

Language and Style: Subject-Verb Agreement

 COMMON CORE L1

Agreement in number means that if the subject of a clause is singular, the verb must also be singular. A plural subject requires a plural verb. Ensuring that each subject and verb pair is in agreement enables writers to communicate their ideas precisely and clearly to their audience.

Read this sentence from "Marita's Bargain":

> **Virtually all of the advantage that wealthy students have over poor students is the result of differences in the way privileged kids learn while they are *not* in school.**

Note that the verb of each subordinate clause agrees with its subject (students have; kids learn; they are). The subject of the main clause is the indefinite pronoun *all* followed by the prepositional phrase *of the advantage,* making *all* singular in this instance and requiring the use of the singular verb *is.*

Here are some examples of different circumstances affecting subject-verb agreement:

Examples	Situation
Most of the sugar is gone. Most of the cookies were eaten.	**Phrases and clauses between the subject and verb:** Generally, phrases or clauses between the subject and verb do not influence number. **Exception:** The indefinite pronouns *all, any, most, more, none,* and *some* can be either singular or plural, depending whether they refer to a quantity (sugar) or a number of things (cookies). The prepositional phrase or context of the sentence must be used to determine the pronoun's number.
Why has only one student responded so far? On the counter are numerous blank applications.	**Sentences beginning with *Here* or *There*, questions, inverted sentences:** Look for the subject after the verb to make sure that the verb agrees with it.
The rain and wind have decreased. Fish and chips is my favorite dinner. Each book and DVD is available to borrowers.	**Subjects joined by *and*:** Most compound subjects joined by *and* require a plural verb. **Exceptions:** If the compound subject refers to one thing, use a singular verb. Compound subjects preceded by *every, each,* or *many a* require a singular verb.
Neither my reluctance nor your threats are enough to keep me from carrying out the mission.	**Subjects joined by *or, nor, either/or, neither/nor*:** The verb should agree with the part of the subject closest to it.

Practice and Apply Create a two-column chart. List the types of situations governing subject-verb agreement in one column. Copy examples of sentences from Gladwell's essay or write original sentences that illustrate each situation in the second column. Be sure to identify the subject-verb pairs. Explain your examples to a partner.

SCAFFOLDING FOR ELL STUDENTS . . .

Language: Subject-Verb Agreement Before students begin the Practice & Apply activity, divide students into mixed language-ability Jigsaw groups. Instead of two-column charts, students will create three-column charts, including a column for the examples shown above. Have students work together to do the following:

• List each situation from the chart (only the boldface heads need to be listed
• Label the subject and verb in each example sentence, and to underline the part of each sentence that makes it an exemplar of the special situation listed, as in the example below.

S   V

<u>Most of the cookies were eaten.</u>

• Complete the Practice & Apply activity.

Analyze Key Terms

COMMON CORE

RI 4

TEACH

Tell students that writers of informational texts use **key terms** to develop their ideas. Some key terms, like "American Dream," represent broad concepts. Others, like "charter school," belong to specific domain or field of knowledge. In both cases, these terms can be freighted with meanings and emotion. That's why it's important for readers to analyze how an author defines and develops key terms throughout a text.

To demonstrate the wide range of meanings often assigned to key terms, write the term achievement gap on a on the board, over an inverted pyramid like the one below.

- Ask students to supply brief definitions and synonyms that they associate with the word. Add all of these responses to the top tier of the pyramid.

Achievement Gap

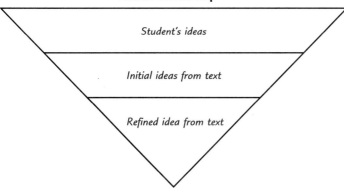

Student's ideas

Initial ideas from text

Refined idea from text

- Then ask a volunteer to read lines 136–145. Ask students to paraphrase the two ideas of the achievement gap summarized in this paragraph

- Next, ask volunteers to take turns reading lines 146–189. Ask students to explain how these paragraphs refine and challenge the earlier ideas about the meaning of the "achievement gap." Write the refined meaning of the term at the bottom of the pyramid.

COLLABORATIVE DISCUSSION

Divide students into groups. Each member of a group takes responsibility for defining a different concept of "public school" from the essay—what public school has meant at different periods in history and parts of the world. Have students complete inverted pyramid charts, in the order in which information is presented in the essay, leaving the bottom tier blank. After about fifteen minutes, bring the class together to define what Gladwell thinks public school should be today.

Determine Central Ideas

COMMON CORE

RI 2

RETEACH

Provide students with this or another sample paragraph.

The ten high schools labeled "most in need of improvement" by the state because of low test scores all have a daily truancy rate averaging almost ten percent. This means that ten out of every one hundred students are missing one or more classes each day. When caught, they have myriad excuses; so do their parents. But the fact is that no excuse can compensate for missed instruction. At some point in the past decades, the idea of education being a privilege was replaced with the perception that it is a right—one that can be taken for granted, and one that requires little responsibility on the part of the person on whom it has been bestowed. This attitude, perpetuated by society, is to blame for much of the absenteeism and consequent failure of students to achieve their potential.

Have students work independently to state the central idea. *(Sample answer: Chronic absenteeism, and the missed opportunities it causes, is symptomatic of a widespread belief that education is not a privilege but a right.)*

 LEVEL UP TUTORIALS Assign the following *Level Up* tutorial: **Main Idea and Supporting Details**

CLOSE READING APPLICATION

Students can apply the skill of determining central ideas to a current magazine or newspaper article. Provide them with a short nonfiction article. Have them work independently to identify one or more central ideas in the article and the details that develop these ideas. Have them explain their strategy to a partner.

Kewauna's Ambition
from How Children Succeed

Nonfiction by Paul Tough

Why This Text

Students sometimes read through a nonfiction text without identifying the author's central ideas, or analyzing how those ideas are supported. "Kewauna's Ambition" provides an opportunity to identify two central ideas by determining the topic of the text and analyzing details within the text. With the help of the close-reading questions, students will discern Tough's most important ideas about education. This close reading will also lead students to the evidence Tough uses to support his ideas.

Background Have students read the background and the information about the author. Introduce the selection by telling students that Paul Tough's book *How Children Succeed* proposes that high test scores are not the only indicator of future success in the world. Tough has identified character traits such as perseverance, curiosity, conscientiousness, optimism, and self-control that are better predictors of future success.

AS YOU READ Ask students to pay attention to the central ideas in Tough's text. How soon into the text can you identify Tough's topic?

Common Core Support

- cite strong and thorough textual evidence
- analyze the development of two or more central ideas
- analyze a complex set of ideas
- determine the meaning of words and phrases as they are used in a text

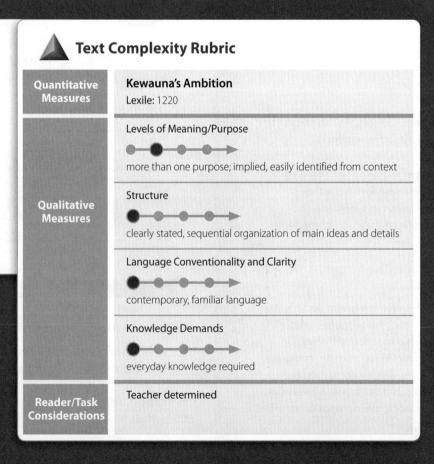

Text Complexity Rubric

Quantitative Measures	**Kewauna's Ambition** Lexile: 1220	
Qualitative Measures	Levels of Meaning/Purpose	more than one purpose; implied, easily identified from context
	Structure	clearly stated, sequential organization of main ideas and details
	Language Conventionality and Clarity	contemporary, familiar language
	Knowledge Demands	everyday knowledge required
Reader/Task Considerations	Teacher determined	

Strategies for CLOSE READING

Determine Central Ideas

Students should read this excerpt carefully all the way through. Close-reading questions at the bottom of the page will help them focus on a thorough analysis of the text. As they read, students should jot down comments or questions about the excerpt in the side margins.

WHEN STUDENTS STRUGGLE . . .

To help students identify Tough's central ideas, have them work in a small group to fill out a chart, such as the one shown below, as they analyze the text.

CITE TEXT EVIDENCE For practice in identifying central ideas, ask students to cite evidence Tough uses to support each central idea.

> *Tough's Topic: helping at-risk students succeed*

> *Central Idea: An underachieving high school student can become a successful college student.*

> *Central Idea: Programs can be put in place to help at-risk students succeed regularly.*

> *Detail: Kewauna started OneGoal in 2009 and learned strategies to help her succeed.*

> *Detail: Kewauna graduated from high school and entered college.*

> *Detail: Kewauna had "non-cognitive" assets, such as grit and not giving up.*

> *Detail: OneGoal has an 85% college-persistence rate.*

Background *"Kewauna's Ambition" is an excerpt from* **Paul Tough's** *book* **How Children Succeed: Grit, Curiosity, and the Hidden Power of Character.** *In his research for this book, Tough met Kewauna Lermar, a 17-year-old student in a program called OneGoal, which works with high schools in Chicago to help at-risk students by teaching them noncognitive skills such as grit and self-control. Kewauna had a chaotic childhood, and she was homeless for a while. When she was 15, she was arrested for punching a police officer. But after a family intervention, Kewauna started working harder at school. With the help of OneGoal teacher Michele Stefel, Kewauna graduated high school and enrolled in college.*

Kewauna's Ambition

***FROM* HOW CHILDREN SUCCEED**

Nonfiction by Paul Tough

CLOSE READ
Notes

1. **READ ▶** As you read lines 1–30, begin to collect and cite text evidence.
   - Underline Kewauna's challenges.
   - Circle key elements of Kewauna's strategy for success.
   - In the margin, use your own words to describe each part of her strategy.

Her first fall at Western Illinois, Kewauna took introductory courses— English 100, Math 100, Sociology 100. None of them was easy for her, but the course she found most challenging was Biology 170, Introduction to Health Careers. The professor was a popular lecturer, so the class was pretty full, and most of the students were upperclassmen. On the first day of class, Kewauna did what Michele Stefel had recommended: she politely introduced herself to the professor before class, and then she sat in the front row which until Kewauna sat down was occupied entirely by white girls. The other African American students all tended to sit at the back, which disappointed Kewauna. ("That's what they *expect* you to do," she said when we talked by phone that fall. "Back in the civil rights movement, if they told you you had to sit in the back, you wouldn't do it.")

Her biology professor used a lot of scientific terms in his lectures that Kewauna wasn't familiar with. So she came up with a strategy: every time he used a word she didn't understand, she wrote it down and put a red star next to it. At the end of the class, she waited until all the other students who wanted to talk to the professor had taken their turns, and then she went through each red-starred word with him, one by one, asking him to explain them.

sits in the front to make her noticeable to her professors

knows when to ask for help

3

---

1. **READ AND CITE TEXT EVIDENCE**

   A **ASK STUDENTS** to cite textual evidence that supports their descriptions of Kewauna's strategy for success. *Students should cite evidence from lines 6 and 7 and line 19 as evidence that Kewauna made herself noticeable to her professors, evidence from lines 14–18 and 21–23 as evidence that Kewauna asks for help, and lines 26–27 as evidence that Kewauna got the help of a tutor.*

CLOSE READ
Notes

finds other students to ask for help

Kewauna spent a lot of time interacting with all her professors, in fact. She
20 was a regular at office hours, and she e-mailed them whenever she wasn't clear
on assignments. She also tried to make one or two acquaintances among the
students in each of her classes, so that if she needed help with homework and
couldn't reach the professor, she'd have someone to ask. Through her
freshman-support program, she found a writing tutor—she had always had
"grammar issues," she told me, as well as trouble with spelling and
punctuation—and she made a practice of going over with her tutor every paper
she wrote before handing it in. Finally, in December, she felt she had
internalized enough about comma splices and dependent clauses, and she
handed in her final English paper without going over it with the writing tutor.
30 She got an A.

He's impressed by her determination to work for a goal that is not immediate.

Still, it was a difficult semester for Kewauna. She was always short of
money and had to economize everywhere she could. At one point, she ran out
of money on her meal card and just didn't eat for two days. She was studying
all the time, it felt like. Every paper was a challenge, and at the end of the
semester, she stayed up practically all night, three nights in a row, studying for
finals. But her hard work was reflected in her final grades that semester: two B
pluses, one A, and, in biology, an A plus. When I spoke to her a few days before
Christmas, she sounded a bit depleted, but proud too. "No matter how
overwhelming it is, no matter how exhausting it is, I'm not going to give up,"
40 she said. "I'm never the type to give up. Even when I played hide-and-go-seek
when I was little, I would be outside till eight o'clock, until I found everyone. I
don't give up on nothing, no matter how hard."

2. **REREAD** Reread lines 5–12. Why do you think Kewauna is disappointed
that the other African American girls sat in the back? Support your answer with
explicit textual evidence.

Kewauna wanted to sit in front and be noticed. She may have felt more comfortable with the other African American girls but they "tended to sit at the back, which disappointed Kewauna."

3. **READ** Read lines 31–50. Circle what the author says most impressed him
about Kewauna. In the margin explain why, in your own words.

4. **REREAD AND DISCUSS** Reread lines 31–50. With a small group, discuss
why Kewauna was successful. What central idea does Tough make about
Kewauna's success in these lines?

CLOSE READ
Notes

There were still seven semesters to go, lots of time for things to go wrong,
for setbacks and mistakes and crises. But Kewauna seemed certain of where she
was heading and why—almost unnervingly so. What was most remarkable to
me about Kewauna was that she was able to marshal her **prodigious**
noncognitive capacity—call it grit, conscientiousness, resilience, or the ability
to delay gratification—all for a distant prize that was, for her, almost entirely
theoretical. She didn't actually *know* any business ladies with briefcases
50 downtown; she didn't even know any college graduates except her teachers.

Not all of Kewauna's fellow OneGoal students are going to take to the deal
with the same **conviction**. And it won't be clear for another couple of years
whether the leadership skills Kewauna and her classmates were taught are
powerful enough to get them through four years of college. But so far,
OneGoal's overall persistence numbers are quite good. Of the 128 students,
including Kewauna, who started OneGoal as juniors at six Chicago high
schools in the fall of 2009, ninety-six were enrolled in four-year colleges as of
March 2012. Another fourteen were enrolled in two-year colleges, for an
overall college-persistence total of 85 percent. Which left only nineteen
60 students who had veered off the track to a college degree: twelve who left
OneGoal before the end of high school, two who joined the military after high
school, two who graduated from high school but didn't enroll in college, and
three who enrolled in college but dropped out in their first six months. The
numbers are less stellar but still impressive for the pilot-program cohort,[1]
students for whom OneGoal was a weekly afterschool class. Three years out of
high school, 66 percent of the students who enrolled in the program as high-
school juniors are still enrolled in college. Those numbers grow more
significant when you recall that OneGoal teachers are deliberately selecting
struggling students who seem especially unlikely to go to college.
70 Jeff Nelson[2] would be the first to admit that what he has created is far from
a perfect solution for the widespread dysfunction of the country's human-
capital[3] pipeline. Ideally, we should have in place an education and social-

prodigious :
huge

conviction:
strong belief

OneGoal teaches students leadership skills.

85% of OneGoal students were in college as of March 2012.

[1] **cohort:** a group of individuals having a statistical factor (as age or class membership) in common in a demographic study.
[2] **Jeff Nelson:** co-founder and CEO of OneGoal.
[3] **human capital:** skills, training, and experience that make an employee valuable in the marketplace.

5. **READ** As you read lines 51–78, summarize what you learn about OneGoal
in the margin.

2. **REREAD AND CITE TEXT EVIDENCE**

B **ASK STUDENTS** to infer the cause of Kewauna's
disappointment, and to support their inference with textual
evidence. *Students can infer from lines 5–6 that Kewauna is using
strategies that will help her get noticed and is not happy that the
other girls who she identifies with racially sit in the back.*

3. **READ AND CITE TEXT EVIDENCE**

C **ASK STUDENTS** to cite the textual evidence that shows why
Tough was impressed by Kewauna. *Students should cite evidence
from lines 45–50.*

4. **REREAD AND DISCUSS USING TEXT EVIDENCE**

D **ASK STUDENTS** to pay attention to the details Tough shares
about Kewauna's success, and make an inference based on these
details. *Students should cite evidence from lines 44–50.*

5. **REREAD AND CITE TEXT EVIDENCE** Remind students that
strong support is the foundation of a good argument.

E **ASK STUDENTS** to read their margin notes to a partner and
then work together to find and cite specific text examples that
support their summaries. *Students can cite evidence from line 53
and lines 56–59.*

Critical Vocabulary: prodigious (line 46) Have students share
their definitions of *prodigious*. Ask them to explain Tough's use
of *prodigious*.

Critical Vocabulary: conviction (line 52) Have students
compare their definitions of *conviction*. Ask them to give
textual evidence of Kewauna's *conviction*. *Students should cite
any evidence that shows Kewauna has a strong belief that she can
succeed (line 44–45).*

FOR ELL STUDENTS Explain that an *acquaintance* is someone
you know, but who is not really a friend.

CLOSE READ
Notes

OneGoal works with disadvantaged students.

support system that produces teenagers from the South Side who *aren't* regularly two or three or four years behind grade level. For now, though, OneGoal and the theories that underlie it seem like a most valuable intervention, a program that, for about fourteen hundred dollars a year per student, regularly turns underperforming, undermotivated, low-income teenagers into successful college students.

6. **◀ REREAD** Reread lines 67–78. How does Tough think OneGoal might be improved? Support your answer with explicit textual evidence.

Tough likes the leadership skills OneGoal teaches but thinks other students (those "who aren't regularly two or three of four years behind grade level") could benefit from being taught these skills.

SHORT RESPONSE

Cite Text Evidence   Identify two of Tough's central ideas, and show how he supports them. Review your reading notes, and be sure to **cite text evidence** from the essay in your response.

Tough asserts that not only can an underachieving high school student become a successful college graduate, but also that programs can be put in place so that this happens regularly. Kewauna and OneGoal are profiled to prove this point. Kewauna started the OneGoal program as a high school junior in 2009. In 2012, as a college freshman, she employed strategies she learned from OneGoal, such as engaging professors and getting a tutor. Tough enumerates her "noncognitive" assets, such as grit and not giving up, to make the point that one need not be born with a great intellect, but can learn character skills that will get one ahead in life. OneGoal's current 85% college-persistence rate suggests that its methods do help students turn their lives around.

6

---

6. REREAD AND CITE TEXT EVIDENCE

F **ASK STUDENTS** to cite textual evidence that supports their answer. *Answers will vary. Students should cite evidence from lines 72–74. Their answer should reflect their interpretation of Tough's "ideal."*

SHORT RESPONSE

Cite Text Evidence   Student responses will vary, but they should cite evidence from the text to support their summary of Tough's central ideas. Students should:

- identify two of Tough's central ideas.
- show how Tough supports his central ideas.
- cite text evidence that illustrates Tough's support for his central ideas.

TO CHALLENGE STUDENTS . . .

For more context, students can listen to "Back to School," episode 474 of the radio program *This American Life.*

ASK STUDENTS to work in groups to report their findings to the class. Have them listen to the episode featuring, among others, Paul Tough and Kewauna Lerma. Suggest that groups focus their reports on topics such as the following:

- What obstacles Kewauna had to overcome.
- What Kewauna did to overcome the obstacles.
- What Paul Tough has found that was not presented in the selection students have read.
- What approaches other than OneGoal are successful in helping students achieve their goals.

DIG DEEPER

With the class, return to Question 4, Reread and Discuss. Have students share the results of their discussions.

ASK STUDENTS whether they were satisfied with the outcome of their small-group discussions. Have each group share their findings about what made Kewauna successful. What textual evidence did students find to support their conclusions?

- Guide each group to share whether they came to a unanimous conclusion about which central idea Tough presented in lines 31–50.
- Ask groups to explain how they determined which details were the most important support Tough provided for his central idea.
- After groups have shared the results of their discussions, ask students whether another groups' contributions to the class discussion helped them improve their conceptualization of Tough's main idea.

ASK STUDENTS to return to their Short Response answer and revise it based on the class discussion.

Don't Eat Fortune's Cookie

Graduation Speech by Michael Lewis

Why This Text?

Speakers and writers rely on readers making inferences to understand meaning beyond what is stated. This lesson examines how a speaker's gestures and tone as well as his words can be used to support these inferences.

Key Learning Objective: The student will be able to cite text evidence to support inferences.

For additional practice:

Background *Title IX, part of the Educational Amendments of 1972, makes it illegal to exclude anyone from participating in any government-funded educational program or activity based on gender. Some people argue that this legislation should put a greater emphasis on single-sex education in public schools. However, in 2001, senators Kay Bailey Hutchison (R-TX) and Barbara Mikulski (D-MD) worked with other legislators to introduce a single-sex education offerings. Recently, Kay Ford had to defend their amendment. The following article appeared in The Wall Street Journal on October 16, 2012.*

A Right to Choose Single-Sex Education

Opinion by Kay Bailey Hutchinson and Barbara Mikulski

Close Reader selection
"A Right to Choose Single-Sex Education,"
Op-ed by Kay Bailey Hutchinson and Barbara Mikulski

COMMON CORE Common Core Standards

RI 1 Cite textual evidence to support inferences.
RI 2 Determine central ideas of a text.
RI 6 Determine an author's point of view or purpose.
W 4 Produce clear and coherent writing.

Text Complexity Rubric

	Don't Eat Fortune's Cookie
Quantitative Measures	**Lexile:** N/A
Qualitative Measures	**Levels of Meaning/Purpose** more than one purpose; implied but easy to infer
	Structure organization of main ideas and details complex, but clearly stated and generally sequential
	Language Conventionality and Clarity contemporary, familiar language
	Knowledge Demands some references to other texts
Reader/Task Considerations	Teacher determined Vary by individual reader and type of text

TEACH

CLOSE READ

Michael Lewis tackles diverse subjects in his writing, ranging from politics to baseball, but what he likes to focus on and bring out most of all is the human element. He is fascinated by the people who make stories happen through their actions. This interest in people and what they do is conveyed clearly in Lewis's speech to the graduates.

AS YOU VIEW Direct students to use the As You View statement to focus their viewing. Remind students to write down questions that they generate as they are watching the video.

Support Inferences

Tell students that when they make inferences from speeches, they base their assumptions on not only the speaker's words, but also the gestures, facial expressions, pauses, and tone of voice that accompany those words.

A **ASK STUDENTS** why Lewis begins his speech with humor and the request that the students give themselves a round of applause. *(Lewis wants to entertain his audience; he wants to put the students at ease and engage their interest so that they will listen to his words.)*

B **CITE TEXT EVIDENCE** Have students explain how they know that Lewis holds his senior advisor in high regard. *(He describes his advisor as a "really gifted man." He credits this professor with helping him to "become engrossed" in the process of writing the thesis. He devotes a number of sentences to the professor. He uses humor to explain what the professor said to him during the defense of his thesis.)*

COLLABORATIVE DISCUSSION Have pairs share the important ideas that Lewis presents in his speech. Then as a class discuss their relevance to the experience of graduating from college. Accept all reasonable responses.

ASK STUDENTS to share any questions they generated in the course of viewing the video.

Michael Lewis *(b. 1960) is the author of several bestselling books, including* The Blind Side *and* Moneyball, *both of which were made into successful movies. In his first book,* Liar's Poker, *he examines Wall Street practices based on his personal experiences as an investment banker. Lewis is a contributing editor for* Vanity Fair *and writes for* The New York Times *as well as other publications. A graduate of Princeton University, he returned to the school in 2012 during graduation weekend to deliver the baccalaureate address recorded in this video.*

MEDIA ANALYSIS

Don't Eat Fortune's Cookie

Graduation Speech by Michael Lewis

AS YOU VIEW Pay attention to Lewis's ideas about success and rewards.

COLLABORATIVE DISCUSSION What ideas does Lewis express about success and how people are rewarded? With a partner, discuss how these ideas relate to students preparing to graduate from college.

SCAFFOLDING FOR ELL STUDENTS

Support Inferences To help students infer the main idea of Lewis's speech, have them replay the video, pausing as needed to note the following:

- direct advice Lewis gives to the graduates
- examples that Lewis uses to illustrate his advice

ASK STUDENTS What important idea does Lewis want listeners to take from his speech? *(Success is the result of luck, and those who are lucky should help the unlucky.)*

Support Inferences COMMON CORE RI 1

Discuss the importance of tone in making inferences from what a speaker says. To illustrate, write this phrase from Lewis's speech on the board: "the Wall Street we've come to know and love." Elicit from students that if they saw the words written, they might think the speaker intended the statement to be taken literally. As a class, view that part of the speech again. Discuss how the speaker's tone and facial expressions support a different interpretation of those words.

Analyzing the Media   COMMON CORE RI 1, RI 2, RI 6
Possible answers:

1. *His main idea is that luck has a great deal to do with success and that those who are lucky need to help those who are not. He might choose to express this idea to Princeton graduates because they have already profited from luck.*

2. *Sharing his experiences engages listeners' attention and adds credibility since his experiences support his message.*

3. Moneyball *shows that luck plays an important role in the statistics of "astonishing" ball players.*

4. *His description makes it clear that the team leaders, who ate the fourth cookie, thought they deserved it even though they had done nothing to deserve being chosen team leaders and nothing during the group activity to deserve an extra reward.*

5. *His purpose is to persuade the graduates to be humble about their success and to help those who are less fortunate. The content contributes to this purpose by supporting his view that luck plays an important role in success.*

 **Assess It!**

Online Selection Test
• Download an editable ExamView bank.
• Assign and manage this test online.

Support Inferences   COMMON CORE RI 1

Ideas are usually stated explicitly in nonfiction writing. However, there may be some unstated thoughts and feelings that require readers to make **inferences**, or logical assumptions based on evidence in the text. When viewing a recorded speech such as "Don't Eat Fortune's Cookie," you can support your inferences with observations about the speaker's tone and gestures as well as with specific words.

In the following quotation, Michael Lewis describes how he once experienced a speech such as the one he is delivering:

> Thirty years ago I sat where you sat. I must have listened to some older person share his life experiences. I don't remember a word of it. I couldn't even tell you who spoke. And you won't be able to either.

You might infer from the author's words, humorous tone, and smile that although he is speaking at a prestigious event, he doesn't want the audience to think he has an inflated opinion of himself.

Analyzing the Media   COMMON CORE RI 1, RI 2, RI 6, W 4

Cite Text Evidence   Support your responses with evidence from the selection.

1. **Identify** What is the central idea of Lewis's speech? Why might he have chosen to express this idea at a Princeton graduation ceremony?

2. **Analyze** Why does Lewis share his personal experiences at the beginning of the speech? How does this part of the speech affect his credibility?

3. **Analyze** Explain how the discussion of *Moneyball* relates to Lewis's central idea.

4. **Infer** What can you infer from Lewis's vivid description of the way the team leaders ate the extra cookies?

5. **Draw Conclusions** What is Lewis's overall purpose in this speech? How does the specific content of the speech contribute to that purpose?

PERFORMANCE TASK

Writing Activity: Review Write a review of Michael Lewis's address for the alumni newsletter from the viewpoint of a graduate in the audience. Comment on these areas:

• the relevance of his central idea
• the development of his central idea
• the focus and organization of his speech
• the style of his delivery

Assign this performance task.

PERFORMANCE TASK   COMMON CORE W 4

Writing Activity: Review Briefly discuss the elements of a strong review, emphasizing that students need to organize their ideas logically and clearly state their view on the speech. Remind them to include enough of the content to inform readers of the important ideas of the speech. Encourage students to review the video of Lewis's speech to help them identify specific details that will support their critique.

Analyze Ideas and Events

COMMON CORE

RL 3

TEACH

Ask students why it is more difficult to identify the important ideas in a speech we watch, as with this one, than a speech we read, with the printed text in front of us. *(With a live or video speech, audience members have to listen and remember at the same time; they have to store key ideas as the speech continues. With the printed text of a speech, readers can pause to think about key ideas; they can take notes before they continue; they can go back and re-read key passages.)*

Ask students if the Michael Lewis speech concentrates more on ideas or on anecdotes—personal stories about the speaker's life. *(personal anecdotes)* Tell them that they are going to watch the speech a second time. Ask them to pay close attention to the speaker's personal anecdotes. Their task is to remember—without making notes—five major anecdotes, or stories, that Lewis tells about his life.

When the speech is finished, conduct a class brainstorm. List the speech's major anecdotes where all can see them. *(writing a senior thesis; getting a job at Solomon Brothers; writing Liar's Poker; writing Moneyball; the experiment with student groups and cookies)*

Now ask students to help identify an idea, or message, Lewis is trying to convey with each of these anecdotes. Have them write these beside the anecdotes themselves. Answers will vary, but the subject of luck should come up. When it does, encourage students to see the role of luck as a theme, or idea, that connects all of the speaker's stories.

PRACTICE AND APPLY

Using "The Role of Luck" as a heading, students are to make a list of their own personal stories that illustrate the part luck has played in their lives. Tell students they may focus on either good luck, as Lewis does, or bad luck.

COLLABORATIVE DISCUSSION

Direct students, in small groups, to discuss the role of luck in their lives. Ask them to use personal anecdotes to illustrate their ideas.

Round up by asking groups to report on the link between their anecdotes and their ideas about luck.

Remind students that when they encounter personal anecdotes in their reading, they should always look for a message or an idea.

Make Inferences

COMMON CORE

RI 1

RETEACH

Review the ideas about how to make and support inferences in the analysis of recorded speeches. Then present the audio version of a historic speech, for example, an early inauguration address or one of Roosevelt's wartime speeches.

- On the board, write two or three inferences. These might relate to the purpose of the speech, the message, or the mood of the country at the time the speech was given.
- Have students work in small groups to review the speech and identify evidence that supports each of the inferences. Remind them to listen to the tone, pace, and expression of the speaker as well as the words.

 LEVEL UP TUTORIALS Assign the following *Level Up* tutorial: **Making Inferences**

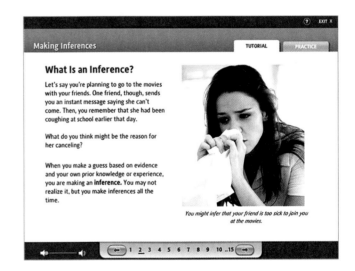

CLOSE READING APPLICATION

Have students view another commencement speech on the Internet with a partner. Ask them to make two inferences and support them with details from the content of the speech as well as the speaker's style. Have pairs present clips of the video along with their analysis in small groups. Have group members evaluate the validity of each pair's inferences.

A Right to Choose Single-Sex Education

Opinion by Kay Bailey Hutchison and Barbara Mikulski

Why This Text

Students sometimes read through an argument without evaluating an author's claim, reasons, or evidence. "A Right to Choose Single-Sex Education" provides an opportunity to evaluate an essay written by two congresswomen regarding public education. With the help of the close-reading questions, students will determine whether Hutchison and Mikulski's claim is clear and specific. This close reading will provide students the opportunity to draw and support inferences from the text.

Background Have students read the background and the information about the author. Introduce the selection by telling students that Kay Bailey Hutchison and Barbara Mikulski were both United States senators when they wrote this opinion. They both strongly believe that a single-sex education option can help some students achieve higher levels of success. In 2001, they worked to reintroduce the option of single-sex education in public schools.

AS YOU READ Ask students to pay attention to the evidence Hutchison and Mikulski offer. What is the first piece of evidence you read that supports their claim?

Common Core Support

- cite strong and thorough textual evidence
- draw inferences from the text
- determine the meaning of words and phrases as they are used in a text

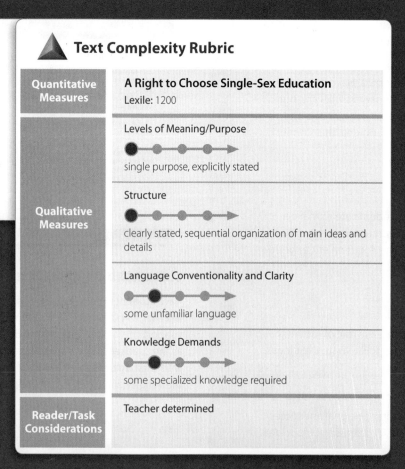

Text Complexity Rubric

Quantitative Measures	**A Right to Choose Single-Sex Education** Lexile: 1200
Qualitative Measures	**Levels of Meaning/Purpose** single purpose, explicitly stated
	Structure clearly stated, sequential organization of main ideas and details
	Language Conventionality and Clarity some unfamiliar language
	Knowledge Demands some specialized knowledge required
Reader/Task Considerations	Teacher determined

Strategies for CLOSE READING

Support Inferences

Students should read this opinion piece carefully all the way through. Close-reading questions at the bottom of the page will help them focus on a thorough analysis of the text. As they read, students should jot down comments or questions about the argument in the side margins.

WHEN STUDENTS STRUGGLE . . .

To help students support inferences drawn from the text, have them work in a small group to fill out a chart, such as the one shown below, as they analyze the text.

CITE TEXT EVIDENCE For practice in supporting inferences, ask students to cite the evidence Hutchison and Mikulski use to support their claim.

INFERENCE: *Allowing single-sex education is important for American students' success.*

SUPPORT:

Reason 1: A 2008 Department of Education study showed that single-sex classrooms decrease distractions and improve student achievement.

Reason 2: Only 59% of girls in mixed classes were scored as proficient on the FCAT, while 75% of girls in single-sex classes achieved proficiency.

Reason 3: Booker T. Washington High School implemented all-boys and all-girls freshman academies. Their graduation rate increased from 55% in 2007 to 81.6% in 2010.

Reason 4: No one has the right to deny students the choice.

Background *Title IX, part of the Educational Amendments of 1972, makes it illegal to exclude anyone from participating in any government-funded educational program or activity based on gender. Some people argue that this legislation should put a permanent end to single-sex education in public schools. However, in 2001, senators Kay Bailey Hutchison (R-TX) and Barbara Mikulski (D-MD) worked with other legislators to reintroduce single-sex education offerings. Recently, they have had to defend their amendment. The following article appeared in* The Wall Street Journal *on October 16, 2012.*

A Right to Choose Single-Sex Education

Opinion by Kay Bailey Hutchinson and Barbara Mikulski

CLOSE READ
Notes

1. **READ ▶** As you read lines 1–33, begin to collect and cite text evidence.
   - In the margin, restate the authors' position in lines 7–12.
   - Underline their claims (lines 13–33).
   - Circle opposing viewpoints.

Education proponents across the political **spectrum** were dismayed by recent attempts to eradicate the single-gender options in public schools in Virginia, West Virginia, Alabama, Mississippi, Maine and Florida. We were particularly troubled at efforts to **thwart** education choice for American students and their families because it is a cause we have worked hard to advance.

A B   Studies have shown that some students learn better in a single-gender environment, particularly in math and science. But federal regulations used to prevent public schools from offering that option. So in 2001 we joined with then-Sen. Hillary Clinton and Sen. Susan Collins to author legislation that allowed public schools to offer single-sex education. It was an epic bipartisan[1] battle against entrenched bureaucracy, but well worth the fight.

10

[1] **bipartisan:** representing, made up of, or organized by members of two political parties.

spectrum:
a wide range

thwart:
stand in the way of

They claim that students have a right to choose single-sex education.

7

---

1. **READ AND CITE TEXT EVIDENCE**

A **ASK STUDENTS** to cite the textual evidence that supports their restatement of the authors' position in lines 7–12. *Students should cite lines 7–8 as evidence that single-gender classrooms help students learn, lines 9–11 as evidence that the authors once championed single-sex education, and line 12 as evidence that the authors continue to support this cause.*

Critical Vocabulary: spectrum (line 1) Have students share their definitions of *spectrum.* Ask them to give examples of elements of "the political spectrum."

Critical Vocabulary: thwart (line 4) Have students compare definitions of *thwart.* Ask them to consider which definition best fits this context, and explain why.

Since our amendment passed, thousands of American children have benefited. Now, though, some civil libertarians are claiming that single-sex public-school programs are discriminatory and thus illegal.

To be clear: The 2001 law did not require that children be educated in single-gender programs or schools. It simply allowed schools and districts to offer the choice of single-sex schools or classrooms, as long as opportunities were equally available to boys and girls. In the vast and growing realm of 20 education research, one central **tenet** has been confirmed repeatedly: Children learn in different ways. For some, single-sex classrooms make all the difference.

Critics argue that these programs promote harmful gender stereotypes. Ironically, it is exactly these stereotypes that the single-sex programs seek to eradicate.

As studies have confirmed—and as any parent can tell you—negative gender roles are often sharpened in coeducational environments. Boys are more likely, for instance, to buy into the notion that reading isn't masculine when they're surrounded by (and showing off for) girls.

30 Girls, meanwhile, have made so much progress in educational achievement that women are overrepresented in postgraduate education. But they still lag in the acquisition of bachelor's and graduate degrees in math and the sciences. It has been demonstrated time and again that young girls are more willing to ask and answer questions in classrooms without boys.

A 2008 Department of Education study found that "both principals and teachers believed that the main benefits of single-sex schooling are decreasing distractions to learning and improving student achievement." The gender slant—the math-is-for-boys, home-EC-is- for-girls trope—is eliminated.

In a three-year study in the mid-2000s, researchers at Florida's Stetson University compared the performance of single-gender and mixed-gender 40 classes at an elementary school, controlling for the likes of class sizes,

tenet:
a belief widely held in common by members of a group or profession

2. ◀ **REREAD AND DISCUSS** Reread lines 7–15. With a small group, discuss your initial responses to the argument. Examine the strengths and weaknesses of their claims. Cite specific examples from the text to support your view.

3. **READ** ▶ As you read lines 34–71, continue to cite textual evidence.
- Circle statistics provided as evidence, and underline the sources of these statistics.
- In the margin, restate the conclusion (lines 64–71).

8

> **No one is arguing that single-sex education is the best option for every student.**

demographics and teacher training. When the children took the Florida Comprehensive Assessment Test (which measures achievement in math and literacy, for instance), the results were striking: Only 59% of girls in mixed classes were scored as proficient, while 75% of girls in single-sex ones achieved proficiency. Similarly, 37% of boys in coeducational classes scored proficient, compared with 86% of boys in the all-boys classes.

Booker T. Washington High School in Memphis, Tenn., the winner of the 2011 Race to the Top High School Commencement Challenge, went to a 81.6% graduation rate in 2010 from a graduation rate of 55% in 2007. 50 Among the changes at the school? Implementing all-girls and all-boys freshman academies.

In Dallas, the all-boys Barack Obama Leadership Academy opened its doors last year. There is every reason to believe it will follow the success of the first all-girls public school, Irma Rangel Young Women's Leadership School, which started in 2004. Irma Rangel, which has been a Texas Education Agency Exemplary School since 2006 also took sixth place at the Dallas Independent School District's 30th Annual Mathematics Olympiad that year.

No one is arguing that single-sex education is the best option for every student. But it is preferable for some students and families, and no one has the 60 right to deny them an option that may work best for a particular child. Attempts to eliminate single-sex education are equivalent to taking away students' and parents' choice about one of the most fundamentally important aspects of childhood and future indicators of success—a child's education.

Lines 58–63 support the primary claim, and include an emotional appeal; a school named after Obama.

Students have a right to choose single-sex education.

9

---

2. **REREAD AND DISCUSS USING TEXT EVIDENCE**

B **ASK STUDENTS** to consider both strengths and weaknesses in the authors' claims, and to cite and explain textual evidence. *Students might say that the authors' claims are unsubstantiated, such as: "Studies have shown…" in line 7. As strengths, they may cite line 13: "Since our amendment passed…" showing legal precedent. They might also point out rallying language such as in lines 11–12.*

3. **READ AND CITE TEXT EVIDENCE**

C **ASK STUDENTS** to explain what inferences they can draw from the evidence cited. *Students should conclude that the statistics in lines 43–46, 47–49, and 54–57 all show that students performed better in single-sex schools.*

Critical Vocabulary: tenet (line 20) Have students compare their definitions of *tenet*.

FOR ELL STUDENTS You may wish to review the different ways to refer to each academic year in America, and their order: freshman (first year), sophomore (second year), junior (third year), and senior (fourth year).

WHEN STUDENTS STRUGGLE . . .
To help students support inferences, ask them to reread lines 47–51. Have them identify the increase in the graduation rate at Booker T. Washington High School from 2007 to 2010. Explain that the authors believe that this is a result of switching to "all-girls" and "all-boys" freshman academies.

CITE TEXT EVIDENCE For practice evaluating evidence, ask students to explain whether this evidence is strong or weak. *Students should see that this is an example of strong evidence, because it is both authoritative and verifiable.*

CLOSE READ
Notes

An appeal is made to national pride in the final paragraph.

Single-sex education is important for our students.

D America once dominated educational attainment among developed countries, but we have fallen disastrously in international rankings. As we seek ways to offer the best education for all our children, in ways that are better tailored to their needs, it seems not just counterproductive but damaging to reduce the options. Single-sex education in public schools will continue to be a voluntary choice for students and their families. To limit or eliminate single-
70 sex education is irresponsible. To take single-sex education away from students who stand to benefit is unforgivable.

4. **◀ REREAD** Reread lines 34–71. Make notes in the margin for the following.
   * Evaluate the strength of the evidence presented.
   * Restate in the margin the authors' positions in lines 58–63.
   * Explain the appeal made in the final pararaph.

SHORT RESPONSE

Cite Text Evidence Explain whether or not the authors convinced you of the value of same-sex education. Review your reading notes and evaluate the strength and effectiveness of the claims and evidence presented. **Cite text evidence** to support your response.

Answers will vary but students should recognize that the authors think that some students may do better in single-sex schools. The authors cite statistics from the Florida Comprehensive Assessment Test where "Only 59% of girls in mixed classes where scored as proficient, while 75% of girls in single-sex ones achieved proficiency." The authors also state that "no one has the right to deny" students an option. Students should cite evidence from the text to support their position.

10

4. **REREAD AND CITE TEXT EVIDENCE** Remind students that they sometimes have to draw inferences, or logical assumptions, based on evidence in the text.

D **ASK STUDENTS** what inference they can draw from the information presented in the first sentence on this page (lines 64–65.) *Students should infer that the authors are appealing to their readers' sense of national pride when drawing attention to American education's decline in international rankings.*

SHORT RESPONSE

Cite Text Evidence Student responses will vary, but they should cite evidence from the text to support their explanations. Students should:

* support inferences from the text that explain the authors' claim.
* evaluate the strength of the evidence.
* explain whether or not they are personally convinced by the argument.

TO CHALLENGE STUDENTS . . .

To explore an opposing viewpoint to Hutchison's and Mikulski's, have students research online the American Civil Liberties Union's (ACLU's) opinion on Title IX and sex-segregated schools.

ASK STUDENTS to explain the ACLU's position on sex-segregated schools. *The ACLU does not support single-sex schools. Have students present the points that the ACLU uses to support its position. Students should include some or all of the following points: Title IX benefits both girls and boys; federally-funded single-sex schools are illegal; support for single-sex schools is based on old stereotypes and questionable science; there is evidence that single-sex schools do not improve student performance.*

DIG DEEPER

With the class, return to Question 2, Reread and Discuss. Have students share the results of their discussions.

ASK STUDENTS whether they were satisfied with the outcome of their small-group discussions. Have each group share their initial responses to the argument as well as their initial assessments of the strengths and weaknesses of the claims. What textual evidence did students find to support their conclusions?

* Guide each group to share whether they came to a unanimous conclusion about the strength of the argument. If not, have groups share the variety of opinions that emerged from their discussion.
* Ask groups to share the textual evidence that seemed the most compelling. Ask students to explain what made this particular evidence strong.
* After groups have shared the results of their discussions, ask whether any students' perceptions of the argument changed as they read on to the end of the article. Ask them to explain how the authors' evidence convinced them, or failed to convince them.

ASK STUDENTS to return to their Short Response answer and revise it based on the class discussion.

The Secret to Raising Smart Kids

Science Article by Carol S. Dweck

Why This Text?

Students encounter arguments in many forms, from impassioned blog posts to reasoned debates. This lesson examines an argument about two ways of viewing intelligence and the scientific research that indicates which one leads to greater success in life.

▶ View It!

Professional Development Podcast:
Teaching Argument

Key Learning Objective: The student will be able to analyze the structure of an argument.

mySmartPlanner Create lesson plans and access resources online.

◌ COMMON CORE Common Core Standards

RI 1 Cite textual evidence to support analysis and inferences.

RI 2 Provide a summary of the text.

RI 5 Analyze and evaluate the structure an author uses in his or her exposition or argument.

RI 6 Determine an author's point of view or purpose, analyzing style and content.

RI 10 Read and comprehend literary nonfiction.

W 1c Use words, phrases, and clauses to link sections of the text.

L 1 Demonstrate command of the conventions of standard English grammar and usage.

L 4b Identify patterns of word changes that indicate different meanings.

▲ Text Complexity Rubric

Quantitative Measures	**The Secret to Raising Smart Kids** **Lexile:** 1400L
Qualitative Measures	**Levels of Meaning/Purpose** ●—●—●—●—●→ more than one purpose; implied, easily identified from context
	Structure ●—●—●—●—●→ implicit compare-contrast text structure
	Language Conventionality and Clarity ●—●—●—●—●→ some unfamiliar, academic, or domain-specific words
	Knowledge Demands ●—●—●—●—●→ several references or allusions to other texts
Reader/Task Considerations	Teacher determined Vary by individual reader and type of text

CLOSE READ

AS YOU READ Direct students to use the As You Read note to focus their reading. Remind them to write down any questions they generate during reading.

Analyze Style (LINES 1-10)

 COMMON CORE RI6

Tell students that an argument is a type of writing that seeks to convince readers to accept the writer's ideas or to take a certain action. To achieve their purpose, authors must present their ideas clearly to readers.

A **ASK STUDENTS** to characterize Dweck's style and use of language. What do her word choices and sentence structures suggest about the audience she is hoping to convince? *(Dweck's style is straightforward. She avoids overly long or complex sentences and chooses words from common usage. This suggests that she wrote her article for a general audience.)*

Analyze Structure: Argument (LINES 11–32)

 COMMON CORE RI 5, RI 10

Explain that the author's position on an issue, or the **claim,** often appears at the beginning of the argument. The claim and details that elaborate on it may be signaled by words and phrases such as *however, on the other hand,* and *but.*

B **CITE TEXT EVIDENCE** Ask students to cite the commonly accepted assumption that Dweck's claim opposes. *("[M]any people assume that possessing superior intelligence or ability…is a recipe for success.")*

CRITICAL VOCABULARY

implicit: The author states that early success in school leads students to hold the unspoken belief that they have a certain amount of intelligence.

ASK STUDENTS what ideas they associate with an implicit belief. *(It may be deeply held and never be questioned.)*

innate: One theory is that a person's intelligence level is determined at birth.

ASK STUDENTS how the theory of innate intelligence can be harmful both to good students and to those who struggle. *(Those who excel might fail to develop a good work ethic; those who struggle might give up.)*

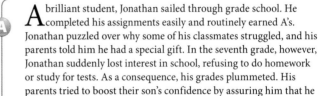

The Secret to Raising Smart Kids

Science Article by Carol S. Dweck

AS YOU READ Pay attention to the details that explain two different mind-sets about intelligence and learning.

A A brilliant student, Jonathan sailed through grade school. He completed his assignments easily and routinely earned A's. Jonathan puzzled over why some of his classmates struggled, and his parents told him he had a special gift. In the seventh grade, however, Jonathan suddenly lost interest in school, refusing to do homework or study for tests. As a consequence, his grades plummeted. His parents tried to boost their son's confidence by assuring him that he was very smart. But their attempts failed to motivate Jonathan (who is a composite drawn from several children). Schoolwork, their son

10 maintained, was boring and pointless.

B Our society worships talent, and many people assume that possessing superior intelligence or ability—along with confidence in that ability—is a recipe for success. In fact, however, more than 30 years of scientific investigation suggests that an overemphasis on intellect or talent leaves people vulnerable to failure, fearful of challenges and unwilling to remedy their shortcomings.

The result plays out in children like Jonathan, who coast through the early grades under the dangerous notion that no-effort academic achievement defines them as smart or gifted. Such children hold an

20 **implicit** belief that intelligence is **innate** and fixed, making striving to learn seem far less important than being (or looking) smart. This belief also makes them see challenges, mistakes and even the need to exert effort as threats to their ego rather than as opportunities to improve. And it causes them to lose confidence and motivation when the work is no longer easy for them.

Praising children's innate abilities, as Jonathan's parents did, reinforces this mind-set, which can also prevent young athletes or people in the workforce and even marriages from living up to their potential. On the other hand, our studies show that teaching people to

implicit
(ĭm-plĭs′ĭt) *adj.*
understood but not directly stated.

innate
(ĭ-nāt′) *adj.*
possessed at birth.

Image Credits: ©Viktor88/Shutterstock

SCAFFOLDING FOR ELL STUDENTS

Vocabulary: Multiple-Meaning Words Remind students that many English words have more than one possible meaning. Point out the word *brilliant* in line 1. Explain that while this word sometimes means "shining brightly," in this sentence it refers to a student who earns good grades easily and means "very smart and talented."

ASK STUDENTS to locate these multiple-meaning words in the first paragraph: *sailed* (line 1), *gift* (line 4), *plummeted* (line 6), *drawn* (line 9), *maintained* (line 10). Have them use context clues to guess the correct meanings and then check their answers in a dictionary.

Analyze Structure: Argument (LINES 48–77)

COMMON CORE RI 5, RI 10

Tell students that authors explain their claims with reasons.

C CITE TEXT EVIDENCE Have students cite and paraphrase the author's first reason in support of her position. *(The first reason appears in lines 48–50. To paraphrase, students who believe their poor performance is due to a lack of effort are more inclined to persevere than those who believe they lack ability.)*

Explain that in a well-constructed argument, each reason is supported and developed with **evidence,** or facts, examples, and other relevant details.

D ASK STUDENTS to evaluate whether the evidence in lines 60–77 convincingly supports the reason. Why or why not? *(Answers may vary. Some students may say that not enough students were involved in the study to make it valid. Others may think 60 students is enough; that the people involved in the study have valid credentials; and that the author explains the results of their work well.)*

Point out to students that Dweck's argument differs in structure from some arguments in that she is explaining two opposing views of intelligence in detail, using a comparison-contrast pattern of organization to make her points.

ASK STUDENTS how this structure, exemplified in lines 48–77, affects readers' perception of the author as well as of her argument. *(Her detailed explanation of both views gives readers the information they need to assess the logic of her argument and form their own judgments. It shows the author's objectivity and desire to inform.)*

CRITICAL VOCABULARY

engender: The author's experiment proved that emphasizing the importance of effort helped students become more successful.

ASK STUDENTS to summarize how praise should be used to engender success. *(Effort should be praised rather than ability.)*

---

30 have a "growth mind-set," which encourages a focus on effort rather than on intelligence or talent, helps make them into high achievers in school and in life.

The Opportunity of Defeat

I first began to investigate the underpinnings of human motivation—and how people persevere after setbacks—as a psychology graduate student at Yale University in the 1960s. Animal experiments by psychologists Martin Seligman, Steven Maier and Richard Solomon of the University of Pennsylvania had shown that after repeated failures, most animals conclude that a situation is hopeless and beyond their control. After such an experience, the researchers found, an animal
40 often remains passive even when it can effect change—a state they called learned helplessness.

People can learn to be helpless, too, but not everyone reacts to setbacks this way. I wondered:

Why do some students give up when they encounter difficulty, whereas others who are no more skilled continue to strive and learn? One answer, I soon discovered, lay in people's beliefs about why they had failed.

In particular, attributing poor performance to a lack of ability depresses motivation more than does the belief that lack of effort is
50 to blame. In 1972, when I taught a group of elementary and middle school children who displayed helpless behavior in school that a lack of effort (rather than lack of ability) led to their mistakes on math problems, the kids learned to keep trying when the problems got tough. They also solved many of the problems even in the face of difficulty. Another group of helpless children who were simply rewarded for their success on easy problems did not improve their ability to solve hard math problems. These experiments were an early indication that a focus on effort can help resolve helplessness and **engender** success.
60 Subsequent studies revealed that the most persistent students do not ruminate about their own failure much at all but instead think of mistakes as problems to be solved. At the University of Illinois in the 1970s I, along with my then graduate student Carol Diener, asked 60 fifth graders to think out loud while they solved very difficult pattern-recognition problems. Some students reacted defensively to mistakes, denigrating their skills with comments such as "I never did have a good rememory," and their problem-solving strategies deteriorated.

Others, meanwhile, focused on fixing errors and honing their
70 skills. One advised himself: "I should slow down and try to figure this out." Two schoolchildren were particularly inspiring. One, in the wake of difficulty, pulled up his chair, rubbed his hands together, smacked his lips and said, "I love a challenge!" The other, also confronting the hard problems, looked up at the experimenter and approvingly

engender
(ĕn-jĕn′dər) *v.* to bring into existence.

APPLYING ACADEMIC VOCABULARY

reinforce	persistence

As you discuss this article, incorporate the Collection 1 academic vocabulary words *reinforce* and *persistence*. Ask students to explain how **reinforcing** the importance of learners' effort, rather than their ability, leads to increased **persistence** on the learners' part.

declared, "I was hoping this would be informative!" Predictably, the students with this attitude outperformed their **cohorts** in these studies.

cohort
(kō´hôrt´) *n.* a companion or associate.

Two Views of Intelligence

Several years later I developed a broader theory of what separates the two general classes of learners—helpless versus mastery-oriented. I realized that these different types of students not only explain their failures differently, but they also hold different "theories" of intelligence. The helpless ones believe that intelligence is a fixed trait: you have only a certain amount, and that's that. I call this a "fixed mind-set." Mistakes crack their self-confidence because they attribute errors to a lack of ability, which they feel powerless to change. They avoid challenges because challenges make mistakes more likely and looking smart less so. Like Jonathan, such children shun effort in the belief that having to work hard means they are dumb.

The mastery-oriented children, on the other hand, think intelligence is **malleable** and can be developed through education and hard work. They want to learn above all else. After all, if you believe that you can expand your intellectual skills, you want to do just that. Because slipups stem from a lack of effort, not ability, they can be remedied by more effort. Challenges are energizing rather than intimidating; they offer opportunities to learn. Students with such a growth mind-set, we predicted, were destined for greater academic success and were quite likely to outperform their counterparts.

malleable
(măl´ē-ə-bəl) *adj.* able to be shaped or molded.

We validated these expectations in a study published in early 2007. Psychologists Lisa Blackwell of Columbia University and Kali H. Trzesniewski of Stanford University and I monitored 373 students for two years during the transition to junior high school, when the work gets more difficult and the grading more stringent, to determine how their mind-sets might affect their math grades. At the beginning of seventh grade, we assessed the students' mind-sets by asking them to agree or disagree with statements such as "Your intelligence is something very basic about you that you can't really change." We then assessed their beliefs about other aspects of learning and looked to see what happened to their grades.

As we had predicted, the students with a growth mind-set felt that learning was a more important goal in school than getting good grades. In addition, they held hard work in high regard, believing that the more you labored at something, the better you would become at it. They understood that even geniuses have to work hard for their great accomplishments. Confronted by a setback such as a disappointing test grade, students with a growth mind-set said they would study harder or try a different strategy for mastering the material.

The students who held a fixed mind-set, however, were concerned about looking smart with little regard for learning. They had negative views of effort, believing that having to work hard at something

The Secret to Raising Smart Kids **23**

WHEN STUDENTS STRUGGLE...

Have students work in pairs to fill out a chart that contrasts the ways in which students with different mind-sets view their intelligence.

Fixed Mind-set	Growth Mind-set
• Each person has a "fixed" amount of intelligence.	• Intelligence can be expanded through effort.
• Intelligence cannot be developed or changed.	• More challenges lead to more growth.

CLOSE READ

Analyze Structure: Argument (SUBHEADING)

COMMON CORE RI 5

Explain that each subheading in the article is a cue that another reason will be developed in that section.

E **ASK STUDENTS** to explain the focus of the part of the argument covered under this subheading. (*The author explains two mind-sets on intelligence.*)

Analyze Style (LINES 78-88)

COMMON CORE RI 6

Remind students that Dweck is writing for a general audience, not just for specialists in her field.

F **CITE TEXT EVIDENCE** Have students identify ways in which the author clarifies ideas in this paragraph. (*In lines 82-83, the author introduces the term "fixed" as it applies to intelligence and then restates the idea in familiar language.*)

Analyze Structure: Argument (LINES 98-103)

COMMON CORE RI 5

Tell students that when they look at the evidence presented by the author, they need to determine whether it comes from a credible or reliable source.

G **CITE TEXT EVIDENCE** Have students identify one piece of evidence in lines 98–103. Is this evidence reliable? (*The evidence is from a study in which the author took part in 2007. The fact that it is a fairly current study conducted by an authoritative source—professional psychologists—makes it reliable.*)

CRITICAL VOCABULARY

cohorts: Although all the students were the same age, their ideas about intelligence differed.
ASK STUDENTS to explain what researchers might look for in choosing cohorts to participate in a study like this one. (*same age group and grade; similar educational, social, economic circumstances*)

malleable: People who have a growth mind-set believe intelligence can be shaped and developed.
ASK STUDENTS to compare someone's intelligence at ages fifteen and age thirty according to the theory of malleable intelligence. (*If intelligence can be developed, the older person would be more intelligent.*)

Analyze Structure: Argument (LINES 152–168)

 COMMON CORE RI 5

Tell students that making an argument relevant to a wider audience helps increase its persuasiveness.

H **CITE TEXT EVIDENCE** Have students identify details that show the relevance of Dweck's ideas to a broader audience. *(She shows that her theories apply to the workplace, making the point that managers with fixed mind-sets are less willing to benefit from or accept criticism, whereas those with a growth mind-set are more receptive to hearing others' ideas.)*

---

120 was a sign of low ability. They thought that a person with talent or intelligence did not need to work hard to do well. Attributing a bad grade to their own lack of ability, those with a fixed mind-set said that they would study less in the future, try never to take that subject again and consider cheating on future tests.

Such divergent outlooks had a dramatic impact on performance. At the start of junior high, the math achievement test scores of the students with a growth mind-set were comparable to those of students who displayed a fixed mind-set. But as the work became more difficult, the students with a growth mind-set showed greater

130 persistence. As a result, their math grades overtook those of the other students by the end of the first semester—and the gap between the two groups continued to widen during the two years we followed them.

Along with Columbia psychologist Heidi Grant, I found a similar relation between mind-set and achievement in a 2003 study of 128 Columbia freshman premed students who were enrolled in a challenging general chemistry course. Although all the students cared about grades, the ones who earned the best grades were those who placed a high premium on learning rather than on showing that they were smart in chemistry. The focus on learning strategies, effort and

140 persistence paid off for these students.

Confronting Deficiencies

A belief in fixed intelligence also makes people less willing to admit to errors or to confront and remedy their deficiencies in school, at work and in their social relationships. In a study published in 1999 of 168 freshmen entering the University of Hong Kong, where all instruction and coursework are in English, three Hong Kong colleagues and I found that students with a growth mind-set who scored poorly on their English proficiency exam were far more inclined to take a remedial English course than were low-scoring students with a fixed mind-set. The students with a stagnant view of intelligence were

150 presumably unwilling to admit to their deficit and thus passed up the opportunity to correct it.

H A fixed mind-set can similarly hamper communication and progress in the workplace by leading managers and employees to discourage or ignore constructive criticism and advice. Research by psychologists Peter Heslin and Don VandeWalle of Southern Methodist University and Gary Latham of the University of Toronto shows that managers who have a fixed mind-set are less likely to seek or welcome feedback from their employees than are managers with a growth mind-set. Presumably, managers with a growth mind-

160 set see themselves as works-in-progress and understand that they need feedback to improve, whereas bosses with a fixed mind-set are more likely to see criticism as reflecting their underlying level of competence. Assuming that other people are not capable of changing either, executives with a fixed mind-set are also less likely to mentor

24 Collection 1

Strategies for Annotation 🖊 🗐 *Annotate it!*

Analyze Structure: Argument  COMMON CORE RI 5

Tell students that the structure of the author's paragraphs adds to the overall persuasiveness of her text. Have them use their eBook annotation tools to analyze lines 152–168.

- Highlight in yellow the sentence that states the main idea.
- Highlight in blue the sentences that present evidence or facts.
- Highlight in green the concluding sentence. *(lines 166–169)*
- Discuss: How does the main idea of this paragraph relate to the author's overall claim?

A fixed mind-set can similarly hamper communication and progress in the workplace by leading managers and employees to discourage or ignore constructive criticism and advice. Research by psychologists Peter Heslin and Don VandeWalle of Southern Methodist University and Gary Latham of the University of Toronto shows that managers who have a fixed mind-set are less likely to their underlings. But after Heslin, VandeWalle and Latham gave managers a tutorial on the value and principles of the growth mind-set, supervisors became more willing to coach their employees and gave more useful advice.

Mind-set can affect the quality and longevity of personal relationships as well, through people's willingness—or unwillingness—to deal with difficulties. Those with a fixed mind-set are less likely than those with a growth mind-set to broach problems in their relationships and to try to solve them, according to a 2006 study I conducted with psychologist Lara Kammrath of Wilfrid Laurier University in Ontario. After all, if you think that human personality traits are more or less fixed, relationship repair seems largely futile. Individuals who believe people can change and grow, however, are more confident that confronting concerns in their relationships will lead to resolutions.

Proper Praise

How do we transmit a growth mind-set to our children? One way is by telling stories about achievements that result from hard work. For instance, talking about math geniuses who were more or less born that way puts students in a fixed mind-set, but descriptions of great mathematicians who fell in love with math and developed amazing skills engenders a growth mindset, our studies have shown. People also communicate mind-sets through praise. Although many, if not most, parents believe that they should build up a child by telling him or her how brilliant and talented he or she is, our research suggests that this is misguided.

In studies involving several hundred fifth graders published in 1998, for example, Columbia psychologist Claudia M. Mueller and I gave children questions from a nonverbal IQ test. After the first 10 problems, on which most children did fairly well, we praised them. We praised some of them for their intelligence: "Wow...that's a really good score. You must be smart at this." We commended others for their effort: "Wow...that's a really good score. You must have worked really hard."

We found that intelligence praise encouraged a fixed mind-set more often than did pats on the back for effort. Those congratulated for their intelligence, for example, shied away from a challenging assignment—they wanted an easy one instead—far more often than the kids applauded for their effort. (Most of those lauded for their hard work wanted the difficult problem set from which they would learn.) When we gave everyone hard problems anyway, those praised for being smart became discouraged, doubting their ability. And their scores, even on an easier problem set we gave them afterward, declined as compared with their previous results on equivalent problems. In contrast, students praised for their effort did not lose confidence when

CLOSE READ

Support Inferences: Draw Conclusions (LINES 169–179)
 COMMON CORE RI 1

Remind students that when they read arguments, they need to draw their own conclusions from the details presented to help them assess the validity of the author's reasons or claim.

I ASK STUDENTS what the author is suggesting about the correlation between mind-set and personal happiness. (*People with a growth mind-set are more likely to try to work on and improve their relationships, thus leading to greater happiness for themselves. Those with a fixed mind-set do not see the point of trying to resolve issues; failure to remedy problematic relationships will lead to personal unhappiness.*)

Analyze Structure: Argument (LINES 180–189)
COMMON CORE RI 5

Explain that authors may offer a counterargument in which they address possible objections or opposing views.

J ASK STUDENTS what possible objection this paragraph could be seen as addressing. (*The information in this paragraph explains how to instill a growth mind-set in a child. This could be seen as a possible response to someone saying that it does no good to know about a growth mind-set if one already has a fixed mind-set, or to parents who believe it is their responsibility to build up a child's self-esteem by praising the child's intelligence.*)

SCAFFOLDING FOR ELL STUDENTS

Comprehension: Structure of Argument Guide students to identify the reason developed by the evidence in this section of the article. Use a whiteboard to project lines 180–210. Together, complete these steps:

- Highlight in green the ways that a growth mind-set can be encouraged in children.
- Highlight in yellow the results of encouraging this mind-set.
- On a note, state the reason that the author gives in this section. (*Encouraging a growth mind-set makes students perform better.*)

Analyze Structure: Argument (LINES 220–236)

COMMON CORE RI 5

Tell students that sound evidence is evidence that can be verified, or backed up by another source. Explain that in the case of anecdotal evidence, readers must decide whether it is persuasive based on the connections the author makes as well as their own knowledge.

K **CITE TEXT EVIDENCE** Have students explain whether the evidence in lines 220–227 is convincing. Why or why not? *(This evidence is presented not as an official study but as an informal account of an experience the author had. It is believable and therefore could be accepted as support for the author's argument, although facts and figures offering more concrete proof would increase the persuasiveness of this part of the text.)* Have students identify evidence in this part of the article that is verifiable. *(In line 233, the author gives specific examples of "geniuses" whose accomplishments were achieved as a result of hard work. Readers could check the biographies of these people to verify whether or not the author is correct.)*

COLLABORATIVE DISCUSSION Suggest that students focus on the consequences Dweck cites for each mind-set, or how each mind-set affects the lives of the people who have it. Accept all reasonable responses.

ASK STUDENTS to share any questions they generated in the course of reading and discussing the selection.

---

faced with the harder questions, and their performance improved
210 markedly on the easier problems that followed.

Making Up Your Mind-Set

In addition to encouraging a growth mind-set through praise for effort, parents and teachers can help children by providing explicit instruction regarding the mind as a learning machine. Blackwell, Trzesniewski and I recently designed an eight-session workshop for 91 students whose math grades were declining in their first year of junior high. Forty-eight of the students received instruction in study skills only, whereas the others attended a combination of study skills sessions and classes in which they learned about the growth mind-set and how to apply it to schoolwork.

220   In the growth mind-set classes, students read and discussed an article entitled "You Can Grow Your Brain." They were taught that the brain is like a muscle that gets stronger with use and that learning prompts neurons in the brain to grow new connections. From such instruction, many students began to see themselves as agents of their own brain development. Students who had been disruptive or bored sat still and took note. One particularly unruly boy looked up during the discussion and said, "You mean I don't have to be dumb?" . . .

Teaching children such information is not just a ploy to get them to study. People do differ in intelligence, talent and ability. And yet
230 research is converging on the conclusion that great accomplishment, and even what we call genius, is typically the result of years of passion and dedication and not something that flows naturally from a gift. Mozart, Edison, Curie, Darwin and Cézanne were not simply born with talent; they cultivated it through tremendous and sustained effort. Similarly, hard work and discipline contribute much more to school achievement than IQ does.

Such lessons apply to almost every human endeavor. For instance, many young athletes value talent more than hard work and have consequently become unteachable. Similarly, many people accomplish
240 little in their jobs without constant praise and encouragement to maintain their motivation. If we foster a growth mind-set in our homes and schools, however, we will give our children the tools to succeed in their pursuits and to become responsible employees and citizens.

COLLABORATIVE DISCUSSION   With a partner, discuss the most important differences between the two mind-sets Dweck writes about. Cite specific evidence from the text to support your comparison.

WHEN STUDENTS STRUGGLE. . .

To help students to distinguish verifiable facts from those that cannot be verified, list several details from the article on the board. Have students work in pairs to determine whether or not they could look the information up in another source to check its validity.

Model this process by asking students to reread lines 154–159. Point out that the specific names of the psychologists are identified, which would enable someone to look them up and find out whether or not they ever carried out such a study and what their conclusions were.

Analyze Structure: Argument

An **argument** expresses the writer's opinion on an issue or problem and supports it with reasons and evidence. A sound argument includes these elements:

- The **claim** is the statement of the writer's position on an issue or problem. It should be clear and specific. Often the claim is presented near the beginning of an argument, which enables readers to evaluate the strength of the supporting evidence that follows. **Example:** Walking for thirty minutes or more several times a week will significantly improve the quality of a person's life.
- **Reasons** are statements that justify or explain the claim. Valid reasons are accurate and relevant. They support the writer's position and rely on logic rather than emotion. **Example:** Walking has been proven to result in measurable health benefits.
- **Evidence** includes details that support the reasons, such as facts, quotations, examples, statistics, and expert views. To be convincing, the evidence must be sound, relevant, and substantial. **Example:** As a result of walking for thirty minutes a day, enzymes are produced that destroy bad cholesterol.
- Good arguments may also include **counterarguments.** These are arguments that anticipate possible opposing views and answer them. Counterarguments show that the writer has thorough knowledge of the issue and has clearly thought about both sides.

Strong support is the foundation of a good argument. The questions in the chart can help you assess the reasons and evidence in "The Secret to Raising Smart Kids."

Evaluating Support	
Can the information be verified?	Check the accuracy of facts by confirming them in another source, such as a reference work or a trustworthy website. In "The Secret to Raising Smart Kids," Dweck provides dates, locations, and names of professionals involved in the studies she cites.
Is there sufficient evidence?	Insufficient evidence leaves readers with unanswered questions and doubt. The organization of "The Secret to Raising Smart Kids" into separate sections helps readers determine whether each reason is amply supported.
Is the evidence authoritative?	In "The Secret to Raising Smart Kids," much of the evidence comes from studies carried out by psychologists whose credentials establish them as experts in their fields. Reference works, reliable websites, or accredited organizations are also credible sources of information on a topic.
Are the reasons logical?	Watch for errors in logic, such as oversimplifying a complex problem, making a generalization that is too broad or is drawn from too little information, or cause-and-effect fallacies (assuming that because one event followed another, the first event caused the second one to occur).

CLOSE READ

Analyze Structure: Argument

 COMMON CORE RI 5, RI 10

Review the elements of an argument with students. Then have them work together to find examples of reasons and different types of evidence.

To ensure students understand the terms in the chart, have them define each one based on the example given or other clues. Explain that every single detail in an argument probably will not be authoritative, verifiable, and logical. But, if too much of the evidence does not meet these criteria, then they must question the validity of the writer's position.

Finally, remind students that authors may have more than one purpose for writing. Ask students to identify this author's purposes, drawing their attention to what the structure of the article reveals about what she wants to accomplish. *(Her primary purpose is to convince readers to accept her analysis of the two mind-sets and their consequences. She also wants to inform. Her emphasis in this article is on communicating factual details.)*

Strategies for Annotation   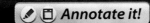 Annotate it!

Analyze Structure: Argument   COMMON CORE RI 5, RI 10

Share these strategies for guided or independent analysis:

- Highlight in pink the author's claim.
- Highlight in yellow the sentences that present reasons for the claim.
- Underline details that support the reasons.
- On a note, consider this question: Does the author include sufficient evidence to support this reason?

A belief in fixed intelligence also makes people less willing to admit to errors or to confront and remedy their deficiencies in school, at work and in their social relationships. In a study published in 1999 of 168 freshmen entering the University of Hong Kong, where all instruction and coursework are in English, three Hong Kong colleagues and I found that students with a growth mind-set who scored poorly

PRACTICE & APPLY

Analyzing the Text COMMON CORE RI 1, RI 5, RI 6, RI 10

Possible answers:

1. *A fixed mind-set, fostered by praising students for their innate ability, can prevent them from achieving their potential, but a growth mind-set, developed by encouraging students' effort, can help them become high achievers in school and in life.*

2. *The author supports her reason by explaining two studies in which she participated that had the goal of finding out why students react differently to setbacks. She includes direct quotations, description of methods used in the studies, and explanation of results.*

3. *Students with a growth mind-set are willing to work harder and tackle challenges because they believe intelligence can be developed. Those with a fixed mind-set want to look smart more than they want to learn, so they will avoid challenges and hard work. The information about the premed students makes the author's argument more convincing because it shows her theories apply to a broader population.*

4. *Dweck says that a fixed mind-set can make people less willing to make changes that will improve their social relationships and work and school performance. This part of the article shows the relevance of her information to everyone, thus broadening its appeal and persuasiveness.*

5. *Dweck says that parents and educators can share stories about people who accomplished great things through hard work, that they should praise children for their effort rather than their ability, and that they should encourage children to see their brains as "learning machines." Giving readers an action plan makes them more receptive to the author's claim.*

6. *The story about Jonathan interests readers and illustrates the author's point clearly, thus encouraging them to read the article.*

7. *Dweck's argument is thorough, explaining her theory about the two mind-sets in detail. She presents several reasons and solid evidence, and she indirectly addresses possible questions and objections.*

8. *The author's style makes the information accessible to readers. She avoids jargon and instead explains results of studies and conclusions using familiar terms.*

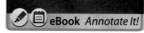

Analyzing the Text COMMON CORE RI 1, RI 5, RI 6, W 1c

Cite Text Evidence Support your responses with evidence from the selection.

1. **Summarize** What is Dweck's claim in this article?

2. **Analyze** In the section entitled "The Opportunity of Defeat," Dweck presents her first reason, which is that students with a growth mind-set show more persistence when faced with obstacles. What evidence does she use to support her view that "attributing poor performance to a lack of ability depresses motivation more than does the belief that lack of effort is to blame"?

3. **Analyze** What idea is supported by the evidence presented in "Two Views of Intelligence"? Why does Dweck include the information about premed students in the last paragraph?

4. **Analyze** What reason does Dweck provide to support her claim in the section entitled "Confronting Deficiencies"? How does this section strengthen her argument?

5. **Analyze** What specific advice does Dweck provide on how parents and educators can influence the mind-sets of children? Explain how this advice could help persuade readers to accept her claim.

6. **Evaluate** Dweck opens her article with the story of a brilliant student named Jonathan who experiences difficulties at school. How effective is this introduction? Give reasons for your opinion.

7. **Evaluate** Does Dweck provide a thorough and balanced argument in her article? Consider the following structural elements in your response: claim, reasons, evidence, counterarguments.

8. **Critique** Is the style of this article appropriate for a persuasive text? Why or why not? Be sure to consider Dweck's word choices and **syntax,** or arrangement of words.

PERFORMANCE TASK

Writing Activity With a partner, write an additional paragraph to be included in one of these sections of the article: "The Opportunity of Defeat," "Two Views of Intelligence," or "Confronting Deficiencies."

- In your paragraph, develop two examples in the context of a high-school setting that support the point the author is making in that part of the article. Your hypothetical examples should be drawn from your own experience and observations and illustrate the characteristics of each mind-set described in that section of the text.

- Use transitional words and phrases to link your paragraph to the main idea.

Assign this performance task.

PERFORMANCE TASK COMMON CORE W 1c

Writing Activity Direct students to reread the section of the article for which they plan to write a paragraph. Encourage them to brainstorm possible examples before choosing one to develop. Remind them to use elements of Dweck's style in their writing

Critical Vocabulary

implicit   innate   engender

cohort   malleable

Practice and Apply Answer each question, explaining your choice.

1. Which is *innate,* a dog's ability to bark or a dog's ability to obey commands?

2. Which is an *implicit* form of communication, a wink or the statement "I'm joking"?

3. Which *engenders* football enthusiasm, a stadium band or the officials?

4. Who is your *cohort,* your aunt in another country or your study partner?

5. What would make taffy *malleable,* freezing it or keeping it out on a warm day?

Vocabulary Strategy: Prefixes with Multiple Meanings

The Critical Vocabulary words *engender* and *innate* are formed with prefixes. Knowing the meaning of a prefix can help you define unfamiliar words. For example, putting together the meaning of the prefix *in-* ("in") with the meaning of the root *nate* ("born") enables you to figure out that *innate* means "inborn," or "possessed at birth." If a prefix has more than one meaning, such as those shown in the chart, use the context of the unfamiliar word to help you confirm its precise definition.

Prefix	Meanings
a-	1. without, not: *amoral* 2. on, in: *aboard*
en-	1. to put into or onto: *encapsulate* 2. to cause to be: *engender*
im-, in-	1. not: *inhumane* 2. in, into, within: *immigrate*
pro-	1. supporting or in favor of: *pronuclear* 2. forward, in front of: *propel* 3. earlier, before: *proactive*

Practice and Apply Write a definition for each underlined word. Explain how context clues help you identify which meaning of the prefix is used.

1. The young boy remained <u>afloat</u> in the rough water.

2. The technician <u>installed</u> the new software on the computer for the nervous customer.

3. A play may begin with a <u>prologue</u> introducing the characters and plot.

4. The charismatic speaker <u>enkindled</u> passion in his audience with his fiery words.

5. After seeing her <u>asymmetrical</u> bangs, she vowed never to cut her own hair again.

PRACTICE & APPLY

Critical Vocabulary   L 4b

Answers:

1. *A dog is born with the innate ability to bark but has to learn commands.*

2. *A wink is a way of implicitly telling someone you are joking.*

3. *The stadium band whips up excitement in the fans.*

4. *A cohort is a companion, so a study partner is a cohort.*

5. *Warm taffy can be shaped, so it is malleable.*

Vocabulary Strategy: Prefixes with Multiple Meanings

1. *on top of the water;* **context clues:** *remained, water*

2. *put in;* **context clues:** *new software, computer*

3. *speech or words that come before;* **context clues:** *begin, introducing*

4. *put fire into, excited;* **context clues:** *charismatic, passion, fiery*

5. *without symmetry, uneven;* **context clues:** *never to cut her own hair again*

Strategies for Annotation  Annotate it!

Prefixes with Multiple Meanings COMMON CORE L 4b

Have students search for words in the article that contain the prefixes in the chart. Ask them to use their eBook annotation tools to do these steps:

- Search for and highlight in pink each word that contains the prefix.
- Reread the surrounding sentences, underlining clues to the word's meaning.
- Review the possible meanings of the prefix as well as the context clues to determine the definition of the word. Write the definition in a note.

People can learn to be helpless, too, but not everyone reacts to setbacks this way. I wondered:

Why do some students give up when they encounter difficulty, whereas others who are no more skilled continue to strive and learn?

PRACTICE & APPLY

Language and Style: Participles and Participial Phrases

To make sure students understand the basic concepts in this lesson, ask them to identify the participles in the three example sentences (*Attributing, confronting, published*) and the noun or pronoun that each participial phrase modifies (*those, The other, study*).

Tell students that they can create a participial phrase by inserting new information into an existing sentence. Or they can combine two sentences. For example:

BEFORE: Most students don't want to appear stupid. They cross their arms and look down when the teacher asks if anyone had trouble understanding the reading.

AFTER: Not wanting to appear stupid, most students cross their arms and look down when the teacher asks if anyone had trouble understanding the reading.

Have volunteers write their "before" and "after" sentences on the board. As a class, discuss the function of each participial phrase and how it contributes to the effectiveness of the sentence.

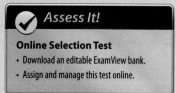

Assess It!

Online Selection Test
- Download an editable ExamView bank.
- Assign and manage this test online.

Language and Style: Participles and Participial Phrases

Participial phrases act as adjectives, modifying nouns or pronouns. A participial phrase includes a **participle** (verb form ending in -*ed* or -*ing*), modifiers, and complements. Writers use participial phrases to add detail that will make their meaning more precise. They also use participial phrases to vary their sentence structure and keep the attention of their readers.

In "The Secret to Raising Smart Kids," the author places participial phrases next to the nouns or pronouns that they modify to make her meaning clear. As a result, the phrases appear in different positions in sentences throughout her article.

A participial phrase that begins a sentence is set off with a comma.

Attributing a bad grade to their own lack of ability, those with a fixed mind-set said that they would study less in the future. . . .

A participial phrase in the middle of a sentence is set off by commas if it contains nonessential information.

The other, **also confronting the hard problems**, looked up at the experimenter. . . .

Most participial phrases that occur at the end of a sentence are not set off by commas if they follow the noun or pronoun they are modifying.

We validated these expectations in a study **published in early 2007**.

A careless writer might have written the last two sentences like this:

The other looked up at the experimenter, also confronting the hard problems. . . .
Published in early 2007 we validated these expectations in a study.

These sentences create confusion because it is not clear which pronoun or noun the participial phrases modify.

Practice and Apply Look back at the paragraph you wrote with a partner in response to this selection's Performance Task. With your partner, rewrite two sentences to include participial phrases. Then compare the before and after versions. Discuss how the use of participial phrases helped you to add detail, improve the clarity of your writing, or vary your sentence structure.

TO CHALLENGE STUDENTS . . .

Evaluate Sentence Structure Explain that there are exceptions to the rule about the best placement for a participial phrase. Display this sentence and have pairs discuss the questions: "In the seventh grade, however, Jonathan suddenly lost interest in school, refusing to do homework or study for tests."

- What is the participial phrase, and what does it modify? (*The phrase "refusing . . . tests" modifies "Jonathan."*)
- Would the sentence be improved by moving the phrase directly after "Jonathan"? Why? (*No; the order of ideas would be less logical.*)
- Is the comma after "school" necessary? Why? (*Yes; it clarifies that the participial phrase does not modify "school" and it marks a natural pause.*)

Summarize a Text

COMMON CORE
RI 2

TEACH

Remind students that summarizing allows readers to focus on a text's key points or main ideas. Summarizing the elements of an argument—claim, reasons, counterarguments, and evidence—makes it possible for readers to evaluate them. Provide these steps to help students summarize an argument:

1. Create a two-column chart. Label the left column "Main Point" and the right column "Explanation."
2. Reread a section of the text. The section may consist of one or more paragraphs.
3. Restate the main point of the section in a few words, recording your answer in the chart.
4. Repeat steps 2 and 3 until you have finished reading the text.
5. Make notes in the "Explanation" column. Your notes can include such labels as "claim," "reason, " "support," or "counterargument."
6. Use the information in the chart to create a short summary that restates the author's claim, reasons, important support, and counterarguments. Make sure your summary represents that author's ideas and does not include personal opinions.

INTERACTIVE WHITEBOARD LESSON
Evaluating an Argument

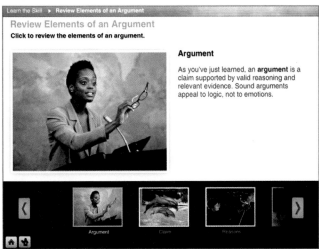

COLLABORATIVE DISCUSSION

Have student pairs summarize "The Secret to Raising Smart Kids." Once pairs have created their summary, conduct a whole-class discussion in which students present the article's key points. Make sure you point out any missing main ideas, or superfluous ideas.

Analyze Structure: Argument

COMMON CORE
RI 5

RETEACH

Review the terms *claim, reasons, evidence,* and *counterargument.* Then give an example of a claim, such as "A fifth year of high school could benefit students academically, financially, and socially."

- Ask students to provide examples of the types of reasons and evidence that might be used to support the claim. *(Sample reason: Students could take college courses that would enable them to get their degree in three years instead of four.)*
- Provide this opposing claim: "By the time they are eighteen, students are ready to be independent and in charge of their own studies." Ask: How could you counter this viewpoint? *(Sample answer: The high percentage of drop-outs in the first year of college suggests that many students are not able to handle the looser structure of college.)*

LEVEL UP TUTORIALS Assign the following *Level Up* tutorial: **Analyzing Arguments**

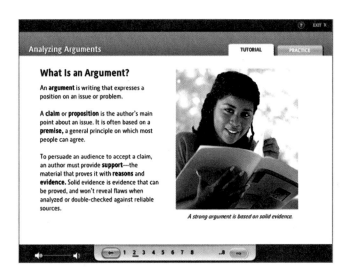

CLOSE READING APPLICATION

Provide students with an editorial. Have students analyze the argument, outlining the claim, reasons, evidence, and counterargument. Ask: Does the writer include enough support to prove the claim? Does he or she do an adequate job of anticipating possible objections?

A Walk to the Jetty
from Annie John

mySmartPlanner Create lesson plans and access resources online.

Novel by Jamaica Kincaid

Why This Text?

To get the most from what they read in text materials and in media, students must analyze the text's language and make valid inferences from it. This lesson explores the impact of Kincaid's specific word choices and helps students draw inferences about characters and events.

Key Learning Objective: The student will be able to analyze the impact of an author's word choices and cite text evidence to support inferences.

For additional practice:

Close Reader selection
"Next Term, We'll Mash You,"
Short Story by Penelope Lively

COMMON CORE — Common Core Standards

RL 1 Cite textual evidence to support inferences.
RL 3 Analyze the impact of the author's choices regarding how to develop elements of a story.
RL 4 Analyze the impact of specific word choices.
RL 10 Read and comprehend literature.
W 3d Use telling details to convey a vivid picture.
L 2 Demonstrate command of the conventions of standard English punctuation.
L 4c Consult reference materials to find etymology.

▲ Text Complexity Rubric

Quantitative Measures	**A Walk to the Jetty** Lexile: 1290L
Qualitative Measures	**Levels of Meaning/Purpose** single level of complex meaning
	Structure few, if any, shifts in point of view
	Language Conventionality and Clarity more complex sentence structure
	Knowledge Demands increased amount of cultural and literary knowledge useful
Reader/Task Considerations	Teacher determined Vary by individual reader and type of text

CLOSE READ

Jamaica Kincaid Have students read the information about the author. Tell them that Kincaid was close to her mother until the birth of her three brothers, which shifted her parents' focus to the boys and their futures. At 17, Kincaid left Antigua to take a job as an au pair in the United States. (An au pair is a young person who moves to another country to do housework or provide child care for a family.) She was supposed to send money back to her family but never did. Despite their difficult relationship, Kincaid and her mother shared a love of reading. In fact, Kincaid loved books so much that she got into trouble stealing money to buy them.

AS YOU READ Direct students to use the As You Read note to focus their reading. Remind them to write down any questions they generate during reading.

Analyze Word Choice

COMMON CORE RL 4

(LINES 1–13)

Explain that the author's use of language in a fictional text creates a distinctive voice for the narrator. Annie John's way of speaking reveals her personality, feelings, and opinions. Her **syntax,** or arrangement of words in sentences, is appropriate for an intelligent, well-educated teenager.

(A) CITE TEXT EVIDENCE Have students read lines 1–10. In what ways do the sentence structures and the choice of words sound like a teenage girl telling about her own life? *(The sentences are somewhat long and rambling, which reflects the way her thoughts might flow as she lies in bed thinking. The informal phrase "for I don't know how long" sounds like everyday speech.)*

Point out that Annie's words often reflect her **tone,** or attitude, toward her situation and the people around her.

(B) ASK STUDENTS to read the sentence in lines 11–13. What is Annie's attitude toward her life in Antigua? *(Her tone is negative, somewhat impatient, and blunt. Staying in Antigua is about the worst thing she can imagine, worse than living "in a cavern and keeping house for seven unruly men.")*

Jamaica Kincaid *(b. 1949) was born Elaine Potter Richardson on the Caribbean island of Antigua in 1949. She left at seventeen to work in New York City. After a series of jobs, she became a writer for* The New Yorker. *In 1985, she published her first novel,* Annie John, *the last chapter of which is "A Walk to the Jetty." Like Kincaid herself, the protagonist is emotionally estranged from her mother at a young age. Kincaid revisits this theme often in her works. She also expresses her abhorrence of British colonial rule in Antigua, most notably in the nonfiction work* A Small Place, *which excited controversy for its deeply angry tone.*

A Walk to the Jetty

from Annie John

Novel by Jamaica Kincaid

AS YOU READ Look for details that tell you how the narrator feels about the people and places in her life.

"My name is Annie John." These were the first words that came into my mind as I woke up on the morning of the last day I spent in Antigua, and they stayed there, lined up one behind the other, marching up and down, for I don't know how long. At noon on that day, a ship on which I was to be a passenger would sail to Barbados, and there I would board another ship, which would sail to England, where I would study to become a nurse. My name was the last thing I saw the night before, just as I was falling asleep; it was written in big, black letters all over my trunk, sometimes followed by my address in
10 Antigua, sometimes followed by my address as it would be in England. I did not want to go to England, I did not want to be a nurse, but I would have chosen going off to live in a cavern and keeping house for seven unruly men rather than go on with my life as it stood. I never wanted to lie in this bed again, my legs hanging out way past the foot of it, tossing and turning on my mattress, with its cotton stuffing all lumped just where it wasn't a good place to be lumped. I never wanted to lie in my bed again and hear Mr. Ephraim driving his sheep to pasture—a signal to my mother that she should get up to prepare my father's and my bath and breakfast. I never wanted to lie in my bed and

(A)

(B)

Close Read Screencasts ▶ View It!

Modeled Discussions

Have students click the *Close Read* icons in their eBooks to access two screencasts in which readers discuss and annotate the following key passages:

- Annie wakes up in her bed for the last time (lines 13–22)
- Annie arrives at the jetty (lines 304–313)

As a class, view and discuss at least one of these videos. Then have students pair up to do an independent close read of an additional passage—Annie takes the launch toward the ship (lines 356–365).

Support Inferences

COMMON CORE RL 1, RL 10

(LINES 23–39)

Remind students that important ideas about characters and events are not always stated directly in a fictional text. Readers must draw **inferences,** or logical conclusions based on details in the text. Valid inferences must be supported by strong and specific textual evidence.

C **CITE TEXT EVIDENCE** Have students read lines 23–39. Ask them what inferences they can draw about Annie's childhood and about her current feelings. Have them cite evidence in the paragraph to support their inferences. (*Annie catalogs items in her room that signify her success in school, people who care about her, and pleasant experiences. She mentions that her father added a room onto the house just for her. At the same time, her "heart could have burst open with joy" because she is leaving all of this behind. Readers can infer that Annie has had a fairly happy childhood, but that she has grown bored with her life in Antigua and is ready for something new.*)

20 hear her get dressed, washing her face, brushing her teeth, and gargling. I especially never wanted to lie in my bed and hear my mother gargling again.

C Lying there in the half-dark of my room, I could see my shelf, with my books—some of them prizes I had won in school, some of them gifts from my mother—and with photographs of people I was supposed to love forever no matter what, and with my old thermos, which was given to me for my eighth birthday, and some shells I had gathered at different times I spent at the sea. In one corner stood my washstand and its beautiful basin of white enamel with blooming red 30 hibiscus painted at the bottom and an urn that matched. In another corner were my old school shoes and my Sunday shoes. In still another corner, a bureau held my old clothes. I knew everything in this room, inside out and outside in. I had lived in this room for thirteen of my seventeen years. I could see in my mind's eye even the day my father was adding it onto the rest of the house. Everywhere I looked stood something that had meant a lot to me, that had given me pleasure at some point, or could remind me of a time that was a happy time. But as I was lying there my heart could have burst open with joy at the thought of never having to see any of it again.

40 If someone had asked me for a little summing up of my life at that moment as I lay in bed, I would have said, "My name is Annie John. I was born on the fifteenth of September, seventeen years ago, at

Image Credits: ©Travelshots/SuperStock

SCAFFOLDING FOR ELL STUDENTS

Vocabulary: Figurative Language Read aloud lines 1–4. Focus on "they stayed there, lined up one behind the other, marching up and down."

- Ask students what the pronoun *they* refers to. (*"the first words that came into my mind"*)
- Point out that this is an example of figurative language, because the words are not literally "marching up and down." Annie means that the words are repeating in her mind.
- Help students interpret other examples of figurative language, including the exaggerated statements in lines 11–13 and lines 37–39.
- Point out that figurative language helps readers to visualize abstract ideas and to understand characters' feelings.

Holberton Hospital, at five o'clock in the morning. At the time I was
born, the moon was going down at one end of the sky and the sun was
coming up at the other. My mother's name is Annie also. My father's
name is Alexander, and he is thirty-five years older than my mother.
Two of his children are four and six years older than she is. Looking
at how sickly he has become and looking at the way my mother now
has to run up and down for him, gathering the herbs and barks that
50 he boils in water, which he drinks instead of the medicine the doctor
has ordered for him, I plan not only never to marry an old man but
certainly never to marry at all. The house we live in my father built
with his own hands. The bed I am lying in my father built with his
own hands. If I get up and sit on a chair, it is a chair my father built
with his own hands. When my mother uses a large wooden spoon to
stir the porridge we sometimes eat as part of our breakfast, it will be
a spoon that my father has carved with his own hands. The sheets on
my bed my mother made with her own hands. The curtains hanging
at my window my mother made with her own hands. The nightie I am
60 wearing, with **scalloped** neck and hem and sleeves, my mother made
with her own hands. When I look at things in a certain way, I suppose
I should say that the two of them made me with their own hands. For
most of my life, when the three of us went anywhere together I stood
between the two of them or sat between the two of them. But then I got
too big, and there I was, shoulder to shoulder with them more or less,
and it became not very comfortable to walk down the street together.
And so now there they are together and here I am apart. I don't see
them now the way I used to, and I don't love them now the way I used
to. The bitter thing about it is that they are just the same and it is I who
70 have changed, so all the things I used to be and all the things I used to
feel are as false as the teeth in my father's head. Why, I wonder, didn't
I see the **hypocrite** in my mother when, over the years, she said that
she loved me and could hardly live without me, while at the same time
proposing and arranging separation after separation, including this
one, which, unbeknownst to her, *I* have arranged to be permanent? So
now I, too, have hypocrisy, and breasts (small ones), and hair growing
in the appropriate places, and sharp eyes, and I have made a vow never
to be fooled again."

    Lying in my bed for the last time, I thought, This is what I add up
80 to. At that, I felt as if someone had placed me in a hole and was forcing
me first down and then up against the pressure of gravity. I shook
myself and prepared to get up. I said to myself, "I am getting up out of
this bed for the last time." Everything I would do that morning until I
got on the ship that would take me to England I would be doing for the
last time, for I had made up my mind that, come what may, the road
for me now went only in one direction: away from my home, away
from my mother, away from my father, away from the everlasting blue
sky, away from the everlasting hot sun, away from people who said to
me, "This happened during the time your mother was carrying you."

scalloped
(skŏl´əpt) *adj.* having
a wavy edge, border,
or design.

hypocrite
(hĭp´ə-krĭt´) *n.* one
who professes good
qualities but does
not demonstrate or
possess them.

A Walk to the Jetty   **33**

WHEN STUDENTS STRUGGLE...

The narration reflects Annie's thoughts, which are sometimes expressed in
sentences with many phrases and clauses. Tell students that if they get lost
in one of these sentences, they should look for the part of the sentence that
has the subject and main verb. Then they can figure out how the other parts
of the sentence modify or describe that part, which is called the main clause.

ASK STUDENTS to read the sentence in lines 47–52 and identify the main
clause. *("I plan not only . . . but certainly never to marry at all")* Discuss how
the other phrases and clauses relate to this main clause. *(They present details
about how Annie's mother must take care of her father and establish why Annie
doesn't want to marry.)*

CLOSE READ

Analyze Word Choice   COMMON CORE RL 4
(LINES 52–62)

Explain that when an author repeats a word or phrase
several times, he or she may be emphasizing an idea
or pointing out similarities between different things.

D **ASK STUDENTS** to read lines 52–62 and identify
the repeated phrase. *("with his/her/their own hands")*
Then ask students to explain what overall meaning
is conveyed by this repetition, and what it reveals
about Annie's attitude toward her life. *(The repetition
of this phrase emphasizes that the family is not wealthy,
since Annie's parents have made so many necessities
by hand instead of buying them. It also suggests that
Annie's parents are intimately involved in every aspect
of her life, a situation that makes her feel smothered and
anxious to break away. Perhaps, in addition to feeling
smothered, Annie is aware that her parents' lives are
defined by hard work and that her own life could also
eventually be defined by work.)*

> ### CRITICAL VOCABULARY
>
> **scalloped**: Annie describes the fancy trim that
> her mother has sewn along the edges of her
> nightgown.
>
> **ASK STUDENTS** who have seen a scallop shell to
> describe what its edges look like. Then have them
> explain why Annie describes the neck, hem, and
> sleeves of her nightgown as being scalloped.
> *(The nightgown has wavy edges, like the edges of a
> scallop shell.)*
>
> **hypocrite**: Annie points out a contradiction
> between her mother's words and actions. Her
> mother says she loves Annie but always seems to
> be arranging for Annie to go away.
>
> **ASK STUDENTS** whether they agree with Annie
> that her mother is a hypocrite, and why. *(Possible
> answer: While her words and actions seem to
> be opposed, Annie's mother is not necessarily a
> hypocrite. Her love for Annie may include wanting her
> to find a better life than she can have in Antigua.)*

Support Inferences

COMMON CORE RL 1, RL 10

(LINES 95–131)

Remind students that they can use details in the text to draw inferences about the characters in a novel, including what the characters are like, how they feel, and what is important to them.

E CITE TEXT EVIDENCE Have students reread Annie's description of the start of her last day in her parents' home (lines 95–131). Ask them what inferences they can draw about Annie's parents, especially her mother. Have them support their inferences with textual evidence. *(Annie's parents are excited and proud that their daughter is starting a new life in England. They have taken great pains to make sure that her last day in Antigua is special and that she is prepared for her journey. Textual evidence includes the following: Annie's father has taken the day off from work; her mother has taken her jewelry and underclothes to the obeah woman to ensure Annie's protection from misfortune; Annie's traveling clothes have been carefully selected and ironed by her mother; her parents have arranged for a special breakfast like the one they usually eat only on Sundays.)*

90 If I had been asked to put into words why I felt this way, if I had been given years to reflect and come up with the words of why I felt this way, I would not have been able to come up with so much as the letter "A." I only knew that I felt the way I did, and that this feeling was the strongest thing in my life.

The Anglican church bell struck seven. My father had already bathed and dressed and was in his workshop puttering around. As if the day of my leaving were something to celebrate, they were treating it as a holiday, and nothing in the usual way would take place. My father would not go to work at all. When I got up, my mother greeted
100 me with a big, bright "Good morning"—so big and bright that I shrank before it. I bathed quickly in some warm bark water that my mother had prepared for me. I put on my underclothes—all of them white and all of them smelling funny. Along with my earrings, my neck chain, and my bracelets, all made of gold from British Guiana, my underclothes had been sent to my mother's obeah[1] woman, and whatever she had done to my jewelry and underclothes would help protect me from evil spirits and every kind of misfortune. The things I never wanted to see or hear or do again now made up at least three weeks' worth of grocery lists. I placed a mark against obeah women,
110 jewelry, and white underclothes. Over my underclothes, I put on an around-the-yard dress of my mother's. The clothes I would wear for my voyage were a dark-blue pleated skirt and a blue-and-white checked blouse (the blue in the blouse matched exactly the blue of my skirt) with a large sailor collar and with a tie made from the same material as the skirt—a blouse that came down a long way past my waist, over my skirt. They were lying on a chair, freshly ironed by my mother. Putting on my clothes was the last thing I would do just before leaving the house. Miss Cornelia came and pressed my hair and then shaped it into what felt like a hundred corkscrews, all lying flat against my head
120 so that my hat would fit properly.

At breakfast, I was seated in my usual spot, with my mother at one end of the table, my father at the other, and me in the middle, so that as they talked to me or to each other I would shift my head to the left or to the right and get a good look at them. We were having a Sunday breakfast, a breakfast as if we had just come back from Sunday-morning services: salt fish and antroba[2] and souse[3] and hard-boiled eggs, and even special Sunday bread from Mr. Daniel, our baker. On Sundays, we ate this big breakfast at eleven o'clock and then we didn't eat again until four o'clock, when we had our big Sunday dinner. It was
130 the best breakfast we ate, and the only breakfast better than that was the one we ate on Christmas morning. My parents were in a festive mood, saying what a wonderful time I would have in my new life, what

---

[1] **obeah** (oʹbē-ə): an African-based religion practiced in the Caribbean.
[2] **antroba:** a blend of crushed eggplant and spices.
[3] **souse:** pickled meat.

SCAFFOLDING FOR ELL STUDENTS

Vocabulary: Phrasal Verbs Tell students that a **phrasal verb** is a verb and another word that function together as one verb. Point out "My father . . . was in his workshop puttering around" in lines 95–96. Explain that *around* usually functions as a preposition, but in this sentence it does not introduce a prepositional phrase. Instead, it forms a phrasal verb with *putter*. To putter around is to keep oneself busy doing unimportant things.

ASK STUDENTS to use context clues to define these phrasal verbs in the selection: *made up* (line 108), *were eating away* (line 134), *taking in* (line 155), *set off* (lines 179–180), *starting out* (line 181), *dressed up* (line 185), *point out* (line 241).

a wonderful opportunity this was for me, and what a lucky person I was. They were eating away as they talked, my father's false teeth making that clop-clop sound like a horse on a walk as he talked, my mother's mouth going up and down like a donkey's as she chewed each mouthful thirty-two times. (I had long ago counted, because it was something she made me do also, and I was trying to see if this was just one of her rules that applied only to me.) I was looking at them with

140 a smile on my face but disgust in my heart when my mother said, "Of course, you are a young lady now, and we won't be surprised if in due time you write to say that one day soon you are to be married."

Without thinking, I said, with bad feeling that I didn't hide very well, "How absurd!"

My parents immediately stopped eating and looked at me as if they had not seen me before. My father was the first to go back to his food. My mother continued to look. I don't know what went through her mind, but I could see her using her tongue to dislodge food stuck in the far corners of her mouth.

150 Many of my mother's friends now came to say goodbye to me, and to wish me God's blessings. I thanked them and showed the proper amount of joy at the glorious things they pointed out to me that my future held and showed the proper amount of sorrow at how much my parents and everyone else who loved me would miss me. My body ached a little at all this false going back and forth, at all this taking in of people gazing at me with heads tilted, love and pity on their smiling faces. I could have left without saying any goodbyes to them and I wouldn't have missed it. There was only one person I felt I should say goodbye to, and that was my former friend Gwen. We had long ago

160 drifted apart, and when I saw her now my heart nearly split in two with embarrassment at the feelings I used to have for her and things I had shared with her. She had now **degenerated** into complete silliness, hardly able to complete a sentence without putting in a few giggles. Along with the giggles, she had developed some other schoolgirl traits that she did not have when she was actually a schoolgirl, so beneath her were such things then. When we were saying our goodbyes, it was all I could do not to say cruelly, "Why are you behaving like such a monkey?" Instead, I put everything on a friendly plain, wishing her well and the best in the future. It was then that she told me that

170 she was more or less engaged to a boy she had known while growing up early on in Nevis, and that soon, in a year or so, they would be married. My reply to her was "Good luck," and she thought I meant her well, so she grabbed me and said, "Thank you. I knew you would be happy about it." But to me it was as if she had shown me a high point from which she was going to jump and hoped to land in one piece on her feet. We parted, and when I turned away I didn't look back.

degenerate
(dĭ-jĕn´ə-rāt´) *v.* to decline in quality.

A Walk to the Jetty **35**

APPLYING ACADEMIC VOCABULARY

appreciation	conform

As you discuss the scene in which Annie says goodbye to the people she knows in Antigua, incorporate the Collection 1 academic vocabulary words *appreciation* and *conform*. Ask students in what ways Annie **conforms** to expectations in this scene, and contrast it with the way Gwen conforms. Have students discuss whether they think Gwen is now completely different than she was when she and Annie were friends, or whether Annie can no longer **appreciate** the qualities she once loved in Gwen.

CLOSE READ

Support Inferences
COMMON CORE RL 1, RL 10
(LINES 139–149)

Tell students that the dialogue in a novel often reveals information about the relationships between characters.

 CITE TEXT EVIDENCE Ask students what they can infer about Annie's relationship with her mother from their conversation in lines 139–149. *(Annie's mother predicts that Annie will soon find someone to marry. When Annie says this is absurd, her mother is shocked. Readers can infer from this conversation that Annie and her mother have different values, and that Annie's mother does not understand her daughter very well.)*

Analyze Word Choice
COMMON CORE RL 4
(LINES 169–176)

Remind students that a **simile** is a figure of speech that compares two fundamentally dissimilar things. An author uses a simile to describe something in a fresh, often surprising way.

G **ASK STUDENTS** to identify the simile in lines 169–176. What two things are compared, and what does this comparison reveal about Annie? *(The simile is in the last sentence, in which Annie compares Gwen's engagement to jumping from a great height and expecting to survive. It shows Annie's attitude toward marriage: she sees great risk and danger in marriage.)*

CRITICAL VOCABULARY

degenerated: Annie describes how Gwen has changed from a trusted and valued friend into someone she scarcely recognizes.

ASK STUDENTS to explain why Annie thinks Gwen has degenerated in the time since they were close friends. *(Annie once felt Gwen was someone worthy of her friendship. Now, Gwen giggles all the time and has "other schoolgirl traits that she did not have when she was actually a schoolgirl." In Annie's opinion, Gwen has become less mature over time instead of growing up.)*

Analyze Word Choice RL 4

(LINES 200–203)

Explain that a **metaphor** is a figure of speech that compares two dissimilar things without using the words *like* or *as*. Authors use metaphors to create fresh, imaginative descriptions.

(H) ASK STUDENTS to read the sentence in lines 200–203 and identify the metaphor. Have them explain why Annie makes this comparison and what it means in the context of her present situation. *(Annie compares her life in Antigua to a dustheap. This comparison reinforces her contemptuous tone toward the life she is leaving behind. She recognizes nothing of value in her past life; it might as well be garbage.)*

Analyze Story Elements: Character Development RL 3

(LINES 204–230)

Point out that the character of Annie's mother is developed mainly through Annie's descriptions of her. As the narrator, Annie presents selected memories of her mother's actions. Readers do not get a complete or unbiased picture of the mother's character, but they can draw their own conclusions about her based on what Annie shares.

(I) CITE TEXT EVIDENCE Have students read Annie's account of her first independent shopping trip in lines 204–230. What details reveal the character of Annie's mother? How has the relationship between mother and daughter changed over time? *(Annie's mother is devoted and proud. She encourages Annie to take on responsibility and learn to do things independently. Details include the careful instructions she gives Annie before she sets out, the fact that Annie wears a "freshly ironed yellow dress" and is allowed to use her mother's talcum powder, and the way that Annie's mother welcomes her home with tears in her eyes and says she is "wonderful and good." Annie seems to have worshipped her mother when she was little, although now she yearns to get away from her.)*

My mother had arranged with a stevedore[4] to take my trunk to the jetty ahead of me. At ten o'clock on the dot, I was dressed, and we set off for the jetty. An hour after that, I would board a launch that would take me out to sea, where I then would board the ship. Starting out, as if for old time's sake and without giving it a thought, we lined up in the old way: I walking between my mother and my father. I loomed way above my father and could see the top of his head. We must have made a strange sight: a grown girl all dressed up in the middle of a morning, in the middle of the week, walking in step in the middle between her two parents, for people we didn't know stared at us. It was all of half an hour's walk from our house to the jetty, but I was passing through most of the years of my life. We passed by the house where Miss Dulcie, the seamstress that I had been apprenticed to for a time, lived, and just as I was passing by, a wave of bad feeling for her came over me, because I suddenly remembered that the months I spent with her all she had me do was sweep the floor, which was always full of threads and pins and needles, and I never seemed to sweep it clean enough to please her. Then she would send me to the store to buy buttons or thread, though I was only allowed to do this if I was given a sample of the button or thread, and then she would find fault even though they were an exact match of the samples she had given me. And all the while she said to me, "A girl like you will never learn to sew properly, you know." At the time, I don't suppose I minded it, because it was customary to treat the first-year apprentice with such scorn, but now I placed on the dustheap of my life Miss Dulcie and everything that I had had to do with her.

We were soon on the road that I had taken to school, to church, to Sunday school, to choir practice, to Brownie meetings, to Girl Guide meetings, to meet a friend. I was five years old when I first walked on this road unaccompanied by someone to hold my hand. My mother had placed three pennies in my little basket, which was a duplicate of her bigger basket, and sent me to the chemist's shop[5] to buy a pennyworth of senna leaves, a pennyworth of eucalyptus leaves, and a pennyworth of camphor. She then instructed me on what side of the road to walk, where to make a turn, where to cross, how to look carefully before I crossed, and if I met anyone that I knew to politely pass greetings and keep on my way. I was wearing a freshly ironed yellow dress that had printed on it scenes of acrobats flying through the air and swinging on a trapeze. I had just had a bath, and after it, instead of powdering me with my baby-smelling talcum powder, my mother had, as a special favor, let me use her own talcum powder, which smelled quite perfumy and came in a can that had painted on it people going out to dinner in nineteenth-century London and was called Mazie. How it pleased me to walk out the door and bend

---

[4] **stevedore:** dock worker who loads and unloads ships.
[5] **chemist's shop:** pharmacy.

SCAFFOLDING FOR ELL STUDENTS

Vocabulary: Idioms Remind students that **idioms** are expressions that mean something different from the literal meaning of the words. Point out "on the dot" (line 179) and "for old time's sake" (line 182) and help students use context to guess their meanings. *("On the dot" means "exactly." "For old time's sake" means "done to recall past customs.")*

Vocabulary: Multiple-Meaning Words Explain that words in English can have different meanings depending on the context. An example is *board* (line 180), which can mean "a flat piece of wood" but here means "to get on a boat."

ASK STUDENTS to look up these words in a dictionary and determine the correct meanings for the selection context: *launch* (line 180), *wave* (line 191), *match* (line 198).

my head down to sniff at myself and see that I smelled just like my
mother. I went to the chemist's shop, and he had to come from behind
the counter and bend down to hear what it was that I wanted to buy,
my voice was so little and timid then. I went back just the way I had
come, and when I walked into the yard and presented my basket
with its three packages to my mother, her eyes filled with tears and
she swooped me up and held me high in the air and said that I was
wonderful and good and that there would never be anybody better. If I
230 had just conquered Persia, she couldn't have been more proud of me.

We passed by our church—the church in which I had been
christened and received and had sung in the junior choir. We passed
by a house in which a girl I used to like and was sure I couldn't live
without had lived. Once, when she had mumps, I went to visit her
against my mother's wishes, and we sat on her bed and ate the cure of
roasted, buttered sweet potatoes that had been placed on her swollen
jaws, held there by a piece of white cloth. I don't know how, but my
mother found out about it, and I don't know how, but she put an end to
our friendship. Shortly after, the girl moved with her family across the
240 sea to somewhere else. We passed the doll store, where I would go with
my mother when I was little and point out the doll I wanted that year
for Christmas. We passed the store where I bought the much-fought-
over shoes I wore to church to be received in. We passed the bank. On
my sixth birthday, I was given, among other things, the present of a
sixpence.[6] My mother and I then went to this bank, and with the

---

[6] **sixpence:** a coin worth six pennies in the old British system, with four farthings
in a penny, twelve pennies in a shilling, and 20 shillings in a pound.

A Walk to the Jetty **37**

CLOSE READ

Support Inferences

 RL 1, RL 10

(LINES 232–239)

Point out that Annie's feelings about her mother are
complex and sometimes contradictory. Some of her
memories show her closeness to her mother, while
others suggest conflict between them.

J CITE TEXT EVIDENCE Ask students to read the
memory Annie shares in lines 232–239. What can
readers infer about Annie's relationship with her
mother from this story? Have students cite specific
evidence for their inferences. *(The story suggests
that Annie resents her mother for meddling in her life.
Annie went to visit her sick friend "against my mother's
wishes." Her mother found out and somehow ended the
friendship; Annie never knew how she did it. Annie tells
this story in a matter-of-fact way, not even mentioning
the friend's name. Still, readers can infer that events like
this would cause tension between mother and daughter
and that they would contribute to Annie's present desire
to escape from her stifling life on the island.)*

SCAFFOLDING FOR ELL STUDENTS

Language: Verb Tenses Point out that the novel is narrated in the
past tense, and that the past perfect tense indicates actions that were
completed before the selection began. Use a whiteboard to project the
sentence in lines 189–195. Invite volunteers to mark it up.

- Underline verbs in the past tense.
- Highlight in green verbs in the past perfect tense.

Explain that once the past perfect tense has been established, the
author may switch to describing past completed actions in the past
tense because it is less awkward and wordy.

most of the years of my life. We <u>passed</u> by the house where Miss

Dulcie, the seamstress that I **had been apprenticed** to for a time, <u>lived</u>,

CLOSE READ

Analyze Word Choice

COMMON CORE **RL 4**

(LINES 260–287)

Remind students that authors choose words carefully so that their writing will convey their intended meaning. Explain that an author might choose to use concrete details and **sensory language,** or words that appeal to readers' senses. Or, an author might choose to use abstract words that name ideas and concepts.

K **CITE TEXT EVIDENCE** Ask students to read lines 260–287. Does Kincaid use mostly concrete or abstract language in this passage? Have students cite specific words and phrases to support their answers. *(Kincaid uses mostly concrete language, including details about the carrot juice, the "small, round, hornrimmed glasses" [line 264], Annie's shielding her eyes from the sun, Annie's gestures with the sunglasses, and the "large porcelain dog—white, with black spots all over and a red ribbon of satin tied around its neck" [lines 277–278].)* Ask students what these details reveal about Annie. *(Annie is observant and curious. She probably feels she has seen all there is to see in Antigua, and now she is ready to move on.)*

Tell students that authors often communicate meaning through **symbols,** or objects that play a role in the story but also represent something beyond themselves.

L **ASK STUDENTS** to think about the sunglasses that Annie's mother finally gets for her. What aspect of Annie's character might the sunglasses symbolize? *(The sunglasses are a symbol of Annie's restlessness and her desire to experience life beyond Antigua. Like so many things that once seemed exciting to her, they are now abandoned in a drawer while she yearns for new experiences.)*

❝ We must have made a strange sight: a grown girl all dressed up in the middle of a morning, in the middle of the week, walking in step in the middle between her two parents. ❞

sixpence I opened my own savings account. I was given a little gray book with my name in big letters on it, and in the balance column it said "6d." Every Saturday morning after that, I was given a sixpence— later a shilling, and later a two-and-sixpence piece—and I would take
250 it to the bank for deposit. I had never been allowed to withdraw even a farthing from my bank account until just a few weeks before I was to leave; then the whole account was closed out, and I received from the bank the sum of six pounds ten shillings and two and a half pence.

We passed the office of the doctor who told my mother three times that I did not need glasses, that if my eyes were feeling weak a glass of carrot juice a day would make them strong again. This happened when I was eight. And so every day at recess I would run to my school gate and meet my mother, who was waiting for me with a glass of juice from carrots she had just grated and then squeezed, and
260 I would drink it and then run back to meet my chums. I knew there was nothing at all wrong with my eyes, but I had recently read a story in *The Schoolgirl's Own Annual* in which the heroine, a girl a few years older than I was then, cut such a figure to my mind with the way she was always adjusting her small, round, hornrimmed glasses that I felt I must have a pair exactly like them. When it became clear that I didn't need glasses, I began to complain about the glare of the sun being too much for my eyes, and I walked around with my hands shielding them—especially in my mother's presence. My mother then bought for me a pair of sunglasses with the exact horn-rimmed frames I wanted,
270 and how I enjoyed the gestures of blowing on the lenses, wiping them with the hem of my uniform, adjusting the glasses when they slipped down my nose, and just removing them from their case and putting them on. In three weeks, I grew tired of them and they found a nice resting place in a drawer, along with some other things that at one time or another I couldn't live without.

We passed the store that sold only grooming aids, all imported from England. This store had in it a large porcelain dog—white, with black spots all over and a red ribbon of satin tied around its neck.

APPLYING ACADEMIC VOCABULARY

accumulate	reinforce

As you discuss Jamaica Kincaid's word choice and distinctive use of language, incorporate the Collection 1 academic vocabulary words *accumulate* and *reinforce.* Ask students to notice the **accumulation** of concrete sensory details over the course of Annie's walk to the jetty. How do these details help readers visualize and understand Annie's childhood? How do they **reinforce** her associations with Antigua, both positive and negative?

The dog sat in front of a white porcelain bowl that was always filled with fresh water, and it sat in such a way that it looked as if it had just taken a long drink. When I was a small child, I would ask my mother, if ever we were near this store, to please take me to see the dog, and I would stand in front of it, bent over slightly, my hands resting on my knees, and stare at it and stare at it. I thought this dog more beautiful and more real than any actual dog I had ever seen or any actual dog I would ever see. I must have outgrown my interest in the dog, for when it disappeared I never asked what became of it. We passed the library, and if there was anything on this walk that I might have wept over leaving, this most surely would have been the thing. My mother had been a member of the library long before I was born. And since she took me everywhere with her when I was quite little, when she went to the library she took me along there, too. I would sit in her lap very quietly as she read books that she did not want to take home with her. I could not read the words yet, but just the way they looked on the page was interesting to me. Once, a book she was reading had a large picture of a man in it, and when I asked her who he was she told me that he was Louis Pasteur and that the book was about his life. It stuck in my mind, because she said it was because of him that she boiled my milk to purify it before I was allowed to drink it, that it was his idea, and that that was why the process was called pasteurization. One of the things I had put away in my mother's old trunk in which she kept all my childhood things was my library card. At that moment, I owed sevenpence in overdue fees.

As I passed by all these places, it was as if I were in a dream, for I didn't notice the people coming and going in and out of them, I didn't feel my feet touch ground, I didn't even feel my own body—I just saw these places as if they were hanging in the air, not having top or bottom, and as if I had gone in and out of them all in the same moment. The sun was bright; the sky was blue and just above my head. We then arrived at the jetty.

My heart now beat fast, and no matter how hard I tried, I couldn't keep my mouth from falling open and my nostrils from spreading to the ends of my face. My old fear of slipping between the boards of the jetty and falling into the dark-green water where the dark-green eels lived came over me. When my father's stomach started to go bad, the doctor had recommended a walk every evening right after he ate his dinner. Sometimes he would take me with him. When he took me with him, we usually went to the jetty, and there he would sit and talk to the night watchman about cricket or some other thing that didn't interest me, because it was not personal; they didn't talk about their wives, or their children, or their parents, or about any of their likes and dislikes. They talked about things in such a strange way, and I didn't see what they found funny, but sometimes they made each other laugh so much that their guffaws would bound out to sea and send back an echo. I was always sorry when we got to the jetty and saw that

CLOSE READ

Analyze Story Elements: Character Development (LINES 287–303)

COMMON CORE RL 3

Remind students that the author develops the character of Annie's mother through the details in Annie's stories about her.

M CITE TEXT EVIDENCE Ask students to read lines 287–303. What does this passage reveal about Annie's mother? What traits do Annie and her mother share? Cite specific details in the text. (*Annie says that her mother "had been a member of the library long before [Annie] was born" and that she went to the library often when Annie was very young. Annie remembers her reading a book about Louis Pasteur. Because of reading about Pasteur, Annie's mother also boils milk to purify it before allowing Annie to drink the milk. Her care with the milk shows an admirable commitment to Annie. Annie's mother is very curious about the world beyond Antigua—a trait she shares with her daughter.*)

Support Inferences

COMMON CORE RL 1, RL 10

(LINES 304–315)

Tell students that they must often make inferences about why characters react to situations the way they do. They should draw upon their understanding of a character's personality and feelings, as well as their own knowledge about people in the real world.

N CITE TEXT EVIDENCE Ask students to read lines 304–315. Why does Annie experience her "old fear" about the jetty in this situation? Have students cite evidence from the story to support their answers. (*Annie is feeling anxious about leaving Antigua. She has spent her walk to the jetty recalling childhood memories in all the places that are familiar to her, and now she is about to sail off into the unknown. She feels strange as she approaches the jetty: "it was as if I were in a dream . . . I didn't feel my feet touch the ground." When she arrives, her heart begins to "beat fast." Her fear of slipping between the boards of the jetty is mainly a reflection of her larger fears about the future.*)

WHEN STUDENTS STRUGGLE . . .

Tell students that when they read a fictional text aloud, they are speaking in the voice of the narrator. Since "A Walk to the Jetty" is told from Annie's point of view, readers should use their voices to express Annie's personality and her feelings about what she is describing.

ASK STUDENTS to form pairs to practice fluent reading.

- Divide the paragraph in lines 204–230 into two sections: lines 204–221 and lines 221–230 (starting with "How it pleased me . . .").
- One partner should read the first section aloud, and then the other partner should read the second section. Listen to how your partner uses his or her voice to express Annie's personality and feelings.
- Switch sections and read the paragraph aloud again.

Analyze Word Choice

COMMON CORE RL 4

(LINES 331–368)

Explain that **parallelism** is the repetition of a grammatical structure to show that two or more things are similar or equally important. An example is "I was leaving them/it forever" in lines 332–333.

 ASK STUDENTS to find at least two more examples of parallelism in lines 331–368 and to explain the effect of each instance. *(Four sentences begin with "I felt" in lines 334–338. Each sentence describes a more torturous sensation, suggesting that Annie's fear is building. In lines 359–368, the phrase "There was" repeatedly introduces details of the island setting. The repetition suggests that Annie feels overwhelmed by all the familiar sights and sounds.)*

Analyze Story Elements: Setting (LINES 359–368)

COMMON CORE RL 3

Tell students that descriptions of a novel's setting can provide insights into a character's feelings.

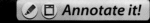 **ASK STUDENTS** to read lines 359–368. What do all these details about the setting reveal about Annie's feelings? *(Annie is noticing details "so familiar that I had long ago stopped paying any attention to them." The details emphasize her feelings of nostalgia now that she is leaving.)*

the night watchman on duty was the one he enjoyed speaking to; it was like being locked up in a book filled with numbers and diagrams and what-ifs. For the thing about not being able to understand and enjoy what they were saying was I had nothing to take my mind off my fear

330 of slipping in between the boards of the jetty.

Now, too, I had nothing to take my mind off what was happening to me. My mother and my father—I was leaving them forever. My home on an island—I was leaving it forever. What to make of everything? I felt a familiar hollow space inside. I felt I was being held down against my will. I felt I was burning up from head to toe. I felt that someone was tearing me up into little pieces and soon I would be able to see all the little pieces as they floated out into nothing in the deep blue sea. I didn't know whether to laugh or cry. I could see that it would be better not to think too clearly about any one thing.

340 The launch was being made ready to take me, along with some other passengers, out to the ship that was anchored in the sea. My father paid our fares, and we joined a line of people waiting to board. My mother checked my bag to make sure that I had my passport, the money she had given me, and a sheet of paper placed between some pages in my Bible on which were written the names of the relatives—people I had not known existed—with whom I would live in England. Across from the jetty was a wharf, and some stevedores were loading and unloading barges. I don't know why seeing that struck me so, but suddenly a wave of strong feeling came over me, and my heart swelled

350 with a great gladness as the words "I shall never see this again" spilled out inside me. But then, just as quickly, my heart shriveled up and the words "I shall never see this again" stabbed at me. I don't know what stopped me from falling in a heap at my parents' feet.

When we were all on board, the launch headed out to sea. Away from the jetty, the water became the customary blue, and the launch left a wide path in it that looked like a road. I passed by sounds and smells that were so familiar that I had long ago stopped paying any attention to them. But now here they were, and the ever-present "I shall never see this again" bobbed up and down inside me. There was

360 the sound of the seagull diving down into the water and coming up with something silverish in its mouth. There was the smell of the sea and the sight of small pieces of rubbish floating around in it. There were boats filled with fishermen coming in early. There was the sound of their voices as they shouted greetings to each other. There was the hot sun, there was the blue sea, there was the blue sky. Not very far away, there was the white sand of the shore, with the run-down houses all crowded in next to each other, for in some places only poor people lived near the shore. I was seated in the launch between my parents, and when I realized that I was gripping their hands tightly I glanced

370 quickly to see if they were looking at me with scorn, for I felt sure that they must have known of my never-see-this-again feelings. But instead my father kissed me on the forehead and my mother kissed me on the

---

Strategies for Annotation ✎ 🗐 *Annotate it!*

Analyze Word Choice

COMMON CORE RL 4

Share these strategies for guided or independent analysis:

- Highlight in yellow the repeated phrases or grammatical structures that create parallelism.
- Underline other words and phrases that show the things that are similar, related, or of equal importance.
- On a note, write the effect that the parallelism has, such as revealing something about the narrator's feelings or emphasizing something about this moment in the story.

everything? I felt a familiar <u>hollow space inside</u>. I felt I was being <u>held down against my will</u>. I felt I was <u>burning up</u> from head to toe. I felt that <u>someone was tearing me up into little pieces</u> and soon I would be able to see all the little pieces as <u>they floated out into nothing</u> in the deep blue sea. I didn't know whether to laugh or cry. I could see mouth, and they both gave over their hands to me, so that I could grip them as much as I wanted. I was on the verge of feeling that it had all been a mistake, but I remembered that I wasn't a child anymore, and that now when I made up my mind about something I had to see it through. At that moment, we came to the ship, and that was that.

> ❝ My mother and my father—I was leaving them forever. My home on an island—I was leaving it forever. ❞

The goodbyes had to be quick, the captain said. My mother introduced herself to him and then introduced me. She told him to
380 keep an eye on me, for I had never gone this far away from home on my own. She gave him a letter to pass on to the captain of the next ship that I would board in Barbados. They walked me to my cabin, a small space that I would share with someone else—a woman I did not know. I had never before slept in a room with someone I did not know. My father kissed me goodbye and told me to be good and to write home often. After he said this, he looked at me, then looked at the floor and swung his left foot, then looked at me again. I could see that he wanted to say something else, something that he had never said to me before, but then he just turned and walked away. My mother said,
390 "Well," and then she threw her arms around me. Big tears streamed down her face, and it must have been that—for I could not bear to see my mother cry—which started me crying, too. She then tightened her arms around me and held me to her close, so that I felt that I couldn't breathe. With that, my tears dried up and I was suddenly on my guard. "What does she want now?" I said to myself. Still holding me close to her, she said, in a voice that raked across my skin, "It doesn't matter what you do or where you go, I'll always be your mother and this will always be your home."
I dragged myself away from her and backed off a little, and then
400 I shook myself, as if to wake myself out of a stupor. We looked at each other for a long time with smiles on our faces, but I know the opposite of that was in my heart. As if responding to some invisible cue, we both said, at the very same moment, "Well." Then my mother turned around and walked out the cabin door. I stood there for I don't know how long, and then I remembered that it was customary to stand on deck and wave to your relatives who were returning to shore. From the deck, I could not see my father, but I could see my mother facing the

CLOSE READ

Analyze Story Elements: Pacing (LINES 378–384)

Point out that a well-written story has appropriate **pacing** throughout. In other words, scenes with a lot of action or intense emotion move along quickly, while sections that feature description or reflection move more slowly.

Q ASK STUDENTS to read lines 378–384. Is the pacing of this scene fast or slow? How does the author create this pace for readers? *(The pacing is fast, which is appropriate because the captain has told everyone to "be quick." The author achieves a faster pace by using shorter sentences than in other parts of the selection. Each sentence begins with a subject and an active verb, emphasizing a quick series of actions.)*

Analyze Word Choice (LINES 389–404)

Tell students that authors choose words with particular **connotations,** or associated feelings, to convey the precise meaning and tone that they intend. For example, "She stormed into the room" conveys a different meaning than "She walked into the room" because *stormed* has connotations of anger.

R CITE TEXT EVIDENCE Have students read lines 389–404, in which Annie says goodbye to her mother. Ask them to note words with strong connotations. What do these word choices reveal about Annie's relationship with her mother? *(Words with strong connotations include "raked" [line 396], "dragged" [line 399], and "stupor" [line 400]. Annie has just been crying in her mother's arms, but suddenly she is on guard. The image of her mother's voice "raking" across Annie's skin suggests that Annie hates the idea that she might not escape her mother or her ties to Antigua. Annie must "drag" herself from her mother's embrace and shake off the "stupor" of feeling close to her. These words suggest that Annie does not trust the warm feelings she has for her mother; even if she is tempted to lose herself in her mother's love, she must force herself to reject it.)*

Analyze Word Choice

 COMMON CORE RL 4

(LINES 413–414)

Remind students that authors use sensory language to create vivid descriptions. These descriptions may also reveal the narrator's thoughts and feelings.

 ASK STUDENTS to read Annie's description of lying down in her cabin after waving goodbye to her parents (lines 413–414). What sensations are readers invited to share with Annie? How do these sensations match her emotions at this moment? *(Annie describes the ship as trembling "as if it had a spring at its very center." Readers can imagine the bouncy, unstable feeling of lying on top of something connected to a giant spring. This physical sensation matches Annie's feelings of uncertainty as she begins her new life among strangers in an unfamiliar country.)*

COLLABORATIVE DISCUSSION Have students form pairs to discuss Annie's perspective on her life. Remind them that her feelings are complex and even contradictory in some ways, so they should review all the evidence and think about which feelings are strongest. Have them share their conclusions with the class as a whole. Accept all reasonable responses.

ASK STUDENTS to share any questions they generated in the course of reading and discussing the selection.

---

ship, her eyes searching to pick me out. I removed from my bag a red cotton handkerchief that she had earlier given me for this purpose, and
410 I waved it wildly in the air. Recognizing me immediately, she waved back just as wildly, and we continued to do this until she became just a dot in the matchbox-size launch swallowed up in the big blue sea.

I went back to my cabin and lay down on my berth. Everything trembled as if it had a spring at its very center. I could hear the small waves lap-lapping around the ship. They made an unexpected sound, as if a vessel filled with liquid had been placed on its side and now was slowly emptying out.

COLLABORATIVE DISCUSSION With a partner, discuss Annie John's view of her life on the island. Cite details from the text that reveal her perspective.

TO CHALLENGE STUDENTS . . .

Compare Points of View Remind students that Annie's first-person narration is subjective. However, the author has provided enough concrete clues for readers to imagine events from a more objective point of view.

ASK STUDENTS to review lines 354–417 and find details that allow them to imagine events as if they are watching a video that does not include Annie's "voice-over." Have them discuss how an outside observer might interpret what is happening. *(Annie clutches her parents' hands, cries in her mother's arms, and waves her handkerchief wildly until the launch disappears. This viewpoint suggests she is very close to her parents and sad to leave Antigua.)*

Support Inferences

COMMON CORE RL 1, RL 10

Inferences are logical assumptions that readers make based on evidence in the text to figure out what is not directly stated. Making inferences enables readers to understand characters' motives, traits, feelings, and relationships. For example, in "A Walk to the Jetty," Annie John's mother goes to the school every day at recess time with fresh-squeezed carrot juice to improve her daughter's eyesight. From the mother's action, readers can infer that she is completely devoted to her daughter. In turn, the fact that Annie is fabricating her eye problems, despite the worry she is causing her mother, enables readers to infer that she doesn't appreciate her mother's devotion and is careless of others' feelings.

When you make inferences about a story, be sure that you can support them with strong textual evidence. Also be aware that authors deliberately leave some matters uncertain. Sometimes this creates tension as readers wonder what might happen later in the story. In other cases, the story is simply open to interpretation. Several different inferences may be equally plausible, but none of them can be proven correct.

Analyze Word Choice

COMMON CORE RL 4

Diction refers to an author's choice of words, including both vocabulary (individual words) and syntax (the order or arrangement of words). In "A Walk to the Jetty," Kincaid creates a distinctive **tone,** or attitude toward a subject, through the diction of her narrator, Annie John. Use the following questions to help you analyze an author's diction:

- **Does the writer choose simple or sophisticated words?** Kincaid makes her seventeen-year-old narrator sound realistic by choosing a suitable level of vocabulary.
- **Does the writer use mostly concrete words, which name specific things, or abstract words that identify concepts?** Kincaid uses concrete words to create fresh, vivid descriptions. For example, as Annie looks around her bedroom, she lists the items that she sees. "In one corner stood my washstand and its beautiful basin of white enamel with blooming red hibiscus painted at the bottom. . . ." These words not only create clear images but also reflect the way Annie John views her surroundings.
- **Does the writer select words with strong connotations, or associated feelings?** When Annie says, "I loomed way above my father," the word *loomed* suggests her emotional distance from him. A more neutral word, such as *stood*, would not have the same effect.
- **Is the writer's syntax formal or informal?** Kincaid varies the length of her sentences, but in general Annie's narration has an informal syntax, following the rhythm of everyday speech. In the third paragraph, Annie offers a summary of her life that mimics the more formal syntax of a school essay.

TEACH

CLOSE READ

Support Inferences

COMMON CORE RL 1, RL 10

Point out that readers combine evidence from the text with their own knowledge when they make inferences. The selection says that Annie John's mother brings carrot juice to Annie's school every day. In addition to noting this textual evidence, readers might ask themselves what would motivate a real person to behave this way. Knowing that a parent's devotion to his or her child often leads the parent to make sacrifices helps readers infer why Annie's mother is willing to spend time each day making and delivering fresh carrot juice.

Analyze Word Choice

COMMON CORE RL 4

Tell students that if an author has made effective word choices, readers should get a strong sense of a first-person narrator's personality and voice. Review each of the bulleted questions with students and make sure they understand the ideas, terms, and examples from the text. Have them reread the first paragraph of the selection (lines 1–22) and discuss whether the vocabulary is simple or sophisticated. *(The paragraph uses simple, everyday words.)*

Strategies for Annotation    *Annotate it!*

Analyze Word Choice

COMMON CORE RL 4

Share these strategies for guided or independent analysis:
- Highlight in blue any words and phrases that reveal Annie's attitude about her life or about other characters.
- Review your highlighting and consider whether the tone is positive or negative in each case. Then think of more precise adjectives to describe the tone.
- On notes, record your description of Annie's tone in each section of the excerpt.

mood, saying what a wonderful time I would have in my new life, what a wonderful opportunity this was for me, and what a lucky person I was. They were eating away as they talked, my father's false teeth making that clop-clop sound like a horse on a walk as he talked, my mother's mouth going up and down like a donkey's as she chewed each mouthful thirty-two times. (I had long ago counted, because it was

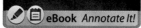

PRACTICE & APPLY

Analyzing the Text <small>COMMON CORE RL 1, RL 3, RL 4</small>

Possible answers:

1. The passage suggests that Annie is angry at her mother for distancing herself from Annie emotionally and arranging for physical distance as well. In response, Annie wants to cut herself off from her parents.

2. These images suggest that Annie feels she has outgrown the island and the people there.

3. Annie's tone is disdainful or annoyed. Her attitude is shown through her comparison of her parents to animals. She says that her father's false teeth make "that clop-clop sound like a horse on a walk as he talked" and her mother's mouth goes "up and down like a donkey's as she chewed each mouthful."

4. The island represents the limitations and frustrations of Annie's childhood. The voyage to England represents leaving her childhood behind and journeying into adulthood and the unknown. Through Annie John, Kincaid is showing that breaking free of one's past can be both painful and necessary.

5. Kincaid uses the walk to the jetty to review important events and people in Annie John's life. These memories reveal how her feelings have changed over the course of her childhood and also suggest that her departure is more painful than she realizes.

6. The words "swelled," "shriveled," and "stabbed" show the extremes of powerful emotion that Annie John is feeling as she thinks about leaving Antigua. She is at one moment ecstatic and the next downcast. The syntax of the sentences causes them to flow quickly and seamlessly, helping readers to understand the pendulum-like swing of these feelings.

7. The simile might suggest that leaving home has filled Annie with conflicting emotions but that the intensity of her feelings will diminish with time.

8. The first-person point of view gives the narrative a sense of intimacy and makes the contrast between Annie's feelings and her outward behavior very clear.

Analyzing the Text <small>COMMON CORE RL 1, RL 3, RL 4, W 3d</small>

 **Cite Text Evidence** Support your responses with evidence from the selection.

1. **Infer** Reread lines 69–78. What do Annie's statements about hypocrisy reveal about her conflict with her mother?

2. **Infer** Referring to her height, Annie says that in bed her legs were "hanging out way past the foot of it" and that she "loomed way above my father and could see the top of his head." What do these details suggest about Annie John's perspective on the island and her life there?

3. **Analyze** Annie describes her parents as the family eats breakfast for the last time together (lines 121–149). What is her tone in this passage? What words convey that attitude?

4. **Analyze** A **symbol** is a person, place, or object that represents something beyond itself. Think about the island setting and Annie John's voyage to England. What might each represent?

5. **Analyze** Much of this selection describes Annie's walk with her parents to the jetty. How does Kincaid use this description to provide insight into Annie's character?

6. **Analyze** In lines 346–350, Annie says that "suddenly a wave of strong feeling came over me, and my heart swelled with a great gladness as the words 'I shall never see this again' spilled out inside me. But then, just as quickly, my heart shriveled up and the words 'I shall never see this again' stabbed at me." Explain how the author's word choices in this passage affect readers' understanding of Annie's emotions.

7. **Draw Conclusions** In the last sentence of the story, Annie compares the "lap-lapping" of the waves to the sound of liquid "slowly emptying out" from a vessel. What does this simile suggest about how leaving home has affected her?

8. **Evaluate** Kincaid uses the first-person point of view to tell Annie's story. Is this an effective technique for developing her narrative? Explain why or why not.

PERFORMANCE TASK

Writing Activity: Letter At the end of the selection, Annie realizes that leaving home is harder than she expected. Write a letter from Annie to her parents after she arrives in England. In the letter, have her reflect on what she has given up and whether she feels the sacrifice was worthwhile.

- Maintain a consistent first-person point of view.
- Include details that develop readers' understanding of Annie's feelings and the circumstances causing those feelings.
- Incorporate elements of Kincaid's style to capture Annie's voice.

Assign this performance task.

PERFORMANCE TASK <small>COMMON CORE W 3d</small>

Writing Activity: Letter Have students draft their letters. Suggest that they review the bulleted questions under Analyze Word Choice on the previous page for ideas on how to mimic Kincaid's style and write in Annie's voice. Then have students exchange their drafts with a partner and give each other constructive feedback. Students may share their final drafts in small groups and discuss the elements that make the letters especially realistic and vivid.

Critical Vocabulary

scalloped   hypocrite   degenerate

Practice and Apply For each Critical Vocabulary word, identify which example below it best illustrates the word's meaning. Be sure to explain why the example you chose is more accurate.

scalloped	hypocrite	degenerate
A skirt is edged with a series of curves.	A person talks about healthy habits but eats only fast food.	Two friends have a big fight but later apologize to each other.
A skirt dips in the back and is shorter in the front.	A person doesn't understand why fast food is not healthy.	Two friends who disagree end up shouting at each other.

Vocabulary Strategy: Etymology

Etymology is the history of a word. Most dictionary entries include etymologies that identify which language the word came from and what the original word meant. The etymology also traces the route by which a word passed into the English language.

The entry below gives the history of the Critical Vocabulary word *hypocrite*. It shows that *hypocrite* comes from an ancient Greek word that meant "to play a part or pretend." From Greek, the word passed into Latin, then French, and finally Middle English. You can see that the meaning of the Greek root is closely related to what *hypocrite* means today.

hyp•o•crite (hĭp´ə-krĭt) *n.* a person given to saying beliefs or feelings that are not genuine. [Middle English *ipocrite,* from Old French, from Late Latin *hypocrite,* from Greek *hupocritēs,* actor, from *hupokrīnesthai,* to play a part, pretend]

Practice and Apply Look up the remaining Critical Vocabulary words—*scalloped, degenerate*—and trace their etymology. Discuss with a partner how closely the original meaning resembles the usage of the word today.

Critical Vocabulary

Answers:
- *scalloped: A skirt is edged with a series of curves.*
- *hypocrite: A person talks about healthy habits but eats only fast food.*
- *degenerate: Two friends who disagree end up shouting at each other.*

Vocabulary Strategy: Etymology

Scalloped comes from the Old French word *escalope,* which means "shell." The modern definition of the word as describing a series of curves along an edge makes sense since many shells have scalloped edges.

Degenerate comes from the Latin word *dēgenerāre,* which means "to deteriorate" or "to depart from one's own kind." The word today is still used in the original sense.

TO CHALLENGE STUDENTS . . .

Explore Nuances of Meaning Point out that the Critical Vocabulary activity—choosing which of two examples correctly expresses a word's meaning—is a good way to check one's working knowledge of a word. Have students work independently to create a similar activity using the Collection 1 academic vocabulary words: *accumulate, appreciation, conform, persistence, reinforce.* Then have them exchange papers with a partner and take each other's quizzes. Encourage students to discuss any examples that do not seem clear and to explore the nuances of meaning that each example brings out.

Language and Style: Dashes

Review the examples in the chart and make sure students understand how each one exemplifies the stated purpose. Then have students look for examples of dashes in the selection and classify them according to their purposes. Examples include the following:

- Lines 16–19, 99–103 (to amplify or extend an idea)
- Lines 248–250, 342–346 (in place of parentheses)

Invite pairs to share with the class some of the sentences they revised and to explain how the dashes clarified the meaning or affected the tone of the writing.

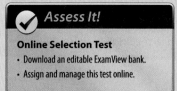

Assess It!

Online Selection Test
- Download an editable ExamView bank.
- Assign and manage this test online.

Language and Style: Dashes

In "A Walk to the Jetty," Kincaid uses dashes in many of her sentences. This chart explains some grammatical functions of the dash.

Purpose	Example
to amplify or extend an idea	She would not visit the library again—even though she still owed sevenpence for overdue books.
to show an abrupt break in thought or speech	When it was time to leave—and this annoyed Annie so much—her parents lingered over their breakfast.
in place of parentheses	Her outfit for the trip—a dark-blue skirt and checked blouse—had been carefully ironed.

Kincaid also uses dashes as a style element. With them she helps readers "hear" the narrator's tone and focus on important ideas.

Read this sentence from the story:

Big tears streamed down her face, and it must have been that—for I could not bear to see my mother cry—which started me crying, too.

The dashes in this sentence interrupt the description of an emotional scene and make the narrator's excuse the focus of the sentence. She wants to justify her tears and make sure that there is no confusion about why she is crying. At the same time, the dashes suggest that the narrator is impatient or annoyed with her mother for leading her to display this weakness.

Now consider the effect of replacing the dashes with parentheses or commas.

Big tears streamed down her face, and it must have been that (for I could not bear to see my mother cry) which started me crying, too.

Big tears streamed down her face, and it must have been that, for I could not bear to see my mother cry, which started me crying, too.

The use of parentheses or commas changes the tone, making the narrator seem almost apologetic rather than defiant. Her excuse for crying is no longer the most important idea in the sentence. Rather, readers are left with the impression of the mother's grief and the narrator's response.

Practice and Apply Look back at the letter that you wrote from the point of view of Annie John in response to this selection's Performance Task. Insert dashes into existing sentences or add sentences with dashes that amplify or extend an idea, show an interruption, or take the place of parentheses. Share your sentences with a partner and discuss how the insertion of dashes affects their tone or meaning.

Analyze Story Elements: Setting

COMMON CORE
RL 3

TEACH

Remind students that in a short story, the **setting** is the place and time in which the plot moves forward. In "A Walk to the Jetty," the setting plays an especially important role:

- Specific places in Antigua provide structure and movement for the narrative.
- These places encourage the rich, sensory language that brings Annie John's story to life.
- These places trigger important memories for Annie John, helping readers to fully understand her.

PRACTICE AND APPLY

Read aloud lines 231–253, from Annie John's last walk before departing Antigua. Point out that the action of the story is the walk itself but that the doctor's office—part of the **setting**—reminds Annie John of a memory so that as she walks along, she tells us about something in her past.

Have students reread lines 254–303, as Annie John continues her walk toward the jetty. Before they begin, point out how line 254 begins: "We passed the office of the doctor . . ." Remind them that the preceding paragraph begins in a similar way: "We passed by our church . . ." As students read, they are to make a list of the major places Annie John describes as her walk continues. Ask them to look for sentences beginning with "We passed."

Have students share their list of settings. Make a list for the entire class to see. *(the doctor's office, the store with a porcelain dog, the library)* Ask if the author describes any of these settings; they will notice that she does not. Ask: What happens when Annie John "passes by" a place? *(Each place reminds her of a story that happened there. The doctor's office leads to a story about eyesight, carrot juice, and glasses; the store to a story about a porcelain dog; the library to Annie's memory of being there with her mother.)*

Point out that the author is using the story's setting to help her structure the plot. Each of the important places along her walk triggers a memory. Each of these memories makes up an episode in the story's plot. Ask students to think of a place they frequently pass by, a place that reminds them of events that happened there. To demonstrate again the connection between setting and plot, have them share places they regularly pass by and the memories those places trigger.

 If students need further instruction, use this *Interactive Whiteboard Lesson:* **Role of Setting**

Analyze Word Choice: Tone

COMMON CORE
RL 4

RETEACH

Review the term **tone.** In a work of fiction, tone is the narrator's attitude toward events and characters. An author conveys the narrator's tone by choosing words and phrases that help readers infer the narrator's feelings and opinions.

- Have students reread Annie's reflections upon waking up in her bed, lines 13–22.
- Ask: Overall, does Annie feel positive or negative about the experience of waking up in Antigua each morning? *(negative)*
- Have students point out specific words and phrases that suggest her negative tone. *(Examples include the repetition of "I never wanted to . . . again," "tossing and turning," "lumped just where it wasn't a good place to be lumped," and the emphasis on her mother's "gargling.")*
- Ask students to think of more precise adjectives to describe Annie's negative tone. *(scornful, impatient, weary, bored)*

 LEVEL UP TUTORIALS Assign the following *Level Up* tutorial: **Tone**

CLOSE READING APPLICATION

Students can apply the skill to another story or novel they have read. Have them select a passage that strongly conveys the narrator's tone and then identify the specific word choices that create that tone. Students may share their analyses in pairs or small groups.

Next Term, We'll Mash You

Short Story by Penelope Lively

Why This Text

Students often have difficulty fully comprehending stories in which they have to make inferences about what happens. "Next Term, We'll Mash You" is such a story. In it, the reader has to draw his or her own inferences about events that happen and about the characters and their feelings. With the help of the close-reading questions, students will analyze the language the author uses to describe the setting and the characters. This close reading will help students gain a deeper understanding of the story's theme.

Background Have students read the background and information about the author. Point out that Lively's quote about her school suggests that her school was not devoted to academics. Explain that the selection students are going to read is about a private British boys' boarding school—and that the story only hints at what is really going on. As students read, they should heed what Penelope Lively herself said: "Getting to know someone else involves curiosity about where they have come from, who they are."

AS YOU READ Ask students to pay attention to words that set the mood; much of the story can be inferred from subtle hints.

Common Core Support

- cite strong and thorough textual evidence

- make inferences and support them with text evidence

- analyze the impact of specific word choices

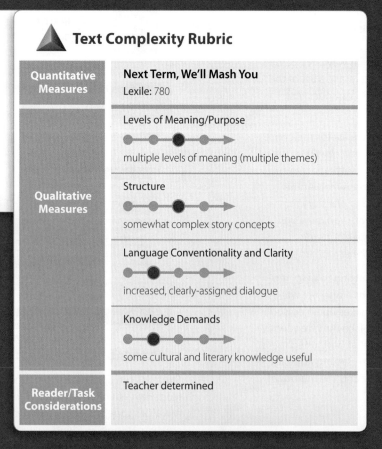

Text Complexity Rubric

Quantitative Measures	**Next Term, We'll Mash You** Lexile: 780
Qualitative Measures	Levels of Meaning/Purpose — multiple levels of meaning (multiple themes)
	Structure — somewhat complex story concepts
	Language Conventionality and Clarity — increased, clearly-assigned dialogue
	Knowledge Demands — some cultural and literary knowledge useful
Reader/Task Considerations	Teacher determined

Strategies for CLOSE READING

Support Inferences

Students should read this story carefully all the way through. Close-reading questions at the bottom of the page will help them draw inferences where the text leaves matters uncertain. As they read, students should jot down comments or questions about the text in the margins.

WHEN STUDENTS STRUGGLE . . .

To help students make and support inferences in "Next Term, We'll Mash You," have them work in small groups to fill out a chart like the one shown below.

CITE TEXT EVIDENCE For practice in supporting inferences drawn from the text, ask students to draw an inference from each text example.

Text Example	Inference
". . . and the child two paces behind." (lines 32–33)	Charles is not at all eager to see the school.
"Sally Wilcox doesn't let you forget that." (lines 77–78)	The mother is jealous of Sally Wilcox.
"And other things, of course. Background and all that stuff." (lines 87–88)	The father is insecure about his own background, and feels inferior.
"They help themselves to his name . . ." (line 127)	The boys are insistent and one-sided with their questions.

Background Penelope Lively *was born in Cairo, Egypt, in 1933. At the age of twelve she moved to England, where she attended The Downs, a boarding school. "I was excruciatingly unhappy for four years," Lively says of her boarding school experience. She also notes, "The school was rigorously devoted to the improvement of its girls' lacrosse and netball." Boarding schools are fairly common in England. It is sometimes argued that expensive and exclusive boarding schools perpetuate an "old boy network" of social entitlement in English society.*

Next Term, We'll Mash You

Short Story by Penelope Lively

CLOSE READ
Notes

1. **READ ▷** As you read lines 1–33, begin to collect and cite text evidence.

   • Underline descriptive words and phrases in lines 1–7.
   • In the margin, describe the mood of the first paragraph.
   • Underline some of the descriptive words in lines 29–33.
   • In the margin, describe your impression of the school.

(A) Inside the car it was quiet, the noise of the engine even and **subdued**, the air just the right temperature, the windows tight-fitting. The boy sat on the back seat, a box of chocolates, unopened, beside him, and a comic, folded. The trim Sussex[1] landscape flowed past the windows: cows, white-fenced fields, highly priced period houses. The sunlight was glassy, remote as a colored photograph. The backs of the two heads in front of him swayed with the motion of the car.

His mother half-turned to speak to him. "Nearly there now, darling."

The father glanced downwards at his wife's wrist. "Are we all right
10 for time?"

"Just right. Nearly twelve."

"I could do with a drink. Hope they lay something on."[2]

"I'm sure they will. The Wilcoxes say they're awfully nice people. Not really the schoolmaster-type at all, Sally says."

[1] **Sussex:** a county on the southeast coast of England.
[2] **lay something on:** have a reception with drinks and/or snacks.

subdued:
quiet,
controlled

The mood is
constrained,
uncomfortable,
and distant.

11

---

1. **READ AND CITE TEXT EVIDENCE** Remind students that an author's word choice can help set the mood or atmosphere in a story. The choice of a single specific word—with its particular meaning within a context—can have a big effect on a reader's understanding; a collection of well-chosen words can definitely establish a tone or feeling.

(A) ASK STUDENTS to cite evidence in order to explain what mood the author has established. *Students should underline many of the adjectives, and note that collectively they set up an atmosphere that is very controlled: it is quiet and everything is in order. Adjectives such as "tight-fitting, unopened, folded" and "trim" suggest an almost unnatural and disturbing sterility.*

Critical Vocabulary: subdued (line 1) Ask students to share their definitions of *subdued*.

CLOSE READ
Notes

The man said, "He's an Oxford chap."

"Is he? You didn't say."

"Mmn."

"Of course, the fees are that much higher than the Seaford place."

B

"Fifty quid³ or so. We'll have to see."

20   The car turned right, between white gates and high, dark, tight-clipped hedges. The whisper of the road under the tires changed to the crunch of gravel. The child, staring sideways, read black lettering on a white board:

"St. Edward's Preparatory School. Please Drive Slowly." He shifted on the seat, and the leather sucked at the bare skin under his knees, stinging.

The mother said, " It's a lovely place. Those must be the playing fields. Look, darling, there are some of the boys." She clicked open her handbag, and the sun caught her mirror and flashed in the child's eye; the comb went through her hair and he saw the grooves it left, neat as distant ploughing.

"Come on, then, Charles, out you get."

The school seems bleak and strict.

30   The building was red brick, early nineteenth century, spreading out long arms in which windows glittered blackly. Flowers, trapped in neat beds, were alternate red and white. They went up the steps, the man, the woman, and the child two paces behind.

The woman, the mother, smoothing down a skirt that would be ridged

Mother is thinking of herself, not of her son.

C

from sitting, thought: I like the way they've got the maid all done up properly. The little white apron and all that. She's foreign, I suppose. Au pair.⁴ Very nice. If he comes here, there'll be Speech Days and that kind of thing. Sally Wilcox says it's quite dressy—she got that cream linen coat for coming down here. You can see why it costs a bomb. Great big grounds and only an hour and a half

40   from London.

---

³ **quid:** slang for pounds, British monetary unit.
⁴ **au pair:** foreign person who does domestic work for room and board and for an opportunity to learn the language of her employers.

---

2. ◄ **REREAD**   Reread lines 19–33. Do you think Charles is likely to agree with his mother that, "It's a lovely place"? Support your inference with explicit textual evidence.

Charles may be intimidated by the new school and the new students he will eventually meet.

3. **READ** ►   As you read lines 34–111, continue to cite textual evidence.

• Circle the parents' unspoken thoughts.
• In the margin, make inferences based on the parents' thoughts.

12

They went into a room looking out into a terrace. Beyond, dappled lawns, gently shifting trees, black and white cows grazing behind iron railings. Books, leather chairs, a table with magazines—*Country Life, The Field, The Economist.* "Please, if you would wait here. The Headmaster won't be long."

Alone, they sat, inspected. "I like the atmosphere, don't you, John?"

"Very pleasant, yes." Four hundred a term, near enough. You can tell it's a cut above the Seaford place, though, or the one at St. Albans. Bob Wilcox says quite a few City people send their boys here. One or two of the merchant

50   bankers, those kind of people. It's the sort of contact that would do no harm at all. You meet someone, get talking at a cricket match or what have you . . . Not at all a bad thing.

Father is more concerned with furthering his career than his son's education.

"All right, Charles? You didn't get sick in the car, did you?"

The child had black hair, slicked down smooth to his head. His ears, too large, jutted out, transparent in the light from the window, laced with tiny, delicate veins. His clothes had the shine and crease of newness. He looked at

D

the books, the dark brown pictures, his parents, said nothing.

"Come here, let me tidy your hair."

The door opened. The child hesitated, stood up, sat, then rose again with his father.

60   "Mr. and Mrs. Manders? How very nice to meet you—I'm Margaret Spokes, and will you please forgive my husband who is tied up with some wretch who broke the cricket pavilion window and will be just a few more minutes. We try to be organized but a schoolmaster's day is always just that bit unpredictable. Do please sit down and what will you have to revive you after that beastly drive?⁵ is that right?"

"Hampstead⁶ really," said the mother. "Sherry would be lovely." She worked over the headmaster's wife from shoes to hairstyle, pricing and assessing. Shoes old but expensive—Russell and Bromley. Good skirt. Blouse could be Marks and Sparks—not sure. Real pearls. Super Victorian ring. She's not gone to any

70   particular trouble—that's just what she'd wear anyway. You can be confident, with a voice like that, of course. Sally Wilcox says she knows all sorts of people.

Mother judges people based on their clothes.

The headmaster's wife said, "I don't know how much you know about us. Prospectuses⁷ don't tell you a thing, do they? We'll look round everything in a minute, when you've had a chat with my husband. I gather you're friends of the Wilcoxes, by the way. I'm awfully fond of Simon—he's down for Winchester, of course, but I expect you know that."

---

⁵ **Finchley:** part of the London borough of Barnet.
⁶ **Hampstead:** part of the London borough of Camden—and a much more desirable place to live.
⁷ **prospectuses:** brochures.

13

---

2. (**REREAD AND CITE TEXT EVIDENCE**)   Tell students that there is no direct evidence for how Charles feels in lines 19–33, but the author has used certain words and has described certain actions that let the reader infer how he might feel.

B **ASK STUDENTS** to cite text evidence that lets them infer how Charles feels. *They may refer to the seat leather stinging his skin (line 24); the sun flashing in his eye (line 27); the flowers "trapped" in their beds (line 31); and Charles walking behind his parents (line 33)—obviously not excited to be there.*

3. (**READ AND CITE TEXT EVIDENCE**)

C **ASK STUDENTS** to compare and refine the inferences they wrote in the margin about Charles's parents. *Students will probably infer that Charles's father is more interested in what the school can do for him, and Charles's mother is more concerned with appearances than with her son's future.*

The mother smiled over her sherry. Oh, I know that all right. Sally Wilcox doesn't let you forget that.

"And this is Charles? My dear, we've been forgetting all about you! In a
80 minute I'm going to borrow Charles and take him off to meet some of the boys because after all you're choosing a school for him, aren't you, and not for you, so he ought to know what he might be letting himself in for and it shows we've got nothing to hide."

The parents laughed. The father, sherry warming his guts, thought that this was an amusing woman. Not attractive, of course, a bit homespun, but impressive all the same. Partly the voice, of course; it takes a bloody expensive education to produce a voice like that. And other things, of course. Background and all that stuff.

"I think I can hear the thud of the Fourth Form coming in from games,
90 which means my husband is on the way, and then I shall leave you with him while I take Charles off to the common-room."

For a moment the three adults centered on the child, looking, judging. The mother said, "He looks so hideously pale, compared to those boys we saw outside."

"My dear, that's London, isn't it? You just have to get them out, to get some color into them. Ah, here's James. James—Mr. and Mrs. Manders. You remember, Bob Wilcox was mentioning at Sports Day . . ."

The headmaster reflected his wife's style, like paired cards in Happy Families. His clothes were mature rather than old, his skin well-scrubbed, his
100 shoes clean, his **geniality** untainted by the least condescension. He was genuinely sorry to have kept them waiting, but in this business one lurches from one minor crisis to the next . . . And this is Charles? Hello, there, Charles. His large hand rested for a moment on the child's head, quite extinguishing the thin, dark hair. It was as though he had but to clench his fingers to crush the skull. But he took his hand away and moved the parents to the window, to observe the mutilated cricket pavilion, with **indulgent** laughter.

And the child is borne away by the headmaster's wife. She never touches him or tells him to come, but simply bears him away like some relentless tide, down corridors and through swinging glass doors, towing him like a frail craft,
110 not bothering to look back to see if he is following, confident in the strength of magnetism, or obedience.

The father believes that a person with an expensive education commands attention and impresses others.

geniality:
friendliness

indulgent:
lenient, permissive

---

4. ◀ **REREAD** Reread lines 52–59 and 79–111. What picture of Charles is emerging? What can you infer about how he feels about being at the school?

He is feeling ignored, trapped, and afraid.

14

And delivers him to a room where boys are scattered among inky tables and rungless chairs and sprawled on a mangy carpet. There is a scampering, and a rising, and a silence falling, as she opens the door.

"Now this is the Lower Third, Charles, who you'd be with if you come to us in September. Boys, this is Charles Manders, and I want you to tell him all about things and answer any questions he wants to ask. You can believe about half of what they say, Charles, and they will tell you the most fearful lies about the food, which is excellent."

120 The boys laugh and groan; **amiable**, exaggerated groans. They must like the headmaster's wife: There is licensed repartee.[8] They look at her with bright eyes in open, eager faces. Someone leaps to hold the door for her, and close it behind her. She is gone.

The child stands in the center of the room, and it draws in around him. The circle of children contracts, faces are only a yard or so from him; strange faces, looking, assessing.

Asking questions. They help themselves to his name, his age, his school. Over their heads he sees beyond the window an inaccessible world of shivering trees and high racing clouds and his voice which has floated like a feather in
130 the dusty schoolroom air dies altogether and he becomes mute, and he stands in the middle of them with shoulders humped, staring down at feet: grubby plimsolls[9] and kicked brown sandals. There is a noise in his ears like rushing water, a torrential din out of which voices boom, blotting each other out so that he cannot always hear the words. Do you? they say, and Have you? And What's your? and the faces, if he looks up, swing into one another in kaleidoscopic patterns and the floor under his feet is unsteady, lifting and falling.

And out of the noises comes one voice that is complete, that he can hear. "Next term, we'll mash you," it says. "We always mash new boys."

And a bell goes, somewhere beyond doors and down corridors, and
140 suddenly the children are all gone, clattering away and leaving him there with the heaving floor and the walls that shift and swing, and the headmaster's wife comes back and tows him away, and he is with his parents again, and they are getting into the car, and the high hedges skim past the car windows once more, in the other direction, and the gravel under the tires changes to black tarmac.

"Well?"

---

[8] **licensed repartee:** approved witty replies.
[9] **plimsolls:** sneakers.

---

amiable:
friendly, likable

The boy warns Charles they will beat him up. Charles does nothing.

---

5. **READ** ▶ As you read lines 112–161, continue to cite textual evidence.

• Underline details that describe the room "where boys are scattered."
• Underline Charles's reactions to the other students.
• Circle the threat one student makes. In the margin, explain what you think this threat means and describe Charles's response.

15

---

4. **REREAD AND CITE TEXT EVIDENCE**

D **ASK STUDENTS** to cite additional text evidence in lines 52–59 and 79–111 that lets them infer how Charles feels. *In line 56, Charles does not respond to his parents; in line 93 his mother makes a mean remark about him; in lines 103–106 the only attention he gets is having a large, threatening hand placed on his head. He probably feels left out, trapped, and nervous.*

Critical Vocabulary: geniality (line 100) Have students explain the meaning of *geniality*, and ask them about the headmaster's geniality. *It is directed to Charles's parents.*

Critical Vocabulary: indulgent (line 106) Ask students why the headmaster's laughter is *indulgent*. *A boy has damaged the pavilion, but the headmaster is tolerant of the misbehavior.*

5. **READ AND CITE TEXT EVIDENCE** Charles is left on his own with the boys of the Lower Third (boys of around 10 years old—Charles's age).

E **ASK STUDENTS** to infer the reasons for Charles's reactions. *Students should note that the room "draws in around him" and he stands "with shoulders humped." Charles is so anxious that the floor appears to move under his feet and sounds blur. He is terrified, even before he hears that he will be beaten up next term.*

Critical Vocabulary: amiable (line 120) Have students explain how the word *amiable* lets the reader know what the boys' groans sound like. *The groans are cartoonish and good-natured.*

FOR ELL STUDENTS Explain that "borrowing someone" means to take a person away from what they were doing or from the company they were with. In this selection, Charles is "borrowed" to be introduced to some other boys.

CLOSE READ
Notes

"I liked it, didn't you?" The mother adjusted the car around her, closing windows, shrugging into her seat.

"Very pleasant, really. Nice chap."

"I liked him. Not quite so sure about her."

150   "It's pricey, of course."

"All the same . . ."

"Money well spent, though. One way and another."

"Shall we settle it, then?"

"I think so. I'll drop him a line."

The mother pitched her voice a notch higher to speak to the child in the back of the car.

"Would you like to go there, Charles? Like Simon Wilcox. Did you see that lovely gym, and the swimming pool? And did the other boys tell you all about it?"

160   The child does not answer. He looks straight ahead of him, at the road coiling beneath the bonnet of the car. His face is haggard with anticipation.

6. **◀ REREAD AND DISCUSS** Reread lines 137–161. With a small group, make an inference about why Charles does not tell his parents about the boy's threat. How might the parents have reacted if Charles had told them? Use evidence from the text to support your opinions.

SHORT RESPONSE

Cite Text Evidence Compare Charles's outlook on the school with that of his parents. What specific phrases does Lively use to build an understanding of what drives the characters? **Cite text evidence** to support your analysis.

We learn about Charles through descriptions of the environment and of his physical feelings. Phrases such as "spreading out long arms in which windows glittered blackly," which describe the exterior of the school, let us know that Charles feels trapped and afraid. By contrast, the words and thoughts of the parents are given directly. The father values the social connections of a prestigious education. When Charles's mother works over "the headmaster's wife from shoes to hairstyle," we know she is more concerned about appearances than she is interested in her son's feelings.

16

TO CHALLENGE STUDENTS . . .

A small detail in "Next Term, We'll Mash You," is used to illustrate the headmaster's composure and understanding. A boy has broken the cricket pavilion window. Tell students that cricket is a team game first played in the sixteenth century in England, and that the pavilion is a wooden building in which team members have dressing rooms. Although cricket is not very popular in the United States, it is said to be the world's second most popular sport (after soccer).

ASK STUDENTS to research cricket to get a reasonable idea of the game: what the players' roles are, what the purpose of the game is, how it is played, and how it is scored. Have students first learn a little about the game, and then watch some online videos that show cricket being played. (There are also online videos that explain the game.)

Have students use what they find out about the game of cricket to make inferences about boys' boarding schools like the one in "Next Term, We'll Mash You."

6. (REREAD AND DISCUSS USING TEXT EVIDENCE)

(F) **ASK STUDENTS** to assign a reporter for each group to present its response. *Building on their previous inferences, students may think that Charles is embarrassed about not sticking up for himself when he is threatened (line 138). As he also feels alienated, and his parents are not including him in the discussion (lines 145–154), he may not think that telling his parents would make a difference.*

SHORT RESPONSE

Cite Text Evidence Students' responses should include text evidence that supports their positions. They should:

- explain how the author's word choices and descriptions allow the reader to make inferences about the characters.
- explain how the dialogue reveals the characters' motivations.
- use the text evidence to compare Charles' outlook with that of his parents.

DIG DEEPER

1. With the class, return to Question 2, Reread. Have students share their responses.

ASK STUDENTS to cite the text evidence that led to their inferences about Charles's reaction to the school.

- Have students explain why they inferred that Charles would not find the school "a lovely place." Point out that there is nothing directly stated that shows he might be uncomfortable. What hints does the author give?

- Have students reread the story from the beginning to line 33. How does the mood continue through the story? How does Charles contribute to the mood? *The story gives a feeling of the characters being trapped in the car, and then the school itself seems to trap them: it spreads out "long arms," and even the flowers are "trapped." Charles says not a word; he is as "remote" as the glassy sunlight. In some ways, it seems as though the author is writing the story from Charles's point of view.*

2. With the class, return to Question 6, Reread and Discuss. Have students share the results of their discussion.

ASK STUDENTS how they think Charles's parents might have reacted had he told them about the boy's threat.

- Have students analyze the conversation Charles's parents have in the car. What can you tell about the parents?

- Ask students the following questions to help them make an inference: What do the parents focus on? Why does the mother express doubt about the headmaster's wife? How interested in Charles's opinion are they? Are they likely to take the threat to Charles seriously, and if they do, are they likely to consider it very important?

ASK STUDENTS to return to their Short Response answer and revise it based on the class discussion.

CLOSE READING NOTES

ILE

Drama by Eugene O'Neill

Why This Text?

Students regularly encounter dramas in TV series, movies, and even Internet videos and podcasts. These may include a full range of dramatic elements or just a few. This lesson explores the dramatic elements of conflict and symbolism in a short drama.

▶ **View It!**

Professional Development Podcast:

Text-Dependent Analysis

Key Learning Objective: The student will be able to analyze elements of a drama, including conflict and symbolism.

COMMON CORE Common Core Standards

RL 1 Cite strong and thorough textual evidence to support analysis.

RL 2 Determine themes of a text.

RL 3 Analyze elements of a drama.

RL 4 Determine figurative meanings.

RL 6 Analyze point of view (irony).

W 4 Produce clear and coherent writing appropriate to task.

SL 1a Come to discussions prepared.

L 1a Apply the understanding that usage is a matter of convention.

L 3 Apply knowledge to understand how language functions in different contexts.

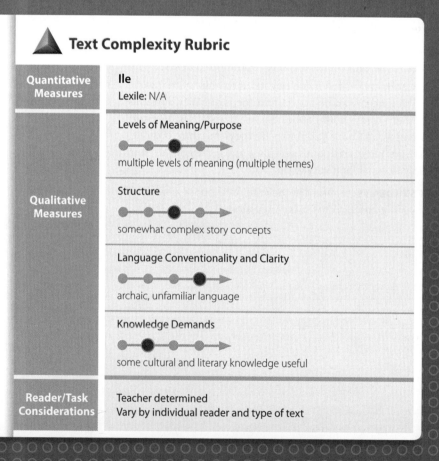

▲ Text Complexity Rubric

Quantitative Measures

Ile
Lexile: N/A

Levels of Meaning/Purpose

multiple levels of meaning (multiple themes)

Qualitative Measures

Structure

somewhat complex story concepts

Language Conventionality and Clarity

archaic, unfamiliar language

Knowledge Demands

some cultural and literary knowledge useful

Reader/Task Considerations

Teacher determined
Vary by individual reader and type of text

TEACH

CLOSE READ

For more context and historical background, students can view the video in their eBooks.

Eugene O'Neill Have students read the background information about the author and the play. Note that O'Neill is one of the most accomplished playwrights in American history. *Ile* is not one of his most famous or honored dramas, but it is one of the early plays that attracted attention to his work and led to his extraordinary career on Broadway during the next two decades.

Critics suggest that several of the characters in *Ile* are similar to famous characters in O'Neill's later plays, especially the character of Mrs. Keeney. She may reflect O'Neill's mother, whose erratic behavior and drug addiction inspired a major character *in Long Day's Journey into Night*. The conflicts within families, as shown by the conflict between Captain and Mrs. Keeney, became a recurring theme in his plays. *Ile* also demonstrates O'Neill's ability to use symbols to expand his meanings beyond the immediate circumstances of the play.

AS YOU READ Direct students to use the As You Read tip to help them focus their reading. Remind them to note any questions they have as they read.

ILE

Drama by Eugene O'Neill

Eugene O'Neill *(1888–1953) won the Nobel Prize for Literature as well as four Pulitzer Prizes. Brooks Atkinson, theater critic for the New York Times, credited him with transforming American drama into a serious art form. Until his late twenties, however, he seemed destined for obscurity.*

O'Neill was born in New York City. His father was a popular touring actor whose profession resulted in an insecure life for the family. As a young man, O'Neill lacked direction. He was expelled from Princeton University; tried a series of occupations, including that of a sailor; and then finally began to write. In 1916, his play Bound East for Cardiff *was produced in New York by the Provincetown Players, launching his literary career.*

The play Ile, *written in 1917, is one of several one-act plays about the sea that O'Neill wrote during this early period. He based the characters and plot on actual residents of Provincetown, Massachusetts: Captain Cook and his wife, Viola, who went to sea with her husband for two years. After Viola returned home, she was never the same.*

O'Neill's literary output between 1920 and 1943 included 20 full-length plays as well as shorter works. Most of his plays explore tragic themes and troubled relationships. Mourning Becomes Electra *(1931) sets the Greek tragedy* Oresteia *in Civil War–era New England. The Iceman Cometh (1939) suggests that without illusions, people cannot escape despair. His autobiographical play* Long Day's Journey into Night *(1941) reveals the searing pain of O'Neill's family life, including his mother's drug addiction. He did not want the play performed until 25 years after his death. However, its first production in 1956 earned O'Neill his fourth Pulitzer Prize.*

AS YOU READ Pay attention to the clues that reveal Captain Keeney's character.

Image Credits: (b) ©General Photographic Agency/Hulton Archive/Getty Images; (t) ©Radius Images/Corbis

SCAFFOLDING FOR ELL STUDENTS

Vocabulary: Context Clues Read aloud the background information about Eugene O'Neill while students follow along in the text. When you have finished, invite them to point out words and phrases in each paragraph that are unclear or confusing. Discuss context clues that could help them figure out the meanings. For example, the phrase "destined for obscurity" at the end of the first paragraph is preceded by "however," which indicates a contrast. (*Earlier sentences tell about the awards and praise that O'Neill had earned by the end of his successful career. Therefore, "destined for obscurity" means the opposite—"unlikely to be successful or famous."*)

Analyze Drama Elements: Symbol (LINE 18)
 COMMON CORE RL 3

Note that a playwright can use a tangible object on the stage as a **symbol** for something beyond itself, such as an idea about the characters or their situation.

A ASK STUDENTS to review the stage directions in lines 1–33 with a focus on the sewing basket mentioned in line 18. Ask them to describe why the sewing basket stands out and what they think it might symbolize. *(The remainder of the set is described as very basic, utilitarian, and rough. The sewing basket is owned by a woman, so it may symbolize a woman's influence on or intrusion into this male atmosphere.)*

Analyze Drama Elements: Conflict (LINES 42–53)
 COMMON CORE RL 3

Introduce the concept of **conflict** by explaining that a drama, like all good stories, involves characters facing problems and trying to solve them. These conflicts can be **internal,** when a character struggles with his or her own thoughts and feelings. They can also be **external,** when a character comes into conflict with another character(s), nature, or society.

B CITE TEXT EVIDENCE Have students reread lines 42–53 and identify text evidence that suggests the Steward is experiencing some kind of conflict. *(The stage directions say that the Steward's "manner is sullen and angry," and that he hears something that "makes his face darken and he mutters a furious curse." These clues indicate a conflict, but its source is unclear.)*

Analyze Language: Dialect (LINES 63–66)
 COMMON CORE L 1a, L 3

Explain that **dialect** is a type of language spoken in a particular place. O'Neill uses dialect throughout *Ile* to make the drama lively and believable.

C ASK STUDENTS to restate lines 63–66 in modern English. How does the use of dialect reinforce the time period and setting? *("Oh, it's you. Why are you cold? If you'd stay by the stove like you should, your teeth wouldn't chatter." The dialect reinforces that the play is set in the late 1800s. It sounds authentic for sailors on a ship.)*

CHARACTERS

BEN, *the cabin boy*	**SLOCUM**, *second mate*
THE STEWARD	**MRS. KEENEY**
CAPTAIN KEENEY	**JOE**, *a harpooner*

Members of the crew of the steam whaler Atlantic Queen.

SCENE—CAPTAIN KEENEY's cabin on board the steam whaling ship Atlantic Queen—a small, square compartment about eight feet high with a skylight in the center looking out on the poop deck. On the left (the stern of the ship) a long bench with rough cushions is built in against the wall. In front of the bench, a table. Over the bench, several
10 curtained portholes.

In the rear, left, a door leading to the captain's sleeping quarters. To the right of the door a small organ, looking as if it were brand new, is placed against the wall.

A On the right, to the rear, a marble-topped sideboard. On the sideboard, a woman's sewing basket. Farther forward, a doorway leading to the
20 companion way, and past the officer's quarters to the main deck.

In the center of the room, a stove. From the middle of the ceiling a hanging lamp is suspended. The walls of the cabin are painted white.

There is no rolling of the ship, and the light which comes through the skylight is sickly and faint, indicating one of those gray days of calm when ocean and sky
30 are alike dead. The silence is unbroken except for the measured tread of some one walking up and down on the poop deck overhead.

It is nearing two bells—one o'clock—in the afternoon of a day in the year 1895.

At the rise of the curtain there is a moment of intense silence. Then the STEWARD enters and commences to
40 clear the table of the few dishes which still remain on it after the CAPTAIN's dinner. He is an old, grizzled man dressed in dungaree pants, a sweater, and a woolen cap with ear flaps. His manner is sullen and angry. He stops stacking up the plates and casts a quick glance upward at the skylight; then tiptoes over to the closed door in rear and listens with his ear pressed to the crack.
50 What he hears makes his face darken and he mutters a furious curse. There is a noise from the doorway on the right and he darts back to the table.

BEN enters. He is an over-grown, gawky boy with a long, pinched face. He is dressed in sweater, fur cap, etc. His teeth are chattering with the cold and he hurries to the stove, where he stands for a moment shivering, blowing on his hands, slapping them against his sides, on the
60 verge of crying.

THE STEWARD (*In relieved tones—seeing who it is*). Oh, 'tis you, is it? What're ye **C** shiverin' 'bout? Stay by the stove where ye belong and ye'll find no need of chatterin'.

WHEN STUDENTS STRUGGLE . . .

To help students visualize the play as they read it, work with them to draw a sketch of the stage as it is described in lines 1–33. Create a top view and/or a front view of the stage and indicate the locations of the doors, the table, the organ, the sideboard, and so on. Discuss the other set directions related to the lighting and wall colors and how the set and stage directions help give the play a clear atmosphere or mood.

BEN. It's c-c-cold. (*Trying to control his chattering teeth—derisively.*) Who d'ye think it were—the Old Man?

70 **THE STEWARD** (*Makes a threatening move—BEN shrinks away*). None o' your lip, young un, or I'll learn ye. (*More kindly.*) Where was it ye've been all o' the time—the fo'c's'tle?[1]

BEN. Yes.

THE STEWARD. Let the Old Man see ye up for'ard monkeyshinin' with the hands and ye'll get a hidin' ye'll not forget in a hurry.

80 **BEN.** Aw, he don't see nothin'. (*A trace of awe in his tones—he glances upward.*) He just walks up and down like he didn't notice nobody—and stares at the ice to the no'the'ard.

THE STEWARD (*The same tone of awe creeping into his voice*). He's always starin' at the ice. (*In a sudden rage, shaking his fist at the skylight.*) Ice, ice, ice! Damn him and damn the ice!

90 Hold-in' us in for nigh on a year—nothin' to see but ice—stuck in it like a fly in molasses!

BEN (*Apprehensively*). Ssshh! He'll hear ye.

THE STEWARD (*Raging*). Aye, damn him, and damn the Arctic seas, and damn this stinkin' whalin' ship of his, and damn me for a fool to ever

100 ship on it! (*Subsiding as if realizing the uselessness of this outburst—shaking his head—slowly, with deep conviction.*) He's a hard man—as hard a man as ever sailed the seas.

BEN (*Solemnly*). Aye.

THE STEWARD. The two years we all signed up for are done this day. Blessed Christ! Two years o' this dog's life, and

no luck in the fishin', and the hands half starved with the food runnin'

110 low, rotten as it is; and not a sign of him turnin' back for home! (*Bitterly.*) Home! I begin to doubt if ever I'll set foot on land again, (*Excitedly.*) What is it he thinks he' goin' to do? Keep us all up here after our time is worked out till the last man of us is starved to death or frozen? We've grub enough hardly to last out the voyage back if we started now. What are the men goin' to

120 do 'bout it? Did ye hear any talk in the fo'c's'tle?

BEN (*Going over to him—in a half whisper*). They said if he don't put back south for home today they're goin' to mutiny.

THE STEWARD (*With grim satisfaction*). Mutiny? Aye, 'tis the only thing they can do; and serve him right after the manner he's treated them—'s if they

130 wern't no better nor dogs.

BEN. The ice is all broke up to s'uth'ard. They's clear water 's far 's you can see. He ain't got no excuse for not turnin' back for home, the men says.

THE STEWARD (*Bitterly*). He won't look no-wheres but no'the'ard where they's only the ice to see. He don't want to see no clear water. All he thinks on is gittin' the ile[2]—'s if it was our fault he ain't had

140 good luck with the whales. (*Shaking his head.*) I think the man's mighty nigh losin' his senses.

BEN (*Awed*). D'you really think he's crazy?

THE STEWARD. Aye, it's the punishment o' God on him. Did ye ever hear of a man who wasn't crazy do the things he does? (*Pointing to the door in rear.*) Who but a man that's mad would

150 take his woman—and as sweet a woman

---
[1] **forecastle** (fōk′səl): the top deck near the bow (front) of a ship.

[2] **ile** (īl): a regional pronunciation of "oil."

Ile **49**

Analyze Language: Dialect (LINES 80–84)

COMMON CORE L 1a, L 3

Explain that another characteristic of dialect is that it may not follow the standard conventions of written or spoken English.

D **ASK STUDENTS** to restate lines 80–84 using standard English. Ask them what the use of this dialect tells the audience about Ben. *("He doesn't see anything. He just walks up and down as if he doesn't notice anybody—and stares at the ice to the north." Ben's dialect, which does not follow the standard conventions of English, may indicate that he is not well educated or comes from a poor background.)*

Analyze Drama Elements: Conflict (LINES 88–103)

COMMON CORE RL 3

Note that the Steward's dialogue in lines 88–92 indicates a conflict with nature.

E **ASK STUDENTS** to describe the Steward's feelings about the ice and the sailors' ability to combat it. *(The Steward is frustrated and angry. He feels that the sailors are helpless to do anything about their situation—the ship is stuck in the ice "like a fly in molasses.")*

Point out that the short speech in lines 95–103 might qualify as a "rant" that identifies and expresses anger about several different conflicts.

F **CITE TEXT EVIDENCE** Have students identify specific words within the Steward's speech that indicate an internal conflict, conflicts with another character and with nature, and a possible conflict between a character and society. *(The words "damn him" and "damn this stinkin' whalin' ship of his" indicate conflict with the captain, while "damn the Arctic seas" reveals a conflict with nature. The Steward also calls himself "a fool," suggesting an internal conflict: he knows he is partially to blame for his own misery. The Steward's statement that the captain is "as hard a man as ever sailed the seas" may indicate a conflict between the captain and society, since a person who is "hard" lacks compassion for others and is not likely to get along with them.)*

SCAFFOLDING FOR ELL STUDENTS

Comprehension: Dialect Tell students that the dialect in this play will be challenging to read. Some vocabulary is specific to life on a whaling ship in the 1800s. There are many idioms and figurative expressions. Grammar is often unusual or incorrect. Many words are clipped. Tell students that an apostrophe represents one or more missing letters, and review some examples: *'tis* ("it is"), *shiverin'* ("shivering"), and so on. Point out some archaic words, such as *ye* ("you") and *nigh on* ("nearly"). Explain that reading the text aloud is a strategy that can help readers figure out the meaning from the sound of the words. Read the first page of dialogue aloud. Pause after each character's speech. Ask volunteers to rephrase the line in standard English.

Analyze Drama Elements: Character (LINES 145–170)

Explain that the initial dialogue between Ben and the Steward provides background for the plot. It sets up the play's major conflicts and introduces important characters and their personality traits.

G CITE TEXT EVIDENCE Have students reread lines 145–170 and describe the character of Mrs. Keeney through these two characters' eyes. What change have they observed in her? *(Ben and the Steward see Mrs. Keeney as a sympathetic figure who helped improve the atmosphere on board—"'Twould of been hell on board without her." They note that she has become "like she is" and has "near lost her mind.")*

Analyze Drama Elements: Conflict (LINES 175–181)

Explain that internal conflict can be indicated by a character's actions and words or by descriptions of a character by other characters.

H CITE TEXT EVIDENCE Direct students to reread lines 175–181 and identify evidence of internal conflict within Mrs. Keeney. *(Lines 179–180 clearly indicate internal conflict because Mrs. Keeney "cries to herself without makin' no noise." This behavior suggests she is struggling with her own thoughts and feelings.)*

---

as ever was—on a stinkin' whalin' ship to the Arctic seas to be locked in by the rotten ice for nigh on a year, and maybe lose her senses forever—for it's sure she'll never be the same again.

BEN (*Sadly*). She useter be awful nice to me before—(*His eyes grow wide and frightened.*) she got—like she is.

THE STEWARD. Aye, she was good to all of us. 'Twould have been hell on board without her; for he's a hard man—a hard, hard man—a driver if there ever was one. (*With a grim laugh.*) I hope he's satisfied now—drivin' her on till she's near lost her mind. And who could blame her? 'Tis a God's wonder we're not a ship full of crazed people—with the damned ice all the time, and the quiet so thick you're afraid to hear your own voice.

BEN (*With a frightened glance toward the door on right*). She don't never speak to me no more—jest looks at me 's if she didn't know me.

THE STEWARD. She don't know no one—but him. She talks to him—when she does talk—right enough.

BEN. She does nothin' all day long now but sit and sew—and then she cries to herself without makin' no noise. I've seen her.

THE STEWARD. Aye, I could hear her through the door a while back.

BEN (*Tiptoes over to the door and listens*). She's cryin' now.

THE STEWARD (*Furiously—shaking his fist*). God send his soul to hell for the devil he is! (*There is the noise of some one coming slowly down the companionway stairs. THE STEWARD hurries to his stacked up dishes. He is so nervous from fright that he knocks off the top one, which falls and breaks on the floor. He stands aghast, trembling with dread. BEN is violently rubbing off the organ with a piece of cloth which he has snatched from his pocket. CAPTAIN KEENEY appears in the doorway on right and comes into the cabin,*

Image Credits: ©Library of Congress

Strategies for Annotation 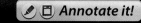 *Annotate it!*

Analyze Drama Elements: Character

Explain that a playwright's stage directions can describe a character. Have students use their eBook annotation tools to identify details in lines 197–210 that describe Captain Keeney's physical appearance and personality.

- Highlight in yellow physical descriptions of Captain Keeney.
- Highlight in green details that help describe his personality.
- On a note, write how these descriptions reinforce what the audience learns about the captain from Ben's conversation with the Steward.

account of the enormous proportions of his shoulders and chest. His face is massive and deeply lined, with gray-blue eyes of a bleak hardness, *and a* tightly clenched, thin-lipped mouth. *His thick hair is long and gray. He is dressed in a*

removing his fur cap as he does so. He is a man of about forty, around five-ten in height but looking much shorter on account of the enormous proportions of his shoulders and chest. His face is massive and deeply lined, with gray-blue eyes of a bleak hardness, and a tightly clenched, thin-lipped mouth. His thick hair is long and gray. He is dressed in a heavy blue jacket and blue pants stuffed
210 into his seaboots.

(He is followed into the cabin by the SECOND MATE, a rangy six-footer with a lean weather-beaten face. The MATE is dressed about the same as the captain. He is a man of thirty or so.)

KEENEY (Comes toward the STEWARD— with a stern look on his face. The STEWARD is visibly frightened and the stack of dishes rattles in his trembling
220 hands. KEENEY draws back his fist and the STEWARD shrinks away. The fist is gradually lowered and KEENEY speaks slowly). 'Twould be like hitting a worm. It is nigh on two bells, Mr. Steward, and this truck not cleared yet.

THE STEWARD (Stammering). Y-y-yes, sir.

KEENEY. Instead of doin' your rightful work ye've been below here gossipin' old
230 woman's talk with that boy. (To BEN, fiercely.) Get out o' this, you! Clean up the chart room. (BEN darts past the MATE to the open doorway.) Pick up that dish, Mr. Steward!

THE STEWARD (Doing so with difficulty). Yes, sir.

KEENEY. The next dish you break, Mr. Steward, you take a bath in the Bering Sea at the end of a rope.

240 **THE STEWARD** (Tremblingly). Yes, sir. (He hurries out. The SECOND MATE walks slowly over to the CAPTAIN.)

MATE. I warn't 'specially anxious the man at the wheel should catch what I wanted to say to you, sir. That's why I asked you to come below.

KEENEY (Impatiently). Speak your say, Mr. Slocum.

MATE (Unconsciously lowering his voice).
250 I'm afeard there'll be trouble with the hands by the look o' things. They'll likely turn ugly, every blessed one o' them, if you don't put back. The two years they signed up for is up to-day.

KEENEY. And d'you think you're tellin' me somethin' new, Mr. Slocum? I've felt it in the air this long time past. D'you think I've not seen their ugly looks and the grudgin' way they worked?
260 (The door in rear is opened and MRS. KEENEY stands in the doorway. She is a slight, sweet-faced little woman primly dressed in black. Her eyes are red from weeping and her face drawn and pale. She takes in the cabin with a frightened glance and stands as if fixed to the spot by some nameless dread, clasping and unclasping her hands nervously. The two men turn and look at her.)

270 **KEENEY** (With rough tenderness). Well, Annie?

MRS. KEENEY (As if awakening from a dream). David, I—(She is silent. The MATE starts for the doorway.)

KEENEY (Turning to him—sharply). Wait!

MATE. Yes, sir.

KEENEY. D'you want anything, Annie?

MRS. KEENEY (After a pause, during
280 which she seems to be endeavoring to collect her thoughts). I thought maybe— I'd go up on deck, David, to get a breath of fresh air. (She stands humbly awaiting his permission. He and the MATE exchange a significant glance.)

Ile **51**

APPLYING ACADEMIC VOCABULARY

accumulate	reinforce

As you discuss *Ile*, incorporate the Collection 1 academic vocabulary words *accumulate* and *reinforce*. To consider the idea that the plot is driven by conflict, ask students to identify evidence of conflict that **accumulates** over the course of the drama. Ask them to cite specific lines that **reinforce** conflicts that have been established earlier in the play.

Analyze Drama Elements: Character (LINES 197–210)

COMMON CORE RL 3

Explain that a playwright's description of a character's physical appearance can enhance or reinforce previous indications of the character's personality, even before the character opens his or her mouth.

CITE TEXT EVIDENCE Have students identify details in lines 197–210 that reinforce the personality of Captain Keeney as described by Ben and the Steward. *(They have described Captain Keeney as a "hard man," and both seem afraid of him. The stage directions indicate that Keeney is large and powerful by describing "the enormous proportions of his shoulders and chest" and his "massive" face. The description of his eyes and mouth reinforce Keeney's "bleak hardness.")*

Analyze Drama Elements: Conflict (LINES 228–239)

COMMON CORE RL 3

O'Neill shows that much of the conflict stems from the relationship between the captain and the crew.

ASK STUDENTS to reread lines 228–239, which indicate the relationship between the captain and the Steward and also reflect the broader relationship between the captain and other crew members. Ask them to describe these relationships and one source of conflict in the drama. *(These lines indicate that the captain has total power on the ship. He is comfortable using that power to order crew members about harshly and threaten them with severe punishment.)*

Analyze Drama Elements: Character (LINES 261–268)

COMMON CORE RL 3

In these lines, O'Neill provides the first physical description of Mrs. Keeney, although Ben and the Steward have already described some of her personality traits and recent changes.

CITE TEXT EVIDENCE Have students reread lines 261–268 to identify details that reinforce the idea that Mrs. Keeney is experiencing severe internal conflict. *(Lines 263–264 indicate she has been crying. The way she "stands . . . clasping and unclasping her hands nervously" suggests she is very anxious and uncertain.)*

Ile **51**

Analyze Drama Elements: COMMON CORE RL 3
Symbol (LINES 298–314; 358–361)

Explain that a symbol can mean different things to different characters.

L ASK STUDENTS to describe what the clear water to the south of the ship symbolizes for Mrs. Keeney and for the captain. *(For Mrs. Keeney, the clear water symbolizes the possibility of returning to a more normal life at home. For Captain Keeney, it symbolizes giving up; if he turns around and sails home, he would be admitting defeat.)*

Tell students that O'Neill introduces another symbol in the dialogue between Keeney and the Mate that will be further developed later in the play.

M ASK STUDENTS to suggest what they think the importance of the "ile" is for Captain Keeney, since he declares it is not money that motivates his stubborn pursuit of whale oil. *(The "ile" must mean something to Captain Keeney personally. It must symbolize some type of success.)*

KEENEY. It's too cold, Annie. You'd best stay below to-day. There's nothing to look at on deck—but ice.

MRS. KEENEY (*Monotonously*). I
290 know—ice, ice, ice! But there's nothing to see down here but these walls. (*She makes a gesture of loathing.*)

KEENEY. You can play the organ, Annie.

MRS. KEENEY (*Dully*). I hate the organ. It puts me in mind of home.

KEENEY (*A touch of resentment in his voice*). I got it jest for you.

L MRS. KEENEY (*Dully*). I know. (*She
300 turns away from them and walks slowly to the bench on left. She lifts up one of the curtains and looks through a porthole; then utters an exclamation of joy.*) Ah, water! Clear water! As far as I can see! How good it looks after all these months of ice! (*She turns round to them, her face transfigured with joy.*) Ah, now I must go upon deck and look at it, David.

KEENEY (*Frowning*). Best not to-day, Annie. Best wait for a day when the sun
310 shines.

MRS. KEENEY (*Desperately*). But the sun never shines in this terrible place.

KEENEY (*A tone of command in his voice*). Best not to-day, Annie.

MRS. KEENEY (*Crumbling before this command—abjectly*). Very well, David. (*She stands there staring straight before her as if in a daze. The two men look at her uneasily.*)

320 **KEENEY** (*Sharply*). Annie!

MRS. KEENEY (*Dully*). Yes, David.

KEENEY. Me and Mr. Slocum has business to talk about—ship's business.

MRS. KEENEY. Very well, David. (*She goes slowly out, rear, and leaves the door three-quarters shut behind her.*)

KEENEY. Best not have her on deck if they's goin' to be any trouble.

MATE. Yes, sir.

330 **KEENEY.** And trouble they's goin' to be. I feel it in my bones. (*Takes a revolver from the pocket of his coat and examines it.*) Got your'n?

MATE. Yes, sir.

KEENEY. Not that we'll have to use 'em—not if I know their breed of dog—jest to frighten' em up a bit. (*Grimly.*) I ain't never been forced to use one yit; and trouble I've had by land and
340 by sea 's long as I kin remember, and will have till my dyin' day, I reckon.

MATE (*Hesitatingly*). Then you ain't goin'—to turn back?

KEENEY. Turn back! Mr. Slocum, did you ever hear o' me pointin' s'uth for home with only a measly four hundred barrel of ile in the hold?

MATE (*Hastily*). No, sir—but the grub's gittin' low.

350 **KEENEY.** They's enough to last a long time yit, if they're careful with it; and they's plenty o' water.

MATE. They say it's not fit to eat—what's left; and the two years they signed on fur is up to-day. They might make trouble for you in the courts when we git home.

KEENEY. To hell with' em! Let them make what law trouble they kin. I don't
360 give a damn' bout the money. I've got to git the ile! (*Glancing sharply at the MATE.*) You ain't turnin' no damned sea lawyer, be you, Mr. Slocum? **M**

MATE (*Flushing*). Not by a hell of a sight, sir.

KEENEY. What do the fools want to go home fur now? Their share o' the four

---

SCAFFOLDING FOR ELL STUDENTS

Vocabulary: Idioms Explain that O'Neill uses many idioms and figurative phrases as part of the characters' dialect. These expressions make the dialogue vivid and realistic, but they can be hard for English learners to understand. Work with students to infer meanings for expressions like these using context clues:

- Line 331: "I feel it in my bones" *("I know it")*
- Lines 336–337: "not if I know their breed of dog" *("since I know what they are like")*
- Lines 368–369: "wouldn't keep 'em in chewin' terbacco" *("is not much money")*

hundred barrel wouldn't keep 'em in chewin' terbacco.

370 **MATE** (*Slowly*). They wants to git back to their folks an' things, I s'pose.

KEENEY (*Looking at him searchingly*). 'N you want to turn back, too. (*The MATE looks down confusedly before his sharp gaze.*) Don't lie, Mr. Slocum. It's writ down plain in your eyes. (*With grim sarcasm.*) I hope, Mr. Slocum, you ain't agoin' to jine the men agin me.

MATE (*Indignantly*). That ain't fair, sir, 380 to say sich things.

KEENEY (*With satisfaction*). I warn't much afeard o' that, Tom. You been with me nigh on ten year and I've learned ye whalin'. No man kin say I ain't a good master, if I be a hard one.

MATE. I warn't thinkin' of myself, sir—'bout turnin' home, I mean. (*Desperately.*) But Mrs. Keeney, sir— seems like she ain't jest satisfied up 390 here, ailin' like—what with the cold an' bad luck an' the ice an' all.

KEENEY (*His face clouding—rebukingly but not severely*). That's my business, Mr. Slocum. I'll thank you to steer a clear course o' that. (*A pause.*) The ice'll break up soon to no'th'ard. I could see it startin' to-day. And when it goes and we git some sun Annie'll perk up. (*Another pause—then he bursts forth:*) It ain't the 400 damned money what's keepin' me up in the Northern seas, Tom. But I can't go back to Homeport with a measly four hundred barrel of ile. I'd die fust. I ain't never come back home in all my days without a full ship. Ain't that truth?

MATE. Yes, sir; but this voyage you been icebound, an'—

KEENEY (*Scornfully*). And d'you s'pose any of 'em would believe that—any o' 410 them skippers I've beaten voyage after voyage? Can't you hear 'em laughin' and

sneerin'—Tibbots 'n' Harris' n' Simms and the rest—and all o' Homeport makin' fun o' me? "Dave Keeney what boasts he's the best whalin' skipper out o' Homeport comin' back with a measly four hundred barrel of ile?" (*The thought of this drives him into a frenzy, and he smashes his fist down on* 420 *the marble top of the sideboard.*) Hell! I got to git the ile, I tell you. How could I figger on this ice? It's never been so bad before in the thirty year I been acomin' here. And now it's breakin' up. In a couple o' days it'll be all gone. And they's whale here, plenty of 'em. I know they is and I ain't never gone wrong yit. I got to git the ile! I got to git it in spite of all hell, and by God, I 430 ain't agoin' home till I do git it! (*There is the sound of subdued sobbing from the door in rear. The two men stand silent for a moment, listening. Then KEENEY goes over to the door and looks in. He hesitates for a moment as if he were going to enter—then closes the door softly. JOE, the harpooner, an enormous six-footer with a battered, ugly face, enters from right and stands waiting for the captain* 440 *to notice him.*)

KEENEY (*Turning and seeing him*). Don't be standin' there like a gawk, Harpooner. Speak up!

JOE (*Confusedly*). We want—the men, sir—they wants to send a depitation aft to have a word with you.

KEENEY (*Furiously*). Tell 'em to go to— (*Checks himself and continues grimly.*) Tell 'em to come. I'll see 'em.

450 **JOE.** Aye, aye, sir. (*He goes out.*)

KEENEY (*With a grim smile*). Here it comes, the trouble you spoke of, Mr. Slocum, and we'll make short shift of it. It's better to crush such things at the start than let them make headway.

Ile **53**

Analyze Drama Elements: Conflict (LINES 370–391; 420–430)

COMMON CORE RL 3

Explain that although the Mate is a minor character, O'Neill's dialogue indicates that he experiences some internal conflict in his thoughts about the voyage.

 CITE TEXT EVIDENCE Direct students to reread lines 370–391 and identify evidence for an internal conflict within the Mate. (*The Mate vigorously objects when Keeney suggests he might join the other men [lines 379–380]. However, in his next line of dialogue, the Mate expresses his sympathy for Mrs. Keeney as an argument for turning toward home. He is torn between his loyalty to the captain and his recognition of the suffering that the captain's actions have caused Mrs. Keeney.*)

Point out that O'Neill uses the ice immobilizing the ship as a part of an external conflict for Captain Keeney.

 ASK STUDENTS to reread lines 420–430 and identify the type of conflict that Keeney describes. (*Keeney indicates an external conflict with nature. He seems to feel betrayed when he says, "How could I figger on this ice? It's never been so bad before in the thirty year I been acomin' here." As a sea captain, he is used to dealing with the elements of nature, but this time he fears he will be defeated by the ice.*)

APPLYING ACADEMIC VOCABULARY

appreciation	conform	persistence

As you discuss *Ile,* incorporate the Collection 1 academic vocabulary words *appreciation, conform,* and *persistence.* As you consider the symbolism of the "ile," ask students what motivates Captain Keeney's **persistence** in the voyage and what kind of **appreciation** he expects if he brings home a full ship of oil. In discussing the internal conflict shown by the Mate, ask students how he **conforms** to his expected role regardless of his conflicted feelings.

Analyze Drama Elements: Conflict (LINES 495–503)

Note that Captain Keeney's rule on the ship may fall outside of the boundaries established by society.

P CITE TEXT EVIDENCE Ask students to review lines 495–503 and identify details that indicate an external conflict between Captain Keeney and society. *(Keeney asserts, "We're at sea now and I'm the law on this ship." He doesn't recognize the power of the "law courts" even though his crew and even his Mate recognize that his actions are probably illegal.)*

Analyze Drama Elements: Character (LINES 507–509)

Point out that Mrs. Keeney appears to observe the confrontation between the crew and the captain but does not take part in it.

Q ASK STUDENTS to review what they know about Mrs. Keeney and explain how they would expect her to react to the confrontation. *(Because she has been portrayed as weak and unstable, she will probably be shocked and disturbed by the confrontation.)*

Analyze Drama Elements: Conflict (510–521)

Explain that this physical conflict is a natural result of the conflicts between Captain Keeney and the crew that have been developed in earlier dialogue.

R CITE TEXT EVIDENCE Have students list the crew's grievances that have led up to this physical conflict. *(The two-year contract they signed for the voyage has now expired, the captain will not turn for home, and the food they are getting is "rotten.")*

MATE (*Worriedly*). Shall I wake up the First and Fourth, sir? We might need their help.

KEENEY. No, let them sleep. I'm well able to handle this alone, Mr. Slocum. (*There is the shuffling of footsteps from outside and five of the crew crowd into the cabin, led by* JOE. *All are dressed alike—sweaters, seaboots, etc. They glance uneasily at the* CAPTAIN, *twirling their fur caps in their hands.*)

KEENEY (*After a pause*). Well? Who's to speak fur ye?

JOE (*Stepping forward with an air of bravado*). I be.

KEENEY (*Eyeing him up and down coldly*). So you be. Then speak your say and be quick about it.

JOE (*Trying not to wilt before the* CAPTAIN'S *glance and avoiding his eyes*). The time we signed up for is done to-day.

KEENEY (*Icily*). You're tellin' me nothin' I don't know.

JOE. You ain't pintin' fur home yit, far's we kin see.

KEENEY. No, and I ain't agoin' to till this ship is full of ile.

JOE. You can't go no further no'the with the ice afore ye.

KEENEY. The ice is breaking up.

JOE (*After a slight pause during which the others mumble angrily to one another*). The grub we're gittin' now is rotten.

KEENEY. It's good enough fur ye. Better men than ye are have eaten worse. (*There is a chorus of angry exclamations from the crowd.*)

JOE (*Encouraged by this support*). We ain't agoin' to work no more less you puts back for home.

KEENEY (*Fiercely*). You ain't, ain't you?

JOE. No; and the law courts'll say we was right.

KEENEY. To hell with your law courts! We're at sea now and I'm the law on this ship. (*Edging up toward the harpooner.*) And every mother's son of you what don't obey orders goes in irons. (*There are more angry exclamations from the crew.* MRS. KEENEY *appears in the doorway in rear and looks on with startled eyes. None of the men notice her.*)

JOE (*With bravado*). Then we're agoin' to mutiny and take the old hooker home ourselves. Ain't we, boys? (*As he turns his head to look at the others,* KEENEY's *fist shoots out to the side of his jaw.* JOE *goes down in a heap and lies there.* MRS. KEENEY *gives a shriek and hides her face in her hands. The men pull out their sheath knives and start a rush, but stop when they find themselves confronted by the revolvers of* KEENEY *and the* MATE.)

KEENEY (*His eyes and voice snapping*). Hold still! (*The men stand huddled together in a sullen silence.* KEENEY's *voice is full of mockery.*) You've found out it ain't safe to mutiny on this ship, ain't you? And now git for'ard where ye belong, and—(*He gives* JOE's *body a contemptuous kick.*) Drag him with you. And remember the first man of ye I see shirkin' I'll shoot dead as sure as there's a sea under us, and you can tell the rest the same. Git for'ard now! Quick! (*The men leave in cowed silence, carrying* JOE *with them.* KEENEY *turns to the* MATE *with a short laugh and puts his revolver back in his pocket.*) Best get up on deck, Mr. Slocum, and see to it they don't try none of their skulkin' tricks. We'll have to keep an eye peeled from now on. I know' em.

WHEN STUDENTS STRUGGLE...

To help students understand the complex relationship and the conflict between Captain Keeney and his wife, have them work in pairs to fill out a two-column chart like the one shown on page 55 to contrast the reasons that Captain Keeney did not want Mrs. Keeney to come on the voyage with the reasons that Mrs. Keeney wanted to. Encourage them to cite text evidence to explain their thoughts. When the charts are complete, ask volunteers to describe how this information affects their view of each character and of the Keeneys' relationship.

MATE. Yes, sir. (*He goes out, right.* KEENEY *hears his wife's hysterical weeping and turns around in surprise— then walks slowly to her side.*)

KEENEY (*Putting an arm around her shoulder—with gruff tenderness*). There, there, Annie. Don't be afeard. It's all past and gone.

550 **MRS. KEENEY** (*Shrinking away from him*). Oh, I can't bear it! I can't bear it any longer!

KEENEY (*Gently*). Can't bear what, Annie?

MRS. KEENEY (*Hysterically*). All this horrible brutality, and these brutes of men, and this terrible ship, and this prison cell of a room, and the ice all around, and the silence. (*After this*
560 *outburst she calms down and wipes her eyes with her handkerchief.*)

KEENEY (*After a pause during which he looks down at her with a puzzled frown*). Remember, I warn't hankerin' to have you come on this voyage, Annie.

MRS. KEENEY. I wanted to be with you, David, don't you see? I didn't want to wait back there in the house all alone as I've been doing these last six years
570 since we were married—waiting, and watching, and fearing—with nothing to keep my mind occupied—not able to go back teaching school on account of being Dave Keeney's wife. I used to dream of sailing on the great, wide, glorious ocean. I wanted to be by your side in the danger and vigorous life of it all. I wanted to see you the hero they make you out to be in Homeport. And
580 instead—(*Her voice grows tremulous.*) All I find is ice and cold—and brutality! (*Her voice breaks.*)

KEENEY. I warned you what it'd be, Annie. "Whalin' ain't no ladies' tea party," I says to you, and "you better

stay to home where you've got all your woman's comforts." (*Shaking his head.*) But you was so set on it.

MRS. KEENEY (*Wearily*). Oh, I know it
590 isn't your fault, David. You see, I didn't believe you. I guess I was dreaming about the old Vikings in the story books and I thought you were one of them.

KEENEY (*Protestingly*). I done my best to make it as cozy and comfortable as could be. (MRS. KEENEY *looks around her in wild scorn.*) I even sent to the city for that organ for ye, thinkin' it might be soothin' to ye to be playin' it times
600 when they was calms and things was dull like.

MRS. KEENEY (*Wearily*). Yes, you were very kind, David. I know that. (*She goes to left and lifts the curtains from the porthole and looks out—then suddenly bursts forth:*) I won't stand it—I can't stand it—pent up by these walls like a prisoner. (*She runs over to him and throws her arms around him, weeping.*
610 *He puts his arm protectingly over her shoulders.*) Take me away from here, David! If I don't get away from here, out of this terrible ship, I'll go mad! Take me home, David! I can't think any more. I feel as if the cold and the silence were crushing down on my brain. I'm afraid. Take me home!

KEENEY (*Holds her at arm's length and looks at her face anxiously*). Best go to
620 bed, Annie. You ain't yourself. You got fever. Your eyes look so strange like. I ain't never seen you look this way before.

MRS. KEENEY (*Laughing hysterically*). It's the ice and the cold and the silence—they'd make any one look strange.

KEENEY (*Soothingly*). In a month or two, with good luck, three at the most,
630 I'll have her filled with ile and then

Reasons Captain Keeney did not want Mrs. Keeney to come on the voyage	Reasons Mrs. Keeney wanted to come on the voyage
He understood that whaling voyages were not "cozy and comfortable" (line 595).	She didn't want to "wait back there in the house all alone" (line 568).
He knew that there were times on whaling voyages that were "dull like" (line 601).	She dreamed of "sailing on the great, wide, glorious ocean" (lines 575–576).
	She wanted to see her husband as "the hero" (line 578).

Analyze Drama Elements: Conflict (LINES 566–582)   COMMON CORE RL 3

Remind students that one kind of external conflict is a conflict between a character and society. A character who does not conform to society's expectations often pays a price.

S CITE TEXT EVIDENCE Ask students to review Mrs. Keeney's reasons for wanting to come on the voyage. What evidence do her words provide of a conflict between herself and the 19th-century society in which she lives? (*Mrs. Keeney's conflict with society is that she has been forced to choose between marriage and meaningful work, and her lack of choices has made her miserable. She used to be a teacher, but now that she is married, she cannot "go back teaching school on account of being Dave Keeney's wife." She finds life as a homemaker stressful and boring, "with nothing to keep [her] mind occupied." Had she been able to keep working as a teacher, she never would have come on this disastrous voyage.*)

Analyze Point of View: Irony (LINES 594–597)   COMMON CORE RL 6

Explain that **verbal irony** is a contrast between what is stated and what is true.

T ASK STUDENTS to explain the verbal irony in these lines and how Mrs. Keeney helps the audience realize the irony. (*Captain Keeney says he has tried to make the ship "cozy and comfortable," while the audience realizes that the conditions are harsh and far from comfortable. Mrs. Keeney helps the audience see the irony through O'Neill's stage direction that she "looks around her in wild scorn."*)

Analyze Drama Elements: COMMON CORE RL 3
Conflict (LINES 633–640)

In these lines, Mrs. Keeney suggests that the captain is in conflict with the basic rules and expectations of society.

 ASK STUDENTS to reread lines 633–640 to determine how Mrs. Keeney feels that Captain Keeney's actions would be judged by the rest of society. *(She describes his actions as "cruel" and "brutal" and suggests that anyone else would turn back because there is "no excuse" for extending the voyage. She believes that society would judge his actions as heartless.)*

Analyze Drama Elements: COMMON CORE RL 3
Symbol (LINES 654–664)

Explain that a writer may use a symbol that is not clearly understood by a character. In these lines, the captain struggles to define what a full ship of oil means to him.

V **CITE TEXT EVIDENCE** Direct students to reread lines 654–664 and identify stage directions and dialogue that suggest that the deeper meaning of a "full ship" is not clear to Captain Keeney himself. *(The stage directions say Keeney is "struggling to express his meaning." At the end of his speech, he acknowledges that his words are not expressing a clear meaning, because he stops abruptly and asks, "Don't you see my meanin', Annie?")*

---

we'll give her everything she'll stand and pint for home.

U

MRS. KEENEY. But we can't wait for that—I can't wait. I want to get home. And the men won't wait. They want to get home. It's cruel, it's brutal for you to keep them. You must sail back. You've got no excuse. There's clear water to the south now. If you've a heart at all you've
640 got to turn back.

KEENEY (*Harshly*). I can't, Annie.

MRS. KEENEY. Why can't you?

KEENEY. A woman couldn't rightly understand my reason.

MRS. KEENEY (*Wildly*). Because it's a stupid, stubborn reason. Oh, I heard you talking with the second mate. You're afraid the other captains will sneer at you because you didn't come
650 back with a full ship. You want to live up to your silly reputation even if you do have to beat and starve men and drive me mad to do it.

V

KEENEY (*His jaw set stubbornly*). It ain't that, Annie. Them skippers would never dare sneer to my face. It ain't so much what any one'd say—but—(*He hesitates, struggling to express his meaning.*) You see—I've always done it—since my first
660 voyage as skipper. I always come back—with a full ship—and—it don't seem right not to—somehow. I been always first whalin' skipper out o' Homeport, and—Don't you see my meanin', Annie? (*He glances at her. She is not looking at him but staring dully in front of her, not hearing a word he is saying.*) Annie! (*She comes to herself with a start.*) Best turn in, Annie, there's a good woman. You
670 ain't well.

MRS. KEENEY (*Resisting his attempts to guide her to the door in rear*). David! Won't you please turn back?

KEENEY (*Gently*). I can't, Annie—not yet awhile. You don't see my meanin'. I got to git the ile.

MRS. KEENEY. It'd be different if you needed the money, but you don't. You've got more than plenty.

680 **KEENEY** (*Impatiently*). It ain't the money I'm thinkin' of. D'you think I'm as mean as that?

MRS. KEENEY (*Dully*). No—I don't know—I can't understand—(*Intensely*). Oh, I want to be home in the old house once more and see my own kitchen again, and hear a woman's voice talking to me and be able to talk to her. Two years! It seems so long ago—as if I'd
690 been dead and could never go back.

KEENEY (*Worried by her strange tone and the far-away look in her eyes*). Best go to bed, Annie. You ain't well.

MRS. KEENEY (*Not appearing to hear him*). I used to be lonely when you were away. I used to think Homeport was a stupid, monotonous place. Then I used to go down on the beach, especially when it was windy and the breakers
700 were rolling in, and I'd dream of the fine free life you must be leading. (*She gives a laugh which is half a sob.*) I used to love the sea then. (*She pauses; then continues with slow intensity:*) But now—I don't ever want to see the sea again.

KEENEY (*Thinking to humor her*). 'Tis no fit place for a woman, that's sure. I was a fool to bring ye.

710 **MRS. KEENEY** (*After a pause—passing her hand over her eyes with a gesture of pathetic weariness*). How long would it take us to reach home—if we started now?

KEENEY (*Frowning*). 'Bout two months, I reckon, Annie, with fair luck.

SCAFFOLDING FOR ELL STUDENTS

Language: Verb Usage Focus students' attention on the verbs used by Captain and Mrs. Keeney. The captain's dialect often includes incorrect verb forms. Display text from their conversation on a whiteboard. Have students highlight correct verb forms in green and incorrect ones in pink. Discuss how to revise for standard usage.

> and I thought you were one of them.
>
> **KEENEY** (*Protestingly*). I done my best
>
> to make it as cozy and comfortable as

W MRS. KEENEY (*Counts on her fingers—then murmurs with a rapt smile*). That would be August, the latter
720 part of August, wouldn't it? It was on the twenty-fifth of August we were married, David, wasn't it?

KEENEY (*Trying to conceal the fact that her memories have moved him—gruffly*). Don't you remember?

MRS. KEENEY (*Vaguely—again passes her hand over her eyes.*) My memory is leaving me—up here in the ice. It was so long ago. (*A pause—then she smiles*
730 *dreamily.*) It's June now. The lilacs will be all in bloom in the front yard—and the climbing roses on the trellis to the side of the house—they're budding. (*She suddenly covers her face with her hands and commences to sob.*)

KEENEY (*Disturbed*). Go in and rest, Annie. You're all wore out cryin' over what can't be helped.

X MRS. KEENEY (*Suddenly throwing her*
740 *arms around his neck and clinging to him*). You love me, don't you, David?

KEENEY (*In amazed embarrassment at this outburst*). Love you? Why d'you ask me such a question, Annie?

MRS. KEENEY (*Shaking him—fiercely*). But you do, don't you, David? Tell me!

KEENEY. I'm your husband, Annie, and you're my wife. Could there be aught but love between us after all these
750 years?

MRS. KEENEY (*Shaking him again—still more fiercely*). Then you do love me. Say it!

KEENEY (*Simply*). I do, Annie.

MRS. KEENEY (*Gives a sigh of relief—her hands drop to her sides. Keeney regards her anxiously. She passes her hand across her eyes and murmurs half to herself:*) I sometimes think if we could only have
760 had a child. (KEENEY *turns away from her, deeply moved. She grabs his arm and turns him around to face her—intensely.*) And I've always been a good wife to you, haven't I, David?

KEENEY (*His voice betraying his emotion*). No man has ever had a better, Annie.

Image Credits: ©Frank Krahmer/Fuse/Getty Images

lle **57**

TO CHALLENGE STUDENTS . . .

Examine Arguments Have students analyze the conversation between Captain and Mrs. Keeney in lines 546–794. What strategies or types of argument does each character use to try to persuade the other to accept his or her point of view? For example, in lines 611–617, Mrs. Keeney appeals to her husband's pity by telling him that the voyage is driving her mad.

ASK STUDENTS to individually chart the various appeals and arguments the characters make. Then have them meet with partners or in small groups to share their findings and discuss what this conversation reveals about the Keeneys' relationship. Can they imagine a way for the conflict to be resolved?

TEACH

CLOSE READ

Analyze Drama Elements: **RL 3**
Symbol (LINES 717–735)

Note that Mrs. Keeney increasingly connects the ice with her lack of mental stability.

W **CITE TEXT EVIDENCE** Ask students to review the dialogue in lines 717–735. What does Mrs. Keeney say that makes a connection between being stuck in the ice and her own mental state? (*She says, "My memory is leaving me—up here in the ice. It was so long ago." She sees the ice as affecting her memory. It also makes time seem to go very slowly.*)

Analyze Drama Elements: **RL 3**
Character (LINES 739–766)

Point out that a close reading of the dialogue between two characters can reveal many details about their relationship. A single remark can instantly change the audience's perception of the characters' relationship.

X **ASK STUDENTS** to review the dialogue in lines 739–766, in which Mrs. Keeney makes a desperate attempt to connect with her husband emotionally. What new fact does Mrs. Keeney reveal, and how does it change the audience's understanding of the Keeneys' relationship? (*Mrs. Keeney says, "I sometimes think if we could only have had a child." The captain is "deeply moved" by this statement and turns away from her to hide his emotion. The audience now realizes that the Keeneys would have liked to start a family, and that their inability to do so remains very painful for both of them. Both the characters and the audience wonder if the marriage might have turned out differently if Mrs. Keeney had had a child to occupy her time at home and had never come on the voyage. A child might also have softened some of Captain Keeney's harsher tendencies and made him less focused on filling his ship with whale oil.*)

lle **57**

Analyze Drama Elements: Conflict (LINES 800–824)

 COMMON CORE RL 3

As the end of the play draws near, several of Captain Keeney's conflicts are resolved.

Y **ASK STUDENTS** what conflicts are resolved in this passage. What impact do the latest events have on the conflict between Captain Keeney and his wife? (*When the ice breaks up, Captain Keeney is free to pursue whales in the north. His external conflict with nature is resolved. Also, the Mate reports that the sailors are "meek as lambs" since the confrontation between them and the captain, so Keeney's conflict with his crew appears to be over. However, his decision to continue the whale hunt rather than turning homeward means that his conflict with his wife will continue.*)

MRS. KEENEY. And I've never asked for much from you, have I, David? Have I?

KEENEY. You know you could have all I got the power to give ye, Annie.

MRS. KEENEY (*Wildly*). Then do this this once for my sake, for God's sake—take me home! It's killing me, this life—the brutality and cold and horror of it. I'm going mad. I can feel the threat in the air. I can hear the silence threatening me—day after gray day and every day the same. I can't bear it. (*Sobbing*). I'll go mad, I know I will. Take me home, David, if you love me as you say. I'm afraid. For the love of God, take me home! (*She throws her arms around him, weeping against his shoulder. His face betrays the tremendous struggle going on within him. He holds her out at arm's length, his expression softening. For a moment his shoulders sag, he becomes old, his iron spirit weakens as he looks at her tear-stained face.*)

KEENEY (*Dragging out the words with an effort*). I'll do it, Annie—for your sake—if you say it's needful for ye.

MRS. KEENEY (*With wild joy—kissing him*). God bless you for that, David! (*He turns away from her silently and walks toward the companionway. Just at that moment there is a clatter of footsteps on the stairs and the SECOND MATE enters the cabin.*)

 MATE (*Excitedly*). The ice is breakin' up to no'the'ard, sir. There's a clear passage through the floe, and clear water beyond, the lookout says. (KEENEY *straightens himself like a man coming out of a trance.* MRS. KEENEY *looks at the* MATE *with terrified eyes.*)

KEENEY (*Dazedly—trying to collect his thoughts*). A clear passage? To no'the'ard?

MATE. Yes, sir.

KEENEY (*His voice suddenly grim with determination*). Then get her ready and we'll drive her through.

MATE. Aye, aye, sir.

MRS. KEENEY (*Appealingly*). David!

KEENEY (*Not heeding her*). Will the men turn to willin' or must we drag 'em out?

MATE. They'll turn to willin' enough. You put the fear o' God into 'em, sir. They're meek as lambs.

KEENEY. Then drive 'em—both watches. (*With grim determination.*) They's whale t'other side o' this floe and we're going to git 'em.

MATE. Aye, aye, sir. (*He goes out hurriedly. A moment later there is the sound of scuffling feet from the deck outside and the* MATE's *voice shouting orders.*)

KEENEY (*Speaking aloud to himself—derisively*). And I was agoin' home like a yaller dog!

MRS. KEENEY (*Imploringly*). David!

KEENEY (*Sternly*). Woman, you ain't adoin' right when you meddle in men's business and weaken' em. You can't know my feelin's. I got to prove a man to be a good husband for ye to take pride in. I got to git the ile, I tell ye.

MRS. KEENEY (*Supplicatingly*). David! Aren't you going home?

KEENEY (*Ignoring this question—commandingly*). You ain't well. Go and lay down a mite. (*He starts for the door.*) I got to git on deck. (*He goes out. She cries after him in anguish:*) David! (*A pause. She passes her hand across her eyes—then commences to laugh hysterically and goes to the organ. She sits down and starts to play wildly an old hymn.* KEENEY *reenters from the doorway to the deck and stands looking at*

WHEN STUDENTS STRUGGLE . . .

Have pairs brainstorm possible symbolic meanings for the directions north and south from Captain Keeney's perspective and from Mrs. Keeney's.

Symbol	Meaning for Captain Keeney	Meaning for Mrs. Keeney
North ("no'the'ard")	whales, a full ship of "ile," success, courage	more ice, loneliness, her husband's disregard for her, possible madness
South ("s'uth")	defeat, cowardice, going against his principles	open water, home, comfort, sanity

her angrily. He comes over and grabs her roughly by the shoulder.)

KEENEY. Woman, what foolish mockin' is this? *(She laughs wildly and he starts back from her in alarm.)* Annie! What is it? *(She doesn't answer him. KEENEY's voice trembles.)* Don't you know me, 860 Annie? *(He puts both hands on her shoulders and turns her around so that he can look into her eyes. She stares up at him with a stupid expression, a vague smile on her lips. He stumbles away from her, and she commences softly to play the organ again.)*

KEENEY *(Swallowing hard—in a hoarse whisper, as if he had difficulty in speaking).* You said—you was a-goin' 870 mad—God! *(A long wail is heard from the deck above.)* Ah bl-o-o-o-ow! *(A moment later the MATE's face appears through the skylight. He cannot see MRS. KEENEY.)*

MATE *(In great excitement).* Whales, sir—a whole school of 'em—off the star'b'd quarter 'bout five mile away—big ones!

KEENEY *(Galvanized into action).* Are 880 you lowerin' the boats?

MATE. Yes, sir.

KEENEY *(With grim decision).* I'm a-comin' with ye.

MATE. Aye, aye, sir. *(Jubilantly.)* You'll git the ile now right enough, sir. *(His head is withdrawn and he can be heard shouting orders.)*

890 **KEENEY** *(Turning to his wife).* Annie! Did you hear him? I'll git the ile. *(She doesn't answer or seem to know he is there. He gives a hard laugh, which is almost a groan.)* I know you're foolin' me. Annie. You ain't out of your mind—*(Anxiously.)* be you? I'll git the ile now right enough—jest a little while longer, Annie—then we'll turn hom'ard. I can't turn back now, you see that, don't ye? I've got to git the ile. *(In sudden terror.)* Answer me! You ain't 900 mad, be you? *(She keeps on playing the organ, but makes no reply. The MATE's face appears again through the skylight.)*

MATE. All ready, sir. *(KEENEY turns his back on his wife and strides to the doorway, where he stands for a moment and looks back at her in anguish, fighting to control his feelings.)*

MATE. Comin', sir?

KEENEY *(His face suddenly grown hard 910 with determination).* Aye. *(He turns abruptly and goes out. MRS. KEENEY does not appear to notice his departure. Her whole attention seems centered in the organ. She sits with half-closed eyes, her body swaying a little from side to side to the rhythm of the hymn. Her fingers move faster and faster and she is playing wildly and discordantly as*

(The Curtain Falls)

COLLABORATIVE DISCUSSION   What are Captain Keeney's predominant character traits? With a partner, discuss whether these qualities are necessary for a ship's captain to have. Cite specific textual evidence to support your ideas.

Ile   **59**

CLOSE READ

Analyze Drama Elements: Character (LINES 855–883)

COMMON CORE RL 3

Point out that the events at the end of the play crystallize Captain Keeney's character traits.

 CITE TEXT EVIDENCE Have students identify dialogue and stage directions in lines 855–883 that reveal Keeney's character traits. *(Lines 859–860 and 867–870 indicate his horror that Mrs. Keeney is apparently going mad because of the voyage and his actions. He loves and feels responsible for her, yet he sticks to his quest for a full ship of oil. When he says with "grim decision," "I'm a-comin' with ye," it's clear that his determination to succeed is central to his character.)*

Determine Themes (LINES 888–919)
COMMON CORE RL 2

Explain that a well-structured play often ends with a dramatic scene that reinforces key **themes**—ideas about people or life that the playwright wants to convey through the events of the drama. The image of Mrs. Keeney playing the organ wildly and discordantly while the captain and crew prepare to head north leaves a powerful impression on the audience while also clarifying important ideas that have been developed throughout the play.

 ASK STUDENTS to reread lines 909–919 and suggest themes illustrated by this concluding scene. *(Possible answers: The quest for personal pride and success can take a toll on loved ones. People don't appreciate what's most important to them until it is gone. Love for another person cannot alter one's most basic personal qualities.)*

TO CHALLENGE STUDENTS . . .

Analyze Structure Ask students to consider the fact that the voyage of the *Atlantic Queen* has been going on for two years when the play begins, and it continues after the curtain falls. Ask students, in small groups, to discuss these questions and then share their ideas with the class:

• Why did O'Neill choose to begin and end the play exactly where he did? How do his choices create a satisfying drama that feels complete in one act?

• Suppose you wanted to expand the play into three acts. What additional events or scenes would you include to create dramatic tension, explore the characters more fully, and end with a logical resolution?

COLLABORATIVE DISCUSSION Have student pairs discuss the specific actions and words that illustrate Captain Keeney's character traits. Suggest that they make a list of qualities important for a ship's captain or any other leader in a dangerous or stressful environment and compare this list with the captain's traits. Ask them to decide if they would like to serve in a position under Captain Keeney or someone like him and to explain their answer. Accept all reasonable responses.

ASK STUDENTS to share any questions they generated in the course of reading and discussing the selection.

CLOSE READ

Analyze Drama Elements: Conflict RL 3

Review the terms for different types of conflict. Have students provide more examples of each—another one from *Ile* or one they might encounter in real life. *(Possible examples: Character vs. Self: Mate struggles with loyalty to Captain Keeney; student must decide whether to help out a friend or study for an exam. Character vs. Character: The sailors want to return now that their contract is up, Keeney refuses; two students vie for a position in student government. Character vs. Nature: The open water to the south creates a conflict for Captain Keeney because he now has "no excuse" not to return. A student battles extreme heat to get in shape for a sport. Character vs. Society: Social norms kept Mrs. Keeney from teaching after she was married, leaving her with no occupation. A student opposes a particular use of class money while others support it.)*

Analyze Drama Elements: Symbol RL 3

Discuss the idea that a person, place, or object can represent something beyond itself. Ask students to identify some everday examples of objects that hold symbolic meanings. *(Possible examples: American flag, Statue of Liberty, a medal or trophy awarded for athletic or other types of achievement)* Have students suggest other things in *Ile* that could symbolize the domestic life Annie has left behind. *(The curtains on the portholes [lines 9–10]; Annie's sewing basket [line 18]; her kitchen with the sound of a woman's voice [lines 686–687])*

Analyze Drama Elements: Conflict RL 3

The action of any play is driven by **conflict,** or a struggle between opposing forces. The plot unfolds as the play's characters try to solve problems that stem from the conflict. **Internal conflict** occurs within a character's own mind. **External conflict** exists between a character and an outside force. The following list provides details about the specific kinds of conflict you may find in the play *Ile*.

- **Character Versus Self** A character with an internal conflict struggles to reconcile opposing values, desires, needs, or emotions in order to act or make a decision. The character's words and actions reveal this conflict to the audience.
- **Character Versus Character** A conflict between two characters is external. Although a fight is the most obvious sign of external conflict, often there is more subtle tension between characters that is revealed through dialogue and the characters' actions and reactions. For example, Annie exerts pressure on her husband when she reminds him of their anniversary and asks him if he loves her.
- **Character Versus Nature** Another type of external conflict occurs when a character is pitted against nature. The sailors are in conflict with the ice that traps them. This conflict with nature leads to other issues, including the confrontation between the crew and the captain.
- **Character Versus Society** Sometimes what a character wants puts him or her in direct opposition to what society considers acceptable. This kind of external conflict may result in the character's being ostracized by his or her community.

Analyze Drama Elements: Symbol RL 3

A **symbol** is a person, place, or object that represents something beyond itself. Some commonplace symbols are easy to interpret. For example, the Garden of Eden symbolizes innocence. Other symbols are invented by authors to have meaning within the context of a specific literary work. To understand them, readers must analyze how they relate to characters, plot, and theme.

Eugene O'Neill incorporates several symbols into his play. One is the organ Captain Keeney bought for his wife, "thinkin' it might be soothin' to ye to be playin' it." The organ might symbolize the domestic life in which Annie feels comfortable, in contrast to the captain's harsher world aboard the ship. Annie's wild playing at the end shows that these worlds are incompatible.

Strategies for Annotation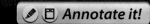

Analyze Drama Elements: Conflict RL 3

Review with students the four types of internal and external conflict. Then have them use their eBook annotation tools to identify specific stage directions and lines of dialogue that clearly indicate each type of conflict:

- Highlight in yellow evidence of characters' internal conflicts.
- Highlight in green evidence of external conflicts between characters.
- Highlight in blue evidence of character-versus-nature conflicts.
- Highlight in pink evidence of character-versus-society conflicts.

> **JOE** (*With bravado*). Then we're agoin' to mutiny and take the old hooker home ourselves. Ain't we, boys? (*As he turns his head to look at the others,* KEENEY's *fist shoots out to the side of his jaw.* JOE *goes down in a heap and lies there.* MRS.

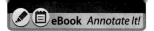

Analyzing the Text

COMMON CORE RL 1, RL 3, W 4, SL 1a

Cite Text Evidence Support your responses with evidence from the selection.

1. **Analyze** What information does O'Neill reveal in the exchange between the Steward and Ben? How does this first scene set the **mood,** or atmosphere, of the play?

2. **Infer** Review the stage directions that describe the confrontation between the crew members and Captain Keeney (lines 461–537). What is the men's attitude toward the captain? What insight into the captain's character do the stage directions provide?

3. **Interpret** When Mrs. Keeney questions why Captain Keeney won't turn back, he replies, "It ain't so much what any one'd say—but. . . .You see—I've always done it— since my first voyage as a skipper. I always come back—with a full ship—and it don't seem right not to—somehow." What does the full ship of oil symbolize for him?

4. **Analyze** Mrs. Keeney convinces the captain to turn the ship around, but he abruptly changes his mind when he learns that the ice is breaking up. What internal conflict of the captain's is revealed in this section of the play?

5. **Analyze** Why is Mrs. Keeney on the ship? How does this information influence your opinion about the conflict between the captain and his wife?

6. **Analyze** Ice is an important symbol in the play. Does it have the same meaning for all of the characters, or does it symbolize different things? Explain your response.

PERFORMANCE TASK

Speaking Activity The captain and Mrs. Keeney have different perspectives on life. In a small group, examine the following lines of dialogue. Discuss how they reveal the conflict between the two characters' viewpoints. Together, write a summary of your discussion and present it to the class.

- "I used to dream of sailing on the great, wide, glorious ocean. I wanted to be by your side in the danger and vigorous life of it all. I wanted to see you the hero. . . ." [Mrs. Keeney]

- "I warned you what it'd be, Annie. 'Whalin' ain't no ladies' tea party,' I says to you." [Captain Keeney]

- "You see I didn't believe you. I guess I was dreaming about the old Vikings in the story books and I thought you were one of them." [Mrs. Keeney]

PRACTICE & APPLY

Analyzing the Text

COMMON CORE RL 1, RL 3

Possible answers:

1. *The dialogue informs the audience that the ship is in the Arctic and has been trapped in ice for nearly a year. The conflict of being trapped in the ice is causing the sailors to think of mutiny as they believe the captain is "mad." The Steward and Ben also reveal that Mrs. Keeney accompanied her husband and is now in danger of losing her senses. Their nervous behavior, anxious expressions, and dialogue set up an atmosphere of dread.*

2. *The stage directions describe the men as glancing "uneasily at the captain, twirling their fur caps in their hands." Joe avoids the captain's eyes. From these descriptions, readers can see that the men are intimidated by the captain and uncomfortable in his presence. The captain shows no fear, even though outnumbered. He glares "icily" at them, knocks Joe out with one blow, and holds his revolver on them. These details show that he is a hard man, willing to do what it takes to keep his ship in order.*

3. *The oil is a symbol of his professional pride, his inner strength, and the meaning in his life.*

4. *His internal conflict is choosing between doing what is best for his wife and protecting his own pride.*

5. *Mrs. Keeney wanted to come on the voyage; her husband did not want her to. He says, "Remember, I warn't hankerin' to have you come on this voyage, Annie." The fact that she insisted on coming makes us more sympathetic toward him because he knew that the reality would be too hard for her; she did not listen to him.*

6. *The ice presents an obstacle that all of the characters want to overcome. For the captain, the ice symbolizes a challenge that he must meet in order to prove his manhood. For Mrs. Keeney, the ice symbolizes the intractability and coldness that she has come to see in her husband's character. For the ship's crew, the ice symbolizes their powerlessness, not only in the face of nature but also in challenging the captain's wishes.*

Assign this performance task.

PERFORMANCE TASK

COMMON CORE W 4, SL 1a

Speaking Activity Encourage all members of each group to contribute their thoughts to the discussion. Consider directing students to go around the circle so that each person can comment on one or more of the bulleted lines of dialogue. Suggest that the group select one person to take notes on the discussion in preparation for creating the written summary. The group may select a person to deliver the summary using a blind draw or other random selection technique.

Language and Style: Dialect

 COMMON CORE L 1a, L 3

Point out that a particular pattern of speech or dialect can help show the personality of a character (such as a character who always speaks hurriedly in incomplete sentences) or suggest something about a character's background (such as a very formal and proper style of speech that may suggest some years of education or exposure to a high level of society). Ask students why O'Neill chose to have Mrs. Keeney speak in standard English. What details about her character make this an appropriate choice? *(Mrs. Keeney is a former school teacher who would have had formal education for her career. Therefore, it makes sense that she would speak standard English.)*

Answers:

Students' dialogues should show an understanding of the captain and Mrs. Keeney and their points of view. They should also mimic the distinct dialect of each character.

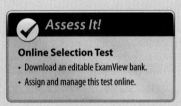

Assess It!

Online Selection Test
- Download an editable ExamView bank.
- Assign and manage this test online.

Language and Style: Dialect

 COMMON CORE L 1a, L 3

Dialect is a type of language spoken in a particular place by a certain group of people. Writers use dialect to evoke a specific setting or to develop characters. In *Ile*, the title itself, which means "oil," is part of the dialect spoken by the characters in the play. The dialect helps establish the setting as the late 1800s. It also creates realism. The language fits the rough-and-ready men who battle the elements of nature. In contrast, O'Neill chooses to have Mrs. Keeney speak in more standard English.

Read the following dialogue from the play:

> **Let the Old Man see ye up for'ard monkeyshinin' with the hands and ye'll get a hidin' ye'll not forget in a hurry.**

Then compare the effect of the dialect with this statement written in standard English:

> **Don't let the Captain see you wasting time with the crew members; you will get in trouble.**

This second version lacks the authenticity of the first. It could have been spoken anywhere by anyone, whereas the original version establishes a sense of place, time, and character.

This chart identifies some of the characteristics of the dialect found in this play:

Characteristic	Example
The dialect includes specialized vocabulary words and colloquial expressions. Readers can use context to help them define these words and phrases.	"It is nigh on two bells, Mr. Steward, and this truck not cleared yet."
The grammatical constructions do not follow the standard conventions of written and spoken English.	"She don't never speak to me no more . . ."
Some terms, such as "ile," and the lack of a final g on progressive verb forms reflect a regional pronunciation.	"She's cryin' now."

Practice and Apply With a partner, write four lines of dialogue between Captain Keeney and Mrs. Keeney. This dialogue should occur directly after she witnesses his confrontation with the crew members; it may include specific details about what upset her as well as the captain's explanation for his actions. Be sure to incorporate characteristics of the captain's dialect and Mrs. Keeney's pattern of speech, and have the dialogue reflect what you know about their characters and the plot. Share your dialogue with a partner.

INTERACTIVE WHITEBOARD LESSON
Analyze Theme

 COMMON CORE
RL 2

Learn the Skill ▸ Tips for Analyzing Theme

Tips for Analyzing Theme

Use these sentence frames to analyze the themes of a novel, story, or drama you've read recently.

The text _____ by _____ is about the topic _____. The title suggests _____.

The conflict revolves around _____.
It is resolved when _____.

The main characters display these traits: _____.
By the end of the text, they learn _____.

The following symbol appears in the story: _____.
This symbol represents _____.

Through these clues, the writer expresses the following themes: _____
_____.

TEACH

After students have read *Ile*, prepare them to discuss how multiple themes in the play develop and interact. If your class needs to review the concept of theme, start at Screen 4: Theme in Literature. (If students are likely to struggle with theme, start the lesson at Screen 1.)

Begin leading the students through the Whiteboard Lesson from Screen 5 to Screen 11. Have students take turns reading it aloud, and have them offer their ideas about the details on each screen, including the **title, setting, plot and conflict, characters,** and **important statements.** Click on each of these elements on the story screens to help students respond.

After working through Screen 11: Tips for Analyzing Theme, skip to Screen 16, where students have a chance to analyze symbolism as it relates to theme. (Symbolism is an important element in *Ile*.)

PRACTICE AND APPLY

Leave Screen 11: Tips for Analyzing Theme on display to guide students as they work in small groups to analyze themes in *Ile*.

- Remind students to refer to the annotations they made in their eBooks during their earlier study of the play.
- After fifteen minutes of discussion, bring the groups together to present their analyses of the play's theme.
- Finally, pose these questions to the class: How do the themes you have discovered interact with each other? *(One key theme, that pride and ambition can lead to disaster, creates a toxic mix with another theme, that love often blinds us to our beloved's true character.)*

Analyze Drama Elements: Symbol

 COMMON CORE
RL 3

RETEACH

Review the definition of *symbol:* a person, place, object, or activity that represents something beyond itself. Ask students what these examples might symbolize:

- Winter *(a time of reduced activity; a hardship to be survived; death)*
- Spring *(a time of growth; a new beginning)*
- A thunderstorm *(a chaotic time; the power of nature)*
- The U.S. Capitol building *(the power and strength of government; democracy)*

Remind students that symbols may mean different things to different characters. Have students use the Web Diagram from the *Interactive Graphic Organizers* to identify the various meanings of ice to the characters in *Ile*. They should label the center circle "Ice" and three outside circles as "Captain Keeney," "Mrs. Keeney," and "The crew." *(Sample answers: Captain Keeney—a threat to his pride; Mrs. Keeney—the hardness of her husband's character; The crew—their helplessness against Captain Keeney's power)*

 LEVEL UP TUTORIALS Assign the following *Level Up* tutorial: **Symbols and Allegories**

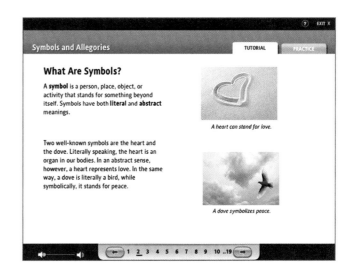

CLOSE READING APPLICATION

Students can apply the skill to another play or story they have read. Have them review their chosen text and identify symbols. Invite them to share their ideas with the class, explaining how each thing takes on symbolic meaning in the context of the story.

COMPARE MEDIA
Media Versions of *ILE*

Opera by Ezra Donner   Production Image

Why These Texts?

Students often encounter stories that have multiple interpretations in different media. This lesson looks at the way in which a drama is interpreted in an operatic adaptation and a stage production.

Key Learning Objective: The student will be able to compare and analyze how a drama is interpreted in different media.

Common Core Standards

RL 1 Cite strong and thorough textual evidence to support analysis.
RL 7 Analyze multiple interpretations of a drama.
W 4 Produce clear and coherent writing.
SL 1 Participate in collaborative discussions.
SL 4 Present information, findings, and evidence.
SL 6 Adapt speech to a variety of contexts and tasks.

Text Complexity Rubric

	Ile (opera version)	Ile (production image)
Quantitative Measures	Lexile: N/A	Lexile: N/A
Qualitative Measures	Levels of Meaning/Purpose — multiple levels of meaning (multiple themes)	Levels of Meaning/Purpose — N/A
	Structure — adapted from the original print source	Structure — adapted from the original print source
	Language Conventionality and Clarity — increased unfamiliar language	Language Conventionality and Clarity — N/A
	Knowledge Demands — single perspective with unfamiliar aspects	Knowledge Demands — single perspective with unfamiliar aspects
Reader/Task Considerations	Teacher determined — Vary by individual reader and type of text	Teacher determined — Vary by individual reader and type of text

TEACH

CLOSE READ

AS YOU VIEW Direct students to use the As You View question to focus their viewing.

Analyze Interpretations of Drama: Operatic Interpretation

COMMON CORE RL 7

Point out that music can be used to highlight meaning or direct the audience's attention to the action on the stage.

ASK STUDENTS to listen carefully to the music in the section of the video from 2:45 to 4:00. How does the music highlight Annie's feelings when she discusses her house and when she asks Captain Keeney whether he loves her? *(The music is soft and flowing when she discusses the house, reflecting her pleasant memories, and it becomes louder and more intense when she asks about his love, highlighting her passion.)*

Tell students that **mood** is the feeling or atmosphere created in a work. In this opera, the performers' voices and the accompanying music work together to create the mood of the opera.

ASK STUDENTS TO describe the mood at the end of the opera. How is this mood created? *(The mood at the end of the opera is disturbing. This mood is created by Annie's wild laughter as well as by the harsh chords of the music.)*

COLLABORATIVE DISCUSSION Have students jot down ideas about the mood independently before meeting with their partners to discuss the elements that contribute to the mood. Accept all reasonable responses.

ASK STUDENTS to share any questions they generated in the course of viewing the selection.

MEDIA ANALYSIS

Media Versions of *ILE*

Opera by Ezra Donner   Production Image

AS YOU VIEW Consider how the music of the opera helps convey the story. Write down any questions you generate during viewing.

Image Credits: (t) ©Egor Arkhipov/Shutterstock; (b) ©Ezra Donner

COLLABORATIVE DISCUSSION How would you describe the overall mood, or feeling, of the opera? With a partner, discuss which elements of the performance contribute to this atmosphere. Cite examples from the video to support your ideas.

SCAFFOLDING FOR ELL STUDENTS

Analyze Interpretations of a Drama The video begins just after the mutiny scene. Have students reread lines 546–919 in the play. Then have them watch the video at least twice to appreciate details of the production.

- For the first viewing, tell students to follow along closely with the subtitles but also to pay attention to how the music brings out the characters' emotions. They should pause or rewind the video as needed to understand the actors' words.

- For the second viewing, tell students to glance at the subtitles as a guide, but to pay more attention to the music and to the actors' movements. What do these features add to the drama?

Analyze Interpretations of Drama: Operatic Interpretation

 COMMON CORE RL 7

Discuss the points made in the instruction, drawing students' attention to each example given. Then organize the class into three groups. Assign each group one of these elements: mood, character, dialogue. Have groups review the opera, tracking the way in which music affects understanding of their element. Have them then present their observations to the class. Use the groups' insights to draw conclusions about the impact of the music in this opera on the audience's perception of character, dialogue, and mood.

Analyzing the Text and Media

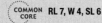 **COMMON CORE** RL 7, W 4, SL 6

Possible answers:

1. *Annie Keeney's dialogue is often accompanied by plaintive, pleading music that conveys feelings of sadness. As a result, the audience perceives her as a sympathetic character.*

2. *The music is central to developing the characters. For example, Captain Keeney's lines are sung in a loud, powerful, dominant voice, conveying the impression of his character as strong and in control. The music at the end, somewhat discordant, heightens the audience's understanding of Annie's breakdown.*

3. *In the opera, the conflict is simplified, becoming a struggle between Captain Keeney, who wants to continue the voyage, and his wife, who wants him to turn back. In the opera, it is not clear why he is so adamant about continuing the voyage. In the play, the additional lines develop his internal conflict more fully, showing that he is not indifferent to his wife's suffering but that he must be true to himself as well. The oil represents his whole concept of himself, not just a means of making a living.*

Analyze Interpretations of Drama: Operatic Interpretation

 COMMON CORE RL 7

Music is the key element in any opera. It helps communicate the story by influencing the audience's interpretation of the characters' words and actions:

- Music sets the **mood**, or emotional atmosphere, of a scene, affecting how the audience feels. Fast music may create a feeling of urgency; slow music may set a somber or sad mood. For example, in *Ile*, a series of quick, emphatic notes intensifies the mood of excitement when the mate announces that the ice is breaking up.
- Music influences the way the audience feels about a **character**. If uplifting music is played when a character enters, the audience may perceive that character in a more positive way.
- Music can be used to draw attention to **dialogue** as well as to a character's gestures or movements. For example, when Captain Keeney goes back on deck after his decision to keep sailing, the music fades, focusing the audience's attention on Annie's actions.

Analyzing the Text and Media

 COMMON CORE RL 7, W 4, SL 6

Cite Text Evidence Support your responses with evidence from the selection.

1. **Analyze** What emotion is conveyed by the music that accompanies much of Annie Keeney's dialogue? How might this music influence the way the audience perceives her character?

2. **Analyze** How do the music and performers' singing contribute to your understanding of the characters? Cite specific examples from the video.

3. **Compare** The opera version of the discussion between Captain Keeney and his wife omits several passages of dialogue, including his explanation of why he has to get the oil and his reminder that he asked her not to come on the voyage. How do these omissions affect the way the audience understands the central conflict?

PERFORMANCE TASK

Writing Activity: Critique Is the opera version of *Ile* a faithful interpretation of O'Neill's play?

- Prepare a written response to the question, citing specific examples to support your view.

- Identify classmates with opposing viewpoints. Take turns presenting your responses to the class.

- As a class, decide which viewpoint is most compelling.

Assign this performance task.

PERFORMANCE TASK

 COMMON CORE W 4, SL 6

Writing Activity: Critique Students' critiques should show whether the opera version conveys the same ideas of character, plot, and theme as the original play, citing specific examples to support their views.

AS YOU VIEW This image shows a scene from a 2009 production of *Ile* that was staged during the summer on a 19th-century schooner docked at the Mystic Seaport Museum in Connecticut. Compare the actors, costumes, and set in the photograph with the images you had in your mind after reading O'Neill's play. Write down any questions you generate as you view the image.

COLLABORATIVE DISCUSSION With a partner, discuss your reaction to the production shown in the photograph. Which scene from O'Neill's play is most likely represented in the image? What specific choices did the director make in staging it? Cite evidence from both the play and the photograph to support your points.

Image Credits: ©Mystic Seaport

CLOSE READ

AS YOU VIEW Direct students to use the As You View directions to focus their viewing. Remind them to write down any questions they generate as they examine the photograph.

Analyze Interpretations of Drama: Casting and Staging

COMMON CORE RL 7

Tell students that several actors may vie for one character's role. The director chooses the actor that matches his or her vision of the play.

Ⓐ **ASK STUDENTS** what the choice of the actor for Mrs. Keeney suggests about the director's interpretation of O'Neill's play. *(The director is leaning toward a traditional interpretation, since the actress matches the image projected by the original text.)*

Explain that the staging, which includes set design and/or location, can affect how the audience feels about what is happening.

Ⓐ **ASK STUDENTS** how the set of this play affects the mood. *(The setting on a schooner makes the mood less dismal than, for example, the dark, barren stage of the opera version.)*

COLLABORATIVE DISCUSSION Encourage students to support their reactions with specific details from the photograph, such as costuming, setting, and casting. Accept all reasonable responses.

ASK STUDENTS to share any questions they generated in the course of viewing the selection.

WHEN STUDENTS STRUGGLE . . .

Draw a Venn diagram or comparison-contrast matrix on the board. Work with students to compare these elements of the two versions of *Ile* using details from the opera and the production still:

- costuming
- staging
- casting

ASK STUDENTS how they would describe the interpretation presented by each adaptation.

TEACH

Analyze Interpretations of Drama: Casting and Staging

 COMMON CORE RL 7

To make sure students understand the concepts of casting and staging, organize them into small groups. As a class, list the names of popular actors and actresses on the board. Then organize students into groups and have them complete these activities:

- Choose an actor to play Captain Keeney and an actress to play his wife. Explain why you cast these actors in the roles and how they further your interpretation of the play.

- Explain where you would set the play and why.

Have groups present their explanations. Use discussion of their choices to reinforce the ideas about casting and staging in the instruction.

Analyzing the Text and Media

COMMON CORE RL 7, SL 4

Possible answers:

1. *The casting is traditional in that Annie Keeney is played by a woman of a similar age to O'Neill's character. Her costume and demeanor make her appear authentic for the time period. The Captain, too, is dressed in a way that fits the original setting. He is a commanding presence, just as O'Neill's captain is. The choice of an African American actor is probably a departure from how O'Neill imagined the character.*

2. *By staging the play on an actual schooner, the audience can more easily enter into the experience of being at sea. They experience the sensations associated with being on board a ship. However, the deck of the schooner offers a view of the shoreline and harbor. This setting could dilute the intensity produced by O'Neill's vision of a claustrophobic and barren cabin. The audience might find it harder to empathize with the desperation of characters, who are trapped in the cabin and trapped in the ice.*

 Assess It!

Online Selection Test
- Download an editable ExamView bank.
- Assign and manage this test online.

Analyze Interpretations of Drama: Casting and Staging

 COMMON CORE RL 7

Before staging a play, directors must decide how they want to interpret the original work. They might choose to stay true to the writer's vision of the characters and setting. Or they might decide on a more radical interpretation of these elements. Their interpretation determines the casting and staging.

- **Casting** involves choosing actors to play the specific roles. The director's criteria for a particular character may include age, gender, personality, and physical appearance. The photograph of the production of *Ile* in Mystic, Connecticut, shows how one director chose to "see" the characters of Captain and Mrs. Keeney.

- **Staging** depends on where and when the director envisions the action taking place. The setting of a play might be created by elaborate sets within a theater. The photograph from the Mystic production shows the choice of an outdoor location that is meaningful to the play and produces the effect the director wants.

Even if audience members do not consciously think about a play's casting and staging, both elements contribute to their reactions to the play and their interpretation of its meaning.

Analyzing the Text and Media

COMMON CORE RL 7, SL 4

Cite Text Evidence   Support your responses with evidence from the selection.

1. **Analyze** In what ways is the casting consistent with O'Neill's text? In what ways does the casting depart from the text?

2. **Analyze** What is the director's purpose in staging the play on an actual schooner anchored off the Connecticut coast? How might this staging, compared to a more traditional theater staging, change the play's impact on the audience?

PERFORMANCE TASK

Media Activity: Set Design How would you stage O'Neill's play?

- With a partner, decide on your vision of the setting of O'Neill's play. Write a brief explanation of the reasons you would choose this setting.

- Draw or find images of the set design that would be used in your staging of the play.

- Present your set design to the class, explaining the reasons behind your decisions.

Assign this performance task.

PERFORMANCE TASK

Media Activity: Set Design Suggest that students review the play before making decisions about how they would stage it. They may wish to create their set design on a computer and project it for the class to see.

Cite Textual Evidence

COMMON CORE

RL 1

TEACH

Before students begin the Performance Task for writing a critique, teach them about the special types of textual evidence they will need to cite. In a performance, like the excerpt from the concert opera *Ile*, textual evidence includes not only the **script** (or libretto, as the text of an opera is known), but these elements:

Music is the central part of any operatic production but can play a role in any stage production of a drama. It sets the mood that the work will convey to the audience and highlights characters' words and actions. The casting of the **performers** as well as the performers' interpretation of the text—including tone, volume, gestures, and movement—provide evidence to support your interpretation and analysis of a production. The director's **staging**—choices about where to perform, as well as the lighting, costumes, props, and scenery—provide evidence to support your response to a production.

PRACTICE AND APPLY

Play the first three minutes of the *Ile* concert opera excerpt, asking students to look for evidence that sheds light on Captain Keeney's character. Use the *Evidence* boxes in the Conclusions Chart from the Interactive Graphic Organizers for Reading website to organize students' responses in four categories. Sample responses are provided:

Libretto: *"To hell with your law courts. We're at sea now, and I'm the law on this ship!"*

Music: *Music stops while the captain says these lines, but his singing grows louder as he declares he is the law.*

Performer: *Keeney sits and coils the rope that Joe flung at him; but soon explodes in anger, striking Joe.*

Staging: *The Mate stands meekly in the background; Mrs. Keeney looks like she wants to hide from a coming storm.*

Conclusions: *Captain Keeney comes across as a powerful man with a current of anger flowing just under the surface. His attempt to control his anger is reflected in his coiling the rope as he and Joe argue. While the music in the segment sounds ominous, its absence when he leaps to his feet—declaring that "I'm the law on this ship"—highlights the force of his will, and the other actors' cowering movements show that they fear him.*

Have students work in groups to interpret another segment of the opera, using the graphic organizer, and citing textual evidence in their concluding paragraph.

Participate in Collaborative Discussions

COMMON CORE

SL 1

TEACH

- After students complete the first two steps of the Performance Task on set design (before the class presentation), have partners review the steps for sharing their work within the context of a collaborative discussion:
- **Step 1: Come to discussions prepared** Review the details of your proposed setting, including your reasons for your choice of staging, props, lighting, and scenery. Make sure you can cite evidence from the text to support your choices, or can make a persuasive case for any dramatic departure from the setting described in the drama. Gather your images and be sure their connection to your written explanations is clear.
- **Step 2: Promote civil, democratic discussions** Once you have convened your collaborative group, decide what you want to accomplish and in what time frame. For instance, you may set the goal of taking the best ideas from each partners' set designs to create one collaborative design. Or you may decide simply to improve each others' designs through constructive feedback. In either case, make sure that every individual in the group has a chance to present his or her ideas as well as respond to others'.
- **Step 3: Respond to questions and challenge ideas** Ask questions that clarify, verify, or challenge each other's set design proposals. Respond constructively, offering ways to extend and refine each other's set design concepts.
- **Step 4: Synthesize comments and resolve contradictions** If your group has decided to join forces in creating one set design with the best of each pairing's ideas, create a plan to revise the written description and images. Otherwise, if the contradictions between the various visions are insurmountable, each pair should sum up feedback received on how to improve their set designs.

COLLABORATIVE DISCUSSION

Direct each pair of set-design partners to form a group with one or two other pairs of students to review each other's set designs. Students should follow the guidelines above until they have reached a consensus on how to proceed with their design. Give students time to incorporate changes before presenting their two-person or collaborative-group set designs to the class.

INTERACTIVE LESSON Have students complete the tutorials in this lesson: **Participating in Collaborative Discussions**

Present Information to Support a Viewpoint

SL 4

TEACH

After students complete the written portion of the Performance Task, have them prepare their critiques for informal oral presentation. Provide students with the following guidelines for presenting their work:

Step 1: Use your written critique as the basis of your presentation.

- Review your textual evidence. Whether or not you believe the opera is a faithful interpretation of O'Neill's play, you must cite textual evidence from both works to support your viewpoint. Remember that evidence from a musical performance will include relevant details about music, the performance of the singers, and the directors' staging.

- Evaluate and revise your organization. Help your audience understand why you do or do not believe the opera is a faithful interpretation of the original by drawing a clear comparison between passages from the play to their execution on the stage.

- Read the draft aloud to yourself or a partner, paying special attention to where you can improve the rhythm or impact of your language through varied sentence structure and parallelism.

- Highlight the key points you want to make. Plan to deliver your point of view and supporting evidence from memory, using your paper to jog your memory.

Step 2: Rehearse your speech in front of a partner, if possible. Glance at your script to jog your memory, but avoid reading it word for word. Ask your partner for feedback to improve your presentation.

Step 3: Make your presentation as you rehearsed it, keeping your partner's feedback in mind. Speak clearly and maintain eye contact as much as possible.

INFORMAL PRESENTATION

Have students prepare their presentations using the guidelines above. Pair students with opposing viewpoints, both to provide feedback during rehearsal and for paired presentation. Remind audience members to listen actively, take notes, and provide polite feedback after each pair of presentations.

 INTERACTIVE LESSON Have students complete the tutorials in this lesson: **Giving a Presentation**

Analyze Interpretations of Drama

RL 7

RETEACH

Discuss the elements of drama and the way in which each director may interpret them, stamping his or her own vision of the original text on the film or stage production. Choose a popular and appropriate film or stage production that most students have seen. Have each group analyze the impact of the casting and staging on their understanding of and feeling about the movie or play. Prompt their discussions with these questions:

- How does the actor playing the main role make you react to the character? Why? Which other characters are well cast? Explain.

- What is the predominant setting of the film or play? What mood does this setting convey?

- Do the casting and staging enhance the story or take away from it? Explain.

 LEVEL UP TUTORIALS Assign the following *Level Up* tutorial: **Elements of Drama**

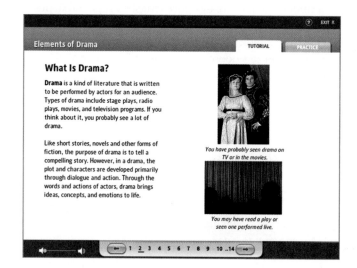

CLOSE READING APPLICATION

Present a video clip from an adaptation of a well-known play. Then have students read the text. Ask them to work in groups to compare and contrast the original text with the film version.

Interactive Lessons

If you need help with...
- **Writing an Argument**
- **Participating in Collaborative Discussions**

Debate an Issue

This collection focuses on the sacrifices people make to achieve success. In the anchor text "Marita's Bargain," the author describes a school in which the days are longer, summer vacation is shorter, and students are very successful. With a group of classmates, conduct a debate on whether *all* students should have longer school days and shorter vacations.

Each team in an effective debate

- takes a clear position, either for or against the idea of students spending more time in school
- selects relevant evidence from "Marita's Bargain" and one or more other texts in the collection to support the claims
- follows an orderly format in which speakers from each team take turns presenting their claims, counterclaims, reasons, and evidence
- communicates ideas formally and objectively, using clear and precise language
- engages in a thoughtful, well-reasoned exchange of ideas in which participants respond to diverse perspectives, build on each other's ideas, and evaluate the reasoning of other speakers

COMMON CORE

SL 1a–d Initiate and participate in a range of collaborative discussions, building on others' ideas and expressing their own.

SL 3 Evaluate a speaker's point of view, reasoning, and use of evidence and rhetoric.

PLAN

Get Organized Work with your classmates to prepare for the debate.

- With a show of hands, identify which students would like to argue for more time in school and which would like to argue against. If the two groups are unequal, some students will need to switch sides so that each team has about the same number of members.
- Select one student to be the moderator for the debate. The moderator will play a neutral role, promoting a civil discussion.
- Create a format for your debate—a schedule that shows the order in which members of each team will speak and for how many minutes. It will be the moderator's job to keep the debate moving along on schedule.

myNotebook

Use the annotation tools in your eBook to find evidence that supports your position. Save each piece of evidence to your notebook.

ACADEMIC VOCABULARY

As you build your argument on the issue of how much time students should spend in school, be sure to use these words.

accumulate

appreciation

conform

persistence

reinforce

DEBATE AN ISSUE

COMMON CORE SL 1a-d, SL 3

Introduce students to the Performance Task by reading the introductory paragraph with them and reviewing the criteria for what makes an effective debate. Remind students that a debate is a productive and balanced argument about both sides of an issue.

PLAN

GET ORGANIZED

View It!

Professional Development Podcast:

Performance Task

As they prepare for the debate, tell students to consider and research both sides of the issue. To argue convincingly either for or against longer school days and shorter vacations, students must be familiar with both sides of the issue. It's also important that the moderator be familiar with both sides so that he or she can introduce the issue and keep the debate on track.

PRODUCE

BUILD YOUR ARGUMENT

Remind students that the purpose of a debate is similar to the purpose of writing an argument: to persuade others to accept a claim about an issue by providing valid reasons and sufficient evidence. Review the types of text evidence students should use to support their claim:

- Examples: specific details or events from the texts
- Quotations: specific words, phrases, and sentences presented word-for-word from the texts and attributed to the author
- Summaries: important information from the texts summed up in their own words

- Get together with your team and choose at least two texts from this collection, including "Marita's Bargain," that you will use to support your position.
- Divide into smaller groups or pairs to review the texts and identify specific reasons and evidence you can use to support your position.
- Discuss other reasons and evidence from your own knowledge and experience that can also be used to support your claim.

PRODUCE

my WriteSmart

Build Your Argument Working with your whole team, organize the reasons and evidence you have accumulated into an effective argument.

Working with your peers, develop a debate plan in *my*WriteSmart. Your group should focus on getting ideas down, rather than on perfecting the language.

- Write a clear statement of your claim or position.
- Outline the main reasons that support your claim.
- Sort through the evidence you have collected from "Marita's Bargain," the other texts, and your own experience. Match each piece of evidence with the reason it most clearly supports.
- Think about the counterclaims the other team will likely make to refute your ideas. Plan the counterarguments you will make to challenge their counterclaims.
- Assign a debate role for each member of the team. One member will introduce the team's claim with supporting reasons and evidence. Other team members will exchange questions with a member of the opposing team to clarify and challenge reasoning. The last member will present a strong closing argument.
- Each debate team member should write out or make notes on the part of the argument he or she will present.
- Draft a closing statement that your last speaker will use to reinforce the strongest reasons for your position.

Practice for the Debate A debate is more than a series of prepared statements read aloud. Participants listen closely to what all speakers say so that they can respond appropriately and build on others' ideas. Use the chart on the following page to review the characteristics of an effective debate. Then divide your team into two groups to practice for a lively exchange of ideas.

my **WriteSmart**

Have your group of peers review your contributions to the debate plan in *my*WriteSmart. Ask them to note any reasons that do not support the claim or that lack sufficient evidence.

- Assign one group to argue for your team's position and the other to argue against it.
- Take turns speaking in a format similar to the one you have planned for the real debate.
- The first speaker in each group should clearly state a position and provide reasons and evidence to support it. Subsequent speakers should provide additional support.
- Pay attention to what each speaker says, and be prepared to modify your own statement to respond to new ideas.
- The last speakers should summarize their groups' positions.
- When your practice debate is over, evaluate each other's reasoning and use of evidence. Discuss how you can improve your performance in the actual debate.

Hold the Debate With guidance from your moderator, carry out the format you agreed on.

- The moderator should begin by introducing the topic of the debate and then recognizing speakers, alternating between the two teams.
- Remember to maintain a respectful tone toward your fellow debaters, even when you disagree with their ideas.
- Take notes during the debate, identifying points of disagreement and noting any errors in reasoning or insufficient evidence from the other team. Be prepared to address these flaws when it is your turn to speak.
- When the debate is over, express appreciation for your opponents' work. Then vote on whether extending the amount of time students spend in school is a good idea.
- Discuss the reasons and evidence that you found most compelling, and why.

PERFORMANCE TASK A

REVISE

PRACTICE FOR THE DEBATE

As students practice, remind them to avoid slang and colloquialisms and to use a respectful, academic tone as they present their side on the issue. Students should also practice using their debate notes while maintaining eye contact with the audience.

PRESENT

HOLD THE DEBATE

Students may want to videotape their debates. Videotaping will allow them to critique themselves on their delivery and to focus on their use of text evidence to support their side's claim.

PERFORMANCE TASK A

Have students look at the chart to offer a self-evaluation of the three main categories, including their assessment of their level of performance. Ask them to set goals for the next time they might do a similar task. What areas will they work on? Students can also work with their debate teams to complete this evaluation.

COLLECTION 1 TASK A
DEBATE

	Ideas and Evidence	Organization	Language
ADVANCED	• The claim clearly states a position on a substantive topic or issue. • The debater's background research is noticeably thorough and accurate. • Valid reasons and relevant evidence from the texts convincingly support the claim. • Opposing claims are anticipated and effectively rebutted with counterclaims. • The concluding section effectively summarizes the claim.	• The reasons and textual evidence are organized consistently and logically throughout the argument. • Varied transitions logically connect reasons and textual evidence to the speaker's claim.	• The speaker uses an appropriately formal style and an objective, or controlled, tone. • The debater speaks with confidence, clarity, and precision and completely keeps the audience's attention. • Grammar and usage are correct.
COMPETENT	• The claim adequately states a position on an issue or topic. • The debater's research on the issue or topic is mostly thorough, but could be more extensive. • Most reasons and evidence from the texts support the speaker's claim, but they could be more convincing. • Opposing claims are anticipated, but the counterclaims need to be developed more. • The concluding section restates the claim.	• The organization of reasons and textual evidence is confusing in a few places. • A few more transitions are needed to connect reasons and textual evidence to the debater's claim.	• The style is informal in a few places, and the tone is defensive at times. • The debater speaks with some confidence and clarity and mostly keeps the audience's attention. • Some grammatical and usage errors are repeated in the argument.
LIMITED	• The claim identifies an issue, but the speaker's position is not clearly stated. • The debater's research on the topic or issue is obviously limited. • The reasons and evidence from the texts are not always logical or relevant. • Opposing claims are anticipated but not addressed logically. • The concluding section includes an incomplete summary of the claim.	• The organization of reasons and textual evidence is logical in some places, but it often doesn't follow a pattern. • Many more transitions are needed to connect reasons and textual evidence to the debater's position.	• The style becomes informal in many places, and the tone is often dismissive of the opposing team's viewpoints. • The debater speaks with uncertainty and minimally holds the audience's attention. • Grammar and usage are incorrect in many places, but the debater's ideas are still clear.
EMERGING	• The introduction and the statement of the claim are missing. • The debater shows little or no evidence of researching the issue or topic. • Significant supporting reasons and evidence from the texts are missing. • Opposing claims are neither anticipated nor rebutted. • The concluding section is missing.	• An organizational strategy is not used; reasons and textual evidence are presented randomly. • Transitions are not used, making the debater's argument difficult to understand.	• The style is inappropriate, and the tone is disrespectful and combative. • The speaker sounds monotonous and does not capture the audience's attention. • Many grammatical and usage errors change the meaning of the debater's ideas.

COLLECTION 1
PERFORMANCE TASK B

Interactive Lessons

If you need help with...
• **Writing as a Process**
• **Using Textual Evidence**

PERFORMANCE TASK B

Write a Compare-Contrast Essay

The texts in this collection show the price some people are willing to pay to fulfill their ambitions. In the anchor text, "A Walk to the Jetty," the narrator goes abroad so she can get ahead in life, despite her painfully conflicted feelings about leaving behind her family and home. Write an essay in which you compare and contrast Annie John's experience with that of another character or person profiled in the collection. Discuss the sacrifices these individuals make and whether they are worth it.

COMMON CORE

W 2 Write informative/ explanatory texts.
W 4 Produce clear and coherent writing.
W 5 Develop writing by planning, revising, editing, rewriting.
W 9 Draw evidence from literary or informational texts.

An effective compare-contrast essay

- Includes a controlling idea that shows how Annie John's experience is similar to and different from that of another character or person in a collection text
- engages readers by introducing the topic with an interesting observation, quotation, or detail from one of the texts
- has an effective organization, such as subject-by-subject or point-by-point comparison
- develops the comparison with thorough evidence from "A Walk to the Jetty" and the other chosen text
- has a concluding section that synthesizes information from both texts and leaves the reader with an interesting insight

PLAN

Gather Evidence The foundation of your essay will be a close analysis of two texts.

- Reread the anchor text "A Walk to the Jetty" and take notes about Annie's ambition and the price she pays for it. Note concrete details that will help readers understand her character, her dreams, and her feelings.
- Then review the other texts in the collection and choose a character or person who offers interesting points for comparison with Annie. Note relevant details from that text as well.
- Use a Venn diagram or another graphic organizer to make important connections and distinctions between Annie and the other character or person.

myNotebook

Use the annotation tools in your eBook to find details for your comparison. Save each detail in your notebook.

ACADEMIC VOCABULARY

As you write your compare-contrast essay, be sure to use these words.

accumulate
appreciation
conform
persistence
reinforce

WRITE A COMPARE-CONTRAST ESSAY

COMMON CORE W 2, W 4, W 5, W 9

Introduce students to the Performance Task by reading the introductory paragraph with them and reviewing the criteria for what makes an effective compare-contrast essay. Note that their completed essays should include a controlling idea, sufficient textual evidence to support the controlling idea, an effective organizational structure, and correct use of language conventions.

PLAN

GATHER EVIDENCE

View It!

Professional Development Podcast:

Teaching Argument

Have students list possible connections and distinctions between Annie John and another character or person in the collection. If there are more similarities than differences, suggest students choose a different person or character to compare with Annie John.

PERFORMANCE TASK B

PLAN

GET ORGANIZED

Suggest that students outline their essays using both organizational patterns:

- Block Structure: discusses all of the points relating to the first subject before moving on to the second subject
- Point-by-Point Structure: compares or contrasts both subjects, one point at a time

Students should choose the structure that is most effective in presenting their controlling ideas and textual evidence.

PRODUCE

DRAFT YOUR ESSAY

Encourage students to focus their first drafts on getting down their ideas. Remind them to include specific, relevant details and examples from the texts to support each point of comparison. Once they are sure their essays are organized logically, they can focus on refining the language.

Get Organized Organize your details and evidence in an outline.

- Develop a controlling idea that will establish the focus of your comparison. Be prepared to refine your controlling idea as you draft your essay.

- Decide what organizational pattern you will use for your essay. Will you write everything you have to say about Annie John first, and then write about the other person or character (subject by subject)? Or, will you discuss one point as it relates to both Annie John and the other subject, and then move on to the next point (point by point)?

- Use your organizational pattern to sort the textual evidence you have gathered into a logical order.

- Select an interesting quotation or detail to introduce your essay.

- Jot down some ideas for your concluding section.

PRODUCE

Draft Your Essay Write a draft of your essay, following your outline.

*my***WriteSmart**

Write your rough draft in *my*WriteSmart. Focus on getting your ideas down, rather than on perfecting your choice of language.

- In the introduction, express your controlling idea and introduce the subjects of your essay and the points you will compare. Be sure to give readers enough information to appreciate your controlling idea even if they are not familiar with the texts.

- Present your details, quotations, and examples from the texts in logically ordered paragraphs.

- Remember to use transitions to clarify the relationships among ideas in your writing. Transitions that are commonly used to compare and contrast include *similarly, however, on the other hand, by contrast,* and *in the same way.*

- Establish and maintain a formal style by avoiding contractions and slang. Adopt a neutral attitude to convey an objective tone in your analysis.

- Write a final paragraph that synthesizes the ideas you have presented in the body of your essay. Explain why you think the sacrifices made by the individuals you have discussed were or were not worth the pain they involved, and draw your own conclusion about personal ambition.

Improve Your Draft Use the chart on the following page to review the characteristics of an effective compare-contrast essay. Then revise your draft to make sure it is clear, coherent, and engaging. Ask yourself these questions as you revise:

*my*WriteSmart

Have your partner or a group of peers review your draft in *my*WriteSmart. Ask your reviewers to note any evidence that does not support the controlling idea.

- Does my introduction grab readers' attention? Have I stated my controlling idea clearly?

- Have I presented relevant evidence from the texts to support the main points of my comparison?

- Have I shown both similarities and differences between Annie John and the other individual?

- Do I need more transitions to link the sections of my essay?

- Have I maintained a formal style, avoiding slang and nonstandard English?

- Have I used varied sentence beginnings and structures to hold my readers' attention?

- Does my conclusion synthesize information from the body of my essay and provide a satisfying ending?

PRESENT

Exchange Essays When your final draft is completed, exchange essays with a partner. Read your partner's essay and provide feedback. Reread the criteria for an effective compare-contrast essay and ask the following questions:

- Which aspects of the essay are particularly strong?

- Which areas could be improved?

PERFORMANCE TASK B

REVISE

IMPROVE YOUR DRAFT

Remind students that revising means evaluating the development, organization, and language of their essays. Have students exchange papers with a partner and use the chart on the following page to evaluate each other's compare-contrast essays. Students should discuss whether their partner's points of comparison and contrast are clear, and provide concrete suggestions for improvement.

PRESENT

EXCHANGE ESSAYS

Provide students with other options for presenting their essays, such as adapting and presenting their essays as an informative speech. Students might also organize a group discussion in which they and several classmates talk about their essays.

Have students look at the chart to offer a self-evaluation of the three main categories, including their assessment of their level of performance. Ask them to set goals for the next time they might do a similar task. What areas will they work on? Students can also work with partners to complete this evaluation.

COLLECTION 1 TASK B
COMPARE-CONTRAST ESSAY

	Ideas and Evidence	Organization	Language
ADVANCED	• The introduction is appealing; the controlling idea clearly identifies the subjects and sets up points for comparison and contrast. • Concrete, relevant details and examples from the texts skillfully support each key point. • The concluding section effectively synthesizes the ideas, summarizes the points of comparison and contrast, and leaves the reader with a thought-provoking idea.	• Key points and supporting textual evidence are organized logically, effectively, and consistently throughout the essay. • Varied transitions successfully show the relationships between ideas.	• The essay has an appropriately formal style and a knowledgeable, objective tone. • Language is precise and effectively emphasizes similarities and differences. • Sentence beginnings, lengths, and structures vary and have a rhythmic flow. • Spelling, capitalization, and punctuation are correct. • Grammar and usage are correct.
COMPETENT	• The introduction could be more engaging; the controlling idea identifies the subjects and sets up one or two points for comparison and contrast. • One or two key points need more textual support. • The concluding section synthesizes most of the ideas and summarizes most points of comparison and contrast, but offers no new insight.	• The organization of key points and supporting textual evidence is confusing in a few places. • A few more transitions are needed to connect ideas.	• The style becomes informal in a few places, and the tone does not always communicate confidence. • Most language is precise. • Sentence beginnings, lengths, and structures vary somewhat. • Several spelling, capitalization, and punctuation mistakes occur. • Some grammatical and usage errors are repeated in the essay.
LIMITED	• The introduction is commonplace; the controlling idea identifies the subjects and only hints at the points of comparison and contrast. • Evidence from the texts supports some key points but is often too general. • The concluding section gives an incomplete summary of the points of comparison and contrast and restates the controlling idea.	• Most key points are organized logically, but many supporting details from the texts are out of place. • More transitions are needed throughout the comparison to connect ideas.	• The style is informal in many places, and the tone communicates a superficial understanding of the subjects. • Language is repetitive or vague at times. • Sentence structures barely vary, and some fragments or run-on sentences are present. • Spelling, capitalization, and punctuation are often incorrect but do not make reading the essay difficult. • Grammar and usage are incorrect in many places, but the writer's ideas are still clear.
EMERGING	• The appropriate elements of an introduction are missing. • Evidence from the texts is irrelevant or missing. • An identifiable concluding section is missing.	• A logical organization is not apparent; ideas are presented randomly. • Transitions are not used, making the comparison-contrast essay difficult to understand.	• The style is informal, and the tone is inappropriate. • Language is inaccurate, repetitive, and vague. • Repetitive sentence structure, fragments, and run-on sentences make the writing monotonous and difficult to follow. • Spelling, capitalization, and punctuation are incorrect throughout. • Many grammatical and usage errors change the meaning of the writer's ideas.

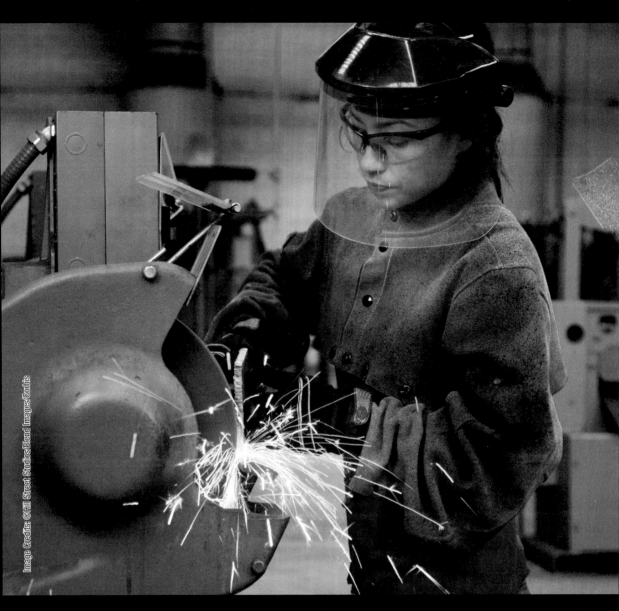

Gender Roles

Like it or not, today we are all pioneers. . . . The old rules are no longer reliable guides to work out modern gender roles.

—Stephanie Coontz

PLAN

CONNECTING WORD AND IMAGE

ASK STUDENTS to discuss how the collection opener image and the collection quotation work together to create a connection.

PERFORMANCE TASK PREVIEW

Point out to students that they will complete two performance tasks at the end of the collection. The performance tasks will require them to further analyze the selections in the collection and to synthesize ideas about these analyses. They will present their findings in a variety of products.

ACADEMIC VOCABULARY

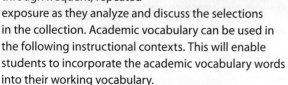

Professional Development Podcast:
Academic Vocabulary

Students can acquire facility with the academic vocabulary words through frequent, repeated exposure as they analyze and discuss the selections in the collection. Academic vocabulary can be used in the following instructional contexts. This will enable students to incorporate the academic vocabulary words into their working vocabulary.

- Collaborative Discussion at the end of each selection
- Analyzing the Text questions for each selection
- Selection-level Performance Task
- Vocabulary instruction (for Critical Vocabulary and/or for Vocabulary Strategy)
- Language and Style
- End-of-collection Performance Task for all selections in the collection

ASK STUDENTS to review the Academic Vocabulary word list for this collection. You may wish to pronounce each word aloud, so students hear the correct pronunciation. Then, discuss the definitions and the related forms for each word. Remind students that they will encounter these five academic vocabulary words throughout the collection.

Gender Roles

This collection explores the traditional roles of men and women as well as changes in gender roles that have occurred in recent decades.

hmhfyi.com

COLLECTION

PERFORMANCE TASK Preview

At the end of this collection, you will have the opportunity to complete two tasks:

- Write an essay about understanding between men and women.
- Discuss changes in gender roles that you foresee in the coming decade.

ACADEMIC VOCABULARY

Study the words and their definitions in the chart below. You will use these words as you discuss and write about the texts in this collection.

Word	Definition	Related Forms
bias (bī´əs) *n.*	predisposition toward; preference for one thing over another	biased
complementary (kŏm´plə-měn´tə-rē) *adj.*	completing; forming a whole	complement, complementarity
exploit (ĭk-sploit´) *v.*	to take advantage of; to use for selfish or unethical purposes	exploitation, exploitative
inclinations (ĭn´klə-nā´shəns) *n.*	leanings toward; propensities for	incline, inclinable
predominance (prĭ-dŏm´ə-nəns) *v.*	superiority in control, force, or influence	predominate, predominant

Image Credit: ©Hill Street Studios/Blend Images/Corbis

USING COLLECTIONS YOUR WAY

Use the following information, along with the charts on the following pages, to help you decide how you want to introduce the collection. Based on your teaching style, your students' interests, or your instructional goals, you may want to structure this collection in various ways. You may choose different entry points each time you teach the collection.

"I stress the importance of language and style."

The setting of this short story by **Mohammed Naseehu Ali** takes the reader to Ghana, introducing parts of the society and developing characters that show aspects of the culture. The imagery and sensory words build a vivid picture of live in a particular neighborhood.

Mohammed Naseehu Ali (b. 1971) was born in Ghana, a country in western Africa. He came to the United States in 1988 at the age of 16 to pursue his education, graduating from Bennington College in Vermont. Although he lives in New York City, the roots of his writing are in Ghana. He wants "to document the history of the Ghanaian people, so that civilization doesn't only see Africa and African people as an exotic people—but as normal people." "Mallam Sile" is from The Prophet of Zongo Street, his first published collection. It is set in a fictional Muslim neighborhood in Ghana.

Mallam Sile

Short Story by Mohammed Naseehu Ali

AS YOU READ Take note of the details that help you understand the character of Mallam Sile. Write down any questions you generate during reading.

He was popularly known as *mai tea*, or the tea seller. His shop was situated right in the navel of Zongo Street—a stone's throw from the chief's assembly shed and adjacent to the kiosk where Mansa BBC, the town gossip, sold her provisions. Along with fried eggs and white butter bread, Mallam Sile carried all kinds of beverages: regular black tea, Japanese green tea, Milo, Bournvita, cocoa drink, instant coffee. But on Zongo Street all hot beverages were referred to just as tea, and it was common, therefore, to hear people say, "Mallam Sile, may I have a mug of cocoa tea?" or "Sile, may I have a cup of coffee tea?"

The tea shop had no windows. It was built of *wawa*, a cheap wood easily infested by termites. The floor was uncemented, and heaps of dust rose in the air whenever a customer walked in. Sile protected his merchandise from the dust by keeping everything in plastic bags. An enormous wooden "chop box," the top of which he used as a serving table, covered most of the space in the shop. There was a tall chair behind the chop box for Sile, but he never used it, preferring instead to stand on his feet even when the shop was empty. There were also three benches that were meant to be used only by those who bought

Mallam Sile 93

"I like to connect literature to history."

In this political argument, **Mary Wollstonecraft** uses rhetorical devices to support her claim and refute opposition to the education of women. The presentation of logical reasons and valid evidence is challenging and connects to the history of the rights of women.

Background *In the eighteenth century, the daughters of English gentlemen were mostly taught reading, languages, playing the piano, singing, drawing, and needlework. This was thought to be adequate preparation for their lives as wives, mothers, governesses, or companions to wealthy ladies.*

Mary Wollstonecraft *(1759–1797) is considered by many to be the mother of feminism. Inspired by the ideas of liberal reformers, she wrote about the rights of women and others. Her 1790 book, A Vindication of the Rights of Man, attacked class and privilege; she followed that with A Vindication of the Rights of Woman in 1792.*

from A Vindication of the Rights of Woman

Political Argument by Mary Wollstonecraft

AS YOU READ Look for details that tell you about the nature of women's education in the eighteenth century.

From the Introduction

After considering the historic page, and viewing the living world with anxious solicitude, the most melancholy emotions of sorrowful indignation have depressed my spirits, and I have sighed when obliged to confess, that either nature has made a great difference between man and man, or that the civilization which has hitherto taken place in the world has been very partial. I have turned over various books written on the subject of education, and patiently observed the conduct of parents and the management of schools; but what has been the result?—a profound conviction that the neglected education of my fellow-creatures is the grand source of the misery I deplore; and that women, in particular, are rendered weak and wretched by a variety of concurring causes, originating from one hasty conclusion. The conduct and manners of women, in fact, evidently prove that their minds are not in a healthy state; for, like the flowers which are planted in too rich a soil, strength and usefulness are sacrificed to beauty; and the flaunting leaves, after having pleased a fastidious eye, fade, disregarded on the stalk, long before the season when they ought to have arrived at maturity. One cause of this barren

vindication (vĭn'dĭ-kā'shən) *n.* justification.

A Vindication of the Rights of Woman 113

"I want to concentrate on standards coverage."

This essay by **Scott Russell Sanders** offers an in-depth look at his point of view about the changes in gender roles in the late twentieth century. The author uses events and incidents from his own life to examine ideas about the roles of men and women in society.

Scott Russell Sanders (b. 1945) was born in Tennessee. He won a scholarship to attend Cambridge University, where he acquired his Ph.D. in English. His professional life was spent teaching at Indiana University. Much of his writing focuses on the relationship between humans and nature and on the importance of conservation. Sanders is particularly known for his essays. He says that an essay usually begins "in a state of strong emotion and equally strong puzzlement. Some event, recollection . . . provokes me, and sets me asking questions that drive the writing forward."

The Men We Carry in Our Minds

Essay by Scott Russell Sanders

AS YOU READ Note the experiences that have influenced Sanders's views about men and women.

"This must be a hard time for women," I say to my friend Anneke. "They have so many paths to choose from, and so many voices calling them."

"I think it's a lot harder for men," she replies.

"How do you figure that?"

"The women I know feel excited, innocent, like crusaders in a just cause. The men I know are eaten up with guilt."

We are sitting at the kitchen table drinking sassafras tea, our hands wrapped around the mugs because this April morning is cool and drizzly. "Like a Dutch morning," Anneke told me earlier. She is Dutch herself, a writer and midwife and peacemaker, with the round face and sad eyes of a woman in a Vermeer[1] painting who might be waiting for the rain to stop, for a door to open. She leans over to sniff a sprig of lilac, pale lavender, that rises from a vase of cobalt blue.

"Women feel such pressure to be everything, do everything," I say. "Career, kids, art, politics. Have their babies and get back to the office

[1] **Vermeer:** Johannes Vermeer (1632–1675), a Dutch painter known for his interior household scenes.

The Men We Carry in Our Minds 131

mySmartPlanner | **eBook** | **myNotebook** | | **fyi** hmhfyi.com

Collection 2 Lessons	Media	Teach and Practice	
Student Edition | eBook	▶ Video Links HISTORY A&E	**Close Reading and Evidence Tracking**	
ANCHOR TEXT Narrative Poem by Geoffrey Chaucer **"The Wife of Bath's Tale"** from *The Canterbury Tales*	▶ **Video** *History's Mysteries: The Knights of Camelot* ◀ **Audio** "The Wife of Bath's Tale" from *The Canterbury Tales*	**Close Read Screencasts** • Modeled Discussion 1 (lines 36–44) • Modeled Discussion 2 (lines 299–312) • Close Read application pdf (lines 402–415)	**Strategies for Annotation** • Determine Themes • Analyze Story Elements: Narrator • Usage
CLOSE READER Narrative Poem by Geoffrey Chaucer **"The Pardoner's Tale"**	◀ **Audio** "The Pardoner's Tale"		
Short Story by Mohammed Naseehu Ali **"Mallam Sile"**	◀ **Audio** "Mallam Sile"		**Strategies for Annotation** • Analyze Story Elements: Character Development • Analyze Story Elements: Setting • Adjectives and Adverbs
Poem by Shirley Geok-lin Lim **"My Father's Sadness"**	◀ **Audio** "My Father's Sadness"		**Strategies for Annotation** • Alliteration and Consonance
Political Argument by Mary Wollstonecraft from *A Vindication of the Rights of Woman*	◀ **Audio** from *A Vindication of the Rights of Woman*		**Strategies for Annotation** • Analyze Structure: Counterargument • Language and Style: Sentence Structure
Online Article by Neil MacFarquhar and Dina Salah Amer **"In a Scattered Protest, Saudi Women Take the Wheel"** **News Video** *Saudi Women Defy Driving Ban*	◀ **Audio** "In a Scattered Protest, Saudi Women Take the Wheel" ◀ **Audio** *Saudi Women Defy Driving Ban*		**Strategies for Annotation** • Summarize the Text
ANCHOR TEXT Essay by Scott Russell Sanders **"The Men We Carry in Our Minds"**	◀ **Audio** "The Men We Carry in Our Minds"	**Close Read Screencasts** • Modeled Discussion 1 (lines 36–46) • Close Read application pdf (lines 147–159)	**Strategies for Annotation** • Determine Author's Point of View • Context Clues
CLOSE READER Essay by Lynn Peril from *Pink Think*	◀ **Audio** from *Pink Think*		
Collection 2 Performance Tasks: **A** Write an Informative Essay **B** Participate in a Group Discussion	**fyi** hmhfyi.com	**Interactive Lessons** **A** Writing an Informative Text **A** Writing as a Process	**B** Participating in Collaborative Discussions

	For Systematic Coverage of Writing and Speaking & Listening Standards	Interactive Lessons Writing an Argument Analyzing and Evaluating Presentations	Lesson Assessments Writing an Argument Analyzing and Evaluating Presentations

Assess		Extend	Reteach
Performance Task	**Online Assessment**	**Teacher eBook**	**Teacher eBook**
Writing Activity: Character Analysis	Selection Test	**Analyze Theme > Interactive Whiteboard Lesson >** Theme/Central Idea	**Analyze Story Elements: Narrator > Level Up Tutorial >** Point of View
Writing Activity: Description	Selection Test	**Writing: Use Sensory Language**	**Support Inferences: Draw Conclusions > Level Up Tutorial >** Drawing Conclusions
Speaking Activity: Oral Interpretation	Selection Test	**Analyze Structure > Interactive Whiteboard Lesson >** Poetry: Language and Form	**Determine Figurative Meanings > Level Up Tutorial >** Elements of Poetry
Speaking Activity: Oral Presentation	Selection Test	**Analyze Key Terms**	**Analyze Structure: Counterargument > Level Up Tutorial >** Elements of an Argument
Media Activity: News Video	Selection Test	**Determine Author's Purpose > Interactive Whiteboard Lesson >** Determine Author's Purpose	**Integrate and Evaluate Information > Level Up Tutorial >** Synthesizing Information
Speaking Activity: Debate	Selection Test	**Support Inferences** **Determine Connotative Meanings > Wordsharp: Interactive Vocabulary Tutorial >** Denotative and Connotative Meanings **Speaking and Listening: Challenge Ideas and Conclusions**	**Determine Central Ideas > Level Up Tutorial >** Main Idea and Supporting Details
A Write an Informative Essay **B** Participate in a Group Discussion	Collection Test		

Collection 2 Lessons	COMMON CORE Key Learning Objective	Performance Task
ANCHOR TEXT **Narrative Poem by Geoffrey Chaucer** **"The Wife of Bath's Tale" from *The Canterbury Tales*, p. 77A**	**The student will be able to...** analyze the narrator and the frame-story structure of a narrative poem	Writing Activity: Character Analysis
Lexile 1150L **Short Story by Mohammed Naseehu Ali** **"MallamSile," p. 93A**	**The student will be able to...** analyze setting as a story element and use textual evidence to make inferences and draw conclusions	Writing Activity: Description
Poem by Shirley Geok-lin Lim **"My Father's Sadness," p. 109A**	**The student will be able to...** determine figurative meanings of words and phrases in the context of a poem	Speaking Activity: Oral Interpretation
Political Argument by Mary Wollstonecraft **Lexile 1350L** **from *A Vindication of the Rights of Woman*, p. 113A**	**The student will be able to...** analyze counterarguments and rhetorical devices used in an argument	Speaking Activity: Oral Presentation
Online Article by Neil MacFarquhar **Lexile 1400L** **and Dina Salah Amer "In a Scattered Protest, Saudi Women Take the Wheel," p. 123A** **News Video** ***Saudi Women Defy Driving Ban*, p. 123A**	**The student will be able to...** summarize the main ideas of a news article; analyze ideas and events; and integrate and evaluate information	Media Activity: News Video
ANCHOR TEXT **Lexile 1060L** **Essay by Scott Russell Sanders** **"The Men We Carry in Our Minds," p. 131A**	**The student will be able to...** determine an author's point of view about a complex subject and determine the central ideas of an essay	Speaking Activity: Debate

Collection 2 Performance Tasks:
A Write an Informative Essay
B Participate in a Group Discussion

Vocabulary Strategy	Language and Style	Student Instructional Support	CLOSE READER Selection
Usage	Inverted Sentences	**Scaffolding for ELL Students:** • Interpret Idioms • Support Inferences **When Students Struggle:** • Summarize Important Passages • Use Details to Determine Theme • Complete Sentences **To Challenge Students:** Storyboard a Scene	Narrative Poem by Geoffrey Chaucer *"The Pardoner's Tale,"* p. 92b
Consult a Dictionary	Adjectives and Adverbs	**Scaffolding for ELL Students:** • Language: Punctuation and Print Cues • Transitions: Time Sequence • Analyze Character Description • Understand Figurative Language **When Students Struggle:** • Identify and Use Descriptive Words • Understand Figurative Language **To Challenge Students:** • Analyze a Relationship	
	Alliteration and Consonance	**Scaffolding for ELL Students:** Vocabulary: Multiple-Meaning Words **When Students Struggle:** Determine Figurative Meanings	
Multiple Meanings	Sentence Structure	**Scaffolding for ELL Students:** • Organizational Patterns: Compare/Contrast • Analyze Structure: Counterargument **When Students Struggle:** • Comprehension: Counterarguments • Identify Rhetorical Devices	
		Scaffolding for ELL Students: • Comprehension: Structure • Language: Colloquial Expressions **When Students Struggle:** • Comprehension Support • Concept Support	
Context Clues	Syntax	**Scaffolding for ELL Students:** Analyze Language: Adjectives **When Students Struggle:** • Determine Central Ideas and Supporting Details • Examine Paragraph Structure	Essay by Lynn Peril from *Pink Think*, p. 140b **Lexile 1490L**

mySmartPlanner — Create lesson plans and access resources online.

ANCHOR TEXT EXEMPLAR

The Wife of Bath's Tale *from* The Canterbury Tales

Narrative Poem by Geoffrey Chaucer

Why This Text?

The Canterbury Tales is one of the greatest works in English literature. In this lesson, students are exposed to elements of Chaucer's genius, such as his use of the frame story and multiple narrators to tell his tales.

► View It!

Professional Development Podcast:

Text-Dependent Analysis

Key Learning Objective: The student will be able to analyze the narrator and the frame-story structure of a narrative poem.

For additional practice:

The Pardoner's Tale
from The Canterbury Tales

Close Reader selection
"The Pardoner's Tale"
Narrative Poem by Geoffrey Chaucer

COMMON CORE Common Core Standards

RL 1 Cite textual evidence.

RL 2 Determine two or more themes.

RL 3 Analyze the impact of the author's choices regarding how to relate elements of a story.

RL 5 Analyze how an author's choices contribute to overall structure and meaning.

W 4 Produce clear and coherent writing.

L 1a Apply the understanding that usage can change over time.

L 1b Resolve issues of complex or contested usage.

L 3a Vary syntax for effect.

▲ Text Complexity Rubric

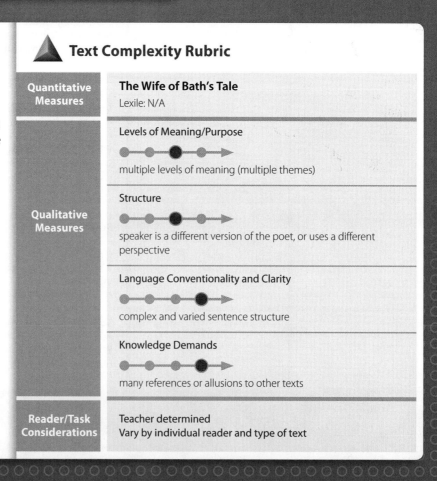

Quantitative Measures	**The Wife of Bath's Tale**
	Lexile: N/A

Qualitative Measures

Levels of Meaning/Purpose

multiple levels of meaning (multiple themes)

Structure

speaker is a different version of the poet, or uses a different perspective

Language Conventionality and Clarity

complex and varied sentence structure

Knowledge Demands

many references or allusions to other texts

Reader/Task Considerations	Teacher determined
	Vary by individual reader and type of text

TEACH

CLOSE READ

The Wife of Bath's Tale
from The Canterbury Tales

Narrative Poem by Geoffrey Chaucer   translated by Nevill Coghill

For more context and historical background, students can view the video "History's Mysteries: The Knights of Camelot" in their eBooks.

Background Have students read the background on *The Canterbury Tales*. Explain that Chaucer's original plan was for each pilgrim to tell two stories on the way to Canterbury and two on the way back, resulting in 120 tales. He did not complete this ambitious plan, writing only 24 tales.

Even though the work is technically unfinished, it shaped the direction of English literature to come. Previously, many characters in literature had been "types," representing ideals. Chaucer creates true individuals who illustrate the best and worst of humanity. His portraits of the various members of medieval society brought together on this pilgrimage are vivid and memorable. He develops these characters through descriptive details, their interactions with each other, and the tales they tell. Some of these tales are familiar to his medieval audience; however, his matching of teller and tale, sometimes ironically, gives these old stories new meaning. This pairing also allows him to achieve deeper characterization through what the story says about the pilgrim who tells it.

Tell students that they will be focusing on Chaucer's structure and the Wife of Bath's role as narrator as they read this tale. Encourage them to also note the way in which Chaucer uses irony to bring out important ideas. Explain that irony is the use of words to express something different from and often opposite to their literal meaning.

Geoffrey Chaucer is often referred to as the "father of English literature." His poetic form in *The Canterbury Tales* became the basis for the heroic couplet, used extensively by later poets. In addition to his use of the vernacular, he also showed poets and writers that humor had a place in literature and could be a valuable tool in conveying insights about society and the human condition.

AS YOU READ Direct students to use the As You Read note to focus their reading.

Background *In 14th-century England, literacy was becoming more widespread and books more easily available. During this period, a number of narrative works were written in Middle English, which was starting to replace French and Latin as the main literary language. They included romances based on the King Arthur legends, short narrative poems known as ballads, and moral tales. The most important one, written in the late 1300s by Geoffrey Chaucer, was a long narrative work called* The Canterbury Tales.

Written mostly in verse, The Canterbury Tales *depicts a group of pilgrims traveling to the shrine of St. Thomas à Becket in Canterbury, England. At the beginning of their journey, the host of a tavern where they stop to rest proposes a story-telling contest, with the winner to receive a free dinner at the tavern.*

The Canterbury Tales *is distinguished by its realism, earthy humor, and shrewd insights into human nature. Chaucer's pilgrims represent a cross-section of medieval society, which allowed him to satirize institutions and practices of his time. The tales are preceded by prologues in which the characters often exchange comments and argue with one another. The selection you will read contains one of Chaucer's best-known tales and an excerpt from its prologue.*

Geoffrey Chaucer *(1342?–1400) held political positions for most of his adult life. In addition to* The Canterbury Tales, *he wrote the tragic verse romance* Troilus and Criseyde. *Upon his death, as a mark of respect, he was buried in Westminster Abbey, an honor rarely given to a commoner.*

AS YOU READ Pay attention to details that reveal the personality of the Wife of Bath. Write down any questions you generate during reading.

The Wife of Bath's Tale   **77**

Close Read Screencasts   **View It!**

Modeled Discussions

Have students click the *Close Read* icons in their eBooks to access two screencasts in which readers discuss and annotate the following key passages:

- ironic commentary on friars (lines 36–44)
- the old woman's response to the knight (lines 299–312)

As a class, view and discuss at least one of these videos. Then have students pair up to do an independent close read of an additional passage—the knight's capitulation (lines 402–415).

Analyze Structure: Frame Story (LINES 1–28)

COMMON CORE RL 5

Point out that the prologue here is part of the frame story in which the pilgrims converse with each other between tales. Their interactions reveal their relationships with one another, ideas about medieval society, and important aspects of their character. Explain that the Wife of Bath has just finished giving an introduction to the tale she is about to tell.

A CITE TEXT EVIDENCE Have students identify lines from this passage that indicate the relationship between the Wife of Bath and the Friar. *(The Friar criticizes the length of the Wife's prologue in the first three lines; she responds at the end of the passage with sarcasm, saying she will proceed "If I have licence from this worthy friar." These lines suggest that they do not care for each other.)*

Have students note that the Friar and the Summoner, a church official who brings people accused of violating church law to ecclesiastical court, also exchange words.

B ASK STUDENTS to describe the tone of the conversation between the Friar and the Summoner. *(It is hostile.)* How do these exchanges affect the portrayals of the pilgrims? *(Their conversations make them seem more human; their personalities are developed through what they say and how they interact.)*

CRITICAL VOCABULARY

preamble: The Friar comments on the Wife's introduction to her tale, which has been lengthy.

ASK STUDENTS what the Friar might be anticipating about the Wife's tale, based on her preamble. *(He might be thinking that her tale will be even longer than her introduction to it.)*

The Wife of Bath's Prologue

The Friar laughed when he had heard all this.
"Well, Ma'am," he said, "as God may send me bliss,
This is a long **preamble** to a tale!"
But when the Summoner heard the Friar rail,
5 "Just look!" he cried, "by the two arms of God!
These meddling friars are always on the prod!
Don't we all know a friar and a fly
Go prod and buzz in every dish and pie!
What do you mean with your 'preambulation'?
10 Amble yourself, trot, do a meditation!
You're spoiling all our fun with your commotion."
The Friar smiled and said, "Is that your motion?
I promise on my word before I go
To find occasion for a tale or so
15 About a summoner that will make us laugh."
"Well, damn your eyes, and on my own behalf,"
The Summoner answered, "mine be damned as well
If I can't think of several tales to tell
About the friars that will make you mourn
20 Before we get as far as Sittingbourne.
Have you no patience? Look, he's in a huff!"
     Our Host called out, "Be quiet, that's enough!
Shut up, and let the woman tell her tale.
You must be drunk, you've taken too much ale.
25 Now, Ma'am, you go ahead and no demur."
"All right," she said, "it's just as you prefer,
If I have licence from this worthy friar."
"Nothing," said he, "that I should more desire."

preamble
(prē´ăm´bəl) *n.*
an introductory
statement.

The Wife of Bath's Tale

When good King Arthur ruled in ancient days
30 (A king that every Briton loves to praise)
This was a land brim-full of fairy folk.
The Elf-Queen and her courtiers joined and broke
Their elfin dance on many a green mead,
Or so was the opinion once, I read,
35 Hundreds of years ago, in days of yore.
But no one now sees fairies any more.
For now the saintly charity and prayer
Of holy friars seem to have purged the air;
They search the countryside through field and stream
40 As thick as motes that speckle a sun-beam,
Blessing the halls, the chambers, kitchens, bowers,
Cities and boroughs, castles, courts and towers,

33 mead: meadow.

40 motes: specks of dust.

41 bowers: bedrooms.

SCAFFOLDING FOR ELL STUDENTS

Interpret Idioms Tell students that they can often define idioms, or phrases that mean something other than what the words say, from context. Point out "as good as dead" in line 66. In lines 63–67, the king decides the knight must die for his crime, and the law says the decision must be carried out. Readers can infer that the phrase means the knight is certain to die.

ASK STUDENTS to work in pairs and use context clues to define "took his leave" in line 92 *("departed or left")* and "all the same" in line 96 *("still, despite his efforts")*. Encourage them to use the same strategy to determine the meanings of other idioms and unfamiliar expressions as they continue reading.

Thorpes, barns and stables, outhouses and dairies,
And that's the reason why there are no fairies.
45 Wherever there was wont to walk an elf
Today there walks the holy friar himself
As evening falls or when the daylight springs,
Saying his matins and his holy things,
Walking his limit round from town to town.
50 Women can now go safely up and down
By every bush or under every tree;
There is no other incubus but he,
So there is really no one else to hurt you
And he will do no more than take your **virtue**.

55   Now it so happened, I began to say,
Long, long ago in good King Arthur's day,
There was a knight who was a lusty liver.
One day as he came riding from the river
He saw a maiden walking all forlorn
60 Ahead of him, alone as she was born.
And of that maiden, spite of all she said,
By very force he took her maidenhead.
        This act of violence made such a stir,
So much petitioning to the king for her,
65 That he condemned the knight to lose his head
By course of law. He was as good as dead
(It seems that then the statutes took that view)
But that the queen, and other ladies too,
Implored the king to exercise his grace
70 So ceaselessly, he gave the queen the case
And granted her his life, and she could choose
Whether to show him mercy or refuse.

        The queen returned him thanks with all her might,
And then she sent a summons to the knight
75 At her convenience, and expressed her will:
"You stand, for such is the position still,
In no way certain of your life," said she,
"Yet you shall live if you can answer me:
What is the thing that women most desire?
80 Beware the axe and say as I require.

        "If you can't answer on the moment, though,
I will concede you this: you are to go
A twelvemonth and a day to seek and learn
Sufficient answer, then you shall return.
85 I shall take gages from you to extort
Surrender of your body to the court."

43 thorpes: villages;
outhouses: sheds.

45 wherever ... elf:
wherever an elf was
accustomed to walk.

49 limit: the area
to which a friar was
restricted in his begging
for donations.

52 incubus (ĭn´kyə-bəs):
an evil spirt belived to
descend on women.

virtue
(vûr´chōō) *n.* purity
or virginity.

**61–62 of that
maiden ...
maidenhead:** in spite of
the maiden's protests,
he robbed her of her
virginity.

85 gages: pledges.

The Wife of Bath's Tale   **79**

APPLYING ACADEMIC VOCABULARY

bias	exploit

As you discuss the Wife's tale, incorporate the Collection 2 academic vocabulary words *bias* and *exploit*. Ask students to explain what **bias** the beginning of the Wife's tale reveals. Then have them talk about the way in which both friars and knights **exploit** their status to get what they want.

Analyze Story Elements: Narrator (LINES 55–72)   COMMON CORE RL 3

Remind students that the Wife of Bath is the narrator of the tale. Explain that readers can make inferences about her traits based on her style of storytelling.

C ASK STUDENTS to explain what aspects of the Wife's narrative style appear in the first part of the tale. *(Her style is straightforward and to the point. She states the knight's crime plainly and without embarrassment.)* What do these elements of her style suggest about her character? *(She is self-assured and does not try to make herself pleasing or inoffensive to others.)*

Analyze Structure: Frame Story (LINE 79)   COMMON CORE RL 5

Tell students that in the prologue to the entire narrative, the Wife of Bath is described as knowing "the remedies for love's mischances, / An art in which she knew the oldest dances." Then have them consider what the queen demands of the knight in the Wife's tale.

D ASK STUDENTS what this line suggests about the Wife's tale. *(It will be about the relationships between men and women. She will share what she knows about love through the events in her tale.)*

> **CRITICAL VOCABULARY**
>
> **virtue:** The Wife suggests that friars are not far removed from the knight she later talks about, preying upon women's chastity. *(lines 57–62)*
>
> ASK STUDENTS what idea about the medieval church is brought out by the Wife's accusation that some friars take women's virtue. *(Some members of the clergy were corrupt.)*

Analyze Story Elements: Narrator (LINES 93–130)

COMMON CORE RL 3

Explain to students that they can make inferences about the Wife's character from the kinds of details she includes in her tale.

E **ASK STUDENTS** to summarize the knight's experience as he travels the land asking people what women want most. What does this part of the tale tell you about the Wife of Bath herself? (*The knight travels far and wide asking people what women want and gets a different answer from every person. This part of the story suggests that the Wife has met many people in her life and understands the way they think. Readers can infer that she herself knows—or believes she knows—the answer to the question and will reveal it through her tale.*)

Remind students that during the Middle Ages, women, other than those of the aristocratic class, had little education.

F **CITE TEXT EVIDENCE** Have students explain how they know the Wife is educated. (*She is familiar with Ovid.*) Ask them why they think Chaucer gave his Wife of Bath this trait. (*He may have wanted to show that women could be as smart or well-educated as men; he is making a point about the competence of the rising middle class.*)

Sad was the knight and sorrowfully sighed,
But there! All other choices were denied,
And in the end he chose to go away
90 And to return after a year and day
Armed with such answer as there might be sent
To him by God. He took his leave and went.

He knocked at every house, searched every place,
Yes, anywhere that offered hope of grace.
95 What could it be that women wanted most?
But all the same he never touched a coast,
Country or town in which there seemed to be
Any two people willing to agree.

Some said that women wanted wealth and treasure,
100 "Honor," said some, some "Jollity and pleasure,"
Some "Gorgeous clothes" and others "Fun in bed,"
"To be oft widowed and remarried," said
Others again, and some that what most mattered
Was that we should be cosseted and flattered.
105 That's very near the truth, it seems to me;
A man can win us best with flattery.
To dance attendance on us, make a fuss,
Ensnares us all, the best and worst of us.

Some say the things we most desire are these:
110 Freedom to do exactly as we please,
With no one to reprove our faults and lies,
Rather to have one call us good and wise.
Truly there's not a woman in ten score
Who has a fault, and someone rubs the sore,
115 But she will kick if what he says is true;
You try it out and you will find so too.
However vicious we may be within
We like to be thought wise and void of sin.
Others assert we women find it sweet
120 When we are thought dependable, discreet
And secret, firm of purpose and controlled,
Never betraying things that we are told.
But that's not worth the handle of a rake;
Women conceal a thing? For Heaven's sake!
125 Remember Midas? Will you hear the tale?

Among some other little things, now stale,
Ovid relates that under his long hair
The unhappy Midas grew a splendid pair
Of ass's ears; as subtly as he might,
130 He kept his foul deformity from sight;

104 cosseted (kŏs´ĭ-tĭd): pampered.

113 ten score: 200.

115 but she will: who will not.

118 void of sin: sinless.

125 Midas: a legendary king of Phrygia, in Asia Minor.

127 Ovid (ŏv´ĭd): an ancient Roman poet whose *Metamorphoses* is a storehouse of Greek and Roman legends.

WHEN STUDENTS STRUGGLE . . .

To help students follow the plot of the Wife's tale, have them work in pairs to summarize important passages in a chart similar to the one shown. Complete the summary for the first passage together, first reading the lines aloud and then modeling how to summarize them.

Point out that the Wife tells the story of Midas (lines 126–156) to make a point about women's ability to keep a secret, but this story is not really part of her tale about the knight. Students may choose to skip this section as they summarize the tale.

Save for his wife, there was not one that knew.
He loved her best, and trusted in her too.
He begged her not to tell a living creature
That he possessed so horrible a feature.

131 **save:** except.

135 And she—she swore, were all the world to win,
She would not do such villainy and sin
As saddle her husband with so foul a name;
Besides to speak would be to share the shame.
Nevertheless she thought she would have died
140 Keeping this secret bottled up inside;
It seemed to swell her heart and she, no doubt,
Thought it was on the point of bursting out.

Fearing to speak of it to woman or man,
Down to a reedy marsh she quickly ran
145 And reached the sedge. Her heart was all on fire

145 **sedge:** marsh grasses.

And, as a bittern bumbles in the mire,
She whispered to the water, near the ground,
"Betray me not, O water, with thy sound!
To thee alone I tell it: it appears

146 **bumbles in the mire:** booms in the swamp. (The bittern, a wading bird, is famous for its loud call.)

150 My husband has a pair of ass's ears!
Ah! My heart's well again, the secret's out!
I could no longer keep it, not a doubt."
And so you see, although we may hold fast
A little while, it must come out at last,
155 We can't keep secrets; as for Midas, well,
Read Ovid for his story; he will tell.

This knight that I am telling you about
Perceived at last he never would find out
What it could be that women loved the best.
160 Faint was the soul within his sorrowful breast,
As home he went, he dared no longer stay;
His year was up and now it was the day.

As he rode home in a dejected mood
Suddenly, at the margin of a wood,
165 He saw a dance upon the leafy floor
Of four and twenty ladies, nay, and more.
Eagerly he approached, in hope to learn
Some words of wisdom ere he should return;
But lo! Before he came to where they were,
170 Dancers and dance all vanished into air!
There wasn't a living creature to be seen
Save one old woman crouched upon the green.
A fouler-looking creature I suppose
Could scarcely be imagined. She arose
175 And said, "Sir knight, there's no way on from here.

CLOSE READ

Analyze Story Elements: Narrator (LINES 153–156)

 COMMON CORE RL 3

Tell students that the Wife's direct comments also provide insight into her character.

 ASK STUDENTS whether the Wife's traits as revealed in this passage make her a likable character. Why or why not? *(In these lines, the Wife shows a sense of humor and the ability to make fun of herself and her gender; this suggests that she would be likable and an asset to the group.)*

Support Inferences: Draw Conclusions (LINES 163–175)

 COMMON CORE RL 1

Explain that in literature, the forest often represents a place untouched by civilization, the home of spirits or other untamed forces of nature.

ASK STUDENTS what they would predict about the Wife's tale based on the scene described in these lines. *(Her tale will contain mystical elements, perhaps an event that cannot be explained logically.)* Point out that this part of the poem relates back to lines 31–49. How might the Wife's inclusion of this passage be interpreted as an insult to the Friar? *(It is suggesting that the "old" religion survives in spite of the efforts of the friars.)*

Lines	Summary
93–98	*The knight travels all over looking for the answer to the queen's question.*
99–122	*He receives a different answer from everyone he asks.*
157–162	*At the end of his year, he still has no answer.*
163–178	*He meets an old woman who offers to help him.*

Analyze Structure: Frame Story (LINES 176–178)

 COMMON CORE RL 5

Tell students that the Wife of Bath has had five husbands. In the General Prologue, her description indicates that although she is no longer young, she still considers herself to be marriage material.

 ASK STUDENTS to explain how these lines might be interpreted in reference to the Wife herself. *(She may be suggesting through the character of the old woman that she still has a lot to offer to her next husband.)*

Analyze Structure: Foreshadowing (LINES 179–196)

COMMON CORE RL 5

Explain that foreshadowing is a literary device that gives clues to what might happen later in the plot.

 ASK STUDENTS how the Wife uses foreshadowing in this part of her tale. *(The old woman forces the knight to make a promise that she will hold him to later in the tale.)* What is the effect of this foreshadowing on readers? *(The foreshadowing builds suspense; readers want to continue reading to find out what the old woman will exact from the knight.)*

Determine Themes

COMMON CORE RL 2

(LINES 211–216)

Explain that Chaucer uses the individual tales to convey ideas about life and the human condition.

K **ASK STUDENTS** what universal idea the knight's answer relates to. *(Women can have the same desire for power over others that men do.)*

CRITICAL VOCABULARY

sovereignty: The answer to the queen's question is that women want to have control over their husbands and lovers.

ASK STUDENTS why this answer, suggesting that women should have sovereignty over certain men, would be particularly significant in the context of the Middle Ages. *(Women did not have the same rights as men or control over their own lives in the way that men did.)*

Tell me what you are looking for, my dear,
For peradventure that were best for you;
We old, old women know a thing or two."

177 peradventure: maybe, possibly.

"Dear Mother," said the knight, "alack the day!
180 I am as good as dead if I can't say
What thing it is that women most desire;
If you could tell me I would pay your hire."
"Give me your hand," she said, "and swear to do
Whatever I shall next require of you
185 —If so to do should lie within your might—
And you shall know the answer before night."
"Upon my honor," he answered, "I agree."
"Then," said the crone, "I dare to guarantee
Your life is safe; I shall make good my claim.
190 Upon my life the queen will say the same.
Show me the very proudest of them all
In costly coverchief or jewelled caul
That dare say no to what I have to teach.
Let us go forward without further speech."
195 And then she crooned her gospel in his ear
And told him to be glad and not to fear.

179 alack the day: an exclamation of sorrow, roughly equivalent to "Woe is me!"

192 coverchief: kerchief; caul (kaul): an ornamental hairnet.

195 gospel: message.

They came to court. This knight, in full array,
Stood forth and said, "O Queen, I've kept my day
And kept my word and have my answer ready."

197 in full array: in all his finery.

200 There sat the noble matrons and the heady
Young girls, and widows too, that have the grace
Of wisdom, all assembled in that place,
And there the queen herself was throned to hear
And judge his answer. Then the knight drew near
205 And silence was commanded through the hall.

200 heady: giddy; impetuous.

201 grace: gift.

The queen gave order he should tell them all
What thing it was that women wanted most.
He stood not silent like a beast or post,
But gave his answer with the ringing word
210 Of a man's voice and the assembly heard:

"My liege and lady, in general," said he,
"A woman wants the self-same **sovereignty**
Over her husband as over her lover,
And master him; he must not be above her.
215 That is your greatest wish, whether you kill
Or spare me; please yourself. I wait your will."

211 liege (lēj): lord.

sovereignty (sŏv´ər-ĭn-tē) *n.* independent rule or authority.

TO CHALLENGE STUDENTS . . .

Storyboard a Scene Would the Wife of Bath's tale make a good movie? Point out that the Wife is telling her story to a group of listeners who must imagine the events she describes. Have students review lines 163–231 and note details that help the audience visualize the scene and that create a fast-paced, dramatic narrative. Ask them to make a storyboard or outline of key moments with notes about how they would film each one. For example, will the camera take in a wide shot or zoom in for a close-up? Invite students to "pitch" their ideas to the class, making the case for why this story would make a great movie.

In all the court not one that shook her head
Or contradicted what the knight had said;
Maid, wife and widow cried, "He's saved his life!"

220 And on the word up started the old wife,
The one the knight saw sitting on the green,
And cried, "Your mercy, sovereign lady queen!
Before the court disperses, do me right!
'Twas I who taught this answer to the knight,
225 For which he swore, and pledged his honor to it,
That the first thing I asked of him he'd do it,
So far as it should lie within his might.
Before this court I ask you then, sir knight,
To keep your word and take me for your wife;
230 For well you know that I have saved your life.
If this be false, deny it on your sword!"

"Alas!" he said, "Old lady, by the Lord
I know indeed that such was my behest,
But for God's love think of a new request,
235 Take all my goods, but leave my body free."
"A curse on us," she said, "if I agree!
I may be foul, I may be poor and old,
Yet will not choose to be, for all the gold
That's bedded in the earth or lies above,
240 Less than your wife, nay, than your very love!"

"My love?" said he. "By heaven, my damnation!
Alas that any of my race and station
Should ever make so foul a misalliance!"
Yet in the end his pleading and defiance
245 All went for nothing, he was forced to wed.

233 behest (bĭ-hĕst´): promise.

242 race and station: family and rank.

243 misalliance (mĭs´ə-lī´əns): an unsuitable marriage.

TEACH

CLOSE READ

Determine Themes

 COMMON CORE **RL 2**

(LINES 220–245)

Point out that the behavior of characters is often used to communicate themes about human nature. This is particularly true when a character undergoes a major change. Have students reread lines 179–187, looking at the way in which the knight responds to the old woman. Then have them read lines 220–245, looking for a change in the knight's attitude toward the old woman.

ASK STUDENTS to describe the contrast between the knight's attitude toward the old woman earlier in the tale (lines 179–197) and his attitude now (lines 220–245). What does the knight's behavior in this passage reveal about his character? *(Earlier in the tale, when he was afraid of losing his life, he was eager to promise the old woman anything. Now he is repelled by her and tries to break his pledge. He shows through his behavior that he doesn't have the strength of character to live up to the terms of his promise.)* Have students discuss what the knight's changed attitude toward the old woman might suggest about human nature. *(Answers will vary, but they might include the following: We often value external beauty above internal beauty; we often try to evade the terms of a difficult promise; it often takes more courage than we have to do the right thing.)*

Strategies for Annotation   ✎ 📖 **Annotate it!**

Determine Themes

COMMON CORE **RL 2**

Encourage students to use their eBook annotation tools.

- Highlight in yellow lines describing the knight's first response to the old woman's demand *(line 187)*.
- Highlight in blue lines that show his reaction when she asks him to honor his pledge.
- On a note, answer this question: What is ironic about the knight's plea that the old woman "leave my body free"? *(His own crime was violating the body of a woman.)*

For well you know that I have saved your life.

If this be false, deny it on your sword.

"Alas!" he said, "Old lady, 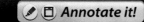by the Lord

I know indeed that such was my behest,

But for God's love think of a new request,

Take all my goods, but leave my body free."

Analyze Story Elements: Narrator (LINES 247–271)

COMMON CORE RL 3

Point out that in lines 247–256, the Wife speaks directly to the other pilgrims.

 ASK STUDENTS to explain the purpose of this digression from her tale. *(The digression allows her to comment ironically on what happens next. In a traditional tale, a wedding would be followed with a celebration, though in this case the knight is so upset by his wife's age and lack of beauty that he wants to "stay hidden like an owl.")*

Make sure students understand that the Wife of Bath is not a member of the noble class but rather belongs to the rising middle class. She lives in a town and is renowned for her weaving of cloth.

 ASK STUDENTS to describe the Wife's attitude toward aristocrats as revealed through what the old woman says in lines 257–271. *(The old woman's words in this part of the text show that the Wife is not intimidated by nobles. She judges them on their behavior, not their titles. If the knight's behavior reflects "the laws of good King Arthur's house," then she is not impressed.)*

Determine Themes (LINES 272–286)

COMMON CORE RL 2

Remind students that theme is brought out through the characters' words and actions.

O ASK STUDENTS to explain the irony of the knight's calling the old woman "low-bred" in the context of this passage. *(He is the one acting "low" or rudely. In fact, it was his low behavior—assaulting a maiden—that got him into trouble at the beginning of the Wife of Bath's Tale.)*

He takes his ancient wife and goes to bed.

    Now peradventure some may well suspect
A lack of care in me since I neglect
To tell of the rejoicing and display
250 Made at the feast upon their wedding-day.
I have but a short answer to let fall;
I say there was no joy or feast at all,

    Nothing but heaviness of heart and sorrow.
He married her in private on the morrow
255 And all day long stayed hidden like an owl,
It was such torture that his wife looked foul.

    Great was the anguish churning in his head
When he and she were piloted to bed;
He wallowed back and forth in desperate style.
260 His ancient wife lay smiling all the while;
At last she said, "Bless us! Is this, my dear,
How knights and wives get on together here?
Are these the laws of good King Arthur's house?
Are knights of his all so contemptuous?
265 I am your own beloved and your wife,
And I am she, indeed, that saved your life;
And certainly I never did you wrong.
Then why, this first of nights, so sad a song?
You're carrying on as if you were half-witted.
270 Say, for God's love, what sin have I committed?
I'll put things right if you will tell me how."

    "Put right?" he cried. "That never can be now!
Nothing can ever be put right again!
You're old, and so abominably plain,
275 So poor to start with, so low-bred to follow;
It's little wonder if I twist and wallow!
God, that my heart would burst within my breast!"

    "Is that," said she, "the cause of your unrest?"

    "Yes, certainly," he said, "and can you wonder?"

280   "I could set right what you suppose a blunder,
That's if I cared to, in a day or two,
If I were shown more courtesy by you.
Just now," she said, "you spoke of gentle birth,
Such as descends from ancient wealth and worth.
285 If that's the claim you make for gentlemen
Such arrogance is hardly worth a hen.

258 piloted: led. (In the Middle Ages, the wedding party typically escorted the bride and groom to their bedchamber.).

259 wallowed: (wŏl´ōd) rolled around; thrashed about.

WHEN STUDENTS STRUGGLE. . .

Make sure students understand that a theme is the author's message to readers, a lesson or idea about life that he or she wants them to take from the work. To facilitate their understanding of theme, have students work in pairs to complete a chart like the one shown, using the details to infer the author's meaning.

P

Whoever loves to work for virtuous ends,
Public and private, and who most intends
To do what deeds of gentleness he can,
290 Take him to be the greatest gentleman.
Christ wills we take our gentleness from Him,
Not from a wealth of ancestry long dim,
Though they **bequeath** their whole establishment
By which we claim to be of high descent.
295 Our fathers cannot make us a bequest
Of all those virtues that became them best
And earned for them the name of gentlemen,
But bade us follow them as best we can.

     "Thus the wise poet of the Florentines,
300 Dante by name, has written in these lines,
For such is the opinion Dante launches:
'Seldom arises by these slender branches
Prowess of men, for it is God, no less,
Wills us to claim of Him our gentleness.'
305 For of our parents nothing can we claim
Save temporal things, and these may hurt and maim.

     "But everyone knows this as well as I;
For if gentility were implanted by
The natural course of lineage down the line,
310 Public or private, could it cease to shine
In doing the fair work of gentle deed?
No vice or villainy could then bear seed.

     "Take fire and carry it to the darkest house
Between this kingdom and the Caucasus,
315 And shut the doors on it and leave it there,
It will burn on, and it will burn as fair
As if ten thousand men were there to see,
For fire will keep its nature and degree,
I can assure you, sir, until it dies.

320   "But gentleness, as you will recognize,
Is not annexed in nature to possessions.
Men fail in living up to their professions;
But fire never ceases to be fire.
God knows you'll often find, if you enquire,
325 Some lording full of villainy and shame.
If you would be esteemed for the mere name
Of having been by birth a gentleman
And stemming from some virtuous, noble clan,
And do not live yourself by gentle deed
330 Or take your father's noble code and creed,

bequeath
(bĭ-kwēth´) *v.* to pass
on to heirs.

299 Florentines: the
people of Florence, Italy.

300 Dante (dän´tā): a
famous medieval Italian
poet. Lines 302–304
refer to a passage in
Dante's most famous
work, *The Divine Comedy.*

306 temporal: worldly,
rather than spiritual.

308 gentility
(jĕn-tĭl´ĭ-tē): the quality
possessed by a gentle, or
noble, person.

314 Caucasus
(kô´kə-səs): a region of
western Asia, between
the Black and Caspian
seas.

322 professions:
beliefs; ideals.

325 lording: lord;
nobleman.

CLOSE READ

Determine Themes
(LINES 287–298)

COMMON CORE RL 2

Have students reread these lines, looking for the
message that Chaucer is conveying.

P **CITE TEXT EVIDENCE** What is the definition
of true nobility, according to the old woman? Cite
details from the text that support this definition.
*(True nobility springs from a quality of gentleness that
makes someone try to live a virtuous and good life. The
old woman points out that "Our fathers cannot make us
a bequest / of all those virtues that . . . earned for them
the name of gentlemen." In other words, noble birth has
nothing to do with true nobility. Instead, "Whoever loves
to work for virtuous ends" is "the greatest gentleman.")*
How does this idea relate back to the knight's original
behavior? *(The knight lacks nobility of spirit, as shown
by the terrible deed he did to the young maiden.)*

CRITICAL VOCABULARY

bequeath: The old woman says that while parents
can hand down their material possessions to their
children, they cannot hand down the virtue that
they have earned from their own behavior.

ASK STUDENTS how a person cultivates gentility
if a parent cannot bequeath it. *(Gentility can be
learned by observing and following the examples
of others, by thinking of others before oneself, or by
setting high standards for behavior and trying to live
up to them.)*

Detail: *Knight assaults a maiden.*		
Detail: *Knight is rude to the old woman.*	→	Theme: *(A person's appearance can be deceiving.)*
Detail: *Knight claims to be a gentleman.*		

Support Inferences

COMMON CORE RL 1

(LINES 345–364)

Remind students that in reading a work of literature they must often combine the details in the text with their own knowledge to make logical assumptions.

Q **ASK STUDENTS** to explain the old woman's function in the tale based on her speech to the knight. *(Her purpose or function is to bring the knight to a greater understanding of what it means to be a good person. She is supposed to reform or redeem him.)* Why does Chaucer make her speech so long? *(The length of this speech gives the knight a chance to absorb what she is saying and gives Chaucer the opportunity to develop his themes. It also adds strength to the argument because the old woman provides many supporting examples and details.)*

"Gentility must come from God alone."

You are no gentleman, though duke or earl.
Vice and bad manners are what make a churl.

    "Gentility is only the renown
For bounty that your fathers handed down,
335 Quite foreign to your person, not your own;
Gentility must come from God alone.
That we are gentle comes to us by grace
And by no means is it bequeathed with place.

    "Reflect how noble (says Valerius)
340 Was Tullius surnamed Hostilius,
Who rose from poverty to nobleness.
And read Boethius, Seneca no less,
Thus they express themselves and are agreed:
'Gentle is he that does a gentle deed.'
345 And therefore, my dear husband, I conclude
That even if my ancestors were rude,
Yet God on high—and so I hope He will—
Can grant me grace to live in virtue still,
A gentlewoman only when beginning
350 To live in virtue and to shrink from sinning.

    "As for my poverty which you reprove,
Almighty God Himself in whom we move,
Believe and have our being, chose a life
Of poverty, and every man or wife,
355 Nay, every child can see our Heavenly King
Would never stoop to choose a shameful thing.
No shame in poverty if the heart is gay,
As Seneca and all the learned say.
He who accepts his poverty unhurt
360 I'd say is rich although he lacked a shirt.
But truly poor are they who whine and fret
And covet what they cannot hope to get.
And he that, having nothing, covets not,
Is rich, though you may think he is a sot.

332 churl (chûrl): low-class person; boor.

339 Valerius (və-lîr´ē-əs): Valerius Maximus, a Roman writer who compiled a collection of historical anecdotes.

340 Tullius (tŭl´ē-əs): surnamed Hostilius (hŏ-stĭl´ē-əs): the third king of the Romans.

342 Boethius (bō-ē´thē-əs): a Christian philosopher of the Dark Ages.; **Seneca** (sĕn´ĭ-kə): an ancient Roman philosopher, writer, teacher, and politician.

364 sot: fool.

SCAFFOLDING FOR ELL STUDENTS

Support Inferences The old woman's speech contains ideas about gentility (courtesy), poverty, and old age. Create mixed language-ability groups and assign each a passage to examine: lines 336–338, lines 361–364, or lines 381–386. Students will need to define several multiple-meaning words in context: *place* in line 338 ("social position"), *taxed* in line 381 ("accused, pointed out a fault"), *breeding* in line 385 ("good manners or behavior that result from training or upbringing"). Ask groups to explain the main idea brought out by each passage. Then, as a class, discuss what the old woman is trying to teach the knight about his treatment of others.

365   "True poverty can find a song to sing.
Juvenal says a pleasant little thing:
'The poor can dance and sing in the relief
Of having nothing that will tempt a thief.'
Though it be hateful, poverty is good,
370 A great incentive to a livelihood,
And a great help to our capacity
For wisdom, if accepted patiently.
Poverty is, though wanting in estate,
A kind of wealth that none calumniate.
375 Poverty often, when the heart is lowly,
Brings one to God and teaches what is holy,
Gives knowledge of oneself and even lends
A glass by which to see one's truest friends.
And since it's no offense, let me be plain;
380 Do not **rebuke** my poverty again.

    "Lastly you taxed me, sir, with being old.
Yet even if you never had been told
By ancient books, you gentlemen engage,
Yourselves in honor to respect old age.
385 To call an old man 'father' shows good breeding,
And this could be supported from my reading.

    "You say I'm old and fouler than a fen.
You need not fear to be a cuckold, then.
Filth and old age, I'm sure you will agree,
390 Are powerful wardens over chastity.
Nevertheless, well knowing your delights,
I shall fulfil your worldly appetites.

    "You have two choices; which one will you try?
To have me old and ugly till I die,
395 But still a loyal, true, and humble wife
That never will displease you all her life,
Or would you rather I were young and pretty
And chance your arm what happens in a city
Where friends will visit you because of me,
400 Yes, and in other places too, maybe.
Which would you have? The choice is all your own."

    The knight thought long, and with a piteous groan
At last he said, with all the care in life,
"My lady and my love, my dearest wife,
405 I leave the matter to your wise decision.
You make the choice yourself, for the provision
Of what may be agreeable and rich

366 Juvenal
(jōō´və-nəl): an ancient
Roman satirist.

373 wanting in estate:
lacking in grandeur.

374 calumniate
(kə-lŭm´nē-āt´):
criticize with false
statements; slander.

rebuke
(rĭ-byōōk´) *v.* to
reprimand or scold.

387 fen: marsh.

388 cuckold (kŭk´əld):
a husband whose wife is
unfaithful.

398 chance your arm:
take your chance on.

The Wife of Bath's Tale   **87**

CLOSE READ

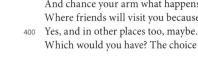

Analyze Story Elements: Narrator (LINES 381–392)

COMMON CORE RL 3

R **ASK STUDENTS** why the narrator's focus is on the old woman rather than the knight in this part of the tale. (*The Wife of Bath is showing that the old woman has much wisdom to impart to the brash knight. It is the old woman who will deliver the theme, or moral, of the tale.*)

Support Inferences

COMMON CORE RL 1

(LINES 402–409)

Remind students that the turning point of a story or narrative poem is the moment of highest tension after which the conflict is resolved or the change in a character can be seen.

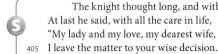

S **ASK STUDENTS** why this is the turning point of the tale. (*After much deliberation, the knight makes the right choice, giving his wife what all women want—sovereignty over their husbands.*) What can be inferred about the knight from what he says in these lines? (*The knight has changed. He has learned to respect others.*)

CRITICAL VOCABULARY

rebuke: The old woman warns the knight not to criticize her condition of poverty again.

ASK STUDENTS why the poet chooses the word *rebuke* rather than a synonym such as *scold.* (Rebuke *has a stronger connotation, showing the firmness of the old woman's warning.*)

CLOSE READ

Determine Themes

COMMON CORE RL 2

(LINES 424–430)

 ASK STUDENTS to explain what message is implied by the old woman's transformation into a young, beautiful woman. (*Positive change will be rewarded; love is transformative.*)

Analyze Story Elements: Narrator (LINES 431–438)

COMMON CORE RL 3

U **CITE TEXT EVIDENCE** Have students discuss what this last stanza of the poem reveals about the Wife of Bath. What details support these conclusions? (*She would like a young husband herself: "may Christ Jesus send/Us husbands meek and young and fresh in bed." She has nothing but hostility toward controlling and miserly husbands, suggesting that at least one of hers had these characteristics:"cut short the lives /Of those who won't be governed by their wives; / And all old, angry niggards of their pence."*)

COLLABORATIVE DISCUSSION Suggest that pairs skim the selection to find details that support their analysis of the Wife of Bath's character. Have them share their analysis of her traits and the ways in which the tale fits her personality. Accept all reasonable responses.

ASK STUDENTS to share any questions they generated in the course of reading and discussing the selection.

In honor to us both, I don't care which;
Whatever pleases you suffices me."

410　　　"And have I won the mastery?" said she,
"Since I'm to choose and rule as I think fit?"
"Certainly, wife," he answered her, "that's it."
"Kiss me," she cried. "No quarrels! On my oath
And word of honor, you shall find me both,
415　That is, both fair and faithful as a wife;
May I go howling mad and take my life
Unless I prove to be as good and true
As ever wife was since the world was new!
And if tomorrow when the sun's above
420　I seem less fair than any lady-love,
Than any queen or empress east or west,
Do with my life and death as you think best.
Cast up the curtain, husband. Look at me!"

　　　And when indeed the knight had looked to see,
425　Lo, she was young and lovely, rich in charms.
In ecstasy he caught her in his arms,
His heart went bathing in a bath of blisses
And melted in a hundred thousand kisses,
And she responded in the fullest measure
430　With all that could delight or give him pleasure.

　　　So they lived ever after to the end
In perfect bliss; and may Christ Jesus send
Us husbands meek and young and fresh in bed,
And grace to overbid them when we wed.
435　And—Jesu hear my prayer!—cut short the lives
Of those who won't be governed by their wives;
And all old, angry niggards of their pence,
God send them soon a very pestilence!

COLLABORATIVE DISCUSSION With a partner, discuss your impression of the Wife of Bath. Explain whether you think her tale is well-suited to her personality.

WHEN STUDENTS STRUGGLE . . .

Have pairs complete these sentences regarding lines 402–430:

- Before the old woman's speech, the knight is . . . (*disrespectful, arrogant, and brutal*)
- After the old woman's speech, the knight is . . . (*more self-aware, respectful, and enlightened*)
- The old woman becomes young and beautiful because . . . (*the knight gives her sovereignty*)
- Through this conclusion, Chaucer shows that . . . (*good behavior is rewarded*)

Analyze Structure: Frame Story COMMON CORE RL 5

The Canterbury Tales has a complex structure that features a **frame story**—a story that surrounds and binds together one or more different narratives in a single work. The frame story in *The Canterbury Tales* is made up of the General Prologue, in which the characters, setting, and storytelling premise are introduced, as well as the main narrator's account of what the pilgrims say and do between each of their tales.

In addition to unifying the tales told by the pilgrims, the frame story provides a vivid portrait of each pilgrim. Through the initial descriptions as well as the later interactions among the pilgrims, readers learn about the places they occupy in medieval society. These interactions enable Chaucer to present insights about practices and institutions in this time period; for example, his portrayals of the clergy and church officials reveal the corruption of the church.

Chaucer also uses the frame story to explore relationships between pilgrims. In "The Wife of Bath's Prologue," the Friar interrupts the Wife of Bath's long account of her five husbands, which prefaces her actual story: "Well, Ma'am, . . . as God may send me bliss,/ This is a long preamble to a tale!" His comment reveals the antagonism between the two of them, which is further developed in the Wife's tale.

Analyze Story Elements: Narrator COMMON CORE RL 3

The **narrator** of a story is the character or voice that relates the story's events to the reader. Chaucer created multiple narrators for *The Canterbury Tales*. The narrator of the frame story describes the pilgrims and records their exchanges with one another. The pilgrims, in turn, narrate their own tales. You can gain insight into the Wife of Bath by examining the following elements in her narration:

Subject and Theme	Direct Statements	Tone
Narrators who are characters in a story usually choose subjects and themes relevant to their own experiences. For example, the Wife of Bath, who has been married five times, tells a tale about relationships between men and women.	Narrators sometimes comment directly on characters and events. The Wife of Bath makes statements on a variety of topics, such as the type of husband she values and the ability of women to keep secrets.	A narrator's tone, or attitude toward a subject, provides clues about the narrator's personality. Usually tone is communicated through word choice and details. Notice the words that the Wife of Bath uses to describe the knight's predicament. What kind of person comes across through this tone?

CLOSE READ

Analyze Structure: Frame Story COMMON CORE RL 5

Make sure students understand the concept of the frame story. Ask them if they can think of other classic or contemporary books or movies that use a frame-story structure. *(The Thousand and One Nights, The Decameron, Citizen Kane, Slumdog Millionaire)*

Analyze Story Elements: Narrator COMMON CORE RL 3

Remind students that the choice of a narrator affects the way in which readers understand plot, character, and even theme. Have them reread the prologue to the Wife's tale (lines 1–28). Ask students how they would describe the narrator in this part of the tale and why. *(The narrator is neutral, offering no opinions and just reporting on the dialogue of the characters.)* Then ask them how the Wife of Bath differs in her style of narration. *(Her personality and personal views are conveyed through her comments and tone.)*

Strategies for Annotation  ✎ 📋 *Annotate it!*

Analyze Story Elements: Narrator COMMON CORE RL 3

Share these strategies for guided or independent analysis:

- Highlight in green passages in which the Wife conveys a distinct tone or attitude.
- Highlight in pink lines that express her direct opinion.
- On a note, explain how her perspective affects readers' understanding of story events, characters, and themes.

"To be oft widowed and remarried," said

Others again, and some that what most mattered

Was that we should be cosseted and flattered.

That's very near the truth, it seems to me;

A man can win us best with flattery.

PRACTICE & APPLY

Analyzing the Text COMMON CORE RL 1, RL 2, RL 3, RL 5

Possible answers:

1. The frame story establishes the hostility between the Friar and the Wife. Therefore, readers understand that the Wife is insulting the Friar through her ironic commentary on the behavior of friars. She ends by accusing friars of taking advantage of maidens in line 54, "And he will do no more than take your virtue," just as the knight does, thus providing a fitting transition into her tale by equating friars and the knight.

2. The answers to the knight's question show that the Wife enjoys being flattered and made a fuss of (lines 105–108); that she doesn't like to have her faults pointed out (lines 111–116); and that she doesn't believe women can keep a secret (lines 120–125).

3. This story serves the purpose of keeping listeners in suspense as they wonder whether the knight will learn the answer or lose his life. It also balances the story of the knight with some humor and the admission that women are not perfect either. Finally, it shows that the Wife is well read and knowledgeable.

4. The Wife's tone is one of amused irony. She says that the knight "wallowed back and forth in desperate style." Ironically, he acts as if the old woman has ruined his life, when in fact she has saved him, a rapist, from the death penalty and now wishes only to please him. The Wife's tone increases his contemptibility and the readers' view of him as not worthy to be called a knight.

5. The old woman is a crone until the knight accepts her for the qualities beneath her foul exterior and gives her sovereignty over her own life. The duality of her character illustrates the importance of looking beneath the surface to find someone's intrinsic qualities and of treating all others with respect. The knight becomes truly noble only when he learns humility and the importance of respecting all others.

6. Essentially the knight is rewarded for a serious crime. Yet, the happy ending may be seen as necessary to show his change and to convey a message about humility and respect.

7. The Wife of Bath is a consummate storyteller. She builds suspense through strategic digressions; she balances the serious parts of the story with humor; she develops significant themes.

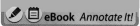

Analyzing the Text COMMON CORE RL 1, RL 2, RL 3, RL 5, W 4

Cite Text Evidence   Support your responses with evidence from the selection.

1. **Identify** The interaction between the Wife of Bath and the Friar in "The Wife of Bath's Prologue" is part of Chaucer's frame story. What connections can be made between this section of the prologue and the tale itself?

2. **Infer** As a narrator, the Wife of Bath comments extensively about the various answers to the knight's question. What do her comments reveal about her own values and ideas? Use evidence from the poem to support your analysis.

3. **Draw Conclusions** The story of Midas appears to be unrelated to the tale of the knight. What narrative purpose or purposes does this digression serve?

4. **Analyze** What is the Wife's tone as she narrates the account of the knight's wedding night? How does her tone influence readers' view of this scene?

5. **Analyze** Chaucer explores the idea that "appearances can be deceiving" through the character of the old woman. How does this theme relate to the earlier events in the tale?

6. **Evaluate** Review the last two stanzas of the poem. Does this happy ending provide a satisfying conclusion, or is it disturbing? Explain your response.

7. **Critique** In "The Wife of Bath's Prologue," the Friar complains about the Wife of Bath's long, rambling preamble. How effective is she at narrating her tale about the knight? Explain your response.

PERFORMANCE TASK

Writing Activity: Character Analysis When the queen demands that the knight find out "What is the thing that women most desire?" he searches for a whole year to find an answer. Does the knight gain understanding of women over the course of the story, or is he still essentially the same as he was at the beginning? Respond to this question by writing a character analysis. Consider the following:

- the knight's initial crime
- his reaction to the old woman after she insists that he marry her
- his response to the choice she offers him on their wedding night

---

Assign this performance task.

PERFORMANCE TASK COMMON CORE W 4

Writing Activity: Character Analysis Have students write their character analyses independently. Remind them to incorporate direct quotations and specific details from the poem to support their view of whether the knight changes. Have students share their essays in small groups.

Critical Vocabulary

preamble	virtue	sovereignty
bequeath	rebuke	

Practice and Apply Use your knowledge of the Critical Vocabulary words to respond to each question.

1. The Wife of Bath chose some of her husbands based on what they could *bequeath* to her. What characteristic did these husbands share?

2. The nuns on the pilgrimage wear clothes that protect their *virtue*. What do their outfits probably look like?

3. After the Friar tells his tale, the Wife of Bath *rebukes* him. What does the Wife think of the tale?

4. As a widow, the Wife of Bath has *sovereignty* over her financial affairs. What can she spend her money on? Explain.

5. Because of the long *preamble*, listeners were prepared for the surprising nature of the tale. Explain why.

Vocabulary Strategy: Usage

The English language is dynamic. New words become part of it; other words are dropped; still others are used in a way that is different from their original or earlier meanings. In line 54 of the poem, Chaucer uses the Critical Vocabulary word *virtue*. "And he will do no more than take your virtue." In this line, *virtue* means "chastity" or "purity." Readers today, however, more commonly interpret *virtue* to mean "a good quality." The chart shows examples of other words found in the poem that are used differently today than they were in Chaucer's time:

Word in the Poem	Meaning in the 14th Century
gentle: "Gentle is he that does a gentle deed."	noble
rude: "even if my ancestors were rude"	of low birth
fair: "And if tomorrow when the sun's above I seem less fair than any lady-love"	beautiful

Practice and Apply Complete the following steps:

1. Define the word in the chart as it is commonly used today.

2. Write a sentence that illustrates a current usage of each word.

3. Work in a small group to identify other words in the poem that have changed their meanings over the years. Share the words and their old and new usages with the class.

PRACTICE & APPLY

Critical Vocabulary

Answers:

1. *Her husbands were wealthy and perhaps old. They could leave money to her.*

2. *Their outfits cover their bodies from head to toe to discourage any impure thoughts.*

3. *She scolds the Friar, showing her disapproval of the tale.*

4. *She can spend her money on anything she chooses since she has control over her finances.*

5. *Before listeners heard the tale, the preamble gave many hints as to what it would be about.*

Vocabulary Strategy: Usage

gentle: *considerate, tender*

rude: *without manners, discourteous*

fair: *light in hair color or complexion; just, unbiased*

Strategies for Annotation ✏️ 🖥️ *Annotate it!*

Usage

Have students use their eBook annotation tools to help them with the third part of the Usage activity.

- Skim the poem, looking for words that are used in an unfamiliar way. Highlight the words in yellow.
- Underline side notes or context clues that help you define the word as it is used in the poem.
- Use a dictionary or other resource to confirm the word's common usage today.

Great was the anguish churning in his head

When he and she were piloted to bed;

He wallowed back and forth in desperate style.

His ancient wife lay smiling all the while;

258 piloted: led

PRACTICE & APPLY

Language and Style: Inverted Sentences

 COMMON CORE L 3a

Have students work in pairs to find other examples of inverted sentences in the Wife's tale. Write them on the board and discuss which elements of the sentences have been reversed from their usual order. *(Examples: line 257—"Great was the anguish churning in his head"; lines 305–306—"For of our parents nothing can we claim / Save temporal things, and these may hurt and maim.")*

Sample answers:

1. *There was the old woman on the green.*

2. *In front of the court stood the knight.*

3. *Foul was she in appearance.*

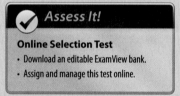

✓ Assess It!

Online Selection Test
- Download an editable ExamView bank.
- Assign and manage this test online.

Language and Style: Inverted Sentences

 COMMON CORE L 3a

An **inverted sentence** is one in which the normal order of a subject followed by a verb is reversed. Notice how Chaucer uses inversion in these lines from the poem:

> This knight that I am telling you about
> Perceived at last he never would find out
> What it could be that women loved the best.
> Faint was the soul within his sorrowful breast,
> As home he went, he dared no longer stay;
> His year was up and now it was the day.

If Chaucer had chosen not to use inversion, his lines might have appeared this way:

> This knight that I am telling you about
> Perceived at last he never would find out
> What it could be that women loved the best.
> His soul within his sorrowful breast was faint,
> As home he went, he dared no longer stay;
> His year was up and now it was the day.

By inverting the sentence in the fourth line, Chaucer preserves his rhyming couplet. Just as importantly he maintains the effective rhythm of his poem. In the second version of the lines with the subject placed before the verb, the rhyme is lost. In addition, the rhythm of the line is stilted and awkward and takes away from the effectiveness of the whole stanza.

Writers of prose also use inversion. Varying sentence structure by reversing the subject-verb order enables writers to refocus the attention of their readers. In addition, inverted sentences add emphasis by building up suspense with words and phrases before arriving at the verb and subject. When inverting sentences in your own writing, it is important to remember to check that the subject and verb agree in number.

Regular Order	Inverted Order
The old woman lurks behind the knights.	Behind the knights lurks the old woman.
The knights travel over the fields and through every village.	Over the fields and through every village travel the knights.

Practice and Apply Write three inverted sentences about events in "The Wife of Bath's Tale."

Analyze Theme

COMMON CORE

RL 2

TEACH

Clarify for students that theme is the underlying message about life or human nature communicated through the elements of a work of fiction. Because the theme is generally implied rather than stated, readers must look closely at the literary elements to discover the author's intended message. In complex or longer works, there may be more than one theme or one interpretation of the meaning.

Discuss with students these ideas related to the analysis of the meaning in the Wife's tale:

- The main **characters** are the knight and the old woman. In the Middle Ages, a highly structured class system existed. The knight was near the top of society, viewed as having high birth and noble qualities. An old woman, without family or resources, would be on the very fringes of society. Their interactions as well as the traits they possess suggest that Chaucer is sending a message related to the idea of rank defining character.

- **Conflict** develops the action in the tale. In the Wife's tale, the knight is central to the conflict, having first violated his supposed ideals and the social mores of his culture. His quest results in internal conflict as he appears to face failure and death. His resistance to honoring his side of the bargain with the old woman then pits him against her. At the end of the tale, he resolves this external conflict, and in doing so, changes, just as his wife does, another clue to Chaucer's theme.

PRACTICE AND APPLY

Have students work with a partner to create a large-scale web diagram that illustrates how ideas derived from character and conflict contribute to an overall theme or themes. Remind them to provide text details that support their analysis of character and conflict. Ask pairs to explain their webs to the class. Compare interpretations of theme. *(Possible themes: People's worth does not depend on their rank; women should have mastery over their own lives. Both are shown through the transformation of the knight who learns to respect others and act in humility.)*

 If students need further instruction, use this *Interactive Whiteboard Lesson:* **Theme/Central Idea.**

Analyze Story Elements: Narrator

COMMON CORE

RI 3

RETEACH

Review the ways in which the narrator's character is revealed through the choice of subject, the tale's theme and tone, and direct comments. Present students with this example:

Little Red Riding Hood wasn't as gullible as she seemed. As she approached the wolf lying in her grandmother's bed, she played it cool, acting as if she didn't know that the big hairy face staring out at her wasn't dear old Grandma. The wolf, caught up in his little playacting, was fooled by her apparent willingness to accept him. That is, until she started pelting him with the under-ripe fruits and vegetables in her basket. One concussion later, he had learned the hard way not to judge a book by its cover.

- Have students identify the narrator's tone. *(The narrator is critical of the wolf and approving of Little Red Riding Hood.)*

- Have students discuss their perception of the narrator based on the clues in this passage. *(The narrator likes strong individuals who stand up for themselves and doesn't like bullies, like the wolf, who take advantage of others.)*

 Assign the following *Level Up* tutorial: **Point of View**

CLOSE READING APPLICATION

Have students return to the description of the Wife of Bath from the General Prologue. Ask them to describe the narrator of this part of the frame story, based on the tone of the Wife's description and the details included.

The Pardoner's Tale

Narrative Poem by Geoffrey Chaucer

Why This Text

Students may be challenged by the story elements in a long narrative poem. "The Pardoner's Tale" will provide students the opportunity to analyze a complex character, the Pardoner, who narrates the tale. With the help of the close-reading questions, students will analyze the techniques Chaucer uses to convey his themes. They will identify and explain Chaucer's use of irony, and explain the narrator's motivations and goals. This close reading will lead students to develop an understanding and appreciation of one of Chaucer's main works.

Background Have students read the background and the information about the author. Tell students that "The Pardoner's Tale" is one of 24 stories narrated by a group of pilgrims traveling through the southeast of England to Canterbury Cathedral. Each story ends up revealing more about the narrator than it does about others.

AS YOU READ Ask students to pay attention to clues to Chaucer's use of irony in his development of the narrator. How soon into the poem can they begin to infer the ethics and morality of the Pardoner?

Common Core Support

- cite strong and thorough textual evidence

- analyze the impact of the author's choices regarding how to relate elements of a story

- analyze how an author's choices concerning how to structure a text add to its meaning

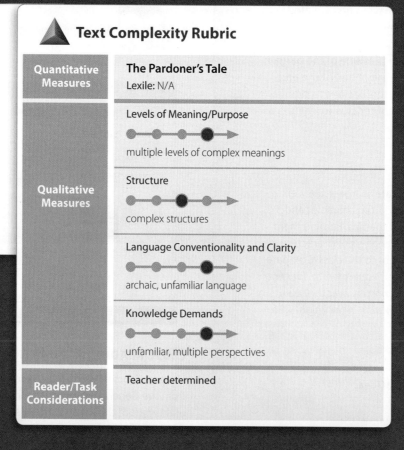

Text Complexity Rubric

Quantitative Measures	**The Pardoner's Tale** Lexile: N/A
Qualitative Measures	Levels of Meaning/Purpose — multiple levels of complex meanings
	Structure — complex structures
	Language Conventionality and Clarity — archaic, unfamiliar language
	Knowledge Demands — unfamiliar, multiple perspectives
Reader/Task Considerations	Teacher determined

Strategies for CLOSE READING

Analyze Story Elements: Narrator

Students should read this narrative poem carefully all the way through. Close-reading questions at the bottom of the page will help them focus on a thorough analysis of the poem. As they read, students should jot down comments or questions about the text in the side margins.

WHEN STUDENTS STRUGGLE . . .

To help students assess the character of the Pardoner, have them work in small groups to fill out a chart like the one shown below.

CITE TEXT EVIDENCE For practice in analyzing the narrator of "The Pardoner's Tale," ask students to cite evidence that offers clues to the Pardoner's morality.

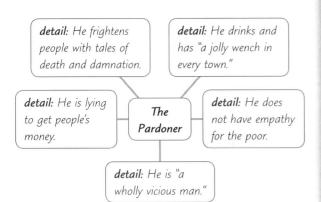

detail: He frightens people with tales of death and damnation.

detail: He drinks and has "a jolly wench in every town."

detail: He is lying to get people's money.

The Pardoner

detail: He does not have empathy for the poor.

detail: He is "a wholly vicious man."

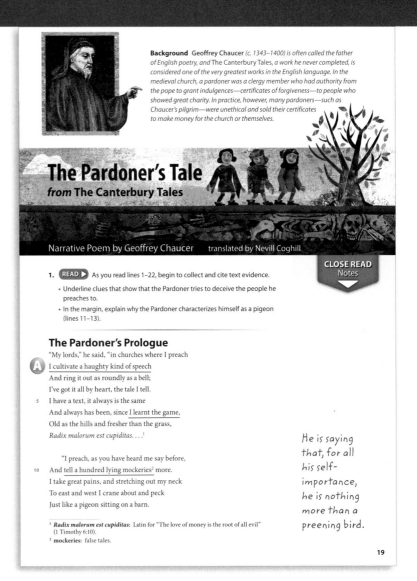

Background Geoffrey Chaucer (c. 1343–1400) is often called the father of English poetry, and The Canterbury Tales, a work he never completed, is considered one of the very greatest works in the English language. In the medieval church, a pardoner was a clergy member who had authority from the pope to grant indulgences—certificates of forgiveness—to people who showed great charity. In practice, however, many pardoners—such as Chaucer's pilgrim—were unethical and sold their certificates to make money for the church or themselves.

The Pardoner's Tale
from The Canterbury Tales

Narrative Poem by Geoffrey Chaucer   translated by Nevill Coghill

CLOSE READ
Notes

1. **READD** As you read lines 1–22, begin to collect and cite text evidence.
   - Underline clues that show that the Pardoner tries to deceive the people he preaches to.
   - In the margin, explain why the Pardoner characterizes himself as a pigeon (lines 11–13).

The Pardoner's Prologue

"My lords," he said, "in churches where I preach
A I cultivate a haughty kind of speech
And ring it out as roundly as a bell;
I've got it all by heart, the tale I tell.
5 I have a text, it always is the same
And always has been, since I learnt the game,
Old as the hills and fresher than the grass,
Radix malorum est cupiditas. . . .[1]

"I preach, as you have heard me say before,
10 And tell a hundred lying mockeries[2] more.
I take great pains, and stretching out my neck
To east and west I crane about and peck
Just like a pigeon sitting on a barn.

[1] *Radix malorum est cupiditas:* Latin for "The love of money is the root of all evil" (1 Timothy 6:10).
[2] *mockeries:* false tales.

He is saying that, for all his self-importance, he is nothing more than a preening bird.

19

1. READ AND CITE TEXT EVIDENCE

A **ASK STUDENTS** to cite evidence that clues the reader in to the character of the Pardoner. *Students should recognize that the Pardoner is telling his listeners right up front how he lies in church to sell pardons and make money. The evidence students cite will vary. Lines 2, 6, 10, and 14 are evidence that he is lying. Lines 19–21 make clear that he wants "to win" and does not care what happens to the immortal souls of his clients.*

CLOSE READ
Notes

My hands and tongue together spin the yarn
15   And all my antics are a joy to see.
The curse of **avarice** and cupidity
Is all my sermon, for it frees the pelf.[3]
Out come the pence,[4] and specially for myself,
(B) For my exclusive purpose is to win
20   And not at all to **castigate** their sin.
Once dead what matter how their souls may fare?
They can go blackberrying, for all I care! . . .

"And thus I preach against the very vice
I make my living out of—avarice.
25   And yet however guilty of that sin
Myself, with others I have power to win
Them from it, I can bring them to repent;
But that is not my principal intent.
Covetousness is both the root and stuff
30   Of all I preach. That ought to be enough.

"Well, then I give examples thick and fast
From bygone times, old stories from the past.
(C) A yokel[5] mind loves stories from of old,
Being the kind it can repeat and hold.
35   What! Do you think, as long as I can preach
And get their silver for the things I teach,
That I will live in poverty, from choice?
That's not the counsel of my inner voice!

[3] **pelf:** riches.
[4] **pence:** pennies.
[5] **yokel:** rustic.

avarice:
greed

castigate:
to criticize

2. **◀ REREAD** Reread lines 19–20. Paraphrase what the Pardoner says. What is his "exclusive purpose"?

The Pardoner's only aim is to get money from people. He does not care about any sins they may have committed.

3. **READ ▶** As you read lines 23–57, continue to cite textual evidence.
- Underline text that reveals what the Pardoner really thinks of those to whom he sells forgiveness.
- Circle statements in which the Pardoner reveals his own character.

20

CLOSE READ
Notes

No! Let me preach and beg from kirk[6] to kirk
40   And never do an honest job of work,
No, nor make baskets, like St. Paul, to gain
A livelihood. I do not preach in vain.
There's no apostle I would **counterfeit**;
I mean to have money, wool and cheese and wheat
45   Though it were given me by the poorest lad
Or poorest village widow, though she had
A string of starving children, all agape.
No, let me drink the liquor of the grape
And keep a jolly wench in every town!

50   "But listen, gentlemen; to bring things down
To a conclusion, would you like a tale?
Now as I've drunk a draft of corn-ripe ale,
By God it stands to reason I can strike
On some good story that you all will like.
(D) 55   For though I am a wholly vicious man
Don't think I can't tell moral tales. I can!
Here's one I often preach when out for winning. . . ."

[6] **kirk:** church.

counterfeit:
imitate

He introduces himself and describes his immoral character, and then explains that he will tell a tale that is moral.

4. **◀ REREAD** Reread lines 50–57. In the margin, summarize the narrator's final comments of the prologue.

SHORT RESPONSE

Cite Text Evidence   Irony is a contrast between expectations and reality. What is ironic about the Pardoner? **Cite text evidence** in your response.

The Pardoner preaches to people to encourage them to buy forgiveness for their sins, but he only cares about getting their money. "Once dead what matter how their souls may fare?" he asks. Despite drawing attention to others' sins, he himself is "a wholly vicious man." He will take from "the poorest lad or poorest village widow" and spend the money on "the liquor of the grape" and "a jolly wench in every town." In the final lines, the corrupt and greedy Pardoner says that he will tell "a moral tale."

21

---

2. **REREAD AND CITE TEXT EVIDENCE**

(B) **ASK STUDENTS** to read their answer aloud to a partner. Have partners discuss and then rewrite their responses, including explicit textual evidence from lines 19–20.

3. **READ AND CITE TEXT EVIDENCE**

(C) **ASK STUDENTS** to cite text evidence that reveals the character of the Pardoner. *Students should recognize that the Pardoner holds others in low regard (lines 33–34 and 44–47). He is guilty of avarice (lines 23–24, 29–30, 35–37, 40, and 55).*

Critical Vocabulary: avarice (line 16) Have students share definitions for *avarice*.

Critical Vocabulary: castigate (line 20) Have students name words that have a similar meaning to *castigate*. *(scold, chasten)*

4. **REREAD AND CITE TEXT EVIDENCE**

(D) **ASK STUDENTS** to cite evidence to support their summaries of the Pardoner's final comments. *Students may cite "though I am a wholly vicious man" from line 55 to support their summaries.*

Critical Vocabulary: counterfeit (line 43) Have students compare definitions for *counterfeit*.

SHORT RESPONSE

Cite Text Evidence   Student responses will vary, but they should cite evidence from the text to support their responses. Students should:

- provide a text-based analysis of what is ironic about the Pardoner.
- cite specific textual evidence of the Pardoner's sins.
- cite the Pardoner's intention to tell "a moral tale."

CLOSE READ Notes

5. **READ** As you read lines 58–107, continue to cite textual evidence.

- In the margin, explain who the Pardoner's tale will be about and who has just been killed (lines 58–72).
- Underline descriptions of and warnings about Death.
- In the margin, explain how the descriptions given by the tavern-knave and the innkeeper personify Death (lines 73–89).

The story will be about three rowdy men. Their friend has just died last night.

The Pardoner's Tale

It's of three rioters[7] I have to tell
Who, long before the morning service bell,
60 Were sitting in a tavern for a drink.
And as they sat, they heard the hand-bell clink
Before a coffin going to the grave;
One of them called the little tavern-knave[8]
And said "Go and find out at once—look spry!—
65 Whose corpse is in that coffin passing by;
And see you get the name correctly too."
"Sir," said the boy, "no need, I promise you;
Two hours before you came here I was told.
He was a friend of yours in days of old,
70 And suddenly, last night, the man was slain,
Upon his bench, face up, dead drunk again.
There came a privy[9] thief, they call him Death,
(E) Who kills us all round here, and in a breath
He speared him through the heart, he never stirred.
75 And then Death went his way without a word.
He's killed a thousand in the present plague,[10]
And, sir, it doesn't do to be too vague
If you should meet him; you had best be wary.
Be on your guard with such an adversary,
80 Be primed to meet him everywhere you go,
That's what my mother said. It's all I know."

---
[7] **rioters:** rowdy people, revelers.
[8] **tavern-knave:** serving boy at an inn.
[9] **privy:** hidden, secretive.
[10] **plague:** Bubonic plague killed at least a quarter of the population of Europe in the mid-14th century.

The **publican** joined in with, "By St. Mary,
What the child says is right; you'd best be wary,
This very year he killed, in a large village
85 A mile away, man, woman, serf at tillage,
Page[11] in the household, children—all there were.
Yes, I imagine that he lives round there.
It's well to be prepared in these alarms,
He might do you dishonor." "Huh, God's arms!"
(F) 90 The rioter said, "Is he so fierce to meet?
I'll search for him, by Jesus, street by street.
God's blessed bones! I'll register a vow!
Here, chaps! The three of us together now,
Hold up your hands, like me, and we'll be brothers
95 In this affair, and each defend the others,
And we will kill this traitor Death, I say!
Away with him as he has made away
With all our friends. God's dignity! Tonight!"

They made their bargain, swore with appetite,
100 These three, to live and die for one another
As brother-born might swear to his born brother.
And up they started in their drunken rage
And made towards this village which the page
And publican had spoken of before.
105 Many and grisly were the oaths they swore,
Tearing Christ's blessed body to a shred;
"If we can only catch him, Death is dead!"

---
[11] **page:** boy servant.

---

publican: innkeeper; tavern owner

The tavern-knave calls Death a "privy-thief" and the publican says that Death probably lives near the village where many have died.

6. **REREAD** Reread lines 90–107. What does the rioters' response to the description of Death tell you about their characters? Cite evidence in your response.

The rioters ask of Death, "Is he so fierce to meet?" They show how foolish and arrogant they are when they decide to "kill" Death.

22   23

---

5. READ AND CITE TEXT EVIDENCE

(E) ASK STUDENTS to cite text evidence to support their explanations of how Death is personified. *Students may cite line 72 "a privy thief, they call him Death" and lines 84–87 which suggest death lives in a nearby town, as well as lines that suggest that Death can be killed, such as line 107.*

FOR ELL STUDENTS Point out that the adjective *spry* is used to describe someone full of energy.

6. REREAD AND CITE TEXT EVIDENCE

(F) ASK STUDENTS to discuss their responses with a partner. Have them quote specific text evidence with line number references to support their analysis of the rioters' characters. *Answers will vary. Students may cite evidence such as in line 90, "Is he so fierce to meet?" or line 96, "we will kill this traitor Death," to show that the rioters are foolish and arrogant.*

Critical Vocabulary: publican (line 82) Have students share definitions of *publican*. Explain that another word for *tavern* is *pub*.

CLOSE READ
Notes

When they had gone not fully half a mile,
Just as they were about to cross a stile,
110 They came upon a very poor old man
Who humbly greeted them and thus began,
"God look to you, my lords, and give you quiet!"
To which the proudest of these men of riot
Gave back the answer, "What, old fool? Give place!
115 Why are you all wrapped up except your face?
Ⓗ Why live so long? Isn't it time to die?"

The old, old fellow looked him in the eye
And said, "Because I never yet have found,
Though I have walked to India, searching round
120 Village and city on my pilgrimage,
Ⓖ One who would change his youth to have my age.
And so my age is mine and must be still
Upon me, for such time as God may will.

"Not even Death, alas, will take my life;
125 So, like a wretched prisoner at strife
Within himself, I walk alone and wait
About the earth, which is my mother's gate,
Knock-knocking with my staff from night to noon
And crying, 'Mother, open to me soon!
130 Look at me, mother, won't you let me in?
See how I wither, flesh and blood and skin!
Alas! When will these bones be laid to rest?
Mother, I would exchange—for that were best—
The wardrobe in my chamber, standing there

The old man personifies Death as a mother, and her house as the earth. His "mother's gate" could be the entrance to the grave.

135 So long, for yours! Aye, for a shirt of hair[12]
To wrap me in!' She has refused her grace,
Whence comes the pallor of my withered face.

"But it dishonored you when you began
To speak so roughly, sir, to an old man,
140 Unless he had injured you in word or deed.
It says in holy writ, as you may read,
'Thou shalt rise up before the **hoary** head
And honor it.' And therefore be it said
'Do no more harm to an old man than you,
145 Being now young, would have another do
When you are old'—if you should live till then.
And so may God be with you, gentlemen,
For I must go whither I have to go."

"By God," the gambler said, "you shan't do so,
150 You don't get off so easy, by St. John!
I heard you mention, just a moment gone,
A certain traitor Death who singles out
And kills the fine young fellows hereabout.
And you're his spy, by God! You wait a bit.
155 Say where he is or you shall pay for it,
By God and by the Holy Sacrament!
I say you've joined together by consent
To kill us younger folk, you thieving swine!"

"Well, sirs," he said, "if it be your design
160 To find out Death, turn up this crooked way
Towards that grove, I left him there today
Under a tree, and there you'll find him waiting.
He isn't one to hide for all your prating.[13]
You see that oak? He won't be far to find.
165 And God protect you that redeemed mankind,
Aye, and amend you!" Thus that ancient man.

hoary: *gray or white with age*

[12]**shirt of hair:** a rough shirt made of animal hair, worn to punish oneself for one's sins.
[13]**prating:** talking at great length; chattering.

7. **READ ▶** As you read lines 108–166, continue to cite textual evidence.

- In the margin, explain who the old man calls Mother and what he calls "my mother's gate" (lines 124–137).
- Circle the ominous words the old man speaks in lines 138–148.
- Underline the old man's instructions about where to find death (lines 149–166).

8. **◀ REREAD AND DISCUSS** Reread lines 108–116. With a small group, discuss the rioters' meeting with the old man. What is ironic about their attitudes toward death?

7. **READ AND CITE TEXT EVIDENCE**

Ⓖ **ASK STUDENTS** to cite text evidence to support their explanation of the old man's references to "Mother," and "my mother's gate." *The man tells the rioters he has sought to be relieved of old age by trading it for youth (line 121) and by seeking out Death (line 124). It is ironic to call Death "mother." He seeks to enter "mother's gate," (line 127), to leave life, and enter death.*

8. **REREAD AND DISCUSS USING TEXT EVIDENCE**

Ⓗ **ASK STUDENTS** to cite text evidence from the poem to support their conclusions about irony in the characters' attitudes toward death. *Students should cite evidence that the rioters would seek to "kill" death in line 107, and then ask an infirm old man "Isn't it time to die?" in line 116.*

FOR ELL STUDENTS Clarify for your ELL students that the verb *wither* means "to become dry and weak."

Critical Vocabulary: hoary (line 142) Have students compare definitions of *hoary*, and explain the meaning of *hoary* as it is used here. Have students explain why a "hoary head" should receive "honor." *A hoary head signifies an older person who is traditionally due respect.*

When they
find money,
they are
distracted
from looking
for Death.

I At once the three young rioters began
To run, and reached the tree, and there they found
J A pile of golden florins[14] on the ground,
170 New-coined, eight bushels of them as they thought.
No longer was it Death those fellows sought,
For they were all so thrilled to see the sight,
The florins were so beautiful and bright,
That down they sat beside the precious pile.
175 The wickedest spoke first after a while.
"Brothers," he said, "you listen to what I say.
I'm pretty sharp although I joke away.
It's clear that Fortune has bestowed this treasure
To let us live in jollity and pleasure.
180 Light come, light go! We'll spend it as we ought.
God's precious dignity! Who would have thought
This morning was to be our lucky day?

"If one could only get the gold away,
Back to my house, or else to yours, perhaps—
185 For as you know, the gold is ours, chaps—
We'd all be at the top of fortune, hey?
But certainly it can't be done by day.
People would call us robbers—a strong gang,
So our own property would make us hang.

---
[14]**florins:** coins.

9. (**READ ▶**) As you read lines 167–204, continue to cite textual evidence.
• In the margin, paraphrase what distracts the rioters from seeking Death.
• In the margin, summarize the plan the rioters make.
• Underline text evidence that supports your summary.

10. (**◀ REREAD**) Reread lines 167–182. What is ironic about this discovery?
How is it different from what you expected?

Instead of finding Death or a beast, the three rioters find gold. It's
ironic they find something positive rather than something deadly.

26

190 No, we must bring this treasure back by night
Some prudent way, and keep it out of sight.
And so as a solution I propose
We draw for lots and see the way it goes;
The one who draws the longest, lucky man,
195 Shall run to town as quickly as he can
To fetch us bread and wine—but keep things dark[15]—
While two remain in hiding here to mark
Our heap of treasure. If there's no delay,
When night comes down we'll carry it away,
200 All three of us, wherever we have planned."

He gathered lots and hid them in his hand
Bidding them draw for where the luck should fall.
It fell upon the youngest of them all,
And off he ran at once towards the town.

205 As soon as he had gone the first sat down
K And thus began a **parley** with the other:
"You know that you can trust me as a brother;
Now let me tell you where your profit lies;
You know our friend has gone to get supplies
210 And here's a lot of gold that is to be
Divided equally amongst us three.
Nevertheless, if I could shape things thus
So that we shared it out—the two of us—
Wouldn't you take it as a friendly act?"

---
[15]**keep things dark:** act in secret, without giving away what has happened.

The youngest
rioter will go
to town to get
some food
while the
other two stay
at the tree to
guard the
money.

parley:
a discussion or
conference

11. (**READ ▶**) As you read lines 205–235, continue to cite textual evidence.
• Underline words the first rioter uses to persuade the other of his plan.
• In the margin, explain the plan the two rioters make (lines 223–235).
• Underline text evidence that supports your explanation.

27

9. READ AND CITE TEXT EVIDENCE

I **ASK STUDENTS** to cite explicit textual evidence to support their summary of the sequence of events that unfolds in lines 167–204. *Students should cite evidence showing that the rioters found a pile of gold (lines 168–169), and stopped looking for death (line 171). They plan to take the gold (line 183), by night (lines 187, 190, 199). The youngest rioter will go to town for "bread and wine" (line 196) while the other two protect the "heap of treasure" (line 198).*

10. REREAD AND CITE TEXT EVIDENCE

J **ASK STUDENTS** to read aloud their response to a partner, then, have partners work together to locate specific textual evidence that supports their response. *Students should cite evidence showing that rioters had set out looking for Death (lines 160–164), and found gold instead (line 169).*

11. READ AND CITE TEXT EVIDENCE

K **ASK STUDENTS** to cite text evidence of how the plot progresses in lines 205–235. *Students should cite evidence that the first rioter is luring the second into some plan (lines 207–218, and 221–222). They plan to kill the youngest one, so they can split the money (lines 226–230 and 234–235).*

Critical Vocabulary: parley (line 206) Have students compare definitions of *parley*, and explain the meaning of *parley* as it is used here. Distinguish between the words *parley* and *parlay*, which sound similar and could be confused. *Parlay* is a betting term which means "a cumulative series of bets."

CLOSE READ Notes

215   "But how?" the other said. "He knows the fact
That all the gold was left with me and you;
What can we tell him? What are we to do?"

    "Is it a bargain," said the first, "or no?
For I can tell you in a word or so
220 What's to be done to bring the thing about."
"Trust me," the other said, "you needn't doubt
My word. I won't betray you, I'll be true."

    "Well," said his friend, "you see that we are two,
And two are twice as powerful as one.
225 Now look; when he comes back, get up in fun
To have a wrestle; then, as you attack,
I'll up and put my dagger through his back
While you and he are struggling, as in game;
Then draw your dagger too and do the same.
230 Then all this money will be ours to spend,
Divided equally of course, dear friend.
Then we can gratify our lusts and fill
The day with dicing[16] at our own sweet will."
Thus these two miscreants[17] agreed to slay
235 The third and youngest, as you heard me say.

    The youngest, as he ran towards the town,
Kept turning over, rolling up and down
Within his heart the beauty of those bright
New florins, saying, "Lord, to think I might
240 Have all that treasure to myself alone!
Could there be anyone beneath the throne
Of God so happy as I then should be?"

---

[16] **dicing:** gambling with dice.
[17] **miscreants:** evildoers, villains.

Two of the rioters plan to kill the youngest one so they can split the money.

12. ◀ **REREAD AND DISCUSS** Reread lines 209–235. With a small group, discuss the frequent references to religion by all three rioters. In what ways do these references to religion connect the rioters to the Pardoner who tells the tale?

28

M   And so the Fiend, our common enemy,
Was given power to put it in his thought
245 That there was always poison to be bought,
And that with poison he could kill his friends.
To men in such a state the Devil sends
Thoughts of this kind, and has a full permission
To lure them on to sorrow and **perdition**;
250 For this young man was utterly content
To kill them both and never to repent.

    And on he ran, he had no thought to tarry,
Came to the town, found an **apothecary**
And said, "Sell me some poison if you will,
255 I have a lot of rats I want to kill
And there's a polecat too about my yard
That takes my chickens and it hits me hard;
But I'll get even, as is only right,
With vermin that destroy a man by night."

260   The chemist answered, "I've a preparation
Which you shall have, and by my soul's salvation
If any living creature eat or drink
A mouthful, ere he has the time to think,
Though he took less than makes a grain of wheat,
265 You'll see him fall down dying at your feet;
Yes, die he must, and in so short a while
You'd hardly have the time to walk a mile,
The poison is so strong, you understand."

perdition: *damnation*

apothecary: *druggist*

The youngest rioter plans to poison the other two, so he can have the money to himself.

13. **READ** ▶ As you read lines 236–295, continue to cite textual evidence.

• Circle references to evil.
• Summarize the plan the youngest rioter makes.
• Underline text evidence in lines 239–251 that supports your summary.

29

---

12. **REREAD AND DISCUSS USING TEXT EVIDENCE**

L **ASK STUDENTS** to look for evidence throughout the poem up to line 235. They should be prepared to cite this evidence in a class discussion. *Students may cite any evidence with religious references, such as lines 89–92, which reference "God," "Jesus," and "God's blessed bones," figuratively connecting the rioters and the Pardoner, who is a clergyman who sells relics, the bones of saints. Students should understand the irony in thanking God (in line 181 "God's precious dignity!") while also plotting to kill one another.*

FOR ELL STUDENTS Encourage your ELL students to think about what the contraction *needn't* means. Ask for a volunteer to express it in other words. (*need not* or *do not need to*).

13. **READ AND CITE TEXT EVIDENCE** Remind students that the Pardoner is telling a story that he will "often preach when out for winning…"

M **ASK STUDENTS** to consider how the Pardoner's references to evil are consistent with his purpose for telling the tale. *Students should find references to evil or the Devil in lines 243, 247, 269, and 277.*

Critical Vocabulary: perdition (line 249) Ask volunteers to read their definitions. Why does the Pardoner include a reference to *perdition*? *Students should recognize that the Pardoner is trying to scare the pilgrims into purchasing his pardons.*

Critical Vocabulary: apothecary (line 253) Have students explain the meaning of *apothecary* as it is used here.

The two rioters kill the youngest rioter and then drink the poisoned wine and die. Rather than killing Death, they are killed by Death.

This cursed fellow grabbed into his hand
270 The box of poison and away he ran
Into a neighboring street, and found a man
Who lent him three large bottles. He withdrew
And deftly poured the poison into two.
He kept the third one clean, as well he might,
275 For his own drink, meaning to work all night
Stacking the gold and carrying it away.
And when this rioter, this devil's clay,
Had filled his bottles up with wine, all three,
Back to rejoin his comrades sauntered he.

280   Why make a sermon of it? Why waste breath?
Exactly in the way they'd planned his death
They fell on him and slew him, two to one.
Then said the first of them when this was done,
"Now for a drink. Sit down and let's be merry,
285 For later on there'll be the corpse to bury."
And, as it happened, reaching for a sup,
He took a bottle full of poison up
And drank; and his companion, nothing loth,[18]
Drank from it also, and they perished both.

290   There is, in Avicenna's[19] long relation
Concerning poison and its operation,
Trust me, no ghastlier section to transcend
What these two wretches suffered at their end.
Thus these two murderers received their due,
295 So did the treacherous young poisoner too.

        O cursed sin! O blackguardly excess!
O treacherous homicide! O wickedness!
O gluttony that lusted on and diced! . . .

[18]**nothing loth:** not at all unwilling.
[19]**Avicenna's:** Avicenna was an 11th-century Islamic physician who wrote descriptions of various poisons and their effects.

14. ◀REREAD Reread lines 280–289. In the margin, explain how each rioter meets his death, and the irony of their deaths.

        Dearly beloved, God forgive your sin
300 And keep you from the vice of **avarice**!
My holy pardon frees you all of this,
Provided that you make the right approaches,
That is with sterling, rings, or silver brooches.
Bow down your heads under this holy bull![20]
305 Come on, you women, offer up your wool!
I'll write your name into my ledger; so!
Into the bliss of Heaven you shall go.
For I'll absolve you by my holy power,
You that make offering, clean as at the hour
310 When you were born. . . . That, sirs, is how I preach.
And Jesu Christ, soul's healer, aye, the leech[21]
Of every soul, grant pardon and relieve you
Of sin, for that is best, I won't deceive you.

        One thing I should have mentioned in my tale,
315 Dear people. I've some relics[22] in my bale
And pardons too, as full and fine, I hope,
As any in England, given me by the Pope.
If there be one among you that is willing
To have my absolution for a shilling[23]
320 Devoutly given, come! and do not harden
Your hearts but kneel in humbleness for pardon;
Or else, receive my pardon as we go.
You can renew it every town or so,
Always provided that you still renew
325 Each time, and in good money, what is due.
It is an honor to you to have found
A pardoner with his credentials sound
Who can absolve you as you ply the spur
In any accident that may occur.

[20]**bull:** an official document from the pope.
[21]**leech:** a physician.
[22]**relics:** the remains of a saint.
[23]**shilling:** a coin worth twelve pence.

avarice:
greed

The Pardoner says that death can come at any time, so people should buy his pardons again and again.

15. READ▶ As you read lines 296–340, continue to cite textual evidence.
  • Circle examples of what the Pardoner offers his listeners.
  • Underline the forms of payment he accepts.
  • In the margin, summarize his final sales pitch.

---

14. **REREAD AND CITE TEXT EVIDENCE**

N **ASK STUDENTS** to cite textual evidence to support their explanations of how each rioter meets Death. *Students should cite line 282 as evidence that the two rioters killed the youngest rioter. They should cite lines 287–289 as evidence that the two remaining rioters drank the poisoned wine and died. So, those who sought to kill Death were instead killed by Death.*

15. **READ AND CITE TEXT EVIDENCE**

O **ASK STUDENTS** to cite text evidence to support their summary of the Pardoner's final sales pitch. *Students should cite evidence showing that the Pardoner tells the other pilgrims that death can come at any time (lines 329–331), so they should buy his pardons again and again (lines 322–323).*

Critical Vocabulary: avarice (line 300) Have students explain the meaning of avarice as it is used here. Ask students to state a theme of the "The Pardoner's Tale" using the word *avarice*. *Students should recognize that Chaucer comments on a corrupt church through the two-faced Pardoner who exemplifies avarice while extorting payment from parishioners who fear punishment for the same sin.*

CLOSE READ
Notes

330 For instance—we are all at Fortune's beck—
Your horse may throw you down and break your neck.
What a security it is to all
To have me here among you and at call
With pardon for the lowly and the great
335 When soul leaves body for the future state!
And I advise our Host here to begin,
The most enveloped of you all in sin.
Come forward, Host, you shall be the first to pay,
And kiss my holy relics right away.
340 Only a groat[24] Come on, unbuckle your purse!

---
[24]**groat:** a silver coin worth less than a shilling.

16. ◀ **REREAD** Reread lines 330–340. What motivation for the Pardoner's telling his tale is revealed in these lines? Cite text evidence in your response.

The Pardoner reminds listeners that they could die at any time. He puts the fear of death and damnation into his listeners so that he can sell them pardons and access to his "holy relics."

SHORT RESPONSE

Cite Text Evidence Relate the story of the rioters to the goal of the Pardoner. How does the tale of the three rioters help the Pardoner make sales? Review your reading notes, and **cite text evidence** in your response.

The tale of the rioters helps the Pardoner in three ways. First, it shows the rioters displaying common "sins" such as drunkenness, disrespect of the aged, and especially greed. Second, it shows that people are vulnerable to "the devil." Third, it shows that people cannot tell when they will die. Calling death a "privy thief" and cautioning, "be primed to meet him everywhere you go," prepares the Pardoner's audience for his sales pitch: "have my absolution for a shilling," so that, "into the bliss of Heaven you shall go."

32

HISTORY

TO CHALLENGE STUDENTS . . .

For more context, and a richer understanding of the fear of death in Chaucer's time, students can view the video "Coroner's Report: Plague" in their eBooks. Explain to students that during the mid-14th century, the Black Death—a massive epidemic of the bubonic plague—swept through Asia and Europe. In Europe alone, about one quarter of the population died.

ASK STUDENTS in what ways the circumstances of plague in Chaucer's time might have made people vulnerable to the tricks of the pardoner and other unscrupulous clergymen. *Students should recognize that Christians would have feared dying without forgiveness for their sins, as doing so would mean eternal damnation. The outbreak of the plague would have led many to seek forgiveness in the form of indulgences. They might have also looked to the supposed power of the pardoner's relics to keep them healthy.*

16. REREAD AND CITE TEXT EVIDENCE

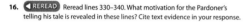 **ASK STUDENTS** to work with a partner to read aloud, discuss, and rewrite their analysis of the Pardoner's motivation for telling his tale. *Students should cite lines 330–331 to show that the Pardoner threatens the listeners with death and damnation, and lines 338–340 as evidence that forgiveness comes at a price.*

SHORT RESPONSE

Cite Text Evidence Student responses will vary, but they should cite evidence from the poem to support their analysis. Students should:

- provide an explanation of how the tale of the three rioters helps the Pardoner make sales.
- describe the rioters' vulnerability to sin, evil, and death.
- cite strong textual evidence to support their response.

DIG DEEPER

1. With the class, return to Question 8, Reread and Discuss. Have students share the results of their discussion.

ASK STUDENTS whether they were satisfied with the outcome of their small-group discussions. Have each group share their conclusions about irony in the characters' attitudes toward death. What compelling evidence did the groups cite from the story to support this opinion?

- Broaden the conversation to include evidence of irony in the old man's relationship to Death. Have students refer to their responses to Question 7, and cite evidence.

- Ask students to contrast the rioters' personification of death with the old man's personification of death. *Students should cite the rioters' personification of death as a traitor to be killed (line 96), and the old man's personification of death as a mother (line 129).* What is ironic, or unexpected about these contrasting points of view?

- After students have shared the results of their group's discussion, ask whether other groups cited examples of irony that they wish they had cited.

2. Now, return to Question 12, Reread and Discuss. Have students share the results of their discussion.

ASK STUDENTS whether they were satisfied with the outcome of their small-group discussions. Have each group share references to religion they identified that connect the rioters to the Pardoner who tells this tale.

- Ask students to take the time to look for further evidence beyond line 235.

- Have students categorize their evidence into three kinds: 1. evidence that the rioters are "sinners," 2. evidence that the rioters are vulnerable to forces of evil, 3. evidence that the rioters might have been well-served by a Pardoner (because they were surprised by death).

ASK STUDENTS to return to their Short Response answer and revise it based on the class discussion.

CLOSE READING NOTES

Mallam Sile

Short Story by Mohammed Naseehu Ali

Why This Text?

Short fiction allows students to briefly enter—and learn from—a world with which they may be unfamiliar. This short story illustrates the relationship between a shopkeeper and his customers in a close-knit Ghanaian neighborhood.

Key Learning Objective: The student will be able to analyze setting as a story element and use textual evidence to make inferences and draw conclusions.

COMMON CORE Common Core Standards

RL 1 Cite textual evidence to support inferences.
RL 2 Determine themes of a text; provide an objective summary of the text.
RL 3 Analyze the impact of the author's choices.
W 3d Use precise words and phrases, telling details, and sensory language to convey a vivid picture of the setting.
W 4 Produce writing appropriate to task, purpose, and audience.
W 10 Write routinely for a range of tasks, purposes, and audiences.
SL 1 Participate in collaborative discussions.
L 1 Demonstrate command of English grammar and usage when writing or speaking.
L 4c Consult general reference materials.
L 4d Verify the preliminary determination of the meaning of a word or phrase.

▲ Text Complexity Rubric

Quantitative Measures	**Mallam Sile** Lexile: 1150L
Qualitative Measures	**Levels of Meaning/Purpose** single level of complex meaning
	Structure no major shifts in chronology; occasional use of flashback
	Language Conventionality and Clarity some unfamiliar language
	Knowledge Demands experience includes unfamiliar aspects
Reader/Task Considerations	Teacher determined Vary by individual reader and type of text

Mohammed Naseehu Ali Have students read the information about the author. Tell them that setting has played an important role in the life of Mohammed Naseehu Ali (mō-häm´ĭd nə-sē´ū ä-lē´), just as it does in his fiction. As a teenager, Ali attended the Interlochen Arts Academy in Michigan. He credits the quiet, snowy winters and long summers of Michigan's Upper Peninsula with fueling his imagination and shaping him as a writer.

AS YOU READ Direct students to use the As You Read note to focus their reading.

Analyze Story Elements: Setting (LINES 1–20)

COMMON CORE RL 3

Point out that the **setting,** or where the action takes place, is often introduced at or near the beginning of a short story. Ali uses vivid details to bring the setting to life for his readers.

 CITE TEXT EVIDENCE Have students read the first two paragraphs. What is the setting, and what specific details does the author use to evoke it? (*The setting is a tea shop on Zongo Street. Details about Zongo Street show it's an important hub housing a meeting hall and the town gossip —whose nickname reveals her broadcasting ability; details about the shop include a list of items sold in the tea shop; the way local customers refer to all hot beverages as "tea;" description of the shop's lack of windows, cheap wood construction, and dirt floor; the fact that the merchandise is in plastic bags; the "chop box" serving table; Sile's "tall chair"; and the three benches for customers.*)

Support Inferences

COMMON CORE RL 1

(LINES 10–12)

Remind students that details in the text offer clues about what the author is trying to convey. Readers can draw upon these clues and their own knowledge to make **inferences**—logical assumptions—about the text.

 ASK STUDENTS to reread lines 10–12 and notice the details the author chose to include about the condition of the tea shop. What inferences can be made about the shop's owner, based on these details? (*The shop's owner is probably poor, since the shop is cheaply constructed.*)

Mohammed Naseehu Ali *(b. 1971) was born in Ghana, a country in western Africa. He came to the United States in 1988 at the age of 16 to pursue his education, graduating from Bennington College in Vermont. Although he lives in New York City, the roots of his writing are in Ghana. He wants "to document the history of the Ghanaian people, so that civilization doesn't only see Africa and African people as an exotic people—but as normal people." "Mallam Sile" is from* The Prophet of Zongo Street, *his first published collection. It is set in a fictional Muslim neighborhood in Ghana.*

Mallam Sile

Short Story by Mohammed Naseehu Ali

AS YOU READ Take note of the details that help you understand the character of Mallam Sile. Write down any questions you generate during reading.

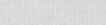

 He was popularly known as *mai tea*, or the tea seller. His shop was situated right in the navel of Zongo Street—a stone's throw from the chief's assembly shed and adjacent to the kiosk where Mansa BBC, the town gossip, sold her provisions. Along with fried eggs and white butter bread, Mallam Sile carried all kinds of beverages: regular black tea, Japanese green tea, Milo, Bournvita, cocoa drink, instant coffee. But on Zongo Street all hot beverages were referred to just as tea, and it was common, therefore, to hear people say, "Mallam Sile, may I have a mug of cocoa tea?" or "Sile, may I have a cup of coffee tea?"

10   The tea shop had no windows. It was built of *wawa*, a cheap wood easily infested by termites. The floor was uncemented, and heaps of dust rose in the air whenever a customer walked in. Sile protected his merchandise from the dust by keeping everything in plastic bags. An enormous wooden "chop box," the top of which he used as a serving table, covered most of the space in the shop. There was a tall chair behind the chop box for Sile, but he never used it, preferring instead to stand on his feet even when the shop was empty. There were also three benches that were meant to be used only by those who bought

Image Credits: (t) ©Christopher Wray-McCann; (b) ©IllFoolish/Shutterstock; (b) ©Jill Ferry Photography/Flickr/Getty Images

Mallam Sile **93**

SCAFFOLDING FOR ELL STUDENTS

Language: Punctuation and Print Cues Tell students that certain clues in the text can help them define unknown words. Share these points:

- A word set in italic type may be a foreign word. It is often followed by a comma and then a simple definition in English.
- A list of items that have something in common may be introduced by a colon. Items are separated by commas.

Work with students to locate these usages in the sentences in line 1, lines 4–6, lines 10–11, lines 31–33, and lines 84–86.

Analyze Story Elements: Setting (LINES 31–35) RL 3

Call students' attention to the fact that local customs may be considered part of the setting. Foreign-language terms that describe these customs are often included in italics.

C CITE TEXT EVIDENCE Ask students to identify where the author weaves cultural references into lines 31–35. *(He mentions the traditional breakfast food kókó da mása, and he spells the English phrase* latest news *"laytes' neus" to reflect the local pronunciation.)* Why might the author include such references in the story? *(It gives the reader more information about the setting and how people of the neighborhood interact.)*

Support Inferences: Draw Conclusions (LINES 45–62) COMMON CORE RL 1

Explain that **conclusions** are general statements readers make based upon inferences supported by the text.

D CITE TEXT EVIDENCE Have students identify details that refer to Mallam Sile's social position and economic status. *(Lines 45–53: He was "a loner without kin." He took a job as a "house servant" and earned "meagre" wages.)* Then ask students to make inferences about why he did not attend his parents' funeral. *(He was too poor to pay for the trip and to give up the wages he would miss while away.)* Ask students to draw conclusions about Mallam Sile's character and his relationship with his parents, citing additional evidence as needed. *(He was a dutiful son. He sent money to his parents when he worked as a house servant, and later he paid for his parents' burial.)*

---

tea, though the idle gossips who crowded the shop and never spent any money occupied the seats most of the time.

Old Sile had an irrational fear of being electrocuted and so he'd never tapped electricity into his shack, as was usually done on Zongo Street. Instead, he used kerosene lanterns, three of which hung from the low wooden ceiling. Sile kept a small radio in the shop, and whenever he had no customers he listened, in meditative silence, to the English programs on GBC 2, as though he understood what was being said. Mallam Sile was fluent only in his northern Sisaala tongue, though he understood Hausa—the language of the street's inhabitants—and spoke just enough pidgin to be able to conduct his business.

C The mornings were usually slow for the tea seller, as a majority of the street folks preferred the traditional breakfast of *kókó da mása*, or corn porridge with rice cake. But, come evening, the shop was crowded with the street's young men and women, who gossiped and talked about the "laytes' neus" in town. Some came to the shop just to meet their loved ones. During the shop's peak hours—from eight in the evening until around midnight—one could hardly hear oneself talk because of the boisterous chattering that went on. But anytime Mallam Sile opened his mouth to add to a conversation people would say, "Shut up, Sile, what do you know about this?" or "Close your beak, Sile, who told you that?" The tea seller learned to swallow his words, and eventually spoke only when he was engaged in a transaction with a customer. But nothing said or even whispered in the shop escaped his sharp ears.

D Mallam Sile was a loner, without kin on the street or anywhere else in the city. He was born in Nanpugu, a small border town in the north. He left home at age sixteen, and, all by himself, journeyed more than nine hundred miles in a cow truck to find work down south in Kumasi—the capital city of Ghana's gold-rich Ashanti region.

Within a week of his arrival in the city, Sile landed a job as a house servant. Although his monthly wages were meagre, he sent a portion of them home to his ailing parents, who lived like paupers in their drought-stricken village. Even so, Sile's efforts were not enough to save his parents from the claws of Death, who took them away in their sleep one night. They were found clinging tightly to each other, as if one of them had seen what was coming and had grabbed onto the other so that they could go together.

The young Sile received the news of his parents' death with mixed emotions. He was sad to lose them, of course, but he saw it as a well-deserved rest for them, as they both had been ill and bedridden for many months. Though Sile didn't travel up north to attend their funeral, he sent money for a decent burial. With his parents deceased, Sile suddenly found himself with more money in his hands. He quit his house-servant job and found another, selling iced *kenkey* in

---

APPLYING ACADEMIC VOCABULARY

exploit	inclinations

As you discuss "Mallam Sile," incorporate the Collection 2 academic vocabulary words *exploit* and *inclinations*. Explore the relationship between Mallam Sile and his customers. Look for evidence in the text to illustrate the shop owner's **inclinations** to behave in a humble and honorable manner toward his customers. Discuss whether the customers **exploit** Sile's goodwill.

Kumasi's central market. Sile kept every pesewa[1] he earned, and two years later he was able to use his savings to open a tea business. It was the first of such establishments on Zongo Street, and would remain the only one for many years to come.

70   Mallam Sile was short—so short, in fact, that many claimed he was a Pygmy. He stood exactly five feet one inch tall. Although he didn't have the broad, flat nose, poorly developed chin, and round head of the Pygmies, he was stout and hairy all over, as they were. A childhood illness that had caused Sile's vision to deteriorate had continued to plague him throughout his adult life. Yet he refused to go to the hospital and condemned any form of medication, traditional or Western. "God is the one who brings illness, and he is the only true healer"—this was Sile's simple, if rather mystical, explanation.

    Sile's small face was covered with a thick, long beard. The wrinkles on his dark forehead and the moistness of his soft, squinted eyes

80 gave him the appearance of a sage, one who had lived through and conquered many adversities in his life. His smile, which stretched from one wrinkled cheek to the other, baring his kola-stained teeth, radiated strength, wisdom, and self-confidence.

    Sile wore the same outfit every day: a white polyester djellabah[2] and its matching *wando*, a loose pair of slacks that tied with strings at the waist. He had eight of these suits, and wore a different one each day of the week. Also, his head was perpetually shaved, and he was never without his white embroidered Mecca hat—worn by highly devout Muslims as a reflection of their submission to Allah. Like most

90 of the street's dwellers, Sile owned just one pair of slippers at a time, and replaced them only when they were worn out beyond repair. An unusual birth defect that caused the tea seller to grow an additional toe on each foot had made it impossible for him to find footwear that fit him properly; special slippers were made for him by Anaba the cobbler, who used discarded car tires for the soles of the shoes he made. The rascals of Zongo Street, led by Samadu, the street's most notorious bully, poked at Sile's feet and his slippers, which they called *kalabilwala*, a nonsensical term that no one could understand, let alone translate.

100   At forty-six, Mallam Sile was still a virgin. He routinely made passes at the divorcées and widows who came to his shop, but none showed any interest in him whatsoever. "What would I do with a dwarf?" the women would ask, feeling ashamed of having had passes made at them by Sile. A couple of them seemed receptive to tea seller Sile's advances, but everyone knew that they were flirting with him only in order to get free tea.

    Eventually, Sile resigned himself to his lack of success with women. He was convinced that he would die a virgin. Yet late at night,

---

[1] **pesewa** (pə-sā′wə): a small Ghanaian coin.

[2] **djellabah** (je-lä′bə): a long, hooded robe.

CLOSE READ

Support Inferences: Draw Conclusions (LINES 69–106)

COMMON CORE RL 1

Explain that physical description is an element of **characterization,** or the representation of the qualities that make up a literary character.

E   **CITE TEXT EVIDENCE** Have students read lines 69–99 and summarize Mallam Sile's appearance based on evidence from the text. *(He is short, "stout and hairy all over," with squinting eyes and a broad, confident smile, and he has an extra toe on each foot.)* How does Mallam Sile respond to any hardships brought about by his health? *(Instead of seeking medical attention for his poor eyesight, he leaves it up to God, "the only true healer," to heal him [lines 74–77]. Because he does not seem to react to the neighborhood bullies' harrassment [lines 96–99], one might infer that he quietly tolerates their taunts and treatment of him.)* What inferences, if any, can be made based on his response to hardship? *(He is a patient man with strong spiritual beliefs.)*

Point out that a number of inferences can be used together to gain a deeper understanding of a character.

F   **ASK STUDENTS** to infer how the neighborhood women feel about Mallam Sile when he tries to flirt with them (lines 100–106). *(They call him "a dwarf." Some flirt "only in order to get free tea." Therefore, the women are not attracted to him.)* Ask students to use the inference they've made so far to draw conclusions about Mallam Sile's social position in the neighborhood. *(People make fun of him and women reject him, so he doesn't have high social status.)*

WHEN STUDENTS STRUGGLE . . .

Have students work in pairs to list words and short phrases the author uses to describe Mallam Sile's physical and emotional characteristics. Assign one student to read aloud lines 69–106 while the other student takes notes using a table like the one below. Then have students discuss and answer these questions about Mallam Sile, citing evidence from their tables:

What does he look like?	How does he feel about himself?	How does the neighborhood feel about him?

Support Inferences: Draw Conclusions (LINES 109–132)

 COMMON CORE RL 1

Explain that fictional characters, like people in real life, sing songs to express their emotions. Readers can draw conclusions about Mallam Sile based on the love song he sings.

G **CITE TEXT EVIDENCE** What does Mallam Sile want, and why is it difficult for him to find it? Cite details from the song as well as what you already know about his situation. *(He is "looking for love" but doesn't know where to find it. Sile feels that he deserves love and would be able to find it among his own people in the north. Because he is a foreigner in the city, no one appreciates his best qualities. He is being judged by the size of his "knife" rather than the size of his "heart.")*

Analyze Story Elements: Setting (LINES 109–110)

 COMMON CORE RL 3

Tell students that descriptions of a story's characters can contribute to readers' understanding of the setting.

H **CITE TEXT EVIDENCE** Have students reread lines 109–110. What words does the author use to describe visitors to the tea shop? *("customers, idlers, and rumormongers")* How does the author describe their living conditions? *("shanties"; "bug-ridden grass mattresses")* What do these details add to readers' understanding of the setting? *(They underscore the fact that it is a very poor neighborhood. Although the story takes place in a city, it is unlike cities that readers in the United States and other developed countries are likely to be familiar with. The author may also want to make a connection between the penny-pinching habits of the customers and their meager living conditions.)*

> Eventually, Sile resigned himself to his lack of success with women. He was convinced that he would die a virgin.

G after all the customers, idlers, and rumormongers had left the shop to **H**
110 seek refuge in their shanties and on their bug-ridden grass mattresses, Sile could be heard singing love songs, hoping that a woman somewhere would respond to his passionate cries:

> A beautiful woman, they say,
> Is like an elephant's meat.
> 115 And only the man with the sharpest knife
> Can cut through.
> That's what they say.
>
> Young girl, I have no knife,
> I am not a hunter of meat,
> 120 And I am not savage.
> I am only looking for love.
> This is what I say.
>
> Up north where I am from,
> Young girls are not what they are here.
> 125 Up north where I am from,
> People don't judge you by your knife.
> They look at the size of your heart.
>
> Young girl, I don't know what you look like.
> I don't know where to look for you.
> 130 I don't even know who you are, young girl.
> All I know is: my heart is aching.
> Oh, oh, oh! My heart is aching for you.

WHEN STUDENTS STRUGGLE . . .

Help students interpret the figurative language in Mallam Sile's song. Display lines 113–127 on a whiteboard. Discuss these questions:

- What is compared to a beautiful woman? *("an elephant's meat")* Who can cut through this meat? *("the man with the sharpest knife")*
- What does the singer mean when he says, "I have no knife?" *(He does not have what it takes to win the love of a beautiful woman.)*
- How are things different "up north"? *(People judge others by the size of their hearts, or the goodness of their souls, rather than their "knives," or more superficial qualities such as wealth or good looks.)*

Sile's voice rang with melancholy when he sang his songs. But still the rascals derided him. "When are you going to give up, Sile?" they would say. "Can't you see that no woman would marry you?"

"I have given up on them long, long ago," he would reply. "But I am never going to give up on myself!"

"You keep fooling yourself," they told him, laughing.

The rascals' mocking didn't end there. Knowing that Mallam Sile couldn't see properly, they often used fake or banned cedi[3] notes to purchase tea from him at night. The tea seller pinned the useless bills to the walls of his shop as if they were good-luck charms. He believed that it was hunger—and not mischief—that had led the rascals to cheat him. And, since he considered it inhuman to refuse a hungry person food, Mallam Sile allowed them to get away with their frauds.

To cool off the hot tea for his customers, Sile poured the contents of one mug into another, raising one over the other. The rascals would push Sile in the middle of this process, causing the hot liquid to spill all over his arms. The tea seller was never angered by such pranks. He merely grinned and, without saying a word, wiped off the spilled tea and continued to serve his customers. And when the rascals blew out the lanterns in the shop, so as to steal bread and Milo while he was trying to rekindle the light, Sile accepted that, too. He managed to rid his heart of any ill feelings. He would wave his short arms to anyone who walked past his shop, and shout, by way of greeting, "How are the heavens with you, boy?" Sile called everyone "boy," including women and older people, and he hardly ever uttered a sentence without referring to the heavens.

He prided himself on his hard work, and smiled whenever he looked in the mirror and saw his dwarfish body and ailing eyes, two abnormalities that he had learned to love. A few months before the death of his parents, he had come to the conclusion that if Allah had made him any differently he would not have been Mallam Sile—and Mallam Sile was an individual whom Sile's heart, mind, and spirit had come to accept and respect. This created within him a peace that made it possible for him not only to tolerate the rascals' ill treatment but also to forgive them. Though in their eyes Sile was only a buffoon.

One sunny afternoon during the dry season, Mallam Sile was seen atop the roof of his shack with hammers, saws, pliers, and all kinds of building tools. He lingered there all day long like a stray monkey, and by dusk he had dismantled all the aluminum roofing sheets that had once sheltered him and his business. He resumed work early the following morning, and by about one-thirty, before *azafar*, the first of the two afternoon prayers, Sile had no place to call either home or tea shop—he had demolished the shack down to its dusty floor.

At three-thirty, after *la-asar*, the second afternoon worship, Mallam Sile moved his personal belongings and all his tea

---

[3] **cedi** (sā´dē): basic unit of currency in Ghana.

Mallam Sile **97**

CLOSE READ

Support Inferences

(LINES 139–158)

Tell students that they can make inferences based on how characters think, what they say, and how they behave.

CITE TEXT EVIDENCE Ask students to read lines 139–158. What is Mallam Sile's response to the teasing and mocking of the "rascals" in his tea shop? *(He believes that "hunger—and not mischief" makes the "rascals" cheat him, and he can't let a person go hungry. He is "never angered by such pranks" but only smiles in response.)* Then ask students to make inferences about Mallam Sile's character based on his reactions. *(Possible answers: Mallam Sile is a patient man to put up with such teasing. He wants to avoid conflict, so he takes the abuse.)*

Determine Themes

COMMON CORE **RL 1, RL 2**

(LINES 159–167)

Remind students that a **theme** is a message about life or human nature communicated through a fictional work. Details about a character that are surprising or seemingly contradictory often point to a theme.

ASK STUDENTS to read lines 159–167. What contradictions are presented in this passage? *(Sile likes what he sees in the mirror, a "dwarfish body and ailing eyes," because that is the way Allah made him. Sile has "within him a peace" that allows him to forgive other people's cruelty, but others interpret this as weakness and consider him "a buffoon.")* What theme might these details suggest? *(The key to happiness is accepting yourself even when others misunderstand and reject you.)*

SCAFFOLDING FOR ELL STUDENTS

Understand Time Transitions Point out "One sunny afternoon during the dry season" in line 168. Explain that this phrase introduces specific events on a particular day. Much of the story up until this point has described events that might have taken place almost any day of Sile's life in the tea shop. Words such as "never" (lines 16, 149), "routinely" (line 100), and "often" (line 140) and the use of verbs with "would" (lines 135, 136, 147, 154) signal events in a normal routine. Line 168 signals the start of the main plot of the story. Going back to line 168, have students identify other time transitions in the paragraph. What do these transitions help readers understand about the action? *(They show that Sile has dismantled his shop with speed and efficiency.)*

Analyze Story Elements: Setting COMMON CORE RL 3
(LINES 186–219)

Tell students that elements of **setting**, such as how neighborhood residents typically interact, can contribute to other story elements, such as plot and conflict.

K **CITE TEXT EVIDENCE** Have students identify details in lines 186–219 that show how the neighborhood communicates information in a harmful way. Ask whether they think these developments will result in conflict *(They spread rumors that Sile is "constructing a mini-market," which creates "bad blood" between Sile and another shopkeeper [lines 188–192]. Another rumor says that Sile has traveled north for "black medicine" for his eyesight [lines 217–219]. Students might reasonably predict that conflict between Sile and the neighbors will arise.)*

Support Inferences COMMON CORE RL 1
(LINES 212–215)

Tell students that readers can make inferences from **dialogue,** or the exact words spoken by characters, to understand the characters' personalities and their relationships with others.

L **CITE TEXT EVIDENCE** Ask students to read the dialogue in lines 212–215. Ask students what they can infer about Abongo's personality based on the dialogue. *(He is unfriendly and does adhere to the credo that "the customer is always right.")* Have students cite dialogue and other evidence from the text supporting their inferences. *(Abongo is "generally abhorred" [line 204]; he has been known to chase a customer out of his shop "brandishing his bullwhip and cursing after him" [lines 212–213]; Abongo calls a customer "you bastard son of a bastard woman" [line 215].)*

CRITICAL VOCABULARY

paraphernalia: While he is rebuilding his shop, Mallam Sile moves all of the items he uses to make tea to the chief's palace. **ASK STUDENTS** why the tea seller might wish to move his paraphernalia elsewhere while he is building. *(to keep his necessary items safe so that they will not be stolen or damaged during construction)*

---

paraphernalia to a room in the servants' quarters of the chief's palace. The room had been arranged for him by the chief's wazir, or right-hand man, who was sympathetic to the tea seller.

During the next two days, Mallam Sile ordered plywood and planks of *odum*, a wood superior to the *wawa* used for the old shop. He also ordered a few bags of cement and truckloads of sand and stones, and immediately began building a new shack, much bigger than the first.

The street folks were shocked by Sile's new building—they wondered where he had got the money to embark on such an enterprise. Sile was rumored to be constructing a mini-market store to compete with Alhaji Saifa, the owner of the street's provision store. (And though the tea seller denied the rumor, it rapidly spread up and down the street, eventually creating bad blood between Sile and Alhaji Saifa.)

It took three days for Mallam Sile to complete work on the new shop's foundation, and an additional three weeks for him to erect the wooden walls and the aluminum roofing sheets. While Sile was busy at work, passersby would call out, "How is the provision store coming?" or "*Mai tea*, how is the mansion coming?" Sile would reply simply, "It is coming well, boy. It will be completed soon, *Inshallah*."[4] He would grin his usual wide grin and wave his short hairy arms, and then return to his work.

Meanwhile, as the days and weeks passed, the street folks grew impatient and somewhat angry at the closing of Sile's shop. The nearest tea shack was three hundred metres away, on Zerikyi Road—and not only that but the owner of the shack, Abongo, was generally abhorred. And for good reason. Abongo, also a northerner, was quite unfriendly even to his loyal customers. He maintained a rigid no-credit policy, and made customers pay him even before they were served. No one was an exception to this policy—even if he or she was dying of hunger. And, unlike Sile, Abongo didn't tolerate idlers or loud conversation in his shop. If a customer persisted in chatting, Abongo reached for the customer's mug, poured the contents in a plastic basin, and refunded his money. He then chased the customer out of the shop, brandishing his bullwhip and cursing after him, "If your mama and papa never teach you manners, I'll teach you some! I'll sew those careless lips of yours together, you bastard son of a bastard woman!"

As soon as work on the shop was completed, Sile left for his home town. Soon afterward, yet another rumor surfaced: it was said that the tea seller had travelled up north in search of "black medicine" for his bad eyesight.

Sile finally returned one Friday evening, some six weeks after he'd begun work on the shop, flanked by a stern woman who looked to be in her late thirties and was three times larger than the tea seller. The

paraphernalia
(păr´ə-fər-nāl´yə) *n.* necessary equipment or utensils.

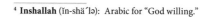

[4] **Inshallah** (ĭn-shä´lə): Arabic for "God willing."

woman, whose name was Abeeba, turned out to be Mallam Sile's wife. She was tall and massive, with a face as gloomy as that of someone mourning a dead relative. Like her husband, Abeeba said very little to people in or out of the shop. She, too, grinned and waved her huge arms whenever she greeted people, though, unlike the tea seller, she seemed to have something harder lurking behind her cheerful smile. Abeeba carried herself with the grace and confidence of a lioness, and
230 covered her head and part of her face with an Islamic veil, a practice that had been dropped by most of the married women on Zongo Street.

The rascals asked Sile, when they ran into him at the market, "From where did you get this elephant? Better not get on her bad side; she'll sit on you till you sink into the ground." To this, the tea seller did not say a word.

Exactly one week after Sile's return from his village, he and his wife opened the doors of the new shop to their customers. Among the most talked-about features were the smooth concrete floor and the
240 bright gas lantern that illuminated every corner. In a small wooden box behind the counter, Sile and his wife burned *tularen mayu*, or witches' lavender, a strong yet sweet-smelling incense that doubled as a jinx repellent—to drive bad spirits away from the establishment.

On the first night, the tea shop was so crowded that some customers couldn't find a seat, even with the twelve new metal folding chairs that Sile had bought. The patrons sang songs of praise to the variety of food on the new menu, which included meat pies, brown bread, custard, and Tom Brown, an imported grain porridge. Some of the patrons even went so far as to thank Sile and his wife for
250 relieving them of "Abongo's nastiness." But wise old Sile, who was as familiar with the street folks' cynicism as he was with the palms of his hands, merely nodded and grinned his sheepish grin. He knew that, despite their praise, and despite the smiles they flashed his way, some customers were at that very moment thinking of ways to cheat him.

While Sile prepared the tea and food, Abeeba served and collected the money. Prior to the shop's reopening, Abeeba had tried to convince her husband that they, too, should adopt Abongo's no-credit policy. Sile had quickly frowned upon the idea, claiming that it was inhumane to do such a thing.
260 The tea seller and his wife debated the matter for three days before they came to a compromise. They agreed to extend credit, but only in special cases and also on condition that the debtor swear by the Koran to pay on time; if a debtor didn't make a payment, he or she would not be given any credit in the future. But, even with the new policy in place, it wasn't long before some of the customers reverted to their old habits and began skipping payments. Then an encounter between Abeeba and one of the defaulters changed everything.

Mallam Sile **99**

TO CHALLENGE STUDENTS ...

Analyze a Relationship Are Mallam Sile and Abeeba a match made in heaven? Have students consider the love song that Sile sang earlier in the story and then read closely to find ways in which Abeeba fulfills or does not fulfill his expressed wishes. Have them note evidence of other needs she fulfills for him that he may not have anticipated. Also have them consider what needs Mallam Sile fulfills for Abeeba.

ASK STUDENTS to discuss their ideas in small groups after finishing the story. Invite them to share their conclusions with the class.

CLOSE READ

Analyze Story Elements RL 3
(LINES 220–232, 244–254, 255–267)

Character Development Tell students that authors sometimes use contrast between two characters to create an effect or to make a point.

M ASK STUDENTS to summarize Abeeba's appearance based on details in lines 220–232. *(She is a tall, massive woman with a gloomy expression and a very confident air.)* Ask students to recall Mallam Sile's appearance and compare it to his wife's. *(Physically, they are opposites. He is small. She is large. They are both quiet and smile at customers, but Abeeba's smile is "harder." Sile shows his religious devotion by wearing a Mecca cap; she by wearing a traditional Islamic veil.)* Why might the author choose to give Sile a wife that appears, at first, to be very different from him? *(The author may want to surprise readers, to create dramatic tension by making readers wonder what this all means, or to show that Sile is open-minded about what constitutes beauty.)*

Setting While Sile's shop was closed, the atmosphere of the neighborhood seemed to point to an inevitable conflict.

N ASK STUDENTS to review lines 244–254 and discuss whether their predictions about the apparent conflict brewing in the neighborhood during Sile's absence came to pass. *(Apparently not; the customers' seem happy with the new shop and relieved to be free of "Abongo's nastiness.")* Ask students to identify what the earlier details about the neighbors' gossip reveal about the author's purpose. *(Ali's goal in the passage was to create a richly evocative setting, including its sometimes toxic atmosphere.)*

Character Development Explain that when an author introduces a new character, that character will often act as a **catalyst**, or an agent of change.

O CITE TEXT EVIDENCE Ask students to read lines 255–267 and identify any changes to the way the new tea shop is run. *(There is a change to the credit policy [lines 261–264].)* Who is the catalyst in bringing about the changes? *(Abeeba)* Why do you think Mallam Sile was willing to make these changes? *(He made an effort to "compromise," so perhaps he wanted to make his new wife happy but still live according to his beliefs.)*

CLOSE READ

Analyze Story Elements: Character Development

COMMON CORE   RL 2, RL 3

(LINES 268–294)

Tell students that writers show how characters interact with one another both to develop the characters and to move the action along.

P **CITE TEXT EVIDENCE** Ask students to read lines 268–280. Have them identify the words and phrases that help characterize Samadu. What sort of character is he? *(Words and phrases include "muscular," "wrestling contests," "'power,'" "tortured and even killed . . . pets or domestic animals," "harassed their children . . . until he was appeased with cash or goods." He is tough and dangerous—a real bully.)* What do his interactions say about his place in the community? *(He uses fear to secure his position.)* What might his importance be to the story? *(His introduction creates tension and suggests that the conflict is building.)*

Explain that the introduction of an **antagonist**—a character who opposes the story's main character—signals a rise in dramatic tension.

Q **ASK STUDENTS** to read lines 281–294. In what ways does Samadu present a challenge for Mallam Sile and Abeeba? *(He refuses to pay the money he owes. Sile and his wife differ on how to handle the situation, which creates tension between them.)* Is Samadu an antagonist? Why? *(Yes, he is an antagonist because he opposes Mallam Sile, the main character.)*

CRITICAL VOCABULARY

pugnacious: The author introduces Samadu, an aggressive bully who owes Mallam Sile money but refuses to pay.

ASK STUDENTS why a bully would be a pugnacious person. *(Bullies are aggressive and would likely be pugnacious, or inclined to fight.)*

P

270

What took place was this: Samadu, the **pugnacious** sixteen-year-old whose fame had reached every corner of the city, was the tough guy of Zongo Street. He was of medium height, muscular, and a natural-born athlete. For nine months running, no one in the neighborhood had managed to put Samadu's back to the ground in the haphazard wrestling contests held beside the central market's latrine. Samadu's "power" was such that parents paid him to protect their children from other bullies at school. He was also known for having tortured and even killed the livestock of the adults who denounced him. If they didn't have pets or domestic animals, he harassed their children for several days until he was appeased with cash or goods. Some parents won Samadu's friendship for their children by bribing him with gifts

280 of money, food, or clothing.

Q

Samadu, of course, was deeply in debt to Mallam Sile—he owed him eighty cedis, about four dollars. Early one Tuesday morning, Mallam Sile's wife showed up at Samadu's house to collect the money. Abeeba had tried to collect the debt amicably, but after her third futile attempt she had suggested to Sile that they use force to persuade the boy to pay. Sile had responded by telling his wife, "Stay out of that boy's way—he is dangerous. If he has decided not to pay, let him keep it. He will be the loser in the end."

"But, Mallam, it is an insult what he is doing," Abeeba argued. "I

290 think people to whom we have been generous should only be generous in return. I am getting fed up with their ways, and the sooner the folks

pugnacious
(pŭg-nāʹshəs) *adj.*
belligerent, inclined
to quarrel.

Image Credits: ©Ariadne Van Zandbergen/Lonely Planet Images/Getty Images

SCAFFOLDING FOR ELL STUDENTS

Analyze Character Description Using a whiteboard, read aloud lines 268–280, pausing at words that help identify Samadu as a bully. Highlight and discuss the meaning of each word. Have students use some of the highlighted words to write or say aloud a summary of Samadu's description. *(Samadu is a muscular bully who uses his power to harass and intimidate other people.)* Read aloud the rest of the page, stopping as needed to explain words such as *debt, futile,* and *dangerous.* Explain that *fed up* (line 291) means "unwilling to accept a bad situation any longer." Help students explain how Samadu creates a conflict or problem. *(Samadu won't pay his debts, and Abeeba wants to force him.)*

here know that even the toad gets sick of filling his belly with the same dirty pond water every day, the better!" Though Sile wasn't sure what his wife meant, he let the matter drop.

When Abeeba arrived at Samadu's house, a number of housewives and young women were busily doing their morning chores in and around the compound—some sweeping and stirring up dust, others fetching water from the tap in the compound's center or lighting up charcoal pots to warm the food left over from the previous night.
300 Abeeba greeted them politely and asked to be shown to the tough guy's door. The women tried to turn Abeeba away, as they feared that Samadu would humiliate her in some way. But Abeeba insisted that she had important business with him, and so the housewives reluctantly directed her to Samadu's room, which, like all the young men's rooms, was situated just outside the main compound.

The usual tactic that the street's teen-age boys used when fighting girls or women was to strip them of the wrapper around their waist, knowing that they would be reluctant to continue fighting half-naked. But Abeeba had heard young boys in the shop discussing Samadu's
310 bullying ways and had come prepared for anything. She wore a sleeveless shirt and a pair of tight-fitting khaki shorts, and, for the first time ever, she had left her veil at home.

"You rogue! If you call yourself a man, come out and pay your debt!" Abeeba shouted, as she pounded on Samadu's door.

"Who do you think you are, ruining my sleep because of some useless eighty cedis?" Samadu screamed from inside.

"The money may be useless, but it is certainly worthier than you, and that's why you haven't been able to pay, you rubbish heap of a man!" Abeeba's voice was coarse and full of menace. The veins on her
320 neck stood out, like those of the *juju* fighters at the annual wrestling contest. Her eyes moved rapidly inside her head, as though she were having a fit of some sort.

One of the onlookers, a famished-looking housewife, pleaded with the tea seller's wife, "Go back to your house, woman. Don't fight him, he will disgrace you in public." Another woman in the background added, "What kind of a woman thinks she can fight a man? Be careful, oh!"

Abeeba didn't pay any attention to the women's **admonitions**. Just then, a loud bang was heard inside the room. The door swung
330 open, and Samadu stormed out, his face red with anger. "No one gets away with insulting me. No one!" he shouted. There was a line of dried drool on his right cheek, and whitish mucus had gathered in the corners of his eyes. "You ugly elephant-woman. After I am done with you today, you'll learn a lesson or two about why women don't grow beards!"

"Ha, you teach me a lesson? You?" Abeeba said. "I, too, will educate you about the need to have money in your pocket before you flag the candy man!" With this, she lunged at Samadu.

admonition
(ăd´mə-nĭsh´ən) *n.* critical advice.

Mallam Sile **101**

SCAFFOLDING FOR ELL STUDENTS

Understand Figurative Language Point out the **proverb,** or traditional saying, in lines 292–293. Tell students that the proverb uses the toad in a figurative way to say something about people. Help them restate the proverb's meaning. *(Even a humble person, like a tea seller, gets tired of taking abuse every day.)*

ASK STUDENTS to rephrase these figurative statements: "you'll learn . . . beards" in lines 334–335 *(After I beat you up, you'll understand that men are stronger than women)*; "have money . . . candy man" in lines 337–338 *(Don't make claims you can't support with action).*

CLOSE READ

Analyze Story Elements: Character Development (LINES 295–305)

 COMMON CORE RL 3

Explain that character **motivation** is the reason or reasons behind a character's behavior.

R **ASK STUDENTS** to read lines 295–305. What details show how the women of the compound feel about Samadu? *(They are afraid of Samadu. They try to turn Abeeba away [line 301] and they point her "reluctantly" [line 304] to his room).* What might be their motivation for trying to protect Abeeba? *(Possible answers: They don't want any trouble in their compound. They feel that if Samadu humiliates Abeeba, it will be humiliating for other women in the community as well. They know firsthand how terrible Samadu is and they feel frightened for Abeeba.)*

Support Inferences: Draw Conclusions (LINES 306–312)

COMMON CORE RL 1

Remind students to keep in mind important information they learn throughout the story, using it to draw conclusions as the story develops.

S **ASK STUDENTS** to recall Abeeba's description when she was first introduced in the story. How has Abeeba changed as she confronts Samadu? *(At first she wore an Islamic veil covering her head and most of her face [lines 230–232]; she now wears a sleeveless shirt, tight shorts, and no veil.)* What significance, if any, does this alteration have? *(By wearing clothing less modest than she is used to, Abeeba shows she is serious about her mission to make Samadu pay her.)* What conclusions can you draw concerning Abeeba's character at this point in the story? *(She is a strong, determined person. She is willing to fight, and possibly suffer, for what she believes in.)*

CRITICAL VOCABULARY

admonition: Abeeba ignores the women's advice to leave Samadu alone and go home.

ASK STUDENTS why the women give Abeeba admonitions concerning Samadu. *(They think Abeeba doesn't realize how dangerous Samadu is, so they warn her to stay away from him.)*

Analyze Story Elements: Pacing (LINES 346–370)

 COMMON CORE RL 3

Tell students that to craft an exciting action scene, the author must control the **pacing,** or the rate at which the action progresses. Even if events unfold quickly, the reader must feel suspense while wondering what will happen next.

T **ASK STUDENTS** to read lines 346–370. Have students **summarize** the fight and the crowd's reactions, showing how dominance shifts between Samadu and Abeeba. *(Abeeba dodges Samadu's first punches; Samadu stumbles; Abeeba seizes and punches him, hushing the crowd; Samadu jabs Abeeba's stomach and frees himself; he dances like a boxer; the crowd chants; Abeeba watches him; the women slap at their thighs, moving to the rhythm of the chanting; the boys boo Abeeba and call her names.)* How does the author control the pacing in this scene? *(by alternating descriptions of the fight with descriptions of the crowd's reaction to the fight)*

Support Inferences: Draw Conclusions (LINES 381–385)

 COMMON CORE RL 1

Suggest that when a crowd behaves as a unit, it effectively becomes a character with feelings, behavior, and motivation.

 CITE TEXT EVIDENCE Have students cite details from lines 381–385 that show the crowd behaving as one person. *(It boos at her, "Wooh, ugly rhinoceros.")* How does the crowd feel about Abeeba's dominance? *(It disapproves.)* What conclusions can you draw about crowd behavior from the passage? *(The emotion of a crowd spreads like a contagion, despite how individuals—like the women who begged Abeeba not to fight—may feel.)*

CRITICAL VOCABULARY

extricate: At one point in the fight, Samadu manages to free himself from Abeeba's grip.

ASK STUDENTS the importance of Samadu's being able to **extricate** himself from Abeeba's grip. *(By breaking free, he has another chance to win the fight.)*

The women placed their palms on their breasts, and their bodies 340 shook with dread. "Where are the men on the street? Come and separate the fight, oh! Men, come out, oh!" they shouted. The children in the compound, though freshly aroused from sleep, hopped about excitedly, as if they were watching a ritual. Half of them called out, "*Piri pirin-pi!,*" while the other half responded, "*Wein son!,*" as they chanted and cheered for Samadu.

Samadu knew immediately that if he engaged Abeeba in a wrestling match she would use her bulky mass to force him to the ground. His strategy, therefore, was to throw punches and kicks from a safe distance, thereby avoiding close contact. But Abeeba was a lot 350 quicker than he imagined, and she managed to dodge the first five punches he threw. He threw a sixth punch, and missed. He stumbled over his own foot when he tried to connect the seventh, and landed inches from Abeeba. With blinding quickness, she seized him by the sleeping wrapper tied around his neck and began to punch him. The exuberant crowd was hushed by this unexpected turn of events.

But Samadu wasn't heralded as the street's tough guy for nothing. He threw a sharp jab at Abeeba's stomach and succeeded in releasing himself from her grip by deftly undoing the knot of his sleeping cloth. He was topless now, clad only in a pair of corduroy knickers. He 360 danced on his feet, swung his arms, and moved his torso from side to side, the way true boxers do. The crowd got excited again and picked up the fight song, "*Piri pirin-pi, Wein son! Piri pirin-pi, Wein son!*" Some among them shouted "Ali! Ali! Ali!" as Samadu danced and pranced, carefully avoiding Abeeba, who watched his movements with the keenness of a hungry lioness.

The women in the crowd went from holding their breasts to slapping their massive thighs. They jumped about nervously, moving their bodies in rhythm to the chants. The boys booed Abeeba, calling her all sorts of names for the beasts of the jungle. "Destroy that 370 elephant!" they shouted.

The harder the crowd cheered for Samadu, the fancier his footwork became. He finally threw a punch that landed on Abeeba's left shoulder, though she seemed completely unfazed and continued to chase him around the small circle created by the spectators. When Samadu next threw his fist, Abeeba anticipated it. She dodged, then grabbed his wrist and twisted his arm with such force that he let out a high-pitched cry: "*Wayyo* Allah!" The crowd gasped as the tough guy attempted to **extricate** himself from Abeeba's grip. He tightened all the muscles in his body and craned his neck. But her strength was just too 380 much for him.

The crowd booed, "Wooh, ugly rhinoceros." Then, in a sudden, swift motion, Abeeba lifted the tough guy off the ground, raised him above her head (the crowd booed louder), and dumped him back down like a sack of rice. She then jumped on top of him and began to whack him violently.

extricate
(ĕk´strĭ-kāt´) *v.* to free from difficulty.

The women, now frantic, shouted, "Where are the men in this house? Men, come out, oh! There is a fight!"

A handful of men came running to the scene, followed by many more a few minutes later.

390 Meanwhile, with each punch Abeeba asked, "Where is our money?"

"I don't have it, and wouldn't pay even if I did!" Samadu responded. The men drew nearer and tried to pull Abeeba off, but her grip on Samadu's waistband was too firm. The men pleaded with Abeeba to let go. "I will not release him until he pays us back our money!" she shouted. "And if he doesn't I'll drag his ass all the way to the Zongo police station."

On hearing this, an elderly man who lived in Samadu's compound ran inside the house; he returned a few minutes later with eighty cedis, 400 which he placed in the palm of Abeeba's free hand. With one hand gripping Samadu's waistband, she used the fingers of the other to flip and count the money. Once she was sure the amount was right, she released the boy, giving him a mean, hard look as she left. The crowd watched silently, mouths agape, as though they had just witnessed something from a cinema reel.

Mallam Sile was still engaged in his morning *zikhr*, or meditation, when Abeeba returned to the shack. He, of course, had no inkling of what had taken place. Later, when Abeeba told him that Samadu had paid the money he owed, the tea seller, though surprised, didn't 410 think to ask how this had happened. In his **naïveté**, he concluded that Samadu had finally been entered by the love and fear of God. Abeeba's news therefore confirmed Mallam Sile's long-standing belief that every man was capable of goodness, just as he was capable of evil.

The tea seller's belief was further solidified when he ran into Samadu a fortnight later. The tough guy greeted him politely, something he had never done before. When Mallam Sile related this

naïveté
(nī´ēv-tā´) *n.* lack of knowledge or experience.

> " In a sudden, swift motion, Abeeba lifted the tough guy off the ground, raised him above her head (the crowd booed louder), and dumped him back down like a sack of rice. "

TEACH

CLOSE READ

Analyze Story Elements: Character Development (LINES 390–413)

COMMON CORE RL 3

Tell students that authors sometimes choose to place a character in an extreme situation in order to reveal the character's true nature and core beliefs.

V **CITE TEXT EVIDENCE** What does Abeeba accomplish by winning the fight with Samadu? *(His debt is paid, although by an elderly man [lines 398–399].)* Ask students to identify what Abeeba's win reveals about her true nature. *(She holds onto Samadu until she counts the money, and she gives him a hard look before leaving the scene. She is a strong person, and a cunning one, who understands the ways of the world.)* What does Mallam Sile's reaction (lines 406–413) reveal about his character? *(He is not as worldly as his wife, and he is more accepting of events and people.)*

CRITICAL VOCABULARY

naïveté: Because he has no idea about what really happened, Mallam Sile credits God with Samadu's sudden morality.

ASK STUDENTS how Mallam Sile reveals his naïveté. *(He believes that the fear of God, rather than a fear of Abeeba, got Samadu's debts paid.)*

Strategies for Annotation  *Annotate it!*

Analyze Story Elements: Character Development

COMMON CORE RL 3

Share these strategies for guided or independent analysis:

- Highlight in green key words and phrases that reveal one character's behavior or nature.
- Use a contrasting color, such as yellow, to highlight key words that reveal another character's behavior or nature.
- On a note, use highlighted words to summarize each character's true nature.

released the boy, giving him a mean, hard look as she left. The crowd watched silently, mouths agape, as though they had just witnessed something from a cinema reel.

Mallam Sile was still engaged in his morning *zikhr*, or meditation, when Abeeba returned to the shack. He, or course, had no inkling of what had taken place. Later, when Abeeba told him that Samadu

Support Inferences: Draw Conclusions (LINES 416–440)

Tell students that they can use interactions between characters to make inferences about their beliefs.

 CITE TEXT EVIDENCE Have students identify a specific detail that reveals Mallam Sile's beliefs about dealing with conflict. *("fire . . . 'worsens rather than extinguishes the original flame.'")* How does Abeeba feel about her husband's approach to conflict? What evidence from the text supports your inference? *(She respects it but thinks it is ineffective. She "restrained herself from telling him the truth" and "knew that Sile would be quite displeased with her methods.")* Based upon your inferences, what conclusions, if any, can you draw about Abeeba's role in her marriage? *(She will do whatever she can to bring her husband happiness and success.)*

Explain to students that details found in a story's ending often provide evidence for understanding the story as a whole.

X **ASK STUDENTS** to read lines 426–440. What is troubling Mallam Sile at the beginning of the passage? *(Everyone is calling his wife "the man checker" and paying credit on time. They are treating him with unusual respect, and he doesn't know why.)* How does Sile ease his troubled mind? *(He prays.)* What conclusions does he come to? *(He believes that God has cured his neighbors of their prejudice against him and that they have finally accepted him "just as he was created.")* How does the author want readers to feel about Mallam Sile? How do you know? *(The author wants readers to like Sile and to enjoy his success. He presents Sile's struggles sympathetically.)*

COLLABORATIVE DISCUSSION Have students form pairs to discuss and create a list of specific character traits of Mallam Sile and Abeeba. Then ask pairs to compare and contrast Sile's traits with those of his wife. Finally, have pairs share their conclusions with the class as a whole. Accept all reasonable responses.

ASK STUDENTS to share any questions they generated in the course of reading and discussing the selection.

---

to his wife, she restrained herself from telling him the truth. Abeeba knew that Sile would be quite displeased with her methods. Just a week ago, he had spoken to her about the pointlessness of using fire to 420 put out fire, of how it "worsens rather than extinguishes the original flame." Abeeba prayed that no one else would tell her husband about her duel with Samadu, although the entire city seemed to know about it by now. Tough guys from other neighborhoods came to the tea shop just to steal a glance at the woman who had conquered the tough guy of Zongo Street.

Then one night during the fasting month of Ramadan,[5] some two months after the fight, a voice in Mallam Sile's head asked, "Why is everyone calling my wife 'the man checker'? How come people I give credit to suddenly pay me on time? Why am I being treated with such 430 respect, even by the worst and most stubborn rascals on the street?" Sile was lying in bed with his wife when these questions came to him. But, in his usual fashion, he didn't try to answer them. Instead, he drew in a deep breath and began to pray. He smiled and thanked Allahu-Raheemu, the Merciful One, for curing the street folks of the prejudice they had nursed against him for so long. Mallam Sile also thanked Allah for giving his neighbors the will and the courage to finally accept him just as he was created. He flashed a grin in the darkness and moved closer to his slumbering wife. He buried his small body in her massive, protective frame and soon fell into a deep, 440 dreamless sleep.

---

[5] **Ramadan:** a month-long religious event that features fasting during daylight hours.

COLLABORATIVE DISCUSSION With a partner, describe Mallam Sile. Discuss his major character traits and how those traits compare and contrast with his wife's traits. Cite specific textual evidence from the story to support your ideas.

APPLYING ACADEMIC VOCABULARY

complementary	predominance

As you discuss the story, incorporate the Collection 2 academic vocabulary words *complementary* and *predominance*. Explore the relationship between Mallam Sile and Abeeba by asking students how the husband and wife have **complementary** strengths and personalities. Have students discuss how Abeeba came to have **predominance** over Samadu, and how that affected Mallam Sile's relationship with other customers in the future.

Analyze Story Elements: Setting

 COMMON CORE RL 3

In "Mallam Sile," the **setting** involves not only the specific location of Zongo Street in Kumasi, Ghana, but also the culture of the Ghanaian Muslims who live and work there. Their beliefs, social structure, religious practices, and customs infuse the story. This **cultural setting** is important for understanding the conflicts experienced by the main characters, Mallam Sile and his wife, who depart from the social norms of their neighbors. The setting is also related to the story's theme.

The author, Mohammed Naseehu Ali, conveys a vivid sense of Mallam Sile's world at the beginning of the story: "He was popularly known as *mai tea,* or the tea seller. His shop was situated right in the navel of Zongo Street—a stone's throw from the chief's assembly shed and adjacent to the kiosk where Mansa BBC, the town gossip, sold her provisions." These first sentences draw readers into the intimacy of this neighborhood in which everyone knows everyone else's business and talks about it. In addition, details such as the term *mai tea,* the reference to the chief's assembly shed, and even Mansa's nickname "BBC" after the British Broadcasting Corporation, establish the cultural context and help readers to understand its predominance in the story.

Support Inferences: Draw Conclusions

 COMMON CORE RL 1

Readers use evidence from a text and their own knowledge to make **inferences,** logical assumptions about something that is not directly stated in the text. For example, the phrase "situated right in the navel of Zongo Street" might lead readers to infer that Mallam's tea shop is central to the life of the residents of Zongo Street. Sometimes the evidence in a text leaves matters uncertain, and readers must understand that their inferences are only guesses.

Conclusions are more general statements about a text. They often are based on inferences that the reader has already made. For example, after reading "Mallam Sile," readers can use details from the story and inferences they have made to draw a conclusion about the author's purpose for choosing the setting of Kumasi, Ghana.

Details	Inferences	Conclusion
The story is set in Kumasi, Ghana, where the author is from.	Ghana is important to the author.	The author wants others to know about the Ghanaian way of life and what makes it special.
The description of the setting is vivid and realistic.	The author wants readers to be able to visualize what life in Ghana is like.	

Mallam Sile **105**

Analyze Story Elements: Setting

COMMON CORE RL 3

Help students understand the various aspects of a setting. Explain that in the case of "Mallam Sile," details about the neighborhood—its physical description, its people and their interactions, its local customs—come together to create the cultural setting. As an example, ask students to notice how frequently the author provides local terms and expressions, such as *mai tea.* Point out that by calling attention to the story's setting from the beginning, the author lets the reader know that it will play an important role in understanding the story's theme.

Support Inferences: Draw Conclusions

COMMON CORE RL 1

Tell students that the act of reading is really a conversation, one between author and reader. Point out that any details provided by the author —concerning setting, characterization, or plot—are part of that conversation. Readers participate in the conversation by making inferences supported by such details. Help students understand how inferences and conclusions differ: One can *infer* that Mallam Sile and his wife depart from the social norms of their neighbors because they are outsiders. One can *conclude* that outsiders tend to have a difficult time fitting into new cultural settings.

Analyze Story Elements: Setting

 COMMON CORE RL 3

Have students identify words and phrases that describe setting. Encourage them to use their eBook annotation tools to do the following:

- Highlight in blue each word or phrase that describes the story's setting.
- Review your highlighting. Does each detail describe physical setting, local characters, or customs and cultural practices?
- On a note, summarize your impression of the setting.

the town gossip, sold her provisions. Along with fried eggs and white butter bread, Mallam Sile carried all kinds of beverages: regular black tea, Japanese green tea, Milo, Bournvita, cocoa drink, instant coffee. But on Zongo Street all hot beverages were referred to just as tea, and it was common, therefore, to hear people say, "Mallam Sile, may I have a mug of cocoa tea?" or "Sile, may I have a cup of coffee tea?"

Analyzing the Text   COMMON CORE RL 1, RL 2

Possible answers:

1. *Words and phrases such as "crowded with the street's young men and women," "one could hardly hear oneself talk," and "boisterous chattering" show that the tea shop is lively. Speech is central to Ghanaian culture, conveying ideas, news, and emotions and strengthening connections within the community.*

2. *Mallam may be seen as "foreign" because he is from the north. He is also "fluent only in his northern Sisaala tongue," which means he has difficulty communicating. Mallam's different appearance may set him apart. This treatment of Mallam shows that he is isolated and lonely. It also shows that Zongo Street society, like others, is leery of those who are different.*

3. *Mallam is a devout Muslim, as shown by his wearing of the Mecca hat. His religious beliefs make him tolerant of those who owe him money. He does not fight back when bullied or ridiculed. He accepts what he is because Allah made him: "he had come to the conclusion that if Allah had made him any differently he would not have been Mallam Sile." As a result of his nature, customers take advantage of Mallam Sile.*

4. *He may build the shop because he needs a better place to bring his new wife. Or, it may represent a new start for him, which his wife also takes part in. Building the tea shop represents the end of "making do" for Mallam Sile and is the point at which he starts to gain his neighbors' respect.*

5. *This scene creates the basis for Mallam's transition in the community from a position of weakness to a position of strength. Abeeba shouts insults to start the battle: "You rogue! If you call yourself a man, come out and pay your debt!" The scene develops understanding of Abeeba's strength and determination. The crowd's reaction shows the public's involvement in private affairs: "The women in the crowd . . . jumped about nervously, moving their bodies in rhythm to the chants." Abeeba's victory leaves the community speechless in astonishment.*

6. *One possible theme is that without a voice, a person is lost and alone. The story's setting in a city neighborhood emphasizes the closeness of the community and therefore the isolation and alienation of Mallam. Abeeba becomes Mallam's voice, speaking up for him and earning him respect.*

7. *He may understand his wife's role on an emotional level, for as he gives thanks to God for bringing about the changes, he snuggles close to his wife and falls into a contented sleep.*

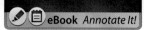
eBook *Annotate It!*

Analyzing the Text   COMMON CORE RL 1, RL 3, W 3d, W 4, SL 1

Cite Text Evidence   Support your responses with evidence from the selection.

1. **Analyze** What words and phrases evoke a sense of the liveliness of Mallam's tea shop? What is revealed about the importance of speech in the Ghanaian culture from this description of the setting?

2. **Infer** Mallam is told to "shut up" whenever he tries to speak, so that eventually "the tea seller learned to swallow his words." Why is Mallam treated in this way? What does this behavior towards Mallam add to readers' understanding of both his character and Ghanaian society?

3. **Cause and Effect** How does Mallam's religion shape his character? How do these aspects of his character lead to conflict? Include details from the text to support your explanation.

4. **Infer** Why does Mallam Sile build a new tea shop? In what way might this be seen as a turning point in the story?

5. **Draw Conclusions** The fight between Abeeba and Samadu is developed in great detail. Why does the author include this scene in the story? Cite details from the story to support your conclusion.

6. **Analyze** What is the **theme**, or underlying message, of the story? How is it related to the setting?

7. **Draw Conclusions** At the end of the story, Mallam Sile questions the changes in his neighbors' attitude toward him as he lies in bed next to his wife. How much does he understand about her role in forcing these changes? Explain your response.

PERFORMANCE TASK

Writing Activity: Description   Using Ali's style as a model, write two or three paragraphs describing a familiar setting that is a gathering place in your school or community.

- Include specific sensory details that convey a vivid picture of your setting as well as its atmosphere.

- Organize your details in a way that allows readers to perceive the relationship of setting elements to each other.

- Share and discuss your description in a small group.

Assign this performance task.

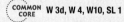

PERFORMANCE TASK   COMMON CORE W 3d, W 4, W10, SL 1

Writing Activity: Description   Have students focus on a specific setting as they draft their descriptions. Teach the lesson on sensory language on page 108a to help students create vivid descriptions. Have students form pairs or small groups to discuss each other's completed drafts. Ask them to be specific in their praise by pointing out which words are effective and offering tips on how to make descriptions more vivid and organization more coherent.

Critical Vocabulary

COMMON CORE L 4c, L 4d

paraphernalia	pugnacious	admonition	extricate	naïveté

Practice and Apply Complete each sentence in a way that reflects the meaning of the Critical Vocabulary word.

1. Abeeba stopped pestering customers to pay their bills after Mallam Sile's *admonition* to her because . . .

2. Mallam worried about confronting the *pugnacious* Samadu because . . .

3. Mallam needed new cupboards to hold his tea-making *paraphernalia* because . . .

4. The women warned Abeeba that she might not be able to *extricate* herself from Samadu's grasp because . . .

5. Mallam's *naïveté* enabled bullies to exploit him because . . .

Vocabulary Strategy: Consult a Dictionary

Although readers often use the context clues in a text that point to the meaning of an unfamiliar word to help them define it, they need to consult dictionaries to find other information about words or to verify meanings. Both print and digital **dictionaries** include the pronunciation, part of speech, etymology, and precise meanings of a word. Sometimes the entry will also identify synonyms or antonyms for the word. Look at the entry for the Vocabulary word *paraphernalia*.

entry word	etymology	part of speech	synonym	definition

par•a•pher•na•lia (păr´ə-fər-nāl´yə) *pl. n. (used with singular or plural verb)* 1. Personal belongings. 2. The articles used in a particular activity; equipment. See synonyms at *equipment*. 3. A married woman's personal property exclusive of her dowry, according to common law. [Medieval Latin *paraphernālia*, neuter pl. of *paraphernālis*, pertaining to the *parapherna*, a married woman's property exclusive of her dowry, from Greek: *para-*, beyond + *phernē*, dowry]

Practice and Apply Use a dictionary to answer these questions about the Critical Vocabulary words.

1. Which meaning of *paraphernalia* is most closely related to the word's origin?

2. What is the meaning of the Latin root from which *extricate* is formed?

3. Where is the long *a* sound in *naïveté*?

4. Based on its dictionary definition, is the connotation of *admonition* "harsh" or "gentle"?

5. What is a synonym for *pugnacious*?

PRACTICE & APPLY

Critical Vocabulary

COMMON CORE L 4c, L 4d

Possible answers:

1. *she did not want to flout his warning directly.*

2. *Samadu was strong and tough.*

3. *his equipment was covered in dust from the floor.*

4. *he could hang on very tightly.*

5. *they could take advantage of his innocence.*

Vocabulary Strategy: Consult a Dictionary

Answers:

1. *It is the third meaning, which refers to a married woman's personal property.*

2. *It comes from the Latin word meaning "hindrances" or "perplexities."*

3. *The long a sound is in the last syllable.*

4. Admonition *has a connotation of being gentle.*

5. *A synonym for* pugnacious *is belligerent.*

TO CHALLENGE STUDENTS . . .

Explore Multiple Meanings Allow students to familiarize themselves with alternative definitions of the Critical Vocabulary words *admonition* and *naïveté.* Ask them to do the following:

- Look up each word in a dictionary. Identify a meaning for each word other than that used in the context of the selection. *(admonition: kind but earnest reproof;* naïveté: *a naïve statement or act)*

- Write a sample sentence for the alternative meaning of the word. *(The toddler ignored his mother's admonition to leave the cat alone. Buying that magic bean was sheer naïveté.)*

ASK STUDENTS to share their findings and sentences with a partner.

Language and Style: Adjectives and Adverbs

 COMMON CORE L 1

Explain to students that adjectives and adverbs make descriptive writing more enjoyable and memorable for the reader. Write *adjectives* and *adverbs* on the board, and then direct students to lines 69–99, a passage that describes Mallam Sile's appearance. Ask volunteers to identify adjectives and adverbs as you record them on the board. Have students familiarize themselves with the differences between adjectives and adverbs by asking them to suggest **synonyms,** or words with similar meanings, for each word on the board.

Answers:

Invite volunteers to share their revisions with the class. Explain how the use of adjectives and adverbs affects the vividness of the imagery. (Accept any revision of the Performance Task activity that includes more specific adjectives and adverbs.)

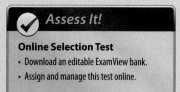

Online Selection Test
- Download an editable ExamView bank.
- Assign and manage this test online.

Language and Style: Adjectives and Adverbs

 COMMON CORE L 1

Adjectives are words used to modify nouns or pronouns. They are located close to the word they modify or come after a linking verb. **Adverbs** are words used to modify verbs, other adverbs, or adjectives. Some may end in *-ly*; others do not.

Adjectives tell . . .	Adverbs tell . . .
which one: *That* cat is mine.	**when:** Call me *later*.
what kind: We ordered *pink* cupcakes.	**where:** We stayed *inside* during the storm.
how many: The bride invited *two hundred* guests.	**how:** He spoke *angrily*.
how much: We needed *less* dirt than we anticipated.	**to what extent:** The acrobat was *very* agile.

Adjectives and adverbs can be valuable tools for a writer. Ali's skillful use of them brings his setting and characters to life in "Mallam Sile."

Read this sentence from the story.

> **Although he didn't have the broad, flat nose, poorly developed chin, and round head of the Pygmies, he was stout and hairy all over, as they were.**

The author could instead have written the sentence this way:

> **He didn't have the nose, chin, and head of the Pygmies, but he looked like them in other ways.**

In contrast to the original sentence, which creates a vivid image in readers' minds of both Pygmies and Mallam Sile, the second version is dull and unhelpful to readers. The lack of descriptive adjectives and adverbs gives them nothing to visualize.

In addition to choosing modifiers for the specific meaning they impart, Ali also chooses adverbs and adjectives for their connotation and level of intensity. For example, he describes the noise in the tea shop as "boisterous chattering," using the more intense *boisterous* instead of the less powerful synonym *loud*.

Practice and Apply Return to the descriptive paragraphs about a familiar setting that you wrote in response to this selection's Performance Task. Revise your paragraphs to include more specific adjectives and adverbs. Compare the "before" and "after" versions of your sentences with a partner and discuss the effect of your revisions.

Strategies for Annotation 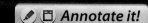 Annotate it!

Adjectives and Adverbs

 COMMON CORE L 1

Have students analyze lines 69–99 by using eBook annotation tools to complete these steps:

- Highlight each adjective.
- Underline each adverb.
- Review the annotations. Notice how each word creates vivid images or helps clarify ideas.
- Use notes to record your overall impression of the passage.

Sile wore the same outfit every day: a white polyester djellabah and its matching *wando*, a loose pair of slacks that tied with strings at the waist. He had eight of these suits, and wore a different one each day of the week. Also, his head was perpetually shaved, and he was never without his white embroidered Mecca hat—worn by highly devout Muslims as a reflection of their submission to Allah. Like most

Writing: Use Sensory Language

COMMON CORE

W 3d

TEACH

Before students begin their Performance Tasks, remind them that in their discussion of "Mallam Sile," they have noted the ways in which Ali brings the setting, action, and characters to life with vivid sensory details. Review that sensory details are those that appeal to the five senses and enable readers to experience the story as if they were present within it.

Clarify that the effectiveness of sensory language hinges on the precision with which the words are chosen. Writers must decide what image they want to create and select nouns, verbs, adjectives, and adverbs that evoke that mental picture. If words are well chosen, the description may appeal to more than one sense. Discuss these points that students should keep in mind:

- **Use concrete details.** Concrete words refer to things in the physical world that can be experienced by the senses. For example, instead of "He looked like he had just woken up," Ali writes: "There was a line of dried drool on his right cheek and whitish mucus had gathered in the corners of his eyes."

- **Use specific words.** Specific words name individuals within a larger classification. For example, Mallam Sile doesn't just burn some incense; he burns "witches' lavender, a strong yet sweet-smelling incense . . ."

- **Use literary devices.** Comparisons in the form of metaphors and similes can evoke feelings as well as mental images. "Abeeba carried herself with the grace and confidence of a lioness . . ." Onomatopoeic words evoke distinct sounds and sensations. Abeeba "whacks" Samadu; the women are "slapping their massive thighs."

PRACTICE AND APPLY

Remind students that they will be evoking a sense of a place in their descriptive paragraphs. To prepare, have them work in pairs to rewrite each of the bland statements listed below in a way that appeals to the senses. Have pairs volunteer their sentences to the class.
1. The cafeteria table was dirty. 2. The cafeteria was noisy.
3. Smells came from the cafeteria kitchen. 4. I stepped in something on the cafeteria floor. *(Sample answers: Stained napkins and puddles of melted ice cream littered the table. Girls' high-pitched shrieks competed with the clanging of trays. The aroma of freshly roasted corn wafted into the dining area. The soft blob of chocolate pudding oozed over my shoe.)*

Support Inferences: Draw Conclusions

COMMON CORE

RL 1

RETEACH

Review the terms *evidence, inference,* and *conclusion.* To comprehend a literary work, readers can use textual evidence, or details from the text, to make inferences, or logical guesses, about the text based on evidence and the reader's own knowledge. Readers may then use one or more inferences to draw conclusions, which are general statements about a text.

- Ask students to reread lines 392–405.
- Ask: Why does the elderly man pay Samadu's debt? *(He is afraid Abeeba will continue to beat Samadu.)*
- Tell students that in answering the question, they made an inference. Ask: What evidence supports your inference? *(Abeeba says, "I will not release him until he pays us back our money!")*
- Ask students to use their inferences to draw a conclusion about community life within the compound. *(People within the compound care about the well-being of its members, even the bullies.)*

 LEVEL UP TUTORIALS Assign the following *Level Up* tutorial: **Drawing Conclusions**

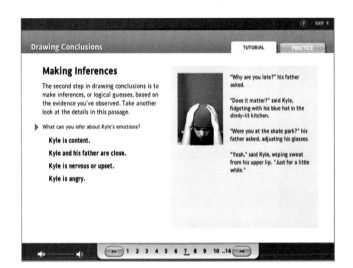

CLOSE READING APPLICATION

Students can apply the skill to lines 414–425. Have pairs respond to the following: Abeeba hopes her husband will not find out about her fight with Samadu. What can you infer about Abeeba's feelings toward Mallam Sile? What conclusion can you draw about men's and women's roles in the culture in which they live?

*my*SmartPlanner   Create lesson plans and access resources online.

My Father's Sadness

Poem by Shirley Geok-lin Lim

Why This Text?

Each student has a unique relationship with one or more parents or caretakers. Rarely are these relationships simple or easily understood. This lesson explores a father-child relationship and how it can be illuminated through the figurative language of poetry.

Key Learning Objective: The student will be able determine figurative meanings of words and phrases in the context of a poem.

Common Core Standards

RL 1 Cite textual evidence to support analysis.
RL 2 Determine themes of a text.
RL 4 Determine figurative meanings.
RL 5 Analyze an author's choices concerning how to structure a text.
SL 6 Adapt speech to a variety of contexts and tasks.
L 3 Understand how language functions in different contexts.
L 5a Interpret figures of speech in context.

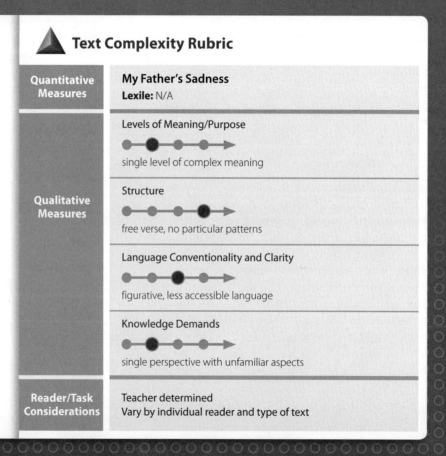

Text Complexity Rubric

Quantitative Measures	**My Father's Sadness** **Lexile:** N/A	
Qualitative Measures	Levels of Meaning/Purpose	single level of complex meaning
	Structure	free verse, no particular patterns
	Language Conventionality and Clarity	figurative, less accessible language
	Knowledge Demands	single perspective with unfamiliar aspects
Reader/Task Considerations	Teacher determined Vary by individual reader and type of text	

Shirley Geok-lin Lim Have students read the information about the author. Explain that Shirley Geok-lin (gyŏk-lin) Lim's "difficult childhood" included a violent home and abandonment by her mother at an early age. Lim's first poem, which she wrote at age 10, was published in the local newspaper; she knew by age 11 that she wanted to be a poet. In her memoir *Among the White Moon Faces*, she recounts some of the difficulties she faced as an immigrant to the United States, where she often did not feel welcomed or accepted.

AS YOU READ Direct students to use the As You Read tip to help them focus their reading.

Determine Figurative Meanings (LINE 2)

COMMON CORE RL 4, L 5a

Point out that poems often include statements that do not make sense if the words are taken literally. Instead, the words have a **figurative meaning** that goes beyond their everyday meaning. Using figurative language is a way for poets to show readers a fresh perspective on a familiar subject.

A **ASK STUDENTS** to reread line 2. What is the literal meaning of this statement? What is the figurative meaning, or the poet's real message? *(The literal meaning is that the father is physically dying as a result of his responsibility. The figurative meaning is that his responsibilities are taking away his youth, either by making him look and feel older or by taking time away from the activities a young person would naturally want to pursue.)*

Shirley Geok-lin Lim *(b. 1944) was born in Malacca, Malaysia. She came to the United States to pursue her education and now teaches at the University of California at Santa Barbara. Lim is a prolific writer, publishing poems, novels, short stories, memoirs, criticism, and other nonfiction works. But she considers herself first and foremost a poet. In 1980, she was the first woman and the first Asian to win the Commonwealth Poetry Prize. In her writing, she explores themes such as identity, transitions, race, gender, and relationships, referring to and drawing from her difficult childhood.*

My Father's Sadness

Poem by Shirley Geok-lin Lim

AS YOU READ Examine the poem for clues that reveal how the speaker views the father's life. Write down any questions you generate during reading.

My father's sadness appears in my dreams. **A**
His young body is dying of responsibility.
So many men and women march out of his mouth
each time he opens his heart for fullness,
5 he is shot down; so many men and women
like dragons' teeth[1] rising in the instance
of his lifetime. He is an oriental. He claims
paternity. But in his dreams he is a young body
with only his life before him.

---

[1] **dragons' teeth:** an allusion to a Greek myth in which a dragon's teeth, when planted, grow into fierce warriors.

Image Credits:(t) Portrait of Shirley Geok-Lin Lim; (b) ©Houghton Mifflin Harcourt

SCAFFOLDING FOR ELL STUDENTS

Vocabulary: Multiple-Meaning Words Remind students that many words in English have different meanings depending on how they are used. Point out *instance* in line 6. Students may be familiar with its use to mean "example," as in the phrase *for instance*. Here its meaning is closer to "event"; the father's lifetime is an event with a beginning and an end.

ASK STUDENTS to work in pairs to determine the contextual meanings of *fullness* in line 4 ("satisfaction of an appetite or need"), *claims* in line 7 ("accepts"), *before* in line 9 ("ahead of, in the future"), and *host* in line 18 ("organism that supports the life of another").

Determine Figurative Meanings (LINES 13–16)

COMMON CORE RL 4, L 5a

Explain that in order to understand the figurative meaning intended by the writer, readers first need to understand the literal meanings of words. In this case, readers need to understand *clay, silicone* (or *silicon*), and *hour-glass*. Make sure students understand that *silicone* refers to the element silica, which often occurs in the form of a fine sand.

B **ASK STUDENTS** to reread the sentence and explain both the literal and the figurative meaning. *(In literal terms, the father's body is a clay figure that breaks down into a fine sand and slips through an hour-glass. The figurative meaning is that the father's responsibility for his many children is causing him to deteriorate.)* How might the children each contribute a bit more to the father's "breaking"? *(Each child adds more economic and emotional responsibility, which he may not have the resources or the strength to completely fulfill.)*

COLLABORATIVE DISCUSSION Before students pair off, briefly discuss the nature of dreams with them. *(Dreams don't always make logical sense, but while we're dreaming, we don't mind; we make the leaps with them. Images in dreams are often absurd, even ridiculous. Things happen that "can't happen.")*

Next, have students pair off and discuss the image of the father the speaker sees in dreams (lines 3–9). Afterwards, conduct a class discussion during which pairs contribute their ideas. *(The dream pictures many men and women marching out of the father's mouth "like dragon's teeth." When the father opens his mouth, he "is shot down." In the poem, life and responsibility overwhelm the father. The dream reinforces the reader's image of the father as overwhelmed.)*

Finally, direct students to re-read the remainder of the poem and make a list of images that have the feeling of a dream. *(the image of the father broken, "his body crumbling to a drizzle of silicone / in the hour glass" [lines 13–16]; the image of the father as "a bull under the axle" [line 17]; the image of a "mangrove netted by lianas" [line 18])*

ASK STUDENTS to share any questions they generated in the course of reading and discussing the selection.

10 My father's sadness masks my face. It is hard
   to see through his tears, his desires drum in my chest.
   I tense like a young man with a full moon
   and no woman in sight. My father broke
   with each child, finer and finer, the clay
15 of his body crumbling to a drizzle of silicone
   in the hour-glass. How hard it is
   to be a father, a bull under the axle,
   the mangrove[2] netted by lianas,[3] the host
   perishing of its lavishness.

---

[2] **mangrove:** a tree that grows along the shore in tropical areas.
[3] **lianas** (lē-ä´nəz): long vines that grow in tropical forests and often climb around trees.

COLLABORATIVE DISCUSSION What is the image of the father that the speaker sees in dreams? With a partner, discuss how this image conveys the speaker's perspective on the father's life. Cite specific textual evidence from the poem to support your ideas.

Image Credits: ©Michael DeFreitas/Robert Harding World Imagery/Getty Images

WHEN STUDENTS STRUGGLE . . .

To help students grasp the poet's basic message, direct their attention to the final lines of the poem, lines 16–19. Explain that here the poet speaks directly of her meaning—"How hard it is / to be a father"—and then follows this direct statement with more figurative language. Ask them to review the footnotes to understand references to the "mangrove" and "lianas." Then discuss ways that a tree—"the host" —might perish from its "lavishness." Ask students to relate this image to the father who is "dying of responsibility" in line 2.

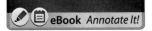

Determine Figurative Meanings

COMMON CORE RL 4, L 5a

Figurative language is language that communicates ideas beyond the literal meaning of the words. Shirley Geok-lin Lim uses figurative language in the form of **similes** and **metaphors** to evoke images of the father and the speaker's perceptions of him in "My Father's Sadness."

| A **simile** compares two dissimilar things using the word *like* or *as*. | "I tense like a young man with a full moon / and no woman in sight." (lines 12–13) |
| A **metaphor** compares two things directly, without using *like* or *as*. | "How hard it is to be a father, / a bull under the axle" (lines 16–17) |

To understand the figurative language in the chart, identify what the things that are compared have in common. In the simile, the speaker and the young man both feel the tension of being frustrated. In the metaphor, the father and the bull are both burdened by heavy labor.

Analyzing the Text

COMMON CORE RL 1, RL 4, L 5a, SL 6

Cite Text Evidence Support your responses with evidence from the selection.

1. **Interpret** What theme about fatherhood is developed in the first stanza? Explain how the poet uses figurative language to convey this meaning.

2. **Cite Evidence** What is the **tone**, or attitude, of the speaker toward the father? How do the details in lines 10–13 communicate this tone?

3. **Analyze** Explain how the metaphor in lines 13–16 contributes to the theme of the poem.

4. **Evaluate** Are lines 18–19, "the mangrove netted by its lianas, the host perishing of its lavishness," an effective ending for the poem? Support your view by explaining both the literal image created by the lines as well as their figurative meaning.

PERFORMANCE TASK

Speaking Activity: Oral Interpretation Prepare an oral reading of the poem:

- On a copy of the poem, highlight important words and phrases that you want to emphasize in your reading to bring out your interpretation.

- Present your reading in a small group. Discuss similarities and differences in the oral interpretations presented by you and your classmates.

PERFORMANCE TASK

COMMON CORE SL 6

Speaking Activity: Oral Interpretation If necessary, model two different readings of the opening lines of the poem to show students how intonation, pacing, and emphasis can influence the effects of an oral presentation. Go over different ways to mark up a copy of the poem. Note that each student can use a unique system as long as it is easily understood by the reader. Their final readings should show evidence of preparation and rehearsal.

PRACTICE & APPLY

Determine Figurative Meanings

 COMMON CORE RL 4, L 5a

Review the definitions and examples in the chart. Then ask students to provide both a simile and a metaphor related to their school day and explain why each comparison makes sense. *(Sample responses: I ran like a rabbit to get to class—the speaker and the rabbit both move very quickly. The assignment was a lead weight around my neck—the assignment and a lead weight both slow the speaker down or limit the speaker's freedom.)*

Analyzing the Text

COMMON CORE RL 1, RL 2, RL 4, L 5a

Possible answers:

1. *The poet presents the idea that being a father takes a toll on a man. In order to be a father, he must relinquish his youth and his own dreams. The poet uses the words "dying" and "shot down" to show that the responsibility of children takes away from the father's life. The poet also presents the image of men and women marching out of his mouth "like dragon's teeth rising" to suggest that the relationship between a man and his children is not easy. It can be adversarial. While the father is proud to claim paternity, he must surrender himself to do it.*

2. *The speaker's tone is sympathetic and compassionate. These feelings are brought out by the speaker's association of him- or herself with the father: "his desires drum in my chest." The speaker understands what the father feels inside—"like a young man with a full moon / and no woman in sight"—but also can see what the father has become, broken "with each child, finer and finer."*

3. *The metaphor shows the physical deterioration of the father with each child, each new responsibility. The "clay" of his body breaks down. The second part of this comparison suggests that the father's time is running out. His sands of life are drizzling through the hour-glass. A father gives his life for his children.*

4. *This metaphor leaves a powerful image in readers' minds that reinforces the theme. Readers envision a tropical shrub or tree covered in clinging vines that wind around it and are supported by it. Figuratively, this image shows the parasitical nature of children—their needs and demands eventually overwhelm the host, or the father.*

Language and Style: Alliteration and Consonance

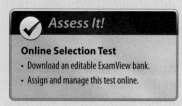COMMON CORE L 3

Remind students that poets can experiment with different types of language and literary devices to produce a desired effect. Devices such as alliteration and consonance add to both the literal and the figurative meanings of the words used.

Possible answers:

Students' lines of poetry should include alliteration and consonance in a way that illustrates their understanding of the two devices. Encourage them to read their work aloud to hear the effects of these sound devices.

> **✓ Assess It!**
>
> **Online Selection Test**
> - Download an editable ExamView bank.
> - Assign and manage this test online.

Language and Style: Alliteration and Consonance

COMMON CORE L 3

In a poem, the sound and language are complementary. A poem's meaning relies on both. In her poem, Lim uses the sound devices **alliteration** and **consonance** to create a particular mood, or feeling, and to emphasize ideas.

Sound Devices in Poetry	
Alliteration is the repetition of consonant sounds at the beginning of words.	"So many men and women march out of his mouth" (line 3)
Consonance is the repetition of consonant sounds within and at the end of words.	"My father's sadness appears in my dreams." (line 1)

In the first example in the chart, the *m* is repeated. This alliteration adds emphasis to the words. It also draws readers' attention to the startling image presented. In the second example, the *s* sound is repeated at the end of several words. This consonance slows the line, helping to create a mood of sadness, which reinforces the poem's meaning.

Lim weaves both devices into several of her lines. Read lines 4–5 from the poem:

> each time he opens his heart for fullness,
> he is shot down; so many men and women

Together the alliteration and the consonance create a link between the sounds of the two lines. The repetition of the initial consonant *h* in the words *he, his, heart,* and *he* again in the second line helps connect the ideas, while the slower pace established by the *s* at the end of several words is brought to an abrupt halt by the use of the word *down,* which repeats none of the sounds. The word ends the pattern, helping to convey the harsh ending of the father's hopes as well.

Practice and Apply In the style of Lim, write four lines of a poem about a particular person. Incorporate alliteration and consonance. Share your lines with a partner and discuss the effectiveness of your devices in creating mood and meaning.

Strategies for Annotation

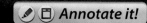 ✎ 🗐 *Annotate it!*

Alliteration and Consonance

Have students look for more examples of alliteration and consonance in the poem. Encourage them to use their eBook annotation tools to do the following:

- Highlight repeated consonant sounds at the beginning of words in green.
- Highlight consonant sounds that create consonance in blue.
- Read the poem aloud, emphasizing the highlighted consonant sounds. What effect do they create?

> My father's sadness masks my face. It is hard
>
> to see through his tears, his desires drum in my chest.
>
> I tense like a young man with a full moon

Analyze Structure

TEACH

Discuss the difference between a traditionally structured poem and one that is organic in form. Make sure students understand that while a traditional poem abides by rules governing line length, stanza structure, and patterns of rhyme and rhythm, organic form has no rules. Point out that Lim chose to write "My Father's Sadness" in free verse, a form of organic poetry.

Tell students that free verse often sounds more fluid and less stilted than highly structured lines because of its irregular line length, irregular rhythm and rhyme, and lack of uniform stanzas. Explain that poets who write in free verse use some of these features as well as other techniques to ensure that the sound of their words creates the meaning that they desire. Advise students to keep these ideas in mind:

- The poet's use or lack of **punctuation** imposes rhythm. For example, punctuation at the end of lines creates a more abrupt rhythm; enjambment, or carrying over a sentence or clause over a line break, contributes to a more flowing rhythm.
- **Line length** may be used to emphasize ideas or capture the attention of readers. For example, a short line after a series of long lines will stand out.
- Literary devices such as **alliteration** and **repetition** can be used to convey tone, create mood, affect rhythm, or intensify meaning.

PRACTICE AND APPLY

Project "My Father's Sadness" on the whiteboard. Have students respond to these questions.

- How does the punctuation in lines 7 and 8 affect the rhythm and tone? *(Periods create short sentences that end in the middle of lines. These sentences intensify the rhythm because of their abruptness. This, in turn, contributes to a forceful tone.)*
- How does the enjambment in lines 13–16 affect the meaning conveyed in those lines? *(These lines show continuity, which reinforces the idea that the father's process of deterioration was continuous, happening bit by bit after each child. Enjambment also stresses key words here: "broke," "clay," "and "silicone.")*
- Examine line 11. How does the poet convey a sense of power and urgency in this line? *(alliteration of the "d")*

 INTERACTIVE LESSON If students need further instruction, use this *Interactive Whiteboard Lesson:* **Poetry: Language and Form.**

Determine Figurative Meanings

RETEACH

 LEVEL UP TUTORIALS Assign the following *Level Up* tutorial: **Elements of Poetry**

Review the definitions in the tutorial: *speaker, traditional and free verse poetry, sound devices, imagery, figurative language.* Ask students to answer these questions for "My Father's Sadness":

- Who is the speaker? *(a person remembering his or her father)*
- Is it traditional poetry or free verse? How do you know? *(free verse because is has no set pattern of rhyming words, line lengths, or stanza lengths)*
- What sound devices are used? *(alliteration, consonance)*
- What are some examples of the imagery used? *(The father is compared to a frustrated young man, a bull, and a mangrove tree.)*
- What types of figurative language are used? *(similes, metaphors)*

CLOSE READING APPLICATION

Have students use the elements of poetry to analyze favorite song lyrics. They can download lyrics from the Internet and then judge whether they work as poetry. If not, challenge students to revise the lyrics by adding sound devices and figurative language. Ask volunteers to share their work with the class.

from A Vindication of the Rights of Woman

Political Argument by Mary Wollstonecraft

Why This Text?

Students regularly encounter political arguments in print, broadcast and digital media, and in person at school and in their community. This lesson explores a political argument about education for women.

▶ **View It!**

Professional Development Podcast:

Teaching Argument

Key Learning Objective: The student will be able to analyze counterarguments and rhetorical devices used in an argument.

Common Core Standards

RI 1 Cite textual evidence.

RI 4 Determine the meaning of words and phrases.

RI 5 Analyze the structure an author uses in her argument.

RI 6 Determine an author's point of view or purpose.

RI 10 Read and comprehend literary nonfiction.

SL 6 Adapt speech to a variety of contexts and tasks.

L 1 Demonstrate command of the conventions of standard English.

L 4a Use context as a clue to the meaning of a word or phrase.

L 4d Verify the preliminary determination of the meaning of a word or phrase.

▲ Text Complexity Rubric

Quantitative Measures	**A Vindication of the Rights of Woman** Lexile: 1350L
Qualitative Measures	**Levels of Meaning/Purpose**  more than one purpose; implied, easily identified from context
	Structure  organization of main ideas and details complex but mostly explicit; may exhibit disciplinary traits
	Language Conventionality and Clarity complex and varied sentence structure
	Knowledge Demands complex social studies concepts
Reader/Task Considerations	Teacher determined Vary by individual reader and type of text

Mary Wollstonecraft Have students read the background and information about the author. Explain that Mary Wollstonecraft was one of seven children in a struggling middle-class English family who supplemented her limited formal education with extensive reading on her own. While running a school in London with her sisters, she met a group of liberal reformers who gave her a broader perspective on her personal struggle for liberation. Her pamphlet, *Thoughts on the Education of Daughters,* was published in 1787.

AS YOU READ Instruct students to use the As You Read directions to focus their reading and to write down any questions that occur to them as they read.

Analyze Style: Rhetorical Devices (LINES 1–6)

COMMON CORE **RI 6**

Inform students that rhetorical devices appear throughout Wollstonecraft's argument. Define rhetorical devices as techniques that writers use to enhance arguments and effectively convey ideas.

One such device is antithesis. **Antithesis** puts sharply contrasting words, phrases, clauses, or sentences near one another to emphasize a point, often using a parallel grammatical structure.

 CITE TEXT EVIDENCE Ask students to reread lines 1–6 and identify where Wollstonecraft uses antithesis. What is her purpose in using antithesis in this passage? *(lines 4–6; by juxtaposing the contrasting terms "nature" and "civilization," Wollstonecraft suggests that she will explore these two influences as they relate to women's education and their place in society.)*

CRITICAL VOCABULARY

vindication: Wollstonecraft's title suggests that her purpose is to defend the rights of women.

CITE TEXT EVIDENCE Ask students what evidence Wollstonecraft provides in lines 1–18 to support the idea that the vindication of the rights of women is necessary. *(Their education has been neglected [lines 9–10]. They've been "rendered weak and wretched" [lines 10–11].)*

Background *In the eighteenth century, the daughters of English gentlemen were mostly taught reading, languages, playing the piano, singing, drawing, and needlework. This was thought to be adequate preparation for their lives as wives, mothers, governesses, or companions to wealthy ladies.*

Mary Wollstonecraft *(1759–1797) is considered by many to be the mother of feminism. Inspired by the ideas of liberal reformers, she wrote about the rights of women and others. Her 1790 book,* A Vindication of the Rights of Man, *attacked class and privilege; she followed that with* A Vindication of the Rights of Woman *in 1792.*

from A Vindication of the Rights of Woman

Political Argument by Mary Wollstonecraft

AS YOU READ Look for details that tell you about the nature of women's education in the eighteenth century.

From the Introduction

After considering the historic page, and viewing the living world with anxious solicitude, the most melancholy emotions of sorrowful indignation have depressed my spirits, and I have sighed when obliged to confess, that either nature has made a great difference between man and man, or that the civilization which has hitherto taken place in the world has been very partial. I have turned over various books written on the subject of education, and patiently observed the conduct of parents and the management of schools; but what has been the result?—a profound conviction that the neglected
10 education of my fellow-creatures is the grand source of the misery I deplore; and that women, in particular, are rendered weak and wretched by a variety of concurring causes, originating from one hasty conclusion. The conduct and manners of women, in fact, evidently prove that their minds are not in a healthy state; for, like the flowers which are planted in too rich a soil, strength and usefulness are sacrificed to beauty; and the flaunting leaves, after having pleased a fastidious eye, fade, disregarded on the stalk, long before the season when they ought to have arrived at maturity. One cause of this barren

vindication
(vĭn´dĭ-kā´shən) *n.* justification.

Image Credits: (t) ©Corbis; (b) ©Houghton Mifflin Harcourt

SCAFFOLDING FOR ELL STUDENTS

Antithesis *Antithesis* sounds more intimidating than it is. Help students understand the antithesis in lines 4–6 by having volunteers paraphrase the two-part statement in everyday language. To help students visualize the two extremes expressed by the antithesis, write the paraphrases in a chart like the one below:

either	or
nature did not make all men equal	*the benefits of civilization have been unfairly distributed between men and women*

Tell students that to identify later instances of antithesis, they should look for antonyms, or words with opposite meanings, or phrases that show a contrast, such as *either/or.*

Analyze Structure

COMMON CORE **RI 5, RI 10**

(LINES 18–49)

Explain that, in an **argument,** the speaker or writer presents one or more **claims,** or positions, on a specific issue and supports them with reasons and evidence. A claim can be directly stated or inferred.

B **ASK STUDENTS** to summarize the claim Wollstonecraft asserts and supports in lines 18–37. *(Women have been denied the right to improve their minds by a "false system of education.")*

Explain that strong arguments include **counterarguments,** or arguments that anticipate and address opposing claims. Counterarguments show that the speaker or writer can disprove or answer the opposition's objections.

C **CITE TEXT EVIDENCE** Have students cite the opposing viewpoint that Wollstonecraft identifies in lines 43–49. How does she concede, or admit, this viewpoint and how does she argue against it? *(In lines 43–47, she concedes that women are inferior in the realm of physical strength. In lines 48–49, she argues that men try to extend this natural inferiority by making women believe they are too weak to be anything other than objects of desire.)*

Analyze Style: Rhetorical Devices (LINES 54–57)

COMMON CORE **RI 6**

Explain that Wollstonecraft uses rhetorical questions—questions to which no answer is expected—as a rhetorical device to emphasize meaning and evoke an emotional response.

D **ASK STUDENTS** the purpose of the rhetorical question in lines 54–57. *(Wollstonecraft uses the question to introduce the topic of women acquiring virtues and talents often deemed "manly.")*

CRITICAL VOCABULARY

abrogated: Wollstonecraft admits that the "law of nature" relating to man's superiority in physical strength has not been invalidated.

ASK STUDENTS what kind of a law might be abrogated in favor of women. *(a law that seeks to discriminate against women)*

B 20 blooming I attribute to a false system of education, gathered from the books written on this subject by men who, considering females rather as women than human creatures, have been more anxious to make them alluring mistresses than affectionate wives and rational mothers; and the understanding of the sex has been so bubbled by this specious homage,[1] that the civilized women of the present century, with a few exceptions, are only anxious to inspire love, when they ought to cherish a nobler ambition, and by their abilities and virtues exact respect.

30 In a treatise,[2] therefore, on female rights and manners, the works which have been particularly written for their improvement must not be overlooked; especially when it is asserted, in direct terms, that the minds of women are enfeebled by false refinement; that the books of instruction, written by men of genius, have had the same tendency as more frivolous productions; and that . . . they are treated as a kind of subordinate beings, and not as a part of the human species, when improvable reason is allowed to be the dignified distinction which raises men above the brute creation, and puts a natural scepter in a feeble hand.

C 40 Yet, because I am a woman, I would not lead my readers to suppose that I mean violently to agitate the contested question respecting the quality or inferiority of the sex; but as the subject lies in my way, and I cannot pass it over without subjecting the main tendency of my reasoning to misconstruction, I shall stop a moment to deliver, in a few words, my opinion. In the government of the physical world it is observable that the female in point of strength is, in general, inferior to the male. This is the law of nature; and it does not appear to be suspended or **abrogated** in favor of woman. A degree of physical superiority cannot, therefore, be denied—and it is a noble prerogative! But not content with this natural preeminence, men endeavor to sink us still lower merely to render us alluring objects for a moment; and 50 women, intoxicated by the adoration which men, under the influence of their senses, pay them, do not seek to obtain a durable interest in their hearts, or to become the friends of the fellow creatures who find amusement in their society.

abrogate
(ăb´rə-gāt´) *v.* to revoke or nullify.

D I am aware of an obvious inference: from every quarter have I heard exclamations against masculine women; but where are they to be found? If by this appellation men mean to inveigh against their ardor[3] in hunting, shooting, and gaming, I shall most cordially join in the cry; but if it be against the imitation of manly virtues, or, more properly speaking, the attainment of those talents and virtues, the 60 exercise of which ennobles the human character, and which raise

---

[1] **bubbled by this specious homage** (spē´shəs hŏm´ĭj): deceived by this false honor.

[2] **treatise:** a formal, detailed article or book on a particular subject.

[3] **If by . . . inveigh** (ĭn-vā´) **against their ardor:** if by this term ("masculine women") men mean to condemn some women's enthusiasm.

APPLYING ACADEMIC VOCABULARY

bias	exploit

As you discuss the Wollstonecraft argument, incorporate the following Collection 2 academic vocabulary words: *bias* and *exploit*. To probe the argument, ask students to cite the evidence Wollstonecraft provides that there is **bias** against women in society. In addition, ask students to explain Wollstonecraft's argument that men have sought to **exploit** their strengths at the expense of women.

females in the scale of animal being, when they are comprehensively termed mankind; all those who view them with a philosophic eye must, I should think, wish with me, that they may every day grow more and more masculine. . . .

My own sex, I hope, will excuse me, if I treat them like rational creatures, instead of flattering their *fascinating* graces, and viewing them as if they were in a state of perpetual childhood, unable to stand alone. I earnestly wish to point out in what true dignity and human happiness consists—I wish to persuade women to endeavor to acquire
70 strength, both of mind and body, and to convince them that the soft phrases, **susceptibility** of heart, delicacy of sentiment, and refinement of taste, are almost synonymous with epithets[4] of weakness, and that those beings who are only the objects of pity and that kind of love, which has been termed its sister, will soon become objects of contempt. . . .

susceptibility
(sə-sĕp´tə-bĭl´ĭ-tē) *n.*
vulnerability, or
the likeliness to be
affected.

The education of women has, of late, been more attended to than formerly; yet they are still reckoned a frivolous sex, and ridiculed or pitied by the writers who endeavor by satire or instruction to improve them. It is acknowledged that they spend many of the first years of
80 their lives in acquiring a smattering of accomplishments;[5] meanwhile strength of body and mind are sacrificed to libertine[6] notions of beauty, to the desire of establishing themselves—the only way women can rise in the world—by marriage. And this desire making mere animals of them, when they marry they act as such children may be expected to act: they dress; they paint, and nickname God's creatures. Surely these weak beings are only fit for a seraglio![7] Can they be expected to govern a family with judgment, or take care of the poor babes whom they bring into the world?

If then it can be fairly deduced from the present conduct of
90 the sex, from the prevalent fondness for pleasure which takes place of ambition and those nobler passions that open and enlarge the soul; that the instruction which women have hitherto received has only tended, with the constitution of civil society, to render them insignificant objects of desire—mere propagators of fools!—if it can be proved that in aiming to accomplish them, without cultivating their understandings, they are taken out of their sphere of duties, and made ridiculous and useless when the short-lived bloom of beauty is over, I presume that *rational* men will excuse me for endeavoring to persuade them to become more masculine and respectable.

---

[4] **epithets** (ĕp´ə-thĕts´): descriptive terms.
[5] **accomplishments:** This term, when applied to women, designated only those achievements then considered suitable for middle- and upper-class women, such as painting, singing, playing a musical instrument, and embroidery.
[6] **libertine** (lĭb´ər-tēn´): indecent or unseemly.
[7] **seraglio** (sə-răl´yō): harem.

A Vindication of the Rights of Woman **115**

SCAFFOLDING FOR ELL STUDENTS

Analyze Structure: Counterargument Explain that *counter–* means "against." A *counterargument* is made against another argument, or claim. It is part of a pattern that starts with acknowledging an opposing claim and is often introduced by a signal phrase, such as "Many have pointed out . . ." or "It is true that . . ." Read lines 76–80 aloud.

- Ask: In what lines does Wollstonecraft acknowledge the opposing claim? *(Lines 79–80: "It is acknowledged that . . .")* What does Wollstonecraft admit? *(that women do receive education)* Where does Wollstonecraft make a counterargument to this claim? *(lines 80–88)*

Read lines 80–88 aloud, pausing after each to have a volunteer paraphrase the meaning. Have a volunteer summarize the counterargument.

Analyze Language
(LINES 65–75)

Explain that sarcasm is a mocking or joking tone that may be used to emphasize a point by saying the opposite of what is meant.

E **ASK STUDENTS** to reread lines 65–75 and interpret what Wollstonecraft really means in the first sentence of the paragraph. *(She believes women are fully rational and speaks to them as such.)* Then ask students at whom Wollstonecraft directs this sarcastic remark? Why does she do so? *(She directs the remark at those, especially men, who believe women are irrational or childlike and incapable of serious thought. She wants to challenge this idea and encourage both men and women to believe that women should seek to improve their minds and strengthen their bodies.)*

Analyze Structure
(LINES 79–99)

Explain that in an argument a writer must support the claim, or conclusion, with reasons, statements that justify an action or opinion, and evidence, specific facts, examples, and opinions that support a claim.

F **CITE TEXT EVIDENCE** Ask students to identify the claim in lines 76–99 and the reasons and evidence that Wollstonecraft uses to support it. *(Claim: women should become more masculine and respectable [line 99]; Support: emphasis on acquiring accomplishments and being beautiful turns women into frivolous creatures unable to be strong wives and mothers [lines 80–88]; their education turns them into "insignificant objects of desire" and leaves them with nothing of value once their beauty has faded [lines 89–97])*

CRITICAL VOCABULARY

susceptibility: Wollstonecraft believes that women's vulnerability is generally seen as a sign of weakness.

ASK STUDENTS how women might exhibit "susceptibility of heart" and why it might be seen as a weakness. *(They are likely to be affected by other people's needs and problems and might be seen as easily taken advantage of.)*

A Vindication of the Rights of Woman **115**

Analyze Structure: Counterargument

 COMMON CORE RI 5

(LINES 106–111)

Tell students that before presenting a counterargument, writers first identify or imply the opposing viewpoint or claim.

G **CITE TEXT EVIDENCE** Ask students to reread lines 106–111 and restate the opposing claim that Wollstonecraft identifies in this paragraph. *(The purpose of women's education is to make them pleasing [lines 110–111].)*

Analyze Style: Rhetorical Devices

 COMMON CORE RI 6

(LINES 114–136)

Remind students to continue looking for examples of antithesis as they read. Also have them look for analogies. Remind students that an **analogy** is a detailed comparison between dissimilar things to explain an unfamiliar idea in terms of a familiar one.

H **CITE TEXT EVIDENCE** Ask students to reread lines 114–136 and identify an example of analogy and an example of antithesis. Then ask them to explain how each device strengthens Wollstonecraft's counterargument. *(Analogy: compares women's charms to "oblique sunbeams" that will fade in time [lines 114–117], which supports the idea that an education focused on pleasing leaves women with nothing when their beauty fades; Antithesis: "a mistress; the chaste wife and mother" (lines 133–134), which emphasizes again that pleasing men is the task of a mistress not of a wife and mother, for whom pleasing should be only "the polish of her virtues.")*

CRITICAL VOCABULARY

congenial: Wollstonecraft suggests that women may make themselves sick and unhappy by spending too much time thinking about the happiness of agreeable people.

ASK STUDENTS why a woman who thinks about "the happiness enjoyed by congenial souls" too much might become discontent. *(Comparing herself to others may make her feel inadequate.)*

---

100   Indeed the word masculine is only a bugbear:[8] there is little reason to fear that women will acquire too much courage or fortitude; for their apparent inferiority with respect to bodily strength, must render them, in some degree, dependent on men in the various relations of life; but why should it be increased by prejudices that give a sex to virtue, and confound simple truths with sensual reveries?[9]

From Chapter 2

Youth is the season for love in both sexes; but in those days of thoughtless enjoyment provision should be made for the more important years of life, when reflection takes place of sensation. But Rousseau,[10] and most of the male writers who have followed his steps, 110 have warmly inculcated that the whole tendency of female education ought to be directed to one point: to render them[11] pleasing.

    Let me reason with the supporters of this opinion who have any knowledge of human nature, do they imagine that marriage can eradicate the habitude of life? The woman who has only been taught to please will soon find that her charms are oblique sunbeams, and that they cannot have much effect on her husband's heart when they are seen every day, when the summer is passed and gone. Will she then have sufficient native energy to look into herself for comfort, and cultivate her dormant faculties? or, is it not more rational to expect 120 that she will try to please other men; and, in the emotions raised by the expectation of new conquests, endeavor to forget the mortification her love or pride has received? When the husband ceases to be a lover— and the time will inevitably come, her desire of pleasing will then grow languid, or become a spring of bitterness; and love, perhaps, the most evanescent of all passions, gives place to jealousy or vanity.

    I now speak of women who are restrained by principle or prejudice; such women, though they would shrink from an intrigue with real abhorrence, yet, nevertheless, wish to be convinced by the homage of gallantry that they are cruelly neglected by their husbands; 130 or, days and weeks are spent in dreaming of the happiness enjoyed by **congenial** souls till their health is undermined and their spirits broken by discontent. How then can the great art of pleasing be such a necessary study? it is only useful to a mistress; the chaste wife, and serious mother, should only consider her power to please as the polish of her virtues, and the affection of her husband as one of the comforts that render her talk less difficult and her life happier. But, whether she be loved or neglected, her first wish should be to make herself

congenial
(kən-jēn´yəl) *adj.*
agreeable,
sympathetic.

---

[8] **bugbear:** an object of exaggerated fear.

[9] **confound . . . reveries** (rĕv´ə-rēz): confuse simple truths with men's sexual daydreams.

[10] **Rousseau** (rōō-sō´): The Swiss-born French philosopher Jean-Jacques Rousseau (1712–1778) presented a plan for female education in his famous 1762 novel *Émile.*

[11] **them:** that is, females.

WHEN STUDENTS STRUGGLE...

To guide comprehension of the counterarguments (and help students answer item 5 on page 120), have pairs fill out a chart like the one shown, following these steps:

- Reread and discuss the introduction to understand the author's claim: *Women should seek respect for their abilities rather than love for their beauty.*

- Look for statements that reflect an opposite point of view: *Women should seek to be beautiful and pleasing.* Continue reading to see how Wollstonecraft argues against these viewpoints.

Because the language and sentence structure are so complex, suggest that students pause after each paragraph to paraphrase the main idea and determine how this information might fit into their chart.

respectable, and not to rely for all her happiness on a being subject to like infirmities with herself.

140   The worthy Dr. Gregory fell into a similar error. I respect his heart; but entirely disapprove of his celebrated Legacy to his Daughters.[12] . . .

He actually recommends **dissimulation**, and advises an innocent girl to give the lie to her feelings, and not dance with spirit, when gaiety of heart would make her feet eloquent without making her gestures immodest. In the name of truth and common sense, why should not one woman acknowledge that she can take more exercise than another? or, in other words, that she has a sound constitution; and why, to damp innocent vivacity, is she darkly to be told that men
150   will draw conclusions which she little thinks of? Let the libertine draw what inference he pleases; but, I hope, that no sensible mother will restrain the natural frankness of youth by instilling such indecent cautions. Out of the abundance of the heart the mouth speaketh; and a wiser than Solomon[13] hath said, that the heart should be made clean, and not trivial ceremonies observed, which it is not very difficult to fulfil with scrupulous exactness when vice reigns in the heart.

Women ought to endeavor to purify their heart; but can they do so when their uncultivated understandings make them entirely dependent on their senses for employment and amusement, when no
160   noble pursuit sets them above the little vanities of the day, or enables them to curb the wild emotions that agitate a reed over which every passing breeze has power? To gain the affections of a virtuous man, is affectation necessary? Nature has given woman a weaker frame than man; but, to ensure her husband's affections, must a wife, who by the exercise of her mind and body whilst she was discharging the duties of a daughter, wife, and mother, has allowed her constitution to retain its natural strength, and her nerves a healthy tone, is she, I say, to condescend to use art and feign a sickly delicacy in order to secure her husband's affection? Weakness may excite tenderness, and gratify
170   the arrogant pride of man; but the lordly caresses of a protector will not gratify a noble mind that pants for, and deserves to be respected. Fondness is a poor substitute for friendship! . . .

Besides, the woman who strengthens her body and exercises her mind will, by managing her family and practicing various virtues, become the friend, and not the humble dependent of her husband; and if she, by possessing such substantial qualities, merit his regard, she

---

[12] **Dr. Gregory . . . Daughters:** In his 1774 work *A Father's Legacy for His Daughters*, John Gregory (1724–1773) offered a plan for female education that remained popular for decades.

[13] **a wiser than Solomon:** King David, reputed author of many psalms in the Bible and the father of King Solomon, who was known for his wisdom. The words that follow draw on ideas in Psalm 24, which states that only those with "clean hands, and a pure heart" shall ascend into Heaven.

Opposing Viewpoints	Wollstonecraft's Counterarguments
A common viewpoint in Wollstonecraft's day: More education will make women too masculine.	Talent and virtue do not belong to just one sex. All humans should have strong minds and bodies. Women should seek to be respectable rather than desirable.
Rousseau's viewpoint	
Dr. Gregory's viewpoint	

margin:

dissimulation
(dĭ-sĭm′yə-lā′shən) *n.* deceit or pretense.

TEACH

CLOSE READ

Analyze Language COMMON CORE RI 4, RI 6
(LINES 162–163)

Explain that an author's word choices not only convey meaning but also add to the power and beauty of the text.

ASK STUDENTS to reread lines 162–163 and explain the meaning of *affection* and *affectation*. (*affection means "love"; affectation means "acting in an artificial way"*) Then invite students to explain how these word choices strengthen Wollstonecraft's writing. (*By using these words that look and sound very similar but that have very different meanings, Wollstonecraft creates a sentence with poetic sound and rhythm that communicates her ideas in a memorable way.*)

Analyze Structure: Counterargument (LINES 163–172) COMMON CORE RI 5

Tell students that authors or speakers may return to particular claims and counterarguments throughout the course of an argument in order to emphasize a particular point or introduce new support.

CITE TEXT EVIDENCE Ask students to reread lines 163–172 and identify the earlier opposing viewpoint that is restated here. If students are unsure, suggest that they reread lines 43–45. ("*Nature has given woman a weaker frame than man*" [lines 163–164]). Then have students summarize Wollstonecraft's counterarguments. (*If a woman has stayed as healthy and strong as she can in mind and body, she should not have to appear weaker than she is in order to gain her husband's affection.*)

CRITICAL VOCABULARY

dissimulation: Wollstonecraft argues against Dr. Gregory, who recommends deceit to young girls as an appropriate way to please men.

ASK STUDENTS why Wollstonecraft is opposed to dissimulation by young girls or women. (*She does not believe girls and women should conceal their true feelings or mental and physical strengths in order to be pleasing to men.*)

Analyze Language

COMMON CORE RI 4

(LINES 179–202)

Tell students that Wollstonecraft wrote during the Enlightenment, a period in history when intellectuals emphasized reason more than emotion or faith.

 CITE TEXT EVIDENCE Ask students to reread lines 179–202 and identify the places where Wollstonecraft appeals to logic and reason. *(lines 188, 195, 199–202)* Discuss why she placed such emphasis on reason and an appeal to rational people in her argument about education for women. *(Wollstonecraft argues that she developed her ideas by using the reason that God gave her, and that rational people should understand that women have as much need for and are just as capable as men in developing their reason. In this way, she applies the ideas of other intellectuals of her age to the issue of women's rights.)*

Analyze Style: Rhetorical Devices (LINES 207–213)

COMMON CORE RI 6

Remind students that analogies compare things that are similar in some way but are otherwise dissimilar.

 CITE TEXT EVIDENCE Ask students to identify and explain two examples of analogies in lines 207–213. *(Women's desire to be loved rather than respected is compared to the slavish relationship of subjects to absolute monarchs. [lines 207–210]; Women who are not free are compared to exotic plants [lines 211–213].)* Then ask how these analogies add to the persuasiveness of Wollstonecraft's argument. *(These vivid images drive home the point that women must be encouraged to develop all their talents and virtues.)*

COLLABORATIVE DISCUSSION Have students pair up and discuss specific evidence that reflects Wollstonecraft's view of the reasoning guiding the education of women and the harm that results from this reasoning. Then have them share their conclusions with the class as a whole. Accept all reasonable responses.

ASK STUDENTS to share any questions they generated in the course of reading and discussing the selection.

---

will not find it necessary to conceal her affection, nor to pretend to an unnatural coldness of constitution to excite her husband's passions. . . .

 If all the faculties of woman's mind are only to be cultivated as
180 they respect her dependence on man; if, when a husband be obtained, she have arrived at her goal, and meanly proud rests satisfied with such a paltry crown, let her grovel contentedly, scarcely raised by her employments above the animal kingdom; but, if, struggling for the prize of her high calling, she look beyond the present scene, let her cultivate her understanding without stopping to consider what character the husband may have whom she is destined to marry. Let her only determine, without being too anxious about present happiness, to acquire the qualities that ennoble a rational being, and a rough inelegant husband may shock her taste without destroying her
190 peace of mind. She will not model her soul to suit the frailties of her companion, but to bear with them: his character may be a trial, but not an impediment to virtue. . . .

These may be termed Utopian dreams. Thanks to that Being who impressed them on my soul, and gave me sufficient strength of mind to dare to exert my own reason, till, becoming dependent only on him for the support of my virtue, I view, with indignation, the mistaken notions that enslave my sex.

I love man as my fellow; but his scepter, real, or usurped, extends not to me, unless the reason of an individual demands my homage;
200 and even then the submission is to reason, and not to man. In fact, the conduct of an accountable being must be regulated by the operations of its own reason; or on what foundation rests the throne of God?

It appears to me necessary to dwell on these obvious truths, because females have been insulated, as it were; and, while they have been stripped of the virtues that should clothe humanity, they have been decked with artificial graces that enable them to exercise a short-lived tyranny. Love, in their bosoms, taking place of every nobler passion, their sole ambition is to be fair, to raise emotion instead of inspiring respect; and this ignoble desire, like the servility in absolute
210 monarchies, destroys all strength of character. Liberty is the mother of virtue, and if women be, by their very constitution, slaves, and not allowed to breathe the sharp invigorating air of freedom, they must ever languish like exotics,[14] and be reckoned beautiful flaws in nature.

---

[14] **languish** (lăng′gwĭsh) **like exotics:** wilt like plants grown away from their natural environment.

COLLABORATIVE DISCUSSION What does Wollstonecraft see as the rationale guiding the education of women in her society? With a partner, discuss the harm that she thinks results from this view of education. Cite specific textual evidence from the essay to support your ideas.

WHEN STUDENTS STRUGGLE . . .

To help students identify rhetorical devices used in Wollstonecraft's argument, have them work in pairs to add examples to a chart like the one shown, using the clues shown on the chart.

Rhetorical Device	Examples
analogies: comparison, often signaled by like or as	"they must ever languish like exotics" (lines 212–213)
antithesis: ideas that are opposites placed close together	"they have been stripped . . ., they have been decked" (lines 205–206)
rhetorical questions: don't require answers; emphasize meaning and emotion	"on what foundation rests the throne of God?" (line 202)

Analyze Structure: Counterarguments

 COMMON CORE RI 5, RI 10

In an argument, writers support their **claims,** or positions on an issue, by presenting logical reasons and valid evidence. Writers may also include **counterarguments** in which they anticipate opposing views and refute them. Mary Wollstonecraft provides several counterarguments in her argument, which show that she has thought about the issue from all sides. Her counterarguments acknowledge her opponents' perspective, making readers who might disagree with her more open to her ideas.

Examine Wollstonecraft's counterargument in lines 43–49: "In the government of the physical world it is observable that the female in point of strength is, in general, inferior to the male . . . But not content with this natural preeminence, men endeavor to sink us still lower merely to render us alluring objects for a moment. . . ." Wollstonecraft starts by agreeing that men do have a physical advantage over women. Then she points out that this advantage is limited to their strength, so it does not justify keeping women in an inferior status in which they merely serve as attractive and charming ornaments for the pleasure of men.

Analyze Style: Rhetorical Devices

 COMMON CORE RI 6

In her argument, Mary Wollstonecraft uses a variety of **rhetorical devices.** The devices shown in the chart make her points clearer and more persuasive.

Rhetorical Device	Example
Analogies are detailed comparisons made between dissimilar things to explain an unfamiliar idea in terms of a familiar one.	Wollstonecraft develops an analogy in her introduction that helps to explain her view of how inadequate or "false" education affects the lives of women.
Antithesis juxtaposes sharply contrasting words, phrases, clauses, or sentences to emphasize a point, often using a parallel grammatical structure.	In speaking of Dr. Gregory, Wollstonecraft says, "I respect his heart; but entirely disapprove of his celebrated Legacy to his Daughters."
Rhetorical questions are questions inserted into a text to which no answer is expected. They emphasize meaning and evoke an emotional response.	Wollstonecraft asks, "Can they [women] be expected to govern a family with judgment or take care of the poor babes whom they bring into the world?"

CLOSE READ

Analyze Structure: Counterarguments

 COMMON CORE RI 5, RI 10

Help students understand the terms **claim** and **counterargument.** Explain that opposing views are claims made by those who disagree with the author's claims. In structuring a counterargument, a writer or speaker may state or imply a counterclaim (a claim that refutes the opposing view) and support that with reasons and evidence.

Have students review the example of Wollstonecraft's counterargument in lines 43–49. Guide them to see that Wollstonecraft generally claims that women are *not* inferior to men and that she is anticipating and answering the claim that women are inferior to men in physical strength.

Analyze Style: Rhetorical Devices

 COMMON CORE RI 6

Define **rhetorical devices** as techniques that writers use to enhance arguments and effectively convey ideas. Have students review the three types of rhetorical devices and the related examples. Explain that analogies are often signaled by the words *like* or *as.* Ask students what words or phrases are sharply contrasted in the example of antithesis. *("respect" and "entirely disapprove")*

Strategies for Annotation 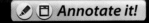 Annotate it!

Analyze Structure: Counterargument

 COMMON CORE RI 5, RI 10

Share these strategies for guided or independent analysis:

- Highlight in yellow the claims that Wollstonecraft makes.
- Highlight in blue the opposing claims that Wollstonecraft identifies.
- Underline reasons and evidence that support Wollstonecraft's argument.
- On a note summarize Wollstonecraft's counterarguments.

Youth is the season for love in both sexes; but in those days of thoughtless enjoyment provision should be made for the more important years of life, when reflection takes place of sensation. But Rousseau, and most of the male writers who have followed his steps, have warmly inculcated that the whole tendency of female education ought to be directed to one point: to render them pleasing.

Analyzing the Text $\overset{\text{COMMON}}{\text{CORE}}$ RI 1, RI 5, RI 6

Possible answers:

1. *Claim: women should be educated in a way that makes them strong mentally, physically, and emotionally. Reasons: Their present education makes them "entirely dependent upon their senses" and may lead them to immoral behavior or at least to a bitter marital relationship; making them stronger will lead them to be better wives and mothers; they will become more virtuous if their character is developed.*

2. *This analogy compares women to flowers forced in a greenhouse. Like the flowers, the women peak too soon and then fade and languish on the stem for the rest of their lives, never reaching their full potential. By making this comparison, Wollstonecraft helps readers to understand her view that teaching women only to be refined and beautiful, pleasing to the eye, condemns them to lead meaningless, barren lives.*

3. *By changing the intonation of her prose through the use of questions, Wollstonecraft captures and refocuses her readers' attention. The question structure also allows her to convey a tone of disbelief and scorn that such advice (to dissemble and pretend infirmity where it doesn't exist) could even be considered legitimate. She uses words such as "vanities," "wild emotions," "affectation," and "feign" to reinforce this tone.*

4. *Antithesis; Wollstonecraft shows how education will help women maintain their own nobility of character even if they find themselves in a less than ideal marriage. The educated woman will still be able to live a life of worth and dignity because she will not be trying to cater to the baseness of her husband but will find a way to tolerate his qualities.*

5. *Improved education will make women better wives and mothers; they will become more masculine only in the sense of becoming more virtuous. Since women are without the physical strength of men, they will still be dependent on men in several ways. Rousseau: the superficiality of a life geared toward pleasing men has no happy ending; a woman's allure will fail to keep the attention of her husband in time and she will then be forced to turn to other men for her due adoration or become bitter and jealous. Dr. Gregory: his advice is demeaning and an insult to truth and common sense.*

6. *Wollstonecraft says that to deny equal education to women is to keep them enslaved and deny them liberty. By using these specific terms she is linking her argument to the lofty ideals already embraced by the intellectual leaders of the day. This strategy increases the effectiveness of her argument by relating it to the more universal issue of liberty for all.*

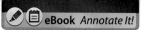

Analyzing Text $\overset{\text{COMMON}}{\text{CORE}}$ RI 1, RI 5, RI 6, SL 6

Cite Text Evidence Support your responses with evidence from the selection.

1. **Identify** What is Mary Wollstonecraft's claim in her argument? Identify three reasons that she provides to support this claim.

2. **Analyze** What analogy does Wollstonecraft present in the first paragraph of her argument? How does this analogy clarify the point she is making?

3. **Analyze** Wollstonecraft includes a series of rhetorical questions in lines 157–168. How does her use of this device contribute to her purpose?

4. **Analyze** What rhetorical device does Wollstonecraft use in lines 190–192? What idea is emphasized by the use of this device?

5. **Analyze** What reasons does Wollstonecraft offer to refute the following opposing views in her counterarguments?
   - the concern that improved education will make women too masculine (lines 76–105)
   - Rousseau's contention that the purpose of education for females is to make them more pleasing to men (106–139)
   - Dr. Gregory's belief that women should dissemble, or hide their true feelings and energies (lines 140–172).

6. **Connect** In the eighteenth century, intellectuals in Europe and the American colonies promoted the expansion of liberty and equality. Reread lines 193–213 of Wollstonecraft's argument. In what ways does she appeal to these ideals in support of her argument for reforming women's education?

PERFORMANCE TASK

Speaking Activity: Oral Presentation Present an oral response to the views and ideas expressed in Wollstonecraft's argument.

To prepare your response, jot down answers to these and other questions:

- Which of Wollstonecraft's views are still relevant?
- What evidence can you present in a counterargument to ideas of Wollstonecraft's with which you disagree?
- What ideas might Wollstonecraft have added if she had written the argument today?

- Develop speaking notes that present your ideas using a logical organization.
- Support your major points with details and evidence.
- Rehearse your speech with a partner, giving each other feedback.

Assign this performance task.

PERFORMANCE TASK $\overset{\text{COMMON}}{\text{CORE}}$ SL 6

Speaking Activity: Oral Presentation Have students work in pairs. Direct them to reread the argument and discuss the questions with their partner. Tell them to prepare detailed speaking notes that include their major points and supporting details. Their oral responses should show evidence of preparation and rehearsal as well as knowledge of the text.

Critical Vocabulary

COMMON CORE L 4a, L 4d

vindication	abrogate	susceptibility
congenial	dissimulation	

Practice and Apply Answer each question, referring to the Critical Vocabulary words in your response.

1. If someone writes an editorial in favor of a new tax on junk food, is the editorial a *vindication* or *dissimulation* of the tax proposal?

2. Did women in the eighteenth century show *susceptibility* or *dissimulation* when they accepted men's view of themselves as helpless and frail?

3. If someone's rights were *abrogated,* would that person's response be *congenial?* Explain.

Vocabulary Strategy: Multiple Meanings

Many words in English have more than one meaning. For example, the dictionary entry for the Vocabulary word *vindication* lists several definitions. To determine which meaning matches the way the word is used in the title of the argument, readers must use context clues. The remaining words in the title, as well as what readers know about the content of the text, can help them figure out that *vindication* means "justification." The chart presents two meanings of the Vocabulary word *congenial.* Notice how the context clues in the sentences help to reveal the intended meaning.

Definition	Example
"having the same tastes, habits, or temperament"	When sharing a room at college, it helps if you and your roommate have <u>congenial</u> living habits.
"friendly and sociable"	Although our host was outwardly <u>congenial</u>, I sensed he was ready for us to leave.

Practice and Apply The following words from the argument have multiple meanings: *conduct, render, exact, sound.* Complete these steps for each word:

1. Identify two of its meanings.

2. Write a sentence illustrating each meaning, including context clues.

3. Exchange sentences with a partner and use the context clues to define the word as it is used in each sentence.

PRACTICE & APPLY

Critical Vocabulary

COMMON CORE L 4a, L 4d

Possible answers:

1. *The editorial would be a vindication of his or her position, since an editorial in favor of something offers justification for it.*

2. *They showed susceptibility because they were influenced to believe this view of themselves. They showed dissimulation, playing along with a false idea in order to please those who had power over them.*

3. *Most likely the person would not be agreeable to the abolition of his or her rights.*

Vocabulary Strategy: Multiple Meanings

Students may identify the following definitions. Sentences should reflect the definitions students identify and include context clues that will help their partners define the words.

conduct: 1. (n.) manage, control; 2. (v.) to lead or guide

render: 1. (v.) to submit for consideration or payment; 2. (v.) to make available

exact: 1. (adj.) precise; 2. (v.) extort

sound: 1. (adj.) in good condition; 2. (n.) a distinctive noise

Language and Style: Sentence Structure

 COMMON CORE L1

Have students review the chart and notice the difference in purpose between the two types of conjunctions. Explain that coordinating conjunctions may join two independent clauses—clauses that can stand by themselves as complete sentences—to form compound sentences, such as the second example in the chart. Subordinating conjunctions link subordinate clauses to independent clauses to form complex sentences, such as those shown in the chart.

If time permits, explain that subordinating conjunctions introduce only one type of subordinate clause— the adverb clause. Noun and adjective clauses are introduced by relative pronouns *(who, whom, whose, which, or that)*.

Possible answers: *Students' revisions to their speaking notes should demonstrate understanding of the function of conjunctions and should improve the flow and clarity of their sentences.*

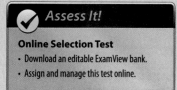

Assess It!

Online Selection Test
- Download an editable ExamView bank.
- Assign and manage this test online.

Language and Style: Sentence Structure

 COMMON CORE L1

Wollstonecraft expresses her ideas in long, detailed sentences that rely heavily on **coordinating** and **subordinating conjunctions** to connect words, phrases, and clauses smoothly in a way that shows the relationships between ideas.

Coordinating Conjunctions	Purpose	Sample Sentences
and, but, for, nor, or, so, yet	connect words or groups of words that have the same function in a sentence	We were so close <u>yet</u> so far. They lost the debate, <u>but</u> they still believed in themselves.

Subordinating Conjunctions	Purpose	Sample Sentences
after, although, as, as if, because, before, if, since, so that, than, though, unless, until, when, whenever, where, wherever, while	introduce subordinate clauses—clauses that cannot stand by themselves as complete sentences	<u>Although</u> they read her essay, they were not convinced. She was sorry <u>that</u> she had not published it sooner.

Read this sentence from the argument:

> I love man as my fellow; but his scepter, real, or usurped, extends not to me, unless the reason of an individual demands my homage; and even then the submission is to reason, and not to man.

The author could have chosen to write the same ideas in this way:

> I love man as my fellow. His scepter, real, or usurped, extends not to me. The reason of an individual may demand my homage. The submission is to reason. The submission is not to man.

The elimination of the conjunctions *but, unless,* and *and* makes it harder for readers to understand the relationships between the ideas.

Practice and Apply Look back at the notes you created for your oral response to the argument when you completed this selection's Performance Task. Insert conjunctions that help to clarify the relationship between ideas. Present your changes to a partner and discuss how they improve the flow and clarity of your speech.

Strategies for Annotation

 Annotate it!

Language and Style: Sentence Structure

COMMON CORE L1

Have students select a passage from Wollstonecraft's essay to explore how she uses conjunctions to create relationships between ideas. Encourage them to use their eBook annotation tools to do the following:

- Highlight in yellow each coordinating conjunction.
- Highlight in pink subordinating conjunctions and relative pronouns.
- On a note indicate the relationship between the words, phrases, or clauses joined by the conjunction.

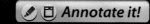

After considering the historic page, and viewing the living world with anxious solicitude, the most melancholy emotions of sorrowful indignation have depressed my spirits, and I have sighed when obliged to confess, that either nature has made a great difference between man and man, or that the civilization which has hitherto taken place in the world has been very partial.

Analyze Key Terms

RI 4

TEACH

Review with students the author's purpose in this essay: to persuade readers of the need to educate women in a way that will prepare them to be strong in mind, body, and character. Explain that in her argument Wollstonecraft relies on certain words, or key terms, to help convey her meaning. Each time she uses the term, what she means becomes clearer and more defined. Tell students that analyzing key terms helps readers to probe an author's meaning more deeply:

- To identify key terms, look for words that closely relate to the author's main idea and that occur frequently. For example, the terms "rational" and "masculine" are integral to the development of Wollstonecraft's argument.
- Track the frequency of the word and the context in which it is used each time. Examine what new ideas are associated with each reuse and how the author expands the word's meaning within the context of the argument.
- State the definition of the term as it emerges in the text. Express how understanding this term provides insight into the author's main idea, perspective, or purpose.

COLLABORATIVE DISCUSSION

Write these words and line references on the board:

- *rational:* lines 22, 65, 78, 119, 188
- *masculine:* lines 55, 64, 99, 100

Have students work with a partner to trace and analyze the use of each term over the course of the essay. Ask them to share in small groups their final understanding of what the author means by each concept as well as the way it helps to bring out the central idea. *(Rational: The word* rational *epitomizes what Wollstonecraft believes should result from women's education. Women should be governed by reason; as rational beings they will have the discipline to cope with life's challenges, refrain from destructive behaviors, and make decisions on the basis of logic rather than affection. Masculine: To Wollstonecraft "masculine women" are those that are noble and strong in spirit. They have qualities that make them able to be independent and do what is right. It has nothing to do with manly pursuits such as hunting or the exercise of physical strength.)*

Analyze Structure: Counterargument

RI 5

RETEACH

Review the terms *claim, reasons, evidence, opposing claims,* and *counterargument.* Then give an example of a claim, such as "Cities should have more bike lanes."

- Ask students to provide examples of types of reasons and evidence that might be used to support the claim. *(Sample reason: Bike lanes help the environment by reducing use of fossil fuels.)*
- Provide the following opposing claim: "Bike lanes lead to more accidents between bikes and cars." Ask: How could you counter this viewpoint? *(Sample answer: Find statistics that show that bike lanes actually make travel safer for bikes and cars.)*

LEVEL UP TUTORIALS Assign the following *Level Up* tutorial: **Elements of an Argument.**

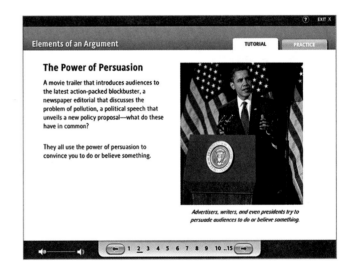

CLOSE READING APPLICATION

Students can apply the skill to a current magazine or newspaper editorial. Have them work independently to outline the claim, support, opposing claim, and counterargument. Ask: Does the writer include enough support to prove the claim? Does he or she adequately anticipate possible objections?

*my*SmartPlanner — Create lesson plans and access resources online.

In a Scattered Protest, Saudi Women Take the Wheel

Saudi Women Defy Driving Ban

Online Article by Neil MacFarquhar and Dina Salah Amer   News Video

Why These Texts?

As members of the global community, students must frequently rely on online information and videos for information about events. These lessons demonstrate how to summarize important ideas in an online article and how to analyze the ideas in a video to determine the filmmaker's view of the event and his or her message.

Key Learning Objective: The student will be able to summarize the main ideas of a news article; analyze ideas and events in a video; and integrate and evaluate information.

COMMON CORE Common Core Standards

RI 1 Cite textual evidence.

RI 2 Determine two or more central ideas of a text; provide an objective summary.

RI 3 Analyze a complex set of ideas or sequence of events.

RI 4 Determine the meaning of words and phrases in a text.

RI 5 Analyze the effectiveness of the structure an author uses.

RI 6 Determine an author's point of view or purpose.

RI 7 Integrate and evaluate multiple sources of information.

SL 1 Participate in discussions.

SL 2 Integrate multiple sources of information presented in diverse formats and media.

SL 5 Make use of digital media in presentations.

Text Complexity Rubric

	In a Scattered Protest, Saudi Women Take the Wheel	Saudi Women Defy Driving Ban
Quantitative Measures	Lexile: 1400L	Lexile: N/A
Qualitative Measures	**Levels of Meaning/Purpose** — more than one purpose; implied, easily identified from context	**Levels of Meaning/Purpose** — single topic
	Structure — organization of main ideas and details complex, but clearly stated and generally sequential	**Structure** — conventional
	Language Conventionality and Clarity — straightforward sentence structure	**Language Conventionality and Clarity** — contextual ambiguous language
	Knowledge Demands — some specialized knowledge required	**Knowledge Demands** — some specialized knowledge required
Reader/Task Considerations	Teacher determined — Vary by individual reader and type of text	Teacher determined — Vary by individual reader and type of text

TEACH

CLOSE READ

AS YOU READ Direct students to use the As You Read note to focus their reading.

Summarize the Text
COMMON CORE RI 2

(LINES 1–13)

Explain to students that pausing at intervals to summarize a text they are reading can help them monitor their comprehension. Tell them that summarizing involves identifying the most important ideas in a paragraph or passage.

A **CITE TEXT EVIDENCE** Have students identify the topic of the article. *(This article tells about a driving protest by Saudi women.)* How was the event different from what organizers anticipated? *(Confrontations between protesters and police were minimal; the protest was smaller than organizers thought it might be.)*

Analyze Author's Purpose (LINES 14–22)
COMMON CORE RI 6

Remind students that authors include details that will help them accomplish their purpose. Paying attention to the kinds of details authors include helps readers understand the authors' purpose.

B **ASK STUDENTS** to reread lines 13–21. Why do the authors include these specific details about Maha al-Qahtani? What impression does this part of the article create of the participants in the protest? *(The purpose of the authors in including this information is to show that ordinary women took part in the protest and that they were very brave.)*

MEDIA ANALYSIS

News Coverage of a Women's Rights Campaign

In a Scattered Protest, Saudi Women Take the Wheel

from **The New York Times,** June 17, 2011
Online Article by Neil MacFarquhar and Dina Salah Amer, Cairo

AS YOU READ Pay attention to details about the reasons for the protest. Write down any questions you generate during reading.

Several dozen women drove in defiance of the law in major cities of Saudi Arabia on Friday, according to reports on social media and by an informal network of activists in the country. There appeared to be few confrontations reported with either the traffic or morals police, and at least half a dozen women who were stopped were escorted home and admonished not to drive again, said activists reached by telephone.

From its inception in April, the protest against the longstanding ban was far smaller than initially anticipated, but it was not meant to 10 be a mass driving effort. Rather, women with legal driver's licenses from other countries were urged to run mundane errands—going to the grocery store, perhaps—in order to underscore the fact that it should be normal for women to drive.

Maha al-Qahtani, an information technology specialist for the government, drove around the capital, Riyadh, for 45 minutes with her husband, Mohamed, a human rights activist, in the car. She braced for a siren after passing each of about five police cars, she said, but they ignored her.

"I woke up today believing with every part of me that this is my 20 right, I woke up believing this is my duty, and I was no longer afraid," said Mrs. Qahtani, adding that she had brought a change of clothes and a prayer rug with her in case she was detained.

SCAFFOLDING FOR ELL STUDENTS

Comprehension: Structure Explain that in a news article, the most important information is often presented in the beginning. Project the first two paragraphs on the whiteboard. Have students use different-colored highlighters to identify the answers to these questions in the first two paragraphs:

- What happened?
- When and where did the event happen?
- Why did the event happen?
- Who was involved?

Then have students summarize the information.

CLOSE READ

Analyze Word Choice

(LINES 27–29)

Point out the idiomatic expression "jumped the gun."

C **ASK STUDENTS** what connotation this phrase holds and why the authors chose to express their idea in this way. (*The phrase suggests impulsive or thoughtless behavior. By using this phrase, the authors are showing the depth of the disappointment and possibly anger that the other supporters felt toward Manal al-Sharif.*)

Summarize the Text

(LINES 30–37)

Explain to students that they should not include their personal opinions in a summary. However, they should include opinions expressed in the text if they are central ideas.

D **ASK STUDENTS** to explain how the issue of women driving is related to the Saudi conservatives' feelings toward the West. (*The conservatives equate women driving with Western influences; they despise the West.*)

Support Inferences: Draw Conclusions (LINES 42–55)

Tell students that when they draw conclusions they use information in a text as well as their own prior knowledge to come to a broad understanding of a situation or event.

E **CITE TEXT EVIDENCE** Have students explain the conclusion the authors want them to reach from the details in this part of the text. Have them explain the evidence that leads to this conclusion. (*Although some men in Saudi Arabia are staunchly conservative, others support women's efforts to achieve more freedom. The comments by Abu Alkhair support this conclusion.*)

❝❝I woke up believing this is my duty, and I was no longer afraid.❞❞

Manal al-Sharif, a 32-year-old single mother, started the call for the June 17 protest in April with a Facebook page. But after posting videos of herself driving around Al Khobar in the Eastern Province, she was arrested in late May and jailed for nine days—a punishment that was stricter than expected. Many supporters were disappointed, feeling that she had jumped the gun and jeopardized them all by taking a confrontational approach.

30 Women driving remains a sensitive issue in Saudi Arabia. For religious conservatives, it is a kind of Alamo, with the ban a sign that the kingdom still holds to its traditions and has not caved to Western pressure.

The ruling family has been especially dependent on this base of supporters in recent months as protests erupted across the region and has been mute as the mufti, the highest religious figure in the kingdom, rolled out a fatwa[1] banning protests.

Many Saudi activists considered the treatment meted out to Ms. Sharif a warning from the monarchy against trying to organize any 40 kind of movement via social media. The initiative for women to drive was the strongest effort so far in the kingdom inspired by the regional climate.

"Women in Saudi Arabia see other women in the Middle East making revolutions, women in Yemen and Egypt at the forefront of revolutions, being so bold, toppling entire governments," said Waleed Abu Alkhair, whose wife drove around Jidda. "The women of Saudi Arabia looked at themselves and they realized, 'Wow! We can't even drive!' "

Mr. Abu Alkhair said he knew about many women who drove, 50 and aside from one being questioned by the police for two hours, none were bothered. Once the campaign had been announced there were frequent threats by opponents to punish female drivers either by beating them or by smashing their cars.

---

[1] **fatwa:** a ruling or opinion on Islamic law.

124 Collection 2

APPLYING ACADEMIC VOCABULARY

predominance	inclinations

As you discuss this online article, incorporate the following Collection 2 academic vocabulary words: *predominance* and *inclinations*. Have students examine all of the reasons for the **predominance** of male drivers in Saudi Arabia. Then have them explain the circumstances leading to the increased **inclination** of Saudi women to protest.

"We want women to keep fighting this fight and to be free," he said. "It will help to liberate the entire society."

In the weeks after Ms. Sharif's arrest, a debate erupted between conservative clerics and their followers and the kingdom's increasingly outspoken women. Opponents largely argued that Saudi society was not ready, that a woman should not be thrown into the wilds of Saudi
60 driving habits or be held responsible for any accidents.

Worse, opponents argued, it would lead to the public mingling of the sexes. Supporters mocked the clerics for putting everything in a sexual context and asked why it was O.K. for Saudi women to be driven around by an army of some 800,000 male drivers imported from Southeast Asia.

Although the arrest of Ms. Sharif discouraged women from driving, the fact that it enlivened the debate was in contrast to the first (and last) such protest in November 1990. Clerics branded the 47 women amoral and the royal family confiscated their passports, firing
70 those working for the government. Many went into isolation for their own safety.

In addition to religious opposition there is widespread suspicion in the country that those who control the visa process—and in Saudi

In a Scattered Protest, Saudi Women Take the Wheel **125**

CLOSE READ

Summarize the Text
 RI 2

(LINES 58–78)

Tell students that summarizing involves distinguishing between important ideas and less important details.

F CITE TEXT EVIDENCE Have students restate the key points in this part of the article. *(Those who support the driving ban believe that women are not ready to cope with Saudi traffic and that driving would lead to "public mingling of the sexes." Those who are against the ban argue that requiring women to hire male drivers leads to "mingling" of the sexes and that many women cannot afford the expense of hiring a driver.)*

WHEN STUDENTS STRUGGLE...

Comprehension Support: Tell students that when they summarize, they should read the text carefully to get the "gist" or basic idea that is being conveyed. They should not include every detail. Model the strategy by projecting lines 58–60 on the whiteboard. Read the lines aloud. Then ask students what this sentence is saying about the opponents' view of women driving in Saudi Arabia. *(Driving in Saudi Arabia is too challenging for women.)* Project the rest of the text on this page, one paragraph at a time. Have students work in pairs to restate each main idea in their own words. Prompt them as needed by helping them identify which details are minor and therefore should not be included.

Summarize the Text

COMMON CORE RI 2

(LINES 84–96)

Remind students that when they paraphrase, they restate an idea in their own words. Point out the direct quotations in this part of the text. Explain that unless a quotation captures the essence of a passage or of an entire text, it should not be included in a summary. Instead, the idea that is expressed in a quotation should be paraphrased.

(G) **ASK STUDENTS** what idea is brought out by Amira Kashgary in the last paragraph. *(Women are not going to give up the struggle until they achieve their goal of having the freedom to drive whenever they want to do so.)*

COLLABORATIVE DISCUSSION Have students review the article to find specific details that support their assessment of the protest's effectiveness. Ask them to share their opinions with the class. Accept all reasonable responses.

ASK STUDENTS to share any questions they generated in the course of reading and discussing the selection.

Arabia that means the princes of the ruling family—have made a business out of controlling the black market in visas for drivers, which can cost more than $3,000 apiece.

Many young married women decry the fact that they cannot afford that, not to mention the driver's salary, about $600 a month.

The more liberal princes support allowing women to drive.

80 Prince Talal bin Abdul-Aziz al-Saud, 79 years old and long among the most outspoken members of the royal family, argues that such reforms lag because the leading members of the family have failed to yield any power or influence to younger generations.

(G) "Bravo to the women!" the prince said in an interview. "Why should women drive in the countryside and not in the cities?" (Women have long driven in rural areas.)

King Abdullah and other royals have said in interviews with foreign reporters that they expected Saudi women to drive one day soon but have done little lately.

90 "Saudi Arabian women are going to have to fight for our rights, men are not going to just hand them over to us," said Amira Kashgary, a professor who drove through Jidda on Friday for 45 minutes with her 21-year-old daughter. Women are tired of being stranded or missing appointments because their drivers disappear for the day, Professor Kashgary said. "We want to drive today, tomorrow, and every day—it's not a one-day show. We want to make it a norm."

COLLABORATIVE DISCUSSION With a partner, discuss how and why the participants organized the protest. Was the protest effective? Cite specific textual evidence from the article to support your ideas.

SCAFFOLDING FOR ELL STUDENTS

Language: Colloquial Expressions Point out that the quotations in the last paragraph, as well as other parts of the text, include colloquial, or everyday, expressions. Remind students that they can use other words in the text to help them define these phrases. Using the whiteboard, project the last paragraph of the article. Have volunteers complete these steps:

- Highlight these two expressions in different colors: "one-day show," "a norm."
- For each expression, highlight in the same color words that suggest its meaning.

ASK STUDENTS what the meaning is of each underlined expression. Then ask them what other words and phrases in the article they can define by using this strategy.

Summarize the Text

 COMMON CORE RI 2

When readers summarize a text, they use their own words to tell what it is about. A **summary** includes only the central ideas and most important details of a text. It follows the order of the original text and is written in a way that is objective and accurate. Readers may summarize paragraphs, passages, or entire selections to help them clarify meaning or remember essential information.

Compare these two summaries of the first paragraph of the article. Note the differences that make the second summary more accurate than the first.

Summary	Analysis
Dozens of women drove in Saudi Arabia according to reports. Some were stopped, but there were not a lot of confrontations, or so activists said. The women who participated were brave.	This summary copies much of the original text, merely leaving out some words to shorten the length. Too many unimportant details are included as well as a statement of the writer's opinion.
A planned protest against the ban on female drivers in Saudi Arabia drew dozens of women but passed without serious incident for participants.	This summary retells the major ideas of the first paragraph in the writer's own words and eliminates unimportant details. The writer maintains an objective tone.

Analyzing the Media

COMMON CORE RI 1, RI 2, RI 4, RI 5, RI 6

Cite Text Evidence Support your responses with evidence from the selection.

1. **Analyze** What does driving represent to Saudi women? Why is it "a kind of Alamo" to supporters of the ban?

2. **Analyze** What is the purpose of this article? How do the authors accomplish their purpose? Explain.

3. **Evaluate** Think about how the authors structure their article. Why is this structure effective?

4. **Summarize** What are the central ideas in this article? Write a brief summary that includes those ideas and the most important details.

In a Scattered Protest, Saudi Women Take the Wheel **127**

TEACH

CLOSE READ

Summarize the Text

COMMON CORE RI 2

Have students point out the unimportant details in the first summary. (*"Some were stopped"; "or so activists said"; "The women who participated were brave."*)

Analyzing the Media

COMMON CORE RI 1, RI 2, RI 4, RI 5, RI 6

Possible answers:

1. *To the women of Saudi Arabia, driving represents freedom and independence. To the religious conservatives who support the driving ban, it is a last stand, or "a kind of Alamo" against the intrusion of Western values.*

2. *The purpose is to inform readers of the protest and the state of civil liberties for women in Saudi Arabia. The authors include facts and quotations.*

3. *First, the authors explain the protest. Then they look at the opposition to it. This structure gives readers the context of the protest and the history behind it.*

4. *The protest against the driving ban for Saudi women drew several dozen participants. It passed without incident, although women were initially fearful of possible consequences. The efforts of the women were inspired by the events in other Arab countries. The right to drive is still strongly opposed by the conservative leaders and members of the royal family. However, Saudi women and the men who support them appear to be ready to continue their struggle.*

Strategies for Annotation ✎ 📋 *Annotate it!*

Summarize the Text

 COMMON CORE RI 2

Have students use their eBook annotation tools to complete these steps, either independently or in groups.

- Highlight sentences in pink throughout the article that seem to include key points.
- On a note, explain these key ideas in your own words.

"Women in Saudi Arabia see other women in the Middle East making revolutions, women in Yemen and Egypt at the forefront of revolutions, being so bold, toppling entire governments," said Waleed Abu Alkhair, whose wife drove around Jidda. "The women of Saudi

In a Scattered Protest, Saudi Women Take the Wheel **127**

AS YOU VIEW Direct students to use the As You View note to focus their reading.

Analyze Ideas and Events COMMON CORE RI 3

Remind students that filmmakers make choices about which visual, sound, and text elements will help them communicate their ideas about the events they are portraying.

ASK STUDENTS to consider why these filmmakers chose not to edit or polish their final product. What effect does the "amateur" nature of the film have on viewers? Explain. *(The choppiness of the video shows that it was shot by people associated with the protest. Letting the participants speak for themselves, without a journalist narrating the video, has a greater impact because it shows firsthand how much the participants want the rest of the world to understand their efforts to achieve freedom. Viewers can infer that those behind the camera are taking serious risks by filming the protest. Viewers can infer also that the protest is a grassroots effort with a serious agenda.)* Point out the appearance of the woman interviewed first and the background that she is filmed against. What impression does this shot create? *(This woman's face cannot be seen at all, suggesting that she does not want to be recognized. The background is neutral, giving away nothing about her identity. These elements give the impression that there might be repercussions for someone who speaks out against the driving ban.)*

COLLABORATIVE DISCUSSION Have students explain whether they would have understood the ideas in this video as clearly if they had not first read the article. Why or why not? *(Answers will vary, but students will likely recognize how difficult the video would be if they hadn't first read about protests against the Saudi driving ban.)* Then have students explain other reasons why multiple sources of information are helpful in understanding an issue. Accept all reasonable responses.

ASK STUDENTS to share any questions they generated in the course of viewing and discussing the selection.

Saudi Women Defy Driving Ban

News Video
June 23, 2011

AS YOU VIEW Consider how the depiction of the protest in the news video is similar to and different from the article. Write down any questions you generate during viewing.

COLLABORATIVE DISCUSSION With a partner, think about whether the video explains all aspects of the issue behind the protest. Discuss why multiple sources of information are helpful in understanding an issue. Cite specific elements of the video to support your ideas.

Image Credits: ©ITN Source

WHEN STUDENTS STRUGGLE . . .

Concept Support To guide students' comprehension of the filmmakers' choices in this video, draw a two-column chart on the board with the headings "Segment" and "Effect." Then replay the video, pausing after each segment of the film. As a class, write a description of each segment in a row of the chart. Ask students to explain how that part of the film affects their understanding of the protest.

Have students return to this chart to help them answer the Analyzing the Media questions.

Analyze Ideas and Events

The way events or ideas are presented in a video, even one not produced by professional filmmakers, influences how the audience perceives them. Examining some of the elements of the video clip "Saudi Women Defy Driving Ban" will help viewers understand the filmmakers' purpose and message more clearly.

Element	Analysis
Opening/Closing Shots	The camera in the opening sequence is placed to reflect the driver's view of the road. The closing shot is of the note left on the car with the broken side mirror, requesting that Azza Al-Shamasi not drive. What do these choices by the filmmakers suggest about the perspective from which they want viewers to understand the events?
Types of Images	The women in the video are each wearing a *niqab*, a veil covering the face and hair that is worn by some Muslim women. The filmmakers also include images of the road, the note, the smashed mirror, and Azza's hands. Think about the message sent by these images and how they build upon the central idea of the film.
Interviews	The women are the only ones who speak in the video. Compare their comments and tones. What ideas do the filmmakers want viewers to learn from these interviews?

Analyzing the Media

COMMON CORE RI 1, RI 3

Cite Text Evidence   Support your responses with evidence from the selection.

1. **Analyze** Do the opening and closing shots suggest a bias, or an inclination to one side of the story, on the part of the filmmakers? Explain.

2. **Compare** What views do both women who are interviewed share? How do their comments affect the audience's sense of where their efforts might lead?

3. **Infer** At one point, the camera zooms in on Azza's hands. What idea is conveyed by this image?

Saudi Women Defy Driving Ban   **129**

APPLYING ACADEMIC VOCABULARY

bias	exploit

While discussing the video, incorporate the following Collection 2 academic vocabulary words: *bias* and *exploit*. Ask students to consider the **bias** that an American audience would have before even watching the video. Then have them discuss how the makers of the video could **exploit** this bias to gain support for their cause.

Analyze Ideas and Events   COMMON CORE RI 3

Discuss with students how changes in any of the elements listed might have affected the impact of the film. For example, what if the women in the film did not speak, and a commentator explained what was happening? What if the film ended immediately after the last interview, instead of returning to the note? Lead students to draw conclusions about the importance of a filmmaker's choices.

Analyzing the Media   COMMON CORE RI 1, RI 3

Possible answers:

1. *The opening shot is of a woman being filmed driving a car. The choice of this image to begin the video suggests that the filmmakers want viewers to see events from the perspective of the women involved, which illustrates a bias, or definite leaning toward one side of the event. The same is true for the closing shot. The note reinforces the idea that the women show bravery in pursuing their efforts despite opposition.*

2. *Both women share a surprisingly optimistic attitude toward the reactions to their driving; Azza explains that she has been left alone while driving, suffering only one minor incident, which does not seem to have upset her. Sara says she believes that there is support, even from conservatives. These comments give the audience the feeling that the efforts of these women may lead to some positive results.*

3. *Although Azza's demeanor is calm and assured, the shot of her hands suggests that she is more nervous or anxious than she appears. This image tells the audience that it takes courage for these women to stand up for their freedom and drive in a society that does not allow it.*

PRACTICE & APPLY

CLOSE READ

Integrate and Evaluate Information

Review key terms with students, such as *purpose, perspective,* and *validity.* Then have students work in small groups to compare the purpose, perspective, and meaning of the two selections. Remind them to cite specific examples and other evidence to support their comparison.

Analyzing the Media

Possible answers:

1. *Both the article and the video clip share insights into the women who protest the ban by driving; both point out that there is support for their efforts, even in the conservative climate; and both note the risk of hiring unknown drivers. However, the article presents more context, or background, which helps readers understand the Saudi Arabian views on women driving. The video gives few facts, focusing mainly on the experiences of the two women, providing a more intimate look at the people affected by the law. These differences show that the article's purpose is to inform, while the video's purpose is to persuade viewers that the "protesters" are simply women who want the right to drive.*

2. *The article and the video are complementary. Taken together, they give a fuller view of the event. The article focuses on communicating facts and gives some insights into the participants; the video develops a greater sense of the people behind the event.*

3. *News articles in reputable newspapers provide readers with a credible source of information; they are fact-checked and well-researched. Videos, such as the one seen here, can help viewers understand the feelings and opinions of the individuals involved in an event. Multiple methods of conveying information reach different audiences and present different perspectives on issues and events. In this way, a more complete and balanced understanding can be achieved.*

Integrate and Evaluate Information

Both the news article and the video clip present information on the Saudi women's protest. As a reader/viewer, you must integrate the ideas that are communicated and evaluate their accuracy and credibility in order to form your own understanding. To do this, examine these aspects of each source of information:

- Purpose: The choice of medium is often dictated by the intended purpose of the piece. For example, the authors chose to write a news article because they wanted to inform readers of what took place in Saudi Arabia. Readers would expect to find facts in the article.

- Perspective: The perspective, or viewpoint, of the piece determines the content. For example, to convey a certain perspective in the video, specific images were used. Being aware of the perspective can help viewers or readers recognize bias.

- Meaning: If sources of information convey similar ideas, then readers/viewers can be more confident that the ideas are valid. If there are major differences, readers or viewers have to decide what the discrepancies mean about the validity of the information.

Analyzing the Media

Cite Text Evidence Support your responses with evidence from the selections.

1. **Compare** What central ideas are conveyed by both the article and the video clip? What do the differences reveal about the purpose of each?

2. **Analyze** Are the article and the video clip complementary or conflicting? Explain, citing specific examples.

3. **Compare** What are the advantages of each medium? Why is it important to have a choice of methods for conveying information?

PERFORMANCE TASK

Media Activity: News Video With a partner, produce your own news video on a local or school event.

- Decide on your purpose. Then organize your ideas for written, visual, and sound elements.
- Using available video equipment, shoot footage of relevant sites, events, or people; include interviews with participants or those affected by the event.
- Create your script and decide on sound effects.
- Put all of your elements together, editing to create a unified story.
- Present to the class. Have class members comment on how well you achieved your purpose.

Assign this performance task.

PERFORMANCE TASK

Media Activity: News Video If students need prompting, suggest a list of possible topics that they might film. Remind them that their purpose may be to inform, entertain, or persuade. What they show and how they show it will determine whether they accomplish their purpose. After each presentation, have the class discuss the perspective from which the subject is viewed and what they learned about the event from the video.

INTERACTIVE WHITEBOARD LESSON

Determine Author's Purpose

COMMON CORE · RI 6

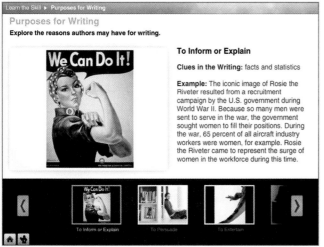

Learn the Skill ▶ Purposes for Writing

Purposes for Writing
Explore the reasons authors may have for writing.

We Can Do It!

To Inform or Explain

Clues in the Writing: facts and statistics

Example: The iconic image of Rosie the Riveter resulted from a recruitment campaign by the U.S. government during World War II. Because so many men were sent to serve in the war, the government sought women to fill their positions. During the war, 65 percent of all aircraft industry workers were women, for example. Rosie the Riveter came to represent the surge of women in the workforce during this time.

To Inform or Explain   To Persuade   To Entertain

TEACH

Before students begin their their Media Activity: News Video Performance Task, remind them that they need to determine the purpose and perspective of their videos. Share these suggestions with them:

- **Purpose:** First, choose a topic. The subject of your video will help you decide whether you want to inform, entertain, or persuade. Your purpose must fit your subject. In other words, a serious news event, like an incident of vandalism in the town square, lends itself to informing or persuading, rather than entertaining. You may have more than one purpose; just be sure to define them in advance.

- **Perspective:** Determine what you feel about your topic and what you want your audience to feel. Your perspective is linked to your purpose. If you want to inform, then you should maintain an objective perspective. If you want to persuade, you need to choose the elements that will convey your opinion on the subject.

- **Content:** Choose your material based on your purpose and perspective.

COLLABORATIVE DISCUSSION

Have students sketch out their subject, purpose, and perspective in small groups. Encourage group members to provide constructive feedback.

Integrate and Evaluate Information

COMMON CORE · RI 7

RETEACH

Discuss with students the reasons to draw information from more than one source. Then give students an example of a topic: "The Impact on the Environment of the Gas Drilling Method Called Fracking."

- Ask students to provide examples of sources from which they might take information on this topic. *(reference works, news articles, web sites, interviews, news programs, scientific journals)* Ask them how they would evaluate the validity of these sources, knowing that there are many special interest groups involved in the issue. *(They would look for sources sponsored by neutral or objective organizations; they would compare facts between sources.)*

- Then have students explain formats that they might use for integrating their information into a report or presentation. *(In addition to text, a report might include graphs, charts, tables, photographs, diagrams, and even video clips, if they are doing a multimedia presentation.)*

LEVEL UP TUTORIALS Assign the following *Level Up* tutorial: **Synthesizing Information**

? EXIT X

Synthesizing Information   TUTORIAL   PRACTICE

What Is Synthesizing?

Suppose you just watched your favorite football team play on TV. Afterward, you read news articles about the players and listened to radio interviews with the coach. Each of these sources gives you different information about a single topic: a football game.

After considering all this information, along with what you already know about the sport, you come up with a new idea—a strategy that could help the team win its next game. This process is called **synthesizing**.

You synthesize by pulling together information from different sources.

◀ 1 **2** 3 4 5 6 7 8 9 10 ..12 ▶

CLOSE READING APPLICATION

Provide students with two articles or an article and a web site on the same topic. Ask: What similar ideas are brought out in each? Do these sources validate each other's information? Do they share a similar purpose and perspective? If not, how do the differences affect the kind of information included?

mySmartPlanner Create lesson plans and access resources online.

ANCHOR TEXT

The Men We Carry in Our Minds

Essay by Scott Russell Sanders

Why This Text?

This lesson explores the provocative issue of gender inequality and the writer's evolving perspective on the issue. Close reading of this personal essay will require students to determine the author's point of view; at the same time, it will challenge them to determine their own point of view about the subject.

▶ *View It!*

Professional Development Podcast:
Teaching Point of View

For additional practice:

Close Reader selection
from *Pink Think* by Lynn Peril

Key Learning Objective: The student will determine an author's point of view about a complex subject and determine the central ideas of an essay.

COMMON CORE — Common Core Standards

RI 1 Cite textual evidence.
RI 2 Determine two or more central ideas; provide an objective summary.
RI 3 Analyze a set of ideas.
RI 4 Determine the meaning of words and phrases.
RI 6 Determine author's point of view or purpose.
SL 1c Challenge ideas and conclusions.
SL 3 Evaluate a speaker's point of view, reasoning, and use of evidence and rhetoric.
SL 4 Present information, findings, and evidence.
W 1 Write arguments to support claims.
L 3a Vary syntax for effect; apply an understanding of syntax when reading.
L 4a Use context as a clue to the meaning of a word or phrase.

▲ Text Complexity Rubric

Quantitative Measures	**The Men We Carry in Our Minds** Lexile: 1060L
Qualitative Measures	**Levels of Meaning/Purpose** multiple purposes; implied, subtle, and difficult to determine
	Structure organization of main ideas and details complex, but clearly stated and generally sequential
	Language Conventionality and Clarity less straightforward sentence structure
	Knowledge Demands somewhat complex concepts
Reader/Task Considerations	Teacher determined Vary by individual reader and type of text

CLOSE READ

Background Have students read the background and information about the author. By 1984, when this essay was published, more and more female lawmakers and professionals were making their mark on society, and some laws to support women's equality had been passed. A woman had been appointed to the Supreme Court in 1981, and, in the presidential election of 1984, a woman was chosen as a vice presidential candidate. More families were beginning to have two wage earners in order to support a middle-class lifestyle. Social relationships were in flux, and gender roles were being re-examined.

AS YOU READ Direct students to use the As Your Read note to focus their reading. Tell them to note any questions they have as they read.

Determine Author's Point of View (LINES 1–7)
COMMON CORE **RI 6**

Explain that writers often begin essays informally, with an anecdote, or, as in this case, a casual conversation. This is an opportunity for them to introduce an issue and suggest the beliefs and values they might explore in their essay.

 CITE TEXT EVIDENCE Have students reread lines 1–7. Then ask what ideas the author is likely to explore in his essay, based on the conversation between the author and his female friend. *(whether he, like the other men Anneke describes, "[is] eaten up with guilt" [line 7])*

Scott Russell Sanders *(b. 1945) was born in Tennessee. He won a scholarship to attend Cambridge University, where he acquired his Ph.D. in English. His professional life was spent teaching at Indiana University. Much of his writing focuses on the relationship between humans and nature and on the importance of conservation. Sanders is particularly known for his essays. He says that an essay usually begins "in a state of strong emotion and equally strong puzzlement. Some event, recollection . . . provokes me, and sets me asking questions that drive the writing forward."*

The Men We Carry in Our Minds

Essay by Scott Russell Sanders

AS YOU READ Note the experiences that have influenced Sanders's views about men and women.

Image Credits: (t) ©Scott Russell Sanders; (b) ©Holly Wilmeth/Aurora Photos/Corbis

"This must be a hard time for women," I say to my friend Anneke. "They have so many paths to choose from, and so many voices calling them."

"I think it's a lot harder for men," she replies.

"How do you figure that?"

"The women I know feel excited, innocent, like crusaders in a just cause. The men I know are eaten up with guilt."

We are sitting at the kitchen table drinking sassafras tea, our hands wrapped around the mugs because this April morning is cool
10 and drizzly. "Like a Dutch morning," Anneke told me earlier. She is Dutch herself, a writer and midwife and peacemaker, with the round face and sad eyes of a woman in a Vermeer[1] painting who might be waiting for the rain to stop, for a door to open. She leans over to sniff a sprig of lilac, pale lavender, that rises from a vase of cobalt blue.

"Women feel such pressure to be everything, do everything," I say. "Career, kids, art, politics. Have their babies and get back to the office

---

[1] **Vermeer:** Johannes Vermeer (1632–1675), a Dutch painter known for his interior household scenes.

The Men We Carry in Our Minds **131**

Close Read Screencasts ▶ View It!

Modeled Discussions

Have students click the *Close Read* icons in their eBooks to access a screencast in which readers discuss and annotate the following key passage:

- the origins of Sanders' ideas about men and women (lines 36–46)

As a class, view and discuss this video. Then have students pair up to do an independent close read of an additional passage—Sanders' description of the true "grievances" of women as he came to understand them (lines 147–159).

Determine Central Ideas RI 2

(LINES 34–46)

Tell students that a central idea is the most important point, or message, that an author wants to get across in a written work. Some works have several central ideas. These can be determined by examining key details.

B **ASK STUDENTS** to reread lines 34–46. Then ask them to identify the central idea that emerges from the author's response to Anneke's statement in lines 34–35. (*Where he grew up was similar in its "sexual patterns" to the early people of the Stone Age; he shared a past with people with limited ideas.*)

Determine Author's Point of View (LINES 47-58) COMMON CORE RI 6

Explain that one way an author reveals his or her point of view is by examining its origin in past experiences.

C **CITE TEXT EVIDENCE** Have students cite an example from the text of how Sanders's early views of men were shaped. (*by watching black convicts and their white guards, "the brute toiling animal and the boss" [lines 47–58]*)

CRITICAL VOCABULARY

discredited: According to Anneke, men are no longer confident in their relations with women. **ASK STUDENTS** why Anneke thinks that men have been discredited. (*They have thought and acted wrongly with regard to women.*)

acrid: Sanders explains that the prisoners had no choice but to inhale the acrid dust. **ASK STUDENTS** to describe possible results from breathing in the acrid dust. (*The dust comes from a poison and might have long-lasting health effects.*)

marginal: The male laborers Sanders describes lived very hard lives. The marginal farmers produced just enough to keep going but little or nothing more. **ASK STUDENTS** to explain how the marginal farmer is an example of a "brute toiling animal" (lines 57–58). (*Like a "toiling" animal—an ox or a draft horse—a marginal farmer does mind-numbing work, to the point of exhaustion, just to feed himself and his family.*)

---

a week later. It's as if they're trying to overcome a million years' worth of evolution in one lifetime."

"But we help one another. We don't try to lumber on alone, like so 20 many wounded grizzly bears, the way men do." Anneke sips her tea. I gave her the mug with owls on it, for wisdom. "And we have this deep-down sense that we're in the *right*—we've been held back, passed over, used—while men feel they're in the wrong. Men are the ones who've been **discredited**, who have to search their souls."

I search my soul. I discover guilty feelings aplenty—toward the poor, the Vietnamese, Native Americans, the whales, an endless list of debts—a guilt in each case that is as bright and unambiguous as a neon sign. But toward women I feel something more confused, a snarl of shame, envy, wary tenderness, and amazement. This muddle 30 troubles me. To hide my unease I say, "You're right, it's tough being a man these days."

"Don't laugh." Anneke frowns at me, mournful-eyed, through the sassafras steam. "I wouldn't be a man for anything. It's much easier being the victim. All the victim has to do is break free. The persecutor has to live with his past."

 How deep is that past? I find myself wondering after Anneke has left. How much of an inheritance do I have to throw off? Is it just the beliefs I breathed in as a child? Do I have to scour memory back through father and grandfather? Through St. Paul?[2] Beyond 40 Stonehenge and into the twilit caves? I'm convinced the past we must contend with is deeper even than speech. When I think back on my childhood, on how I learned to see men and women, I have a sense of ancient, dizzying depths. The back roads of Tennessee and Ohio where I grew up were probably closer, in their sexual patterns, to the campsites of Stone Age hunters than to the genderless cities of the future into which we are rushing.

The first men, besides my father, I remember seeing were black convicts and white guards, in the cottonfield across the road from our farm on the outskirts of Memphis. I must have been three or four. 50 The prisoners wore dingy gray-and-black zebra suits, heavy as canvas, sodden with sweat. Hatless, stooped, they chopped weeds in the fierce heat, row after row, breathing the **acrid** dust of boll-weevil poison. The overseers wore dazzling white shirts and broad shadowy hats. The oiled barrels of their shotguns flashed in the sunlight. Their faces in memory are utterly blank. Of course those men, white and black, have become for me an emblem of racial hatred. But they have also come to stand for the twin poles of my early vision of manhood—the brute toiling animal and the boss.

When I was a boy, the men I knew labored with their bodies. They 60 were **marginal** farmers, just scraping by, or welders, steelworkers,

---

discredit
(dĭs-krĕd´ĭt) *v.*
to damage the reputation of.

acrid
(ăk´rĭd) *adj.* strongly unpleasant in smell or taste.

marginal
(mär´jə-nəl) *adj.* just meeting a very low standard of success.

---

[2] **St. Paul:** an influential first-century Christian teacher and writer who, in the view of some theologians, reinforced the secondary status of women in the early church.

132 Collection 2

SCAFFOLDING FOR ELL STUDENTS

Analyze Language: Adjectives Students may find it difficult to understand multiple modifiers not separated by commas or conjunctions. Tell students that this essay contains many **adjectives**—modifiers that describe and expand the meaning of nouns and pronouns. Briefly review these parts of speech. Then display this sentence:

- "The overseers wore dazzling white shirts and broad shadowy hats." (*line 53*)

Ask students to identify the nouns and the adjectives in the sentence. Point out that the nouns are modified by more than one adjective. Then have students repeat the sentence aloud, with either a pause for a comma between adjectives or with the word *and* separating the modifiers. Finally, have students use this strategy to help them unpack the meaning of another sentence in the text that contains nouns modified by multiple adjectives.

carpenters; they swept floors, dug ditches, mined coal, or drove trucks, their forearms ropy with muscle; they trained horses, stoked furnaces, built tires, stood on assembly lines wrestling parts onto cars and refrigerators. They got up before light, worked all day long whatever the weather, and when they came home at night they looked as though somebody had been whipping them. In the evenings and on weekends they worked on their own places, tilling gardens that were lumpy with clay, fixing broken-down cars, hammering on houses that were always too drafty, too leaky, too small.

70   The bodies of the men I knew were twisted and maimed in ways visible and invisible. The nails of their hands were black and split, the hands tattooed with scars. Some had lost fingers. Heavy lifting had given many of them finicky backs and guts weak from hernias. Racing against conveyor belts had given them ulcers. Their ankles and knees ached from years of standing on concrete. Anyone who had worked for long around machines was hard of hearing. They squinted, and the skin of their faces was creased like the leather of old work gloves. There were times, studying them, when I dreaded growing up. Most of them coughed, from dust or cigarettes, and most of them drank cheap
80 wine or whiskey, so their eyes looked bloodshot and bruised. The fathers of my friends always seemed older than the mothers. Men wore out sooner. Only women lived into old age.

     As a boy I also knew another sort of men, who did not sweat and break down like mules. They were soldiers, and so far as I could tell

WHEN STUDENTS STRUGGLE...

To help students determine central ideas and supporting details, have them complete a cluster diagram for lines 70–82. Students may work in small groups to list key details that help them infer a central idea. Then have them discuss how this central idea contributes to their understanding of how the author's experiences and observations influence his point of view.

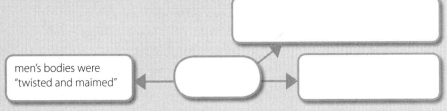

men's bodies were "twisted and maimed"

CLOSE READ

Determine Author's Point of View (LINES 65–82)

Tell students that an author's **style,** or way of using language, can convey his or her point of view in a unique way. Students can analyze and appreciate a writer's style by paying attention to the way the writer arranges the words in sentences (**syntax**), and the choice of words that convey his or her attitude toward the subject (**tone**).

D **CITE TEXT EVIDENCE** Have students reread lines 65–82. Then ask them what the author's style in this section suggests about his point of view toward his subject. *(He is sympathetic to the laborers who, when they "came home at night, . . . looked as though somebody had been whipping them" [lines 65–66]; "their eyes looked bloodshot and bruised" [line 80].)*

Tell students that an author's point of view can often be inferred from the details he or she includes and from the observations he or she makes about them. It can also be directly stated.

E **CITE TEXT EVIDENCE** Ask students what Sanders thinks that he, as a man, might experience in the future, based on the details in lines 78–82. *(He might not age as well or live as long as most women. Text evidence that reveals this point of view includes his statement that he "dreaded growing up" [line 78] and his observation that "men wore out sooner" [lines 81–82].)*

Determine Central Ideas

Point out that visual elements, such as the photograph on p. 133, can often help reinforce central ideas.

F **ASK STUDENTS** how the photograph helps support the central idea in the text. *(The central idea is that the men's bodies were damaged by many years of grueling physical labor. The men in the photograph look exhausted, and the dirt on their hands and faces is deeply ingrained.)*

Image Credits: ©Reporters Associes/Gamma-Rapho/Getty Images

TEACH

CLOSE READ

Determine Central Ideas RI 2

(LINES 98–102)

Tell students that an essay can contain several central ideas that connect with and build on each other.

G **CITE TEXT EVIDENCE** Have students reread lines 98–102. Then ask them what these sentences suggest about the connection between the soldiers and the earlier description of the laborers. *(By comparing soldiers to hammers, Sanders suggests that they are simply tools being put to use by others; these others are probably the same "boss" referred to in line 58. The two types of men that Sanders knew were connected by the fact that they were not the boss; as "warriors and toilers, they fulfilled the "chief destinies for men" [lines 101-102].)*

Determine Author's Point of View (LINES 110–124) RI 6

Tell students personal essays may often begin with generalizations and then shift to a more individual focus.

H **CITE TEXT EVIDENCE** Ask students how Sanders's essay shifts to a more personal focus in lines 110–124. Have them cite text evidence that shows this shift. *(It shifts to men he knew personally—his father, young men at school, and other boys who joined the Army or "labored with their bodies." His father did "move up," into an office, but because he had once been a "toiler," his body gave out early and he died before he got very old [lines 110–124].)*

> ### CRITICAL VOCABULARY
>
> **savvy**: The savvy lawyers, politicians, and other men have a destiny other than "warriors and toilers."
>
> **ASK STUDENTS** to explain the difference between the savvy men and the "warriors and toilers" Sanders has already described. *(The savvy men do not labor with their bodies; they do not kill, and they are not killed.)*

---

they scarcely worked at all. During my early school years we lived on a military base, an arsenal in Ohio, and every day I saw GIs in the guardshacks, on the stoops of barracks, at the wheels of olive drab Chevrolets. The chief fact of their lives was boredom. Long after I left the Arsenal I came to recognize the sour smell the soldiers gave off as
90 that of souls in limbo. They were all waiting—for wars, for transfers, for leaves, for promotions, for the end of their hitch—like so many braves waiting for the hunt to begin. Unlike the warriors of older tribes, however, they would have no say about when the battle would start or how it would be waged. Their waiting was broken only when they practiced for war. They fired guns at targets, drove tanks across the churned-up fields of the military reservation, set off bombs in the wrecks of old fighter planes. I knew this was all play. But I also felt certain that when the hour for killing arrived, they would kill. When the real shooting started, many of them would die. This was what
100 soldiers were *for*, just as a hammer was for driving nails. **G**

Warriors and toilers: those seemed, in my boyhood vision, to be the chief destinies for men. They weren't the only destinies, as I learned from having a few male teachers, from reading books, and from watching television. But the men on television—the politicians, the astronauts, the generals, the **savvy** lawyers, the philosophical doctors, the bosses who gave orders to both soldiers and laborers— seemed as remote and unreal to me as the figures in tapestries. I could no more imagine growing up to become one of these cool, potent creatures than I could imagine becoming a prince.
110 A nearer and more hopeful example was that of my father, who had escaped from a red-dirt farm to a tire factory, and from the assembly line to the front office. Eventually he dressed in a white shirt and tie. He carried himself as if he had been born to work with his mind. But his body, remembering the earlier years of slogging work, began to give out on him in his fifties, and it quit on him entirely before he turned sixty-five. Even such a partial escape from man's fate as he had accomplished did not seem possible for most of the boys I knew. They joined the Army, stood in line for jobs in the smoky plants, helped build highways. They were bound to work as their fathers had
120 worked, killing themselves or preparing to kill others.

A scholarship enabled me not only to attend college, a rare enough feat in my circle, but even to study in a university meant for the children of the rich. Here I met for the first time young men who had assumed from birth that they would lead lives of comfort and power. And for the first time I met women who told me that men were guilty of having kept all the joys and privileges of the earth for themselves. I was baffled. What privileges? What joys? I thought about the maimed, dismal lives of most of the men back home. What had they stolen from their wives and daughters? The right to go five days a week, twelve
130 months a year, for thirty or forty years to a steel mill or a coal mine? The right to drop bombs and die in war? The right to feel every leak in

savvy
(săv´ē) *adj.* shrewd, confidently clever.

134 Collection 2

APPLYING ACADEMIC VOCABULARY

exploit	predominance

As you discuss the essay, incorporate the following Collection 2 academic vocabulary words: *exploit* and *predominance*. Ask students in what way the "toilers and warriors"—the laborers and the soldiers—may have been **exploited**. Discuss the **predominant** viewpoint on gender inequality that Sanders found at college. Have them cite evidence from the text to support their answers.

> ## " Warriors and toilers: those seemed, in my boyhood vision, to be the chief destinies for men. "

the roof, every gap in the fence, every cough in the engine, as a wound they must mend? The right to feel, when the lay-off comes or the plant shuts down, not only afraid but ashamed?

I was slow to understand the deep grievances of women. This was because, as a boy, I had envied them. Before college, the only people I had ever known who were interested in art or music or literature, the only ones who read books, the only ones who ever seemed to enjoy a sense of ease and grace were the mothers and daughters. Like the
140 menfolk, they fretted about money, they scrimped and made-do. But, when the pay stopped coming in, they were not the ones who had failed. Nor did they have to go to war, and that seemed to me a blessed fact. By comparison with the narrow, ironclad days of fathers, there was an expansiveness, I thought, in the days of mothers. They went to see neighbors, to shop in town, to run errands at school, at the library, at church. No doubt, had I looked harder at their lives, I would have envied them less. It was not my fate to become a woman, so it was easier for me to see the graces. Few of them held jobs outside the home, and those who did filled thankless roles as clerks and waitresses.
150 I didn't see, then, what a prison a house could be, since houses seemed to me brighter, handsomer places than any factory. I did not realize—because such things were never spoken of—how often women suffered from men's bullying. I did learn about the wretchedness of abandoned wives, single mothers, widows; but I also learned about the wretchedness of lone men. Even then I could see how exhausting it was for a mother to cater all day to the needs of young children. But if I had been asked, as a boy, to choose between tending a baby and tending a machine, I think I would have chosen the baby. (Having now tended both, I know I would choose the baby.)
160 So I was baffled when the women at college accused me and my sex of having cornered the world's pleasures. I think something like my bafflement has been felt by other boys (and by girls as well) who grew up in dirt-poor farm country, in mining country, in black ghettos, in Hispanic barrios, in the shadows of factories, in Third World nations—any place where the fate of men is as grim and bleak as the fate of women. Toilers and warriors. I realize now how

The Men We Carry in Our Minds **135**

CLOSE READ

Determine Author's Point of View (LINES 160–166)   COMMON CORE RI 6

Remind students that an author's point of view can be formed not only by his or her personal experiences but also by how those experiences relate to a wider worldview.

ASK STUDENTS to reread lines 160–166 and explain why Sanders was baffled by women's accusations against men. (*He sees that men as well as women suffer in many parts of the world.*)

WHEN STUDENTS STRUGGLE . . .

To aid students' comprehension, guide them to break down the long paragraph on page 135 into two sections. Tell students that in the first half of the paragraph, from lines 135–146, Sanders explains why he used to envy women. In the second part of the paragraph, after the transition in lines 146–147, Sanders describes the causes of some women's "deep grievances." Have students explain to a partner at least two reasons for Sanders's ideas in each part of the paragraph.

Point out that there are several serial commas in this paragraph, used to separate adjectives, phrases, and clauses. Help students understand the meaning of these long sentences by reading them aloud, showing them how the ideas in each part of the series are related.

Determine Central Ideas RI 2

(LINES 172-181)

Explain that an essay's title can often suggest its central idea.

J CITE TEXT EVIDENCE Have students reread lines 172–181 and identify the reference to the essay's title in this paragraph. Then ask them to summarize the central idea of the essay. *("The women I met at college . . . did not carry in their minds the sort of men I had known in my childhood." Men and women "carry" ideas about different kinds of men, depending on their personal experiences and circumstances.)*

Determine Author's RI 6
Point of View (LINE 188)

Remind students that the development of an author's point of view is often a process, the conclusion of which is expressed at the end of a piece of writing.

K CITE TEXT EVIDENCE Is Sanders any clearer about whether or not he should feel guilty, whether or not he is a "persecutor" or a "victim"? Cite examples from the text. *(Yes, because he has reframed the question: "I wasn't an enemy, in fact or in feeling. I was an ally "[line 188].)*

COLLABORATIVE DISCUSSION Have students discuss specific textual evidence that shows how Sanders's point of view has developed over time. Then have them share the main points of their discussion with the class as a whole. Accept all reasonable responses.

ASK STUDENTS to share any questions they generated in the course of reading and discussing the selection.

---

ancient these identities are, how deep the tug they exert on men, the undertow of a thousand generations. The miseries I saw, as a boy, in the lives of nearly all men I continue to see in the lives of many—the
170 body-breaking toil, the tedium, the call to be tough, the humiliating powerlessness, the battle for a living and for territory.

When the women I met at college thought about the joys and privileges of men, they did not carry in their minds the sort of men I had known in my childhood. They thought of their fathers, who were bankers, physicians, architects, stockbrokers, the big wheels of the big cities. These fathers rode the train to work or drove cars that cost more than any of my childhood houses. They were attended from morning to night by female helpers, wives and nurses and secretaries. They were never laid off, never short of cash at month's end, never lined up
180 for welfare. These fathers made decisions that mattered. They ran the world.

The daughters of such men wanted to share in this power, this glory. So did I. They yearned for a say over their future, for jobs worthy of their abilities, for the right to live at peace, unmolested, whole. Yes, I thought, yes yes. The difference between me and these daughters was that they saw me, because of my sex, as destined from birth to become like their fathers, and therefore as an enemy to their desires. But I knew better. I wasn't an enemy, in fact or in feeling. I was an ally. If I had known, then, how to tell them so, would they have believed me?
190 Would they now?

COLLABORATIVE DISCUSSION With a partner, discuss how Sanders's views have developed over time.

Determine Author's Point of View

 COMMON CORE RI 6

"The Men We Carry in Our Minds" is a **personal essay**, a particular type of writing in which writers express their points of view on subjects by reflecting on events or incidents in their own lives. Sanders's essay is informal; it starts with a casual conversation between the writer and a female friend. This discussion in which Anneke calls men "persecutors" prompts the writer to think about how his perception of male roles and responsibilities has been shaped by his past experiences. In this passage he describes the men of his childhood:

> The bodies of the men I knew were twisted and maimed in ways visible and invisible. The nails of their hands were black and split, the hands tattooed with scars. Some had lost fingers.

Through these details and the words he chooses—*twisted, maimed, split*, and *scars*—Sanders's perspective on the lives of the men he knew is clearly conveyed to readers.

Determine Central Ideas

 COMMON CORE RI 2

A **central idea** is an important point about a topic that the writer wants to convey. In this essay, Sanders presents more than one central idea as he reflects on the role of men in society from his own perspective as well as the perspectives of his female friends. By the end of his essay, he has reconciled the ideas conveyed by both viewpoints. He comes to a new understanding of gender roles, as well as the way in which people's past lives shape their present outlooks.

To identify a central idea implied in a paragraph, passage, or selection, examine the details that the writer includes. Consider what point about the topic these details communicate. Then express that idea in a statement.

In this example notice how the details from one of the paragraphs in the essay develop the main idea:

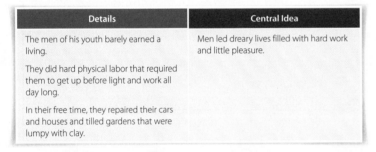

Details	Central Idea
The men of his youth barely earned a living.	Men led dreary lives filled with hard work and little pleasure.
They did hard physical labor that required them to get up before light and work all day long.	
In their free time, they repaired their cars and houses and tilled gardens that were lumpy with clay.	

TEACH

CLOSE READ

Determine Author's Point of View

 COMMON CORE RI 6

Review the instructions and the example passage with students, making sure that they understand how to determine author's point of view. Then have them work in pairs to find other places in the essay where Sanders describes experiences that have affected his perception of male roles and responsibilities.

Determine Central Ideas

 COMMON CORE RI 2

Tell students that an essay can contain several central ideas. To determine the essay's central ideas, have students work through these steps:

- Divide the essay into sections and have students work in small groups to identify the central idea of each section and to list details that support the idea.
- Have students share the central ideas of each section and discuss how these ideas relate or contribute to the overall central ideas of the essay.

Strategies for Annotation   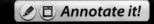 ✎ 🗐 *Annotate it!*

Determine Author's Point of View

Share these strategies for guided or independent analysis:

Have students locate passages with details that convey the author's perspective about the lives of men he knew growing up.

- Highlight in yellow details that create a clear image of these men.
- Underline words describing the men's fate.
- On a note, write the author's point of view as suggested by the description.

> wine or whiskey, so their eyes looked bloodshot and bruised. The fathers of my friends <u>always seemed older</u> than the mothers. Men <u>wore out sooner</u>. Only women lived into old age.

PRACTICE & APPLY

Analyzing the Text   RI 1, RI 2, RI 3, RI 4, RI 6

Possible answers:

1. *Sanders expects Anneke to agree that life is hard for women today. However, Anneke thinks that men are so burdened with guilt over what they have done to women that it is hard for them to get past it. Sanders sees the lives of men as just plain hard—"maimed" and "dismal."*

2. *Sanders contrasts the "sexual patterns" of his past—and humanity's past—with the imminent future. In the past, gender roles were sharply defined—men were hunters, and it can be inferred that women tended the "home" and children. In "genderless cities," such distinct roles will not exist—neither men nor women will be "victims" or "perpetrators."*

3. *Through the years, men have enjoyed a disproportionate share of privilege and power.*

4. *When Sanders was young, he perceived that many men are trapped in lives that offer few choices and no reprieve from their burdens of making a living and taking care of their families. The phrase "I dreaded growing up" captures his negative and almost fearful view of the kind of life he might expect to lead.*

5. *In this paragraph Sanders shows where his views on gender were first developed. As a youth, he envied women. Although their lives were plagued by some of the same problems as the men faced, they had more freedom and flexibility. They didn't have to go to war. As Sanders grew older, he began to develop a more realistic view of the nature of women's lives.*

6. *At the beginning of the essay, Sanders is confused by the idea that men's lives could ever be seen as more desirable than a woman's. He moves from this confusion to the realization that many men share women's envy of the "power-brokers," and he concludes that men and women should be allies in their struggle to achieve power and autonomy. He suggests that women need to move beyond their preconceptions to recognize this, too.*

7. *Sanders' descriptive words and phrases bring scenes and people to life. He draws an especially vivid portrait of the men he knew, using similes, such as "the skin . . . was creased like the leather of old work gloves" (line 77), and sensory details, such as "their eyes looked bloodshot and bruised" (line 80).*

8. *Students' answers may vary. Some students may feel the title is limiting because Sanders touches on several themes.*

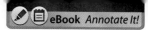

Analyzing the Text  RI 1, RI 2, RI 3, RI 4, RI 6, W 1, SL 3, SL 4

Cite Text Evidence   Support your responses with evidence from the selection.

1. **Identify** The term **irony** describes a contrast between expectation and reality. What is ironic about Anneke's statement that life is a lot harder for men?

2. **Interpret** Explain what Sanders means by the phrases "Stone Age hunters" and "genderless cities" in this quotation: "The back roads of Tennessee and Ohio where I grew up were probably closer, in their sexual patterns, to the campsites of Stone Age hunters than to the genderless cities of the future into which we are rushing" (lines 43–46).

3. **Analyze** What central idea about how women view gender roles is conveyed through Anneke's comments and the author's descriptions of his female friends in college?

4. **Analyze** What does the phrase "I dreaded growing up" reveal about the author's perspective on the men he observed in his youth?

5. **Draw Conclusions** Why does Sanders include the paragraph about the women in his childhood (lines 135–159)? How does the contrast between men's and women's lives in this paragraph help support his central idea about men?

6. **Analyze** How does Sanders reconcile his understanding of what men's lives are like with the perspective of his female friends?

7. **Evaluate** Reread lines 59–82. Identify elements of Sanders's style in this passage. **Style** is the distinctive way in which a writer uses language. How effective is Sanders's style in conveying his point of view?

8. **Critique** Is the title "The Men We Carry in Our Minds" appropriate for the essay? Explain why or why not.

PERFORMANCE TASK

Speaking Activity: Debate Sanders presents varying views on gender roles in his essay. As a class, debate which view has more validity and relevance today.

1. Form a team with classmates to support one of the positions.

2. Create an outline stating your claim and identifying the evidence that supports this claim.

3. Take turns presenting each argument and answering questions from the listeners.

4. Students in the audience should write an evaluation of the persuasiveness of each side's argument and decide the "winner" of the debate.

Assign this performance task.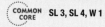

PERFORMANCE TASK   COMMON CORE SL 3, SL 4, W 1

Speaking Activity: Debate Students on each team should present a well-organized and supported argument. Students in the audience should be able to support their evaluations with specific examples from each team's argument.

Critical Vocabulary

discredit   acrid   marginal   savvy

Practice and Apply   Explain which choice accurately fits the meaning of the Critical Vocabulary word.

1. Is a *savvy* professional easily exploited or hard to deceive? Explain.

2. Would peppermint tea or burning rubber have an *acrid* odor?

3. If investigators *discredit* a politician, is the politician likely to get reelected or voted out of office?

4. Does a *marginal* worker enjoy a rich lifestyle or live on a small amount of money?

Vocabulary Strategy: Context Clues

When readers encounter an unfamiliar word, they can use context clues to determine its meaning. **Context clues** are the words, phrases, or sentences that surround an unfamiliar word. Sometimes a clue will be in the same sentence. Other times readers must look before or after the sentence to find the familiar words that help them decide on the meaning of the unknown word. The chart shows the context clues in the essay that could be used to define vocabulary words:

Context Clues	
Quotation	**Clue**
"...while men feel they're in the wrong. Men are the ones who've been *discredited,* who have to search their souls."	"in the wrong"
"They were *marginal* farmers, just scraping by, or welders..."	"just scraping by"

Practice and Apply   Return to the essay to find context clues that define each of these words: *lumber* (line 19), *maimed* (line 70), *potent* (line 108), *expansiveness* (line 144).

1. Write the definition based on the clues.

2. Use each word in an original sentence.

PRACTICE & APPLY

Critical Vocabulary

Answers:

1. *A savvy professional is shrewd and knowledgeable. Therefore, he or she would be hard to deceive.*

2. *Burning rubber has a sharp stinging smell.*

3. *If someone is proven to be in the wrong, it is unlikely he or she would be reelected.*

4. *A marginal worker is one who is barely hanging on and most likely living on less money.*

Vocabulary Strategy: Context Clues

Answers:

1. *lumber: "wounded grizzly bears" (context clue), to walk slowly and heavily (definition); maimed: "twisted," "scars" (context clues), disfigured, hurt (definitions); potent: "cool," "prince" (context clues), powerful (definition); expansiveness: "narrow ironclad"(context clue), having space (definition).*

2. *lumber: We watched John lumber down the street on his crutches; maimed: The trapeze artist was maimed by a bad fall; potent: An expensive car can be a potent symbol; expansiveness: The museum's large rooms had a feeling of expansiveness.*

Strategies for Annotation   ✏ 🗐 *Annotate it!*

Context Clues

Have students locate the sentences containing the words *discredit, acrid, marginal,* and *savvy.* Encourage them to use their eBook annotation tools to do the following:

- Highlight in green each vocabulary word.
- Reread the surrounding sentences, looking for clues to the word's meaning. Underline any context clues, such as examples, synonyms, or antonyms.
- Review your annotations and try to infer the word's meaning.

down sense that <u>we are in the *right*</u>—we've been held back, passed over, used—while men feel <u>they're in the wrong</u>. Men are the ones who've been discredited, who have to search their souls.

Language and Style: Syntax

COMMON CORE L 3a

Review the literary element of **tone,** which is a writer's attitude toward the subject. Tone can be either formal or informal, depending on the writer's purpose. A writer creates tone through word choice and sentence structure (syntax).

Possible answers:

Paragraphs should use each type of syntax identified in the chart.

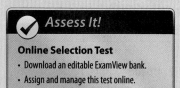

Assess It!

Online Selection Test
- Download an editable ExamView bank.
- Assign and manage this test online.

Language and Style: Syntax

COMMON CORE L 3a

Syntax refers to the way words are arranged in a sentence. Writers use syntax to establish the tone of their writing—for example, the use of complex sentence structures can help create a formal tone. Varying syntax can also make writing more engaging or emphasize certain ideas. The chart shows examples of how Sanders varies his syntax.

Syntax	Purpose	Example
Alternating between short and long sentences	to make writing more engaging	"I search my soul. I discover guilty feelings aplenty—toward the poor, the Vietnamese, Native Americans, the whales, an endless list of debts—a guilt in each case that is as bright and unambiguous as a neon sign."
Sentence fragments	to create an informal tone	"What privileges? What joys?"
Parallel structure	to emphasizes ideas	"Before college, the only people I had ever known who were interested in art or music or literature, the only ones who read books, the only ones who ever seemed to enjoy a sense of ease and grace were the mothers and daughters."

Practice and Apply Write a paragraph in which you express your reaction to the essay, using all three of the types of syntax identified in the chart. Compare your use of varied syntax with a partner.

Determine Connotative Meanings

COMMON CORE

RI 4

TEACH

Tell students that good writers choose their words with deliberation, considering both the denotation—dictionary definition—and the **connotation**, those feelings or ideas associated with a word. Point out that the denotation is easily determined by checking the word in a print or digital dictionary, but connotation can be more elusive. Review these strategies for determining connotation:

- **Use context clues.** Examine the surrounding words to see what feeling or impression they convey. *The warm, gentle rays of the sun filtering into the room immediately lifted her spirits and gave her a sense of elation.*

- **Replace with synonyms.** Contrast the "before-and-after" sentences to understand the shade of meaning brought out by the original word choice. *She was crushed by her test results. / She was disappointed in her test results.*

- **Consider the sound of the word.** To reinforce a negative connotation, writers may choose words that sound harsh or discordant. To enhance a positive connotation, writers may choose softer-sounding words. *The villain's face, a map of scabs and leaking pustules, was imprinted on her memory. / The child's dewy complexion was smooth and unblemished.*

 PARA-INTERACTIVE For additional instruction and guided practice, send students, individually or in groups, to Wordsharp: Interactive Vocabulary Tutorial: **Denotative and Connotative Meanings**

PRACTICE AND APPLY

Project lines 70–82 on the whiteboard.

- Call on volunteers to highlight words with strong connotations. *(twisted, maimed, black, split, scars, finicky, squinted, leather, bruised, wore out)*

- Have students work in pairs to determine each word's connotation. Have them explain how they arrived at the meaning.

As a class, discuss what ideas both the denotations and the connotations convey. What main point does the author communicate in this paragraph? *(The men in his childhood were physically and emotionally damaged by their lives.)*

Determine Central Ideas

COMMON CORE

RI 2

RETEACH

Review the definition of **central idea** (an important point that an author wants to convey about a subject). Explain out that to identify the central idea of a piece, students must look carefully for details and evaluate how they work together to develop a larger idea. Provide students with another personal essay, such as Zora Neal Hurston's "How It Feels to Be Colored Me," E. B. White's "Once More to the Lake," Virginia Woolf's "Death of a Moth," or Annie Dillard's "Total Eclipse."

- Read a section of the essay aloud, and then ask students to identify the central idea of that section.

- Ask students to name details that help to support this central idea.

 LEVEL UP TUTORIALS Assign the following *Level Up* tutorial: **Main Idea and Supporting Details**

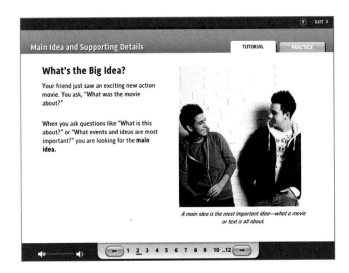

CLOSE READING APPLICATION

Students can apply the skill to one of the other essays listed above, or to a selection on the *FYI* website. Have them work independently or with a partner to highlight details that help them determine the central ideas of individual paragraphs and sections, and then the overall central ideas.

from Pink Think

Essay by Lynn Peril

Why This Text

Lynn Peril's essay presents her point of view about the role women were expected to conform to in the 1940s to the 1970s. Contemporary young readers of the essay may be unfamiliar with the culture that promoted the values that Peril mocks. With the help of the close-reading questions, students will determine the author's point of view and analyze the examples she uses to support it. This close reading will lead students to fully comprehend the author's perspective.

Background Have students read the background and information about Lynn Peril and her book *Pink Think*. Point out that this essay is from the introduction to *Pink Think* and it focuses on American attitudes from the 1940s to the 1970s towards "ideas and attitudes about what constituted proper female behavior." Have students consider how those attitudes have changed.

AS YOU READ Ask students to pay attention to the rhetorical devices used to advance the author's viewpoint. How do they help the author gain support from her readers?

Common Core Support

- cite strong and thorough textual evidence
- determine an author's central ideas
- determine an author's point of view
- analyze how an author's style contributes to the text

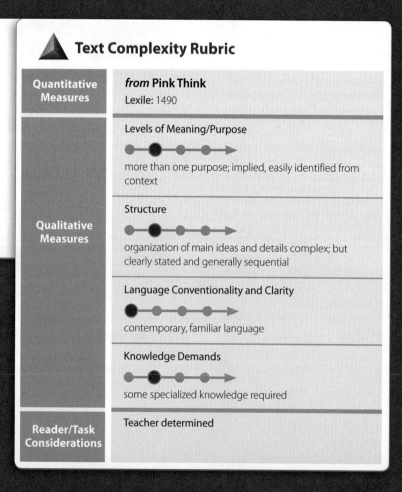

◣ Text Complexity Rubric

Quantitative Measures	*from* Pink Think
	Lexile: 1490

Qualitative Measures

Levels of Meaning/Purpose

more than one purpose; implied, easily identified from context

Structure

organization of main ideas and details complex; but clearly stated and generally sequential

Language Conventionality and Clarity

contemporary, familiar language

Knowledge Demands

some specialized knowledge required

Reader/Task Considerations

Teacher determined

Strategies for CLOSE READING

Determine Author's Point of View

Students should read this essay carefully all the way through. Close-reading questions at the bottom of the page will help them determine the author's point of view. As they read, students should jot down comments or questions about the text in the margins.

WHEN STUDENTS STRUGGLE . . .

To help students analyze "Pink Think," have them work in small groups to fill out a chart like the one shown below.

CITE TEXT EVIDENCE For practice in determining an author's point of view, ask students to cite text evidence that reveals it.

Text Evidence	How It Reveals the Author's Point of View
"charm" (line 18) "personality" (line 19) "experts" (line 21) "feminine charm" (line 59)	The author is mocking the values described in these terms.
"It was almost as if the men and women . . . modern world." (lines 32–34) If only all women . . . would be fine." (lines 42–44)	The author finds these views unbelievable.
". . . such helplessness adds to her appearance of femininity." (line 17) ". . . no greater destiny than to glory in their own femininity." (lines 48–49)	The author ridicules the pursuit of these ideals.
". . . femininity was necessary for catching and marrying a man . . ." (lines 50–51) ". . . motherhood and housewifery as women's only meaningful career . . ." (line 58)	The author believes women have a much greater role in society than merely marrying and raising children.

Background *Author* **Lynn Peril** *has been described as a mild-mannered civil servant by day, and a serious—but lighthearted—proponent of womens' rights all of the time. The following essay comes from the introduction to her book* Pink Think: Becoming a Woman in Many Uneasy Lessons, *"a pop-culture history of the perilous path to achieving the feminine ideal."*

from **Pink Think**

Essay by Lynn Peril

CLOSE READ
Notes

1. **READD** As you read lines 1–20, begin to collect and cite text evidence.
   - Underline text in the first paragraph that explain what *pink think* is.
   - Circle stereotypes of femininity.
   - In the margin, note language that hints at the writer's point of view.

A Pink think is a set of ideas and attitudes about what **constitutes** proper female behavior; a groupthink that was consciously or not adhered to by advice writers, manufacturers of toys and other consumer products, experts in many walks of life, and the public at large, particularly during the years spanning the mid-twentieth century—but enduring even into the twenty-first century. Pink think assumes there is a standard of behavior to which all women, no matter their age, race, or body type, must aspire.

B "Femininity" is sometimes used as a code word for this mythical standard,
10 which suggests that women and girls are always gentle, soft, delicate, nurturing beings made of sugar and spice and everything nice. But pink think is more than a stereotyped vision of girls and women as poor drivers who are afraid of mice and snakes, adore babies and small dogs, talk incessantly on the phone, and are incapable of keeping secrets. Integral to pink think is the belief that one's success as a woman is grounded in one's allegiance to such behavior. For example, a woman who fears mice isn't necessarily following the dictates of pink think. On the other hand, a woman who isn't afraid of mice but pretends

constitutes:
makes up; comprises

Phrases such as "mythical standard" and "stereotyped vision" let you know the writer's point of view.

33

1. **READ AND CITE TEXT EVIDENCE** Tell students that authors often do not express their points of view directly. They may build their arguments using language that influences readers' opinions.

   A **ASK STUDENTS** to explain the examples of rhetorical language that the author uses. *Students may cite "mythical standard" in line 8 that shows the author thinks the standard is make-believe; "stereotyped vision" in line 11 lets the reader know that the author finds certain accepted ideas about women to be typecast.*

   Critical Vocabulary: constitutes (line 1) Have students share their definitions of *constitutes*, and ask them what noun has the same root and how its meaning relates to the verb. *The noun* constitution *means "makeup or composition" of something— what it is composed of.*

to be because she thinks such helplessness adds to her appearance of femininity is toeing the pink think party line. When you hear the words "charm" or "personality" in the context of successful womanhood, you can almost always
20   be sure you're in the presence of pink think.

While various self-styled "experts" have been advising women on their "proper" conduct since the invention of the printing press, the phenomenon defined here as pink think was particularly pervasive from the 1940s to the 1970s. These were fertile years for pink think, a cultural mindset and consumer behavior rooted in New Deal[1] prosperity yet culminating with the birth of women's liberation. During this time, pink think permeated popular books and magazines aimed at adult women, while little girls absorbed rules of feminine behavior while playing games like the aforementioned Miss Popularity. Meanwhile, prescriptions for ladylike dress, deportment, and mindset seeped
30   into child-rearing manuals, high school home economics textbooks, and guides for bride, homemaker, and career girl alike.

panacea:
a solution for all problems or difficulties

    It was almost as if the men and women who wrote such books viewed proper feminine behavior as a **panacea** for the ills of a rapidly changing modern world. For example, myriad articles in the popular press devoted to the joys of housewifery helped coerce Rosie the Riveter[2] back into the kitchen when

[1] **New Deal:** series of economic programs passed between 1933 and 1936 that were meant to stimulate the economy after the Great Depression.
[2] **Rosie the Riveter:** a cultural icon in the U.S. who represented the women who worked in factories during World War II.

2. ◀ REREAD   Reread lines 8–20. Note the words or phrases that are in quotes. Why does the author use quotation marks with these words or phrases?

She is being sarcastic. She wants to emphasize that these words and phrases are examples of pink think and not real traits that women must necessarily possess.

3. READ ▶   As you read lines 21–44, continue to cite textual evidence.
- Circle products from the 1940s and 1970s that contained pink think ideas.
- Underline examples of what women were expected to be like during the "early cold war years."
- In the margin on the next page, describe women's expected role.

34

> ❝ *If only all women behaved like our Ideal Woman . . . then everything would be fine.* ❞

her hubby came home from the war and expected his factory job back. During the early cold war years, some home economics texts seemed to suggest that knowing how to make hospital corners and a good tuna casserole were the only things between Our Way of Life and communist incursion. It was patriotic to
40   be an exemplary housewife. And pink-thinking experts of the sixties and seventies, trying to maintain this ideal, churned out reams of pages that countered the onrushing tide of the women's movement. If only all women behaved like our Ideal Woman, the experts seemed to say through the years, then everything would be fine.

    You might even say that the "problem with no name" that Betty Friedan wrote about in *The Feminine Mystique* (1963) was a virulent strain of pink-thinkitis. After all, according to Friedan, "the problem" was in part engendered by the experts' insistence that women "could desire no greater destiny than to glory in their own femininity"—a pink think **credo**.
50   The pink think of the 1940s to 1970s held that femininity was necessary for catching and marrying a man, which was in turn a prerequisite for childbearing—the ultimate feminine fulfillment. This resulted in little girls playing games like Mystery Date[3] long before they were ever interested in boys. It made home economics a high school course and college major, and suggested a teen girl's focus should be on dating and getting a boyfriend. It made beauty,

[3] **Mystery Date:** a board game marketed to girls aged 6–14. The object of the game was to be ready for a date by assembling three matching cards to make an outfit appropriate for the date.

Women had a secondary role: in the kitchen, at home, doing household chores.

Pink-thinkitis is an illness caused by focusing solely on being feminine.

credo:
belief, principle

4. ◀ REREAD AND DISCUSS   Reread lines 21–44. With a small group, identify and discuss Peril's central idea in these paragraphs.

5. READ ▶   As you read lines 45–65, continue to cite textual evidence.
- In the margin, explain in your own words what the author means by "pink-thinkitis."
- Underline text that describes other principles of "pink think."

35

---

2. REREAD AND CITE TEXT EVIDENCE   You may want to point out that there is a modern term for quotation marks used in a way that is not meant to imply an actual quotation: *scare quotes.*

Ⓑ **ASK STUDENTS** to compare their responses. *Students will probably state that the author is mocking these ideals by putting them in quotes.*

3. READ AND CITE TEXT EVIDENCE

Ⓒ **ASK STUDENTS** why women had been appreciated for working outside the home during World War II. *Students should note that because men were overseas during the war, women were needed to do the work the men had previously been doing at home. When the war was over, the men wanted their jobs back.*

Critical Vocabulary: panacea (line 33) Have students share definitions of *panacea.* Point out that the root *pan-* is Greek for "all," and is found in words such as *Pan-American* and *pantheism.*

4. REREAD AND DISCUSS USING TEXT EVIDENCE

Ⓓ **ASK STUDENTS** to compare central ideas. *Some will cite lines 42–44 or "proper feminine behavior" was "a panacea for the ills of a rapidly changing modern world."*

5. READ AND CITE TEXT EVIDENCE

Ⓔ **ASK STUDENTS** what Peril thinks causes "pink-thinkitis." *"Pink-thinkitis" is caused by so-called "experts" pushing their stereotyped ideas of what a woman should be.*

Critical Vocabulary: credo (line 49) Ask students to identify words with the same root as *credo* and explain how they relate to the meaning of *credo.* The words credible *and* credibility *mean "believable" and "the quality of inspiring belief."*

FOR ELL STUDENTS Clarify that the word *hubby* is an informal way to shorten *husband.*

CLOSE READ
Notes

mandatory:
required

charm, and submissive behavior of **mandatory** importance to women of all ages in order to win a man's attention and hold his interest after marriage. It promoted motherhood and housewifery as women's only meaningful career,
60 and made sure that women who worked outside the home brought "feminine charm" to their workplaces lest a career make them too masculine.

Not that pink think resides exclusively alongside antimacassars[4] and 14.4 modems in the graveyard of outdated popular culture: Shoes, clothing, and movie stars may go in and out of style with astounding rapidity, but attitudes have an unnerving way of hanging around long after they've outlived their usefulness—even if they never had any use to begin with.

[4] **antimacassars:** small cloths placed over the arms of furniture such as chairs or couches to prevent wear or soiling.

6. **◀ REREAD** Reread lines 61–65. Why does Peril use the phrase "the graveyard of outdated popular culture" to refer to pink think?

She is comparing pink think to things that deserved to go out of style and implying that pink think was a pointless set of ideas.

SHORT RESPONSE

Cite Text Evidence Review your reading notes to identify elements of Peril's style. What words and phrases best suggest her perspective, or point of view, on pink think? **Cite textual evidence** in your response.

Peril calls pink think "groupthink" and refers to "pink-thinkitis"— negative terms. She uses quotes to mock: "experts"; "sugar and spice and everything nice." She presents evidence showing that people thought of women as nothing more than concepts. Peril lists different ways that women were told through various media how to be an exemplary housewife. She ends the essay by grouping pink think with other items of "outdated popular culture." This analogy is effective in allowing readers to identify with her ideas—and support them.

36

---

6. **REREAD AND CITE TEXT EVIDENCE**

(F) ASK STUDENTS to analyze the phrase "the graveyard of outdated popular culture" (line 62). *A graveyard is a place for things that have died, things that are outdated and no longer have any use; "popular culture" suggests fads that are trivial and transitory.*

Critical Vocabulary: mandatory (line 56) Have students share their definitions of *mandatory*. Ask students why the author uses the word here. *She is pointing out that the concepts listed were not only expected, but were required by society.*

SHORT RESPONSE

Cite Text Evidence Students should:

- identify the author's point of view.
- cite evidence the author uses to support her argument.
- give examples of rhetorical devices that advance the author's point of view.

TO CHALLENGE STUDENTS . . .

To deepen student's understanding of women's roles in American society during World War II, have them work in groups and research Rosie the Riveter and related topics online.

ASK STUDENTS to report on what they learned about women workers during the war. Why were women important in the war effort? *Without women, there would not be enough workers since so many men were in the military.* Did most women work in factories? *No, most of them worked in the service sector. About 3 million women worked in factories.* Did women rush to get jobs at the outbreak of war? *No, the government started a propaganda campaign to encourage them.* How did men regard women workers? *They gradually began to accept them as coworkers.*

DIG DEEPER

With the class, return to Question 4, Reread and Discuss. Have groups share their responses to the question.

ASK STUDENTS about the details that the author supplies to support her central idea in lines 21–44.

- Have students discuss the ideas about women's roles put forward from the 1940s through the 1970s. How did proponents of pink think appeal to women? *They flooded the market with publications aimed at women—books and magazines that assumed that their audience was complicit in the pink think culture. They extolled the joys of being a housewife, and suggested that this role was patriotic.*

- Ask students why the author includes such details as "knowing how to make hospital corners and a good tuna casserole." *These skills are presented as being trivial, and the idea that they are important is being mocked.*

ASK STUDENTS to return to their Short Response answer and revise it based on the class discussion.

COLLECTION 2
PERFORMANCE TASK A

Interactive Lessons

If you need help with...
• **Writing an Informative Text**
• **Writing as a Process**

Write an Informative Essay

COMMON CORE

W 2 Write informative/explanatory texts.
W 4 Produce clear and coherent writing.
W 9 Draw evidence from literary or informational texts.

This collection focuses on gender roles through a variety of viewpoints and genres as well as from a range of cultures and time periods. In the anchor text "The Wife of Bath's Tale," a knight goes on a year-long quest to find out what women most desire in life. What does Chaucer suggest about the ability of people to understand someone of the opposite sex? Write an informative essay about understanding between men and women, drawing on "The Wife of Bath's Tale" and two other selections in this collection.

An effective informative essay includes

- an introduction with a clearly stated controlling idea about understanding between men and women
- a logically structured body that thoroughly develops the topic with relevant examples, concrete details, quotations, and other evidence
- transitions to clarify the relationships between ideas about understanding the opposite sex and the evidence you gathered from the texts
- a conclusion that follows from the ideas conveyed in the body of the essay
- precise use of language with appropriate tone and style for an informative essay

PLAN

Analyze the Texts Reread "The Wife of Bath's Tale" and take notes on what Chaucer is trying to convey about our ability to understand someone of the opposite sex. Consider the ways in which gender bias might affect how we perceive others. Does our inclination to make generalizations about the opposite sex prevent us from understanding each other? Pay attention to specific details, quotations, and examples from the text. Then review two other chosen texts in the collection, noting any relevant evidence from those texts. Synthesize your findings to form a controlling idea.

*my*Notebook

Use the annotation tools in your eBook to find evidence about understanding between men and women. Save each piece of evidence to your notebook.

WRITE AN INFORMATIVE ESSAY

COMMON CORE W 2, W 4, W 9

Introduce students to the Performance Task by reading the introductory paragraph with them and reviewing the criteria for an effective informative essay. Work with students to distill the prompt into a simple question, such as *Can men and women ever really understand each other?*

PLAN

ANALYZE THE TEXTS

View It!

Professional Development Podcast:
Performance Task

Once student have finished their review of "The Wife of Bath's Tale," suggest that they write a possible controlling idea based on the evidence they have identified. They can use this idea to help them choose which additional texts to review for supporting evidence. After reviewing the other selections, they can refine the controlling idea to fit the evidence from all three texts.

PLAN

GET ORGANIZED

Tell students that organizing details, quotations, and examples in a logical way is essential to writing an effective informative essay. Remind them that all of the text evidence they include should be relevant to their controlling idea. Review the second bulleted point and make sure students understand the organizational patterns that are described.

PRODUCE

DRAFT YOUR ESSAY

Tell students that they should establish a clear link between the controlling idea in their draft introductions and the main idea of each supporting paragraph. They can make these connections through transitions. In turn, they must fully explain the connection of any text evidence they present to the idea it supports.

Get Organized Organize your details and evidence in an outline.

- Choose the textual evidence that is the most relevant to your controlling idea.
- Decide what organizational pattern you will use for your essay. For example, will you present your first idea about the ability of men and women to understand each other, citing evidence from all three texts, and then move on to the next idea? Or, will you discuss the texts one at a time, presenting all your ideas and evidence for one selection before turning to the next selection?
- Use your organizational pattern to sort textual evidence into a logical order.
- Select an interesting quotation or detail from one of the texts to accompany the statement of your controlling idea in the introduction.
- List some ideas for your concluding section. Think about how you can relate your topic to a broader concept regarding gender biases or the roles of men and women that your audience can easily relate to.

ACADEMIC VOCABULARY

As you write your informative essay, be sure to use these words.

bias
complementary
exploit
inclinations
predominance

> **PRODUCE**

Draft Your Essay Write a draft of your essay, following your outline.

- Introduce your controlling idea about understanding the opposite sex. Present your topic in an interesting way that will make readers want to continue reading. Remember that you must take an objective approach to the topic; you are not making an argument or stating your opinion.
- Present your details, facts, quotations, and examples from the texts in logically ordered paragraphs.
- Use appropriate transitions to create cohesion between sections of your essay and to clarify relationships between your topic and the provided evidence.
- Write a concluding section that summarizes the main points of your topic. Include a closing statement that relates the topic to your audience.

As you draft your informative essay, keep in mind that you should use formal language; avoid slang or contractions.

my **WriteSmart**

Write your rough draft in *my*WriteSmart. Focus on getting your ideas down, rather than on perfecting your choice of language.

REVISE

Improve Your Draft Revise your draft to make sure it is clear, coherent, and engaging. Use the chart on the following page to review the characteristics of a well-writen informative essay. Then, ask yourself these questions as you revise:

- Have I introduced my topic clearly? Does my introduction engage the reader?

- Have I presented relevant evidence from the texts to support the central ideas in my essay?

- Is my essay logically organized? Are transitions from section to section smooth and easy to follow? Do I need to clarify how the central ideas are connected to the evidence from the texts? Do my sentence structures give my writing a a rhythmic flow?

- Have I maintained an objective viewpoint throughout the essay?

- Have I used a formal style of English appropriate for an informative essay?

- Does my conclusion follow logically from the body and provide a satisfying ending?

*my*WriteSmart

Have your partner or a group of peers review your draft in *my*WriteSmart. Ask your reviewers to note any evidence that does not support the central ideas.

PRESENT

Present Your Essay When your final draft is completed, present your essay to a small group. Your classmates will listen attentively, take notes, and ask questions. Group members should pay attention to whether or not the presenter maintained an objective tone throughout the essay and point out aspects of the presenter's essay that are particularly strong, as well as areas that could be improved.

REVISE

IMPROVE YOUR DRAFT

Suggest that students use the criteria in the chart Collection 2, Task A: Informative Essay on page 144 to rank their essay in each of the three categories. Then they can focus their revisions on the category that needs the most improvement.

PRESENT

PRESENT YOUR ESSAY

Other options for sharing students' essays include
- posting them on the school's website
- hosting another class for a panel discussion of ideas raised in the essays

IDEAS AND EVIDENCE

Have students look at the chart to assess their level of performance in the Ideas and Evidence category. Have them evaluate the facts, concrete details, quotations (if any), and text evidence cited in their essay for relevancy and accuracy. Ask them to set goals for the next time they write an informative essay. What areas will they work to improve? What strategies might help them achieve their goals?

COLLECTION 2 TASK A
INFORMATIVE ESSAY

	Ideas and Evidence	Organization	Language
ADVANCED	• The introduction is intriguing and informative; the controlling idea clearly identifies a compelling topic. • The topic is strongly developed with relevant facts, concrete details, interesting quotations, and examples from the texts. • The concluding section capably follows from and supports the ideas presented.	• The organization is effective and logical throughout the essay. • Transitions are well crafted and successfully connect related ideas.	• The writing reflects a formal style and an objective, knowledgeable tone. • Language is vivid and precise. • Sentence beginnings, lengths, and structures vary and have a rhythmic flow. • Spelling, capitalization, and punctuation are correct. • Grammar and usage are correct.
COMPETENT	• The introduction could do more to attract the reader's curiosity; the controlling idea identifies a topic. • One or two key points could use additional support in the form of relevant facts, concrete details, quotations, and examples from the texts. • The concluding section mostly follows from and supports the ideas presented.	• The organization is confusing in a few places. • A few more transitions are needed to connect related ideas.	• The style is inconsistent in a few places, and the tone is subjective at times. • Vague language is used in a few places. • Sentence beginnings, lengths, and structures vary somewhat. • Some spelling, capitalization, and punctuation mistakes occur. • Some grammatical and usage errors are repeated in the essay.
LIMITED	• The introduction provides some information about a topic but does not include a controlling idea. • Most key points need additional support in the form of relevant facts, concrete details, quotations, and examples from the texts. • The concluding section is confusing and does not follow from the ideas presented.	• The organization is confusing in some places and often doesn't follow a pattern. • More transitions are needed throughout to connect related ideas.	• The style is too informal; the tone conveys subjectivity and a lack of understanding of the topic. • Vague, general language is used in many places. • Sentence structures barely vary, and some fragments or run-on sentences are present. • Spelling, capitalization, and punctuation are often incorrect but do not make reading the essay difficult. • Grammar and usage are incorrect in many places, but the writer's ideas are still clear.
EMERGING	• The appropriate elements of an introduction are missing. • Facts, details, quotations, and examples from the texts are missing. • The essay lacks an identifiable concluding section.	• A logical organization is not used; information is presented randomly. • Transitions are not used, making the essay difficult to understand.	• The style and tone are inappropriate for the essay. • Language is too vague or general to convey the information. • Repetitive sentence structure, fragments, and run-on sentences make the writing monotonous and difficult to follow. • Spelling, capitalization, and punctuation are incorrect throughout. • Many grammatical and usage errors change the meaning of the writer's ideas.

PERFORMANCE TASK B

Participate in a Group Discussion

COMMON CORE

This collection explores traditional roles of men and women as well as changes in gender roles that have occurred in recent decades. Look back at the texts and think about how gender roles have evolved over time. In the anchor text "The Men We Carry in Our Minds," Scott Russell Sanders offers a nuanced view of feminism, arguing that the jobs that were once monopolized by men were not always so enviable. Over the past few decades, women have pushed hard to break down social barriers, and men's roles have also been changing. What changes do you foresee in gender roles over the next ten years? Talk about your ideas in a group discussion, drawing on Sanders's essay and at least one other collection text in your response.

SL 1a–d Initiate and participate effectively in a range of collaborative discussions with diverse partners, building on others' ideas and expressing their own clearly and persuasively.

Participants in an effective group discussion

- present well-founded predictions based on ideas in "The Men We Carry in Our Minds" and one or more other collection texts

- provide quotations or examples to support their predictions

- make clear, logical, and well-developed connections among the texts' views of gender roles

- respond thoughtfully to the ideas of others in the group, adapting or expanding upon their own ideas or politely challenging others' assertions

- pay attention to fairness and engagement, taking turns and asking questions to ensure participation of all group members

PLAN

Get Organized Work with your classmates to prepare for the discussion.

my **Notebook**

Use the annotation tools in your eBook to find evidence about changing gender roles. Save each piece of evidence to your notebook.

- Get together with your group and choose at least one other text from this collection, in addition to "The Men We Carry in Our Minds," that you will use to have a discussion about how gender roles will change in the future.

- Decide on roles for the discussion. You will need a moderator, a note-taker, and a presenter. The moderator will keep the conversation moving forward and ensure a friendly discussion in which all members participate equally. The note-taker will write down the central ideas from the discussion. The presenter will summarize the discussion to the rest of the class.

PARTICIPATE IN A GROUP DISCUSSION

COMMON CORE SL 1a–d

Introduce the Performance Task by reading the introductory paragraph with students and reviewing the criteria for effective group discussion on this page. Tell students that they will have a preliminary meeting with their group to decide which selections to discuss. Then they will analyze the texts independently to prepare for the actual discussion.

PLAN

GET ORGANIZED

Suggest that students choose a total of two or three selections to discuss so that group members can complete their analysis in time for the discussion. If there is disagreement about which texts to discuss, students should take a vote or use another fair method to reach a decision.

▶ **View It!**

Professional Development Podcast:
Performance Task

PERFORMANCE TASK B

PLAN

CREATE AN OUTLINE

Students' outlines provide a written record of their work that you may use, along with their participation in the discussion, to assess their performance on the task. If you plan to collect the outlines for this purpose, let students know in advance.

PRODUCE

HAVE THE DISCUSSION

Remind students to refer to their outlines as they present their ideas and evidence, but also to engage in authentic conversation. They should maintain eye contact when speaking to other students and listen closely to what others have to say. The discussion is a chance for them to gain new perspectives on the issue based on their classmates' analysis of the texts.

Students may want to videotape their discussions. Videotaping will allow them to critique themselves on their discussion skills and their use of text evidence to support their ideas.

- Set rules regarding how and when the moderator or other group members will ask questions or interject ideas.

Analyze the Texts Work individually to review the chosen texts. Reread "The Men We Carry in Our Minds" and take notes about how Sanders conveys his view on gender roles. Gather evidence from the text and note any specific details, quotations, or examples. Then review and take notes on your other chosen text(s). Pay attention to ways in which the texts may make suggestions about the continued evolution of gender roles in the next ten years. Will we see a change in the predominance of men in positions of power? Will existing gender biases change or disappear? Will women continue to break barriers to equality?

Create an Outline Organize your predictions and evidence in a detailed outline.

- Write down your ideas and predictions about future gender roles.
- Sort through the evidence you have collected from the texts. Match each piece of evidence with one of your predictions.
- Think of questions that your group members may ask, and be prepared to answer them.
- Draft a closing statement that you will make when it is your last turn to speak.

ACADEMIC VOCABULARY

As you plan your discussion on the issue of changing gender roles, use these words.

bias
complementary
exploit
inclinations
predominance

> PRODUCE

Have the Discussion With guidance from your moderator, hold your discussion.

- Join your group members to have a lively exchange of ideas.
- Maintain a respectful tone toward your fellow group members, even when you disagree with their ideas.
- Listen closely to what all speakers say so that you can respond appropriately and ask relevant questions.
- Take notes throughout the discussion, even though the note-taker will be keeping track of the central ideas that are introduced and developed.

my **WriteSmart**

Write your outline in *my*WriteSmart. Follow a logical outline format, so your notes are easy to refer to later.

Evaluate the Discussion

When your discussion is over, evaluate each other's predictions. Refer to the chart on the following page to review the characteristics of an effective discussion.

- First, talk about the reasons and evidence that you found most compelling, and why.
- Then, synthesize the ideas expressed by the group and resolve any contradictions, if possible.
- As a group, decide on the most important points from the discussion that the presenter will report back to the class.

Present to the Class

The presenter will summarize the group discussion for the rest of the class. Invite your classmates to ask questions about the discussion. Either the presenter or other group members can respond.

my WriteSmart

Before your discussion, exchange the outlines you created in *my*WriteSmart with another group member. Ask your reviewer to note any evidence that does not support the prediction.

REVISE

EVALUATE THE DISCUSSION

As students evaluate their discussion, encourage them to consider both the content and the presentation. Were the predictions logical and well supported by text evidence? Did the discussion flow smoothly, with all participants showing respect for other group members? Were disagreements handled to everyone's satisfaction?

PRESENT

PRESENT TO THE CLASS

If students have videotaped their discussions, they could include one or two clips as part of their presentation to the class. These clips could later be added to the school's website as part of a page summarizing the activity.

PERFORMANCE TASK B

LANGUAGE

Have students look at the chart to evaluate their level of performance in the Language category. Have them consider how well they used formal English and cited relevant details from the texts to support their ideas, and whether they maintained a respectful tone during the discussion. Ask them to set goals for the next time they participate in a group discussion. How will they improve their participation?

COLLECTION 2 TASK B
GROUP DISCUSSION

	Ideas and Evidence	Organization	Language
ADVANCED	• The participant clearly states a valid generalization or prediction and supports it with strong, relevant ideas and well-chosen evidence from the texts and personal experience. • The participant carefully evaluates others' evidence and reasoning and responds with insightful comments and questions. • The participant synthesizes the analysis of the texts to help listeners understand the prediction.	• The participant's remarks are based on a well-organized outline or notes that clearly identify the prediction and the supporting ideas and evidence. • Ideas are presented in a logical order with effective transitions to show the connections between ideas. • The participant concludes with a statement that reinforces the prediction and includes the ideas that have emerged from the discussion.	• The participant adapts speech to the context of the discussion, using appropriately formal English to discuss the texts and ideas. • The participant consistently quotes accurately from the texts to support ideas. • The participant consistently maintains a polite and thoughtful tone throughout the discussion.
COMPETENT	• The participant states a prediction and supports it with relevant ideas and evidence from the texts and personal experience. • The participant evaluates others' evidence and reasoning and responds with appropriate comments and questions. • The participant synthesizes some ideas and links to the prediction.	• The participant's remarks are based on an outline or notes that identify the prediction, supporting ideas, and evidence. • Ideas are presented in a logical order and linked with transitions. • The participant concludes with a statement that reinforces the prediction.	• The participant mostly uses formal English to discuss literature and ideas. • The participant mostly quotes accurately from the texts to support ideas. • The participant maintains a polite and thoughtful tone throughout most of the discussion.
LIMITED	• The participant states a reasonably clear prediction and supports it with some ideas and evidence. • The participant's response to others' comments shows limited evaluation of the evidence and reasoning. • The participant does not synthesize but simply repeats the prediction in a vague way.	• The participant's remarks reflect an outline or notes that may identify the prediction but do not organize ideas and evidence very effectively. • Ideas are presented in a somewhat disorganized way with few transitions. • The participant makes a weak concluding statement that does little to reinforce the prediction.	• The participant uses some formal and some informal English to discuss the texts and ideas. • The participant's quotations and examples sometimes do not accurately reflect the texts. • The participant occasionally forgets to maintain a polite tone when responding to others' comments and questions.
EMERGING	• The participant's prediction is unclear; ideas and evidence are not coherent. • The participant does not evaluate others' evidence and reasoning. • The participant does not synthesize.	• The panelist does not follow an outline or notes that organize ideas and evidence. • Ideas are presented in a disorganized way with no transitions. • The panelist's remarks lack any kind of conclusion or summary.	• The panelist uses informal English and/or slang, resulting in ideas that are not clearly expressed. • The panelist's quotations and examples do not accurately reflect the texts. • The panel member does not maintain a polite tone when responding to others' comments and questions.

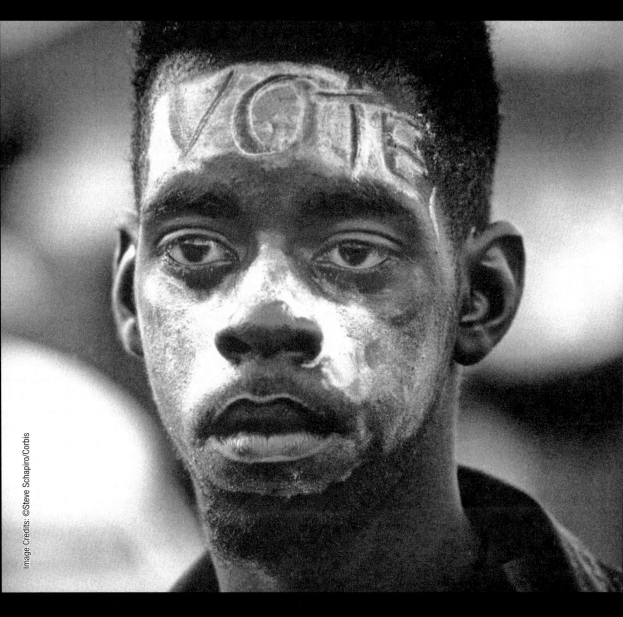

Voices of Protest

PLAN

Voices of Protest

This collection represents nearly three centuries of opposition to injustice, addressing problems such as tyranny, hunger, and pollution.

CONNECTING WORD AND IMAGE

ASK STUDENTS to discuss how the collection opener image and the collection quotation work together to create a connection.

PERFORMANCE TASK PREVIEW

Point out to students that they will complete two performance tasks at the end of the collection. The performance tasks will require them to further analyze the selections in the collection and to synthesize ideas about these analyses. They will present their findings in a variety of products.

COLLECTION

PERFORMANCE TASK Preview

At the end of this collection, you will have the opportunity to complete two tasks:

• Participate in a group discussion about the nature of injustice and ways to end it.

• Using "A Modest Proposal" as a model, write a satire on a topic discussed in one of the selections.

ACADEMIC VOCABULARY

View It!

Professional Development Podcast:

Academic Vocabulary

Students can acquire facility with the academic vocabulary words through frequent, repeated exposure as they analyze and discuss the selections in the collection. Academic vocabulary can be used in the following instructional contexts. This will enable students to incorporate the academic vocabulary words into their working vocabulary.

• Collaborative Discussion at the end of each selection
• Analyzing the Text questions for each selection
• Selection-level Performance Task
• Vocabulary instruction (for Critical Vocabulary and/or for Vocabulary Strategy)
• Language and Style
• End-of-collection Performance Task for all selections in the collection

ASK STUDENTS to review the Academic Vocabulary word list for this collection. You may wish to pronounce each word aloud, so students hear the correct pronunciation. Then, discuss the definitions and the related forms for each word. Remind students that they will encounter these five academic vocabulary words throughout the collection.

ACADEMIC VOCABULARY

Study the words and their definitions in the chart below. You will use these words as you discuss and write about the texts in this collection.

Word	Definition	Related Forms
controversy (kŏn´trə-vûr´sē) *n.*	public disagreement, argument	controversial, controvert
convince (kən-vĭns´) *n.*	persuade or lead to agreement by means of argument	convict, conviction
ethics (ĕth´ĭks) *n.*	rules of conduct or set of principles	ethical, ethicist
radical (răd´ĭ-kəl) *adj.*	extreme; desirous of change in established institutions or practices	radicalism, radicalize
tension (tĕn´shən) *n.*	mental strain or excitement	tense, tensive

150

USING COLLECTIONS YOUR WAY

Use the following information, along with the charts on the following pages, to help you decide how you want to introduce the collection. Based on your teaching style, your students' interests, or your instructional goals, you may want to structure this collection in various ways. You may choose different entry points each time you teach the collection.

"I require my students to do a lot of research."

The cause-and-effect relationships discussed in this essay by **Terry Tempest Williams** provide opportunities for students to do additional research about possible connections between nuclear testing and cancer.

Terry Tempest Williams (b. 1955) was raised by a large Mormon family in Utah. Both Utah and Mormonism have influenced her writing. Her book Refuge: An Unnatural History of Family and Place, from which the selection is taken, tells about her mother's cancer diagnosis, and the unprecedented rise of the Great Salt Lake that flooded a wildlife refuge. This link between people and nature is one that Williams often explores in her writing. Her concern for the environment has led her to testify before Congress.

The Clan of One-Breasted Women
Essay by Terry Tempest Williams

AS YOU READ Look for the details that the author includes to show how her family and nature are engaged in the same struggle.

I belong to a Clan of One-Breasted Women. My mother, my grandmothers, and six aunts have all had mastectomies. Seven are dead. The two who survive have just completed rounds of chemotherapy and radiation.

I've had my own problems: two biopsies for breast cancer and a small tumor between my ribs diagnosed as a "borderline malignancy."

This is my family history.

Most statistics tell us breast cancer is genetic, hereditary, with rising percentages attached to fatty diets, childlessness, or becoming pregnant after thirty. What they don't say is living in Utah may be the greatest hazard of all.

We are a Mormon family with roots in Utah since 1847. The "word of wisdom" in my family aligned us with good foods—no coffee, no tea, tobacco, or alcohol.[1] For the most part, our women were finished having their babies by the time they were thirty. And only one faced

[1] **The "word of wisdom" . . . alcohol:** law of the Mormon religion concerning health, as revealed by the Prophet Joseph Smith in 1833.

The Clan of One-Breasted Women **187**

"I want to challenge my students to the utmost."

This satire by **Jonathan Swift** was originally written to bring about reform. Although many people today read it as a story, it challenges students to consider the history and effects of political corruption in eighteenth-century Ireland.

Background In the 1720s, the Catholics in Ireland suffered from the repressive rule of England, which stripped them of their rights and forced them into poverty. Their misery increased with a series of crop failures; many had to beg or face starvation. Swift wrote "A Modest Proposal" to protest England's policies in Ireland.

Jonathan Swift (1667–1745) was born of English parents in Dublin, Ireland. He became an Anglican priest and a writer, whose satires took aim at injustice and vice. He is probably best known for Gulliver's Travels. This satire is now enjoyed as a story, although Swift wrote it as a criticism of political corruption.

A Modest Proposal
for preventing the children of poor people in Ireland from being a burden to their parents or country, and for making them beneficial to the public

Satire by Jonathan Swift

AS YOU READ Pay attention to details that Swift includes to make his proposal sound convincing. Note questions you have during reading.

It is a melancholy object to those who walk through this great town[1] or travel in the country, when they see the streets, the roads, and cabin doors, crowded with beggars of the female sex, followed by three, four, or six children, all in rags and importuning every passenger for an alms.[2] These mothers, instead of being able to work for their honest livelihood, are forced to employ all their time in strolling to beg sustenance for their helpless infants, who, as they grow up, either turn thieves for want[3] of work, or leave their dear native country to fight for the Pretender[4] in Spain, or sell themselves to the Barbadoes.[5]

[1] **this great town:** Dublin, Ireland.
[2] **importuning** (ĭm'pôr-tōōn'ĭng) . . . **alms** (ämz): begging from every passerby for a charitable handout.
[3] **want:** lack; need.
[4] **Pretender:** James Edward Stuart, who claimed the English throne, from which his now deceased father, James II, had been removed in 1688. Because James II and his son were Catholic, the common people of Ireland were loyal to them.
[5] **sell . . . Barbadoes:** To escape poverty, some Irish migrated to the West Indies, obtaining money for their passage by agreeing to work as slaves on plantations there for a set period.

A Modest Proposal **199**

"I like to use visual media as a starting point."

The text and photographs in **Alison Wright's** piece of photojournalism prompt readers and viewers to consider aspects of poverty in the United States. The photographs and the captions show an uncompromising view of people trying to survive in difficult conditions.

Alison Wright is a photojournalist whose work has taken her around the world. Her photographs capture people struggling for survival and coping with human-rights issues. She also records traditions of changing cultures to preserve them. Her pictures have appeared in many publications including National Geographic magazine. In addition, her photos and writing have been published in several books. One of her books recounts her recovery after surviving a life-threatening bus accident in Laos.

MEDIA ANALYSIS

Third World America
Photojournalism by Alison Wright

AS YOU VIEW Notice details in the photographs that provide insight into the living conditions of the people shown in them.

This project covers an array of social and ethnic borders: the black families of the Mississippi Delta who live in the first town started after slavery was abolished; the struggles of a single woman raising three children on the minimum wage while working at Wendy's in Ohio; the food bank in Appalachia where 800 cars a day line up for groceries; migrant workers who live in Texas and raise children in this country so they can have a better life as American citizens; Indians on a Navaho reservation who instill a cultural sense of pride to their children in the native powwows, yet have no running water or electricity in their basic hogans.

The face of poverty in this country is not the rail thin visage as in developing countries, but due to such a poor innutritious diet, obesity is a ubiquitous problem. Children's health is so affected that diabetes is prevalent, and many are overweight with severe psychological problems. With the cost of living outweighing the average income, many families across America are just one pay check away from being on the edge, especially when it comes to healthcare issues.

Third World America **213**

mySmartPlanner | **eBook** | **my**Notebook | **my** WriteSmart | fyi hmhfyi.com

Collection 3 Lessons	Media	Teach and Practice
Student Edition | eBook	▶ Video Links	**Close Reading and Evidence Tracking**
ANCHOR TEXT — Speech by Martin Luther King Jr. Speech on the Vietnam War, 1967	▶ **Video** *LBJ: Civil Rights and Vietnam* ◀ **Audio** Speech on the Vietnam War, 1967	**Close Read Screencasts** • Modeled Discussion 1 (lines 14–24) • Modeled Discussion 2 (lines 219–228) • Close Read application pdf (lines 494–505)	**Strategies for Annotation** • Analyze Language • Delineate and Evaluate an Argument: Inductive Reasoning • Use Suffixes
CLOSE READER — Speech by Shirley Chisholm "People and Peace, not Profits and War"	◀ **Audio** *"People and Peace, not Profits and War"*		
Essay by Thomas Paine from "The Crisis" Essay by Henry David Thoreau from "Civil Disobedience"	◀ **Audio** from "The Crisis" ◀ **Audio** from "Civil Disobedience"		**Strategies for Annotation** • Analyze Foundational Documents • Vocabulary Strategy: Clarify Precise Meaning • Delineate and Evaluate an Argument
Essay by Terry Tempest Williams "The Clan of One-Breasted Women"	▶ **Video** *Expedition Inspiration* ◀ **Audio** "The Clan of One-Breasted Women"		**Strategies for Annotation** • Determine Author's Purpose • Analyze Ideas and Events: Cause and Effect • Denotation and Connotation
ANCHOR TEXT — Satire by Jonathan Swift "A Modest Proposal"	◀ **Audio** "A Modest Proposal"	**Close Read Screencasts** • Modeled Discussion 1 (lines 25–33) • Modeled Discussion 2 (lines 186–193) • Close Read application pdf (lines 278–288)	**Strategies for Annotation** • Analyze Author's Point of View: Satire
CLOSE READER — Satire by Joel Stein "Who Speaks for the 1%?"	◀ **Audio** "Who Speaks for the 1%?"		
Photojournalism by Alison Wright "Third World America"	◀ **Audio** "Third World America"		
Poem by Martín Espada "Imagine the Angels of Bread"	◀ **Audio** "Imagine the Angels of Bread"		
CLOSE READER — Poem by Derek Walcott "Elsewhere"	◀ **Audio** "Elsewhere"		
Collection 3 Performance Tasks: **A** Participate in a Group Discussion **B** Write a Satire	fyi hmhfyi.com	**Interactive Lessons** **A** Participating in Collaborative Discussions **A** Using Textual Evidence	**B** Writing an Argument **B** Writing as a Process

	For Systematic Coverage of Writing and Speaking & Listening Standards	Interactive Lessons Conducting Research Evaluating Sources	Lesson Assessments Conducting Research Evaluating Sources

Assess		Extend	Reteach
Performance Task	**Online Assessment**	**Teacher eBook**	**Teacher eBook**
Writing Activity: Review	Selection Test	**Analyze Style: Rhetorical Devices**	**Delineate and Evaluate an Argument: Inductive Reasoning > Level Up Tutorial >** Analyzing Arguments
Writing Activity: Letter Research Activity: Report Speaking Activity: Role Play	Selection Test	**Support Inferences > Interactive Whiteboard Lesson >** Making Inferences	**Delineate and Evaluate an Argument > Level Up Tutorial >** Elements of an Argument
Media Activity: Report	Selection Test	**Determine Author's Point of View > Interactive Whiteboard Lesson >** Author's Purpose and Perspective	**Analyze Ideas and Events: Cause and Effect > Level Up Tutorial >** Cause-and-Effect Organization **Para-Interactive >** Nonfiction Selection
Writing Activity: Context Guide	Selection Test	**Analyze and Evaluate Structure > Interactive Whiteboard Lesson >** Evaluating Arguments	**Analyze Author's Point of View: Satire > Level Up Tutorial >** Irony
Media Activity: Photo Essay	Selection Test	**Determine Author's Purpose**	**Integrate and Evaluate Information > Level Up Tutorial >** Analyzing Visuals
Writing Activity: Poem	Selection Test	**Language: Repetition and Parallelism**	**Analyze Word Choice: Tone > Level Up Tutorial >** Tone
A Participate in a Group Discussion **B** Write a Satire	Collection Test		

Collection 3 Lessons	Key Learning Objective	Performance Task
ANCHOR TEXT **Speech by Martin Luther King Jr.** **Lexile 1290L** **Speech on the Vietnam War, 1967, p. 151A**	**The student will be able to…** delineate and evaluate an argument as well as determine connotative meanings of the language used	Writing Activity: Review
Essay by Thomas Paine **Lexile 1180L** from "The Crisis," p. 169A **Essay by Henry David Thoreau** **Lexile 1200L** from "Civil Disobedience," p. 169A	**The student will be able to…** analyze foundational documents and delineate and evaluate arguments	Writing Activity: Letter Research Activity: Report Speaking Activity: Role Play
Essay by Terry Tempest Williams **Lexile 990L** **"The Clan of One-Breasted Women," p. 187A**	**The student will be able to…** analyze cause and effect and cite text evidence to support inferences	Media Activity: Report
ANCHOR TEXT **Satire by Jonathan Swift** **Lexile 1590L** **"A Modest Proposal," p. 199A**	**The student will be able to…** analyze satire and its historical context	Writing Activity: Context Guide
Photojournalism by Alison Wright **Lexile 1260L** **"Third World America," p. 213A**	**The student will be able to…** integrate and evaluate information presented in words and photographs	Media Activity: Photo Essay
Poem by Martín Espada **"Imagine the Angels of Bread," p. 217A**	**The student will be able to…** analyze the impact of word choice on meaning and tone in the poem	Writing Activity: Poem

Collection 3 Performance Tasks:
A Participate in a Group Discussion
B Write a Satire

Vocabulary Strategy	Language and Style	Student Instructional Support	CLOSE READER Selection
Suffixes	Imperative Mood	**Scaffolding for ELL Students:** • Clarify Historical Context • Language: Pronoun Referents • Use Prefixes • Language: Punctuation Cues **When Students Struggle:** • Examine Chronological Order • Analyze Reasons and Evidence • Summarize Paragraphs **To Challenge Students:** • Analyze Tone and Purpose • Explore Connections	Speech by Shirley Chisholm "People and Peace, not Profits and War," p. 168b **Lexile 1150L**
Clarify Precise Meaning	Combining Sentences	**Scaffolding for ELL Students:** • Vocabulary: Multiple-Meaning Words and Idioms • Language: Punctuation and Print Cues • Vocabulary: Prefixes **When Students Struggle:** • Summarize Paragraphs • Analyze Cause-and-Effect Organization • Clarify Meaning **To Challenge Students:** • Gather Information • Examine Persuasive Techniques	
Denotation and Connotation	Gerunds and Gerund Phrases	**Scaffolding for ELL Students:** • Culture: Background • Vocabulary: Idiomatic Expressions • Vocabulary Support **When Students Struggle:** Understand Cause and Effect **To Challenge Students:** Evaluate Author's Style	
Context Clues	Active and Passive Voice	**Scaffolding for ELL Students:** • Vocabulary: Context Clues • Language: Verb Tense **When Students Struggle:** • Identify Problem-Solution Organization • Analyze Reasons • Use Active and Passive Voice **To Challenge Students:** Analyze Metaphorical Language	Satire by Joel Stein "Who Speaks for the 1%?," p. 212b **Lexile 1080L**
		Scaffolding for ELL Students: Culture: Comprehension Support **When Students Struggle:** Analyze Photographs	
		Scaffolding for ELL Students: Analyze Word Choice **When Students Struggle:** Find Main Idea	Poem by Derek Walcott "Elsewhere," p. 220b

Speech on the Vietnam War, 1967

*my*SmartPlanner — Create lesson plans and access resources online.

Speech by Martin Luther King Jr.

Why This Text?

In this historic speech, Martin Luther King Jr. presents a compelling argument about the need for change in American policy. This lesson guides students in an evaluation of the reasoning and language he uses to persuade his listeners.

View It!

Professional Development Podcast:

Teaching Argument

Key Learning Objective: The student will be able to delineate and evaluate an argument as well as determine connotative meanings of the language used.

For additional practice:

People and **Peace,** not **Profits** and **War**

Close Reader selection
"People and Peace, not Profits and War"
Speech by Shirley Chisholm

COMMON CORE Common Core Standards

RI 1 Cite textual evidence.

RI 4 Determine the meaning of words and phrases used in a text, including connotative meanings.

RI 5 Analyze and evaluate the effectiveness of the structure an author uses.

RI 6 Determine an author's point of view or purpose.

RI 8 Delineate and evaluate the reasoning in seminal U.S. texts.

RI 9 Analyze foundational U.S. documents of historical and literary significance.

RI 10 Read and comprehend literary nonfiction.

W 9b Apply *grades 11–12 Reading Standards* to literary nonfiction.

L 3 Apply knowledge of language.

L 4b Identify and correctly use patterns of word changes.

▲ Text Complexity Rubric

Quantitative Measures	**Speech on the Vietnam War, 1967** Lexile: 1290L
Qualitative Measures	**Levels of Meaning/Purpose** ●—●—●—●—► multiple levels of meaning (multiple themes)
	Structure ●—●—●—●—► organization of main ideas and details complex but mostly explicit; may exhibit disciplinary traits
	Language Conventionality and Clarity ●—●—●—●—► figurative, symbolic language
	Knowledge Demands ●—●—●—●—► somewhat complex social studies concepts
Reader/Task Considerations	Teacher determined Vary by individual reader and type of text

TEACH

CLOSE READ

For more context and historical background, students can view the video ""LBJ: Civil Rights and Vietnam" in their eBooks.

Martin Luther King Jr. Have students read the biographical information on Martin Luther King Jr. Explain that in 1967, opposition to the war in Vietnam was just beginning. U.S. involvement was escalating; the first combat troops had been sent over in 1965 to support the government of South Vietnam against the communist North Vietnam and its allies in the south, the Viet Cong. Criticism of the U.S. government's policy by such a leading figure was not welcome. Martin Luther King Jr.'s stance antagonized the White House and made some of the other leaders of the civil rights movement concerned that he might be jeopardizing support for their agenda.

AS YOU READ Direct students to use the As You Read note to focus their reading.

Delineate and Evaluate an Argument: Inductive Reasoning (LINES 1–13)

 COMMON CORE RI 8

Explain to students that the audience of a speech dictates the kind of language and ideas that the speaker includes in order to achieve his or her purpose.

Ⓐ ASK STUDENTS to reread the last two lines of the first paragraph. What does King's explanation that he does "not wish to speak with Hanoi and the National Liberation Front, but rather to my fellow Americans" suggest about his purpose in this speech? *(He doesn't want to say what "the enemy" should do; rather he wants to explain what Americans need to do.)* Why does King use the phrase "my fellow Americans"? *(This phrase shows his solidarity with those to whom he is speaking.)*

CRITICAL VOCABULARY

facile: King believes that the fact of his ministry and dedication to civil rights makes his desire to speak about Vietnam easy to understand.

ASK STUDENTS what King is implying about the war in Vietnam by saying its connection to the struggle to gain civil rights is facile. *(The civil rights struggle is an effort to right injustice; the war in Vietnam is unjust and distracts Americans from the need to address the civil rights of their fellow citizens.)*

 VIDEO

Martin Luther King Jr. (1929–1968), *a Baptist minister and social activist, was the most prominent leader of the civil rights movement from the mid-1950s until his assassination in 1968. He was committed to using nonviolent protest to end legal discrimination and segregation in the United States. His efforts aided in the passage of the Civil Rights Act of 1964 and the Voting Rights Act of 1965. In the mid-1960s, he grew concerned about the involvement of the United States in the Vietnam War. He gradually became more vocal in his opposition to the war, giving this speech on April 4, 1967, at the Riverside Church in New York City.*

Speech on the Vietnam War, 1967

Speech by Martin Luther King Jr.

AS YOU READ Look for connections between King's opposition to the war and his civil rights work. Note any questions you have as you read.

 Ⓐ

I come to this platform tonight to make a passionate plea to my beloved nation. This speech is not addressed to Hanoi or to the National Liberation Front.[1] It is not addressed to China or to Russia. Nor is it an attempt to overlook the ambiguity of the total situation and the need for a collective solution to the tragedy of Vietnam. Neither is it an attempt to make North Vietnam or the National Liberation Front paragons of virtue, nor to overlook the role they must play in the successful resolution of the problem. While they both may have justifiable reasons to be suspicious of the good faith of the United

10 States, life and history give eloquent testimony to the fact that conflicts are never resolved without trustful give and take on both sides. Tonight, however, I wish not to speak with Hanoi and the National Liberation Front, but rather to my fellow Americans.

Since I am a preacher by calling, I suppose it is not surprising that I have seven major reasons for bringing Vietnam into the field of my moral vision. There is at the outset a very obvious and almost **facile**

---
[1] **National Liberation Front:** also known as the Viet Cong, revolutionary fighters in South Vietnam.

facile
(făs´əl) *adj.* easy to make or understand.

Image Credits: (t) ©ASSOCIATED PRESS; (b) ©Bettmann/Corbis

Speech on the Vietnam War, 1967 **151**

Close Read Screencasts ▶ View It!

Modeled Discussions

Have students click the *Close Read* icons in their eBooks to access two screencasts in which readers discuss and annotate the following key passages:

- King's justification for speaking on Vietnam (lines 14–24)
- King's defense of the Viet Cong (lines 219–228)

As a class, view and discuss at least one of these videos. Then have students pair up to do an independent close read of an additional passage—King's exhortation to action (lines 494–505).

CLOSE READ

Delineate and Evaluate an Argument: Inductive Reasoning (LINES 18–29)

COMMON CORE RI 8

Tell students that when they evaluate an argument, they need to look at whether the reasons that the speaker gives for his or her position are logical. Logical reasons make sense intellectually and are based on fact rather than emotion.

 ASK STUDENTS to explain the first reason that King gives for taking a stand on Vietnam. *(The war is draining resources from the programs that help the poor in the United States.)* Is this a logical reason for his view that the war should be stopped? Why or why not? *(Yes. It makes sense that funding an expensive war would necessitate cuts elsewhere in the budget.)*

Determine Connotative Meanings (LINES 34–37)

COMMON CORE RI 4

Tell students that the connotations of words, or feelings and ideas associated with them, can help a speaker sway the opinions of his or her listeners.

 ASK STUDENTS why King chooses to use "crippled" rather than the words "hurt" or "held back." *("Crippled" has a much stronger connotation. It suggests that society has deliberately inflicted irreparable harm upon these young men, which has resulted in their loss of potential and full social and economic health.)* How does the use of this word intensify the point he is making in this sentence? *(This word draws attention to the irony that the young men, who have been damaged by denial of their own rights, are being victimized a second time as they are sent to Vietnam to fight for the very same rights they have been denied at home.)*

CRITICAL VOCABULARY

eviscerated: King says that the war has literally taken out what is most important in the programs so painstakingly constructed.

ASK STUDENTS what feelings are conveyed by the word *eviscerated*. *(This word is powerful, showing that King believes these programs have been gutted, leaving nothing useful behind.)*

---

connection between the war in Vietnam and the struggle I and others have been waging in America. A few years ago there was a shining moment in that struggle. It seemed as if there was a real promise of hope for the poor, both black and white, through the poverty program.[2] There were experiments, hopes, new beginnings. Then came the buildup in Vietnam, and I watched this program broken and **eviscerated** as if it were some idle political plaything of a society gone mad on war. And I knew that America would never invest the necessary funds or energies in rehabilitation of its poor so long as adventures like Vietnam continued to draw men and skills and money like some demonic, destructive suction tube. So I was increasingly compelled to see the war as an enemy of the poor and to attack it as such.

> **eviscerate**
> (ĭ-vĭs´ə-rāt´) *v.* to remove the necessary or important parts of.

Perhaps a more tragic recognition of reality took place when it became clear to me that the war was doing far more than devastating the hopes of the poor at home. It was sending their sons and their brothers and their husbands to fight and to die in extraordinarily high proportions relative to the rest of the population. We were taking the black young men who had been crippled by our society and sending them eight thousand miles away to guarantee liberties in Southeast Asia which they had not found in southwest Georgia and East Harlem. So we have been repeatedly faced with the cruel irony of watching Negro and white boys on TV screens as they kill and die together for a nation that has been unable to seat them together in the same schools. So we watch them in brutal solidarity burning the huts of a poor village, but we realize that they would hardly live on the same block in Chicago. I could not be silent in the face of such cruel manipulation of the poor.

My third reason moves to an even deeper level of awareness, for it grows out of my experience in the ghettos of the North over the last three years, especially the last three summers. As I have walked among the desperate, rejected, and angry young men, I have told them that Molotov cocktails[3] and rifles would not solve their problems. I have tried to offer them my deepest compassion while maintaining my conviction that social change comes most meaningfully through nonviolent action. But they asked, and rightly so, "What about Vietnam?" They asked if our own nation wasn't using massive doses of violence to solve its problems, to bring about the changes it wanted. Their questions hit home, and I knew that I could never again raise my voice against the violence of the oppressed in the ghettos without having first spoken clearly to the greatest purveyor of violence in the world today: my own government. For the sake of those boys, for the

---

[2] **poverty program:** legislation, often called the "War on Poverty." enacted in 1964 during Lyndon Johnson's administration.

[3] **Molotov cocktails:** home-made incendiary weapons made by filling breakable bottles with a flammable liquid, attaching and lighting wicks, and throwing them at a target.

SCAFFOLDING FOR ELL STUDENTS

Clarify Historical Context Read aloud lines 30–44. Tell students that in this part of the speech, King is referring to the hardships of black Americans. Explain that the Civil Rights Act of 1964 ended legal discrimination and segregation. But years of being denied equal opportunities for education, housing, and jobs had trapped many African Americans in a cycle of poverty from which they were unable to escape. They lacked political power, having only recently with the Voting Act of 1965 achieved unrestricted access to the polls. As a result, they had few representatives guarding their interests.

ASK STUDENTS how King sees the Vietnam War as another form of discrimination against poor African Americans.

sake of this government, for the sake of the hundreds of thousands
60 trembling under our violence, I cannot be silent.

For those who ask the question, "Aren't you a civil rights leader?"
and thereby mean to exclude me from the movement for peace, I have
this further answer. In 1957, when a group of us formed the Southern
Christian Leadership Conference, we chose as our motto: "To save
the soul of America." We were convinced that we could not limit
our vision to certain rights for black people, but instead affirmed the
conviction that America would never be free or saved from itself until
the descendants of its slaves were loosed completely from the shackles
they still wear. In a way we were agreeing with Langston Hughes, that
70 black bard of Harlem, who had written earlier:

> O, yes, I say it plain,
> America never was America to me,
> And yet I swear this oath—
> America will be!

Now it should be incandescently clear that no one who has any
concern for the integrity and life of America today can ignore the
present war. If America's soul becomes totally poisoned, part of the
autopsy must read "Vietnam." It can never be saved so long as it
destroys the deepest hopes of men the world over. So it is that those
80 of us who are yet determined that "America will be" are led down the
path of protest and dissent, working for the health of our land.

As if the weight of such a commitment to the life and health of
America were not enough, another burden of responsibility was placed
upon me in 1964. And I cannot forget that the Nobel Peace Prize[4]
was also a commission, a commission to work harder than I had ever
worked before for the brotherhood of man. This is a calling that takes
me beyond national allegiances.

But even if it were not present, I would yet have to live with the
meaning of my commitment to the ministry of Jesus Christ. To me,
90 the relationship of this ministry to the making of peace is so obvious
that I sometimes marvel at those who ask me why I am speaking
against the war. Could it be that they do not know that the Good
News[5] was meant for all men—for communist and capitalist, for
their children and ours, for black and for white, for revolutionary and
conservative? Have they forgotten that my ministry is in obedience to
the one who loved his enemies so fully that he died for them? What
then can I say to the Vietcong[6] or to Castro or to Mao as a faithful
minister of this one? Can I threaten them with death or must I not
share with them my life?

---

[4] **Nobel Peace Prize:** an annual award given to an individual who best promotes
international friendship, reduces military forces, and fosters peaceful relations.
King won the prize in 1964.

[5] **Good News:** the Gospels, or the written accounts of Jesus and his teachings.

[6] **Vietcong:** the National Liberation Front, South Vietnamese revolutionaries.

APPLYING ACADEMIC VOCABULARY

radical	ethics

As you discuss the King speech, incorporate the following Collection 3
academic vocabulary words: *radical* and *ethics*. Ask students to explain why
King's position on the Vietnam War would have been seen as **radical** in 1967.
Then have them discuss King's **ethics** and how they shape his response to
this war.

CLOSE READ

Delineate and Evaluate an Argument: Inductive Reasoning (LINES 61–81)

COMMON CORE RI 8

Remind students that convincing arguments often
include counterarguments, which provide answers
to possible opposing views on the issue. Presenting
counterarguments shows that the speaker has
thought about the issue from both sides.

D CITE TEXT EVIDENCE Have students explain
what opposing view King is addressing in this
counterargument. *(In lines 61–63, he explains that he is
responding to those who would say that as a civil rights
leader, he should not be involved in antiwar efforts.)* Ask
students to summarize his argument. *(He says that his
concern is for all of America's people. Since this war is
poisoning them all, he must speak out.)*

Support Inferences (LINES 82–87)

COMMON CORE RI 1

Tell students that the details in a persuasive speech
are chosen with deliberation. Details appeal to
listeners and enlist their support for a position.

E ASK STUDENTS to reread these lines. Have them
explain the effect of King mentioning his Nobel
Prize. *(The fact that King won a Nobel Prize increases
his prestige and would help his audience view him as
someone with authority and knowledge.)*

Analyze Structure (LINES 88–99)

COMMON CORE RI 5

Tell students that an effective way to structure an
argument is to state a reason clearly and then to
explain and defend the reason stated.

F ASK STUDENTS what important reason King
gives in lines 89-92 for opposing the war in Vietnam.
*(In lines 89–92, King states that his stance is part of who
he is as a minister.)* Ask students to summarize King's
defense of the reason he states. *(The Christian belief
in peace extends to all human beings, including the
Vietnamese Americans who were fighting in the war.)*

Determine Connotative Meanings (LINES 107–110)

 COMMON CORE RI 4

Tell students that the context in which a word is used can affect its connotation.

G **ASK STUDENTS** whether King uses the word *nationalism* in a positive or negative sense in this sentence. (*The connotation of* nationalism *in this sentence is negative.*) Have students explain what ideas are associated with the word *nationalism*. (*Nationalism in this sentence suggests a view of the world that is narrow and emphasizes a nation at the expense of its citizens and the citizens of other nations.*)

Delineate and Evaluate an Argument: Inductive Reasoning (LINES 123–138)

 COMMON CORE RI 8

Clarify for students that although many arguments begin with the statement of the speaker's claim followed by reasons and evidence, an argument based on inductive reasoning has the reverse structure. Reasons and evidence are presented before the conclusion.

H **ASK STUDENTS** what kind of evidence King presents in this part of his argument. (*He presents facts about Vietnam's struggle for independence and America's resistance to Vietnam's independence.*) Remind students that sound arguments are based on valid evidence. Ask them how they could determine whether this information is valid. (*They could verify the facts in a reference book, a history book, or on a reliable web site.*)

CRITICAL VOCABULARY

indigenous: King says that the United States prevented a government run by the Vietnamese themselves from taking power.

ASK STUDENTS to explain the reasons that King would see an indigenous government as advantageous to Vietnam. (*Officials native to a land know more about the people whom they govern. They understand the culture. They have a sense of the most pressing needs and issues facing the country. They are also invested in the outcomes of their policies.*)

---

100 Finally, as I try to explain for you and for myself the road that leads from Montgomery[7] to this place, I would have offered all that was most valid if I simply said that I must be true to my conviction that I share with all men the calling to be a son of the living God. Beyond the calling of race or nation or creed is this vocation of sonship and brotherhood. Because I believe that the Father is deeply concerned, especially for His suffering and helpless and outcast children, I come tonight to speak for them. This I believe to be the privilege and the burden of all of us who deem ourselves bound by allegiances and loyalties which are broader and deeper than nationalism and which go

110 beyond our nation's self-defined goals and positions. We are called to speak for the weak, for the voiceless, for the victims of our nation, for those it calls "enemy," for no document from human hands can make these humans any less our brothers.

And as I ponder the madness of Vietnam and search within myself for ways to understand and respond in compassion, my mind goes constantly to the people of that peninsula. I speak now not of the soldiers of each side, not of the ideologies of the Liberation Front, not of the junta in Saigon, but simply of the people who have been living under the curse of war for almost three continuous decades

120 now. I think of them, too, because it is clear to me that there will be no meaningful solution there until some attempt is made to know them and hear their broken cries.

They must see Americans as strange liberators. The Vietnamese people proclaimed their own independence in 1954—in 1945 rather—after a combined French and Japanese occupation and before the communist revolution in China. They were led by Ho Chi Minh. Even though they quoted the American Declaration of Independence in their own document of freedom, we refused to recognize them. Instead, we decided to support France in its reconquest of her former

130 colony. Our government felt then that the Vietnamese people were not ready for independence, and we again fell victim to the deadly Western arrogance that has poisoned the international atmosphere for so long. With that tragic decision we rejected a revolutionary government seeking self-determination and a government that had been established not by China—for whom the Vietnamese have no great love—but by clearly **indigenous** forces that included some communists. For the peasants this new government meant real land reform, one of the most important needs in their lives.

For nine years following 1945 we denied the people of Vietnam

140 the right of independence. For nine years we vigorously supported the French in their abortive effort to recolonize Vietnam. Before the end of the war we were meeting 80 percent of the French war costs. Even before the French were defeated at Dien Bien Phu, they began to

indigenous
(ĭn-dĭj′ə-nəs) *adj.*
native to a land.

---

[7] **Montgomery:** Alabama city and site of the 1955 bus boycott, a civil-rights protest that brought King to national prominence.

WHEN STUDENTS STRUGGLE . . .

Point out that in lines 123–161 King uses chronological order to organize his explanation of the history of Vietnam since 1945. Remind students that words such as *then, following, before,* and *after,* as well as specific dates signal the time relationship between events.

Have students work independently to create a simple timeline of the information included in this part of the text. Have them compare their timelines with a partner. As a class, complete the segment from 1963 (Diem's death) to 1967, drawing from the background provided at the beginning of the selection.

ASK STUDENTS how King views the actions of the United States in Vietnam before the war. Why does he include this information in his speech?

despair of their reckless action, but we did not. We encouraged them with our huge financial and military supplies to continue the war even after they had lost the will. Soon we would be paying almost the full costs of this tragic attempt at recolonization.

After the French were defeated, it looked as if independence and land reform would come again through the Geneva Agreement. But instead there came the United States, determined that Ho should not unify the temporarily divided nation, and the peasants watched again as we supported one of the most vicious modern dictators, our chosen man, Premier Diem.[8] The peasants watched and cringed as Diem ruthlessly rooted out all opposition, supported their **extortionist** landlords, and refused even to discuss reunification with the North. The peasants watched as all of this was presided over by United States influence and then by increasing numbers of United States troops who came to help quell the **insurgency** that Diem's methods had aroused. When Diem was overthrown they may have been happy, but the long line of military dictators seemed to offer no real change, especially in terms of their need for land and peace.

The only change came from America as we increased our troop commitments in support of governments which were singularly corrupt, inept, and without popular support. All the while the people read our leaflets and received the regular promises of peace and democracy and land reform. Now they languish under our bombs and consider us, not their fellow Vietnamese, the real enemy. They move sadly and apathetically as we herd them off the land of their fathers into concentration camps where minimal social needs are rarely met. They know they must move on or be destroyed by our bombs.

So they go, primarily women and children and the aged. They watch as we poison their water, as we kill a million acres of their crops. They must weep as the bulldozers roar through their areas preparing to destroy the precious trees. They wander into the hospitals with at least twenty casualties from American firepower for one Vietcong-inflicted injury. So far we may have killed a million of them, mostly children. They wander into the towns and see thousands of the children, homeless, without clothes, running in packs on the streets like animals. They see the children degraded by our soldiers as they beg for food. They see the children selling their sisters to our soldiers, soliciting for their mothers.

What do the peasants think as we ally ourselves with the landlords and as we refuse to put any action into our many words concerning land reform? What do they think as we test out our latest weapons on them, just as the Germans tested out new medicine and new tortures in the concentration camps of Europe? Where are the

extortionist
(ĭk-stôr´shən-ĭst) *n.*
one who obtains something by force or threat.

insurgency
(ĭn-sûr´jən-sē) *n.*
rebellion or revolt.

---

[8] **Premier Diem** (dē-ĕm´): Ngo Dinh Diem (1901–1963), the first president of South Vietnam in 1955, who was later killed in a military coup.

TO CHALLENGE STUDENTS...

Analyze Tone and Purpose Have students reread lines 162–170. Tell them that King's tone and the details he cites reveal his purpose. Have them use their eBook annotation tools to analyze King's tone. Assign this task:

- Highlight in yellow words that indicate King's feelings about the events in this passage. On a note, explain how the denotation and connotation of each word help to convey King's feeling or attitude.

ASK STUDENTS to describe King's tone and explain how it relates to his purpose. *(His tone is passionate as he illustrates the disconnect between the U.S. rhetoric and its actions. His purpose is to show that America's presence is doing more to destroy the South Vietnamese than the threat from North Vietnam.)*

CLOSE READ

Delineate and Evaluate an Argument: Inductive Reasoning (LINES 148–161)

COMMON CORE RI 8

Explain to students that a strong argument depends on thorough evidence. Sufficient facts, examples, or other details must be provided to support the speaker's reasons and ultimate conclusion.

(I) ASK STUDENTS Why does King provide so much detail about the political history of Vietnam? *(He wants to show how the American interference in Vietnam has undermined the trust of the South Vietnamese.)* Have students evaluate whether these facts support his central idea. *(Yes. By tracing American involvement since 1945, King is proving that Vietnamese resentment of Americans is justified.)*

Determine Connotative Meanings (LINES 166–170)

COMMON CORE RI 4

Remind students that King uses words that will help him achieve his purpose.

(J) CITE TEXT EVIDENCE Have students identify words in these lines that convey judgment and explain the connotation of each word. *("languish" [line 166]; "herd"[line 168]; "concentration camps"[line 169] "Languish" suggests weakness; "herd" suggests that they are being treated like animals; the phrase "concentration camps" evokes memories of the inhumanity of the Germans toward perceived enemies)*

CRITICAL VOCABULARY

extortionist: Under the dictator Diem, the peasants were victimized by unscrupulous landlords. **ASK STUDENTS** how extortionist landlords would profit from the peasants. *(They could demand more than their share of crops; they could force peasants to pay higher rents for the land.)*

insurgency: The Vietnamese rebelled against the methods of their leader Diem. **ASK STUDENTS** to explain the result of the insurgency in South Vietnam. *(American troops came in to help suppress it; although Diem was overthrown, other dictators took his place.)*

Analyze Language

COMMON CORE RI 6

(LINES 189–193)

Rhetorical devices are techniques that writers use to enhance arguments and convey ideas. In this passage, King relies on parallelism, the use of similar grammatical construction to express related ideas. Read the lines aloud to help students hear the device.

K **ASK STUDENTS** to explain with evidence how the use of parallelism enhances King's argument. *(When King uses the phrases "we have destroyed," "we have cooperated," "we have supported," and "we have corrupted," he focuses attention on what the United States has done to the Vietnamese. These phrases show that the United States is responsible for events that have been detrimental to Vietnam.)*

Support Inferences: Draw Conclusions (LINES 202–211)

COMMON CORE RI 1

Remind students that as they read, they make their own judgments based on the evidence presented and their prior knowledge.

L **ASK STUDENTS** what King risks by his sympathetic comments about the Viet Cong and why he might be willing to take that risk. *(By speaking of the Viet Cong, King risks alienating his audience. He takes this risk to contrast the United States against the Viet Cong and to show how the actions of the United States appear from the perspective of the Viet Cong.)*

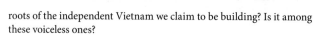

roots of the independent Vietnam we claim to be building? Is it among these voiceless ones?

190 We have destroyed their two most cherished institutions: the family and the village. We have destroyed their land and their crops. We have cooperated in the crushing of the nation's only noncommunist revolutionary political force, the unified Buddhist Church. We have supported the enemies of the peasants of Saigon. We have corrupted their women and children and killed their men.

Now there is little left to build on, save bitterness. Soon the only solid physical foundations remaining will be found at our military bases and in the concrete of the concentration camps we call "fortified hamlets." The peasants may well wonder if we plan to build our new Vietnam on such grounds as these. Could we blame them for such 200 thoughts? We must speak for them and raise the questions they cannot raise. These, too, are our brothers.

Perhaps a more difficult but no less necessary task is to speak for those who have been designated as our enemies. What of the National Liberation Front, that strangely anonymous group we call "VC" or "communists"? What must they think of the United States of America when they realize that we permitted the repression and cruelty of Diem, which helped to bring them into being as a resistance group in the South? What do they think of our condoning the violence which led to their own taking up of arms? How can they believe in 210 our integrity when now we speak of "aggression from the North" as if there were nothing more essential to the war? How can they trust us when now we charge them with violence after the murderous reign of

Image Credits: ©Luis Davilla/The Image Bank/Getty Images

156 Collection 3

Analyze Language

COMMON CORE RI 6

Have students use their eBook annotation tools to analyze the impact of parallelism on King's audience and meaning:

- Find one or more examples of parallelism in the speech up to this point. Highlight the repeated phrases or grammatical structures.
- Underline other words and phrases that show the things that are similar, related, or of equal importance.
- On a note, explain what the parallelism emphasizes. Then use your annotations to conclude what role parallelism has in King's style.

which led to their own taking up of arms? How can they believe in our integrity when now we speak of "aggression from the North" as if there were nothing more essential to the war? How can they trust us when now we charge them with

Diem and charge them with violence while we pour every new weapon of death into their land? Surely we must understand their feelings, even if we do not condone their actions. Surely we must see that the men we supported pressed them to their violence. Surely we must see that our own computerized plans of destruction simply dwarf their greatest acts.

220 How do they judge us when our officials know that their membership is less than 25 percent communist, and yet insist on giving them the blanket name? What must they be thinking when they know that we are aware of their control of major sections of Vietnam, and yet we appear ready to allow national elections in which this highly organized political parallel government will not have a part? They ask how we can speak of free elections when the Saigon press is censored and controlled by the military junta. And they are surely right to wonder what kind of new government we plan to help form without them, the only party in real touch with the peasants. They question our political goals and they deny the reality of a peace

230 settlement from which they will be excluded. Their questions are frighteningly relevant. Is our nation planning to build on political myth again, and then shore it up upon the power of a new violence?

Here is the true meaning and value of compassion and nonviolence, when it helps us to see the enemy's point of view, to hear his questions, to know his assessment of ourselves. For from his view we may indeed see the basic weaknesses of our own condition, and if we are mature, we may learn and grow and profit from the wisdom of the brothers who are called the opposition.

So, too, with Hanoi. In the North, where our bombs now pummel

240 the land, and our mines endanger the waterways, we are met by a deep but understandable mistrust. To speak for them is to explain this lack of confidence in Western words, and especially their distrust of American intentions now. In Hanoi are the men who led the nation to independence against the Japanese and the French, the men who sought membership in the French Commonwealth and were betrayed by the weakness of Paris and the willfulness of the colonial armies. It was they who led a second struggle against French domination at tremendous costs, and then were persuaded to give up the land they controlled between the thirteenth and seventeenth parallel as a

250 temporary measure at Geneva. After 1954 they watched us conspire with Diem to prevent elections which could have surely brought Ho Chi Minh to power over a united Vietnam, and they realized they had been betrayed again. When we ask why they do not leap to negotiate, these things must be remembered.

Also, it must be clear that the leaders of Hanoi considered the presence of American troops in support of the Diem regime to have been the initial military breach of the Geneva Agreement concerning foreign troops. They remind us that they did not begin to send troops

CLOSE READ

Support Inferences: Draw Conclusions (LINES 233–238) COMMON CORE RI 1

Point out that King has spoken of the conflict from the perspective of the South Vietnamese, the Viet Cong, and now the North Vietnamese.

M **ASK STUDENTS** to explain his strategy in looking at the war from these differing perspectives. How does he believe this approach will help him accomplish his purpose? *(He wants to show that it is not only the citizens of the United States who are suffering as a result of the war. It is inflicting grave hardship on others as well. He wants to make the enemy human so that the audience will understand that the war is wrong on many levels. He wants to show that the perspective of the United States about the war is not the only valid one.)*

Delineate and Evaluate an Argument: Inductive Reasoning (LINES 239–254) COMMON CORE RI 8

Explain that in a long speech such as this one, King has the opportunity to make more than one counterargument.

N **CITE TEXT EVIDENCE** Ask students to cite evidence to explain the opposing view and counterargument that King presents in lines 239–254. *(He is responding to those who say it is the North Vietnamese who are prolonging the war by their refusal to negotiate. For example, in line 240–241, King states, "we are met by a deep but understandable mistrust." He asks why the North Vietnamese should negotiate when they have been betrayed so frequently in the past; for example, in lines 250–253, the men from Hanoi realize they "had been betrayed again" when the United States conspired with Diem to prevent a unified Vietnam. In order to effectively counter the opposing view, King lists other times in which the political efforts of North Vietnam were sabotaged by the French and the Americans.)*

SCAFFOLDING FOR ELL STUDENTS

Language: Pronoun Referents Point out the pronoun *they* used in lines 219–232. Remind students that pronouns replace nouns used earlier. To find which noun the pronoun replaces, readers may have to look back to previous lines or paragraphs. Project lines 202 to 232 on the whiteboard. Invite volunteers to mark it up.

- Highlight in yellow the pronoun *they*.
- Underline the sentences that come before the pronoun *they* starts being used.
- Highlight in blue the noun that *they* replaces.

Liberation Front, that strangely anonymous group we call "VC" or "communists"?

Delineate and Evaluate an Argument: Inductive Reasoning (LINES 273–305)

 COMMON CORE RI 8

Remind students that the speaker presents his or her ideas in the order that will be most effective.

O CITE TEXT EVIDENCE Have students explain what topic King chooses to finish this segment of his argument and why. (*King talks about American troops in lines 273–285. He knows that his audience will be receptive and sympathetic to this part of his argument.*) Ask students to look at lines 273–285 and identify the lines that state King's central idea. (*The last lines of this paragraph state that the war is really one that is between the Vietnamese and that the Americans are just helping to further injustice for the poor.*) Have students then state the conclusion that all of these reasons and evidence have been leading to. (*The United States must stop their war against the Vietnamese immediately.*)

Explain to students that speakers may include persuasive techniques in their arguments to influence their listeners to think or feel a certain way. They may appeal to their listeners' sense of ethics, their emotions, such as fear or pity, or to other desires they might have. In this part of his argument, King uses an appeal to authority.

P ASK STUDENTS to describe the possible effect of including the quotation from a Buddhist leader. (*This quotation from an authoritative source validates what King has been saying. It also has the effect of making listeners see their country from a new perspective, as it shows how negatively their actions are viewed by members of the international community.*)

---

in large numbers and even supplies into the South until American
260 forces had moved into the tens of thousands.

Hanoi remembers how our leaders refused to tell us the truth about the earlier North Vietnamese overtures for peace, how the president claimed that none existed when they had clearly been made. Ho Chi Minh has watched as America has spoken of peace and built up its forces, and now he has surely heard the increasing international rumors of American plans for an invasion of the North. He knows the bombing and shelling and mining we are doing are part of traditional pre-invasion strategy. Perhaps only his sense of humor and of irony can save him when he hears the most powerful nation of the world
270 speaking of aggression as it drops thousands of bombs on a poor, weak nation more than eight hundred, or rather, eight thousand miles away from its shores.

O At this point I should make it clear that while I have tried in these last few minutes to give a voice to the voiceless in Vietnam and to understand the arguments of those who are called "enemy," I am as deeply concerned about our own troops there as anything else. For it occurs to me that what we are submitting them to in Vietnam is not simply the brutalizing process that goes on in any war where armies face each other and seek to destroy. We are adding cynicism
280 to the process of death, for they must know after a short period there that none of the things we claim to be fighting for are really involved. Before long they must know that their government has sent them into a struggle among Vietnamese, and the more sophisticated surely realize that we are on the side of the wealthy, and the secure, while we create a hell for the poor.

Somehow this madness must cease. We must stop now. I speak as a child of God and brother to the suffering poor of Vietnam. I speak for those whose land is being laid waste, whose homes are being destroyed, whose culture is being subverted. I speak for the poor of
290 America who are paying the double price of smashed hopes at home, and dealt death and corruption in Vietnam. I speak as a citizen of the world, for the world as it stands aghast at the path we have taken. I speak as one who loves America, to the leaders of our own nation: The great initiative in this war is ours; the initiative to stop it must be ours.

This is the message of the great Buddhist leaders of Vietnam. Recently one of them wrote these words, and I quote:

> Each day the war goes on the hatred increases in the heart of the Vietnamese and in the hearts of those of humanitarian instinct. The Americans are forcing even their friends into becoming
> 300 their enemies. It is curious that the Americans, who calculate so carefully on the possibilities of military victory, do not realize that in the process they are incurring deep psychological and political defeat. The image of America will never again be the image of **P**

WHEN STUDENTS STRUGGLE . . .

To help students manage the complexity of King's argument, display a chart similar to the one shown. Tell them that in this first part of the argument, King uses the negative impact of America's involvement in Vietnam on various groups to lead to a logical conclusion about the war.

- Organize students into small groups and assign each group one of these passages: lines 14–44, 171–201, 219–238, 239–272.
- Have them reread their passage to find evidence supporting each reason in the chart.
- As a class, add their details to the chart. Then direct students to lines 286–294 and complete the chart by filling in the conclusion.

revolution, freedom, and democracy, but the image of violence and militarism.

Unquote.

310 If we continue, there will be no doubt in my mind and in the mind of the world that we have no honorable intentions in Vietnam. If we do not stop our war against the people of Vietnam immediately, the world will be left with no other alternative than to see this as some horrible, clumsy, and deadly game we have decided to play. The world now demands a maturity of America that we may not be able to achieve. It demands that we admit that we have been wrong from the beginning of our adventure in Vietnam, that we have been detrimental to the life of the Vietnamese people. The situation is one in which we must be ready to turn sharply from our present ways. In order to atone for our sins and errors in Vietnam, we should take the initiative in bringing a halt to this tragic war.

I would like to suggest five concrete things that our government 320 should do immediately to begin the long and difficult process of extricating ourselves from this nightmarish conflict:

Number one: End all bombing in North and South Vietnam.

Number two: Declare a unilateral cease-fire in the hope that such action will create the atmosphere for negotiation.

Three: Take immediate steps to prevent other battlegrounds in Southeast Asia by curtailing our military buildup in Thailand and our interference in Laos.

Four: Realistically accept the fact that the National Liberation Front has substantial support in South Vietnam and must thereby 330 play a role in any meaningful negotiations and any future Vietnam government.

Five: Set a date that we will remove all foreign troops from Vietnam in accordance with the 1954 Geneva Agreement. [*Sustained applause*]

Part of our ongoing [*Applause continues*], part of our ongoing commitment might well express itself in an offer to grant asylum to any Vietnamese who fears for his life under a new regime which included the Liberation Front. Then we must make what **reparations** we can for the damage we have done. We must provide the medical aid 340 that is badly needed, making it available in this country if necessary. Meanwhile [*Applause*], meanwhile, we in the churches and synagogues have a continuing task while we urge our government to disengage itself from a disgraceful commitment. We must continue to raise our voices and our lives if our nation persists in its perverse ways in Vietnam. We must be prepared to match actions with words by seeking out every creative method of protest possible.

As we counsel young men concerning military service, we must clarify for them our nation's role in Vietnam and challenge them with

reparations
(rĕp′ə-rā′shəns) *n.* compensation or payment from a nation for damage or injury during a war.

TEACH

CLOSE READ

Delineate and Evaluate an Argument: Inductive Reasoning (LINES 307–334)

COMMON CORE RI 8

Explain to students that King's speech is uniquely structured. In the first part, he presents reasons and evidence that lead to the conclusion about the war in Vietnam. He then elaborates on that conclusion; that conclusion becomes support for a second argument, which he develops next.

Q ASK STUDENTS how the proposals he lists affect his persuasiveness. *(These proposals are concrete steps that the United States can take. They show that King has thought about how his conclusion that the war must end can be implemented on a practical level. They make his argument stronger.)*

CRITICAL VOCABULARY

reparations: To enable Vietnam to recover from this devastating war, America would have to offer payment or some kind of compensation for the damage that it helped to inflict.

ASK STUDENTS to recall what King said about the damage caused by the actions of the U.S. military. Have them explain the form that reparations would take. *(In lines 170–181, King describes the destruction of millions of acres of crops, the razing of trees, the poisoning of water sources, the obliteration of houses, the number of deaths, and the psychological and physical harm suffered by survivors. America would have to help rebuild the economy and the infrastructure and provide extensive medical care to compensate for these acts.)*

Reasons

War is hurting America's poor.

U.S. military action is devastating South Vietnam.

America's involvement creates more problems with the Viet Cong and North Vietnamese than it solves.

Conclusion
America needs to get out of the war between South and North Vietnam.

CLOSE READ

Support Inferences
COMMON CORE **RI 1**

(LINES 349–359)

Remind students that at the time King gave this speech, he was a well-known and well-respected public figure.

R **ASK STUDENTS** why this part of his speech might be considered controversial. *(He is recommending a course of action that will undermine the official policy on Vietnam. His position will influence others to take this action.)*

Delineate and Evaluate an Argument: Inductive Reasoning
COMMON CORE **RI 8**

(LINES 360–391)

Point out that in this part of the speech, King begins building his next argument.

S **CITE TEXT EVIDENCE** Have students identify the line that states the focus of the next part of his speech. *(Lines 372–373. There must be "a significant and profound change in American life and policy.")* Ask students how the argument about ending the war in Vietnam relates to this idea and what support King offers to support his assertion. *(According to King, the war in Vietnam is a symptom of the problem within American society. War cannot be America's solution to protecting their interests overseas; otherwise, there will be a succession of Vietnams. He offers facts, saying that there are advisors in Venezuela, American forces in Guatemala, and military action in Cambodia and Peru.)*

Remind students of the various persuasive techniques that a speaker might use.

T **ASK STUDENTS** what appeal King incorporates in lines 386–388. What is the intended effect of this appeal on his audience? *(He uses an appeal to authority by quoting from President Kennedy. The feelings of respect for Kennedy will transfer to King and give his argument legitimacy.)*

---

the alternative of conscientious objection.[9] [*Sustained applause*] I am
350 pleased to say that this is a path now chosen by more than seventy
students at my own alma mater, Morehouse College, and I recommend
it to all who find the American course in Vietnam a dishonorable and
unjust one. [*Applause*] Moreover, I would encourage all ministers of
draft age to give up their ministerial exemptions and seek status as
conscientious objectors. [*Applause*] These are the times for real choices
and not false ones. We are at the moment when our lives must be
placed on the line if our nation is to survive its own folly. Every man
of humane convictions must decide on the protest that best suits his
convictions, but we must all protest.

360   Now there is something seductively tempting about stopping there
and sending us all off on what in some circles has become a popular
crusade against the war in Vietnam. I say we must enter that struggle,
but I wish to go on now to say something even more disturbing.

The war in Vietnam is but a symptom of a far deeper malady
within the American spirit, and if we ignore this sobering reality
[*Applause*], and if we ignore this sobering reality, we will find
ourselves organizing "clergy and laymen concerned" committees for
the next generation. They will be concerned about Guatemala and
Peru. They will be concerned about Thailand and Cambodia. They
370 will be concerned about Mozambique and South Africa. We will be
marching for these and a dozen other names and attending rallies
without end unless there is a significant and profound change in
American life and policy. [*Sustained applause*] So such thoughts take
us beyond Vietnam, but not beyond our calling as sons of the living
God.

In 1957 a sensitive American official overseas said that it seemed
to him that our nation was on the wrong side of a world revolution.
During the past ten years we have seen emerge a pattern of suppression
which has now justified the presence of U.S. military advisors in
380 Venezuela. This need to maintain social stability for our investments
accounts for the counter-revolutionary action of American forces in
Guatemala. It tells why American helicopters are being used against
guerrillas in Cambodia and why American napalm and Green Beret
forces have already been active against rebels in Peru.

It is with such activity in mind that the words of the late John F.
Kennedy come back to haunt us. Five years ago he said, "Those who
make peaceful revolution impossible will make violent revolution
inevitable." [*Applause*] Increasingly, by choice or by accident, this is
the role our nation has taken, the role of those who make peaceful
390 revolution impossible by refusing to give up the privileges and the
pleasures that come from the immense profits of overseas investments.
I am convinced that if we are to get on the right side of the world

---

[9] **conscientious objection:** the refusal to participate in military actions because of moral or religious beliefs.

APPLYING ACADEMIC VOCABULARY

controversy	tension

To discuss the ideas on these pages, use these Collection 3 academic vocabulary words: *controversy* and *tension*. Ask students why King's speech generated **tension** between him and the government as well as other civil rights leaders. Then have students describe how King would react to the **controversy** over this speech, based on what they know of his approach to the struggle for civil rights.

> ## "The war in Vietnam is but a symptom of a far deeper malady within the American spirit."

revolution, we as a nation must undergo a radical revolution of values. We must rapidly begin [*Applause*], we must rapidly begin the shift from a thing-oriented society to a person-oriented society. When machines and computers, profit motives and property rights, are considered more important than people, the giant triplets of racism, extreme materialism, and militarism are incapable of being conquered.

400 A true revolution of values will soon cause us to question the fairness and justice of many of our past and present policies. On the one hand we are called to play the Good Samaritan on life's roadside, but that will be only an initial act. One day we must come to see that the whole Jericho Road[10] must be transformed so that men and women will not be constantly beaten and robbed as they make their journey on life's highway. True compassion is more than flinging a coin to a beggar. It comes to see that an edifice which produces beggars needs restructuring. [*Applause*]

A true revolution of values will soon look uneasily on the glaring contrast of poverty and wealth. With righteous indignation, it will 410 look across the seas and see individual capitalists of the West investing huge sums of money in Asia, Africa, and South America, only to take the profits out with no concern for the social betterment of the countries, and say, "This is not just." It will look at our alliance with the landed gentry of South America and say, "This is not just." The Western arrogance of feeling that it has everything to teach others and nothing to learn from them is not just.

A true revolution of values will lay hand on the world order and say of war, "This way of settling differences is not just." This business of burning human beings with napalm,[11] of filling our nation's 420 homes with orphans and widows, of injecting poisonous drugs of hate into the veins of peoples normally humane, of sending men home from dark and bloody battlefields physically handicapped and

---

[10]**Jericho Road:** an ancient route between Jerusalem and Jericho. In the New Testament, the Good Samaritan stops on this road to helped an injured robbery victim.

[11]**napalm:** an incendiary fuel used in U.S. bombs to burn Vietnamese opponents.

Speech on the Vietnam War, 1967 **161**

CLOSE READ

Delineate and Evaluate an Argument: Inductive Reasoning (LINES 399–407)
 COMMON CORE RI 8

Have students reread this paragraph, looking at the type of evidence that King presents here.

Ⓤ ASK STUDENTS what King is appealing to in these lines. *(He is appealing to his audience's sense of ethics, their desire to do what is right.)* Why does he allude to the story of the Good Samaritan here? *(It illustrates his point metaphorically; it is familiar to many people.)*

Analyze Language (LINES 408–416)
 COMMON CORE RI 6

Explain that another rhetorical device used by King is repetition. Read this paragraph aloud to enable students to hear the repetition.

Ⓥ ASK STUDENTS what the repetition of the phrase "This is not just" emphasizes. *(By repeating this phrase, King draws attention to the exploitative actions and arrogant attitude of the Western world.)*

WHEN STUDENTS STRUGGLE...

Project lines 399–426. Read the text aloud. Explain that King is expounding on what must happen and what will result from a change in America's values. He wants his audience to understand why this change is needed.

Model how to summarize what he is saying metaphorically in the first paragraph. *(A change of values will lead to rebuilding society in order to eliminate the conditions of poverty and injustice.)* Have students work together to summarize other paragraphs. Provide these sentence stems as prompts: (lines 408–416) *A change of values will lead America to question its exploitation [of other countries for the sake of profit].* (lines 417–426) *A change of values will lead to America no longer using [war as a means of solving problems].*

Delineate and Evaluate an Argument: Inductive Reasoning (LINES 427–444)

 COMMON CORE RI 8

Remind students that they need to look at whether the evidence that King provides in this second part of his argument is thorough and valid.

 CITE TEXT EVIDENCE Ask students to explain how the evidence in this part of his speech differs from the support for his first conclusion. Have them give specific examples and explain if the evidence can be verified. *(He provides many verifiable facts, such as dates and statistics, in the first part of the speech. In this part, he develops his argument with eloquent rhetoric that expresses his assessment of the situation and his beliefs, but because these details are his own insights, there is no way to check whether they are true or not.)*

Determine Connotative Meanings (LINES 451–454)

 COMMON CORE RI 4

 ASK STUDENTS what feelings and ideas King wants his listeners to associate with the phrase "arch antirevolutionaries." *(King uses this term to suggest that Western nations have come to oppose world justice. They have become afraid of change and myopic, unable to see beyond their own thresholds or imagine how to foster the spirit of democratic revolution.)*

> **CRITICAL VOCABULARY**
>
> **recalcitrant**: King is suggesting in this sentence that the instinct to solve problems with war is so entrenched that it will resist efforts to replace it with solutions involving peaceful means.
>
> **ASK STUDENTS** what is implied about the status quo by King's use of the adjective *recalcitrant* to describe it. *(This adjective applies to something with a conscious will. King's use of it in this context suggests that the status quo, or existing state of affairs, is driven by people's wills or desires.)*

---

psychologically deranged, cannot be reconciled with wisdom, justice, and love. A nation that continues year after year to spend more money on military defense than on programs of social uplift is approaching spiritual death. [*Sustained applause*]

America, the richest and most powerful nation in the world, can well lead the way in this revolution of values. There is nothing except a tragic death wish to prevent us from reordering our priorities so that 430 the pursuit of peace will take precedence over the pursuit of war. There is nothing to keep us from molding a **recalcitrant** status quo with bruised hands until we have fashioned it into a brotherhood.

This kind of positive revolution of values is our best defense against communism. [*Applause*] War is not the answer. Communism will never be defeated by the use of atomic bombs or nuclear weapons. Let us not join those who shout war and, through their misguided passions, urge the United States to relinquish its participation in the United Nations. These are days which demand wise restraint and calm reasonableness. We must not engage in a negative anticommunism, 440 but rather in a positive thrust for democracy [*Applause*], realizing that our greatest defense against communism is to take offensive action in behalf of justice. We must with positive action seek to remove those conditions of poverty, insecurity, and injustice, which are the fertile soil in which the seed of communism grows and develops.

These are revolutionary times. All over the globe men are revolting against old systems of exploitation and oppression, and out of the wounds of a frail world, new systems of justice and equality are being born. The shirtless and barefoot people of the land are rising up as never before. The people who sat in darkness have seen a great light. 450 We in the West must support these revolutions.

It is a sad fact that because of comfort, complacency, a morbid fear of communism, and our proneness to adjust to injustice, the Western nations that initiated so much of the revolutionary spirit of the modern world have now become the arch antirevolutionaries. This has driven many to feel that only Marxism has a revolutionary spirit. Therefore, communism is a judgment against our failure to make democracy real and follow through on the revolutions that we initiated. Our only hope today lies in our ability to recapture the revolutionary spirit and go out into a sometimes hostile world declaring eternal hostility to 460 poverty, racism, and militarism. With this powerful commitment we shall boldly challenge the status quo and unjust mores, and thereby speed the day when every valley shall be exalted, and every mountain and hill shall be made low [*Audience:*] (*Yes*); the crooked shall be made straight, and the rough places plain.[12]

A genuine revolution of values means in the final analysis that our loyalties must become ecumenical rather than sectional. Every nation

recalcitrant
(rĭ-kăl′sĭ-trənt) *adj.*
uncooperative and resistant of authority.

---

[12] **every valley shall be . . . plain:** biblical quote from Old Testament book of Isaiah describing the arrival of the Messiah.

SCAFFOLDING FOR ELL STUDENTS

Use Prefixes Write these prefixes and their meanings on the board: *anti-, against; re-, again; in-, not/opposite of.* Explain to students that putting the meaning of the prefix together with the meaning of a base word can help them define an unfamiliar term. Project lines 451–460 on the whiteboard. Have volunteers complete these steps.

- Highlight in blue a word with the prefix "in-." *(injustice; line 443)*
- Highlight in pink a word with the prefix "anti-." *(antirevolutionary; line 454)*
- Highlight in green a word with the prefix "re-." *(recapture; line 458)*

Discuss the meaning of each base word. Then have students define the words, using their knowledge of the prefix. Have them identify other words in this speech that include these prefixes.

must now develop an overriding loyalty to mankind as a whole in order to preserve the best in their individual societies.

This call for a worldwide fellowship that lifts neighborly concern 470 beyond one's tribe, race, class, and nation is in reality a call for an all-embracing and unconditional love for all mankind. This oft misunderstood, this oft misinterpreted concept, so readily dismissed by the Nietzsches[13] of the world as a weak and cowardly force, has now become an absolute necessity for the survival of man. When I speak of love I am not speaking of some sentimental and weak response. I'm not speaking of that force which is just emotional bosh. I am speaking of that force which all of the great religions have seen as the supreme unifying principle of life. Love is somehow the key that unlocks the door which leads to ultimate reality. This Hindu-Muslim-Christian-480 Jewish-Buddhist belief about ultimate reality is beautifully summed up in the first epistle of Saint John: "Let us love one another (Yes), for love is God. (Yes) And every one that loveth is born of God and knoweth God. He that loveth not knoweth not God, for God is love. . . . If we love one another, God dwelleth in us and his love is perfected in us." Let us hope that this spirit will become the order of the day.

We can no longer afford to worship the god of hate or bow before the altar of retaliation. The oceans of history are made turbulent by the ever-rising tides of hate. History is cluttered with the wreckage of nations and individuals that pursued this self-defeating path of hate. 490 As Arnold Toynbee says: "Love is the ultimate force that makes for the saving choice of life and good against the damning choice of death and evil. Therefore the first hope in our inventory must be the hope that love is going to have the last word." Unquote.

We are now faced with the fact, my friends, that tomorrow is today. We are confronted with the fierce urgency of now. In this unfolding conundrum of life and history, there is such a thing as being too late. Procrastination is still the thief of time. Life often leaves us standing bare, naked, and dejected with a lost opportunity. The tide in the affairs of men does not remain at flood—it ebbs. We may cry 500 out desperately for time to pause in her passage, but time is **adamant** to every plea and rushes on. Over the bleached bones and jumbled residues of numerous civilizations are written the pathetic words, "Too late." There is an invisible book of life that faithfully records our vigilance or our neglect. Omar Khayyam[14] is right: "The moving finger writes, and having writ moves on."

We still have a choice today: nonviolent coexistence or violent coannihilation. We must move past indecision to action. We must find new ways to speak for peace in Vietnam and justice throughout the developing world, a world that borders on our doors. If we do not

adamant
(ăd´ə-mənt) *adj.*
inflexible and insistent, unchanging.

---

[13] **Nietzsches** (nē´chəz): a reference to the German philosopher Friedrich Nietzsche (1844–1900), who rejected Christianity and its associated morality.
[14] **Omar Khayyam:** (1048–c. 1132) influential Persian poet and scholar.

Speech on the Vietnam War, 1967 **163**

CLOSE READ

Determine Connotative Meanings (LINES 474–476)

 COMMON CORE RI 4

Y **ASK STUDENTS** how the word *bosh*"conveys King's attitude. *(This word has the connotation of nonsense, a waste of time, showing King's impatience with people's dilution of the meaning of "love.")*

Analyze Language

 COMMON CORE RI 6

(LINES 486–489)

Explain that sometimes persuasive speakers rely on literary devices to help their audiences "see" what they are talking about. One such device is a metaphor, a comparison between two unlike things.

Z **CITE TEXT EVIDENCE** Have students identify the metaphors in these lines and discuss how the use of metaphors affects listeners' understanding of King's message. *(The emotion of hatred is compared to a god who demands worship through violence and retaliation and to the tides in the ocean of history. Countries and individuals have been wrecked upon these tides. These metaphors show how entwined hatred and its results are in the history of the world. They give listeners strong mental images.)*

CRITICAL VOCABULARY

adamant: To emphasize the urgency of acting now rather than waiting, King reminds listeners that time is on an inflexible path; it cannot be halted.

ASK STUDENTS whether King himself could be described as adamant, based on this speech. Have them explain. *(Yes. He is inflexible in his resolve to awaken his listeners to the need for change.)*

SCAFFOLDING FOR ELL STUDENTS

Language: Punctuation Cues Explain that in this part of his speech, King includes quotations, or lines from what others have written or said. Project lines 469–505. Highlight in yellow a colon *(line 481)*, opening and closing quotation marks *(lines 481, 484)*, and a period *(line 485)*. Explain the function and placement of each mark. Invite volunteers to perform these tasks:

- Highlight in blue the punctuation that sets off the second quotation (line 490). Highlight in pink the punctuation that indicates the third quotation (line 504).

ASK STUDENTS to finish this sentence with a quotation from King's speech, using correct punctuation. *As Martin Luther King says . . .*

Delineate and Evaluate an Argument: Inductive Reasoning (LINES 513–539)

COMMON CORE RI 8

Explain that the beginning and the end of a persuasive speech are important. The introduction should capture listeners' attention and lay the groundwork for the argument. The end of the speech should send the audience away with a positive impression of the speaker and the argument and something to remember.

A2 ASK STUDENTS to identify the rhetorical devices that King uses in these last three paragraphs and their effect on the audience. *(He uses rhetorical questions and parallelism. These devices help to fasten the audience's attention on what he is saying, stir up their fervor, and impress his message upon them.)*

COLLABORATIVE DISCUSSION Have students reread the speech, looking for relevant passages. Remind them that King spoke directly to that issue near the beginning of his speech. Accept all reasonable responses.

ASK STUDENTS to share any questions they generated in the course of reading and discussing the selection.

---

510 act, we shall surely be dragged down the long, dark, and shameful corridors of time reserved for those who possess power without compassion, might without morality, and strength without sight.

A2   Now let us begin. Now let us rededicate ourselves to the long and bitter, but beautiful, struggle for a new world. This is the calling of the sons of God, and our brothers wait eagerly for our response. Shall we say the odds are too great? Shall we tell them the struggle is too hard? Will our message be that the forces of American life militate against their arrival as full men, and we send our deepest regrets? Or will there be another message—of longing, of hope, of solidarity with
520 their yearnings, of commitment to their cause, whatever the cost? The choice is ours, and though we might prefer it otherwise, we must choose in this crucial moment of human history.

    As that noble bard of yesterday James Russell Lowell eloquently stated:

> Once to every man and nation comes a moment to decide,
> In the strife of Truth and Falsehood, for the good or evil side;
> Some great cause, God's new Messiah offering each the bloom or
>   blight,
> And the choice goes by forever 'twixt that darkness and that light.
> Though the cause of evil prosper, yet 'tis truth alone is strong
530 > Though her portions be the scaffold, and upon the throne be
>   wrong
> Yet that scaffold sways the future, and behind the dim unknown
> Standeth God within the shadow, keeping watch above his own.

    And if we will only make the right choice, we will be able to transform this pending cosmic elegy into a creative psalm of peace. If we will make the right choice, we will be able to transform the jangling discords of our world into a beautiful symphony of brotherhood. If we will but make the right choice, we will be able to speed up the day, all over America and all over the world, when justice will roll down like waters, and righteousness like a mighty stream. [*Sustained applause*]

COLLABORATIVE DISCUSSION How does King relate the war and the civil rights issues in America? With a partner, discuss how he brings the two movements together. Cite specific textual evidence from the speech to support your ideas.

TO CHALLENGE STUDENTS . . .

Explore Connections Have a volunteer read aloud the excerpt from Lowell's poem in lines 525–533. Organize students into small groups and have them discuss these questions:

- What point is Lowell making?
- How does Lowell's meaning relate to what King is saying?
- Why does King choose to include this excerpt? Does it enhance this part of his argument or detract from it?

Have groups share their analyses with the class.

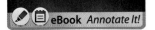

Delineate and Evaluate an Argument: Inductive Reasoning

 COMMON CORE RI 8

In his complex speech, Martin Luther King Jr., wants to persuade listeners to agree with his views about the Vietnam War. To do this, he uses **inductive reasoning**, a method of argument in which the writer first presents evidence about an issue or problem and then draws a conclusion from it. The conclusion presents the writer's belief about what should be done or how the issue or problem should be resolved.

In evaluating an inductive argument, consider the following:

Is the evidence valid?	The facts presented by the writer must be accurate and verifiable. A fact can be verified in an eyewitness account, a newspaper article, an encyclopedia, a history book, or another reputable source.
Is the evidence thorough?	Make sure that the writer has examined enough evidence to support his or her conclusions. Question any generalizations drawn from a small sample of evidence.
Does the conclusion follow logically from the evidence?	Look for errors in logic that would undermine the argument. For example, the writer may oversimplify a complex issue or mistakenly assume that because one event followed another, the first event caused the second one to occur.

Determine Connotative Meanings

 COMMON CORE RI 4

The term **connotation** refers to the shades of meaning associated with a word beyond its basic dictionary definition. Good writers carefully select words with connotations that will help convey their ideas or persuade people. Such choices may include **loaded language**, words with strongly positive or negative connotations. In his speech, Martin Luther King Jr., selects words that will resonate with his listeners—he relies on the words' connotative meanings to convince the audience to feel the way he does about certain issues and ideas.

Read this passage from his speech.

> **And I knew that America would never invest the necessary funds or energies in rehabilitation of its poor so long as adventures like Vietnam continued to draw men and skills and money like some demonic, destructive suction tube.**

The phrase "demonic, destructive suction tube" expresses King's view of the war as a colossal waste of resources. His loaded language suggests that the war is "demonic," or associated with the devil, and that it acts like a destructive machine. In other words, the war represents something evil and inhuman, gobbling up all that is good.

TEACH

CLOSE READ

Delineate and Evaluate an Argument: Inductive Reasoning

 COMMON CORE RI 8

Review with students the ideas about evidence in the chart. Discuss how there must be a clear connection between this evidence and the conclusion that King eventually draws. Ask students to identify the types of evidence that he uses to support and develop his argument in this speech. Have them give examples of each type. *(King uses facts, direct quotations, examples, description, and his personal experiences and observations.)* Have students then work in groups to identify one of the reasons in his speech and assess whether his evidence supporting that reason is valid and thorough.

Determine Connotative Meanings

 COMMON CORE RI 4

Make sure students understand how the connotation of a word differs from its denotation. Point out that "pummel" in line 239 means "to hit or pound." Its connotation, however, is to attack without ceasing, without giving the victim a reprieve. It also has a connotation of bullying in that the one doing the pummeling is superior in strength. Discuss how these connotations affect readers' understanding of the meaning of this sentence.

Strategies for Annotation  *Annotate it!*

Delineate and Evaluate an Argument: Inductive Reasoning

 COMMON CORE RI 8

Have students use their eBook annotation tools to analyze King's argument.

- Highlight in blue King's final conclusion.
- Highlight in pink the most persuasive reasons and evidence he presents in support of this conclusion.
- Work with a partner to evaluate the strength of his argument based on your annotations.

and love. A nation that continues year after year to spend more money on military defense than on programs of social uplift is approaching spiritual death.

Analyzing the Text COMMON CORE RI 1, RI 4, RI 5, RI 6, RI 8, RI 9, RI 10

Possible answers:

1. *King's seven reasons provide a clear context for his controversial position. They help justify his stand against the war by linking it with the civil-rights movement and with his status as a Nobel Prize recipient and clergyman.*

2. *He cites evidence that the U.S. supported French efforts to retake Vietnam, funneled money and troops to keep Diem in power, and then escalated military force to counter opposition to Diem's rule.*

3. *In lines 182–188, King's questions focus attention on violence and suggest that the U.S. is destroying, not rebuilding in Vietnam. The questions beginning on line 203 invite listeners to acknowledge the grievances and motivations of the National Liberation Front.*

4. *King wants his listeners to acknowledge and empathize with the Vietnamese perspective. By delineating the causes of violence, he suggests that North Vietnam is not entirely to blame for its response to what it perceives as U.S. aggression.*

5. *These nonviolent proposals offer a solution to the war King has argued against from the outset.*

6. *Both strategies advocate resistance through nonviolent means. Both responses stand in direct opposition to the government and elicit censure and alienation from mainstream society.*

7. *King concludes that the United States must leave Vietnam and "undergo a radical revolution of values" (line 393) to transform the society into one that prioritizes peace and social justice, not profit and property. King's conclusion is logical in view of the evidence he presents: violence in Vietnam is not working; it only causes greater violence.*

8. *Answers may vary. King uses words such as "hope," "solidarity," "peace," "brotherhood," and "justice." The words that conclude the speech are uplifting, positive, and affirming. They can inspire the audience to act for change.*

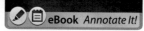 eBook *Annotate It!*

Analyzing the Text   COMMON CORE RI 1, RI 4, RI 5, RI 6, RI 8, RI 9, RI 10, W 9b

Cite Text Evidence Support your responses with evidence from the selection.

1. **Interpret** At the beginning of the speech, why does King explain his reasons for speaking out against the Vietnam War?

2. **Cite Evidence** What evidence does King offer to support his suggestion in line 123 that the United States is not really acting to liberate the Vietnamese people?

3. **Analyze** Questions that are posed for effect, without any expectation of a reply, are called **rhetorical questions.** Explain the effect of this rhetorical device in lines 182–188 and lines 203–214.

4. **Draw Conclusions** Why does King try to help his audience understand the enemy's point of view in lines 202–272?

5. **Analyze** In lines 319–334, King presents five specific steps that the U.S. should take. How do these proposals relate to the preceding part of his argument?

6. **Compare** In the civil rights movement, King and his followers refused to obey racial laws that they considered unjust. How does this strategy compare with his recommendation that young men in the United States become conscientious objectors?

7. **Evaluate** What conclusion does King reach through inductive reasoning? Does this conclusion logically follow from the evidence he has presented? Why or why not?

8. **Evaluate** What words with strongly positive connotations does King use in lines 513–539? Is his use of this loaded language an effective way to end the speech? Expain your response.

PERFORMANCE TASK

Writing Activity: Review What would have been newsworthy about Dr. King's speech in 1967? Write an article about the speech from the viewpoint of a journalist.

- Identify the purpose of the argument and its major points. Then evaluate the evidence presented and the logic of the conclusion reached.

- Include discussion of King's style and the devices that he uses to command attention.

- Use conventions of standard written English.

Assign this performance task.

PERFORMANCE TASK   COMMON CORE W 9b

Writing Activity: Review Have students work in pairs to discuss these elements of King's speech before writing their review independently: his purpose and perspective; the reasons and evidence that he presents to support his conclusion(s); the validity of his conclusion(s); his use of rhetorical devices; the historical significance of his speech; the effectiveness of his structure.

Critical Vocabulary

facile   eviscerate   indigenous   extortionist

insurgency   reparations   recalcitrant   adamant

Practice and Apply Create a semantic map for each Critical Vocabulary word. Use a dictionary or thesaurus as needed. This example is for a word in line 43 of the speech.

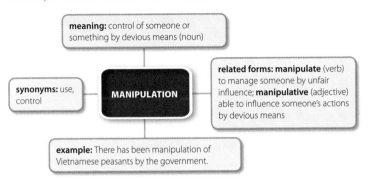

Vocabulary Strategy: Suffixes

Several Critical Vocabulary words have suffixes that indicate their part of speech and meaning. For example, the suffix *-ous* means "relating to or having the quality of." This suffix forms an adjective, as in *indigenous*. Knowing some common suffixes and the part of speech they form will help you define unfamiliar terms.

	Noun suffixes	Adjective suffixes
Suffix **Meaning** **Example**	*-ation, -tion* action, resulting state *desperation*	*-ate* having, characterized by *desperate*
Suffix **Meaning** **Example**	*-ism* belief or doctrine *nationalism*	*-al* of or relating to *national*
Suffix **Meaning** **Example**	*-ence* action or process, quality or state *incandescence*	*-ent* being in a specified state or condition *incandescent*

Practice and Apply Identify a new word that uses a suffix shown in each row of the chart.

- Identify the base, or main word part without the suffix.
- Note the word's part of speech.
- Write a definition for the base word's meaning and the suffix's meaning.
- Write a sentence for each word.

PRACTICE & APPLY

Critical Vocabulary

facile—**meaning:** easy to make or understand; **related words:** facilitate *(v)* make easy; facility *(n)* ability to do something without effort; **synonyms:** easy, effortless; eviscerate—**meaning:** to remove the necessary or important parts of; **related words:** evisceration *(n)* the process of disemboweling or emptying; **synonyms:** disembowel; indigenous—**meaning:** native to a land; **related words:** indigen *(n)* one who is native to an area; **synonyms:** native; extortionist—**meaning:** one who obtains something by force or threat; **related words:** extort *(v)* to obtain through force or other means; extortion *(n)* extraction of something illegally or by force; **synonyms:** blackmailer; insurgency—**meaning:** rebellion or revolt; **related words:** insurgent *(adj)* revolting against an established government; insurgence *(n)* insurrection; **synonyms:** rebellion, revolt, insurrection; reparation— **meaning:** compensation or payment for a wrong that has been committed; **related words:** reparative *(adj)* relating to war compensation; **synonyms:** compensation, remuneration; recalcitrant—**meaning:** uncooperative and resistant to authority; **related words:** recalcitrance *(n)* stubborn resistance to authority; **synonyms:** stubborn, defiant; adamant—**meaning:** inflexible and insistent, unchanging; **related words:** adamantine *(adj)* inflexible; **synonyms:** unyielding, unresponsive

Vocabulary Strategy: Suffixes

Answers:

Responses will vary. Students should identify the base and suffix of each word. Their sentences should reflect understanding of the part of speech of their words.

Strategies for Annotation   🖉 🖹 *Annotate it!*

Use Suffixes

Have students use their eBook annotation tools to assist them with the Vocabulary Strategy activity.

- Identify word forms in the speech that contain the suffixes shown in the chart. Highlight each word in a different color.
- Read the sentence in which each word appears to determine its part of speech.
- Then underline clues to the meaning of the word in the surrounding text.

I come to this platform tonight to make a passionate <u>plea</u> to my <u>beloved</u> nation. This speech is not addressed to Hanoi or to the National Liberation Front. It is not addressed to China or to Russia.

Language and Style: Imperative Mood

COMMON CORE L 3

Point out that using the imperative mood of a verb makes a sentence more forceful. Explain that in a persuasive speech such as this one, the imperative mood can play an important role in capturing listeners' attention and emphasizing ideas.

Sample response:

These are tips that I have found helpful for successful speech-giving. First, prepare a set of speaking notes. Write your main ideas and most important details on large index cards. You should be able to see your notes at a glance. Second, practice in front of a mirror by yourself, incorporating gestures and working on eye contact. Third, ask a friend or family member to listen to your speech. Finally, get a good night's sleep before the big day. If you are well rested, you will be able to do your best.

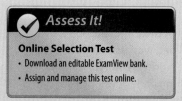

✓ Assess It!

Online Selection Test
- Download an editable ExamView bank.
- Assign and manage this test online.

Language and Style: Imperative Mood

COMMON CORE L 3

The **mood** of a verb shows the way in which a thought or idea is expressed. The **indicative mood** is the one most commonly used in writing to state ideas, opinions, or facts, or to ask questions. The **imperative mood** is used to give orders, make requests, or issue advice. In the imperative mood, the subject is not typically stated but is understood. The chart shows how the same idea is stated in both moods.

Indicative Mood	Imperative Mood
We must stop bombing the countryside.	Stop bombing the countryside.
Would you sign the peace treaty?	Sign the peace treaty.
Returning soldiers should be given jobs.	Give jobs to returning soldiers.

Read these sentences from the speech.

End all bombing in North and South Vietnam.
Set a date that we will remove all foreign troops from Vietnam.

Martin Luther King Jr., could have said the sentences in this way instead:

The government should end all bombing in North and South Vietnam.
The government should set a date that we will remove all foreign troops from Vietnam.

Notice that the mood is changed to indicative in the second set of sentences by adding a subject and helping verb. In these sentences, the emphasis on the verb, or the action, is diluted. As a result, the intensity of the original version is lost, making the sentences less effective in conveying emotion and meaning.

Practice and Apply Rewrite this paragraph, changing some of the sentences to the imperative mood.

These are tips that I have found helpful for successful speech-giving. First, it is important to make sure that you have prepared a set of speaking notes. Your main ideas and most important details should be written on large index cards. You should be able to see your notes at a glance. Second, you should practice in front of a mirror by yourself, incorporating gestures and working on eye contact. Third, it is a good idea to ask a friend or family member to listen to your speech. Finally, you should get a good night's sleep before the big day. If you are well rested, you will be able to do your best.

Analyze Style: Rhetorical Devices

COMMON CORE
RI 6

TEACH

Explain that Martin Luther King Jr. incorporates rhetorical devices, or techniques used to enhance arguments and effectively convey ideas, into his speech. These devices capture the audience's attention and emphasize his meaning. Review the definitions of these rhetorical devices with students:

- **Parallelism** is the use of similar grammatical constructions to express related ideas. Skillful parallelism creates a mesmerizing rhythm, which focuses the audience's concentration on the ideas being expressed. To identify parallelism, look for a series of similar words, phrases, or clauses.

- **Repetition** refers to the use of the same word or phrase more than once. Often these words or phrases represent key ideas that the speaker wants the audience to remember.

- **Antithesis** juxtaposes sharply contrasting words, phrases, clauses, or sentences to emphasize a point, often using parallel grammatical structures. For example, King quotes from President Kennedy: "Those who make peaceful revolution impossible will make violent revolution inevitable." The parallelism of "peaceful revolution" and "violent revolution" highlights the contrast between "peaceful" and "violent."

- **Rhetorical questions** are asked for the purpose of drawing attention to ideas or changing the tempo of the speech. They do not require an answer.

PRACTICE AND APPLY

Project lines 408–416. Ask students to identify one example of antithesis in this paragraph. Remind them that often antithetical statements also illustrate parallelism. *(The antithesis in this paragraph comes in the last sentence, with the contrast between the parallel structures "everything to teach others" and "nothing to learn from them.")* Ask students what idea King emphasizes through his use of antithesis. *(He stresses the idea that a country is like a person who talks—or teaches—but won't listen or learn.)*

Project lines 445–464. Ask students to identify the term that is deliberately repeated in these lines. *(revolution)* Have students discuss what King means by this term and why he repeats it. *(To King, "revolution" means making decisions based on new moralities and values and recognizing that through revolution, democracy was born. The United States needs to recapture that spirit of revolution to help other foundering nations realize their destinies.)*

Delineate and Evaluate an Argument: Inductive Reasoning

COMMON CORE
RI 8

RETEACH

Remind students that drawing a general conclusion, principle, or solution to a problem from observations, examples, or facts is inductive reasoning. Review the process with students by listing these ideas on the board:

1. Just this week another factory closed, eliminating 500 jobs.
2. Unemployment in our area is over thirteen percent.
3. The majority of young people surveyed said that they would not return to this town after college because of the lack of career opportunities.
4. There are state grants available that will give tax breaks to newly established businesses in a region.

Ask students what conclusion can be logically reasoned from these facts and examples. *(Possible answer: To save the dying economy, local officials need to work with the state to attract new businesses and industry to the region.)*

 LEVEL UP TUTORIALS Assign the following *Level Up* tutorial: **Analyzing Arguments**

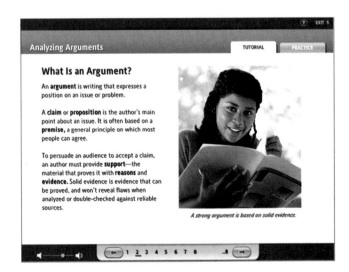

CLOSE READING APPLICATION

Have small groups of students peruse a variety of editorials or persuasive selections from print or online sources. Ask them to choose one that uses inductive reasoning as the basis for the argument. Have groups label the reasons, the evidence, and then the conclusion. Ask them to share their analysis of the argument with another group.

People and Peace, Not Profits and War

Speech by Shirley Chisholm

Why This Text

Students may finish reading an argument without a thorough understanding of the writer's ideas and evidence. Arguments such as this persuasive speech by Shirley Chisholm may use complex inductive reasoning or "loaded language" that becomes clear only with careful study. With the help of the close-reading questions, students will trace and evaluate Chisholm's argument that the money spent on weapons to fight the Vietnam War would be better spent on education and on social programs in our nation.

Background Have students read the background and biographical information about Shirley Chisholm, the first African American congresswoman and one of the founders of the Congressional Black Caucus, an organization representing the African American members of Congress. Introduce the selection by pointing out that Chisholm was an outspoken opponent of social, economic, and racial injustice, the draft, and the Vietnam War.

AS YOU READ Ask students to pay attention to the reasons Chisholm gives to support her position that the money used for weapons to fight the Vietnam War would be better spent on urban education and on social programs. How soon into her speech can students begin to identify her point of view?

Common Core Support

- cite strong and thorough textual evidence
- determine the meaning of words and phrases as they are used in a text, including connotative meanings
- evaluate the effectiveness of the structure of an argument
- delineate and evaluate the reasoning in an argument

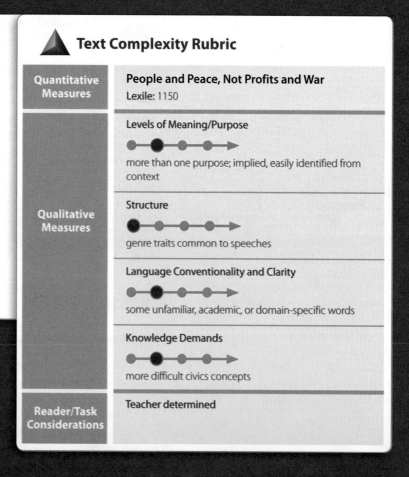

Text Complexity Rubric

Quantitative Measures	**People and Peace, Not Profits and War** Lexile: 1150
Qualitative Measures	**Levels of Meaning/Purpose** more than one purpose; implied, easily identified from context
	Structure genre traits common to speeches
	Language Conventionality and Clarity some unfamiliar, academic, or domain-specific words
	Knowledge Demands more difficult civics concepts
Reader/Task Considerations	Teacher determined

Strategies for CLOSE READING

Delineate and Evaluate an Argument

Students should read this speech carefully all the way through. Close-reading questions at the bottom of the page will help them focus on a thorough analysis of the argument. As they read, students should record comments or questions about the text in the side margins.

WHEN STUDENTS STRUGGLE . . .

To help students follow the reasons Chisholm gives to support her argument about our nation's disproportionate defense spending, have students work in small groups to fill out a chart such as the one shown below as they analyze the speech.

CITE TEXT EVIDENCE For practice in tracing an argument, ask students to cite the evidence Chisholm uses to support each reason for her claim.

CLAIM: The money spent on military weapons to fight the Vietnam War would be better spent on education and social programs.

SUPPORT:

Reason 1: These weapons are "elaborate, unnecessary, and impractical," and the money spent on them could be used toward urban education.

Reason 2: President Nixon delays urban renewal and educational and social programs for the sake of the war effort.

Reason 3: Rather than waiting for a solution to the Vietnam War before spending on education, we should spend on education first before spending on the war.

Reason 4: The war must end now so as not to waste young lives, money, or energy, which are needed in our cities and schools.

Reason 5: The defense industry has spent billions on worthless weapons, which could have been used to support education and social programs.

Reason 6: Distorted priorities must be eliminated so that the nation uses its resources for people and peace, not for profits and war.

Reason 7: The business of America should not be war.

Background Shirley Chisholm (1924–2005) was born in New York City but spent her early years living with her maternal grandmother in Barbados. Committed to education and social justice, Chisholm began her career as a teacher, later becoming the first African American congresswoman, representing New York from 1969–1983. In 1972, despite what she termed "hopeless odds," she became the first African American woman to run for the office of U.S. President. Although unsuccessful in her presidential bid, she served seven terms in Congress, during which time she was a vocal opponent of social injustice, the draft, and the Vietnam War. She gave the following speech on March 26, 1969, to the House of Representatives.

People and Peace, not Profits and War

Speech by Shirley Chisholm

CLOSE READ
Notes

1. **READ ▶** As you read lines 1–24, begin to collect and cite text evidence.
   - Circle the person being addressed at the beginning of the speech.
   - Underline the argument Chisholm makes against defense spending in lines 5–8.
   - Circle the loaded language Chisholm uses to describe the weapons in lines 5–8. In the margin, explain what she wants her listeners to understand.

Mr. Speaker, on the same day President Nixon announced he had decided the United States will not be safe unless we start to build a defense system against missiles, the Head Start[1] program in the District of Columbia was cut back for the lack of money.

(A) As a teacher, and as a woman, I do not think I will ever understand what kind of values can be involved in spending $9 billion—and more, I am sure—on elaborate, unnecessary and impractical weapons when several thousand disadvantaged children in the nation's capital get nothing.

(B) When the new administration took office, I was one of the many
10 Americans who hoped it would mean that our country would benefit from the fresh **perspectives**, the new ideas, the different priorities of a leader who had no part in the mistakes of the past. Mr. Nixon had said things like this: "If our cities are to be livable for the next generation, we can delay no longer in launching new approaches to the problems that beset them and to the tensions

[1] **Head Start:** a federal agency that offers educational programs for children age 3 to 5, and a variety of services for their families.

She wants her listeners to agree that money for weapons should be spent on education.

perspectives: *viewpoints*

39

---

1. READ AND CITE TEXT EVIDENCE

(A) ASK STUDENTS to read their margin notes to a partner and then write one response that best states Chisholm's argument about defense spending in lines 5–8, using specific evidence from the text. *Students should emphasize that Chisholm uses loaded language by describing the weapons of war as being "elaborate, unnecessary, and impractical," in the hope of persuading her congressional audience to agree with her viewpoint.*

Critical Vocabulary: perspectives (line 11) Have students share their definitions of *perspectives*. Why does she use the word to introduce what she had hoped the new administration would bring to the office of President? *She had hoped that Nixon would bring a fresh viewpoint to the office since he had not taken part in the mistakes of the Vietnam War.*

CLOSE READ
Notes

that tear them apart." And he said, "When you cut expenditures for education, what you are doing is shortchanging the American future."

But frankly, I have never cared too much what people say. What I am interested in is what they do. We have waited to see what the new administration is going to do. The pattern is now becoming clear. Apparently
20 launching those new programs can be delayed for a while, after all. It seems we have to get some missiles launched first. Recently the new secretary of commerce spelled it out. The secretary, Mr. Stans, told a reporter that the new administration is "pretty well agreed it must take time out from major social objectives" until it can stop inflation.

The new secretary of health, education, and welfare, Robert Finch, came to the Hill[2] to tell the House Education and Labor Committee that he thinks we should spend more on education, particularly in city schools. But, he said, unfortunately we cannot "afford" to, until we have reached some kind of honorable solution to the Vietnam War. I was glad to read that the
30 distinguished Member from Oregon [Mrs. Green] asked Mr. Finch this: "With the crisis in education, and the crisis in our cities, can we wait to settle the war? Shouldn't it be the other way around? Unless we can meet the crisis in education, we really can't afford the war."

Finch claims we cannot afford education expenses until the Vietnam War is settled honorably.

C

---
[2] **Hill:** Capitol Hill, the center of the United States federal government.

Secretary of Defense Melvin Laird came to Capitol Hill, too. His mission was to sell the antiballistic missile[3] insanity to the Senate. He was asked what the new administration is doing about the war. To hear him, one would have thought it was 1968, that the former secretary of state was defending the former policies, that nothing had happened, a president had never decided not to run because he knew the nation would reject him in despair over this tragic war we
40 have blundered into. Mr. Laird talked to being prepared to spend at least two more years in Vietnam.

D Two more years, Two more years of hunger for Americans, of death for our best young men, of children here at home suffering the lifelong handicap of not having a good education when they are young. Two more years of high taxes collected to feed the cancerous growth of a Defense Department budget that now consumes two-thirds of our federal income.

Two more years of too little being done to fight our greatest enemies—poverty, prejudice, and neglect—here in our own country. Two more years of fantastic waste in the Defense Department and of penny pinching on social
50 programs. Our country cannot survive two more years, or four, of these kinds of policies. It must stop this year—now.

E F Now, I am not a **pacifist.** I am deeply, unalterably opposed to this war in Vietnam. Apart from all other considerations—and there are many—the main

pacifist:
someone opposed to war

---
[3] **antiballistic missile:** a weapon that intercepts and destroys ballistic missiles.

---

2. ◀ REREAD Reread lines 9–24. How does Chisholm use inductive reasoning to support her argument? What conclusion does she draw from the evidence she presents?

She presents facts about defense spending and then highlights the disparity between the money being spent on weapons and the lack of funding for disadvantaged children. She also shows the disparity between President Nixon's words and deeds. She draws the conclusion that money for war materials will be spent before promised social programs are funded.

3. READ ▶ As you read lines 25–51, continue to cite textual evidence.
• Underline the opposing viewpoint Chisholm references in lines 25–33, and restate it in the margin.
• Circle the repetitive phrase Chisholm uses in lines 42–51.
• Underline the loaded language Chisholm uses in lines 42–51.

4. ◀ REREAD Reread lines 42–51. How does Chisholm's use of repetition and her use of loaded language contribute to the persuasive power of the speech? Support your answer with explicit textual evidence.

The repetition of "Two more years" highlights the speaker's emotions and ideas, making the tone of the speech more emphatic. Loaded language, such as "cancerous growth of a Defense Department budget," and "children here at home suffering the lifelong handicap" helps listeners understand the dangers of neglecting social programs in favor of military spending.

5. READ ▶ As you read lines 52–73, continue to cite textual evidence. Underline the main argument the author makes about the need for ending the Vietnam War, and restate it in the margin.

40

41

---

2. **REREAD AND CITE TEXT EVIDENCE**

B **ASK STUDENTS** to cite evidence that Chisholm presents to support her conclusion that something must be done about unfair defense spending. *Students should cite evidence from lines 9–16 and 18–24.*

3. **READ AND CITE TEXT EVIDENCE**

C **ASK STUDENTS** to read their margin notes to a partner and then write one response that best states the opposing viewpoint Chisholm cites in lines 25–33, using textual evidence. *Although Finch thinks the nation should spend more on urban education, he claims it cannot afford to, until the war is settled honorably.*

FOR ELL STUDENTS Explain that *take time out* (line 23) is an idiomatic expression meaning "to pause from doing something." Ask students to look for other time expressions and cite them in the margin.

4. **REREAD AND CITE TEXT EVIDENCE**

D **ASK STUDENTS** to evaluate the effectiveness of the repetitive phrase *Two more years* and of the use of loaded language in lines 42–51. *The repetition of* Two more years *in lines 42, 44, 47, 48, and 50 presents an emotional appeal to the audience to end the war now. Loaded language and connotative meanings, such as "cancerous growth" (line 45) and "penny pinching" (line 49), contribute to the persuasive tone and power of the speech.*

5. **READ AND CITE TEXT EVIDENCE**

E **ASK STUDENTS** to read their margin notes to a partner and then write one response that best states Chisholm's central argument about the need to end the war now, citing specific textual evidence. *Students should cite evidence from lines 52–55.*

Critical Vocabulary: pacifist (line 52) Have students explain *pacifist* as Chisholm uses it in her argument.

We cannot waste the lives of young people fighting in the war, the money being spent on weaponry, or the energy we need to put into our cities and schools.

fact is that we cannot squander the lives, the money, the energy that we need desperately here, in our cities, in our schools.

I wonder whether we cannot reverse our whole approach to spending. For years, we have given the military, the defense industry, a blank check. New weapons systems are dreamed up, billions are spent, and many times they are found to be impractical, inefficient, unsatisfactory, even worthless. What do we do then? We spend more money on them. But with social programs, what do we do? Take the Job Corps.[4] Its failure has been mercilessly exposed and criticized. If it had been a military research and development project, they would have been ready to pour more billions after those that had been wasted on it.

The case of Pride, Inc.,[5] is interesting. This vigorous, successful black organization here in Washington, conceived and built by young, inner-city men, has been ruthlessly attacked by its enemies in the government, in this Congress. At least six auditors from the General Accounting Office were put to work investigating Pride. They worked seven months and spent more than $100,000. They uncovered a fraud. It was something less than $2,100. Meanwhile, millions of dollars—billions of dollars, in fact—were being spent by the Department of Defense, and how many auditors and investigators were checking into their negotiated contract? Five.

We Americans have come to feel that it is our mission to make the world free. We believe that we are the good guys everywhere—in Vietnam, in Latin

[4] **Job Corps:** a federally funded free education and training program that helps young people learn a career, earn a high-school diploma or GED, and find a good job.
[5] **Pride, Inc.:** a program of food distribution for poor African Americans in Washington, DC, begun after the 1968 riots there.

6. **◀ REREAD AND DISCUSS** Reread lines 52–73. With a small group, discuss whether the evidence Chisholm presents is sufficient to support her conclusion that the government's money is unfairly spent.

7. **READ ▶** As you read lines 74–94,
• underline the inductive reasoning that Chisholm uses to support her claim in lines 84–94.
• circle the conclusion she draws from the evidence she presents.
• in the margin, restate her conclusion in your own words.

42

America, wherever we go. We believe that we are the good guys at home, too. When the Kerner Commission[6] told white America what black America had always known, that prejudice and hatred built the nation's slums, maintain them, and profit by them, white America would not believe it. But it is true. Unless we start to fight and defeat the enemies of poverty and racism in our own country and make our talk of equality and opportunity ring true, we are exposed as hypocrites in the eyes of the world when we talk about making other people free.

I am deeply disappointed at the clear evidence that the number-one priority of the new administration is to buy more and more weapons of war, to return to the era of the Cold War, to ignore the war we must fight here—the war that is not optional. There is only one way, I believe, to turn these policies around. The Congress can respond to the mandate that the American people have clearly expressed. They have said, "End this war. Stop the waste. Stop the killing. Do something for your own people first." We must find the money to "launch the new approaches," as Mr. Nixon said. We must force the administration to rethink its distorted, unreal scale of priorities. Our children, our jobless men, our deprived, rejected, and starving fellow citizens must come first.

For this reason, I intend to vote "No" on every money bill that comes to the floor of this House that provides any funds for the Department of Defense— any bill whatsoever—until the time comes when our values and priorities have

Chisholm concludes that Congress should end the war and find money for social programs in the United States.

[6] **Kerner Commission:** an 11-member commission established to investigate the causes of the 1967 race riots in the U.S.

8. **◀ REREAD** Reread lines 74–83. What idea is Chisholm emphasizing by repeating the term "good guys"?

Americans are considered to be the "good guys," champions of freedom abroad and at home; the use of this loaded language is ironic because it is these same "good guys" who are charged with building, maintaining, and profiting from the nation's slums.

9. **READ ▶** As you read lines 95–105, continue to cite textual evidence.
• Underline Chisholm's promise to her listeners.
• Circle text explaining the reason she gives for her decision.
• Underline the parallel statements that Chisholm makes.

43

---

6. **REREAD AND DISCUSS USING TEXT EVIDENCE**

F ASK STUDENTS to appoint a reporter for each group. Ask students to cite specific textual evidence and line numbers to support their position. *Students should cite evidence from lines 52–63 and 65–73.*

7. **READ AND CITE TEXT EVIDENCE** Explain that Chisholm supports her argument throughout the text by presenting evidence of a problem, drawing a conclusion, and then suggesting a solution.

G ASK STUDENTS to cite evidence that supports Chisholm's conclusion about the need to end the Vietnam War. *Students should cite specific evidence from lines 84–94.*

8. **REREAD AND CITE TEXT EVIDENCE**

H ASK STUDENTS to evaluate the effectiveness of the repetition of the term *good guys* that Chisholm uses to depict the role of Americans in the world. *Students should point out that the repetition emphasizes the part that Americans have played in promoting freedom, but that the term is ironic since these "good guys" have allowed inequality, prejudice, and hatred to exist in this nation.*

9. **READ AND CITE TEXT EVIDENCE**

I ASK STUDENTS to cite the specific word choice (including loaded words and connotative meanings) as well as textual evidence that Chisholm uses to explain her decision to vote "No" on further defense spending. *Students should cite specific textual evidence from lines 98–101.*

CLOSE READ Notes

been turned rightside up again, until the monstrous waste and the shocking profits in the defense budget have been eliminated and our country starts to
100 use its strength, its tremendous resources, for people and peace, not for profits and war.

It was Calvin Coolidge, I believe, who made the comment that "the business of America is business." We are now spending $80 billion a year on defense. That is two-thirds of every tax dollar. At this time, gentlemen, the business of America is war, and it is time for a change.

10. ◀ **REREAD** Reread lines 102–105. Then, restate Chisholm's final comment.

She declares that America's business is war, not business, and that this must change.

SHORT RESPONSE

Cite Text Evidence Evaluate Chisholm's speech against the Vietnam War. Did she convince you that the money being spent on the Vietnam War could be better spent on social programs, such as education? Review your reading notes and **cite text evidence** in your response.

Chisholm gives many convincing reasons to support her argument. She states that the nation's priorities are wrong—that defense spending, the number-one priority, should go toward battling the crises in education and the cities. She uses clear, inductive reasoning to make her argument and to try to persuade her audience, but she also employs loaded language and other emotional appeals which detract from factual evidence. Her evidence is reasonable and sufficient to warrant her conclusion.

44

TO CHALLENGE STUDENTS . . .

For more context about the life and legacy of Shirley Chisholm, including her decision to run for the Democratic presidential nomination in 1972, students can view the video *Shirley Chisholm Runs for Presidential Nomination* in their eBooks.

ASK STUDENTS to work in small groups to listen to Chisholm's speech. One student in each group should be the transcriber, and then groups should analyze the speech and outline Chisholm's main points.

- What does Chisholm see as some main problems in the United States in 1972? *She points out that there are many people who are suffering poverty and hardship through no fault of their own. There are working poor who cannot support their families. In addition, minorities and women are underpaid as sources of labor. The main recipients of welfare, Chisholm says, are the giant corporations in the defense industry, utility companies, railroads, and airlines. They receive more of the taxpayers' money than do the "so-called welfare recipients"— people who cannot find jobs or get training.*

- What does Chisholm suggest can be done? *She says that the nation needs the brain-power of minorities and women, and that they should be allowed to use their talents to help the nation grow. She wants a more inclusive society.*

Encourage students to continue their research to find out more about Chisholm's legacy.

---

10. REREAD AND CITE TEXT EVIDENCE

J **ASK STUDENTS** to reread the last paragraph of Chisholm's speech so that they can put her final comment into their own words. How do lines 102–105 add power to her argument? How do her parallel statements in these four lines help to convince her audience to adopt her point of view? *Students should cite explicit textual evidence from lines 102–105.*

SHORT RESPONSE

Cite Text Evidence Student responses will vary, but students should cite specific examples and evidence from the text to support their positions. Students should:

- explain whether or not they agree with Chisholm's argument.
- give reasons for their point of view.
- cite specific evidence from the text to support their reasons.

DIG DEEPER

With the class, return to Question 6, Reread and Discuss. Have students share the results of their discussion.

ASK STUDENTS whether they were satisfied with the outcome of their small-group discussions. Have each group share their opinion on whether Chisholm presented sufficient evidence to support her conclusion. What compelling evidence did the groups cite from the speech to support this opinion?

- Guide students to tell whether there was any convincing evidence cited by group members holding the opposite opinion. If so, why didn't that evidence sway the group?

- Encourage groups to explain how they decided whether or not they had found sufficient evidence in the text to support their opinion. Did everyone in the group agree as to what made the evidence sufficient? How did the group resolve any disagreements or differences of opinion?

- After students have shared the results of their group's discussion, ask whether another group shared any findings they wish they had considered.

ASK STUDENTS to return to their Short Response answer to revise it based on the class discussion.

CLOSE READING NOTES

from The Crisis

from Civil Disobedience

Essay by Thomas Paine

Essay by Henry David Thoreau

Why These Texts?

In the coming years, students will start voting and contemplating service to their country, accepting both the privileges and responsibilities of being an adult citizen. This lesson explores ideas about citizens' responsibilities to the government and to their own conscience.

View It!

Professional Development Podcast:

Teaching Argument

Key Learning Objective: The student will be able to analyze foundational documents and delineate and evaluate arguments.

COMMON CORE Common Core Standards

RI 1 Cite textual evidence.

RI 2 Determine central ideas.

RI 3 Analyze complex ideas.

RI 4 Determine the meanings of words and phrases including figurative meanings.

RI 6 Determine author's point of view.

RI 8 Delineate and evaluate reasoning and arguments in works of public advocacy.

RI 9 Analyze foundational U.S. documents.

W 2b Convey complex ideas and develop the topic thoroughly.

W 3d Use precise words and phrases.

W 4 Produce clear and coherent writing.

W 9 Draw evidence from texts to support analysis, reflection, and research.

SL 1a Come to discussions prepared.

L 3a Vary syntax for effect.

L 4c Consult general reference materials.

 Text Complexity Rubric

	The Crisis	Civil Disobedience
Quantitative Measures	Lexile: 1180L	Lexile: 1200L
Qualitative Measures	**Levels of Meaning/Purpose** more than one purpose; implied but easy to infer	**Levels of Meaning/Purpose** multiple purposes; implied, subtle, and difficult to determine
	Structure organization of main ideas and details complex but mostly explicit	**Structure** more than one text structure
	Language Conventionality and Clarity complex and varied sentence structure	**Language Conventionality and Clarity** increased unfamiliar, academic, or domain-specific words
	Knowledge Demands somewhat complex social studies concepts	**Knowledge Demands** complex civics concepts
Reader/Task Considerations	Teacher determined Vary by individual reader and type of text	Teacher determined Vary by individual reader and type of text

TEACH

CLOSE READ

Thomas Paine Have students read the information about the author. Tell them that Paine is considered to be one of the great writers of political propaganda. His passionate views were usually meant to influence and persuade people to take action. *Common Sense* was an influential document that helped lead to the Declaration of Independence. Although there were thousands of copies sold, Paine refused to take any profits from the sale so that as many cheap copies as possible could be distributed. After the Revolutionary War, he was given a small farm in New York as a reward for his efforts, but he found little luck with jobs or government positions. By the time of his death in 1809, few people remembered his important contributions to the American Revolution. It wasn't until the mid-1900s that Paine was again recognized for the power of his words.

Henry David Thoreau Have students read the information about the author. Explain that Thoreau, like Paine, is more widely recognized and admired today than he was at the end of his life. After graduating from Harvard University, he spent much of his early adult life working in his father's pencil-making business to support himself. Fortunately, he became friends with a more wealthy and well-known writer, Ralph Waldo Emerson, who also lived in Concord, Massachusetts. Emerson helped him publish poems, essays, and reviews in a magazine they founded. In his later years, Thoreau became an active and outspoken abolitionist, helping slaves escape through Massachusetts to Canada as a part of the Underground Railroad. His work became very popular in the 1950s and 1960s as people protested government actions during the civil rights movement and the Vietnam War. The practice of Thoreau's brand of nonviolence to achieve political goals continues to this day.

from The Crisis   *from* Civil Disobedience

Essay by Thomas Paine   Essay by Henry David Thoreau

Thomas Paine (1737–1809) *came to America from London in 1774 and rapidly made a name for himself as a revolutionary writer. Embracing the colonists' cause, in 1776 he wrote* Common Sense, *a 50-page pamphlet that attacked the injustices of hereditary rule and advocated independence. His pamphlet sold 120,000 copies in three months. Later that year, he began to publish his "Crisis" papers, the first of which is included here. Paine wrote this essay while he was camped with troops from the Colonial Army following a retreat. General Washington ordered his officers to read the essay aloud to the troops to boost their morale. Once the war was over, Paine left for Europe, where similar movements were underway. There, however, he offended many with his brashness and alienated others with his last published work,* The Age of Reason, *which attacked organized religion. Upon returning to America in 1802, he had few friends left. He lived the rest of his life in poverty and obscurity.*

Henry David Thoreau (1817–1862) *published only two books before his death at the age of 44. Neither book sold well, but in the years following his death, his renown grew. Today he is highly regarded for both his nature writing and his political ideas. The nonviolent principles he espouses in* Civil Disobedience *have influenced activists throughout the world, including Mohandas Gandhi and Martin Luther King Jr. Thoreau lived a life of nonconformity, refusing to do anything that conflicted with the dictates of his own conscience. For example, he refused to pay his poll tax to protest the war in Mexico and slavery. As a result, he spent a night in jail, which he refers to in this essay.*

Compare Texts **169**

SCAFFOLDING FOR ELL STUDENTS

Vocabulary: Multiple-Meaning Words and Idioms Explain that because this text was written in the 1700s, some familiar words have unfamiliar meanings. Paine also uses unfamiliar idioms. Remind students that using **context clues** (the meanings of surrounding words and sentences) or consulting dictionaries can help them determine meaning. Point out *try* in the opening line: "These are the times that try men's souls." Note that Paine refers to a "crisis" and some who will "shrink" from duty while others will "stand it." These clues help students understand *try* as "challenge."

ASK STUDENTS to use context clues or a dictionary to identify the correct meaning of these multiple meaning words and idioms: *consolation* (line 5), *proper* (line 8), *decent* (line 30), *highwayman* and *housebreaker* (line 35), and *lay your shoulders to the wheel* (line 59).

AS YOU READ Direct students to use the As You Read note to focus their reading. Remind them to write down any questions they generate during reading.

Analyze Foundational Documents (LINES 10–15)

COMMON CORE RI 9

Explain that propagandists like Paine use a variety of **rhetorical features,** or persuasive techniques, to influence readers. One of these involves quoting or referring to an **authority** that the writer's audience respects.

A **ASK STUDENTS** to reread lines 10–15. How and why does Paine refer to God in line 15? *(Paine appeals to his audience's respect for God's authority. He asserts that God would object to British statements of their power and suggests that the British are claiming a power that only God can have when they say they can bind Americans "in all cases whatsoever.")*

CRITICAL VOCABULARY

tyranny: Paine uses this emotional word to describe British rule.

ASK STUDENTS to use lines 10-15 and the footnote to explain why British rule might be considered tyranny. *(The Declaratory Act of 1766 gave British parliament broad powers over the American colonies.)*

resolution: Note that this noun is also synonymous with "resolve," both indicating strength of purpose.

ASK STUDENTS what type of resolution Paine thinks is necessary to recover the territory that Howe's forces have ravaged during the past month. *(He refers to "the spirit of the Jersies a year ago"; this same spirit can win the territory back.)*

calamities: Paine emphasizes hardships and dangers of war by referring to them as things to avoid.

ASK STUDENTS to identify two calamities that Paine describes in the same sentence. *(Paine refers to "military destruction" in line 28 and to the possibility that people might "perish" in line 29.)*

AS YOU READ Think about how Paine catches and keeps your attention with his writing. Write down any questions you generate during reading.

from The Crisis
by Thomas Paine

These are the times that try men's souls: The summer soldier and the sunshine patriot will, in this crisis, shrink from the service of his country; but he that stands it NOW, deserves the love and thanks of man and woman. **Tyranny**, like hell, is not easily conquered; yet we have this consolation with us, that the harder the conflict, the more glorious the triumph. What we obtain too cheap, we esteem too lightly:— 'Tis dearness only that gives every thing its value. Heaven knows how to set a proper price upon its goods; and it would be strange indeed, if so celestial an article as FREEDOM should not
10 be highly rated. Britain, with an army to enforce her tyranny, has declared, that she has a right (*not only to* TAX) but "to BIND us in ALL CASES WHATSOEVER,"[1] and if *being bound in that manner* is not slavery, then there is not such a thing as slavery upon earth. Even the expression is impious, for so unlimited a power can only belong to God.

   Whether the Independence of the Continent was declared too soon, or delayed too long, I will not now enter into as an argument; my own simple opinion is, that had it been eight months earlier, it would have been much better. We did not make a proper use of last
20 winter, neither could we, while we were in a dependant state. However, the fault, if it were one, was all our own; we have none to blame but ourselves. But no great deal is lost yet; all that Howe has been doing for this month past is rather a ravage than a conquest which the spirit of the Jersies a year ago would have quickly repulsed, and which time and a little **resolution** will soon recover.

   I have as little superstition in me as any man living, but my secret opinion has ever been, and still is, that God almighty will not give up a people to military destruction, or leave them unsupportedly to perish, who had so earnestly and so repeatedly sought to avoid
30 the **calamities** of war, by every decent method which wisdom could invent. Neither have I so much of the infidel in me, as to suppose, that he has relinquished the government of the world, and given us up to the care of devils; and as I do not, I cannot see on what grounds the king of Britain can look up to heaven for help against us: A common murderer, a highwayman, or a housebreaker, has as good a pretense as he. . . .

tyranny
(tĭr´ə-nē) *n.* oppressive rule by an absolute power.

resolution
(rĕz´ə-loō´shən) *n.* determination.

calamity
(kə-lăm´ĭ-tē) *n.* a disaster or catastrophe.

---

[1] **"to BIND us in ALL CASES WHATSOEVER":** a reference to wording in the Declaratory Act of 1766, in which the British parliament asserted its "power and authority" to make and enforce laws over the American colonies.

TO CHALLENGE STUDENTS . . .

Gather Information Have pairs of students reread lines 16–25 to understand what circumstances of 1776 Paine addresses in the second paragraph. Have students conduct brief research on the Internet to gather historical facts about the conflicts over the Declaration of Independence ("Whether the Independence of the Continent was declared too soon, or delayed too long") and early losses in the war ("All that [the British General] Howe has been doing for this month past . . .").

ASK STUDENTS to present their research to the class along with their research notes in an outline or bulleted list.

> ## "The harder the conflict, the more glorious the triumph."

I once felt all that kind of anger, which a man ought to feel, against the mean principles that are held by the Tories:[2] A noted one, who kept a tavern at Amboy,[3] was standing at his door, with as pretty a
40 child in his hand, about eight or nine years old, as most I ever saw, and after speaking his mind as freely as he thought was prudent, finished with this unfatherly expression, *"Well! give me peace in my day."* Not a man lives on the Continent but fully believes that a separation must some time or other finally take place, and a generous parent would have said, *"If there must be trouble, let it be in my day, that my child may have peace;"* and this single reflection, well applied, is sufficient to awaken every man to duty. Not a place upon earth might be so happy as America. Her situation is remote from all the wrangling world, and she has nothing to do but trade with them. A man may
50 easily distinguish in himself between temper and principle, and I am as confident, as I am that God governs the world, that America will never be happy until she gets clear of foreign dominion. Wars, without ceasing, will break out until that period arrives, and the Continent must in the end be conqueror; for, though the flame of liberty may sometimes cease to shine, the coal never can expire. . . .

I turn with the warm ardor of a friend to those who have nobly stood, and are yet determined to stand the matter out: I call not upon a few, but upon all; not on this State or that State, but on every State; up and help us; lay your shoulders to the wheel; better have too much
60 force than too little, when so great an object is at stake. Let it be told to the future world, that in the depth of winter, when nothing but hope and virtue could survive, that the city and the country, alarmed at one common danger, came forth to meet and to repulse it. Say not, that thousands are gone, turn out your tens of thousands; throw not the burden of the day upon Providence, but *"shew your faith by your works,"* that God may bless you. It matters not where you live, or what rank of life you hold, the evil or the blessing will reach you all. The far

---

[2] **the mean principles . . . Tories:** the small-minded beliefs of those colonists who remain loyal to Great Britain.

[3] **Amboy:** probably Perth Amboy, a town in New Jersey.

CLOSE READ

Analyze Foundational Documents (LINES 26–36)   COMMON CORE RI 9

Tell students that persuasive writers may use several persuasive techniques in the same paragraph. In these lines, Paine again appeals to authority as he invokes God. Writers may also make **emotional appeals** by using words or analogies with strong positive or negative connotations.

B **CITE TEXT EVIDENCE** Have students reread lines 26–36. Have them identify the lines in which Paine uses an emotional analogy and explain why it is so powerful. *(Lines 33–36 compare "the king of Britain" to a criminal who might murder the readers or steal their belongings. This analogy plays on the fears Paine's audience may have had about the increasing control that Britain is exerting over the colonies.)*

Another rhetorical device that is used in lines 37–47 is an **ethical appeal,** which invokes the audience's sense of right and wrong.

C **CITE TEXT EVIDENCE** Have students reread lines 37–47. Ask them to identify the words and reasoning that Paine uses in his ethical appeal. What does he imply? *(He starts his ethical appeal by discussing the "mean principles" in line 38 that are held by the Tories. Paine says that seeking peace now is "unfatherly" (line 42), while working for freedom now in line 44 is the approach of a "generous parent" (line 44). His point is that in considering whether to seek peace with Britain, people should think about their "duty" (line 47) to the next generation. He implies that the Continental Army must continue fighting.)*

WHEN STUDENTS STRUGGLE . . .

Have students form groups of three and direct their attention to lines 37–55. Ask each student to come up with a one-line summary of part of a paragraph to share with his or her group. Have groups share their work with the class.

ASK STUDENTS to summarize the following lines:

- Lines 37–47 ending with ". . . to duty." *(We should fight today so our children can have peace tomorrow.)*
- Lines 47–49 ending with ". . . with them." *(America has a chance to be a wonderful place if it can be peaceful.)*
- Lines 49–55 *(America will never be peaceful until is independent.)*

Analyze Foundational Documents (LINES 77–86)

COMMON CORE RI 9

Paine uses **parallel structure,** the repetition of similar grammatical structures, to emphasize his ideas.

 CITE TEXT EVIDENCE Have students cite examples of parallel structure in lines 81–84. *("whether he who does it, is a king or a common man; my countryman or not my countryman? Whether it is done by an individual villain or an army of them?")* Ask which grammatical elements are repeated. *(A clause beginning with "whether" is repeated once; throughout the passage are noun phrases joined by "or.")* Ask what previous passage these lines echo, and why Paine returns to the ideas here. *(Paine again compares the king to a criminal. Many people likely viewed the king as a person they must obey. By comparing the king to a criminal, Paine breaks through this respectful attitude to convince his audience to support independence from Britain.)*

Determine Figurative Meaning (LINES 99–101)

COMMON CORE RI 4

One persuasive technique is the use of **figurative language**—language that departs from the literal meaning of words. Writers use forms of it, such as **analogies,** to emphasize ideas and evoke emotions.

 ASK STUDENTS to explain the comparisons that Paine makes to British war tactics in lines 99–101. What point is the author making? What emotion does this passage evoke? *(Paine says that General Howe's attempt to get Americans to surrender shows he has the "cunning of the fox" while his military attacks are like the "violence of the wolfe." Paine points out that the British are treacherous. The passage evokes fear and caution.)*

CRITICAL VOCABULARY

signifies: Explain that *signify,* as an intransitive verb meaning "to matter," is rarely used today . **ASK STUDENTS** to use different forms of *signify* to recast this phrase. *(Possible answers: "What is the significance . . ." or "Why is it significant . . . "*

solace: Paine indicates that gaining comforting with the hope of mercy is "madness." **ASK STUDENTS** why the people need to "solace themselves." *(They believe that Americans will lose the war or that they will improve their standing if they surrender to General Howe now rather than later.)*

---

and the near, the home counties and the back, the rich and the poor, shall suffer or rejoice alike. The heart that feels not now, is dead: The
70 blood of his children shall curse his cowardice, who shrinks back at a time when a little might have saved the whole, and made *them* happy. I love the man that can smile in trouble, that can gather strength from distress, and grow brave by reflection. 'Tis the business of little minds to shrink; but he whose heart is firm, and whose conscience approves his conduct, will pursue his principles unto death. My own line of reasoning is to myself as strait and clear as a ray of light. Not all the treasures of the world, so far as I believe, could have induced me to support an offensive war, for I think it murder; but if a thief break into my house, burn and destroy my property, and kill or threaten to kill
80 me, or those that are in it, and to "*bind me in all cases whatsoever,*" to his absolute will, am I to suffer it? What **signifies** it to me, whether he who does it, is a king or a common man; my countryman or not my countryman? whether it is done by an individual villain, or an army of them? If we reason to the root of things we shall find no difference; neither can any just cause be assigned why we should punish in the one case, and pardon in the other. Let them call me rebel, and welcome, I feel no concern from it; but I should suffer the misery of devils, were I to make a whore of my soul by swearing allegiance to one, whose character is that of a sottish, stupid, stubborn, worthless,
90 brutish man. I conceive likewise a horrid idea in receiving mercy from a being, who at the last day shall be shrieking to the rocks and mountains to cover him, and fleeing with terror from the orphan, the widow and the slain of America.

There are cases which cannot be overdone by language, and this is one. There are persons too who see not the full extent of the evil that threatens them; they **solace** themselves with hopes that the enemy, if they succeed, will be merciful. It is the madness of folly to expect mercy from those who have refused to do justice; and even mercy, where conquest is the object, is only a trick of war: The cunning of
100 the fox is as murderous as the violence of the wolfe; and we ought to guard equally against both. Howe's first object is partly by threats and partly by promises, to terrify or seduce the people to deliver up their arms, and receive mercy. The ministry recommended the same plan to Gage, and this is what the Tories call making their peace; "*a peace which passeth all understanding*" indeed! A peace which would be the immediate forerunner of a worse ruin than any we have yet thought of. Ye men of Pennsylvania, do reason upon those things! Were the back counties to give up their arms, they would fall easy prey to the Indians, who are all armed: This perhaps is what some Tories would not be
110 sorry for. Were the home counties to deliver up their arms, they would be exposed to the resentment of the back counties, who would then have it at their power to chastise their defection at pleasure. And were any one State to give up its arms, that State must be garrisoned by all Howe's army of Britons and Hessians to preserve it from the anger of

signify
(sĭg´nə-fī´) *v.* to have meaning or importance.

solace
(sŏl´ĭs) *v.* give comfort or relief to.

SCAFFOLDING FOR ELL STUDENTS . . .

Language: Punctuation and Print Cues Tell students that because this text was written in the 1700s, it features language constructions that are no longer common. Direct students to lines 66–75. Discuss the two instances where Paine uses a negative construction to introduce a sentence—"It matters not where . . ." in line 66 and "The hearts that feels not . . ." in line 69. Help students paraphrase the sentences.

ASK STUDENTS to form pairs to practice fluent reading.

- Pairs should take turns reading aloud sentences. Have students pay attention to punctuation to help them read phrases fluently.
- Ask volunteers to read the passage aloud, providing emphasis, pacing, and intonation to make the passage into a rousing speech.

the rest. Mutual fear is a principal link in the chain of mutual love, and woe be the State that breaks the compact. Howe is mercifully inviting you to barbarous destruction, and men must be either rogues or fools that will not see it. I dwell not upon the vapours of imagination; I bring reason to your ears; and in language, as plain as A, B, C, hold up

120   truth to your eyes.

    I thank God that I fear not. I see no real cause for fear. I know our situation well, and can see the way out of it. While our army was collected, Howe dared not risk a battle, and it is no credit to him that he decamped from the White Plains, and waited a mean opportunity to ravage the defenceless Jersies; but it is great credit to us, that, with an handful of men, we sustained an orderly retreat for near an hundred miles, brought off our ammunition, all our field-pieces, the greatest part of our stores, and had four rivers to pass. None can say that our retreat was precipitate, for we were near three weeks in

130   performing it, and the country might have time to come in. Twice we marched back to meet the enemy and remained out till dark. The sign of fear was not seen in our camp, and had not some of the cowardly and disaffected inhabitants spread false alarms through the country, the Jersies had never been ravaged. Once more we are again collected and collecting; our new army at both ends of the Continent is recruiting fast, and we shall be able to open the next campaign with sixty thousand men, well armed and clothed. This is our situation, and who will may know it. By perseverance and fortitude we have the prospect of a glorious issue; by cowardice and submission, the sad

140   choice of a variety of evils—a ravaged country—a depopulated city— habitations without safety, and slavery without hope—our homes turned into barracks and bawdy-houses for Hessians, and a future race to provide for whose fathers we shall doubt of. Look on this picture, and weep over it!—and if there yet remains one thoughtless wretch who believes it not, let him suffer it unlamented.

COLLABORATIVE DISCUSSION To whom is Paine addressing his essay? With a partner, discuss those characteristics of Paine's writing that make his essay effective for his audience. Cite specific textual evidence from the essay to support your ideas.

WHEN STUDENTS STRUGGLE...

Analyze Cause-and-Effect Organization Direct students to lines 107–120. Explain that Paine attempts to persuade readers by describing a cause *(Americans giving up arms)* and many of its possible effects. Have students complete a cluster diagram that identifies the effects Paine lists if Americans give up their arms to the British.

Cause:
Americans giving up arms

Effect:
defeat by Indians

Effect:
fighting among counties

Effect:
breaking chain of mutual love

CLOSE READ

Analyze Foundational Documents (LINES 121–145)

COMMON CORE RI 9

Tell students that persuasive writers often repeat or state their central idea or theme in the closing paragraph or lines of a text.

F **ASK STUDENTS** Ask students to identify what type of an appeal Paine uses in lines 121–134 and how it is different from the other appeals in the text. *(In these lines, Paine suggests a theme through an appeal to the emotion of bravery, instead of fear. To bolster his audience's will to fight on, Paine recites what he sees as successes—or at least the lack of defeats—to suggest that Americans have no reason to fear the British.)*

Point out that parallel structure has been a key rhetorical device in this document.

G **CITE TEXT EVIDENCE** Direct students to reread lines 137–145. Ask them to identify the lines in which Paine uses parallelism to describe different possibilities for the future. *(In lines 138–139, Paine balances the fruits won by "perseverance and fortitude" against the results of "cowardice and submission.")*

COLLABORATIVE DISCUSSION Have students pair up and discuss specific examples of language, techniques, and devices Paine uses to make his essay appealing to "the common man." Have partners jointly write a short summary of their discussion and then call on volunteers from each pair to share their summaries with the class.

ASK STUDENTS to share any questions they generated in the course of reading and discussing the selection.

Analyze Foundational Documents COMMON CORE RI 9

Review the types of appeals persuasive writers can use as well as the specific rhetorical features of Paine's writing to be sure that students understand the terms and examples. This essay was intended for the troops and other colonists either supporting the Revolution or considering it. Paine selected the types of appeals that would be most effective for this audience.

Ask students to evaluate the importance and prevalence of each type of appeal in the essay.

- Emotional appeals *(Paine uses many emotional appeals, especially those comparing the king to a criminal and using loaded language to honor Americans and denigrate the British and Hessians.)*
- Ethical appeals *(Paine repeatedly suggests that the Revolution is righteous, compared to wrongful British and Tory actions.)*
- Appeals to association *(This is least important in the essay with only a reference to Paine being "a friend" to those who keep supporting the Revolution.)*
- Appeals to authority *(Paine often suggests that God is siding with the Americans against the British, who are compared to devils and criminals.)*

Analyze Foundational Documents COMMON CORE RI 9

Through his essay, Thomas Paine hopes to persuade those colonists who have not yet done so to take up arms against the British and for the rest to keep faith with the cause. To achieve his patriotic purpose, he incorporates a number of persuasive techniques.

Technique	Example
Emotional appeals are attempts to persuade by eliciting strong feelings, such as pity or fear. These appeals rely on **loaded language,** words with strong positive or negative connotations.	Paine's use of phrases such as "flame of liberty" in line 54 helps to stir feelings of patriotism in his readers.
Ethical appeals call upon readers' sense of right and wrong.	Paine's story of a father in Amboy in lines 37–47 appeals to readers' ethics.
Appeals to association imply that one will gain acceptance or prestige by taking the writer's position.	"I turn with the warm ardor of a friend to those who have nobly stood . . ."
Appeals to authority call upon experts or others who warrant respect.	"My secret opinion is that God almighty will not give up a people to military destruction . . ."

In addition to these persuasive techniques, Paine's literary style includes these rhetorical devices that strengthen his meaning:

Parallel structure	Analogy	Repetition
Paine uses similar grammatical constructions to express ideas of equal importance. Notice in this quotation that the parallel structure emphasizes the reward of persevering through hard conflict: "yet we have this consolation with us, that the harder the conflict, the more glorious the triumph."	In lines 75–86, Paine makes a point-by-point comparison between two situations to present the war from another perspective.	To emphasize meaning and add intensity to the rhythm of his prose, Paine repeats words and phrases, as in this quotation: "I thank God that I fear not. I see no real cause for fear."

Analyze Foundational Documents COMMON CORE RI 9

Share these strategies for guided or independent analysis:

- Highlight in blue words and phrases that use an emotional appeal to readers.
- Highlight in green words and phrases that use an ethical appeal.
- Highlight in yellow words and phrases that appeal to an association for acceptance or prestige.
- Highlight in pink words and phrases that use an appeal to authority to help persuade readers.

of man and woman. Tyranny, like hell, is not easily conquered; yet we have this consolation with us, that the harder the conflict, the more glorious the triumph. What we obtain too cheap, we esteem too lightly:—'Tis dearness only that gives every thing its value. Heaven knows how to set a proper price upon its goods; and it would be strange indeed, if so celestial an article as FREEDOM

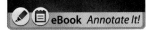
eBook *Annotate It!*

Analyzing the Text

Cite Text Evidence   Support your responses with evidence from the selection.

1. **Interpret** The opening sentence of this essay is one of the most famous in American literature. Explain the point that Paine is making here. Which word choices help make the sentence memorable?

2. **Identify** Find examples of loaded language in lines 1–15. To which emotions do these words appeal?

3. **Infer** What is Paine calculating will be the result of the ethical appeal he uses in lines 37–47? Explain.

4. **Analyze** A writer's **tone** is his or her attitude toward a subject. What is Paine's tone in lines 56–71? What persuasive and rhetorical techniques help convey this tone?

5. **Analyze** What analogy does Paine make in lines 75–86? What conclusion does he want readers to draw from this analogy?

6. **Analyze** According to Paine in lines 101–120, what would happen if colonists acceded to Howe's demand to relinquish their arms? What does he want to persuade readers about in this passage?

7. **Evaluate** Reread lines 121–138. What is Paine's purpose in including these details about the war? Is this an effective way to conclude his essay? Explain.

PERFORMANCE TASK

Writing Activity: Letter Paine read this essay to General Washington's troops to boost their morale. Imagine that you are one of the soldiers. Write a letter to a family member back home, explaining how you felt upon hearing it.

- Analyze the impact of the speech on you as a listener. Refer to the parts of the speech that you found memorable and why.
- Use conventions of standard written English.

Assign this performance task.

PERFORMANCE TASK

COMMON CORE — W 4

Writing Activity: Letter Discuss with students the historical context and the privations faced by soldiers in the Continental Army. Remind students to develop a tone appropriate to a friendly letter and include specific details that support their message about how Paine's essay affected them from the perspective of a soldier.

PRACTICE & APPLY

Analyzing the Text

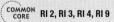 RI 2, RI 3, RI 4, RI 9

Possible answers:

1. *Paine points out that genuine patriotism lies in the commitment and endurance one shows during times of adversity, not just in favorable circumstances. Breezy phrases such as "summer soldier" and "sunshine patriot" belittle those who won't serve in the difficult times. They appeal to the audience's sense of shame, or pride. No self-respecting colonists like being called a "summer soldier."*

2. *Examples include "shrink," "love," "tyranny," "hell," "glorious," "triumph," "celestial," "slavery," "impious," and "God." They appeal to the audience's belief in faith, freedom, and justice, since many came to America to escape religious intolerance, tyranny, and injustice.*

3. *The ethical appeal highlights the idea that the Tory father in Amboy puts his own needs above those of his child. He implies that those who side with the Tories are doing a disservice to their children. His audience will shy away from such an association.*

4. *Paine's tone is one of passionate moral conviction. It is conveyed through loaded language, such as "nobly," "great," "virtue," repulse it," "suffer," "rejoice," and "curse." He also uses repetition and parallel structure for emphasis. He includes an appeal to association, "Let it be told to the future world . . . " in lines 60–64; an appeal to authority, "throw not the burden of the day upon Providence . . . " in lines 64–66; "but 'shew your faith by your works,' that God may bless you"; and an ethical appeal, "but he whose heart is firm . . ." in lines 74–75.)*

5. *He compares the British to a thief breaking into a house, destroying property, and harming the inhabitants. He wants readers to conclude that the British must be fought off, just as a homeowner would fight for his family and property against a thief.*

6. *If the back counties surrendered their arms, they would be in danger from the Indians. If the home counties surrendered their arms, they would be "exposed to the resentment of the back counties," and "if one State gives up arms, then that State would have to be protected from the anger of the rest." This passage reinforces one of Paine's major ideas in the essay: that the colonies must remain unified in order to achieve victory.*

7. *Paine's purpose is to show that the situation is far from hopeless and that the colonists have acquitted themselves well. Paine includes these details to reassure those who don't want to sacrifice themselves to a losing cause. It is an effective way to keep up the morale of those who are fighting already.*

PRACTICE & APPLY

Critical Vocabulary 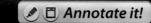 COMMON CORE L 4c

Answers:

1. *antonyms*

2. *synonyms*

3. *synonyms*

4. *antonyms*

5. *synonyms*

Vocabulary Strategy: Clarify Precise Meaning

Answers:

1. *act of destruction*

2. *affection, love*

3. *win over, tempt*

4. *sound sense*

Critical Vocabulary

COMMON CORE L 4c

tyranny	resolution	calamity
signify	solace	

Practice and Apply Explain whether the words in each pair are synonyms or antonyms. Use a dictionary to check your work if necessary.

1. resolution/weakness

2. solace/comfort

3. tyranny/oppression

4. calamity/good fortune

5. signify/matter

Vocabulary Strategy: Clarify Precise Meaning

Some words have several meanings that may be closely related. To find out the precise meaning of a word as it is used in a sentence, readers need to look at the context of the word, or the words and phrases surrounding it, and consult a print or digital dictionary.

The Critical Vocabulary word *resolution* has a number of definitions. In this sentence from the essay, "and which time and a little resolution will soon recover," the adjective "little" tells readers that it is something that can be measured. Looking in the dictionary confirms that *resolution* means "the condition or quality of being firmly determined."

Use of the dictionary can help readers to extend their understanding of words and be more exact in the way that they define them.

Practice and Apply Use the dictionary as well as context clues to define each of the italicized words in these sentences from the essay.

1. "All that Howe has been doing for this month past is rather a *ravage* than a conquest."

2. "I turn with a warm *ardor* of a friend to those who have nobly stood, and are yet determined to stand the matter out. . . ."

3. "Howe's first object is partly by threats and partly by promises, to terrify or *seduce* the people to deliver up their arms."

4. "I bring *reason* to your ears; and in language, as plain as A, B, C, hold up truth to your eyes."

Strategies for Annotation 🖉 🖹 *Annotate it!*

Vocabulary Strategy: Clarify Precise Meaning

COMMON CORE L 4c

Share these strategies for guided or independent analysis:

- Highlight in yellow words or phrases that are unfamiliar or have multiple meanings.
- Highlight in green any context clues that help establish meaning.
- After determining a precise meaning by consulting a general reference source as necessary, add a note that shows the definition as the word or phrase is used here.

to awaken every man to duty. Not a place upon earth might be so happy as America. Her situation is remote from all the wrangling world, and she has nothing to do but trade with them.

> quarreling, fighting

AS YOU READ Direct students to use the As You Read note to focus their reading.

Delineate and Evaluate an Argument (LINES 8–17)

 COMMON CORE **RI 8**

Remind students that a central part of persuasive writing is making a **claim** and then supporting it with **reasoning** and **evidence**. As they read, they should work to isolate and identify basic claims in persuasive writing and then analyze whether the reasoning the writer uses to support the claim is logical and the evidence is sufficient.

A CITE TEXT EVIDENCE Ask students to reread lines 8–17 to identify with line numbers the claims Thoreau makes and the reasoning or evidence he offers to support them. *(He states that arguments against the standing army should prevail in lines 8–10 but offers no evidence or reasoning for that claim. In lines 12–14, he claims that the government is liable to be "abused and perverted" and then offers as evidence the "Mexican war" that he asserts is "the work of a comparatively few individuals.")*

B ASK STUDENTS to read lines 18–22. What does Thoreau say is the purpose of his essay? What conclusion can the reader draw from this paragraph about Thoreau's argument? *(Thoreau explains that this essay is his way to "make known what kind of government would command his respect." In this case, Thoreau distinguishes himself from the "no-government men" because he argues not for the dissolution of the government but for a better government "at once.")*

C ASK STUDENTS to explain the claim Thoreau makes in lines 23–27 and whether the reasoning is logical. *(He claims that majorities do not rule because they are most likely to be right or fair to the minority. His reasoning states that they rule because they are the physically strongest. Although there is no further evidence given, it does seem logical for students of history to believe that majorities rule because they are the strongest, because in so many cases the minorities under such governments have had to fight long and hard for their rights.)*

AS YOU READ Pay attention to details that tell you how Thoreau feels about government. Write down any questions you generate during reading.

from Civil Disobedience
by Henry David Thoreau

A

I heartily accept the motto, "That government is best which governs least;" and I should like to see it acted up to more rapidly and systematically. Carried out, it finally amounts to this, which also I believe,—"That government is best which governs not at all;" and when men are prepared for it, that will be the kind of government which they will have. Government is at best but an expedient; but most governments are usually, and all governments are sometimes, inexpedient. The objections which have been brought against a standing army, and they are many and weighty, and deserve to

10 prevail, may also at last be brought against a standing government. The standing army is only an arm of the standing government. The government itself, which is only the mode which the people have chosen to execute their will, is equally liable to be abused and perverted before the people can act through it. Witness the present Mexican war,[1] the work of comparatively a few individuals using the standing government as their tool; for, in the outset, the people would not have consented to this measure. . . .

But, to speak practically and as a citizen, unlike those who call themselves no-government men, I ask for, not at once no government,

20 but *at once* a better government. Let every man make known what kind of government would command his respect, and that will be one step toward obtaining it. **B**

C

After all, the practical reason why, when the power is once in the hands of the people, a majority are permitted, and for a long period continue, to rule is not because they are most likely to be in the right, nor because this seems fairest to the minority, but because they are physically the strongest. But a government in which the majority rule in all cases cannot be based on justice, even as far as men understand it. Can there not be a government in which majorities do not virtually

30 decide right and wrong, but conscience?—in which majorities decide only those questions to which the rule of expediency is applicable? Must the citizen ever for a moment, or in the least degree, resign his conscience to the legislator? Why has every man a conscience, then? I think that we should be men first, and subjects afterward. It is not desirable to cultivate a respect for the law, so much as for the right. The only obligation which I have a right to assume is to do at any time

[1] **the present Mexican war:** the 1846–1848 war between Mexico and the United States.

Image Credits: ©Fedorov Oleksiy/Shutterstock

SCAFFOLDING FOR ELL STUDENTS

Analyze Language: Prefixes and Double Negatives Explain that prefixes change the meaning of a root word. Project the sentence in lines 6–8 on a whiteboard. Invite volunteers to mark it up.

- Highlight in green a root word (*expedient*, line 6) that is later modified by a prefix. Discuss its meaning *(an "expedient" is a means to an end, created to meet an urgent need.)*

- In line 8, highlight the root word *expedient* in green and the prefix *in* in yellow. Discuss the new meaning *("inexpedient" is something that does not fit a need).* How does the prefix change the meaning of the word? *(It negates it.)*

Delineate and Evaluate an Argument (LINES 39–48)

COMMON CORE RI 8

In these lines, Thoreau states a premise—a statement on which an argument is based—relating to laws. Remind students to examine the validity of the premises writers use.

D **ASK STUDENTS** to reread lines 39–48. Have them identify Thoreau's premise and analyze whether his reasoning is sound. *(Thoreau says that laws never helped people become more "just;" indeed people are forced to become "agents of injustice" when they follow the law. However, it's reasonable to argue that some laws, like the Civil Rights Act (or, in Thoreau's time, laws in other countries that had already abolished slavery), have helped people become more just. Thoreau offers as evidence soldiers who are peaceable but forced to go to war against their wills. Thoreau is assuming that the reader agrees that war is always unjust, and therefore the soldiers who follow the law are forced to be unjust. Thoreau's conclusion does not follow logically from the support offered. He does not provide adequate support for his statement in line 39 that "Law never made men a whit more just...")*

Analyze Figurative Language

COMMON CORE RI 4, RI 6

(LINES 59–67)

Thoreau uses a variety of rhetorical features that leave little doubt about his point of view. His highly figurative style brims with **loaded language,** words designed to appeal to readers' emotions through strong positive or negative associations.

E **CITE TEXT EVIDENCE** Ask students to identify details in lines 59–67 in which Thoreau compares "the mass of men" who "serve the state" with other things. Students should explain why this section of text is an example of loaded language. *(In line 60, he compares men serving the state to a "machine"; in line 63 to "wood and earth and stones"; and in lines 65–67, to "straw," "a lump of dirt," "horses," and "dogs." This is loaded language because few men would want to compare themselves to inanimate objects such as "wood and earth" or to animals such as "horses and dogs.")*

> ## "The only obligation which I have a right to assume is to do at any time what I think right."

what I think right. It is truly enough said, that a corporation has no conscience; but a corporation of conscientious men is a corporation *with* a conscience. Law never made men a whit more just; and, by

40 means of their respect for it, even the well-disposed are daily made the agents of injustice. A common and natural result of an undue respect for law is, that you may see a file of soldiers, colonel, captain, corporal, privates, powder-monkeys,[2] and all, marching in admirable order over hill and dale to the wars, against their wills, ay, against their common sense and consciences, which makes it very steep marching indeed, and produces a palpitation of the heart. They have no doubt that it is a damnable business in which they are concerned; they are all peaceably inclined. Now, what are they? Men at all? or small movable forts and magazines,[3] at the service of some unscrupulous man in power? Visit

50 the Navy-Yard, and behold a marine, such a man as an American government can make, or such as it can make a man with its black arts[4]—a mere shadow and reminiscence of humanity, a man laid out alive and standing, and already, as one may say, buried under arms with funeral accompaniments, though it may be,—

> "Not a drum was heard, not a funeral note,
> As his corse to the rampart we hurried;
> Not a soldier discharged his farewell shot
> O'er the grave where our hero we buried."[5]

The mass of men serve the state thus, not as men mainly, but as

60 machines, with their bodies. They are the standing army, and the militia, jailers, constables, *posse comitatus*,[6] etc. In most cases there is no free exercise whatever of the judgment or of the moral sense; but they put themselves on a level with wood and earth and stones;

---

[2] **powder-monkeys:** boys with the job of carrying gunpowder to artillery crews.

[3] **magazines:** places where ammunition is stored.

[4] **black arts:** witchcraft.

[5] "**Not a drum . . . we buried**": opening lines of "The Burial of Sir John Moore After Corunna" by the Irish poet Charles Wolfe (1791–1823).

[6] *posse comitatus* (pŏsʹē kŏm-ə-tāʹtəs): group of people that can be called on by the sheriff to help enforce the law [*Latin*, literally, the power of the county].

APPLYING ACADEMIC VOCABULARY

| controversy | ethics |

As you discuss Thoreau's argument, incorporate the Collection 3 academic vocabulary words *controversy* and *ethics*. Ask students why Thoreau's description of his obligation to the law and to government caused **controversy** when originally printed and continue to cause people to disagree today. Discuss the **ethics** of following laws that Thoreau believes make people "agents of injustice."

and wooden men can perhaps be manufactured that will serve the purpose as well. Such command no more respect than men of straw or a lump of dirt. They have the same sort of worth only as horses and dogs. Yet such as these even are commonly esteemed good citizens. Others—as most legislators, politicians, lawyers, ministers, and office-holders—serve the state chiefly with their heads; and, as they rarely

70 make any moral distinctions, they are as likely to serve the Devil, without *intending* it, as God. A very few—as heroes, patriots, martyrs, reformers in the great sense, and *men*—serve the state with their consciences also, and so necessarily resist it for the most part; and they are commonly treated as enemies by it. . . .

Unjust laws exist: shall we be content to obey them, or shall we endeavor to amend them, and obey them until we have succeeded or shall we transgress them at once? Men generally, under such a government as this, think that they ought to wait until they have persuaded the majority to alter them. They think that, if they should

80 resist, the remedy would be worse than the evil. But it is the fault of the government itself that the remedy *is* worse than the evil. *It* makes it worse. Why is it not more apt to anticipate and provide for reform? Why does it not cherish its wise minority? Why does it cry and resist before it is hurt? Why does it not encourage its citizens to be on the alert to point out its faults, and *do* better than it would have them? Why does it always crucify Christ, and excommunicate Copernicus and Luther,[7] and pronounce Washington and Franklin rebels? . . .

If the injustice is part of the necessary friction of the machine of government, let it go, let it go: perchance it will wear smooth, certainly

90 the machine will wear out. If the injustice has a spring, or a pulley, or a rope, or a crank, exclusively for itself, then perhaps you may consider whether the remedy will not be worse than the evil; but if it is of such a nature that it requires you to be the agent of injustice to another, then, I say, break the law. Let your life be a counter-friction to stop the machine. What I have to do is to see, at any rate, that I do not lend myself to the wrong which I condemn. . . .

I meet this American government, or its representative, the state government, directly, and face to face, once a year—no more—in the person of its tax-gatherer; this is the only mode in which a man

100 situated as I am necessarily meets it; and it then says distinctly, Recognize me; and the simplest, most effectual, and, in the present posture of affairs,[8] the indispensablest mode of treating with it on this head, of expressing your little satisfaction with and love for it, is to deny it then. My civil neighbor, the tax-gatherer, is the very man I have to deal with,—for it is, after all, with men and not with parchment

---

[7] **Copernicus** (kō-pûr′nə-kəs) **and Luther:** Radicals in their time, Polish astronomer Nicolaus Copernicus theorized that the sun rather than the Earth was the center of our planetary system; German theologian Martin Luther was a leader in the Protestant Reformation.

[8] **posture of affairs:** situation.

Civil Disobedience **179**

WHEN STUDENTS STRUGGLE . . .

Direct students to lines 80–87 in which Thoreau describes the traits of governments. Ask a volunteer to read them aloud. Have students respond to the following:

- What is the "it" that Thoreau repeatedly refers to in lines 81–87? *(government)*
- In lines 81–85, is Thoreau referring to one particular government, such as the U.S. government at the time? Why or why not? *(At first, he seems to refer to the current government because of the way he uses "we" to describe people's action, but later it seems he is referring to all or many governments.)*
- How do lines 86–87 clarify Thoreau's meaning? *(Thoreau is clearly referring to the traits of all or many governments because he uses the word "it" to refer to the many different governments that responded to Christ, Copernicus, Luther, etc.)*

CLOSE READ

Delineate and Evaluate an Argument (LINES 71–87)

Note that in some persuasive writing, there may be a significant gap between a claim and the evidence supporting it. Writers may **overgeneralize,** or make generalizations that are too broad based on available evidence.

F CITE TEXT EVIDENCE Ask students to reread lines 71–87 and cite specific lines in which Thoreau makes a claim and provides evidence to support it. Have students decide whether the evidence that Thoreau provides is sufficient. *(In lines 71–74, Thoreau claims that those who truly serve the government resist it, and they are treated as enemies. In lines 86–87, Thoreau cites several revered figures from history who were treated by a government as enemies. Although Thoreau cites names, he presents them in rhetorical questions without further details. Therefore, Thoreau's claim that governments "commonly" make enemies of people who resist them might be considered an overgeneralization.)*

Analyze Point of View

(LINES 75–87)

Persuasive writers often use **rhetorical questions** to bolster their own point of view; the answer to these types of questions is supposed to be self-evident. Some writers, however, use rhetorical questions to explore different points of view.

G ASK STUDENTS to reread lines 75–87. Have them identify both types of rhetorical question and explain how Thoreau uses them to advance his argument. *(In lines 75–77, Thoreau uses the second type of rhetorical question, asking readers whether "we" shall obey, change, or disobey unjust laws. Thoreau then explains that people generally think it is better to try to influence the majority to change an unjust law. Thoreau implies that this is not the correct course of action and that the government is at fault for the idea that resisting would result in a situation where the "remedy is worse than the evil." In lines 82–87, he uses the first type of rhetorical question. He does not expect an answer, and his purpose appears to be more to stir emotions than to persuade through logic)*

Analyze Ideas and Events (LINES 104–113)

COMMON CORE   RI 3

In these lines, Thoreau states an idea that will be further developed later in the essay. He moves from theoretical analysis to suggestions for action.

 ASK STUDENTS to reread lines find 104–113. Ask them to describe the actions Thoreau would like people to take and what might be accomplished by the actions. *(Thoreau suggests that his neighbor does not understand "what he is and does as an officer of the government." If Thoreau or others offer some resistance and require the government worker to decide on a course of action, then the government worker would be forced to consider the idea that he is serving an unjust government.)*

Delineate and Evaluate an Argument (LINES 113–117)

COMMON CORE   RI 8

In these lines, Thoreau makes a claim that is a powerful motivation for individual action.

ASK STUDENTS to describe the claim and evidence involved. *(Thoreau claims that if one man would end up in jail because of opposing slavery, it would end slavery in America. He provides no evidence for this claim and therefore his claim is unsupported.)*

Image Credits: ©Keystone-France/Gamma-Keystone/Getty Images

that I quarrel,—and he has voluntarily chosen to be an agent of the government. How shall he ever know well what he is and does as an officer of the government, or as a man, until he is obliged to consider whether he shall treat me, his neighbor, for whom he has respect, as a
110 neighbor and well-disposed man, or as a maniac and disturber of the peace, and see if he can get over this obstruction to his neighborliness without a ruder and more impetuous thought or speech corresponding with his action. I know this well, that if one thousand, if one hundred, if ten men whom I could name,—if ten *honest* men only,—ay, if *one* honest man, in this State of Massachusetts, *ceasing to hold slaves*, were actually to withdraw from this copartnership, and be locked up in the county jail therefor, it would be the abolition of slavery in America. For it matters not how small the beginning may seem to be: what is once well done is done forever. But we love better to talk about it: that
120 we say is our mission. Reform keeps many scores of newspapers in its service, but not one man. . . .

Under a government which imprisons any unjustly, the true place for a just man is also a prison. The proper place today, the only place which Massachusetts has provided for her freer and less desponding spirits, is in her prisons, to be put out and locked out of the State by her own act, as they have already put themselves out by their principles. It is there that the fugitive slave, and the Mexican prisoner on parole, and the Indian come to plead the wrongs of his race should find them; on that separate, but more free and honorable ground,

Strategies for Annotation ✎ 🖯 *Annotate it!*

Delineate and Evaluate an Argument

COMMON CORE   RI 8

Share these strategies for guided or independent analysis:

- Highlight in yellow the repeated words or phrases used to focus a reader's attention.
- Highlight in green any use of hyperbole, or exaggeration, to emphasize a point.
- Highlight in blue claims made by Thoreau that need to be supported.

For it matters not how small the beginning may seem to be: what is once well done is done forever. But we love better to talk about it: that we say is our mission. Reform keeps many scores of newspapers in its service, but not one man. . . .

Under a government which imprisons any unjustly, the true place for a just man is also a prison. The proper place today, the only place where the State places those who are not *with* her, but *against* her,—the only house in a slave State in which a free man can abide with honor. If any think that their influence would be lost there, and their voices no longer afflict the ear of the State, that they would not be as an enemy within its walls, they do not know by how much truth is stronger than error, nor how much more eloquently and effectively he can combat injustice who has experienced a little in his own person. Cast your whole vote, not a strip of paper merely, but your whole influence. A minority is powerless while it conforms to the majority; it is not even a minority then; but it is irresistible when it clogs by its whole weight. If the alternative is to keep all just men in prison, or give up war and slavery, the State will not hesitate which to choose. If a thousand men were not to pay their tax bills this year, that would not be a violent and bloody measure, as it would be to pay them, and enable the State to commit violence and shed innocent blood. This is, in fact, the definition of a peaceable revolution, if any such is possible. If the tax-gatherer, or any other public officer, asks me, as one has done, "But what shall I do?" my answer is, "If you really wish to do anything, resign your office." When the subject has refused allegiance, and the officer has resigned his office, then the revolution is accomplished. But even suppose blood should flow. Is there not a sort of blood shed when the conscience is wounded? Through this wound a man's real manhood and immortality flow out, and he bleeds to an everlasting death. I see this blood flowing now. . . .

I have paid no poll-tax for six years. I was put into a jail once on this account, for one night; and, as I stood considering the walls of solid stone, two or three feet thick, the door of wood and iron, a foot thick, and the iron grating which strained the light, I could not help being struck with the foolishness of that institution which treated me as if I were mere flesh and blood and bones, to be locked up. I wondered that it should have concluded at length that this was the best use it could put me to, and had never thought to avail itself of my services in some way. I saw that, if there was a wall of stone between me and my townsmen, there was a still more difficult one to climb or break through before they could get to be as free as I was. I did not for a moment feel confined, and the walls seemed a great waste of stone and mortar. I felt as if I alone of all my townsmen had paid my tax. They plainly did not know how to treat me, but behaved like persons who are underbred.[9] In every threat and in every compliment there was a blunder; for they thought that my chief desire was to stand the other side of that stone wall. I could not but smile to see how industriously they locked the door on my meditations, which followed them out again without let or hindrance,[10] and *they* were really all that was dangerous. As they could not reach me, they had resolved

---

[9] **underbred:** ill-mannered.
[10] **without let or hindrance:** without encountering obstacles.

Civil Disobedience **181**

TO CHALLENGE STUDENTS . . .

Examine Persuasive Techniques Direct students to lines 135–141 to examine Thoreau's use of figurative language as a persuasive technique. Have students discuss these questions in groups and then have groups share their ideas with the class:

- What is Thoreau's attitude towards voting with "a strip of paper merely? (*By using the qualifier "merely," Thoreau minimizes the importance of a paper ballot.*)

- What implied metaphor does Thoreau create in these lines? (*He compares subjecting oneself to incarceration to voting.*)

- In lines 139–141, what problems does Thoreau think would be solved if "all just men" required imprisonment? (*war and slavery*) Is Thoreau naïve? Explain. (*Answers will vary.*)

CLOSE READ

Delineate and Evaluate an Argument (LINES 141–153)

COMMON CORE RI 8

In these lines, Thoreau uses an analogy, linking two things that are literally very different. It is up to readers to decide in each case whether such a comparison withstands scrutiny, or whether it is a **false analogy,** or one that doesn't hold up because of critical differences in the subjects.

J **ASK STUDENTS** to reread lines 141–153. Have them describe the analogy Thoreau makes in these lines to support his idea that people should "combat injustice." Ask them to decide if this is an accurate or false analogy. (*Thoreau equates the wounds from a violent revolution with those of a peaceable revolution since both involve "blood shed." Students may judge this a false analogy since the wounds from a violent revolution are literal and may cause actual death rather than figurative death; others may find the analogy holds up, citing a belief that the death of the soul is worse than physical death.*)

Determine Figurative Meaning (LINES 166–167)

COMMON CORE RI 4

In this sentence, Thoreau uses **paradox,** or a seemingly contradictory statement to suggest an important truth.

K **ASK STUDENTS** to explain why lines 166–167 are an example of paradox. (*Thoreau is alone among his "townsmen" because he has not paid his tax. Yet he feels alone among them because he believes that he alone had "paid my tax." He equates standing up to government and paying the consequences as an appropriate tax, and not the payment of money to the government.*)

Delineate and Evaluate an Argument (LINES 173–178)

COMMON CORE RI 8

Thoreau uses more analogies in these lines to make a strong emotional appeal to readers.

 CITE TEXT EVIDENCE Ask students to reread lines 173–178. Identify the analogies and explain how Thoreau's night in prison affected his thinking. *(He compares the government to boys who will abuse a person's dog because they cannot "come at some person" in lines 173–175, to a "half-witted" person in line 176, and to "a lone woman" in lines 176–177. Lines 177–178 explain that Thoreau "lost all my remaining respect" for the government and "pitied it.")*

Determine Figurative Meaning (LINES 186–188)

COMMON CORE RI 4

Thoreau often makes implied comparisons rather than directly stating that one thing is like another.

 ASK STUDENTS to whom Thoreau implicitly compares the government in lines 186–188. *("Your money or your life" is a quotation associated with robbers. Thoreau is suggesting the government is on the same level as common criminals.)*

COLLABORATIVE DISCUSSION Provide students a few minutes to review the text and take notes before they begin discussion with their partner. They might also write a sentence or two that summarizes their thoughts prior to discussion. Basically, Thoreau would prefer that there be no government. He feels that government forces people to do things that are against their consciences.

ASK STUDENTS to share any questions they generated in the course of reading and discussing the selection.

to punish my body; just as boys, if they cannot come at some person against whom they have a spite, will abuse his dog. I saw that the State was half-witted, that it was timid as a lone woman with her silver spoons, and that it did not know its friends from its foes, and I lost all my remaining respect for it, and pitied it.

180 Thus the State never intentionally confronts a man's sense, intellectual or moral, but only his body, his senses. It is not armed with superior wit or honesty, but with superior physical strength. I was not born to be forced. I will breathe after my own fashion. Let us see who is the strongest. What force has a multitude? They only can force me who obey a higher law than I. They force me to become like themselves. I do not hear of *men* being *forced* to live this way or that by masses of men. What sort of life were that to live? When I meet a government which says to me, "Your money or your life," why should I be in haste to give it my money? It may be in a great strait, and not know what to do: I cannot help that. It must help itself; do as I do. It

190 is not worth the while to snivel about it. I am not responsible for the successful working of the machinery of society. I am not the son of the engineer. I perceive that, when an acorn and a chestnut fall side by side, the one does not remain inert to make way for the other, but both obey their own laws, and spring and grow and flourish as best they can, till one, perchance, overshadows and destroys the other. If a plant cannot live according to its nature, it dies; and so a man.

COLLABORATIVE DISCUSSION With a partner, discuss Thoreau's beliefs about government. Cite specific textual evidence from the essay to support your ideas.

APPLYING ACADEMIC VOCABULARY

radical	tension

As you discuss Thoreau's argument, incorporate the Collection 3 academic vocabulary words *radical* and *tension*. As a summary, ask students whether Thoreau's ideas seem **radical**. Refer students to the final lines of the essay, lines 192–196, and ask them to describe the **tension** Thoreau sees as inherent in nature and in relationships between individuals and the government.

Delineate and Evaluate an Argument

 COMMON CORE RI 8

"Civil Disobedience" is a work of public advocacy—that is, it seeks to influence the opinions or attitudes of the general public to bring about change. To evaluate Thoreau's argument, it is necessary to examine each of the elements shown in the chart.

Claim	After identifying the claim, readers need to look at whether it is convincingly supported by reasons and evidence. Illogical reasoning or insufficient evidence can undermine the credibility of the claim.
Reasoning	**Premises:** Premises are statements from which a conclusion is drawn or upon which the argument is based. To evaluate the soundness of Thoreau's reasoning, it is helpful to question the legitimacy of his premises. For example: • Is the general principle that "government is best which governs least" sound? • Can a government function if it lets all people obey their own conscience? • Is civil disobedience—breaking laws and refusing to pay taxes—always preferable to legal efforts to reform government, such as voting and petitioning? **Logical errors:** A writer may sound convincing but base his or her conclusions on errors in logic, such as these: • non sequitur: a conclusion that does not follow logically from the proof offered in support of it • false analogy: a comparison that doesn't hold up because of major differences between the subjects • overgeneralization: a generalization that is too broad
Evidence	The facts, examples, and other details have to be valid, authoritative, relevant, sufficient, and up to date.

For example, to analyze the first five lines of "Civil Disobedience," readers must first consider the validity of the premise "That government is best which governs least." If this premise is not sound—in other words, if there are exceptions to this statement—then any reasoning based on it is flawed also. Thoreau draws a conclusion based on that statement, which is that "government is best which governs not at all." In evaluating this conclusion, readers must decide whether Thoreau offers proof that supports it, or whether it is a non sequitur.

By questioning the validity of Thoreau's premises and examining the relationships between evidence and conclusions, readers will be able to ascertain the soundness of his argument.

Civil Disobedience **183**

 TEACH

CLOSE READ

Delineate and Evaluate an Argument

COMMON CORE RI 8

Review the terms and definitions to be sure students understand them and their relationships. For example, **claims** may be supported with **reasoning** alone, or with reasoning supported by **evidence.** In examining reasoning, students need to analyze **premises** and possible **logical errors.**

In examining evidence, students need to judge whether it is valid (or truthful), authoritative (coming from a reputable, expert source), relevant (applicable to the subject of the claim), sufficient (strong or numerous enough to prove a claim), and up to date. In modern persuasive writing, evidence may involve scientific studies, polls, personal interviews, or statistics. Note, however, that Thoreau does not cite any of these types of evidence and relies primarily instead on what he believes to be logical reasoning.

Discuss the idea of a premise as the first part of this "if-then" construction: "If this is true, then that is true." Often, a writer does not state a premise as directly as Thoreau does in lines 1–5. In many cases, readers must work backward to identify the writer's premise. For example, direct students to Thoreau's claim in lines 36–37 that "The only obligation I have a right to assume is to do at any time what I think is right." Ask them to identify a premise that underlies this claim. *(An individual's judgment or needs are more important than the needs of the majority of a group.)* Discuss whether this is a valid premise. Explain that readers' belief or disbelief in a particular premise may affect their entire analysis of a piece of writing or an idea.

 **Strategies for Annotation** **Annotate it!**

Delineate and Evaluate an Argument

COMMON CORE RI 8

Share these strategies for guided or independent analysis:

• Highlight in blue claims the author makes.
• Underline evidence or reasoning used to support the claim.
• Highlight in green evidence or reasoning that you feel is sufficient to support the claim.
• Highlight in pink evidence that is insufficient to support the claim or reasoning that is not logical, valid, or reasonable.

whole vote, not a strip of paper merely, but your whole influence. A minority is powerless while it conforms to the majority; it is not even a minority then; but it is irresistible when it clogs by its whole weight. If the alternative is to keep all just men in prison, or give up war and slavery, the State will not hesitate which to choose. If a thousand men were not to pay their tax bills this year, that would not be a violent and bloody measure, as it would be to pay them, and enable the State to

Analyzing the Text COMMON CORE RI 2, RI 3, RI 8

Possible answers:

1. Thoreau believes that the majority hold control because they are the strongest physically, not because they have right on their sides. Therefore, they are able to impose their wills upon the minority, which is not just. This leads into Thoreau's claim that it is necessary, therefore, for thinking men to resist acts of government that they see as immoral.

2. Thoreau claims his only obligation to the government is to do what he thinks is right. The best government, therefore, would be one that does the least to force him to act in any way contrary to his thoughts and judgments.

3. Thoreau presents judgments and generalizations: military men follow orders blindly without exercising independent thought. Those who serve the state with their heads "are as likely to serve the Devil . . . as God." He does offer examples of some honored men who "serve the state with their conscience"; that is, resist it (Christ, Copernicus, etc.).

4. Thoreau says that some injustices will work themselves out. However, if the injustice of a government requires its citizens to be unjust toward others, then it is necessary to break the law. "Let your life be a counter-friction to stop the machine." In the third paragraph of the essay, Thoreau presents his ideas about resisting the government; this paragraph helps to qualify and explain the conditions under which that resistance should take place and the fact that some injustice can be tolerated.

5. Thoreau is convincing when he argues that truth holds power and that people should not fear to withhold support from an unjust government. He is not as convincing when he argues that a thousand people should go to jail. He offers this impractical solution without significant logical or factual support.

6. He is free as he stands imprisoned in the jail, because his conscience and his spirit are free.

7. This example conveys the message that people should live and die according to their own laws and the laws of nature. This effectively communicates the idea that Thoreau is trying to convey, although this idea is not necessary supported by evidence or logic.

 eBook *Annotate It!*

Analyzing the Text COMMON CORE RI 2, RI 3, RI 8, W 9

Cite Text Evidence   Support your responses with evidence from the selection.

1. **Interpret** Why does Thoreau believe that "a government in which the majority rule in all cases cannot be based on justice, even as far as men understand it"?

2. **Analyze** What claim does Thoreau make about his obligation as a citizen? How does this claim relate to the premise, "That government is best which governs least"?

3. **Cite Evidence** What reasons and evidence does Thoreau offer to justify his view that the people who truly serve the state are those who often resist it?

4. **Analyze** How do the ideas expressed in lines 88–96 help to qualify or clarify some of Thoreau's earlier points?

5. **Evaluate** In lines 122–153, Thoreau argues that civil disobedience is an effective way of bringing about change. How convincing is this argument? Explain.

6. **Analyze** A statement that seems to contradict itself but nevertheless suggests an important truth is called a **paradox**. What is paradoxical about Thoreau's observations of the night he spent in prison?

7. **Critique** At the end of the excerpt, Thoreau uses an analogy of an acorn and a chestnut to convey his point about human nature. Is this an effective way to communicate his message? Why or why not?

PERFORMANCE TASK

Research Activity: Report How did later activists, such as Martin Luther King Jr., or Mohandas Gandhi, interpret the principles set forth by Thoreau in "Civil Disobedience"?

- Find sources that explain the connection between the activist you have chosen and Thoreau. Identify key similarities and differences in their approaches to nonviolent resistance.

- Organize your ideas into a report. Include charts or other text features to convey your important ideas.

- Document your sources.

- Use the conventions of standard written English.

Assign this performance task.

PERFORMANCE TASK COMMON CORE W 9

Research Activity: Report Brainstorm with students a list of social movements. Have them use Internet or print resources to research information for a brief introduction that summarizes the work of their chosen activist. Have partners share their first drafts for review and suggestions. Students' final reports should show the ways in which their chosen activist interpreted and acted upon the principles developed in Thoreau's essay.

Language and Style: Combining Sentences

 COMMON CORE L 3a

A series of short sentences can result in a terse style that fails to clearly show the relationship between ideas. One way writers can combine their sentences is by connecting two or more complete sentences with one of these coordinating conjunctions:

Coordinating Conjunction	Sample Sentence
and: builds upon or adds to an idea	Walden is an account of his years spent in nature, <u>and</u> Civil Disobedience presents his political philosophy.
but: shows opposition or contrast	Paine's rhetoric is fiery and intense, <u>but</u> Thoreau chose a more measured style.
or: identifies a choice	Would you like to write a report on the historical controversy surrounding Paine, <u>or</u> would you prefer to create a poster about the radical theories of Thoreau?

In his essay "Civil Disobedience," Thoreau uses coordinating conjunctions to build compound sentences that show how the ideas in each sentence relate to each other. By combining ideas, he creates a smooth, rhythmical prose.

Read this sentence from the essay.

> Government is at best but an expedient; but most governments are usually, and all governments are sometimes, inexpedient.

This compound sentence could have been written as a series of simple sentences:

> Government is at best but an expedient. Most governments are usually inexpedient. All governments are sometimes inexpedient.

Breaking the sentence into three separate statements takes away the elegance of Thoreau's style. The three sentences are functional but bland. They have a choppy rhythm, and to convey the correct meaning they must repeat the adjective "inexpedient." Thoreau's meaning is weakened as well with the loss of the conjunction "but," which helps emphasize the point that most governments are inexpedient rather than expedient.

Practice and Apply Return to the report about Thoreau's influence on later activists that you wrote in response to this selection's Performance Task, or return to another essay you have recently written. Find places where you could create a smoother flow and clarify your meaning by combining sentences with a coordinating conjunction. Remember to include a comma before the conjunction. Share the changes you make with a partner.

Language and Style: Combining Sentences

 COMMON CORE L 3a

Review the examples to make sure students understand that these conjunctions are used to connect two independent clauses. The intent is to make a piece of writing flow smoothly. However, students should choose carefully when to use them, since shorter, discrete sentences are sometimes a better choice. In certain cases, combining sentences can actually make the ideas less clear.

Review these examples from the essay and ask students to determine the two ideas that are combined and decide whether the combination is effective.

- Lines 151–153 "Through this wound . . . an everlasting death." *(a man bleeds through the wound, a man bleeds to death; effective combination)*
- Lines 179–180 "Thus the State . . . his senses." 16–19, 23–28 *(State does not confront a man's sense, State confronts a man's body; effective combination)*
- Lines 107–113 "How shall he ever . . . with his action." *(a government man should have to consider how he treats his neighbor, he should have to consider what he needs to do to do his job; this combination makes a very complex sentence that is hard to understand)*

Invite volunteers to share with the class some of the sentences they combined and to explain how they improved the writing's flow.

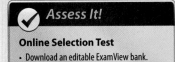

✓ Assess It!

Online Selection Test
- Download an editable ExamView bank.
- Assign and manage this test online.

PRACTICE & APPLY

Analyze Foundational Documents

COMMON CORE RI 9

Note that Paine advocates the formation of a new government that will not treat its citizens tyrannically, while Thoreau suggests that the government that has been formed is doing exactly that. These two documents show the diversity of thought that has been a central part of the development of the United States and its government and culture.

Analyzing the Text

COMMON CORE RI 1, RI 6, RI 9

Possible answers:

1. *Paine's tone throughout his essay is fiery, emphatic, and passionate, and is oratorical in its tone as much as literary. This tone is appropriate because he wants to stir a similar passion in his readers and must reach them with his own emotion. Thoreau's tone is more contemplative and shows less awareness of his audience. This tone fits his purpose, to justify his own actions and explain his view of the individual's responsibility to resist immoral government.*

2. *Paine's style depends heavily on rhetorical devices that help stir reader's emotions. He uses loaded words, such as "shrink," "love," "tyranny," "hell," "glorious," "triumph," "Heaven," "celestial," "slavery," "impious," and "God." He uses parallel structure for effect, e.g., "What we obtain too cheap, we esteem too lightly." He alternates longer statements with short dramatic declarations, and creates a literary style that is powerful and intense. Thoreau also uses some rhetorical devices. In this passage, parallel structure and repetition applied to rhetorical questions create rhythm and build a sense of urgency. He includes repetition elsewhere as well ("If the injustice...") and makes his point in the second paragraph through the use of an analogy. His sentences are longer, building upon ideas with successive phrases and clauses. His style leads readers to reflection rather than emotion.*

3. *Responses will vary. Elements of Paine's essay can be and have been applied to many situations where rebels, resistance fighters, and underdogs have faced difficult odds. Thoreau's essay, inspired by his resistance to the Mexican-American War, has aged well, and has certainly been more influential to subsequent generations than it was in his own day.*

---

from The Crisis
from Civil Disobedience

 eBook *Annotate It!*

Analyze Foundational Documents

COMMON CORE RI 9

By comparing foundational documents from different periods in American history, readers can gain insight into how important ideas evolved over time and how they were influenced by historical events.

Thomas Paine and Henry David Thoreau both argue for resistance to injustice in their essays, but in different ways. Paine argues that the colonists must be united in opposition to the British. Thoreau argues that individuals must follow their own consciences, even if it means opposing the majority. Paine argues in favor of war; Thoreau advocates nonviolent resistance through refusing to cooperate. Both works, however, have had a major impact on political thought and movements in America and around the world.

Analyzing the Text

COMMON CORE RI 1, RI 6, RI 9, W 2b, SL 1a

Cite Text Evidence Support your responses with evidence from the selections.

1. **Analyze** Compare the **tone**, or attitude of the author toward his subject, in each work, citing details to show how it is conveyed. Explain how the tone relates to each author's purpose.

2. **Compare** Examine lines 1–15 of "The Crisis" and lines 75–96 of "Civil Disobedience." Compare elements of each author's style, including the use of **rhetorical devices**, such as repetition and parallel structure.

3. **Analyze** Discuss the influence of the historical context on each author's philosophy of resistance, and explain whether their ideas transcend this historical context.

PERFORMANCE TASK

Speaking Activity: Role Play What would Paine and Thoreau have to say about some of today's political issues?

- Working in a group, decide on two or three current events. Develop questions pertaining to these issues and work together to prepare answers from both writers' perspectives, citing specific evidence.

- Choose two members to represent Paine and Thoreau. In a whole-class setting, ask the prepared questions of the two students, who should respond in their roles.

- Invite other class members to ask questions. As a class, summarize the relevance of each writer's approach to current issues.

Assign this performance task.

 *my* WriteSmart

PERFORMANCE TASK

COMMON CORE W 2b, SL 1a

Speaking Activity: Role Play As group members discuss hypothetical responses by Paine and Thoreau, they should support their views with examples from the essays. Suggest that each group summarize key ideas from each essay to help the students role-playing the two writers answer questions not covered in their original groups. Students' responses should reflect their writer's philosophy and a solid grasp of the current events chosen as topics.

Support Inferences

COMMON CORE

RI 1

TEACH

In persuasive texts, writers usually state their claims explicitly, but the premise on which a claim is based may need to be inferred, and there may be any number of smaller points about which readers are left to make inferences. Review with students the two building blocks of inference:

- **Prior Knowledge** When reading historical documents, students may start out with limited knowledge of the historical context from which a text arose. Impress upon students the importance of reading introductory background or biographical material that accompanies historical texts, as well as all footnotes.

- **Textual Evidence** Authors may offer only indirect clues to some of their positions. Readers need to pay close attention to ways a subject is treated to infer a writer's position. For example, a writer may use loaded language or make positive or negative analogies about an idea or position without stating his or her thoughts directly.

PRACTICE AND APPLY

Ask students to make inferences concerning the following issues and identify prior knowledge used as well as textual evidence to support the inference:

- What is Paine's attitude towards Tories? *(Paine strongly disagrees with all Tory positions; Prior knowledge: Tories supported the British position before and during the Revolutionary War while Paine was a strong advocate of American independence; Textual evidence: In lines 37–47, Paine suggests Tories who want peace now do a disservice to their children who will not have peace. In lines 103–105, he suggests that support by the Tories for Americans giving up their arms would result in "worse ruin" than anything previously.)*

- What is Thoreau's attitude towards the Mexican War and war in general? *(Thoreau strongly opposes the Mexican War and war in general; Prior knowledge: The Mexican War was being fought at the time Thoreau wrote Civil Disobedience; Textual Evidence: In lines 14–17, he describes the war as "the work of a comparatively few individuals. In lines 41–46, he suggests that soldiers are marching "against their will" and "their common sense and consciences." In line 141, he suggests that the government might be pressured to "give up war.")*

 INTERACTIVE LESSON If students need further instruction, use this Interactive Whiteboard Lesson: **Making Inferences**

Delineate and Evaluate an Argument

COMMON CORE

RI 8

RETEACH

 LEVEL UP TUTORIALS Assign the following *Level Up* tutorial: **Elements of an Argument**

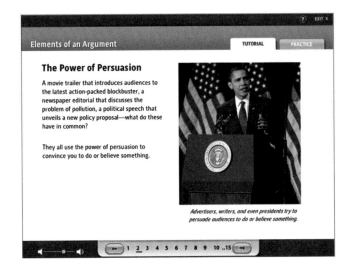

Review the terms *claim, premise, reasons, evidence, opposing claims,* and *counterargument.* Then give an example of a claim, such as "Everyone in a town should share the cost of children's education equally."

- Ask students to provide examples of types of reasons and evidence that might be used to support the claim. *(Sample reason: Good education will help everyone through an improved local economy and lower crime rate.)*

- Provide the following opposing claim: "Only people with kids in school should pay for education." Ask: How could you counter this viewpoint? *(Sample counterargument: Dollars spent on education now mean fewer dollars spent on combating poverty and crime later—costs that would be borne by the whole community anyway.)*

CLOSE READING APPLICATION

Students can apply the skill to another persuasive text. Have them select a newspaper editorial or a blog post that strongly advocates a position. Then have them identify the basic claims, the premises that underlie them, reasons and evidence that are used for support, and any opposing claims and counterarguments used. After their analysis, they should decide if the text was persuasive or not.

*my*SmartPlanner Create lesson plans and access resources online.

The Clan of One-Breasted Women

Essay by Terry Tempest Williams

Why This Text?

An essay is a vehicle for the exchange of ideas. This lesson examines events in the author's life that led her to the realizations about the impact of human actions on the environment that she shares in this essay.

Key Learning Objective: The student will be able to analyze cause and effect and cite text evidence to support inferences.

COMMON CORE Common Core Standards

RI 1 Cite textual evidence to support inferences.

RI 3 Analyze ideas or events and explain how ideas or events interact and develop.

RI 4 Determine the meaning of words and phrases as they are used in a text.

RI 6 Determine an author's point of view or purpose.

RI 7 Integrate and evaluate multiple sources of information.

W 7 Conduct short research projects.

W 8 Gather relevant information from multiple print and digital sources.

SL 5 Make use of digital media in presentations.

L 1 Demonstrate command of the conventions of standard English.

L 3 Apply knowledge of language to make effective choices for meaning or style.

L 5b Analyze nuances in the meanings of words with similar denotations.

▲ Text Complexity Rubric

Quantitative Measures	**The Clan of One-Breasted Women** Lexile: 990L
Qualitative Measures	**Levels of Meaning/Purpose** more than one purpose; implied, easily identified from context
	Structure organization of main ideas and details is highly complex; not explicit, must be inferred by the reader
	Language Conventionality and Clarity contemporary, familiar language
	Knowledge Demands some specialized knowledge required
Reader/Task Considerations	Teacher determined Vary by individual reader and type of text

CLOSE READ

Terry Tempest Williams Have students read the biographical information about the author. Tell students that Williams's work on behalf of the environment has led her to receive numerous awards, including the Robert Marshall Award from the Wilderness Society—the highest honor the society gives to a private citizen. Her passion for the environment stems from her vision that land is the essential connection to life for all who live on this planet. Although her views about preserving the land have, in the past, put her at odds with state and federal officials, she is fearless about speaking out, believing that it is her responsibility to do so.

AS YOU READ Direct students to use the As You Read note to focus their reading. Remind them to write down any questions they generate during reading.

Analyze Ideas and Events: Cause and Effect (LINES 1–17)

 COMMON CORE RI 3

Tell students that to accomplish his or her purpose, an author must decide the most effective way to present ideas and/or events so that readers can clearly see how they relate to each other and understand how they interact to develop a central point. Explain that in this essay, the author has chosen to convey her main idea by illustrating a cause-and-effect relationship between events.

 ASK STUDENTS to identify the effect that the author presents in the first paragraphs. *(The effect is the prevalence of cancer in her family.)* Ask them what they would anticipate about the cause of this occurrence from reading the last two paragraphs, lines 8–17. *(The cause is not what one might think. It is something other than what statistics suggest is often the cause.)* Have students discuss why the author begins her essay by identifying the effect first. *(It shows the severity of the effect; it captures readers' attention.)*

Terry Tempest Williams *(b. 1955) was raised by a large Mormon family in Utah. Both Utah and Mormonism have influenced her writing. Her book* Refuge: An Unnatural History of Family and Place, *from which the selection is taken, tells about her mother's cancer diagnosis, and the unprecedented rise of the Great Salt Lake that flooded a wildlife refuge. This link between people and nature is one that Williams often explores in her writing. Her concern for the environment has led her to testify before Congress.*

The Clan of One-Breasted Women

Essay by Terry Tempest Williams

AS YOU READ Look for the details that the author includes to show how her family and nature are engaged in the same struggle.

A

I belong to a Clan of One-Breasted Women. My mother, my grandmothers, and six aunts have all had mastectomies. Seven are dead. The two who survive have just completed rounds of chemotherapy and radiation.

I've had my own problems: two biopsies for breast cancer and a small tumor between my ribs diagnosed as a "borderline malignancy."

This is my family history.

Most statistics tell us breast cancer is genetic, hereditary, with rising percentages attached to fatty diets, childlessness, or becoming

10 pregnant after thirty. What they don't say is living in Utah may be the greatest hazard of all.

We are a Mormon family with roots in Utah since 1847. The "word of wisdom" in my family aligned us with good foods—no coffee, no tea, tobacco, or alcohol.[1] For the most part, our women were finished having their babies by the time they were thirty. And only one faced

---

[1] **The "word of wisdom" . . . alcohol:** law of the Mormon religion concerning health, as revealed by the Prophet Joseph Smith in 1833.

Image Credits: (t) ©Chad Hurst/WireImage/Getty Images; (b) ©Purestock/Getty Images

The Clan of One-Breasted Women **187**

SCAFFOLDING FOR ELL STUDENTS

Culture: Background Provide this background to facilitate understanding the essay:

- Point out, on a map of the U.S., the proximity of Utah to Nevada. Explain that the author lives in Utah; the nuclear testing to which she refers took place in Nevada.

- Explain that the Mormons—a religious group—originated in New York but traveled west to find a place where they could practice their religion without opposition. They settled in Salt Lake City, Utah, in 1869. Tell students that the author includes details about Mormon beliefs to bring out a central idea of her essay.

ASK STUDENTS to identify the Mormon law that the author mentions in lines 12–14. Ask: How does it relate to the author's family history of cancer?

Analyze Ideas and Events: RI 3
Cause and Effect (LINES 35–59)

Tell students that authors may not explicitly connect certain ideas or events but may imply a relationship through the position of details in the text.

B **ASK STUDENTS** what link the author suggests by mentioning her mother's death at the beginning of this passage. (*The author mentions her mother's death, one assumes from cancer, and then is told about an enormous explosion that rained ashes on their car. The implication is that this explosion may have been connected to the cancer.*)

CRITICAL VOCABULARY

anomaly: The author's family saw the prevalence of cancer in their women as simply an unusual or freakish occurrence.

ASK STUDENTS why this view that their high rate of cancer was an anomaly made sense in 1971. (*There was very little research on cancer compared to what has been done now.*)

stoic: The women accepted that they had cancer without complaining.

ASK STUDENTS why the author views the stoic attitude of her relatives negatively. (*She may think that they could have understood their disease better if they had asked questions and refused to accept it.*)

---

breast cancer prior to 1960. Traditionally, as a group of people, Mormons have a low rate of cancer.

Is our family a cultural **anomaly**? The truth is, we didn't think about it. Those who did, usually the men, simply said, "bad genes."
20   The women's attitude was **stoic**. Cancer was part of life. On February 16, 1971, the eve of my mother's surgery, I accidently picked up the telephone and overheard her ask my grandmother what she could expect.

"Diane, it is one of the most spiritual experiences you will ever encounter."

I quietly put down the receiver.

Two days later, my father took my brothers and me to the hospital to visit her. She met us in the lobby in a wheelchair. No bandages were visible. I'll never forget her radiance, the way she held herself in a
30   purple velvet robe, and how she gathered us around her.

"Children, I am fine. I want you to know I felt the arms of God around me."

We believed her. My father cried. Our mother, his wife, was thirty-eight years old.

A little over a year after Mother's death, Dad and I were having dinner together. He had just returned from St. George, where the Tempest Company was completing the gas lines that would service southern Utah. He spoke of his love for the country, the sandstoned landscape, bare-boned and beautiful. He had just finished hiking the
40   Kolob trail in Zion National Park. We got caught up in reminiscing, recalling with fondness our walk up Angel's Landing on his fiftieth birthday and the years our family had vacationed there.

Over dessert, I shared a recurring dream of mine. I told my father that for years, as long as I could remember, I saw this flash of light in the night in the desert—that this image had so permeated my being that I could not venture south without seeing it again, on the horizon, illuminating buttes and mesas.

"You did see it," he said.

"Saw what?"
50   "The bomb. The cloud. We were driving home from Riverside, California. You were sitting on Diane's lap. She was pregnant. In fact, I remember the day, September 7, 1957. We had just gotten out of the Service.[2] We were driving north, past Las Vegas. It was an hour or so before dawn, when this explosion went off. We not only heard it, but felt it. I thought the oil tanker in front of us had blown up. I pulled over and suddenly, rising from the desert floor, we saw it, clearly, this golden-stemmed cloud, the mushroom. The sky seemed to vibrate with an eerie pink glow. Within a few minutes, a light ash was raining on the car."

anomaly
(ə-nŏmʹə-lē) *n.*
peculiarity; an unusual example.

stoic
(stōʹĭk) *adj.* enduring difficulty without expressing emotion or complaint.

---

[2] **the Service:** many Mormons volunteer to serve as missionaries for a two-year period, during which they attempt to convert others to their faith.

188 Collection 3

APPLYING ACADEMIC VOCABULARY

convince	ethics

As you discuss the author's conversation with her father, incorporate the Collection 3 academic vocabulary words *convince* and *ethics*. Ask students what her father's revelation **convinces** the author of concerning the cancer in her family. Discuss what set of **ethics** guided the decision to test nuclear weapons in the desert and whether the author sees this justification as acceptable.

Image Credits: ©Time Life Pictures/Department Of Energy (DOE)/Getty Images

C 60 I stared at my father.

  "I thought you knew that," he said. "It was a common occurrence in the fifties."

  It was at this moment that I realized the deceit I had been living under. Children growing up in the American Southwest, drinking contaminated milk from contaminated cows, even from the contaminated breasts of their mothers, my mother—members, years later, of the Clan of One-Breasted Women.

D It is a well-known story in the Desert West, "The Day We Bombed Utah," or more accurately, the years we bombed Utah: above ground 70 atomic testing in Nevada took place from January 27, 1951, through July 11, 1962. Not only were the winds blowing north covering "low-use segments of the population" with fallout and leaving sheep dead in their tracks, but the climate was right. The United States of the 1950s was red, white, and blue. The Korean War was raging. McCarthyism[3] was **rampant**. Ike[4] was it, and the cold war was hot. If you were against nuclear testing, you were for a communist regime.

  Much has been written about this "American nuclear tragedy." Public health was secondary to national security. The Atomic Energy

rampant
(răm´pənt) *adj.*
growing wildly without restraint or limit.

---

[3] **McCarthyism:** criticizing and denouncing people for their belief or sympathy for Communism, often without evidence, as practiced by Senate committees led by Joseph McCarthy of Wisconsin.

[4] **Ike:** Dwight David Eisenhower (1890–1969) World War II military leader and President of the U.S. between 1953 and 1961.

The Clan of One-Breasted Women **189**

SCAFFOLDING FOR ELL STUDENTS

Vocabulary: Idiomatic Expressions Remind students that some words and phrases can mean something other than the literal meaning of the words. Project lines 68–76. Invite volunteers to mark the text.

- Highlight idiomatic expressions in blue. *("red, white, and blue"; "Ike was it"; "the cold war was hot")*
- Underline clues that explain the context of these phrases. *("Korean War," "McCarthyism," "against nuclear testing," "for a communist regime")*

ASK STUDENTS to work together to define the phrases in context. *(red, white, and blue: "fervently patriotic"; Ike was it: "the president was highly popular"; the cold war was hot: "the cold war was raging fiercely")*

Analyze Perspective   **RI 6**
(LINES 60–67)

Remind students that an author's view on events is shown through his or her choice of language and details.

C CITE TEXT EVIDENCE Ask students how the author would describe this moment in her life. How does she convey this perspective through her language? *(This moment is a horrifying epiphany. It is knowledge that will change her life. She conveys this perspective through the way she uses repetition and parallelism to emphasize the word "contaminated" and the idea of being poisoned—"drinking contaminated milk from contaminated cows. . . .")*

Determine Author's   COMMON CORE **RI 6**
Purpose (LINES 68–76)

Tell students that as they read an essay, they should consider the reason that the author includes certain details.

D ASK STUDENTS to explain the purpose of the specific dates in this paragraph. *(These dates prove that nuclear testing took place place during the time that she and her relatives would have been affected by it.)*

CRITICAL VOCABULARY

rampant: The author says that, in the 1950s in the United States, fear of communism was out of control, encouraged by people like Joseph McCarthy.

ASK STUDENTS to explain the cause-and-effect relationship between the rampant fear of communism and the nuclear testing. *(This fear stemmed from the belief that the United States was vulnerable to attack by communist regimes, so government officials and others wanted to be ready to attack first or defend themselves.)*

Analyze Ideas and Events: RI 3
Cause and Effect (LINES 90–100)

Remind students that although this essay is not persuasive, the author does need readers to believe in the cause-and-effect relationships that she is using to develop her main ideas. To validate these relationships, she includes specific factual details.

E **ASK STUDENTS** how the tone in this passage affects their perception of the information presented. *(The author's tone is objective, which suggests that this information is factual and has serious implications.)* Have students discuss the relationship between these ideas and preceding parts of the essay. *(The ideas presented in this passage help to prove the connection between nuclear testing and the incidence of cancer. They make the author's interpretation of the circumstances legitimate and give it weight.)*

Support Inferences RI 1

(LINES 101–106)

Tell students that they can infer a person's motivation and aspects of their character from what they say.

F **ASK STUDENTS** to explain the author's purpose in including this direct quotation from Mrs. Allen. What important idea about the litigants is revealed through her words? *(The author is showing that the victims were not motivated by the desire for government money as compensation; many of them simply wanted others to avoid similar fates. They were gentle, accepting people who normally would not question authority, but extreme circumstances had forced them into this role.)*

> ❝Children . . . drinking contaminated milk from contaminated cows, even from the contaminated breasts of their mothers.❞

Commissioner, Thomas Murray, said, "Gentlemen, we must not let
80 anything interfere with this series of tests, nothing."

Again and again, the American public was told by its government, in spite of burns, blisters, and nausea, "It has been found that the tests may be conducted with adequate assurance of safety under conditions prevailing at the bombing reservations." Assuaging public fears was simply a matter of public relations. "Your best action," an Atomic Energy Commission booklet read, "is not to be worried about fallout." A news release typical of the times stated, "We find no basis for concluding that harm to any individual has resulted from radioactive fallout."

90 On August 30, 1979, during Jimmy Carter's presidency, a suit was filed, *Irene Allen* v. *The United States of America*. Mrs. Allen's case was the first on an alphabetical list of twenty-four test cases, representative of nearly twelve hundred plaintiffs seeking compensation from the United States government for cancers caused by nuclear testing in Nevada.

Irene Allen lived in Hurricane, Utah. She was the mother of five children and had been widowed twice. Her first husband, with their two oldest boys, had watched the tests from the roof of the local high school. He died of leukemia in 1956. Her second husband died of
100 pancreatic cancer in 1978.

In a town meeting conducted by Utah Senator Orrin Hatch, shortly before the suit was filed, Mrs. Allen said, "I am not blaming the government, I want you to know that, Senator Hatch. But I thought if my testimony could help in any way so this wouldn't happen again to any of the generations coming up after us . . . I am happy to be here this day to bear testimony of this."

God-fearing people. This is just one story in an anthology of thousands.

On May 10, 1984, Judge Bruce S. Jenkins handed down his
110 opinion. Ten of the plaintiffs were awarded damages. It was the first time a federal court had determined that nuclear tests had been the cause of cancers. For the remaining fourteen test cases, the proof

WHEN STUDENTS STRUGGLE . . .

To guide students' comprehension of the important causes and effects in the text, organize students into small groups and have them reread lines 90–141. Then ask them to complete a chart similar to the one shown to map the relationships between the events in this passage.

of causation was not sufficient. In spite of the split decision, it was considered a landmark ruling. It was not to remain so for long.

In April 1987, the Tenth Circuit Court of Appeals overturned Judge Jenkins's ruling on the ground that the United States was protected from suit by the legal doctrine of sovereign immunity, a centuries-old idea from England in the days of absolute monarchs.

120 In January 1988, the Supreme Court refused to review the Appeals Court decision. To our court system it does not matter whether the United States government was irresponsible, whether it lied to its citizens, or even that citizens died from the fallout of nuclear testing. What matters is that our government is immune: "The King can do no wrong."

In Mormon culture, authority is respected, obedience is revered, and independent thinking is not. I was taught as a young girl not to "make waves" or "rock the boat."

"Just let it go," Mother would say. "You know how you feel, that's what counts."

130 For many years, I have done just that—listened, observed, and quietly formed my own opinions, in a culture that rarely asks questions because it has all the answers. But one by one, I have watched the women in my family die common, heroic deaths. We sat in waiting rooms hoping for good news, but always receiving the bad. I cared for them, bathed their scarred bodies, and kept their secrets. I watched beautiful women become bald as Cytoxan, cisplatin, and Adriamycin[5] were injected into their veins. I held their foreheads as they vomited green-black bile, and I shot them with morphine when the pain became inhuman. In the end, I witnessed their last peaceful 140 breaths, becoming a midwife to the rebirth of their souls.

The price of obedience has become too high.

The fear and inability to question authority that ultimately killed rural communities in Utah during atmospheric testing of atomic weapons is the same fear I saw in my mother's body. Sheep. Dead sheep. The evidence is buried.

I cannot prove that my mother, Diane Dixon Tempest, or my grandmothers, Lettie Romney Dixon and Kathryn Blackett Tempest, along with my aunts developed cancer from nuclear fallout in Utah. But I can't prove they didn't.

150 My father's memory was correct. The September blast we drove through in 1957 was part of Operation Plumbbob, one of the most intensive series of bomb tests to be initiated. The flash of light in the night in the desert, which I had always thought was a dream, developed into a family nightmare. It took fourteen years, from 1957 to 1971, for cancer to manifest in my mother—the same time, Howard L. Andrews, an authority in radioactive fallout at the National

---

[5] **Cytoxan, cisplatin, and Adriamycin** (sī-tŏk´săn, sĭs-plă´tn, and ă-drē´ă-mī´sĭn): drugs used in chemotherapy to treat cancer.

CLOSE READ

Support Inferences RI 1

(LINES 115–124)

Remind students that reasonable inferences are based on logical interpretation of the evidence.

G ASK STUDENTS to explain the implications of the court's action of claiming immunity for the government. *(The original verdict would have opened the floodgates for lawsuits.)* How does the author view this overturning of Judge Jenkins's ruling? *(She sees it as a betrayal.)*

Analyze Ideas and Events: COMMON CORE RI 3
Cause and Effect (LINES 130–141)

Tell students that not all cause-and-effect relationships consist of one cause leading to one effect. Sometimes multiple causes bring about an effect; sometimes an effect becomes the cause of another event or several events.

H ASK STUDENTS to explain the implied change in the author in this part of the essay. What has brought about this change? *(As a result of the knowledge that the author has and the suffering that her family has gone through, she rejects the idea that she must be silent and obedient.)* Discuss the significance of the statement "The price of obedience has become too high." *(She is saying that lives have been sacrificed because no one questioned authority.)*

nuclear testing ▶ cancer in many families ▶ lawsuits ▶ denial of responsibility by government ▶ change in author's attitude

Analyze Ideas and Events: Cause and Effect (LINES 160–164)

COMMON CORE RI 3

Have students reread what the author says about Mormon culture in lines 125–129.

 ASK STUDENTS what idea is suggested by the phrase "member of a border tribe" (lines 163–164). Why does the author anticipate this outcome of her actions? *(Mormons do not question. Therefore, if she chooses to question and defy authority, she may be ostracized from her community of believers.)* What is shown by her willingness to accept this consequence? *(She has the courage of her convictions; finding the truth and stopping the damage are more important to her than continuing to conform.)*

Determine Author's Purpose (LINES 188–200)

COMMON CORE RI 6

Explain that to accomplish his or her purpose, an author might include a variety of details such as facts, examples, and description.

CITE TEXT EVIDENCE Ask students what kind of details the author includes in this part of the essay. Have them give examples. *(She includes descriptive details that create vivid images of the effects of the nuclear tests, such as "Rocks were hot from the inside out.")* Have students explain what the author accomplishes through the use of these details. *(She shows the destructive effects of these tests on nature. She shows how the nuclear blasts kill the land. She reinforces the idea that they cannot be seen as positive in any way.)*

Institutes of Health, says radiation cancer requires to become evident. The more I learn about what it means to be a "downwinder," the more questions I drown in.

160   What I do know, however, is that as a Mormon woman of the fifth generation of Latter-day Saints, I must question everything, even if it means losing my faith, even if it means becoming a member of a border tribe among my own people. Tolerating blind obedience in the name of patriotism or religion ultimately takes our lives.

When the Atomic Energy Commission described the country north of the Nevada Test Site as "virtually uninhabited desert terrain," my family and the birds at Great Salt Lake were some of the "virtual uninhabitants."

One night, I dreamed women from all over the world circled a blazing
170   fire in the desert. They spoke of change, how they hold the moon in their bellies and wax and wane with its phases. They mocked the presumption of even-tempered beings and made promises that they would never fear the witch inside themselves. The women danced wildly as sparks broke away from the flames and entered the night sky as stars.

And they sang a song given to them by Shoshone grandmothers:

Ah ne nah, nah	Consider the rabbits
nin nah nah—	How gently they walk on the earth—
ah ne nah, nah	Consider the rabbits
nin nah nah—	How gently they walk on the earth—
Nyaga mutzi	We remember them
oh ne nay—	We can walk gently also—
Nyaga mutzi	We remember them
oh ne nay—	We can walk gently also—

180

The women danced and drummed and sang for weeks, preparing themselves for what was to come. They would reclaim the desert for the sake of their children, for the sake of the land.

A few miles downwind from the fire circle, bombs were being tested. Rabbits felt the tremors. Their soft leather pads on paws and
190   feet recognized the shaking sands, while the roots of mesquite and sage were smoldering. Rocks were hot from the inside out and dust devils hummed unnaturally. And each time there was another nuclear test, ravens watched the desert heave. Stretch marks appeared. The land was losing its muscle.

The women couldn't bear it any longer. They were mothers. They had suffered labor pains but always under the promise of birth. The red hot pains beneath the desert promised death only, as each bomb became a stillborn. A contract had been made and broken between human beings and the land. A new contract was being drawn by the
200   women, who understood the fate of the earth as their own.

SCAFFOLDING FOR ELL STUDENTS

Vocabulary Support Explain that a play on words occurs when a writer or speaker uses both meanings of a word to make a point. Draw students' attention to the word *virtually* in line 166. Tell students that in this sentence, it means "for all practical purposes." In other words, according to the commission, the land was practically or almost uninhabited.

Point out that the author uses the word *virtual* (line 167) in responding to this description. Explain that *virtual* in this sentence means "not real." The author is saying that although the government may have seen the region as virtually uninhabited, the virtual uninhabitants—the author and her family—are very real, indeed.

ASK STUDENTS what point the author wants to make about the government's decision through this word play.

Under the cover of darkness, ten women slipped under a barbed-wire fence and entered the contaminated country. They were trespassing. They walked toward the town of Mercury, in moonlight, taking their cues from coyote, kit fox, antelope squirrel, and quail. They moved quietly and deliberately through the maze of Joshua trees. When a hint of daylight appeared they rested, drinking tea and sharing their rations of food. The women closed their eyes. The time had come to protest with the heart, that to deny one's genealogy[6] with the earth was to commit treason against one's soul.

210   At dawn, the women draped themselves in mylar, wrapping long streamers of silver plastic around their arms to blow in the breeze. They wore clear masks, that became the faces of humanity. And when they arrived at the edge of Mercury, they carried all the butterflies of a summer day in their wombs. They paused to allow their courage to settle.

The town that forbids pregnant women and children to enter because of radiation risks was asleep. The women moved through the streets as winged messengers, twirling around each other in slow motion, peeking inside homes and watching the easy sleep of men and 220   women. They were astonished by such stillness and periodically would utter a shrill note or low cry just to verify life.

The residents finally awoke to these strange **apparitions**. Some simply stared. Others called authorities, and in time, the women were apprehended by wary soldiers dressed in desert fatigues. They were taken to a white, square building on the other edge of Mercury. When asked who they were and why they were there, the women replied, "We are mothers and we have come to reclaim the desert for our children."

The soldiers arrested them. As the ten women were blindfolded and handcuffed, they began singing:

230   *You can't forbid us everything*
You can't forbid us to think—
You can't forbid our tears to flow
And you can't stop the songs that we sing.

The women continued to sing louder and louder, until they heard the voices of their sisters moving across the mesa:

Ah ne nah, nah
nin nah nah—
Ah ne nah, nah
nin nah nah—
240   *Nyaga mutzi*
oh ne nay—
Nyaga mutzi
oh ne nay—

---

[6] **genealogy:** Mormons believe that their connections with ancestors are eternal, and that those who have died can still become members of the church.

apparition
(ăp´ə-rĭsh´ən) *n.*
an unexpected, unexplained vision; a ghostly image of a person.

The Clan of One-Breasted Women   **193**

Analyze Ideas and Events: COMMON CORE RI 3
Cause and Effect (LINES 247–260)

Tell students that the events in the essay have been leading up to this final action.

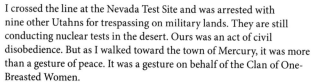 **ASK STUDENTS** to explain why the author's participation in the protest is significant. (*The protest is the result of all that she has witnessed and learned about the effects of nuclear testing on the environment and on humans; it is a rejection of the values that she was brought up with, which stressed acceptance rather than action.*)

Support Inferences COMMON CORE RI 1

(LINES 261–273)

Tell students that another form of making inferences is to predict what might happen in the future. By looking at text details that show what someone thinks or feels or how he or she has changed, they can make logical assumptions about that person's later actions.

(N) ASK STUDENTS to explain how this protest changes the author. (*It makes her unafraid of speaking out against what is wrong.*) Have students discuss what they think the protest signals for the author. Have them explain the details that support their prediction. (*It signals the start of her mission to act on her conscience regardless of the personal consequences. The reference to the Joshua trees pointing to the Promised Land suggests the link between the author's actions and what she hopes to achieve. Her memory of her mother also implies that she will continue speaking out.*)

COLLABORATIVE DISCUSSION Have students answer the questions independently, identifying support from the essay, before sharing their ideas with a partner. Ask pairs to discuss their insights in small groups. Accept all reasonable responses.

ASK STUDENTS to share any questions they generated in the course of reading and discussing the selection.

"Call for reinforcements," one soldier said.

"We have," interrupted one woman, "we have—and you have no idea of our numbers."

(M) 250 I crossed the line at the Nevada Test Site and was arrested with nine other Utahns for trespassing on military lands. They are still conducting nuclear tests in the desert. Ours was an act of civil disobedience. But as I walked toward the town of Mercury, it was more than a gesture of peace. It was a gesture on behalf of the Clan of One-Breasted Women.

As one officer cinched the handcuffs around my wrists, another frisked my body. She found a pen and a pad of paper tucked inside my left boot.

"And these?" she asked sternly.

"Weapons," I replied.

Our eyes met. I smiled. She pulled the leg of my trousers back over my boot.

260 "Step forward, please," she said as she took my arm.

We were booked under an afternoon sun and bused to Tonopah, Nevada. It was a two-hour ride. This was familiar country. The Joshua trees standing their ground had been named by my ancestors, who believed they looked like prophets pointing west to the Promised Land. These were the same trees that bloomed each spring, flowers appearing like white flames in the Mojave. And I recalled a full moon in May, when Mother and I had walked among them, flushing out mourning doves and owls.

The bus stopped short of town. We were released.

270 The officials thought it was a cruel joke to leave us stranded in the desert with no way to get home. What they didn't realize was that we were home, soul-centered and strong, women who recognized the sweet smell of sage as fuel for our spirits.

COLLABORATIVE DISCUSSION In Williams's view, what has caused her family's health problems? What is this same cause doing to the landscape? With a partner, discuss what point the author is making by linking the two consequences to the same cause. Cite specific textual evidence from the essay to support your ideas.

TO CHALLENGE STUDENTS . . .

Evaluate Author's Style Explain to students that one of the characteristics of the author's style in this essay is the use of metaphors to compare two things not normally thought of as alike. To analyze the impact of this literary device on the author's meaning, have pairs do the following and then share their analyses with the class:

- Locate significant metaphors in the text. (*lines 139–140, 193–200, 210–215*)
- Explain what each compares.
- Identify points of similarity between the metaphors.
- Discuss how the metaphors underscore the author's central idea.

Support Inferences

Inferences are logical assumptions that readers make based on details in the text as well as what they know from their own experiences. Making inferences enables readers to understand thoughts and feelings that are not directly stated in the text. Sometimes these unstated thoughts and feelings are fairly easy to infer; in other cases, the author deliberately leaves matters uncertain.

In the following quotation, Williams describes seeing her mother after her cancer surgery:

> She met us in the lobby . . . I'll never forget her radiance, the way she held herself in a purple velvet robe, and how she gathered us around her.

Williams's use of the word *radiance* and the details she includes might lead readers to infer that her mother was a very strong woman with a deep faith; that it was important to her mother to reassure the family that she was all right; and that Williams actually believed her mother might survive.

Analyze Ideas and Events: Cause and Effect

COMMON CORE RI 3

To understand how the author moves from "blind obedience" to "civil disobedience," readers must examine the **cause-and-effect** relationship between the events. In a cause-and-effect relationship, one or more actions or events cause another action or event to occur. As this organizer shows, the major events in the essay all contribute to the author's changed attitude and her deliberate act of protest.

TEACH

CLOSE READ

Support Inferences

COMMON CORE RI 1

Have students review the inferences they have made in their discussion of the essay about the author's feelings, beliefs, and interpretation of events. Ask them to infer the reason that the author wrote this essay. *(She wrote this essay to expose how the government's actions in testing nuclear bombs has had and will continue to have disastrous consequences for nature and the population.)* Have students identify the most compelling evidence in support of their inferences.

Analyze Ideas and Events: Cause and Effect

COMMON CORE RI 3

Ask students to define both *cause* and *effect*. Make sure they understand that authors do not always present causes first and effects later. As in this essay, the author might manipulate the order to convey ideas more effectively.

Organize students into groups and have them identify causes and their effects other than those listed in the chart. Have them work together to create a diagram that clearly shows the relationships among the events.

Strategies for Annotation 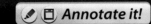 **Annotate it!**

Analyze Ideas and Events: Cause and Effect

 COMMON CORE RI 3

Have students use their eBook annotation tools to trace cause-and-effect relationships in the essay. Have them do the following:

- Highlight in green events that are the causes of other events.
- Highlight in blue effects of earlier events.
- On a note, match causes and effects and explain how they are related to other causes and effects in the essay. Then discuss how presenting her ideas and the events in cause-and-effect relationships affects the author's meaning.

> I told my father that for years, as long as I could remember, I saw this flash of light in the night in the desert—that this image had so permeated by being

Cause of father's revelation that family had been exposed to radioactive fallout.

Analyzing the Text

COMMON CORE RI 1, RI 3, RI 4, RI 6

Possible answers:

1. The attitude that can be inferred is that the author's mother and grandmother accept their illness as spiritual, or the will of God. We can also infer this as a possible explanation of why the government's testing of bombs continued without protest for so long. The author may also want readers to understand a deeply ingrained tradition of "blind obedience."

2. After watching the women die, she writes, "The price of obedience has become too high." Because participating in the protest could lead to alienation from her culture, it was necessary that she reconcile her beliefs with that possibility.

3. The realization that her mother, grandmothers, and aunts died probably as a result of nuclear fallout moves Williams from acceptance to rebellion. Her epiphany comes with her father's revelation of the source of the golden light: "It was at this moment that I realized the deceit I had been living under."

4. Her tone is ironic, her attitude displeased. She chooses quotes from government documents that reveal deceit, such as "Your best action is not to be worried about fallout."

5. The dream connects the women and the earth. What happens to them is happening to the earth on a far greater scale. Readers understand that not only are individuals suffering, but the source of all life is becoming barren, and "to deny one's genealogy with the earth was to commit treason against one's soul."

6. Imagery emphasizes the destruction brought about by nuclear testing. For example, the author describes caring for her mother and aunts with words and phrases that appeal to the senses of sight and touch. ("I . . . bathed their scarred bodies. . . . I held their foreheads as they vomited green-black bile. . . .") She also uses imagery to demonstrate the impact of the explosions. ("Their soft leather pads on paws and feet recognized the shaking sands, while the roots of mesquite and sage were smoldering.")

7. The author wields her pen and paper as weapons, as she says to the officer. Her essay and her participation in the protest both draw attention to the problem. She is not keeping quiet and not accepting the situation. Her essay and the protest both demonstrate the need for change.

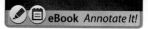
eBook *Annotate It!*

Analyzing the Text

COMMON CORE RI 1, RI 3, RI 4, RI 6, RI 7, W 7, W 8, SL 5

Cite Text Evidence Support your responses with evidence from the selection.

1. **Infer** What can readers infer about the ethics and attitudes of the Mormon faith from what the author shares about her mother and grandmother? Why does the author want readers to understand the Mormon culture?

2. **Analyze** Explain how the author's perspective on her Mormon faith changes. Why must this shift occur before she can participate in the protest?

3. **Cause/Effect** Which event or moment has the greatest effect on the author's decision to protest? Cite details from the essay that support your response.

4. **Analyze** What is the author's **tone**, or attitude, toward the government? What words and phrases convey her tone?

5. **Analyze** What is the author's purpose in including her dream in the essay? How does this dream affect readers' understanding of the author's feelings and the protest itself?

6. **Cite Evidence** In this essay, the author presents facts, but she also uses **imagery**, words and phrases that create vivid sensory perceptions for readers. Explain how imagery heightens readers' understanding of important parts of the essay. Cite specific examples to support this analysis.

7. **Synthesize** Terry Tempest Williams has described her writing by saying, "I write through my biases of gender, geography, and culture." How does this point of view influence both her writing and her social activism? Explain what the essay and her protest at the Nevada Test Site have in common.

PERFORMANCE TASK

Media Activity: Report With a small group, present a multimedia report on the nuclear testing in Utah.

- Research the topic, using reliable web sites, reference books, and other resources. Remember to document your sources and write notes in your own words.

- Decide on the major point you want to convey through your presentation. Create a storyboard to help organize the visual, audio, and verbal elements of your report.

- Present your report to the class.

Assign this performance task.

PERFORMANCE TASK

COMMON CORE RI 7, W 7, W 8, SL 5

Media Activity: Report Remind students to check copyright restrictions when they choose visual and audio elements for their presentation. Encourage them to incorporate charts, tables, or graphs that they have created to help organize their information. Suggest that they rehearse their presentation to enable them to create smoother transitions and to make sure that their main idea is conveyed.

Critical Vocabulary

 COMMON CORE L 5b

| anomaly | stoic | rampant | apparition |

Practice and Apply Answer each question, referring to the meaning of the Critical Vocabulary word in the statement.

1. The woman was *stoic* during her controversial testimony. How did she behave?

2. The girl thought she saw an *apparition* in her bedroom. How did she react? Why?

3. The disease was *rampant* in the area. Were public health officials worried or not? Explain.

4. The pickpocketing incident in the neighborhood was an *anomaly*. Should more police be assigned to the neighborhood in response? Explain why or why not.

Vocabulary Strategy: Denotation and Connotation

In her essay, Williams states, "McCarthyism was rampant." The Critical Vocabulary word *rampant* means "uncontrolled or out of hand." *Rampant* has many synonyms including "wild," "excessive," "riotous," or "unchecked." The author chose *rampant*, however, because it is associated with something harmful or malicious. While the **denotation**, or dictionary definition of a word, is important, a word's **connotation**—ideas and feelings associated with it—helps convey the author's tone or attitude. The chart includes other words from the essay that were chosen for their connotations.

	Word	Example	Denotation	Connotation
	revered	"Obedience is revered."	held in deep respect	sacred
	inhuman	"The pain became inhuman."	not ordinary; cruel	beyond a person's ability to survive
	heave	"Ravens watched the desert heave."	shift or raise with great effort; throw	violent; painful

Practice and Apply For each word in the chart, identify a synonym—a word with the same denotation. Follow these steps:

1. Write the synonym and define it.

2. Use the synonym in a sentence.

3. Explain how the connotation of the new word differs from the connotation of the original.

PRACTICE & APPLY

Critical Vocabulary COMMON CORE L 5b

Possible answers:

1. *She showed no emotion as she testified calmly.*

2. *She was frightened; she thought she saw a ghost or something unreal.*

3. *They were worried because there was nothing they could do to stop it.*

4. *Because the case was an exception, it is unlikely that more police are needed to prevent future cases.*

Vocabulary Strategy: Denotation and Connotation

Possible answers:

1. **prized:** *highly valued*

2. **monstrous:** *beastly or dreadful*

3. **erupt:** *flare up or arise*

Student sentences and explanations will vary, but they should demonstrate the proper meaning of each synonym and show how its connotations differ from the original words. Students may need to use a dictionary to locate synonyms and pinpoint their connotations.

Strategies for Annotation ✎ 📖 *Annotate it!*

Denotation and Connotation COMMON CORE L 5b

Have students use their eBook tools to complete the Vocabulary Strategy activity by doing the following:

Highlight *revered, inhuman,* and *heave* in the text. Underline words in the surrounding text that help you understand their connotations. Identify two or more synonyms for each word, using context, a dictionary, or a thesaurus. Replace the word in the original sentence with each synonym. Reread the surrounding text to determine how the synonym's connotation differs from that of the original word.

> devils hummed <u>unnaturally</u>. And each time there was another nuclear test, ravens watched the desert heave. Stretch marks <u>appeared. The land was losing its muscle.</u>

Language and Style: Gerunds and Gerund Phrases

 COMMON CORE L1, L3

Clarify for students that both participles and gerunds end in *-ing*. Explain that participles function as adjectives, however, while gerunds take the place of nouns. To check whether a word is a gerund, students should see if they can substitute a noun for it.

Possible answers: *Students should use the conventions of standard English grammar to include gerunds or gerund phrases in their multimedia reports. Discussions should address whether the use of gerunds did make the text livelier.*

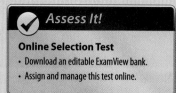

Assess It!

Online Selection Test
- Download an editable ExamView bank.
- Assign and manage this test online.

Language and Style: Gerunds and Gerund Phrases

 COMMON CORE L1, L3

Gerunds are verb forms that end in *-ing* and are used as nouns. **Gerund phrases** include the gerund plus its modifiers and complements. As this chart shows, gerunds and gerund phrases can appear in any part of a sentence where a noun could be used.

Part of the sentence	Example
subject	**Bombing in Utah** was at its height in the 1950s.
direct object	The women finished **chanting**.
indirect object	The women gave **petitioning** a try.
subject complement	Her cure for tension was **writing in her journal**.
object of the preposition	She thought for a long time before **protesting at the site**.

Williams uses gerunds and gerund phrases in her essay. Read these sentences from the essay.

> We got caught up in reminiscing . . .

> Tolerating blind obedience in the name of patriotism or religion ultimately takes over our lives.

The author could instead have replaced the gerunds with nouns:

> We got caught up in our memories . . .

> The toleration of blind obedience in the name of patriotism or religion ultimately takes over our lives.

Although both versions of each sentence say the same thing, notice that the use of a gerund makes the sentences livelier. The *-ing* form of the verb creates a sense of motion and energy that helps to keep the readers' attention.

Practice and Apply Return to the multimedia report that you created in response to this selection's Performance Task. Identify places where you could replace a noun with a gerund or gerund phrase to make your speaking more lively. Discuss your changes with a partner.

Determine Author's Point of View

COMMON CORE
RI 6

TEACH

Explain that to every piece of nonfiction writing, an author brings his or her view of the subject. What the author thinks about the topic is colored by his or her experiences, feelings, and values. This perspective may, in fact, be the reason the author chooses the particular topic to write about.

Tell students that determining the author's perspective enables them to decide whether or not they share it. It also allows them to evaluate the validity and objectivity of the ideas presented as well as ensure that they fully understand the author's central points. Explain that they can identify the author's perspective by looking at both the explicit and implicit meanings.

- **Explicit:** Sometimes, the author will include sentences that directly state what he or she thinks about the subject. These statements may contain words that express feelings or judgments.
- **Implicit:** Most frequently, the author's perspective must be inferred from the language and content of the work. Strongly connotative words, sensory language, and the syntax of the writing provide clues to what the author thinks. The perspective is also implied by the kinds of information that the author includes as well as what is omitted.

PRACTICE AND APPLY

Project lines 81–89 on the board. Ask students how they would describe the author's perspective on the government's actions in the 50s, 60s, and beyond. *(She sees the government as responsible for what happened; she is very angry.)* Have students explain how they determined that perspective from this paragraph. *(The author deliberately includes details of the government's actions at this time; they show how the government misled the public. She mainly lets the facts speak for themselves; but her statement, "Assuaging public fears was simply a matter of public relations," is clearly sarcastic.)*

INTERACTIVE WHITEBOARD LESSON If students need further instruction, use this Interactive Whiteboard Lesson: **Author's Purpose and Perspective.**

Analyze Ideas and Events: Cause and Effect

COMMON CORE
RI 3

RETEACH

Review the important ideas related to cause-and-effect relationships, reminding students that the author develops her central idea by presenting this connection between the events in her essay.

- Direct students to one of the texts that they have previously read, such as "Speech on the Vietnam War, 1967," "The Secret to Raising Smart Kids," "Marita's Bargain," or "A Vindication of the Rights of Woman."
- Ask students to work together to identify a cause-and-effect relationship in the text that helps bring out the author's central idea. Call on pairs or groups to explain how the central idea is developed through establishing this connection between events.

LEVEL UP TUTORIALS Assign the following *Level Up* tutorial: **Cause-and-Effect Organization**

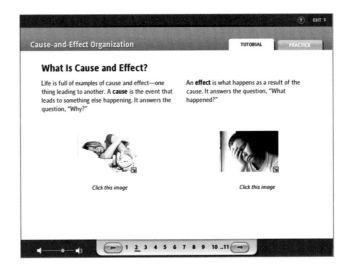

CLOSE READING APPLICATION

Have students read an article, essay, or other brief nonfiction text independently. Ask them to identify the relationships between the ideas. Remind them that ideas or events can be related by cause and effect, problem-solution, comparison-contrast, or sequence.

Direct students to the FYI site to find a nonfiction selection to use in the Close Reading Application.

ANCHOR TEXT

A Modest Proposal

mySmartPlanner Create lesson plans and access resources online.

Satire by Jonathan Swift

Why This Text?

It is important for students to recognize satire when they encounter it in various forms of media. This lesson explores the characteristic elements of satire through analysis of Swift's exposure of the cruel practices of the English.

 ▶ *View It!*

Professional Development Podcast:

Text Complexity

Key Learning Objective: The student will be able to analyze satire and its historical context.

For practice and application:

Close Reader selection
"Who Speaks for the 1%?"
Satire by Joel Stein

 COMMON CORE

Common Core Standards

RL 6 Analyze a case in which grasping point of view requires distinguishing what is directly stated from what is really meant (e.g., satire).

RI 3 Analyze ideas or events.

RI 4 Determine the meaning of words and phrases.

RI 5 Analyze and evaluate the effectiveness of the structure an author uses.

RI 6 Determine an author's point of view or purpose.

RI 7 Integrate and evaluate multiple sources of information.

RI 10 Read and comprehend literary nonfiction.

W 4 Produce clear and coherent writing.

L 3a Vary syntax for effect.

L 4a Use context as a clue to the meaning of a word or phrase.

L 4d Verify the meaning of a word or phrase.

L 5a Interpret figures of speech in context.

▲ Text Complexity Rubric

Quantitative Measures	**A Modest Proposal** Lexile: 1590L
Qualitative Measures	**Levels of Meaning/Purpose**  multiple levels of complex meanings
	Structure organization of main ideas and details is highly complex; not explicit, must be inferred by the reader
	Language Conventionality and Clarity ambiguous language requiring inferences
	Knowledge Demands cultural or literary knowledge essential to understanding
Reader/Task Considerations	Teacher determined Vary by individual reader and type of text

CLOSE READ

Background Have students read the background information. Tell them that Irish society in the eighteenth century was divided into three major classes: the "Protestant Ascendancy," who were the British landowners; the Anglo-Irish, born of English parents in Ireland, who had some status in society; and the Catholics, who had no position, no land, and no rights. Swift was Anglo-Irish; from this vantage point he could see the harm being done to Ireland by the English as well as the need for the Irish to unify in order to fight this repression.

Jonathan Swift Tell students that Swift established his reputation with his early satires, including *A Tale of a Tub*, which satirized both religion and the learning of the day. Many of these works were published under the pseudonym of Isaac Bickerstaff. After years of moving back and forth from England to Ireland, Swift finally settled in Ireland in 1713, becoming the dean of St. Patrick's Cathedral in Dublin. He chafed at being back in Ireland at first, feeling exiled from London, but then became the champion of the Irish through his satires.

AS YOU READ Direct students to use the As You Read note to focus their reading.

Comprehend Literary Nonfiction: Historical Context (LINES 1–9)

COMMON CORE **RI 10**

Point out that the details in the first paragraph begin to depict the problem that the "modest proposal" will seek to solve.

Ⓐ **CITE TEXT EVIDENCE** What picture of the economic situation in Ireland is created by the details in the paragraph? Explain. *(There is widespread poverty, shown by the many "beggars of the female sex" who lack the money to feed their children. The children are "all in rags" and can expect an equally hopeless future in which they steal for a living, die in war, or work on plantations far from home [lines 7–9].)* What is the effect of presenting this description of the problem at the beginning of the essay? *(After becoming aware of such deplorable conditions, readers will be anxious to find out about a possible solution.)*

Background In the 1720s, the Catholics in Ireland suffered from the repressive rule of England, which stripped them of their rights and forced them into poverty. Their misery increased with a series of crop failures; many had to beg or face starvation. Swift wrote "A Modest Proposal" to protest England's policies in Ireland.

Jonathan Swift (1667–1745) was born of English parents in Dublin, Ireland. He became an Anglican priest and a writer, whose satires took aim at injustice and vice. He is probably best known for *Gulliver's Travels. This satire is now enjoyed as a story, although Swift wrote it as a criticism of political corruption.*

A Modest Proposal

for preventing the children of poor people in Ireland from being a burden to their parents or country, and for making them beneficial to the public

Satire by Jonathan Swift

AS YOU READ Pay attention to details that Swift includes to make his proposal sound convincing. Note questions you have during reading.

Ⓐ It is a melancholy object to those who walk through this great town[1] or travel in the country, when they see the streets, the roads, and cabin doors, crowded with beggars of the female sex, followed by three, four, or six children, all in rags and importuning every passenger for an alms.[2] These mothers, instead of being able to work for their honest livelihood, are forced to employ all their time in strolling to beg sustenance for their helpless infants, who, as they grow up, either turn thieves for want[3] of work, or leave their dear native country to fight for the Pretender[4] in Spain, or sell themselves to the Barbadoes.[5]

---

[1] **this great town:** Dublin, Ireland.

[2] **importuning** (ĭm´pôr-tōōn´ĭng) . . . alms (ämz): begging from every passerby for a charitable handout.

[3] **want:** lack; need.

[4] **Pretender:** James Edward Stuart, who claimed the English throne, from which his now deceased father, James II, had been removed in 1688. Because James II and his son were Catholic, the common people of Ireland were loyal to them.

[5] **sell . . . Barbadoes:** To escape poverty, some Irish migrated to the West Indies, obtaining money for their passage by agreeing to work as slaves on plantations there for a set period.

A Modest Proposal **199**

Close Read Screencasts ▶ View It!

Modeled Discussions

Have students click the *Close Read* icons in their eBooks to access two screencasts in which readers discuss and annotate the following key passages:

- development of the narrator's persona (lines 25–33)
- reasons in favor of the proposal (lines 186–193)

As a class, view and discuss at least one of these videos. Then have students pair up to do an independent close read of an additional passage—the narrator's final plea to readers (lines 278–288).

Comprehend Literary Nonfiction: Historical Context (LINES 10–21)

COMMON CORE RI 10

Ask students to use what they know about the conditions in Ireland to infer ideas.

 B **ASK STUDENTS** why the number of young children is "in the present deplorable state of the kingdom a very great additional grievance." *(Ireland has suffered crop failures for several seasons; famine is rife, meaning that the growth of the population will only create more hardship and suffering.)*

Tell students that authors may exaggerate the truth for emphasis.

C **ASK STUDENTS** to explain the exaggeration in lines 13–16 and its purpose. *(The idea of erecting a statue to the one who solves the children's problem exaggerates how important that person would be; at the same time, it stresses how great the problem is.)*

Analyze Author's Point of View: Satire (LINES 22–39)

COMMON CORE RL 6, RI 6

Clarify that satire aims to ridicule a group's weakness or wrongdoing in the hope of effecting positive change. Explain that to deliver his satire, Swift creates a fictional narrator. The narrator's traits and attitude are key to understanding Swift's meaning.

D **ASK STUDENTS** what impression they get of the narrator in lines 22–39. *(He says he has studied the issue for a long time; he sounds businesslike, sincere. But he describes mothers and infants as if they are farm animals; he discusses poverty as an easily fixed economic (not human) problem. By pretending an exaggerated indifference to suffering, he sets himself up as one who sounds reasonable but cannot be trusted.)*

CRITICAL VOCABULARY

prodigious: The number of children being born into poverty is overwhelmingly great.
ASK STUDENTS how Swift's focus on the prodigious number of children affects readers' understanding of the situation in Ireland. *(It makes the problem seem more heartbreaking and severe.)*

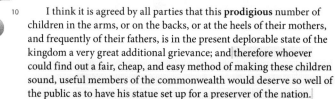

10   I think it is agreed by all parties that this **prodigious** number of children in the arms, or on the backs, or at the heels of their mothers, and frequently of their fathers, is in the present deplorable state of the kingdom a very great additional grievance; and therefore whoever could find out a fair, cheap, and easy method of making these children sound, useful members of the commonwealth would deserve so well of the public as to have his statue set up for a preserver of the nation.

    But my intention is very far from being confined to provide only for the children of professed beggars; it is of a much greater extent, and shall take in the whole number of infants at a certain age who are born 20 of parents in effect as little able to support them as those who demand our charity in the streets.

    As to my own part, having turned my thoughts for many years upon this important subject, and maturely weighed the several schemes of other projectors,[6] I have always found them grossly mistaken in their computation. It is true, a child just dropped from its dam[7] may be supported by her milk for a solar year, with little other nourishment; at most not above the value of two shillings, which the mother may certainly get, or the value in scraps, by her lawful occupation of begging; and it is exactly at one year old that I propose 30 to provide for them in such a manner as instead of being a charge upon their parents or the parish, or wanting food and raiment for the rest of their lives, they shall on the contrary contribute to the feeding, and partly to the clothing, of many thousands.

    There is likewise another great advantage in my scheme, that it will prevent those voluntary abortions, and that horrid practice of women murdering their bastard children, alas, too frequent among us, sacrificing the poor innocent babes, I doubt,[8] more to avoid the expense than the shame, which would move tears and pity in the most savage and inhuman breast.

40   The number of souls in this kingdom being usually reckoned one million and a half, of these I calculate there may be about two hundred thousand couples whose wives are breeders; from which number I subtract thirty thousand couples who are able to maintain their own children, although I apprehend there cannot be so many under the present distresses of the kingdom; but this being granted, there will remain an hundred and seventy thousand breeders. I again subtract fifty thousand for those women who miscarry, or whose children die by accident or disease within the year. There only remain an hundred and twenty thousand children of poor parents annually born. The 50 question therefore is, how this number shall be reared and provided for, which, as I have already said, under the present situation of affairs, is utterly impossible by all the methods hitherto proposed. For we can

prodigious (prə-dĭj´əs) *adj.* remarkably great; huge.

---
[6] **projectors:** persons who propose public projects or plans.
[7] **dam** (dăm): female parent. The term is used mostly for farm animals.
[8] **doubt:** suspect.

SCAFFOLDING FOR ELL STUDENTS

Vocabulary: Context Clues Remind students that they can use context clues to help define multiple-meaning words. Point out the word *sound* in line 15. Write these definitions on the board: 1. (n.) a noise; 2. (adj.) in good condition; 3. (n.) a body of water. Draw students' attention to the context clue "useful" in the sentence, which helps them identify the second meaning as the correct one.

ASK STUDENTS to use context clues and a dictionary to help them determine the meanings of these additional words: *charge* (line 30), *move* (line 38), *maintain* (line 43).

> ❝ Whoever could find out a fair, cheap, and easy method of making these children sound, useful members of the commonwealth would deserve so well of the public. ❞

neither employ them in handicraft or agriculture; we neither build houses (I mean in the country) nor cultivate land. They can very seldom pick up a livelihood by stealing till they arrive at six years old, except where they are of towardly parts;[9] although I confess they learn the **rudiments** much earlier, during which time they can however be looked upon only as probationers, as I have been informed by a principal gentleman in the county of Cavan, who protested to me that

60   he never knew above one or two instances under the age of six, even in a part of the kingdom so renowned for the quickest proficiency in that art.

    I am assured by our merchants that a boy or girl before twelve years old is no salable commodity; and even when they come to this age they will not yield above three pounds, or three pounds and half a crown at most on the Exchange; which cannot turn to account[10] either to the parents or the kingdom, the charge of nutriment and rags having been at least four times that value.

    I shall now therefore humbly propose my own thoughts, which I
70   hope will not be liable to the least objection.

    I have been assured by a very knowing American of my acquaintance in London, that a young healthy child well nursed is at a year old a most delicious, nourishing, and wholesome food, whether stewed, roasted, baked, or boiled; and I make no doubt that it will equally serve in a fricassee or a ragout.[11]

    I do therefore humbly offer it to public consideration that of the hundred and twenty thousand children, already computed, twenty thousand may be reserved for breed,[12] whereof only one fourth part to be males, which is more than we allow to sheep, black cattle, or
80   swine; and my reason is that these children are seldom the fruits of marriage, a circumstance not much regarded by our savages, therefore one male will be sufficient to serve four females. That the remaining

rudiment:
(ro͞o′də-mənt) *n.* basic principle or aspect.

---

[9] **are of towardly** (tôrd′lē) **parts:** have a promising talent.
[10] **turn to account:** earn a profit; benefit; prove useful.
[11] **fricassee** (frĭk′ə-sē′) . . . **ragout** (ră-go͞o′): types of meat stews.
[12] **reserved for breed:** kept for breeding (instead of being slaughtered).

A Modest Proposal   **201**

APPLYING ACADEMIC VOCABULARY

radical	convince

As you discuss the proposal, incorporate the Collection 3 academic vocabulary words *radical* and *convince*. Ask students to discuss the reason that Swift's proposal in this essay is so **radical.** Then have them explain the means by which the narrator seeks to **convince** readers of the thought that has gone into the proposed solution.

Comprehend Literary Nonfiction: Historical Context (LINES 54–62)

 COMMON CORE RI 10

Explain to students that Swift satirizes the way the English view the Irish by incorporating details that suggest the narrator shares the same perspective.

E **ASK STUDENTS** what generalization about the poor in Ireland they can infer from these lines. *(that they often support themselves by stealing)* Have students discuss how Swift uses this view to make a further point about the conditions in Ireland. *(He satirically condemns the English for their callous attitude toward the Irish poor. He also suggests that some Irish may have to turn to stealing since they cannot be employed in industries or agriculture.)*

Analyze Author's Point of View: Satire (LINES 69–82)

COMMON CORE RL 6, RI 6

Point out that having described the problem, the narrator puts forth his proposed solution. Have students look for **verbal irony,** a discrepancy between what is said and what is meant. Swift uses this device to convey his satire in this part of the essay.

F **CITE TEXT EVIDENCE** Have students explain how the narrator's introduction increases the impact of the proposal on readers. *(The introduction suggests that the proposal will be innocuous, not "liable to the least objection." Instead, the proposal that children be sold for food is horrifying.)* Ask students what the extreme nature of the proposal implies about the English treatment of the Irish. *(It is inhumane. The English give the Irish no more regard than "sheep, black cattle, or swine." They are destroying the Irish people and robbing them of their future.)*

CRITICAL VOCABULARY

rudiments: The narrator says that even though young children know the basic principles of stealing, they cannot always execute them successfully until they are at least six years old.

ASK STUDENTS to explain the connotation of rudiments. *(It sounds formal and makes stealing seem like a profession that requires training.)*

Analyze Author's Point of View: Satire (LINES 83–93)

COMMON CORE RL 6, RI 6

Point out to students that the thoroughness with which Swift develops the proposal increases the effectiveness of his satire.

 CITE TEXT EVIDENCE Ask students to identify the details that make the proposal sound practical. *(The narrator explains the number of meals that a single child might supply [lines 86–90] and what a child might be expected to weigh at the end of a year [lines 91–93].)* What effect on readers does Swift intend the sensible approach of his narrator to have? *(When readers think about the fact that infants are being discussed as sources of food, they are repelled.)*

Analyze Language

COMMON CORE RI 4

(LINES 94–96)

Remind students that authors use metaphorical language to add layers of meaning.

H **ASK STUDENTS** to identify the metaphor in these lines. What does Swift mean by it? *(He says the landlords "have already devoured most of the parents" of the children who would be sold for food. In other words, the landlord system is so unjust that it has already consumed the lives of the Irish.)*

CRITICAL VOCABULARY

collateral: The narrator shows the additional advantages of his proposal in an effort to show why it should be adopted.

ASK STUDENTS what "collateral" advantage Swift satirizes here and why. *(The collateral advantage ridiculed here is that in addition to providing tasty meals, the use of children as food would reduce the number of Catholics. This argument is designed to satirize the British bias against Irish Catholicism.)*

---

 hundred thousand may at a year old be offered in sale to the persons of quality and fortune through the kingdom, always advising the mother to let them suck plentifully in the last month, so as to render them plump and fat for a good table. A child will make two dishes at an entertainment for friends; and when the family dines alone, the fore or hind quarter will make a reasonable dish, and seasoned with a little pepper or salt will be very good boiled on the fourth day, especially in

90 winter.

I have reckoned upon a medium that a child just born will weigh twelve pounds, and in a solar year if tolerably nursed increaseth to twenty-eight pounds.

I grant this food will be somewhat dear, and therefore very proper for landlords, who, as they have already devoured most of the parents, seem to have the best title to the children.

Infant's flesh will be in season throughout the year, but more plentiful in March, and a little before and after. For we are told by a grave author, an eminent French physician,[13] that fish being a prolific[14]

100 diet, there are more children born in Roman Catholic countries about nine months after Lent[15] than at any other season; therefore, reckoning a year after Lent, the markets will be more glutted than usual, because the number of popish infants is at least three to one in this kingdom; and therefore it will have one other **collateral** advantage, by lessening the number of Papists[16] among us.

I have already computed the charge of nursing a beggar's child (in which list I reckon all cottagers, laborers, and four fifths of the farmers), to be about two shillings per annum, rags included; and I believe no gentleman would repine to give ten shillings for the carcass

110 of a good fat child, which, as I have said, will make four dishes of excellent nutritive meat, when he hath only some particular friend or his own family to dine with him. Thus the squire will learn to be a good landlord, and grow popular among the tenants; the mother will have eight shillings net profit, and be fit for work till she produces another child.

Those who are more thrifty (as I must confess the times require) may flay the carcass; the skin of which artificially dressed will make admirable gloves for ladies, and summer boots for fine gentlemen.

As to our city of Dublin, shambles[17] may be appointed for this

120 purpose in the most convenient parts of it, and butchers we may be assured will not be wanting; although I rather recommend buying the

collateral
(kə-lăt´ər-əl)
adj. additional, accompanying.

---

[13]**grave . . . physician:** François Rabelais (răb´ə-lā´), a 16th-century French satirist.

[14]**prolific:** promoting fertility.

[15]**Lent:** Catholics traditionally do not eat meat during Lent, the 40 days leading up to Easter, and instead eat a lot of fish.

[16]**popish** (pō´pĭsh) . . . Papists: hostile or contemptuous terms referring to Roman Catholics.

[17]**shambles:** slaughterhouses.

202 Collection 3

WHEN STUDENTS STRUGGLE . . .

Remind students that the essay follows a problem-solution organization. First, the narrator presents a problem; then, he offers a solution. Display a chart like the one shown here. Have students work in groups to identify what they learn in lines 1–115 about the problem and solution.

Have groups volunteer details for the class chart. Use the completed chart to clarify students' understanding of the satirical nature of the essay. Remind them that Swift is outraged about the way the English laws and other practices force the Irish to live in poverty. He feels the English victimize the Irish; to prove his point, he takes the concept of victimization to a ridiculous and unbelievable extreme.

children alive, and dressing them hot from the knife as we do roasting pigs.

A very worthy person, a true lover of his country, and whose virtues I highly esteem, was lately pleased in discoursing on this matter to offer a refinement upon my scheme. He said that many gentlemen of this kingdom, having of late destroyed their deer, he conceived that the want of venison might be well supplied by the bodies of young lads and maidens, not exceeding fourteen years
130 of age nor under twelve, so great a number of both sexes in every county being now ready to starve for want of work and service; and these to be disposed of by their parents, if alive, or otherwise by their nearest relations. But with due deference to so excellent a friend and so deserving a patriot, I cannot be altogether in his sentiments; for as to the males, my American acquaintance assured me from frequent experience that their flesh was generally tough and lean, like that of our schoolboys, by continual exercise, and their taste disagreeable; and to fatten them would not answer the charge. Then as to the females, it would, I think with humble submission, be a loss to the public,
140 because they soon would become breeders themselves; and besides, it is not improbable that some **scrupulous** people might be apt to censure such a practice (although indeed very unjustly) as a little bordering upon cruelty; which, I confess, hath always been with me the strongest objection against any project, how well soever intended.

But in order to justify my friend, he confessed that this expedient was put into his head by the famous Psalmanazar, a native of the island Formosa,[18] who came from thence to London above twenty years ago, and in conversation told my friend that in his country when any young person happened to be put to death, the executioner sold the carcass
150 to persons of quality as a prime dainty; and that in his time the body of a plump girl of fifteen, who was crucified for an attempt to poison the emperor, was sold to his Imperial Majesty's prime minister of state, and other great mandarins of the court, in joints from the gibbet,[19] at four hundred crowns. Neither indeed can I deny that if the same use were made of several plump young girls in this town, who without one single groat[20] to their fortunes cannot stir abroad without a chair,[21] and appear at the playhouse and assemblies in foreign fineries which they never will pay for, the kingdom would not be the worse.

Some persons of a desponding spirit are in great concern about
160 that vast number of poor people who are aged, diseased, or maimed, and I have been desired to employ my thoughts what course may be

scrupulous:
(skrōō′pyə-ləs) *adj.*
honorable; moral.

---

[18]**Psalmanazar** (săl′mə-năz′ər) . . . Formosa (fôr-mō′sə): a French imposter in London who called himself George Psalmanazar and pretended to be from Formosa (now Taiwan), where, he said, cannibalism was practiced.

[19]**gibbet** (jĭb′ĭt): gallows.

[20]**groat:** an old British coin worth four pennies.

[21]**cannot stir . . . chair:** cannot go outside without using an enclosed chair carried on poles by two men.

A Modest Proposal   **203**

Problem:		**Solution:**
too many poor children who suffer from lack of food and adequate shelter	▶	sell one-year-old babies to gentlemen and landlords who will use them for food

CLOSE READ

Comprehend Literary Nonfiction: Historical Context (LINES 133–158)

COMMON CORE RI 10

Remind students that Swift wrote this essay in 1729. His references to people of different cultures and nationalities reflect some of the misconceptions of the day.

🄸 **ASK STUDENTS** what they can infer about Europeans' views of Americans from the narrator's reference to his American acquaintance in lines 71–74 and in this passage. *(Americans were thought to be crude and barbaric; Swift takes this view to an extreme by depicting Americans as individuals who casually resort to cannibalism.)*

Explain that Swift takes advantage of every opportunity to satirize the political and social practices of this time period. Encourage students to use the details in lines 145–158 to determine Swift's criticism.

🄹 **ASK STUDENTS** to summarize Psalmanazar's story from his country. *(A 15-year-old girl who had been executed was sold as meat to the imperial court.)* What does Swift find reprehensible about those who are wealthy or favored in society? *(They appear unconcerned about the suffering of others.)*

CRITICAL VOCABULARY

scrupulous: The narrator adds to the satire by suggesting that people who object to the eating of adolescents but not to the eating of infant children could be considered ethical.

ASK STUDENTS to explain the irony in Swift's use of the word in this context. *(The word itself means* principled *or* morally right, *but here the narrator is describing a practice that is clearly evil and immoral.)*

CLOSE READ

Integrate and Evaluate Information

COMMON CORE RI 7

Have students examine the illustration on this page. Point out that art may be used as a way to convey criticism of a group, practice, or institution.

 ASK STUDENTS how this sketch reinforces ideas that Swift has expressed in his essay. Have them explain, citing details from the illustration.
(In this illustration, diners who are already well-fed are greedily devouring huge portions of meat. They might represent the English, who have exploited the Irish but still want more.)

204 Collection 3

APPLYING ACADEMIC VOCABULARY

controversy	ethics

Have students discuss the illustration on this page, incorporating the Collection 3 academic vocabulary words *controversy* and *ethics*. Ask students what Swift suggests about the **ethics** of men such as those pictured here through his constant references to them as consumers of babies. Would the inclusion of a sketch such as this one in Swift's original essay have ignited **controversy**? Why or why not?

taken to ease the nation of so grievous an encumbrance. But I am not in the least pain upon that matter, because it is very well known that they are every day dying and rotting by cold and famine, and filth and vermin, as fast as can be reasonably expected. And as to the younger laborers, they are now in almost as hopeful a condition. They cannot get work, and consequently pine away for want of nourishment to a degree that if at any time they are accidentally hired to common labor, they have not strength to perform it; and thus the country and

170 themselves are happily delivered from the evils to come.

I have too long digressed, and therefore shall return to my subject. I think the advantages by the proposal which I have made are obvious and many, as well as of the highest importance.

For first, as I have already observed, it would greatly lessen the number of Papists, with whom we are yearly overrun, being the principal breeders of the nation as well as our most dangerous enemies; and who stay at home on purpose to deliver the kingdom to the Pretender, hoping to take their advantage by the absence of so many good Protestants, who have chosen rather to leave their

180 country than stay at home and pay tithes against their conscience to an Episcopal curate.[22]

Secondly, the poorer tenants will have something valuable of their own, which by law may be made liable to distress,[23] and help to pay their landlord's rent, their corn and cattle being already seized and money a thing unknown.

Thirdly, whereas the maintenance of an hundred thousand children, from two years old and upwards, cannot be computed at less than ten shillings a piece per annum, the nation's stock will be thereby increased fifty thousand pounds per annum, besides the profit

190 of a new dish introduced to the tables of all gentlemen of fortune in the kingdom who have any refinement in taste. And the money will circulate among ourselves, the goods being entirely of our own growth and manufacture.

Fourthly, the constant breeders, besides the gain of eight shillings sterling per annum by the sale of their children, will be rid of the charge of maintaining them after the first year.

Fifthly, this food would likewise bring great custom to taverns, where the vintners will certainly be so prudent as to procure the best receipts[24] for dressing it to perfection, and consequently have

200 their houses frequented by all the fine gentlemen, who justly value themselves upon their knowledge in good eating; and a skillful cook, who understands how to oblige his guests, will contrive to make it as expensive as they please.

---

[22]**Protestants . . . curate** (kyŏŏr´ĭt): Swift is criticizing absentee Anglo-Irish landowners who lived—and spent their income from their property—in England.

[23]**distress:** seizure of a person's property for the payment of debts.

[24]**receipts:** recipes.

A Modest Proposal **205**

WHEN STUDENTS STRUGGLE . . .

Point out that on this page the narrator presents five reasons that his proposal should be adopted. Organize students into small groups and assign each a reason. Ask them to explain who the narrator thinks would benefit and why. As needed, prompt them with the sentence frame: ___ would benefit because ___. *(Reason 1: Protestants; there would be fewer Catholics. Reason 2: The poor; they would have something else [their babies] to give to the landlords for rent. Reason 3: The nation; it would have fewer poor children to care for. Reason 4: Poor parents; they wouldn't have the expense of taking care of their children. Reason 5: Tavern owners; they could attract more customers.)* Discuss with students the irony underlying each reason and how it illustrates Swift's point about the exploitation of the poor.

CLOSE READ

Analyze Author's Point of View: Satire (LINES 174–185) COMMON CORE RL 6, RI 6

Remind students that in order to understand the satire, readers must recognize the irony in what a writer expresses.

L ASK STUDENTS to explain the irony in the statement that the Irish "stay at home on purpose to deliver the kingdom to the Pretender." *(The irony lies in the fact that the Irish have no choice but to stay at home, since they have few resources to take them anywhere else. Also, in their current state of deprivation they would be incapable of coming to the aid of anyone, including an outcast king.)* Have students discuss how the narrator's tone in lines 182–185 conveys irony. *(The narrator is enthusiastic on behalf of the tenants, who will now be able to pay their landlords by selling their infant children as food. The exaggerated enthusiasm of this passage helps readers see a genuine outrage on behalf of the poor that contrasts with the literal meaning of the narrator's words.)*

Analyze Ideas (LINES 186–203) COMMON CORE RI 3

Point out that the narrator, in the role of a concerned citizen offering a solution to a serious problem, offers several numbered reasons in support of his proposal.

M ASK STUDENTS to summarize the cost-benefit analysis the narrator offers in lines 186–196. *(The sale of infant children as food will increase the gross national product; it will improve the lives of the poor because they will have fewer children to support.)* Have students discuss what Swift is satirizing here. *(Speaking of selling babies in terms of the profit they will yield and the money their deaths will save satirizes the English view of the Irish as less than human, as worth no more sympathy than agricultural products.)*

> " No gentleman would repine to give ten shillings for the carcass of a good fat child. "

Analyze Author's Point of View: Satire (LINES 204–232)

 COMMON CORE RL 6, RI 6

Tell students that a **stereotype** is a sweeping generalization about a group or an institution.

 CITE TEXT EVIDENCE Have students reread lines 204–214. Have them identify the narrator's stereotype of the Irish and cite the details that reveal it. *(The narrator expresses the English view of the Irish as amoral and brutal. He says his proposal "would increase the care and tenderness of mothers" because their children would now have a monetary value. He imagines that the mothers would compete to see "which of them could bring the fattest child to the market." He also suggests that only the cash value of a child would induce Irish husbands not to "beat or kick" their pregnant wives.)* How might this stereotype be used by the English as justification for their behavior? *(Holding such a stereotype enables the English to treat the Irish as subhuman beings.)*

CRITICAL VOCABULARY

inducement: The narrator says that being able to sell their babies would encourage people in the lower classes to marry.

ASK STUDENTS what Swift hopes his entire essay will be an inducement to. *(He hopes it will lead to reforms that will improve the lives of the Irish poor.)*

Sixthly, this would be a great **inducement** to marriage, which all wise nations have either encouraged by rewards or enforced by laws and penalties. It would increase the care and tenderness of mothers toward their children, when they were sure of a settlement for life to the poor babes, provided in some sort by the public, to their annual profit instead of expense. We should see an honest emulation among
210 the married women, which of them could bring the fattest child to the market. Men would become as fond of their wives during the time of their pregnancy as they are now of their mares in foal, their cows in calf, or sows when they are ready to farrow; nor offer to beat or kick them (as is too frequent a practice) for fear of a miscarriage.

Many other advantages might be enumerated. For instance, the addition of some thousand carcasses in our exportation of barreled beef, the propagation of swine's flesh, and improvement in the art of making good bacon, so much wanted among us by the great destruction of pigs, too frequent at our tables, which are no way
220 comparable in taste or magnificence to a well-grown, fat, yearling child, which roasted whole will make a considerable figure at a lord mayor's feast or any other public entertainment. But this and many others I omit, being studious of brevity.

Supposing that one thousand families in this city would be constant customers for infants' flesh, besides others who might have it at merry meetings, particularly weddings and christenings, I compute that Dublin would take off annually about twenty thousand carcasses, and the rest of the kingdom (where probably they will be sold somewhat cheaper) the remaining eighty thousand.
230 I can think of no one objection that will possibly be raised against this proposal, unless it should be urged that the number of people will be thereby much lessened in the kingdom. This I freely own, and it was indeed one principal design in offering it to the world. I desire the reader will observe, that I calculate my remedy for this one individual kingdom of Ireland and for no other that ever was, is, or I think ever can be upon earth. Therefore let no man talk to me of other expedients: of taxing our absentees at five shillings a pound: of using neither clothes nor household furniture except what is of our

inducement: (ĭn-dōōs´mənt) *n.* an incentive or stimulus.

Strategies for Annotation ✏ 🖫 *Annotate it!*

Analyze Author's Point of View: Satire

COMMON CORE RL 6, RI 6

Tell students that Swift uses **loaded language,** words and phrases that arouse the emotions, to shock his readers. Have students use their eBook annotation tools for analysis of this device in lines 204–265:

- Highlight in pink examples of loaded language, words and phrases deliberately used to make readers feel emotion.
- On a note, explain Swift's purpose in that part of the text for using the language and how it contributes to the effectiveness of his satire.

the married women, which of them could bring the fattest child to the market. Men would become as fond of their wives during the time of their pregnancy as they are now of their mares in foal, their cows in calf, or sows when they are ready to farrow; nor offer to beat or kick

own growth and manufacture: of utterly rejecting the materials and
instruments that promote foreign luxury: of curing the expensiveness
of pride, vanity, idleness, and gaming in our women: of introducing a
vein of parsimony,[25] prudence, and temperance: of learning to love our
country, in the want of which we differ even from Laplanders and the
inhabitants of Topinamboo:[26] of quitting our animosities and factions,
nor acting any longer like the Jews, who were murdering one another
at the very moment their city was taken:[27] of being a little cautious not
to sell our country and conscience for nothing: of teaching landlords
to have at least one degree of mercy toward their tenants: lastly, of
putting a spirit of honesty, industry, and skill into our shopkeepers;
who, if a resolution could now be taken to buy only our native goods,
would immediately unite to cheat and exact upon us in the price, the
measure, and the goodness, nor could ever yet be brought to make one
fair proposal of just dealing, though often and earnestly invited to it.

Therefore I repeat, let no man talk to me of these and the like
expedients,[28] till he hath at least some glimpse of hope that there will
ever be some hearty and sincere attempt to put them in practice.

But as to myself, having been wearied out for many years with
offering vain, idle, visionary thoughts, and at length utterly despairing
of success, I fortunately fell upon this proposal, which, as it is wholly
new, so it hath something solid and real, of no expense and little
trouble, full in our own power, and whereby we can incur no danger
in disobliging England. For this kind of commodity will not bear
exportation, the flesh being of too tender a consistence to admit a long
continuance in salt, although perhaps I could name a country which
would be glad to eat up our whole nation without it.

After all, I am not so violently bent upon my own opinion as to
reject any offer proposed by wise men, which shall be found equally
innocent, cheap, easy, and effectual. But before something of that kind
shall be advanced in contradiction to my scheme, and offering a better,
I desire the author or authors will be pleased maturely to consider two
points. First, as things now stand, how they will be able to find food
and raiment for an hundred thousand useless mouths and backs. And
secondly, there being a round million of creatures in human figure
throughout this kingdom, whose sole subsistence put into a common
stock[29] would leave them in debt two millions of pounds sterling,
adding those who are beggars by profession to the bulk of farmers,

---

[25]**parsimony** (pär´sə-mō´nē): frugality; thrift.

[26]**Topinamboo** (tŏp´ĭ-năm´bōō): an area in Brazil supposedly inhabited by wild
savages.

[27]**Jews . . . taken:** In A.D. 70, during a Jewish revolt against Roman rule, the
inhabitants of Jerusalem, by fighting among themselves, made it easier for the
Romans to capture the city.

[28]**let no man . . . expedients:** In his writings, Swift had suggested "other
expedients" without success.

[29]**common stock:** ordinary stock in a company or business venture.

A Modest Proposal **207**

CLOSE READ

Analyze Author's Point of View: Satire (LINES 257–265)

COMMON CORE RL 6, RI 6

Tell students that although Swift expresses his ideas through the voice of the narrator, at times he betrays his own feelings about the issue.

ASK STUDENTS to identify two places in the paragraph where Swift expresses a hint of his own voice, his own feelings. *(The reference to being weary [line 257] and the statement that "I could name a country which would be glad to eat up our whole nation" [lines 264-265] sound more like Swift himself, who was, indeed, tired from his efforts to bring about reform and who believed that England was interested only in further exploiting Ireland.)*

TO CHALLENGE STUDENTS . . .

Analyze Metaphorical Language Discuss with students how Swift has used metaphors of consumption throughout his essay, including the one in lines 262–265. Have students work in pairs to identify the "devouring" language used throughout the essay. Ask them to analyze the political implications of that language and explain why Swift uses it to describe the relationship between England and Ireland. Have pairs contribute their insights to a class discussion.

Analyze Author's Point of View: Satire (LINES 289–295)

 COMMON CORE RL 6, RI 6

Point out that the final paragraph is the narrator's last chance to convince readers to accept his proposal.

P CITE TEXT EVIDENCE Ask students what the narrator says about his motivation in making this proposal. What evidence does he cite in support? *(He says that his motive is only to promote the public good [lines 291-293]. He claims to have no selfish motive because his children are too old to be sold and he will not be having any more [lines 293–295].)* Have students discuss what Swift is satirizing in this conclusion. *(He is satirizing anyone who claims to have the best interests of the Irish poor at heart while betraying a callous and inhumane attitude toward them.)*

COLLABORATIVE DISCUSSION Have students work independently to identify specific facts, examples, figures, and other details the narrator advances to promote the legitimacy of his proposal. Then have them discuss how these facts and figures actually undermine the narrator's "modest proposal," instead of convincing readers that he is right.

ASK STUDENTS to share any questions they generated in the course of reading and discussing the selection.

cottagers, and laborers, with their wives and children who are beggars in effect; I desire those politicians who dislike my overture, and may perhaps be so bold to attempt an answer, that they will first ask the
280 parents of these mortals whether they would not at this day think it a great happiness to have been sold for food at a year old in the manner I prescribe, and thereby have avoided such a perpetual scene of misfortunes as they have since gone through by the oppression of landlords, the impossibility of paying rent without money or trade, the want of common sustenance, with neither house nor clothes to cover them from the inclemencies of the weather, and the most inevitable prospect of entailing the like or greater miseries upon their breed forever.

I profess, in the sincerity of my heart, that I have not the least
290 personal interest in endeavoring to promote this necessary work, having no other motive than the public good of my country, by advancing our trade, providing for infants, relieving the poor, and giving some pleasure to the rich. I have no children by which I can propose to get a single penny; the youngest being nine years old, and my wife past childbearing.

COLLABORATIVE DISCUSSION With a partner, discuss how Swift increases the impact of his satire by making his proposal appear legitimate. Cite specific textual evidence from the essay in support.

SCAFFOLDING FOR ELL STUDENTS

Language: Verb Tense Project lines 278–288 on a whiteboard, explaining that this sentence contains present, future, and present perfect verbs. Mark one example before inviting volunteers to highlight the rest. Guide students to recognize what each tense indicates.

- Highlight present-tense verbs in yellow. *(action taking place in the present)*

- Highlight future-tense verbs in pink. *(action that will take place in the future)*

- Highlight verbs in the present perfect tense in blue. *(action completed in the present)*

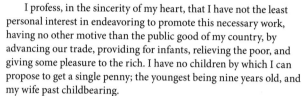

manner I prescribe, and thereby have avoided such a perpetual scene of misfortunes as they have since gone through by the oppression of

Analyze Author's Point of View: Satire

COMMON CORE RL 6, RI 6

Satire is a literary technique in which institutions, practices, or behaviors are ridiculed for the purpose of bringing about reform. The effectiveness of satire depends on the ability of readers to distinguish between what is directly stated and what is really meant.

Although some satirical works are lighthearted and humorous, in "A Modest Proposal," Swift's satire is dark and scathing. He shows his contempt for England's policies in Ireland through the outrageousness of his proposal. To develop his satire, he relies on several literary devices, including the two described in the chart.

Device	Example
Verbal irony occurs when a writer says the opposite of what is meant.	The title of Swift's essay, "A Modest Proposal," is an example of verbal irony because the actual proposal is outrageous rather than reasonable.
Understatement occurs when the writer says less than is expected or appropriate.	Swift says that a plan to hunt boys and girls 12 to 14 years old might be criticized as "a little bordering upon cruelty."

Comprehend Literary Nonfiction: Historical Context

COMMON CORE RI 10

Some literary works, particularly satires, can be more fully appreciated if readers understand the **historical context**—the conditions or events that inspired them. "A Modest Proposal" conveys a universal message about injustice, but its true purpose is to serve as an indictment of English policies in Ireland.

To comprehend Swift's satire, you should examine the footnotes that explain 18th-century references. In addition, keep in mind that at the time Swift was writing, Irish Catholics could not vote, hold public office, buy land, or receive an education. Land was mostly owned by English or Anglo-Irish Protestants, many of whom were absentee landlords. Tenants were forced to pay rent to these landlords, even during the years when the crops failed. Little money paid to the English found its way back into the Irish economy. Swift had protested these injustices before the publication of "A Modest Proposal." In fact, he actually presented the solutions that he ironically dismisses in lines 236–241 of the satire, but his ideas were not accepted. "A Modest Proposal" was his last great published satire that attempted to right the wrongs he saw.

TEACH

CLOSE READ

Analyze Author's Point of View: Satire

COMMON CORE RL 6, RI 6

To make sure that students understand and can recognize verbal irony and understatement, organize them into small groups. Have them review the essay looking for examples of both. Together, complete a chart on the board with the examples contributed by each group. Discuss how the tone of the narrator is designed to deepen the irony; he presents each statement as serious, but readers understand Swift's ironic intent. As a class, discuss the idea that each example conveys.

Comprehend Literary Nonfiction: Historical Context

COMMON CORE RI 10

Have students work in pairs to find references in the essay to the various injustices suffered by Irish Catholics in the early 1700s and the economic practices that kept them repressed and deprived. Discuss how knowing the historical context helps them understand and interpret Swift's satire. For example, his reference to the plump young ladies in "foreign fineries" (line 157) makes more sense when readers know that those who profited from Ireland's industries spent their money elsewhere, thus doubly depriving the Irish economy.

Strategies for Annotation    *Annotate it!*

Analyze Author's Point of View: Satire

COMMON CORE RL 6, RI 6

Share these strategies for guided or independent analysis:

- Highlight examples of verbal irony in green.
- Review your highlighting and analyze what Swift is criticizing through this irony.
- Highlight examples of understatement in pink.
- On a note, explain how the understatement conveys Swift's point.

they are every day dying and rotting by cold and famine, and filth and vermin, as fast as can be reasonably expected. And as to the younger laborers, they are now in almost as hopeful a condition.

PRACTICE & APPLY

Analyzing the Text

Possible answers:

1. The tone is very matter-of-fact and businesslike. For example, he says, "a young healthy child well nursed is at a year old a most delicious, nourishing, and wholesome food" and "I have already computed the charge of nursing a beggar's child." His tone, combined with the absurdity of the content, heightens the satire's effectiveness.

2. The idea is that the Irish could be exploited and harvested like livestock as a matter of business. Statistical data develops the idea because it is a component of such a business analysis.

3. In lines 69–70, the narrator says he will "humbly propose" his ideas and that he expects them not to provoke "the least objection," but his proposal involves cannibalizing the children of people he considers inferior, which is both arrogant and highly objectionable. Lines 124–144 introduce "a very worthy person" but then address the unworthy topic of replacing venison with the flesh of older children. In 159–170, Swift sees the country as "happily delivered from the evils to come." This is ironic because he supposes the sufferers would happily cease to exist because their problems would also cease.

4. In lines 71–74 and lines 135–138, Swift uses hyperbole to characterize Americans as barbaric and cannibalistic. His remarks about his American friend are both humorous and shocking because they suggest the man has had "frequent experience" with eating children and has eaten them in many ways—"stewed, roasted, baked, or broiled."

5. Swift's purpose is to reveal the economic, moral, and social failure of England's unethical policies in Ireland. The "digression" is presented as an afterthought but actually reveals the depth of suffering inflicted by England's policies, which Swift wants to reform.

6. Swift rejects proposals that he actually believes are right and reasonable solutions. By denouncing them within the context of satire, he actually enhances their legitimacy.

7. Swift may intend to show that a humanistic awareness is, by its very nature, an important component of addressing social problems. The scientific approach is objective and detached. Swift likely feared that it could be as heartless as the attitudes he satirizes here.

Analyzing the Text

Cite Text Evidence Support your responses with evidence from the selection.

1. **Analyze** Swift uses a fictional narrator to present the proposal in his essay. Describe the tone of this narrator toward the ideas he is proposing, citing words and phrases that reveal his attitude. How does this tone contribute to the effectiveness of the satire?

2. **Infer** What idea about the English view of the Irish does Swift convey through his use of words such as *breeder, carcasses,* and *flesh*? How does his inclusion of statistical data develop this idea?

3. **Analyze** Discuss examples of verbal irony in the following passages:
    *   lines 69–70 ("I shall now . . . least objection.")
    *   lines 124–144 ("A very worthy . . . soever intended.")
    *   lines 159–170 ("Some persons . . . evils to come.")

4. **Analyze** Another device that Swift uses to develop his satire is **hyperbole**, a figure of speech in which the truth is exaggerated for emphasis or to create humor. Identify an example of hyperbole in Swift's essay and describe its effect.

5. **Analyze** Swift says that he has "digressed" in lines 159–170. Explain how this digression actually serves his purpose of exposing English injustice.

6. **Draw Conclusions** Reread lines 236–256, in which Swift dismisses alternate "expedients" as impractical. What point does he make by referring to his own proposals in this way?

7. **Connect** The period from the late 1600s through the 1700s is known as the Enlightenment, a time when many writers promoted scientific reasoning as a means of solving social problems. Swift was often critical of such writers. How is this historical context reflected in "A Modest Proposal"?

PERFORMANCE TASK

Writing Activity: Context Guide Working with a partner, reread the essay to identify a section where you need more historical context to understand Swift's references.

*   With your partner, research the history behind a certain reference or passage in the text.
*   Record the line numbers of your reference or passage and your sources on a sheet of paper.
*   Take notes about your findings and write a short summary statement.

*   Review your work for accuracy and standard English grammar and usage. Then share it with the class.
*   Gather all notes and summaries into a "Context Guide" folder to help other students who read "A Modest Proposal."

Assign this performance task.

PERFORMANCE TASK

Writing Activity: Context Guide Review the text with the class as needed to find sections that assume an awareness of historical context for full understanding. List possible passages on the board and suggest that students choose one to ensure that there is as little overlapping as possible. Remind them to use reference works, credible websites, and history textbooks to find their information. Encourage them to check two sources for accuracy.

Critical Vocabulary

prodigious	rudiment	collateral
scrupulous	inducement	

Practice and Apply Choose the situation that fits the meaning of the Critical Vocabulary word. Explain your decision.

1. If you have a *prodigious* talent for satire, would people reject your work or want to read it?

2. What would be an *inducement* to the English to settle in Ireland, the offer of land or the inability to understand the language?

3. What is a *rudiment* of farming, grinding the wheat or preparing the soil?

4. If a landlord is *scrupulous*, would he live on site or visit his tenants every few years?

5. What is *collateral* damage from a famine, higher food prices or diseased crops?

Vocabulary Strategy: Context Clues

Context clues are often found in the words and sentences around an unknown term. A context clue may consist of definition or restatement of the meaning of the unfamiliar word, an example following the word, a comparison or contrast, or a nearby synonym. The unknown word's position or function in a sentence can also be a clue.

For example, the placement and suffix of the Critical Vocabulary word *prodigious* in line 10 tell you that it is an adjective. Knowing this makes the word easier to define. The Vocabulary word *inducement* appears in this sentence with the context clue "encouraged": "Sixthly, this would be a great inducement to marriage, which all wise nations have either encouraged by rewards or enforced by laws and penalties." After using context clues to get a preliminary understanding of a word, you can verify the word's meaning by looking it up in a dictionary.

Practice and Apply Use the context clues in each sentence to define the italicized words from the essay. Check your meanings in a dictionary.

1. Their *sustenance*, a bland potato soup, kept them alive through the winter.

2. He *reckoned* the cost of raising a child, computing it to the penny.

3. The *inclemency* of the country's weather, the bitter wind and constant rain, added to the misery of those who lacked shelter.

4. Those who crave such a delicacy would not *repine* for an instant at the thought of spending the money.

PRACTICE & APPLY

Critical Vocabulary

Answers:

1. *They would want to read works by a great talent.*

2. *The offer of land would encourage the English to come to Ireland.*

3. *A basic principle of farming is that the soil must be prepared before the crops are planted.*

4. *He would live on site, to more carefully look out for his tenants' welfare.*

5. *According to the principle of supply and demand, a shortage of food would have the side effect of leading to higher prices.*

Vocabulary Strategy: Context Clues

Answers:

1. Sustenance *means "necessary nourishment or means of sustaining life."*

2. Reckoned *means "calculated."*

3. Inclemency *means "storminess or mercilessness."*

4. Repine *means "complain or be unhappy."*

Word Sharp   Have students complete the tutorial(s) in this lesson: **Context Clues: Synonym and Restatement.**

SCAFFOLDING FOR ELL STUDENTS

Vocabulary: Context Clues Write the first Practice and Apply sentence on the board. Invite volunteers to mark it up.

- Underline the suffix *-ance.*
- Highlight in yellow the context clues.

Point out that the suffix indicates that *sustenance* is a noun. Guide students to define it as "food" or "source of nourishment" using the context clue "potato soup."

ASK STUDENTS to work in pairs to complete the exercise. Circulate around the room to check that they are implementing the strategy successfully.

PRACTICE & APPLY

Language and Style: Active and Passive Voice

COMMON CORE L 3a

Give students additional practice in forming the active and passive voices by writing these verbs on the board: *avoid, propose.* Invite volunteers to write two sentences for each that show passive and active voice. *(Sample answers: The passers-by avoided the beggar. / The beggar was avoided by most passers-by. / The politician proposed abolishing the tax. / Abolishing the tax was proposed by the politician.)*

Possible answers:

Students' sentences should demonstrate an understanding of the passive and active voices. Comparisons of the two forms should demonstrate the stronger, more engaging qualities of the sentences containing active verbs.

 If students need further instruction, use *GrammarNotes Lesson 11:* **Using Active and Passive Voice.**

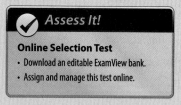

✓ **Assess It!**

Online Selection Test
- Download an editable ExamView bank.
- Assign and manage this test online.

Language and Style: Active and Passive Voice

COMMON CORE L 3a

Swift uses both active and passive voice in his essay. When a verb is in the **active voice**, the subject performs the action. When the verb is in the **passive voice**, the subject is the receiver of the action. The passive voice is formed with the verb *to be* and the past participle of a verb. Typically, the active voice is preferred because it conveys more energy and is more direct. To develop a more formal tone fitting for his proposal, however, Swift turns to the passive voice.

Read these sentences from the essay.

> It is agreed by all parties that this prodigious number of children . . . is a very great additional grievance.

> I am assured by our merchants that a boy or girl before twelve years old is no salable commodity.

Swift could have chosen to use the active voice in both sentences:

> All parties agree that this prodigious number of children . . . is a very great additional grievance.

> Our merchants assure me that a boy or girl before twelve years old is no salable commodity.

Altering the verb from passive to active makes the writing more vigorous and less like the bureacratic language that might be used in a real proposal. Sometimes, the passive voice is preferred for other reasons as explained in the chart.

Uses of Passive Voice	
Purpose	**Example**
to emphasize the receiver of the action	The truce was shattered by the accidental firing.
when the doer of the action is not known or not important	The votes were counted.

Practice and Apply Write four sentences about "A Modest Proposal" in passive voice. Exchange sentences with a partner and rewrite each other's sentences in active voice. Compare the differences between the two versions.

WHEN STUDENTS STRUGGLE . . .

Project these sentences on the board:

The proposal _____ by the narrator. (present)

The profit _____ carefully by the narrator. (calculate)

Readers _____ by Swift's essay. (shock)

It _____ a brilliant satire by critics today. (consider)

Have students complete each sentence with the passive voice. Then guide them to identify the word that will be the subject of the sentence in the active voice. Provide sentence stems and have students complete them independently. Discuss the differences.

Analyze and Evaluate Structure

COMMON CORE
RI 5

TEACH

Discuss with students how the structure of Swift's essay contributes to its effectiveness. Because it is presented as a serious argument, it succeeds in its intent of catching readers' attention and emphasizing both the problem and the lack of solutions. Review these structural elements with students:

- **Problem:** In this type of argument, the problem is presented first with an explanation of its causes. This makes readers aware of the pressing need to solve the problem.

- **Claim:** The claim is the statement that reveals the writer's position on the issue and his or her belief about what should be done. In this essay, the claim takes the form of a proposal, or a proposed solution to the problem already set forth.

- **Reasons:** To convince readers to accept the claim, writers give logical reasons, or statements that justify and defend their view of the solution.

- **Evidence:** To be convincing, reasons must be supported with evidence. This evidence may include description, examples, statistics, facts, the testimony of experts, or other relevant details.

- **Counterargument:** An argument is made more persuasive if the writer anticipates objections to his or her argument and answers them in advance.

COLLABORATIVE DISCUSSION

Have students work in pairs to identify and evaluate each component of an argument in Swift's essay. Have them discuss how this organization clarifies and strengthens his satire. *(Problem and causes: lines 1–68; Claim: lines 70-90; Reasons and evidence: lines 171–223; Counterargument: lines 230–256)*

 If students need further instruction, use this *Interactive Whiteboard Lesson:* **Evaluating Arguments.**

Analyze Author's Point of View: Satire

COMMON CORE
RL 6,
RI 6

RETEACH

Review these terms related to satire: *verbal irony, understatement, hyperbole.* Then have students return to the illustration on page 204.

- Ask students to work together to write captions for the illustration that use verbal irony, understatement, and hyperbole.

- Have them share their examples with the class. *(Sample answers: Verbal irony: The problems of the poor weighed heavily on the minds of the banquet guests. Understatement: We just stopped by for a light snack. Hyperbole: He had the appetite of fifty men and inhaled his dinner in the blink of an eye.)*

- Discuss how the illustration provides a satirical comment on the topic of the essay as well.

 LEVEL UP TUTORIALS Assign the following *Level Up* tutorial: **Irony**

CLOSE READING APPLICATION

Have students work independently to find an example of modern satire, such as an article in a publication that parodies newspapers, a cartoon, or even a clip from a satirical news show. Have them explain what is being satirized and the techniques used to convey this satire.

Who Speaks for the 1%?

Article by Joel Stein

Why This Text

Some students may have difficulty fully comprehending satirical texts—texts with a literal meaning very different from the author's intended meaning. The article "Who Speaks for the 1%?" is such a text. On the surface, the author seems to defend the very wealthy and to criticize the middle class and poor for causing the financial recession. With the help of the close-reading questions, students will analyze the author's claims and arguments to develop a clear understanding of the author's real message, which is in fact very different from what it appears to be.

Background Have students read the background information about the Occupy Wall Street movement. Explain that "Wall Street" refers to the financial district in New York City located on Wall Street and on surrounding streets. There, billions of dollars are invested daily in companies around the world. The people who invest these large sums of money are generally wealthy and become even richer through their investments. The Occupy movement occurred in the midst of the financial recession that began in the United States in 2008 and that resulted in widespread unemployment.

AS YOU READ Ask students to pay close attention to the claims the author makes while developing his argument. Encourage students to consider whether or not the author really means what he says.

Common Core Support

- determine an author's point of view or purpose
- read and comprehend literary nonfiction
- distinguish what is stated in text from what is really meant

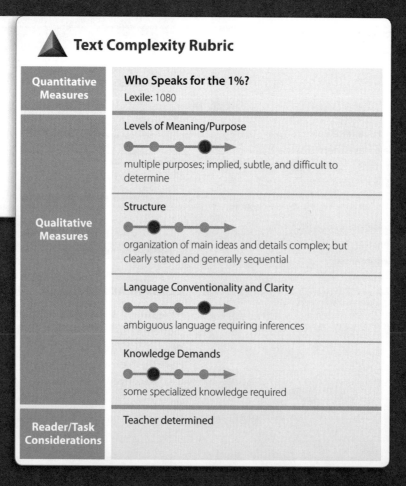

Text Complexity Rubric

Quantitative Measures

Who Speaks for the 1%?
Lexile: 1080

Qualitative Measures

Levels of Meaning/Purpose

multiple purposes; implied, subtle, and difficult to determine

Structure

organization of main ideas and details complex; but clearly stated and generally sequential

Language Conventionality and Clarity

ambiguous language requiring inferences

Knowledge Demands

some specialized knowledge required

Reader/Task Considerations

Teacher determined

Strategies for CLOSE READING

Analyze Author's Point of View: Satire

Students should read this article carefully all the way through. Close-reading questions at the bottom of the page will guide them to an understanding of the text. As they read, students should jot down comments or questions about the text in the margins.

WHEN STUDENTS STRUGGLE . . .

To help students determine the author's point of view in "Who Speaks for the 1%?," have them work in small groups to fill out a chart like the one shown below.

CITE TEXT EVIDENCE For practice in grasping the author's point of view, ask students to explain the difference between what the author says and what the author means.

What the Author Says	What the Author Means
"I don't like the top 1% of anything." (line 1)	The examples that the author gives (intelligence, fun, and thoughtfulness) to prove his point are clearly things people value and appreciate. This tells the reader that the author does not mean it when he says that he doesn't "like the top 1% of anything."
"Part of the reason I'm defending the 1% is that . . . the 1% are available for some serious networking." (lines 18–20)	The examples the author gives to prove his point (Kathy Griffin and Mark Cuban) are so ridiculous that you know his defense of the 1% is not serious and that what he means is actually the opposite.
". . . these days the 1% don't live that differently than the middle class does." (lines 31–32)	The examples that the author gives to prove his point (wine, cars, TV, and movie watching habits) are so silly that the reader immediately knows he is not being serious and means just the opposite of what he says.

Background In September 2011, protestors calling themselves Occupy Wall Street encamped in Zuccotti Park in New York City. The group's slogan "We are the 99%" took aim at the power of the rich (the 1%) and the systems that further their interests. The Occupy movement quickly spread to other cities and countries, addressing the growing income inequality between the wealthiest 1% and the rest of the population. In the following satire, journalist Joel Stein takes a stab at speaking for the 1%.

Who Speaks for the 1%?

Article by Joel Stein

CLOSE READ
Notes

1. **READ ▶** As you read lines 1–11, begin to collect and cite text evidence.

   • Circle the opening statement of the article.
   • In the margin, explain the verbal irony in lines 1–2.
   • Underline the use of exaggeration in lines 5–8, and in the margin, explain what the author is ridiculing.

Ⓐ I don't like the top 1% of anything. Intelligence? Boring! Fun? Exhausting! Thoughtfulness? Annoying! Hairiness? Too hairy!

So I get why the Occupy Wall Street protesters gained momentum with their slogan WE ARE THE 99%. Everyone loves the 99%. You can have a beer with the 99%. You can eat with your hands in front of the 99%. You can talk about TV shows with the 99% without them telling you that while they don't think there's anything wrong with TV, if they had one, they would watch it literally all the time, so it's better to just not keep one in the house.

Ⓑ 10 But I've met some of the top 1%, and on average, they're interesting, generous and charming. You know who is in the top 1%? Tom Hanks. You know who is in the bottom 99%? Not Tom Hanks.

His complaints are the opposite of what one expects.

He is ridiculing snobbery about TV habits.

45

1. **READ AND CITE TEXT EVIDENCE** Remind students that writers of satire often use verbal irony (statements in which what is said is the opposite of what is meant) and exaggeration to express their meaning.

   Ⓐ ASK STUDENTS to describe in their own words what the author says in lines 1 and 2. *He says intelligence bores him, having fun is tiring, sensitive people get on his nerves, and hairiness is too hairy.* How can you tell that the author is being ironic? *The examples he gives of the top 1% are nonsensical.*

He thinks of the 1% as necessary, and the 99 percenters as boring.

It's not just that we admire the 1%. We need them. The 1% started Time Inc., creating my job. They founded Stanford, where I went to college. They funded Facebook and my mortgage. They created the Bill & Melinda Gates Foundation, bankrolled most great art, paid for medical research and created genius grants. No one has ever woken up early to gather around a TV to watch a wedding of two 99 percenters.

Part of the reason I'm defending the 1% is that while all the other journalists waste their time with the Occupy Wall Street losers, the 1% are available for some serious networking. But when I started talking to them, I learned that for all their supposed power, they are now too afraid to stand up for themselves. When I asked Kathy Griffin[1] to explain why she and her fellow 1 percenters are a boon to society, she said, "I wouldn't touch that topic with a 10-foot pole made out of $100 bills I made from Suddenly Susan Season 2." Mark Cuban,[2] the billionaire owner of the Dallas Mavericks who isn't even afraid of NBA refs, said, "I think there are financial engineers that add no value and fit the Occupy Wall Street stereotypes. They are the 1% of the 1% that mess it up for everyone." In other words, Cuban is going with the rallying cry, "We are the 99.99%."

[1] **Kathy Griffin:** a popular comedienne who appeared on the TV show *Suddenly Susan.*
[2] **Mark Cuban:** American businessman and investor. As owner of the Dallas Mavericks, Cuban has been fined numerous times by the National Basketball Association (NBA) for critical statements about the league and its referees.

2. ◀ REREAD Reread lines 9–11. Why does the author use Tom Hanks as an example of the 1%? How are these lines sarcastic? Support your answer with explicit textual evidence.

He uses Tom Hanks as an example of the 1% and claims he is "interesting, generous and charming." He assumes his readers also like Hanks and agree that he possesses those qualities. The author's only claim about the 99% is they are "not Tom Hanks" which is sarcastic because it doesn't say anything about who makes up the 99%.

3. READ ▶ As you read lines 12–29, continue to cite textual evidence.

- Circle the author's references to himself in lines 12–17.
- In the margin, explain his point of view in lines 12–17.
- Underline the words and phrases in lines 18–29 that express judgment of others.

46

I get that we need someone to blame.

So I guess it's up to me to point out that all this anger about income inequality is misplaced because, unlike any other time in history, these days the 1% don't live that differently than the middle class does. Never before has $10 wine tasted so much like $1,000 bottles—and the $10 bottles come with pictures of cute animals! A $15,000 car breaks down as rarely as one that costs $250,000 and has far more cup holders. The middle class and the rich watch the same stuff on TV and in movie theaters, have equal access to Wikipedia and pay the same college graduates to do nothing but make us complicated coffee drinks. It is so difficult for the 1% to live differently that they have to collect art. Collecting art is so boring, there aren't any reality shows about it.

I get that we need someone to blame. Everyone loves the banker when they're borrowing and hates him when they have to pay him back. They also hate him when he claims to have mixed up the orange $500s with the light peach $100s and suddenly has a lot of cash even though he owns only Vermont and Oriental Avenues. I don't know a lot about banking. But I do not believe that the worldwide recession was caused by financial derivatives created by the 1% who tricked the innocent 99%. I believe it was created by the great wide middle class who took out loans to live out the techno-bling dream we deified in rap songs and reality TV. Credit-card debt went up 75% from 1997 to 2007. We're now a nation of really poor people with a lot of frequent-flier miles.

The Tea Party and Occupy Wall Street are both right: We need government to get smaller and bigger. I'd argue for slashing middle-class entitlements but also adding services for migrant workers and that new poverty-stricken

He blames the middle class for taking out loans and using credit cards.

4. ◀ REREAD AND DISCUSS Reread lines 12–29. With a small group, discuss the author's use of examples from popular culture to advance his point of view. How do these examples add to the satire?

5. READ ▶ As you read lines 30–63, continue to cite textual evidence. Underline examples the author gives of the supposed similarities between the 1% and the middle class. In the margin, explain who he blames for income inequality.

47

---

2. **REREAD AND CITE TEXT EVIDENCE**

B **ASK STUDENTS** why they think Tom Hanks is in the top 1%. *He is a very successful movie star, so he is very rich.* How does the author describe the 99%? What does that imply? *He says they are not Tom Hanks—implying that they are not worth considering.*

3. **READ AND CITE TEXT EVIDENCE** In line 19, the author refers to the Occupy Wall Street protesters as "losers."

C **ASK STUDENTS** if the author really thinks that the Occupy Wall Street protesters are "losers." Remind them to cite text evidence to support their answer. *He gives no explanation for calling the protesters losers and then cites made-up statements by members of the 1%, by implication proving that they and people like them are the real losers.*

4. **REREAD AND DISCUSS USING TEXT EVIDENCE** Ask students to assign a reporter to each group to present its response. Building on the previous analysis of the author's point of view, have students discuss techniques used by the author, such as verbal irony and exaggeration, to communicate his thoughts.

D **ASK STUDENTS** about the examples of the 1% that the author cites in lines 12–17. What do they have in common? *Many of them have personally benefited the author, or they are things that the author himself supports.*

5. **READ AND CITE TEXT EVIDENCE** In lines 40–49, the author says the middle class is to blame for the worldwide recession.

E **ASK STUDENTS** to cite text evidence in lines 40–49 that reveals what the author really thinks. *Students may cite references to the game Monopoly in lines 41–44 or the description in line 49 of a nation "of really poor people with a lot of frequent-flier miles" as examples of evidence the writer is not serious.*

CLOSE READ Notes

He satirizes his own ability to understand the national debt problem.

He makes a satiric indictment of "the besieged 1 percenters."

Muppet, Lily, who has to live on the same street as a monster who shoves cookies into his mouth just to let them fall right out.

But even I, who scored only in the 95th percentile on my math SAT, know that we are not going to dig out of our nation's debt just by jacking up taxes on the 1%. Raising their tax rate won't change the overall debt that much. We are **(F)** all going to have to pay more and take less. Except for Lily. That poor girl can have whatever she wants.

60 Until people calm down and realize that, we should do something nice for the besieged 1 percenters. Invite Mark Zuckerberg to join you on FarmVille. Let Rupert Murdoch listen to your voice mail. Watch that silly Oprah network. At least until they get through this hard time.

6. **◀ REREAD** Reread lines 55–63. In the margin, explain who the author is making fun of, and why.

SHORT RESPONSE

Cite Text Evidence What do you think is the author's real point of view on the economic crisis? What is he really satirizing? Review your reading notes, and evaluate the author's style. **Cite evidence from the text** in your response.

The author is satirizing the 1%, and also blaming them for the economic crisis. Although he names well-respected representatives of the 1% (Tom Hanks and Bill Gates, for example), he also puts forward satirical arguments on their behalf that are self-defeating—he proposes that the commodities that the 99% enjoy are as good as those the 1% enjoy; he blames the 99% for being lured into devious loans made attractive by the 1%. The author also mocks the 1% by explaining that they are "besieged," and cleverly points out that he really doesn't have a clue about what he is saying.

48

TO CHALLENGE STUDENTS . . .

To give students more context on the "99%" and the "1%," tell students that the slogan "We are the 99%" was launched by Occupy Wall Street, a movement that began in 2011. The movement protested economic inequality and the influence of government by financial services companies.

ASK STUDENTS to research the Occupy movement and the 2008 financial crisis that had at its center Wall Street investment banks. Have students report on what investment banks do and how they make their money—and how the financial crisis affected the banks and their clients. Students should also report on what Occupy achieved and how far its message traveled.

DIG DEEPER

With the class, return to Question 4, Reread and Discuss. Have students share their responses.

ASK STUDENTS to cite the text evidence that helped them understand the author's point of view and message. Have them cite specific examples of techniques used by the author (such as verbal irony or exaggeration) and explain how those techniques helped them to discern the author's real message.

ASK STUDENTS to return to their answer to the Short Response and revise it based on the class discussion.

---

6. 〔 REREAD AND CITE TEXT EVIDENCE 〕

(F) **ASK STUDENTS** which people the author suggests we should invite into our lives and offer comfort to. *He names Mark Zuckerberg, Rupert Murdoch, and Oprah.* What do these people have in common? What does the author really think? *The people he mentioned are immensely wealthy, and are in no way "besieged." Feeling sorry for them is pointless.*

FOR ELL STUDENTS Explain that *deified* means "made a god of; worshiped." Point out to Spanish-speaking students that it comes from the same root as the Spanish word for *god* (*dios*).

SHORT RESPONSE

Cite Text Evidence Students should:

- explain the author's point of view about the economic crisis.
- explain who or what the author is satirizing.
- evaluate the author's style.

mySmartPlanner Create lesson plans and access resources online.

Third World America

Photojournalism by Alison Wright

Why This Text?

Students regularly encounter photojournalism in print, online, or in broadcast media. This lesson explores photojournalism that uses images and words to present a picture of poverty in America.

Key Learning Objective: The student will be able to integrate and evaluate information presented in words and photographs.

 Common Core Standards

RI 6 Determine an author's purpose.
RI 7 Integrate and evaluate information presented in different media.
SL 4 Present information, conveying a clear and distinct perspective.
SL 5 Make strategic use of digital media in presentations.

Text Complexity Rubric

Quantitative Measures	**Third World America** Lexile: 1260L
Qualitative Measures	**Levels of Meaning/Purpose** 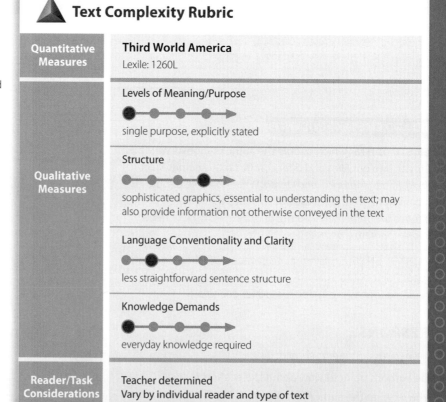 single purpose, explicitly stated
	Structure sophisticated graphics, essential to understanding the text; may also provide information not otherwise conveyed in the text
	Language Conventionality and Clarity less straightforward sentence structure
	Knowledge Demands everyday knowledge required
Reader/Task Considerations	Teacher determined Vary by individual reader and type of text

CLOSE READ

Alison Wright Have students read the information about the photojournalist. Explain that Wright has won prestigious awards for her work, including the Dorothea Lange Award in Documentary Photography and the Lowell Thomas Travel Journalism Award. Wright has also created the Faces of Hope Fund to help children in need around the world receive medical care and education.

AS YOU VIEW Instruct students to use the As You View note to focus their viewing. Remind them to write down any questions they generate as they view the selection.

Integrate and Evaluate Information (LINES 1–17)

 COMMON CORE RI 7

Explain that this selection contains words and images, and students need to bring information from both types of media together to evaluate the author's meaning and purpose. Students will need to make **inferences,** or logical assumptions based on details in the selection and their own knowledge and experience, to reach their conclusions.

Ⓐ CITE TEXT EVIDENCE Ask students to reread lines 1–10 and identify examples of "social and ethnic borders." *("black families of the Mississippi Delta," a single mother working a low-wage job in Ohio, "food bank in Appalachia," "migrant workers . . . in Texas," and "Indians on a Navaho reservation . . . [with] no running water or electricity")* Ask them to explain Wright's purpose in using these examples. *(She wants to show that poverty affects people of many ethnic groups in different parts of the country.)*

Ⓑ ASK STUDENTS to reread lines 11–17 and explain how Wright compares poverty in America to poverty in other parts of the world. *(In developing countries, poor people are thin, but in America, obesity and related health problems are the issue for poor people because they have a diet lacking proper nutrition and can't afford healthcare.)* Then ask students to connect this paragraph to the title. *("Third World" is a term sometimes used to describe the poorest developing countries. Wright suggests that parts of America, one of the wealthiest developed countries, are like the Third World because poverty is a major problem that affects people's health.)*

Alison Wright is a photojournalist whose work has taken her around the world. Her photographs capture people struggling for survival and coping with human-rights issues. She also records traditions of changing cultures to preserve them. Her pictures have appeared in many publications including National Geographic *magazine. In addition, her photos and writing have been published in several books. One of her books recounts her recovery after surviving a life-threatening bus accident in Laos.*

MEDIA ANALYSIS

Third World America

Photojournalism by Alison Wright

AS YOU VIEW Notice details in the photographs that provide insight into the living conditions of the people shown in them.

Ⓐ This project covers an array of social and ethnic borders; the black families of the Mississippi Delta who live in the first town started after slavery was abolished; the struggles of a single woman raising three children on the minimum wage while working at Wendy's in Ohio; the food bank in Appalachia where 800 cars a day line up for groceries; migrant workers who live in Texas and raise children in this country so they can have a better life as American citizens; Indians on a Navaho reservation who instill a cultural sense of pride to their children in the native powwows, yet have no running water or electricity in their basic hogans.

10 The face of poverty in this country is not the rail thin visage as in developing countries, but due to such a poor innutritious diet, obesity is a ubiquitous problem. Children's health is so affected that diabetes is prevalent, and many are overweight with severe psychological problems. With the cost of living outweighing the average income, many families across America are just one pay check away from being on the edge, especially when it comes to healthcare issues. Ⓑ

Image Credits: ©Pete Ryan/Getty Images

Third World America **213**

SCAFFOLDING FOR ELL STUDENTS

Culture: Comprehension Support Have students work in pairs or small groups with native English speakers to read Wright's introduction together. They may wish to refer to a map of the United States and discuss the meanings of these phrases:

- "Mississippi Delta . . . after slavery was abolished"
- "minimum wage while working at Wendy's in Ohio"
- "food bank in Appalachia"
- "migrant workers who live in Texas"
- "Indians on a Navaho reservation . . . native powwows"
- "one pay check away from being on the edge"

CLOSE READ

Integrate and Evaluate Information

COMMON CORE RI 7

Explain that a photographer's choices about what to include in an image—such as people, props, and setting—and the way he or she takes the photograph are tools used to communicate a message.

C **CITE TEXT EVIDENCE** Ask students what the details in the room reveal about the children's lives. *(The furniture is very simple with basic linens on the beds, and part of the ceiling is falling down, showing that they have limited income and resources. The items on the wall show that they try to bring some beauty into their lives. The cross suggests that religion is important to them.)* Why did the photographer choose to photograph the children in a group rather than individually? *(She wants to emphasize that all seven children, who are very close in age, sleep in this one small bedroom and must sleep at least two to each bed.)*

Mood Tell students that **mood** is the atmosphere created in a photograph through lighting, setting, and props. Mood is the way the viewer feels when looking at the photograph. Explain that **captions** may add to or change the viewer's understanding of the photograph.

D **ASK STUDENTS** to cover the caption, study the image only, and describe what they think it shows. What mood has the photographer created? *(Students may say that it shows shoppers at a warehouse store. The long line of people waiting in the stark, shed-like structure suggests an anxious, apprehensive mood. The interaction of the women with the baby in the cart adds some lightness to the mood and suggests a feeling of community.)* Then ask students to read the caption and ask how it affects their understanding of the photograph. *(Students might say that knowing this is a food bank rather than a store makes them realize that these people are dependent on the free food in order for their families to survive. Knowing that the food bank serves such a large number of people per day emphasizes that this long line is not an isolated example and that there are large numbers of poor people in the area.)*

C

Texas: The bedroom for seven children, Rio Grande Valley.

D

Ohio, Appalachia: This foodbank feeds over 1,000 people per day.

214 Collection 3

APPLYING ACADEMIC VOCABULARY

convince	radical

As you discuss Wright's text and photographs, incorporate the Collection 3 academic vocabulary words *convince* and *radical*. To probe Wright's purpose, ask students to explain what Wright might be trying to **convince** viewers to understand about poverty in America. In addition, ask students whether Wright's point of view might be considered **radical,** and why.

Arizona: This family lives in a bus with no electricity or water on a Navaho Indian reservation.

Mississippi Delta: Woman raising her children alone.

COLLABORATIVE DISCUSSION With a partner, share your impressions of the people in the photographs. Cite specific details from the photos to support your discussion.

WHEN STUDENTS STRUGGLE...

To guide students' analysis of each photograph, have them work in pairs to answer these questions, based on 5*W*s and an *H*.

- Who is shown in the photograph?
- What else is shown in the photograph?
- Where was the photograph taken?
- When was the photograph taken?
- Why were these subjects photographed in this particular way?
- How did the photographer pose and light the subjects?

CLOSE READ

Integrate and Evaluate Information

 COMMON CORE RI 7

Invite students again to notice the choices Wright makes in each of her photographs.

E **ASK STUDENTS** to study the photograph of the Navaho family and infer why she might have photographed them from a middle distance rather than more close-up. (*She wanted to show the starkness and isolation of their living situation; from this distance viewers can see their inadequate living quarters against a cold, harsh landscape.*) Then ask why Wright might have chosen to photograph the family outside the bus in winter rather than showing them inside the bus. (*Photographing them in winter reveals how difficult it is to survive with no electricity or water when it is cold and snowy. Photographing the outside of the bus shows the viewer something familiar in an unfamiliar context—a bus is not usually considered a place to live. The outside shot also reveals the generator that may give them a little heat.*)

Explain that a photo essay like this one has a cumulative effect as the photos combine to tell a story and allow viewers to find common themes.

F **CITE TEXT EVIDENCE** Ask students to compare the photo of the woman and her two children with the photo of the seven children in the first photo. What details reveal similarities in their situations? (*In both photographs, the furniture is very basic and rather worn, as are the walls. Both families decorate their walls with items that are meaningful although not of high monetary value.*) Ask students to compare the ways the subjects are posed in the two photographs and what effect this arrangement has. (*Subjects are posed in tight groups, but they are not interacting with each other. Instead, they look directly into the camera with expressions that are stoic, even sad. The mood is one of lonely endurance in the face of great challenge.*)

COLLABORATIVE DISCUSSION Have students jot down their own impressions of the people in the photographs before sharing with a partner. Then have them share their conclusions with the class as a whole.

ASK STUDENTS to share any questions they generated in the course of viewing and discussing the selection.

Integrate and Evaluate Information

Call on volunteers to read aloud the description of each photographic element. Ask students to explain what to look for in their own words.

Analyzing the Media

Possible answers:

1. *Wright's wide angles present her subjects in context to convey the conditions with which they struggle. In the first photograph, viewers see the crumbling ceiling and the children's small beds. The photo of the food bank demonstrates the sheer number of people needing help. The snow and the shabby school bus stun viewers with the reality of what the family must cope with daily. The last photo emphasizes the darkness of the family's life through the darkness of the setting. By including details of setting, Wright imprints her message about poverty on viewers.*

2. *The captions include facts that help viewers better understand the images. They refer to specific sentences in the introduction, helping viewers unify the written and visual information and appreciate the severity of each situation.*

3. *Responses will depend upon the photo selected, but students should support their interpretations and opinions with specific references to visual elements.*

4. *Wright's style might be described as realistic. She avoids special lighting effects to emphasize the grim reality her subjects face. She includes children to show that they are the ones most afflicted by poverty in America. While people remain the focal point of her images, she carefully establishes the background to convey important ideas about their lives. The mood of each photo might be called somber or grim. The expressions on the faces of the subjects reinforce this mood. They face the camera the same way they face their lives, unflinchingly but without much hope.*

Assess It!

Online Selection Test
- Download an editable ExamView bank.
- Assign and manage this test online.

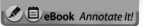

Integrate and Evaluate Information

In her photo essay, Alison Wright uses text and images to communicate her message about poverty in America. In order to appreciate the meaning conveyed by each photo as well as their cumulative effect, viewers need to analyze the following elements:

- **Camera angle:** Does Wright take close-up shots or use a wider angle? How does this choice affect what viewers see in the photographs?
- **Subject:** Does Wright show people in isolation or photograph them in groups? What do their poses suggest about them? How does the surrounding text enhance the information in the photos?
- **Lighting:** A photographer might create an effect through lighting. What choices does Wright make in these photos?
- **Mood:** Through lighting, choice of setting, and props, a photographer can create a particular mood, or atmosphere, that helps convey a message.

Analyzing the Media

Cite Text Evidence   Support your responses with evidence from the selection.

1. **Analyze** Explain why Wright chooses a wider angle from which to view her subjects. How does this view enhance readers' understanding of the context of each photograph?

2. **Analyze** How do the captions add to the effectiveness of the photo essay? What is the relationship between the captions and the introductory text?

3. **Cite Evidence** Choose one photograph, and explain how it communicates Wright's message. Identify details that help convey the meaning.

4. **Critique** Describe the photographer's style as revealed through this series of photographs, commenting on her choice of subjects, the use of lighting, and the mood conveyed by each. How is Wright's style related to her purpose?

PERFORMANCE TASK

Media Activity: Photo Essay With a partner, create your own photo essay to convince an audience of your perspective on an aspect of poverty in the United States.

- Conduct research and find or take photographs to illustrate your point. Be sure to consider copyright restrictions.
- Write a brief preface, assemble the photographs, and write captions.
- Display your photo essay in a gallery in the classroom.

Assign this performance task.

PERFORMANCE TASK

Media Activity: Photo Essay Before students begin collecting their photos, lead a discussion in which volunteers suggest potentially evocative scenes and topics. Remind students that they need not adhere to Alison Wright's style or compositional methods, but they should thoughtfully choose their photos. Their prefaces and captions should inform and contribute to the main idea. Remind students that they need to get permission from any subjects they wish to photograph themselves.

Determine Author's Purpose

RI 6

TEACH

Ask students to consider the work that went into producing Alison Wright's photo essay. She traveled to at least four states—Texas, Ohio, Arizona, and Mississippi. She identified the subjects she wanted to photograph, gained their permission and their trust, and made an effort to set up each photograph to achieve a particular effect. Why did she go to all this trouble? Like the author of a story or an article, a photojournalist has a **purpose** or reason for creating a photo essay. Often this purpose has to do with presenting a specific **point of view** or perspective on some aspect of the world today.

Remind students of the four elements they explored in the lesson: camera angle, subject, lighting, and mood. Point out that a photojournalist's choice of subject provides the most obvious clue to his or her purpose for taking a photograph. Camera angle, lighting, and the mood created by these techniques give further clues to the photographer's point of view on the subject.

PRACTICE AND APPLY

Organize students into small groups. Have each group discuss these questions:

- What does the title of the photo essay suggest about Wright's purpose? *(By juxtaposing "third world" with the name of one of the world's wealthiest nations, Wright is drawing attention to the surprising fact that so much poverty exists in the United States.)*
- Why did Wright choose to include subjects from several different states rather than focusing on a single region? *(This shows that the problem of poverty is widespread. People throughout the country are suffering.)*
- How does the photographer's use of camera angles and lighting support her purpose? *(Wright shoots her subjects from a medium-wide angle so that viewers can see and connect with people's facial expressions but also take in their impoverished surroundings. The lighting, whether interior or exterior, is natural, which also helps viewers connect with the subjects.)*

Have groups share their answers to the questions in a class discussion. Then have the class draw a conclusion about Alison Wright's overall purpose for creating the photo essay.

Integrate and Evaluate Information

RI 7

RETEACH

Review the terms *camera angle, subject, lighting,* and *mood.* Invite students to share an example of a photograph they have recently taken or present an example from a print or online source. Discuss how the terms apply to each photograph by exploring these questions:

- What is the subject of the photograph? Why might the photographer have chosen this subject?
- How would you describe the camera angle? Why might the photographer have chosen to shoot the subject from this particular angle?
- Does the lighting come from the sun or from an artificial source? Does it emphasize something in particular?
- What feelings are conveyed by the photograph?

 LEVEL UP TUTORIALS Assign the following *Level Up* tutorial: **Analyzing Visuals**

CLOSE READING APPLICATION

Students can apply the skill to a photograph from a print or online source. Encourage them to write a paragraph about the photograph in which they include each of the elements they have studied. Ask: What was the photographer's purpose in taking the photograph? How does he or she achieve that purpose?

Imagine the Angels of Bread

Poem by Martín Espada

Why This Text?

Students are probably familiar with orators, journalists, and essayists who seek to expose and address injustice. This lesson explores how poetry can serve as a political tool in this example by award–winning poet Martín Espada.

Key Learning Objective: The student will be able to analyze the impact of word choice on meaning and tone in the poem.

For additional practice:

Worktext selection
"Elsewhere"
Poem by Derek Walcott

COMMON CORE Common Core Standards

RL 1 Cite textual evidence.
RL 4 Analyze the impact of word choices on meaning and tone.
W 10 Write for a range of tasks, purposes, and audiences.
L 3 Apply knowledge of language in different contexts

▲ Text Complexity Rubric

Quantitative Measures	**Imagine the Angels of Bread** Lexile: N/A
Qualitative Measures	**Levels of Meaning/Purpose** multiple levels of meaning (multiple themes)
	Structure free verse, no particular patterns
	Language Conventionality and Clarity more complex descriptions
	Knowledge Demands cultural and literary knowledge essential to understanding
Reader/Task Considerations	Teacher determined Vary by individual reader and type of text

TEACH

CLOSE READ

Martín Espada Have students read the information about the poet. Explain that Espada is the son of a Puerto Rican father and a Jewish mother. His father, Frank, an activist in the civil rights movement during the 1950s and 1960s, frequently took young Martín to meetings and protests. There he learned about the social injustices that many people faced. These experiences, along with his Latino heritage, have informed and shaped Espada's poetry.

AS YOU READ Instruct students to use the As You Read note to focus their reading.

Analyze Word Choice

COMMON CORE **RL 4**

(LINES 1–16)

Explain that poets frequently use descriptive words and phrases that appeal to the senses to create **imagery.** Helping readers tap into their five senses allows them to immerse themselves in the poem's characters, scenes, and situations.

Ⓐ CITE TEXT EVIDENCE Ask students to reread lines 1–16 and identify examples of words and phrases that appeal to different senses—seeing, tasting, touching or feeling, hearing, or smelling. (seeing: *"gazing like admirals," "levitating hands in praise," "shawled refugees," "swollen feet," "raging cops," and "nightsticks splinter in their palms"*; feeling: *"steam in the shower," "swollen feet," "stove-hot, blister the fingers," "splinter in their palms"*; hearing: *"raging cops"*)

Imagery is one technique that writers use to communicate their **tone,** or attitude toward their subject. We often describe tone with adjectives, such as angry, sad, sympathetic, or playful.

Ⓑ ASK STUDENTS to reread lines 6–11 and interpret the speaker's tone when describing refugees and judges. *(The speaker adopts a sympathetic tone toward refugees and a critical tone toward judges.)* Then ask them to describe the overall tone of these lines. *(The tone is hopeful because refugees are going to get back at judges by deporting them.)*

Martín Espada (b. 1957) *was born in Brooklyn, New York. Growing up in a rough neighborhood, he experienced many of the conditions that he writes about in his poetry. Espada says that when he worked as a tenant lawyer, he used law as a political tool, and he uses poetry for the same purpose. A professor at the University of Massachusetts at Amherst, Espada has written several volumes of poetry, including* Imagine the Angels of Bread, *which won an American Book Award. He believes that "poetry humanizes. It makes the abstract concrete. It makes the general specific and particular."*

Imagine the Angels of Bread

Poem by Martín Espada

AS YOU READ Pay attention to images of suffering and injustice in the poem. Write down any questions that you generate during reading.

Ⓐ This is the year that squatters evict landlords,
gazing like admirals from the rail
of the roofdeck
or levitating hands in praise
5 of steam in the shower;
this is the year
that shawled refugees deport judges
who stare at the floor Ⓑ
and their swollen feet
10 as files are stamped
with their destination;
this is the year that police revolvers,
stove-hot, blister the fingers
of raging cops,
15 and nightsticks splinter
in their palms;
this is the year
that darkskinned men
lynched a century ago

Image Credits: ©Melinda Palacio

Imagine the Angels of Bread **217**

SCAFFOLDING FOR ELL STUDENTS

Analyze Word Choice Help students to understand and visualize the images and the scene that the poet creates in each stanza. Model a way of visualizing by reading aloud lines 1–5 and drawing a rough sketch on the board showing what is being described. Point to parts of your sketch to reinforce key words such as *squatter, evict, landlords, admirals, levitating.* Call on a volunteer to summarize the scene.

Have students work in pairs or small groups and follow this model to visualize the remaining stanzas. Encourage them to use English as much as possible when summarizing each scene.

Analyze Word Choice

COMMON CORE **RL 4**

(LINES 29–34)

Explain that writers have many ways of using words to communicate their ideas effectively. Define the following:

- **Repetition** is the use of the same word or phrase more than once. It emphasizes and calls attention to specific ideas.
- **Parallelism** is the use of similar grammatical constructions to express related ideas.

Tell students that these devices provide rhythm, enhance ideas, and organize complex passages. To locate them in the text, students should look for a series of similar words, phrases, or clauses.

C ASK STUDENTS to reread lines 29–34 and identify examples of repetition and parallelism. *("the hands pulling tomatoes" and "the hands canning tomatoes")* Then ask students to identify the types of justice that the "hands" receive and to explain how that justice is expressed with words that reflect parallel ideas. *(The hands pulling tomatoes "uproot the deed to the earth" where the tomatoes grow, while the hands canning tomatoes are "named in the will that owns the . . . cannery." In both instances, the workers receive a legal document indicating ownership of the wealth that comes from their work.)*

20   return to sip coffee quietly
       with the apologizing descendants
       of their executioners.

       This is the year that those
       who swim the border's undertow
25   and shiver in boxcars
       are greeted with trumpets and drums
       at the first railroad crossing
       on the other side;
       this is the year that the hands
30   pulling tomatoes from the vine
       uproot the deed to the earth that sprouts the vine,
       the hands canning tomatoes
       are named in the will
       that owns the bedlam of the cannery;
35   this is the year that the eyes
       stinging from the poison that purifies toilets
       awaken at last to the sight
       of a rooster-loud hillside,
       pilgrimage of immigrant birth;
40   this is the year that cockroaches
       become extinct, that no doctor
       finds a roach embedded
       in the ear of an infant;

APPLYING ACADEMIC VOCABULARY

controversy	tension

As you discuss Espada's poem, incorporate the following Collection 3 academic vocabulary words: *controversy* and *tension*. To explore the tone that Espada conveys, ask students why the poem might cause **controversy** among some audiences. Then ask students to explain how Espada creates **tension** through the images in the poem.

this is the year that the food stamps
45   of adolescent mothers
are auctioned like gold doubloons,
and no coin is given to buy machetes
for the next bouquet of severed heads
in coffee plantation country.

50   If the abolition of slave-manacles
began as a vision of hands without manacles,
then this is the year;
if the shutdown of extermination camps
began as imagination of a land
55   without barbed wire or the crematorium,
then this is the year;
if every rebellion begins with the idea
that conquerors on horseback
are not many-legged gods, that they too drown
60   if plunged in the river,
then this is the year.

So may every humiliated mouth,
teeth like desecrated headstones,
fill with the angels of bread.

COLLABORATIVE DISCUSSION With a partner, discuss how Espada uses imagery to reverse common forms of suffering and injustice in the world. Cite specific examples in the text.

WHEN STUDENTS STRUGGLE...

Guide students to see that within each stanza there is a series of scenes separated by semicolons. Encourage students to use this punctuation cue to divide the poem into smaller chunks and then read to find the main idea in each scene.

- Have students reread the poem with a partner, taking turns reading aloud each scene.
- Tell them to restate the idea of each scene in their own words.
- Encourage them to look for repeated phrases following the semicolons that signal ideas that the poet wants to emphasize.

CLOSE READ

Analyze Word Choice COMMON CORE RL 4
(LINES 44–61)

Explain that poets make frequent use of **figurative language** that communicates beyond the literal meanings of words. Figurative language helps to make unfamiliar ideas more understandable. Define these two common types of figurative language:

- **Simile** is the comparison of two things, using the words *like* or *as*.
- **Metaphor** is a direct comparison of two unlike things that have something in common. It does not use the words *like* or *as*.

D **CITE TEXT EVIDENCE** Ask students to reread lines 44–49, identify examples of simile and metaphor, and describe the tone that this figurative language creates. *(Simile: "food stamps . . . auctioned like gold doubloons"; metaphor: "bouquet of severed heads." The tone is cautionary as the speaker juxtaposes the value of food given to adolescent mothers with the gruesome image of machetes creating bouquets of workers' heads rather than flowers.)*

Explain that writers may signal new ideas when they change patterns of words and phrases, while continuing to use repetition and parallelism.

E **ASK STUDENTS** to reread lines 44–61 and identify where the speaker shifts the tone and interpret the meaning of this shift. *(In line 50, the speaker shifts the tone by structuring the clauses with the pattern "If . . . began [begins] . . . then this is the year." In this way, the speaker says that, although the previous images may seem too idealistic, these historical examples show that all reversals of injustice begin by imagining that change can happen. Hope is grounded in realism.)*

COLLABORATIVE DISCUSSION Have students appropriately identify how Espada reverses each specific example of injustice. Then have them share their conclusions with the class as a whole. Accept all reasonable responses.

ASK STUDENTS to share any questions they have generated in the course of reading the poem.

Analyze Word Choice: Tone COMMON CORE RL 4

Discuss with students how people often communicate attitude through tone of voice. Similarly, poets use words to convey a tone or attitude. Have students reread the lines and see how substituting words with slightly different connotations, such as *gulp* instead of *sip* (line 20) changes the tone of the lines.

Analyzing the Text COMMON CORE RL 1, RL 4

Possible answers:

1. *The simile shows the lowly rising up to power, climbing to roofdecks, where, like admirals on the bridges of flagships, they control all they survey. This simile establishes the central idea that the social order will change to favor the downtrodden.*

2. *In lines 12–16, the words* stove-hot, blister, raging cops, *and* splinter *convey a strong, angry tone, suggesting that that while authority can intimidate as well as protect, violent oppression cannot overcome justice. In lines 26–28, the phrase "greeted with trumpets and drums" suggests a triumphant tone as compassion and justice prevail. The image in lines 36–38 evokes a grim, determined tone as menial workers, "eyes stinging from the poison . . . ," gain vindication. Instead of looking down in subservience, they will look up and beyond at a "rooster-loud hillside."*

3. *The incantatory repetition of "this is the year" creates a tone of prayerful determination and faith. The reversal of that phrase's position in the second-to-last stanza (lines 50–61) adds confidence and emphasis.*

4. *The last stanza presents a concrete image of poverty— broken, chipped teeth. The comparison to headstones evokes the idea that the poor often die before their time. The metaphor "angels of bread" connotes a force, both social and spiritual, that will sustain and uplift the "humiliated." It implies that this force resides within the poor and dispossessed.*

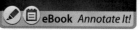 **eBook** *Annotate It!*

Analyze Word Choice: Tone COMMON CORE RL 4

The **tone** of a poem is the speaker's attitude toward the subject. Often tone can be described with a single word, such as *sarcastic, bitter,* or *affectionate.* In some works, such as "Imagine the Angels of Bread," the tone is more complicated because the speaker mixes together hopeful statements with disturbing imagery. As you analyze this poem's tone, consider how the following elements contribute to it:

Word choices and their **connotations** (the thoughts and feelings associated with the words)	For example, *blister* in line 13 has a harsh connotation, while *sip* in line 20 evokes a calm and soothing mood.
Imagery used to depict the subject or action	The poem contains many images associated with oppression, but also more hopeful images such as "levitating hands in praise."

Analyzing the Text COMMON CORE RL 1, RL 4, W 10

Cite Text Evidence   Support your responses with evidence from the selection.

1. **Identify Patterns** Lines 1–3 of the poem include a **simile,** a comparison between two unlike things that uses the word *like* or *as.* What idea does the simile convey? Explain how this simile helps establish a pattern in the poem.

2. **Analyze** Identify the tone in each of the following passages. Cite specific words and images that help create this tone.
   - lines 12–16
   - lines 26–28
   - lines 36–38

3. **Analyze** What words and phrases are repeated in the poem? Explain how this repetition is used to emphasize ideas and emotions.

4. **Draw Conclusions** Reread the poem's last stanza. What is the significance of the phrase "angels of bread" used here and in the title?

PERFORMANCE TASK

Writing Activity: Poem Write a short poem inspired by one of the images or statements in "Imagine the Angels of Bread."

- Decide on a theme, or message, that you want to convey in the poem.
- Choose words and images that create an appropriate tone.
- Read the completed poem to a small group.

Assign this performance task.

PERFORMANCE TASK COMMON CORE W 10

Writing Activity: Poem Discuss the ways in which Espada uses words to paint vivid pictures that represent suffering in society. The immediacy of his images engages readers and makes them anticipate change. Encourage students to extend their chosen images with specific, evocative details, using carefully selected words and phrases to establish an appropriate tone.

Language: Repetition and Parallelism

L 3

TEACH

Explain that an important part of understanding an author's meaning is understanding his **syntax,** or the way he arranges words, phrases, clauses, and sentences. Define these two common elements of syntax:

- **Repetition** is the use of the same sound, word, or phrase more than once. It is often used to reinforce meaning and create a particular rhythm.
- **Parallelism** is the use of similar grammatical constructions to express ideas that are related or equal in importance. The parallel elements may be words, phrases, or clauses. Writers often use repetition of parallel structures to create rhythm and emphasis.

PRACTICE AND APPLY

Display lines 1–22 of the poem on the board or on a device. Have volunteers point out an example of repetition and describe its effect. *("This is the year that . . ." begins each new example. It creates a rhythm like a chant and emphasizes that change is happening now.)*

Then ask volunteers to explain how this repetition is combined with parallelism. *(In each sentence the introductory clause is followed by a clause in the form of subject-verb-object, e.g. "squatters evict landlords," "shawled refugees deport judges," "police revolvers . . . blister the fingers.")*

Display lines 50–61. Call on volunteers to compare the repetition and parallelism in these lines with the previous passage. *("This is the year" is still repeated but the parallel structures have changed so this clause now comes at the end of a sentence structured in the form of "If . . . began as [begins with] . . . then this is the year.")*

Display lines 62–64. Invite students to discuss the poet's purpose in repeating the phrase "angels of bread" from the title in the last line of the poem. *(Repetition ties the poem together. The title asks readers to imagine what "angels of bread" might mean, perhaps those who give food to the hungry. By the end of the poem, the poet has asked readers to imagine how several types of injustice might be reversed. "Angels of bread" takes on a broader meaning of comfort for "every humiliated mouth.")*

Analyze Word Choice: Tone

RL 4

RETEACH

Read aloud the following sentence several times: "I am thrilled about the trip to the museum." For each reading, use a different tone of voice to suggest a different attitude toward the trip to the museum.

- Ask students to suggest words to describe your tone of voice in each example. *(Possible tones: excited, sarcastic)* Discuss how the tone of voice reflected different attitudes toward the trip.
- Then explain that writers choose words carefully in order to communicate different attitudes without people being able to hear the speaker's tone of voice. Invite students to suggest words that might replace *thrilled* to communicate different tones or attitudes. *(Possible responses: happy, excited, bored, annoyed)*

 LEVEL UP TUTORIALS Assign the following *Level Up* tutorial: **Tone**

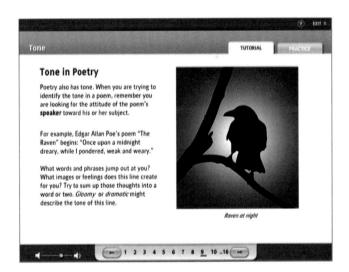

CLOSE READING APPLICATION

Students can apply the skill to another poem from a textbook, library book, or web site. Ask: What words and phrases provide clues to the tone? What is the speaker's tone or attitude toward the subject? Does the tone change in the course of the poem?

After students have analyzed the tone of the poem individually, have them share their ideas with a partner.

Elsewhere

Poem by Derek Walcott

Why This Text

Poets have a lot to say and not a lot of space to say it in—which is why each word is important. Poets use words and imagery to create tone and meaning. Students reading "Elsewhere" may have difficulty with Walcott's nuanced use of language, but because of the emotional weight of the subject and the striking imagery he creates, the meaning comes through loud and clear. With the help of the close-reading questions, students will analyze the language of the poem to find the meaning behind the words.

Background Have students read the background information about Derek Walcott. Explain that, although Walcott's essays and plays have been highly praised, it is his poetry for which he is known worldwide. Walcott draws on his deep commitment to social justice to take on issues of ethnicity, political repression, and cultural inequality. "Elsewhere" is part of a collection of poems called *The Arkansas Testament*, which focuses on the clash of Western and Caribbean cultures.

AS YOU READ Ask students to pay attention to the author's use of figurative language and its impact on tone and meaning. How do the images in the poem help to convey universal truths?

Common Core Support

- cite strong and thorough textual evidence
- determine the figurative meanings of words
- analyze the impact of word choices on meaning and tone

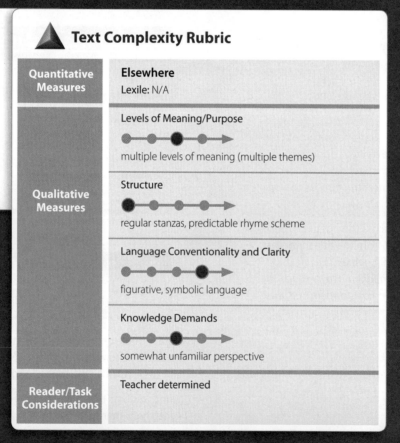

Text Complexity Rubric

Quantitative Measures	**Elsewhere** Lexile: N/A
Qualitative Measures	Levels of Meaning/Purpose multiple levels of meaning (multiple themes)
	Structure regular stanzas, predictable rhyme scheme
	Language Conventionality and Clarity figurative, symbolic language
	Knowledge Demands somewhat unfamiliar perspective
Reader/Task Considerations	Teacher determined

Strategies for CLOSE READING

Analyze Word Choice: Tone

Students should read this poem carefully all the way through. Close-reading questions at the bottom of the page will help them to analyze how the poet's word choices help create the poem's tone and meaning. As they read, students should jot down comments or questions about the text in the margins.

WHEN STUDENTS STRUGGLE . . .

To help students analyze the poem "Elsewhere," have them work in small groups to fill out a chart like the one shown below.

CITE TEXT EVIDENCE For practice in recognizing the effects of word choice and figurative language on tone and meaning, have students use the chart to analyze each example from the text.

Example	Effect
"a field whose sticks are ringed with barbed wire"	This creates a tone of bleakness and repression.
"tired of torture stories"	The poet's choice of words demonstrates the trivialization of the horrific.
"writer . . . who will not read this, or write"	This use of language suggests that the writer is dead, or in jail.
"whatever we write will be stamped twice"	This symbolizes state censorship.
"Fingers grip the cross bars of these stanzas"	This example of personification conveys the chokehold the state has on the poet's artistic freedom.

Background Derek Walcott, *a Caribbean poet and playwright, was raised with his twin brother and sister on the island of Saint Lucia in the West Indies. Of African and European descent, Walcott and his twin brother lost their father, a painter, before they were born. As a young man, Walcott studied writing because he was "madly in love with English," and he published his first poem at the age of 14. Nearly fifty years later, he won the Nobel Prize in Literature. Walcott dedicates this poem to the well-known English poet Stephen Spender, whose poetry, like Walcott's, often focuses on themes of social injustice.*

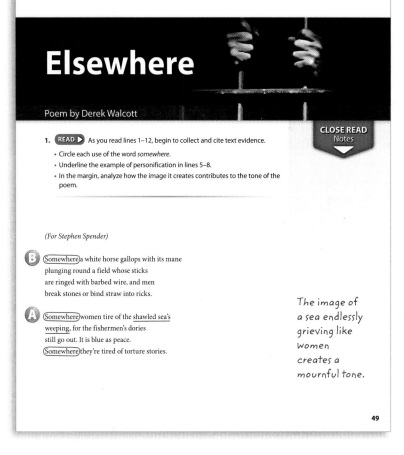

Elsewhere

Poem by Derek Walcott

CLOSE READ Notes

1. **READ ▶** As you read lines 1–12, begin to collect and cite text evidence.
   - Circle each use of the word *somewhere.*
   - Underline the example of personification in lines 5–8.
   - In the margin, analyze how the image it creates contributes to the tone of the poem.

(For Stephen Spender)

B Somewhere a white horse gallops with its mane
plunging round a field whose sticks
are ringed with barbed wire, and men
break stones or bind straw into ricks.

A Somewhere women tire of the shawled sea's
weeping, for the fishermen's dories
still go out. It is blue as peace.
Somewhere they're tired of torture stories.

The image of a sea endlessly grieving like women creates a mournful tone.

49

1. **READ AND CITE TEXT EVIDENCE** Explain that Walcott uses personification to give his words depth, immediacy, and emotional weight.

   A **ASK STUDENTS** to examine the phrase "shawled sea's weeping." What human features does the sea have? *It has a shawl; it is weeping.* What is the sea being compared to? *The sea is being compared to a grieving woman.* What is the effect of this comparison? *It makes the image more "real"; it contributes to the bleak tone.*

   FOR ELL STUDENTS Guide students to understand the meaning of the verb *shawled.* Ask a volunteer to identify the base word, *shawl,* and explain its meaning. Then ask another volunteer to guess what the verb means and why the poet would use it to refer to the sea.

CLOSE READ Notes

Comparing foliage to camouflage creates an image of war.

The writer may be imprisoned and unaware that anyone knows this.

D That somewhere there was an arrest.
10 Somewhere there was a small harvest
of bodies in the truck. Soldiers rest
somewhere by a road, or smoke in a forest.

Somewhere there is the conference rage
at an outrage. Somewhere a page
15 is torn out, and somehow the foliage
no longer looks like leaves but camouflage.

C Somewhere there is a comrade,
a writer lying with his eyes wide open
on a mattress ticking, who will not read
20 this, or write. How to make a pen?

2. **◄ REREAD** Reread lines 1–12. What is the speaker emphasizing by repeating the word *somewhere*? How does the repetition of this word choice affect the meaning and tone of the poem? Support your answer with explicit textual evidence.

The repetitive use of "somewhere" expresses the idea that people are oblivious to the suffering of others taking place somewhere else in the world. The repetition of the word reinforces the speaker's tone of ironic detachment.

3. **READ ►** As you read lines 13–20, continue to cite textual evidence.
- Circle the simile in lines 13–16.
- In the margin, explain the image that this simile creates.
- Underline the subject of lines 17–20. In the margin, state the point the poet is making about this person.

CLOSE READ Notes

> *Somewhere there is a comrade . . . who will not read this, or write.*

E And here we are free for a while, but
elsewhere, in one-third, or one-seventh
of this planet, a summary rifle butt
breaks a skull into the idea of a heaven

25 where nothing is free, where blue air
is paper-frail, and whatever we write
will be stamped twice, a blue letter,
its throat slit by the paper knife of the state.

Through these black bars
30 hollowed faces stare. Fingers
grip the cross bars of these stanzas
and it is here, because somewhere else

"Here" there is a false sense of freedom. "Elsewhere" there is no freedom, just abuse, oppression and censorship. Freedom is fleeting.

4. **◄ REREAD AND DISCUSS** With a small group, discuss the tone of the poem so far. What is the speaker's attitude toward the subject?

5. **READ ►** As you read lines 21–40, continue to cite textual evidence.
- Circle what is happening "here," in line 21.
- Underline what is happening "elsewhere."
- In the margin, compare what is happening "here" with what is happening "elsewhere." What does this comparison say about freedom?

2. **REREAD AND CITE TEXT EVIDENCE** Point out the deliberate choice of the word *somewhere* to refer to places around the world where suffering occurs.

B **ASK STUDENTS** why they think the poet chose this word instead of naming real places. *By keeping the references nameless, he is stressing the fact that these abuses can happen anywhere in the world—and do.*

3. **READ AND CITE TEXT EVIDENCE**

C **ASK STUDENTS** to examine the writer's word choice in lines 17–19. What is Walcott saying about the writer's condition? *The writer is in jail ("lying. . . on a mattress ticking") and is someone we know ("a comrade").* What effect does this image have on the reader? *The fact that we "see" this person makes it more personal and also removed.*

4. **REREAD AND DISCUSS USING TEXT EVIDENCE** Discuss the images "small harvest of bodies in the truck" (lines 10–11) and "the foliage no longer looks like leaves but camouflage" (lines 15–16).

D **ASK STUDENTS** to think about the connotations of the words used in these lines. Which words are warlike? *Students may suggest* camouflage *and* soldiers. Which are peaceful? *Students may suggest* harvest *and* foliage.

5. **READ AND CITE TEXT EVIDENCE**

E **ASK STUDENTS** to explain ". . . elsewhere, in one-third, or one-seventh of this planet. . . " (lines 21–23). Why is the poet intentionally vague? *When referring to atrocities around the world, numbers don't matter: we are only "free for a while."*

CLOSE READ
Notes

*Prisoners'
blank stares
are being
compared to
"fog" and to
numbers in an
address book
that are as
forgotten as
"last year's
massacres."*

 their stares fog into oblivion
thinly, like the faceless numbers
35 that bewilder you in your telephone
diary. Like last year's massacres.

The world is blameless. The darker crime
is to make a career of conscience,
to feel through our own nerves the silent scream
40 of winter branches, wonders read as signs.

6. ◀ **REREAD** As you reread lines 33–40,
• in the margin, explain the two images in lines 33–36.
• underline the personification in the last stanza.

SHORT RESPONSE

Cite Text Evidence   Analyze the impact of specific word choices, including
figurative and connotative meanings of words, on the meaning and tone of
the poem. **Cite text evidence** in your response.

*The repetitive use of the word "somewhere" emphasizes the
speaker's tone of detachment from what goes on "elsewhere." By
using disturbing metaphors, personification, and images such as "a
blue letter, its throat slit by the paper knife of the state" and "a
small harvest of bodies," the speaker stresses a sense of disgust
toward oppressive regimes and toward those who are oblivious to
people's struggles in nameless parts of the world. People who live
"elsewhere" experience a false sense of freedom until they
experience the horror for themselves.*

52

---

6. (**REREAD AND CITE TEXT EVIDENCE**) Have students analyze
the imagery in lines 34–36.

 ASK STUDENTS what is being compared in these lines. *The
numbers in an address book are compared to the names of
massacred people.* In what way are these subjects similar? *They are
both seen as things easily forgotten; the comparison suggests that
violence is treated lightly.*

SHORT RESPONSE

Cite Text Evidence   Students' responses should include text
evidence that supports their positions. They should:

• analyze the poet's use of language and imagery to create meaning.
• cite examples from the text that show how word choice affects
tone.
• cite examples of figurative and connotative language.

TO CHALLENGE STUDENTS . . .

To familiarize students with this author's work, they can read his
famous poem "Love After Love," which can be found online.

ASK STUDENTS to compare the poems in terms of subject, tone,
structure, and language. How do they differ? What do they have in
common? What themes run through his work?

DIG DEEPER

With the class, return to Question 4, Reread and Discuss. Have
groups share their responses to the question.

ASK STUDENTS to revisit lines 10–11, "small harvest of bodies in
the truck," and lines 15–16, "the foliage no longer looks like leaves
but camouflage." Have them focus on the way they categorized
images as "warlike" or "peaceful."

• Have students discuss how the poet juxtaposes these
images. What effect is created by putting them together? *By
juxtaposing the mundane and the horrific, the poet shows how
easy it is to ignore atrocities—both these phrases use unexpected
images to show the horrors around us.*

• What other examples of this kind of juxtaposition can
students find? *Students may suggest "a field whose sticks are
ringed with barbed wire" (lines 2–3), "a summary rifle butt breaks
a skull into the idea of a heaven" (lines 23–24), and "the silent
scream of winter branches" (lines 39–40).*

• How does this juxtaposition reflect the poem's theme?
*Through the use of clashing images, the poet demonstrates
what it feels like when violence breaks into one's comfort zone,
shattering complacency. When these images are put together,
the effect of the violence is infinitely more jarring.*

ASK STUDENTS to return to their Short Response answer and
revise it based on the class discussion.

Participate in a Group Discussion

COMMON CORE

SL 1a–d Initiate and participate in collaborative discussions.
SL 4 Present information, findings, and supporting evidence.

The texts in this collection focus on injustice and the authors' ideas for fighting or eradicating it. Look back at the anchor text "Speech on the Vietnam War, 1967" and at the other texts you have read in the collection. What connections do you see between the examples of injustice explored in each text? Synthesize your ideas in a group discussion, and then write a summary of the discussion.

Participants in a successful group discussion

- present quotations or examples from "Speech on the Vietnam War, 1967" and at least two other collection texts to illustrate ideas about injustice
- make clear, logical, and well-developed connections among the texts' views of injustice
- pose and respond to questions to keep the conversation going
- respond thoughtfully to the ideas of others in the group, adapting or expanding upon their own ideas or politely challenging others' assertions
- write an accurate and objective summary of the discussion

PLAN

Get Organized
Work with your classmates to prepare for the discussion.

- In the anchor text "Speech on the Vietnam War, 1967," Martin Luther King Jr. outlines many intersecting areas of injustice that relate to the war. Get together with your group and choose two other texts from this collection, in addition to King's speech, that you will use to discuss relationships between various examples of injustice.
- Choose a moderator and a note-taker for the discussion. The moderator will keep track of the time and make sure all members participate equally. The note-taker will write down important ideas from the discussion.
- Set deadlines to make sure all tasks related to the discussion can be completed on time. Tasks include analyzing the texts, holding the discussion, and writing summaries.

*my*Notebook

Use the annotation tools in your eBook to find examples of injustice from the selections that you will discuss. Save each example to your notebook.

ACADEMIC VOCABULARY

As you plan your discussion on the issue of injustice, try to use these words.

controversy
convince
ethics
radical
tension

PERFORMANCE TASK A

PARTICIPATE IN A GROUP DISCUSSION

COMMON CORE SL 1a-d, SL 4

Introduce students to the Performance Task by reading the introductory paragraph with them and reviewing the criteria for a successful group discussion that follows it. Tell students that the point of the group discussion will be to take the connections they discovered independently and synthesize them into general ideas about injustice.

PLAN

GET ORGANIZED

▶ **View It!**

Professional Development Podcast:
Performance Task

Point out that students who take on the roles of moderator and note-taker will also be taking part in the discussion. They should analyze the chosen texts independently, along with the other group members.

PERFORMANCE TASK A

PLAN

ANALYZE THE TEXTS

Suggest that students review the notes they took while reading the selections, as well as their answers to "Analyzing the Text" questions for each selection. As they gather information for the discussion, they should be thinking about the connections they need to make, and focus on the most relevant passages in each text rather than rereading each one from start to finish.

PRODUCE

HAVE THE DISCUSSION

Remind students that the point of a discussion is to share ideas. Group members should present their own ideas as clearly and convincingly as possible, but they should also be open to new perspectives. The discussion is an opportunity for them to learn from the work their classmates have done. Emphasize the importance of taking good notes that they can use later to write their summary.

Analyze the Texts Work independently to review your group's chosen texts.

- Reread "Speech on the Vietnam War, 1967" and identify examples of injustice cited by Martin Luther King Jr. Take note of any details or quotations you might want to mention in a discussion about the speech.

- Then review the other chosen texts, also taking notes on examples of injustice.

- Consider how the examples you have identified are related. Do the injustices stem from the same root cause, for example, or do they interact in ways that make the problems grow?

Outline Your Ideas Put your ideas in order so that you can refer to them quickly during the discussion. You might create an outline or use a graphic organizer.

- Write down your central ideas about how the examples of injustice in the three texts are related to each other. State your ideas clearly and concisely so that others will easily understand them.

- Sort through the evidence you have collected from the texts. Match each piece of evidence with the central idea it most clearly supports. Make sure your reasoning is sound enough to convince other group members of your ideas.

- Think of questions that the moderator or other group members may ask you. Be prepared to answer them.

- Develop some suggestions to end the injustices that your group is going to discuss. Recall the steps that Martin Luther King Jr. outlines in lines 322–333 of his speech. You may need to do some additional research on the specific problems before you can suggest reasonable solutions to them.

> PRODUCE

my WriteSmart

Have the Discussion Join your group members to exchange ideas in a discussion.

Write your outline in *my*WriteSmart. Focus on putting your ideas in a logical order.

- The moderator may start the discussion by calling on a student to speak first. After that, everyone in the group should take responsibility for building on others' ideas and posing questions to keep the conversation going.

- Maintain a respectful tone toward your fellow group members, even when you disagree with each other's ideas. It is the moderator's job to ease any tension among group members and keep the discussion focused on the topic.

- Listen closely to what all speakers say so that you can respond appropriately and ask relevant questions.

- If the discussion gets off track, the moderator may ask the note-taker to read back his or her notes on the last relevant part of the conversation.
- Take your own notes throughout the discussion. You will use these notes to write your summary.

REVISE

*my*WriteSmart

Write your summary in *my*WriteSmart. Make sure that you include all of your group's key points.

Evaluate the Discussion Conclude your discussion by evaluating the ideas that have been brought up. Use the chart on the following page to review the characteristics of an effective discussion.

- Discuss the reasons and evidence that you found most compelling.
- Synthesize the ideas expressed by the group and resolve any controversial ideas, if possible.
- Decide on the most important points from the discussion that the note-taker will report back to the class.
- Work independently to write a summary of the conclusions that your group reached and your suggestions for addressing the problems.

PRESENT

Present to the Class The note-taker should summarize the main points from the group discussion for the rest of the class. Then give your classmates a chance to ask questions about your analysis and your suggested solutions. All group members can respond to the questions.

REVISE

EVALUATE THE DISCUSSION

Remind students that a summary includes only main ideas and crucial details. Encourage them to keep their summaries to about one page in length.

PRESENT

PRESENT TO THE CLASS

Emphasize that all students should participate in the class presentation after the note-taker has read his or her summary. The moderator might direct questions from the class to specific students so that everyone has a chance to speak.

PERFORMANCE TASK A

ORGANIZATION

Have students look at the chart to evaluate their level of
performance in the Organization category. Have students
consider the following questions: Are the central ideas
clearly identified? Do the examples connect logically to
the ideas presented? Do they remain focused on the topic?
Discuss areas for improvement and have students outline a
revised summary of the group's conclusions showing more
logical connections between ideas and examples.

COLLECTION 3 TASK A
GROUP DISCUSSION

	Ideas and Evidence	Organization	Language
ADVANCED	• Group members identify clear and relevant examples of injustice from three collection texts, including the King speech. • Students propel discussion by posing thoughtful questions and offering new ideas. • Students offer well-reasoned analysis of the connections between examples. • Students propose reasonable, real-world solutions to the problems discussed.	• The group completes all tasks on schedule. • Group members' remarks are based on well-organized notes that clearly identify their central ideas. • The conversation stays focused on the topic and makes logical connections between ideas and examples. • Group members accurately summarize their discussion in writing and in a class presentation.	• Group members adapt speech to the context of the discussion, using appropriately formal English to discuss texts and ideas. • Students quote accurately from the texts to support ideas. • Students maintain a polite and thoughtful tone throughout the discussion.
COMPETENT	• Group members identify examples of injustice from three collection texts, including the King speech. • Students pose questions and offer new ideas, but the discussion lapses occasionally. • Students analyze some connections between examples. • Students propose solutions to the problems discussed.	• The group completes most tasks on schedule. • Group members' remarks are based on notes that identify their central ideas. • The conversation mostly stays focused on the topic and makes connections between ideas and examples. • Group members adequately summarize their discussion in writing and in a class presentation.	• Group members mostly use formal English to discuss texts and ideas. • Students quote accurately from the texts to support ideas. • Students maintain a polite and thoughtful tone throughout most of the discussion.
LIMITED	• Group members identify a few examples of injustice from collection texts. • The discussion is not fluid, and students depend on the moderator to ask questions. • Students make few connections between the text examples. • Students propose solutions to some of the problems, but the solutions are not practical or appropriate.	• The group completes many tasks late. • Group members' notes do not clearly identify their central ideas. • The conversation wanders off the topic and makes few connections between ideas and examples. • Students' summaries are incomplete or unfocused.	• Group members use some formal and some informal English to discuss texts and ideas. • Students' quotations and examples sometimes do not accurately reflect the texts. • Students sometimes forget to maintain a polite tone when responding to others' comments and questions.
EMERGING	• Group members do not identify clear examples of injustice. • There is no real discussion of ideas; the moderator fails to keep group members engaged. • Students make no connections between the text examples. • Students propose no solutions to the problems, or the solutions are illogical.	• The group seems unaware of deadlines. • Group members do not prepare notes that can help them express their central ideas about the texts. • The conversation is unfocused and makes no connections between ideas and examples. • Students' summaries of the discussion are inaccurate.	• Group members use informal English and/or slang, resulting in ideas that are not clearly expressed. • Students' quotations and examples do not accurately reflect the texts. • Students do not maintain a polite tone when responding to others' comments and questions.

COLLECTION **3**
PERFORMANCE TASK B

Interactive Lessons

If you need help with...
• **Writing an Argument**
• **Writing as a Process**

Write a Satire

This collection focuses on injustice and how it can be overcome. In "A Modest Proposal," Jonathan Swift proposes a satirical solution to one particular injustice as a way of drawing attention to it and exposing its horrors. Using Swift's essay as a model, write a satire on a topic covered in one of the other texts in the collection.

COMMON CORE

W 1 Write arguments.
W 4 Produce clear and coherent writing.
W 5 Develop and strengthen writing.
W 9 Draw evidence from literary or informational texts.

An effective satire

- introduces a particular idea, custom, behavior, or institution to be the target of satire with the goal of convincing readers to change their view of the target or of bringing about social reform

- includes irony, humor, exaggeration, and understatement to show the target in a critical light

- identifies the object of the satire, but makes the reader infer the writer's true perspective on the issue

- uses the form of a problem-solution essay, as in "A Modest Proposal"

- has transitions to link the major sections of the satire and to clarify relationships among ideas

- concludes with a summary or global statement about the issue

- uses precise language with appropriate tone and style for a literary satire

PLAN

Analyze "A Modest Proposal" Reread Swift's essay and take note of the problem-solution format, using the points below to guide you. Model the structure of your own satire after "A Modest Proposal." Your satire should

- clearly identify a problem and its causes

- propose a solution to the problem and explain how to implement it

- provide support for the proposed solution in the form of reasons and evidence

- note other possible solutions and argue against them

myNotebook

Use the annotation tools in your eBook to identify features of the format of Swift's essay. Save each note to your notebook.

PERFORMANCE TASK B

WRITE A SATIRE

COMMON CORE W 1, W 4, W 5, W 9

Introduce students to the Performance Task by reading the introductory paragraph with them and reviewing the criteria for an effective satire. Point out that this writing task will allow them to synthesize what they have learned from analyzing two collection texts. They will apply the satirical style of "A Modest Proposal" to a topic introduced in another selection.

PLAN

ANALYZE "A MODEST PROPOSAL"

► View It!

Professional Development Podcast:

Performance Task

Suggest that students review any notes they made while reading "A Modest Proposal" and their answers to the "Analyzing the Text" questions to help them identify the major parts of the essay.

PERFORMANCE TASK B

PLAN

BRAINSTORM

Point out to students that part of the brainstorming process is figuring out which of several possible topics would be best to write about. They should select a topic that is not only interesting to them but that also gives them plenty of material for developing a rich satire. Remind them that for this kind of essay, they may invent some facts to use as evidence, as Swift invented the remarks of his American acquaintance.

PRODUCE

DRAFT YOUR SATIRE

Tell students that while they are using Swift's essay as a model, their satire should be written in their own unique voice. Encourage them to let their own sense of humor shine through as they draft their satires.

Brainstorm Review the other texts in the collection, paying attention to the types of injustices presented in each text.

- Which of the topics covered in the collection is the most interesting to you? Consider racism, poverty, the effects of war, or another type of injustice.

- Choose one topic and use a graphic organizer to help you generate ideas for your satire.

- Think of the target of your satire as a specific problem, and come up with a satirical solution for it. Gather supporting reasons and evidence. You should also identify other possible solutions and offer opposing arguments.

- Remember that the overall tone of a satire is ironic. That is, the ideas you state directly should be the opposite of what you really mean. Your readers will infer your meaning once they recognize the ironic tone of your writing.

Get Organized Organize your ideas and evidence in an outline.

- Using the organizational pattern of "A Modest Proposal," create an outline of your ideas for the satire.

- Choose which evidence is the most relevant to your topic.

- Use your organizational pattern to sort your textual evidence into a logical order.

- Select a controversial detail or example to introduce the target of your satire in a humorous way.

- List some ideas for your concluding section.

PRODUCE

Draft Your Satire Write a draft of your satire, following your outline.

- Introduce the type of injustice that is the target of your satire. Use humor or exaggeration to draw your reader in. Remember that a satire uses these tools to ridicule or criticize the target.

- Present your problem, solution, alternative solutions, and counterarguments in logically ordered paragraphs.

- Use appropriate transitions to create overall cohesion of the text.

- Write a concluding section that summarizes your central ideas and follows logically from the body of the essay.

ACADEMIC VOCABULARY

As you draft your satire, try to use these words.

controversy
convince
ethics
radical
tension

myWriteSmart

Write your rough draft in *my*WriteSmart. Focus on getting your ideas down, rather than on perfecting your choice of language.

REVISE

Improve Your Draft Revise your draft to make sure it is clear, coherent, and engaging. Ask yourself these questions as you revise:

- Have I introduced my topic clearly? Does my introduction grab readers' attention?

- Have I presented logical reasons and relevant evidence to support the central ideas in my satire?

- Is my satire organized in a way that makes sense? Are transitions from section to section smooth and easy to follow? Do I need to clarify how the central ideas are connected to each other and to the supporting evidence?

- Have I maintained an appropriate tone for a satire, using irony, humor, exaggeration, and understatement to develop my central ideas?

- Have I used a formal style of English appropriate for a satire that is written in an essay format?

- Does my conclusion accurately summarize the issue and present a global statement about the injustice that serves as the target of the satire?

my **WriteSmart**

Have your partner review your draft in *my*WriteSmart. Ask your reviewer to evaluate whether the tone of your essay clearly indicates your satirical intent, and also whether you have organized your ideas effectively.

PRESENT

Exchange Satires When your final draft is completed, exchange satires with a partner. Use the chart on the following page to review the characteristics of an effective satire. Read your partner's satire and provide feedback. Be sure to point out aspects of the satire that are particularly strong, as well as areas that could be improved.

- Is the ironic tone of your partner's essay clear from the first or second paragraph?

- Does the satire present a problem and propose a solution?

- Does your partner use humor, exaggeration, and understatement effectively?

- Was your partner successful in persuading you to change your perspective on the issue?

REVISE

IMPROVE YOUR DRAFT

Point out that even if students are presenting outrageous ideas like those in "A Modest Proposal," their reasons and evidence must be logical. Their partners can help identify any lapses in logic.

PRESENT

EXCHANGE SATIRES

Students may share their satires with a wider audience by creating a class Web page that defines the genre, describes "A Modest Proposal" as a classic example, and includes links to students' essays.

PERFORMANCE TASK B

SATIRE

Have students look at the chart to evaluate their level of performance in each of the three main categories. Then have them examine how well their argument meets the characteristics of the highest level of proficiency. Is the introduction compelling? Do the reasons and evidence support the solution? Is an ironic tone present throughout? Ask students to set goals for the next time they write a satire or a problem-solution essay. What areas will they work to improve?

SATIRE

	Ideas and Evidence	Organization	Language
ADVANCED	• The introduction is compelling; it introduces an injustice and promises a bold but satirical solution. • Relevant reasons and evidence logically support the solution. • Opposing solutions are anticipated and addressed effectively. • Humor, exaggeration, and understatement enhance the satire. • The concluding section effectively summarizes the ideas and clearly emphasizes the advantages of the proposed solution.	• The reasons and evidence are organized consistently and logically throughout the essay. • Varied transitions successfully connect reasons and evidence to the problem and the proposed solution.	• The writing reflects a formal style and an ironic tone. • Sentence beginnings, lengths, and structures vary and have a rhythmic flow. • Spelling, capitalization, and punctuation are correct. • Grammar and usage are correct.
COMPETENT	• The introduction introduces an injustice and promises a solution. • Reasons and evidence support the solution. • Opposing solutions are anticipated and addressed adequately. • The writer uses humor, exaggeration, and/or understatement to create a satirical effect. • The concluding section summarizes ideas and emphasizes the advantages of the proposed solution.	• The organization of reasons and evidence is confusing in a few places. • A few more transitions are needed to connect reasons and evidence to the problem and the proposed solution.	• The style is inconsistent in a few places, and the ironic tone disappears in some passages. • Sentence beginnings, lengths, and structures vary somewhat. • Several spelling, capitalization, and punctuation mistakes occur. • Some grammatical and usage errors are repeated in the description.
LIMITED	• The introduction suggests an injustice and a solution, but the formulation is vague. • Reasons and evidence support the solution but are not sufficient or consistently logical. • Opposing solutions may be acknowledged but are not addressed adequately. • There are a few examples of humor, exaggeration, and/or understatement. • The concluding section summarizes some of the writer's ideas and repeats the proposed solution.	• The organization of reasons and evidence is logical in some places, but it often doesn't follow a pattern. • Many more transitions are needed throughout to connect reasons and evidence to the problem and the proposed solution.	• The style becomes informal in many places, and the ironic tone is very inconsistent. • Sentence structures barely vary, and some fragments or run-on sentences are present. • Spelling, capitalization, and punctuation are often incorrect but do not make reading the essay difficult. • Grammar and usage are incorrect in many places, but the writer's ideas are still clear.
EMERGING	• The introduction hints at an injustice but does not allow readers to see that the essay is a satire. • Reasons and evidence in support of the solution are missing or insufficient. • Opposing solutions are neither acknowledged nor addressed. • Any examples of humor, exaggeration, and/or understatement do not support the purpose of a satire. • The concluding section does not summarize the writer's ideas or reinforce the proposed solution.	• A logical organization is not apparent; ideas are presented randomly. • Transitions are not used, making the essay difficult to understand.	• The style and tone are inappropriate for the essay. • Repetitive sentence structure, fragments, and run-on sentences make the writing monotonous. • Spelling, capitalization, and punctuation are incorrect throughout. • Many grammatical and usage errors change the meaning of the writer's ideas.

Image Credits: ©Rob Howard/Corbis

Seeking Justice, Seeking Peace

"Forgiving means abandoning your right to pay back the perpetrator in his own coin, but it is a loss which liberates the victim."

—Desmond Tutu

PLAN

Seeking Justice, Seeking Peace

hmhfyi.com

This collection raises the issue of whether it is more important to revenge evil acts or end conflict through reconciliation.

CONNECTING WORD AND IMAGE

ASK STUDENTS to discuss how the collection opener image and the collection quotation work together to create a connection.

PERFORMANCE TASK PREVIEW

Point out to students that they will complete two performance tasks at the end of the collection. The performance tasks will require them to further analyze the selections in the collection and to synthesize ideas about these analyses. They will present their findings in a variety of products.

COLLECTION

PERFORMANCE TASK Preview

At the end of this collection, you will have the opportunity to complete two tasks:

- Write an analytical essay that considers how violence intrudes upon and affects the course of people's lives.

- Develop an argumentative essay that addresses the question of whether revenge is ever justifiable.

ACADEMIC VOCABULARY

View It!

Professional Development Podcast:

Academic Vocabulary

Students can acquire facility with the academic vocabulary words through frequent, repeated exposure as they analyze and discuss the selections in the collection. Academic vocabulary can be used in the following instructional contexts. This will enable students to incorporate the academic vocabulary words into their working vocabulary.

- Collaborative Discussion at the end of each selection
- Analyzing the Text questions for each selection
- Selection-level Performance Task
- Vocabulary instruction (for Critical Vocabulary and/or for Vocabulary Strategy)
- Language and Style
- End-of-collection Performance Task for all selections in the collection

ASK STUDENTS TO to review the Academic Vocabulary word list for this collection. You may wish to pronounce each word aloud, so students hear the correct pronunciation. Then discuss the definitions and the related forms for each word. Remind students that they will encounter these five academic vocabulary words throughout the collection.

ACADEMIC VOCABULARY

Study the words and their definitions in the chart below. You will use these words as you discuss and write about the texts in this collection.

Word	Definition	Related Forms
drama (drä´mə) *n.*	a prose or verse composition that is intended to be acted out	dramatic, dramatist, dramatization
integrity (ĭn-tĕg´rĭ-tē) *n.*	quality of being ethically or morally upright	integrate, integration
mediate (mē´dē-āt´) *v.*	to settle differences between two individuals or groups	mediation, mediator
restrain (rĭ-strān´) *v.*	to hold back or control	restraint, restrainedly, restrainer
trigger (trĭg´ər) *v.*	to set off a chain of events	trigger (*n.*)

230

USING COLLECTIONS YOUR WAY

Use the following information, along with the charts on the following pages, to help you decide how you want to introduce the collection. Based on your teaching style, your students' interests, or your instructional goals, you may want to structure this collection in various ways. You may choose different entry points each time you teach the collection.

"I like to teach by comparing texts."

These film versions of *Hamlet* give ample opportunities for students to compare media presentations, and to consider how text and media versions of the play present different aspects of the characters and the plot.

COMPARE TEXT AND MEDIA

MEDIA ANALYSIS

Film Versions of Hamlet

Hamlet (1980)

BBC Shakespeare
Directed by Rodney Bennett

AS YOU VIEW Pay attention to the elements that make each film version unique, and generate a list of questions as you watch.

Compare Text and Media **357**

"I emphasize informational texts."

This article by **Alex Kotlowitz** presents information about a program that is trying to curb, or "interrupt," violence by using a methodology that has been used to treat infectious diseases. This unique perspective about violence prevention, along with specific examples, helps students analyze and draw conclusions.

Alex Kotlowitz *wrote one of the most important books of the twentieth century, according to the New York Public Library. That book, entitled There Are No Children Here, tells the story of two brothers trying to survive in a public housing project in Chicago. Much of his writing, in both books and articles, focuses on topics related to race and poverty. In addition to being a senior lecturer at Northwestern University, he contributes regularly to the New York Times Magazine and other publications. His most recent book is Never a City So Real, a portrait of Chicago.*

Blocking the Transmission of Violence

Feature Article by Alex Kotlowitz

AS YOU READ Pay attention to details that help you understand the connection between infectious diseases and violence.

Last summer, Martin Torres was working as a cook in Austin, Tex., when, on the morning of Aug. 23, he received a call from a relative. His 17-year-old nephew, Emilio, had been murdered. According to the police, Emilio was walking down a street on Chicago's South Side when someone shot him in the chest, possibly the culmination of an ongoing dispute. Like many killings, Emilio's received just a few sentences in the local newspapers. Torres, who was especially close to his nephew, got on the first Greyhound bus to Chicago. He was grieving and plotting **retribution**. "I thought, Man, I'm going to take care of business," he told me recently. "That's how I live. I was going hunting. This is my own blood, my nephew."

Torres, who is 38, grew up in a dicey section of Chicago, and even by the standards of his neighborhood he was a rough character. His nickname was Packman, because he was known to always pack a gun. He was first shot when he was 12, in the legs with buckshot by members of a rival gang. He was shot five more times, including once through the jaw, another time in his right shoulder and the last time—seven years ago—in his right thigh, with a .38-caliber bullet that is still

retribution
(rĕt´rə-byōō´shən) *n.* appropriate punishment or revenge.

Blocking the Transmission of Violence **379**

"I stress the importance of language and style."

This poem by **Wisława Szymborska** discusses the nuances of hatred in terms of how it affects all humanity. The poet uses literary techniques such as repetition and parallelism to convey her tone toward the subject.

Wisława Szymborska *(1923–2012) was born in Poland and remained there throughout her life. She lived modestly, supporting herself with a full-time job at a literary magazine. Though her body of work includes only about 400 poems, it was remarkable enough to be recognized with a Nobel Prize in 1996. In her Nobel lecture, she compared poets to scientists because, just as scientists need to question what they know through rigorous experimentation, poets need to question what they know through writing. Though her poetry is sometimes seen as political, she considered her work to be more prosaic, dealing with ordinary people and life.*

Hatred

Poem by Wisława Szymborska

AS YOU READ Pay attention to the details that characterize hatred. Write down any questions you generate during reading.

See how efficient it still is,
how it keeps itself in shape—
our century's hatred.
How easily it vaults the tallest obstacles.
5 How rapidly it pounces, tracks us down.

It's not like other feelings.
At once both older and younger.
It gives birth itself to the reasons
that give it life.
10 When it sleeps, it's never eternal rest.
And sleeplessness won't sap its strength; it feeds it.

One religion or another—
whatever gets it ready, in position.
One fatherland or another—
15 whatever helps it get a running start.
Justice also works well at the outset
until hate gets its own momentum going.

Hatred **395**

COLLECTION 4 DIGITAL OVERVIEW

*my*SmartPlanner | **eBook** | *my*Notebook | *my*WriteSmart | fyi hmhfyi.com

Collection 4 Lessons	Media	Teach and Practice	
Student Edition | eBook	Video Links HISTORY A&E	**Close Reading and Evidence Tracking**	
ANCHOR TEXT — Drama by William Shakespeare *The Tragedy of Hamlet*	▶ **Video BIOGRAPHY** *Biography: William Shakespeare* ◀) **Audio** *The Tragedy of Hamlet*	**Close Read Screencasts** • Modeled Discussion 1 (Act I, Scene 3, lines 33–42) • Modeled Discussion 2 (Act II, Scene 2, lines 207–221) • Modeled Discussion 3 (Act III, Scene 4, lines 19–32) • Modeled Discussion 4 (Act IV, Scene 4, lines 58–68) • Close Read application pdf (Act V, Scene 2, lines 351-365)	**Strategies for Annotation** pp. 242, 258, 265, 270, 275, 285, 291, 300, 305, 318, 347, 354
CLOSE READER — Drama by William Shakespeare **Excerpt from *Hamlet***	◀) **Audio** excerpt from *Hamlet*		
Film Versions of *Hamlet*	◀) **Audio** Film Versions of *Hamlet*		
Literary Criticism by René Girard "Hamlet's Dull Revenge"	◀) **Audio** "Hamlet's Dull Revenge"		**Strategies for Annotation** • Analyze Structure: Argument • Domain-Specific Words and Phrases
Short Story by Juan Rulfo "Tell Them Not to Kill Me!"	◀) **Audio** "Tell Them Not to Kill Me!"		**Strategies for Annotation** • Analyze Structure • Language and Style: Vary Syntax for Effect
ANCHOR TEXT — Feature Article by Alex Kotlowitz **"Blocking the Transmission of Violence"**	◀) **Audio** "Blocking the Transmission of Violence"	**Close Read Screencasts** • Modeled Discussion 1 (lines 58–67) • Modeled Discussion 2 (lines 188–198) • Close Read application pdf (lines 399–413)	**Strategies for Annotation** • Analyze Ideas and Events • Direct and Indirect Quotations
CLOSE READER — Speech by Wangaa Mathari **Nobel Peace Prize Acceptance Speech**	◀) **Audio** Nobel Peace Prize Acceptance Speech		
Poem by Wisława Szymborska "Hatred"	◀) **Audio** "Hatred"		
Collection 4 Performance Tasks: **A** Write an Analytical Essay **B** Write an Argument	fyi hmhfyi.com **hmhfyi.com**	**Interactive Lessons** **A** Writing an Informative Text **A** Writing as a Process	**B** Writing an Argument **B** Using Textual Evidence

	For Systematic Coverage of Writing and Speaking & Listening Standards	**Interactive Lessons** Using Textual Evidence Using Media in a Presentation	**Lesson Assessments** Using Textual Evidence Using Media in a Presentation

Assess		Extend	Reteach
Performance Task	**Online Assessment**	**Teacher eBook**	**Teacher eBook**
Act I: Writing Activity: Analysis Act II: Speaking Activity: Discussion Act III: Speaking Activity: Performance Act IV: Writing Activity: Journal Entry Act V: Writing Activity: Funeral Speech	Selection Tests, Acts I–V	**Analyze Drama Elements:** Foil	**Analyze Structure: Conflict > Level Up Tutorial >** Characters and Conflict
Media Activity: Trailer	Selection Test	**Analyze Elements of Drama:** Characterization	**Analyze Interpretations of Drama > Level Up Tutorial >** Elements of Drama
Writing Activity: Argument	Selection Test	**Analyze Key Terms > Word Shop >** Specialized Vocabulary	**Analyze Structure > Level Up Tutorial >** Evidence
Speaking Activity: Discussion	Selection Test	**Support Inferences > Interactive Whiteboard Lesson >** Citing Textual Evidence	**Analyze Structure > Level Up Tutorial >** Plot: Sequence of Events
Speaking Activity: Discussion	Selection Test	**Author's Purpose and Perspective > Interactive Whiteboard Lesson >** Author's Purpose and Perspective	**Support Inferences: Draw Conclusions > Level Up Tutorial >** Drawing Conclusions
Writing Activity: Comparison	Selection Test	**Analyze Impact of Word Choice: Tone > Interactive Whiteboard Lesson >** Analyze Impact of Word Choice: Tone **Determine Theme > Interactive Whiteboard Lesson >** Determine Theme **Writing: Use Precise Words and Phrases**	**Determine Figurative Meanings: Personification > Level Up Tutorial >** Figurative Language
A Write an Analytical Essay **B** Write an Argument	Collection Test		

Collection 4 Lessons	Key Learning Objective	Performance Task
ANCHOR TEXT **Drama by William Shakespeare** *The Tragedy of Hamlet,* p. 231A	**The student will be able to…** analyze both the language and structure of the play	Act I: Writing Activity: Analysis Act II: Speaking Activity: Discussion Act III: Speaking Activity: Performance Act IV: Writing Activity: Journal Entry Act V: Writing Activity: Funeral Speech
Film Versions of *Hamlet,* p. 357A	**The student will be able to…** analyze multiple interpretations of a drama to evaluate how each version interprets the text	Media Activity: Trailer
Literary Criticism by René Girard **"Hamlet's Dull Revenge,"** p. 361A **Lexile 1290L**	**The student will be able to…** analyze the structure of an argument and identify its central ideas	Writing Activity: Argument
Short Story by Juan Rulfo **"Tell Them Not to Kill Me!"** p. 369A **Lexile 810L**	**The student will be able to…** analyze author's choices concerning the structure and point of view in a text	Speaking Activity: Discussion
ANCHOR TEXT **Feature Article by Alex Kotlowitz** **"Blocking the Transmission of Violence,"** p. 379A **Lexile 1150L**	**The student will be able to…** analyze ideas and events developed in the text and draw conclusions about them	Speaking Activity: Discussion
Poem by Wisława Szymborska **"Hatred,"** p. 395A	**The student will be able to…** determine the figurative meanings of words and phrases as they are used to personify an idea	Writing Activity: Comparison

Collection 4 Performance Tasks:
A Write an Analytical Essay
B Write an Argument

Vocabulary Strategy	Language and Style	Student Instructional Support	CLOSE READER Selection
	Paradox	**Scaffolding for ELL Students:** pp. 233, 236, 238, 240, 244, 248, 254, 264, 268, 272, 273, 277, 278, 286, 288, 294, 307, 316, 320, 328, 335, 342 **When Students Struggle:** pp. 232, 235, 239, 245, 246, 250, 255, 260, 266, 274, 282, 293, 297, 302, 304, 308, 313, 315, 324, 330, 336, 345, 351 **To Challenge Students:** pp. 234, 252, 257, 259, 271, 279, 287, 295, 301, 306, 317, 326, 340, 352	Drama by William Shakespeare Excerpt from *Hamlet*, p. 356b
		Scaffolding for ELL Students: Comprehension Support **When Students Struggle:** Compare and Contrast: Casting, Set Design, Lighting	
Domain-Specific Words and Phrases		**Scaffolding for ELL Students:** • Language: Print Cues • Vocabulary: Affixes **When Students Struggle:** Comprehension: Indented Quotations **To Challenge Students:** Evaluate the Author's Argument	
	Vary Syntax for Effect	**Scaffolding for ELL Students:** • Language: Contractions • Organizational Patterns: Time Sequence **When Students Struggle:** Comprehension: Time Sequence **To Challenge Students:** Analyze Perspective	
Latin Roots	Direct and Indirect Quotations	**Scaffolding for ELL Students:** • Comprehension: Time Sequence • Vocabulary: Informal Expressions • Language: Phrasal Verbs • Vocabulary: Cognates **When Students Struggle:** • Central Ideas and Characters • Draw Conclusions • Evidence and Conclusion **To Challenge Students:** • Write About Risk	Speech by Wangaa Mathari Nobel Peace Prize Acceptance Speech, p. 394b **Lexile 1210L**
	Repetition and Parallelism	**Scaffolding for ELL Students:** Vocabulary: Idioms **When Students Struggle:** Web Diagram: Visualize	

ANCHOR TEXT # The Tragedy of Hamlet

mySmartPlanner Create lesson plans and access resources online.

Drama by William Shakespeare

Why This Text?

The Tragedy of Hamlet stands as the playwright's innovative response to the revenge drama tradition. In this lesson, students are introduced to the powerful soliloquies that express the hero's conflict and make him a character that has stood the test of time.

▶ **View It!**

Professional Development Podcast:

Text Complexity

Key Learning Objective: The student will be able to analyze both the language and the structure of the play.

For additional practice:

Close Reader selection
Excerpt from "The Tragedy of Hamlet,"
Drama by William Shakespeare

COMMON CORE Common Core Standards

RL 1 Cite textual evidence.
RL 2 Determine two or more themes.
RL 3 Analyze elements of a story or drama.
RL 4 Determine the meaning of words and phrases in the text.
RL 5 Analyze author's choices concerning structure.
RL 6 Analyze a case in which grasping point of view requires distinguishing what is directly stated from what is really meant.
W 1 Write arguments to support claims.
W 4 Produce clear and coherent writing.
W 10 Write routinely over extended time frames and shorter time frames.
SL 1 Participate effectively in collaborative discussions.
SL 6 Adapt speech to a variety of contexts and tasks.
L 5a Interpret figures of speech.

▲ Text Complexity Rubric

Quantitative Measures	**The Tragedy of Hamlet** Lexile: N/A
Qualitative Measures	**Levels of Meaning/Purpose** ●—●—●—**●**→ multiple levels of complex meaning
	Structure ●—●—**●**—●→ some unconventional story structure elements
	Language Conventionality and Clarity ●—●—●—**●**→ archaic, unfamiliar language
	Knowledge Demands ●—●—●—**●**→ cultural and literary knowledge essential to understanding
Reader/Task Considerations	Teacher determined Vary by individual reader and type of text

Shakespearean Drama

Have students read the introduction independently. Discuss with them the ways in which *Hamlet* differs from other Shakespearean tragedies such as *Macbeth*. Elicit from students how that difference most likely contributes to the timelessness of the play.

The Globe Theater

After students read this section, draw their attention to the photograph on page 232. Have volunteers identify each part of the theater shown in the image. Discuss how the structure of the Elizabethan theater affected performances of the plays.

The Players

Have students discuss how the theater has changed since Shakespeare's time. Ask students what kind of event today might be comparable in the diversity of its audience. *(Possible answer: a concert or car race)*

Shakespearean Tragedy

Renaissance Drama

On the board, write these headings: Comedies, Tragedies, Histories. Have students volunteer the titles of Shakespeare's plays they have read or heard of and the category to which each belongs. Provide these additional examples as needed: Comedies: *As You Like It, A Midsummer Night's Dream, Much Ado About Nothing, The Taming of the Shrew.* Tragedies: *Romeo and Juliet, Macbeth, Hamlet, Julius Caesar.* Histories: *Henry V, King John, Richard III.*

Point out that many film versions of these plays have been made over the years. Additionally, many of the plots have been adapted to become the basis of modern movies. For example, the film *Ten Things I Hate About You* owes its story line to *The Taming of the Shrew.* Ask students if they can think of other current films that derive their plots from Shakespeare's dramas.

Shakespearean Drama

Shakespeare wrote *Hamlet* sometime around 1600. The story originated in an old folktale that became part of Denmark's legendary history. Shakespeare may have read a French retelling of the story, but he seems to have based his tragedy mainly on an English play about Hamlet from the 1580s. This earlier play had fallen out of fashion among Elizabethan audiences, but Shakespeare's version was an immediate success. Shakespeare transformed the genre of revenge tragedy by introducing a hero whose insights, doubts, and moral dilemmas often overshadow the play's action. *Hamlet's* psychological complexity helps explain the play's lasting popularity and influence.

The Globe Theater In Shakespeare's time, most plays were performed in outdoor public theaters. These theaters resembled courtyards, with the stage surrounded on three sides by galleries. The most famous theater in London was the Globe, where Shakespeare and his acting company performed. The Globe was a three-story wooden structure that could hold as many as 3,000 people. Plays were performed in the afternoon on a platform stage in the theater's center. The poorer patrons, or "groundlings," stood around the stage to watch the performance. Wealthier patrons sat in the covered galleries. The stage was mostly bare, which allowed for quick changes of scene. A trapdoor gave the stage added flexibility; in *Hamlet* it was used for the Ghost's entrances and exits and also in a scene set around a grave.

The Players Actors worked in close proximity to the groundlings, who stood around the stage, often eating and drinking. If they disapproved of certain characters or lines, they would let the actors know by jeering or even throwing food. The large crowds also attracted pickpockets and other rough elements. The rowdiness of the audiences and the location of theaters near taverns and other unsavory establishments gave theaters, and actors, an immoral reputation. Because the theater was viewed as disreputable, women were not allowed to perform; boys normally played the female roles.

Shakespearean Tragedy

Renaissance Drama During the Middle Ages, English drama focused mainly on religious themes, teaching moral lessons or retelling Bible stories to a populace that by and large could not read. In the Renaissance, however, a revival of interest in ancient Greek and Roman literature led playwrights to model their plays on classical drama. These plays fell into two main categories: comedies and tragedies. In Renaissance England, **comedy** was broadly defined as a dramatic work with a happy ending; many comedies contained humor, but humor was not required. A **tragedy**, in contrast, was a work in which the main character, or **tragic hero**, came to an unhappy end. In addition to comedies and tragedies, Shakespeare wrote plays classified as **histories**, which present stories about England's monarchs.

The Greek Origins of Tragedy

Have students read this section independently. Write the terms *catharsis, hubris,* and *nemesis* on the board. Have students define each term. Then ask them to summarize the relationship among the words and their connection to the tragedy genre.

Characteristics of Tragedy

Ask volunteers to read each row of the chart aloud.

A modern reconstruction of Shakespeare's theater was built near the site of the original Globe. Since opening in 1997, the new Globe has become one of London's most popular tourist attractions. As in the original Globe, performances only take place during the warmer months of the year because the theater is not enclosed.

The Greek Origins of Tragedy Both tragedy and comedy originated in ancient Greece, where plays were performed as part of elaborate outdoor festivals. According to the ancient Greek philosopher Aristotle, tragedy arouses pity and fear in the audience—pity for the hero and fear for all human beings, who are subject to character flaws and an unknown destiny. Seeing a tragedy unfold produces a **catharsis**, or cleansing, of these emotions in the audience. In ancient Greek tragedies, the hero's tragic flaw is often **hubris**—excessive pride that leads the tragic hero to challenge the gods. Angered by such hubris, the gods unleash their retribution, or nemesis, on the hero.

Characteristics of Tragedy The intention of tragedy is to exemplify the idea that human beings are doomed to suffer, fail, or die because of their own flaws, destiny, or fate. As part of this tradition, Shakespeare's tragedies share the following characteristics with the classical Greek tragedies.

Image Credits: ©Fotolia

WHEN STUDENTS STRUGGLE . . .

To help students understand the concept of a tragic hero, ask them to name a famous and well-liked sports figure who suffered public disgrace because of his or her actions. As a class, trace how the person reached the pinnacle of fame through his or her ambition, talent, or physical ability. Then guide students to see how this person's strength became a weakness and led to his or her downfall.

ASK STUDENTS how they feel when a public figure they look up to is revealed to be flawed and suffers a downfall. Do they feel fear on behalf of this figure? Do they feel pity for this figure? Would this figure's story make a good movie about pride and the downfall it can cause?

Characteristics of Tragedy	
The Tragic Hero	• is the main character who comes to an unhappy or miserable end. • is generally a person of importance in society, such as a king or queen. • exhibits extraordinary abilities but also a **tragic flaw**, a fatal error in judgment or weakness of character that leads directly to his or her downfall.
The Plot	• involves a **conflict** between the hero and a person or force, called the **antagonist**, which the hero must battle. Inevitably the conflict contributes to the hero's downfall. • is built upon a series of causally related events that lead to the **catastrophe**, or tragic resolution. This final stage of the plot usually involves the death of the hero. • is resolved when the tragic hero meets his or her doom with courage and dignity, reaffirming the grandeur of the human spirit.
The Theme	• is the central idea conveyed by the work and usually focuses on an aspect of fate, ambition, loss, defeat, death, loyalty, impulse, or desire. Tragedies may contain several themes.

One way in which Shakespearean tragedy differs from classical tragedy is that Shakespeare's tragic works are not uniformly serious. He often eased the intensity of the action by using the device of **comic relief**—a light, mildly humorous scene preceding or following a serious one.

Shakespeare's Conventions of Drama

The printed text of a Shakespeare play is like that of most traditional dramas. The play is divided into **acts** and **scenes**. The **dialogue** is labeled to show who is speaking, and **stage directions**, written in italics and in parentheses, specify the setting (time and place) and how the characters should behave and speak. In addition, Shakespeare typically used the following literary devices in his dramas.

Blank Verse Like many plays written before the 19th century, *Hamlet* is a **verse drama**, a play in which the dialogue consists almost entirely of poetry with a fixed pattern of rhythm, or **meter**. Many English verse dramas are written in **blank verse**, or unrhymed **iambic pentameter**, a meter in which the normal line contains five stressed syllables, each preceded by an unstressed syllable.

A little more than kin and less than kind.

Soliloquy and Aside Shakespeare often used two conventions, the soliloquy and the aside, to give audiences access to characters' private thoughts and feelings.

• A **soliloquy** is a speech that a character makes while alone on stage to reveal his or her thoughts to the audience.

Shakespearean Drama **233**

SCAFFOLDING FOR ELL STUDENTS

Clarify Concepts Write these terms on the board: act, scene, dialogue, stage directions, aside. Discuss the definitions of each. As a class, find the beginning of Act I, Scene 1, as well as examples of stage directions, dialogue, and an aside. Then organize students into mixed-ability groups. Provide each group with sticky notes.

ASK STUDENTS to write each term on a sticky note. Then direct them to Act II and have them attach a note to an example of each element. As a class, review their choices.

Characteristics of Tragedy

Discuss each characteristic with students. Then follow up with these additional insights:

• In order for tragedy to involve the audience's emotions, the tragic hero cannot be a villain. He or she must be someone to whom the audience can relate on some level in order to feel sympathy and horror at his or her downfall.

• Because few audience members are royalty or nobles, the conflict must be one that on some level represents the kind of dilemma that others have struggled with as well. The tragic hero is battling this conflict merely on a bigger stage.

• In most tragedies, as in life itself, the tragic hero must make choices that determine his or her fate. Once the hero is on the chosen path, the outcome can be foreseen.

Shakespeare's Conventions of Drama

Discuss the structure and features of Shakespeare's plays with students, drawing their attention to the bold terms in the text. Have them read the explanation of each literary device. Add these ideas:

Blank Verse

Read a longer passage from the play to help students hear the rhythm created by iambic pentameter. Point out that blank verse echoes the natural rhythms of English. Remind them that thoughts are not always expressed in single end-stopped lines (ending with a mark of punctuation). Sometimes, one sentence flows into several lines and can begin or end in the middle of a line. Explain that not all characters speak in blank verse; sometimes rhymed verse and even prose is used. In those cases, it is important to analyze why the change occurs.

Soliloquy and Aside

Point out that an aside is indicated by the stage directions. Explain that both soliloquies and asides serve the function of revealing a character's thoughts, feelings, attitudes, and personality traits as well as hinting at future plot events.

CLOSE READ

Dramatic Irony

Ask students to give an example of real-life dramatic irony. *(Possible answer: any sort of surprise when the person being surprised is unaware of the event but everyone else knows about it)* Have them explain why they think dramatic irony would be an effective device in a drama. *(Possible answers: It would intensify suspense as the audience waits for the characters to find out the truth; it could lead to misunderstanding and confusion that, in turn, would affect the plot.)*

Foreshadowing

Elicit from students examples of foreshadowing in stories they have read or movies they have seen. Explain that foreshadowing helps to maintain the attention of the audience as well as create suspense and tension.

Shakespearean Language

Read the description of each characteristic aloud. Then write lines 19–22 from Scene 1 on the board. Point out the unusual grammatical forms and word order. Explain that marginal notes help to clarify meaning; in addition, paraphrasing the lines can help readers understand them more clearly. Write these paraphrased lines on the board as an example:

Marcellus: Good night, Francisco. Who is taking your place? (line 19)

Barnado: Is that you, Horatio? (line 22)

- An **aside** is a remark that a character makes in an undertone to the audience or another character but that others on stage are not supposed to hear. A stage direction clarifies that a remark is an aside; unless otherwise specified, the aside is to the audience. Here is an example from *Hamlet*.

> **Polonius.** Fare you well, my lord.
> **Hamlet** [*aside*]. These tedious old fools.

Dramatic Irony Irony is based on a contrast between appearance or expectation and reality. In **dramatic irony**, the audience knows something that one or more characters do not know. For example, the audience knows why Hamlet behaves strangely in much of the play, but most characters are confused by this behavior.

Foreshadowing Foreshadowing is a writer's use of hints or clues to suggest what events will occur later in a work. In Act One, Scene 3, Hamlet's friends are worried after he decides to follow a ghost that appears to be his father. Their reactions provide clues about what the ghost will reveal and also hint at Hamlet's behavior later in the play:

> **Horatio.** He waxes desperate with imagination.
> **Marcellus.** Let's follow. 'Tis not fit thus to obey him.
> **Horatio.** Have after. To what issue will this come?
> **Marcellus.** Something is rotten in the state of Denmark.

Shakespearean Language

The English language in which Shakespeare wrote was quite different from today's. As you read a Shakespearean play, pay attention to the following.

Shakespearean Language	
Grammatical Forms	In Shakespeare's day, people still commonly used the pronouns *thou, thee, thy, thine,* and *thyself* in place of forms of *you.* Verb forms that are now outdated were also in use—*art* for *are* and *cometh* for *comes,* for example.
Unusual Word Order	Shakespeare often put verbs before subjects, objects before verbs, and other sentence parts in positions that now seem unusual. For instance, Polonius advises his son, "Neither a borrower nor a lender be," instead of saying, "Be neither a borrower nor a lender."
Unfamiliar Vocabulary	Shakespeare's vocabulary included many words no longer in use (like *seeling,* meaning "blinding") or words with meanings different from their meanings today (like *choppy,* meaning "chapped"). Shakespeare also coined new words, some of which (like *assassination*) have become a permanent part of the language.

Image Credits: ©Fotolia

TO CHALLENGE STUDENTS . . .

Give students a sense of Shakespeare's genius by having pairs write several lines of blank verse. Suggest that they take these steps:

- Choose a topic. Jot down ideas.
- Rephrase the ideas in lines of iambic pentameter.
- Read them aloud to see how they scan. Mark the stressed and unstressed syllables.

ASK STUDENTS to share their blank verse with the class. Have them discuss the challenges of creating an entire play in this form.

TEACH

CLOSE READ

William Shakespeare Have students read the biographical information about William Shakespeare. Share with them that it is recorded that in 1592, a rival dramatist named Robert Greene jealously referred to Shakespeare as an "upstart crow," showing that already by this time, Shakespeare was gaining recognition for his work.

Career Tell students that Shakespeare's theater company, the Lord Chamberlain's Men, enjoyed the approval of Queen Elizabeth. After her death in 1603, King James I became their patron at which time the company changed its name to the King's Men. Having the patronage of the reigning monarch helped to ensure their domination of the theater scene.

Legacy Remind students that Shakespeare's accomplishments are even more astonishing when the conditions that he had to meet are considered. There had to be enough parts for all of the members of the theater company; the women's parts had to be played by men; and there had to be enough action and excitement to satisfy the demanding audiences of the day. Yet, even working within these parameters, Shakespeare was able to create an astonishing range of plays that all speak to the universal human experience.

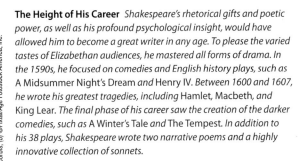

The Tragedy of Hamlet

Drama by William Shakespeare

William Shakespeare (1564–1616) *was born in Stratford-upon-Avon, a market town in central England. His father was a prosperous tradesman. Shakespeare probably attended Stratford's grammar school, where he would have studied Latin and read classical authors. In 1582 he married Anne Hathaway. The next year she gave birth to a daughter, Susanna. Their twins Hamnet and Judith followed in 1585.*

Sometime during the next seven years, Shakespeare found work in London as an actor; he also began to write plays. In 1594 he joined the Lord Chamberlain's Men, which became the most prestigious theater company in London. Shakespeare soon grew affluent from his share in the company's profits. He bought a large house in Stratford, where his wife and children remained.

The Height of His Career *Shakespeare's rhetorical gifts and poetic power, as well as his profound psychological insight, would have allowed him to become a great writer in any age. To please the varied tastes of Elizabethan audiences, he mastered all forms of drama. In the 1590s, he focused on comedies and English history plays, such as* A Midsummer Night's Dream *and* Henry IV. *Between 1600 and 1607, he wrote his greatest tragedies, including* Hamlet, Macbeth, *and* King Lear. *The final phase of his career saw the creation of the darker comedies, such as* A Winter's Tale *and* The Tempest. *In addition to his 38 plays, Shakespeare wrote two narrative poems and a highly innovative collection of sonnets.*

His Legacy *Shakespeare died in Stratford when he was 52 years old. At the time, some of his plays existed in cheap, often badly flawed editions; others had never appeared in print. In 1623, two theater colleagues published a collected edition of his plays known as the First Folio, which ensured the survival of his work. Ben Jonson, a rival playwright, wrote an introduction for the volume in which he declared that Shakespeare "was not of an age, but for all time." Four centuries after Shakespeare's death, his plays, which have been translated into many languages, continue to be performed around the world.*

WHEN STUDENTS STRUGGLE...

To help students familiarize themselves with the cast of characters listed on page 236, organize students into small groups. Ask them to preview the list and create a diagram that shows the relationships among the principal characters. Display a blank family tree to give students an idea of how they might want to structure their own diagram.

ASK STUDENTS to present their organizers to another group and discuss the similarities and differences. Then, together, create a class chart to use as a reference throughout the reading of the play.

TEACH

CLOSE READ

AS YOU READ Direct students to use the As You Read note to focus their reading.

Characters

Read each name aloud, allowing time for students to repeat the names after you.

Then discuss the identifying details given for the principal characters. Tell students that the list is organized in order of importance; the more minor characters appear at the end.

Remind students that the action of a play is driven by conflict, or a struggle between opposing forces. Have students make predictions about possible conflicts based on the details presented for Hamlet, Queen Gertrude, and King Claudius. Write these predictions on the board, and verify or adjust them as the class reads the play.

AS YOU READ More has been written about Hamlet than about any other Shakespearean character. Pay attention to details that show his complexity or that help explain why audiences find him so intriguing. Write down any questions you generate during reading.

CHARACTERS

The Ghost
Hamlet, Prince of Denmark, son of the late King Hamlet and Queen Gertrude
Queen Gertrude, widow of King Hamlet, now married to Claudius
King Claudius, brother to the late King Hamlet
Polonius, councillor to King Claudius
Ophelia, daughter of Polonius
Laertes, son of Polonius
Reynaldo, servant to Polonius
Horatio, Hamlet's friend and confidant

COURTIERS AT THE DANISH COURT

  Voltemand
  Cornelius
  Rosencrantz
  Guildenstern
  Osric
  Gentlemen
  A Lord

DANISH SOLDIERS

  Francisco
  Barnardo
  Marcellus
Fortinbras, Prince of Norway
A Captain in Fortinbras's army
Ambassadors to Denmark from England
Players who take the roles of Prologue, Player King, Player Queen, and Lucianus
  in *The Murder of Gonzago*
Two Messengers
Sailors
Gravedigger
Gravedigger's companion
Doctor of Divinity
Attendants, Lords, Guards, Musicians, Laertes's Followers, Soldiers, Officers

Place: Denmark

SCAFFOLDING FOR ELL STUDENTS

Understand Elliptical Language Explain that in some passages of dialogue, when the characters are engaging in casual conversation, words or phrases might be omitted. Point out "Give you good night" in line 20. Tell students that Francisco relies on the listeners to be able to understand that he means "I give you good night," meaning "I will say goodnight now." On the board, write lines 8–11.

ASK STUDENTS to work in pairs to supply the words that are missing. Invite volunteers to write their completed dialogue on the board. *(For this relief,* **I give you** *much thanks. /* **Not a mouse** *has been stirring.)* Remind students to practice this strategy when they encounter other elliptical language in the play.

ACT I

Scene 1 *A guard platform at Elsinore Castle.*

[*Enter* Barnardo *and* Francisco, *two sentinels.*]

Barnardo. Who's there?

Francisco. Nay, answer me. Stand and unfold yourself.

Barnardo. Long live the King!

Francisco. Barnardo.

5　**Barnardo.** He.

Francisco. You come most carefully upon your hour.

Barnardo. 'Tis now struck twelve. Get thee to bed,
Francisco.

Francisco. For this relief much thanks. 'Tis bitter cold,
And I am sick at heart.

10　**Barnardo.** Have you had quiet guard?

Francisco. Not a mouse stirring.

Barnardo. Well, good night.
If you do meet Horatio and Marcellus,
The rivals of my watch, bid them make haste.

[*Enter* Horatio *and* Marcellus.]

15　**Francisco.** I think I hear them.—Stand ho! Who is there?

Horatio. Friends to this ground.

Marcellus. And liegemen to the Dane.

Francisco. Give you good night.

Marcellus. O farewell, honest soldier. Who hath relieved you?

20　**Francisco.** Barnardo hath my place. Give you good night.

[Francisco *exits.*]

Marcellus. Holla, Barnardo.

Barnardo. Say, what, is Horatio there?

Horatio. A piece of him.

Barnardo. Welcome, Horatio.—Welcome, good Marcellus.

25　**Horatio.** What, has this thing appeared again tonight?

Barnardo. I have seen nothing.

Marcellus. Horatio says 'tis but our fantasy
And will not let belief take hold of him
Touching this dreaded sight twice seen of us.

30　Therefore I have entreated him along

2 unfold yourself: show
who you are.

14 rivals of my watch:
the other soldiers on
guard duty with me.

16–17 Horatio and
Marcellus identify
themselves as friendly to
Denmark (**this ground**)
and loyal subjects of the
Danish king (**the Dane**).

27–33 Marcellus
explains that Horatio
doubts their story about
having twice seen a
ghost (**apparition**), so
he has brought Horatio
to confirm what they
saw (**approve our eyes**).

Hamlet: Act I, Scene 1　**237**

CLOSE READ

Analyze Drama Elements: Setting (LINES 1–9)

 COMMON CORE **RL 3**

Tell students that Shakespeare's plays do not include elaborate stage directions. Specific details of setting are often revealed through the characters' dialogue.

Read lines 1–34 carefully with students, stopping frequently to make sure that all students are following what happens here. Point out how Shakespeare establishes the mood of the scene—with the cold, the late night confusion over the changing of the guard, and the hint that the guards have seen something strange during their late-night watch.

Ⓐ ASK STUDENTS to describe the setting of this scene. *(It takes place on the guard platform at Elsinore Castle at night in the bitter cold.)* Have students reread lines 1–9. What actions and phrases contribute to a mood of foreboding? *(Francisco is the one standing guard. Bernardo is coming to relieve him. As the one standing guard, Francisco should be the one to say something along the lines of "Hark, who goes there?" Instead, the play begins with Bernardo calling out "Who's there?" Bernardo's calling out seems to indicate that he is afraid, and that there is danger of some kind where these men stand guard. Finally, Francisco says that he is "sick at heart." His statement makes the audience wonder why he feels this way.)*

Close Read Screencasts　 ▶ View It!

Modeled Discussions

Have students click the *Close Read* icons in their eBooks to access a screencast in which readers discuss and annotate the following key passage:

- Laertes's warning to his sister (Act I, Scene 3, lines 33–42)

As a class, view and discuss the video.

Analyze Structure:
Conflict (LINES 44–63)

 COMMON CORE **RL 3**

Explain to students that the beginning of a play is known as the exposition, during which the setting, characters, and conflict are introduced. Tell students that opening scenes often hint at future events or ideas through the author's use of foreshadowing.

Read lines 44–63 carefully with students, stopping frequently to make sure that all students are following what happens when the Ghost appears and that they understand who the Ghost resembles.

B ASK STUDENTS to consider what the resemblance of this ghost to the late king of Denmark foreshadows. *(There is a problem related to Hamlet's dead father. Something needs to be resolved before the ghost of Hamlet's father can be at peace.)*

With us to watch the minutes of this night,
That, if again this apparition come,
He may approve our eyes and speak to it.

Horatio. Tush, tush, 'twill not appear.

Barnardo.   Sit down a while,
35   And let us once again assail your ears,
That are so fortified against our story,
What we have two nights seen.

Horatio.   Well, sit we down,
And let us hear Barnardo speak of this.

Barnardo. Last night of all,
40   When yond same star that's westward from the pole
Had made his course t' illume that part of heaven
Where now it burns, Marcellus and myself,
The bell then beating one—

[*Enter* Ghost.]

Marcellus. Peace, break thee off! Look where it comes again.

B   45   **Barnardo.** In the same figure like the King that's dead.

Marcellus [to Horatio]. Thou art a scholar. Speak to it, Horatio.

Barnardo. Looks he not like the King? Mark it, Horatio.

Horatio. Most like. It harrows me with fear and wonder.

Barnardo. It would be spoke to.

Marcellus.   Speak to it, Horatio.

50   **Horatio.** What art thou that usurp'st this time of night,
Together with that fair and warlike form
In which the majesty of buried Denmark
Did sometimes march? By heaven, I charge thee, speak.

Marcellus. It is offended.

Barnardo.   See, it stalks away.

55   **Horatio.** Stay! speak! speak! I charge thee, speak!

[Ghost *exits*.]

Marcellus. 'Tis gone and will not answer.

Barnardo. How now, Horatio, you tremble and look pale.
Is not this something more than fantasy?
What think you on 't?

60   **Horatio.** Before my God, I might not this believe
Without the sensible and true avouch
Of mine own eyes.

Marcellus.   Is it not like the King?

40 star . . . pole: the North Star.

41 his: its.

46–50 It was commonly believed that a ghost could only speak after it was spoken to, preferably by someone learned enough (**a scholar**) to ask the proper questions.

48 harrows: torments.

50 usurp'st: unlawfully takes over.

52 majesty of buried Denmark: the buried King of Denmark.

53 sometimes: formerly.

61–62 Without . . . eyes: without seeing the proof (**avouch**) with my own eyes.

SCAFFOLDING FOR ELL STUDENTS

Clarify Pronoun Referents Explain to students that in this part of the text, more than one pronoun may replace the same noun. Tell students they need to use the context in which the pronouns are used to help them identify the nouns they replace.

Project lines 39–49 on the whiteboard. Read Barnardo's first lines. Circle the word *star* and draw an arrow to the pronouns *his* and *it*. Explain that both pronouns refer to *star*.

ASK STUDENTS to notice where the Ghost enters. Have them identify the pronouns that the characters then use to refer to the Ghost. Invite a volunteer to highlight these pronouns on the board. Remind students that when they are in doubt about a pronoun referent, they should replace the pronoun with the noun to check whether it fits the context.

Horatio. As thou art to thyself.
Such was the very armor he had on
65 When he the ambitious Norway combated.
So frowned he once when, in an angry parle,
He smote the sledded Polacks on the ice.
'Tis strange.

Marcellus. Thus twice before, and jump at this dead hour,
70 With martial stalk hath he gone by our watch.

Horatio. In what particular thought to work I know not,
But in the gross and scope of mine opinion
This bodes some strange eruption to our state.

Marcellus. Good now, sit down, and tell me, he that knows,
75 Why this same strict and most observant watch
So nightly toils the subject of the land,
And why such daily cast of brazen cannon
And foreign mart for implements of war,
Why such impress of shipwrights, whose sore task
80 Does not divide the Sunday from the week.
What might be toward that this sweaty haste
Doth make the night joint laborer with the day?
Who is 't that can inform me?

Horatio.   That can I.
At least the whisper goes so: our last king,
85 Whose image even but now appeared to us,
Was, as you know, by Fortinbras of Norway,
Thereto pricked on by a most emulate pride,
Dared to the combat; in which our valiant Hamlet
(For so this side of our known world esteemed him)
90 Did slay this Fortinbras, who by a sealed compact,
Well ratified by law and heraldry,
Did forfeit, with his life, all those his lands
Which he stood seized of, to the conqueror.
Against the which a moiety competent
95 Was gagèd by our king, which had returned
To the inheritance of Fortinbras
Had he been vanquisher, as, by the same comart
And carriage of the article designed,
His fell to Hamlet. Now, sir, young Fortinbras,
100 Of unimprovèd mettle hot and full,
Hath in the skirts of Norway here and there
Sharked up a list of lawless resolutes
For food and diet to some enterprise
That hath a stomach in 't; which is no other
105 (As it doth well appear unto our state)
But to recover of us, by strong hand

65 Norway: the King of Norway.

66 parle: parley, meeting with an enemy.

67 smote: defeated; **sledded Polacks:** Polish soldiers riding in sleds.

69 jump: exactly.

72–73 This is a bad omen (**bodes some strange eruption**) for Denmark.

74–78 Can anyone explain why the Danes weary themselves each night with sentry duty and why there is so much casting of armaments (**brazen cannon**) and foreign trade (**mart**) for weapons?

81 toward: approaching, in preparation.

90–104 By prior agreement and according to laws governing combat, Hamlet gained all the land that Fortinbras had possessed (**stood seized of**). Hamlet had pledged an equivalent portion (**moiety competent**) of his land, which would have gone to Fortinbras if he won the battle, as was specified in the same agreement. Young Fortinbras, who has an undisciplined character (**unimproved mettle**), has gathered hastily (**Sharked up**) in outlying districts (**skirts**) of Norway a troop of lawless desperadoes to serve in some undertaking that requires courage (**hath a stomach in 't**).

Hamlet: Act I, Scene 1   **239**

Analyze Drama Elements: Plot (LINES 74–108)   COMMON CORE RL 3

Tell students that in a lengthy work, there are often subplots, or less important stories involving minor characters, that will have an impact on the main plot at some point in the play.

Read lines 74–108 carefully with students, stopping frequently to make sure that all students grasp the seeds of the conflict between Denmark and Norway. Let them know that there are two characters named Hamlet and two characters named Fortinbras. The elder Hamlet and the elder Fortinbras are the focus of the little piece of history Horatio relates here. The younger Hamlet will be the hero of the play.

C ASK STUDENTS what the audience learns from Marcellus's question to Horatio. (*Denmark is preparing to defend itself from an attack by young Fortinbras.*) How does Marcellus's description of a military build-up as well as Horatio's response affect the mood of this scene? (*Both speeches add to the uneasy feeling that something is amiss in Denmark.*)

Explain that when a minor character is mentioned early in the play, he or she may prove to be important later.

D ASK STUDENTS to describe Fortinbras based on what Horatio says. (*Fortinbras is a man of quick action and courage who wants to regain the lands his father lost.*)

WHEN STUDENTS STRUGGLE...

Tell students that in lines 84–108, Horatio provides background information on a possible threat to Denmark. Help them understand this subplot by completing a cause-and-effect chart, using the marginal notes as well as the text.

King Hamlet defeated King Fortinbras and took his land.	*Young Fortinbras wants the land back and is planning to attack.*	*Denmark is preparing to defend itself against this attack.*

CLOSE READ

Analyze Word Choice   COMMON CORE RL 4

(LINES 116–129)

Remind students that an **allusion** is an indirect reference to a place, historical figure, or work of literature that helps the author convey an important idea.

Read lines 116–129 carefully with students. Explain the allusion to Julius Caesar and help students to picture the scene Horatio describes in these lines.

Ⓔ ASK STUDENTS to explain the significance of Horatio's allusions to ancient Rome and Julius Caesar. What is he suggesting through this reference? *(Horatio explains that before Julius Caesar was assassinated, the ghosts of the dead broke out of their graves and walked the streets of Rome. Horatio mentions other omens preceding Caesar's murder. Horatio says that there are similar signs and omens in Denmark, hinting that bad things will happen.)*

Analyze Drama Elements: COMMON CORE RL 3
Character (LINES 130–143)

Point out that a character's actions and words define him or her. Read lines 130–144 carefully with students and check for understanding.

Ⓕ CITE TEXT EVIDENCE Ask students to explain the traits that Horatio possesses. Have them support their ideas with details from the text. *(Horatio is courageous. He demands that the Ghost speak to him; he refuses to back down, repeating "Speak to me" and "O speak." He interrogates the Ghost about its purpose in appearing, saying "If thou art privy to thy country's fate, / Which happily foreknowing may avoid, / O, speak!"*

SCAFFOLDING FOR ELL STUDENTS

Analyze Language Project lines 116–129 on the whiteboard. Invite volunteers to mark up the text:

- Highlight in blue images of supernatural occurrences.
- Underline words that suggest death or destruction.

ASK STUDENTS what Horatio is suggesting that the Ghost foreshadows through his reference to what happened to ancient Rome.

And terms compulsory, those foresaid lands
So by his father lost. And this, I take it,
Is the main motive of our preparations,
110   The source of this our watch, and the chief head
Of this posthaste and rummage in the land.

Barnardo. I think it be no other but e'en so.
Well may it sort that this portentous figure
Comes armèd through our watch so like the king
115   That was and is the question of these wars.

Horatio. A mote it is to trouble the mind's eye.
In the most high and palmy state of Rome,
A little ere the mightiest Julius fell,
The graves stood tenantless, and the sheeted dead
120   Did squeak and gibber in the Roman streets;
As stars with trains of fire and dews of blood,
Disasters in the sun; and the moist star,
Upon whose influence Neptune's empire stands,
Was sick almost to doomsday with eclipse.
125   And even the like precurse of feared events,
As harbingers preceding still the fates
And prologue to the omen coming on,
Have heaven and earth together demonstrated
Unto our climatures and countrymen.

[*Enter* Ghost.]

130   But soft, behold! Lo, where it comes again!
I'll cross it though it blast me.—Stay, illusion!

[*It spreads his arms.*]

If thou hast any sound or use of voice,
Speak to me.
If there be any good thing to be done
135   That may to thee do ease and grace to me,
Speak to me.
If thou art privy to thy country's fate,
Which happily foreknowing may avoid,
O, speak!
140   Or if thou hast uphoarded in thy life
Extorted treasure in the womb of earth,
For which, they say, you spirits oft walk in death,
Speak of it.

[*The cock crows.*]

Stay and speak!—Stop it, Marcellus.

Marcellus. Shall I strike it with my partisan?

145   **Horatio.** Do, if it will not stand.

110 head: source.

111 rummage: bustle.

113 Well . . . sort: it may be fitting.

116 mote: dust speck.

117 palmy: thriving.

119 sheeted: wrapped in shrouds.

120 gibber: chatter.

122 disasters: menacing signs; **moist star:** the moon, which controls the Earth's tides.

123 Neptune: Roman god of the sea.

125–129 A similar foreshadowing (**precurse**) has occurred in Denmark, where a terrible event (**omen**) was preceded by signs that were like forerunners (**harbingers**) announcing the approach of someone.

130 soft: be quiet, hold off.

131 cross: confront.

138 happily . . . avoid: perhaps (**happily**) may be avoided if known in advance.

141 extorted: ill-gotten.

144 partisan: a long-handled weapon.

The graves stood tenantless, and the sheeted dead
Did squeak and gibber in the Roman streets;
As stars with trains of fire and dews of blood,
Disasters in the sun; and the moist star,

Barnardo. 'Tis here.

Horatio. 'Tis here.

[Ghost *exits*.]

Marcellus. 'Tis gone.
We do it wrong, being so majestical,
150   To offer it the show of violence,
For it is as the air, invulnerable,
And our vain blows malicious mockery.

Barnardo. It was about to speak when the cock crew.

Horatio. And then it started like a guilty thing
155   Upon a fearful summons. I have heard
The cock, that is the trumpet to the morn,
Doth with his lofty and shrill-sounding throat
Awake the god of day, and at his warning,
Whether in sea or fire, in earth or air,
160   Th' extravagant and erring spirit hies
To his confine, and of the truth herein
This present object made probation.

Marcellus. It faded on the crowing of the cock.
Some say that ever 'gainst that season comes
165   Wherein our Savior's birth is celebrated,
This bird of dawning singeth all night long;
And then, they say, no spirit dare stir abroad,
The nights are wholesome; then no planets strike,
No fairy takes, nor witch hath power to charm,
170   So hallowed and so gracious is that time.

Horatio. So have I heard and do in part believe it.
But look, the morn in russet mantle clad
Walks o'er the dew of yon high eastward hill.
Break we our watch up, and by my advice
175   Let us impart what we have seen tonight
Unto young Hamlet; for, upon my life,
This spirit, dumb to us, will speak to him.
Do you consent we shall acquaint him with it
As needful in our loves, fitting our duty?

180   **Marcellus.** Let's do 't, I pray, and I this morning know
Where we shall find him most convenient.

[*They exit*.]

---

154 started: made a sudden movement.

160 extravagant and erring: wandering out of bounds.

162 made probation: demonstrated.

164–165 ever . . . celebrated: just before Christmas.

168 strike: put forth an evil influence.

169 takes: bewitches.

TEACH

CLOSE READ

Analyze Structure

COMMON CORE **RL 5**

(LINES 148–181)

Tell students that playwrights make deliberate choices about how to structure their plays in order to communicate their meaning and achieve the desired impact.

Read lines 148–181 with students. Stop after each chunk of dialogue by Horatio and Marcellus and ask students to summarize what they are saying about the appearance of the Ghost.

Point out that by the end of the first scene, Hamlet, the play's hero, has not yet appeared.

G ASK STUDENTS to explain the purpose of the first scene. What ideas does Shakespeare want the audience to understand before meeting the main characters? (*The first scene fills in the background on the Ghost and the political situation with Norway. It establishes the idea in the audience's mind that there is something wrong in Denmark. It builds suspense.*) As the scene draws to a close, what does Horatio say that he and the guards should do next and why? (*Horatio says they should tell Hamlet about the Ghost. He thinks that even though the Ghost would not speak to him and the guards, it might speak to Hamlet.*) Given how Scene 1 closes, ask students to predict what might happen in Act II. (*Answers will vary, but students will likely expect to meet Hamlet and to see more of or find out more about the Ghost.*)

CLOSE READ

Analyze Drama Elements: Character (sc. 2 LINES 1–38)

COMMON CORE RL 3

Call students' attention to the setting and audience of this speech. Remind them that characters have a purpose for what they say that is often revealed through the words in which they express themselves.

Read the King's opening speech carefully with your students. Stop at line 14 and discuss what he has said about his brother's death and his marriage to his brother's widow. Stop as necessary during the remainder of this speech to discuss details of the conflict between Denmark and Norway. Remind students that they've heard about this conflict already; Horatio speaks of it in Scene 1, lines 74–108.

H **ASK STUDENTS** why Claudius addresses his brother's death and his remarriage in the first part of his speech. *(He wants to establish that he feels the proper emotions of grief, and he wants to show that his marriage to Gertrude is both personally and politically necessary.)* How does the second part of the speech differ from the first? *(He takes care of state business in the second part, explaining his plan for dealing with the threat from Fortinbras.)* What impression does Claudius wish to create through this speech? *(He comes across as a competent ruler in his desire to avoid war and come to a peaceful settlement. He conveys sincere grief for his brother and the purest of motives in marrying his widowed sister-in-law.)*

Scene 2 *A state room at the castle.*

[*Flourish. Enter* Claudius, *King of Denmark,* Gertrude the Queen, the Council, *as* Polonius, *and his son* Laertes, Hamlet, *with others, among them* Voltemand *and* Cornelius.]

H

King. Though yet of Hamlet our dear brother's death
The memory be green, and that it us befitted
To bear our hearts in grief, and our whole kingdom
To be contracted in one brow of woe,
5　Yet so far hath discretion fought with nature
That we with wisest sorrow think on him
Together with remembrance of ourselves.
Therefore our sometime sister, now our queen,
Th' imperial jointress to this warlike state,
10　Have we (as 'twere with a defeated joy,
With an auspicious and a dropping eye,
With mirth in funeral and with dirge in marriage,
In equal scale weighing delight and dole)
Taken to wife. Nor have we herein barred
15　Your better wisdoms, which have freely gone
With this affair along. For all, our thanks.
Now follows that you know. Young Fortinbras,
Holding a weak supposal of our worth
Or thinking by our late dear brother's death
20　Our state to be disjoint and out of frame,
Colleaguèd with this dream of his advantage,
He hath not failed to pester us with message
Importing the surrender of those lands
Lost by his father, with all bonds of law,
25　To our most valiant brother—so much for him.
Now for ourself and for this time of meeting.
Thus much the business is: we have here writ
To Norway, uncle of young Fortinbras,
Who, impotent and bedrid, scarcely hears
30　Of this his nephew's purpose, to suppress
His further gait herein, in that the levies,
The lists, and full proportions are all made
Out of his subject; and we here dispatch
You, good Cornelius, and you, Voltemand,
35　For bearers of this greeting to old Norway,
Giving to you no further personal power
To business with the King more than the scope
Of these dilated articles allow.

[*Giving them a paper.*]

Farewell, and let your haste commend your duty.

8 our sometime sister: my former sister-in-law. (Claudius uses the royal "we.")

9 jointress: a woman who owns property with her husband.

11–12 With . . . eye: with one eye reflecting good fortune and the other eye, sorrow; **dirge:** a song of mourning.

21 Colleaguèd . . . advantage: connected with this false hope of his superior position.

23 Importing: relating to.

29 impotent: helpless.

30–33 Since Fortinbras has obtained all of his troops and supplies from Norway, Claudius has asked the King of Norway to stop him from proceeding further.

37 To business: to negotiate.

38 dilated articles: detailed instructions.

Strategies for Annotation　🖊 📖 *Annotate it!*

Analyze Character
COMMON CORE RL 4

Have students use their eBook annotation tools to analyze Claudius's speech and what it reveals about his character.

- Highlight in green the words that refer to King Hamlet's death or emotions related to that event.
- Highlight in yellow the words that refer to Claudius's marriage or emotions related to it.
- Underline phrases that include both positive and negative words.
- Review your annotations. On a note, explain what you might infer from Claudius's balance of emotions in this speech.

That we with wisest sorrow think on him …
Therefore our sometime sister, now our queen,
Th' imperial jointress to this warlike state,
Have we (as 'twere with a defeated joy, With an
auspicious and a dropping eye, With mirth in
funeral and with dirge in marriage,

Laurence Olivier's 1948 film *Hamlet*. Background: Hamlet (Laurence Olivier). Foreground, left to right: Claudius (Basil Sidney), Gertrude (Eileen Herlie), Polonius (Felix Aylmer).

40 **Cornelius/Voltemand.** In that and all things will we show our duty.

King. We doubt it nothing. Heartily farewell.

[Voltemand *and* Cornelius *exit.*]

And now, Laertes, what's the news with you?
You told us of some suit. What is 't, Laertes?
You cannot speak of reason to the Dane
45 And lose your voice. What wouldst thou beg, Laertes,
That shall not be my offer, not thy asking?
The head is not more native to the heart,
The hand more instrumental to the mouth,
Than is the throne of Denmark to thy father.
50 What wouldst thou have, Laertes?

Laertes.   My dread lord,
Your leave and favor to return to France,
From whence though willingly I came to Denmark
To show my duty in your coronation,

45 lose your voice: waste your breath.

47 native: closely connected.

Hamlet: Act I, Scene 2 **243**

CLOSE READ

Support Inferences   COMMON CORE **RL 1**

(sc. 2 PHOTOGRAPH)

Tell students that film directors use actors' positions on stage, gestures, and posture to convey ideas about the characters they are portraying.

I ASK STUDENTS to look at the photograph and say what perception of Hamlet's character is developed in this scene. Why? *(Hamlet is off by himself. He appears very isolated from the others—not involved in their conversation or in the activities of the King and his court.)*

Analyze Drama Elements: COMMON CORE **RL 3**
Character (sc. 2 LINES 42–50)

Point out that although Hamlet is present at court, Claudius chooses to address Laertes next rather than his nephew.

J CITE TEXT EVIDENCE Have students explain how they would describe Claudius's attitude toward Laertes. What details support their description? *(Claudius appears very fond of Laertes, who is the son of his councillor Polonius. He says that he will do whatever he can for Laertes. "What wouldst thou beg, Laertes,/That shall not be my offer, not thy asking?")* Ask students what they might infer from Claudius's action of turning to Laertes first. *(He may fear a confrontation with Hamlet. Hamlet may be at a distance from Claudius, unwilling to engage in conversation with him.)*

APPLYING ACADEMIC VOCABULARY

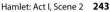

integrity	trigger

As you discuss the characters and events in Act I, incorporate the following Collection 4 academic vocabulary words: *integrity* and *trigger*. Ask students to look for details that reveal Hamlet's view of his uncle's **integrity**. Have them also discuss how the Ghost **triggers** the action by his appearance.

Analyze Drama Elements: Conflict (sc. 2 LINES 62–95)

COMMON CORE RL 3

Remind students that although they cannot see the actions or facial expressions accompanying the characters' words, they can hear the tone in which the dialogue is spoken by looking carefully at the choice of words and their arrangement.

 ASK STUDENTS to describe the tone of Hamlet's aside after Claudius greets him as "my cousin Hamlet and my son." Why might he feel this way? *(Hamlet shows veiled animosity toward Claudius, perhaps because the King has married Hamlet's mother.)* Why does the Queen urge Hamlet to cast "thy nighted color off"? *(Hamlet's dark mourning attire is a reminder of her husband's recent death and a sign that her son has not adjusted to her hasty marriage to Claudius. She wants her son to accept his father's death and to be cheerful about his mother's re-marriage.)* What does Hamlet imply when he says that outward signs of mourning "are actions that a man might play"? *(He may be saying that although the Queen and Claudius play the part of mourning his father, in fact, they feel no real grief. He also makes it very clear that his own mourning is both inward and outward—that he feels genuine grief inside that surpasses the grief his dark clothing indicates.)* Finally, and most important, ask students to describe the conflict they see between Hamlet on one side and, on the other side, his uncle, the King, and his mother, the Queen. *(Hamlet appears to be mired in grief over his father's recent death. He appears to resent how cheerful his mother and his uncle are while they clearly wish for him to get over his father's death and move on.)*

Yet now I must confess, that duty done,
55 My thoughts and wishes bend again toward France
And bow them to your gracious leave and pardon.

King. Have you your father's leave? What says Polonius?

Polonius. Hath, my lord, wrung from me my slow leave
By laborsome petition, and at last
60 Upon his will I sealed my hard consent.
I do beseech you give him leave to go.

King. Take thy fair hour, Laertes. Time be thine,
And thy best graces spend it at thy will.—
But now, my cousin Hamlet and my son—

65 **Hamlet** [*aside*]. A little more than kin and less than kind.

King. How is it that the clouds still hang on you?

Hamlet. Not so, my lord; I am too much in the sun.

Queen. Good Hamlet, cast thy nighted color off,
And let thine eye look like a friend on Denmark.
70 Do not forever with thy vailèd lids
Seek for thy noble father in the dust.
Thou know'st 'tis common; all that lives must die,
Passing through nature to eternity.

Hamlet. Ay, madam, it is common.

Queen.   If it be,
75 Why seems it so particular with thee?

Hamlet. "Seems," madam? Nay, it is. I know not "seems."
'Tis not alone my inky cloak, good mother,
Nor customary suits of solemn black,
Nor windy suspiration of forced breath,
80 No, nor the fruitful river in the eye,
Nor the dejected havior of the visage,
Together with all forms, moods, shapes of grief,
That can denote me truly. These indeed "seem,"
For they are actions that a man might play;
85 But I have that within which passes show,
These but the trappings and the suits of woe.

King. 'Tis sweet and commendable in your nature, Hamlet,
To give these mourning duties to your father.
But you must know your father lost a father,
90 That father lost, lost his, and the survivor bound
In filial obligation for some term
To do obsequious sorrow. But to persever
In obstinate condolement is a course
Of impious stubbornness. 'Tis unmanly grief.
95 It shows a will most incorrect to heaven,

60 Upon . . . consent: I reluctantly agreed to his wishes.

64 cousin: kinsman.

65 Hamlet plays off two meanings of **kind:** "loving" and "natural." He does not resemble Claudius in nature or feel a son's affection for him.

67 sun: the sunlight of royal favor (also a pun on **son,** suggesting annoyance at Claudius's use of the word).

68 nighted color: dark mood.

70 vailèd lids: lowered eyes.

74 Hamlet plays off two meanings of **common:** "universal" and "vulgar."

75 particular: special, personal.

77–83 'Tis not . . . truly: My feelings are not limited to my black mourning clothes, heavy sighs, tears, downcast expression, and other outward signs of grief.

89–94 Claudius says that a surviving son must dutifully mourn (**do obsequious sorrow**) for a while, but to remain stubbornly in grief (**obstinate condolement**) beyond that appropriate period is perverse.

SCAFFOLDING FOR ELL STUDENTS

Identify Prefixes Remind students that prefixes are word parts attached to the beginning of a base word. Explain that recognizing prefixes can help them to figure out the meaning of a word. Point out the prefix *un-* in line 94. Tell students that *un-* means "not." Someone who is unmanly is not manly or strong.

ASK STUDENTS to list words that contain the prefix *un-* on page 245. Have them work together to define the words, using their knowledge of the prefix as well as the context of the word. *(Possible answers: unfortified [line 96]: not strengthened; unschooled [line 117]: not educated; unprevailing [line 107]: not dominant or not shared by others; unforced [line 123]: not forced, freely offered; unprofitable [line 133]: not profitable or worthwhile; unweeded [line 123]: not weeded, not cared for)*

A heart unfortified, a mind impatient,
An understanding simple and unschooled.
For what we know must be and is as common
As any the most vulgar thing to sense,
100 Why should we in our peevish opposition
Take it to heart? Fie, 'tis a fault to heaven,
A fault against the dead, a fault to nature,
To reason most absurd, whose common theme
Is death of fathers, and who still hath cried,
105 From the first corse till he that died today,
"This must be so." We pray you, throw to earth
This unprevailing woe and think of us
As of a father; for let the world take note,
You are the most immediate to our throne,
110 And with no less nobility of love
Than that which dearest father bears his son
Do I impart toward you. For your intent
In going back to school in Wittenberg,
It is most retrograde to our desire,
115 And we beseech you, bend you to remain
Here in the cheer and comfort of our eye,
Our chiefest courtier, cousin, and our son.

Queen. Let not thy mother lose her prayers, Hamlet.
I pray thee, stay with us. Go not to Wittenberg.

120 **Hamlet.** I shall in all my best obey you, madam.

King. Why, 'tis a loving and a fair reply.
Be as ourself in Denmark.—Madam, come.
This gentle and unforced accord of Hamlet
Sits smiling to my heart, in grace where of
125 No jocund health that Denmark drinks today
But the great cannon to the clouds shall tell,
And the King's rouse the heaven shall bruit again,
Respeaking earthly thunder. Come away.

[*Flourish. All but* Hamlet *exit.*]

Hamlet. O, that this too, too sullied flesh would melt,
130 Thaw, and resolve itself into a dew,
Or that the Everlasting had not fixed
His canon 'gainst self-slaughter! O God, God,
How weary, stale, flat, and unprofitable
Seem to me all the uses of this world!
135 Fie on 't, ah fie! 'Tis an unweeded garden
That grows to seed. Things rank and gross in nature
Possess it merely. That it should come to this:
But two months dead—nay, not so much, not two.
So excellent a king, that was to this

96 unfortified: unstrengthened against adversity.

99 As . . . sense: as the most common experience.

104 still: always.

105 corse: corpse.

107 unprevailing: not yielding to persuasion.

108–112 Claudius claims that he offers (**impart toward**) Hamlet, who is next in line (**most immediate**) to succeed to the throne, all the love that the most affectionate father feels for his son.

113 Wittenberg University (founded in 1502) was famous for being the school of German theologian Martin Luther, whose challenge to Roman Catholic doctrine started the Reformation.

114 retrograde: contrary.

125–128 Claudius boasts that he will not merely drink a happy toast (**jocund health**) that day, but a deep drink (**rouse**) accompanied by fanfare, which heaven will echo with thunder.

129 sullied: stained, defiled.

132 canon: law.

139–140 Hamlet says that comparing his father to Claudius would be like comparing the sun god **Hyperion** to a **satyr** (a mythical creature, half man and half goat, associated with lechery).

Hamlet: Act I, Scene 2 **245**

WHEN STUDENTS STRUGGLE . . .

Tell students that when they read a speech from a play aloud, they should be speaking in the voice of that character. To read Hamlet's soliloquy, they should use their voices to express his depression at the situation in which he finds himself, his grief over the loss of his father, and his anger at his mother. Read aloud several lines of the soliloquy to model how to convey emotion through volume, tone, expression, and pace. Have pairs practice reading.

- Divide the speech into two parts: lines 129–136, lines 136–159.
- One partner should read the first section aloud, and then the other partner should read the second section. Listen to how your partner uses his or her voice to express Hamlet's feelings.

CLOSE READ

Support Inferences
COMMON CORE RL 1

(sc. 2 LINES 106–128)

Review the strategy of making inferences with students, explaining that they need to look at the context as well as the specific details to make an educated guess about what is not directly stated.

Read with students the exchange between Claudius and Hamlet, and also between Gertrude and Hamlet. Make sure they understand what the King and Queen want from Hamlet.

L ASK STUDENTS to explain Claudius's purpose in his speech to Hamlet. Does he feel he accomplishes this purpose? Why or why not? *(Claudius's purpose is to win Hamlet over to his side and get him to stay at court instead of returning to Wittenberg. Claudius interprets Hamlet's reply that he will obey his mother's request as a sign that he has succeeded in his purpose. Claudius says, "Why, 'tis a loving and a fair reply." He then urges the court to join him in a great celebration.)*

Analyze Structure: Soliloquy (sc. 2 LINES 129–159)
COMMON CORE RL 5

Point out to students that this is the first of Hamlet's soliloquies. Remind them that a soliloquy often occurs at a moment of high emotion for the character; through his or her words, the character's inner conflict, thoughts, and feelings are revealed to the audience.

Before discussing this soliloquy, have students work in pairs to paraphrase the speech, translating Hamlet's words into standard English.

M CITE TEXT EVIDENCE Ask students what this speech reveals about the reason for Hamlet's attitude toward Claudius and his mother. *(Hamlet blames his mother for her unfaithfulness to his father's memory and her willingness to remarry so quickly. He says, "frailty, thy name is woman!" and emphasizes the "wicked speed" with which she fell into "incestuous sheets." With each restatement of this idea, the length of time shortens. He sees his uncle as a lecher, taking advantage of this frailty.)* What does he resolve to do about this situation? *(He says that he will remain silent.)*

Analyze Drama Elements: Character (sc. 2 LINES 160–184)

CITE TEXT EVIDENCE Have students explain how they know that Hamlet thinks highly of Horatio. *(He calls him "my good friend." He says that by being critical of himself, Horatio is doing Hamlet's ear a violence.)*

Have students explain Hamlet's mocking, ironic humor in lines 178–179. *(Hamlet knows that Horatio has come home for the elder Hamlet's funeral. When he says, "I think it was to see my mother's wedding," he is being sarcastic about how soon his mother re-married after his father's death.)* Have students paraphrase lines 181–182 and explain the element of humor in Hamlet's words here. *(Paraphrase: It was thrifty of my mother to re-marry so soon, Horatio. That way, the meats that were baked and served at my father's funeral could be served as cold cuts at the wedding reception. The humor: Again, Hamlet is making a joke at the expense of his mother and her hasty marriage to Claudius.)* Finally, ask students why Hamlet might joke like this with Horatio and what his wisecracks about his mother's wedding reveal about him. *(Hamlet clearly sees Horatio as a trusted friend with whom he can make jokes about painful personal matters. What Hamlet reveals about himself is that he has a sharp sense of humor that he doesn't mind aiming at himself and that he seems almost as upset about his mother's marriage to Claudius as about his father's death.)*

Hamlet is one of the most challenging pieces of literature students of any age are likely to encounter. Most students will struggle with the characters, the dialogue, and the hero's complexity. To give all your students an early grasp of Hamlet himself, use "When Students Struggle . . ." (on this page) with all students.

---

140   Hyperion to a satyr; so loving to my mother
      That he might not beteem the winds of heaven
      Visit her face too roughly. Heaven and earth,
      Must I remember? Why, she would hang on him
      As if increase of appetite had grown
145   By what it fed on. And yet, within a month
      (Let me not think on 't; frailty, thy name is woman!),
      A little month, or ere those shoes were old
      With which she followed my poor father's body,
      Like Niobe, all tears—why she, even she
150   (O God, a beast that wants discourse of reason
      Would have mourned longer!), married with my uncle,
      My father's brother, but no more like my father
      Than I to Hercules. Within a month,
      Ere yet the salt of most unrighteous tears
155   Had left the flushing in her gallèd eyes,
      She married. O, most wicked speed, to post
      With such dexterity to incestuous sheets!
      It is not, nor it cannot come to good.
      But break, my heart, for I must hold my tongue.

      [*Enter* Horatio, Marcellus, *and* Barnardo.]

160   **Horatio.** Hail to your lordship.

      Hamlet. I am glad to see you well.
      Horatio—or I do forget myself!

      Horatio. The same, my lord, and your poor servant ever.

      Hamlet. Sir, my good friend. I'll change that name with you.
165   And what make you from Wittenberg, Horatio?—Marcellus?

      Marcellus. My good lord.

      Hamlet. I am very glad to see you. [*To* Barnardo.] Good
      even, sir.—
      But what, in faith, make you from Wittenberg?

170   **Horatio.** A truant disposition, good my lord.

      Hamlet. I would not hear your enemy say so,
      Nor shall you do my ear that violence
      To make it truster of your own report
      Against yourself. I know you are no truant.
175   But what is your affair in Elsinore?
      We'll teach you to drink deep ere you depart.

      Horatio. My lord, I came to see your father's funeral.

      Hamlet. I prithee, do not mock me, fellow student.
      I think it was to see my mother's wedding.

180   **Horatio.** Indeed, my lord, it followed hard upon.

141 beteem: allow.

147 or ere: before.

149 Niobe: a Greek mythological figure who continued weeping for her slaughtered children even after she was turned to stone.

155 Had . . . eyes: had stopped reddening her inflamed (**gallèd**) eyes.

157 incestuous: Marriage between a widow and her late husband's brother was often considered incestuous in Shakespeare's time and was prohibited by church law.

163 Horatio refers to himself as a "servant" out of respect for Hamlet.

169 what . . . from: what are you doing away from.

173 truster: believer.

180 hard upon: soon after.

WHEN STUDENTS STRUGGLE . . .

Tell students that conflict is the basis of action in a drama as the character tries to resolve his or her problem. To guide students' understanding of both Hamlet's character and the conflicts he is experiencing, have them reread lines 65–159. Have them then fill out a chart similar to the one on page 247, explaining each conflict that Hamlet's words reveal and the details that show the conflict.

Prompt students as needed by directing them to specific passages.

Hamlet. Thrift, thrift, Horatio. The funeral baked meats
Did coldly furnish forth the marriage tables.
Would I had met my dearest foe in heaven
Or ever I had seen that day, Horatio!
185 My father—methinks I see my father.

Horatio. Where, my lord?

Hamlet.   In my mind's eye, Horatio.

Horatio. I saw him once. He was a goodly king.

Hamlet. He was a man. Take him for all in all,
I shall not look upon his like again.

190 **Horatio.** My lord, I think I saw him yesternight.

Hamlet. Saw who?

Horatio. My lord, the King your father.

Hamlet.   The King my father?

Horatio. Season your admiration for a while
With an attent ear, till I may deliver
195 Upon the witness of these gentlemen
This marvel to you.

Hamlet.   For God's love, let me hear!

Horatio. Two nights together had these gentlemen,
Marcellus and Barnardo, on their watch,
In the dead waste and middle of the night,
200 Been thus encountered: a figure like your father,
Armèd at point exactly, cap-à-pie,
Appears before them and with solemn march
Goes slow and stately by them. Thrice he walked
By their oppressed and fear-surprisèd eyes
205 Within his truncheon's length, whilst they, distilled
Almost to jelly with the act of fear,
Stand dumb and speak not to him. This to me
In dreadful secrecy impart they did,
And I with them the third night kept the watch,
210 Where, as they had delivered, both in time,
Form of the thing (each word made true and good),
The apparition comes. I knew your father;
These hands are not more like.

Hamlet.   But where was this?

Marcellus. My lord, upon the platform where we watch.

215 **Hamlet.** Did you not speak to it?

Horatio.   My lord, I did,
But answer made it none. Yet once methought

181–182 The funeral . . . tables: Leftovers from the funeral were served cold at the marriage feast.

183 dearest: most hated.

184 Or ever: before.

187 goodly: fine, admirable.

193–194 Season . . . ear: Control your astonishment for a moment and listen carefully.

201 Armèd . . . cap-à -pie: armed properly in every detail, from head to foot.

205 Within his truncheon's length: no farther away than the length of his short staff.

205–206 distilled . . . fear: reduced almost to jelly by fear.

207–208 This . . . did: They told me this in terrified (**dreadful**) secrecy.

210 delivered: asserted.

CLOSE READ

Support Inferences

COMMON CORE RL 1

(sc. 2 LINES 185–213)

Read this exchange between Horatio and Hamlet with your students. Be sure they notice the change in Hamlet when Horatio mentions having seen the ghost of his father.

ⓐ ASK STUDENTS to explain in detail what Horatio tells Hamlet in lines 197–213. If necessary, conduct a line-by-line class paraphrase of Horatio's report on the sighting of the ghost of Hamlet's father. Then, ask students to explain why Horatio might be so detailed in his account. *(He needs to convince Hamlet that the Ghost does, indeed, exist.)*

Internal Conflict	External Conflict
grieves for his father (line 85: "But I have that within which passes show,/ These but the trappings and the suits of woe.")	*dislikes his uncle (line 67: "A little more than kin and less than kind.")*
feels depressed about his life (line 133: "How weary, stale, flat, and unprofitable/Seem to me all the uses of this world!")	*feels anger toward his mother for remarrying so quickly (line 146: "frailty, thy name is woman!")*

CLOSE READ

Analyze Drama Elements: Character (sc. 2 LINES 229–244)

COMMON CORE RL 3

Remind students that, like people in real life, characters do not always react as expected.

(P) ASK STUDENTS to explain Hamlet's reaction upon hearing the news of the Ghost. What do his numerous questions suggest about his feelings? *(Hamlet seems more curious than afraid. He wants to know the specific details of the Ghost's appearance and demeanor. He may, in fact, want to see the Ghost because it represents the father that he misses.)*

It lifted up its head and did address
Itself to motion, like as it would speak;
But even then the morning cock crew loud,
220 And at the sound it shrunk in haste away
And vanished from our sight.

217–218 did...speak: began to move as if it were going to speak.

219 even then: just then.

Hamlet.   'Tis very strange.

Horatio. As I do live, my honored lord, 'tis true.
And we did think it writ down in our duty
To let you know of it.

225 **Hamlet.** Indeed, sirs, but this troubles me.
Hold you the watch tonight?

All.   We do, my lord.

Hamlet. Armed, say you?

All.   Armed, my lord.

Hamlet.   From top to toe?
All My lord, from head to foot.

Hamlet. Then saw you not his face?

(P) 230 **Horatio.** O, yes, my lord, he wore his beaver up.

230 beaver: movable front piece of a helmet.

Hamlet. What, looked he frowningly?

Horatio. A countenance more in sorrow than in anger.

Hamlet. Pale or red?

Horatio. Nay, very pale.

Hamlet.   And fixed his eyes upon you?

235 **Horatio.** Most constantly.

Hamlet.   I would I had been there.

Horatio. It would have much amazed you.

Hamlet. Very like. Stayed it long?

Horatio. While one with moderate haste might tell a hundred.

Barnardo/Marcellus. Longer, longer.

238–239 While... hundred: for as long as one could count (**tell**) to one hundred at a moderate pace.

240 **Horatio.** Not when I saw 't.

Hamlet.   His beard was grizzled, no?

240 grizzled: gray.

Horatio. It was as I have seen it in his life,
A sable silvered.

242 A sable silvered: black hair with white hair mixed through it.

Hamlet.   I will watch tonight.
Perchance 'twill walk again.

Horatio.   I warrant it will.

SCAFFOLDING FOR ELL STUDENTS

Recognize Verb Forms Tell students that as they read the play, they will encounter irregular forms of verbs. Explain that they can use context clues to help them identify the familiar form of the verb. Direct students' attention to the word *crew* in line 219. Guide students to understand that this word means "crowed," based on the clue "loud" that follows it.

ASK STUDENTS to use context clues to identify the familiar form of these verbs: *writ* (line 223), *hap* (line 249).

Hamlet. If it assume my noble father's person,

245 I'll speak to it, though hell itself should gape
And bid me hold my peace. I pray you all,
If you have hitherto concealed this sight,
Let it be tenable in your silence still;
And whatsomever else shall hap tonight,

250 Give it an understanding but no tongue.
I will requite your loves. So fare you well.
Upon the platform, 'twixt eleven and twelve,
I'll visit you.

    All.   Our duty to your Honor.

    Hamlet. Your loves, as mine to you. Farewell.

    [*All but* Hamlet *exit.*]

255 My father's spirit—in arms! All is not well.
I doubt some foul play. Would the night were come!
Till then, sit still, my soul. Foul deeds will rise,
Though all the earth o'erwhelm them, to men's eyes.

    [*He exits.*]

    Scene 3 *Polonius's chambers.*

    [*Enter* Laertes *and* Ophelia, *his sister.*]

    Laertes. My necessaries are embarked. Farewell.
And, sister, as the winds give benefit
And convey is assistant, do not sleep,
But let me hear from you.

    Ophelia.   Do you doubt that?

5   **Laertes.** For Hamlet, and the trifling of his favor,
Hold it a fashion and a toy in blood,
A violet in the youth of primy nature,
Forward, not permanent, sweet, not lasting,
The perfume and suppliance of a minute,

10 No more.

    Ophelia.   No more but so?

    Laertes.   Think it no more.
For nature, crescent, does not grow alone
In thews and bulk, but, as this temple waxes,
The inward service of the mind and soul
Grows wide withal. Perhaps he loves you now,

15 And now no soil nor cautel doth besmirch
The virtue of his will; but you must fear,
His greatness weighed, his will is not his own,
For he himself is subject to his birth.
He may not, as unvalued persons do,

---

248 tenable: held.

249 whatsomever: whatever; **hap:** happen.

251 I . . . loves: I will reward your devotion.

256 doubt: suspect.

6 fashion . . . blood: a temporary enthusiasm and an amorous whim.

7 in . . . nature: at the beginning of its prime.

8 Forward: early blooming.

9–10 The . . . more a sweet but temporary diversion.

11–14 A growing person does not only increase in strength (**thews**) and size, but as the body grows (**this temple waxes**), the inner life (**inward service**) of mind and soul grows along with it.

15 cautel: deceit.

17 His . . . weighed: if you consider his high position.

Hamlet: Act I, Scene 3 **249**

CLOSE READ

Analyze Structure: Conflict (sc. 2 LINES 244–258)

 COMMON CORE RL 3

Q ASK STUDENTS to explain why Hamlet urges his friends to keep the news of the Ghost secret. *(He wants to find out what it has to say first.)* Have them discuss what is foreshadowed by his comment that "All is not well. / I doubt some foul play." *(Hamlet thinks the Ghost denotes that some dark deed was done, which is why the spirit has returned. He may even suspect that his father's death was not natural.)*

Analyze Drama Elements: Character (sc. 3 LINES 5–24)

 COMMON CORE RL 3

Remind students that their father's position as advisor to Claudius means that Ophelia and Laertes are present at court and in close proximity to Hamlet when he is there.

R CITE TEXT EVIDENCE Have students describe Laertes's attitude toward Ophelia. Have them identify details that support this assessment. *(Laertes is watchful towards Ophelia. In this speech, he warns Ophelia to be careful not to trust Hamlet's affections. "For Hamlet, and the trifling of his favor, / Hold it a fashion and a toy in blood . . . not permanent, sweet, not lasting.")* Have students explain the reasons Laertes gives Ophelia for not trusting Hamlet's love. *(Laertes says Hamlet's love is youthful passion and won't last [lines 5–10]. He also suggests that because Hamlet is a prince, he cannot love or marry by choice. As evidence, students might cite line 17 ["His greatness weighed, his will is not his own."] and lines 19–21 ["He may not, as unvalued persons do, / Carve for himself, for on his choice depends / The safety and the health of this whole state."])* Explain that royal marriages were often political alliances made not out of love but out of political expediency.

Analyze Language

 COMMON CORE RL 4

(sc. 2 LINES 33–51)

Tell students that images included in characters' speeches are used to heighten the impact and meaning.

S **ASK STUDENTS** to explain how the images in Laertes's speech relate to his message. *(The images of diseased infants and contagious diseases of the young suggest that young love can be as dangerous as disease itself.)* Ask students to explain the role images play in Ophelia's reply to her brother. *(She says that by insisting she resist Hamlet, Laertes has shown her "the steep and thorny way to heaven" [line 48]. She adds that Laertes should follow his own advice. He should resist young love too, instead of taking "the primrose path of dalliance" [line 50].)*

Polonius's speech to Laertes [lines 55–81] is one of the most famous passages in all of Shakespeare. Consider having all of your students participate in the activity described in "When Students Struggle . . ." on pages 250–251.

---

20   Carve for himself, for on his choice depends
     The safety and the health of this whole state.
     And therefore must his choice be circumscribed
     Unto the voice and yielding of that body
     Whereof he is the head. Then, if he says he loves you,
25   It fits your wisdom so far to believe it
     As he in his particular act and place
     May give his saying deed, which is no further
     Than the main voice of Denmark goes withal.
     Then weigh what loss your honor may sustain
30   If with too credent ear you list his songs
     Or lose your heart or your chaste treasure open
     To his unmastered importunity.
     Fear it, Ophelia; fear it, my dear sister,
     And keep you in the rear of your affection,
35   Out of the shot and danger of desire.
     The chariest maid is prodigal enough
     If she unmask her beauty to the moon.
     Virtue itself 'scapes not calumnious strokes.
     The canker galls the infants of the spring
40   Too oft before their buttons be disclosed,
     And, in the morn and liquid dew of youth,
     Contagious blastments are most imminent.
     Be wary, then; best safety lies in fear.
     Youth to itself rebels, though none else near.

45   **Ophelia.** I shall the effect of this good lesson keep
     As watchman to my heart. But, good my brother,
     Do not, as some ungracious pastors do,
     Show me the steep and thorny way to heaven,
     Whiles, like a puffed and reckless libertine,
50   Himself the primrose path of dalliance treads
     And recks not his own rede.

     Laertes.   O, fear me not.

     [*Enter* Polonius.]

     I stay too long. But here my father comes.
     A double blessing is a double grace.
     Occasion smiles upon a second leave.

55   **Polonius.** Yet here, Laertes? Aboard, aboard, for shame!
     The wind sits in the shoulder of your sail,
     And you are stayed for. There, my blessing with thee.
     And these few precepts in thy memory
     Look thou character. Give thy thoughts no tongue,
60   Nor any unproportioned thought his act.
     Be thou familiar, but by no means vulgar.
     Those friends thou hast, and their adoption tried,

20 Carve: choose.

22–24 And . . . head: His choice must be limited (**circumscribed**) by the opinion and consent (**voice and yielding**) of Denmark.

30 credent: trustful, **list:** listen to.

31–32 your chaste . . . importunity: lose your virginity to his uncontrolled pleading.

34 keep . . . affection: Don't go as far as your emotions would lead.

39 canker galls: cankerworm destroys; **infants:** early flowers.

40 buttons: buds; **disclosed:** opened.

42 contagious blastments: withering blights, harm or injury, catastrophes.

44 Youth . . . near: Youth by nature is prone to rebel.

46–51 Ophelia warns him not to act like a hypocritical pastor, preaching virtue and abstinence while leading a life of promiscuity and ignoring his own advice.

58–65 Polonius tells Laertes to write down (**character**) these few rules of conduct (**precepts**) in his memory. He should keep his thoughts to himself and not act on any unfit (**unproportioned**) thoughts, be friendly but not vulgar, remain loyal to friends proven (**tried**) worthy of being accepted but not shake hands with every swaggering youth (**unfledged courage**) who comes along.

WHEN STUDENTS STRUGGLE . . .

Explain to students that Polonius's speech in lines 55–81 contains some advice to a son who is leaving home. Help them to increase their comprehension of Shakespeare's language by organizing them into small groups and assigning them a passage to paraphrase.

Before students begin the activity, remind them that they will first identify the idea that is being communicated and then they will rephrase it in their own words. Point out that the marginal notes have paraphrased the first set of lines for them.

After students have completed their paraphrases, add them to a chart similar to the one on page 251.

Ophelia (Jean Simmons)

Image Credits: ©John Kobal Foundation/Moviepix/Getty Images

Grapple them unto thy soul with hoops of steel,
But do not dull thy palm with entertainment
65　Of each new-hatched, unfledged courage. Beware
Of entrance to a quarrel, but, being in,
Bear 't that th' opposèd may beware of thee.
Give every man thy ear, but few thy voice.
Take each man's censure, but reserve thy judgment.
70　Costly thy habit as thy purse can buy,
But not expressed in fancy (rich, not gaudy),
For the apparel oft proclaims the man,
And they in France of the best rank and station
Are of a most select and generous chief in that.
75　Neither a borrower nor a lender be,
For loan oft loses both itself and friend,
And borrowing dulls the edge of husbandry.
This above all: to thine own self be true,
And it must follow, as the night the day,
80　Thou canst not then be false to any man.
Farewell. My blessing season this in thee.

Laertes. Most humbly do I take my leave, my lord.

Polonius. The time invests you. Go, your servants tend.

Laertes. Farewell, Ophelia, and remember well
85　What I have said to you.

73–74 And they . . . that: Upper-class French people especially show their refinement and nobility in their choice of apparel.

77 husbandry: thrift, proper handling of money.

81 Polonius hopes that his advice will ripen (**season**) in Laertes.

83 invests: is pressing.

Passage	Paraphrase
65–67	Choose your arguments wisely.
68–69	Listen to everyone but be careful of what you say. Take criticism graciously but do not judge others yourself.
70–74	Buy clothes that are of good quality but not flashy. Remember you will be judged on the way you look.
75–77	Avoid asking for money or letting someone borrow it because you can lose friends over it or become too extravagant in your habits.
78–80	Be yourself. Be true to yourself.

CLOSE READ

Analyze Author' Choices: Character (sc. 3 LINES 65–81)

COMMON CORE　RL 3

Tell students that a skillful playwright creates characters that are realistic in their motivations and emotions.

T **ASK STUDENTS** to identify the purpose of Polonius's speech to Laertes. What ideas are conveyed about the character of Polonius through his words? *(Polonius wants to give Laertes some parting advice about how to conduct himself while he is in France. His advice shows Polonius to be a concerned father. It also shows Polonius to be a wordy man, one who seems to like hearing himself talk and who is his own best audience)*

Analyze Word Choice

COMMON CORE **RL 4**

(sc. 3 LINES 100–113)

Tell students that although they may associate a play on words with lighthearted dialogue, characters may use puns also to emphasize important ideas.

Ⓤ ASK STUDENTS what point Polonius wants to make through his play on the word *tender*. *(He echoes Laertes's warning to stay away from Hamlet.)* What is the tone of his comments to Ophelia? How does this tone affect the audience's view of Hamlet? Explain. *(His tone is serious, impatient, and almost angry. He conveys this tone through words such as "go to, go to." His attitude makes the audience wonder about Hamlet's character and trustworthiness.)* How does this passage lend to the developing view of Polonius? *(It lends to the perception of Polonius as a wordy man who loves listening to himself talk.)*

Ophelia. 'Tis in my memory locked,
And you yourself shall keep the key of it.

Laertes. Farewell.

[Laertes *exits*.]

Polonius. What is 't, Ophelia, he hath said to you?

90 **Ophelia.** So please you, something touching the Lord Hamlet.

Polonius. Marry, well bethought.
'Tis told me he hath very oft of late
Given private time to you, and you yourself
Have of your audience been most free and bounteous.

95 If it be so (as so 'tis put on me,
And that in way of caution), I must tell you
You do not understand yourself so clearly
As it behooves my daughter and your honor.
What is between you? Give me up the truth.

100 **Ophelia.** He hath, my lord, of late made many tenders
Of his affection to me.

Polonius. Affection, puh! You speak like a green girl
Unsifted in such perilous circumstance.
Do you believe his "tenders," as you call them?

105 **Ophelia.** I do not know, my lord, what I should think.

Polonius. Marry, I will teach you. Think yourself a baby
That you have ta'en these tenders for true pay,
Which are not sterling. Tender yourself more dearly,
Or (not to crack the wind of the poor phrase,
110 Running it thus) you'll tender me a fool.

Ophelia. My lord, he hath importuned me with love
In honorable fashion—

Polonius. Ay, "fashion" you may call it. Go to, go to!

Ophelia. And hath given countenance to his speech, my lord,
115 With almost all the holy vows of heaven.

Polonius. Ay, springes to catch woodcocks. I do know,
When the blood burns, how prodigal the soul
Lends the tongue vows. These blazes, daughter,
Giving more light than heat, extinct in both
120 Even in their promise as it is a-making,
You must not take for fire. From this time
Be something scanter of your maiden presence.
Set your entreatments at a higher rate
Than a command to parle. For Lord Hamlet,
125 Believe so much in him that he is young,
And with a larger tether may he walk

91 Marry: a mild oath, shortened from "by the Virgin Mary."

95 put on: told to.

100–110 Tenders: offers (lines 100 and 107). Polonius uses the word in line 107 to refer to coins that are not legal currency (**sterling**). He then warns Ophelia to offer (**tender**) herself at a higher rate (**more dearly**), or she will tender Polonius a fool—meaning either that she will present herself as a fool, that she will make him look like a fool, or that she will give him a grandchild.

116 springes . . . woodcocks: snares to catch birds that are easily caught.

117 prodigal: lavishly.

118–121 These blazes . . . fire: These blazes, which lose their light and heat almost immediately, should not be mistaken for fire.

123–135 Polonius, metaphorically referring to Ophelia as a besieged castle, tells her not to enter into negotiations (**entreatments**) for surrender merely because the enemy wants to meet (**parle**) with her. Hamlet's vows are go-betweens (**brokers**) that are not like their outward appearance; these solicitors (**implorators**) of sinful petitions (**unholy suits**) speak in pious terms in order to deceive. Polonius orders her never to disgrace (**slander**) a moment of her time by speaking to Hamlet.

TO CHALLENGE STUDENTS . . .

Consider Points of View What is Hamlet like when looked at through a different lens? Have students analyze the character of Hamlet as he is presented through the eyes of Laertes and Polonius. Have them identify words and phrases that evoke these characters' views of him. Then ask students to discuss these questions in small groups:

• Does the portrayal of Hamlet by Laertes and Polonius match your impression of his character as seen in this act? Explain.

• Considering Hamlet is the future king of Denmark, why would Laertes and Polonius oppose his attentions to Ophelia? What might their underlying motives be?

Than may be given you. In few, Ophelia,
Do not believe his vows, for they are brokers,
Not of that dye which their investments show,
130 But mere implorators of unholy suits,
Breathing like sanctified and pious bawds
The better to beguile. This is for all:
I would not, in plain terms, from this time forth
Have you so slander any moment leisure
135 As to give words or talk with the Lord Hamlet.
Look to 't, I charge you. Come your ways.

Ophelia. I shall obey, my lord.

[*They exit.*]

Scene 4 *A guard platform at the castle.*

[*Enter* Hamlet, Horatio, *and* Marcellus.]

Hamlet. The air bites shrewdly; it is very cold.

Horatio. It is a nipping and an eager air.

Hamlet. What hour now?

Horatio. I think it lacks of twelve.

5 **Marcellus.** No, it is struck.

Horatio. Indeed, I heard it not. It then draws near the season
Wherein the spirit held his wont to walk.

[*A flourish of trumpets and two pieces goes off.*]

What does this mean, my lord?

Hamlet. The King doth wake tonight and takes his rouse,
10 Keeps wassail, and the swagg'ring upspring reels;
And, as he drains his draughts of Rhenish down,
The kettledrum and trumpet thus bray out
The triumph of his pledge.

Horatio. Is it a custom?

15 **Hamlet.** Ay, marry, is 't,
But, to my mind, though I am native here
And to the manner born, it is a custom
More honored in the breach than the observance.
This heavy-headed revel east and west
20 Makes us traduced and taxed of other nations.
They clepe us drunkards and with swinish phrase
Soil our addition. And, indeed, it takes
From our achievements, though performed at height,
The pith and marrow of our attribute.
25 So oft it chances in particular men
That for some vicious mole of nature in them,

1 **shrewdly:** keenly.

2 **eager:** cutting.

9–13 The King stays up tonight drinking and dancing wildly; as he drinks down a glass of wine, kettledrums and trumpets play.

17 to the manner born: familiar since birth with this custom.

19–24 This drunken festivity makes us standered and blamed by other nations. They call us drunkards and pigs, soiling our good name. Even when we do something outstanding, the essence of our reputation (**pith and marrow of our attribute**) is lost through drunkenness.

26 mole: defect.

Hamlet: Act I, Scene 4   **253**

CLOSE READ

Support Inferences

(sc. 3 LINES 132–137)

Explain that students can use their knowledge of human nature to infer what characters might be feeling in certain situations.

V ASK STUDENTS what ultimatum Polonius delivers to Ophelia. (*He tells her not to waste another minute talking to or interacting with Hamlet.*) Based on what Ophelia has previously said about Hamlet, what emotions might her statement in line 137 conceal? (*She is obviously fond of Hamlet and has hopes for their relationship. Therefore, obeying her father will create a conflict for her. She may be concealing dismay or disappointment.*)

Analyze Drama Elements: Character

(sc. 4 LINES 9–13)

Remind students that characters are developed not only through what they say and do but through others' reactions to them. Explain that when differing views of the same character are presented, audiences must weigh the evidence to decide which assessment is more valid.

W CITE TEXT EVIDENCE Have students explain the picture of Claudius that Hamlet's comments paint. (*Claudius appears in these lines as someone who drinks and parties without limits.*) Have students compare their first impression of Claudius to the image presented here. (*In the opening scene of Act II, Claudius projects the image of a thoughtful, restrained, trustworthy ruler—the opposite of the self-indulgent libertine Hamlet describes here.*)

Analyze Drama Elements: Character (sc. 4 LINES 41–59)

COMMON CORE RL 3

Remind students that so far they have seen Hamlet at court, in the presence of the King and Queen; Hamlet in a very private setting, voicing painful thoughts in his first soliloquy; and Hamlet in a relaxed social setting, talking with Horatio. Here, for the first time, they see Hamlet in the presence of his father's ghost.

 CITE TEXT EVIDENCE Have students describe Hamlet's emotional state in lines 41–59 and point to phrases in this speech that illustrate his mood. *(Hamlet is extremely agitated. His choice of words shows agitation, including "goblin damned" [line 42], "blasts from hell" [line 43], and the description of skeletal remains bursting out of their graves [lines 49–50]. He uses insistent constructions, as with "I will speak to thee" [line 46].)* Have students briefly characterize Hamlet as seen at court, then alone with his own thoughts, and when he is with Horatio. Have them explain how his behavior here adds to the play's developing impression of Hamlet. *(Answers will vary, but in the opening scene at court, Hamlet is a grieving man who wants those around him to believe that his grief is genuine. Alone, he is a man in anguish, tortured by the death of his father and his mother's hasty re-marriage to his uncle. With Horatio, he is genuine and at ease. Here, he is emotionally distraught. Shakespeare depicts Hamlet as a complex human being, whose behavior and emotions vary with the situation at hand.)*

As in their birth (wherein they are not guilty,
Since nature cannot choose his origin),
By the o'ergrowth of some complexion
30 (Oft breaking down the pales and forts of reason),
Or by some habit that too much o'erleavens
The form of plausive manners—that these men,
Carrying, I say, the stamp of one defect,
Being nature's livery or fortune's star,
35 His virtues else, be they as pure as grace,
As infinite as man may undergo,
Shall in the general censure take corruption
From that particular fault. The dram of evil
Doth all the noble substance of a doubt
40 To his own scandal.

[*Enter* Ghost.]

Horatio.   Look, my lord, it comes.

Hamlet. Angels and ministers of grace, defend us!
Be thou a spirit of health or goblin damned,
Bring with thee airs from heaven or blasts from hell,
Be thy intents wicked or charitable,
45 Thou com'st in such a questionable shape
That I will speak to thee. I'll call thee "Hamlet,"
"King," "Father," "Royal Dane." O, answer me!
Let me not burst in ignorance, but tell
Why they canonized bones, hearsèd in death,
50 Have burst their cerements; why the sepulcher,
Wherein we saw thee quietly interred,
Hath oped his ponderous and marble jaws
To cast thee up again. What may this mean
That thou, dead corse, again in complete steel,
55 Revisits thus the glimpses of the moon,
Making night hideous, and we fools of nature
So horridly to shake our disposition
With thoughts beyond the reaches of our souls?
Say, why is this? Wherefore? What should we do?

[Ghost *beckons.*]

60 **Horatio.** It beckons you to go away with it
As if it some impartment did desire
To you alone.

Marcellus.   Look with what courteous action
It waves you to a more removèd ground.
But do not go with it.

Horatio.   No, by no means.

65 **Hamlet.** It will not speak. Then I will follow it.

29–32 Hamlet describes reason as a castle whose fortified walls are broken by the excessive growth of a natural trait or by a corrupting habit.

34 nature's ... star: which they are born with or acquire.

35 His virtues else: their other virtues.

38–40 The dram ... scandal: A small amount of evil blots out all of a person's good qualities.

45 questionable: capable of responding to questions.

48–50 tell ... cerements: Tell me why your bones, which were placed in a coffin and received a proper church burial, have escaped from their burial clothes.

57 horridly... disposition: disturb us terribly.

61–62 As if...alone: as if it has something to tell you on your own.

SCAFFOLDING FOR ELL STUDENTS

Understand Contractions Explain to students that Shakespeare uses contractions to maintain the rhythm of his poetry. A contraction is a shortened form of a word or words in which an apostrophe takes the place of the omitted letters.

Project lines 27–46 on the whiteboard. Invite volunteers to mark up the text:

- Highlight in blue contractions that are shortened forms of verbs.
- Highlight in green contractions that are words made shorter by dropping one or more letters.

ASK STUDENTS to work in pairs to rewrite each word with the letters restored.

Horatio. Do not, my lord.

Hamlet. Why, what should be the fear?
I do not set my life at a pin's fee.
And for my soul, what can it do to that,
Being a thing immortal as itself?
70 It waves me forth again. I'll follow it.

Horatio. What if it tempt you toward the flood, my lord?
Or to the dreadful summit of the cliff
That beetles o'er his base into the sea,
And there assume some other horrible form
75 Which might deprive your sovereignty of reason
And draw you into madness? Think of it.
The very place puts toys of desperation,
Without more motive, into every brain
That looks so many fathoms to the sea
80 And hears it roar beneath.

Hamlet. It waves me still.—Go on, I'll follow thee.

Marcellus. You shall not go, my lord.

[*They hold back* Hamlet.]

Hamlet. Hold off your hands.

Horatio. Be ruled. You shall not go.

Hamlet. My fate cries out
And makes each petty arture in this body
85 As hardy as the Nemean lion's nerve.
Still am I called. Unhand me, gentlemen.
By heaven, I'll make a ghost of him that lets me!
I say, away!—Go on. I'll follow thee.

[Ghost *and* Hamlet *exit.*]

Horatio. He waxes desperate with imagination.

90 **Marcellus.** Let's follow. 'Tis not fit thus to obey him.

Horatio. Have after. To what issue will this come?

Marcellus. Something is rotten in the state of Denmark.

Horatio. Heaven will direct it.

Marcellus. Nay, let's follow him.

[*They exit.*]

---

67 pin's fee: the value of a pin.

71–76 Horatio is worried that the Ghost might lead Hamlet toward the sea (**flood**) or to the top of the cliff that hangs (**beetles**) over the sea, and then take on some horrible appearance that would drive Hamlet insane.

77 toys of desperation: irrational impulses.

84 arture: artery.

85 Nemean lion's nerve: the sinews of a mythical lion strangled by Hercules.

87 lets: hinders.

91 Have after: Let's go after him.

CLOSE READ

Analyze Structure: Conflict (sc. 4 LINES 66–80)

 COMMON CORE RL 3

Point out that conflicting motives can put good friends in conflict.

ASK STUDENTS to explain Hamlet's motive—what he wants—in lines 66–70. (*Hamlet wants to pursue the ghost of his father, even at risk to his own personal safety. He says, "I do not set my life at a pin's fee."*) Note that Horatio doesn't want Hamlet to pursue the Ghost. Ask students: Why not? What is he afraid might happen to Hamlet if he follows the Ghost? (*Horatio is afraid the Ghost will transform itself into such a "horrible form" [line 74] that it "might deprive your sovereignty of reason / And draw you into madness."*)

Analyze Drama Elements: Character (sc. 4 LINES 82–89)

 COMMON CORE RL 3

Point out that sometimes in drama, conflict reveals character.

Z **ASK STUDENTS** to describe the conflict between Horatio and Hamlet in these lines. (*Horatio wants Hamlet to stay; Hamlet wants to follow the Ghost.*) What does Hamlet's behavior here make Horatio fear? (*Hamlet is so agitated that Horatio fears he might be temporarily mad. Horatio says about Hamlet, "He waxes desperate with imagination" [line 89].*)

WHEN STUDENTS STRUGGLE...

Read aloud lines 83–88 and discuss with students the intensity with which Hamlet expresses his desire to follow the Ghost. Remind them that characters, like real people, have their own reasons for wanting to do things.

Have students work in small groups to identify all of the possible motivations that Hamlet might have for following the Ghost. Remind them to consider what they already know about Hamlet. Have students share their motivations. (*Possible answers: he hopes to find out more about his father's afterlife; he wants to know why the Ghost keeps appearing; he thinks the Ghost can tell him why his mother married Claudius so quickly; he thinks the Ghost might have other information that relates to Hamlet's life and Denmark.*)

Analyze Drama Elements RL 1

(sc. 5 LINES 1–24)

Tell students that Elizabethan drama included some special effects; however, the dialogue of the characters was essential to creating the atmosphere desired by the playwright.

A2 **ASK STUDENTS** what mood is created by the words of the Ghost. (*His reference to "sulf'rous and tormenting flames" and his warning that the tale he could tell about life beyond death would "freeze thy young blood" and make "thy two eyes, like stars, start from their spheres" evoke an atmosphere of horror and foreboding. His words evoke images of hell and eternal torment.*) What does the Ghost say is his ultimate destination? Why? (*He is going to be consigned to the flames "till the foul crimes done in my days of nature / Are burnt and purged away."*) How does the information that the Ghost reveals influence the audience's impression of Hamlet's father? (*He did not lead a blameless life.*)

Analyze Structure: Conflict RL 3

(sc. 5 LINES 25–32)

Draw students' attention to the fact that the major conflict of the play is about to be introduced. Return to the predictions that they made initially about the conflict and remind them to verify or adjust these predictions as they read this passage.

B2 **ASK STUDENTS** what the revelation made by the Ghost means for Hamlet. (*He must seek revenge on the man who murdered him.*) Ask students why knowing that his father was murdered might create a conflict for Hamlet. (*Answers will vary but might include the fact that seeking revenge will put Hamlet in conflict with whoever murdered his father.*)

Scene 5 *Another part of the fortifications.*

[*Enter* Ghost *and* Hamlet.]

Hamlet. Whither wilt thou lead me? Speak. I'll go no further.

Ghost. Mark me.

Hamlet.   I will.

Ghost.   My hour is almost come
When I to sulf'rous and tormenting flames
Must render up myself.

Hamlet.   Alas, poor ghost!

5 **Ghost.** Pity me not, but lend thy serious hearing
To what I shall unfold.

Hamlet. Speak. I am bound to hear.

Ghost. So art thou to revenge, when thou shalt hear.

Hamlet. What?

10 **Ghost.** I am thy father's spirit.
Doomed for a certain term to walk the night
And for the day confined to fast in fires
Till the foul crimes done in my days of nature
Are burnt and purged away. But that I am forbid
15 To tell the secrets of my prison house,
I could a tale unfold whose lightest word
Would harrow up thy soul, freeze thy young blood,
Make thy two eyes, like stars, start from their spheres,
Thy knotted and combinèd locks to part,
20 And each particular hair to stand an end,
Like quills upon the fearful porpentine.
But this eternal blazon must not be
To ears of flesh and blood. List, list, O list!
If thou didst ever thy dear father love—

25 **Hamlet.** O God!

Ghost. Revenge his foul and most unnatural murder.

Hamlet. Murder?

Ghost. Murder most foul, as in the best it is,
But this most foul, strange, and unnatural.

30 **Hamlet.** Haste me to know 't, that I, with wings as swift
As meditation or the thoughts of love,
May sweep to my revenge.

Ghost.   I find thee apt;
And duller shouldst thou be than the fat weed
That roots itself in ease on Lethe wharf,

7 bound: obligated.

13 crimes: sins.

17 harrow up: tear up, disturb.

18 Make . . . spheres: make your two eyes like stars jump from their assigned places in the universe.

19 knotted . . . locks: carefully arranged hair.

20 an end: on end.

21 fearful porpentine: frightened porcupine.

22–23 The Ghost says he must not describe life beyond death to a living person.

28 as . . . is: which murder in general (**it**) is at the very least.

32–35 I find . . . this: I think you are willing, and you would have to be duller than the thick weed that grows on the banks of Lethe (the river of forgetfulness in the underworld) to not be roused by this.

256 Collection 4

35 Wouldst thou not stir in this. Now, Hamlet, hear.
   'Tis given out that, sleeping in my orchard,
   A serpent stung me. So the whole ear of Denmark
   Is by a forgèd process of my death
   Rankly abused. But know, thou noble youth,
40 The serpent that did sting thy father's life
   Now wears his crown.

   Hamlet. O, my prophetic soul! My uncle!

   Ghost. Ay, that incestuous, that adulterate beast,
   With witchcraft of his wit, with traitorous gifts—
45 O wicked wit and gifts, that have the power
   So to seduce!—won to his shameful lust
   The will of my most seeming-virtuous queen.
   O Hamlet, what a falling off was there!
   From me, whose love was of that dignity
50 That it went hand in hand even with the vow
   I made to her in marriage, and to decline
   Upon a wretch whose natural gifts were poor
   To those of mine.
   But virtue, as it never will be moved,
55 Though lewdness court it in a shape of heaven,
   So, lust, though to a radiant angel linked,
   Will sate itself in a celestial bed
   And prey on garbage.
   But soft, methinks I scent the morning air.
60 Brief let me be. Sleeping within my orchard,
   My custom always of the afternoon,
   Upon my secure hour thy uncle stole,
   With juice of cursèd hebona in a vial,
   And in the porches of my ears did pour
65 The leprous distilment, whose effect
   Holds such an enmity with blood of man
   That swift as quicksilver it courses through
   The natural gates and alleys of the body,
   And with a sudden vigor it doth posset
70 And curd, like eager droppings into milk,
   The thin and wholesome blood. So did it mine,
   And a most instant tetter barked about,
   Most lazar-like, with vile and loathsome crust
   All my smooth body.
75 Thus was I, sleeping, by a brother's hand
   Of life, of crown, of queen at once dispatched,
   Cut off, even in the blossoms of my sin,
   Unhouseled, disappointed, unaneled,
   No reck'ning made, but sent to my account
80 With all my imperfections on my head.

36 orchard: garden.

37–39 So...abused:
Thus all of Denmark
is deceived by a false
account of my death.

43 adulterate:
adulterous.

54–58 The Ghost
compares virtue, which
remains pure even if
indecency courts it in a
heavenly form, with lust,
which grows weary of a
virtuous marriage and
seeks depravity.

63 hebona: a poisonous
plant.

64 porches: entrances.

65 leprous distilment:
a distilled liquid that
causes disfigurement
similar to that caused by
leprosy.

69–71 doth . . . blood:
The poison curdles the
blood like something
sour dropped into milk.

72–74 most instant . . .
body: An eruption of
sores (tetter) instantly
covered my smooth
body, leper-like (lazar-
like), with a vile crust
like the bark on a tree.

76 dispatched:
deprived.

77–80 The Ghost
regrets that he had no
chance to receive the
last rites of the church;
he died with all his sins
unabsolved.

Hamlet: Act I, Scene 5 **257**

Determine Themes

COMMON CORE RL 2

(sc. 5 LINES 35–71)

Tell students that they can determine the playwright's essential messages once they have read the play in its entirety. Explain that the playwright develops these themes throughout the play, however. As students read this passage, encourage them to think about the message that Shakespeare might be conveying about human nature.

Ⓒ **ASK STUDENTS** how the real cause of King Hamlet's death differs from the "official" version. *(The official version is that a serpent stung him as he was sleeping. The real version is that Claudius poured poison in the king's ear.)* Have students consider the connotations of the word *serpent*. What ideas about Claudius are suggested by this word? *(Claudius is evil and sneaky.)* Have students recall Claudius's words about the dead king and his actions following his death. What theme is suggested by the revelation of the truth behind the king's death? *(Appearances are deceiving. A look of virtue can hide an evil heart.)*

TO CHALLENGE STUDENTS . . .

Examine Structure Why is the Ghost an important device in this play? Have students reread the Ghost's account of the circumstances surrounding the king's death. Organize students into small groups and ask them to do the following:

- Identify and discuss the way in which the images and events evoke the story of Adam and Eve in the Garden of Eden.

- Explain why Shakespeare develops these parallels.

- Discuss how these comparisons connect to a possible theme.

CLOSE READ

Analyze Drama Elements   RL 3

(sc. 5 LINES 85–89)

Point out that sometimes a comment that seems insignificant can play an important part in the way a play develops. Ask them to notice how much of what the Ghost says focuses on Claudius as the villain who poisoned him. And the Ghost's request of Hamlet is to exact revenge on Claudius. Then the Ghost makes a brief request regarding Hamlet's mother.

D2 **ASK STUDENTS** to restate in their own words what the Ghost asks Hamlet to do about his mother. *(The Ghost says Hamlet should leave her alone; he should let her be punished by her own conscience in this life and by God after she dies.)* Ask students why it might be hard for Hamlet to obey his father's wish that he not punish his mother. *(Hamlet has expressed great anger and frustration and disgust about his mother because of her hasty marriage to Claudius. Since she is married to the man who killed his father, Hamlet might also consider her partly to blame for his father's death.)*

O horrible, O horrible, most horrible!
If thou hast nature in thee, bear it not.
Let not the royal bed of Denmark be
A couch for luxury and damnèd incest.

85   But, howsomever thou pursues this act,
Taint not thy mind, nor let thy soul contrive
Against thy mother aught. Leave her to heaven
And to those thorns that in her bosom lodge
To prick and sting her. Fare thee well at once.

90   The glowworm shows the matin to be near
And 'gins to pale his uneffectual fire.
Adieu, adieu, adieu. Remember me.

[*He exits.*]

Hamlet. O all you host of heaven! O earth! What else?
And shall I couple hell? O fie! Hold, hold, my heart,

95   And you, my sinews, grow not instant old,

84 luxury: lust.

86–89 The Ghost tells Hamlet not to think of revenge against his mother.

90 matin: morning.

94 couple: add.

Image Credits: ©Nat Farbman/Time Life Pictures/Getty Images

258   Collection 4

Strategies for Annotation   ✏️ 🗒️ *Annotate it!*

Analyze Language    RL 4

Have students use their eBook annotation tools to analyze the Ghost's speech.

- Highlight in pink words with strongly negative connotations.
- Underline words that describe Hamlet's uncle and mother.
- On a note, write the effect of the highlighted and underlined words and phrases on the reader and audience.
- In a small group, discuss the purpose of the Ghost's speech as revealed through his word choice.

Though lewdness court it in a shape of heaven,

So, lust, though to a radiant angel linked,

Will sate itself in a celestial bed

And prey on garbage. . . .

With juice of cursèd hebona in a vial, . . .

The leprous distilment, whose effect

Holds such an enmity with blood of man

But bear me stiffly up. Remember thee?
Ay, thou poor ghost, whiles memory holds a seat
In this distracted globe. Remember thee?
Yea, from the table of my memory
100 I'll wipe away all trivial, fond records,
All saws of books, all forms, all pressures past,
That youth and observation copied there,
And thy commandment all alone shall live
Within the book and volume of my brain,
105 Unmixed with baser matter. Yes, by heaven!
O most pernicious woman!
O villain, villain, smiling, damnèd villain!
My tables—meet it is I set it down
That one may smile and smile and be a villain.
110 At least I am sure it may be so in Denmark.

[*He writes.*]

So, uncle, there you are. Now to my word.
It is "adieu, adieu, remember me."
I have sworn 't.

[*Enter* Horatio *and* Marcellus.]

Horatio. My lord, my lord!

115 **Marcellus.** Lord Hamlet.

Horatio. Heavens secure him!

Hamlet. So be it.

Marcellus. Illo, ho, ho, my lord!

Hamlet. Hillo, ho, ho, boy! Come, bird, come!

120 **Marcellus.** How is 't, my noble lord?

Horatio.   What news, my lord?

Hamlet. O, wonderful!

Horatio. Good my lord, tell it.

Hamlet.   No, you will reveal it.

Horatio. Not I, my lord, by heaven.

Marcellus.   Nor I, my lord.

Hamlet. How say you, then? Would heart of man once think it?
125 But you'll be secret?

Horatio/Marcellus. Ay, by heaven, my lord.

Hamlet. There's never a villain dwelling in all Denmark
But he's an arrant knave.

98 globe: head.

99–105 Hamlet vows to erase from the slate (**table**) of his memory all foolish notes (**fond records**), wise sayings (**saws**) he copied from books, and past impressions (**pressures past**) so that the Ghost's command will live in his mind unmixed with ordinary, insignificant thoughts.

119 Hamlet responds to Marcellus's greeting (**illo, ho, ho**) with the call of a falconer to his hawk.

128 arrant knave: thoroughly dishonest person.

Hamlet: Act I, Scene 5   **259**

CLOSE READ

Analyze Drama Elements: Character (sc. 5 LINES 106–110)

COMMON CORE RL 3

E2 ASK STUDENTS to read Hamlet's oath very carefully and to notice how faithfully and thoroughly he vows to seek the revenge the Ghost wants. Ask them to identify one thing Hamlet says that runs counter to what the Ghost asked of him. What does this statement reveal about Hamlet? (*Immediately after swearing to get revenge for his father's death, Hamlet exclaims, "O most pernicious woman!" The Ghost asked him to leave his mother out of it, but it seems clear that it will be difficult for Hamlet to obey this part of the Ghost's request. He appears to be almost as upset about his mother's marriage to Claudius as about the news his father was murdered by Claudius.*)

TO CHALLENGE STUDENTS...

Analyze Author's Choices What is reality? Discuss with students how the character of the Ghost poses an essential question that shapes the play. Point out that the Ghost may be "real" in the sense of truly bringing a message to Hamlet from his father. Or, the Ghost may not be what it seems.

Have students debate the function of the Ghost, supporting their view with details from the text. Have them explore what it means for Hamlet if the Ghost is real and if it is not. How will the answer to this question affect Hamlet's future actions? Can the question be answered?

Ask students to share their insights in a class discussion.

Analyze Drama Elements: RL 3
Character (sc. 5 LINES 148–170)

Ask students to concentrate on Hamlet's agitated behavior after the Ghost departs and Hamlet joins Horatio and Marcellus.

F2 **ASK STUDENTS** to infer why Hamlet doesn't tell the others what the Ghost has told him and why he swears them to silence. *(Hamlet is too upset about what the Ghost has told him to tell anyone yet, and though Horatio is his close friend, he doesn't know Marcellus well and might not wish to say anything in front of him. He might also wish to seek his revenge alone.)* Inform students that when the Ghost speaks [lines 155, 161, and 167], many critics believe that only Hamlet hears the Ghost and that he is so agitated by this point that the Ghost saying "Swear" is an aural hallucination. Have students read this scene closely, finding evidence that only Hamlet hears the Ghost. *(Horatio and Marcellus say nothing to indicate they have heard the Ghost, yet surely hearing the Ghost speak would upset or frighten them. In line 170, when Horatio says, "O day and night, but this is wondrous strange," he could easily be talking about Hamlet's wild behavior and not the Ghost.)* Finally, if line 170 is about Hamlet's behavior and not about the Ghost, it indicates that Horatio is concerned about his friend. Ask students to remember this moment in the play as they observe Hamlet's behavior in Act II.

Horatio. There needs no ghost, my lord, come from the grave.
130 To tell us this.

    Hamlet.   Why, right, you are in the right.
And so, without more circumstance at all,
I hold it fit that we shake hands and part,
You, as your business and desire shall point you
(For every man hath business and desire,
135 Such as it is), and for my own poor part,
I will go pray.

131 circumstance: elaboration.

    Horatio. These are but wild and whirling words, my lord.

    Hamlet. I am sorry they offend you, heartily;
Yes, faith, heartily.

    Horatio.   There's no offense, my lord.

140   **Hamlet.** Yes, by Saint Patrick, but there is, Horatio,
And much offense, too. Touching this vision here,
It is an honest ghost—that let me tell you.
For your desire to know what is between us,
O'ermaster 't as you may. And now, good friends,
145 As you are friends, scholars, and soldiers,
Give me one poor request.

142 honest: genuine.

    Horatio. What is 't, my lord? We will.

    Hamlet. Never make known what you have seen tonight.

F2   **Horatio/Marcellus.** My lord, we will not.

150   **Hamlet.** Nay, but swear 't.

    Horatio. In faith, my lord, not I.

    Marcellus. Nor I, my lord, in faith.

    Hamlet. Upon my sword.

    Marcellus.   We have sworn, my lord, already.

    Hamlet. Indeed, upon my sword, indeed.

153 The hilt of a sword, shaped like a cross, was often used for swearing oaths.

155   **Ghost** [*cries under the stage*]. Swear.

    Hamlet. Ha, ha, boy, sayst thou so? Art thou there, truepenny?
Come on, you hear this fellow in the cellarage.
Consent to swear.

156 truepenny: honest fellow.

    Horatio.   Propose the oath, my lord.

    Hamlet. Never to speak of this that you have seen,
160 Swear by my sword.

    Ghost [*beneath*]. Swear.

    Hamlet. *Hic et ubique*? Then we'll shift our ground.
Come hither, gentlemen,

162 *Hic et ubique*: here and everywhere (Latin).

WHEN STUDENTS STRUGGLE . . .

To help students' comprehension, suggest that they summarize the important events in the plot. Have them work together to complete these steps:

1. Review the act.
2. Note major events in a sequence chart similar to the one on page 261.
3. Write two or three sentences explaining the events.

ASK STUDENTS to share their summaries in small groups. Have them review these summaries before beginning Act II.

And lay your hands again upon my sword.
165 Swear by my sword
Never to speak of this that you have heard.

Ghost [*beneath*]. Swear by his sword.

Hamlet. Well said, old mole. Canst work i' th' earth so fast?
A worthy pioner! Once more remove, good friends.

170 **Horatio.** O day and night, but this is wondrous strange.

Hamlet. And therefore as a stranger give it welcome.
There are more things in heaven and earth, Horatio,
Than are dreamt of in your philosophy. But come.
Here, as before, never, so help you mercy,
175 How strange or odd some'er I bear myself
(As I perchance hereafter shall think meet
To put an antic disposition on)
That you, at such times seeing me, never shall,
With arms encumbered thus, or this headshake,
180 Or by pronouncing of some doubtful phrase,
As "Well, well, we know," or "We could an if we would."
Or "If we list to speak," or "There be an if they might,"
Or such ambiguous giving-out, to note
That you know aught of me—this do swear,
185 So grace and mercy at your most need help you.

Ghost [*beneath*]. Swear.

Hamlet. Rest, rest, perturbèd spirit.—So, gentlemen,
With all my love I do commend me to you,
And what so poor a man as Hamlet is
190 May do t' express his love and friending to you,
God willing, shall not lack. Let us go in together,
And still your fingers on your lips, I pray.
The time is out of joint. O cursèd spite
That ever I was born to set it right!
195 Nay, come, let's go together.

[*They exit.*]

169 pioner: digger, miner.

171 Hamlet tells Horatio to welcome, or accept, the night's events as one would welcome a stranger.

173 your philosophy: the general subject of philosophy (not a particular belief of Horatio's).

174–185 Hamlet reveals that he may have to disguise himself with strange behavior (**antic disposition**); he has them swear not to make any gestures or hints that would give him away.

188–191 Hamlet says that he entrusts himself to them and will do his best to reward them.

193 The . . . joint: Everything is in disorder.

CLOSE READ

Analyze Structure: Conflict (sc. 5 LINES 174–185)

 COMMON CORE RL 3

Remind students that dramatic irony involves a situation in which the audience knows more than one or more of the characters know.

ASK STUDENTS to explain the deception Hamlet asks his friends to agree to. (*He tells them that in the future he might "put an antic disposition on" [line 177], meaning that he might behave as if he's mad.*) What does the audience know that Hamlet's friends do not about his motives? (*He has not told them the Ghost's story that Claudius murdered his father.*) Since Horatio and Marcellus are missing important information, how might this affect their perception of Hamlet as Act I draws to a close? (*Horatio and Marcellus don't know why Hamlet would act mad. Instead, his behavior has been so odd, especially if only Hamlet heard the Ghost saying "Swear," that Horatio and Marcellus could easily believe that Hamlet is not in his right mind as Act I ends.*)

The Ghost appears and is seen by Horatio.

Hamlet confronts the reality of his mother's remarriage.

Laertes and Polonius tell Ophelia to reject Hamlet's advances.

Hamlet learns from the Ghost the truth about his father's death.

Hamlet resolves to take revenge and conceal his motives behind a mask of madness.

PRACTICE & APPLY

Analyzing the Text COMMON CORE RL 1, RL 3, RL 4

Possible answers:

1. The opening scene creates a dark, suspenseful, and foreboding mood. Details include the late night, the cold, and the guards' fear and confusion.

2. Ostensibly he expresses concern that the person "most immediate to our throne" cannot overcome his unhealthy "unprevailing woe." However, Claudius might also want to keep close watch on Hamlet to forestall any plot against him.

3. Claudius portrays himself as an able statesman, a competent ruler, and a fond husband. However, Hamlet says he is "no more like my father / than I to Hercules" (lines 152–153). The contrast suggests that the outward appearance may mask inner corruption.

4. Hamlet seems extremely depressed. His world appears "weary, stale, flat, and unprofitable," and suicidal thoughts of "self slaughter" have crossed his mind.

5. Laertes's statement means that Hamlet is subject to, or must obey, the responsibilities and obligations of his rank. Laertes is warning Ophelia that even if Hamlet loves her now, he may not be able to marry her if his princely duties demand otherwise. The word subject can also mean "one who owes loyalty to a king or prince." This suggests a paradox: Hamlet is both prince and subject, since he cannot make his own decisions as "unvalued persons" can.

6. Hamlet is in the throes of depression over his mother's treachery but lacks an outlet for his feelings. By consigning Gertrude to her own punishment, the Ghost eliminates the stigma of matricide and enables Hamlet to wipe away all doubt and softness in order to avenge his father's murder.

7. Hamlet tells Horatio that he plans to act mad in order to catch Claudius out. This dramatic irony will enable the audience to see behind Hamlet's apparent madness to the intent beneath it, while Claudius and others may just think he has lost his mind.

8. Hamlet would have rather not been given the task, saying "O cursed spite, / That ever I was born to set it right!" Doubts remain: he may lack the heart to kill Claudius in cold blood; he cannot be sure that the Ghost's story is accurate; he may not wish to risk his own soul by carrying out this vengeance.

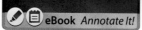 **eBook** *Annotate It!*

Analyzing the Text COMMON CORE RL 1, RL 3, RL 4, W 4

Cite Text Evidence   Support your responses with evidence from the selection.

1. **Analyze** What **mood,** or atmosphere, does Shakespeare establish in Scene 1? Which details help create this mood?

2. **Infer** In Scene 2, Claudius urges Hamlet to stay at court instead of returning to Wittenberg. What might he be concerned about?

3. **Compare** How do Hamlet's comments about Claudius in Scene 2 contrast with the impression Claudius conveys of himself through his speeches? What does this contrast suggest about life at the Danish court?

4. **Draw Conclusions** Reread lines 129–159 of Scene 2. What does this soliloquy suggest about Hamlet's state of mind at this point in the play?

5. **Interpret** Many of Shakespeare's characters use puns in their speech. A **pun** is a play on the multiple meanings of a word or on two words that sound alike but have different meanings. Throughout *Hamlet*, notes in the margin explain many puns that would be unfamiliar to a modern audience. Although puns are often associated with humor, they can also be an effective way to convey serious meaning. For example, in his conversation with Ophelia in Scene 3, Laertes says that Hamlet "himself is subject to his birth" (line 18). Explain how Laertes's statement is enriched by his drawing on two separate meanings of the word *subject*.

6. **Infer** In Scene 5, the Ghost speaks harshly about Gertrude. Why does he insist that Hamlet not take any action against her?

7. **Predict** In lines 175–177 of Scene 5, Hamlet tells Horatio and Marcellus that he might soon have to pretend to act strangely. What does this comment suggest about how he will try to carry out his revenge?

8. **Draw Conclusions** What do lines 193–195 in Scene 5 reveal about Hamlet's attitude toward the responsibility given to him by the Ghost? Why does he feel this way?

PERFORMANCE TASK

Writing Activity: Analysis In Act I, we learn about Hamlet's relationship with his uncle, and we also learn about Ophelia's relationship with her father. Write a brief essay in which you compare the two relationships.

- First, analyze Hamlet's interaction with Claudius in Scene 2, lines 64–128.

- Next, analyze Ophelia's interaction with Polonius in Scene 3, lines 89–137.

- Summarize the key similarities and differences in these relationships.

Assign this performance task.

PERFORMANCE TASK COMMON CORE W 4

Writing Activity: Analysis Have student pairs assume roles and read both dialogues aloud. Ask them to note ways in which the tone of each interaction reveals details about the relationship and to consider the actual feelings that may lie beneath the words. Then let partners develop a list of similarities and differences that they can incorporate into their analyses.

TEACH

CLOSE READ

Analyze Drama Elements: Character (LINES 1–24)

COMMON CORE RL 3

Point out that this scene further develops the audience's understanding of the character of Polonius. Tell students that his character traits will have a major impact on what happens later in the play.

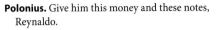 **ASK STUDENTS** to explain what Polonius wants Reynaldo to do. How is Reynaldo to do this? *(Polonius wants Reynaldo to find out if Laertes is behaving himself. Reynaldo is to do this by indirectly accusing Laertes of various indiscretions.)* What do Polonius's actions reveal about his character? *(He has a devious mind; he likes spying; he also does not trust his son.)*

ACT II

Scene 1 *Polonius's chambers.*

[*Enter old* Polonius *with his man* Reynaldo.]

Polonius. Give him this money and these notes, Reynaldo.

Reynaldo. I will, my lord.

Polonius. You shall do marvelous wisely, good Reynaldo,
Before you visit him, to make inquire
5 Of his behavior.

Reynaldo.   My lord, I did intend it.

Polonius. Marry, well said, very well said. Look you, sir,
Inquire me first what Danskers are in Paris;
And how, and who, what means, and where they keep,
What company, at what expense; and finding
10 By this encompassment and drift of question
That they do know my son, come you more nearer
Than your particular demands will touch it.
Take you, as 'twere, some distant knowledge of him,
As thus: "I know his father and his friends
15 And, in part, him." Do you mark this, Reynaldo?

Reynaldo. Ay, very well, my lord.

Polonius. "And, in part, him, but," you may say, "not well.
But if 't be he I mean, he's very wild,
Addicted so and so." And there put on him
20 What forgeries you please—marry, none so rank
As may dishonor him, take heed of that,
But, sir, such wanton, wild, and usual slips
As are companions noted and most known
To youth and liberty.

Reynaldo.   As gaming, my lord.

25 **Polonius.** Ay, or drinking, fencing, swearing,
Quarreling, drabbing—you may go so far.

Reynaldo. My lord, that would dishonor him.

Polonius. Faith, no, as you may season it in the charge.
You must not put another scandal on him
30 That he is open to incontinency;
That's not my meaning. But breathe his faults so quaintly
That they may seem the taints of liberty,

6–12 Polonius tells him to start by asking general questions, because he will find out more through this roundabout approach (**encompassment**) than by asking specific questions about Laertes.

13 Take you: assume.

19–20 put on . . . please: accuse him of whatever faults you wish to make up; **rank:** gross.

22 wanton: reckless.

23–24 As are . . . liberty: that are commonly associated with youth and freedom.

24 gaming: gambling.

26 drabbing: going to prostitutes.

28 you . . . charge: You can soften (**season**) the charge by the way you state it.

30 incontinency: habitual sexual misconduct (as opposed to an occasional lapse).

31–36 Polonius tells him to describe Laertes's faults so subtly that they will seem the faults that come with independence (**taints of liberty**), the sudden urges of an excited mind, a wildness in untamed blood that occurs in most men.

Close Read Screencasts

Modeled Discussions

Have students click the *Close Read* icons in their eBooks to access a screencast in which readers discuss and annotate the following key passage:

- Polonius's attempt to discern the cause of Hamlet's madness (Act II, Scene 2, lines 207–221)

As a class, view and discuss the video.

Determine Themes

COMMON CORE RL 2

(LINES 62–66)

Have students recall Hamlet's own plan, devised in Scene 5 of the first act.

B **ASK STUDENTS** how Polonius's strategy and Hamlet's are similar. *(Hamlet will pretend to be mad in order to gain the truth about his father's murder. Reynaldo will pretend to know that Laertes has committed certain follies in order to find out the truth about his behavior. Both will use "… indirections [to] find directions out.")*

The flash and outbreak of a fiery mind,
A savageness in unreclaimèd blood,
35 Of general assault.

Reynaldo. But, my good lord—

Polonius. Wherefore should you do this?   **37 Wherefore:** why.

Reynaldo. Ay, my lord, I would know that.

Polonius. Marry, sir, here's my drift,
40 And I believe it is a fetch of wit.   **40 fetch of wit:** clever move.
You, laying these slight sullies on my son,
As 'twere a thing a little soiled i' th' working,   **41–46** Polonius wants Reynaldo to put these small stains (**sullies**) on his son's reputation—similar to the way in which cloth might be dirtied when it is handled—and then ask the person whether he has seen Laertes engaged in the offenses Reynaldo has mentioned (**prenominate crimes**).
Mark you, your party in converse, him you would
   sound,
Having ever seen in the prenominate crimes
45 The youth you breathe of guilty, be assured
He closes with you in this consequence: **46 He closes . . . consequence:** he agrees with you in the following way.
"Good sir," or so, or "friend," or "gentleman,"
According to the phrase or the addition   **48 addition:** form of address.
Of man and country—

Reynaldo.   Very good, my lord.

50 **Polonius.** And then, sir, does he this, he does—what was I
about to say? By the Mass, I was about to say something.
Where did I leave?

Reynaldo. At "closes in the consequence," at "friend, or
so, and gentleman."

55 **Polonius.** At "closes in the consequence"—ay, marry—
He closes thus: "I know the gentleman.
I saw him yesterday," or "th' other day"
(Or then, or then, with such or such), "and as you say,
There was he gaming, there o'ertook in 's rouse,   **59 o'ertook in 's rouse:** overcome by drink.
60 There falling out at tennis"; or perchance
"I saw him enter such a house of sale"—
Videlicet, a brothel—or so forth. See you now   **62 Videlicet:** namely.
Your bait of falsehood take this carp of truth;
And thus do we of wisdom and of reach,   **64–66 we of . . . out:** we who have wisdom and intelligence (**reach**) find things out indirectly, through roundabout courses (**windlasses**) and indirect tests (**assays of bias**).
65 With windlasses and with assays of bias,
By indirections find directions out.
So by my former lecture and advice
Shall you my son. You have me, have you not?

Reynaldo. My lord, I have.

Polonius.   God be wi' you. Fare you well.   **71–73** Polonius tells him to observe Laertes's behavior personally and to see that Laertes practices his music.
70 **Reynaldo.** Good my lord.

Polonius. Observe his inclination in yourself.

SCAFFOLDING FOR ELL STUDENTS

Identify Quotations Explain to students that words and phrases enclosed in quotation marks indicate the exact speech of someone. Tell students that in this part of the scene, Polonius tells Reynaldo to listen for what friends or acquaintances of Laertes might say about him. To make sure Reynaldo understands his instructions, Polonius uses specific examples of their possible comments. Point out the phrases in quotation marks in line 47.

ASK STUDENTS to work in pairs to identify the direct quotations that Polonius uses as examples in lines 55–61. Have students read them aloud. Discuss their meaning in the context of Polonius's speech.

Reynaldo. I shall, my lord.

Polonius. And let him ply his music.

Reynaldo. Well, my lord.

75 **Polonius.** Farewell.

[Reynaldo *exits.*]

[*Enter* Ophelia.]

How now, Ophelia, what's the matter?

Ophelia. O, my lord, my lord, I have been so affrighted!

Polonius. With what, i' th' name of God?

Ophelia. My lord, as I was sewing in my closet,
Lord Hamlet, with his doublet all unbraced,
80 No hat upon his head, his stockings fouled,
Ungartered, and down-gyvèd to his ankle,
Pale as his shirt, his knees knocking each other,
And with a look so piteous in purport
As if he had been loosèd out of hell
85 To speak of horrors—he comes before me.

Polonius. Mad for thy love?

Ophelia. My lord, I do not know,
But truly I do fear it.

Polonius. What said he?

Ophelia. He took me by the wrist and held me hard.
Then goes he to the length of all his arm,
90 And, with his other hand thus o'er his brow,
He falls to such perusal of my face
As he would draw it. Long stayed he so.
At last, a little shaking of mine arm,
And thrice his head thus waving up and down,
95 He raised a sigh so piteous and profound
As it did seem to shatter all his bulk
And end his being. That done, he lets me go,
And, with his head over his shoulder turned,
He seemed to find his way without his eyes,
100 For out o' doors he went without their helps
And to the last bended their light on me.

Polonius. Come, go with me. I will go seek the King.
This is the very ecstasy of love,
Whose violent property fordoes itself
105 And leads the will to desperate undertakings
As oft as any passions under heaven
That does afflict our natures. I am sorry.
What, have you given him any hard words of late?

78 **closet:** private room.

79 **doublet all
unbraced:** jacket entirely
unfastened.

80 **fouled:** dirty.

81 **down-gyvèd to his
ankle:** fallen down to his
ankles (like a prisoner's
ankle chains, or gyves).

83 **purport:** expression.

96 **bulk:** body.

101 **to the last . . . me:**
kept his eyes upon me
the whole time.

103–107 Polonius says
that the violent nature
(**property**) of this love
madness (**ecstasy**)
often leads people to do
something desperate.

TEACH

CLOSE READ

Analyze Structure: Conflict (LINES 78–101)

COMMON CORE RL 3

Tell students that in the second act of a Shakespearean drama, the action rises as the conflict becomes more evident and more intense and the characters struggle to resolve it.

C ASK STUDENTS to reread Ophelia's description of Hamlet in lines 78–85. Ask how his appearance is related to the Ghost's revelation in Act I, Scene 5, line 26. (*The Ghost revealed that Hamlet's father was murdered by his uncle. Hamlet resolves to act mad in order to learn more about this situation. His disheveled appearance here is part of his act.*) Have students discuss possible motives for his behavior in lines 88–101. (*He is developing the impression of his madness. He is wondering whether or not he can trust Ophelia with the truth.*)

Strategies for Annotation

✎ 🖫 **Annotate it!**

Analyze Drama Elements

COMMON CORE RL 3

Have students use their eBook annotation tools to analyze Hamlet's behavior in lines 78–101.

- Highlight in pink details of Hamlet's appearance. *(lines 79–84)*
- Highlight in yellow lines that describe Hamlet's actions.
- Highlight in blue details that show Hamlet's emotions.
- On a note, explain what might be inferred from these details about his reasons for going to see Ophelia.

And, with his other hand thus o'er his brow,

He falls to such perusal of my face

As he would draw it. Long stayed he so.

At last, a little shaking of mine arm,

He raised a sigh so piteous and profound

As it did seem to shatter all his bulk

Analyze Drama Elements: Character (LINES 109–121) COMMON CORE RL 3

Point out that in this part of the scene, Ophelia and Polonius are drawn into Hamlet's deception.

D ASK STUDENTS what Ophelia and Polonius believe about Hamlet's condition. *(They think that Ophelia's rejection of him has driven him to madness.)* Ask students what feeling Polonius's comment "But beshrew my jealousy" expresses. Have them discuss whether Ophelia feels the same. Why or why not? *(Polonius says that he feels guilty for misreading the situation. He believed that Hamlet's intentions were to take advantage of Ophelia. If he feels guilty, then Ophelia must feel doubly so since she is the one who actually rejected him. Her previous conversations with Laertes and her father show her to be trusting, affectionate, and obedient, making it likely that she would bear the burden of guilt very heavily.)*

Analyze Drama Elements COMMON CORE RL 3

(sc. 2 LINES 1–18)

Remind students that one of the reasons that playwrights use dramatic irony is to add a layer of meaning to character's words and actions.

E ASK STUDENTS what is ironic about the King sending for Rosencrantz and Guildenstern. *(The audience knows that Hamlet is just acting. The King is using Hamlet's two good friends to spy on him in the hopes that Hamlet will not be suspicious.)* Have students discuss why the King might be worried about Hamlet's behavior. *(The King may wonder if Hamlet knows more than he thinks about what Claudius has done; he may be concerned because Hamlet's mother is so worried; he may see Hamlet as a threat because of his unpredictability.)*

D **Ophelia.** No, my good lord, but as you did command
110 I did repel his letters and denied
His access to me.

Polonius. That hath made him mad.
I am sorry that with better heed and judgment
I had not coted him. I feared he did but trifle
And meant to wrack thee. But beshrew my jealousy!
115 By heaven, it is as proper to our age
To cast beyond ourselves in our opinions
As it is common for the younger sort
To lack discretion. Come, go we to the King.
This must be known, which, being kept close,
    might move
120 More grief to hide than hate to utter love.
Come.

[*They exit.*]

Scene 2 *The castle.*

[*Flourish. Enter* King *and* Queen, Rosencrantz *and*
Guildenstern *and* Attendants.]

E **King.** Welcome, dear Rosencrantz and Guildenstern.
Moreover that we much did long to see you,
The need we have to use you did provoke
Our hasty sending. Something have you heard
5 Of Hamlet's transformation, so call it,
Sith nor th' exterior nor the inward man
Resembles that it was. What it should be,
More than his father's death, that thus hath put him
So much from th' understanding of himself
10 I cannot dream of. I entreat you both
That, being of so young days brought up with him
And sith so neighbored to his youth and havior,
That you vouchsafe your rest here in our court
Some little time, so by your companies
15 To draw him on to pleasures, and to gather
So much as from occasion you may glean,
Whether aught to us unknown afflicts him thus
That, opened, lies within our remedy.

Queen. Good gentlemen, he hath much talked of you,
20 And sure I am two men there is not living
To whom he more adheres. If it will please you
To show us so much gentry and goodwill
As to expend your time with us awhile
For the supply and profit of our hope,

113 coted: observed.

114 wrack: ruin, seduce; **beshrew my jealousy:** curse my suspicious nature.

115–118 It is as natural for old people to go too far (**cast beyond ourselves**) with their suspicions as it is for younger people to lack good judgment.

119–120 Polonius decides that although it may anger the King, he must be told about this love because keeping it a secret might create even more grief.

6 Sith . . . man: since neither his appearance nor his personality.

10–18 Because Rosencrantz and Guildenstern were childhood friends with Hamlet and are so familiar with his past and his usual manner (**havior**), Claudius asks them to agree to stay (**vouchsafe your rest**) at court awhile to cheer Hamlet up and find out whether he is troubled by something that Claudius is unaware of.

18 opened: revealed.

22 gentry: courtesy.

24 For . . . hope: to aid and fulfill our wishes.

266 Collection 4

WHEN STUDENTS STRUGGLE . . .

Help students to understand the events set in motion by Hamlet's decision to act mad by having them complete a cause-and-effect chart similar to the one on page 267. They should use the details on these pages to identify the ways in which his behavior affects the other characters and the action.

ASK STUDENTS to share their charts. Then ask them what effect Hamlet is hoping that his behavior will lead to. *(that he will be able to find out more about what Claudius did)*

25   Your visitation shall receive such thanks
       As fits a king's remembrance.

       Rosencrantz.   Both your Majesties
       Might, by the sovereign power you have of us,
       Put your dread pleasures more into command
       Than to entreaty.

       Guildenstern.   But we both obey,
30   And here give up ourselves in the full bent
       To lay our service freely at your feet,
       To be commanded.

       King. Thanks, Rosencrantz and gentle Guildenstern.

       Queen. Thanks, Guildenstern and gentle Rosencrantz.
35   And I beseech you instantly to visit
       My too much changèd son. Go, some of you,
       And bring these gentlemen where Hamlet is.

       Guildenstern. Heavens make our presence and our
          practices
       Pleasant and helpful to him!

       Queen.   Ay, amen!

       [Rosencrantz *and* Guildenstern *exit with some* Attendants.]

       [*Enter* Polonius.]

40   **Polonius.** Th' ambassadors from Norway, my good lord,
       Are joyfully returned.

       King. Thou still hast been the father of good news.

       Polonius. Have I, my lord? I assure my good liege
       I hold my duty as I hold my soul,
45   Both to my God and to my gracious king,
       And I do think, or else this brain of mine
       Hunts not the trail of policy so sure
       As it hath used to do, that I have found
       The very cause of Hamlet's lunacy.

50   **King.** O, speak of that! That do I long to hear.

       Polonius. Give first admittance to th' ambassadors.
       My news shall be the fruit to that great feast.

       King. Thyself do grace to them and bring them in.

       [Polonius *exits.*]

       He tells me, my dear Gertrude, he hath found
55   The head and source of all your son's distemper.

       Queen. I doubt it is no other but the main—
       His father's death and our o'erhasty marriage.

29–32 Guildenstern promises that they will devote themselves entirely (**in the full bent**) to the service of the King and Queen.

38 practices: doings (sometimes used to mean "trickery").

42 still: always.

47–48 Hunts . . . do: does not follow the path of political shrewdness as well as it used to.

52 fruit: dessert.

56 the main: the main matter.

Hamlet: Act II, Scene 2   **267**

CLOSE READ

Analyze Drama Elements: Character (sc. 2 LINES 40–55)

COMMON CORE   RL 3

Point out that, in a drama, dialogue is used to indicate characters' relationships to each other.

F CITE TEXT EVIDENCE Ask students to describe the relationship between Polonius and Claudius and its effect upon the characters' actions. *(Polonius looks up to Claudius; he will do whatever he can to please him. This is shown by his equating of his "gracious king" with his God and his comment that "I hold my duty as I hold my soul." Claudius sees Polonius as someone loyal to him who will do his bidding.)*

Cause:	Effect:
Hamlet acts mad.	Ophelia believes it is her fault.
	Hamlet's mother is worried.
	Hamlet's mother and Claudius send for Rosencrantz and Guildenstern.

Analyze Drama Elements: Character COMMON CORE RL 3
(sc. 2 LINES 60–80)

Remind students that ideas about character may be brought out through comparing and contrasting their traits.

G CITE TEXT EVIDENCE Ask students to recall what they know about Fortinbras from Scene 2 of Act I. Then have them note the additional details they learn about him in Voltemand's report. How is he similar to Hamlet? How is he different? *(Their situations are similar. Both lost their fathers through murder and both saw their uncles succeed to the throne. The major difference, however, is that Fortinbras actively sought revenge. Hamlet has not yet acted on his pledge to avenge his father's death.)*

Determine Themes COMMON CORE RL 2

(sc. 2 LINES 81–85)

Point out that this scene shows Claudius in his public persona, conducting official business on behalf of the state.

H ASK STUDENTS what ideas about the "public" Claudius this scene brings out. *(He is skillful at the affairs of state. He is gracious to those who serve him.)* Have students explain how this public persona contrasts with his private nature as the audience understands it. What possible theme is brought out through this contrast? *(His public persona is beyond reproach. His private nature, on the other hand, is corrupt. One idea is that again a virtuous appearance hides a corrupt reality. Also, the fact that Claudius is the leader of Denmark suggests that his corruption affects the state. That is why "something is rotten.")*

King. Well, we shall sift him.

[*Enter* Ambassadors Voltemand *and* Cornelius *with* Polonius.]

Welcome, my good friends.
Say, Voltemand, what from our brother Norway?

60 **Voltemand.** Most fair return of greetings and desires.
Upon our first, he sent out to suppress
His nephew's levies, which to him appeared
To be a preparation 'gainst the Polack,
But, better looked into, he truly found
65 It was against your Highness. Whereat, grieved
That so his sickness, age, and impotence
Was falsely borne in hand, sends out arrests
On Fortinbras, which he, in brief, obeys,
Receives rebuke from Norway, and, in fine,
70 Makes vow before his uncle never more
To give th' assay of arms against your Majesty.
Whereon old Norway, overcome with joy,
Gives him three-score thousand crowns in annual fee
And his commission to employ those soldiers,
75 So levied as before, against the Polack,
With an entreaty, herein further shown,

[*He gives a paper.*]

That it might please you to give quiet pass
Through your dominions for this enterprise,
On such regards of safety and allowance
80 As therein are set down.

King. It likes us well,
And, at our more considered time, we'll read,
Answer, and think upon this business.
Meantime, we thank you for your well-took labor.
Go to your rest. At night we'll feast together.
85 Most welcome home!

[*Voltemand and Cornelius exit.*]

Polonius. This business is well ended.
My liege, and madam, to expostulate
What majesty should be, what duty is,
Why day is day, night night, and time is time
Were nothing but to waste night, day, and time.
90 Therefore, since brevity is the soul of wit,
And tediousness the limbs and outward flourishes,
I will be brief. Your noble son is mad.
"Mad" call I it, for, to define true madness,

58 sift him: question Polonius carefully.

59 brother: fellow king.

61 Upon our first: as soon as we brought up the matter.

67 borne in hand: deceived; **arrests:** orders to desist.

69 in fine: finally.

71 give ... against: challenge militarily.

77–80 give ... down: allow troops to move through Denmark for this expedition, under the conditions set down for Denmark's security and Fortinbras's permission.

80 likes: pleases.

81 our more considered time: a more suitable time for consideration.

86–89 To inquire into (**expostulate**) the nature of one's duty to the crown would be a waste of time, like trying to figure out the reason for day, night, and time.

90 brevity ... wit: intelligent speech should be concise.

91 flourishes: decorations.

SCAFFOLDING FOR ELL STUDENTS

Identify Subject and Verb Point out that many sentences in *Hamlet* are long and complicated. Explain that identifying the main subject, verb, and objects in such sentences is a good strategy for understanding their meaning. Display lines 72–80.

Have pairs pick out the main subject and verb (*Norway, gives*), the direct objects (*crowns, commission*), and the indirect object (*him*). Highlight or circle those words in the sentence. Then, as a class, sort out the modifying phrases and clauses, identifying those that tell about the subject (*overcome with joy*) and the direct objects (*in annual fee, to employ those soldiers ...*). Point out that the adjective clause (*that it might please you ...*) modifies the word *entreaty*. Encourage students to apply this strategy when they encounter long, complicated sentences.

What is 't but to be nothing else but mad?
95 But let that go.

Queen.   More matter with less art.

Polonius. Madam, I swear I use no art at all.
That he's mad, 'tis true; 'tis true 'tis pity,
And pity 'tis 'tis true—a foolish figure,
But farewell it, for I will use no art.
100 Mad let us grant him then, and now remains
That we find out the cause of this effect,
Or, rather say, the cause of this defect,
For this effect defective comes by cause.
Thus it remains, and the remainder thus.
105 Perpend.
I have a daughter (have while she is mine)
Who, in her duty and obedience, mark,
Hath given me this. Now gather and surmise.

[*He reads.*] *To the celestial, and my soul's idol, the*
110 *most beautified Ophelia—*

That's an ill phrase, a vile phrase; "beautified" is a
vile phrase. But you shall hear. Thus: [*He reads.*]
In her excellent white bosom, these, etc.—

Queen. Came this from Hamlet to her?

115 **Polonius.** Good madam, stay awhile. I will be faithful.

[*He reads the letter.*]

          Doubt thou the stars are fire,
              Doubt that the sun doth move,
          Doubt truth to be a liar,
              But never doubt I love.
120 *O dear Ophelia, I am ill at these numbers. I have not*
art to reckon my groans, but that I love thee
best, O most best, believe it. Adieu.
                  Thine evermore, most dear lady, whilst
                      this machine is to him, Hamlet.

125 This, in obedience, hath my daughter shown me,
And more above, hath his solicitings,
As they fell out by time, by means, and place,
All given to mine ear.

King. But how hath she received his love?

130 **Polonius.** What do you think of me?

King. As of a man faithful and honorable.

Polonius. I would fain prove so. But what might you
    think,

96–99 The Queen asks
Polonius to make his
point without such a
display of rhetoric (**art**).
He claims to be speaking
plainly about the matter,
but then he can't resist
making a figure of
speech that even he
describes as foolish.

105 **Perpend:** consider.

108 **gather and
surmise:** draw your own
conclusions.

114–115 The Queen
doubts Hamlet would
use such formal and
flowery language;
Polonius assures her
he will read the letter
accurately.

116 **Doubt:** suspect.

120 **ill at these
numbers:** bad at writing
in verse.

121 **reckon:** count, put
into metrical verse.

123–124 **whilst . . . to
him:** while I am still in
this body (**machine**).

126–128 **more
above . . . ear:** In
addition, she has told
me all the details of his
solicitations as they
occurred.

TEACH

CLOSE READ

Analyze Drama Elements: COMMON CORE RL 1
Character (sc. 2 LINES 85–128)

Tell students to pay close attention to the developing
character of Polonius in this scene.

 CITE TEXT EVIDENCE In line 90, as he explains
to the King and Queen why he thinks Hamlet is
mad, Polonius says that "brevity is the soul of wit."
Ask students to explain the irony in this statement.
*(Polonius has already spoken five lines, and he's still
introducing his subject. He is not being brief. There is
little wit or intelligence in this long-winded speech.)*
As Polonius continues (lines 96–113), ask students
to cite more evidence of his tendency to be wordy.
*(He speaks for eighteen lines in this second speech,
but he still has not begun to explain why he thinks
Hamlet is mad.)* Finally, ask students what it reveals
about Polonius that he reads aloud Hamlet's letter to
Ophelia (lines 116–124). *(Polonius might be sincere in
wanting to explain why he thinks Hamlet is mad, but he
clearly lacks respect for the privacy of others, even his
own daughter and son.)*

Analyze Word Choice RL 4

(sc. 2 LINES 133–152)

Direct students to reread Polonius's speech to Claudius and Gertrude, noting how the various literary techniques affect their understanding of his words.

 ASK STUDENTS to describe the tone of the first part of this speech. To what comment of Claudius's is he responding? *(Polonius is insulted. He is responding to Claudius's question about whether Ophelia received Hamlet's love.)* Have students discuss the tone of the last part of the speech. Ask them to identify literary techniques that help to convey this tone. *(The tone is vehement and certain. Parallelism and repetition help to make him sound more emphatic.)*

Analyze Drama Elements: 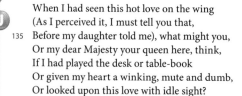 RL 3
Character (sc. 2 LINES 157–169)

ASK STUDENTS how Polonius's suggestion further illustrates his character. *(As seen earlier in the act, Polonius favors deceptive approaches to get at the truth. He tells the King that they will eavesdrop on Hamlet and Ophelia to ascertain whether she is the cause of his madness.)*

When I had seen this hot love on the wing
(As I perceived it, I must tell you that,
135   Before my daughter told me), what might you,
Or my dear Majesty your queen here, think,
If I had played the desk or table-book
Or given my heart a winking, mute and dumb,
Or looked upon this love with idle sight?
140   What might you think? No, I went round to work,
And my young mistress thus I did bespeak:
"Lord Hamlet is a prince, out of thy star.
This must not be." And then I prescripts gave her,
That she should lock herself from his resort,
145   Admit no messengers, receive no tokens;
Which done, she took the fruits of my advice,
And he, repelled (a short tale to make),
Fell into a sadness, then into a fast,
Thence to a watch, thence into a weakness,
150   Thence to a lightness, and, by this declension,
Into the madness wherein now he raves
And all we mourn for.

   King [*to* Queen].   Do you think 'tis this?

   Queen. It may be, very like.

   Polonius. Hath there been such a time (I would fain
     know that)
155   That I have positively said "'Tis so,"
When it proved otherwise?

   King.   Not that I know.

   Polonius. Take this from this, if this be otherwise.
If circumstances lead me, I will find
Where truth is hid, though it were hid, indeed,
160   Within the center.

   King.   How may we try it further?

   Polonius. You know sometimes he walks four hours
     together
Here in the lobby.

   Queen.   So he does indeed.

   Polonius. At such a time I'll loose my daughter to him.
[*To the* King.] Be you and I behind an arras then.
165   Mark the encounter. If he love her not,
And be not from his reason fall'n thereon,
Let me be no assistant for a state,
But keep a farm and carters.

   King.   We will try it.

137 played . . . table-book: kept this knowledge hidden within me.

138 given . . . winking: closed the eyes of my heart.

139 with idle sight: saw without really noticing.

142 star: sphere.

143 prescripts: orders.

144 resort: visits.

147–152 Polonius describes the stages of Hamlet's decline: he grew sad, then stopped eating, then suffered from sleeplessness (**a watch**), then turned weak and light-headed, and finally became mad.

157 The actor playing Polonius might point from his head to his shoulder or make a similar gesture while speaking this line.

160 the center: the Earth's center, the most inaccessible place; **try:** test.

163 loose: turn loose (as an animal might be released for mating).

164 arras: a tapestry hung in front of a wall.

Strategies for Annotation 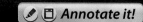   Annotate it!

Analyze Word Choice RL 4

Have students use their eBook tools to analyze how literary techniques contribute to tone in lines 140–152:

- Highlight examples of repetition in blue.
- Highlight examples of parallel structure in yellow.
- Read the highlighted lines and phrases aloud to hear the tone.
- On a note, explain what feeling or attitude on the part of the speaker is conveyed through the use of these techniques.

> And he, repelled (a short tale to make),
>
> Fell into a sadness, then into a fast,
>
> Thence to a watch, thence into a weakness,
>
> Thence to a lightness, and, by this declension,
>
> Into the madness wherein now he raves

[*Enter* Hamlet *reading on a book*.]

Queen. But look where sadly the poor wretch comes reading.

170 **Polonius.** Away, I do beseech you both, away.
I'll board him presently. O, give me leave.

[King *and* Queen *exit with* Attendants.]

How does my good Lord Hamlet?

Hamlet. Well, God-a-mercy.

Polonius. Do you know me, my lord?

175 **Hamlet.** Excellent well. You are a fishmonger.

Polonius. Not I, my lord.

Hamlet. Then I would you were so honest a man.

Polonius. Honest, my lord?

Hamlet. Ay, sir. To be honest, as this world goes, is to
180 be one man picked out of ten thousand.

Polonius. That's very true, my lord.

**171 board him
presently:** speak to him
at once.

175 fishmonger: fish
seller.

Hamlet: Act II, Scene 2 **271**

Image Credits: ©Nat Farbman/Time Life Pictures/Getty Images

Analyze Drama Elements RL 3

(sc. 2 LINES 173–181)

Remind students that as they read this scene dramatic irony enables them to have an advantage over Polonius: as readers and members of the play's audience, they know about Hamlet's plan to pretend madness. Polonius does not.

L ASK STUDENTS to explain Hamlet's purpose in this conversation. *(He intends to demonstrate his madness to Polonius. He also intends to tease and taunt Polonius.)* Ask students what he suggests about Polonius in line 177 that shows to the informed audience that he is not insane. *(He questions the honesty of Polonius. Polonius has been shown to be devious; therefore, this question is a valid one.)*

TO CHALLENGE STUDENTS...

Synthesize Meaning What words in this dialogue show Hamlet's opinion of Polonius? Point out that this dialogue between Polonius and Hamlet functions on a dual level: Polonius sees little sense in what Hamlet says to him, while Hamlet is using their conversation as a chance to insult Polonius and reveal how much he knows about him.

Have pairs analyze the puns and the meaning of lines 173–221. Have them consult sources that will help them to interpret specific terms in the passage.

Ask students to compare their analyses in small groups and discuss the importance of this dialogue in developing an understanding of Hamlet's character and the role he is playing.

Analyze Drama Elements: Character

COMMON CORE RL 3

(sc. 2 LINES 182–219)

Tell students that this exchange between Hamlet and Polonius works on two levels. On one level, Polonius, working on behalf of the King, engages Hamlet in conversation to learn more about his madness. On another level, Hamlet taunts and insults Polonius with madness as his cover.

 CITE TEXT EVIDENCE Read this passage with your students. Stop at line 206. Ask students to reread lines 198–206 and then explain how Hamlet's words can come across both as crazy talk and as insults to Polonius. *(Crazy talk: Instead of answering Polonius sensibly, Hamlet rambles about old men and their infirmities, leading up to a nonsense statement about aging backward by walking like a crab. Insulting talk: In his exaggerated description of old men, Hamlet clearly includes Polonius as the kind of old man he describes.)* Read lines 207–219 with students. Before asking them questions, clear up any confusion they have about meaning in these lines. Then, ask them to cite evidence that Polonius understands there is more to Hamlet's talk than simple nonsense. *(Polonius says "Though this be madness, yet there is / method in't." [lines 207–208] and "How / pregnant sometimes his replies are." [lines 210–211])* Finally, ask students to point out further evidence that Polonius is a devious character. *(In lines 213-215, Polonius plans again to spy on someone—this time a meeting of Hamlet and Ophelia.)*

Hamlet. For if the sun breed maggots in a dead dog, being a good kissing carrion—Have you a daughter?

Polonius. I have, my lord.

185 **Hamlet.** Let her not walk i' th' sun. Conception is a blessing, but, as your daughter may conceive, friend, look to 't.

Polonius [*aside*]. How say you by that? Still harping on my daughter. Yet he knew me not at first; he said I
190 was a fishmonger. He is far gone. And truly, in my youth, I suffered much extremity for love, very near this. I'll speak to him again.—What do you read, my lord?

Hamlet. Words, words, words.

195 **Polonius.** What is the matter, my lord?

Hamlet. Between who?

Polonius. I mean the matter that you read, my lord.

Hamlet. Slanders, sir; for the satirical rogue says here that old men have gray beards, that their faces are
200 wrinkled, their eyes purging thick amber and plum-tree gum, and that they have a plentiful lack of wit, together with most weak hams; all which, sir, though I most powerfully and potently believe, yet I hold it not honesty to have it thus set down; for
205 yourself, sir, shall grow old as I am, if, like a crab, you could go backward.

Polonius [*aside*]. Though this be madness, yet there is method in 't.—Will you walk out of the air, my lord?

Hamlet. Into my grave?

210 **Polonius.** Indeed, that's out of the air. [*Aside.*] How pregnant sometimes his replies are! A happiness that often madness hits on, which reason and sanity could not so prosperously be delivered of. I will leave him and suddenly contrive the means of
215 meeting between him and my daughter.—My lord, I will take my leave of you.

Hamlet. You cannot, sir, take from me anything that I will more willingly part withal—except my life, except my life, except my life.

220 **Polonius.** Fare you well, my lord.

Hamlet [*aside*]. These tedious old fools.

[*Enter* Guildenstern *and* Rosencrantz.]

183 a good kissing carrion: good flesh for kissing. (Hamlet seems to be reading at least part of this sentence from his book.)

185 Conception: understanding, being pregnant.

188 harping on: sticking to the subject of.

195 matter: subject matter. (Hamlet plays off another meaning, "the basis of a quarrel.")

201 wit: understanding.

204 honesty: good manners.

208 Polonius asks him to come out of the open air.

211 pregnant: full of meaning; **happiness:** talent for expression.

SCAFFOLDING FOR ELL STUDENTS

Understand Dashes Explain to students that dashes have a variety of functions. In dialogue, a dash can be used for these reasons: to indicate an interruption; to show a change in the person being addressed; to show that the speaker has lost his or her train of thought; to signal a sudden change of subject; to include comments that are afterthoughts. Read aloud lines 182–183, using your voice to show how the dash affects tone and timing.

ASK STUDENTS what the dash in line 183 tells readers. *(that the speaker has changed the subject abruptly)* Have students identify the function of the dashes in the rest of the dialogue on this page. *(lines 192, 207, and 215: to indicate that Polonius changes from talking to himself to talking to Hamlet; line 218: to add afterthoughts.)*

Polonius. You go to seek the Lord Hamlet. There he is.

Rosencrantz [*to* Polonius]. God save you, sir.

[Polonius *exits*.]

Guildenstern. My honored lord.

225 **Rosencrantz.** My most dear lord.

Hamlet. My excellent good friends! How dost thou, Guildenstern? Ah, Rosencrantz! Good lads, how do you both?

Rosencrantz. As the indifferent children of the earth.

230 **Guildenstern.** Happy in that we are not overhappy. On Fortune's cap, we are not the very button.

Hamlet. Nor the soles of her shoe?

Rosencrantz. Neither, my lord.

Hamlet. Then you live about her waist, or in the middle
235 of her favors?

Guildenstern. Faith, her privates we.

Hamlet. In the secret parts of Fortune? O, most true!

She is a strumpet. What news?

Rosencrantz. None, my lord, but that the world's
240 grown honest.

Hamlet. Then is doomsday near. But your news is not true. Let me question more in particular. What have you, my good friends, deserved at the hands of Fortune that she sends you to prison hither?

245 **Guildenstern.** Prison, my lord?

Hamlet. Denmark's a prison.

Rosencrantz. Then is the world one.

Hamlet. A goodly one, in which there are many confines, wards, and dungeons, Denmark being
250 one o' th' worst.

Rosencrantz. We think not so, my lord.

Hamlet. Why, then, 'tis none to you, for there is nothing either good or bad but thinking makes it so. To me, it is a prison.

255 **Rosencrantz.** Why, then, your ambition makes it one. 'Tis too narrow for your mind.

229 indifferent: ordinary.

234–238 Hamlet exchanges sexual puns with his childhood friends. References to Fortune's sexual favors and private parts lead up to the traditional saying that the unfaithful Fortune is a prostitute (**strumpet**).

249 confines: places of confinement; **wards:** cells.

Hamlet: Act II, Scene 2 **273**

CLOSE READ

Analyze Drama Elements COMMON CORE RL 3

(sc. 2 LINES 224–244)

Have students note that all of these encounters between characters take place in the same setting. Point out that this enables the audience to focus on Hamlet throughout.

 ASK STUDENTS what Hamlet's exchange of comments suggests about his feelings for Rosencrantz and Guildenstern. *(He is almost lighthearted in this exchange, as if the sight of his two friends cheers him up.)* How does the mood of their conversation change after line 241? Explain. *(Hamlet is struck by the word "honest" and that might be when he begins to wonder at their motives.)*

SCAFFOLDING FOR ELL STUDENTS

Understand Elliptical Language Remind students that when they read dialogue, they must sometimes fill in missing words in order to understand the speaker's meaning. Point out line 229 in which Rosencrantz replies to Hamlet's question. Explain that the subject and verb are both missing from this fragment. Read the line with the missing sentence parts inserted: *We are as the indifferent children of the earth.*

ASK STUDENTS to work in pairs to rewrite the fragments in lines 230, 232, 233, and 239–240. Have them take turns reading their rewritten lines aloud.

Analyze Structure: Conflict (sc. 2 LINES 270–297)

  COMMON CORE **RL 3**

Tell students to observe the pressure Hamlet applies to Rosencrantz and Guildernstern. Ask them to read Hamlet's lines closely to see if he is still pretending to be mad or if he has dropped the pretense.

Ⓞ ASK STUDENTS to explain what Hamlet wants from Rosencrantz and Guildenstern and why they resist giving him a straight answer. *(Hamlet wants them to confirm his suspicion that, instead of coming freely to visit him, they were sent for by the King and Queen. Since they were asked to spy on Hamlet and spying on him would violate their friendship, Rosencrantz and Guildenstern would naturally resist telling him the truth. Telling him they were sent for will also compromise their role as spies.)* Ask students whether Hamlet is still pretending to be mad during this part of the scene and to cite evidence to support their answer. *(Hamlet seems to have dropped the pretense of madness entirely here. He speaks directly and earnestly to his friends. He asks them honestly, as friends, to tell him the truth. In his dialogue, there is none of the teasing and wordplay that he displayed in the scene with Polonius.)*

Hamlet. O God, I could be bounded in a nutshell and count myself a king of infinite space, were it not that I have bad dreams.

260 **Guildenstern.** Which dreams, indeed, are ambition, for the very substance of the ambitious is merely the shadow of a dream.

Hamlet. A dream itself is but a shadow.

Rosencrantz. Truly, and I hold ambition of so airy and
265 light a quality that it is but a shadow's shadow.

Hamlet. Then are our beggars bodies, and our monarchs and outstretched heroes the beggars' shadows. Shall we to th' court? For, by my fay, I cannot reason.

Rosencrantz/Guildenstern. We'll wait upon you.

270 **Hamlet.** No such matter. I will not sort you with the rest of my servants, for, to speak to you like an honest man, I am most dreadfully attended. But, in the beaten way of friendship, what make you at Elsinore?

275 **Rosencrantz.** To visit you, my lord, no other occasion.

Hamlet. Beggar that I am, I am even poor in thanks; but I thank you, and sure, dear friends, my thanks are too dear a halfpenny. Were you not sent for? Is it your own inclining? Is it a free visitation? Come,
280 come, deal justly with me. Come, come; nay, speak.

Guildenstern. What should we say, my lord?

Hamlet. Anything but to th' purpose. You were sent for, and there is a kind of confession in your looks which your modesties have not craft
285 enough to color. I know the good king and queen have sent for you.

Rosencrantz. To what end, my lord?

Hamlet. That you must teach me. But let me conjure you by the rights of our fellowship, by the consonancy
290 of our youth, by the obligation of our everpreserved love, and by what more dear a better proposer can charge you withal: be even and direct with me whether you were sent for or no.

Rosencrantz [*to* Guildenstern]. What say you?

295 **Hamlet** [*aside*]. Nay, then I have an eye of you.—If you love me, hold not off.

Guildenstern. My lord, we were sent for.

260–262 Guildenstern says that the apparently substantial aims of ambition are even less substantial than dreams.

266–267 Hamlet says that according to their logic, only beggars would have real bodies (since they lack ambition), and monarchs and ambitious (**outstretched**) heroes would be the shadows of beggars.

268 fay: faith.

269 wait upon: escort. (Hamlet takes the word to mean "serve" and replies that he would not categorize them with his servants.)

278 too dear a halfpenny: too costly at a halfpenny.

279 free: voluntary.

282 Hamlet sarcastically asks them to give him anything but a straight answer.

285 color: disguise.

288–289 conjure you: ask you earnestly.

289–290 consonancy of our youth: our closeness when we were young.

291–292 by what . . . withal: by whatever you hold more valuable, which someone more skillful than me would use to urge you with.

295 Hamlet reminds them that he is watching.

274 Collection 4

WHEN STUDENTS STRUGGLE . . .

Tell students that reading dialogue aloud can help them to hear and understand the emotions of the characters. Read aloud lines 270–297 with expression as students follow along in their texts.

ASK STUDENTS what tone they hear in Hamlet's voice. Why? *(He becomes increasingly insistent. He may also sound hopeful that his friends will tell the truth about why they have come to the castle.)* Ask students how Rosencrantz and Guildenstern sound. Why? *(They sound awkward and flustered. They don't know whether to tell the truth or lie.)* Point out to students that this scene shows how much Hamlet suspects about what is going on in the castle.

Hamlet. I will tell you why; so shall my anticipation prevent your discovery, and your secrecy to the
300 King and Queen molt no feather. I have of late, but wherefore I know not, lost all my mirth, forgone all custom of exercises, and, indeed, it goes so heavily with my disposition that this goodly frame, the earth, seems to me a sterile promontory; this
305 most excellent canopy, the air, look you, this brave o'er-hanging firmament, this majestical roof, fretted with golden fire—why, it appeareth nothing to me but a foul and pestilent congregation of vapors. What a piece of work is a man, how noble in reason,
310 how infinite in faculties, in form and moving how express and admirable; in action how like an angel, in apprehension how like a god: the beauty of the world, the paragon of animals—and yet, to me, what is this quintessence of dust? Man delights
315 not me, no, nor women neither, though by your smiling you seem to say so.

Rosencrantz. My lord, there was no such stuff in my thoughts.

Hamlet. Why did you laugh, then, when I said "man
320 delights not me"?

Rosencrantz. To think, my lord, if you delight not in man, what Lenten entertainment the players shall receive from you. We coted them on the way, and hither are they coming to offer you service.

325 **Hamlet.** He that plays the king shall be welcome—his Majesty shall have tribute on me. The adventurous knight shall use his foil and target, the lover shall not sigh gratis, the humorous man shall end his part in peace, the clown shall make those laugh
330 whose lungs are tickle o' th' sear, and the lady shall say her mind freely, or the blank verse shall halt for 't. What players are they?

Rosencrantz. Even those you were wont to take such delight in, the tragedians of the city.

335 **Hamlet.** How chances it they travel? Their residence, both in reputation and profit, was better both ways.

Rosencrantz. I think their inhibition comes by the means of the late innovation.

Hamlet. Do they hold the same estimation they did
340 when I was in the city? Are they so followed?

Rosencrantz. No, indeed are they not.

298–299 shall my . . . discovery: My saying it first will spare you from revealing your secret.

300 molt no feather: will not be diminished.

304 promontory: a rock jutting out from the sea.

305 brave: splendid.

306 fretted: adorned.

308 congregation: gathering.

309 piece of work: work of art or fine craftsmanship.

311 express: exact, expressive.

312 apprehension: understanding.

314 quintessence of dust: essence, or most refined form, of dust.

322 Lenten entertainment: meager, or spare, reception.

323 coted: passed.

325–332 The king shall receive his praise, the knight shall use his sword and shield, the lover shall not sigh for nothing, the eccentric (**humorous**) character shall play his part in peace, the clown shall make those laugh who do so easily, and the lady shall speak without restraint, or else the blank verse (which has five metrical feet) will limp (**halt**) because of it.

CLOSE READ

Determine Themes

COMMON CORE RL 2

(sc. 2 LINES 298–316)

Explain that this passage contains one of the best-known passages in the play—Hamlet's description of the world as he sees it, from "this goodly frame" (line 310) to "this quintessence of dust" (line 314).

P CITE TEXT EVIDENCE Have students point out contrasts in the images Hamlet uses to develop this passage. (*"this goodly frame the earth" vs. "a sterile promontory"; the sky, described as a canopy, a "majestical roof / fretted with golden fire" vs. "a foul and pestilent congregaton of vapors"; the exalted image of a human being as "the paragon of animals" vs. "this quintessence of dust."*) Ask if, as he speaks, Hamlet believes in the positive or the negative images he creates. (*Negative images of the earth as a sterile environment, the air as foul, and human beings as made of dust carry the weight in Hamlet's mind here. Hamlet gives them more weight. Each time he spins a positive image, he undercuts it with a negative image, and he ends emphatically by asking, "and yet, to / me, what is this quintessence of dust?"*) What is the theme of this speech? (*Answers should address the idea that external beauty and nobility of character are ruined by internal rot.*) Have students connect Hamlet's theme to themes that have arisen so far in the play. (*There is a hint of this theme at the end of Act I, Scene 4, when Marcellus says, "Something is rotten in the state of Denmark." The theme is evident in Claudius, a king who appears to be noble but who has murdered his brother to become king. The theme is evident elsewhere, too, in characters such as Polonius, who puts on the appearance of an honest man, but who connives and spies in a devious and dishonest fashion.*)

Strategies for Annotation

 Annotate it!

Analyze Drama Elements

COMMON CORE RL 3

Have students use their eBook annotation tools to analyze Hamlet's speech.

- Highlight in green details that show Hamlet's awareness of the world's beauty and man's potential.
- Highlight in blue phrases and lines that express his feelings toward both.
- On a note, explain why he feels as he does and how his view of mankind prevents him from acting on his feelings.

What a piece of work is a man, how noble in reason,

how infinite in faculties, in form and moving

how express and admirable; in action how like an

angel, in apprehension how like a god: the beauty

of the world, the paragon of animals—and yet, to

me, what is this quintessence of dust? Man delights

CLOSE READ

Analyze Drama Elements RL 3

(sc. 2 LINES 321–373)

Read the dialogue about the arrival of the troupe of actors. Point out that this is one of the lighter moments in the play, a break from the continuing tensions of this long scene. Point out also that, despite the lightness of the moment, the presence of the actors supports the plays concern with appearances. Actors pretend; they play a part, much as Hamlet does when he pretends to be mad, or as Claudius does, pretending to be a good king when he is in fact a murderer.

Q ASK STUDENTS to reread lines 368–373 and then explain what Hamlet says here about his uncle, the current King of Denmark. *(Claudius is like actors who are unpopular one day and popular the next. When Hamlet's father was alive, people would make faces at Claudius to express their dislike. Now that he is king, they pay a high price for miniature portraits of him.)* Ask students to relate this passage to the play's themes. *(Hamlet's concern with a pretended admiration for a likeness of the King echoes the play's concern with pretense and false appearances.)*

Hamlet. How comes it? Do they grow rusty?

Q

Rosencrantz. Nay, their endeavor keeps in the wonted pace. But there is, sir, an aerie of children, little
345 eyases, that cry out on the top of question and are most tyrannically clapped for 't. These are now the fashion and so berattle the common stages (so they call them) that many wearing rapiers are afraid of goose quills and dare scarce come thither.

350 **Hamlet.** What, are they children? Who maintains 'em? How are they escoted? Will they pursue the quality no longer than they can sing? Will they not say afterwards, if they should grow themselves to common players (as it is most like, if their means are no better),
355 their writers do them wrong to make them exclaim against their own succession?

Rosencrantz. Faith, there has been much to-do on both sides, and the nation holds it no sin to tar them to controversy. There was for a while no
360 money bid for argument unless the poet and the player went to cuffs in the question.

Hamlet. Is 't possible?

Guildenstern. O, there has been much throwing about of brains.

365 **Hamlet.** Do the boys carry it away?

Rosencrantz. Ay, that they do, my lord—Hercules and his load too.

Hamlet. It is not very strange; for my uncle is King of Denmark, and those that would make mouths at
370 him while my father lived give twenty, forty, fifty, a hundred ducats apiece for his picture in little. 'Sblood, there is something in this more than natural, if philosophy could find it out.

[*A flourish for the* Players.]

Guildenstern. There are the players.

375 **Hamlet.** Gentlemen, you are welcome to Elsinore. Your hands, come then. Th' appurtenance of welcome is fashion and ceremony. Let me comply with you in this garb, lest my extent to the players, which, I tell you, must show fairly outwards,
380 should more appear like entertainment than yours. You are welcome. But my uncle-father and aunt-mother are deceived.

337–349 The players had to leave the city due to competition from a company of boy actors—a nest (**aerie**) of young hawks (**little eyases**) who are loudly applauded for their shrill performances. Many fashionable patrons are afraid to attend the public theaters (**common stages**) where adult actors play, fearing satirical attacks from the pens of those who write for the boy actors.

351 escoted: provided for.

351–352 pursue . . . sing: perform only until their voices change.

353 common: adult.

356 succession: future work as actors.

358 tar: provoke.

359–361 no money . . . question: the only profitable plays were satires about this rivalry.

366–367 Ay . . . load: Yes, they've won over the whole theater world.

368–371 Hamlet says that people who made faces (**mouths**) at his uncle while his father was alive now pay up to 100 gold coins for his miniature portrait.

375–381 Hamlet tells Rosencrantz and Guildenstern that since fashion and ceremony should accompany a welcome, he wants to observe these formalities with them so it will not appear that the players get a better reception than they do.

Guildenstern. In what, my dear lord?

385 **Hamlet.** I am but mad north-north-west. When the wind is southerly, I know a hawk from a handsaw.

[*Enter* Polonius.]

Polonius. Well be with you, gentlemen.

Hamlet. Hark you, Guildenstern, and you too—at each ear a hearer! That great baby you see there is not yet out of his swaddling clouts.

390 **Rosencrantz.** Haply he is the second time come to them, for they say an old man is twice a child.

Hamlet. I will prophesy he comes to tell me of the players; mark it.—You say right, sir, a Monday morning, 'twas then indeed.

395 **Polonius.** My lord, I have news to tell you.

Hamlet. My lord, I have news to tell you: when Roscius was an actor in Rome—

Polonius. The actors are come hither, my lord.

Hamlet. Buzz, buzz.

400 **Polonius.** Upon my honor—

Hamlet. Then came each actor on his ass.

Polonius. The best actors in the world, either for tragedy, comedy, history, pastoral, pastoral-comical, historical-pastoral, tragical-historical,
405 tragical-comical-historical-pastoral, scene individable, or poem unlimited. Seneca cannot be too heavy, nor Plautus too light. For the law of writ and the liberty, these are the only men.

Hamlet. O Jephthah, judge of Israel, what a treasure
410 hadst thou!

Polonius. What a treasure had he, my lord?

Hamlet. Why,

> One fair daughter, and no more,
> The which he lovèd passing well.

415 **Polonius** [*aside*]. Still on my daughter.

Hamlet. Am I not i' th' right, old Jephthah?

Polonius. If you call me "Jephthah," my lord: I have a daughter that I love passing well.

Hamlet. Nay, that follows not.

420 **Polonius.** What follows then, my lord?

384–385 Hamlet says he is only mad when the wind blows in a certain direction; at other times he can tell one thing from another.

389 swaddling clouts: cloth used to wrap a newborn baby.

397 Roscius: a famous Roman actor.

399 Hamlet dismisses the announcement as old news.

406 Seneca: a Roman writer of tragedies.

406–407 Plautus: a Roman writer of comedies; **For the . . . liberty:** for plays that follow strict rules of dramatic composition as well as more loosely written plays.

409–426 Jephthah: a biblical figure who sacrifices his beloved daughter after making a thoughtless vow (see Judges 11). Hamlet quotes lines from a ballad based on this story.

TEACH

CLOSE READ

Analyze Drama Elements: Character (sc. 2 LINES 384–415)

COMMON CORE RL 3

R **ASK STUDENTS** to notice that although no one else knows about Hamlet's plan to feign madness, what Hamlet says in lines 384–385 gives him away to Rosencrantz and Guildenstern. Then ask students how Hamlet changes when Polonius enters. (*Hamlet is back to feigning madness.*) Have students discuss what the audience realizes about the conversation that Polonius does not. Ask them to give an example that illustrates this lack of realization on the part of Polonius. (*Polonius is so busy trying to analyze what Hamlet says that he does not realize that he is being made fun of. When Hamlet makes wisecracks about a biblical figure and his daughter, Polonius jumps to the conclusion, again, that Hamlet's madness is explained by his fixation on Ophelia.*)

SCAFFOLDING FOR ELL STUDENTS

Interpret Idiomatic Expressions Remind students that idiomatic expressions have a meaning other than what their words say. Review the strategy of using context clues to help define these phrases. Point out the expression "much to-do" in line 357 and help students use the context to guess its meaning. (*argument; controversy*)

ASK STUDENTS to use context clues to help them define these expressions: (line 361) "went to cuffs" (*fought it out*); (line 363) "throwing about of brains" (*satirizing; insulting*); (line 365) "carry it away" (*succeed*).

Analyze Structures: Conflict (sc. 2 LINES 454–455)

COMMON CORE RL 3

Have students note Hamlet's relationship with the players and familiarity with their work.

 ASK STUDENTS why Hamlet chooses that particular speech for the actor to recite. *(He connects the story of a grieving son wreaking revenge on his father's killer to himself.)*

Hamlet. Why,
          As by lot, God wot
and then, you know,
          It came to pass, as most like it was—
425 the first row of the pious chanson will show you
more, for look where my abridgment comes.

[*Enter the* Players.]

You are welcome, masters; welcome all.—I am glad
to see thee well.—Welcome, good friends.—O my
old friend! Why, thy face is valanced since I saw
430 thee last. Com'st thou to beard me in Denmark—
What, my young lady and mistress! By'r Lady,
your ladyship is nearer to heaven than when I saw
you last, by the altitude of a chopine. Pray God
your voice, like a piece of uncurrent gold, be not
435 cracked within the ring. Masters, you are all
welcome. We'll e'en to 't like French falconers, fly
at anything we see. We'll have a speech straight.
Come, give us a taste of your quality. Come, a passionate
speech.

440 **First Player.** What speech, my good lord?

Hamlet. I heard thee speak me a speech once, but it
was never acted, or, if it was, not above once; for
the play, I remember, pleased not the million: 'twas
caviary to the general. But it was (as I received it,
445 and others whose judgments in such matters cried
in the top of mine) an excellent play, well digested
in the scenes, set down with as much modesty as
cunning. I remember one said there were no sallets
in the lines to make the matter savory, nor no matter
450 in the phrase that might indict the author of
affectation, but called it an honest method, as
wholesome as sweet and, by very much, more
handsome than fine. One speech in 't I chiefly
loved. 'Twas Aeneas' tale to Dido, and thereabout
455 of it especially when he speaks of Priam's slaughter.
If it live in your memory, begin at this line—let me
see, let me see:
          The rugged Pyrrhus, like th' Hyrcanian beast—
'tis not so; it begins with Pyrrhus:
460   *The rugged Pyrrhus, he whose sable arms,*
          Black as his purpose, did the night resemble
          When he lay couchèd in th' ominous horse,
          Hath now this dread and black complexion smeared
          With heraldry more dismal. Head to foot,

425 the first . . . chanson: the first stanza of the religious song.

429 valanced: fringed (with a beard).

431–435 All female roles were played by boys. Hamlet fears that this boy's voice might crack onstage, since he has grown by the height of a thick-soled shoe.

436–437 fly . . . see: take on anything.

437 straight: right away.

444 caviary to the general: like caviar, which is unappreciated by most people.

446 digested: arranged.

447 modesty: restraint.

448 cunning: skill, **sallets:** spicy bits, racey jests.

454–455 Pyrrhus, son of the Greek hero Achilles, killed King Priam to revenge the death of his father during the Trojan War. Aeneas tells the story to Dido, the Queen of Carthage, in Virgil's *Aeneid*.

458 Hyrcanian beast: a tiger.

462 couchèd: concealed; **ominous horse:** wooden horse used by the Greeks to enter Troy.

278 Collection 4

SCAFFOLDING FOR ELL STUDENTS

Analyze Metaphorical Language Explain to students that sometimes one thing is described in terms of another. Project lines 438–449 on the whiteboard. Then ask a volunteer to mark up the text:

- Highlight words that appeal to the sense of taste.
- Underline the noun that is being described with these words.

ASK STUDENTS what idea about the play is conveyed through this metaphor.

the play, I remember, pleased not the million: 'twas

caviary to the general. But it was (as I received it,

and others whose judgments in such matters cried

in the top of mine) an excellent **play,** well digested

465 *Now is he total gules, horridly tricked*
With blood of fathers, mothers, daughters, sons,
Baked and impasted with the parching streets,
That lend a tyrannous and a damnèd light
To their lord's murder. Roasted in wrath and fire,
470 *And thus o'ersizèd with coagulate gore,*
With eyes like carbuncles, the hellish Pyrrhus
Old grandsire Priam seeks.
So, proceed you.

Polonius. 'Fore God, my lord, well spoken, with good
475 accent and good discretion.

First Player.   *Anon he finds him*
Striking too short at Greeks. His antique sword,
Rebellious to his arm, lies where it falls,
Repugnant to command. Unequal matched,
480 *Pyrrhus at Priam drives, in rage strikes wide;*
But with the whiff and wind of his fell sword
Th' unnervèd father falls. Then senseless Ilium,
Seeming to feel this blow, with flaming top
Stoops to his base, and with a hideous crash
485 *Takes prisoner Pyrrhus' ear. For lo, his sword,*
Which was declining on the milky head
Of reverend Priam, seemed i' th' air to stick.
So as a painted tyrant Pyrrhus stood
And, like a neutral to his will and matter,
490 *Did nothing.*
But as we often see against some storm
A silence in the heavens, the rack stand still,
The bold winds speechless, and the orb below
As hush as death, anon the dreadful thunder
495 *Doth rend the region; so, after Pyrrhus' pause,*
Arousèd vengeance sets him new a-work,
And never did the Cyclops' hammers fall
On Mars's armor, forged for proof eterne,
With less remorse than Pyrrhus' bleeding sword
500 *Now falls on Priam.*
Out, out, thou strumpet Fortune! All you gods
In general synod take away her power,
Break all the spokes and fellies from her wheel,
And bowl the round nave down the hill of heaven
505 *As low as to the fiends!*

Polonius. This is too long.

Hamlet. It shall to the barber's with your beard.—
Prithee say on. He's for a jig or a tale of bawdry, or
he sleeps. Say on; come to Hecuba.

---

465 **total gules:** all red;
tricked: adorned.

467 The blood is baked
and crusted (**impasted**)
from the heat of the
burning streets.

470 **o'ersizèd:** smeared
over.

471 **carbuncles:** fiery
red stones.

479 **Repugnant to:**
resisting.

482 **unnervèd:**
strengthless; **senseless
Ilium:** the inanimate
fortress of Troy.

485 **Takes . . . ear:**
captures Pyrrhus'
attention.

488–490 **So . . .
nothing:** Pyrrhus stood
still like a tyrant in a
painting, suspended
between his intentions
and taking the actions
that would fulfill them.

492 **rack:** mass of high
clouds.

497 **Cyclops:** one-eyed
giants who worked for
Vulcan, the Roman god
of metalworking.

498 **Mars:** Roman god
of war; **for proof eterne:**
to last for eternity.

502 **synod:** assembly.

503 **fellies:** section of a
wheel's rim.

504 **nave:** hub of a
wheel.

508–509 **He's for . . .
sleeps:** Unless he's
hearing a comic song
and dance (**jig**) or a
bawdy tale, he falls
asleep.

509 **Hecuba:** Priam's
wife.

CLOSE READ

Analyze Word Choice   COMMON CORE RL 4

(sc. 2 LINES 465–472)

Remind students that Hamlet's words have been his
weapon so far throughout the play. Have them look
at the descriptive words and phrases for their literal as
well as connotative meanings.

🅣 **CITE TEXT EVIDENCE** Ask students what words
are used to describe Pyrrhus as he pursues his quest
of revenge. What purpose does this language serve
for Hamlet? *(Pyrrhus is described as "roasted in wrath
and fire," "o'ersized with coagulate gore," "with eyes like
carbuncles," and "hellish." Hamlet may be using this
language to remind himself of what he needs to become
in order to carry out his revenge or what he will become
if he does.)*

TO CHALLENGE STUDENTS . . .

Compare and Analyze Ideas What kind of language is appropriate for a
ghost? Have students think about the word choices Shakespeare made to
bring his character of the Ghost "alive." Point out that the language in lines
465–472 echoes that used by the Ghost in his description of purgatory or
hell in lines 10–24 of Scene 5 in Act I.

Have students compare the language in the two passages, identifying
words that evoke similar images or emotions. Then have them use their
comparison and the significance of the earlier passage to answer this
question in a paragraph or two: *In what way is Pyrrhus what Hamlet fears he
will become if he avenges his father?*

Analyze Drama Elements: COMMON CORE RL 3
Plot (sc. 2 LINES 543–546)

Remind students that in a tragedy, such as this one, suspense is an important element.

Ⓤ ASK STUDENTS to explain how the suspense is heightened by Hamlet's comment to the actor. *(The title of the play that he requests they perform suggests that he plans to confront Claudius with evidence of his wrongdoing. Thus the audience is left to wonder whether this ploy will work and what will happen.)*

---

510 **First Player.** *But who, ah woe, had seen the moblèd queen—*

Hamlet. "The moblèd queen"?

Polonius. That's good. "Moblèd queen" is good.

First Player. *Run barefoot up and down, threat'ning the flames*
With bisson rheum, a clout upon that head
515 *Where late the diadem stood, and for a robe,*
About her lank and all o'erteemèd loins
A blanket, in the alarm of fear caught up—
Who this had seen, with tongue in venom steeped,
'Gainst Fortune's state would treason have pronounced.
520 *But if the gods themselves did see her then*
When she saw Pyrrhus make malicious sport
In mincing with his sword her husband's limbs,
The instant burst of clamor that she made
(Unless things mortal move them not at all)
525 *Would have made milch the burning eyes of heaven*
And passion in the gods.

Polonius. Look whe'er he has not turned his color and has tears in 's eyes. Prithee, no more.

Hamlet. 'Tis well. I'll have thee speak out the rest of
530 this soon.—Good my lord, will you see the players well bestowed? Do you hear, let them be well used, for they are the abstract and brief chronicles of the time. After your death you were better have a bad epitaph than their ill report while you live.

535 **Polonius.** My lord, I will use them according to their desert.

Hamlet. God's bodykins, man, much better! Use every man after his desert and who shall 'scape whipping? Use them after your own honor and dignity.
540 The less they deserve, the more merit is in your bounty. Take them in.

Polonius. Come, sirs.

 Hamlet. Follow him, friends. We'll hear a play tomorrow. [*As Polonius and* Players *exit,* Hamlet *speaks to*
545 *the* First Player.] Dost thou hear me, old friend? Can you play "The Murder of Gonzago"?

First Player. Ay, my lord.

Hamlet. We'll ha 't tomorrow night. You could, for a need, study a speech of some dozen or sixteen

510 **moblèd:** her face was muffled.

514 **bisson rheum:** blinding tears; **clout:** cloth.

516 **o'erteemèd:** worn out from childbearing.

519 **'Gainst ... pronounced:** would have proclaimed treasonous statements against Fortune's rule.

525 **milch:** milky, moist with tears.

527 **whe'er:** whether.

532 **abstract:** summary.

537 **God's bodykins:** by God's little body.

548 **ha 't:** have it.

550　lines, which I would set down and insert in 't,
　　could you not?

First Player. Ay, my lord.

Hamlet. Very well. Follow that lord—and look you mock
him not. [First Player *exits*.] My good friends, I'll leave
555　you till night. You are welcome to Elsinore.

Rosencrantz. Good my lord.

Hamlet. Ay, so, good-bye to you.

[Rosencrantz *and* Guildenstern *exit*.]

　　　　　　　　　　　　　　Now I am alone.

　　O, what a rogue and peasant slave am I!
　　Is it not monstrous that this player here,
560　But in a fiction, in a dream of passion,
　　Could force his soul so to his own conceit
　　That from her working all his visage wanned,
　　Tears in his eyes, distraction in his aspect,
　　A broken voice, and his whole function suiting
565　With forms to his conceit—and all for nothing!
　　For Hecuba!
　　What's Hecuba to him, or he to Hecuba,
　　That he should weep for her? What would he do
　　Had he the motive and the cue for passion
570　That I have? He would drown the stage with tears
　　And cleave the general ear with horrid speech,

**561–562 Could . . .
wanned:** could force
his soul into such
agreement with his
thoughts that his soul
made his face turn pale.

**564–565 his whole . . .
conceit:** all of his activity
creating outward
appearances that
express his thoughts.

571 cleave . . . speech:
pierce everyone's ears
with horrible words.

CLOSE READ

Analyze Structure: Soliloquy (sc. 2 LINES 557–614)

COMMON CORE **RL 5**

Discuss with students how soliloquies fulfill a variety
of functions in the play. Explain that in this soliloquy,
Hamlet directly expresses his conflict. In doing so, he is
able to conceive a plan that might resolve it for him.

V **ASK STUDENTS** to read lines 558–574 closely
and carefully. What quality does the actor possess
that Hamlet feels he does not? *(Hamlet points out that
the actor could summon true emotion over a fictional
character. He cannot summon that depth of emotion over
the terrible wrong done to his own father.)* Read lines
574–597 with students and discuss the various ways in
which Hamlet insults himself for not acting to avenge
his father's murder. Then, read lines 597–607 and ask
students to explain Hamlet's plan here. *(Hamlet will
have the actors do a play with a murder "something like
the murder of my father." During the play, he will study
Claudius to see if the King reveals his guilt.)* Read the
remainder of the soliloquy with your students. Ask
them what reason or excuse Hamlet gives himself for
putting on the play before taking his revenge. *(The
ghost he has seen could be a devil taking the form of his
father to deceive him. The play will give him a way to
test Claudius and see if the Ghost has told him the truth.)*
Finally, ask students if they accept Hamlet's reasoning
at the close of the soliloquy or if they think he's simply
giving himself another excuse to delay. *(Answers
will vary, but students will likely have noticed Hamlet's
tendency to delay, to talk instead of acting.)*

APPLYING ACADEMIC VOCABULARY

drama	trigger

As you discuss the conclusion of Act II, incorporate the following Collection
4 academic vocabulary words: *drama* and *trigger*. Ask students how Hamlet
anticipates the **drama** will **trigger** the exposure of his uncle's guilt. Have
students discuss whether they agree, based on what they know of the
character of Claudius.

Make mad the guilty and appall the free,
Confound the ignorant and amaze indeed
The very faculties of eyes and ears. Yet I,
575 A dull and muddy-mettled rascal, peak
Like John-a-dreams, unpregnant of my cause,
And can say nothing—no, not for a king
Upon whose property and most dear life
A damned defeat was made. Am I a coward?
580 Who calls me "villain"? breaks my pate across?
Plucks off my beard and blows it in my face?
Tweaks me by the nose? gives me the lie i' th' throat
As deep as to the lungs? Who does me this?
Ha! 'Swounds, I should take it! For it cannot be
585 But I am pigeon-livered and lack gall
To make oppression bitter, or ere this
I should have fatted all the region kites
With this slave's offal. Bloody, bawdy villain!
Remorseless, treacherous, lecherous, kindless villain!
590 O vengeance!
Why, what an ass am I! This is most brave,
That I, the son of a dear father murdered,
Prompted to my revenge by heaven and hell,
Must, like a whore, unpack my heart with words
595 And fall a-cursing like a very drab,
A scullion! Fie upon 't! Foh!
About, my brains!—Hum, I have heard
That guilty creatures sitting at a play
Have, by the very cunning of the scene,
600 Been struck so to the soul that presently
They have proclaimed their malefactions.
For murder, though it have no tongue, will speak
With most miraculous organ. I'll have these players
Play something like the murder of my father
605 Before mine uncle. I'll observe his looks;
I'll tent him to the quick. If he do blench,
I know my course. The spirit that I have seen
May be a devil, and the devil hath power
T' assume a pleasing shape; yea, and perhaps,
610 Out of my weakness and my melancholy,
As he is very potent with such spirits,
Abuses me to damn me. I'll have grounds
More relative than this. The play's the thing
Wherein I'll catch the conscience of the King.

[*He exits.*]

572 appall the free: terrify the innocent.

575 muddy-mettled: weak-spirited; **peak:** mope.

576 John-a-dreams: a dreamy idler; **unpregnant of:** not roused to action by.

579 defeat: destruction.

582–583 gives . . . lungs: calls me a complete liar.

584 'Swounds: by Christ's wounds (an oath).

585 pigeon-livered: meek as a pigeon.

587 kites: birds of prey.

588 offal: entrails.

589 kindless: unnatural.

591 brave: admirable.

595 drab: prostitute.

596 scullion: kitchen servant.

597 About: get to work.

599 cunning of the scene: skill of the performance.

600 presently: immediately.

601 malefactions: crimes.

606 tent . . . quick: probe him in his most vulnerable spot; **blench:** flinch.

612–613 grounds . . . this: a more solid basis for acting than the Ghost's words.

WHEN STUDENTS STRUGGLE . . .

To help students understand Hamlet's conflict, write these lines on the board, replacing the text in parentheses with blank lines for students to fill in:

- Hamlet does not want to kill his uncle because *(he is not sure his uncle is guilty.)*
- The Ghost may not *(have told the truth.)*
- If he *(kills an innocent man,)* he will be a murderer.

ASK STUDENTS to work in pairs to complete the statements. Then ask them how the players (actors) will help Hamlet resolve this conflict.

 **eBook** *Annotate It!*

Analyzing the Text

COMMON CORE RL 1, RL 3, RL 4, SL 1

Cite Text Evidence Support your responses with evidence from the selection.

1. **Infer** In the opening scene of Act II, how does Polonius want Reynaldo to check on Laertes's conduct? What does this instruction suggest about Polonius's character?

2. **Analyze** In a play, **dramatic irony** occurs when the audience knows something that a character does not know. In lines 88–111 of Scene 1, Ophelia tells Polonius what took place when Hamlet visited her. Explain why this passage is an example of dramatic irony.

3. **Infer** Reread Hamlet's exchange with Polonius in Scene 2, lines 172–219. Polonius says of Hamlet's responses, "Though this be madness, yet there is method in 't." What is the method, or purpose, of Hamlet's behavior in this interaction?

4. **Interpret** In line 246 of Scene 2, Hamlet says to Guildenstern that "Denmark's a prison." Explain that remark in the context of Hamlet's present situation, considering also the role of Rosencrantz and Guildenstern.

5. **Compare** In Scene 2, lines 368–371, Hamlet compares Claudius to a company of boy actors who have chased the adult actors from the city. What does Claudius have in common with the boy actors?

6. **Compare** The play discussed by Hamlet and the players (Scene 2, lines 453–526) tells the story of Pyrrhus seeking revenge on Priam. What are the parallels between this tale and Hamlet's own quest for revenge? What does the conclusion of the tale foreshadow for Hamlet?

7. **Analyze** Summarize Hamlet's comments about the First Player's performance in Scene 2, lines 558–588. What internal conflict is expressed in this soliloquy?

8. **Draw Conclusions** At the end of Act II, Hamlet reveals his plan for testing Claudius's guilt. Why might Shakespeare have chosen to have him use a theatrical performance for this purpose?

PERFORMANCE TASK

Speaking Activity: Discussion Why is Hamlet so cautious?

- Jot down ideas about Hamlet's pretending to be mad and about his plan to test Claudius's guilt.

- In a small group, discuss why Hamlet takes these measures. Consider what might happen if instead he tried to immediately take revenge.

- Summarize the group discussion and present your ideas to the class.

 Assign this performance task.

PERFORMANCE TASK

COMMON CORE SL 1

Speaking Activity: Discussion Before dividing the class into small discussion groups, conduct a brief whole-class discussion on the nature of revenge. Elicit volunteers' opinions on whether or when revenge might be justified. Suggest that any differences of students' opinion might reflect Hamlet's own conflict and caution as he tries to reconcile his conflicted feelings with his "responsibility" to avenge his father's death.

Analyzing the Text COMMON CORE RL 1, RL 3, RL 4

Possible answers:

1. *Polonius wants Reynaldo to check on his son by having him spread falsehoods about him in order to see if they are true. It suggests Polonius's ruthlessness and duplicity.*

2. *Although the characters believe that Hamlet acted this way because he is mad for the love of Ophelia, the audience knows Hamlet is acting crazy as a cover while he plans his revenge.*

3. *Hamlet's purpose is to mislead and deceive Polonius, because he knows that Polonius will report back to the King and Queen. He mocks Polonius's honesty and age, warns him about Ophelia, and alludes to his weariness of life.*

4. *Hamlet feels penned in by enemies and those who spy on him, including his two old friends. He has to imprison his thoughts and feelings in the semblance of madness and trust no one.*

5. *Like the boy actors who have profited from their newfound preeminence and notoriety, Claudius's stature and the value of his image has increased since his brother's demise.*

6. *Pyrrhus is unable to complete the act of revenge, just as Hamlet is unable to kill Claudius. Pyrrhus then finds a renewed spirit of vengeance and, without remorse, slays Priam. This foreshadows that Hamlet may also find the motivation necessary to complete his task.*

7. *Hamlet is impressed by the actor's ability to feign emotion and apparent sincerity on cue. It demonstrates his own inability to summon the conviction necessary to consummate the vengeance that his situation demands.*

8. *Hamlet believes that "The Murder of Gonzago," by its "very cunning," will cause a "soul-struck" Claudius to reveal his guilt. Shakespeare may be commenting on the ability of theater to convey and instill real emotion in an audience; conversely, he may be commenting on the artifice of revenge itself. Putting a play within the play also supports the theme of pretense and false appearance.*

Analyze Drama Elements: Plot (LINES 1–49)

 COMMON CORE RL 3

Discuss with students how they can expect this act to produce more complications as Hamlet tries to resolve his conflict.

A **CITE TEXT EVIDENCE** Read lines 1–14 with students. Ask them to sum up the report from Rosencrantz and Guildenstern and then have them explain what they say about Hamlet in line 8. *(They have not been able to determine the cause of Hamlet's madness. By saying that he has a "crafty madness," they indicate that Hamlet's behavior doesn't appear to be pure madness but appears to be "crafty" or purposeful.)* Read lines 15–28 with students. Ask them to comment on the dramatic irony in these lines by explaining what they know that the characters onstage during these lines do not know. *(As members of the audience, students know that Hamlet has planned to have the actors do a play resembling the murder of his father, that Hamlet plans this play as a test for the King, and that Hamlet plans to observe the King to see if he gives away his guilt.)* Read lines 28–49 with students. Ask them what is being set up here and what plan it fulfills from Act II. *(The King and Polonius are preparing to spy on Ophelia and Hamlet to see if she is the cause of his madness. Polonius suggested this act of spying in Act II, when he first mentioned his theory that Hamlet had gone mad because Ophelia, obeying her father, had stopped seeing him.)*

ACT III

Scene 1 *The castle.*

[*Enter* King, Queen, Polonius, Ophelia, Rosencrantz, Guildenstern, *and* Lords.]

King. And can you by no drift of conference
Get from him why he puts on this confusion,
Grating so harshly all his days of quiet
With turbulent and dangerous lunacy?

5 **Rosencrantz.** He does confess he feels himself distracted,
But from what cause he will by no means speak.

Guildenstern. Nor do we find him forward to be sounded,
But with a crafty madness keeps aloof
When we would bring him on to some confession
10 Of his true state.

Queen.   Did he receive you well?

Rosencrantz. Most like a gentleman.

Guildenstern. But with much forcing of his disposition.

Rosencrantz. Niggard of question, but of our demands
    Most free in his reply.

15 **Queen.** Did you assay him to any pastime?

Rosencrantz. Madam, it so fell out that certain players
We o'erraught on the way. Of these we told him,
And there did seem in him a kind of joy
To hear of it. They are here about the court,
20 And, as I think, they have already order
This night to play before him.

Polonius.   'Tis most true,
And he beseeched me to entreat your Majesties
To hear and see the matter.

King. With all my heart, and it doth much content me
25 To hear him so inclined.
Good gentlemen, give him a further edge
And drive his purpose into these delights.

Rosencrantz. We shall, my lord.

[Rosencrantz *and* Guildenstern *and* Lords *exit.*]

King.   Sweet Gertrude, leave us too,
For we have closely sent for Hamlet hither,
30 That he, as 'twere by accident, may here
Affront Ophelia.
Her father and myself (lawful espials)

1 drift of conference: steering of conversation.

7 forward to be sounded: interested in being questioned.

12 forcing of his disposition: effort.

13–14 Niggard . . . reply: Reluctant to talk, but willing to answer our questions.

15 assay: tempt.

17 o'erraught: overtook.

26 give . . . edge: sharpen his interest.

29 closely: privately.

31 Affront: meet.

32 espials: spies.

Close Read Screencasts ▶ View It!

Modeled Discussions

Have students click the *Close Read* icons in their eBooks to access a screencast in which readers discuss and annotate the following key passage:

- Hamlet's murder of Polonius (Act III, Scene 4, lines 19–32)

As a class, view and discuss the video.

Will so bestow ourselves that, seeing unseen,
We may of their encounter frankly judge
35 And gather by him, as he is behaved,
If't be th' affliction of his love or no
That thus he suffers for.

Queen.   I shall obey you.
And for your part, Ophelia, I do wish
That your good beauties be the happy cause
40 Of Hamlet's wildness. So shall I hope your virtues
Will bring him to his wonted way again,
To both your honors.

Ophelia.   Madam, I wish it may.

[*Queen exits.*]

Polonius. Ophelia, walk you here.—Gracious, so please you,
We will bestow ourselves. [*To Ophelia.*] Read on this book,
45 That show of such an exercise may color
Your loneliness.—We are oft to blame in this
('Tis too much proved), that with devotion's visage
And pious action we do sugar o'er
The devil himself.

50 **King** [*aside*]. O, 'tis too true!
How smart a lash that speech doth give my conscience.
The harlot's cheek beautied with plast'ring art
Is not more ugly to the thing that helps it
Than is my deed to my most painted word.
55 O heavy burden!

Polonius. I hear him coming. Let's withdraw, my lord.

[*They withdraw.*]

[*Enter Hamlet.*]

Hamlet. To be or not to be—that is the question:
Whether 'tis nobler in the mind to suffer
The slings and arrows of outrageous fortune,
60 Or to take arms against a sea of troubles
And, by opposing, end them. To die, to sleep—
No more—and by a sleep to say we end
The heartache and the thousand natural shocks
That flesh is heir to—'tis a consummation
65 Devoutly to be wished. To die, to sleep—
To sleep, perchance to dream. Ay, there's the rub,
For in that sleep of death what dreams may come,
When we have shuffled off this mortal coil,
Must give us pause. There's the respect
70 That makes calamity of so long life.
For who would bear the whips and scorns of time,

---

35 as is behaved: according to his behavior.

43 Gracious: Your Grace (addressing the King).

44–49 Polonius tells Ophelia to read a religious book to provide an excuse for being alone. He remarks that many people are guilty of using worship and a devout appearance to cover their sins.

50–55 Claudius compares the heavy makeup that covers up the flaws on a prostitute's cheek to the beautiful words that cover his crime.

57 To be: To exist, to continue living.

59 slings: something thrown or shot.

64 consummation: final ending.

66 rub: obstacle.

68 shuffled . . . coil: cast aside the turmoil of life.

69–70 There's . . . life: That is the consideration that makes us endure misery (**calamity**) for such a long time.

71 time: life in this world.

TEACH

CLOSE READ

Analyze Drama Elements: Character (LINES 50–55)   COMMON CORE RL 3

Remind students that during an aside, a character may voice his or her thoughts but that, as in a movie voice-over, no one else onstage can hear these thoughts.

B CITE TEXT EVIDENCE Ask what Claudius reveals here and how what he says might be connected to what the Ghost has told Hamlet. (*Claudius reveals that he feels a punishing guilt about something. Given what the Ghost has said, the audience will likely conclude that he feels guilty because he has murdered his brother, the previous king, Hamlet's father.*) Ask students to relate Claudius's aside to the play's theme. (*Claudius compares what he has done to "the harlot's cheek beautied with plast'ring art"—something attractive to appearance but ugly beneath. This is a theme of the play, that often what looks good is rotten inside*)

Strategies for Annotation   Annotate it!

Analyze Language   COMMON CORE RL 4

Have students use their eBook annotation tools to analyze the meaning in Hamlet's soliloquy.

- Highlight in pink what it is "to be."
- Highlight in yellow his fears about what it is "not to be."
- On a note explain how Hamlet's fears intensify his conflict.

And, by opposing, end them. To die, to sleep—

No more—and by a sleep to say we end

The heartache and the thousand natural shocks

That flesh is heir to—'tis a consummation

Devoutly to be wished. To die, to sleep—

To sleep, perchance to dream. Ay, there's the rub,

For in that sleep of death what dreams may come,

Analyze Language: Soliloquy (LINES 57–89)

 COMMON CORE RL 4

Point out that students will recognize the famous first line of this soliloquy.

C **CITE TEXT EVIDENCE** Read lines 57–61 with students. Ask them what Hamlet means when he says "To be or not to be." *(He wants to know if it's better to quietly suffer life's difficulty—"the slings and arrows of outrageous fortune"—or to stand up against trouble.)* Read lines 61–83 with students; stop frequently to check for understanding. Ask what Hamlet wishes for when he says, "To die, to sleep" [line 61]. *(His wish here is that death could be a peaceful escape from life's suffering.)* Ask students to explain why Hamlet fears escaping life by committing suicide. *(We don't know what happens after death. It might not bring peace. We bear suffering in life because we fear what comes after death.)* Finally, ask students to paraphrase lines 84–89 and explain how these lines apply to Hamlet's situation in the play. *(Paraphrase: Conscience turns us into cowards. Our firm resolve to act turns weak when we think about the consequences. Thus, important projects or plans are set aside, and inaction replaces action. Application: Hamlet wants to avenge his father's death, but thinking about it makes him hesitate. He is smart enough to be aware that the more he thinks about revenge, the less likely he will be to take revenge.)*

Analyze Drama Elements: Character (89–111)

 COMMON CORE RL3

Explain to students that close attention to this dialogue will reveal Hamlet's shifting tone.

D **ASK STUDENTS** to describe Hamlet's tone as he initially speaks to Ophelia. *(Hamlet is gentle and sincere. He asks Ophelia to remember his sins as she prays.)* What gesture accompanies Ophelia's words in lines 98–103? How does her action affect the tone of Hamlet's responses? Explain. *(She tries to give him his letters and other tokens back. As a result, Hamlet's tone becomes agitated and insulting.)*

Th' oppressor's wrong, the proud man's contumely,
The pangs of despised love, the law's delay,
The insolence of office, and the spurns
75 That patient merit of th' unworthy takes,
When he himself might his quietus make
With a bare bodkin? Who would fardels bear,
To grunt and sweat under a weary life,
But that the dread of something after death,
80 The undiscovered country from whose bourn
No traveler returns, puzzles the will
And makes us rather bear those ills we have
Than fly to others that we know not of?
Thus conscience does make cowards of us all,
85 And thus the native hue of resolution
Is sicklied o'er with the pale cast of thought,
And enterprises of great pitch and moment
With this regard their currents turn awry
And lose the name of action.— Soft you now,
90 The fair Ophelia.— Nymph, in thy orisons
Be all my sins remembered.

Ophelia.   Good my lord,
How does your Honor for this many a day?

Hamlet. I humbly thank you, well.

Ophelia. My lord, I have remembrances of yours
95 That I have longèd long to redeliver.
I pray you now receive them.

Hamlet. No, not I. I never gave you aught.

Ophelia. My honored lord, you know right well you did,
And with them words of so sweet breath composed
100 As made the things more rich. Their perfume lost,
Take these again, for to the noble mind
Rich gifts wax poor when givers prove unkind.
There, my lord.

Hamlet. Ha, ha, are you honest?

105 **Ophelia.** My lord?

Hamlet. Are you fair?

Ophelia. What means your lordship?

Hamlet. That if you be honest and fair, your honesty
should admit no discourse to your beauty.

110 **Ophelia.** Could beauty, my lord, have better commerce
than with honesty?

72 contumely: insults, expressions of contempt.

73 despised: unreturned.

74 office: officials.

74–75 spurns . . . takes: the insults that people of merit receive from the unworthy.

76–77 When . . . bodkin: when he might settle his accounts (**his quietus make**) with merely a dagger (**a bare bodkin**)—that is, end his unhappiness by killing himself.

77 fardels: burdens.

80 bourn: boundary.

81 puzzles: paralyzes.

85 native hue: natural color.

86 cast: shade.

87–89 pitch and moment: height and importance; **with this regard:** for this reason.

89 Soft you: be quiet, enough.

90 orisons: prayers.

104 honest: truthful, chaste.

108 Your honesty . . . beauty: Your chastity should not allow itself to be influenced by your beauty.

110 commerce: dealings.

SCAFFOLDING FOR ELL STUDENTS

Understand Multiple-Meaning Words Tell students that some of the words in the dialogue between Ophelia and Hamlet have more than one meaning. Point out the word *long* in line 95. Discuss with students how its context, following the verb *longed*, which itself means "wanted or desired to," can help them to figure out that it means "great duration of time."

ASK STUDENTS to work together to define these multiple-meaning words, using context clues as well as a dictionary: (line 96) "pray" *(ask)*; (line 102) "wax" *(become)*; (line 106) "fair" *(beautiful)*.

Image Credits: ©Mondadori/Getty Images

Hamlet. Ay, truly, for the power of beauty will sooner transform honesty from what it is to a bawd than the force of honesty can translate beauty into his
115 likeness. This was sometime a paradox, but now the time gives it proof. I did love you once.

Ophelia. Indeed, my lord, you made me believe so.

Hamlet. You should not have believed me, for virtue cannot so inoculate our old stock but we shall relish
120 of it. I loved you not.

Ophelia. I was the more deceived.

Hamlet. Get thee to a nunnery. Why wouldst thou be a breeder of sinners? I am myself indifferent honest, but yet I could accuse me of such things that it
125 were better my mother had not borne me: I am very proud, revengeful, ambitious, with more offenses at my beck than I have thoughts to put them in, imagination to give them shape, or time to act them in. What should such fellows as I do
130 crawling between earth and heaven? We are arrant knaves all; believe none of us. Go thy ways to a nunnery. Where's your father?

Ophelia. At home, my lord.

114 his: its.

115 This ... paradox: This once went against the common viewpoint.

116 time: the present age.

118–120 Hamlet's metaphor is of grafting a branch onto a fruit tree: If virtue is grafted onto his sinful nature, the fruit of the grafted tree will still taste of his old nature.

122 nunnery: convent (sometimes used as a slang word for "brothel").

123 indifferent honest: reasonably virtuous.

127 beck: command.

Hamlet: Act III, Scene 1   **287**

Analyze Structure: Conflict (LINES 112–133)

COMMON CORE   RL 3

Have students recall what Hamlet feels toward his mother and why. Explain that his view of women, specifically Ophelia, is colored by his disillusionment with his mother and her marriage to Claudius.

E ASK STUDENTS why Hamlet blames beauty for the loss of a woman's honesty. *(His mother's beauty led her to be seduced by Claudius and betray his father; Ophelia's beauty makes her a pawn for her father.)* Ask students to explain Hamlet's dilemma in this dialogue, shown through his contradictory declarations about love. *(He does not know whether Ophelia is truly what she seems, an innocent victim of her father's schemes, or if she is like his mother, guilty of being dishonest in every sense of the word.)* Why is Hamlet's question to Ophelia about where her father is a turning point in their dialogue? *(He is offering her a chance to align herself with him and tell the truth.)*

TO CHALLENGE STUDENTS...

Evaluate Characterization How does Shakespeare use Ophelia's character to advance the plot? What character traits does she have that make this possible? Discuss how Ophelia is a catalyst for Hamlet's emotional displays. Her role is significant, but her character is harder to define.

- Have students work in small groups to review her appearances in the first three acts, noting what she says and how she interacts with others. Have them use the details as the basis of a character analysis.

- Have groups present their analyses to the class. Discuss points of similarity and difference. Then, as a class, debate the question of whether Ophelia is a victim, and, if so, of whom.

Analyze Drama Elements: COMMON CORE RL 3
Character (LINES 134–153)

Ask students to observe the change in Hamlet after Ophelia tells him that her father is "at home" (line 133). Tell them he might suspect Polonius is spying on them, and that often when the play is performed, an offstage noise precedes Hamlet's question, "Where's your father?" (line 132).

F ASK STUDENTS to reread Hamlet's speeches to Ophelia. Ask: What sincere emotion drives him in these speeches? Explain, citing text details. *(Hamlet's fears about the treachery of women are confirmed with Ophelia's lie about where her father is. He says they make "monsters" of wise men and deceive. "God hath given you one face and you make yourselves another." He is disappointed, disgusted, and disillusioned. But he disguises his truth in the rantings of a madman.)*

Analyze Drama Elements: COMMON CORE RL 3
Plot (LINES 154–174)

Remind students that a character's words and actions can have a profound effect on others.

G CITE TEXT EVIDENCE Have students identify details that show how upset Ophelia is after talking to Hamlet. Have them explain why. *(She is stricken that Hamlet has lost his reason. She says, "O, woe is me / T' have seen what I have seen, see what I see!")* What effect does Hamlet's exchange with Ophelia have on Claudius? *(He is not convinced that Hamlet is mad as a result of love. He fears there is something else wrong that could prove troublesome to him. He decides to send Hamlet to England.)*

SCAFFOLDING FOR ELL STUDENTS

Analyze Character Project lines 145–153 on the whiteboard. Invite volunteers to mark up the text:

- Highlight in yellow Hamlet's criticism of women.
- Underline the lines that accuse them of dishonesty.

ASK STUDENTS why Hamlet is so angry at Ophelia. Of what does he suspect her?

Hamlet. Let the doors be shut upon him that he may
135 play the fool nowhere but in 's own house. Farewell.

Ophelia. O, help him, you sweet heavens!

Hamlet. If thou dost marry, I'll give thee this plague
for thy dowry: be thou as chaste as ice, as pure as
snow, thou shalt not escape calumny. Get thee to a
140 nunnery, farewell. Or if thou wilt needs marry,
marry a fool, for wise men know well enough what
monsters you make of them. To a nunnery, go, and
quickly too. Farewell.

Ophelia. Heavenly powers, restore him!

145 **Hamlet.** I have heard of your paintings too, well
enough. God hath given you one face, and you
make yourselves another. You jig and amble, and
you lisp; you nickname God's creatures and make
your wantonness your ignorance. Go to, I'll no
150 more on 't. It hath made me mad. I say we will
have no more marriage. Those that are married
already, all but one, shall live. The rest shall keep
as they are. To a nunnery, go.

[*He exits.*]

Ophelia. O, what a noble mind is here o'erthrown!
155 The courtier's, soldier's, scholar's, eye, tongue, sword,
Th' expectancy and rose of the fair state,
The glass of fashion and the mold of form,
Th' observed of all observers, quite, quite down!
And I, of ladies most deject and wretched,
160 That sucked the honey of his musicked vows,
Now see that noble and most sovereign reason,
Like sweet bells jangled, out of time and harsh;
That unmatched form and stature of blown youth
Blasted with ecstasy. O, woe is me
165 T' have seen what I have seen, see what I see!

King [*advancing with* Polonius]. Love? His affections do
not that way tend;
Nor what he spake, though it lacked form a little,
Was not like madness. There's something in his soul
O'er which his melancholy sits on brood,
170 And I do doubt the hatch and the disclose
Will be some danger; which for to prevent,
I have in quick determination
Thus set it down: he shall with speed to England
For the demand of our neglected tribute.
175 Haply the seas, and countries different,

139 calumny: slander, defamation.

142 monsters: horned cuckolds (men whose wives are unfaithful).

148 nickname: find new names for.

148–149 make ... ignorance: use ignorance as an excuse for your waywardness.

155–158 Ophelia starts her description of Hamlet's former self by evoking the princely ideal of statesman, soldier, and scholar. He was the hope and ornament (**expectancy and rose**) of Denmark, a model of behavior and appearance for other people, respected (**observed**) by all who looked upon him.

163–164 blown ... ecstasy: youth in full bloom withered by madness.

166 affections: feelings.

168–171 Claudius says that Hamlet's melancholy broods on something like a bird sits on an egg; he fears that some danger will hatch from it.

---

enough. God hath given you one face, and you

make yourselves another. You jig and amble, and

you lisp; you nickname God's creatures and make

your wantonness your ignorance. Go to, I'll no

With variable objects, shall expel
This something-settled matter in his heart,
Whereon his brains still beating puts him thus
From fashion of himself. What think you on 't?

177 This . . . heart: this unknown thing that has settled in his heart.

180 **Polonius.** It shall do well. But yet do I believe
The origin and commencement of his grief
Sprung from neglected love.— How now, Ophelia?
You need not tell us what Lord Hamlet said;
We heard it all.— My lord, do as you please,
185 But, if you hold it fit, after the play
Let his queen-mother all alone entreat him
To show his grief. Let her be round with him;
And I'll be placed, so please you, in the ear
Of all their conference. If she find him not,
190 To England send him, or confine him where
Your wisdom best shall think.

187 be round: speak plainly.

189 find him not: does not learn what is disturbing him.

    King.   It shall be so.
Madness in great ones must not unwatched go.

[*They exit.*]

Scene 2 *The castle.*

[*Enter* Hamlet *and three of the* Players.]

Hamlet. Speak the speech, I pray you, as I pronounced
it to you, trippingly on the tongue; but if you mouth
it, as many of our players do, I had as lief the town-crier
spoke my lines. Nor do not saw the air too
5 much with your hand, thus, but use all gently; for in
the very torrent, tempest, and, as I may say, whirlwind
of your passion, you must acquire and beget
a temperance that may give it smoothness. O, it
offends me to the soul to hear a robustious, periwig-
10 pated fellow tear a passion to tatters, to very rags,
to split the ears of the groundlings, who for the
most part are capable of nothing but inexplicable
dumb shows and noise. I would have such a fellow
whipped for o'erdoing Termagant. It out-
15 Herods Herod. Pray you, avoid it.

3 I had as lief: I would just as soon.

9 robustious: boisterous.

9–10 periwig-pated: wig-wearing.

11 groundlings: the spectators who paid the cheapest price for admittance to the theater and stood in an open area in front of the stage.

14–15 Termagant, Herod: noisy, violent figures from early drama.

    Player. I warrant your Honor.

Hamlet. Be not too tame neither, but let your own discretion
be your tutor. Suit the action to the word,
the word to the action, with this special observance,
20 that you o'erstep not the modesty of nature. For
anything so o'erdone is from the purpose of playing,
whose end, both at the first and now, was and
is to hold, as 'twere, the mirror up to nature, to

20 modesty: moderation.

21 is from: strays from.

Hamlet: Act III, Scene 2 **289**

APPLYING ACADEMIC VOCABULARY

mediate	restrain

As you discuss Hamlet's interaction with the players, incorporate the
following Collection 4 academic vocabulary words: *mediate* and *restrain*.
Ask students why Hamlet pleads with the players to **restrain** themselves
while acting. Then have them discuss how Horatio's task during the play
is to **mediate**.

CLOSE READ

Analyze Drama Elements: Character (LINES 180–192)

 COMMON CORE RL 3

Tell students that while some characters are
complex and multi-faceted, others have fewer
dimensions and act in a way that manifests one
particular trait consistently.

 ASK STUDENTS how Polonius's new plan is in
keeping with his character as it has been developed
through the play. Have them cite details in support.
(*Polonius is reluctant to let go of his theory about
why Hamlet appears mad. Instead he wants to create
yet another trap and hide in the hopes of confirming
his suspicions. This plan shows his love of intrigue as
well as his determination to be right.*) Ask students
why they think Claudius agrees. (*He is just generally
suspicious of Hamlet now and wants him to be
monitored as much as possible.*)

Determine Themes

COMMON CORE RL 2

(Sc. 2 LINES 1–25)

Tell students that in this part of the scene, what is
real converges with what is false, or acted. Have
them read carefully to see how Shakespeare blurs
the line between appearance and reality.

 CITE TEXT EVIDENCE Have students explain
why Hamlet objects to overacting. (*Overacting
turns emotions false; it will "tear a passion to tatters"
[line 10].*) Why is it fitting that Hamlet be giving
the actors advice about how to act? (*He has been
acting for much of the play. He is concerned about the
difference between what is false and what is genuine.
He is concerned about how bad people cover for
themselves with a good act.*) Have students explain
what Hamlet means by "the purpose of playing, /
whose end, both at the first and now, was and / is to
hold, as 'twere, the mirror up to nature." Why does
he want to emphasize that for this play? (*He reminds
the players that the purpose of a play is to appear real.
That is particularly important for this play, which is to
reveal Claudius's crime by portraying it.*)

Support Inferences

 COMMON CORE RL 1

(Sc. 2 LINES 48–53)

Remind students to make inferences about a character's traits, reasons for doing something, and inner thoughts and feelings from what he or she says and does.

 ASK STUDENTS to explain Hamlet's motives in sending Polonius, Rosencrantz, and Guildenstern to help the players. *(He wants them out of the way so that he can speak to Horatio privately.)*

---

 show virtue her own feature, scorn her own image,
25 and the very age and body of the time his form and
   pressure. Now this overdone or come tardy off,
   though it makes the unskillful laugh, cannot but make
   the judicious grieve, the censure of the which one
   must in your allowance o'erweigh a whole theater
30 of others. O, there be players that I have seen play
   and heard others praise (and that highly), not to
   speak it profanely, that, neither having th' accent of
   Christians nor the gait of Christian, pagan, nor
   man, have so strutted and bellowed that I have
35 thought some of nature's journeymen had made
   men, and not made them well, they imitated
   humanity so abominably.

   Player. I hope we have reformed that indifferently
   with us, sir.

40 **Hamlet.** O, reform it altogether. And let those that
   play your clowns speak no more than is set down
   for them, for there be of them that will themselves
   laugh, to set on some quantity of barren spectators
   to laugh too, though in the meantime some necessary
45 question of the play be then to be considered.
   That's villainous and shows a most pitiful ambition
   in the fool that uses it. Go make you ready.

   [Players *exit.*]

   [*Enter* Polonius, Guildenstern, *and* Rosencrantz.]

   How now, my lord, will the King hear this piece of
   work?

50 **Polonius.** And the Queen too, and that presently.

   Hamlet. Bid the players make haste. [Polonius *exits.*]
   Will you two help to hasten them?

   Rosencrantz. Ay, my lord.

   [*They exit.*]

   Hamlet. What ho, Horatio!

   [*Enter* Horatio.]

55 **Horatio.** Here, sweet lord, at your service.

   Hamlet. Horatio, thou art e'en as just a man
   As e'er my conversation coped withal.

   Horatio. O, my dear lord—

   Hamlet.   Nay, do not think I flatter,
   For what advancement may I hope from thee

24 scorn: something scornful.

25–26 the very... pressure: a true impression of the present.

26 come tardy off: done inadequately.

27 the unskillful: those lacking in judgment.

28–30 the censure... others: You should value the opinion of a single judicious theatergoer over an entire audience that lacks judgment.

38 indifferently: fairly well.

42 of them: some among them.

43 barren: dull-witted.

56–57 Hamlet says that Horatio is as honorable as any man he has ever dealt with.

60   That no revenue hast but thy good spirits
     To feed and clothe thee? Why should the poor be flattered?
     No, let the candied tongue lick absurd pomp
     And crook the pregnant hinges of the knee
     Where thrift may follow fawning. Dost thou hear?
65   Since my dear soul was mistress of her choice
     And could of men distinguish, her election
     Hath sealed thee for herself. For thou hast been
     As one in suffering all that suffers nothing,
     A man that Fortune's buffets and rewards
70   Hast ta'en with equal thanks; and blessed are those
     Whose blood and judgment are so well commeddled
     That they are not a pipe for Fortune's finger
     To sound what stop she please. Give me that man
     That is not passion's slave, and I will wear him
75   In my heart's core, ay, in my heart of heart,
     As I do thee.—Something too much of this.—
     There is a play tonight before the King.
     One scene of it comes near the circumstance
     Which I have told thee of my father's death.
80   I prithee, when thou seest that act afoot,
     Even with the very comment of thy soul
     Observe my uncle. If his occulted guilt
     Do not itself unkennel in one speech,
     It is a damnèd ghost that we have seen,
85   And my imaginations are as foul
     As Vulcan's stithy. Give him heedful note,
     For I mine eyes will rivet to his face,
     And, after, we will both our judgments join
     In censure of his seeming.

     Horatio.   Well, my lord.
90   If he steal aught the whilst this play is playing
     And 'scape detecting, I will pay the theft.

     [*Sound a flourish.*]

     Hamlet. They are coming to the play. I must be idle.
     Get you a place.

     [*Enter Trumpets and Kettle Drums. Enter* King, Queen,
     Polonius, Ophelia, Rosencrantz, Guildenstern, *and other*
     Lords *attendant with the* King's guard *carrying torches.*]

     King. How fares our cousin Hamlet?

95   **Hamlet.** Excellent, i' faith, of the chameleon's dish. I
     eat the air, promise-crammed. You cannot feed
     capons so.

62 candied: flattering.

63 crook...knee: bend the ready joint of the knee (kneel down).

64 thrift: profit.

68 one...nothing: one who experiences everything but is harmed by nothing.

71 blood: passions; **commeddled:** blended.

72 pipe: small wind instrument.

73 stop: a hole in a wind instrument that controls sound.

81 Even...soul: with your most searching observation.

82–86 Hamlet says that if Claudius's hidden (**occulted**) guilt does not reveal (**unkennel**) itself with the speech Hamlet wrote, then the Ghost is in league with the devil and Hamlet's thoughts about Claudius are as foul as the forge of the Roman god of metalworking.

89 censure of his seeming: judgment of how he looks and behaves.

92 be idle: play the fool, be unoccupied.

94–97 Hamlet, taking **fares** to mean "feeds," answers that he eats promises. (Chameleons were said to feed on air.)

CLOSE READ

Analyze Drama Elements: COMMON CORE RL 1
Character (sc. 2 LINES 58–89)

Ask students to consider Horatio's role in the play as they read this passage.

Ⓚ **ASK STUDENTS** to study lines 65-76 closely. Hamlet says that since he was old enough to choose a friend, he has chosen Horatio. What quality does he admire in his friend? *(Horatio takes "Fortune's buffets and rewards" objectively, with calm and detachment. He is not "passion's slave.")* When Hamlet tells Horatio about the play he has asked the actors to perform, what does he want from Horatio during the performance and why? *(Hamlet wants Horatio to watch Claudius closely to see if he betrays guilt in the murder of Hamlet's father. Hamlet needs a trusted and objective witness to help him determine if the Ghost can be trusted.)*

Strategies for Annotation   ✏️ 🗂 *Annotate it!*

Analyze Drama Elements: Plot   COMMON CORE RL 3

Have students use their eBook annotation tools to analyze Hamlet's speech to Horatio.

- Highlight in pink the details that describe Horatio's attributes.
- Underline the words that suggest the opposite quality.
- Use the annotations to contrast Horatio with the others, such as Rosencrantz and Guildenstern, that surround Hamlet.

> That they are not 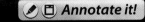 a pipe for Fortune's finger
>
> To sound what stop she please. Give me that man
>
> That is not passion's slave, and I will wear him
>
> In my heart's core, ay, in my heart of heart,
>
> As I do thee.—Something too much of this.—

Analyze Structure: Conflict (sc. 2 LINES 100–123)

 COMMON CORE **RL 3**

As students read these lines, ask them to keep in mind what Polonius said about Hamlet in Act II, Scene 2, lines 207–208: "Though this be madness, yet there is / method in it." Ask students to observe Hamlet's "method" both with Polonius and with Ophelia.

L ASK STUDENTS to describe Hamlet's "madness" with Polonius and to explain how and why it changes when he is with Ophelia. *(Hamlet teases Polonius almost lightheartedly and makes fun of him as a fool. With Ophelia, Hamlet turns crude, making sexual jokes. His conflict with Polonius stems from his disrespect of him as a wordy fool; his conflict with Ophelia stems from feeling betrayed by her as a woman.)*

Analyze Language

 COMMON CORE **RL 4**

(sc. 2 LINES 125–132)

Tell students that in addition to dramatic irony, Shakespeare also uses verbal irony, in which a character says one thing but means another.

M CITE TEXT EVIDENCE Have students identify examples of verbal irony in Hamlet's lines to Ophelia. Ask them to explain his real meaning. *(Hamlet makes a joke about "how cheerfully my / mother looks, and my father died within 's two hours." But he indicates serious disapproval of his mother for marrying so quickly after his father's death. Hamlet makes another joke on the same subject, his father dead "two months ago, and not forgotten yet." Again, he is clearly appalled by how quickly a woman might forget the promises she has made to a man.)*

King. I have nothing with this answer, Hamlet. These words are not mine.

100 **Hamlet.** No, nor mine now. [*To* Polonius.] My lord, you played once i' th' university, you say?

Polonius. That did I, my lord, and was accounted a good actor.

Hamlet. What did you enact?

105 **Polonius.** I did enact Julius Caesar. I was killed i' th' Capitol. Brutus killed me.

Hamlet. It was a brute part of him to kill so capital a calf there.—Be the players ready?

108 calf: fool.

Rosencrantz. Ay, my lord. They stay upon your patience.

110 **Queen.** Come hither, my dear Hamlet, sit by me.

Hamlet. No, good mother. Here's metal more attractive.

111 metal more attractive: a substance more magnetic.

[Hamlet *takes a place near* Ophelia.]

Polonius [*to the* King]. Oh, ho! Do you mark that?

Hamlet. Lady, shall I lie in your lap?

Ophelia. No, my lord.

115 **Hamlet.** I mean, my head upon your lap?

Ophelia. Ay, my lord.

Hamlet. Do you think I meant country matters?

117 country matters: something coarse or indecent, which a rustic from the country might propose.

Ophelia. I think nothing, my lord.

Hamlet. That's a fair thought to lie between maids' legs.

120 **Ophelia.** What is, my lord?

Hamlet. Nothing.

Ophelia. You are merry, my lord.

Hamlet. Who, I?

Ophelia. Ay, my lord.

125 **Hamlet.** O God, your only jig-maker. What should a man do but be merry? For look you how cheerfully my mother looks, and my father died within 's two hours.

125 Hamlet sarcastically refers to himself as the best jig (comical song and dance) performer.

Ophelia. Nay, 'tis twice two months, my lord.

Hamlet. So long? Nay, then, let the devil wear black, for 130 I'll have a suit of sables. O heavens, die two months ago, and not forgotten yet? Then there's hope a great man's memory may outlive his life half a year. But, by'r Lady, he must build churches, then, or else shall

129–130 Hamlet sarcastically suggests giving up his mourning clothes for luxurious clothing trimmed with furs.

he suffer not thinking on, with the hobby-horse, whose
135 epitaph is "For oh, for oh, the hobby-horse is forgot."

[*The trumpets sound. Dumb show follows.*]

[*Enter a* King *and a* Queen, *very lovingly, the* Queen
*embracing him and he her. She kneels and makes show of
protestation unto him. He takes her up and declines his head
upon her neck. He lies him down upon a bank of flowers.
She, seeing him asleep, leaves him. Anon comes in another*
man, *takes off his crown, kisses it, pours poison in the
sleeper's ears, and leaves him. The* Queen *returns, finds
the* King *dead, makes passionate action. The poisoner
with some three or four come in again, seem to condole
with her. The dead body is carried away. The poisoner
woos the* Queen *with gifts. She seems harsh awhile but in
the end accepts his love.*]

[Players *exit.*]

Ophelia. What means this, my lord?

Hamlet. Marry, this is miching mallecho. It means mischief.

Ophelia. Belike this show imports the argument of the
140 play.

[*Enter* Prologue.]

Hamlet. We shall know by this fellow. The players cannot
keep counsel; they'll tell all.

Ophelia. Will he tell us what this show meant?

Hamlet. Ay, or any show that you will show him. Be
145 not you ashamed to show, he'll not shame to tell
you what it means.

Ophelia. You are naught, you are naught. I'll mark the
play.

Prologue.

            For us and for our tragedy,
150   Here stooping to your clemency,
            We beg your hearing patiently.

[*He exits.*]

Hamlet. Is this a prologue or the posy of a ring?

Ophelia. 'Tis brief, my lord.

Hamlet. As woman's love.

[*Enter the* Player King *and* Queen.]

155 **Player King.** *Full thirty times hath Phoebus' cart gone round
Neptune's salt wash and Tellus' orbèd ground,*

134 not thinking on:
being forgotten;
hobby-horse: a horse-
and-rider figure who
once performed in
morris and may-day
dances. Such traditions
had been disappearing.

Dumb show: a scene
without dialogue.

138 miching mallecho:
sneaking misdeed. (The
Spanish word **malhecho**
means "misdeed.")

139 Belike: perhaps;
argument: plot.

147 naught: naughty,
indecent.

152 posy of a ring: a
motto inscribed in a
ring.

155–160 The Player
King says that they have
been united in love and
marriage for 30 years.
Phoebus' cart: the sun
god's chariot; **Neptune's
salt wash:** the ocean;
Tellus: Roman goddess
of the earth; **Hymen:**
god of marriage.

Hamlet: Act III, Scene 2   **293**

CLOSE READ

Support Inferences

COMMON CORE   RL 1

(sc. 2 LINES 135–140)

Direct students to read the description of the
pantomime that occurs before the play. Remind them
that Hamlet most likely arranged for this part of the
performance ahead of time.

N **ASK STUDENTS** to explain the function of this
dumb show in Hamlet's plan. (*The pantomime gives
an overview of what is to happen in the play. Seeing it,
Claudius should become nervous and less able to control
his reactions during the play itself.*)

WHEN STUDENTS STRUGGLE . . .

Read the italicized description of the pantomime to students. Discuss how it
relates to what the Ghost told Hamlet at the end of Act I. Then have students
work with a partner to explain possible effects of the play on the King, using
these sentence stems:

1. If the King is guilty, he will . . .
2. If the King is not guilty, he will . . .

ASK STUDENTS to share their completed sentences. Then ask them what
each reaction would mean for the play's plot.

TEACH

Support Inferences

COMMON CORE RL 1

(sc. 2 LINES 161–186)

Tell students that *Hamlet* is known for its "play within a play." As students read it, remind them to look for the parallels between the actors' play and the plot and characters of the play itself.

Ⓞ **CITE TEXT EVIDENCE** Have students explain how the marriage of the King and Queen is depicted. Ask them to discuss the purpose of this scene. (*The King and Queen are shown to be devoted to each other. The Queen says that "You are so sick of late, / . . . That I distrust you." She also cries out that it is "treason" to even think of marrying again when her husband dies. "A second time I kill my husband dead / When second husband kisses me in bed." Hamlet possibly wants to remind his mother of the devotion she professed to his father.*)

And thirty dozen moons with borrowed sheen
About the world have times twelve thirties been
Since love our hearts and Hymen did our hands
160 Unite commutual in most sacred bands.

Player Queen. *So many journeys may the sun and moon
Make us again count o'er ere love be done!
But woe is me! You are so sick of late,
So far from cheer and from your former state,*
165 *That I distrust you. Yet, though I distrust,
Discomfort you, my lord, it nothing must.
For women fear too much, even as they love,
And women's fear and love hold quantity,
In neither aught, or in extremity.*
170 *Now what my love is, proof hath made you
know, And, as my love is sized, my fear is so:
Where love is great, the littlest doubts are fear;
Where little fears grow great, great love grows there.*

Player King. *Faith, I must leave thee, love, and shortly too.*
175 *My operant powers their functions leave to do.
And thou shalt live in this fair world behind,
Honored, beloved; and haply one as kind
For husband shalt thou—*

Player Queen.   *O, confound the rest!
Such love must needs be treason in my breast.*
180 *In second husband let me be accurst.
None wed the second but who killed the first.*

Hamlet. That's wormwood!

Player Queen. *The instances that second marriage move
Are base respects of thrift, but none of love.*
185 *A second time I kill my husband dead
When second husband kisses me in bed.*

Player King. *I do believe you think what now you speak,
But what we do determine oft we break.
Purpose is but the slave to memory,*
190 *Of violent birth, but poor validity,
Which now, the fruit unripe, sticks on the tree
But fall unshaken when they mellow be.
Most necessary 'tis that we forget
To pay ourselves what to ourselves is debt.*
195 *What to ourselves in passion we propose,
The passion ending, doth the purpose lose.
The violence of either grief or joy
Their own enactures with themselves destroy.
Where joy most revels, grief doth most lament;*
200 *Grief joys, joy grieves, on slender accident.*

165 distrust you: am worried about you.

168–169 And women's...extremity: Women love and fear in equal measure, loving and fearing either too much or hardly at all.

175 My...do: My vital powers are no longer functioning.

176 behind: after I'm gone.

182 wormwood: a bitter herb.

183–184 The instances...love: People marry a second time for profit, not for love.

189–190 Our intentions are dependent on our memory; they are powerful at first but have little durability (**validity**).

193–194 Most...debt: We inevitably forget promises we have made to ourselves.

197–200 When the violence of extreme grief or joy ceases, so too does the willingness to act upon these emotions. People who feel extreme grief also feel extreme joy, and one passion is likely to follow another without much cause (**on slender accident**).

SCAFFOLDING FOR ELL STUDENTS

Analyze Language Project lines 174–181 on the whiteboard.
Then ask volunteers to mark up the text:

- Underline the last sound in each line.
- Highlight the first two words that sound the same in yellow, the second two in blue, the third set in green, and the last in pink.

ASK STUDENTS to read each line after you, emphasizing the rhyme. Ask how the sound of the rhyme affects the mood created by the verse.

> **Player Queen. O,** *confound the* <u>rest!</u>
>
> *Such love must needs be treason in my* <u>breast.</u>
>
> *In second husband let me be* <u>accurst.</u>
>
> *None wed the second but who killed the* <u>first.</u>

This world is not for aye, nor 'tis not strange
That even our loves should with our fortunes change;
For 'tis a question left us yet to prove
Whether love lead fortune or else fortune love.
205 The great man down, you mark his favorite flies;
The poor, advanced, makes friends of enemies.
And hitherto doth love on fortune tend,
For who not needs shall never lack a friend,
And who in want a hollow friend doth try
210 Directly seasons him his enemy.
But, orderly to end where I begun:
Our wills and fates do so contrary run
That our devices still are overthrown;
Our thoughts are ours, their ends none of our own.
215 So think thou wilt no second husband wed,
But die thy thoughts when thy first lord is dead.

Player Queen. *Nor earth to me give food, nor heaven light,*
Sport and repose lock from me day and night,
To desperation turn my trust and hope,
220 *An anchor's cheer in prison be my scope.*
Each opposite that blanks the face of joy
Meet what I would have well and it destroy.
Both here and hence pursue me lasting strife,
If, once a widow, ever I be wife.

225 **Hamlet.** If she should break it now!

201 for aye: forever.

205 The great...flies:
When a great man's
fortune falls, his closest
friend abandons him.

206 advanced: moving
up in life.

207 hitherto: to this
extent.

**210 Directly seasons
him:** immediately
changes him into.

213 devices still: plans
always.

218 Sport...night: May
the day deny (**lock from**)
me its pastimes and
night its rest.

220 An anchor's cheer:
a religious hermit's fare.

221–222 May each
obstacle that turns the
face of joy pale meet
and destroy everything
that I wish to see
prosper (**what I would
have well**).

Image Credits: ©Nat Farbman/Time Life Pictures/Getty Images

Hamlet: Act III, Scene 2 **295**

CLOSE READ

Support Inferences

COMMON CORE **RL 1**

(sc. 2 LINES 211–224)

CITE TEXT EVIDENCE Have students summarize the Player King's statement and the Player Queen's response. What can the audience infer about each speaker's attitude toward human nature. *(The Player King says that no matter what we intend, fate will prove us wrong; that the Queen may think she will not remarry if he dies but that when he dies, she will forget her promise. The audience can infer that he has a realistic understanding of human nature. By contrast, the Player Queen insists that she will remain faithful to him if he dies. The audience can infer that she believes in the strength of a promise and that she has an optimistic, even naive view of human nature.)*

TO CHALLENGE STUDENTS...

Explore Plot Twists How does *Hamlet* explore ideas related to both meanings of *acting*: "committing an action" and "presenting a false appearance"? Ask students to discuss these points in small groups to understand Shakespeare's themes:

- In what way is Hamlet both acting and not acting? How do both behaviors lead to conflict?
- What other characters act in the play? How does this also create conflict for Hamlet?
- What is the irony of having real actors stage a performance that reflects reality?

Have groups share their insights in a class discussion.

Analyze Structure: Conflict (sc. 2 LINES 228–244)

COMMON CORE **RL 3**

Point out that although nothing sinister has happened yet in the play, the stage is set. In this interval, Hamlet has a chance to gauge the reactions of his mother and uncle.

Q ASK STUDENTS what the comment of Hamlet's mother in line 231 suggests about her perception of the play. (*Her comment that the Queen protests too much suggests both that she recognizes overacting and that she does not recognize herself in the portrayal.*) Ask students to explain Hamlet's purpose in lines 238–244. (*He is increasing the pressure on his uncle by reiterating the plot of the play while ironically suggesting that it has nothing to do with anyone present.*)

Player King. '*Tis deeply sworn. Sweet, leave me here awhile.*
My spirits grow dull, and fain I would beguile
The tedious day with sleep.

[*Sleeps.*]

Player Queen.   *Sleep rock thy brain,*
And never come mischance between us twain.

[*Player Queen exits.*]

230 **Hamlet.** Madam, how like you this play?

Queen. The lady doth protest too much, methinks.

Hamlet. O, but she'll keep her word.

King. Have you heard the argument? Is there no offense in 't?

235 **Hamlet.** No, no, they do but jest, poison in jest. No offense i' th' world.

King. What do you call the play?

Hamlet. "The Mousetrap." Marry, how? Tropically. This play is the image of a murder done in Vienna.
240 Gonzago is the duke's name, his wife Baptista. You shall see anon. 'Tis a knavish piece of work, but what of that? Your Majesty and we that have free souls, it touches us not. Let the galled jade wince; our withers are unwrung.

[*Enter Lucianus.*]

245 This is one Lucianus, nephew to the king.

Ophelia. You are as good as a chorus, my lord.

Hamlet. I could interpret between you and your love, if I could see the puppets dallying.

Ophelia. You are keen, my lord, you are keen.

250 **Hamlet.** It would cost you a groaning to take off mine edge.

Ophelia. Still better and worse.

Hamlet. So you mis-take your husbands.—Begin, murderer. Pox, leave thy damnable faces and begin.
255 Come, the croaking raven doth bellow for revenge.

Lucianus. *Thoughts black, hands apt, drugs fit, and*
* time agreeing,*
Confederate season, else no creature seeing,
Thou mixture rank, of midnight weeds collected,
With Hecate's ban thrice blasted, thrice infected,

---

231 doth protest too much: overstates her case, makes too many assurances.

233 argument: plot.

238 Tropically: metaphorically.

242 free: guilt-free.

243–244 Let... unwrung: a proverbial expression that means, "Let the guilty flinch; our consciences do not bother us."

246 chorus: a character who explains what will happen in a play.

247–252 An "interpreter" is a narrator in a puppet show. Hamlet says that he could explain what is going on between Ophelia and her lover if he caught them together. When she comments that he is **keen** (sharp, penetrating), he responds with wordplay (using **keen** to mean "sexually aroused") that she finds even more witty but also more offensive.

253 mis-take: take falsely. A reference to the marriage vow to take a husband "for better, for worse."

257 Time is my ally, (**Confederate**) and only witness.

259 Hecate's ban: the curse of Hecate, goddess of witchcraft.

260 *Thy natural magic and dire property*
On wholesome life usurp immediately.

[*Pours the poison in his ears.*]

Hamlet. He poisons him i' th' garden for his estate.
His name's Gonzago. The story is extant and written
in very choice Italian. You shall see anon how
265 the murderer gets the love of Gonzago's wife.

[*Claudius rises.*]

Ophelia. The King rises.

Hamlet. What, frighted with false fire?

Queen. How fares my lord?

Polonius. Give o'er the play.

270 **King.** Give me some light. Away!

Polonius. Lights, lights, lights!

[*All but* Hamlet *and* Horatio *exit.*]

Hamlet. *Why, let the strucken deer go weep,*
The hart ungallèd play.
For some must watch, while some must sleep:
275 *Thus runs the world away.*
Would not this, sir, and a forest of feathers (if the
rest of my fortunes turn Turk with me) with two
Provincial roses on my razed shoes, get me a fellowship
in a cry of players?

280 **Horatio.** Half a share.

Hamlet. A whole one, I.
For thou dost know, O Damon dear,
This realm dismantled was
Of Jove himself, and now reigns here
285 *A very very—pajock.*

Horatio. You might have rhymed.

Hamlet. O good Horatio, I'll take the ghost's word for
a thousand pound. Didst perceive?

Horatio. Very well, my lord.

290 **Hamlet.** Upon the talk of the poisoning?

Horatio. I did very well note him.

Hamlet. Ah ha! Come, some music! Come, the
recorders!
For if the King like not the comedy,
295 *Why, then, belike he likes it not, perdy.*
Come, some music!

261 usurp: steal.

267 false fire: the discharge of a gun loaded without shot.

273 ungallèd: uninjured.

277–279 turn Turk with me: turn against me. Elizabethan theater costumes often included feathers worn on hats and ribbon rosettes on shoes. A fellowship is a share or partnership in a theater company.

282 Damon: in Roman mythology the friend of Pythias.

285 pajock: either "peacock," which had a reputation for lust and cruelty, or "patchock," a savage person. (Presumably the rhyme Horatio hints at is **ass**.)

293 recorders: flute-like wooden wind instruments.

295 perdy: by God (from the French **par dieu**).

Hamlet: Act III, Scene 2 **297**

CLOSE READ

Analyze Structure: Conflict (sc. 2 LINES 256–271)

COMMON CORE RL 3

Remind students of Hamlet's comment at the end of Act II: "the play's the thing / Wherein I'll catch the conscience of the King."

R **ASK STUDENTS** if Hamlet has succeeded. Has he "caught the conscience of the King"? Explain. *(Claudius reacted dramatically to the portrayal of the murder of the King, providing Hamlet with evidence of his guilt.)* Ask students what effect Claudius's reaction might have on Hamlet's conflict and on the play's developing action. *(By providing evidence that the Ghost is honest and Claudius is guilty of murder, Claudius's reaction puts pressure on Hamlet to fulfill his promise to avenge his father's murder. The action of the play will follow what Hamlet does now that he has seen evidence of Claudius's guilt.)*

WHEN STUDENTS STRUGGLE . . .

Direct students to reread lines 256 to 271. Ask them why Claudius's reaction shows he is guilty. *(If he had not killed his brother, then the play's plot would have meant nothing to him. He wouldn't have known the significance of the poison being poured in the ear.)* Have students then reread lines 287–291. Ask them how Hamlet feels upon seeing the King's reaction. *(He is elated. He knows now the Ghost was right.)* Have students discuss what they think Hamlet will do next, based on what he has learned from this scene.

Analyze Drama Elements RL 3

(sc. 2 LINES 299–325)

Have students read what Hamlet says in this conversation to discover how the revelation brought about by the play has affected him.

S **CITE TEXT EVIDENCE** Ask students to describe Hamlet's mood in this passage. What details convey his feelings? *(Hamlet is flippant and plays on words, making a joke of his uncle's anger and refusing to respond seriously to what Rosencrantz and Guildenstern say. He is clearly elated at the success of his scheme.)*

[*Enter* Rosencrantz *and* Guildenstern.]

Guildenstern. Good my lord, vouchsafe me a word
with you.

Hamlet. Sir, a whole history.

300 **Guildenstern.** The King, sir—

Hamlet. Ay, sir, what of him?

Guildenstern. Is in his retirement marvelous distempered.

Hamlet. With drink, sir?

Guildenstern. No, my lord, with choler.

305 **Hamlet.** Your wisdom should show itself more richer
to signify this to the doctor, for for me to put him
to his purgation would perhaps plunge him into
more choler.

Guildenstern. Good my lord, put your discourse into
310 some frame and start not so wildly from my affair.

Hamlet. I am tame, sir. Pronounce.

Guildenstern. The Queen your mother, in most great
affliction of spirit, hath sent me to you.

Hamlet. You are welcome.

315 **Guildenstern.** Nay, good my lord, this courtesy is not
of the right breed. If it shall please you to make me
a wholesome answer, I will do your mother's commandment.
If not, your pardon and my return shall
be the end of my business.

320 **Hamlet.** Sir, I cannot.

Rosencrantz. What, my lord?

Hamlet. Make you a wholesome answer. My wit's diseased.
But, sir, such answer as I can make, you
shall command—or, rather, as you say, my mother.
325 Therefore no more but to the matter. My mother,
you say—

Rosencrantz. Then thus she says: your behavior hath
struck her into amazement and admiration.

Hamlet. O wonderful son that can so 'stonish a mother!
330 But is there no sequel at the heels of this mother's
admiration? Impart.

Rosencrantz. She desires to speak with you in her closet
ere you go to bed.

302 distempered: upset. (Hamlet takes it in the sense of "drunk.")

304 choler: anger. (Hamlet takes it in the sense of "biliousness.")

307 purgation: cleansing of the body of impurities; spiritual cleansing through confession.

310 frame: order; **start:** shy away like a nervous or wild horse.

318 pardon: permission to leave.

328 admiration: wonder.

332 closet: private room.

298 Collection 4

APPLYING ACADEMIC VOCABULARY

drama	integrity

As you discuss the remainder of Scene 2 and Scene 3, incorporate the following Collection 4 academic vocabulary words: *drama* and *integrity*. Have students explain the events that the **drama** sets into motion. Then have them discuss how Hamlet's actions in this act are an attempt to assess the **integrity** of those around him.

Hamlet. We shall obey, were she ten times our mother.
335 Have you any further trade with us?

Rosencrantz. My lord, you once did love me.

Hamlet. And do still, by these pickers and stealers.

337 pickers and stealers: hands (from the Church catechism, "To keep my hands from picking and stealing").

Rosencrantz. Good my lord, what is your cause of distemper? You do surely bar the door upon your
340 own liberty if you deny your griefs to your friend.

Hamlet. Sir, I lack advancement.

Rosencrantz. How can that be, when you have the voice of the King himself for your succession in Denmark?

345 **Hamlet.** Ay, sir, but "While the grass grows"—the proverb is something musty.

345–346 The rest of the stale (**musty**) proverb is "the horse starves," suggesting that Hamlet cannot wait so long.

[*Enter the* Players *with recorders.*]

O, the recorders! Let me see one. [*He takes a recorder and turns to* Guildenstern.] To withdraw with you: why do you go about to recover the
350 wind of me, as if you would drive me into a toil?

348–350 withdraw: speak privately. Hamlet uses a hunting metaphor: The hunter moves to the windward side of the prey, causing it to flee toward a net (**toil**).

Guildenstern. O, my lord, if my duty be too bold, my love is too unmannerly.

Hamlet. I do not well understand that. Will you play upon this pipe?

355 **Guildenstern.** My lord, I cannot.

Hamlet. I pray you.

Guildenstern. Believe me, I cannot.

Hamlet. I do beseech you.

Guildenstern. I know no touch of it, my lord.

360 **Hamlet.** It is as easy as lying. Govern these ventages with your fingers and thumb, give it breath with your mouth, and it will discourse most eloquent music. Look you, these are the stops.

360 ventages: stops, or finger holes, on the recorder.

Guildenstern. But these cannot I command to any
365 utt'rance of harmony. I have not the skill.

Hamlet. Why, look you now, how unworthy a thing you make of me! You would play upon me, you would seem to know my stops, you would pluck out the heart of my mystery, you would sound me
370 from my lowest note to the top of my compass; and there is much music, excellent voice, in this little organ, yet cannot you make it speak. 'Sblood,

369–375 sound me: play upon me like an instrument, investigate me; **compass:** an instrument's range; **organ:** musical instrument; **fret me:** annoy me (also punning on **frets,** the raised bars for fingering a stringed instrument).

Hamlet: Act III, Scene 2 **299**

CLOSE READ

Determine Theme

COMMON CORE RL 2

(sc. 2 LINES 347–375)

Have students note the language Hamlet uses in this passage. Remind them that figures of speech reinforce the ideas about lying, pretense, and deception apparent in so much of the play.

ASK STUDENTS to explain what Hamlet means when he says playing the recorder is as easy as lying (line 360). (*He means that, like playing a recorder, lying is as easy as opening your mouth and using your breath to make sounds. In the case of lying, a person can easily create a pretty impression to mask underlying ugliness.*) Ask students to study lines 366–375 and then explain how, aside from lying, he thinks Guildenstern is "playing" him. (*Guildenstern is playing Hamlet by spying on him, by trying to get information out of him the way a musician would get music out of a recorder. He is pretending to be a friend, all the while undermining what real friendship means.*)

Analyze Drama Elements: Character COMMON CORE RL 3
(sc. 2 LINES 377–386)

Ask students to read Hamlet's lines closely to see how his behavior changes when Polonius enters the scene.

U CITE TEXT EVIDENCE Have students contrast Hamlet's attitude toward Polonius here with his attitude toward Guildenstern just before Polonius's entrance. *(Hamlet changes from agitated and angry with Guildenstern to flippant and teasing with Polonius. He suggests that a cloud looks like a camel, a weasel, and a whale. His motive could be to make a fool of Polonius, who agrees to each of Hamlet's absurd suggestions. Still, the change in Hamlet is sudden and dramatic.)*

T do you think I am easier to be played on than a pipe? Call me what instrument you will, though
375 you can fret me, you cannot play upon me.

[*Enter* Polonius.]

God bless you, sir.

Polonius. My lord, the Queen would speak with you, and presently.

Hamlet. Do you see yonder cloud that's almost in
380 shape of a camel?

Polonius. By th' Mass, and 'tis like a camel indeed.

U Hamlet. Methinks it is like a weasel.

Polonius. It is backed like a weasel.

Hamlet. Or like a whale.

385 **Polonius.** Very like a whale.

Hamlet. Then I will come to my mother by and by.

[*Aside.*] They fool me to the top of my bent.—I will come by and by.

Polonius. I will say so.

390 **Hamlet.** "By and by" is easily said. Leave me, friends.

[*All but* Hamlet *exit.*]

V 'Tis now the very witching time of night,
When churchyards yawn and hell itself breathes out
Contagion to this world. Now could I drink hot blood
And do such bitter business as the day
395 Would quake to look on. Soft, now to my mother.
O heart, lose not thy nature; let not ever
The soul of Nero enter this firm bosom.
Let me be cruel, not unnatural.
I will speak daggers to her, but use none.
400 My tongue and soul in this be hypocrites:
How in my words somever she be shent,
To give them seals never, my soul, consent.

[*He exits.*]

387 fool…bent: make me play the fool to the limits of my ability.

388 by and by: before long.

397 Nero: a Roman emperor who put his mother to death.

401–402 Hamlet tells himself that however much she is rebuked (**shent**) in his words, he must not put those words into action (**give them seals**).

Strategies for Annotation ✎ 🗐 *Annotate it!*

Analyze Language COMMON CORE RL 4

Have students use their eBook annotation tools to analyze Hamlet's soliloquy.

- Highlight in green examples of personification.
- Highlight in pink metaphors.
- Highlight in blue allusions.
- Underline words with powerful connotations.
- Review your annotations. In a small group, discuss what the images and words tell you about Hamlet's mood and purpose.

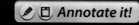

O heart, lose not thy nature; let not ever

The soul of Nero enter this firm bosom.

Let me be cruel, not unnatural.

I will speak daggers to her, but use none.

Scene 3 *The castle.*

[*Enter* King, Rosencrantz, *and* Guildenstern.]

King. I like him not, nor stands it safe with us
To let his madness range. Therefore prepare you.
I your commission will forthwith dispatch,
And he to England shall along with you.
5   The terms of our estate may not endure
Hazard so near 's as doth hourly grow
Out of his brows.

Guildenstern.   We will ourselves provide.
Most holy and religious fear it is
To keep those many many bodies safe
10 That live and feed upon your Majesty.

Rosencrantz. The single and peculiar life is bound
With all the strength and armor of the mind
To keep itself from noyance, but much more
That spirit upon whose weal depends and rests
15 The lives of many. The cess of majesty
Dies not alone, but like a gulf doth draw
What's near it with it; or it is a massy wheel
Fixed on the summit of the highest mount,
To whose huge spokes ten thousand lesser things
20 Are mortised and adjoined, which, when it falls,
Each small annexment, petty consequence,
Attends the boist'rous ruin. Never alone
Did the king sigh, but with a general groan.

King. Arm you, I pray you, to this speedy voyage,

25 For we will fetters put about this fear,
Which now goes too free-footed.

Rosencrantz.   We will haste us.

[Rosencrantz *and* Guildenstern *exit.*]

[*Enter* Polonius.]

Polonius. My lord, he's going to his mother's closet.
Behind the arras I'll convey myself
To hear the process. I'll warrant she'll tax him home;
30 And, as you said (and wisely was it said),
'Tis meet that some more audience than a mother,
Since nature makes them partial, should o'erhear
The speech of vantage. Fare you well, my liege.
I'll call upon you ere you go to bed
35 And tell you what I know.

King.   Thanks, dear my lord.

[Polonius *exits.*]

1 him: his behavior.

3 forthwith dispatch: have prepared at once.

5 The terms of our estate: my position as king.

6 near 's: near us.

11 single and peculiar: individual and private.

13 noyance: harm.

14 weal: well-being.

15 cess: cessation, decease.

16 gulf: whirlpool.

17–22 Rosencrantz alludes to Fortune's massive (**massy**) wheel, with the king traditionally shown on the top; when the king falls, everyone connected with him plunges as well.

24 Arm you: prepare yourself.

29 process: proceedings; **tax him home:** strongly rebuke him.

31 meet: fitting.

33 of vantage: in addition.

Hamlet: Act III, Scene 3   **301**

TO CHALLENGE STUDENTS . . .

Determine Figurative Meanings How do comparisons help authors convey ideas and emotions? Have students discuss the simile in lines 15–17 with a partner. *(The downfall or death of a king is compared to a whirlpool that draws in others. This shows the importance of the throne to the well being of the country.)* Have students use this simile and the metaphor that follows to answer these questions in small groups:

- What do these figures of speech illustrate about the Renaissance view of the monarch?

- How do these figures of speech provide insight into the motives of Rosencrantz and Guildenstern? How should they be classified in the play—as villains or pawns of the King?

CLOSE READ

Analyze Language: Soliloquy (sc. 2 LINES 391–402)

 COMMON CORE **RL 4**

Read this soliloquy aloud. Have students consider how the language in this speech reveals Hamlet's state of mind.

V **ASK STUDENTS** how the setting of this speech relates back to events in Act I. What is the significance of this connection? *(It is midnight, the same hour at which the Ghost appeared to Hamlet. Just as the Ghost evoked images of hell, so too Hamlet's words in the first lines depict an atmosphere of evil and horror.)* **What feeling is revealed by Hamlet's comment that "Now could I drink hot blood"? What other words convey this state of mind?** *(He feels empowered and ready to do what he has to in order to find the truth. He is filled with the cruelty of violence and must control it in order not to be like Nero, who put his mother to death. He wants to "speak daggers to her, but use none.")* **How do his words here violate the spirit of the final demand the Ghost made of him?** *(The Ghost told Hamlet to leave his mother to her own conscience and to God's punishment. But here, even though Hamlet says he will not do physical harm to his mother, clearly he plans to punish her verbally.)*

Analyze Language

 COMMON CORE **RL 4**

(sc. 3 LINES 24–26)

Point out that this scene advances the plot at a quick pace as characters react to the previous events. Tell students that in giving his instructions, the King uses language to disguise his intent and feelings.

W **ASK STUDENTS** to explain the King's metaphor. *(By sending Hamlet away, he will arrest or stop the threat to his throne. Right now, Hamlet has the potential to seriously harm him.)* **What does his use of this metaphor reveal?** *(After seeing the play, he clearly fears that Hamlet may try to harm him.)*

Analyze Language: Soliloquy (sc. 3 LINES 36–72)

COMMON CORE RL 4

Direct students to read this speech carefully. Point out that it provides rare insight into the King's thoughts and feelings.

X CITE TEXT EVIDENCE Have students identify details in the speech that show evidence of the King's feelings of guilt. *(He says his act "smells to heaven." His "stronger guilt defeats my strong intent." He cries out "O wretched state!" "O bosom black as death!" "O limed soul, that, struggling to be free, / Art more engaged!")* Ask students what he knows he should do to lessen these feelings of guilt. How does this realization lead to his conflict? *(He knows he must relinquish what he gained from the crime, but he cannot. That is his conflict.)*

O, my offense is rank, it smells to heaven;
It hath the primal eldest curse upon 't,
A brother's murder. Pray can I not,
Though inclination be as sharp as will.
40 My stronger guilt defeats my strong intent,
And, like a man to double business bound,
I stand in pause where I shall first begin
And both neglect. What if this cursèd hand
Were thicker than itself with brother's blood?
45 Is there not rain enough in the sweet heavens
To wash it white as snow? Whereto serves mercy
But to confront the visage of offense?
And what's in prayer but this twofold force,
To be forestallèd ere we come to fall,
50 Or pardoned being down? Then I'll look up.
My fault is past. But, O, what form of prayer
Can serve my turn? "Forgive me my foul murder"?
That cannot be, since I am still possessed
Of those effects for which I did the murder:
55 My crown, mine own ambition, and my queen.
May one be pardoned and retain th' offense?
In the corrupted currents of this world,
Offense's gilded hand may shove by justice,
And oft 'tis seen the wicked prize itself
60 Buys out the law. But 'tis not so above:
There is no shuffling; there the action lies
In his true nature, and we ourselves compelled,
Even to the teeth and forehead of our faults,
To give in evidence. What then? What rests?
65 Try what repentance can. What can it not?
Yet what can it, when one cannot repent?
O wretched state! O bosom black as death!
O limèd soul, that, struggling to be free,
Art more engaged! Help, angels! Make assay.
70 Bow, stubborn knees, and heart with strings of steel
Be soft as sinews of the newborn babe.
All may be well.

[*He kneels.*]

[*Enter* Hamlet.]

Hamlet. Now might I do it pat, now he is a-praying,
And now I'll do 't.

[*He draws his sword.*]

                    And so he goes to heaven,
75 And so am I revenged. That would be scanned:
A villain kills my father, and for that,

37 primal eldest curse: the curse of Cain (the son of Adam and Eve who murdered his brother Abel).

46–47 Whereto... offense: What purpose does mercy serve other than to oppose condemnation?

56 th' offense: the benefits of the crime.

57–64 In the corrupt ways (**currents**) of this world, a rich offender can push aside justice, and often the law is bribed with stolen wealth. But that isn't the case in heaven, where there is no evasion (**shuffling**); the true nature of every deed lies exposed, and we must testify against ourselves.

64 rests: remains.

68 limèd: trapped like a bird caught in quicklime (a sticky substance).

69 engaged: entangled; **Make assay:** Make an attempt (addressed to himself).

73 pat: conveniently.

75 would be scanned: needs to be looked at carefully.

WHEN STUDENTS STRUGGLE...

To help students better comprehend the meaning of the King's speech, display a chart similar to the one on page 303.

- Read each of these sets of lines aloud as students follow along in their books: 36–43, 51–56, 66–72.
- Give students time after the reading of each set of lines to work with a partner to identify the main idea.
- Call on pairs to state the main idea. Then record it in the class chart.

ASK STUDENTS to explain the King's major conflict. *(He feels guilt but not enough to relinquish what he gained through the murder.)*

I, his sole son, do this same villain send
To heaven.
Why, this is hire and salary, not revenge.
80 He took my father grossly, full of bread,
With all his crimes broad blown, as flush as May;
And how his audit stands who knows save heaven.
But in our circumstance and course of thought
'Tis heavy with him. And am I then revenged
85 To take him in the purging of his soul,
When he is fit and seasoned for his passage?
No.
Up sword, and know thou a more horrid hent.

[*He sheathes his sword.*]

When he is drunk asleep, or in his rage,
90 Or in th' incestuous pleasure of his bed,
At game a-swearing, or about some act
That has no relish of salvation in 't—
Then trip him, that his heels may kick at heaven,
And that his soul may be as damned and black
95 As hell, whereto it goes. My mother stays.
This physic but prolongs thy sickly days.

[*Hamlet exits.*]

King [*rising*]. My words fly up, my thoughts remain
     below;
Words without thoughts never to heaven go.

[*He exits.*]

Scene 4 *The Queen's private chamber.*

[*Enter* Queen *and* Polonius.]

Polonius. He will come straight. Look you lay home to him.
Tell him his pranks have been too broad to bear with
And that your Grace hath screened and stood between
Much heat and him. I'll silence me even here.
5 Pray you, be round with him.

Hamlet [*within*]. Mother, mother, mother!

Queen. I'll warrant you. Fear me not. Withdraw,
I hear him coming.

[*Polonius hides behind the arras.*]

[*Enter* Hamlet.]

Hamlet. Now, mother, what's the matter?

10 **Queen.** Hamlet, thou hast thy father much offended.

Hamlet. Mother, you have my father much offended.

79 hire and salary: something Claudius should pay me to do.

80–84 Hamlet complains that his father was killed without allowing him spiritual preparation (**grossly**). He was immersed in worldly pleasures and his sins were in full bloom. Only heaven knows how his final account stands, but from Hamlet's perspective his father's sins seem a heavy burden.

86 seasoned: prepared.

88 know thou a more horrid hent: wait to be grasped on a more horrible occasion.

95 stays: awaits me.

96 physic: medicine (referring to the postponement of revenge or to Claudius's act of prayer).

1 straight: right away; **lay home to:** strongly rebuke.

2 broad: unrestrained.

5 round: blunt.

Lines	Main Idea
36–43	He knows that killing his brother was a terrible crime.
51–56	He wants forgiveness, but he doesn't want to give up what he gained through his action.
66–72	He feels despair over the wretched state of his soul, and then calls upon the angels for help and kneels to pray.

CLOSE READ

Analyze Structure: Conflict (sc. 3 LINES 74–98)

 COMMON CORE RL 3

Point out that a character's actions determine the direction that a play takes. Have students read this passage, noting the decision that Hamlet makes here.

 ASK STUDENTS why Hamlet doesn't kill Claudius when he sees him alone and undefended. (*Hamlet sees that Claudius is praying. Believing that prayer might grant the King forgiveness for murder, Hamlet delays. He wants Claudius to die damned for murder and go straight to hell to be punished for eternity.*) **How do the King's lines at the end of the scene make Hamlet's decision ironic?** (*Claudius knows that because he isn't willing to give up his throne or his wife, his prayer is futile. If Hamlet acted now, he would get the kind of revenge he wants.*)

Analyze Language

COMMON CORE RL 4

(sc. 4 LINES 9–11)

Remind students that Hamlet intends to use his words as "daggers."

ASK STUDENTS how Hamlet's play on words establishes the reason he has come to see his mother. (*He tells her that she has offended his father, showing that he means to confront her with her wrongdoing.*)

CLOSE READ

Determine Theme COMMON CORE RL 2

(sc. 4 LINES 19–21)

Remind students that a symbol is an object that stands for something greater than itself.

A2 **ASK STUDENTS** what the mirror represents. Have them explain how this symbol illustrates what Hamlet is trying to do throughout the play. *(Hamlet uses the mirror to force his mother to look at the truth of her actions. It represents the reality beneath surface appearances. Throughout the play, Hamlet struggles to answer the question of what is real.)*

Analyze Structure: Conflict COMMON CORE RL 3

(sc. 4 LINES 22–26)

Explain to students that Act III includes an event that means the tragic hero is committed to a path of action that will lead to tragedy, often for others as well as himself.

B2 **ASK STUDENTS** why the killing of Polonius is a turning point for Hamlet. *(Killing Polonius is a rash and impetuous act. Hamlet has just seen Claudius praying, so he must know that the King is not behind the arras, that this murderous act has nothing to do with avenging his father's death. By killing Polonius, Hamlet makes an outlaw of himself and loses control of his own plot. He has turned himself from a righteous hero pursuing justice into a foolish fugitive from justice.)*

Image Credits: ©Nat Farbman/Time Life Pictures/Getty Images

Queen. Come, come, you answer with an idle tongue.

> **12 idle:** foolish.

Hamlet. Go, go, you question with a wicked tongue.

Queen. Why, how now, Hamlet?

Hamlet. What's the matter now?

15 **Queen.** Have you forgot me?

> **15 forgot me:** forgotten who I am; **rood:** cross.

Hamlet. No, by the rood, not so.
You are the Queen, your husband's brother's wife,
And (would it were not so) you are my mother.

Queen. Nay, then I'll set those to you that can speak.

A2 **Hamlet.** Come, come, and sit you down; you shall not budge.
20 You go not till I set you up a glass
Where you may see the inmost part of you.

> **20 glass:** mirror.

B2 **Queen.** What wilt thou do? Thou wilt not murder me?
Help, ho!

Polonius [*behind the arras*]. What ho! Help!

25 **Hamlet.** How now, a rat? Dead for a ducat, dead.

> **25 Dead for a ducat:** I'll wager a ducat that I kill him; I'll kill him for a ducat.

[*He kills* Polonius *by thrusting a rapier through the arras.*]

Polonius [*behind the arras*]. O, I am slain!

Queen. O me, what hast thou done?

WHEN STUDENTS STRUGGLE . . .

To make sure students understand the concept of a turning point, draw this diagram on the board, placing the murder of Polonius at the top.

ASK STUDENTS what this diagram shows about the events that will follow. *(They will have negative consequences for Hamlet; they will not lead to a happy ending.)*

Hamlet. Nay, I know not. Is it the King?

Queen. O, what a rash and bloody deed is this!

Hamlet. A bloody deed—almost as bad, good mother,
30   As kill a king and marry with his brother.

Queen. As kill a king?

Hamlet.   Ay, lady, it was my word.

[*He pulls* Polonius' *body from behind the arras.*]

Thou wretched, rash, intruding fool, farewell.
I took thee for thy better. Take thy fortune.
Thou find'st to be too busy is some danger.

[*To* Queen.]

35   Leave wringing of your hands. Peace, sit you down,
And let me wring your heart; for so I shall
If it be made of penetrable stuff,
If damnèd custom have not brazed it so
That it be proof and bulwark against sense.

40   **Queen.** What have I done, that thou dar'st wag thy tongue
In noise so rude against me?

Hamlet.   Such an act
That blurs the grace and blush of modesty,
Calls virtue hypocrite, takes off the rose
From the fair forehead of an innocent love
45   And sets a blister there, makes marriage vows
As false as dicers' oaths—O, such a deed
As from the body of contraction plucks
The very soul, and sweet religion makes
A rhapsody of words! Heaven's face does glow
50   O'er this solidity and compound mass
With heated visage, as against the doom,
Is thought-sick at the act.

Queen.   Ay me, what act
That roars so loud and thunders in the index?

Hamlet. Look here upon this picture and on this,
55   The counterfeit presentment of two brothers.
See what a grace was seated on this brow,
Hyperion's curls, the front of Jove himself,
An eye like Mars' to threaten and command,
A station like the herald Mercury
60   New-lighted on a heaven-kissing hill,
A combination and a form indeed
Where every god did seem to set his seal
To give the world assurance of a man.

34 too busy: too much of a busybody.

38–39 If...sense: if habitual wickedness (**damnèd custom**) has not so hardened (**brazed**) your heart that it has become armor (**proof**) and fortification against feeling (**sense**).

47 contraction: the marriage contract.

48 sweet religion: marriage vows.

49 rhapsody: senseless jumble.

49–52 Heaven's face looks down shamefully and is sick with sorrow.

53 index: introduction.

55 counterfeit presentment: portraits.

57 Hyperion: the sun god; **front:** brow.

59–60 A station...hill: a stance like that of the winged messenger of the gods.

Hamlet: Act III, Scene 4   **305**

CLOSE READ

Analyze Drama Elements: Character (sc. 4 LINES 29–52)

Have students consider how the killing of Polonius may have affected Hamlet.

C2 CITE TEXT EVIDENCE Have students identify the lines that suggest Hamlet may suspect his mother of conspiring to kill his father. *(In lines 29–30, Hamlet compares killing Polonius to being almost as bad as killing a king and marrying his brother.)* Ask them to characterize Hamlet's behavior and his tone in this confrontation. Has he momentarily gone mad? If so, how does his behavior contrast with scenes where he was playing at madness? (*Starting with the murder of Polonius, Hamlet's behavior in this scene grows increasingly irrational. The rush of overwrought images in lines 41–52 make Hamlet sound as if he has temporarily taken leave of his senses. Before, audiences could see he was in control, taunting Polonius or manipulating Rosencrantz and Guildenstern. Here, there is no control over the way he rages at his mother.*)

Analyze Word Choices

(sc. 4 LINES 54–89)

D2 ASK STUDENTS how Hamlet's increasing vehemence is revealed through the literary devices that Shakespeare uses in this speech. *(His tone of anger is emphasized by the repetition of questions, the use of the simile that compares his uncle to a "mildewed ear," the parallel structure of "eyes without feeling," "ears without hands," and the metaphorical comparisons.)*

Strategies for Annotation

Analyze Language

Have students use their eBook annotation tools to analyze Hamlet's speech to his mother:

- Highlight in yellow the description Hamlet gives of his father. On a note, explain what is revealed about Hamlet's view of his father through these details.
- Highlight in blue the simile that Hamlet uses to describe his uncle. On a note, explain the ideas conveyed by this simile, referring to the marginal notes.
- Review the annotations. In a small group, discuss Hamlet's purpose in this speech as well as his views of both his father and his uncle.

This was your husband. Look you now what follows.

Here is your husband, like a mildewed ear

Blasting his wholesome brother. Have you eyes?

Could you on this fair mountain leave to feed

And batten on this moor? Ha! Have you eyes?

Analyze Drama Elements COMMON CORE RL 3

(sc. 4 LINES 90–105)

Point out that Hamlet is becoming increasingly carried away by his own eloquence in this dialogue.

E2 **ASK STUDENTS** what the Queen's comments in lines 90–93 reveal about Hamlet's purpose. *(He has succeeded in making her see herself and her actions.)* What is Hamlet's motive in continuing to attack her verbally? *(He wants to hurt his mother as much as she has hurt him by her actions.)*

This was your husband. Look you now what follows.
65　Here is your husband, like a mildewed ear
　　Blasting his wholesome brother. Have you eyes?
　　Could you on this fair mountain leave to feed
　　And batten on this moor? Ha! Have you eyes?
　　You cannot call it love, for at your age
70　The heyday in the blood is tame, it's humble
　　And waits upon the judgment; and what judgment
　　Would step from this to this? Sense sure you have,
　　Else could you not have motion; but sure that sense
　　Is apoplexed; for madness would not err,
75　Nor sense to ecstasy was ne'er so thralled,
　　But it reserved some quantity of choice
　　To serve in such a difference. What devil was 't
　　That thus hath cozened you at hoodman-blind?
　　Eyes without feeling, feeling without sight,
80　Ears without hands or eyes, smelling sans all,
　　Or but a sickly part of one true sense
　　Could not so mope. O shame, where is thy blush?
　　Rebellious hell,
　　If thou canst mutine in a matron's bones,
85　To flaming youth let virtue be as wax
　　And melt in her own fire. Proclaim no shame
　　When the compulsive ardor gives the charge,
　　Since frost itself as actively doth burn,
　　And reason panders will.

90　**Queen.** O Hamlet, speak no more!
　　Thou turn'st my eyes into my very soul,
　　And there I see such black and grainèd spots
　　As will not leave their tinct.

　　Hamlet.　　　　　　Nay, but to live
　　In the rank sweat of an enseamèd bed,
95　Stewed in corruption, honeying and making love
　　Over the nasty sty!

　　Queen. O, speak to me no more!
　　These words like daggers enter in my ears.
　　No more, sweet Hamlet!

　　Hamlet.　　　　　　A murderer and a villain,
100　A slave that is not twentieth part the tithe
　　Of your precedent lord; a vice of kings,
　　A cutpurse of the empire and the rule,
　　That from a shelf the precious diadem stole
　　And put it in his pocket—

105　**Queen.** No more!

　　Hamlet. A king of shreds and patches—

65–66 Hamlet uses the metaphor of a mildewed ear of grain that is blighting (**blasting**) a nearby healthy plant.

68 batten on: grow fat from feeding on; **moor:** barren land.

70 heyday in the blood: sexual excitement.

72–78 Hamlet says that her senses must be paralyzed, because madness would let her choose correctly between Claudius and Hamlet's father. He wonders what devil tricked her in a game.

80 sans all: without the other senses.

82 so mope: be so dazed.

83–89 If hell can stir up rebellion in an older woman's bones, then in young people virtue should be like a candle melting in its own flame.

92 grainèd: ingrained, indelible.

93 leave their tinct: lose their color, fade.

94 enseamèd: greasy, sweaty.

100 tithe: tenth part.

101 vice: buffoon. (The Vice was a clownish villain in medieval morality plays.)

102 cutpurse: thief.

103 diadem: crown.

106 shreds and patches: referring to the patchwork costume of clowns or fools.

TO CHALLENGE STUDENTS . . .

Draw Conclusions How might using a particular word in different contexts help an author emphasize certain ideas? Point out the use of the word *rank* in line 94. Tell students that this word occurs several times throughout the play, including in these passages: Act I, sc. 2, line 136; Act I, sc. 5, line 39; Act II, sc. 1, line 20; Act III, sc. 2, line 258; Act III, sc. 3, line 36; Act III, sc. 4, lines 154, 158.

Have students return to each passage to examine the context of the word. Then have them discuss how the word's meaning and the frequency with which it occurs relates to the idea of pervasive corruption that underlies the play.

[Enter Ghost.]

Save me and hover o'er me with your wings,
You heavenly guards!— What would your gracious figure?

Queen. Alas, he's mad.

110 **Hamlet.** Do you not come your tardy son to chide,
That, lapsed in time and passion, lets go by
Th' important acting of your dread command?
O, say!

Ghost. Do not forget. This visitation
115 Is but to whet thy almost blunted purpose.
But look, amazement on thy mother sits.
O, step between her and her fighting soul.
Conceit in weakest bodies strongest works.
Speak to her, Hamlet.

Hamlet. How is it with you, lady?

120 **Queen.** Alas, how is 't with you,
That you do bend your eye on vacancy
And with th' incorporal air do hold discourse?
Forth at your eyes your spirits wildly peep,
And, as the sleeping soldiers in th' alarm,
125 Your bedded hair, like life in excrements,
Start up and stand an end. O gentle son,
Upon the heat and flame of thy distemper
Sprinkle cool patience! Whereon do you look?

Hamlet. On him, on him! Look you how pale he glares.
130 His form and cause conjoined, preaching to stones,
Would make them capable. [*To the* Ghost.] Do not look upon me,
Lest with this piteous action you convert
My stern effects. Then what I have to do
Will want true color—tears perchance for blood.

135 **Queen.** To whom do you speak this?

Hamlet. Do you see nothing there?

Queen. Nothing at all; yet all that is I see.

Hamlet. Nor did you nothing hear?

Queen. No, nothing but ourselves.

140 **Hamlet.** Why, look you there, look how it steals away!
My father, in his habit as he lived!
Look where he goes even now out at the portal!

[Ghost *exits.*]

111 **lapsed in time and passion:** having let time pass and my passion cool.

116 **amazement:** bewilderment, shock.

118 **Conceit:** imagination.

122 **incorporal:** immaterial.

124–126 Like soldiers awakened by an alarm, your smoothly laid (**bedded**) hair—as if there were life in this outgrowth (**excrements**)—jumps up and stands on end.

130 **conjoined:** joined together.

131 **them capable:** the stones responsive.

132–133 **convert… effects:** alter the stern impression I give.

134 **want:** lack.

141 **in his habit as he lived:** in the clothes he wore when alive.

CLOSE READ

Support Inferences

COMMON CORE RL 1

(sc. 4 LINES 107–145)

Point out that the Ghost has not been seen since Act I. Have students read to note the significance of this visit.

F2 **ASK STUDENTS** what the Ghost's comment in lines 114–119 reveals about his reason for appearing. (*He is there to remind Hamlet of his "blunted purpose"—to get revenge—and to ask Hamlet to comfort his mother, not to make her feel worse.*) What does the Queen say to indicate that Hamlet is hallucinating the Ghost? (*She says to Hamlet, "you do bend your eye on vacancy" [line 121]. In lines 135–140, she repeatedly says that she does not see the Ghost. Finally, in line 143, she insists that her son is hallucinating: "This is the very coinage of your brain."*)

SCAFFOLDING FOR ELL STUDENTS

Understand Dramatic Irony Project lines 120–135 on the whiteboard. Then ask volunteers to mark up the text:

- Highlight in pink the questions that the Queen asks Hamlet.
- Highlight in green what Hamlet replies.
- Highlight in yellow the comments that Hamlet directs to the Ghost.

ASK STUDENTS to explain the dramatic irony of this scene. What can the audience see that the Queen cannot? How does she interpret Hamlet's actions?

Queen. Alas, how is 't with you,

That you do bend your eye on vacancy

And with th' incorporal air do hold discourse?

Forth at your eyes your spirits wildly peep,

Analyze Drama Elements: Character (SC. 4 LINES 146–178)

 COMMON CORE RL 3

 G2 CITE TEXT EVIDENCE Ask students to comment on Hamlet's speeches to his mother here in light of the Ghost's request that he comfort her. *(Hamlet appears to be incapable of leaving his mother to her own conscience. He devotes most of two long speeches to reminding her of her sins and insisting she show repentance by not spending the night with Claudius. Hamlet is still not in control of himself. He is not taking command of the act of revenge the Ghost has reminded him of.)*

F2

Queen. This is the very coinage of your brain.
This bodiless creation ecstasy
145 Is very cunning in.

    Hamlet.   Ecstasy?
My pulse as yours doth temperately keep time
And makes as healthful music. It is not madness
That I have uttered. Bring me to the test,
And I the matter will reword, which madness
150 Would gambol from. Mother, for love of grace,
Lay not that flattering unction to your soul
That not your trespass but my madness speaks.
It will but skin and film the ulcerous place,
Whiles rank corruption, mining all within,
155 Infects unseen. Confess yourself to heaven,
Repent what's past, avoid what is to come,
And do not spread the compost on the weeds

G2

To make them ranker. Forgive me this my virtue,
For, in the fatness of these pursy times,
160 Virtue itself of vice must pardon beg,
Yea, curb and woo for leave to do him good.

    Queen. O Hamlet, thou hast cleft my heart in twain!

    Hamlet. O, throw away the worser part of it,
And live the purer with the other half!
165 Good night. But go not to my uncle's bed.
Assume a virtue if you have it not.
That monster, custom, who all sense doth eat,
Of habits devil, is angel yet in this,
That to the use of actions fair and good
170 He likewise gives a frock or livery
That aptly is put on. Refrain tonight,
And that shall lend a kind of easiness
To the next abstinence, the next more easy;
For use almost can change the stamp of nature
175 And either . . . the devil or throw him out
With wondrous potency. Once more, good night,
And, when you are desirous to be blest,
I'll blessing beg of you. For this same lord

    [*Pointing to* Polonius.]

I do repent; but heaven hath pleased it so
180 To punish me with this and this with me,
That I must be their scourge and minister.
I will bestow him and will answer well
The death I gave him. So, again, good night.
I must be cruel only to be kind.

144–145 Madness (**ecstasy**) is very skillful at creating this kind of hallucination (**bodiless creation**).

148–155 Hamlet tells his mother to make him repeat his description word for word, a test that madness would skip (**gambol**) away from. He asks her not to use his madness rather than her misdeeds to explain this visitation; such a soothing ointment (**unction**) would merely cover up the sore on her soul, allowing the infection within to grow unseen.

158 this my virtue: my virtuous talk.

159 fatness: grossness; **pursy:** flabby, bloated.

161 curb: bow; **leave:** permission.

167–171 Custom, which consumes our awareness of the evil we habitually do, can also make us grow used to performing good actions.

174 stamp of nature: the traits we are born with.

175 A word seems to be missing in this line.

180 this: Polonius.

181 their scourge and minister: heaven's agent of retribution.

182 answer well: explain.

WHEN STUDENTS STRUGGLE . . .

Guide students' comprehension of plot by having them complete a sequence chart that includes the important events in scenes 2 and 3.

ASK STUDENTS to quickly skim scenes 2 and 3, raising their hands to volunteer ideas about important events. List their contributions on the board. Then work together to order them chronologically, identifying when they occur and who is involved.

185 This bad begins, and worse remains behind.
One word more, good lady.

Queen. What shall I do?

Hamlet. Not this by no means that I bid you do:
Let the bloat king tempt you again to bed,
Pinch wanton on your cheek, call you his mouse,
190 And let him, for a pair of reechy kisses
Or paddling in your neck with his damned fingers,
Make you to ravel all this matter out
That I essentially am not in madness,
But mad in craft. 'Twere good you let him know,
195 For who that's but a queen, fair, sober, wise,
Would from a paddock, from a bat, a gib,
Such dear concernings hide? Who would do so?
No, in despite of sense and secrecy,
Unpeg the basket on the house's top,
200 Let the birds fly, and like the famous ape,
To try conclusions, in the basket creep
And break your own neck down.

Queen. Be thou assured, if words be made of breath
And breath of life, I have no life to breathe
205 What thou hast said to me.

Hamlet. I must to England, you know that.

Queen. Alack,
I had forgot! 'Tis so concluded on.

Hamlet. There's letters sealed; and my two schoolfellows,
Whom I will trust as I will adders fanged,
210 They bear the mandate; they must sweep my way
And marshal me to knavery. Let it work,
For 'tis the sport to have the enginer
Hoist with his own petard; and 't shall go hard
But I will delve one yard below their mines
215 And blow them at the moon. O, 'tis most sweet
When in one line two crafts directly meet.
This man shall set me packing.
I'll lug the guts into the neighbor room.
Mother, good night indeed. This counselor
220 Is now most still, most secret, and most grave,
Who was in life a foolish prating knave.—
Come, sir, to draw toward an end with you.
Good night, mother.

[*They exit*, Hamlet *tugging in* Polonius.]

---

185 remains behind: is still to come.

188 bloat: bloated.

189 mouse: a term of endearment.

190 reechy: filthy.

191 paddling in: fingering on.

194 in craft: by clever design or action.

194–202 Although Hamlet has asked his mother not to let Claudius use sexual attentions to unravel the secret that Hamlet is only pretending to be mad, he now sarcastically urges her to go ahead and tell Claudius. He refers to a story about an ape that died trying to imitate the flight of birds it released from a cage, hinting that the Queen will get hurt if she lets out her secret.

208–211 Rosencrantz and Guildenstern have been commanded to escort Hamlet to some treachery.

212–213 to have… petard: to have the maker of military devices blown up (**hoist**) by his own bomb (**petard**).

213–214 and 't… I will: unless I have bad luck I will; **mines:** tunnels.

216 crafts: plots, crafty schemes.

217 Polonius's death will force Hamlet to leave in a hurry.

222 to draw toward an end: to finish up.

CLOSE READ

Drama Elements: Character (sc. 4 LINES 186–223)

 COMMON CORE RL 3

Remind students that killing Polonius was the turning point for Hamlet. As they read the last page of Act III, ask them to look for further evidence of change in Hamlet.

H2 ASK STUDENTS to explain why Hamlet doesn't want Gertrude to be intimate with Claudius again. What is Hamlet afraid might happen? (*He's afraid that if his mother spends time with the King, she will slip up and let him know that Hamlet is only pretending to be mad.*) As the scene closes and Hamlet prepares to drag Polonius from the room, how does he refer to the dead man? What do his words about the dead man reveal about Hamlet? (*Hamlet says about Polonius, "I'll lug the guts into the neighbor room" [line 218]. Then, he says of Polonius, "This counselor / Is now most still, most secret, and most grave, / Who was in life a foolish prating knave." For a man who prides himself on sensitivity, referring to Polonius as "guts" is remarkably callous. And though Polonius was "a foolish prating knave," referring to him in this manner after having murdered him shows Hamlet to have little feeling for anything outside his own personal agenda.*)

Scene 2: The King shows his guilt by leaving the play.

Scene 2: The King arranges to send Hamlet to England.

Scene 3: Hamlet passes up a chance to kill the King.

Scene 3: Hamlet confronts his mother.

Scene 3: Hamlet kills Polonius.

Scene 3: Hamlet sees the Ghost.

PRACTICE & APPLY

Analyzing the Text 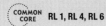 COMMON CORE RL 1, RL 4, RL 6

Possible answers:

1. *His aside tells the audience that he did, indeed, kill his brother.*

2. *Hamlet is cruel to Ophelia, insulting her both in this part of the scene and later, during the play. His crudeness also suggests his disgust with her, which has its source in the disgust he feels for his mother because she married Claudius soon after her husband's death.*

3. *Hamlet admires Horatio's stolid practicality, honesty, and faithfulness. As Hamlet's trusted confidante, Horatio hears the prince's true feelings and plans, thereby allowing Shakespeare to convey such information to his audience.*

4. *Hamlet ostensibly speaks about the play when he says "no offense i' th' world," but he conveys his awareness of the King's treachery and the Queen's disloyalty, which he finds very offensive indeed.*

5. *Hamlet says that playing beautiful music on a recorder is as easy as blowing through it and fingering the stops. In fact, this cannot be done without skill and knowledge of the instrument, any more than Guildenstern can get Hamlet to open up ("Though you can fret me, you cannot play upon me."). His anger reveals his distrust of Rosencrantz and Guildenstern, which has markedly grown since his warm greeting of the pair in Act II.*

6. *The Ghost lamented that since he died "with all my imperfections on my head," he is now destined to burn his unforgiven sins away. Hamlet is determined that Claudius, too, not go directly to heaven, as he would if he were murdered while at prayers.*

7. *Gertrude expresses guilt for marrying Claudius inappropriately (lines 91–93). However, she does not seem to know of his role in the murder, and when Hamlet presses her on that point, she says, "Alas, he's mad."*

8. *Through these events, Shakespeare suggests that thinking and plotting about revenge only makes it more difficult to carry out, since there is no logical reason for pursuing it. Revenge is a thoughtless act motivated by emotion.*

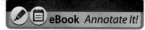 **eBook** *Annotate It!*

Analyzing the Text

COMMON CORE RL 1, RL 4, RL 6, SL 1

Cite Text Evidence Support your responses with evidence from the selection.

1. **Interpret** What does Claudius's aside in Scene 1, lines 50–55, reveal about him?

2. **Draw Conclusions** Hamlet's command "Get thee to a nunnery" (Scene 1, line 122) can be interpreted in two ways. Either he wants Ophelia to retreat to a convent, safe from the corruption of the world, or he thinks she is so tainted that she belongs in a brothel. Choose the interpretation that is best supported by his behavior toward her in this scene, and explain your choice. What has caused him to feel this way?

3. **Analyze** Reread lines 58–76 in Scene 2. What does Hamlet admire about Horatio? How does Shakespeare use Horatio to help develop the play's plot?

4. **Analyze** When a character says one thing but means another, it is called **verbal irony.** Find an example of verbal irony in Hamlet's conversation with Claudius and Gertrude in Scene 2, lines 230–236. What message is Hamlet really conveying?

5. **Analyze** An **extended metaphor** is a metaphor in which two things are compared at length and in various ways. Review Hamlet's dialogue in Scene 2, lines 353–375. In what ways does he compare himself to a musical instrument? Is his attitude toward Rosencrantz and Guildenstern consistent with his behavior toward them in Act II, Scene 2, or does this speech signal a change? Explain.

6. **Identify Patterns** How does Hamlet's refusal to kill Claudius while he is praying relate back to what the Ghost said about the circumstances of his own death in Act I, Scene 5?

7. **Draw Conclusions** Hamlet confronts his mother in Scene 4, and she responds with expressions of guilt. Does she seem to realize that Claudius murdered Hamlet's father? Explain why or why not.

8. **Synthesize** Soon after Hamlet decides against killing Claudius while he is praying, he mistakes Polonius for the King and kills him without hesitation. What does this combination of events suggest about revenge?

PERFORMANCE TASK

Speaking Activity: Performance Act out a brief scene or a section of a longer scene.

- In a small group, choose a scene and decide which role will be played by each member.

- Read the scene aloud. Discuss the motivation of each character.

- Decide where performers will enter or exit and where they will stand while reciting the dialogue. Read the stage directions to determine if any sound or lighting effects are needed.

- Perform the scene in front of the class.

Assign this performance task.  my WriteSmart

PERFORMANCE TASK

 COMMON CORE SL 1

Speaking Activity: Performance To avoid repetition, have each group choose a different scene or assign scenes yourself. Allow the "actors" to read, rather than memorize, their lines. Evaluate their performance on the basis of delivery and appropriate interpretation of content and context.

TEACH

CLOSE READ

Analyze Drama Elements: Plot (LINES 1–32)

Briefly review the plot of Act III. Remind students that the entire action of the third act transpires in the space of an hour or so—including action leading up to the play within a play, the play itself, and the aftermath. Explain that the action in Act IV will move forward faster, as consequences unfold from the killing of Polonius.

 ASK STUDENTS to listen as you read aloud lines 1–32. Ask them why the playwright might have had Rosencrantz and Guildenstern enter as the scene begins, although they have no lines before they exit. (*As they enter and exit, then enter again shortly, Rosencrantz and Guildenstern help contribute to the agitation, the hectic pacing of the opening scene.*) Ask students to describe the Queen's mental state and the King's reaction to her news. How do their emotions affect the opening scene's tone and pace? (*Gertrude is highly distraught over Hamlet's madness and the murder of Polonius. Claudius, too, is distraught. Their volatile emotional state makes for a tense, fast-moving opening scene.*) As the King, it is Claudius's duty to see that justice is done for the murder of Polonius. Does he set the wheels of justice in motion? How does his handling of this crime affect his image with the play's audience? (*At this point, Claudius shows no interest in justice. He wants to get Hamlet out of the way and use his position as King to "countenance and excuse" [line 32] what Hamlet has done. Here is a man in cover-up mode, a far cry from the dignified King who appears at the beginning of Act II.*)

ACT IV

Scene 1 *The Castle.*

[*Enter* King *and* Queen, *with* Rosencrantz *and* Guildenstern.]

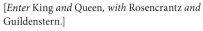

King. There's matter in these sighs; these profound heaves
You must translate; 'tis fit we understand them.
Where is your son?

Queen. Bestow this place on us a little while.

[Rosencrantz *and* Guildenstern *exit*.]

5 Ah, mine own lord, what have I seen tonight!

King. What, Gertrude? How does Hamlet?

Queen. Mad as the sea and wind when both contend
Which is the mightier. In his lawless fit,
Behind the arras hearing something stir,
10 Whips out his rapier, cries "A rat, a rat,"
And in this brainish apprehension kills
The unseen good old man.

King.   O heavy deed!
It had been so with us, had we been there.
His liberty is full of threats to all—
15 To you yourself, to us, to everyone.
Alas, how shall this bloody deed be answered?
It will be laid to us, whose providence
Should have kept short, restrained, and out of haunt
This mad young man. But so much was our love,
20 We would not understand what was most fit,
But, like the owner of a foul disease,
To keep it from divulging, let it feed
Even on the pith of life. Where is he gone?

Queen. To draw apart the body he hath killed,
25 O'er whom his very madness, like some ore
Among a mineral of metals base,
Shows itself pure: he weeps for what is done.

King. O Gertrude, come away!
The sun no sooner shall the mountains touch
30 But we will ship him hence; and this vile deed
We must with all our majesty and skill
Both countenance and excuse.—Ho, Guildenstern!

[*Enter* Rosencrantz *and* Guildenstern.]

Friends both, go join you with some further aid.
Hamlet in madness hath Polonius slain,

1 **matter:** significance.

11 **brainish apprehension:** frenzied belief.

17–19 Claudius worries that the death will be blamed on him (**laid to us**) because he should have had the foresight (**providence**) to keep Hamlet restrained (**short**) and isolated (**out of haunt**).

22 **divulging:** being revealed.

25–26 O're . . . mineral: vein of gold in a mine.

32 **countenance:** accept.

33 **some further aid:** others who can help.

Close Read Screencasts

Modeled Discussions

Have students click the *Close Read* icons in their eBooks to access the screencast in which readers discuss and annotate the following key passage:

- Hamlet's steeling of himself to act (Act IV, Scene 4, lines 58–68)

As a class, view and discuss the video.

Image Credits: ©John Kobal Foundation/Moviepix/Getty Images

312 Collection 4

35 And from his mother's closet hath he dragged him.
Go seek him out, speak fair, and bring the body
Into the chapel. I pray you, haste in this.

[Rosencrantz *and* Guildenstern *exit*.]

B 40 Come, Gertrude, we'll call up our wisest friends
And let them know both what we mean to do
And what's untimely done. . . .
Whose whisper o'er the world's diameter,
As level as the cannon to his blank
Transports his poisoned shot, may miss our name
And hit the woundless air. O, come away!
45 My soul is full of discord and dismay.

[*They exit*.]

Scene 2 *The Castle.*

[*Enter* Hamlet.]

Hamlet. Safely stowed.

Gentlemen [*within*]. Hamlet! Lord Hamlet!

Hamlet. But soft, what noise? Who calls on Hamlet?
O, here they come.

[*Enter* Rosencrantz, Guildenstern, *and others*.]

5 **Rosencrantz.** What have you done, my lord, with the
dead body?

Hamlet. Compounded it with dust, whereto 'tis kin.

Rosencrantz. Tell us where 'tis, that we may take it
thence
And bear it to the chapel.

Hamlet. Do not believe it.

10 **Rosencrantz.** Believe what?

C **Hamlet.** That I can keep your counsel and not mine
own. Besides, to be demanded of a sponge, what
replication should be made by the son of a king?

Rosencrantz. Take you me for a sponge, my lord?

15 **Hamlet.** Ay, sir, that soaks up the King's countenance,
his rewards, his authorities. But such officers do
the King best service in the end. He keeps them like
an ape an apple in the corner of his jaw, first
mouthed, to be last swallowed. When he needs

40–44 Some words are missing after "untimely done" in line 40. Many editors insert "So haply slander" or a similar phrase. Claudius is hoping that slander, which hits as directly as a cannon fired at point-blank range hits its target, will miss the royal household.

6 compounded: mixed. Hamlet alludes to Genesis 3.19: "dust thou art, and unto dust shalt thou return."

12 demanded of: questioned by.

13 replication: response.

15 countenance: favor.

17–18 like an ape . . . jaw: as an ape keeps food in the corner of its mouth.

Hamlet: Act IV, Scene 2 **313**

CLOSE READ

Analyze Drama Elements: Character (LINES 38–45)

Explain that Shakespeare develops many different characters in his plays. Some are very complex, like Hamlet, showing differing sides which provoke mixed reactions. Other characters are more consistent in their actions or thoughts, showing a single overriding characteristic repeatedly and sometimes becoming an archetype for a single set of interests.

B **CITE TEXT EVIDENCE** which shows the King's overriding concern about maintaining his political power. *(Lines 43–44 indicate that he is concerned that what people say concerning Polonius' death will not affect "our name" or reputation and not endanger his hold on the throne.)*

Analyze Structure: Conflict (sc. 2 LINES 9–21)

Ask students to observe Hamlet closely as Act IV unfolds.

C **ASK STUDENTS** to compare Hamlet's behavior with Rosencrantz and Guildenstern to the way he treated them in Act II. *(As in Act II, Hamlet teases and taunts Rosencrantz and Guildenstern, though sometimes in the earlier act, his teasing seemed lighthearted. Here, there is no lightness to Hamlet's treatment of his old friends. He seems purely to despise them.)* Ask students to explain Hamlet's meaning when he calls Rosencrantz a sponge. *(Like a sponge, Rosencrantz "soaks up the King's countenance, / his rewards, his authorities," meaning that Rosencrantz enjoys being liked by the King, being in his presence, getting a vicarious thrill out of the King's power. Hamlet also says that once the King is done with this sponge, he'll squeeze it dry, meaning that when he no longer needs a sponge, Rosencrantz will be done for.)*

WHEN STUDENTS STRUGGLE . . .

Direct students to lines 38–45. Note the missing words mentioned in the side note for lines 40–44 and read the passage aloud, substituting the words "so haply slander" as suggested in the note. Discuss the concerns that the King mentions here. *(He is worried about what others will think and say about the death of Polonius and about how it will affect his power as King.)*

Discuss how this speech helps illustrate the character of the King as he has been portrayed previously. *(The King has been shown to be someone most concerned with his own power and how to keep it. This speech reinforces his scheming and planning to gain and keep power.)*

TEACH

CLOSE READ

Analyze Drama Elements: RL 3
Character (sc. 2 LINES 22–31)

Read this short exchange aloud with students. Concentrate on the tone of the speakers.

 ASK STUDENTS to describe Hamlet's tone here. Is he back to feigning madness, as he did in Act II? *(For someone who has just committed murder and then fallen into a mad rage at his mother, Hamlet has an oddly joking tone in this first scene. This kind of behavior could be an effect of shock. He could be feigning madness. Or it might be in his character simply to indulge in word play and make jokes.)*

Determine Theme RL 2
(sc. 3 LINES 4–5)

Remind students that a skillful playwright weaves themes into the dialogue subtly.

 ASK STUDENTS to discuss the theme echoed in these lines by Claudius. *(One of the play's themes reflects on pleasant appearances and the unpleasantness that lies beneath. In this case, we have the appearance of a popular and handsome young prince, though Claudius knows the reality—that the prince is a cold-blooded murderer.)* Ask students to comment on the irony that Claudius is making this statement. *(Claudius is dismayed by Hamlet as a popular murderer, but that's exactly what Claudius is. He seems unaware of the comparison here, but that makes it all the more powerful.)*

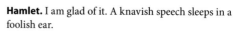

C 20 what you have gleaned, it is but squeezing you, and, sponge, you shall be dry again.

Rosencrantz. I understand you not, my lord.

D **Hamlet.** I am glad of it. A knavish speech sleeps in a foolish ear.

25 **Rosencrantz.** My lord, you must tell us where the body is and go with us to the King.

Hamlet. The body is with the King, but the King is not with the body. The King is a thing—

Guildenstern. A "thing," my lord?

30 **Hamlet.** Of nothing. Bring me to him. Hide fox, and all after!

[*They exit.*]

Scene 3 *The castle.*

[*Enter* King *and two or three.*]

King. I have sent to seek him and to find the body.
How dangerous is it that this man goes loose!
Yet must not we put the strong law on him.
E He's loved of the distracted multitude,
5 Who like not in their judgment, but their eyes;
And, where 'tis so, th' offender's scourge is weighed,
But never the offense. To bear all smooth and even,
This sudden sending him away must seem
Deliberate pause. Diseases desperate grown
10 By desperate appliance are relieved
Or not at all.

[*Enter* Rosencrantz.]

How now, what hath befallen?

Rosencrantz. Where the dead body is bestowed, my lord,
We cannot get from him.

King.   But where is he?

Rosencrantz. Without, my lord; guarded, to know your pleasure.

15 **King.** Bring him before us.

Rosencrantz.   Ho! Bring in the lord.

[*They enter with* Hamlet.]

F **King.** Now, Hamlet, where's Polonius?

Hamlet. At supper.

King. At supper where?

23 sleeps in: is meaningless to.

27–30 Hamlet may be playing off the idea that the king occupies two "bodies": his own mortal body and the office of kingship. Claudius is a king of no account (**of nothing**); the office of kingship does not belong to him.

30 Hide fox . . . after: a cry from a children's game such as hide-and-seek.

4–5 He's loved . . . eyes: He's loved by the confused masses, who choose not by judgment but by appearance.

6 scourge: punishment.

7 To bear . . . even: to manage everything smoothly and evenly.

9 Deliberate pause: carefully thought out.

9–11 Diseases . . . all: Desperate diseases require desperate remedies.

19–21 Hamlet says that a group of crafty (**politic**) worms are dining on him.

314 Collection 4

APPLYING ACADEMIC VOCABULARY

| integrity | restrain |

As you discuss the opening pages, incorporate the Collection 4 academic vocabulary words: *integrity* and *restrain*. Ask students to suggest whether the King shows any **integrity**, especially in relationship to his opening speech of Scene 3, lines 1–11. In discussing the development of the plot, ask students to discuss what efforts Hamlet has made throughout the play to **restrain** himself from showing his strong feelings and how effective those efforts have been.

Hamlet. Not where he eats, but where he is eaten. A
20 certain convocation of politic worms are e'en at
him. Your worm is your only emperor for diet. We
fat all creatures else to fat us, and we fat ourselves
for maggots. Your fat king and your lean beggar is
but variable service—two dishes but to one table.
25 That's the end.

King. Alas, alas!

Hamlet. A man may fish with the worm that hath eat
of a king and eat of the fish that hath fed of that
worm.

30 **King.** What dost thou mean by this?

Hamlet. Nothing but to show you how a king may go
a progress through the guts of a beggar.

King. Where is Polonius?

Hamlet. In heaven. Send thither to see. If your messenger
35 find him not there, seek him i' th' other place
yourself. But if, indeed, you find him not within
this month, you shall nose him as you go up the
stairs into the lobby.

King [*to* Attendants]. Go, seek him there.

40 **Hamlet.** He will stay till you come.

[*Attendants exit.*]

King. Hamlet, this deed, for thine especial safety
(Which we do tender, as we dearly grieve
For that which thou hast done) must send thee hence
With fiery quickness. Therefore prepare thyself.
45 The bark is ready, and the wind at help,
Th' associates tend, and everything is bent
For England.

Hamlet. For England?

King. Ay, Hamlet.

50 **Hamlet.** Good.

King. So is it, if thou knew'st our purposes.

Hamlet. I see a cherub that sees them. But come, for
England.
Farewell, dear mother.

King. Thy loving father, Hamlet.

---

21 Your...diet: Worms have the last word when it comes to eating.

24 but variable service: only different courses (of a meal).

32 progress: royal journey.

42 tender: regard, hold dear.

45–47 Claudius says that the sailing vessel (**bark**) is ready, the wind is favorable (**at help**), his fellow travellers wait (**tend**) for him, and everything is ready (**bent**).

52 cherub: angel of knowledge.

Hamlet: Act IV, Scene 3 **315**

TEACH

CLOSE READ

Determine Figurative Meanings (sc. 3 LINES 17–32)

 COMMON CORE RL 4

Explain that one method Shakespeare uses to make a point is the use of extended **metaphors** in which a direct comparison is made and then the comparison is explored over an extended section of lines.

F CITE TEXT EVIDENCE Ask students to reread lines 18–32 to identify lines in which a metaphor is established and extended. Ask them to describe the meanings of this metaphor. *(In lines 18–25, Hamlet says that Polonius is at dinner, but he's the food. He's being eaten by maggots. Lines 27–32 extend the metaphor by suggesting that a king, when he is dead, might be eaten by worms, which could be used to catch a fish that would in turn be eaten by a beggar.)*

Analyze Drama Elements: Character (sc. 3 LINES 34–40)

 COMMON CORE RL 3

Before reading these lines with students, point out the grimly humorous tone of the passage you have read and discussed with them (above).

G CITE TEXT EVIDENCE Ask students to read these lines closely and then describe Hamlet's attitude toward the King and toward Polonius here. *(Hamlet has a joking attitude, but he is also cold, cruel, and callous. In lines 35–36, Hamlet suggests that the King can essentially go to hell—"th' other place"—to seek Polonius' body if it is not in heaven. He makes a joke of death by saying the stink of Polonius's decomposing body will help Claudius find him. He further mocks Claudius, Polonius, and death by noting that the King's attendants don't need to hurry to find the body because "He will stay till you come.")*

WHEN STUDENTS STRUGGLE . . .

To help students comprehend the contradictions and conflicts within Hamlet, direct them to his exchange with the King in lines 17–38. Have students discuss the following questions:

- What does Hamlet's general attitude appear to be to killing Polonius? *(He seems unconcerned and flippant, not answering the King's questions directly and making word play such as in line 19 about Polonius' death.)*
- What deeper thoughts does Hamlet convey at the same time? *(He considers that all men are mortal and that both kings and beggars are eaten by worms in the end. He shows his penchant for introspection even at the same time as he is treating the King and Polonius disrespectfully.)*

TEACH

CLOSE READ

Analyze Language: Soliloquy (sc. 3 LINES 61–71)

 COMMON CORE RL 4

Explain that a variety of major characters in Shakespeare's plays speak soliloquies, not just the single main character. Remind students that soliloquies are often used so that characters can speak their thoughts to the audience in the same way a third person narrator might describe a character's thoughts in a novel or short story.

H CITE TEXT EVIDENCE Ask students to reread lines 61–71. Have them identify and analyze lines which use figurative language to explain the King's deepest thoughts about Hamlet. *(In lines 69–71, the King uses a simile to compare Hamlet to a disease or "hectic in my blood" that will prevent "my joys" until Hamlet's death "tis done.")* What previously unrevealed plan for Hamlet does Claudius reveal here, and how does it reflect on his character? *(Claudius is sending a sealed letter with Hamlet, asking the King of England to put Hamlet to death. Claudius may feel guilt over his crimes, but he is willing to commit more of them to maintain his grip on power.)*

Analyze Drama Elements: Foil (sc. 4 LINES 1–7)

COMMON CORE RL 3

Explain that a **foil** is a character whose actions contrast sharply with those of another character. Because Hamlet is the central character in the play, other characters may serve as a foil to bring his actions into sharper focus.

I ASK STUDENTS to reread lines 1–7 and consider the introduction of the character Fortinbras. Ask them to compare the character traits expressed in this short speech by Fortinbras with the character shown by Hamlet up until this point. *(Fortinbras appears forceful, certain, and willing to state his intentions plainly. Hamlet up to this point has been responding to the actions of others, uncertain, and unwilling or unable to express his intentions to the Danish king.)*

Hamlet. My mother. Father and mother is man and wife,
55   Man and wife is one flesh, and so, my mother.—
Come, for England.

[*He exits.*]

King. Follow him at foot; tempt him with speed aboard.
Delay it not. I'll have him hence tonight.
Away, for everything is sealed and done
60   That else leans on th' affair. Pray you, make haste.

[*All but the* King *exit.*]

And England, if my love thou hold'st at aught
(As my great power thereof may give thee sense,
Since yet thy cicatrice looks raw and red
After the Danish sword, and thy free awe
65   Pays homage to us), thou mayst not coldly set
Our sovereign process, which imports at full,
By letters congruing to that effect,
The present death of Hamlet. Do it, England,
For like the hectic in my blood he rages,
70   And thou must cure me. Till I know 'tis done,
Howe'er my haps, my joys were ne'er begun.

[*He exits.*]

Scene 4 *Near the coast of Denmark.*

[*Enter* Fortinbras *with his army over the stage.*]

Fortinbras. Go, Captain, from me greet the Danish king.
Tell him that by his license Fortinbras
Craves the conveyance of a promised march
Over his kingdom. You know the rendezvous.
5   If that his Majesty would aught with us,
We shall express our duty in his eye;
And let him know so.

Captain. I will do 't, my lord.

Fortinbras. Go softly on.

[*All but the* Captain *exit.*]

[*Enter* Hamlet, Rosencrantz, Guildenstern, *and others.*]

10   **Hamlet.** Good sir, whose powers are these?

Captain. They are of Norway, sir.

Hamlet. How purposed, sir, I pray you?

Captain. Against some part of Poland.

Hamlet. Who commands them, sir?

15   **Captain.** The nephew to old Norway, Fortinbras.

57 at foot: closely.

60 leans on: is related to.

61–68 Claudius says that if the King of England values his friendship, he will not ignore Claudius's command to have Hamlet killed immediately.

69 hectic: fever.

71 Howe'er my haps: whatever my fortunes.

2 license: permission.

3 the conveyance of: escort during.

5–7 Fortinbras says that if the King wishes to see him, he will show his respect in person (**in his eye**).

9 softly: slowly, carefully.

10 powers: forces.

316   Collection 4

SCAFFOLDING FOR ELL STUDENTS

Understand Punctuation: Apostrophe Review the general uses of an apostrophe *(to form possessives and to indicate missing letters in contractions)*. Remind students that Shakespeare wrote in iambic pentameter which only allows ten syllables per line. To do this, he used contractions or omitted letters to shorten a word by a syllable.

Ask students to give the uses of the apostrophe, the omitted letter(s), and the word's full spelling, and count the number of syllables in each line that has the apostrophe.

- Line 61 "hold'st" *(e is omitted from "holdest" which is an archaic usage, 10 syllables)*
- Line 70 "'tis" *(i is omitted from "it is," 10 syllables)*

Hamlet. Goes it against the main of Poland, sir,
Or for some frontier?

Captain. Truly to speak, and with no addition,
We go to gain a little patch of ground
20 That hath in it no profit but the name.
To pay five ducats, five, I would not farm it;
Nor will it yield to Norway or the Pole
A ranker rate, should it be sold in fee.

Hamlet. Why, then, the Polack never will defend it.

25 **Captain.** Yes, it is already garrisoned.

Hamlet. Two thousand souls and twenty thousand ducats
Will not debate the question of this straw.
This is th' impostume of much wealth and peace,
That inward breaks and shows no cause without
30 Why the man dies.—I humbly thank you, sir.

Captain. God be wi' you, sir.

[*He exits.*]

Rosencrantz. Will 't please you go, my lord?

Hamlet. I'll be with you straight. Go a little before.

[*All but Hamlet exit.*]

How all occasions do inform against me
35 And spur my dull revenge. What is a man
If his chief good and market of his time
Be but to sleep and feed? A beast, no more.
Sure He that made us with such large discourse,
Looking before and after, gave us not
40 That capability and godlike reason
To fust in us unused. Now whether it be
Bestial oblivion or some craven scruple
Of thinking too precisely on th' event
(A thought which, quartered, hath but one part wisdom
45 And ever three parts coward), I do not know
Why yet I live to say "This thing's to do,"
Sith I have cause, and will, and strength, and means
To do 't. Examples gross as earth exhort me:
Witness this army of such mass and charge,
50 Led by a delicate and tender prince,
Whose spirit with divine ambition puffed

16 the main: the main part.

18 Truly ... addition: to speak plainly.

21 To pay ... it: I would not pay even five ducats a year to rent it.

23 ranker: higher; **in fee:** outright.

27 Will not ... straw: are not enough to settle this trifling dispute.

28 impostume: puss-filled swelling.

29 without: on the outside.

34 inform against: denounce.

36 market: profit.

38–41 Sure He ... unused: God would not have given us such a considerable power of reasoning to let it grow moldy from lack of use.

42–43 Bestial ... event: beast-like forgetfulness or cowardly hesitation from thinking too carefully about the outcome.

48 gross: obvious.

TO CHALLENGE STUDENTS ...

Interpret Shakespeare from a Modern Perspective What makes Shakespeare intriguing from a literary standpoint? Discuss the idea that Shakespeare's language can create both surprising understandings and magnificent, timeless images, but can also pose a significant challenge to comprehension and interest. Challenge students to rewrite one of the following passages using modern language more easily understood but which retains the meanings and vivid imagery created by Shakespeare.

- Act IV, Scene 4, lines 16–31
- Act IV, Scene 4, lines 34–48 ending with " ... To do 't."

When writing is complete, ask volunteers to share their work with the class.

CLOSE READ

Determine Themes

(sc. 4 LINES 16–31)

Often, Hamlet has given voice to this play's concern with appearances and reality. Both the character and the play seem deeply disillusioned by the rot and rankness that can lie at the core of a physically attractive person who appears to be decent and honest. Here, Hamlet turns from individuals to whole countries—and a larger sense of futility.

J CITE TEXT EVIDENCE Have students reread lines 16–31 and identify the theme in Hamlet's words and attitude. (*Answers will vary but should touch upon the idea that, without reason, humans will waste much on things that aren't worth the expense, like Fortinbras's army fighting "to gain a little patch of ground / That hath in it no profit but the name."*)

Analyze Language: Soliloquy

(sc. 4 LINES 34–58)

Remind students that Hamlet's previous soliloquy came in Act II—before the play, before Claudius revealed his guilt, before Hamlet murdered Polonius and confronted his mother. Ask them to examine this soliloquy for evidence of change.

K ASK STUDENTS to sum up Hamlet's thinking in lines 34–48. (*Fortinbras's impending attack against Poland is one of the "occasions [that] do inform against me / And spur my dull revenge." Hamlet speaks of the emptiness of life if all we do is eat and sleep like animals and waste our minds [lines 35–41]. He worries that thinking too much makes one a coward [lines 43–45] and asks why he hasn't acted to avenge his father's murder [lines 45–48]).* Have them sum up what Hamlet thinks of Fortinbras, lines 48–58. (*Fortinbras is willing to defend his honor over something as minor as "an eggshell" [line 55]. His greatness lies in defending his honor. Implicitly, Hamlet condemns himself for not having the courage to act that he sees in the Norwegian prince.*)

Analyze Language: Soliloquy (sc. 4 LINES 58–68)

COMMON CORE RL 4

Shakespeare allows Hamlet to use this soliloquy to analyze himself and to express his thoughts for the future.

Ⓛ CITE TEXT EVIDENCE Have students reread lines 58–68 and identify lines in which Shakespeare clearly indicates Hamlet's feelings about himself and how he plans to act in the future. *(In lines 58–67, Hamlet judges himself to be worthy of "shame" because he stands idle, despite just cause for revenge, while Fortinbras risks "The imminent death of twenty-thousand men" for "a fantasy, a trick of fame," a piece of land not big enough to bury the soldiers who will die capturing it. In lines 67–68, Hamlet vows that he will take bloody action in the future.)* Ask students if they believe Hamlet's closing vow. Ask for evidence to support their response. *(Responses will vary. But students will likely see Hamlet as a man who delays and delays and delays, all the while talking about action. They will see that Hamlet is on the way to some kind of exile, that despite his resolution, in England he will have no opportunity to avenge his father's murder. They might see the vow itself as hollow: Hamlet speaks not of action but of words. He says, "O from this time forth / My thoughts be bloody or be nothing worth!")*

Ⓚ
Makes mouths at the invisible event,
Exposing what is mortal and unsure
To all that fortune, death, and danger dare,
55 Even for an eggshell. Rightly to be great
Is not to stir without great argument,
But greatly to find quarrel in a straw
When honor's at the stake. How stand I, then,
That have a father killed, a mother stained,
60 Excitements of my reason and my blood,
Ⓛ
And let all sleep, while to my shame I see
The imminent death of twenty thousand men
That for a fantasy and trick of fame
Go to their graves like beds, fight for a plot
65 Whereon the numbers cannot try the cause,
Which is not tomb enough and continent
To hide the slain? O, from this time forth
My thoughts be bloody or be nothing worth!

[*He exits.*]

Scene 5 *The castle.*

Ⓜ
[*Enter* Horatio, Queen, *and a* Gentleman.]

Queen. I will not speak with her.

Gentleman. She is importunate,
Indeed distract; her mood will needs be pitied.

Queen. What would she have?

5 **Gentleman.** She speaks much of her father, says she hears
There's tricks i' th' world, and hems, and beats her
    heart,
Spurns enviously at straws, speaks things in doubt
That carry but half sense. Her speech is nothing,
Yet the unshaped use of it doth move
10 The hearers to collection. They aim at it
And botch the words up fit to their own thoughts;
Which, as her winks and nods and gestures yield them,
Indeed would make one think there might be thought,
Though nothing sure, yet much unhappily.

15 **Horatio.** 'Twere good she were spoken with, for she
    may strew
Dangerous conjectures in ill-breeding minds.

Queen. Let her come in.

[Gentleman *exits.*]

[*Aside*] To my sick soul (as sin's true nature is),
Each toy seems prologue to some great amiss.

52 Makes mouths . . . event: makes scornful faces at the unforeseeable outcome.

55–58 True greatness does not lie in refraining from action when there is no great cause but in the willingness to fight whenever honor is at stake.

63 fantasy and trick of fame: illusion of honor.

65–67 Whereon . . . slain: The disputed land does not have enough room for so many men to battle on and is too small a burial ground to hold those who will be killed.

3 distract: distracted; **mood . . . pitied:** state of mind must be pitied.

6 tricks: deception.

7 Spurns enviously at straws: takes offense at trifles; **in doubt:** without clear meaning.

8–11 Although Ophelia speaks nonsense, her confused manner of speaking moves her listeners to gather some meaning by patching her words together to fit their conjectures.

16 ill-breeding: intent on making trouble.

19 toy: trifle; **amiss:** misfortune.

Strategies for Annotation   ✎ 🖥 *Annotate it!*

Analyze Language: Soliloquy and Aside

COMMON CORE RL 4

Share these strategies for guided or independent analysis:

- Highlight in yellow soliloquies in the play.
- Highlight in blue any asides in the play.
- Underline any figurative or powerful language.
- On a note, identify whether the language is a simile, metaphor, allusion, or simply powerful or vivid language.

The imminent death of twenty thousand men

That for a fantasy and trick of fame

 simile

Go to their graves like beds, fight for a plot

Whereon the numbers cannot try the cause,

Which is not tomb enough and continent

 powerful language

To hide the slain? O, from this time forth

My thoughts be bloody or be nothing worth!

20 So full of artless jealousy is guilt,
It spills itself in fearing to be spilt.

[*Enter Ophelia distracted.*]

Ophelia. Where is the beauteous Majesty of Denmark?

Queen. How now, Ophelia?

Ophelia [*sings*]. *How should I your true love know*
25 *From another one?*
By his cockle hat and staff
And his sandal shoon.

Queen. Alas, sweet lady, what imports this song?

Ophelia. Say you? Nay, pray you, mark.
30 [*Sings.*] *He is dead and gone, lady,*
He is dead and gone;
At his head a grass-green turf,
At his heels a stone.

Oh, ho!

35 **Queen.** Nay, but Ophelia—

Ophelia. Pray you, mark.

[*Sings.*] *White his shroud as the mountain snow—*

[*Enter King.*]

Queen. Alas, look here, my lord.

Ophelia [*sings*]. *Larded all with sweet flowers;*
40 *Which bewept to the ground did not go*
With true-love showers.

King. How do you, pretty lady?

Ophelia. Well, God dild you. They say the owl was a
baker's daughter. Lord, we know what we are but
45 know not what we may be. God be at your table.

King. Conceit upon her father.

Ophelia. Pray let's have no words of this, but when
they ask you what it means, say you this:
[*Sings.*] *Tomorrow is Saint Valentine's day,*
50 *All in the morning betime,*
And I a maid at your window,
To be your Valentine.
Then up he rose and donned his clothes
And dupped the chamber door,
55 *Let in the maid, that out a maid*
Never departed more.

King. Pretty Ophelia—

20–21 Guilt is so full of clumsy suspicion (**artless jealousy**) that it reveals (**spills**) itself through fear of being revealed.

26 cockle hat: a hat with a scallop shell (worn by pilgrims to show that they had been to an overseas shrine).

27 shoon: shoes.

28 imports: means.

39 Larded: decorated.

41 showers: tears

43 God dild you: God yield, or reward, you.

43–44 Ophelia refers to a legend about a baker's daughter who was turned into an owl because she refused to give Christ bread.

46 Conceit: brooding.

49–67 This song refers to the ancient custom that the first maiden a man sees on St. Valentine's Day will be his sweetheart.

54 dupped: opened.

Hamlet: Act IV, Scene 5 **319**

Analyze Drama Elements: Plot (sc. 5 LINES 1–21)

COMMON CORE RL 3

Tell students that by letting his hero be taken away, Shakespeare has taken a great risk with his play. In Hamlet's absence, the plot must go on.

M CITE TEXT EVIDENCE Read lines 1–21 aloud with students. Point out that this scene begins not with action but with news of offstage developments. Ask them to summarize the news. *(Ophelia has gone mad. She speaks of her father, but she is incoherent. She wants to see the Queen, though the Queen appears afraid to see her.)* Ask students to infer the cause of Ophelia's madness and to support their inferences with evidence from the play. *(Ophelia could be mad with grief over her father's murder. In early scenes with him, she was loyal and obedient to Polonius and seemed to genuinely love him. Another cause of her madness might be Hamlet, who professed love for her but then, during his pretended madness, treated her cruelly, and later, in a rash act that has had him exiled, murdered her father.)*

Analyze Drama Elements: Character (sc. 5 LINES 22–56)

COMMON CORE RL 3

Ask students to observe Ophelia closely during her first appearance since her father's death and the news that she has gone mad.

N ASK STUDENTS to find evidence in Ophelia's spoken lines and songs that her father's death and Hamlet's cruelty are on her mind. *(She sings of a man who is dead and buried, of his grave and the flowers on it—clear references to the death of Polonius. Her first song [lines 24–25] could be related to Hamlet: "How should I your true love know / From another one?" Her last song [lines 49–56] is a bawdy lyric about a lover who uses and then leaves women. Though Hamlet treated her as if she'd betrayed him, she might have experienced his cruel treatment earlier in the play as betrayal, and surely killing her father is beyond even casual betrayal.)*

Determine Theme and Analyze Structure:
Conflict (sc. 5 LINES 76–97)

COMMON CORE **RL 2, RL 3**

Ask students to observe Claudius closely for any signs of change.

○ ASK STUDENTS to reread lines 76–87 and identify the events that are causing emotional and moral conflict for Claudius. *(the murder of Polonius; Hamlet's exile to England; the people of Denmark "muddied, / Thick, and unwholesome in their thoughts and whispers" over Polonius's death and the fact that the King has had him quickly buried; Ophelia's madness.)* In lines 88–95, Claudius delivers news the audience has not yet heard. What is this news and how does it add to the conflicts Claudius experiences at this moment in the play? *(Ophelia's brother Laertes has secretly returned from France, clearly upset by his father's death. Laertes' return increases the pressure on Claudius because as son and brother, he will want answers about his father's death and his sister's madness.)* Ask students to examine the entire speech and the closing lines for evidence of a change in the King. *(This is the most distraught language Claudius has used in the presence of another character. He sounds as upset as he did earlier, in his Act III soliloquy, when he agonized over his crime and his inability to repent. The bad news coming at him is like a dagger, "a murd'ring piece" stabbing him "in many places" [line 96].)*

Ophelia. Indeed, without an oath, I'll make an end on 't:
[*Sings.*] *By Gis and by Saint Charity,*
60   *Alack and fie for shame,*
Young men will do 't, if they come to 't;
      By Cock, they are to blame.
Quoth she "Before you tumbled me,
      You promised me to wed."
65 He answers:
"So would I 'a done, by yonder sun,
      An thou hadst not come to my bed."

King. How long hath she been thus?

Ophelia. I hope all will be well. We must be patient,
70 but I cannot choose but weep to think they would
lay him i' th' cold ground. My brother shall know
of it. And so I thank you for your good counsel.
Come, my coach! Good night, ladies, good night,
sweet ladies, good night, good night.

[*She exits.*]

75 **King.** Follow her close; give her good watch, I pray you.

[Horatio *exits.*]

O, this is the poison of deep grief. It springs
All from her father's death, and now behold!
O Gertrude, Gertrude,
When sorrows come, they come not single spies,
80 But in battalions: first, her father slain;
Next, your son gone, and he most violent author
Of his own just remove; the people muddied,
Thick, and unwholesome in their thoughts and
      whispers
For good Polonius' death, and we have done but
      greenly
85 In hugger-mugger to inter him; poor Ophelia
Divided from herself and her fair judgment,
Without the which we are pictures or mere beasts;
Last, and as much containing as all these,
Her brother is in secret come from France,
90 Feeds on his wonder, keeps himself in clouds,
And wants not buzzers to infect his ear
With pestilent speeches of his father's death,
Wherein necessity, of matter beggared,
Will nothing stick our person to arraign
95 In ear and ear. O, my dear Gertrude, this,
Like to a murd'ring piece, in many places
Gives me superfluous death.

59 Gis: Jesus.

62 Cock: a substitution for "God" in oaths.

63 tumbled: had sexual intercourse with.

79 spies: soldiers sent ahead as scouts.

82 muddied: confused.

84–85 Claudius says that he has only acted foolishly (**greenly**) by burying Polonius in haste and secrecy.

89–95 Laertes, who has secretly returned from France, is clouded by suspicion and does not lack gossipers who spread rumors of his father's death. And in the absence of facts, the need for some explanation means that Claudius will be accused of the crime.

96 murd'ring piece: a cannon that can kill many men simultaneously with its scattered shot.

97 Gives . . . death: kills me over and over.

SCAFFOLDING FOR ELL STUDENTS

Understand Language: Possessives Review the process of forming possessive nouns in English *(adding an apostrophe and an s in most cases or possibly just an apostrophe for a noun ending in s).*

ASK STUDENTS to review the following possessives and identify the two words which are linked by the possessive and an alternate way of saying the same thing.

- Scene 5 line 78 "father's" *(father and death, the death of her father)*
- Scene 5 line 84 "Polonius'" *(Polonius and death, the death of Polonius)*
- Scene 5 line 93 "father's" *(father and death, the death of his father)*
- Scene 5 line 206 "Christians'" *(Christians and souls, the souls of Christians)*

[*A noise within.*]

Queen. Alack, what noise is this?

King. Attend!
100 Where is my Switzers? Let them guard the door.

[*Enter a* Messenger.]

What is the matter?

Messenger. Save yourself, my lord.
The ocean, overpeering of his list,
Eats not the flats with more impiteous haste
Than young Laertes, in a riotous head,
105 O'erbears your officers. The rabble call him "lord,"
And, as the world were now but to begin,
Antiquity forgot, custom not known,
The ratifiers and props of every word,
They cry "Choose we, Laertes shall be king!"
110 Caps, hands, and tongues applaud it to the clouds,
"Laertes shall be king! Laertes king!"

[*A noise within.*]

Queen. How cheerfully on the false trail they cry.
O, this is counter, you false Danish dogs!

King. The doors are broke.

[*Enter* Laertes *with others.*]

115 **Laertes.** Where is this king?—Sirs, stand you all without.

All. No, let's come in!

Laertes. I pray you, give me leave.

All. We will, we will.

Laertes. I thank you. Keep the door. [*Followers exit.*] O,
thou vile king,
120 Give me my father!

Queen. Calmly, good Laertes.

Laertes. That drop of blood that's calm proclaims me
bastard,
Cries "cuckold" to my father, brands the harlot
Even here between the chaste unsmirchèd brow
Of my true mother.

King. What is the cause, Laertes,
125 That thy rebellion looks so giant-like?—
Let him go, Gertrude. Do not fear our person.
There's such divinity doth hedge a king
That treason can but peep to what it would,

100 Switzers: Swiss bodyguards.

102–105 Laertes is overpowering Claudius's officers as quickly as the ocean, rising above its boundary (**list**), floods the level ground.

106–108 as the world . . . word: as if the world had just begun, and ancient tradition and custom, which should confirm and support everything one says, were both forgotten.

110 Caps: caps thrown into the air.

113 counter: a hunting term that means "to follow a trail in the wrong direction."

121–124 Laertes says that no true son could be calm about his father's murder—that being calm would in effect prove that son to be a bastard.

122 cuckold: a man whose wife is unfaithful.

124 true: faithful.

CLOSE READ

Analyze Drama Elements: Foil (sc. 5 LINES 102–120)

 COMMON CORE RL 3

Review the definition of a **foil** as a character whose traits contrast with those of another character, even though the two characters may be facing similar situations.

P ASK STUDENTS to reread lines 102–120. Have them consider this initial description of Laertes, identify the similarities in the situation facing both Laertes and Hamlet, and tell how their character traits are clearly different. *(Both Hamlet and Laertes have lost a father and arrive in Denmark to find out the circumstances related to the death. Hamlet is described as beloved by the people but has not rallied any support from them and has not prepared to take any action. Laertes arrives at the castle with a band of followers who wish him to be king, and he is clearly willing to take action, even defying the King in a very public setting.)*

Analyze Drama Elements:
Foil (sc. 5 LINES 135–141)   COMMON CORE RL 3

Explain that characters in dramas often reveal themselves through impassioned speech. This speech by Laertes shows his passion and his intent.

 ASK STUDENTS to reread lines 135–141. Have them describe Laertes' strongly stated, public intentions and compare them with the way that Hamlet has approached the issue of his father's death. *(Laertes is determined to get revenge for his father even if it means renouncing his "allegiance" and "conscience and grace," and risking "damnation." Hamlet desires a bloody revenge but has not managed to state his intentions to anyone or state his absolute dedication to it regardless of bad results such as "damnation.")*

Acts little of his will.—Tell me, Laertes,
130 Why thou art thus incensed.—Let him go,
   Gertrude.—
Speak, man.

Laertes. Where is my father?

King. Dead.

Queen. But not by him.

King.   Let him demand his fill.

135 **Laertes.** How came he dead? I'll not be juggled with.
To hell, allegiance! Vows, to the blackest devil!
Conscience and grace, to the profoundest pit!
I dare damnation. To this point I stand,
That both the worlds I give to negligence,
140 Let come what comes, only I'll be revenged
Most throughly for my father.

King. Who shall stay you?

Laertes. My will, not all the world.
And for my means, I'll husband them so well
145 They shall go far with little.

King.   Good Laertes,
If you desire to know the certainty
Of your dear father, is 't writ in your revenge
That, swoopstake, you will draw both friend and
   foe,
Winner and loser?

150 **Laertes.** None but his enemies.

King. Will you know them, then?

Laertes. To his good friends thus wide I'll ope my arms
And, like the kind life-rend'ring pelican,
Repast them with my blood.

King.   Why, now you speak
155 Like a good child and a true gentleman.
That I am guiltless of your father's death
And am most sensibly in grief for it,
It shall as level to your judgment 'pear
As day does to your eye.
                [*A noise within*] Let her come in.

160 **Laertes.** How now, what noise is that?

[*Enter* Ophelia.]

 O heat, dry up my brains! Tears seven times salt
Burn out the sense and virtue of mine eye!

126–129 Claudius tells Gertrude not to fear for his personal safety; so much divinity protects (**doth hedge**) a king that treason can only peer (**peep**) from afar at what it would like to do.

135 juggled with: played with, deceived.

144 husband: manage, conserve.

148 swoopstake: a gambling term that means taking all the stakes on the gambling table.

153 pelican: traditionally thought to feed its young with its own blood.

157 sensibly: feelingly.

158 level: plain.

162 virtue: power.

APPLYING ACADEMIC VOCABULARY

mediate	trigger

As you discuss the opening pages, incorporate the Collection 4 academic vocabulary words: *mediate* and *trigger*. Ask students to review the confrontation between Laertes and the King and how the Queen tries to **mediate** their conflict. In discussing Ophelia's madness, ask students what emotions she **triggers** in Laertes by her behavior.

By heaven, thy madness shall be paid with weight
Till our scale turn the beam! O rose of May,
165   Dear maid, kind sister, sweet Ophelia!
O heavens, is 't possible a young maid's wits
Should be as mortal as an old man's life?
Nature is fine in love, and, where 'tis fine,
It sends some precious instance of itself
170   After the thing it loves.

Ophelia [*sings*]. *They bore him barefaced on the bier,*
   Hey non nonny, nonny, hey nonny,
   And in his grave rained many a tear.
Fare you well, my dove.

175   **Laertes.** Hadst thou thy wits and didst persuade revenge,
It could not move thus.

Ophelia. You must sing "A-down a-down"—and you
"Call him a-down-a."—O, how the wheel becomes
it! It is the false steward that stole his master's
180   daughter.

Laertes. This nothing's more than matter.

Ophelia. There's rosemary, that's for remembrance.
Pray you, love, remember. And there is pansies,
that's for thoughts.

185   **Laertes.** A document in madness: thoughts and
remembrance fitted.

Ophelia. There's fennel for you, and columbines.
There's rue for you, and here's some for me; we
may call it herb of grace o' Sundays. You must
190   wear your rue with a difference. There's a daisy. I
would give you some violets, but they withered all
when my father died. They say he made a good end.
[*Sings.*] *For bonny sweet Robin is all my joy.*

Laertes. Thought and afflictions, passion, hell itself
195   She turns to favor and to prettiness.

Ophelia [*sings*].
And will he not come again?
And will he not come again?
   No, no, he is dead.
   Go to thy deathbed.
200   *He never will come again.*

   His beard was as white as snow,
   All flaxen was his poll.
   He is gone, he is gone,
   And we cast away moan.
205   *God 'a mercy on his soul.*

163–164 In his vow to revenge Ophelia's madness, Laertes uses the image of weights being placed on a scale to make it tilt in the opposite direction.
168–169 fine in: refined by; **instance:** token (suggesting that Ophelia has sent her sanity into the grave with her father).
175 persuade: argue rationally for.
176 move thus: have such an effect.
177–178 Ophelia assigns refrains to the others so they can join in the singing.
178 the wheel: perhaps referring to the refrain or a spinning wheel that accompanies the singing.
181 This . . . matter: This nonsense has more meaning than rational speech.
182–192 Rosemary was used to symbolize remembrance at funerals. **Pansies**, a name derived from the French word for thought, **pensée**, was associated with courtship. Ophelia also mentions **fennel** (flattery), **columbines** (adultery or ingratitude), **rue** (repentance, sorrow), the **daisy** (dissembling, false love) and **violets** (faithfulness).
185–186 Laertes finds a lesson (**document**) in Ophelia's linking of thoughts and remembrance.
194 Thought: melancholy; **passion:** suffering.
202 flaxen: pale yellow; **poll:** head.
204 cast away: scatter uselessly.

CLOSE READ

Analyze Drama Elements: Foil (sc. 5 LINES 161–170)

COMMON CORE RL 3

Remind students that they have seen passionate anger and an insistence on justice in Laertes in this scene. Ask them to examine lines 161–170 for evidence of other emotions.

R **CITE TEXT EVIDENCE** Ask students to characterize Laertes' emotional state here and to comment again on Laertes as a foil to Hamlet. (*Emotional state: Where before Laertes' was passionately angry, here his emotions turn to horror and intense sympathy for his sister in her stricken state. He begins by invoking tears: "Tears seven times salt / Burn out the sense and virtue of mine eye." He pays tribute to her: "O rose of May, / Dear maid, kind sister, sweet Ophelia!" Foil to Hamlet: Hamlet has shown little of the kindred feeling we see here in Laertes, little sympathy for the plight of others. In fact, Hamlet has been singularly cruel to Ophelia, the woman he supposedly loves, singularly indifferent to her fate.*)

Analyze Drama Elements: **COMMON CORE RL 3**
Foreshadowing

(sc. 5 LINES 209–226)

A common technique to build tension in drama for following scenes is **foreshadowing** which leads readers or viewers to guess at what might happen later.

S CITE TEXT EVIDENCE Ask students to reread lines 209–226 to identify lines which foreshadow future events. *(Claudius promises Laertes satisfaction and even hints at a future event of some kind: "we shall jointly labor with your soul / To give it due content" [lines 218–219]. In speaking of the justice Laertes demands, the King states further: "where th' offense is, let the great ax fall" [line 225]. These statements foreshadow a plot of some kind to bring down Hamlet.)*

And of all Christians' souls, I pray God. God be
wi' you.

[*She exits.*]

Laertes. Do you see this, O God?

King. Laertes, I must commune with your grief,
210   Or you deny me right. Go but apart,
Make choice of whom your wisest friends you will,
And they shall hear and judge 'twixt you and me.
If by direct or by collateral hand
They find us touched, we will our kingdom give,
215   Our crown, our life, and all that we call ours,
To you in satisfaction; but if not,
Be you content to lend your patience to us,
And we shall jointly labor with your soul
To give it due content.

Laertes.   Let this be so.
220   His means of death, his obscure funeral
(No trophy, sword, nor hatchment o'er his bones,
No noble rite nor formal ostentation)
Cry to be heard, as 'twere from heaven to earth,
That I must call 't in question.

King.   So you shall,
225   And where th' offense is, let the great ax fall.
I pray you, go with me.

[*They exit.*]

Scene 6 *The castle.*

[*Enter* Horatio *and others.*]

Horatio. What are they that would speak with me?

Gentleman. Seafaring men, sir. They say they have letters for you.

Horatio. Let them come in. [*Gentleman exits.*] I do not
5   know from what part of the world I should be
greeted, if not from Lord Hamlet.

[*Enter* Sailors.]

Sailor. God bless you, sir.

Horatio. Let Him bless thee too.

Sailor. He shall, sir, an 't please Him. There's a letter
10   for you, sir. It came from th' ambassador that was
bound for England—if your name be Horatio, as I
am let to know it is.

213 collateral: indirect.

214 find us touched: find me implicated.

221–222 The traditional burial ceremony (**ostentation**) for a knight included hanging his helmet, sword, and a tablet displaying his coat of arms (**hatchment**) over the tomb.

224 That I . . . question: so that I must demand an explanation.

9 an 't: if it.

10 th' ambassador: Hamlet.

WHEN STUDENTS STRUGGLE . . .

To develop reading fluency, have pairs of students read lines 209–226 aloud by alternating sentences. Direct them to pay attention to commas for pacing, but especially concentrate on periods to help define ideas and to alert them when to change readers. When one reading is complete, they should read the passage again with the other student reading the first sentence. When two readings are complete, have students summarize the content of the passage and share their summaries with the class. Discuss differing opinions on what the King and Laertes are saying in the passage.

[*He hands* Horatio *a letter.*]

Horatio [*reads the letter*]. *Horatio, when thou shalt*
have overlooked this, give these fellows some means
15 *to the King. They have letters for him. Ere we*
were two days old at sea, a pirate of very warlike
appointment gave us chase. Finding ourselves too
slow of sail, we put on a compelled valor, and in the
grapple I boarded them. On the instant, they got
20 *clear of our ship; so I alone became their prisoner.*
They have dealt with me like thieves of mercy, but
they knew what they did: I am to do a good turn
for them. Let the King have the letters I have sent,
and repair thou to me with as much speed as thou
25 *wouldst fly death. I have words to speak in thine*
ear will make thee dumb; yet are they much too
light for the bore of the matter. These good fellows
will bring thee where I am. Rosencrantz and
Guildenstern hold their course for England; of
30 *them I have much to tell thee. Farewell.*
He that thou knowest thine, Hamlet.

Come, I will give you way for these your letters
And do 't the speedier that you may direct me
To him from whom you brought them.

[*They exit.*]

Scene 7 *The castle.*

[*Enter* King *and* Laertes.]

King. Now must your conscience my acquittance seal,
And you must put me in your heart for friend,
Sith you have heard, and with a knowing ear,
That he which hath your noble father slain
5   Pursued my life.

Laertes.   It well appears. But tell me
Why you proceeded not against these feats,
So criminal and so capital in nature,
As by your safety, greatness, wisdom, all things else,
You mainly were stirred up.

10 **King.** O, for two special reasons,
Which may to you perhaps seem much unsinewed,
But yet to me they're strong. The Queen his mother
Lives almost by his looks, and for myself
(My virtue or my plague, be it either which),

14 **overlooked:** read;
means: means of access.

16–17 **pirate . . .**
appointment: pirate
ship well equipped for
warfare.

21 **thieves of mercy:**
merciful thieves.

22 **they knew what**
they did: their actions
were calculated.

24 **repair:** come.

27 **light . . . bore:**
inadequate for the
importance.

32 **way:** means of
access.

1 **my acquittance seal:**
confirm my innocence.

3 **Sith:** since.

7 **capital:** punishable by
death.

8 **safety:** concern for
your safety.

9 **mainly:** greatly.

11 **unsinewed:** weak.

Analyze Drama Elements: **RL 3**
Plot (sc. 6 LINES 13–31)

Note that sometimes playwrights rely on outside
events to advance the plot. In some cases, they may
include highly improbable events.

ASK STUDENTS to examine Hamlet's letter to
Horatio, to summarize the events related in the letter,
and to comment on their plausibility. (*Hamlet's letter*
says that the ship he was traveling on was attacked by
pirates, that he was the only one captured, and that the
ship carrying Rosencrantz and Guildenstern continued
to England, while Hamlet persuaded the pirates to bring
him back to Denmark and release him. Students may
recognize this as a rather implausible turn of events but
one that is necessary for the plot to advance and bring
Hamlet back to the Danish court.)

CLOSE READ

Analyze Drama Elements: Plot

COMMON CORE RL 3

(sc. 7 LINES 10–36)

As Scene 7 begins, Laertes asks Claudius why he has done nothing to bring Hamlet to justice. As Claudius answers Laertes and the two interact, Shakespeare moves the plot forward.

 ASK STUDENTS to read lines10–25 closely and sum up the reasons—or excuses—Claudius gives Laertes. *(Claudius provides two reasons for having delayed punishment of Hamlet. The first is that "the Queen his mother / Lives almost by his looks" [lines 12–13]. In other words, Claudius has delayed justice because his wife loves her son. The second is "the great love the general gender bear him" [line 19]: Hamlet is so popular with Danish citizens that where he has vices, they see "graces" [line 22].)* Ask students to notice that Laertes remains determined, saying "my revenge will come" [line 30]. Finally, ask students to examine lines 31–36 and indentify foreshadowing in what Claudius says. *(Here again, Claudius hints at satsifaction for Laertes: "You shortly shall hear more" [line 34].)*

---

15 She is so conjunctive to my life and soul
That, as the star moves not but in his sphere,
I could not but by her. The other motive
Why to a public count I might not go
Is the great love the general gender bear him,
20 Who, dipping all his faults in their affection,
Work like the spring that turneth wood to stone,
Convert his gyves to graces, so that my arrows,
Too slightly timbered for so loud a wind,
Would have reverted to my bow again,
25 But not where I have aimed them.

Laertes. And so have I a noble father lost,
A sister driven into desp'rate terms,
Whose worth, if praises may go back again,
Stood challenger on mount of all the age
30 For her perfections. But my revenge will come.

King. Break not your sleeps for that. You must not think
That we are made of stuff so flat and dull
That we can let our beard be shook with danger
And think it pastime. You shortly shall hear more.
35 I loved your father, and we love ourself,
And that, I hope, will teach you to imagine—

[*Enter a* Messenger *with letters.*]

How now? What news?

Messenger.   Letters, my lord, from Hamlet.
These to your Majesty, this to the Queen.

King. From Hamlet? Who brought them?

40 **Messenger.** Sailors, my lord, they say. I saw them not.
They were given me by Claudio. He received them
Of him that brought them.

King.   Laertes, you shall hear them.—
Leave us.

[Messenger *exits.*]

[*Reads.*] *High and mighty, you shall know I am set*
45 *naked on your kingdom. Tomorrow shall I beg*
leave to see your kingly eyes, when I shall (first
asking your pardon) thereunto recount the occasion
of my sudden and more strange return. Hamlet.
What should this mean? Are all the rest come back?
50 Or is it some abuse and no such thing?

Laertes. Know you the hand?

---

15 conjunctive: closely joined.

16 star...sphere: In Shakespeare's time, it was believed that each planet moves around the Earth in a hollow sphere.

18 count: account, indictment.

19–25 Claudius says that the common people (**general gender**), through their love for Hamlet, act like a spring with such a high concentration of lime that wood placed in it will become petrified; they change his limitations (**gyves**) into attractive qualities, so that the strong wind of their approval would blow back any arrows that Claudius might shoot at Hamlet.

27 terms: condition.

28–30 Whose worth ... perfections: If praises can recall Ophelia's former self, her worth placed her at the top of the age.

45 naked: destitute, defenseless.

50 Claudius wonders if this is a deception and no such thing has occurred.

TO CHALLENGE STUDENTS...

Change Point of View How would parts of the play change if told from a different perspective? Direct students to review the King's explanation of his reasons for doing nothing about Hamlet's killing of Polonius in Scene 7, lines 10–25. Discuss the King's character and whether students trust his words of explanation.

Challenge students to write a journal entry from the point of view of the King in which he discusses the possible actions he might have taken against Hamlet and why he chose to delay any actions against him. If students' don't believe his explanations, they should detail what they believe his real motives were. If they do believe his explanation, they should explain them in the journal entry. They should try to mimic the King's speaking style in their journal entry. When work is complete, ask volunteers to share their work with the class.

Image Credits: ©Hulton Archive/Getty Images

King. 'Tis Hamlet's character. "Naked"—
And in a postscript here, he says "alone."
Can you advise me?

55 **Laertes.** I am lost in it, my lord. But let him come.
It warms the very sickness in my heart
That I shall live and tell him to his teeth
"Thus didst thou."

King.   If it be so, Laertes
(As how should it be so? how otherwise?),
60 Will you be ruled by me?

Laertes.   Ay, my lord,
So you will not o'errule me to a peace.

King. To thine own peace. If he be now returned,
As checking at his voyage, and that he means
No more to undertake it, I will work him
65 To an exploit, now ripe in my device,
Under the which he shall not choose but fall;
And for his death no wind of blame shall breathe,
But even his mother shall uncharge the practice
And call it accident.

70 **Laertes.** My lord, I will be ruled,
The rather if you could devise it so
That I might be the organ.

King.   It falls right.
You have been talked of since your travel much,

52 **character:** handwriting.

61 **So:** as long as.

63 **checking at:** turning away from.
65 **device:** devising.

68 **uncharge the practice:** not blame the plot.

72 **organ:** agent, instrument.

Hamlet: Act IV, Scene 7 **327**

CLOSE READ

Determine Figurative Meanings (sc. 7 LINES 56–58)

COMMON CORE RL 4

Explain that in certain cases, Shakespeare uses very surprising combinations of images to make a characterization memorable.

Ⓥ **ASK STUDENTS** to examine lines 56–58 and describe the surprising imagery used by Shakespeare to illustrate Laertes' feeling. *(In line 56, Laertes describes something happening which "warms" his "heart." However, it is not the pleasant feeling that might come from a welcome visit of a loved one, but one which warms the "sickness in my heart"—the opportunity to confront Hamlet face-to-face, clearly with violence in mind. Here Shakespeare combines warmth of heart with sickness of heart and warm-hearted anticipation with a desire for violence.)*

CLOSE READ

Analyze Drama Elements: Character COMMON CORE RL 3
(sc. 7 LINES 98–109)

Explain that characters may be developed by other characters' descriptions of them. Students need to assess whether the other character is a reliable witness and provides accurate descriptions.

Ⓦ CITE TEXT EVIDENCE Ask students to examine lines 98–109 and identify the lines which describe Hamlet's character. Ask them if they think this description is accurate and why. *(Hamlet is described as filled with "envy" at the description of Laertes' skill at fencing [lines 105–108]. Although the King has no love for Hamlet, this description is consistent with Hamlet's behavior in the play thus far. He has displayed an obsessive concern with his own image in front of others.)*

And that in Hamlet's hearing, for a quality
75 Wherein they say you shine. Your sum of parts
Did not together pluck such envy from him
As did that one, and that, in my regard,
Of the unworthiest siege.

Laertes. What part is that, my lord?

80 **King.** A very ribbon in the cap of youth—
Yet needful too, for youth no less becomes
The light and careless livery that it wears
Than settled age his sables and his weeds,
Importing health and graveness. Two months since
85 Here was a gentleman of Normandy.
I have seen myself, and served against, the French,
And they can well on horseback, but this gallant
Had witchcraft in 't. He grew unto his seat,
And to such wondrous doing brought his horse
90 As had he been encorpsed and demi-natured
With the brave beast. So far he topped my thought
That I in forgery of shapes and tricks
Come short of what he did.

Laertes.   A Norman was 't?

King. A Norman.

95 **Laertes.** Upon my life, Lamord.

King.   The very same.

Laertes. I know him well. He is the brooch indeed
And gem of all the nation.

King. He made confession of you
And gave you such a masterly report
100 For art and exercise in your defense,
And for your rapier most especial,
That he cried out 'twould be a sight indeed
If one could match you. The 'scrimers of their nation
He swore had neither motion, guard, nor eye,
105 If you opposed them. Sir, this report of his
Did Hamlet so envenom with his envy
That he could nothing do but wish and beg
Your sudden coming-o'er, to play with you.
Now out of this—

Laertes.   What out of this, my lord?

75–84 The rest of Laertes's qualities combined did not inspire as much envy in Hamlet as this one, which ranks lowest in Claudius's regard. Yet this quality is important even if only a mere decoration (**very ribbon**), because light, carefree clothes (**livery**) are as well-suited to youth as more richly trimmed or sober clothes (**his sables and his weeds**) are to old age, suggesting well-being and dignity.

87 can well: are skillful.

90–91 encorpsed . . . beast: as if he and the horse shared the same body, a double-natured beast (like the mythical centaur, half man and half horse).

91–93 His feats surpassed the ability of Claudius's imagination to reconstruct them.

96 brooch: ornament.

98 made confession of: testified about.

100 art . . . defence: skill and practice in fencing.

103 'scrimers: fencers.

108 play: fence.

SCAFFOLDING FOR ELL STUDENTS

Understand Time Sequence Point out that in lines 80–109, the King lays out the background for a plan to kill Hamlet. Ask students to identify the lines which indicate what time period the King is discussing. *(line 84 "Two months since")* Then direct their attention to Hamlet's actions as described in lines 105–109 and discuss those actions. When did Hamlet's actions occur? *(also two months before)* Why are these previous actions by Hamlet important? *(The King believes he can trick Hamlet into a fencing match with Laertes which will prove deadly to Hamlet.)*

110 **King.** Laertes, was your father dear to you?
Or are you like the painting of a sorrow,
A face without a heart?

Laertes.   Why ask you this?

King. Not that I think you did not love your father,
But that I know love is begun by time
115 And that I see, in passages of proof,
Time qualifies the spark and fire of it.
There lives within the very flame of love
A kind of wick or snuff that will abate it,
And nothing is at a like goodness still;
120 For goodness, growing to a pleurisy,
Dies in his own too-much. That we would do
We should do when we would; for this "would"
    changes
And hath abatements and delays as many
As there are tongues, are hands, are accidents;
125 And then this "should" is like a spendthrift sigh,
That hurts by easing. But to the quick of th' ulcer:
Hamlet comes back; what would you undertake
To show yourself indeed your father's son
More than in words?

Laertes.   To cut his throat i' th' church.

130 **King.** No place indeed should murder sanctuarize;
Revenge should have no bounds. But, good Laertes,
Will you do this? Keep close within your chamber.
Hamlet, returned, shall know you are come home.
We'll put on those shall praise your excellence
135 And set a double varnish on the fame
The Frenchman gave you; bring you, in fine, together
And wager on your heads. He, being remiss,
Most generous, and free from all contriving,
Will not peruse the foils, so that with ease,
140 Or with a little shuffling, you may choose
A sword unbated, and in a pass of practice
Requite him for your father.

Laertes.   I will do 't,
And for that purpose I'll anoint my sword.
I bought an unction of a mountebank
145 So mortal that, but dip a knife in it,
Where it draws blood no cataplasm so rare,

114 begun by time: created by circumstance.

119 nothing . . . still: Nothing remains at the same level of goodness.

120 pleurisy: excess.

121 his own too-much: its own excess.

121–122 That we . . . would: If one wishes to do something, one should act right away.

123 abatements: lessenings.

125–126 spendthrift sigh . . . easing: an allusion to the idea that sighing brings temporary relief but weakens the heart.

130 should murder sanctuarize: should protect a murderer from punishment.

134 put on those shall: arrange for people to.

136 in fine: finally.

137 remiss: carelessly unsuspicious.

138 generous: noble-minded

141 unbated: not blunted; **pass of practice:** treacherous thrust.

144–149 Laertes bought from a quack doctor an ointment (**unction**) so deadly that no medical dressing (**cataplasm**) can save anyone scratched by it.

Hamlet: Act IV, Scene 7 **329**

Analyze Drama Elements: Character (sc. 7 LINES 110–129)

As they examine this exchange between Claudius and Laertes ask students to keep in mind what they know about each character.

 ASK STUDENTS to describe how Claudius baits Laertes and what these lines reveal about the King's character. *(Claudius questions whether Laertes really loved his father [lines 110–112] and wonders aloud if his love won't fade with time [lines 116-121]. Baiting Laertes in this fashion shows that Claudius has a shrewd understanding of Laertes. He knows that by questioning Laertes' love for his father, he will sharpen Laertes' determination to avenge Polonius' death. He all but assures that when he tells Laertes that Hamlet has returned and asks what Laertes is willing to do, Laertes says "To cut his throat i' th' church.")*

Analyze Drama Elements: Plot (sc. 6 LINES 130–142)

Remind students that Claudius has hinted at coming vengeance for Laertes.

 ASK STUDENTS to sum up the plan Claudius pitches to Laertes. *(The King will set up a fencing match for Laertes and Hamlet. While Hamlet isn't looking, Laertes will choose an un-blunted sword so that he can fatally wound Hamlet.)* How does Laertes respond and what does his response reveal about his character? *(Laertes says "I will do 't." His behavior in this scene reveals that he is willing to do whatever it takes, even by dishonest means, to avenge his father's death.)*

Analyze Drama Elements   COMMON CORE RL 3

(sc. 7 LINES 166–187)

At this point in the play, the Queen arrives with news of another death. Read this passage with your students. Ask them to pay close attention to the Queen's description of the death she reports.

Ⓩ **CITE TEXT EVIDENCE** Point out how Shakespeare uses vivid sensory language to paint a picture of what happens offstage. Ask students to identify images and sensory details in the Queen's story of Ophelia's death and to explain how it contributes to the scene. *(Sensory language includes "hoar leaves in the glassy stream" [line 170] and the description of Ophelia "on the pendant boughs her coronet weeds / Clamb'ring to hang" when "an envious sliver broke" and "down her weedy trophies and herself / Fell in the weeping brook" [lines 175-178]. The Queen's descriptive language helps the audience visualize an important event.)* Point out that Shakespeare is taking liberties here. The Queen wouldn't likely have observed Ophelia's drowning. If there had been a witness, she would have called out to Ophelia and tried to help her. The point of this scene is not realism. The point is to create a vivid word picture for the audience.

Collected from all simples that have virtue
Under the moon, can save the thing from death
That is but scratched withal. I'll touch my point
150   With this contagion, that, if I gall him slightly,
It may be death.

King.   Let's further think of this,
Weigh what convenience both of time and means
May fit us to our shape. If this should fail,
And that our drift look through our bad performance,
155   'Twere better not assayed. Therefore this project
Should have a back or second that might hold
If this did blast in proof. Soft, let me see.
We'll make a solemn wager on your cunnings—
I ha 't!
160   When in your motion you are hot and dry
(As make your bouts more violent to that end)
And that he calls for drink, I'll have prepared him
A chalice for the nonce, whereon but sipping,
If he by chance escape your venomed stuck,
165   Our purpose may hold there.—But stay, what noise?

[*Enter* Queen.]

Queen. One woe doth tread upon another's heel,
So fast they follow. Your sister's drowned, Laertes.

Laertes. Drowned? O, where?

Queen. There is a willow grows askant the brook
170   That shows his hoar leaves in the glassy stream.
Therewith fantastic garlands did she make
Of crowflowers, nettles, daisies, and long purples,
That liberal shepherds give a grosser name,
But our cold maids do "dead men's fingers" call them.
175   There on the pendant boughs her coronet weeds
Clamb'ring to hang, an envious sliver broke,
When down her weedy trophies and herself
Fell in the weeping brook. Her clothes spread wide,
And mermaid-like awhile they bore her up,
180   Which time she chanted snatches of old lauds,
As one incapable of her own distress
Or like a creature native and endued
Unto that element. But long it could not be
Till that her garments, heavy with their drink,
185   Pulled the poor wretch from her melodious lay
To muddy death.

Laertes.   Alas, then she is drowned.

Queen. Drowned, drowned.

---

150 gall: injure.

153 fit us to our shape: suit our purposes.

153–155 If the plot should fail and our intentions are exposed, it would be better if we never attempted it.

156 back: backup.

157 blast in proof: blow up while tested.

158 cunnings: skills.

159 ha 't: have it.

163 A chalice for the nonce: a cup of wine for the occasion.

164 stuck: thrust.

169 askant: slanting over

170 his hoar: its gray.

171 Therewith . . . make: she used the willow twigs to make elaborate wreaths.

172 long purples: orchids.

173 liberal: free-spoken.

174 cold: chaste.

175 pendant boughs: overhanging branches; **coronet:** made into a wreath or crown.

176 envious sliver: malicious branch.

180 lauds: hymns.

181 incapable: unaware.

182 native and endued: naturally adapted.

WHEN STUDENTS STRUGGLE . . .

To increase comprehension, provide language support for the passage in which the King explains his plan for killing Hamlet in lines 152–165.

ASK STUDENTS to paraphrase the following phrases and discuss their meaning. Students should use the side notes to assist them. Help students to understand the meaning of the passage as necessary.

- Line 153 "convenience both of time and means" *(opportunities)*
- Line 154 "our drift look through our bad performance" *(our plan is revealed)*
- Line 164 "venomed stuck" *(a thrust with a poisoned fencing sword)*
- Line 165 "Our purpose may hold there" *(we may still accomplish our purpose)*

Analyze Drama Elements: Character RL 4

(sc. 7 LINES 194–197)

This final statement of the act provides another clue to the King's character.

A2 **ASK STUDENTS** to describe how these lines confirm one aspect of the King's character. *(The King has repeatedly shown that he is more interested in his own concerns than anyone else's. These lines indicate that he thinks more about his own efforts to control Laertes than how Laertes might react to the death of his sister.)*

Laertes. Too much of water hast thou, poor Ophelia,
And therefore I forbid my tears. But yet
190 It is our trick; nature her custom holds,
Let shame say what it will. When these are gone,
The woman will be out.—Adieu, my lord.
I have a speech o' fire that fain would blaze,
But that this folly drowns it.

[*He exits.*]

King.   Let's follow, Gertrude.
195 How much I had to do to calm his rage!
Now fear I this will give it start again.
Therefore, let's follow.

[*They exit.*]

189–192 Laertes says that tears are a natural trait (**trick**), which shame cannot prevent. When all his tears are shed, the womanly part of him will be gone.

Image Credits: ©John Kobal Foundation/Moviepix/Getty Images

Analyzing the Text 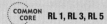 COMMON CORE RL 1, RL 3, RL 5

Possible answers:

1. *As a result of Polonius's death, Hamlet is sent away, Laertes comes back to try to take over the throne and then to seek revenge, Ophelia goes mad and drowns. Laertes and the King plot Hamlet's death.*

2. *Claudius realizes he must get Hamlet out of Denmark because he represents a serious threat to him and Gertrude. However, Hamlet is beloved by the people, so Claudius must act carefully and avoid the appearance that Hamlet is being sent away abruptly or for the wrong reasons.*

3. *Hamlet doesn't trust the King—and with good reason. So far in Act III, his behavior with the King has been flippant. The same appears to be true here in Scene 4. In a way, he's taunting the King, pretending not to care where he goes or why.*

4. *Hamlet conflates an honorable action with quick, brave action at the least effrontery ("to find quarrel in a straw when honor's at the stake"). Hamlet innately resists such an attitude, but "all occasions do inform against" him and force him to reconsider his position.*

5. *Ophelia is disturbed by more than her father's death. Her songs about young women betrayed by untrustworthy lovers make it clear that she feels twice betrayed by Hamlet—first because he has spurned her love and second because he has murdered her father.*

6. *Both Fortinbras and Laertes serve as foils because they are able to summon the resolution to act—Fortinbras to win possession of a meaningless plot of land, Laertes to vindicate his father's death. The contrast emphasizes Hamlet's hesitation and intellectualizing of a situation rather than reacting with emotion.*

7. *The two messages excite suspense on the part of the audience and increase the pace of the plot. Horatio's letter clarifies past exploits and alludes to secrets and plots to come; Claudius's letter inspires suspicion and spurs him to action.*

8. *By staging Hamlet's "accidental" death during a fencing match, the King avoids hurting his wife by taking direct action against her son. Laertes, too, can safely avenge the deaths of his father and sister while also appearing blameless. Incorporating poison into the plan presents a disadvantage in that it might cause more than one death or the death of the wrong person.*

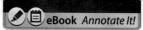 eBook *Annotate It!*

Analyzing the Text

COMMON CORE RL 1, RL 3, RL 5, W 1

Cite Text Evidence   Support your responses with evidence from the selection.

1. **Cause/Effect** What sequence of events is triggered by the killing of Polonius?

2. **Interpret** What does Claudius's speech at the beginning of Scene 3 (lines 1–11) reveal about the difficult situation he is in?

3. **Draw Conclusions** Reread lines 41–52 in Scene 3. Hamlet has already confided to his mother at the end of Act III that Rosencrantz and Guildenstern have been assigned to lead him into a trap. What does it suggest about his character that he now appears eager to go with them?

4. **Interpret** Reread lines 48–58 in Scene 4. Paraphrase the view of honor that Hamlet praises in the speech. Is this view consistent with his other comments in the scene? Why or why not?

5. **Interpret** Ophelia has fallen into madness following the death of her father. In Scene 5, do her statements and singing suggest she is only disturbed by his death, or is something else troubling her? Explain.

6. **Compare** A **foil** is a character whose traits contrast with those of another character. Very often a minor character is used as a foil to emphasize traits of the main character. Explain how the following characters serve as foils to Hamlet:
   • Fortinbras
   • Laertes

7. **Draw Conclusions** Hamlet sends two letters announcing his return to England, one to Horatio and one to Claudius. Why might Shakespeare have chosen to have him send the letter to Horatio even though it is not needed to advance the plot?

8. **Analyze** In Scene 7, lines 130–142, Claudius describes an elaborate scheme to kill Hamlet. What advantages does this scheme have for both him and Laertes? Based on what has happened so far in the play, what might be a disadvantage of the scheme?

PERFORMANCE TASK

Writing Activity: Journal Entry Write a journal entry by either Rosencrantz or Guildenstern about their mission to take Hamlet to England.

- Describe Hamlet's behavior toward his old friends and the events that led to Claudius's decision to send him away.

- Consider the limited knowledge that Rosencrantz and Guildenstern have about these events. Only include information that your character would be aware of.

- Use an informal, intimate style appropriate for a journal entry.

Assign this performance task.

PERFORMANCE TASK

 COMMON CORE W 1

Writing Activity: Journal Entry Have students describe the personal qualities of Rosencrantz and Guildenstern, and ask them to share their opinions about whether or not the pair could have known the contents of Claudius's letter. Explain that journal entries should reflect the attributes, attitude, and experiences of its author.

ACT V

Scene 1 *A churchyard.*

[*Enter* Gravedigger *and* Another.]

Gravedigger. Is she to be buried in Christian burial, when she willfully seeks her own salvation?

Other. I tell thee she is. Therefore make her grave straight. The crowner hath sat on her and finds it
5 Christian burial.

Gravedigger. How can that be, unless she drowned herself in her own defense?

Other. Why, 'tis found so.

Gravedigger. It must be se offendendo; it cannot be else.
10 For here lies the point: if I drown myself wittingly, it argues an act, and an act hath three branches—it is to act, to do, to perform. Argal, she drowned herself wittingly.

Other. Nay, but hear you, goodman delver—

15 **Gravedigger.** Give me leave. Here lies the water; good. Here stands the man; good. If the man go to this water and drown himself, it is (will he, nill he) he goes; mark you that. But if the water come to him and drown him, he drowns not himself. Argal, he
20 that is not guilty of his own death shortens not his own life.

Other. But is this law?

Gravedigger. Ay, marry, is 't—crowner's 'quest law.

Other. Will you ha' the truth on 't? If this had not
25 been a gentlewoman, she should have been buried out o' Christian burial.

Gravedigger. Why, there thou sayst. And the more pity that great folk should have count'nance in this world to drown or hang themselves more than
30 their even-Christian. Come, my spade. There is no ancient gentlemen but gard'ners, ditchers, and grave-makers. They hold up Adam's profession.

Other. Was he a gentleman?

Gravedigger. He was the first that ever bore arms.

35 **Other.** Why, he had none.

---

1 Christian burial: Suicides were not allowed Christian funeral rites. The Gravedigger assumes that Ophelia killed herself.

2 salvation: probably a blunder for **damnation**.

4 straight: immediately; **crowner:** coroner; **sat on her:** held an inquest into her death; **finds it:** gave a verdict allowing.

9 se offendendo: a blunder for **se defendendo**, a legal term meaning "in self-defense."

12 Argal: a blunder for Latin **ergo**, "therefore."

13 wittingly: intentionally.

14 goodman: a title used before the name of a profession or craft; **delver:** digger.

17 will he, nill he: willy-nilly, whether he wishes it or not.

23 'quest: inquest.

27 thou sayst: you speak the truth.

28 count'nance: privilege.

30 even-Christian: fellow Christians.

32 hold up: keep up.

34 bore arms: had a coat of arms (the sign of a gentleman).

Analyze Drama Elements: Comic Relief (LINES 1–30)

 COMMON CORE RL 2, RL 3

Remind students that Act III ends with the murder of Polonius, Act IV with news of Ophelia's death. *Hamlet* is a very serious play, a tragedy, that begins with the ghost of a murdered king and returns regularly to events or thoughts related to death. Audiences can only take so much of this heavy stuff. They need relief, and Shakespeare knew that. He was a master at comic relief, even of turning very serious subjects into the material for humor.

A **ASK STUDENTS** to read this page with an eye for inappropriate humor. Ask them to identify the serious subject the gravediggers discuss here. *(They talk about whether Ophelia's drowning was suicide and, if she died by suicide, whether she should have a Christian burial.)* Ask students to identify elements of grim humor in the dialogue. *(In line 6, the Gravedigger asks a wisecracking question about whether Ophelia "drowned herself in her own defense." In the lines that follow, he follows a goofy line of reasoning about suicide by drowning. In lines 28–30, he makes a joke about rich people being allowed "to drown or hang themselves more than their even-Christian.")* Finally, ask students to point out a scene of grim or inappropriate humor from Act IV. *(In Act IV, Scene 3, Hamlet makes numerous brutal jokes about the dead body of Polonius, even about the worms and maggots that consume a dead body.)*

Close Read Screencasts   *View It!*

Modeled Discussions

Have students pair up and do an independent close read of the following passage—Hamlet's dying words (Act V, Scene 2, lines 351-365).

As a class, discuss the passage.

Determine Theme ⟨COMMON CORE RL 2⟩

(LINES 42–61)

Note that the Gravedigger's humor continues as the scene progresses, but inform students that comic relief can convey a theme as well as serious dialogue.

B **CITE TEXT EVIDENCE** Read lines 42–61 aloud with students. Ask them to sum up the joking riddle the Gravedigger develops in these lines. *(The riddle: "What is he that builds stronger than either the mason, the shipwright, or the carpenter?" After a grimly humorous digression [lines 44–50] about the gallows-maker, the punch line is "a grave-maker. The houses he makes last till doomsday" [line 60].)* Ask students what idea about death the first two pages of this scene might convey and how this idea relates to themes already expressed by the play and its hero. *(Answers will vary, but themes might include: Death is the ultimate joke on human beings. Death awaits us all; it is the great equalizer. Hamlet touched on a similar theme in Act IV, Scene 3, during his brutal jokes about Polonius' body: One day all of us will rot, kings and beggars alike.)*

Determine Figurative Meanings ⟨COMMON CORE RL 4⟩ (LINES 57–58)

Point out that in Shakespeare's plays, even uneducated and comic figures such as the Gravedigger often use vivid figurative language.

C **ASK STUDENTS** to reread lines 57–58 and ask them to identify the type of figurative language used, the things being compared, and how the image adds to the comic effect of the scene. *(The Gravedigger uses an indirect metaphor that suggests that the Other's brains are a slow donkey that cannot be speeded up by a beating. The Gravedigger has shown himself to be quick-witted even though he is uneducated, so essentially calling the Other stupid shows the Gravedigger raising himself above the Other as he digs a grave.)*

Gravedigger. What, art a heathen? How dost thou understand the scripture? The scripture says Adam digged. Could he dig without arms? I'll put another question to thee. If thou answerest me not to the
40 purpose, confess thyself—

Other. Go to!

Gravedigger. What is he that builds stronger than either the mason, the shipwright, or the carpenter?

Other. The gallows-maker; for that frame outlives a
45 thousand tenants.

Gravedigger. I like thy wit well, in good faith. The gallows does well. But how does it well? It does well to those that do ill. Now, thou dost ill to say the gallows is built stronger than the church. Argal, the
50 gallows may do well to thee. To 't again, come.

Other. "Who builds stronger than a mason, a shipwright, or a carpenter?"

Gravedigger. Ay, tell me that, and unyoke.

Other. Marry, now I can tell.

55 **Gravedigger.** To 't.

Other. Mass, I cannot tell.

[*Enter* Hamlet *and* Horatio *afar off.*]

Gravedigger. Cudgel thy brains no more about it, for your dull ass will not mend his pace with beating. And, when you are asked this question next, say "a
60 grave-maker." The houses he makes lasts till doomsday. Go, get thee in, and fetch me a stoup of liquor.

[*The* Other Man *exits and the* Gravedigger *digs and sings.*]
In youth when I did love, did love,
*   Methought it was very sweet*
To contract—O—the time for—a—my behove,
65 *   O, methought there—a—was nothing—a—meet.*

Hamlet. Has this fellow no feeling of his business? He sings in grave-making.

Horatio. Custom hath made it in him a property of easiness.

70 **Hamlet.** 'Tis e'en so. The hand of little employment hath the daintier sense.

Gravedigger [*sings*].
*   But age with his stealing steps*
*   Hath clawed me in his clutch,*

41 Go to: go on (an expression of impatience).

44 frame: structure

48–50 Now, thou . . . to thee: Since you blasphemously say that the gallows is stronger than the church, you may be headed for the gallows.

53 unyoke: stop work for the day.

56 Mass: by the Mass.

57–58 The Gravedigger tells him to stop beating his brains to figure it out, because a beating won't make a slow donkey pick up its pace.

62–123 The Gravedigger sings a version of a popular Elizabethan song, with some added grunts (**O** and **a**), as he works.

68–69 Custom . . . easiness: Habit has made it easy for him.

71 hath the daintier sense: is more sensitive.

And hath shipped me into the land,
75   *As if I had never been such.*

[*He digs up a skull.*]

Hamlet. That skull had a tongue in it and could sing once. How the knave jowls it to the ground as if 'twere Cain's jawbone, that did the first murder! This might be the pate of a politician which this
80 ass now o'erreaches, one that would circumvent God, might it not?

Horatio. It might, my lord.

Hamlet. Or of a courtier, which could say "Good morrow, sweet lord! How dost thou, sweet lord?"
85 This might be my Lord Such-a-one that praised my Lord Such-a-one's horse when he went to beg it, might it not?

Horatio. Ay, my lord.

Hamlet. Why, e'en so. And now my Lady Worm's,
90 chapless and knocked about the mazard with a sexton's spade. Here's fine revolution, an we had the trick to see 't. Did these bones cost no more the breeding but to play at loggets with them? Mine ache to think on 't.

Gravedigger [*sings*].
95   *A pickax and a spade, a spade,*
  For and a shrouding sheet,
  O, a pit of clay for to be made
  For such a guest is meet.

[*He digs up more skulls.*]

Hamlet. There's another. Why may not that be the
100 skull of a lawyer? Where be his quiddities now, his quillities, his cases, his tenures, and his tricks? Why does he suffer this mad knave now to knock him about the sconce with a dirty shovel and will not tell him of his action of battery? Hum, this fellow
105 might be in 's time a great buyer of land, with his statutes, his recognizances, his fines, his double vouchers, his recoveries. Is this the fine of his fines and the recovery of his recoveries, to have his fine pate full of fine dirt? Will his vouchers vouch him
110 no more of his purchases, and double ones too, than the length and breadth of a pair of indentures? The very conveyances of his lands will scarcely lie in this box, and must th' inheritor himself have no more, ha?

---

77 jowls: dashes.

79–81 The skull, which the Gravedigger gets the better of, might have been the head (**pate**) of a schemer who would have tried to get the better of God.

90 chapless: missing the lower jaw; **mazard:** head.

91 revolution: turn of Fortune's wheel; **an:** if.

92 trick: ability.

92–94 Hamlet asks whether the cost of bringing up these people was so low that one may play a game with their bones.

100 quiddities: subtle arguments, quibbles.

101 quillities: subtle distinctions; **tenures:** terms for the holding of property.

103 sconce: head.

104–114 Hamlet lists different legal terms related to the buying and holding of property. **Fines** were documents involved in the transfer of estates; Hamlet also uses the word to refer to the "end result" of the lawyer's legal work and his "elegant" head filled with "small particles" of dirt. He plays similarly off the meanings of other terms.

CLOSE READ

Determine Theme

(LINES 76–114)

Explain that this long set of observations by Hamlet is inspired by the Gravedigger's immunity to the respect Hamlet feels should be given to the dead. Point out the irony in Hamlet saying the Gravedigger has "no feeling of his business" [line 66]: Hamlet himself made a series of jokes about the dead Polonius and how his corpse would decompose

Ⓓ CITE TEXT EVIDENCE Ask students to examine lines 76–114. Ask them to identify the lines that most clearly express Hamlet's deepest thoughts on death and to paraphrase them. *(In lines 92–93, Hamlet wonders at the idea that people are carefully brought up and go through so much in life yet their bones still end up as if they were playthings in a game of "loggets.")*

Determine Figurative Meanings (LINES 101–104)

Explain that Shakespeare has Hamlet use a wide variety of vivid language to express his shock and wonderment about the fact that a person's bones no longer have any of the value or power that they did when they belonged to a living person.

Ⓔ ASK STUDENTS to examine lines 101–104, and then explain what Hamlet means here and why these lines are appropriate for Hamlet's consideration of a skull that he imagines may be that of a lawyer. *(Hamlet suggests that the Gravedigger may be committing the legal offense of "battery" against the lawyer by knocking his head with a shovel, but the lawyer no longer has any legal or other power because of his death.)*

SCAFFOLDING FOR ELL STUDENTS

Multiple-Meaning Words Explain that Shakespeare often used words with multiple meanings as part of his word play and frequent puns. In lines 107–109, he uses the word *fine* to indicate four different meanings in a single sentence. Remind them that they may need to use a dictionary to find another meaning of a word if it isn't familiar.

- "Is this the fine . . ." (*This is an archaic use indicating the end result of something—the lawyer's life*)
- ". . . . of his fines . . ." (*This is another archaic usage related to documents in the sale of real estate.*)

Analyze Drama Elements: **RL 3**
Wordplay (LINES 120–138)

Ask students to think about how often they've seen wordplay in Hamlet, especially from the hero. During scenes when Hamlet pretends madness, he makes puns and frequently plays on the multiple meanings of some English words.

F **ASK STUDENTS** to examine lines 120–138 and to concentrate on the shifting meanings of the words Hamlet and the Gravedigger use. Ask them to discuss the play on *lie* in lines 124–131. *(Both speakers acknowledge that one can "lie" or recline in a grave; Hamlet accuses the Gravedigger of telling a "lie" or untruth.)* Ask students to discuss the play on *man* and *woman* in lines 132–138. *(Hamlet uses "man" to mean person. When the Gravedigger says the grave is not for a man, Hamlet asks, "What woman then?" The Gravedigger's punch line takes "man" or "woman" to be a living person and says, "One that was a woman, sir, but rest her soul, she's dead.")* Ask students to discuss how wordplay here and elsewhere in Hamlet might be related to the play's themes. *(In wordplay, as in the plot of Hamlet and in many of the hero's musings, things are not what they seem.)*

---

115 **Horatio.** Not a jot more, my lord.

Hamlet. Is not parchment made of sheepskins?

Horatio. Ay, my lord, and of calves' skins too.

Hamlet. They are sheep and calves which seek out assurance in that. I will speak to this fellow.—
120 Whose grave's this, sirrah?

Gravedigger. Mine, sir.

[*Sings.*] O, a pit of clay for to be made
       For such a guest is meet.

Hamlet. I think it be thine indeed, for thou liest in 't.

125 **Gravedigger.** You lie out on 't, sir, and therefore 'tis not yours. For my part, I do not lie in 't, yet it is mine.

Hamlet. Thou dost lie in 't, to be in 't and say it is thine. 'Tis for the dead, not for the quick; therefore thou liest.

130 **Gravedigger.** 'Tis a quick lie, sir; 'twill away again from me to you.

Hamlet. What man dost thou dig it for?

Gravedigger. For no man, sir.

Hamlet. What woman then?

135 **Gravedigger.** For none, neither.

Hamlet. Who is to be buried in 't?

Gravedigger. One that was a woman, sir, but, rest her soul, she's dead.

Hamlet. How absolute the knave is! We must speak
140 by the card, or equivocation will undo us. By the Lord, Horatio, this three years I have took note of it: the age is grown so picked that the toe of the peasant comes so near the heel of the courtier, he galls his kibe.—How long hast thou been grave
145 maker?

Gravedigger. Of all the days i' th' year, I came to 't that day that our last King Hamlet overcame Fortinbras.

Hamlet. How long is that since?

Gravedigger. Cannot you tell that? Every fool can tell
150 that. It was that very day that young Hamlet was born—he that is mad, and sent into England?

Hamlet. Ay, marry, why was he sent into England?

119 assurance in that: safety in legal documents.

120 sirrah: a term used to address inferiors.

125 out on 't: outside of it.

130 quick: living.

139 absolute: strict, precise.

140 by the card: accurately; **equivocation:** use of words that are vague or have more than one meaning.

142–144 The present age has grown so refined (**picked**) that hardly any distinction remains between a peasant and a courtier; the peasant walks so closely that he chafes (**galls**) the courtier's sore heel (**kibe**).

WHEN STUDENTS STRUGGLE . . .

Explain that there are several characters in Shakespeare's plays who have little education and social standing but show their intelligence by engaging in wordplay with those of the higher classes. The Gravedigger spars with Hamlet in lines 120–131 and uses the multiple meanings of *lie* to answer Shakespeare literally without giving him the answer Hamlet wants. Discuss why this type of scene and character might be popular with the audiences of Shakespeare's plays. *(Audiences for Shakespeare's plays included upper-class people who paid a higher price for tickets and lower-class people who did not get seats but stood on the floor of the theater. Those standing probably appreciated the idea that a lower-class person could be shown to be intelligent and able to frustrate an upper-class person through the use of words.)*

Gravedigger. Why, because he was mad. He shall
recover his wits there. Or if he do not, 'tis no great
155 matter there.

Hamlet. Why?

Gravedigger. 'Twill not be seen in him there. There the
men are as mad as he.

Hamlet. How came he mad?

160 **Gravedigger.** Very strangely, they say.

Hamlet. How "strangely"?

Gravedigger. Faith, e'en with losing his wits.

Hamlet. Upon what ground?

Gravedigger. Why, here in Denmark. I have been sexton
165 here, man and boy, thirty years.

Hamlet. How long will a man lie i' th' earth ere he rot?

Gravedigger. Faith, if he be not rotten before he die
(as we have many pocky corses nowadays that will
scarce hold the laying in), he will last you some eight
170 year or nine year. A tanner will last you nine year.

Hamlet. Why he more than another?

Gravedigger. Why, sir, his hide is so tanned with his
trade that he will keep out water a great while; and
your water is a sore decayer of your whoreson
175 dead body. Here's a skull now hath lien you i' th'
earth three-and-twenty years.

Hamlet. Whose was it?

Gravedigger. A whoreson mad fellow's it was. Whose
do you think it was?

180 **Hamlet.** Nay, I know not.

Gravedigger. A pestilence on him for a mad rogue! He
poured a flagon of Rhenish on my head once. This
same skull, sir, was, sir, Yorick's skull, the King's
jester.

185 **Hamlet.** This?

Gravedigger. E'en that.

Hamlet [*taking the skull*]. Let me see. Alas, poor Yorick!
I knew him, Horatio—a fellow of infinite jest, of
most excellent fancy. He hath bore me on his back
190 a thousand times, and now how abhorred in my
imagination it is! My gorge rises at it. Here hung
those lips that I have kissed I know not how oft.

163 ground: cause.
(The Gravedigger takes
it in the sense of "land.")

168 pocky: rotten,
infected with syphilis.

**169 scarce hold the
laying in:** barely hold
together until they are
buried.

**174–175 your . . .
body:** Water is a terrible
(**sore**) decayer of vile
(**whoreson**) corpses.

175 lien you: lain.

Hamlet: Act V, Scene 1   **337**

CLOSE READ

Analyze Point of View: Irony (LINES 149–165)

COMMON CORE   RL 6

Ask students to review the definition of **dramatic
irony** before examining the passage.

 ASK STUDENTS to explain the dramatic irony
of the situation here, and to discuss how the irony
contributes to the continuing humor of Scene 1 and
to Shakespeare's developing characterization of
Hamlet. (*The audience realizes that the Gravedigger
is speaking to "young Hamlet" but the Gravedigger
does not recognize him. The fact that the Gravedigger
is making jokes about Hamlet's sanity while Hamlet is
actually onstage gives the audience even more room
for laughter. The fact that Hamlet doesn't give away
his identity shows that he is in on the joke, and that
sometimes he can take a joke at his own expense.*)

Determine Theme
COMMON CORE   RL 2

(LINES 166–176)

Explain that even minor characters, such as the
Gravedigger, can help develop a theme through their
thoughts and actions.

ASK STUDENTS to examine lines 166–176. Ask
them to explain how this exchange helps advance
the development of a theme related to death.
(*Hamlet and the Gravedigger focus on the physical
processes that occur after death. The Gravedigger even
makes light of the process by light-heartedly noting
that "a tanner" may be preserved longer because of
his trade. This exchange emphasizes that as important
as life may be, the physical body is at the mercy of the
elements after death, just as the skulls and bones were
in Hamlet's previous ruminations.*)

Determine Theme

COMMON CORE RL 2

(LINES 187–219)

Note that in these lines, it is Hamlet who expands on his thoughts about death—by commenting on the skull of someone he once knew and by posing hypothetical questions.

🅘 **CITE TEXT EVIDENCE** Read lines 187–219 aloud with your students. Stop as necessary to discuss Hamlet's meaning and how it relates to the play's themes. Ask them to identify lines that most clearly state Hamlet's thoughts on death. Ask them to describe how these thoughts relate to his thoughts expressed in lines 76–114 when he considers the Gravedigger's treatment of skulls. *(In lines 187–199, Hamlet remembers the King's jester, Yorick, while he holds and observes Yorick's skull. In line 206, Hamlet observes that everyone's dead body returns to "base uses." In lines 216–219, Hamlet suggests that the body of the great Caesar might be used to "stop a hole" in a wall to keep the wind out. These thoughts build on the idea that people's bodies are nothing more than physical elements subject to decay and that this decay awaits all humans, even the most powerful.)*

Where be your gibes now? your gambols? your songs? your flashes of merriment that were wont to
195 set the table on a roar? Not one now to mock your own grinning? Quite chapfallen? Now get you to my lady's chamber, and tell her, let her paint an inch thick, to this favor she must come. Make her laugh at that.—Prithee, Horatio, tell me one thing.

200 **Horatio.** What's that, my lord?

Hamlet. Dost thou think Alexander looked o' this fashion i' th' earth?

Horatio. E'en so.

Hamlet. And smelt so? Pah!

[*He puts the skull down.*]

205 **Horatio.** E'en so, my lord.

Hamlet. To what base uses we may return, Horatio! Why may not imagination trace the noble dust of Alexander till he find it stopping a bunghole?

Horatio. 'Twere to consider too curiously to consider so.

210 **Hamlet.** No, faith, not a jot; but to follow him thither, with modesty enough and likelihood to lead it, as thus: Alexander died, Alexander was buried, Alexander returneth to dust; the dust is earth; of earth we make loam; and why of that loam whereto
215 he was converted might they not stop a beer barrel? Imperious Caesar, dead and turned to clay, Might stop a hole to keep the wind away.

193 gibes: taunts; **gambols:** pranks.

196 chapfallen: down in the mouth, missing the lower jaw.

197–198 let her . . . come: Even if she covers her face with an inch of makeup, eventually she will have this appearance (**favor**).

201 Alexander: Alexander the Great.

208 bunghole: a hole in a keg or barrel for pouring liquid.

209 curiously: minutely, closely.

211 modesty: moderation.

214 loam: a mixture of clay, sand, and straw used for plastering.

216 Imperious: imperial.

Image Credits: ©John Kobal Foundation/Moviepix/Getty Images

O, that that earth which kept the world in awe
Should patch a wall t' expel the winter's flaw!

219 flaw: gust of wind.

[*Enter* King, Queen, Laertes, Lords attendant, *and the corpse of* Ophelia, *with a* Doctor of Divinity.]

220 But soft, but soft awhile! Here comes the King,
The Queen, the courtiers. Who is this they follow?
And with such maimèd rites? This doth betoken
The corse they follow did with desp'rate hand
Fordo its own life. 'Twas of some estate.
225 Couch we awhile and mark.

[*They step aside.*]

Laertes. What ceremony else?

Hamlet. That is Laertes, a very noble youth. Mark.

Laertes. What ceremony else?

Doctor. Her obsequies have been as far enlarged
230 As we have warranty. Her death was doubtful,
And, but that great command o'ersways the order,
She should in ground unsanctified been lodged
Till the last trumpet. For charitable prayers
Shards, flints, and pebbles should be thrown on her.
235 Yet here she is allowed her virgin crants,
Her maiden strewments, and the bringing home
Of bell and burial.

Laertes. Must there no more be done?

Doctor.   No more be done.
We should profane the service of the dead
240 To sing a requiem and such rest to her
As to peace-parted souls.

Laertes.   Lay her i' th' earth,
And from her fair and unpolluted flesh
May violets spring! I tell thee, churlish priest,
A minist'ring angel shall my sister be
245 When thou liest howling.

Hamlet [*to* Horatio].   What, the fair Ophelia?

Queen. Sweets to the sweet, farewell!
She scatters flowers.
I hoped thou shouldst have been my Hamlet's wife;
I thought thy bride-bed to have decked, sweet maid,
250 And not have strewed thy grave.

Laertes.   O, treble woe
Fall ten times treble on that cursèd head
Whose wicked deed thy most ingenious sense

222 maimèd: incomplete.

224 Fordo: destroy; **some estate:** high rank.

225 Couch . . . mark: Let us conceal ourselves awhile and observe.

229–233 The priest says he has performed her funeral rites to the extent allowed under church law. The manner of her death was suspicious, and if the King's orders hadn't overruled the procedures, she would have remained buried in unsanctified ground until Judgment Day.

233 For: instead of.

234 Shards: pieces of broken pottery; **should be:** would have been.

235 virgin crants: wreaths placed on the coffin as a sign of virginity.

236 strewments: flowers strewn on a grave.

236–237 bringing . . . burial: being laid to rest in consecrated ground with church bells tolling.

240–241 such rest . . . souls: pray for her to have the same rest as those who died in peace.

245 howling: in hell.

252–253 thy most . . . thee of: deprived you of your excellent mind.

CLOSE READ

Drama Elements: Character (LINES 241–258)

COMMON CORE RL 3

Remind students of the rage and determination they witnessed in Laertes in Act IV. Remind them that he said he was willing to cut Hamlet's throat in a church and that he agreed to a dishonest means of assuring Hamlet's death. Remind them that, since Hamlet is present, they will likely see Laertes as a foil to the play's hero again.

ASK STUDENTS to examine lines 241–258 for evidence of Laertes' emotional state. (*Laertes feels grief for his sister in these lines, a grief so strong it overtakes him and he leaps into her grave, asking to be buried with her.*) Ask students if they see any evidence of the anger Laertes showed in Act IV. (*Laertes is clearly a caring brother, a man who genuinely loved his sister. His grief over her death is so strong here that it seems to have replaced the anger he displayed in Act IV.*)

APPLYING ACADEMIC VOCABULARY

trigger	restrain

As you discuss the events surrounding Ophelia's burial, incorporate the Collection 4 academic vocabulary words *trigger* and *restrain*. Ask students to describe why Ophelia's death **triggers** a debate and confrontation between Laertes and the Doctor. Ask students to explain why the Doctor **restrains** Laertes and others from performing further religious rites for Ophelia.

Analyze Drama Elements: Character COMMON CORE RL 3 (LINES 258–290)

Remind students that when they first saw Hamlet, in Act I, Scene 2, he was wearing black in mourning for his father. Hold a brief review discussion of Hamlet's behavior in that scene—how he insisted that his grief was real, both outside and inside, along with the implication that others did not experience genuine grief. Finally, remind students that although the audience and other characters have known of Ophelia's death since late in Act IV, Hamlet does not know of her death until he realizes that he is observing her funeral.

 ASK STUDENTS to examine lines 258–290 to determine what motivates Hamlet's behavior here. Ask them to suggest what, besides grief and shock, might cause him to act out as he does. *(Answers will vary, but Hamlet's behavior in this scene is like an exaggerated version of his first appearance, where he showed a need to convince those around him that his grief was genuine, perhaps more genuine than the grief of others. Clearly, he is competing with Laertes, whose words of grief motivate him to reveal himself. In lines 280–290, Hamlet itemizes the ways Laertes might show grief, each time insisting that he can do the same. Given how badly Hamlet treated Ophelia in earlier scenes, he might also be feeling guilt here—and trying to disguise or assuage his guilt by expressing grief instead.)*

Deprived thee of!—Hold off the earth awhile,
Till I have caught her once more in mine arms.

[*Leaps in the grave.*]

255   Now pile your dust upon the quick and dead,
Till of this flat a mountain you have made
T' o'ertop old Pelion or the skyish head
Of blue Olympus.

   Hamlet [*advancing*]. What is he whose grief
Bears such an emphasis, whose phrase of sorrow
260   Conjures the wand'ring stars and makes them stand
Like wonder-wounded hearers? This is I,
Hamlet the Dane.

   Laertes [*coming out of the grave*].

               The devil take thy soul!

   Hamlet. Thou pray'st not well.

[*They grapple.*]

   I prithee take thy fingers from my throat,
265   For though I am not splenitive and rash,
Yet have I in me something dangerous,
Which let thy wisdom fear. Hold off thy hand.

   King. Pluck them asunder.

   Queen. Hamlet! Hamlet!

270   **All.** Gentlemen!

   Horatio. Good my lord, be quiet.

[*Hamlet and Laertes are separated.*]

   Hamlet. Why, I will fight with him upon this theme
Until my eyelids will no longer wag!

   Queen. O my son, what theme?

275   **Hamlet.** I loved Ophelia. Forty thousand brothers
Could not with all their quantity of love
Make up my sum. What wilt thou do for her?

   King. O, he is mad, Laertes!

   Queen. For love of God, forbear him.

280   **Hamlet.** 'Swounds, show me what thou't do.
Woo't weep, woo't fight, woo't fast, woo't tear thyself,
Woo't drink up eisel, eat a crocodile?
I'll do 't. Dost thou come here to whine?
To outface me with leaping in her grave?
285   Be buried quick with her, and so will I.
And if thou prate of mountains, let them throw

257 Pelion: In Greek mythology, giants placed Mount Pelion on top of Mount Ossa in an attempt to reach the top of Mount Olympus, home of the gods.

260–261 wand'ring stars: planets; **wonder-wounded:** struck with amazement.

265 splenitive: quick-tempered.

279 forbear him: leave him alone.

281 Woo't: wilt thou.

282 eisel: vinegar.

285 quick: alive.

TO CHALLENGE STUDENTS . . .

Update Cultural References Who loved Ophelia more? Refer students to the speeches that Laertes and Hamlet make in describing their love for Ophelia in lines 255–258 and 280–290. Discuss the reasons they make these speeches and if these arguments are persuasive. *(Each is trying to prove his love for Ophelia by describing the suffering or discomfort he would go through for her sake. Both sound like idle boasts of young men caught up in a competition to prove their love with hyperbole.)*

Challenge students to rewrite each speech using modern references to what they might do to prove their love for Ophelia. They might include references to mountains as in the original or use different references. They can also change the tasks that Hamlet says he would endure to something else more modern, but just as unpleasant.

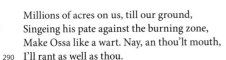

Millions of acres on us, till our ground,
Singeing his pate against the burning zone,
Make Ossa like a wart. Nay, an thou'lt mouth,
290 I'll rant as well as thou.

   Queen.   This is mere madness;
And thus awhile the fit will work on him.
Anon, as patient as the female dove
When that her golden couplets are disclosed,
His silence will sit drooping.

   Hamlet.   Hear you, sir,
295 What is the reason that you use me thus?
I loved you ever. But it is no matter.
Let Hercules himself do what he may,
The cat will mew, and dog will have his day.

   [Hamlet *exits.*]

   King. I pray thee, good Horatio, wait upon him.

   [Horatio *exits.*]

300 [*To* Laertes.] Strengthen your patience in our last
        night's speech.
We'll put the matter to the present push.—
Good Gertrude, set some watch over your son.—
This grave shall have a living monument.
An hour of quiet shortly shall we see;
305 Till then in patience our proceeding be.

   [*They exit.*]

Scene 2 *The hall of the castle.*

[*Enter* Hamlet *and* Horatio.]

Hamlet. So much for this, sir. Now shall you see the
        other.
You do remember all the circumstance?

Horatio. Remember it, my lord!

Hamlet. Sir, in my heart there was a kind of fighting
5   That would not let me sleep. Methought I lay
Worse than the mutines in the bilboes. Rashly—
And praised be rashness for it: let us know,
Our indiscretion sometime serves us well
When our deep plots do pall; and that should learn us
10 There's a divinity that shapes our ends,
Rough-hew them how we will—

   Horatio.   That is most certain.

**288 Singeing his . . .
zone:** burning its head in
the sphere of the Sun's
orbit.

289 Ossa: See note
to line 257, **an thou'lt
mouth:** if you rant.

290 mere: utter.

292–294 Soon Hamlet
will fall as silent as a
dove after its twin baby
birds (**couplets**) are
hatched.

299 wait upon:
accompany.

**301 to the present
push:** into immediate
action.

1 see the other: hear
the rest of the story.

6 mutines: mutineers;
bilboes: shackles, chains.

8 indiscretion: hasty
actions.

9 pall: falter; **learn:**
teach.

10–11 There's a . . . will:
A divine power guides
our destinies, despite
our clumsy attempts to
fashion them ourselves.

CLOSE READ

Analyze Drama Elements: COMMON CORE RL 3
Plot (sc. 1 LINES 300–305)

Note that the King always seems to remain attentive
to his plans and to ways to maintain his power.

L **ASK STUDENTS** to examine lines 300–305 and
explain why they are important in the development
of the plot. *(The King needs Laertes to remain patient
so that Hamlet can be killed according to their scheme
using an un-blunted, poisoned sword. He reminds him
of that and suggests that they will put the plan into
immediate action. He also needs Gertrude to watch
over Hamlet to be sure he is available for the scheme
and does not take some rash action before it can be
put in motion. Finally, the rhyming couplet with which
Claudius closes the scene shows him to be a calm
and dignified ruler, though the audience knows that
beneath the surface, Claudius is not a dignified man.)*

Analyze Drama Elements: COMMON CORE RL 3

Plot (sc. 2 LINES 12–47)

Point out that significant action has occurred offstage. Here, with Horatio as his confidant, Hamlet fills us in on the adventure at sea. To insure that the audience understands these actions, Hamlet describes the events to Horatio.

Ⓜ ASK STUDENTS to examine lines 12–47. Direct them to summarize the events Hamlet describes. *(On his sea journey to England, Hamlet stole the secret packet carried by Rosencrantz and Guildenstern and opened it to read the contents. He found that the King had directed the English authorities to execute him immediately upon his arrival. He then wrote a forgery asking that the English execute Rosencrantz and Guildenstern.)* Ask students to discuss how discovering the King's letter is useful to Hamlet. *(Hamlet knows the King means for him to die. If he is to take his revenge, he must get to the King before the King gets to him.)* Finally, ask students to discuss the forged letter Hamlet left with Rosencrantz and Guildenstern. How does it connect to the play's themes and what does it reveal about Hamlet? *(The forged letter echoes the idea that life is a cruel cosmic joke on all of us. It shows in Hamlet a capacity for singular cruelty. Rosencrantz and Guildenstern were tools of the King—and fools—but they gave no evidence of evil, of deserving the death Hamlet sets up for them.)*

Hamlet. Up from my cabin,
My sea-gown scarfed about me, in the dark
 Groped I to find out them; had my desire,
15 Fingered their packet, and in fine withdrew
To mine own room again, making so bold
(My fears forgetting manners) to unfold
Their grand commission; where I found, Horatio,
A royal knavery—an exact command,
20 Larded with many several sorts of reasons
Importing Denmark's health and England's too,
With—ho!—such bugs and goblins in my life,
That on the supervise, no leisure bated,
No, not to stay the grinding of the ax,
25 My head should be struck off.

Horatio. Is 't possible?

Hamlet. Here's the commission. Read it at more leisure.

[*Handing him a paper.*]

But wilt thou hear now how I did proceed?

Horatio. I beseech you.

Hamlet. Being thus benetted round with villainies,
30 Or I could make a prologue to my brains,
They had begun the play. I sat me down,
Devised a new commission, wrote it fair—
I once did hold it, as our statists do,
A baseness to write fair, and labored much
35 How to forget that learning; but, sir, now
It did me yeoman's service. Wilt thou know
Th' effect of what I wrote?

Horatio. Ay, good my lord.

Hamlet. An earnest conjuration from the King,
As England was his faithful tributary,
40 As love between them like the palm might flourish,
As peace should still her wheaten garland wear
And stand a comma 'tween their amities,
And many suchlike ases of great charge,
That, on the view and knowing of these contents,
45 Without debatement further, more or less,
He should those bearers put to sudden death,
Not shriving time allowed.

Horatio. How was this sealed?

Hamlet. Why, even in that was heaven ordinant.
I had my father's signet in my purse,
50 Which was the model of that Danish seal;

13 scarfed: wrapped.

14 them: Rosencrantz and Guildenstern.

15 Fingered: stole; **in fine:** finally.

20 Larded: embellished.

21 importing: concerning.

22 bugs . . . life: imaginary terrors in my remaining alive.

23 on the supervise: upon reading this; **no leisure bated:** without hesitation.

24 stay: wait for.

30–31 Before Hamlet had time to consider what to do, his brains started working out a plan.

33–36 Like a politician, Hamlet once considered it beneath him to write neatly (as a clerk would), but his handwriting gave him substantial service.

39 tributary: a nation controlled by another.

41 still: always; **wheaten garland:** symbol of peace and prosperity.

42 stand . . . amities: join their friendships.

43 suchlike . . . charge: similar legal phrases of great import beginning with "whereas." (Hamlet is ridiculing official language.)

47 shriving time: time for confession and absolution of sins.

48 ordinant: controlling events.

50 model: likeness.

SCAFFOLDING FOR ELL STUDENTS

Reading Support: Read Aloud Explain that Hamlet tells a straightforward story of his actions on the ship to England in lines 12–25. Review the side notes that help explain some of the language and then read the passage aloud, stopping after a sentence or an extended phrase to discuss the meaning. Then read the passage aloud again with a volunteer acting out Hamlet's actions as he describes them. When that reading is complete, ask a student volunteer to do another reading with another volunteer doing the acting. Discuss the importance of this passage in the plot. *(Hamlet discovers that the King has sent him to England to be executed. This knowledge spurs Hamlet to his final actions.)*

Folded the writ up in the form of th' other,
Subscribed it, gave 't th' impression, placed it safely,
The changeling never known. Now, the next day
Was our sea-fight; and what to this was sequent
55 Thou knowest already.

Horatio. So Guildenstern and Rosencrantz go to 't.

Hamlet. Why, man, they did make love to this employment.
They are not near my conscience. Their defeat
Does by their own insinuation grow.
60 'Tis dangerous when the baser nature comes
Between the pass and fell incensèd points
Of mighty opposites.

Horatio. Why, what a king is this!

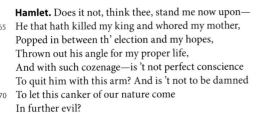

Hamlet. Does it not, think thee, stand me now upon—
65 He that hath killed my king and whored my mother,
Popped in between th' election and my hopes,
Thrown out his angle for my proper life,
And with such cozenage—is 't not perfect conscience
To quit him with this arm? And is 't not to be damned
70 To let this canker of our nature come
In further evil?

Horatio. It must be shortly known to him from England
What is the issue of the business there.

Hamlet. It will be short. The interim's mine,
75 And a man's life's no more than to say "one."
But I am very sorry, good Horatio,
That to Laertes I forgot myself,
For by the image of my cause I see
The portraiture of his. I'll court his favors.
80 But, sure, the bravery of his grief did put me
Into a tow'ring passion.

Horatio.   Peace, who comes here?

[*Enter* Osric, *a courtier.*]

Osric. Your lordship is right welcome back to Denmark.

Hamlet. I humbly thank you, sir. [*Aside to* Horatio.]
Dost know this waterfly?

85 **Horatio** [*aside to* Hamlet]. No, my good lord.

Hamlet [*aside to* Horatio]. Thy state is the more gracious,
for 'tis a vice to know him. He hath much land,
and fertile. Let a beast be lord of beasts and his
crib shall stand at the king's mess. 'Tis a chough,
90 but, as I say, spacious in the possession of dirt.

52 **Subscribed . . . impression:** signed and sealed it.

53 **changeling:** substitution.

54 **what to this was sequent:** what followed.

58 **defeat:** destruction.

59 **insinuation:** worming their way in.

60–62 **'Tis . . . opposites:** It is dangerous for inferior people to come between the fiercely thrusting sword points of mighty antagonists.

66 The Danish king was elected by a small group of electors.

68 **cozenage:** deception.

69 **quit:** pay back.

70–71 **come/In:** grow into.

74–75 Hamlet says that although he only has a short time in which to act, a man's life is also brief, lasting no longer than it takes to count to one.

78 **image:** likeness.

80 **bravery:** showiness.

88–89 **Let a . . . mess:** If a man owns a lot of livestock, no matter how much he resembles them, he may eat at the king's table.

89 **chough:** chattering bird.

Hamlet: Act V, Scene 2   **343**

CLOSE READ

Analyze Structure: Conflict (sc. 2 LINES 64–71)

COMMON CORE RL 3

Remind students that throughout the play, Hamlet has revealed that he is conflicted about getting revenge against Claudius, and by his actions—or lack of action—he has revealed that he is hesitant about doing what the Ghost has asked of him.

N ASK STUDENTS to examine lines 64–71. Direct them to analyze Hamlet's statements in these lines and whether they indicate a change in his attitude toward Claudius and toward his own quest for vengeance. (*Because Hamlet has discovered the truth about the King's plans for him to be executed, Hamlet no longer feels hesitation about his resolve to "quit him"– kill Claudius–with his own hand. He also feels he would be "damned" if he allowed "this canker of our nature" to do further evil. Hamlet no longer feels conflicted or hesitant about killing the King.*)

Analyze Point of View: Satire (sc. 2 LINES 82–90)

COMMON CORE RL 6

Provide the definition of **satire**—ridiculing ideas, customs, behaviors, or institutions to improve society. Explain that Hamlet's interactions with Osric are repeated instances of satire. This use of satire at the expense of the upper classes was another reason Shakespeare was popular with those at the lower ends of the social ladder.

O CITE TEXT EVIDENCE Ask students to examine lines 82–90 and identify lines in which Hamlet ridicules Osric. They should also identify lines that criticize a social custom. (*In line 84, Osric is compared to a "waterfly" and in line 89 to a chattering bird. Hamlet observes in lines 87–89 that people with a large amount of livestock are welcome at the King's table, regardless of their intelligence.*)

Analyze Point of View:

Satire (sc. 2 LINES 91–101)

  COMMON CORE RL 6

Shakespeare continues his satire of wealthy courtiers in these lines.

 ASK STUDENTS to examine lines 91–101 and explain how Hamlet exposes Osric as a subject for ridicule. *(Osric suggests that he shouldn't put his hat on because it is hot. Hamlet comments that it is cold and Osric agrees. Then Hamlet notes that it is "sultry and hot" and Osric agrees again. This shows that Osric is not expressing his true thoughts, but instead kissing up to a prince.)*

Analyze Point of View:

Satire (sc. 2 LINES 106–121)

COMMON CORE RL 6

This bit of satire relies on the audience to remember the regular manner of Hamlet's speech.

 ASK STUDENTS to examine lines 106–121 and identify the characteristic of Osric that Hamlet is making light of. *(In answer to a simple question about Osric's business, Osric launches into a long and unnecessarily flattering description of Laertes. Hamlet responds in the same way, with overwrought language, to mock Osric. Because this speech is so unlike Hamlet's previous statements, it is clear that he is ridiculing Osric.)*

Osric. Sweet lord, if your lordship were at leisure, I should impart a thing to you from his Majesty.

Hamlet. I will receive it, sir, with all diligence of spirit. Put your bonnet to his right use: 'tis for the head.

95 **Osric.** I thank your lordship; it is very hot.

Hamlet. No, believe me, 'tis very cold; the wind is northerly.

Osric. It is indifferent cold, my lord, indeed.

Hamlet. But yet methinks it is very sultry and hot for 100 my complexion.

Osric. Exceedingly, my lord; it is very sultry, as 'twere—I cannot tell how. My lord, his Majesty bade me signify to you that he has laid a great wager on your head. Sir, this is the matter—

105 **Hamlet.** I beseech you, remember.

[*He motions to* Osric *to put on his hat.*]

Osric. Nay, good my lord, for my ease, in good faith. Sir, here is newly come to court Laertes—believe me, an absolute gentleman, full of most excellent differences, of very soft society and great showing. 110 Indeed, to speak feelingly of him, he is the card or calendar of gentry, for you shall find in him the continent of what part a gentleman would see.

Hamlet. Sir, his definement suffers no perdition in you, though I know to divide him inventorially would 115 dozy th' arithmetic of memory, and yet but yaw neither, in respect of his quick sail. But, in the verity of extolment, I take him to be a soul of great article, and his infusion of such dearth and rareness as, to make true diction of him, his semblable is his mirror, 120 and who else would trace him, his umbrage, nothing more.

Osric. Your lordship speaks most infallibly of him.

Hamlet. The concernancy, sir? Why do we wrap the gentleman in our more rawer breath?

125 **Osric.** Sir?

Horatio [*aside to* Hamlet]. Is 't not possible to understand in another tongue? You will to 't, sir, really.

Hamlet [*to* Osric]. What imports the nomination of this gentleman?

130 **Osric.** Of Laertes?

93–106 Men commonly wore their hats indoors but removed them in the presence of superiors. Hamlet mocks not only this show of respect but also Osric's insistence on agreeing with everything Hamlet says.

98 indifferent: somewhat.

100 complexion: temperament.

110–112 Among his compliments, Osric calls Laertes the map or guide (**card or calendar**) of good breeding, one who contains in him (**the continent of**) all the qualities a gentleman would look for.

113–121 Hamlet, mocking Osric's flowery speech, says that nothing has been lost in Osric's definition of Laertes, but the calculations needed to make an inventory of Laertes's excellences would be dizzying, and even then one would fail to capture him. He goes on to say that the only true likeness (**semblable**) of Laertes is his reflection in a mirror, and anyone who wanted to copy him would be nothing more than his shadow (**umbrage**).

123–124 Hamlet asks why they are speaking about Laertes.

128 What imports ... of: for what purpose are you mentioning.

344 Collection 4

Horatio [*aside*]. His purse is empty already; all 's golden words are spent.

Hamlet. Of him, sir.

Osric. I know you are not ignorant—

135 **Hamlet.** I would you did, sir. Yet, in faith, if you did, it would not much approve me. Well, sir?

Osric. You are not ignorant of what excellence Laertes is—

Hamlet. I dare not confess that, lest I should compare
140 with him in excellence. But to know a man well were to know himself.

Osric. I mean, sir, for his weapon. But in the imputation laid on him by them, in his meed he's unfellowed.

Hamlet. What's his weapon?

145 **Osric.** Rapier and dagger.

Hamlet. That's two of his weapons. But, well—

Osric. The King, sir, hath wagered with him six Barbary horses, against the which he has impawned, as I take it, six French rapiers and poniards, with their
150 assigns, as girdle, hangers, and so. Three of the carriages, in faith, are very dear to fancy, very responsive to the hilts, most delicate carriages, and of very liberal conceit.

Hamlet. What call you the "carriages"?

155 **Horatio** [*aside to* Hamlet]. I knew you must be edified by the margent ere you had done.

Osric. The carriages, sir, are the hangers.

Hamlet. The phrase would be more germane to the matter if we could carry a cannon by our sides. I
160 would it might be "hangers" till then. But on. Six Barbary horses against six French swords, their assigns, and three liberal-conceited carriages—that's the French bet against the Danish. Why is this all "impawned," as you call it?

165 **Osric.** The King, sir, hath laid, sir, that in a dozen passes between yourself and him, he shall not exceed you three hits. He hath laid on twelve for nine, and it would come to immediate trial if your lordship would vouchsafe the answer.

170 **Hamlet.** How if I answer no?

---

131 all 's: all his.

136 approve: commend.

142–143 In the reputation others have given him, his merit (**meed**) is unmatched.

145 Rapier and dagger: a type of fencing with a rapier (sword) held in the right hand and a dagger in the left.

147–153 Against Claudius's wager, Laertes has staked six rapiers and daggers, along with their accessories, such as straps (**hangers**) to hold the swords onto a sword belt (**girdle**), and so forth. Three of the hangers are fancifully designed, well adjusted, finely crafted, and have an elaborate design.

155–156 Horatio jokes that he knew Hamlet would seek explanation in a marginal note.

159 cannon by our sides: an affected term for "hanger," *carriage* normally refers to the wheeled base of a cannon.

165 laid: wagered.

166 passes; bouts, exchanges; **him:** Laertes.

169 vouchsafe the answer: accept the challenge.

CLOSE READ

Analyze Point of View: Satire (sc. 2 LINES 147–164)

 COMMON CORE RL 6

Osric again serves as the subject of a bit of light-hearted satire before the tragic events of the final scene unfold. Remind students of the comic relief that began the act.

(R) CITE TEXT EVIDENCE Ask student to examine lines 147–164 and identify the lines in which Hamlet ridicules the affected speech of Osric. (*In line 154, Hamlet asks Osric what he means by "carriages." In line 157, Osric reveals that he is using a glorified word for the "hangers" used to hang swords from a belt. In lines 157–160, Hamlet suggests that the use of the word "carriages" is unwarranted and that Osric is using it improperly.*)

WHEN STUDENTS STRUGGLE . . .

Discuss the definition of satire (ridiculing ideas, customs, behaviors, or institutions to improve society) and how it could affect society. Ask students to identify any movies or TV shows they have seen that use satire and how they think the writers hoped that society would change because of them.

Have students review the following lines and identify what is being ridiculed and how Shakespeare would like society to change.

- Scene 2, lines 91–104 (*courtiers who will agree to anything a lord says even if it is contradictory; he would like courtiers to be more forthright*)

- Scene 2, lines 106–124 (*courtiers' flowery speech; he would like people to speak more plainly*)

Analyze Point of View: Satire (sc. 2 LINES 182–194)

Hamlet pokes fun at Osric and an entire social group.

S **ASK STUDENTS** to examine lines 182–194 and summarize Hamlet's thoughts on a group of courtiers who have become popular during this period. *(Hamlet suggests that "many more of the same breed" as Osric have little substance but make their way through high society with empty words that are no more than "bubbles" that will burst when questioned.)*

Analyze Drama Elements: Foreshadowing

(sc. 2 LINES 204–224)

Remind students that foreshadowing can build tension in the audience about events to follow.

T **CITE TEXT EVIDENCE** Ask students to examine lines 204–224 for evidence of foreshadowing. *(Horatio, Hamlet's friend and an objective, trustworthy character, says of Hamlet's coming duel with Laertes, "You will lose, my lord." Hamlet replies that he will win but undercuts this assertion by saying, "thou wouldst not think how ill all's here about my heart." Finally, Hamlet delivers a fatalistic little speech about "the fall of a sparrow," saying that if death doesn't come now, it will come later.)*

Osric. I mean, my lord, the opposition of your person in trial.

Hamlet. Sir, I will walk here in the hall. If it please his Majesty, it is the breathing time of day with me.
175 Let the foils be brought, the gentleman willing, and the King hold his purpose, I will win for him, an I can. If not, I will gain nothing but my shame and the odd hits.

Osric. Shall I deliver you e'en so?

180 **Hamlet.** To this effect, sir, after what flourish your nature will.

Osric. I commend my duty to your lordship.

 Hamlet. Yours. [*Osric exits.*] He does well to commend it himself. There are no tongues else for 's turn.

185 **Horatio.** This lapwing runs away with the shell on his head.

Hamlet. He did comply, sir, with his dug before he sucked it. Thus has he (and many more of the same breed that I know the drossy age dotes on) only
190 got the tune of the time, and, out of an habit of encounter, a kind of yeasty collection, which carries them through and through the most fanned and winnowed opinions; and do but blow them to their trial, the bubbles are out.

[*Enter a Lord.*]

195 **Lord.** My lord, his Majesty commended him to you by young Osric, who brings back to him that you attend him in the hall. He sends to know if your pleasure hold to play with Laertes, or that you will take longer time.

200 **Hamlet.** I am constant to my purposes. They follow the King's pleasure. If his fitness speaks, mine is ready now or whensoever, provided I be so able as now.

Lord. The King and Queen and all are coming down.

205 **Hamlet.** In happy time.

Lord. The Queen desires you to use some gentle entertainment to Laertes before you fall to play.

Hamlet. She well instructs me.

[*Lord exits.*]

Horatio. You will lose, my lord.

174 breathing time of day: usual time for exercise.

175 foils: swords with blunt tips.

182 commend: present to your favor.

185 lapwing: A bird that supposedly left its nest soon after hatching and ran around with its shell on its head—probably a reference to Osric's hat.

187–194 After joking that Osric paid courtesies to his mother's nipple before nursing, Hamlet complains that Osric and his type, popular in this worthless age, have only picked up a fashionable manner of speaking (**the tune of the time**) and a frothy collection of phrases that help them move through refined society (**fanned and winnowed opinions**), but the bubbles burst as soon as they are tested.

201–202 If his . . . whensoever: I am ready at his convenience.

205 In happy time: a polite phrase of welcome.

206 use some gentle entertainment: show some courtesy.

210 Hamlet. I do not think so. Since he went into France, I
have been in continual practice. I shall win at the
odds; but thou wouldst not think how ill all's here
about my heart. But it is no matter.

Horatio. Nay, good my lord—

215 Hamlet. It is but foolery, but it is such a kind of gaingiving
as would perhaps trouble a woman.

Horatio. If your mind dislike anything, obey it. I will
forestall their repair hither and say you are not fit.

Hamlet. Not a whit. We defy augury. There is a special
220 providence in the fall of a sparrow. If it be now, 'tis
not to come; if it be not to come, it will be now; if
it be not now, yet it will come. The readiness is all.
Since no man of aught he leaves knows, what is 't
to leave betimes? Let be.

*[A table prepared. Enter Trumpets, Drums, and Officers
with cushions, King, Queen, Osric, and all the state, foils,
daggers, flagons of wine, and Laertes.]*

225 King. Come, Hamlet, come and take this hand from me.

[He puts Laertes' hand into Hamlet's.]

Hamlet [*to* Laertes]. Give me your pardon, sir. I have
done you wrong;
But pardon 't as you are a gentleman. This presence
knows,
And you must needs have heard, how I am punished
With a sore distraction. What I have done
230 That might your nature, honor, and exception
Roughly awake, I here proclaim was madness.
Was 't Hamlet wronged Laertes? Never Hamlet.
If Hamlet from himself be ta'en away.
And when he's not himself does wrong Laertes,
235 Then Hamlet does it not; Hamlet denies it.
Who does it, then? His madness. If 't be so,
Hamlet is of the faction that is wronged;
His madness is poor Hamlet's enemy.
Sir, in this audience
240 Let my disclaiming from a purposed evil
Free me so far in your most generous thoughts
That I have shot my arrow o'er the house
And hurt my brother.

Laertes. I am satisfied in nature,
245 Whose motive in this case should stir me most
To my revenge; but in my terms of honor
I stand aloof and will no reconcilement

215–216 gaingiving:
misgiving.

218 repair: coming.

219–224 Hamlet rejects
augury (attempting to
foresee the future by
interpreting omens) and
declares that since the
death of even a sparrow
is not left to chance,
he is ready to accept
any circumstances he
encounters; his death
will come sooner or later.
He concludes that since
man knows nothing
about the life he leaves
behind, what does it
matter if he leaves early?

227 presence: royal
assembly.

229 sore distraction:
severe confusion.

230 exception:
disapproval.

237 faction: party.

240 purposed evil:
intentional harm.

242 That I have: as if
I had.

244–250 Laertes is
satisfied in regard to his
own feelings (**nature**),
but in regard to his
honor he will wait until
men experienced in such
matters have given their
authoritative judgment
(**voice and precedent**)
in favor of reconciliation,
which would allow him
to keep his reputation
undamaged (**name
ungored**).

Hamlet: Act V, Scene 2 **347**

CLOSE READ

Analyze Structure: Conflict (sc. 2 LINES 226–243)

COMMON CORE RL 3

In these lines, Hamlet expresses his own
interpretation of his character and the events related
to Polonius' death.

U ASK STUDENTS to examine lines 226–243 in
which Hamlet tries to explain his actions to Laertes.
Students should summarize his thoughts and assess
whether this explanation is plausible or sufficient.
*(Hamlet blames his actions on madness and inadvertent
consequences from his actions. This is a curious
explanation since Hamlet has repeatedly claimed that
his madness has been an act to allow him to investigate
his father's death. He accepts no responsibility for
himself—the wrong was "Never Hamlet" but instead
what replaced Hamlet when Hamlet was "ta'en away.")*

Determine Figurative Meanings (sc. 2 LINES 241–243)

COMMON CORE RL 4

Hamlet uses certain figures of speech to justify his
actions.

V ASK STUDENTS to examine lines 241–243,
identify the figure of speech used and how the
comparison serves to justify Hamlet's actions.
*(Hamlet uses a simile to compare himself to an innocent
boy who hurts his brother by mistake and without
malice. The comparison portrays Hamlet as blameless in
Polonius' death.)*

Strategies for Annotation   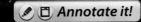 *Annotate it!*

Determine Figurative Meanings

COMMON CORE RL 4

Share these strategies for guided or independent analysis:

- Highlight in blue any similes or metaphors.
- Highlight in pink any allusions or strong language.
- On notes, explain the meaning of the figurative language.

Osric. I commend my duty to your lordship.

Hamlet. Yours. [*Osric exits.*] He does well to commend

it himself. There are no tongues else for 's turn.

Horatio. This lapwing runs away with the shell on his head.

Hamlet. He did comply, sir, with his dug before he

sucked it. Thus has he (and many more of the same

Osric is a
tiny young
bird, barely
hatched

Analyze Drama Elements: Plot (sc. 2 LINE 264)

 COMMON CORE RL 3

Explain that a single line of dialogue and a single action can be crucial to the plot.

W ASK STUDENTS to examine line 264 and explain why Shakespeare includes it in the play and what purpose it serves in advancing the plot. *(Laertes requests another sword until he gets the one he wants, reminding the audience that it is crucial that he has the sword that the King has poisoned.)*

Till by some elder masters of known honor
I have a voice and precedent of peace
250 To keep my name ungored. But till that time
I do receive your offered love like love
And will not wrong it.

Hamlet.   I embrace it freely
And will this brothers' wager frankly play.—
Give us the foils. Come on.

Laertes.   Come, one for me.

255 **Hamlet.** I'll be your foil, Laertes; in mine ignorance
Your skill shall, like a star i' th' darkest night,
Stick fiery off indeed.

Laertes.   You mock me, sir.

Hamlet. No, by this hand.

King. Give them the foils, young Osric. Cousin Hamlet,
260 You know the wager?

Hamlet.   Very well, my lord.
Your Grace has laid the odds o' th' weaker side.

King. I do not fear it; I have seen you both.
But, since he is better, we have therefore odds.

Laertes. This is too heavy. Let me see another.

253 frankly: without any hard feelings.

255 foil: metallic background used to display a jewel (punning on **foils**, referring to the blunted swords).

257 Stick fiery off: stand out brilliantly.

260–261 Hamlet comments that Claudius has bet on (**laid the odds o'**) the weaker fencer. Claudius expresses confidence in Hamlet, but says he has arranged a handicap (**odds**) for Laertes because he has improved.

Hamlet dueling with Laertes (Terence Morgan)

348 Collection 4

APPLYING ACADEMIC VOCABULARY

drama	integrity

As you discuss the upcoming swordplay, incorporate the Collection 4 academic vocabulary words *drama* and *integrity*. Ask students to suggest how this coming action differs from much of the rest of the play and enhances the **drama.** Ask students to assess the **integrity** of the main characters—the King, the Queen, Laertes, Hamlet—as the climax approaches.

265 **Hamlet.** This likes me well. These foils have all a length?

Osric. Ay, my good lord.

[*Prepare to play.*]

King. Set me the stoups of wine upon that table.—
If Hamlet give the first or second hit
Or quit in answer of the third exchange,
270 Let all the battlements their ordnance fire.
The King shall drink to Hamlet's better breath,
And in the cup an union shall he throw,
Richer than that which four successive kings
In Denmark's crown have worn. Give me the cups,
275 And let the kettle to the trumpet speak,
The trumpet to the cannoneer without,
The cannons to the heavens, the heaven to earth,
"Now the King drinks to Hamlet." Come, begin.
And you, the judges, bear a wary eye.

[*Trumpets the while.*]

280 **Hamlet.** Come on, sir.

Laertes. Come, my lord.

[*They play.*]

Hamlet. One.

Laertes. No.

Hamlet. Judgment!

285 **Osric.** A hit, a very palpable hit.

Laertes. Well, again.

King. Stay, give me drink.—Hamlet, this pearl is thine.
Here's to thy health.

[*He drinks and then drops the pearl in the cup. Drum,
trumpets, and shot.*]

Give him the cup.

Hamlet. I'll play this bout first. Set it by awhile.
290 Come. They play. Another hit. What say you?

Laertes. A touch, a touch. I do confess 't.

King. Our son shall win.

Queen. He's fat and scant of breath.
Here, Hamlet, take my napkin; rub thy brows.
The Queen carouses to thy fortune, Hamlet.

[*She lifts the cup.*]

295 **Hamlet.** Good madam.

265 likes me: pleases me; **have all a length:** are all the same length.

269 quit ... exchange: gets back at Laertes by scoring the third hit.

272 union: pearl.

275 kettle: kettledrum.

292 fat: sweaty

293 napkin: handkerchief.

Hamlet: Act V, Scene 2 **349**

CLOSE READ

Analyze Drama Elements: Plot (sc. 2 LINES 267–279)

 COMMON CORE RL 3

Explain that Shakespeare uses the King's directions here to remind the audience of important elements of the plot.

X CITE TEXT EVIDENCE Ask students to examine lines 267–279 and identify lines that notify the audience of an important bit of stagecraft needed to advance the plot. (*In lines 271–274, the King suggests he will give Hamlet a cup containing a valuable pearl for his success in any of the first three rounds of swordplay. It is obvious that the pearl is meant to mark the cup that is poisoned to cause Hamlet's death.*)

Analyze Point of View: Irony (sc. 2 LINES 287–288)

 COMMON CORE RL 6

Ask student to review the definition of **verbal irony** before answering the question.

Y ASK STUDENTS to examine lines 287–288 and explain why this is an example of verbal irony. (*The King gives Hamlet the poisoned cup, hoping that it will kill him while voicing the words "Here's to your health." The King means the opposite of his words but cannot speak his meaning out loud.*)

Analyze Drama Elements: RL 3
Foil (sc. 2 LINES 301–309)

Explain that ever since his return, the character of Laertes has functioned as a foil for the character of Hamlet.

Z **ASK STUDENTS** to examine lines 301–309 and explain how they illustrate a contrast between the character of Hamlet and the character of Laertes. *(In these lines, Laertes expresses some misgivings about his actions because of his conscience, but proceeds with the plan to kill Hamlet despite them. Hamlet was not moved to action until he was absolutely convinced of the rightness of his actions by discovering the King's letter ordering his execution.)*

Analyze Drama Elements: RL 3
Character (sc. 2 LINE 315)

Note that some characters in Shakespearean drama are moved to a self-realization as they approach death.

A2 **ASK STUDENTS** to examine line 315 and explain how it indicates a change in the character of Laertes. *(Laertes acknowledges that he is "killed with mine own treachery." Before his impending death, he probably would not have classified his actions as "treachery" but rather as a justifiable means of seeking revenge for his father, Polonius.)*

King. Gertrude, do not drink.

Queen. I will, my lord; I pray you pardon me.

[*She drinks.*]

King [*aside*]. It is the poisoned cup. It is too late.

Hamlet. I dare not drink yet, madam—by and by.

300 **Queen.** Come, let me wipe thy face.

Laertes [*to* Claudius]. My lord, I'll hit him now.

King.   I do not think 't.

Laertes [*aside*]. And yet it is almost against my conscience.

Hamlet. Come, for the third, Laertes. You do but dally.
I pray you pass with your best violence.
305 I am afeard you make a wanton of me.

Laertes. Say you so? Come on. [*Play.*]

Osric. Nothing neither way.

Laertes. Have at you now!

[Laertes *wounds* Hamlet. *Then in scuffling they change rapiers, and* Hamlet *wounds* Laertes.]

King. Part them. They are incensed.

310 **Hamlet.** Nay, come again.

[*The* Queen *falls.*]

Osric. Look to the Queen there, ho!

Horatio. They bleed on both sides.—How is it, my lord?

Osric. How is 't, Laertes?

Laertes. Why as a woodcock to mine own springe, Osric.

[*He falls.*]

315 I am justly killed with mine own treachery.

Hamlet. How does the Queen?

King.   She swoons to see them bleed.

Queen. No, no, the drink, the drink! O, my dear Hamlet!

The drink, the drink! I am poisoned. [*She dies.*]

Hamlet. O villainy! Ho! Let the door be locked.

[Osric *exits.*]

320 Treachery! Seek it out.

304 pass: thrust.

305 make a wanton of me: indulge me as if I were a spoiled child.

314 Laertes says he's been caught like a **woodcock** (a proverbially stupid bird) in his own trap.

Laertes. It is here, Hamlet. Hamlet, thou art slain.
No med'cine in the world can do thee good.
In thee there is not half an hour's life.
The treacherous instrument is in thy hand,
325 Unbated and envenomed. The foul practice
Hath turned itself on me. Lo, here I lie,
Never to rise again. Thy mother's poisoned.
I can no more. The King, the King's to blame.

Hamlet. The point envenomed too! Then, venom, to
    thy work. [*Hurts the* King.]
330 All Treason, treason!

King. O, yet defend me, friends! I am but hurt.

Hamlet. Here, thou incestuous, murd'rous, damnèd Dane,
Drink off this potion. Is thy union here?

[*Forcing him to drink the poison.*]

Follow my mother.

[King *dies.*]

Laertes.   He is justly served.
335 It is a poison tempered by himself.
Exchange forgiveness with me, noble Hamlet.
Mine and my father's death come not upon thee,
Nor thine on me.

[*Dies.*]

Hamlet. Heaven make thee free of it. I follow thee.—
340 I am dead, Horatio.—Wretched queen, adieu.—
You that look pale and tremble at this chance,
That are but mutes or audience to this act,
Had I but time (as this fell sergeant, Death,
Is strict in his arrest), O, I could tell you—
345 But let it be.—Horatio, I am dead.
Thou livest; report me and my cause aright
To the unsatisfied.

Horatio.   Never believe it.
I am more an antique Roman than a Dane.
Here's yet some liquor left.

[*He picks up the cup.*]

Hamlet.   As thou'rt a man,
350 Give me the cup. Let go! By heaven, I'll ha 't.
O God, Horatio, what a wounded name,
Things standing thus unknown, shall I leave behind me!
If thou didst ever hold me in thy heart,
Absent thee from felicity awhile

325 unbated: not blunted; **practice:** trick.

333 union: a pun on the meanings "pearl" and "marriage." (Claudius is joining his wife in death.)

335 tempered: mixed.

342 mutes: silent observers (literally, actors without speaking parts).

343 fell sergeant: cruel arresting officer.

348 more an antique Roman: a reference to the Roman idea that suicide can be an honorable action following a defeat or the death of a loved one.

354 Absent thee from felicity: deny yourself the pleasure of death.

Hamlet: Act V, Scene 2 **351**

CLOSE READ

Analyze Drama Elements: Character (sc. 2 LINES 327–334)

Explain that extreme events may create extreme changes in characters as well.

B2 ASK STUDENTS to examine lines 327–334 and explain how they indicate a final change in Hamlet. *(When Hamlet realizes that the King is responsible for his mother's death as well as his own death from the rigged sword fight, Hamlet moves to kill the King, an action he has been contemplating since the early part of the play.)*

Determine Figurative Meanings (sc. 2 LINES 343–344)

Shakespeare's figurative language again provides a vivid image in the moments before Hamlet's death. Remind students that **personification** is a figure of speech in which human qualities are given to an object, animal, or idea.

C2 ASK STUDENTS to examine lines 343–344, identify the figure of speech used, and explain how the comparison serves to illustrate Hamlet's situation. *(Hamlet uses personification to illustrate the finality of his situation by suggesting that Death is a human "sergeant" who will not release an arrested person. Hamlet indicates he will not escape death.)*

WHEN STUDENTS STRUGGLE . . .

Explain that the action in the final scene is fast and furious and that most actions serve as a cause of a further effect. To insure comprehension, complete the following exercise with students.

ASK STUDENTS to identify the effects of the following actions:

- Gertrude drinks from the wrong cup *(she dies because of Claudius' treachery towards Hamlet)*
- Laertes wounds Hamlet with the poisoned dagger *(Hamlet wounds Laertes also and both die of the poison)*
- Laertes explains the King's treachery before dying *(Hamlet stabs the King and forces him to drink poison and the King dies)*

Analyze Drama Elements: **RL 3**

Plot (sc. 2 LINES 376–383)

Explain that the arrival of the Ambassador from England helps to wrap up the plot of the play.

D2 **CITE TEXT EVIDENCE** Ask students to examine lines 376–383 and identify lines that notify the audience of important events that have occurred off stage. Students should explain the importance of these events. *(Line 380 indicates that other people who were a part of the treachery, the messengers Rosencrantz and Guildenstern, have been executed, as Hamlet directed in his forged letter. This event wraps up the effects of the plot, reaching back to the death of the elder King Hamlet with the deaths of everyone involved.)*

---

355 And in this harsh world draw thy breath in pain
To tell my story.

[*A march afar off and shot within.*]

What warlike noise is this?

[*Enter* Osric.]

Osric. Young Fortinbras, with conquest come from Poland,
To th' ambassadors of England gives
This warlike volley.

Hamlet.   O, I die, Horatio!
360 The potent poison quite o'ercrows my spirit.
I cannot live to hear the news from England.
But I do prophesy th' election lights
On Fortinbras; he has my dying voice.
So tell him, with th' occurrents, more and less,
365 Which have solicited—the rest is silence.
O, O, O, O!

[*Dies.*]

Horatio. Now cracks a noble heart. Good night, sweet
  prince,
And flights of angels sing thee to thy rest.

[*March within.*]

Why does the drum come hither?

[*Enter* Fortinbras *with the* English Ambassadors *with
Drum, Colors, and* Attendants.]

370 **Fortinbras.** Where is this sight?

Horatio. What is it you would see?
If aught of woe or wonder, cease your search.

Fortinbras. This quarry cries on havoc. O proud Death,
What feast is toward in thine eternal cell
375 That thou so many princes at a shot
So bloodily hast struck?

D2 **Ambassador.**   The sight is dismal,
And our affairs from England come too late.
The ears are senseless that should give us hearing
To tell him his commandment is fulfilled,
380 That Rosencrantz and Guildenstern are dead.
Where should we have our thanks?

Horatio.   Not from his mouth,
Had it th' ability of life to thank you.
He never gave commandment for their death.
But since, so jump upon this bloody question,

357–359 Fortinbras, returning triumphant from Poland, has saluted the English ambassadors with a volley of gunfire.

360 o'ercrows: triumphs over (like the winner in a cockfight).

362–363 Hamlet predicts that Fortinbras will be elected the new Danish king and gives him his vote (**voice**).

364 occurrents: occurrences.

365 solicited: prompted, brought about. (Hamlet dies before finishing this thought.)

373 This heap of dead bodies (**quarry**) proclaims a massacre (**cries on havoc**).

374 toward: in preparation.

381 his: Claudius's.

384 so jump upon this bloody question: so soon after this bloody quarrel.

TO CHALLENGE STUDENTS . . .

Consider Characterization What would have happened if one of the main characters had survived? Note that Hamlet dies a dramatic and painful death from a wound from the poisoned sword inflicted by Laertes. When Fortinbras arrives, he finds the bodies of the King, the Queen, Laertes, and Hamlet, and the English ambassador arrives to announce the deaths of Rosencrantz and Guildenstern.

Challenge students to imagine and write a different ending to the play. Imagine that one of the characters somehow survives the carnage through a spilled drink or a missed sword thrust. They should describe how the character changes (if at all) from the tragedies surrounding Hamlet and his father and mother and what actions they take. Have pairs of students exchange their work and discuss any questions.

385 You from the Polack wars, and you from England,
Are here arrived, give order that these bodies
High on a stage be placed to the view,
And let me speak to th' yet unknowing world
390 How these things came about. So shall you hear

Of carnal, bloody, and unnatural acts,
Of accidental judgments, casual slaughters,
Of deaths put on by cunning and forced cause,
And, in this upshot, purposes mistook
395 Fall'n on th' inventors' heads. All this can I
Truly deliver.

Fortinbras. Let us haste to hear it
And call the noblest to the audience.
For me, with sorrow I embrace my fortune.
I have some rights of memory in this kingdom,
Which now to claim my vantage doth invite me.

400 **Horatio.** Of that I shall have also cause to speak,
And from his mouth whose voice will draw on more.
But let this same be presently performed
Even while men's minds are wild, lest more mischance
On plots and errors happen.

Fortinbras. Let four captains
405 Bear Hamlet like a soldier to the stage,
For he was likely, had he been put on,
To have proved most royal; and for his passage,
The soldier's music and the rite of war
Speak loudly for him.
410 Take up the bodies. Such a sight as this
Becomes the field but here shows much amiss.
Go, bid the soldiers shoot.

[*They exit, marching, after the which a peal of ordnance are shot off.*]

COLLABORATIVE DISCUSSION With a partner, discuss the reasons why Hamlet continues to capture the interest of critics and readers four centuries after his creation. Cite evidence from the play to support your opinion.

387 stage: platform.

390 carnal, bloody, and unnatural acts: Claudius's murder of his brother and marriage to Gertrude.

391 accidental judgments, casual slaughters: punishments that occurred by chance.

392 put on: instigated; **forced:** contrived.

395 deliver: tell the story of.

398–399 Fortinbras says he has some unforgotten claims to Denmark, and this is a favorable time to present them.

401 from his mouth . . . more: the words of Hamlet, whose decision will influence other votes.

402 presently: immediately.

403–404 lest more . . . happen: lest other trouble occur in addition to these plots and accidents.

406 put on: enthroned, and so put to the test.

407 passage: death.

411 field: field of battle.

CLOSE READ

Determine Theme
COMMON CORE **RL 2**

(sc. 2 LINES 389–395)

Explain that in the closing actions of a play, characters may summarize what has happened and make some judgment on them. These comments may spark the audience to think about another theme.

 ASK STUDENTS to examine lines 389–395. Ask them to consider Horatio's words and suggest a theme expressed in them. (*Horatio's words review the entire series of events that have resulted in the total destruction of the Danish royal court. They include Claudius' actions to kill the elder King Hamlet, Claudius' action to retain his power, Hamlet's actions in killing Polonius, and the events of the final scene involving Laertes, Hamlet, and the King and Queen. This recitation may spur the audience to think about human nature and the susceptibility of human beings to the base instincts that create "carnal, bloody, and unnatural acts.")*

Analyze Drama Elements: Foil
COMMON CORE **RL 3**

(sc. 2 LINES 396–399)

Note that Fortinbras continues as a foil to the character of Hamlet even after his death.

ASK STUDENTS to examine lines 396–399 and explain how he serves as a foil to the character of Hamlet. (*Fortinbras is straightforward and decisive in his intention to "hear" the events that have transpired. Because of the events, he is also able to move directly toward ruling the kingdom because of his "rights of memory." This contrasts with Hamlet, who was never able to hear a clear story of the events related to the murder of his father and was never able to move clearly towards the leadership of the country.*)

COLLABORATIVE DISCUSSION Have small groups discuss their reactions to Hamlet and the differing nature of his character. The numerous facets of his personality and conflict and subsequent behavior both mystify and intrigue readers.

ASK STUDENTS to share any questions they generated in the course of reading and discussing the selection.

Analyze Language: Soliloquy COMMON CORE RL 4

Ask students to identify the soliloquies that are memorable to them from *Hamlet*. Discuss the reasons soliloquies are memorable if they are written well. *(The speaker of the soliloquy is not distracted or affected by other characters or events and is able to identify and describe ideas or emotions that have not been revealed in speech or actions in the presence of others.)* Note that in modern dramas on TV, movies, or on stage, soliloquies are no longer a common dramatic device.

Analyze Drama Elements: Conflict COMMON CORE RL 3

Encourage students to answer each question as Hamlet would have.

- **The Ghost** *(an emissary of truth)*
- **The deed and his soul** *(His soul is absolved because his actions were necessary for righteous revenge.)*
- **His conscience** *(He could not live with his conscience if he did not take action.)*
- **Corruptibility and nobility** *(Each is apparent and neither is triumphant.)*

Analyze Language: Soliloquy COMMON CORE RL 4

A **soliloquy** is a long speech performed in a drama by a character alone on the stage. Hamlet delivers seven soliloquies in the first four acts of the play. These soliloquies perform multiple functions: they develop Hamlet's character; they expose his internal conflict; they foreshadow the action to come; they present his perspective on the other characters and events; and they communicate themes. In these speeches, Hamlet speaks the truth as he sees it; no deception is necessary.

Hamlet's language in these speeches is rich and powerful; his words draw the audience into his state of mind and remain memorable long after the play is over. To achieve this lasting impact, Shakespeare uses a variety of techniques.

Language in Hamlet's Soliloquies	
Figures of speech: metaphors, similes, and personification	Act III, Scene 2, 391–393: "'Tis now the very witching time of night, / When churchyards yawn and hell itself breathes out / Contagion to this world." The personification emphasizes Hamlet's heightened awareness of the evil around him.
Allusions	Act I, Scene 2, 139–140: "So excellent a king, that was to this / Hyperion to a satyr. . . ." Hamlet alludes to Hyperion, the sun god, to make the point that his father had integrity—unlike Claudius, whom he compares to a satyr, a mythical half-goat, half-man figure associated with lechery.
Powerful imagery; careful word choices	Act III, Scene 2, 393–395: "Now could I drink hot blood / And do such bitter business as the day / Would quake to look on." The sensory details show the intensity of Hamlet's feelings.

Analyze Drama Elements: Conflict COMMON CORE RL 3

In contrast with many of Shakespeare's tragic heroes, Hamlet's conflicts often result in inaction rather than action. As the play opens, Hamlet is already suffering a profound disillusionment about the nature of women. His subsequent encounter with the Ghost darkens his vision further. Still, he cannot surrender himself to the duty demanded by the Ghost until he has resolved his inner conflict by answering the questions that plague him:

- Is the Ghost an emissary of truth or deception?
- How will the deed affect the fate of his soul?
- How will he live with his conscience if he does or does not kill Claudius?
- How can one reconcile the corruption and nobility within human nature?

By answering these questions, Hamlet achieves the resolution that he needs to act.

Strategies for Annotation 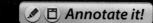 *Annotate it!*

Analyze Structure: Conflict COMMON CORE RL 3

Share these strategies for guided or independent analysis:

- Highlight in yellow lines related to the Ghost and his truth or deception.
- Underline lines that are determined to be truthful by the end of the play.
- Highlight in blue lines related to Hamlet's conscience.
- Write a note that indicates Hamlet's feelings about his conscience.

He that hath killed my king and whored my mother,

Popped in between th' election and my hopes,

Thrown out his angle for my proper life,

And with such cozenage—is 't not perfect conscience

To quit him with this arm? And is 't not to be damned

To let this canker of our nature come

In further evil?

> Hamlet feels he needs to kill the King to live with his conscience.

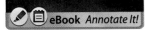  **eBook** *Annotate It!*

Analyzing the Text

COMMON CORE   RL 1, RL 2, RL 3, RL 4, RL 5, RL 6, W 10, SL 6

Cite Text Evidence Support your responses with evidence from the selection.

1. **Analyze** Review Hamlet's encounter with the Gravedigger and his thoughts about Yorick at the beginning of Act V. Why might Shakespeare have chosen to include this darkly humorous scene here?

2. **Interpret** Why does Hamlet quarrel with Laertes at Ophelia's grave? What does this conflict clarify about his feelings?

3. **Infer** In the story he tells Horatio at the start of Act V, Scene 2, what qualities does Hamlet show that he has not displayed previously?

4. **Analyze** Ideas, customs, behaviors, or institutions are ridiculed in **satire** for the purpose of improving society. Satirists often use irony, wordplay, and exaggeration to poke fun at their targets. Reread Hamlet's exchange of words with Osric in Scene 2, lines 82–184. What customs or behavior is Hamlet ridiculing? Identify examples of techniques used in this satirical passage.

5. **Compare** Reread Hamlet's speech in Scene 2, lines 219–224. How do these thoughts about fate differ from his attitude in earlier speeches?

6. **Infer** As he is dying, Hamlet urges Horatio to stay alive and tell his story. Why is this so important to Hamlet?

7. **Analyze** Choose a soliloquy in the play, such as the famous "To be or not to be" speech in Act III, Scene 1, lines 57–89. Summarize the ideas in the soliloquy, and discuss the literary techniques Shakespeare uses to express them. Provide specific examples.

8. **Draw Conclusions** A **theme** is the central idea that a writer wishes to convey to the audience. Use specific details to explain what message *Hamlet* conveys about each of these subjects:
   • revenge
   • fate
   • the human condition

PERFORMANCE TASK

Speaking Activity: Funeral Speech If you were invited to speak at Hamlet's funeral, what would you say?

• Think about your overall impression of Hamlet's character. What were his admirable qualities, and what were his flaws? What motivated his actions?

• Write a brief speech that you would deliver at Hamlet's funeral. Address the events that led up to his death. Sum up your conclusions about him in a way that fits the occasion.

• Deliver your speech to a small group of classmates.

Assign this performance task.

PERFORMANCE TASK   COMMON CORE   W 10, SL 6

Writing Activity: Funeral Speech Explain that a funeral speech, or eulogy, cites the good qualities of the deceased, often through anecdotes and reminiscences. Students' speeches should reflect thoughtful analysis of Hamlet's character, motivations, and actions, and should include language appropriate for such a somber occasion.

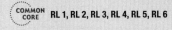

PRACTICE & APPLY

Analyzing the Text   COMMON CORE   RL 1, RL 2, RL 3, RL 4, RL 5, RL 6

Possible answers:

1. *The gravediggers' scene provides comic relief, but it also offers a meditation on the nature of death. All are reduced to dust and bones, no matter what their status. This scene shows that Hamlet no longer seeks death, but now accepts it as life's natural conclusion.*

2. *Hamlet objects to Laertes's expression of emotion, particularly when compared to his own feelings. Their quarrel reveals Hamlet's need to outdo Laertes in his show of grief.*

3. *Hamlet shows that he has become a man of action rather than reflection. He altered the king's letter to cause the deaths of Rosencrantz and Guildenstern (lines 38–47), and then escaped from the ship.*

4. *Through Osric, Shakespeare satirizes the effete "European" fashions of upper society. He exaggerates his obsequiousness (lines 95–104), mocks Osric's pompous language (lines 113–127), and mocks his attire and manner with puns (line 180, 190).*

5. *This speech shows that Hamlet embraces his fate and no longer tries to anticipate the consequences of his actions. He realizes that he has a destiny that will dictate what happens to him here and hereafter.*

6. *Hamlet fears that "things standing thus unknown" will never be understood unless Horatio tells the story and prevents "more mischance on plots and errors" from happening. Horatio symbolizes truth, an antidote to the corruption and deception of other characters.*

7. *In Scene 1, lines 57–89, Hamlet ponders what lies after death. Shakespeare uses parallel structure to echo the balancing of Hamlet's thoughts. He employs metaphors and personification to contrast Hamlet's images of what life has to offer with what is unknown about death, describing "the slings and arrows of outrageous fortune," "a sea of troubles," "the whips and scorns of time," and concluding that "conscience does make cowards of us all." His fear of the unknown ultimately "puzzles the will" and makes "enterprises of great pitch" "lose the name of action."*

8. *Through the deaths of all involved in elements of revenge, Shakespeare shows it is a waste. He implies the dominance of fate; that everyone has a role, and each must accept it. Hamlet shows the paradox of human nature in the way in which our better impulses conflict with our desires. Through this dichotomy, Shakespeare explores how our ideas of the afterlife shape our mortal actions.*

Language and Style: Paradox

 COMMON CORE L 5a

Emphasize that paradoxical expression, including oxymorons, are ways to grab the attention of the audience because they combine clearly opposing attributes of a situation. Discuss the idea that Hamlet himself is a paradoxical character who exhibits widely divergent characteristics: impulsiveness and careful planning, tenderness and extreme violence, attraction to Ophelia and disgust with Ophelia, etc.

Possible answers:

Individual insertions of paradoxes into the funeral speeches will vary. Invite volunteers to share with the class paradoxical references or expressions they have used in their funeral speeches.

1. **(Hamlet)** *This paradox is in reference to excessive drinking that occurs at the King's late-night celebrations. By saying that among the people, the habit of excessive drinking is more honored in the breach than in the observance, Hamlet suggests that Danish citizens are not excessive drinkers.*

2. **(Polonius)** *Polonius says that by asking misleading questions that are false accusations against his son, they will find out the truth of his behavior.*

3. **(Hamlet)** *Hamlet says this to his mother, meaning that to force her to face the truth and save herself, he has to be cruel.*

Assess It!

Online Selection Test
- Download an editable ExamView bank.
- Assign and manage this test online.

Language and Style: Paradox

 COMMON CORE L 5a

A **paradox** is a statement that is seemingly contradictory but actually reveals a truth. Shakespeare uses this literary device frequently in *Hamlet*. By expressing ideas paradoxically, he is able to convey subtle meanings and reinforce the audience's understanding of the duplicitous nature of many of the characters and their actions.

In Act I, Scene 2, Claudius's first speech features examples of paradox and **oxymoron** (a paradox condensed into a brief phrase):

> Have we (as 'twere with a defeated joy,
> With an auspicious and a dropping eye,
> With mirth in funeral and with dirge in marriage,
> In equal scale weighing delight and dole)
> Taken to wife.

He speaks of "defeated joy," "mirth in funeral," "dirge in marriage," and "weighing delight and dole." These paradoxical expressions tell those assembled that he views his marriage and accession to the throne as a mixed blessing, achieved at the expense of his brother's life. The use of paradox also hints at his own contradictory nature: outwardly virtuous, inwardly scheming and self-centered.

Hamlet also uses paradoxical language in the play. For example, in Act II, Scene 2, lines 309–320, he describes humankind in idealistic terms ("how noble in reason, how infinite in faculties . . . in action how like an angel, in apprehension how like a god") but ends the speech with the dismissive remark, "and yet, to me, what is this quintessence of dust? Man delights not me. . . ." This paradox emphasizes Hamlet's obsession with human corruption.

Note these other instances of paradox in the play:

- **Hamlet:** "it is a custom / More honored in the breach than the observance" (Act I, Scene 4, lines 17–18)
- **Polonius:** "Your bait of falsehood takes this carp of truth; / And thus do we of wisdom and of reach, / With windlasses and with assays of bias, / By indirections find directions out." (Act II, Scene 1, lines 63–66)
- **Hamlet:** "I must be cruel only to be kind." (Act III, Scene 4, line 184)

Practice and Apply Review the context of each example of paradox listed. With a partner, discuss the meaning of each paradox and examine how it deepens the audience's understanding of the character or situation. Then look back at the funeral speech you wrote for the Performance Task that follows Act V. Insert a reference to one of the paradoxes from the play, or create your own paradoxical expression about Hamlet's life.

Analyze Drama Elements: Foil

COMMON CORE

RL 3

TEACH

Review the idea that a **foil** is a way for a playwright to highlight a character's traits by providing another character with opposing or differing traits. Shakespeare uses both Laertes and Fortinbras as foils for Hamlet. Their words and actions allow the audience to think more deeply about Hamlet.

PRACTICE AND APPLY

To highlight differences among the three characters, have students create and fill in a character chart similar to the one shown below. For each character trait, students should support their ideas by citing one or more scenes or speeches from the play. Following are examples:

Character	Trait	Text Support
Laertes	decisive	Act IV, Scene 5, lines 100–120
	not stopped by conscience	Act V, Scene 2, lines 302–308
Fortinbras	direct in action and speech	Act IV, Scene 4, lines 1–7
	able to act to take leadership	Act V, Scene 2, lines 396–399
Hamlet	indecisive	Act III, Scene 1, lines 57–91
	evasive in speech and action	Act IV, Scene 2, lines 11–31

Analyze Structure: Conflict

COMMON CORE

RL 3

RETEACH

 LEVEL UP TUTORIALS Assign the following *Level Up* tutorial: **Characters and Conflict**

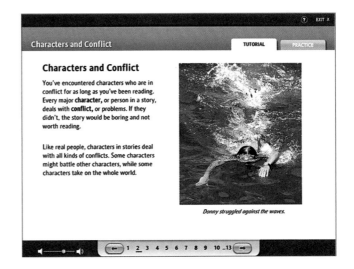

Donny struggled against the waves.

Lead a discussion of Hamlet's *internal* and *external conflicts*. (Review the terms if needed.) Have pairs answer these questions:

- What is Hamlet's major internal conflict? How do you know? *(Hamlet's major internal conflict is that his father has died and he is unsure about how because in Act I [lines 44–63], the Ghost seems to indicate that the King is not at peace.)*

- What are some external conflicts that resulted from Hamlet's internal conflicts? *(Sample answer: He came into conflict with his mother, stepfather, and friends. In his effort to resolve his internal conflict about his father's death, he entered into conflicts with other characters in the play.)*

- How are some of Hamlet's conflicts resolved in Act V? *(Because Hamlet discovers the exact nature of the King's plans, he no longer feels conflicted about killing him. This resolves the conflict caused by his guilty feelings and conscience.)*

Discuss students' answers as a group.

CLOSE READING APPLICATION

Have students identify a personal issue that creates internal and external conflict. Have them research it using print or online resources to write a paragraph about why they may feel internal conflict related to it or why it might create external conflict.

from The Tragedy of Hamlet

Drama by William Shakespeare

Why This Text

Although Hamlet is a prince of an ancient kingdom, he is also a young person caught up in circumstances beyond his control. He is a son who has lost a beloved father and who resents and distrusts his mother's new husband—a situation all too understandable to many people today. With the help of the close-reading questions, students will analyze the conflicts that Hamlet faces at the beginning of the play. This close reading will lead students to an understanding of how Shakespeare sets up his tragedy.

Background Have students read the background about *The Tragedy of Hamlet* and its author, William Shakespeare. Tell students that, as was customary at that time, Shakespeare used an existing story as the basis for *Hamlet*. Evidence seems to point to the existence of earlier plays about Hamlet by other playwrights. There were also much older chronicles that told the story (perhaps real, perhaps legendary) of a Danish prince named Amleth.

AS YOU READ Remind students that drama, like fiction, generally depends on a conflict. Which characters seem to be in conflict with one another? What events take place that create or could lead to a conflict faced by the characters?

 Common Core Support

- cite strong and thorough textual evidence
- analyze the impact of the author's choices for the development and relationship of elements of the drama (setting, action, characters)
- analyze the impact of specific word choices

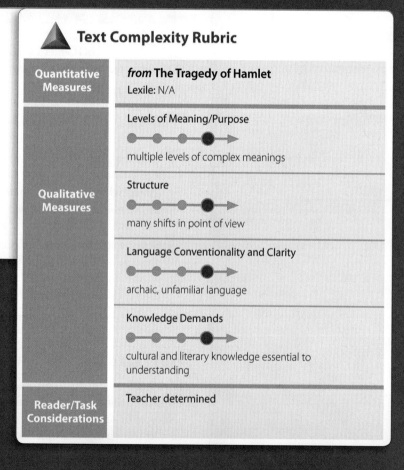

Text Complexity Rubric

Quantitative Measures	*from* The Tragedy of Hamlet
	Lexile: N/A

Qualitative Measures	
	Levels of Meaning/Purpose — multiple levels of complex meanings
	Structure — many shifts in point of view
	Language Conventionality and Clarity — archaic, unfamiliar language
	Knowledge Demands — cultural and literary knowledge essential to understanding

Reader/Task Considerations	Teacher determined

Strategies for CLOSE READING

Analyze Structure: Conflict

Students should read Act I, Scenes 1 and 2 carefully all the way through. Close-reading questions will help them understand how Shakespeare sets up events that foreshadow conflict for the characters, especially Hamlet. As they read, students should jot down comments or questions about the text in the margins.

WHEN STUDENTS STRUGGLE . . .

To help students understand how characters' dialogue reveals conflict, have them work in small groups to fill out a chart like the one shown below.

CITE TEXT EVIDENCE For practice in analyzing conflict, ask students to give text examples and identify the event that seems to create or foreshadow conflict for one or more characters.

Character's Words	Point of Conflict

Horatio
"If thou art privy to thy
    country's fate,
Which happily foreknowing
    may avoid,
O, speak!"
(Act I, Scene 1, lines 137–139)
	The ghost might have come to warn of something bad that is about to happen to Denmark.

Hamlet
"Within a month,
Ere yet the salt of most
    unrighteous tears,
Had left the flushing in her
    galled eyes,
She married. Oh, most wicked
    speed, . . . "
(Act I, Scene 2, lines 153–156)
	Hamlet shows his disgust and disdain for his mother, who has remarried within a month of his father's death.

Background *Written by* **William Shakespeare,** The Tragedy of Hamlet *is considered one of the greatest dramas ever written. It's a political thriller, a murder mystery, and a tragic tale of vengeance. Set in Denmark, the play revolves around Prince Hamlet's quest for revenge. As the play opens, Hamlet's father has died and his uncle Claudius has swiftly married Hamlet's mother Gertrude and pronounces himself the new king. Horatio, Hamlet's friend, joins two guards at the castle wall.*

from
THE TRAGEDY OF
HAMLET

Drama by William Shakespeare

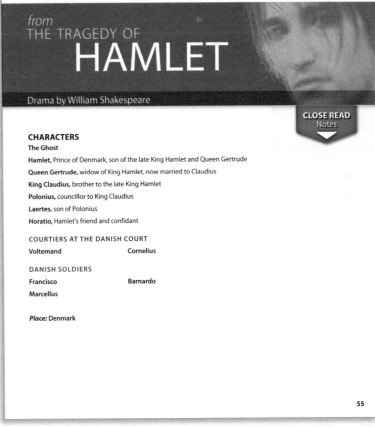

CLOSE READ
Notes

CHARACTERS
The Ghost

Hamlet, Prince of Denmark, son of the late King Hamlet and Queen Gertrude

Queen Gertrude, widow of King Hamlet, now married to Claudius

King Claudius, brother to the late King Hamlet

Polonius, councillor to King Claudius

Laertes, son of Polonius

Horatio, Hamlet's friend and confidant

COURTIERS AT THE DANISH COURT

Voltemand   **Cornelius**

DANISH SOLDIERS

Francisco   **Barnardo**

Marcellus

Place: **Denmark**

55

1. **READ** ▶ As you read lines 1–37, begin to collect and cite text evidence.

- Underline clues that identify an important event that has already occurred.
- In the margin, explain what the section reveals about the government or social structure of the country.

ACT I

Scene 1 • A guard platform at Elsinore Castle.

A [*Enter* Barnardo *and* Francisco, *two sentinels.*]
Barnardo. Who's there?
Francisco. Nay, answer me. Stand and unfold[1] yourself.
Barnardo. Long live the King!
Francisco. Barnardo.
5 **Barnardo.** He.
Francisco. You come most carefully upon your hour.
Barnardo. 'Tis now struck twelve. Get thee to bed, Francisco.
Francisco. For this relief much thanks. 'Tis bitter cold, And I am sick at heart.
10 **Barnardo.** Have you had quiet guard?
Francisco. Not a mouse stirring.
Barnardo. Well, good night.
If you do meet Horatio and Marcellus,
The rivals of my watch,[2] bid them make haste.
[*Enter* Horatio *and* Marcellus.]
15 **Francisco.** I think I hear them.—Stand ho! Who is there?
Horatio. Friends to this ground.
Marcellus. And liegemen to the Dane.[3]
Francisco. Give you good night.
Marcellus. O farewell, honest soldier. Who hath relieved you?
20 **Francisco.** Barnardo hath my place. Give you good night.
[*Francisco exits.*]
Marcellus. Holla, Barnardo.
Barnardo. Say, what, is Horatio there?
Horatio. A piece of him.
Barnardo. Welcome, Horatio.—Welcome, good Marcellus.
25 **Horatio.** What, has this thing appeared again tonight?

[1] **unfold:** identify.
[2] **rivals of my watch:** the others on guard duty with me.
[3] **liegemen to the Dane:** loyal subjects of the Danish king.

Denmark is ruled by a king, to whom the subjects owe loyalty.

56

B **Barnardo.** I have seen nothing.
Marcellus. Horatio says 'tis but our fantasy
And will not let belief take hold of him
Touching this dreaded sight twice seen of us.
30 Therefore I have entreated him along
With us to watch the minutes of this night,
That, if again this **apparition** come,
He may approve our eyes[4] and speak to it.
Horatio. Tush, tush, 'twill not appear.
Barnardo. Sit down awhile,
35 And let us once again assail your ears,
That are so fortified against our story,
What we have two nights seen.
Horatio. Well, sit we down,
And let us hear Barnardo speak of this.
Barnardo. Last night of all,
40 When yond same star that's westward from the pole
Had made his course t'illume that part of heaven
Where now it burns, Marcellus and myself,
The bell then beating one—
[*Enter* Ghost.]
C **Marcellus.** Peace, break thee off! Look where it comes again.
45 **Barnardo.** In the same figure like the King that's dead.
Marcellus (*to* Horatio). Thou art a scholar. Speak to it, Horatio.
Barnardo. Looks he not like the King? Mark it, Horatio.

[4] **approve our eyes:** confirm what we have seen.

apparition: a ghostly figure

2. **◀ REREAD** Reread lines 27–37. What conflicting opinions do Marcellus and Horatio express? What does Marcellus hope will change Horatio's view?

Marcellus is sure he has seen a ghost, but Horatio doesn't believe him. Marcellus hopes that Horatio will be convinced by seeing the ghost himself.

3. **READ** ▶ As you read lines 38–73, continue to cite textual evidence.

- Underline text that shows which man has changed his mind about the "apparition."
- In the margin, explain how Shakespeare gives the events a dynamic pacing rather than just having characters present information.

57

---

1. **READ AND CITE TEXT EVIDENCE** Shakespeare begins the play subtly and mysteriously. At first, it's hard to tell what is about to happen.

A **ASK STUDENTS** what happens in lines 1–25. Ask them where the first hint of an unusual event shows up. What do they learn from that moment? *Horatio asks if "this thing" has "appeared again tonight." It seems as if something unnatural, or at least something that is not a person, has already been seen.*

FOR ELL STUDENTS Explain that the idiom *make haste* (line 14) is equivalent to "hurry up."

2. **REREAD AND CITE TEXT EVIDENCE**

B **ASK STUDENTS** in what two ways we learn of Horatio's first opinion about the ghost. *Students should identify Marcellus's description of Horatio's skepticism (lines 27–29) and Horatio's own statement of disbelief (line 34).*

3. **READ AND CITE TEXT EVIDENCE**

C **ASK STUDENTS** to look at lines 38–48. What effect does the entrance of the ghost have on the pacing and mood of the scene, compared to earlier, when the characters were just standing and talking? *The scene becomes more active, fast paced, and tense.*

Critical Vocabulary: apparition (line 32) Ask students to share their definitions of *apparition*. Ask them how the word choice contributes to the mood of the scene.

CLOSE READ
Notes

As Barnardo is telling how the ghost appeared earlier, he is interrupted by the entrance of the actual ghost, a much more shocking and dynamic way for audiences to experience it.

Horatio. Most like. It harrows me with fear and wonder.

(D) Barnardo. It would be spoke to.

Marcellus.   Speak to it, Horatio.

50 **Horatio.** What art thou that usurp'st[5] this time of night,
Together with that fair and warlike form
In which the majesty of buried Denmark[6]
Did sometimes[7] march? By heaven, I charge thee, speak.

Marcellus. It is offended.

Barnardo.   See, it stalks away.

55 **Horatio.** Stay! speak! speak! I charge thee, speak!

[Ghost *exits*.]

Marcellus. 'Tis gone and will not answer.

Barnardo. How now, Horatio, you tremble and look pale.
Is not this something more than fantasy?
What think you on 't?

60 **Horatio.** Before my God, I might not this believe
Without the sensible and true avouch[8]
Of mine own eyes.

Marcellus.   Is it not like the King?

Horatio. As thou art to thyself.
Such was the very armor he had on

65 When he the ambitious Norway[9] combated.
So frowned he once when, in an angry parle,[10]
He smote the sledded Polacks on the ice.
'Tis strange.

Marcellus. Thus twice before, and jump[11] at this dead hour,

70 With martial stalk hath he gone by our watch.

---
[5] **usurp'st:** unlawfully takes over.
[6] **the majesty of buried Denmark:** the buried King of Denmark.
[7] **sometimes:** formerly.
[8] **avouch:** proof.
[9] **Norway:** the king of Norway; Shakespeare often refers to the ruler of a country by the country's name.
[10] **parle:** meeting with an enemy.
[11] **jump:** exactly.

---

4. **◀ REREAD** Reread lines 57–73. What mood has Shakespeare established so far? Cite textual evidence in your response.

The appearance of the ghost has obviously unsettled everyone. After seeing it, Horatio says that he believes that it portends some disturbance to "our state."

58

CLOSE READ
Notes

" Is not this something more than fantasy? "

Horatio. In what particular thought to work I know not,
But in the gross and scope of mine opinion
This bodes some strange eruption[12] to our state.

Marcellus. Good now, sit down, and tell me, he that knows,

75 Why this same strict and most observant watch
So nightly toils the subject of the land,[13]
And why such daily cast of **brazen** cannon
And foreign mart[14] for implements of war,
Why such impress[15] of shipwrights, whose sore task

80 Does not divide the Sunday from the week.
What might be toward[16] that this sweaty haste
Doth make the night joint laborer with the day?
Who is 't that can inform me?

Horatio.   That can I.

(E) At least the whisper goes so: our last king,

85 Whose image even but now appeared to us,
Was, as you know, by Fortinbras of Norway,
Thereto pricked on by a most emulate pride,
Dared to the combat; in which our valiant Hamlet
(For so this side of our known world esteemed him)

90 Did slay this Fortinbras, who by a sealed compact,[17]
Well ratified by law and heraldry,

brazen:
loud and resonant

The apparition seems to be the ghost of King Hamlet.

---
[12]**eruption:** an outbreak, often of something evil.
[13]**subject of the land:** the ordinary Danish people.
[14]**mart:** trade.
[15]**impress:** forced service.
[16]**toward:** approaching, in preparation.
[17]**sealed compact:** prior agreement.

---

5. **READ ▶** As you read lines 74–129, continue to cite textual evidence.
- Underline sentences that talk about the dead king of Norway, the elder Fortinbras.
- Circle text that refers to the dead king's son, the younger Fortinbras.
- In the margin, explain the connection between the ghost and King Hamlet.

59

---

4. **REREAD AND CITE TEXT EVIDENCE**

(D) ASK STUDENTS to reread lines 44–59. What lines tell how Horatio reacts on seeing the ghost? *Horatio says that it "harrows me with fear and wonder" (line 48), and Barnardo describes him as pale and trembling (line 57).*

FOR ELL STUDENTS Clarify the multiple meanings of the verb *charge* (line 53). Explain that familiar meanings are "to pay with a credit card" and "to attack," but in this context the verb means "to command or instruct with authority."

5. **READ AND CITE TEXT EVIDENCE** This play refers to two men named Fortinbras (father and son) and two men named Hamlet (also father and son). The dead King Hamlet mentioned here is not the play's title character but his father. The dead King Fortinbras, king of Norway, also had a son named after himself.

(E) ASK STUDENTS to look at lines 84–111. How do these lines explain who is who? Which men are dead? Which man is alive? *Students should be aware that the late King Hamlet killed ("did slay") King Fortinbras (the father) in battle. King Hamlet is of course also dead. Young Fortinbras is alive.*

Critical Vocabulary: brazen (line 77) In this case, two possible meanings of *brazen* might apply: "loud and resonant" and "made of brass." Have students discuss how the playwright seems to have conveyed two shades of meaning simultaneously.

CLOSE READ Notes

Did forfeit, with his life, all those his lands
Which he stood seized of, to the conqueror.
Against the which a moiety competent[18]
95 Was gagèd[19] by our king, which had[20] returned
To the inheritance of Fortinbras
Had he been vanquisher, as, by the same comart
And carriage of the article designed, [21]
His fell to Hamlet. Now, sir, young Fortinbras,
100 Of unimproved mettle[22] hot and full,
Hath in the skirts of Norway here and there
Sharked up[23] a list of lawless resolutes
For food and diet to some enterprise
That hath a stomach in 't; which is no other
105 (As it doth well appear unto our state)
But to recover of us, by strong hand
And terms compulsatory, those foresaid lands
So by his father lost. And this, I take it,
Is the main motive of our preparations,
110 The source of this our watch, and the chief head
Of this posthaste and rummage in the land.
Barnardo. I think it be no other but e'en so.
Well may it sort that this **portentous** figure
Comes armed through our watch so like the king
115 That was and is the question of these wars.
(F) Horatio. A mote it is to trouble the mind's eye.
In the most high and palmy state of Rome,
A little ere the mightiest Julius[24] fell,
The graves stood tenantless, and the sheeted dead
120 Did squeak and gibber in the Roman streets;
As stars with trains of fire and dews of blood,
Disasters in the sun; and the moist star,[25]
Upon whose influence Neptune's empire stands,
Was sick almost to doomsday with eclipse.

portenteous:
foreboding,
ominous

---

[18]**moiety competent:** equivalent portion.
[19]**gagèd:** pledged.
[20]**had:** would have.
[21]**comart and carriage of the article designed:** agreement.
[22]**unimproved mettle:** undisciplined character
[23]**sharked up:** gathered hastily.
[24]**the mightiest Julius:** Julius Caesar, ruler of ancient Rome, who was assassinated.
[25]**the moist star:** the Moon.

60

CLOSE READ Notes

125 And even the like precurse of feared events,
As harbingers preceding still the fates
And prologue to the omen coming on,
Have heaven and earth together demonstrated
Unto our climatures[26] and countrymen.
[*Enter* Ghost.]
(G) 130 But soft, behold! Lo, where it comes again!
I'll cross it though it blast me.—Stay, illusion!
[*It spreads his arms.*]
If thou hast any sound or use of voice,
Speak to me.
If there be any good thing to be done
135 That may to thee do ease and grace to me,
Speak to me.
If thou art privy to thy country's fate,
Which happily[27] foreknowing may avoid,
O, speak!
140 Or if thou hast uphoarded in thy life
Extorted treasure in the womb of earth,
For which, they say, you spirits oft walk in death,
Speak of it.

They want to
know about
Denmark's
fate and also
if the ghost
has buried
any treasure.

---

[26]**climatures:** land.
[27]**happily:** perhaps.

---

6. **(◀ REREAD)** Reread lines 116–129. What is the effect of including the references to Julius Caesar's assassination in ancient Rome? Cite textual evidence in your response.

Horatio's descriptions of the supernatural events surrounding
Caesar's murder—the "tenantless" graves and the "sheeted dead"
wandering the streets of Rome—may foreshadow or serve as a
"prologue to the omen" that could afflict the Danes.

7. **(READ ▶)** As you read lines 130–181, continue to cite textual evidence.

• Underline the soldiers' attempts to engage the ghost and their descriptions of its actions.
• In the margin, explain what the soldiers want to learn from the ghost.

61

Critical Vocabulary: portentous (line 113) Ask students to share their definitions of *portentous*. Ask them how the word choice contributes to the mood of the scene.

FOR ELL STUDENTS Students may have trouble with lines 140–143. Explain that Barnardo asks the Ghost if it has any buried treasure somewhere because he has heard this often makes ghosts restless. Ask students what they think the archaic word *uphoard* means here. *to hoard up; to gather up*

6. **REREAD AND CITE TEXT EVIDENCE**

(F) ASK STUDENTS how Shakespeare sets up two parallel situations, one in the past and one in the present. *Horatio says that supernatural happenings such as the dead leaving their graves predicted Caesar's death. The appearance of Hamlet's ghost might be a parallel supernatural warning of something about to happen in Denmark.*

7. **READ AND CITE TEXT EVIDENCE**

(G) ASK STUDENTS to reread lines 130–140. What does Horatio say the ghost's appearance might mean? *Horatio hopes that the ghost will warn them if something bad is going to happen.*

CLOSE READ Notes

[*The cock crows.*]

Stay and speak!—Stop it, Marcellus.

Marcellus. Shall I strike it with my partisan?[28]

145 **Horatio.** Do, if it will not stand.

Barnardo. 'Tis here.

Horatio. 'Tis here.

[Ghost *exits.*]

Marcellus. 'Tis gone.

We do it wrong, being so majestical,

150 To offer it the show of violence,

For it is as the air, invulnerable,

And our vain blows malicious mockery.

Barnardo. It was about to speak when the cock crew.

Horatio. And then it started[29] like a guilty thing

155 Upon a fearful summons. I have heard

The cock, that is the trumpet to the morn,

Doth with his lofty and shrill-sounding throat

Awake the god of day, and at his warning,

Whether in sea or fire, in earth or air,

160 Th' extravagant and **erring** spirit hies

To his confine, and of the truth herein

This present object made probation.[30]

Marcellus. It faded on the crowing of the cock.

Some say that ever 'gainst that season comes

165 Wherein our Savior's birth is celebrated,

This bird of dawning singeth all night long;

And then, they say, no spirit dare stir abroad,

The nights are wholesome; then no planets strike,[31]

No fairy takes, nor witch hath power to charm,

170 So hallowed and so gracious is that time.

Horatio. So have I heard and do in part believe it.

But look, the morn in russet mantle clad

Walks o'er the dew of yon high eastward hill.

Break we our watch up, and by my advice

175 Let us impart what we have seen tonight

Unto young Hamlet; for, upon my life,

This spirit, dumb to us, will speak to him.

erring:
mistaken

[28]**partisan:** a weapon.
[29]**started:** made a sudden movement.
[30]**made probation:** demonstrated.
[31]**no planets strike:** no planets put forth an evil influence.

62

CLOSE READ Notes

Do you consent we shall acquaint him with it

As needful in our loves, fitting our duty?

180 **Marcellus.** Let's do 't, I pray, and I this morning know

Where we shall find him most convenient.

[*They exit.*]

Scene 2 • *A state room at the castle.*

[*Flourish. Enter* Claudius, *King of Denmark,* Gertrude *the Queen,* the Council, *as* Polonius, *and his son* Laertes, Hamlet, *with others, among them* Voltemand *and* Cornelius.]

King. Though yet of Hamlet our[32] dear brother's death

The memory be green, and that it us befitted

To bear our hearts in grief, and our whole kingdom

To be contracted in one brow of woe,

5 Yet so far hath discretion fought with nature

That we with wisest sorrow think on him

Together with remembrance of ourselves.

Therefore our sometime sister,[33] now our queen,

Th' imperial jointress[34] to this warlike state,

10 Have we (as 'twere with a defeated joy,

With an auspicious and a dropping eye,[35]

With mirth in funeral and with dirge in marriage,

In equal scale weighing delight and dole)

Taken to wife. Nor have we herein barred

15 Your better wisdoms, which have freely gone

With this affair along. For all, our thanks.

[32]**our:** the "royal we," referring to oneself.
[33]**our sometime sister:** my former sister-in-law.
[34]**jointress:** a woman who owns property with her husband.
[35]**an auspicious and a dropping eye:** one eye showing good fortune and the other showing sorrow.

The funeral of the dead King Hamlet took place at the same time as the wedding of Hamlet's widow, Gertrude, and the new King, Claudius.

8. ◀ **REREAD AND DISCUSS** Reread lines 171–181. In a small group, discuss how this last exchange of dialogue between Horatio and Marcellus advances the plot. Cite textual evidence in your discussion.

9. **READ** ▶ As you read Scene 2, lines 1–50, continue to cite text evidence.

• Underline examples of contradictory statements (lines 1–15).

• In the margin, tell what two events this set of contradictory elements describes.

• In the margin, explain what Claudius says that confirms what Horatio told the sentries earlier about Denmark.

63

Critical Vocabulary: erring (line 160) In this case, two possible meanings of *erring* might apply: "mistaken" (making an error), and the older meaning of "wandering" (related to the word *errant*). Have students discuss which meaning seems more relevant to the action of the ghost as shown in this scene, and as commented on by the characters. Suggest that students consider the context clue "hies (hurries) to his confine (the place where he is normally confined)."

FOR ELL STUDENTS Point out the words *'tis, th',* and *'gainst,* and explain the purpose of the apostrophe in each case. *The apostrophe takes the place of missing letters. In* 'tis *it's the* i *for "it is"; in* th' *it's the* e *for* the; *and in* 'gainst *it's the* a *for* against.

8. **REREAD AND DISCUSS USING TEXT EVIDENCE** This is the first mention of "young Hamlet," the title character.

🄗 **ASK STUDENTS** who Marcellus, Barnardo, and Horatio think that the ghost is. How does this assumption make their plan seem logical? *The men think that the ghost is the dead king. It is logical that they want to tell the king's son about it.*

9. **READ AND CITE TEXT EVIDENCE**

🄘 **ASK STUDENTS** to reread lines 1–9 of Scene 2. What background information does Claudius give in these lines? *King Hamlet, Claudius's brother, has died (line 1). Claudius has married the widowed queen, Gertrude ("our sometime sister, now our queen,") and become king.*

Now follows that you know. Young Fortinbras,
Holding a weak supposal of our worth
Or thinking by our late dear brother's death
20 Our state to be disjoint and out of frame,
Colleagued with this dream of his advantage,
He hath not failed to pester us with message
Importing[36] the surrender of those lands
Lost by his father, with all bonds of law,
25 To our most valiant brother—so much for him.
Now for ourself and for this time of meeting.
Thus much the business is: we have here writ
To Norway, uncle of young Fortinbras,
Who, impotent and bedrid, scarcely hears
30 Of this his nephew's purpose, to suppress
His further gait herein, in that the levies,[37]
The lists, and full proportions are all made
Out of his subject;[38] and we here dispatch
You, good Cornelius, and you, Voltemand,
35 For bearers of this greeting to old Norway,
Giving to you no further personal power
To business with the King more than the scope
Of these **dilated** articles allow.
[*Giving them a paper.*]
Farewell, and let your haste commend your duty.
40 **Cornelius/Voltemand.** In that and all things will we show our duty.
King. We doubt it nothing. Heartily farewell.
[Voltemand *and* Cornelius *exit.*]

[36]**importing:** relating to.
[37]**levies:** gathered troops.
[38]**out of his subject:** from the King's own subjects.

Claudius gives the same history of war between Denmark and Norway as Horatio did earlier.

dilated:
expanded, widened

10. **◀ REREAD** Reread lines 17–38. One key theme of *Hamlet* is the nature of relationships between fathers and sons. What other father-son pairing seems to parallel that of Prince Hamlet and his father, King Hamlet?

Prince Hamlet has lost his father, King Hamlet. Fortinbras has lost his father, Fortinbras the elder, who was also a king. Both sons seem not to have inherited the kingship; in both Norway and Denmark, an uncle is on the throne.

64

And now, Laertes, what's the news with you?
You told us of some suit. What is 't, Laertes?
You cannot speak of reason to the Dane
45 And lose your voice. What wouldst thou beg, Laertes,
That shall not be my offer, not thy asking?
The head is not more native to the heart,
The hand more instrumental to the mouth,
Than is the throne of Denmark to thy father.
50 What wouldst thou have, Laertes?
Laertes.   My dread lord,
Your leave and favor to return to France,
From whence though willingly I came to Denmark
To show my duty in your coronation,
Yet now I must confess, that duty done,
55 My thoughts and wishes bend again toward France
And bow them to your gracious leave and pardon.
King. Have you your father's leave? What says Polonius?
Polonius. Hath, my lord, wrung from me my slow leave
By laborsome petition, and at last
60 Upon his will I sealed my hard consent.
I do beseech you give him leave to go.
King. Take thy fair hour, Laertes. Time be thine,
And thy best graces spend it at thy will.—
But now, my cousin[39] Hamlet and my son—
65 **Hamlet** [*aside*]. A little more than kin and less than kind.
King. How is it that the clouds still hang on you?
Hamlet. Not so, my lord; I am too much in the sun.
Queen. Good Hamlet, cast thy nighted color off,
And let thine eye look like a friend on Denmark.
70 Do not forever with thy vailèd lids
Seek for thy noble father in the dust.
Thou know'st 'tis common; all that lives must die,
Passing through nature to eternity.

[39]**cousin:** kinsman.

This shows that he probably guards his thoughts and feelings closely—out of anger, grief, or distrust of the people around him.

11. **READ ▶** As you read lines 51–86, continue to cite textual evidence.

• Underline the first words spoken by Hamlet, and in the margin explain why his first words might be delivered as an aside.

• In the margin, explain how King Claudius, the Queen, Prince Hamlet, and the dead King are related to one another.

65

---

10. REREAD AND CITE TEXT EVIDENCE

Ⓙ **ASK STUDENTS** to think about what they learned in the first scene about King Fortinbras and his son. Remind students that Shakespeare often uses the country's name to mean the king himself (line 28). Who is the king of Norway in this scene? What has happened to the previous king? Who else has lost a king who is also his father? *The present king of Norway is the younger Fortinbras's uncle. The previous king, Fortinbras the elder, died in battle. This has also happened to Hamlet the younger, who lost his father, the king of Denmark. Young Hamlet's uncle is now king of Denmark.*

Critical Vocabulary: dilated (line 38) Have students discuss whether "expanded" or "widened" would be a better meaning for the context of the line.

11. READ AND CITE TEXT EVIDENCE

Students who are familiar with television soap operas, or *telenovelas,* might see a connection to the tangled family relationships that provide drama in *Hamlet.* The difference is that this is a royal family, so that power as well as family ties are at issue. When a family goes through such a chaotic period, there are bound to be effects on the children, even if they are older teenagers or young adults.

Ⓚ **ASK STUDENTS** what emotions Hamlet's behavior shows. *Students may think of grief, anger, and mistrust, especially of Claudius.*

CLOSE READ
Notes

CLOSE READ
Notes

Prince Hamlet is the son of Queen Gertrude and the dead king. Claudius was the King's brother, but has married Gertrude and become King. Prince Hamlet is his nephew and stepson.

Hamlet. Ay, madam, it is common.
Queen.   If it be,
75 Why seems it so particular with thee?
Hamlet. "Seems," madam? Nay, it is. I know not "seems."
'Tis not alone my inky cloak, good mother,
Nor customary suits of solemn black,
Nor windy suspiration of forced breath,
80 No, nor the fruitful river in the eye,
Nor the dejected havior of the visage,
Together with all forms, moods, shapes of grief,
That can denote me truly. These indeed "seem,"
For they are actions that a man might play;
85 But I have that within which passes⁴⁰ show,
These but the trappings and the suits of woe.
King. 'Tis sweet and commendable in your nature, Hamlet,
To give these mourning duties to your father.
But you must know your father lost a father,
90 That father lost, lost his, and the survivor bound
In filial obligation for some term
To do obsequious sorrow. But to persever
In obstinate condolement is a course
Of impious stubbornness. 'Tis unmanly grief.

⁴⁰**passes:** goes beyond.

95 It shows a will most incorrect to heaven,
A heart unfortified, a mind impatient,
An understanding simple and unschooled.
For what we know must be and is as common
As any the most vulgar thing to sense,
100 Why should we in our **peevish** opposition
Take it to heart? Fie, 'tis a fault to heaven,
A fault against the dead, a fault to nature,
To reason most absurd, whose common theme
Is death of fathers, and who still hath cried,
105 From the first corse⁴¹ till he that died today,
"This must be so." We pray you, throw to earth
This unprevailing woe and think of us
As of a father; for let the world take note,
You are the most immediate to our throne,
110 And with no less nobility of love
Than that which dearest father bears his son
Do I impart toward you. For your intent
In going back to school in Wittenberg,
It is most retrograde to our desire,
115 And we beseech you, bend you to remain
Here in the cheer and comfort of our eye,
Our chiefest courtier, cousin, and our son.
Queen. Let not thy mother lose her prayers, Hamlet.
I pray thee, stay with us. Go not to Wittenberg.
120 **Hamlet.** I shall in all my best obey you, madam.
King. Why, 'tis a loving and a fair reply.
Be as ourself in Denmark.—Madam, come.
This gentle and unforced accord of Hamlet
Sits smiling to my heart, in grace whereof

⁴¹**corse:** corpse.

peevish: discontented, bad-tempered

Both the King and the Queen present a united front and urge Hamlet to stop grieving for his dead father.

12. ◀ REREAD Reread lines 76–86. According to Hamlet, how does his behavior reflect his innermost feelings? Cite textual evidence in your response.

Hamlet says that his grief is real and that his real feelings surpass the emotions he displays. He says that what he feels within himself goes beyond what shows on the outside.

13. READ ▶ As you read lines 87–128, continue to cite textual evidence.
- Underline the feelings Claudius claims to have for Hamlet.
- In the margin, compare the King's words to Hamlet with the Queen's earlier speech to Hamlet.

14. ◀ REREAD Reread line 120. Why does Hamlet use formal language to cover his feelings? What significance might lie in the fact that he addresses only one person?

He expresses no feelings, so neither the king nor the queen can be sure he really wants to stay. Hamlet addresses only Gertrude. This could show his resentment toward Claudius.

66

67

---

12. **REREAD AND CITE TEXT EVIDENCE**

L **ASK STUDENTS** what the queen is advising Hamlet to do. How do Hamlet's words in lines 76–86 show whether or not he will take her advice? *She advises him that he's been mourning for too long and should move on. It's plain in his answer that his grief is too deep to end soon.*

13. **READ AND CITE TEXT EVIDENCE**

M **ASK STUDENTS** to read lines 106–117. What words does Claudius use to describe family relationships? To whom do they refer? *He uses the words* father, dearest father, son, cousin *(meaning "kinsman"),* son. *Claudius uses all the references to* father *to mean himself. He refers to Hamlet with the words* son *and* cousin.

FOR ELL STUDENTS Explain that the word *havior* (line 81) is an abbreviation of a more common word. Challenge students to guess which one. *behavior*

14. **REREAD AND CITE TEXT EVIDENCE**

N **ASK STUDENTS** to look at lines 118–120. In these lines, which person—Gertrude or Hamlet—sounds more sincere? *Gertrude seems the most sincere. She talks as a mother to her son. Hamlet doesn't sound very personal. He talks as someone promising obedience, perhaps (with the use of the word* madam*) a subject obeying his queen.*

Critical Vocabulary: peevish (line 100) Ask students to share their definitions of *peevish*. Ask them how this word shows Claudius's opinion of Hamlet's feelings.

125 No jocund health[42] that Denmark drinks today
But the great cannon to the clouds shall tell,
And the King's rouse[43] the heaven shall bruit[44] again,
Respeaking earthly thunder. Come away.
[*Flourish. All but Hamlet exit*]
Hamlet. O, that this too, too sullied[45] flesh would melt,
130 Thaw, and resolve itself into a dew,
Or that the Everlasting had not fixed
His canon[46] 'gainst self-slaughter! O God, God,
How weary, stale, flat, and unprofitable
Seem to me all the uses of this world!
135 Fie on 't, ah fie! 'Tis an unweeded garden
That grows to seed. Things rank and gross in nature
Possess it merely.[47] That it should come to this:
But two months dead—nay, not so much, not two.

O So excellent a king, that was to this

140 Hyperion to a satyr;[48] so loving to my mother
That he might not beteem[49] the winds of heaven
Visit her face too roughly. Heaven and earth,
Must I remember? Why, she would hang on him
As if increase of appetite had grown
145 By what it fed on. And yet, within a month
(Let me not think on 't; frailty, thy name is woman!),
A little month, or ere those shoes were old
With which she followed my poor father's body,

[42]**jocund health:** happy toast.
[43]**rouse:** deep drink.
[44]**bruit:** announce.
[45]**sullied:** stained, defiled.
[46]**canon:** law.
[47]**merely:** entirely.
[48]**Hyperion to a satyr:** In ancient Greek mythology, Hyperion embodied light and wisdom, while a satyr was half man, half goat.
[49]**beteem:** allow.

15. **READ** As you read lines 129–159, continue to cite textual evidence.

• Underline text that compares the dead King Hamlet and Claudius.
• In the margin, restate the accusations Hamlet makes against Claudius and against his mother.

68

Like Niobe, all tears—why she, even she
150 (O God, a beast that wants discourse of reason[50]
Would have mourned longer!), married with my uncle,
My father's brother, but no more like my father
Than I to Hercules. Within a month,
Ere yet the salt of most unrighteous tears
155 Had left the flushing in her galled eyes,
She married. O, most wicked speed, to post
With such dexterity to incestuous sheets!
It is not, nor it cannot come to good.
But break, my heart, for I must hold my tongue.
[*Enter Horatio, Marcellus, and Barnardo.*]

R P 160 **Horatio.** Hail to your lordship.
Hamlet. I am glad to see you well.
Horatio—or I do forget myself!
Horatio. The same, my lord, and your poor servant ever.
Hamlet. Sir, my good friend. I'll change that name with you.
165 And what make you from[51] Wittenberg, Horatio?—Marcellus?
Marcellus. My good lord.
Hamlet. I am very glad to see you. [*To Barnardo.*]
Good even, sir.—
But what, in faith, make you from Wittenberg?

[50]**wants discourse of reason:** lacks the ability to reason.
[51]**what make you from:** what are you doing away from.

16. **REREAD** Reread lines 158–159. In what way do these lines sum up the conflict Hamlet feels? Cite textual evidence in your response.

Hamlet's heart is breaking over the grief he feels about his father's death and his mother's swift remarriage. His mother and the new king have criticized his mourning, and he feels that he cannot voice his true feelings.

17. **READ** As you read lines 160–196, continue to cite textual evidence.

• Underline an example of Hamlet's use of sarcasm.
• In the margin, tell what Hamlet is bitter about that makes him utter such a sarcastic response.
• Circle the lines that show a change in Hamlet's demeanor. In the margin, explain what news seems to bring new life to him.

69

Hamlet doesn't think Claudius worthy of the dead King. Hamlet accuses his mother of disloyalty for marrying so soon after her husband's death.

---

15. **READ AND CITE TEXT EVIDENCE** Lines 129–159 present the first of Hamlet's soliloquies. These private thoughts, which Hamlet says to himself but shares with the audience, give insight into his frame of mind.

O ASK STUDENTS in what ways does Hamlet describe his father, the dead king, Claudius, the current king, and Gertrude. *Hamlet describes his father as "so excellent a king" and "so loving to my mother"—in other words, both a fine king and a fine man. Claudius is described as a very low man in comparison. He is as far away in quality from Hamlet the older as a satyr is from Hyperion. Hamlet describes Gertrude as disloyal to her late husband by remarrying with "most wicked speed" (line 156).*

16. **REREAD AND CITE TEXT EVIDENCE**

P ASK STUDENTS why Hamlet feels that he must hold his tongue (line 159). *He might feel that he must hold his tongue because he has no power to oppose or even criticize his stepfather, who is king.*

17. **READ AND CITE TEXT EVIDENCE**

Q ASK STUDENTS in what way does the meeting between Hamlet, Horatio, Marcellus, and Barnardo connect to events in Scene 1. *Horatio and Marcellus planned at the end of Scene 1 to tell Hamlet about seeing the ghost. Here, they carry out that plan.*

CLOSE READ
Notes

CLOSE READ
Notes

> *He was a man. Take him for all in all, I shall not look upon his like again.*

Horatio. I saw him once. He was a goodly king.

Hamlet. He was a man. Take him for all in all,
I shall not look upon his like again.

190 **Horatio.** My lord, I think I saw him yesternight.

Hamlet. Saw who?

Horatio. My lord, the King your father.

Hamlet. The King my father?

Horatio. Season your admiration for a while
With an attent ear, till I may deliver
195 Upon the witness of these gentlemen
This marvel to you.

Hamlet. For God's love, let me hear!

Horatio. Two nights together had these gentlemen,
Marcellus and Barnardo, on their watch,
In the dead waste and middle of the night,
200 Been thus encountered: a figure like your father,
Armèd at point exactly, cap-à-pie,[52]
Appears before them and with solemn march
Goes slow and stately by them. Thrice he walked
By their (oppressed) and (fear-surprisèd) eyes
205 Within his truncheon's length, whilst they, (distilled)
(Almost to jelly with the act of fear,)
Stand dumb and speak not to him. This to me
In dreadful secrecy impart they did,
And I with them the third night kept the watch,
210 Where, as they had delivered, both in time,
Form of the thing (each word made true and good),
The apparition comes. I knew your father;
These hands are not more like.

[52]**cap-à-pie:** head to foot.

Hamlet's demeanor changes when Horatio says he has seen Hamlet's father.

170 **Horatio.** A truant disposition, good my lord.

Hamlet. I would not hear your enemy say so,
Nor shall you do my ear that violence
To make it truster of your own report
Against yourself. I know you are no truant.
175 But what is your affair in Elsinore?
We'll teach you to drink deep ere you depart.

Horatio. My lord, I came to see your father's funeral.

Hamlet. I prithee, do not mock me, fellow student.
I think it was to see my mother's wedding.
180 **Horatio.** Indeed, my lord, it followed hard upon.

Hamlet. Thrift, thrift, Horatio. The funeral baked meats
Did coldly furnish forth the marriage tables.
Would I had met my dearest foe in heaven
Or ever I had seen that day, Horatio!
185 My father—methinks I see my father.

Horatio. Where, my lord?

Hamlet. In my mind's eye, Horatio.

He is bitter that his mother's wedding occurred so soon after the funeral of his father.

◀ **REREAD AND DISCUSS** Reread lines 161–176. In a small group, discuss Hamlet's state of mind. What words would you use to describe his behavior and his reactions to the situation he finds himself in? Explain whether you think his response to this situation is understandable. Cite explicit evidence from the text in your discussion.

18. **READ ▶** As you read lines 197–258, continue to cite textual evidence.

• Circle words that convey feelings of fear.
• Underline text that shows Horatio's assurance that the event took place.
• In the margin, explain how Hamlet's reaction and questions show what kind of a thinker he is.

REREAD AND DISCUSS USING TEXT EVIDENCE

R **ASK STUDENTS** to reread lines 161–176. What is the relationship between Hamlet and Horatio? How is Hamlet's behavior toward Horatio and the other two men different from his earlier behavior toward Claudius and Gertrude? *Horatio is a fellow student from Wittenberg (line 165). In court, Hamlet barely spoke, and when he did it was with formality that barely hid his anger and bitterness. His speech to Horatio in lines 171–176 is open and friendly. Students may say that Hamlet feels he can trust these men more than he can his mother or Claudius.*

FOR ELL STUDENTS Some of your Spanish-speaking students may recognize the word *truant* from a similar Spanish word, *truhán*. Point out that in English *truant* is used to describe someone who misses school, while the Spanish false cognate refers to someone who is an ill-intentioned trickster.

18. **READ AND CITE TEXT EVIDENCE**

S **ASK STUDENTS** to read lines 213–242. What kind of information is Hamlet interested in hearing from Horatio? How precise are Hamlet's questions? *Hamlet asks for detailed, specific information, such as what the ghost's facial expression was like, what color his hair was, and how long he stayed. His questions seem sensible and precise. They are questions that could verify a resemblance between the ghost and his father. They show that Hamlet is really paying attention.*

Hamlet. But where was this?

Marcellus. My lord, upon the platform where we watch.

215 **Hamlet.** Did you not speak to it?

Horatio. My lord, I did,
But answer made it none. Yet once methought
It lifted up its head and did address
Itself to motion, like as it would speak;
But even then the morning cock crew loud,

220 And at the sound it shrunk in haste away
And vanished from our sight.

Hamlet. 'Tis very strange.

Horatio. As I do live, my honored lord, 'tis true.
And we did think it writ down in our duty
To let you know of it.

225 **Hamlet.** Indeed, sirs, but this troubles me.
Hold you the watch tonight?

All. We do, my lord.

Hamlet. Armed, say you?

All. Armed, my lord.

Hamlet. From top to toe?

All. My lord, from head to foot.

Hamlet. Then saw you not his face?

230 **Horatio.** O, yes, my lord, he wore his beaver[53] up.

Hamlet. What, looked he frowningly?

Horatio. A countenance more in sorrow than in anger.

Hamlet. Pale or red?

Horatio. Nay, very pale.

Hamlet. And fixed his eyes upon you?

235 **Horatio.** Most constantly.

Hamlet. I would I had been there.

Horatio. It would have much amazed you.

Hamlet. Very like. Stayed it long?

Horatio. While one with moderate haste might tell[54] a hundred.

Barnardo/Marcelius. Longer, longer.

240 **Horatio.** Not when I saw 't.

Hamlet. His beard was grizzled, no?

---

[53]**beaver:** the movable front piece of a helmet.
[54]**tell:** count to.

Hamlet seems to believe the men, and his detailed questions show that he is a clear, precise thinker.

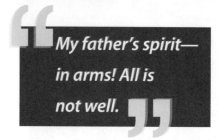

> *My father's spirit—in arms! All is not well.*

Horatio. It was as I have seen it in his life,
A sable silvered.

Hamlet. I will watch tonight.
Perchance 'twill walk again.

Horatio. I warrant it will.

Hamlet. If it assume my noble father's person,

245 I'll speak to it, though hell itself should gape
And bid me hold my peace. I pray you all,
If you have hitherto concealed this sight,
Let it be **tenable** in your silence still;
And whatsomever else shall hap tonight,

250 Give it an understanding but no tongue.
I will requite your loves. So fare you well.
Upon the platform, 'twixt eleven and twelve,
I'll visit you.

All. Our duty to your Honor.

Hamlet. Your loves, as mine to you. Farewell.
[*All but* Hamlet *exit.*]

255 My father's spirit—in arms! All is not well.
I doubt[55] some foul play. Would the night were come!
Till then, sit still, my soul. Foul deeds will rise,
Though all the earth o'erwhelm them, to men's eyes.
[*He exits.*]

---

[55]**doubt:** suspect.

tenable:
defensible

72

73

Critical Vocabulary: tenable (line 248) Students may find the meanings "defensible" and "capable of being maintained" in a dictionary. In Shakespeare's time, *tenable* could mean "kept back" or "withheld." (The word *tenable* comes from the French verb *tenir*, meaning "to hold.") Have students consider what that meaning might convey that Hamlet is instructing the men to do (keep the ghost incident a secret).

CLOSE READ
Notes

19. ◀ REREAD Reread lines 213–258. What details does Hamlet want to know about this father's ghost? Why does he find the answers convincing? Support your response with explicit textual evidence.

He asks about the place where the ghost appeared and for how long it stayed. He also asks precise questions about whether the ghost indeed resembled the dead King—face, beard, armor—and how it behaved, including whether it spoke. The answers are so detailed and vivid that Hamlet seems convinced that the ghost really appeared.

SHORT RESPONSE

Cite Text Evidence Who is Hamlet? What have you learned about him so far? Explain the person Hamlet appears to be at this point in the play. **Cite text evidence** to support your response.

Hamlet is a conflicted young man. He has just lost his father, King Hamlet, and his mother, only two months after her husband's death, has married Claudius, her husband's brother. Even though Hamlet is clearly grief stricken, his mother and Claudius urge him to cheer up. Claudius tells Hamlet that his "obstinate condolement is a course of impious stubbornness." He and Hamlet's mother also refuse to let Hamlet return to his studies in Wittenberg, and poor Hamlet replies, "I shall in all my best obey you, madam," as he is now trapped in his miserable surroundings. Hamlet's only source of comfort is the possibility of seeing his father's ghost, but he suspects his future will be grim, and ends Scene 2 ominously predicting "foul deeds will rise."

74

---

19. REREAD AND CITE TEXT EVIDENCE

Ⓣ **ASK STUDENTS** what text evidence they found in lines 213–258 to support their answers. *Hamlet asks where the men saw the ghost (line 213), whether they spoke (line 215), and what the ghost looked like (lines 229, 231, 233, 241). He finds the answers convincing because the men are acting out of duty (line 223) and furnish believable details.*

SHORT RESPONSE

Cite Text Evidence   Students' responses should include text evidence that supports their positions. They should:

- explain the circumstances in which Hamlet finds himself at the beginning of the play.
- analyze sources of conflict for Hamlet.
- identify the action he decides to take at the end of Scene 2 and his thoughts about what might happen next.

TO CHALLENGE STUDENTS . . .

Shakespeare's plays are traditionally divided into three categories: comedies, histories, and tragedies. In Shakespeare's time, a comedy was a story or play that had a happy ending; it wasn't necessarily funny. Shakespeare's histories, all named for kings, dealt specifically with English historical characters. His plays featuring other historical characters, such as *Julius Caesar* or *Macbeth*, were grouped with the tragedies.

ASK STUDENTS to work in small groups that will each research a play from one of the three categories. (They should not include *Hamlet*.) Have each group read a synopsis of the play it has chosen and write a paragraph or two from their research telling about a main problem or conflict featured in the play and how that conflict is resolved. Have groups compare their findings with those of other students.

DIG DEEPER

With the class, return to Question 4, Reread. Have students share their responses.

ASK STUDENTS to cite the text evidence that led to their description of the mood at the beginning of the play.

- Have students reread lines 1–73 and notice how Shakespeare uses pacing to create suspense. How do we gradually find out about the ghost? *Only at line 25 is there a hint of something that has appeared, but it is not described. As the men tell Horatio about what they saw, the ghost shows up (line 44).*
- Ask what word choices Shakespeare makes to build the mood. *He uses phrases like* this dreaded sight. *(line 29), and* It harrows me with fear and wonder *(line 48).*
- Ask how the characters' reactions to the ghost help intensify the mood. *Barnardo calls it "this dreaded sight" When Horatio sees the ghost for himself, he feels "fear and wonder," and he is seen to "tremble and look pale" (line 57).*

ASK STUDENTS to return to their Reread answer and revise it based on the class discussion.

Film Versions of *Hamlet*

mySmartPlanner Create lesson plans and access resources online.

Why These Texts?

Great works of literature are often interpreted by multiple film directors, each of whom brings a unique vision to the story and the characters. This lesson explores a scene from *Hamlet* as it is portrayed in two film versions from 1980 and 2009.

Key Learning Objective: The student will be able to analyze multiple interpretations of a drama to evaluate how each version interprets the text.

COMMON CORE Common Core Standards

RL 3 Analyze the impact of the author's choices regarding how to develop and relate elements of a drama (e.g., characters).

RL 7 Analyze multiple interpretations of a drama, evaluating how each version interprets the source text.

SL 5 Make strategic use of digital media in presentations.

Text Complexity Rubric

	Hamlet (1980)	Hamlet (2009)
Quantitative Measures	Lexile: N/A	Lexile: N/A
Qualitative Measures	**Levels of Meaning/Purpose** multiple levels of complex meanings	**Levels of Meaning/Purpose** multiple levels of complex meanings
	Structure closely aligned with the original print source	**Structure** closely aligned with the original print source
	Language Conventionality and Clarity archaic, unfamiliar language	**Language Conventionality and Clarity** archaic, unfamiliar language
	Knowledge Demands cultural and literary knowledge essential to understanding	**Knowledge Demands** cultural and literary knowledge essential to understanding
Reader/Task Considerations	Teacher determined Vary by individual reader and type of text	Teacher determined Vary by individual reader and type of text

CLOSE READ

AS YOU VIEW Direct students to use the As You View note to focus their viewing.

Analyze Interpretations of Drama

COMMON CORE RL 7

Tell students that when interpreting *Hamlet* as a film, much is left to the discretion of the director. Remind them that at the beginning of the play, Hamlet is a student, probably in his twenties.

ASK STUDENTS to consider the actor cast as Hamlet and discuss whether his age, hair coloring, and build suit the character. *(Possible answer: The actor seems older than Hamlet should be, but his build and looks suit Hamlet.)* Then ask what character traits of Hamlet's this actor might have been chosen to emphasize. *(Possible answer: The actor's age and stature make him seem contemplative, and Hamlet is a pensive man. The director might also have chosen this actor because he is more experienced, and Hamlet is a difficult character to play.)*

Point out that actors work with directors to decide how they will deliver their lines.

ASK STUDENTS what the actor's facial expressions, movements, and gestures during the soliloquy convey about the character of Hamlet. *(The actor twists his face and moves around the stage, at one point sitting down and putting his head in his hands. These movements and gestures help convey the complexity of the character and the emotional turmoil he is enduring.)* Point out that during the soliloquy, the actor looks into the camera as he speaks. Ask students what effect this has. *(The viewer is pulled into the drama and is able to see each expression and emotion on the actor's face.)*

Explain that camera angles and close-ups also help tell a story. For example, filming a character from a low angle makes him or her seem more imposing, while filming from a high angle makes the character seem smaller. Point out that the camera moves toward Hamlet as he speaks.

ASK STUDENTS what effect this has. *(It emphasizes what Hamlet says and makes it more dramatic.)*

MEDIA ANALYSIS

Film Versions of Hamlet

Hamlet (1980)

BBC Shakespeare
Directed by Rodney Bennett

AS YOU VIEW Pay attention to the elements that make each film version unique, and generate a list of questions as you watch.

Image Credits: (t) ©STILLFX/Shutterstock; (b) ©BBC Motion Gallery

Compare Text and Media **357**

SCAFFOLDING FOR ELL STUDENTS

Comprehension Support Remind students of the events in Act I, Scene 2, or have them review their notes to recall the basic situation and events. Then have them watch the film clips at least twice to appreciate details of each production.

- For the first viewing, have students notice the actors chosen to play each part. Ask them to also note the costumes. What differences do they notice between the two productions? Which interpretation more closely matches their own vision of the characters?

- For the second viewing, tell students to pay attention to the set and the lighting. What do these features add to the drama?

Analyze Interpretations of Drama

COMMON CORE RL 7

Explain to students that the **mood** of a film is the atmosphere that is established. Point out that mood is created with lighting, set design, and costume design.

ASK STUDENTS how the setting helps establish the mood of the 2009 film. *(The ballroom in black, white, and gray makes the set seem stark. The formal gowns and reflective floors also help establish a chilly mood.)* Ask students to explain how this mood is different from the mood established in the 1980 film. *(The mood in the 1980 film is more gloomy.)*

Remind students that directors and actors have great freedom in determining how actors will deliver lines.

ASK STUDENTS to describe the actor's movements and gestures in this version of the soliloquy. *(The actor weeps, squatting and then on his knees, rocking slightly, his head down.)* Then ask how these gestures help convey Hamlet's state of mind. *(They make Hamlet seem weak and broken, completely overcome with grief.)* Ask how this portrayal differs from that in the 1980 film. *(In that film, Hamlet does not weep as much, and he does not break down. He seems more composed.)*

Explain that **point of view** in a film is determined by camera angle and that it can shift quickly, from the point of view of one character to another or to an omniscient point of view. Point out the black and white camera shots, like those of a security camera.

ASK STUDENTS what point of view these shots may represent. *(They may represent the point of view of someone spying or watching from afar, or they may represent an omniscient point of view.)*

COLLABORATIVE DISCUSSION Have pairs discuss the details that led them to prefer one version over the other. Then invite pairs to share their ideas with the class.

ASK STUDENTS to share any questions they generated in the course of viewing and discussing the selections.

Hamlet (2009)

BBC Shakespeare
Directed by Gregory Doran

COLLABORATIVE DISCUSSION Which version did you prefer? Why? With a partner, discuss the overall effect of each film version and the details that contribute to its impact. Cite specific evidence from the clips to support your ideas.

APPLYING ACADEMIC VOCABULARY

restrain	integrity

As you discuss the two films, incorporate the Collection 4 academic vocabulary words *restrain* and *integrity*. To probe the effectiveness of the two actors in conveying Hamlet's character traits, ask students if one scene better retains the **integrity** of the original *Hamlet* than the other. Does one scene seem to take more liberties with the printed version, or are both faithful to the original? Then ask them to describe how the actors differ in their attempts to **restrain** their anger and contempt for Claudius. Ask if one of the actors showed more restraint than the other.

Analyze Interpretations of Drama

COMMON CORE RL 7

For a director, the chance to make a film of one of Shakespeare's plays is both a great opportunity and a great risk. Although Shakespeare sometimes included descriptions of characters or setting in the dialogue, his texts have few stage directions, and those usually provide only basic information, such as indicating a trumpet flourish. As a result, the director has little guidance but a great deal of freedom to imagine the play's details. Many of Shakespeare's plays have been adapted into more than one film, allowing audiences to experience multiple interpretations of the same play and to evaluate how well each version interprets the source text.

Each director has a personal vision of the film he or she wants to make. This concept is determined by the way the director interprets the play, the film's purpose and intended audience, previous versions of the play, and the particular subject matter of the play. To realize his or her vision, the director must make decisions that include casting, set design, and lighting.

Elements of Film Adaptation

Casting refers to the selection of actors to play the parts. Actors may be chosen based on how their appearance and age fit the image that the director has of the characters. They must also be able to bring out the characters' traits in the way the director envisions. For example, directors casting *Hamlet* would most likely choose actors of different ages for the roles of Hamlet and his mother, since that relationship is an established part of the play. The choice of actors is crucial to the success of the production; the actors determine how the audience responds to the characters and to the film as a whole. Directors may stay true to type or cast against type, perhaps choosing a female Hamlet or an actor whose race or ethnicity differs from what would be expected for a character. In the two clips seen here, the same actor, Patrick Stewart, was chosen to play the role of Claudius.

Set design refers to the scenery, props, furniture, and physical location that create the setting for the film. The set design may be traditional, modern, futuristic, or primitive, or it may spring from the imagination of the director. The setting in which the action of the film takes place is important to the director's interpretation. It also affects how the audience reacts. Consider the effect of the spacious, modern set of the 2009 film, for example, compared to the set of the 1980 version, which is crowded with furniture and actors. How does each set shape your impression of the Danish court and the interaction among the characters?

Lighting can have a major influence on the mood and perception of character and action. Dim lighting conveys an air of mystery or gloominess and obscures actors' features and actions. Bright lighting cheers up the atmosphere and highlights actors' movements and expressions. In the 2009 film version, the reflective floor creates an interesting play of light and shadow that rivets the audience's attention on Hamlet's gestures and words during his soliloquy.

CLOSE READ

Analyze Interpretations of Drama

COMMON CORE RL 7

Help students understand the elements of film adaptation, reviewing each element and how it affects the film. Then divide students into three groups and have them watch both film clips. Ask one group to note casting choices in the films and how the choices affect the interpretation of the characters. Ask another group to note the set design in both films and how this establishes mood and moves the plot. Ask the third group to note the lighting in both films and discuss how this element affects mood and the audience's perception of the characters. Have each group present their findings to the class, citing specific examples from each film to support their conclusions.

WHEN STUDENTS STRUGGLE . . .

Display a generic comparison-contrast chart and help students compare the following elements from the 1980 and 2009 films:

- Casting
- Set design
- Lighting

You may use three Venn diagrams, one for each point of comparison, or a two-column chart with three rows, one for each bullet point above.

ASK STUDENTS how each film helps them understand Shakespeare's play.

PRACTICE & APPLY

Analyzing the Text and Media

COMMON CORE RL 7

Possible answers:

1. *The actors are dressed in elaborate costumes that suggest what the nobility wore in Shakespeare's day. To approach the king and queen on their thrones, one must walk between rows of courtiers. This conveys a formal feeling consistent with court protocol in 1600.*

2. *The costumes are strikingly different. Most of the men wear dark business suits, and the women are in modern dresses. The polished granite floors, dark pillars, and snowball lights also feel modern. The large, open set creates coldness and distance between the characters. By contrast, the crowded set in the 1980 film makes the court seem claustrophobic.*

3. *Jacobi's Hamlet has an air of confidence and shows more obvious bitterness in the tone of his voice and in his gestures and expressions. Tennant's Hamlet is haunted and intense. He appears less confident as he lurks in the background. His anguish is more internal.*

4. *In both performances, Stewart commands the room. He is a leader. His 2009 performance, however, is more subtle. His delivery is more deliberate, conveying an impression of great intelligence and shrewdness. In the 1980 film, he speaks quickly and assertively, so that the effect is of forcefulness and impatience.*

5. *The impression of Horatio developed in the text is that of a concerned friend who wants to spare Hamlet additional grief as he informs him about the ghost. Both film Horatios show their friendship to Hamlet; the 2009 Horatio is particularly warm and caring.*

6. *The lighting is dim, with shadows cast on actors and parts of the set. This reflects the darkness of Hamlet's mourning and perhaps the darkness within Claudius's nature. Text references to Hamlet's "nighted color" and "inky cloak" make the darkness appropriate.*

7. *The 1980 Gertrude is more demonstrative and appears more dependent on Claudius. The 2009 Gertrude is elegant and dignified. She appears even more concerned for Hamlet, looking anxiously toward him for much of the scene.*

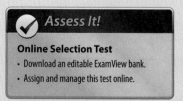

✓ Assess It!

Online Selection Test
- Download an editable ExamView bank.
- Assign and manage this test online.

Analyzing the Text and Media

COMMON CORE RL 7, SL 5

Cite Text Evidence   Support your responses with evidence from the selections.

1. **Analyze** Describe the setting of the 1980 BBC adaptation. What time and place are indicated by the set and costumes?

2. **Compare** In what ways is the setting of the 2009 adaptation different from the setting of the earlier film? How might audiences respond to each setting?

3. **Interpret** Consider the two actors who play Hamlet. What does each one emphasize about Hamlet's personality and his relationships with the other characters? Explain your response.

4. **Compare** How are Patrick Stewart's performances in the two films similar to and different from each other?

5. **Infer** Reread lines 160-180 in Act I, Scene 2 of the play. What can you infer about Horatio's appearance and personality from Shakespeare's text? How does each director's casting of Horatio either confirm or upend these assumptions?

6. **Analyze** What mood is evoked by the lighting in the 1980 film? Is this mood consistent with the atmosphere in the same scene in Shakespeare's text? Explain.

7. **Critique** In the absence of stage directions, how does each actress playing Gertrude use voice and gesture to mediate matters between Hamlet and Claudius? Where do they use similar choices? Where do their choices differ? Cite specific evidence in to support your response.

PERFORMANCE TASK

Media Activity: Trailer Which film version would you endorse? With a partner, complete these activities.

- Identify your reasons for preferring one film over the other.
- Develop a storyboard for a trailer to be shown in theaters, "plugging" the film you have chosen.

- Match images from the film with each of your reasons. Express your ideas in a way that is specific and engaging.
- Create a video version of your trailer or refine your storyboard for presentation to the class.
- Show your trailer to the class.

Assign this performance task.

PERFORMANCE TASK

COMMON CORE SL 5

Media Activity: Trailer Have pairs view their chosen film and identify scenes that support their reasons for endorsing it. Explain that a storyboard, like a comic strip, shows each shot in a video or multimedia story. Storyboards may show screen shots or drawings of images students have chosen. If students decide to create a trailer, direct them to the Internet for movie trailer ideas. Ask partners to share their completed trailers or storyboards with the class.

Analyze Elements of Drama: Characterization

COMMON CORE
RL 3

TEACH

Remind students that in a written story, **characterization** refers to all the methods the author uses to show readers what a character is like. Explain that characters in a film drama are introduced to the audience and their traits are revealed through the following methods:

- The character's dress and mannerisms help introduce the character's traits. For example, the 1980 Hamlet is dressed like a prince, providing a clue to his status, but his brooding countenance also reveals a great deal. Similarly, the 2009 Hamlet's agitated manner reveals his fragile psyche.

- The character's lines reveal much about the character's traits. Shakespeare's soliloquies, in particular, provide the playwright the opportunity to introduce his characters and to explore the inner thoughts and conflicts that help propel the plot. For example, Hamlet's soliloquy in Act I, Scene 2, reveals the emotional conflict he has endured, as well as his feelings for his mother and Claudius.

- Characters are also introduced through the lines of other characters. Hamlet, for example, is criticized by Claudius for mourning his father too long. Claudius's criticism seems to imply that Hamlet is immature and overly emotional, traits that are developed later in the play. Likewise, Hamlet's reaction to Horatio reveals his fondness for his friend. It also tells us something about Horatio.

COLLABORATIVE DISCUSSION

Direct students to work in groups to discuss how either Hamlet, Claudius, or Gertrude is introduced and developed in one of the film versions of the scene. Remind students to look at the characters' mannerisms and dress, their lines, and the lines other characters speak about them. Ask them to consider how each method helps them learn more about the character, and to discuss which method is the most reliable in revealing information about a character.

Analyze Interpretations of Drama

COMMON CORE
RL 7

RETEACH

Direct students to watch all or part of one of the following pairs of movies:

- *Pygmalion* (1938) and *My Fair Lady* (1964)
- *The Three Musketeers* (1993) and *The Three Musketeers* (2011)
- *Jane Eyre* (1996) and *Jane Eyre* (2011)

Group students according to the film they viewed and have them discuss the casting, set design, and lighting in each film. Ask them to consider the following questions:

- How did the casting choices in each film influence your impression of the main characters?

- How did the set design and lighting choices reflect the characters' traits and develop the mood of each film?

 LEVEL UP TUTORIALS Assign the following *Level Up* tutorial: **Elements of Drama**

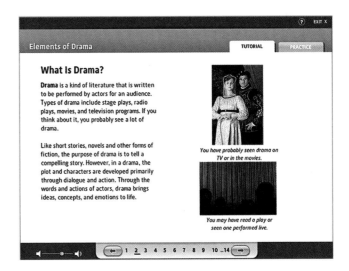

CLOSE READING APPLICATION

Students can read the opening scenes of *Pygmalion* by George Bernard Shaw or the opening chapters of Alexandre Dumas's *The Three Musketeers*, or Charlotte Brontë's *Jane Eyre,* and then compare the text to the film version, using the same points of comparison provided in the bulleted list above.

Hamlet's Dull Revenge

Literary Criticism by René Girard

Why This Text?

Criticism is a kind of argument that students encounter whenever they read a movie, book, or music review. Having just read *Hamlet,* they will have the background knowledge they need to analyze and appreciate René Girard's literary criticism.

View It!

Professional Development Podcast:

Text Complexity

Key Learning Objective: The student will be able to analyze the structure of an argument and identify its central ideas.

Common Core Standards

RI 1 Cite textual evidence.
RI 2 Determine central ideas; provide an objective summary.
RI 4 Determine the meaning of words and phrases as they are used in a text.
RI 5 Analyze and evaluate the structure an author uses in his or her argument.
W 1 Write arguments to support claims, using valid reasoning and relevant and sufficient evidence.
L 6 Acquire and use academic and domain-specific words and phrases.

Text Complexity Rubric

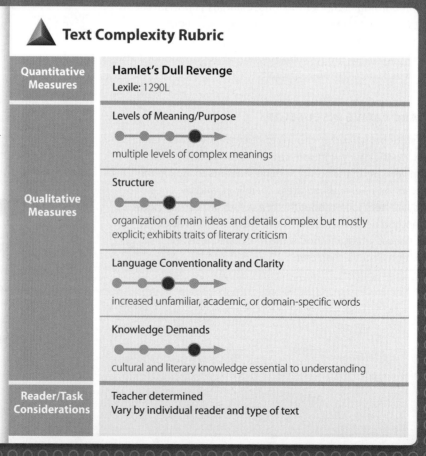

Quantitative Measures

Hamlet's Dull Revenge
Lexile: 1290L

Levels of Meaning/Purpose

multiple levels of complex meanings

Qualitative Measures

Structure

organization of main ideas and details complex but mostly explicit; exhibits traits of literary criticism

Language Conventionality and Clarity

increased unfamiliar, academic, or domain-specific words

Knowledge Demands

cultural and literary knowledge essential to understanding

Reader/Task Considerations

Teacher determined
Vary by individual reader and type of text

CLOSE READ

AS YOU READ Direct students to use the As You Read suggestion to focus their reading.

Analyze Structure: Argument (LINES 1–24)

 COMMON CORE RI 2, RI 5

Inform students that an argument usually begins with a **claim,** a statement of the author's position on an issue. To find the claim, students should look for a central idea in the first few paragraphs. They can then verify whether this idea is the author's claim by reading on to see whether the idea is supported by reasons and evidence throughout the entire argument.

Ⓐ **CITE TEXT EVIDENCE** Ask students to identify the central idea in lines 1–24. *(In* Hamlet, *Shakespeare uses the form of a revenge tragedy to show how tedious revenge is while also giving his audience the katharsis it craves in a revenge play.)* What value does Girard see in identifying Shakespeare's "double goal" (line 21)? Cite specific support. *(It will clarify some "unexplained details" [line 22] and "the function of many obscure scenes" [line 23].)*

CRITICAL VOCABULARY

genre: The author compares revenge tragedies to television "thrillers."

ASK STUDENTS what these two genres have in common. *(Both forms have predictable elements but still create excitement and suspense for the audience.)*

double entendre: The author suggests that Shakespeare has two goals in mind for his play.

ASK STUDENTS to explain the *double entendre* that the author describes. *(Shakespeare's first goal is to denounce revenge theatre, and his second is to give "his mass audience the* katharsis *it demands," thus making his revenge play a success.)*

Hamlet's Dull Revenge

Literary Criticism by René Girard

AS YOU READ Pay attention to details that reveal how Girard views Hamlet's character. Write down any questions you have as you read.

Ⓐ *H*amlet belongs to the **genre** of the revenge tragedy, as hackneyed and yet inescapable in Shakespeare's days as the "thriller" in ours to a television writer. In *Hamlet* Shakespeare turned this necessity for a playwright to go on writing the same old revenge tragedies into an opportunity to debate almost openly for the first time the questions I have tried to define. The weariness with revenge and *katharsis*[1] which can be read, I believe, in the margins of the earlier plays must really exist because, in *Hamlet,* it moves to the center of the stage and becomes fully articulated.

10 Some writers who were not necessarily the most unimaginative found it difficult, we are told, to postpone for the whole duration of the lengthy Elizabethan play an action which had never been in doubt in the first place and which is always the same anyway. Shakespeare can turn this tedious chore into the most brilliant feat of theatrical *double entendre* because the tedium of revenge is really what he wants to talk about, and he wants to talk about it in the usual Shakespearean fashion; he will denounce the revenge theater and all its works with the utmost daring without denying his mass audience the *katharsis* it demands, without depriving himself of the dramatic success which is

20 necessary to his own career as a dramatist.

If we assume that Shakespeare really had this double goal in mind, we will find that some unexplained details in the play become intelligible and that the function of many obscure scenes becomes obvious.

Ⓑ In order to perform revenge with conviction, you must believe in the justice of your own cause. This is what we noted before, and the revenge seeker will not believe in his own cause unless he believes in

genre
(zhän´rə) *n.* a category within an art form, based on style or subject.

double entendre
(dŭb´əl än-tän´drə) *n.* an expression having a double meaning.

---

[1] **katharsis:** catharsis, the elimination of tension through the release of repressed emotions.

SCAFFOLDING FOR ELL STUDENTS

Language: Print Cues Explain to students that italics are used in the essay for different purposes. For example:

- to indicate direct quotations
- to emphasize certain words and phrases
- to distinguish a work (*Hamlet*) from a character's name (Hamlet)
- to indicate words from other languages

ASK STUDENTS to scan the essay and look for italicized words. Then have them use context to determine which purpose the italics serve in each case.

Determine Central Ideas COMMON CORE RI 2

(LINES 25–44)

Remind students that a **central idea** is the main point that an author wants to convey in a section of text. Readers can sometimes determine the central idea by examining details and then inferring the main point.

 ASK STUDENTS to reread lines 25–44. Hamlet wants to get revenge for his father's murder, but his father was a murderer himself. What central idea is the author supporting with this detail? *(The central idea is that, for revenge to be justified, the victim must be guilty and the "victim's victim" must be innocent. Since Hamlet's father was a murderer, killing Claudius does not achieve justice, and Hamlet's "own revenge will look like still another link" in "an already long chain" of crimes [lines 42–43].)*

Analyze Structure: Argument COMMON CORE RI 5

(LINES 51–70)

The **reasons** an author gives to support a claim must themselves be supported by **evidence,** such as details and examples from the play.

C CITE TEXT EVIDENCE What is the reason that neither Shakespeare nor Hamlet can give up revenge, even though they are tired of it? What evidence does the author provide to support this reason? *(Shakespeare must provide the tragedy's "vicarious victims" [line 66] or he loses his audience and "his identity as a playwright" [lines 68–69]. Hamlet feels pressure to do his "sacred duty" [line 52], although he cannot fully justify his revenge. Hamlet "does not believe in his play half as much as the critics do" [line 60]. Neither Hamlet nor Shakespeare can fulfill the expectations of their critics.)*

CRITICAL VOCABULARY

entails: A justifiable act of revenge assumes certain facts about the person who will be targeted.

ASK STUDENTS what the decision to get revenge on a victim entails. *(The revenge seeker must be sure of the guilt of an intended victim and the innocence of that victim's victim.)*

 B

the guilt of his intended victim. And the guilt of that intended victim
entails in turn the innocence of that victim's victim. If the victim's
30   victim is already a killer and if the revenge seeker reflects a little
too much on the circularity of revenge, his faith in vengeance must
collapse.

    This is exactly what we have in *Hamlet.* It cannot be without a
purpose that Shakespeare suggests the old Hamlet, the murdered
king, was a murderer himself. In the various sources of the play there
may be indications to that effect, but Shakespeare would have omitted
them if he had wanted to strengthen the case for revenge. However
nasty Claudius may look, he cannot look nasty enough if he appears
in a context of previous revenge; he cannot generate, as a villain, the
40   absolute passion and dedication which is demanded of Hamlet. The
problem with Hamlet is that he cannot forget the context. As a result,
the crime by Claudius looks to him like one more link in an already
long chain, and his own revenge will look like still another link,
perfectly identical to all the other links.

    In a world where every ghost, dead or alive, can only perform the
same action, revenge, or clamor for more of the same from beyond
the grave, all voices are interchangeable. You can never know with
certainty which ghost is addressing whom. It is one and the same thing
for Hamlet to question his own identity and to question the ghost's
50   identity, and his authority.

C   To seek singularity in revenge is a vain enterprise but to shrink
from revenge, in a world which looks upon it as a "sacred duty" is to
exclude oneself from society, to become a nonentity once more. There
is no way out for Hamlet and he shifts endlessly from one impasse to
the other, unable to make up his mind because neither choice makes
sense.

    If all characters are caught in a cycle of revenge that extends in all
directions beyond the limits of its action, *Hamlet* has no beginning
and no end. The play collapses. The trouble with the hero is that
60   he does not believe in his play half as much as the critics do. He
understands revenge and the theater too well to assume willingly a role
chosen for him by others. His sentiments are those, in other words,
which we have surmised in Shakespeare himself. What the hero feels
in regard to the act of revenge, the creator feels in regard to revenge as
theater.

    The public wants vicarious victims and the playwright must
oblige. Tragedy is revenge. Shakespeare is tired of revenge, and yet
he cannot give it up, or he gives up his audience and his identity as a
playwright. Shakespeare turns a typical revenge topic, *Hamlet,* into a
70   meditation on his predicament as a playwright. . . .

    What Hamlet needs, in order to stir up his vengeful spirit, is a
revenge theater more convincing than his own, something less half-
hearted than the play Shakespeare is actually writing. Fortunately
for the hero and for the spectators who are eagerly awaiting their

entail
(ĕn-tāl´) *v.* involve as
a consequence.

APPLYING ACADEMIC VOCABULARY

restrain	trigger

As you discuss Girard's analysis, incorporate the Collection 4 academic vocabulary words *restrain* and *trigger.* Discuss why Shakespeare had to **restrain** himself—and Hamlet—from enacting revenge for the duration of a very long play. Describe the **trigger**—Laertes's passionate act of mourning—that finally gives Hamlet the determination to act.

final bloodbath, Hamlet has many opportunities to watch rousing spectacles during his play and he tries to generate even more, in a conscientious effort to put himself in the right mood for the murder of Claudius. Hamlet must receive from someone else, a mimetic[2] model, the impulse which he does not find in himself. This is what he tried to
80 achieve with his mother, we found, and he did not succeed. He is much more successful with the actor who impersonates for him the role of Hecuba. It becomes obvious, at this point, that the only hope for Hamlet to accomplish what his society—or the spectators—require, is to become as "sincere" a showman as the actor who can shed real tears when he pretends to be the queen of Troy!

> Is it not monstrous that this player here,
> But in a fiction, in a dream of passion,
> Could force his soul so to his own conceit
> That from her working all his visage wanned,
90 Tears in his eyes, distraction in's aspect,
> A broken voice, and his whole function suiting
> With forms to his conceit? And all for nothing!
> For Hecuba!
> What's Hecuba to him or he to Hecuba,
> That he should weep for her? What would he do
> Had he the motive and the cue for passion
> That I have?

Another catchy example for Hamlet comes from the army of Fortinbras on its way to Poland. The object of the war is a worthless
100 speck of land. Thousands of people must risk their lives:

> Even for an eggshell. Rightly to be great
> Is not to stir without great argument,
> But greatly to find quarrel in a straw
> When Honor's at the stake.

The scene is as ridiculous as it is sinister. It would not impress Hamlet so much if the hero truly believed in the superiority and urgency of his cause. His words constantly betray him, here as in the scene with his mother. As a cue for passion, his revenge motif is no more compelling, really, than the cue of an actor on the stage. He too
110 must *greatly . . . find quarrel in a straw*, he too must stake everything *even for an eggshell.*

The effect of the army scene obviously stems, at least in part, from the large number of people involved, from the almost infinite multiplication of the example which cannot fail to increase its mimetic attraction enormously. Shakespeare is too much a master of mob effects not to remember at this point the cumulative effect of mimetic models. In order to whip up enthusiasm for the war against Claudius,

---
[2] **mimetic:** relating to imitation.

CLOSE READ

Analyze Structure: Argument (LINES 86–104)

 COMMON CORE RI 5

Tell students that in literary criticism, a writer often quotes extensively from the work to provide evidence for his or her claim.

D **ASK STUDENTS** to reread lines 86–104. What is the value of quoting directly from the play instead of merely summarizing the dialogue? (*In general, a direct quotation provides more convincing evidence in literary criticism than a paraphrase, though the significance of a given passage must be clearly explained. In this instance, Hamlet's voice comes alive in the dialogue and makes his dilemma seem more urgent.*) Why does the author provide these examples in this order? (*The examples show Hamlet's progression toward having the ability to fulfill his revenge on Claudius.*)

Determine Central Ideas (LINES 98–122)

 COMMON CORE RI 2

Remind students that direct quotations from the play can be used to suggest or support a central idea.

E **ASK STUDENTS** to reread lines 98–122. Then point out the excerpt from the play in lines 101–104. Why is Fortinbras's army a "catchy example for Hamlet" (line 98)? (*Fortinbras's army gives Hamlet the idea that enthusiasm can exist even in pursuit of a worthless end.*) What central idea can be inferred from this example? (*The army shows Hamlet that, in order to act, he does not need to be rational or even to stand on firm moral ground.*)

SCAFFOLDING FOR ELL STUDENTS

Vocabulary: Affixes Explain that prefixes and suffixes (together called affixes) are word parts that change a word's meaning. Some words can have more than one affix. Write *unimaginative* (line 10) on the board. Have students identify and define the base word. (*imagine, "to create a mental image of something"*) Explain that the prefix *un-* means "not," and the suffix *-ive* means "tending toward." Thus, the word means, roughly, "not tending to create mental images." (*Example: An unimaginative playwright is not very creative.*) Distribute a list of affixes and their meanings. As they read, students can look for words with affixes, and then find the base words. Explain that even if students don't know the meaning of an affix, identifying the base word can help their understanding of the essay.

Determine Central Ideas (LINES 134–136)

COMMON CORE RI 2

Tell students that examples are used to point to a central idea; for that reason, they tend also to relate to each other.

F CITE TEXT EVIDENCE Ask students to consider how Laertes is like the actor who played Hecuba. What word in this sentence about Laertes links back to the author's description of the actor in lines 80–85? *(Hamlet noted that the actor was "sincere" in his performance as Hecuba [line 84]. Likewise, Laertes "can perform with the utmost sincerity all the actions his social milieu demands, even if they contradict each other" [lines 135–136].)* What does this similarity suggest? *(In both cases, the "sincerity" is full of human emotion but is not grounded in reason or reality. This is a kind of sincerity that Hamlet might be able to achieve in his revenge, even though he knows that killing Claudius makes little sense.)*

Analyze Structure: Argument (LINES 137–148)

COMMON CORE RI 5

Explain that in a strong argument every example is relevant to the claim.

G ASK STUDENTS to reread lines 137–148. How does this section of the essay relate to the author's argument? *(The author says that Laertes "can mourn the useless death of a human being at one minute and the next he can uselessly kill a dozen more if he is told that his honor is at stake" [lines 137–139]. Laertes has much in common with Shakespeare's audience and critics: none question the validity of revenge.)*

CRITICAL VOCABULARY

emulation: The author explains that Hamlet is moved to action by Laertes's example.

ASK STUDENTS to explain why Hamlet is especially driven toward emulation of Laertes. *(Laertes is Hamlet's peer—he is about Hamlet's age and is a privileged member of the court. When Hamlet sees him react with such passion to the death of his sister, Hamlet feels ashamed that he has not had a similarly passionate response to his own father's murder.)*

---

the same irrational contagion is needed as in the war against Poland. The type of mimetic incitement from which Hamlet "benefits" at this
120 point resembles very much the kind of spectacle which governments never fail to organize for their citizenry when they have decided it is time to go to war: a rousing military parade.

But it is not the actor, ultimately, or the army of Fortinbras; it is Laertes, I believe, who determines Hamlet to act. Laertes provides the most persuasive spectacle not because he provides the "best" example but because his situation parallels that of Hamlet. Being Hamlet's peer, at least up to a point, his passionate stance constitutes the most powerful challenge imaginable. In such circumstances, even the most apathetic man's sense of **emulation** must rise to such a pitch that the
130 sort of disaster that the fulfillment of the revenge demands can finally be achieved.

The simple and unreflective Laertes can shout to Claudius "give me my father" and then leap into his sister's grave in a wild demonstration of grief. Like a well-adjusted gentleman or a consummate actor, he can perform with the utmost sincerity all the actions his social milieu demands, even if they contradict each other. He can mourn the useless death of a human being at one minute and the next he can uselessly kill a dozen more if he is told that his honor
140 is at stake. The death of his father and sister are almost less shocking to him than the lack of pomp and circumstance at their burial. At the rites of Ophelia, Laertes keeps asking the priest for "more ceremony." Laertes is a formalist[3] and he reads the tragedy of which he is a part very much like the formalists of all stripes. He does not question the validity of revenge. He does not question the literary *genre*. He does not question the relationship between revenge and mourning. These are not valid critical questions to him; they never enter his mind, just as it never occurs to most critics that Shakespeare himself could question the validity of revenge.

Hamlet watches Laertes leap into Ophelia's grave and the effect
150 on him is electrifying. The reflective mood of the conversation with Horatio gives way to a wild imitation of the rival's theatrical mourning. At this point, he has obviously decided that he, too, would act according to the demands of society, that he would become another Laertes in other words. He, too, as a result, must leap into the grave of one who has already died, even as he prepares other graves for those still alive:

> 'Swounds, show me what thou'lt do.
> Woo't weep? Woo't fight? Woo't fast? Woo't tear thyself?
> Woo't drink up eisel? Eat a crocodile?
160 I'll do't. Dost thou come here to whine?
> To outface me with leaping in her grave?

emulation
(ĕmʹyə-lāʹshən) *n.* competitive imitation.

---

[3] **formalist:** one who strictly adheres to accepted rules and conventions.

WHEN STUDENTS STRUGGLE . . .

To guide students' comprehension of this part of the argument, point out the indented quotations. Explain that these are used to support the central idea that Hamlet needs to find a model to imitate in order to accomplish his revenge. Help them summarize the main point of each quotation:

- Lines 86–97: Hamlet wonders if he can be as sincere as the actor seems to be.
- Lines 101–104: Hamlet knows that Fortinbras makes foolish decisions, but at least he is able to act.
- Lines 157–163: Hamlet is inspired when Laertes leaps into Ophelia's grave.

Have students discuss which model Hamlet finally imitates, and why.

Be buried quick with her, and so will I.
....
I'll rant as well as thou. . . .

Shakespeare can place these incredible lines in the mouth of
Hamlet without undermining the dramatic credibility of what follows.
Following the lead of Gertrude, the spectators will ascribe the outburst
to "madness."

> This is mere madness.
> And thus awhile the fit will work on him.
> 170 Anon, as patient as the female dove
> When that her golden couplets are disclosed,
> His silence will sit drooping.

A little later Hamlet himself, now calmly determined to kill Claudius,
will recall the recent outburst in most significant words:

> I am very sorry, good Horatio,
> That to Laertes I forgot myself,
> For by the image of my cause I see
> The portraiture of his. I'll court his favors.
> But, sure, the bravery of his grief did put me
> 180 Into a towering passion.

Like all victims of mimetic suggestion, Hamlet reverses the
true **hierarchy** between the other and himself. He should say: "by
the image of *his* cause I see the portraiture of *mine*." This is the
correct formula, obviously, for all the spectacles that have influenced
Hamlet. The actor's tears and the military display of Fortinbras were
already presented as mimetic models. In order to realize that Laertes,
too, functions as a model, the last two lines are essential. The cool
determination of Hamlet, at this point, is the transmutation[4] of the
"towering passion" which he had vainly tried to build up before and
190 which Laertes has finally communicated to him through the "bravery
of his grief." This transmutation is unwittingly predicted by Gertrude
when she compares Hamlet to the dove who becomes quiet after she
has laid her eggs. Gertrude only thinks of Hamlet's previous changes
of mood, as sterile as they were sudden, but her metaphor suggests a
more tangible accomplishment, the birth of something portentous:

> Anon, as patient as the female dove
> When that her golden couplets are disclosed,
> His silence will sit drooping.

> **hierarchy**
> (hī′ə-rär′kē) *n.* a
> ranking of status
> within a group.

---
[4] **transmutation:** an alteration or conversion into another form.

COLLABORATIVE DISCUSSION With a partner, discuss whether you
agree with Girard's assessment of Hamlet's character. Cite specific
textual evidence from the essay to support your ideas.

Hamlet's Dull Revenge **365**

TO CHALLENGE STUDENTS . . .

Evaluate the Author's Argument Near the beginning of his essay, Girard
says that his analysis will help clarify "some unexplained details" and "the
function of many obscure scenes."

ASK STUDENTS to identify the details and scenes from *Hamlet* that Girard
cites as evidence in his argument. Do students agree that these parts of
the play are "unexplained" and "obscure" *without* Girard's explanation that
Shakespeare sought to denounce revenge theater and the very idea of
revenge? Have students formulate some thoughts independently and then
share their ideas in pairs or small groups.

CLOSE READ

Determine Central Ideas (LINES 166–180)

A literary critic can use the varying perspectives of
different characters to suggest a single, central idea.

ASK STUDENTS to reread lines 166–180. Gertrude
refers to Hamlet's outburst as "madness" (line 167),
while he describes it as a "towering passion" (line 180).
What central idea does Girard infer from the different
descriptions of Hamlet's behavior? *(Both versions
of Hamlet's behavior have been an imitation of the
passions he has witnessed around him, though finally he
has worked up enough of that borrowed passion to act.)*

Analyze Structure: Argument (LINES 196–198)

Tell students that every choice an author makes is for
a reason.

ASK STUDENTS to reread lines 196–198. Point
out that Girard ends his essay by repeating the last
three lines of Gertrude's speech. Why does he do
this? Does this repetition strengthen his argument?
*(The repetition emphasizes that Hamlet's "drooping"
is now calm deliberation, not the passive, pliant mood
following earlier outbursts.)*

CRITICAL VOCABULARY

hierarchy: At Ophelia's funeral, Laertes shows a
higher degree of passion than Hamlet has been
able to muster.

ASK STUDENTS how Hamlet confuses the
hierarchy between him and Laertes. *(Laertes'
passion is the model that Hamlet imitates, not the
reverse; thus, Laertes "passion" is at the higher level.)*

COLLABORATIVE DISCUSSION Have partners share
ideas about whether Girard's ideas about Hamlet's
character ring true. Have them cite reasons and
examples that Girard uses to support his assessment.
Then have them share their ideas with the class.

ASK STUDENTS to share any questions they generated
in the course of reading and discussing the selection.

TEACH

CLOSE READ

Analyze Structure: Argument

COMMON CORE RI 5

Review the elements of an argument with students. Then have them outline the structure of the argument they have just read, including the claim, Girard's reasoning, and the evidence he provides to support his reasoning.

Note that the body of Girard's essay does not follow the familiar pattern of reason #1, evidence, reason #2, evidence, etc. Instead, Girard presents his reasoning over a series of paragraphs, including the key idea that Hamlet seeks mimetic examples to spur his passion. Girard then demonstrates that episodes in the drama provide increasingly strong mimetic examples for Hamlet.

Determine Central Ideas

COMMON CORE RI 2

Remind students that making inferences means combining what they already know with what they find in their reading. Reinforce that it is possible to infer central ideas from details.

Review the graphic organizer with students. Have them complete a similar graphic organizer to show how details from lines 132–148 support a central idea. (*Laertes "does not question the validity of revenge"* [lines 143–144].)

Analyze Structure: Argument

COMMON CORE RI 5

In his critical essay, Girard makes an **argument** about Shakespeare's motivations in writing *Hamlet*. Following a traditional structure for argument, Girard's essay begins with a **claim**, or statement of position on an issue. It includes **reasons** for making the claim. The reasoning is supported by **evidence**—in this case, examples from the text. In a persuasive argument, reasons flow logically from the evidence because the evidence is strong and relevant. When you analyze the structure of an argument and the way it is developed, these kinds of questions can help you assess the validity of the argument:

- What is Girard's claim?
- Does Girard support his claim with reasons? Are the reasons arranged logically, in a way that becomes increasingly convincing and engaging?
- Does Girard cite evidence from the drama to support his reasoning? Is the evidence both relevant and adequate?
- Are there any inconsistencies in Girard's argument?

Determine Central Ideas

COMMON CORE RI 2

In his literary criticism "Hamlet's Dull Revenge," Girard develops central ideas related to the character of Hamlet and the Elizabethan theater. **Central ideas** are important points that an author wants to convey about a topic. In an argument, you can think of the claim and the supporting reasons as the central ideas. Readers can determine these central ideas by reading the details in each section of the essay and then inferring the major point—or in the case of argument, the reason—being advanced in that section. The graphic organizer shows how details from lines 71–97 of the essay support a central idea.

Detail

Hamlet cannot get motivated to carry out his act of revenge.

Detail

He sees that the actor playing Hecuba has more emotion than he does.

Central Idea

Hamlet needs a model, or example, of behavior to persuade him to act.

This central idea is one part of the reasoning that supports Girard's claim. Examining how the claim and other central ideas interact and build on one another can help the reader understand Girard's complex and subtle literary analysis.

Strategies for Annotation 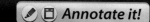 *Annotate it!*

Analyze Structure: Argument

COMMON CORE RI 1, RI 5

Encourage students to use their eBook annotation tools to do the following:

- Highlight a reason in yellow.
- Highlight supporting evidence in green.
- On a note, explain whether the evidence is adequate and relevant.
- Look for additional details in the surrounding text that might further support the reason.

final bloodbath, Hamlet has many opportunities to watch rousing spectacles during his play and he tries to generate even more, in a conscientious effort to put himself in the right mood for the murder of Claudius. Hamlet must receive from someone else, a mimetic model, the impulse which he does not find in himself.

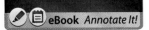 eBook *Annotate It!*

Analyzing the Text

Cite Text Evidence   Support your responses with evidence from the selection.

1. **Summarize** What claim does Girard develop in this essay?

2. **Analyze** What is Girard's explanation for why Hamlet fails to take revenge swiftly? What does he argue is the link between this behavior and revenge theater?

3. **Draw Conclusions** What central idea does Girard begin to develop in lines 25–70?

4. **Analyze** What is Girard's tone toward Shakespeare and his play? Explain how his feelings are revealed through his language as well as his choice of details.

5. **Evaluate** Girard provides three examples of the models that he claims Hamlet needs to work up a taste for vengeance. Identify these examples and discuss how their presentation within the argument strengthens or diminishes Girard's claims.

6. **Critique** According to Girard, what is the relationship between the character of Laertes and revenge theater? Is this interpretation of Laertes' role convincing? Why or why not?

7. **Evaluate** Review the lines spoken by Hamlet that Girard cites. Do these lines effectively support his perspective on Hamlet's state of mind? Explain.

8. **Summarize** Trace the reasoning that Girard uses to support his overall claim, showing the relationships among the central ideas.

9. **Analyze** What is the "something portentous" that Gertrude's birth metaphor refer to in line 195? In Girard's view, how might the phrase be applied to Shakespeare's play as well?

PERFORMANCE TASK

Writing Activity: Argument Does Girard succeed in presenting a valid interpretation of Shakespeare's play *Hamlet*?

- Write a sentence or two summarizing Girard's interpretation.
- Decide whether or not he convincingly supports this reading of the play in his essay.

- Give reasons for your claim and use details from the essay to provide evidence for your opinion.
- Use conventions of standard written English.

Assign this performance task.

PERFORMANCE TASK

Writing Activity: Argument Begin with a class discussion that elicits students' own interpretations of *Hamlet*. Encourage students to validate their own opinions with reasons and textual evidence. Explain that there is no single "correct" interpretation, and that students need not agree with Girard's claim in order to address its validity. When writing their arguments, students should cite Girard's central ideas and the examples he uses to support them.

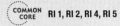

PRACTICE & APPLY

Analyzing the Text

Possible answers:

1. *Girard claims that Shakespeare had dual motives in Hamlet: to achieve a dramatic success with a play about revenge while at the same time making the point that revenge theater was flawed (lines 15–20).*

2. *Girard argues that Hamlet is not fully convinced that Claudius deserves to die, since his victim, Hamlet's father, may not have been entirely blameless. In that case, carrying out revenge would make Hamlet as guilty as Claudius. Girard says that Hamlet's feelings about revenge illustrate what Shakespeare felt about revenge theater—he no longer believed in it.*

3. *The idea is that Shakespeare's play shows how he understood the problems of revenge theater and revenge itself. Lines 29–35, among others, clearly support this point.*

4. *Girard adopts an admiring tone toward Shakespeare for fashioning a complex and successful play in a genre he no longer believed in. His rationale for scenes that might otherwise not make sense; his direct statements about Shakespeare's skill (such as "Shakespeare can place these incredible lines in the mouth of Hamlet without undermining the dramatic credibility of what follows"); and his choice of words and phrases all help to reveal his attitude.*

5. *He cites the actor (line 81), the army (line 99), and Laertes (line 123) as "mimetic incitements" for Hamlet. Their sequential presentation, from the tangential to the strongest, provides increasing support for his claims.*

6. *Girard implies that Shakespeare uses Laertes to represent or personify revenge theater. Girard calls Laertes "a formalist," one who observes the outward forms of revenge without questioning the validity of the act, the genre, or the relationship between revenge and mourning. Laertes's character enables Shakespeare to pose such questions.*

7. *The quotations show how each model is a catalyst for Hamlet's introspection and eventual change of heart.*

8. *Girard claims that by resisting the social impetus that demands revenge and perpetuates violence, Hamlet reveals Shakespeare's own revulsion toward revenge theater. He cites examples of models that represent how all remain trapped in an inescapable cycle.*

9. *"The birth of something portentous," or awe-inspiring, is both Hamlet's decision to act and Shakespeare's play itself, which excites wonder and awe at his artistry.*

PRACTICE & APPLY

Critical Vocabulary

COMMON CORE L 6

Possible answers:

1. entail, *because it refers to a necessary or required consequence*

2. genre, *of which* drama *and* novel *are examples*

3. emulation, *which connotes copying someone else in a spirit of competition*

4. hierarchy, *which refers to organization by status or rank*

5. double entendre, *because it indicates more than one meaning*

Vocabulary Strategy: Domain-Specific Words and Phrases

Answers:

For words not defined in footnotes, students' definitions should resemble the following:

tragedy: *a drama in which the protagonist's downfall is brought about through a tragic flaw or moral weakness*
hero: *the protagonist in a tragedy*
motif: *dominant theme*
metaphor: *an implied, figurative comparison between unlike things*

The use of the terms in relation to the play will vary.

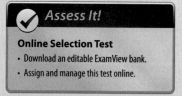

Assess It!

Online Selection Test
- Download an editable ExamView bank.
- Assign and manage this test online.

Critical Vocabulary

COMMON CORE L 6

genre	double entendre	entail
emulation	hierarchy	

Practice and Apply Work with a partner and discuss which Critical Vocabulary word is most closely associated with the italicized word in each sentence and why.

1. Which word is most closely associated with *requirement*? Why?

2. Which word goes with *drama* or *novel*? Why?

3. Which word is associated with *rivalry*? Why?

4. Which word goes with *rank*? Why?

5. Which word might be associated with *ambiguity*? Why?

Vocabulary Strategy: Domain-Specific Words and Phrases

To convey his precise meaning, Girard uses **domain-specific words**, terms that are related to the field of literary criticism. The Critical Vocabulary words *genre* and *double entendre* are two examples of this specialized vocabulary. Many times domain-specific words are footnoted. If the words are not explained, following these steps will help you define them.

1. Look closely at the context in which the term is used for familiar phrases or words that give clues to its meaning.

2. Identify word parts—roots, prefixes, or suffixes—as well as the word's part of speech, and use them to help define the term.

3. Consult a print or digital dictionary to determine the exact meaning of the term, referring to a specialized dictionary if necessary.

Practice and Apply Work with a partner to complete these activities.

1. Review this list of words that Girard uses in his essay: *tragedy, katharsis, hero, mimetic, motif, formalist, metaphor.*

2. Use the footnotes, context clues, word parts, and a dictionary to define each word as it applies to literature or literary criticism.

3. Use three of the words to discuss an aspect of the play *Hamlet* with a partner.

Strategies for Annotation

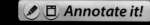 **Annotate it!**

Domain-Specific Words and Phrases

COMMON CORE L 6

Have students locate these words in the text: *villain* (line 39); *spectacles* (line 76); *cue* (line 108). Share these strategies for independent analysis:

- Highlight the word in pink.
- Look for context clues. Highlight these in blue.
- Underline any word parts that might help you define the term.
- On a note, write the definition of the word. Verify the definition in a dictionary or other reference work.

nasty Claudius may look, he cannot look nasty enough if he appears in a context of previous revenge; he cannot generate, as a villain, the absolute passion and dedication which is demanded of Hamlet. The problem with Hamlet is that he cannot forget the context. As a result, the crime by Claudius looks to him like one more link in an already

villain: wrongdoer; criminal

Analyze Key Terms

COMMON CORE

RI 4

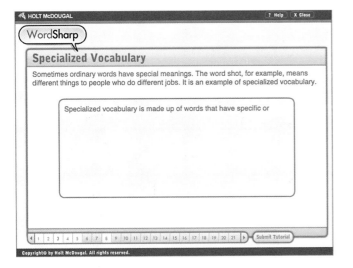

TEACH

Explain that students can have a broader comprehension of a text by clearly understanding the meaning of key terms as they are used by the author.

Review the following key terms from the essay:

- *revenge tragedy* (line 1); *revenge theater* (line 17); *context* (line 39); *spectacle(s)* (line 76); *mimetic* (line 78)

Model how students can analyze how the author uses and refines the meaning of a term by analyzing the context surrounding the word in each instance. For example:

mimetic: "relating to imitation"

- "mimetic model" (line 78): Hamlet does not find the "impulse" for action in himself (line 79). He must copy it from another source—a model.
- "mimetic attraction" (line 114) and "mimetic incitement" (line 119): *contagion* (line 118) suggests the intensity of the imitation of passion that occurs in an angry mob.
- "mimetic suggestion" (line 181): Hamlet is a "victim" of his identification with and imitation of Laertes.

Readers can conclude that the term *mimetic*, as used by Girard, involves imitation that is powerfully motivated by impulses not under the victim's control.

PRACTICE AND APPLY

Have students define each term above. Then have them identify at least one example of each term in the text and analyze how the author uses and refines its meaning over the course of the text.

Analyze Structure

COMMON CORE

RI 5

RETEACH

Review what students have learned about the importance of providing good evidence to build a strong argument. Tell them that as they read and write arguments, they should be able to:

- understand the importance of evidence in writing
- recognize different kinds of evidence
- distinguish between facts and opinions
- evaluate the relevance and reliability of a piece of evidence

 LEVEL UP TUTORIALS Assign the following *Level Up* tutorial: **Evidence**

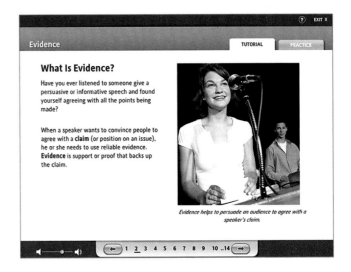

After they have completed the tutorial, make sure students understand the idea of "relevance." Ask which of the following pieces of evidence might be relevant to Girard's argument:

- Hamlet's reaction when he first finds out about his father's murder
- dialogue between Laertes and Ophelia
- excerpts from the play within the play

Students should give reasons for their answers.

CLOSE READING APPLICATION

Ask students to apply the skill to another argumentative text. Have them identify the claim, reasons, and evidence, and explain whether the evidence is relevant and why. If not, they should say what kind of evidence might be more relevant and convincing.

my**SmartPlanner** Create lesson plans and access resources online.

Tell Them Not to Kill Me!

Short Story by Juan Rulfo   Translated by George D. Schade

Why This Text?

This short story explores the ideas of the importance of fathers, vengeance, fear, and justice through shifting points of view and flashbacks. Rulfo's structural choices and the use of irony convey a sense of the main character and the fact that he has not changed despite (or perhaps because of) hardship and fear.

Key Learning Objective: The student will be able to analyze author's choices concerning the structure and point of view in a text.

 Common Core Standards

RL 1 Cite textual evidence.
RL 2 Determine two or more themes of a text.
RL 3 Analyze author's choices.
RL 5 Analyze how an author's choices concerning structure create effects.
RL 6 Analyze point of view, distinguishing what is directly stated from what is really meant (irony).
SL 1a Come to discussions prepared.
L 3a Vary syntax for effect.

 Text Complexity Rubric

Quantitative Measures

Tell Them Not to Kill Me!
Lexile: 810L

Qualitative Measures

Levels of Meaning/Purpose

single level of complex meaning

Structure

several shifts in chronology; use of flashback and flash–forward.

Language Conventionality and Clarity

less straightforward sentence structure

Knowledge Demands

somewhat unfamiliar perspective

Reader/Task Considerations

Teacher determined
Vary by individual reader and type of text

TEACH

CLOSE READ

Background Have students read the background and information about the author, Juan Rulfo (hwän rül'fō). Tell students that Mexico was plagued by civil war from about 1910–1920, with disorganized violence continuing after that time. This story explores violence at a more personal level, speaking to how violence on a societal level affects the behavior of individuals.

AS YOU READ Direct students to use the As You Read instruction to focus their reading. Remind them to write down any questions they generate during reading.

Analyze Point of View:
Irony (LINES 10–14)

COMMON CORE · RL 6

Remind students that an author can use point of view to help readers understand the thoughts of the characters. One way to present point of view is through irony. **Irony** is a contrast between expectations, which can be based on initial impressions, and reality. Authors use irony to present ideas in memorable ways and to help their readers discover truths in the characters.

Ⓐ **ASK STUDENTS** what the dialogue in lines 10–14 implies about the father and son. What initial impression of the son and the father does the author create? *(The dialogue gives the impression that the son is cold-hearted and selfish, because he refuses to try to save his father. The father is more sympathetic because he appears to be desperate and helpless to save himself. The point of view used in this opening scene gives an initial impression of the old man's character and predicament.)*

Juan Rulfo (1918–1986) *was a Mexican writer. He wrote only one novel and a book of short stories, but they have earned him recognition as one of the finest writers in twentieth-century Latin America. His style, which is characterized by shifting points of view, flashbacks, and a stream-of-consciousness technique, influenced other Latin American authors, including well-known novelist Gabriel García Márquez. Rulfo's childhood and family life were disrupted by political conflict that wracked Mexico in the 1920s; his stories are primarily set in that time period and reflect the hardship and violence that characterized rural Mexicans' struggle to survive.*

Tell Them Not to Kill Me!

Short Story by Juan Rulfo   translated by George D. Schade

Image Credits: (t) ©GDA/AP Images; (b) ©PBNJ Productions/Corbis

AS YOU READ Make predictions about the main character in the story. Write down any questions you generate during reading.

"Tell them not to kill me, Justino! Go on and tell them that. For God's sake! Tell them. Tell them please for God's sake."

"I can't. There's a sergeant there who doesn't want to hear anything about you."

"Make him listen to you. Use your wits and tell him that scaring me has been enough. Tell him please for God's sake."

"But it's not just to scare you. It seems they really mean to kill you. And I don't want to go back there."

"Go on once more. Just once, to see what you can do."

10 "No. I don't feel like going. Because if I do they'll know I'm your son. If I keep bothering them they'll end up knowing who I am and will decide to shoot me too. Better leave things the way they are now."

Ⓐ "Go on, Justino. Tell them to take a little pity on me. Just tell them that."

Justino clenched his teeth and shook his head saying no.

And he kept on shaking his head for some time.

"Tell the sergeant to let you see the colonel. And tell him how old I am—How little I'm worth. What will he get out of killing me?"

SCAFFOLDING FOR ELL STUDENTS

Language: Contractions Tell students that contractions—shortened versions of one or two words—are used in informal writing, reflecting the sound of conversational English.

Full Form	Contraction
They will	They'll
Can not	Can't
I am	I'm

Have students identify contractions as they read and write out the full form of each one to ensure comprehension.

Varying Syntax

COMMON CORE RL 5, L 3a

(LINES 27–32)

Remind students that **syntax,** the arrangement of words in a sentence, is one way that authors communicate ideas. Discuss how stylistic choices such as varying sentence length and the use of subordinate clauses can affect the reader's emotional experience of a piece of writing.

 CITE TEXT EVIDENCE Have students reread lines 27–32. Ask them to describe the way the author varies the syntax in this passage. *(A series of short, abrupt sentences are followed by a much longer one.)* Then ask why the author chose this style. What information is conveyed to the reader? *(The short sentences describing Juvencio's behavior while tied to the post convey his desperation and fear. The longer sentence that closes the paragraph conveys his own desire to live a longer life, to survive as long as he can.)*

Analyze Structure

COMMON CORE RL 5

(LINES 59–63)

Explain to students that an author will sometimes shift the point of view to change the way readers view the characters. Remind students that **first-person point of view** is used to tell the story from the perspective of one character. On the other hand, the **third-person point of view narrator** is either omniscient—revealing the thoughts and feelings of all the characters—or limited—presenting the story from the perspective of one character.

C **ASK STUDENTS** what happens at line 59 that affects how they perceive the characters. What new information does the reader get from lines 59–63? *(At line 59, there is a transition from third- to first-person narration. The shift to first-person creates an intimacy between the reader and Juvencio. His tone is cold and callous. The reader learns that he doesn't feel remorse for his actions; he justifies it by saying "he killed one of my yearlings" and then goes on to complain that his attempts to bribe the judge didn't work. Readers begin to lose sympathy for Juvencio.)*

Nothing. After all he must have a soul. Tell him to do it for the blessed
20 salvation of his soul."

Justino got up from the pile of stones which he was sitting on and walked to the gate of the corral. Then he turned around to say, "All right, I'll go. But if they decide to shoot me too, who'll take care of my wife and kids?"

"Providence will take care of them, Justino. You go there now and see what you can do for me. That's what matters."

They'd brought him in at dawn. The morning was well along now and he was still there, tied to a post, waiting. He couldn't keep still.
He'd tried to sleep for a while to calm down, but he couldn't. He wasn't
30 hungry either. All he wanted was to live. Now that he knew they were really going to kill him, all he could feel was his great desire to stay alive, like a recently resuscitated man.

Who would've thought that old business that happened so long ago and that was buried the way he thought it was would turn up? That business when he had to kill Don Lupe. Not for nothing either, as the Alimas tried to make out, but because he had his reasons. He remembered: Don Lupe Terreros, the owner of the Puerta de Piedra— and besides that, his compadre—was the one he, Juvencio Nava, had to kill, because he'd refused to let him pasture his animals, when he was
40 the owner of the Puerta de Piedra and his compadre too.

At first he didn't do anything because he felt compromised. But later, when the drought came, when he saw how his animals were dying off one by one, plagued by hunger, and how his compadre Lupe continued to refuse to let him use his pastures, then was when he began breaking through the fence and driving his herd of skinny animals to the pasture where they could get their fill of grass. And Don Lupe didn't like it and ordered the fence mended, so that he, Juvencio Nava, had to cut open the hole again. So, during the day the hole was stopped up and at night it was opened again, while the stock
50 stayed there right next to the fence, always waiting—his stock that before had lived just smelling the grass without being able to taste it.

And he and Don Lupe argued again and again without coming to any agreement.

Until one day Don Lupe said to him, "Look here, Juvencio, if you let another animal in my pasture, I'll kill it."

And he answered him, "Look here, Don Lupe, it's not my fault that the animals look out for themselves. They're innocent. You'll have to pay for it, if you kill them."

And he killed one of my yearlings.
60 This happened thirty-five years ago in March, because in April I was already up in the mountains, running away from the summons. The ten cows I gave the judge didn't do me any good, or the lien on my house either, to pay for getting me out of jail. Still later they used up what was left to pay so they wouldn't keep after me, but they kept

---

APPLYING ACADEMIC VOCABULARY

mediate	integrity

As you discuss Rulfo's short story, incorporate the following Collection 4 academic vocabulary words: *mediate* and *integrity*. Ask students why Juvencio's son refuses to try to **mediate** between the old man and his captors. As you dig deeper into the story, ask students which characters, if any, have **integrity,** and why.

"All he could feel was his great desire to stay alive, like a recently resuscitated man."

after me just the same. That's why I came to live with my son on this other piece of land of mine which is called Palo de Venado. And my son grew up and got married to my daughter-in-law Ignacia and has had eight children now. So it happened a long time ago and ought to be forgotten by now. But I guess it's not.

70   I figured then that with about a hundred pesos everything could be fixed up. The dead Don Lupe left just his wife and two little kids still crawling. And his widow died soon afterward too—they say from grief. They took the kids far off to some relatives. So there was nothing to fear from them.

    But the rest of the people took the position that I was still summoned to be tried just to scare me so they could keep on robbing me. Every time someone came to the village they told me, "There are some strangers in town, Juvencio."

    And I would take off to the mountains, hiding among the
80 madrone thickets and passing the days with nothing to eat but herbs. Sometimes I had to go out at midnight, as though the dogs were after me. It's been that way my whole life. Not just a year or two. My whole life.

    And now they'd come for him when he no longer expected anyone, confident that people had forgotten all about it, believing that he'd spend at least his last days peacefully. "At least," he thought, "I'll have some peace in my old age. They'll leave me alone."

    He'd clung to this hope with all his heart. That's why it was hard for him to imagine that he'd die like this, suddenly, at this time of life,
90 after having fought so much to ward off death, after having spent his best years running from one place to another because of the alarms, now when his body had become all dried up and leathery from the bad days when he had to be in hiding from everybody.

    Hadn't he even let his wife go off and leave him? The day when he learned his wife had left him, the idea of going out in search of her didn't even cross his mind. He let her go without trying to find out at all who she went with or where, so he wouldn't have to go down to the

---

SCAFFOLDING FOR ELL STUDENTS

Organizational Patterns: Time Sequence Remind students to look for **signal words** showing shifts in time *and* point of view to sequence events:

- *Before, after, afterward, first, then, finally*: Have students look at line 81 as you read it aloud, emphasizing the word *after*. Read aloud lines 88–93. Compare the uses of *after* in line 81 and line 90. (In line 81 it is an adverb meaning "behind, or following"; in line 90 it means "subsequent to.")

- Remind students to look for pronouns to decide the point of view, as well as words that signal sequence. For example, in lines 79–83, the pronoun *I* shows that this part of the story is being told by Juvencio.

CLOSE READ

Analyze Structure
COMMON CORE RL 1, RL 5

(LINES 81–86)

Tell students that an author will often structure a story by shifting the point of view and by manipulating the timing of events. For example, an author might include a flashback. Through **flashback,** a narrator relates events from a time before the beginning of the story.

D   **CITE TEXT EVIDENCE** Ask students to observe the shifts in point of view and timing that occur in lines 81–86. (*The narrator shifts back to third-person, and the time moves from a flashback to the present.*) Then ask students to consider the effects of these shifts on the reader's point of view. (*The first-person narration reveals Juvencio as prideful and defensive, focusing on justifying his past acts and expressing anger at his victim and the society that tried to hold him accountable. For example, lines 81–82 focus on how difficult things were for him when he had to hide from the police. When the narration shifts back to the third person, the reader is brought back to his present predicament, in which he is finally being forced to face his actions and is terrified about the consequences. The tone is less defensive and more sympathetic, inviting readers to empathize with Juvencio again.*)

Analyze Point of View: Irony
COMMON CORE RL 6

(LINES 84–93)

Remind students that irony is the contrast between expectations and reality. In a work of fiction, this contrast may be between the reader's expectations and what actually happens in a story, or it may be a contrast in what the characters expect to happen and what actually happens.

E   **ASK STUDENTS** to explain the **irony** in lines 84–93. (*It is ironic that just when Juvencio expected that he was safe from the law, he was caught. It is also ironic that he spent his entire life on the run only to be caught in the end.*)

Analyze Structure

COMMON CORE RL 5

(LINES 102–104)

Tell students that although the shifts in time sequence may be confusing, Rulfo chose this structure deliberately, to help build suspense and gradually reveal Juvencio's character.

F **ASK STUDENTS** what time period is represented in the paragraph that starts with line 102. *(The time jumps back to the near present, to when Juvencio was captured.)* What is revealed in this paragraph about Juvencio, and why is this important to the story? *(Readers learn that Juvencio was so afraid once he was caught that the police didn't even have to restrain him to make him follow them. This is important because it reveals the cowardly side of Juvencio's character.)*

Analyze Point of View:

COMMON CORE RL 1, RL 3, RL 6

Irony (LINES 107–110)

Tell students that **motivation,** or a character's reasons for behaving the way he or she does, is an important part of understanding point of view. In this selection, Juvencio's motivation also creates irony.

G **CITE TEXT EVIDENCE** Have students look for words and phrases in lines 107–110 that reveal Juvencio's main motivation throughout the story. *("stinging in his stomach" "saw death nearby", "big with fear)* What does this language tell readers about Juvencio's main motivation in this story? *(He is motivated by his fear of death; survival at any cost has been his motivation all along.)* How does this create irony? *(His very motivation to survive is what leads him to kill Don Lupe—with no regard for that man's right to survive—and results in a life of fear and finally death.)*

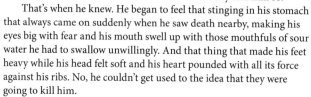

village. He let her go as he'd let everything else go, without putting up a fight. All he had left to take care of was his life, and he'd do that, 100 if nothing else. He couldn't let them kill him. He couldn't. Much less now.

But that's why they brought him from there, from Palo de Venado. They didn't need to tie him so he'd follow them. He walked alone, tied by his fear. They realized he couldn't run with his old body, with those skinny legs of his like dry bark, cramped up with the fear of dying. Because that's where he was headed. For death. They told him so.

That's when he knew. He began to feel that stinging in his stomach that always came on suddenly when he saw death nearby, making his eyes big with fear and his mouth swell up with those mouthfuls of sour 110 water he had to swallow unwillingly. And that thing that made his feet heavy while his head felt soft and his heart pounded with all its force against his ribs. No, he couldn't get used to the idea that they were going to kill him.

There must be some hope. Somewhere there must still be some hope left. Maybe they'd made a mistake. Perhaps they were looking for another Juvencio Nava and not him.

He walked along in silence between those men, with his arms fallen at his sides. The early-morning hour was dark, starless. The wind blew slowly, whipping the dry earth back and forth, which was 120 filled with that odor like urine that dusty roads have.

His eyes, that had become squinty with the years, were looking down at the ground, here under his feet, in spite of the darkness. There in the earth was his whole life. Sixty years of living on it, of holding it tight in his hands, of tasting it like one tastes the flavor of meat. For a

WHEN STUDENTS STRUGGLE . . .

Some students may struggle with following the shifting time sequence of this story. To help ensure comprehension, have students put the key events in the story in the correct sequence on a time line as shown here.

long time he'd been crumbling it with his eyes, savoring each piece as if it were the last one, almost knowing it would be the last.

Then, as if wanting to say something, he looked at the men who were marching along next to him. He was going to tell him loose, to let him go; "I haven't hurt anybody, boys," he was going to
130 say to them, but he kept silent. "A little further on I'll tell them," he thought. And he just looked at them. He could even imagine they were his friends, but he didn't want to. They weren't. He didn't know who they were. He watched them moving at his side and bending down from time to time to see where the road continued.

He'd seen them for the first time at nightfall, that dusky hour when everything seems scorched. They'd crossed the furrows trodding on the tender corn. And he'd gone down on account of that—to tell them that the corn was beginning to grow there. But that didn't stop them.
140 He'd seen them in time. He'd always had the luck to see everything in time. He could've hidden, gone up in the mountains for a few hours until they left and then come down again. Already it was time for the rains to have come, but the rains didn't come and the corn was beginning to wither. Soon it'd be all dried up.

So it hadn't even been worthwhile, his coming down and placing himself among those men like in a hole, never to get out again.

And now he continued beside them, holding back how he wanted to tell them to let him go. He didn't see their faces, he only saw their bodies, which swung toward him and then away from him. So when
150 he started talking he didn't know if they'd heard him. He said, "I've never hurt anybody." That's what he said. But nothing changed. Not one of the bodies seemed to pay attention. The faces didn't turn to look at him. They kept right on, as if they were walking in their sleep.

Then he thought that there was nothing else he could say, that he would have to look for hope somewhere else. He let his arms fall again to his sides and went by the first houses of the village, among those four men, darkened by the black color of the night.

"Colonel, here is the man."
They'd stopped in front of the narrow doorway. He stood with his
160 hat in his hand, respectfully, waiting to see someone come out. But only the voice came out, "Which man?"

"From Palo de Venado, colonel. The one you ordered us to bring in."

"Ask him if he ever lived in Alima," came the voice from inside again.

"Hey, you. Ever lived in Alima?" the sergeant facing him repeated the question.

"Yes. Tell the colonel that's where I'm from. And that I lived there till not long ago."
170 "Ask him if he knew Guadalupe Terreros."

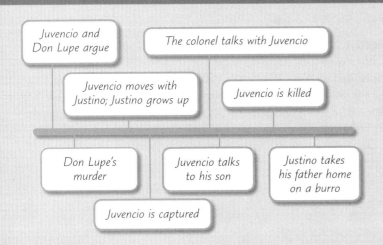

TEACH

CLOSE READ

Analyze Point of View:
Irony (LINES 145–146)

COMMON CORE RL 6

Remind students that irony plays a key role throughout this story.

H **ASK STUDENTS** why it is ironic that Juvencio tries to protect the corn. *(The corn was dying anyway, and in trying to protect it he only got himself caught. In addition, it is ironic that Juvencio has shown that he has cared for little except himself during his lifetime, so showing care for the corn is unexpected.)*

Analyze Language (LINES 151–152)

COMMON CORE RL 4

Have students read line 151–152. Discuss how beginning the sentence with "Not one of the bodies" affects the tone.

I **ASK STUDENTS** What effect does the word choice in this sentence have? How does the effect change if the sentence is rewritten as "None of the men seemed to pay attention."? *(Using the phrase "not one of the bodies" instead of "men" or "people" dehumanizes the people who have captured Juvencio. If Juvencio were the narrator here, the word choice might accord with his self-absorbed viewpoint. Since the narrator here is omniscient, however, the dehumanizing reference to the men suggests a more pervasive attitude of callousness.)*

Analyze Point of View:
Irony (LINES 158–197)

COMMON CORE RL 6

In this long passage, the point of view of the third-person narrator has settled on the Colonel.

J **ASK STUDENTS** why it is ironic that throughout this scene, the Colonel refuses to look at or speak directly to Juvencio. *(Throughout the narrative, Juvencio has pleaded his own case. Here—the only time when telling his own story really counts—he is forced to listen to Colonel tell his side of the story, not allowing another perspective to intervene.)*

Analyze Point of View: Irony (LINES 175–184)

 COMMON CORE RL 6

Discuss with students that authors use irony to maintain tension in a story. Irony allows the author to surprise the reader with unexpected information about characters and events.

K **ASK STUDENTS** what ironic shift is presented in lines 175–176. How does this affect the reader's perception of the person who has captured Juvencio? *(The fact that the person who has captured Juvencio is Don Lupe's son is ironic because earlier in the story, Juvencio notes that Don Lupe's children were taken "far off to live with some relatives," so he wasn't worried about them. Now Juvencio is in danger because of one of the children. A desire for revenge probably drove the Colonel to capture Juvencio.)*

Discuss how the dialogue in lines 180–184 reveals the actual events that have led to Juvencio's situation.

L **ASK STUDENTS** how the description in lines 180–184 affects the reader's point of view. *(The description of Don Lupe's death reveals that he was killed in a brutal way, and died a slow and agonizing death. This fact eliminates any remaining sympathy for Juvencio. It also points to Juvencio's earlier lie that he "never hurt anybody," revealing him as exceptionally dishonest as well as a killer.)*

> " He began to feel that stinging in his stomach that always came on suddenly when he saw death nearby. "

"He says did you know Guadalupe Terreros?"

"Don Lupe? Yes. Tell him that I knew him. He's dead."

Then the voice inside changed tone: "I know he died," it said. And the voice continued talking, as if it was conversing with someone there on the other side of the reed wall.

"Guadalupe Terreros was my father. When I grew up and looked for him they told me he was dead. It's hard to grow up knowing that the thing we have to hang on to take roots from is dead. That's what happened to us.

180 "Later on I learned that he was killed by being hacked first with a machete and then an ox goad[1] stuck in his belly. They told me he lasted more than two days and that when they found him, lying in an arroyo,[2] he was still in agony and begging that his family be taken care of.

"As time goes by you seem to forget this. You try to forget it. What you can't forget is finding out that the one who did it is still alive, feeding his rotten soul with the illusion of eternal life. I couldn't forgive that man, even though I don't know him; but the fact that I know where he is makes me want to finish him off. I can't forgive his

190 still living. He should never have been born."

From here, from outside, all he said was clearly heard. Then he ordered, "Take him and tie him up awhile, so he'll suffer, and then shoot him!"

"Look at me, colonel!" he begged. "I'm not worth anything now. It won't be long before I die all by myself, crippled by old age. Don't kill me!"

"Take him away!" repeated the voice from inside.

---

[1] **ox goad:** a long stick with a pointed end used to control or guide oxen.

[2] **arroyo** (ə-roi´ō): a dry or frequently waterless streambed often found in arid regions.

TO CHALLENGE STUDENTS

Analyze Perspective What can students glean from the story about Justino, Juvencio's son, and how he feels about his father's predicament? Challenge students to rewrite this story from Justino's perspective. How does he feel about his father? Does he feel sadness, pity, regret, or possibly contempt? Would he justify his father's actions or condemn them? Why is he so reluctant to do more to save him? Encourage students to try to write in the same tone and style as Rulfo. Give students the opportunity to share their writing in a small group or with the class.

"I've already paid, colonel. I've paid many times over. They took everything away from me. They punished me in many ways. I've spent about forty years hiding like a leper, always with the fear they'd kill me at any moment. I don't deserve to die like this, colonel. Let the Lord pardon me, at least. Don't kill me! Tell them not to kill me!"

There he was, as if they'd beaten him, waving his hat against the ground. Shouting.

Immediately the voice from inside said, "Tie him up and give him something to drink until he gets drunk so the shots won't hurt him."

Finally, now, he'd been quieted. There he was, slumped down at the foot of the post. His son Justino had come and his son Justino had gone and had returned and now was coming again.

He slung him on top of the burro. He cinched him up tight against the saddle so he wouldn't fall off on the road. He put his head in a sack so it wouldn't give such a bad impression. And then he made the burro giddap, and away they went in a hurry to reach Palo de Venado in time to arrange the wake for the dead man.

"Your daughter-in-law and grandchildren will miss you," he was saying to him. "They'll look at your face and won't believe it's you. They'll think the coyote has been eating on you when they see your face full of holes from all those bullets they shot at you."

COLLABORATIVE DISCUSSION With a partner, discuss the predictions you made as you read the story. Were you surprised by the revelations about Juvencio's past or by the way he died? Cite specific textual evidence to support your ideas.

Tell Them Not to Kill Me! **375**

CLOSE READ

Analyze Structure

COMMON CORE **RL 5**

(LINES 207–214)

Discuss how Rulfo ends the story. Explain to students that authors sometimes structure stories so that readers need to make inferences about the events. This type of structure requires the reader to think about what has already happened, and sometimes read ahead, in order to decide what a passage means.

Ⓜ ASK STUDENTS what effect Rulfo's description in lines 207–210 has on the reader. *(In these lines, the reader needs to infer from the phrase "he'd been quieted" that Juvencio has actually been shot. The changing point of view makes the reader almost believe that he is just tired from pleading for his life and that Justino is just coming back to talk to him again. The structure is disconcerting and unexpected, almost ironic in that Juvencio's end is so much less dramatic than the way he pleaded for his life.)*

Ⓝ CITE TEXT EVIDENCE Ask students to read lines 210–218. Is Justino sad about his father's death? Cite specific evidence from the text to support your answer. *(Justino does not appear to be sad about his father's death. He straps him to the burro in an undignified manner. Even when he puts a sack over Juvencio's head it is "so it wouldn't give such a bad impression," not out of respect for Juvencio. The words he speaks to his dead father as they ride away convey contempt and bitterness more than sadness or respect. He does, however, say "Your daughter-in-law and grandchildren will miss you," indicating some sensitivity.)*

COLLABORATIVE DISCUSSION Have students review their predictions and questions independently before meeting with their partners to discuss the story. Encourage students to cite details from the story to support their ideas.

ASK STUDENTS to share any questions they generated in the course of discussing the selection.

TEACH

CLOSE READ

Analyze Structure COMMON CORE RL 5

As a class, discuss how the story is structured and the narrative techniques that are listed. Have students consider the effects of third-person and first-person point of view. Third-person narration tends to feel more detached, while first-person narration is more subjective and gives the reader insight into the narrator's character not only through what he or she says and does but also through other characters' reactions. Discuss these effects in the context of the selection.

Analyze Point of View: Irony COMMON CORE RL 6

To help students analyze the use of irony in the story, ask them to review the story and recall the predictions they made as they read. Guide the class through the story to identify points that surprised them or proved their predictions wrong. Tell students that the author's ever-shifting point of view was a deliberate choice, inviting readers to question assumptions and expectations while reading. The author uses irony to reveal the disjuncture between Juvencio's self-perception and his perception by other characters (which includes the third-person narrator).

Analyze Structure COMMON CORE RL 5

Authors make deliberate choices about how to structure a story to convey their meaning and to achieve a particular aesthetic, or artistic, impact. Rulfo uses a variety of narrative techniques that affect how readers understand both the plot and the characters of his story.

- **Shifting point of view:** The story begins with a third-person narrator, moves to first person, and then shifts back to third person. To analyze the purpose and effect of these changes, readers should consider what each narrator says, how each perspective relates to the other and to the story as a whole, and how the shifting point of view might affect the reader's response to the story.
- **Flashback:** Flashbacks are accounts of conversations or events that occurred before the beginning of the story. Rulfo's flashbacks help readers understand the main character and important plot points. They also build suspense as they delay the story's climax.
- **Conclusion:** Rulfo's decision to conclude his story abruptly is deliberate. Think about what purpose such a sudden ending might serve.

Analyze Point of View: Irony COMMON CORE RL 6

The point of view from which a story is narrated influences readers' understanding of events and characters. In Rulfo's short story, he shifts between first- and third-person narrators, which enables readers to understand Juvencio's feelings about his present situation, as well as the events that led him there.

Initially, Juvencio is a sympathetic character—a frightened old man talking to his son. As the story develops and readers learn more details, their perceptions of Juvencio change. A contrast develops between expectations and reality. This **irony** can be analyzed by comparing Juvencio's words, and what they suggest about his motives and actions, to the story that emerges as more details unfold. The following passage from the story is a good example.

> I figured then that with about a hundred pesos everything could be fixed up. The dead Don Lupe left just his wife and two little kids still crawling. And his widow died soon afterward too—they say from grief. They took the kids far off to some relatives.

Here, Juvencio presents the wife and children of the murdered Don Lupe as threats that have been neutralized, not as victims deserving compassion. This callous attitude is surprising based on Juvencio's words and actions earlier in the story. It is ironic that the initially sympathetic character of Juvencio actually turns out to be selfish and cold-hearted. As you analyze the story, think about what actually happens versus what you expected to happen.

376 Collection 4

Strategies for Annotation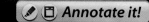

Analyze Structure COMMON CORE RL 5

Share these strategies for guided or independent analysis:

- Highlight in yellow the first line representing a shift from third- to first-person point of view.
- Highlight in blue the shift back to third-person point of view.
- Underline each reference that points to shift in time.
- On a note, record the time sequence in the story.

And he answered him, "Look here, Don Lupe, it's not my fault that the animals look out for themselves. They're innocent. You'll have to pay for it, if you kill them."

And he killed one of my yearlings.

This happened thirty-five years ago in March, because in April I

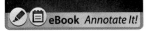
Analyzing the Text

COMMON CORE RL 1, RL 2, RL 3, RL 5, RL 6, SL 1a

Cite Text Evidence Support your responses with evidence from the selection.

1. **Analyze** What impression of the main character and his situation is created by the opening dialogue in which he begs his son to mediate? Explain.

2. **Draw Conclusions** In the story, Juvencio states that "he had to kill Don Lupe." What does this line reveal about how he views his deed? What do his further thoughts in lines 41–101 make clear to readers?

3. **Analyze** How does the author structure the story to reveal the details about Juvencio's life? Does the author use a straightforward chronological order? Explain.

4. **Interpret** Why is the sentence "So there was nothing to fear from them" (line 73–74) ironic? What does it foreshadow?

5. **Evaluate** Identify where the point of view shifts from third person to first person in the story. Why does the author use the first person to have Juvencio narrate this part of the story? Does the change significantly affect the tone of the narrative?

6. **Analyze** Review the details that are revealed about Juvencio's crime prior to line 158. How does each new fact affect readers' perception of his integrity and his character? Explain what makes these revelations ironic.

7. **Cite Evidence** What is ironic about Juvencio's capture and his fierce desire to live? Cite details from the story that illustrate the irony.

8. **Draw Conclusions** Structurally, the dialogue between Juvencio and the Colonel balances the initial conversation between Juvencio and his son. What other purposes does it serve?

9. **Draw Conclusions** Why does the author choose to end the story without describing Juvencio's actual death? Cite details from the story to support your answer.

PERFORMANCE TASK

Speaking Activity: Discussion What is the central theme of this story, and how does the author's use of irony help develop this theme? Jot down details that support your ideas.

- In a small group, discuss the theme you have identified and cite several examples of how the author's use of irony supports this theme.
- As a group, examine the support and decide on the central theme.
- Create a group chart that summarizes your conclusions. Present it to the class.

Assign this performance task.

PERFORMANCE TASK

COMMON CORE RL 2, RL 6, SL 1a

Speaking Activity: Discussion Students should cite text evidence to clearly support their interpretations and generally express them in terms of revenge, duty, and death. Examples of irony that advance the theme are: The only way Juvencio can keep his family alive is to kill another person. One son wants to avenge his father's death; the other son seems unmoved by it. The Colonel's revenge seems inconsequential following the life Juvencio has endured.

PRACTICE & APPLY

Analyzing the Text

COMMON CORE RL 1, RL 2, RL 3, RL 5, RL 6

Possible answers:

1. *With no knowledge of the context, the opening dialogue (lines 1–26) creates an impression of an innocent victim pleading with someone who apparently lacks empathy and sympathy.*

2. *Line 35, along with the description of dying livestock and his attempts to resolve the problem with Don Lupe, indicates that Juvencio feels his action was justified. Readers recognize his rationalization and desperation.*

3. *Rulfo uses flashbacks to take readers from the far past to the recent past before returning to the present. The flashback allows readers to gradually understand Juvencio's circumstances and character.*

4. *This line ironically foreshadows that one of the children Juvencio did not fear actually has him executed.*

5. *By shifting to first person (line 59) Rulfo shows that Juvencio blames everyone but himself for his predicament. His tone of grievance expresses outrage that Don Lupe killed one of his animals, that the villagers took advantage of him, and that he was forced to hide and subsist on herbs.*

6. *As details are revealed (i.e., Don Lupe's orphaned children, the antipathy of the villagers), readers begin to lose sympathy for Juvencio. They gradually realize that all along he has been concerned only for himself. Ironically, by trying to justify his actions, Juvencio ends up condemning himself in the readers' eyes.*

7. *He was captured as he tried to prevent soldiers from trampling his corn; the corn died anyway from lack of rain. His fierce desire to live is ironic because he has wasted his life on the run. And, after depriving two children of their father, Juvencio deprived his own children of their father by trying to save himself.*

8. *This dialogue also reveals the truth about Don Lupe's brutal murder, which eliminates any lingering sympathy readers feel for Juvencio. It also explains why Justino declines to help his father. Finally, it shows that the Colonel feels some compassion, in spite of his desire for justice. He cannot look at Juvencio directly and allows him to have a drink to ease his pain.*

9. *His death is anticlimactic. Its omission leaves readers with the final impression created by the Colonel, an innocent victim of his crime. Further, the execution might stir up lingering feelings of pity by seeing him die. Even his body, in a sack to avoid "a bad impression" is borne without emotion or dignity.*

PRACTICE & APPLY

Language and Style: Vary Syntax for Effect

COMMON CORE L 3a

Review the examples in the chart and make sure students understand the differences in syntax and their effects.

Possible answer:

One puzzling aspect of the story is Rulfo's use of the word compadre, *which means both "buddy" and "godfather" in Spanish. In the context of the story, it's difficult to tell which meaning applies. If it means "buddy," it could justify Juvencio's anger toward Don Lupe, but if it means "godfather," Juvencio's murder could seem more abhorrent.*

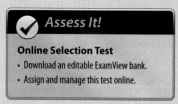

Assess It!

Online Selection Test
- Download an editable ExamView bank.
- Assign and manage this test online.

Language and Style: Vary Syntax for Effect

COMMON CORE L 3a

Syntax refers to the way in which words are arranged in a sentence. To keep readers interested and to draw attention to particular ideas, writers vary their syntax. For example, they might use inverted word order, alternate long sentences with short ones, or even include sentence fragments.

Read this passage from the story.

> And I would take off to the mountains, hiding among the madrone thickets and passing the days with nothing to eat but herbs. Sometimes I had to go out at midnight, as though the dogs were after me. It's been that way my whole life. Not just a year or two. My whole life.

The author could have chosen not to vary the syntax:

> And I would take off to the mountains, hiding among the madrone thickets and passing the days with nothing to eat but herbs. Sometimes I had to go out at midnight, as though the dogs were after me. It's been that way my whole life, not just for a year or two but for my whole life.

The two sentence fragments at the end of the original passage grab readers' attention. They are abrupt and unexpected. The meaning stands out because the syntax is different from the syntax of the previous sentences. In the second version, the two fragments are incorporated into a longer sentence. Visually, they don't catch the readers' attention, nor do they stand out when the sentence is read. The forcefulness of the two ideas is lost.

In formal writing, these methods can be used to vary syntax.

Method to Vary Syntax	Original	Revised
Revise a sentence to begin with a phrase or subordinate clause.	Don Lupe's son gave the old man something to drink out of pity.	Out of pity for the old man, Don Lupe's son gave him something to drink.
Invert the word order.	The old man shuffled along behind the soldiers.	Behind the soldiers shuffled the old man.
Combine two short sentences to clarify the relationship between ideas.	Juvencio becomes less sympathetic as the narrative unfolds. Still, his motive for killing Don Lupe remains vexingly strong.	Although Juvencio becomes less sympathetic as the narrative unfolds, his motive for killing Don Lupe remains vexingly strong.

Practice and Apply Rewrite this paragraph, varying the syntax for effect. Share your rewritten version with a partner and discuss your changes.

> One puzzling aspect of the story is Rulfo's use of the word *compadre*. In Spanish, it means both "buddy" and "godfather." It's difficult to tell from the context of the story which meaning applies. If it means "buddy," it could make Juvencio's anger toward Don Lupe more justified. If it means "godfather," it could make Juvencio's murder more abhorrent.

Strategies for Annotation Annotate it!

Language and Style: Vary Syntax for Effect

COMMON CORE L 3a

Share these strategies to helps students become more aware of the syntax choices in the selection.

- Underline subordinate clauses.
- Highlight in yellow sentence fragments.
- In a note, jot down your observations about the author's syntax choices and their effect.

> And I would take off to the mountains, <u>hiding among the madrone thickets</u> and <u>passing the days with nothing to eat but herbs.</u> Sometimes I had to go out at midnight, <u>as though the dogs were after me.</u> It's been that way my whole life. Not just a year or two. My whole life.

Support Inferences

RL 1

TEACH

Tell students that in a complex story such as "Tell Them Not to Kill Me!," many aspects of the story are not fully explained. To fully understand the story, students will need to make **inferences,** or conclusions about the story's characters, plot, and theme using details from the story and their own knowledge. In addition, initial inferences readers make may be proved wrong as more details emerge. This is especially true in "Tell Them Not to Kill Me!" Advise students to keep in mind the following points:

- First- and third-person narrators offer different perspectives on the same events, as do the different characters in stories. In "Tell Them Not to Kill Me!," readers can make some inferences in the beginning of the story, but as readers learn more through changing narrative viewpoints, inferences may change.
- Valid inferences must be based on evidence in the text, even if the evidence is incomplete.

PRACTICE AND APPLY

Have students reread the Colonel's words about his dead father (lines 176–179). What can you infer about the Colonel's idea of a child's relationship to his father? Cite text evidence to support your answer. *(When he says "It's hard to grow up knowing that the thing we have to hang on to to take roots from is dead." he is expressing how important he feels all fathers are to their children. The father is the "root" that helps the children grow up properly.)*

If students need further instruction, use this *Interactive Whiteboard Lesson:* **Citing Textual Evidence**

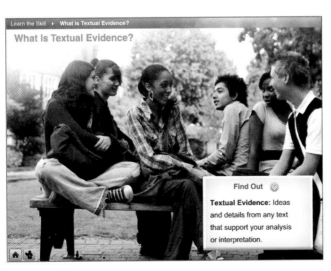

Analyze Structure

RL 5

RETEACH

Review the structural techniques authors use in storytelling. These include making choices about:

- **Time sequence:** Some stories are told chronologically, with events related in the order they happen. Others, like "Tell Them Not to Kill Me!," use flashbacks to move back and forth in time.
- **Narration:** Fiction may use first- second- or third-person narration. "Tell Them Not to Kill Me!" switches from third-person to first-person and back to third-person. The third-person narration shifts focus among various characters.
- **Plot structure:** Authors may use various techniques to build suspense or draw the reader's focus to certain details. In "Tell Them Not to Kill Me!," for example, Rulfo chooses not to describe the story's resolution, leaving this scene to the reader's imagination.

LEVEL UP TUTORIALS If students need further instruction on plot structure and time sequence, including flashback and foreshadowing, assign the following *Level Up* tutorial: **Plot: Sequence of Events**

CLOSE READING APPLICATION

Students can apply the skill to other works of fiction. Have them work independently to read or reread another work of fiction to identify the structural choices the author makes, and their effect on the reader's comprehension of the author's ideas.

*my*SmartPlanner Create lesson plans and access resources online.

ANCHOR TEXT Blocking the Transmission of Violence

Feature Article by Alex Kotlowitz

Why This Text?

In the media and in conversations, students likely encounter discussions about pressing social problems and proposed solutions. This lesson explores one writer's presentation of the problem of violence in our communities and an innovative solution.

► **View It!**
Professional Development Podcast:
Informational Text

For practice and application:

Close Reader selection
"Nobel Peace Prize Acceptance Speech"
Speech by Wangaa Mathari

Key Learning Objective: The student will be able to analyze ideas and events developed in the text and draw conclusions about them.

COMMON CORE Common Core Standards

RI 1 Cite textual evidence to support inferences.
RI 2 Determine central ideas and analyze their development.
RI 3 Analyze ideas or events.
RI 4 Determine the meaning of words and phrases as they are used in a text.
RI 5 Analyze structure.
RI 6 Determine an author's purpose.
SL 1a Come to discussions prepared to stimulate a thoughtful exchange of ideas.
L 2 Demonstrate command of the conventions of standard English.
L 4 Determine or clarify the meaning of unknown words.

▲ Text Complexity Rubric

Quantitative Measures

Blocking the Transmission of Violence
Lexile: 1150L

Qualitative Measures

Levels of Meaning/Purpose

more than one purpose; implied, easily identified from context

Structure

implicit problem–solution text structure

Language Conventionality and Clarity

literal, accessible language

Knowledge Demands

somewhat complex social studies concepts

Reader/Task Considerations

Teacher determined
Vary by individual reader and type of text

CLOSE READ

Alex Kotlowitz (kät´lə-wĭts) Have students read the information about the author. Tell them that this article, which appeared in the *New York Times Magazine* in 2008, inspired filmmaker Steve James to collaborate with Kotlowitz on the award-winning documentary about the CeaseFire program called *The Interrupters*. Kotlowitz conducted the interviews featured in the film.

AS YOU READ Direct students to use the As You Read note to focus their reading. Remind them to write down any questions they generate during reading.

Support Inferences: Draw Conclusions (LINES 1–11)

 COMMON CORE RI 1

Explain to students that a **conclusion** is a judgment or statement of belief based on evidence, experience, and reasoning. Tell them that often they will need to make **inferences,** or logical assumptions, based on the evidence directly stated by the author before they can begin to draw a broader conclusion.

Ⓐ CITE TEXT EVIDENCE Ask students to reread lines 1–11 and state their conclusion about what Torres is planning to do. *(He's planning to track down and kill the person who murdered his nephew.)* Discuss the textual evidence that led them to this conclusion. *(He was "plotting retribution . . . 'going to take care of business,' . . . 'going hunting.'")*

CRITICAL VOCABULARY

retribution: Kotlowitz reports that Martin Torres was planning to avenge his nephew's murder.

ASK STUDENTS why, when there are many ways to seek the punishment of a criminal act, Martin Torres was seeking violent retribution after his nephew's death. *(Seeking revenge for a family member's violent death was probably considered part of Torres's code of honor.)*

Alex Kotlowitz *wrote one of the most important books of the twentieth century, according to the New York Public Library. That book, entitled* There Are No Children Here, *tells the story of two brothers trying to survive in a public housing project in Chicago. Much of his writing, in both books and articles, focuses on topics related to race and poverty. In addition to being a senior lecturer at Northwestern University, he contributes regularly to the* New York Times Magazine *and other publications. His most recent book is* Never a City So Real, *a portrait of Chicago.*

Blocking the Transmission of Violence

Feature Article by Alex Kotlowitz

Image Credits: (b) ©Rebecca Floyd/Graphistock/Corbis; (t) ©Barron Claiborne/Corbis

AS YOU READ Pay attention to details that help you understand the connection between infectious diseases and violence.

Last summer, Martin Torres was working as a cook in Austin, Tex., when, on the morning of Aug. 23, he received a call from a relative. His 17-year-old nephew, Emilio, had been murdered. According to the police, Emilio was walking down a street on Chicago's South Side when someone shot him in the chest, possibly the culmination of an ongoing dispute. Like many killings, Emilio's received just a few sentences in the local newspapers. Torres, who was especially close to his nephew, got on the first Greyhound bus to Chicago. He was grieving and plotting **retribution**. "I thought, Man, I'm going to take
10 care of business," he told me recently. "That's how I live. I was going hunting. This is my own blood, my nephew."

Torres, who is 38, grew up in a dicey section of Chicago, and even by the standards of his neighborhood he was a rough character. His nickname was Packman, because he was known to always pack a gun. He was first shot when he was 12, in the legs with buckshot by members of a rival gang. He was shot five more times, including once through the jaw, another time in his right shoulder and the last time— seven years ago—in his right thigh, with a .38-caliber bullet that is still

retribution
(rĕt´rə-byōō´shən) *n.* appropriate punishment or revenge.

Close Read Screencasts   ▶ **View It!**

Modeled Discussions

Have students click the *Close Read* icons in their eBooks to access two screencasts in which readers discuss and annotate the following key passages:

- first example of how the interrupters work (lines 58–67)
- Slutkin's way of dealing with infectious disease (lines 188–198)

As a class, view and discuss at least one of these videos. Then have students pair up to do an independent close read of an additional passage—a discussion of the relationship between poverty and violence (lines 399–413).

Analyze Ideas and Events COMMON CORE RI 3

(LINES 29–52)

Explain that authors use a variety of techniques to develop their ideas. Providing examples is an effective way to engage readers and introduce complex ideas.

 CITE TEXT EVIDENCE Ask students to reread lines 29–52 and trace the sequence of events that define the relationship between Torres and Hoddenbach. *(They were members of related gangs and first met in prison 17 years before [lines 33–36]; Hoddenbach called Torres when he returned to Chicago after his nephew's death, at the request of Torres's brother [lines 43–46].)* Invite students to discuss the possible purpose of this example involving these two people. *(Kotlowitz introduces the idea that people from similar violent backgrounds might change over time and have different ideas. He also suggests that their shared background is a way for Hoddenbach to approach Torres.)*

Support Inferences: Draw Conclusions COMMON CORE RI 1

(LINES 47–52)

Explain that a key to drawing conclusions is evaluating new evidence as it is presented and judging whether it supports previous inferences or calls them into question.

 ASK STUDENTS to reread lines 47–52 and explain how the details presented affect their understanding of Hoddenbach. *(These lines make it clear that Hoddenbach has changed and now thinks differently from Torres.)* Discuss what questions they might want answered as they continue to read. *(Why did Torres's brother call Hoddenbach? Why has Hoddenbach changed?)*

CRITICAL VOCABULARY

affiliation: Torres still wears earrings to signify his association with a gang.

ASK STUDENTS why Torres may want to display a sign of his gang affiliation even though he is no longer active in the gang. *(He wants to acknowledge his relationship with the gang that helped shape his identity.)*

---

lodged there. On his chest, he has tattooed a tombstone with the name 20 "Buff" at its center, a tribute to a friend who was killed on his 18th birthday. Torres was the head of a small Hispanic gang, and though he is no longer active, he still wears two silver studs in his left ear, a sign of his **affiliation**.

When he arrived in Chicago, he began to ask around, and within a day believed he had figured out who killed his nephew. He also began drinking a lot. . . . He borrowed two guns, a .38 and a .380, from guys he knew. He would, he thought, wait until after the funeral to track down his nephew's assailants.

affiliation
(ə-fĭl´ē-ā´shən) *n.*
association with.

Zale Hoddenbach looks like an ex-military man. He wears his 30 hair cropped and has a trimmed goatee that highlights his angular jaw. He often wears T-shirts that fit tightly around his muscled arms, though he also carries a slight paunch. When he was younger, Hoddenbach, who is also 38, belonged to a gang that was under the same umbrella as Torres's, and so when the two men first met 17 years ago at Pontiac Correctional Center, an Illinois maximum-security prison, they became friendly. Hoddenbach was serving time for armed violence; Torres for possession of a stolen car and a gun (he was, he says, on his way to make a hit). "Zale was always in segregation, in the hole for fights," Torres told me. "He was aggressive." In one scuffle, 40 Hoddenbach lost the sight in his right eye after an inmate pierced it with a shank.[1] Torres and Hoddenbach were at Pontiac together for about a year but quickly lost touch after they were both released.

Shortly after Torres arrived in Chicago last summer, Hoddenbach received a phone call from Torres's brother, the father of the young man who was murdered. He was worried that Torres was preparing to seek revenge and hoped that Hoddenbach would speak with him. When Hoddenbach called, Torres was thrilled. He immediately thought that his old prison buddy was going to join him in his search for the killer. But instead Hoddenbach tried to talk him down, telling 50 him retribution wasn't what his brother wanted. "I didn't understand what the hell he was talking about," Torres told me when I talked to him six months later. "This didn't seem like the person I knew." The next day Hoddenbach appeared at the wake, which was held at New Life Community Church, housed in a low-slung former factory. He spent the day by Torres's side, sitting with him, talking to him, urging him to respect his brother's wishes. When Torres went to the parking lot for a smoke, his hands shaking from agitation, Hoddenbach would follow. "Because of our relationship, I thought there was a chance," Hoddenbach told me. "We were both cut from the same cloth." 60 Hoddenbach knew from experience that the longer he could delay Torres from heading out, the more chance he'd have of keeping him from shooting someone. So he let him vent for a few hours. Then Hoddenbach started laying into him with every argument he could

---

[1] **shank:** a crude, homemade knife.

SCAFFOLDING FOR ELL STUDENTS

Comprehension: Time Sequence Help students analyze the sequences of events in this article. Review these key concepts involving sequence and signal words:

- *Before* and *after:* Explain using examples from students' lives: "I eat breakfast before school. I eat dinner after school."

- *First, then, next, finally:* Read aloud lines 24–28 and model how they can be restated using these words: "First, Torres arrived in Chicago. Then, he began asking about his nephew's death. Next, he began drinking and borrowed two guns. Finally, he decided to wait until after the funeral to track down the killers."

- References to dates or time periods: Point out examples, such as "within a day" (lines 24–25); "When he was younger" (line 32); "17 years ago" (lines 34–35).

Zale Hoddenbach, a CeaseFire interrupter

think of: *Look around, do you see any old guys here? I never seen so many young kids at a funeral. Look at these kids, what does the future hold for them? Where do we fit in? Who are you to step on your brother's wishes?*

The stubborn core of violence in American cities is troubling and perplexing. Even as homicide rates have declined across the country—
70   in some places, like New York, by a remarkable amount—gunplay continues to plague economically struggling minority communities. For 25 years, murder has been the leading cause of death among African-American men between the ages of 15 and 34, according to the Centers for Disease Control and Prevention. . . .

The traditional response has been more focused policing and longer prison sentences, but law enforcement does little to disrupt a street code that allows, if not encourages, the settling of squabbles with deadly force. Zale Hoddenbach, who works for an organization called CeaseFire, is part of an unusual effort to apply the principles of public
80   health to the brutality of the streets. CeaseFire tries to deal with these quarrels on the front end. Hoddenbach's job is to suss out[2] smoldering disputes and to intervene before matters get out of hand. His job title

---

[2] **suss out:** to discover or figure out.

Image Credits: ©Reuben Cox

Blocking the Transmission of Violence **381**

TEACH

CLOSE READ

Analyze Ideas and Events (LINES 68–88)

COMMON CORE RI 3, RI 5

Tell students that Kotlowitz has chosen to use a problem-solution organization to present his ideas about the transmission of violence.

D **CITE TEXT EVIDENCE** Ask students to reread lines 68–88 and identify how the passage reflects Kotlowitz's pattern of organization. *(Lines 68–74 present some statistics about the problem of violence; lines 75–88 present information about some solutions to the problem.)* Then ask students how CeaseFire's solution is different from others. *(CeaseFire tries to stop violence before it starts by applying "principles of public health" to the problem.)*

Support Inferences: Draw Conclusions (LINES 68–74)

COMMON CORE RI 1

Explain that it is important to notice and evaluate different types of evidence in the process of drawing conclusions.

E **ASK STUDENTS** to reread lines 68–74 and describe how the evidence presented in this paragraph compares to the earlier evidence in the selection. *(Kotlowitz shifts from presenting an example of violence to presenting statistics about it.)* Discuss why Kotlowitz might want to use multiple types of evidence. *(The story of Torres and Hoddenbach makes the problem of violence concrete and engaging; statistics show that the problem of violence in certain communities is widespread.)*

Then have students work in mixed language-ability groups to read the article and keep track of the sequence of events using a graphic organizer like this one.

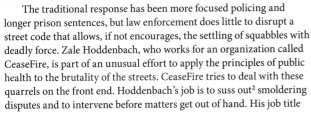

Torres's nephew is killed. ▶ Torres comes to Chicago for revenge. ▶ Hoddenbach talks to Torres.

Analyze Ideas and Events (LINES 89–100)

COMMON CORE RI 2, RI 3, RI 4

Explain that the title of an article often provides a clue to its central ideas.

F **ASK STUDENTS** to reread lines 89–100 and explain the meaning of the phrase "transmission of violence" used in the title. (*The transmission of violence refers to the ways it spreads from one violent event to another in the same way that an infectious disease is transmitted from an infected person to an uninfected person.*) Discuss how this phrase reflects the difference in CeaseFire's approach. (*CeaseFire views violence as a public health problem rather than a moral problem and focuses on containing and changing behavior that transmits violence.*)

Support Inferences: Draw Conclusions (LINES 109–119)

COMMON CORE RI 1

Point out that Kotlowitz uses statements made by people such as Torres, Hoddenbach, and Slutkin to reveal their personalities in the same way that a fiction writer uses dialogue to reveal character. Explain that Kotlowitz also uses other techniques to reveal information about the people in the article.

G **CITE TEXT EVIDENCE** Ask students to reread lines 109–119 and cite examples of different ways that Kotlowitz helps readers understand Slutkin. (*Kotlowitz presents a physical description of Slutkin [lines 111–112] and also presents quotes from two people who work with Slutkin that reflect their observations and analysis of him [lines 113–114, lines 116–119].*) Then ask students what conclusion they draw about Slutkin based on this evidence. (*Slutkin takes an understated approach but is more on top of things than he at first appears to be.*)

CRITICAL VOCABULARY

ruminate: Kotlowitz says interrupters meet to share their thoughts about recent incidents of violence. **ASK STUDENTS** to explain the purpose of interrupters getting together to ruminate about the problem of violence. (*They want to examine the problem from many angles and consider what can be done about it.*)

is violence interrupter, a term that while not artful seems bluntly self-explanatory. Newspaper accounts usually refer to the organization as a gang-intervention program, and Hoddenbach and most of his colleagues are indeed former gang leaders. But CeaseFire doesn't necessarily aim to get people out of gangs—nor interrupt the drug trade. It's almost blindly focused on one thing: preventing shootings.

90   CeaseFire's founder, Gary Slutkin, is an epidemiologist and a physician who for 10 years battled infectious diseases in Africa. He says that violence directly mimics infections like tuberculosis and AIDS, and so, he suggests, the treatment ought to mimic the regimen applied to these diseases: go after the most infected, and stop the infection at its source. "For violence, we're trying to interrupt the next event, the next transmission, the next violent activity," Slutkin told me recently. "And the violent activity predicts the next violent activity like H.I.V. predicts the next H.I.V. and TB predicts the next TB." Slutkin wants to shift how we think about violence from a moral issue (good and bad people) to a public health one (healthful and unhealthful

100 behavior).

    Every Wednesday afternoon, in a Spartan room on the 10th floor of the University of Illinois at Chicago's public-health building, 15 to 25 men—and two women—all violence interrupters, sit around tables arranged in a circle and **ruminate** on the rage percolating in the city. Most are in their 40s and 50s, though some, like Hoddenbach, are a bit younger. All of them are black or Hispanic and in one manner or another have themselves been privy to, if not participants in, the brutality of the streets.

    On a Wednesday near the end of March, Slutkin made a rare

110 appearance; he ordinarily leaves the day-to-day operations to a staff member. Fit at 57, Slutkin has a somewhat disheveled appearance—tie askew, hair uncombed, seemingly forgetful. Some see his presentation as a calculated effort to disarm. "Slutkin does his thing in his Slutkinesque way," notes Carl Bell, a psychiatrist who has long worked with children exposed to neighborhood violence and who admires CeaseFire's work. "He seems kind of disorganized, but he's not." Hoddenbach told me: "You can't make too much of that guy. In the beginning, he gives you that look like he doesn't know what you're talking about."

120   Slutkin had come to talk with the group about a recent high-profile incident outside Crane Tech High School on the city's West Side. An 18-year-old boy was shot and died on the school's steps, while nearby another boy was savagely beaten with a golf club. Since the beginning of the school year, 18 Chicago public-school students had been killed. (Another six would be murdered in the coming weeks.) The interrupters told Slutkin that there was a large police presence at the school, at least temporarily muffling any hostilities there, and that the police were even escorting some kids to and from

ruminate
(rōō′mə-nāt′) *v.* to consider or think about carefully; contemplate.

WHEN STUDENTS STRUGGLE...

To help students keep track of the people described in this article, have them work in pairs to fill out a chart like the one shown. Encourage students to refer to the chart as they read to see if a particular person has been previously mentioned and to add new information as they encounter it. Explain that their purpose is to understand how each person relates to the central ideas of the article.

Depending on your students' needs, you may wish to use a modified Jigsaw approach by assigning groups of students to track particular individuals or categories of individuals, such as people who work for CeaseFire, experts, or law enforcement officials. Students could then summarize what they know about the people they are tracking to other groups.

> ## For violence, we're trying to interrupt the next event, the next transmission, the next violent activity. "

school. They then told him what was happening off the radar in
130 their neighborhoods. There was the continuing discord at another
high school involving a group of girls ("They'd argue with a stop
sign," one of the interrupters noted); a 14-year-old boy with a gang
tattoo on his forehead was shot by an older gang member just out of
prison; a 15-year-old was shot in the stomach by a rival gang member
as he came out of his house; and a former CeaseFire colleague was
struggling to keep himself from losing control after his own sons were
beaten. There was also a high-school basketball player shot four times;
a 12-year-old boy shot at a party; gang members arming themselves
to counter an egging of their freshly painted cars; and a high-ranking
140 gang member who was on life support after being shot, and whose
sister was overheard talking on her cellphone in the hospital, urging
someone to "get those straps together. Get loaded."

These incidents all occurred over the previous seven days. In
each of them, the interrupters had stepped in to try to keep one act
of **enmity** from spiraling into another. Some had more success than
others. Janell Sails prodded the guys with the egged cars to go to a car
wash and then persuaded them it wasn't worth risking their lives over
a stupid prank. At Crane Tech High School, three of the interrupters
fanned out, trying to convince the five gangs involved in the conflict
150 to lie low, but they conceded that they were unable to reach some of the
main players. Many of the interrupters seem bewildered by what they
see as a wilder group of youngsters now running the streets and by a
gang structure that is no longer top-down but is instead made up of
many small groups—which they refer to as cliques—whose members
are answerable to a handful of peers. . . .

It became clear as they delivered their reports that many of the
interrupters were worn down. One of them, Calvin Buchanan, whose
street name is Monster and who just recently joined CeaseFire, showed
the others six stitches over his left eye; someone had cracked a beer
160 bottle on his head while he was mediating an argument between two
men. The other interrupters applauded when Buchanan told them
that, though tempted, he restrained himself from getting even.

enmity
(ĕn´mĭ-tē) *n.* hatred or
hostility towards an
enemy.

Blocking the Transmission of Violence **383**

Name	Identity	Key Details
Zale Hoddenbach	interrupter, works for CeaseFire	former gang leader; knows Torres
Gary Slutkin	founder of CeaseFire	physician; battled infectious disease in Africa

CLOSE READ

Support Inferences: Draw Conclusions (LINES 129–143)

Explain that authors present details to support their central ideas. Analyzing the details gives readers evidence that they can combine with their own experience to make inferences and draw conclusions.

Ⓗ ASK STUDENTS to reread lines 129–143 and describe the types of details that Kotlowitz presents in the passage. (*He lists several violent or potentially violent incidents that occurred in the past week in several neighborhoods.*) Then ask: What is the purpose of presenting these details? (*The list of incidents shows the ongoing and widespread nature of violence, often triggered by seemingly petty disputes or insults.*)

Analyze Ideas and Events (LINES 151–155)

Explain that authors often develop ideas by providing examples to illustrate general principles and by adding information that expands or modifies previously stated ideas.

Ⓘ ASK STUDENTS to reread lines 151–155 and explain how the information presented in the passage continues to develop ideas about the problem of violence that Kotlowitz presented earlier in the article. (*This passage indicates that the interrupters are still dealing with gang violence that can spread quickly and get out of control, but now it may be more difficult to interrupt the violence because the young people are "a wilder group" and there is less hierarchy in the gangs, making it more difficult to work with gang leaders to control actions by gang members.*)

> **CRITICAL VOCABULARY**
>
> **enmity**: Kotlowitz says one act of hostility often leads to another.
>
> **ASK STUDENTS** to explain how CeaseFire tries to interrupt acts of enmity. (*The interrupters try to prevent hostile acts from spreading in a vicious cycle of revenge.*)

Analyze Ideas and Events RI 2, RI 3, RI 5

(LINES 171–182; 186–201)

In problem-solution writing, authors often propose or report on more than one solution to a problem.

J CITE TEXT EVIDENCE Ask students to reread lines 171–182 and identify three possible solutions to the problem of violence. *(Tackle gun safety [lines 172–173]; use school programs to change unsafe behavior [lines 174–175]; take Slutkin's approach of containing violence like an infectious disease [lines 176–177].)* Then ask students which of these three solutions is most fully developed. Have them cite details that show how the idea is developed. *(Slutkin's approach is developed with more details. Kotlowitz summarizes how Slutkin compares his goals for containing violence with the process of containing the spread of AIDS: containment is the first goal and changing behavior is the second.)*

Then explain that in a well-constructed informational article, every passage has a purpose that relates to the article's main idea.

K ASK STUDENTS to reread lines 186–201 and summarize Slutkin's approach to dealing with TB among immigrants from Southeast Asia in San Francisco. *(Slutkin concentrated on the most difficult and active TB cases because these patients were the ones infecting the most people. He used outreach workers from the same ethnic background as the patients to help identify the patients and support them during treatment. His approach resulted in a significant decrease in the number of cases among immigrant populations.)* Then ask them to analyze the purpose of this passage about Slutkin's work in San Francisco. *(The purpose is to show how Slutkin's approach to preventing violence emerged from his work in curbing the transmission of infectious disease.)*

When Slutkin finally spoke, he first praised the interrupters for their work. "Everybody's overreacting, and you're trying to cool them down," he told them. He then asked if any of them had been experiencing jitteriness or fear. He spent the next half-hour teaching stress-reduction exercises. If they could calm themselves, he seemed to be saying, they could also calm others. I recalled what one of the interrupters told me a few weeks earlier: "We helped create the
170 madness, and now we're trying to debug it."

J In the public-health field, there have long been two schools of thought on derailing violence. One focuses on environmental factors, specifically trying to limit gun purchases and making guns safer. The other tries to influence behavior by introducing school-based curricula like antidrug and safe-sex campaigns.

Slutkin is going after it in a third way—as if he were trying to contain an infectious disease. The fact that there's no vaccine or medical cure for violence doesn't dissuade him. He points out that in the early days of AIDS, there was no treatment either. In the short run,
180 he's just trying to halt the spread of violence. In the long run, though, he says he hopes to alter behavior and what's considered socially acceptable.

K Slutkin's perspective grew out of his own experience as an infectious-disease doctor. In 1981, six years out of the University of Chicago Pritzker School of Medicine, Slutkin was asked to lead the TB program in San Francisco. With an influx of new refugees from Cambodia, Laos and Vietnam, the number of cases in the city had nearly doubled. Slutkin chose to concentrate on those who had the most active TB; on average, they were infecting 6 to 10 others a year.
190 Slutkin hired Southeast Asian outreach workers who could not only locate the infected individuals but who could also stick with them for nine months, making sure they took the necessary medication. These outreach workers knew the communities and spoke the languages, and they were able to persuade family members of infected people to be tested. Slutkin also went after the toughest cases—26 people with drug-resistant TB. The chance of curing those people was slim, but Slutkin reckoned that if they went untreated, the disease would continue to spread. "Gary wasn't constrained by the textbook," says Eric Goosby, who worked in the clinic and is now the chief executive of
200 the Pangaea Global AIDS Foundation. Within two years, the number of TB cases, at least among these new immigrants, declined sharply.

Slutkin then spent 10 years in Africa, first in refugee camps in Somalia and then working, in Uganda and other countries, for the World Health Organization to curtail the spread of AIDS. . . . After leaving Africa, Slutkin returned to Chicago, where he was raised and where he could attend to his aging parents. . . . It was 1995, and there had been a series of horrific murders involving children in the city. He was convinced that longer sentences and more police officers had

APPLYING ACADEMIC VOCABULARY

mediate	restrain

As you discuss the selection, incorporate the Collection 4 academic vocabulary words *mediate* and *restrain*. Invite students to give examples of how CeaseFire members work to **mediate** between hostile groups and encourage people to **restrain** themselves from meeting violence with violence.

made little difference. "Punishment doesn't drive behavior," he told
me. "Copying and modeling and the social expectations of your peers
is what drives your behavior."

Borrowing some ideas (and the name) from a successful Boston
program, Slutkin initially established an approach that exists in one
form or another in many cities: outreach workers tried to get youth
and young adults into school or to help them find jobs. These outreach
workers were also doing dispute mediation. . . . One of Slutkin's
colleagues, Tio Hardiman, brought up an uncomfortable truth: the
program wasn't reaching the most **bellicose**, those most likely to
pull a trigger. So in 2004, Hardiman suggested that, in addition to
outreach workers, they also hire men and women who had been deep
into street life, and he began recruiting people even while they were
still in prison. Hardiman told me he was looking for those "right
there on the edge." (The interrupters are paid roughly $15 an hour,
and those working full time receive benefits from the University of
Illinois at Chicago, where CeaseFire is housed.) The new recruits, with
strong connections to the toughest communities, would focus solely
on sniffing out clashes that had the potential to escalate. They would
intervene in potential acts of retribution—as well as try to defuse
seemingly minor spats that might erupt into something bigger, like
disputes over women or insulting remarks.

As CeaseFire evolved, Slutkin says he started to realize how much
it was drawing on his experiences fighting TB and AIDS. "Early
intervention in TB is actually treatment of the most infectious people,"
Slutkin told me recently. "They're the ones who are infecting others.
So treatment of the most infectious spreaders is the most effective
strategy known and now accepted in the world." And, he continued,
you want to go after them with individuals who themselves were once
either infectious spreaders or at high risk for the illness. In the case
of violence, you use those who were once hard-core, once the most
belligerent, once the most uncontrollable, once the angriest. They are
the most convincing messengers. It's why, for instance, Slutkin and his
colleagues asked sex workers in Uganda and other nations to spread
the word to other sex workers about safer sexual behavior. Then,
Slutkin said, you train them, as you would paraprofessionals[3]. . . .

The first step to containing the spread of an infectious disease
is minimizing transmission. The parallel in Slutkin's Chicago work
is thwarting retaliations, which is precisely what Hoddenbach was
trying to do in the aftermath of Emilio Torres's murder. But Slutkin
is also looking for the equivalent of a cure. The way public-health
doctors think of curing disease when there are no drug treatments
is by changing behavior. Smoking is the most obvious example.
Cigarettes are still around. And there's no easy remedy for lung cancer

bellicose
(bĕl´ĭ-kōs´) *adj.*
aggressively inclined
to fight.

---

[3] **paraprofessionals:** specialized workers who assist physicians, attorneys, or
other professionals.

SCAFFOLDING FOR ELL STUDENTS

Vocabulary: Informal Expressions Explain that Kotlowitz sometimes
uses conversational language to describe the lives of people engaged in
violence. He also uses words in a figurative or nonliteral way to present vivid
descriptions. Have pairs read lines 212–244 and use context clues to figure
out the meaning of these phrases:

deep into street life (lines 220–221); *right there on the edge* (lines 222–223);
sniffing out clashes (line 227); *hard-core* (line 239)

ASK STUDENTS what kind of people CeaseFire hired to reach the people
most likely to be violent.

CLOSE READ

Analyze Ideas and Events (LINES 212–227)

COMMON CORE RI 3

Explain that noting when writers introduce new ideas
is important. In a problem-solution article, a new idea
may be another aspect of a problem or solution.

(L) CITE TEXT EVIDENCE Have students reread
lines 212–227 to identify a new problem and a new
solution to the problem of containing violence's
spread. *(Problem: the program using outreach workers
wasn't reaching those likely to commit violence [lines
218–219]; solution: hire people with histories of violence
and ties to the "toughest communities" who had the
ability to identify potential problems and the credibility
to deal with potential troublemakers [lines 220–227].)*

Support Inferences: Draw Conclusions (LINES 231–244)

COMMON CORE RI 1

Explain that Kotlowitz presents Slutkin's rationale
for applying his experience fighting TB and AIDS
to the problem of violence. As he presents Slutkin's
evidence, readers must decide whether Slutkin's
reasoning and conclusions are valid.

(M) ASK STUDENTS to reread lines 231–244 and
interpret the evidence showing how Slutkin applied
his infectious-disease experience to the problem of
violence. *(According to Slutkin, the most effective way
to contain the spread of infectious disease is to treat the
most infectious people and reach them via people who
had previously been highly infectious themselves. He
says this strategy is accepted in the medical community
worldwide. Kotlowitz makes the parallels clear: when
it comes to violence, Slutkin believes in enlisting
people who were once the most violent and angriest in
communities to reach those like that now.)*

CRITICAL VOCABULARY

bellicose: Tio Hardiman realized it was difficult to
reach those most likely to commit violence.

ASK STUDENTS why CeaseFire targets the most
bellicose individuals on the streets. *(They are the
ones most likely to resort to violence in response to
acts of violence or disrespect.)*

Analyze Ideas and Events COMMON CORE RI 2, RI 3

(LINES 253–271)

Explain that Kotlowitz continues to describe how Slutkin applies insights learned as an infectious disease specialist to the problem of violence.

** CITE TEXT EVIDENCE** Ask students to reread lines 253–271 and identify the insight that Slutkin learned while fighting AIDS that he applied to the attempt to change violent behavior. (*"Peer or social pressure is the most effective way to change behavior" [lines 260–261]; Slutkin learned that people were most likely to use condoms if "they think their friends use them" [line 264].*) Then ask students how this insight specifically applies to CeaseFire's work. (*The interrupters have prestige on the street because of their violent pasts and therefore have a good chance of convincing peers that it's okay to walk away from violent confrontations.*)

Support Inferences: Draw Conclusions COMMON CORE RI 1

(LINES 281–290)

Explain that authors may choose to illustrate a general statement with details without explicitly stating how the details relate to the general statement. In those situations, readers need to make inferences.

** ASK STUDENTS** to reread lines 281–290 and interpret why Kotlowitz says, "Relying on hardened types . . . is risky." Have them point to specific details that support their inference. (*It is risky using hardened criminals to try to stop violence because putting them in violent situations might cause them to become violent again. Details: Hoddenbach beat a man and punctured his lungs, was active in a gang, was known for "unmitigated aggression," and served eight years in prison for violent crimes.*)

CRITICAL VOCABULARY

unmitigated: Kotlowitz describes Hoddenbach's aggression as being complete and unrestrained.

ASK STUDENTS what evidence would indicate that someone had unmitigated aggression. (*Someone who had a history of repeated acts of extreme violence and who showed no signs of changing would reveal unmitigated aggression.*)

---

or emphysema. So the best way to deal with the diseases associated with smoking is to get people to stop smoking. In Uganda, Slutkin and his colleagues tried to change behavior by encouraging people to have fewer sexual partners and to use condoms. CeaseFire has a visible public-communications campaign, which includes billboards and bumper stickers (which read, "Stop. Killing. People."). It also holds rallies—or what it calls "responses"—at the sites of killings. But much

260 research suggests that peer or social pressure is the most effective way to change behavior. "It was a real turning point for me," Slutkin said, "when I was working on the AIDS epidemic and saw research findings that showed that the principal determinant of whether someone uses a condom or not is whether they think their friends use them." Daniel Webster, a professor of public health at Johns Hopkins University who has looked closely at CeaseFire, told me, "The guys out there doing the interruption have some prestige and reputation, and I think the hope is that they start to change a culture so that you can retain your status, retain your manliness and be able to walk away from events where

270 all expectations were that you were supposed to respond with lethal force."

As a result, the interrupters operate in a netherworld between upholding the law and upholding the logic of the streets. They're not meant to be a substitute for the police, and indeed, sometimes the interrupters negotiate disputes involving illicit goings-on. They often walk a fine line between mediating and seeming to condone criminal activity. At one Wednesday meeting this past December, the interrupters argued over whether they could dissuade stickup artists from shooting their victims; persuading them to stop robbing people

280 didn't come up in the discussion. . . .

Relying on hardened types—the ones who, as Webster of Johns Hopkins says, have some prestige on the streets—is risky. They have prestige for a reason. Hoddenbach, who once beat someone so badly he punctured his lungs, is reluctant to talk about his past. "I don't want to be seen as a monster," he told me. . . . Hoddenbach always worked. He did maintenance on train equipment and towed airplanes at a private airport. But he was also active in a Hispanic street gang and was known for his **unmitigated** aggression. He served a total of eight years in the state penitentiary, the last stay for charges that included

290 aggravated battery. He was released in 2002.

In January, I was with Slutkin in Baltimore, where he spoke about CeaseFire to a small gathering of local civic leaders at a private home. During the two-hour meeting, Slutkin never mentioned that the interrupters were ex-felons. When I later asked him about that omission, he conceded that talking about their personal histories "is a dilemma. I haven't solved it." I spent many hours with Hoddenbach and the others, trying to understand how they chose to make the transition from gangster to peacemaker, how they put thuggery

unmitigated
(ŭn-mĭt´ĭ-gā´tĭd) *adj.* complete and undiminishing.

WHEN STUDENTS STRUGGLE . . .

Help students make the connections between curing disease and curing the problem of violence.

- Direct them to read lines 249–264 and discuss how they give insight into what Dr. Slutkin wants to do to cure the problem of violence. (*When there is no drug to cure a disease, doctors focus on changing behavior, such as getting people to stop smoking to prevent lung disease or practice safer sex to reduce the spread of AIDS. Dr. Slutkin wants to apply social pressure to change people's behavior and reduce violence.*)

- Encourage them to read the whole passage to see if information that may seem confusing at first (such as references to Uganda) is clarified later on.

CLOSE READ

Gary Slutkin,
founder of CeaseFire

behind them. It is, of course, their street savvy and reputations that
300 make them effective for CeaseFire. (One supporter of the program
admiringly called it "a terrifying strategy" because of the inherent
risks.) Some CeaseFire workers have, indeed, reverted to their
old ways. One outreach worker was fired after he was arrested for
possession of an AK-47 and a handgun. Another outreach worker and
an interrupter were let go after they were arrested for dealing drugs.
Word-of-mouth allegations often circulate, and privately, some in the
police department worry about CeaseFire's workers returning to their
old habits.

        Not all the interrupters I talked to could articulate how they had
310 made the transition. Some, like Hoddenbach, find religion—in his
case, Christianity. He also has four children he feels responsible for,
and has found ways to decompress, like going for long runs. (His
brother Mark speculated that "maybe he just wants to give back what
he took out.") I once asked Hoddenbach if he has ever apologized to
anyone he hurt. We were with one of his old friends from the street,
who started guffawing, as if I had asked Hoddenbach if he ever wore
dresses. "I done it twice," Hoddenbach told us—quickly silencing his
friend and saving me from further embarrassment. (One apology was
to the brother of the man whose lungs he'd punctured; the other was
320 to a rival gang member he shot.) . . .

Blocking the Transmission of Violence   **387**

Support Inferences: Draw Conclusions (LINES 309–320)

 COMMON CORE RI 1

Explain that when writers want readers to draw
certain conclusions, they must present evidence that
is relevant, or related in a meaningful way, to their
central idea.

(P) CITE TEXT EVIDENCE Ask students to reread lines
309–320 and make inferences about what it is like to
be an interrupter, citing text evidence to support their
inferences. *(Being an interrupter is stressful and requires
a lot of motivation, strength, and support. Hoddenbach
is motivated by his faith and his family and helps
relieve stress by running. He has to face uncomfortable
situations with old friends.)*

Analyze Language (LINES 314–317)

 COMMON CORE RI 4

Explain that figurative language is the use of
language in nonliteral ways to help readers
understand unfamiliar situations or ideas. Point out
that Kotlowitz uses a **simile,** a form of figurative
language that compares two things using the word
like or *as*, in lines 316–317.

(Q) ASK STUDENTS to reread lines 314–317 and
interpret the simile. Why might Kotlowitz have used
it in this passage? *(Kotlowitz says that in the eyes of
Hoddenbach's friend, apologizing to someone is as
shameful as a man wearing a dress. Kotlowitz uses the
simile to help readers understand just how big a change
Hoddenbach has made by giving up his old life to
become an interrupter.)*

TO CHALLENGE STUDENTS . . .

Write About Risk Why might it be risky for a former gang leader to
start advocating nonviolence on the streets? Point out that Kotlowitz has
explored the risks to CeaseFire in its use of former hardened criminals as
interrupters, but he has given little space to exploring what kinds of risks the
interrupters themselves might face.

ASK STUDENTS to write one or two paragraphs to explore this question.
Encourage them to draw on evidence from the text as well as their own
knowledge and experience. Then have students share their writings and
discuss their ideas in small groups.

Image Credits: ©Reuben Cox

CLOSE READ

Support Inferences: Draw Conclusions (LINES 321–338)

 COMMON CORE RI 1

Remind students that particular details provide clues that will help them make inferences as they read.

R CITE TEXT EVIDENCE Ask students to reread lines 321–338 and cite details that support inferences about why Torres seems "both grateful to and annoyed at Hoddenbach." *(He is grateful because he knows he respected his brother's wishes [lines 336–338]. At the same time, he is annoyed because he feels he should have done something to avenge his nephew's murder [lines 328–331].)* Then ask them to interpret what the passage reveals about CeaseFire's work. *(It shows that there is an ongoing need for vigilance to prevent the transmission of violence. It shows that someone who is once persuaded against committing a violent act may still be tempted to be violent in the future. Hoddenbach's presence in the car with Torres interrupts the impulse toward violence triggered by listening to a particular song [lines 332–335].)*

Analyze Ideas and Events (LINES 349–367)

COMMON CORE RI 3, RI 6

Explain that authors rarely say why they include specific examples in their writing. Readers must determine how the particular ideas or events serve the author's **purpose** or reason for writing. Remind students that Kotlowitz has presented a variety of evidence throughout the article.

S ASK STUDENTS to reread lines 349–367 and compare the evidence presented in these paragraphs to the evidence in lines 321–348. *(Kotlowitz shifts from presenting and analyzing another example of how CeaseFire works to providing information about how CeaseFire is expanding beyond Chicago. He presents some statistics and also includes the comments of an academic expert who was skeptical about the program.)* Discuss how this new information might serve Kotlowitz's purpose for writing. *(He wants to inform readers by presenting a range of responses to CeaseFire to show that he is not just accepting Slutkin's assertions without corroboration. He balances statistics with anecdotal evidence.)*

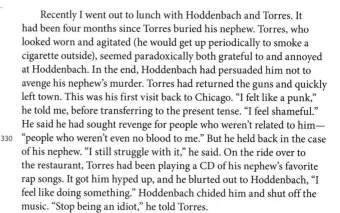

R Recently I went out to lunch with Hoddenbach and Torres. It had been four months since Torres buried his nephew. Torres, who looked worn and agitated (he would get up periodically to smoke a cigarette outside), seemed paradoxically both grateful to and annoyed at Hoddenbach. In the end, Hoddenbach had persuaded him not to avenge his nephew's murder. Torres had returned the guns and quickly left town. This was his first visit back to Chicago. "I felt like a punk," he told me, before transferring to the present tense. "I feel shameful." He said he had sought revenge for people who weren't related to him—
330 "people who weren't even no blood to me." But he held back in the case of his nephew. "I still struggle with it," he said. On the ride over to the restaurant, Torres had been playing a CD of his nephew's favorite rap songs. It got him hyped up, and he blurted out to Hoddenbach, "I feel like doing something." Hoddenbach chided him and shut off the music. "Stop being an idiot," he told Torres.

"Something made me do what Zale asked me to do," Torres said later, looking more puzzled than comforted. "Which is respect my brother's wishes."

When Slutkin heard of Hoddenbach's intervention, he told me:
340 "The interrupters have to deal with how to get someone to save face. In other words, how do you not do a shooting if someone has insulted you, if all of your friends are expecting you to do that? . . . In fact, what our interrupters do is put social pressure in the other direction."

He continued: "This is cognitive dissonance.[4] Before Zale walked up to him, this guy was holding only one thought. So you want to put another thought in his head. It turns out talking about family is what really makes a difference." Slutkin didn't take this notion to the interrupters; he learned it from them. . . .

S Baltimore, Newark and Kansas City, Mo., have each replicated
350 components of the CeaseFire model and have received training from the Chicago staff. In Baltimore, the program, which is run by the city, combines the work of interrupters and outreach workers and has been concentrated in one East Baltimore neighborhood. (The program recently expanded to a second community.) Early research out of the Johns Hopkins Bloomberg School of Public Health shows that in the East Baltimore neighborhood there were on average two shootings a month just before the program started. During the first four months that interrupters worked the streets, there had not been a single incident.
360 "My eyes rolled immediately when I heard what the model was," says Webster of Johns Hopkins, who is studying the Baltimore project. Webster knew the forces the interrupters were up against and considered it wishful thinking that they could effectively mediate disputes. "But when I looked closer at the data," Webster continues,

---

[4] **cognitive dissonance:** having contradictory or conflicting ideas or attitudes.

APPLYING ACADEMIC VOCABULARY

integrity	trigger

As you discuss the selection, incorporate the Collection 4 academic vocabulary words *integrity* and *trigger*. Ask students to explore the reasons why some people might question the interrupters' **integrity** and what kinds of situations might **trigger** the interrupters' return to their old ways.

"The interrupters have to deal with how to get someone to save face."

"and got to know more about who these people were and what they were doing, I became far less skeptical and more hopeful. We're going to learn from it. And it will evolve." George Kelling, a Rutgers professor of criminal justice who is helping to establish an effort in Newark to reduce homicide, helped develop the "broken window" theory of fighting crime: addressing small issues quickly. He says a public-health model will be fully effective only if coupled with other efforts, including more creative policing and efforts to get gang members back to school or to work. But he sees promise in the CeaseFire model. "I had to overcome resistance," Kelling told me, referring to the introduction of a similar program in Newark. "But I think Slutkin's on to something."

Most of the police officials I spoke with, in both Chicago and Baltimore, were grateful for the interrupters. James B. Jackson, now the first deputy superintendent in Chicago, was once the commander of the 11th district, which has one of the highest rates of violent crime in the city. Jackson told me that after his officers investigated an incident, he would ask the police to pull back so the interrupters could mediate. He understood that if the interrupters were associated with the police, it would jeopardize their standing among gang members. "If you look at how segments of the population view the police department, it makes some of our efforts problematic," Baltimore's police commissioner, Frederick H. Bealefeld III, told me. "It takes someone who knows these guys to go in and say, 'Hey, lay off.' We can't do that."

Like many new programs that taste some success, CeaseFire has ambitions that threaten to outgrow its capacity. Slutkin has put much of his effort on taking the project to other cities (there's interest from Los Angeles, Oakland and Wilmington, Delaware, among others), and he has consulted with the State Department about assisting in Iraq and in Kenya. (CeaseFire training material has been made available to the provincial reconstruction teams in Iraq.) Meanwhile, their Chicago project is underfinanced, and the interrupters seem stressed from the amount of work they've taken on. . . .

CLOSE READ

Support Inferences: Draw Conclusions (LINES 377–389)   COMMON CORE RI 1

Remind students to combine their own knowledge and experience with the evidence directly stated in the selection to make inferences and draw conclusions.

T **ASK STUDENTS** to reread lines 377–389 and explain why many police officials "were grateful for the interrupters." *(The police recognize that the interrupters can talk to gang members in ways that the police cannot. Anything that reduces violence in a city makes the police's job easier and also makes the city a safer place, which is a key objective of the police.)*

RI 3, RI 5

Analyze Ideas and Events   COMMON CORE
(LINES 390–398)

Remind students that Kotlowitz has chosen to use a problem-solution organization to present his ideas in this article.

U **ASK STUDENTS** to reread lines 390–398 and explain how the passage reflects Kotlowitz's pattern of organization. *(This passage outlines some of the problems that CeaseFire faces as an organization because it wants to build on its success.)* Then discuss how these problems might affect CeaseFire's work in Chicago. *(The Chicago program may become less effective if it does not have the resources it needs.)*

SCAFFOLDING FOR ELL STUDENTS

Language: Phrasal Verbs Explain that a **phrasal verb** is a verb followed by another word that function together as one verb. Point out "he would get up periodically to smoke a cigarette outside" in lines 323–324. Explain that *get* and *up* are words with multiple meanings and that *up* can be used as several different parts of speech. The two words together form a phrasal verb that can also have multiple meanings. In this sentence, it means "to stand from a seated position."

ASK STUDENTS to use context clues to define these phrasal verbs in the selection: *worn down* (line 157), *brought up* (line 217), *come up* (line 280), *let go* (line 305), *held back* (line 330), *shut off* (line 334), *pull back* (line 382), *lay off* (line 388), and *putting away* (line 422).

Analyze Ideas and Events RI 3

(LINES 399–413)

Encourage students to notice how Kotlowitz develops Slutkin's ideas by restating them and fleshing them out with additional supporting details.

 ASK STUDENTS to reread lines 399–413 and summarize the relationship between poverty and violence. *(The relationship is always changing. Violence is a result of poverty, but violence also reinforces poverty because a community characterized by violence is not one where economic growth is likely.)*

Support Inferences: Draw RI 1
Conclusions (LINES 414–423)

Explain that Slutkin's approach is based on parallels that he sees between fighting infectious disease and fighting violence. As readers draw conclusions, they must decide whether these parallels are relevant and convincing.

W **ASK STUDENTS** to reread lines 414–423 and state a conclusion that Slutkin wants readers to draw. *(Treating violence like a moral problem instead of a public health problem is as misguided as the response to infectious diseases in Chinatown, San Francisco, in the 1880s.)*

CRITICAL VOCABULARY

ubiquity: Kotlowitz says that guns are constantly present in the country's inner cities.

ASK STUDENTS how the ubiquity of guns causes problems in inner cities. *(The constant presence of so many guns increases the likelihood that one violent act will lead to another.)*

COLLABORATIVE DISCUSSION Have students pair up and discuss specific experiences that Dr. Slutkin had in Africa that influenced his work to stop violence. Then have them share their conclusions with the class as a whole. Accept all reasonable responses.

ASK STUDENTS to share any questions they generated in the course of reading and discussing the selection.

390 Collection 4

Slutkin says that it makes sense to purify the water supply if—and only if—you acknowledge and treat the epidemic at hand. In other words, antipoverty measures will work only if you treat violence. It would seem intuitive that violence is a result of economic deprivation, but the relationship between the two is not static. People who have little expectation for the future live recklessly. On the other side of the coin, a community in which arguments are settled by gunshots is unlikely to experience economic growth and opportunity. In his book "The Bottom Billion," Paul Collier argues that one of the characteristics of many developing countries that suffer from entrenched poverty is what he calls the conflict trap, the inability to escape a cycle of violence, usually in the guise of civil wars. Could the same be true in our inner cities, where the **ubiquity** of guns and gunplay pushes businesses and residents out and leaves behind those who can't leave, the most impoverished?

ubiquity
(yōō-bĭk´wĭ-tē) *n.* constant presence or prevalence.

In this, Slutkin sees a direct parallel to the early history of seemingly incurable infectious diseases. "Chinatown, San Francisco in the 1880s," Slutkin says. "Three ghosts: malaria, smallpox and leprosy. No one wanted to go there. Everybody blamed the people. Dirty. Bad habits. Something about their race. Not only is everybody afraid to go there, but the people there themselves are afraid at all times because people are dying a lot and nobody really knows what to do about it. And people come up with all kinds of other ideas that are not scientifically grounded—like putting people away, closing the place down, pushing the people out of town. Sound familiar?"

COLLABORATIVE DISCUSSION How did an infectious disease doctor get involved in stopping violence? With a partner, discuss how Dr. Slutkin's career in Africa connects to what he is doing now in Chicago. Cite specific textual evidence from the article to support your ideas.

390 Collection 4

WHEN STUDENTS STRUGGLE...

- Display a graphic organizer consisting of a box labeled "Conclusion" with arrows leading to it from several outlying boxes.
- Ask: How is violence like an infectious disease? Call on volunteers to answer.
- Enter any reasonable conclusion in the "Conclusion" box.
- Allow students time to reread the selection, individually or in pairs, to find evidence—facts and details—to support the conclusion. As volunteers suggest facts and details, enter them in the outlying boxes.
- Have students evaluate each piece of evidence to see if it leads logically to the conclusion. Revise the wording of the conclusion if necessary.

Analyze Ideas and Events COMMON CORE RI 3

The feature article "Blocking the Transmission of Violence" includes a great deal of information. To enable readers to understand how all the ideas interact and fit together, Alex Kotlowitz chooses a problem-solution organization. The graphic organizer shows how readers can use this organization to help them analyze the development of the author's major points:

Problem of Violence	Solution
• What ideas does the author present about the causes, nature, prevalence, and seriousness of the problem?	• How does the author develop the connection between CeaseFire's solution and the problem of violence?
• What kinds of details does the author use to develop readers' understanding of these ideas?	• What is his purpose in including certain types of details in his explanation of CeaseFire's solution?
• How does the author's structure help to communicate his ideas in this part of the article clearly and effectively?	• How does his conclusion show the significance of the ideas he has presented?

Support Inferences: Draw Conclusions COMMON CORE RI 1

Kotlowitz expects readers to draw their own conclusions from the ideas and details he shares in "Blocking the Transmission of Violence." When readers **draw conclusions**, they use textual evidence as well as their own prior knowledge and experience to make a judgment or statement of belief. Conclusions are often universal in that they can apply to a situation or issue beyond what is in the text.

From the information in this article, readers can draw several conclusions about the problem of violence and possible solutions, using these strategies:

- Examine both the ideas and supporting details that the author includes in his discussion of the problem and solution.
- Use this information to make inferences, or logical assumptions, about specific facets of violence or about CeaseFire.
- Combine the information and your inferences to arrive at a new understanding that applies to the subject beyond the context of this article.

CLOSE READ

Analyze Ideas and Events COMMON CORE RI 3

Review the terms in the graphic organizer that relate to the problem of violence: *causes, nature, prevalence* (how widespread it is), and *seriousness*. Explain that details related to any of these aspects relate to the problem. Then explain that solutions may address any of these aspects and that CeaseFire's solution is based on a particular understanding of the nature of violence. Encourage students to use these clues to help them track the problems and solutions as they analyze the text.

Support Inferences: Draw Conclusions COMMON CORE RI 1

Tell students that drawing conclusions requires that they apply correct reasoning to the textual evidence and combine it with their own relevant knowledge and experience.

- Tell them to read carefully to understand the ideas, examples, and facts the author presents.
- In reading Kotlowitz's article, they should be aware of their own prior knowledge about the problem of violence and consider how the information presented by the author relates to it.
- Suggest that they attempt to answer questions that arise while they read by making inferences.
- Have them review the evidence and the inferences they have made to see what general conclusions they can draw.

 # Strategies for Annotation   ✎ 🖫 *Annotate it!*

Analyze Ideas and Events COMMON CORE RI 3

Have students locate passages where Kotlowitz presents information about problems or solutions related to violence. Encourage them to use their eBook annotation tools to do the following:

- Highlight in pink each problem.
- Highlight in green each solution.
- On a note, explain what aspect of the problem the solution addresses.

colleagues, Tio Hardiman, brought up an uncomfortable truth: the program wasn't reaching the most bellicose, those most likely to pull a trigger. So in 2004, Hardiman suggested that, in addition to outreach workers, they also hire men and women who had been deep into street life, and he began recruiting people even while

> people with the same bkgd. as those caught up in violence have more cred. w/ them

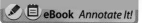

PRACTICE & APPLY

Analyzing the Text 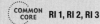 COMMON CORE RI 1, RI 2, RI 3

Possible answers:

1. *As with many acts of violence, revenge motivates Martin Torres, not personal hatred. By placing the episode at the beginning, Kotlowitz illustrates a significant problem in curbing the culture of violence: a code of honor that requires "an eye for an eye."*

2. *This list (lines 122–142) shows that violence occurs everywhere and for every reason. There is no minimum age, no place off limits, no bad reason, and no wrong time as far as perpetrators of violence are concerned. These realizations help readers to appreciate more fully the extent of the problem and also the work that faces the interrupters.*

3. *CeaseFire interrupters try to defuse a situation before it erupts into violence, and they come in after an incident to try to prevent further outbreaks. Their goal is prevention as part of a cure. Law enforcement officials react after the fact. If the situation between the law officials and CeaseFire is cooperative, then their efforts are complementary. Police will stand back to allow interrupters to do their job (lines 377–383).*

4. *The follow-up on the Torres story (line 321) shows that intervention can help. But it also shows the complexity of the culture that demands revenge. Torres knows that he did the right thing by refraining, but at the same time he feels shame for having let his nephew's killer escape unscathed.*

5. *Kotlowitz voices his concern that, although CeaseFire is expanding nationally and internationally, in Chicago it remains underfunded and its staff overwhelmed. He implies that programs can fail by overreaching and losing focus.*

6. *The final two paragraphs reiterate the ideas that a solution/cure for violence has to be found because it won't go away if we ignore it and that the problem persists when people become afraid to go into the areas that are "infected." These ideas harken back to CeaseFire's philosophy and confirm the necessity of trying its approach.*

7. *The author wants readers to see behind the façade of statistics and facts about violence to the people involved, both those involved in the problem and those involved in the solution. These descriptive details bring Torres, Hoddenbach, and Slutkin to life. Readers understand their struggles and roles more clearly as a result.*

Analyzing the Text COMMON CORE RI 1, RI 2, RI 3, SL 1a

Cite Text Evidence   Support your responses with evidence from the selection.

1. **Cause/Effect** What motive triggers Martin Torres's desire to commit an act of violence? Why did the author place this account at the beginning of the article?

2. **Draw Conclusions** What does the list of incidents discussed at the CeaseFire meeting illustrate about the prevalence and nature of violence? What effect is this list likely to have on readers?

3. **Draw Conclusions** Do the functions performed by CeaseFire complement or conflict with those of law enforcement?

4. **Analyze** Why does the author follow up on the story of Martin Torres near the end of his article? What important ideas does this part of the article support?

5. **Infer** What are the author's reasons for including the ideas in lines 391–399? Cite evidence to support your inference.

6. **Identify Patterns** How do the ideas expressed in the last two paragraphs relate to the information in the preceding parts of the article? Explain.

7. **Critique** The author includes many descriptive details about Torres, Hoddenbach, Slutkin, and others. Are such details appropriate for the author's purpose in this article? Why or why not?

PERFORMANCE TASK

Speaking Activity: Discussion In a small group, discuss your conclusions about whether CeaseFire is the type of organization that could work in many different communities confronting the problem of violence.

-   Jot down the ideas from the article that you think offer the most valuable insight into the problems of violence and the potential solutions.
-   Apply the insights from the article to communities beyond Chicago—your own community or a community whose violent conflicts are frequently in the headlines.

-   Bring your notes to a group conversation. Present your conclusions and listen to others' conclusions. As a group, discuss the pros and cons of CeaseFire and write a statement that summarizes the group's ideas.

Assign this performance task.

PERFORMANCE TASK   COMMON CORE SL 1a

Speaking Activity: Discussion Have students work individually to record their thoughts on CeaseFire's possible effectiveness in many different communities by noting ideas from the article and their own insights before meeting in their groups. Suggest that students choose one member of their group to record the pros and cons about CeaseFire that are brought up during the discussion. Each group's summary should reflect the conclusion reached by the group.

Critical Vocabulary

retribution	affiliation	ruminate	enmity
bellicose	unmitigated	ubiquity	

Practice and Apply Complete the sentence in a way that shows your understanding of the Critical Vocabulary word.

1. The *bellicose* expression on his face alerted those around him that . . .

2. The *ubiquity* of thieves in the neighborhood meant . . .

3. It is important to stop displays of *enmity* early on because . . .

4. The ex-convict was proud of his *affiliation* with CeaseFire because . . .

5. They met to *ruminate* on possible solutions before they made a decision because . . .

6. His *unmitigated* rage was frightening because . . .

7. The impulse to seek *retribution* should be restrained because . . .

Vocabulary Strategy: Latin Roots

The Critical Vocabulary words *affiliation* and *bellicose* are both derived from Latin roots. Knowing the meaning of their roots can help readers to define many related words, such as those shown in the chart.

Root/Meaning	Related Words
bellum: war	**bellicose**, belligerence, rebel, rebellious, antebellum
filius: son	**affiliation**, affiliate, filial

Practice and Apply Work with a partner to complete the steps.

1. Define each of the related words in the chart. Use your knowledge of the meaning of their roots. Check your definition in the dictionary to confirm.

2. For each word, write a sentence that includes context clues to help convey the word's meaning.

3. Read your sentences to another pair. Discuss your use of each word.

PRACTICE & APPLY

Critical Vocabulary

Possible answers:

1. *he was angry and likely to fight.*

2. *that its residents would likely be robbed.*

3. *they can lead to other violent actions.*

4. *he was making a difference by associating with the organization.*

5. *they didn't want to overlook any details by acting rashly.*

6. *nothing could reduce it.*

7. *revenge usually leads to more problems.*

Vocabulary Strategy: Latin Roots

Possible answers:

- *belligerence: "hostile attitude"*
- *rebel: "one who acts against authority"; "to act against authority"*
- *rebellious: "having a hostile attitude toward authority"*
- *antebellum: "before a war, especially the American Civil War"*
- *affiliate: "to associate with or become a member of"; "one who associates with an organization or another individual"*
- *filial: "relating to being a son or a child"*

Students' sentences will vary but should demonstrate their understanding of each word's meaning.

SCAFFOLDING FOR ELL STUDENTS

Vocabulary: Cognates English words with Latin roots often have cognates in Romance languages *(e.g. bellicose: belicoso in Spanish and Portuguese; belliqueux in French; bellicoso in Italian)*.

However, some seeming cognates are "false friends." Because the Latin *bello* (meaning "beautiful") looks like *bellum* (meaning "war"), Romance words from these roots can look similar but have different meanings. Readers must use context to figure out which meaning lies at the root of a word. Invite volunteers whose first language is a Romance language to generate words in it related to the roots in the chart. Then have them work with partners to find the English equivalent of each word they generate.

PRACTICE & APPLY

Language and Style: Direct and Indirect Quotations

 COMMON CORE L2

Point out that direct quotations are enclosed in quotation marks unless they run for several lines; then they may be set off from the rest of the text in an indented paragraph, or block quotation. Have students review the examples in the chart and identify the tag in each example (*The writer said; the teen said; said the interrupter*).

Then ask students to review the examples of sentences using indirect quotation and notice how the word *that* connects *said* (or a similar verb) to each indirect quotation.

Remind students that if they use an indirect quotation in a research paper, they should paraphrase the speaker, restating the speaker's ideas in their own words. If they want to directly quote even a phrase, that phrase should be enclosed in quotation marks within the indirect quotation

Possible answers:

When revising direct quotations, students should apply the conventions of standard English grammar to write and punctuate indirect quotations.

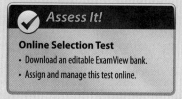

✓ Assess It!

Online Selection Test
- Download an editable ExamView bank.
- Assign and manage this test online.

Language and Style: Direct and Indirect Quotations

COMMON CORE L2

In his article, Alex Kotlowitz includes both direct and indirect quotations. **Direct quotations** are a speaker's exact words. They are set off by quotation marks and usually by a comma. **Indirect quotations** are the writer's restatement of a speaker's words. They are often introduced by *that* and are not punctuated with quotation marks, showing that the exact words are not recorded. Writers will often use indirect quotations when it is the idea they want to convey rather than the expression of the idea.

Kotlowitz includes a direct quotation from Torres in the first paragraph of his article:

> **"I thought, Man, I'm going to take care of business," he told me recently. "That's how I live. I was going hunting. This is my own blood, my nephew."**

The author could have chosen to present most of Torres's comments as an indirect quotation:

> **Torres said to me that he was going to get revenge for his nephew's death. He explained that it was how he lived; he was "going hunting."**

Notice the difference between the two versions. In the first, Torres's own words show his raw emotion. Readers can more clearly hear his voice as he uses the expression "Man" and talks about his "own blood." The second version conveys the idea without the emotion or sense of the speaker's personality.

Kotlowitz uses direct quotations for effect, when restating the speaker's words would dilute their impact. He uses indirect quotations when he wants to integrate the information more smoothly into his own writing and use it to support a point that he is making.

The chart shows different ways to punctuate direct quotations:

Punctuation of Direct Quotations	
with tag at beginning	The writer said, "I saw that in certain groups violence is a way to live up to social expectations."
with tag interrupting the quotation	"He taught us that violence is not a solution," the teen said, "but the way to start another problem."
with tag after the quotation	"We need to mediate in the hopes that we can reach a peaceful settlement," said the interrupter.
to introduce a long quotation	The interrupter told me the philosophy behind CeaseFire: "We want to prevent shootings . . ."

Practice and Apply Return to the article. Copy several of the direct quotations that the author includes. Rewrite them as indirect quotations. Analyze the way the change affects the impact of that part of the article.

Strategies for Annotation 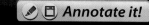 ✏️ 📘 *Annotate it!*

Direct and Indirect Quotations COMMON CORE L2

Share these strategies for guided or independent analysis:

- Highlight in yellow examples of direct quotations.
- Highlight in blue examples of indirect quotations.
- On a note, rewrite the direct quotation as an indirect quotation. Consider how the change affects the impact of that part of the article.

> says that violence directly mimics infections like tuberculosis and AIDS, and so, he suggests, the treatment ought to mimic the regimen applied to these diseases: go after the most infected, and stop the infection at its source. "For violence, we're trying to interrupt the next event, the next transmission, the next violent activity," Slutkin told me

> Slutkin told me that CeaseFire's goal is to interrupt the next event in a chain of violent activity.

INTERACTIVE WHITEBOARD LESSON
Author's Purpose and Perspective

COMMON CORE
RI 6

TEACH

Use the Interactive Whiteboard Lesson to review the steps for determining an author's purpose.

- **Step 1: Explore the Purposes for Writing** Review the four reasons authors may have for writing and the types of clues that help identify each one by exploring the examples in the activity.
- **Step 2: Identify the Basics** Explain that determining an author's purpose begins with identifying the title, text type, subject, and audience of the selection. Students may need to make inferences or logical assumptions about the audience from the content of the selection. Review the example with the class.
- **Step 3: Examine the Details** Explain that the details in a selection provide clues to the author's purpose. Review the example in the activity with the class.

COLLABORATIVE DISCUSSION

Have students work individually to apply the sentence frames in the activity to the selection and then share their responses with a partner. Instruct them to discuss how well the author achieved his purpose.

Support Inferences: Draw Conclusions

COMMON CORE
RI 1

RETEACH

Review the definition of a conclusion as a judgment or statement of belief based on evidence, experience, and reasoning. Then present these two scenarios:

- Sam spends Saturday at his aunt's home and plays with his young cousin, who has a cold. Sam wakes up on Sunday morning with a sore throat.
- Hannah attends a high-school basketball game on Saturday evening and cheers loudly for her team. She wakes up on Sunday morning with a sore throat.

ASK STUDENTS to make inferences about what happened in each scenario and draw conclusions about what Sam and Hannah should do next. *(First scenario: Sam may be coming down with a cold and should take preventive measures. Second scenario: Hannah has overused her voice; she needs to rest it and perhaps drink something soothing for her throat.)*

LEVEL UP TUTORIALS Assign the following *Level Up* tutorial: **Drawing Conclusions**

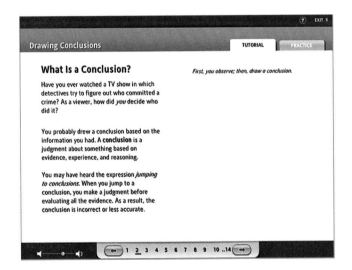

CLOSE READING APPLICATION

Students can apply the skill to a current magazine or newspaper article in print or online. Have them work independently to identify relevant evidence and make inferences about it. Ask: What conclusion do you draw about the topic of the article? What evidence and inferences support your conclusion?

Nobel Peace Prize Acceptance Speech

Speech by Wangari Maathai

Why This Text

Students may leave the text of a speech without a thorough understanding of how the author develops his or her ideas. Acceptance speeches such as this one may have a complex organizational structure that becomes clear only with careful study. With the aid of the close-reading questions, students will trace the organization of Maathai's ideas to help them analyze her main points.

Background Have students read the background and biographical information about Wangari Maathai, the founder of the Green Belt Movement in Kenya. Introduce the speech by telling students that Maathai, a Kenyan environmentalist and political activist, worked alongside the National Council of Women in Kenya (NCWK) to initiate the Green Belt Movement and to provide a forum for rural women to help the environment by planting trees in Kenya and to become self-sufficient.

AS YOU READ Ask students to pay attention to the reasons Maathai gives for founding the Green Belt Movement. How soon into her speech can students begin to identify the problems she hoped to solve by starting the movement?

 COMMON CORE

Common Core Support

- cite strong textual evidence to support inferences drawn from a text

- determine two or more central ideas of a text and analyze their development

- analyze a complex set of ideas and explain how they interact and develop over the course of a text

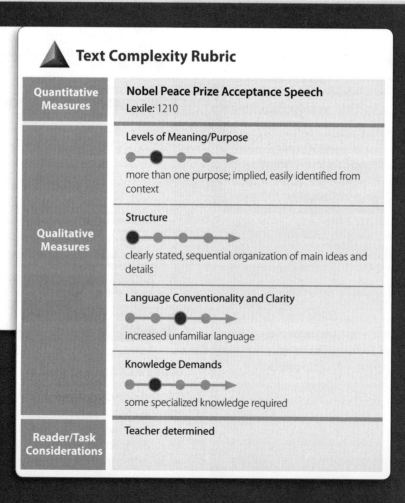

Text Complexity Rubric

Quantitative Measures	**Nobel Peace Prize Acceptance Speech** Lexile: 1210
Qualitative Measures	**Levels of Meaning/Purpose** more than one purpose; implied, easily identified from context
	Structure clearly stated, sequential organization of main ideas and details
	Language Conventionality and Clarity increased unfamiliar language
	Knowledge Demands some specialized knowledge required
Reader/Task Considerations	Teacher determined

Strategies for CLOSE READING

Analyze Ideas and Events

Students should read this speech carefully all the way through. Close-reading questions at the bottom of the page will help them focus on a thorough analysis of the interaction of a complex set of ideas or a series of events. As they read, students should record comments or questions about the text in the side margins.

WHEN STUDENTS STRUGGLE . . .

To help students follow the ideas Maathai presents in her speech, have small groups complete a chart such as the one below to analyze the speech.

CITE TEXT EVIDENCE Explain to students that Maathai uses a problem–solution text structure in her speech. Ask students to cite the evidence Maathai uses in the chart below.

Problem	Solution
Kenya was plagued by conflicts, poverty, environmental damage, and gender inequality.	Green Belt Movement was formed to protect the environment and create equality and income for Kenyan women.
Kenyan women lacked basic needs—firewood, clean water, shelter, income, food.	Maathai started Green Belt Movement to provide women with basic needs.
Kenyans thought their problems could be solved only by outside help, and women did not realize their basic needs depended on a healthy, sustainable environment.	Maathai developed a citizen education program for Kenyans to identify and solve their own problems.
Kenyans were unaware they were harming the environment and society.	Maathai showed people how their actions were damaging the environment and society.

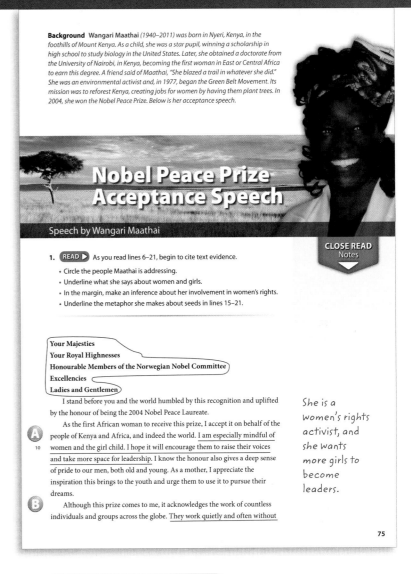

Background Wangari Maathai (1940–2011) was born in Nyeri, Kenya, in the foothills of Mount Kenya. As a child, she was a star pupil, winning a scholarship in high school to study biology in the United States. Later, she obtained a doctorate from the University of Nairobi, in Kenya, becoming the first woman in East or Central Africa to earn this degree. A friend said of Maathai, "She blazed a trail in whatever she did." She was an environmental activist and, in 1977, began the Green Belt Movement. Its mission was to reforest Kenya, creating jobs for women by having them plant trees. In 2004, she won the Nobel Peace Prize. Below is her acceptance speech.

Nobel Peace Prize Acceptance Speech

Speech by Wangari Maathai

CLOSE READ
Notes

1. **READ ▷** As you read lines 6–21, begin to cite text evidence.

- Circle the people Maathai is addressing.
- Underline what she says about women and girls.
- In the margin, make an inference about her involvement in women's rights.
- Underline the metaphor she makes about seeds in lines 15–21.

Your Majesties
Your Royal Highnesses
Honourable Members of the Norwegian Nobel Committee
Excellencies
Ladies and Gentlemen

I stand before you and the world humbled by this recognition and uplifted by the honour of being the 2004 Nobel Peace Laureate.

As the first African woman to receive this prize, I accept it on behalf of the people of Kenya and Africa, and indeed the world. I am especially mindful of women and the girl child. I hope it will encourage them to raise their voices and take more space for leadership. I know the honour also gives a deep sense of pride to our men, both old and young. As a mother, I appreciate the inspiration this brings to the youth and urge them to use it to pursue their dreams.

Although this prize comes to me, it acknowledges the work of countless individuals and groups across the globe. They work quietly and often without

She is a women's rights activist, and she wants more girls to become leaders.

75

1. READ AND CITE TEXT EVIDENCE

A **ASK STUDENTS** to read their margin notes to a partner. *Students should infer from textual evidence that Maathai is an advocate for women's rights, as alluded to in these specific statements from her speech: "I am especially mindful of women and the girl child. I hope it will encourage them to raise their voices and take more space for leadership" (lines 9–11).*

FOR ELL STUDENTS Have ELL students analyze the word *countless* (line 15), identifying the base word and its meaning. *The base word is* count, *meaning "to name one by one to get a total."* Then ask a volunteer to identify the suffix and the meaning it adds to the word. *The suffix is* –less, *meaning "without," so* countless *means "without being able to be counted."*

ASK STUDENTS to look for other words in the text that use the suffix *–less* and its opposite *–ful*, meaning "full of," and cite the words in the margin.

CLOSE READ
Notes

CLOSE READ
Notes

recognition to protect the environment, promote democracy, defend human rights and ensure equality between women and men. By so doing, they plant seeds of peace. I know they, too, are proud today. To all who feel represented by
20 this prize I say use it to advance your mission and meet the high expectations the world will place on us.

This honour is also for my family, friends, partners and supporters throughout the world. All of them helped shape the vision and sustain our work, which was often accomplished under hostile conditions. I am also grateful to the people of Kenya—who remained stubbornly hopeful that democracy could be realized and their environment managed sustainably. Because of this support, I am here today to accept this great honour.

I am immensely privileged to join my fellow African Peace laureates, Presidents Nelson Mandela and F.W. de Klerk, Archbishop Desmond Tutu, the
30 late Chief Albert Luthuli, the late Anwar el-Sadat and the UN Secretary General, Kofi Annan.

I know that African people everywhere are encouraged by this news. My fellow Africans, as we embrace this recognition, let us use it to intensify our commitment to our people, to reduce conflicts and poverty and thereby improve their quality of life. Let us embrace democratic governance, protect human rights and protect our environment. I am confident that we shall rise to the occasion. I have always believed that solutions to most of our problems must come from us.

C In this year's prize, the Norwegian Nobel Committee has placed the
40 critical issue of environment and its linkage to democracy and peace before the

world. For their visionary action, I am profoundly grateful. Recognizing that sustainable development,[1] democracy and peace are indivisible is an idea whose time has come. Our work over the past 30 years has always appreciated and engaged these linkages.

D My inspiration partly comes from my childhood experiences and observations of Nature in rural Kenya. It has been influenced and nurtured by the formal education I was privileged to receive in Kenya, the United States and Germany. As I was growing up, I witnessed forests being cleared and replaced by commercial plantations, which destroyed local biodiversity[2] and the capacity
50 of the forests to conserve water.

Excellencies, ladies and gentlemen,

In 1977, when we started the Green Belt Movement, I was partly responding to needs identified by rural women, namely lack of firewood, clean drinking water, balanced diets, shelter and income.

E Throughout Africa, women are the primary caretakers, holding significant responsibility for tilling the land and feeding their families. As a result, they are often the first to become aware of environmental damage as resources become scarce and incapable of sustaining their families.

The women we worked with recounted that unlike in the past, they were
60 unable to meet their basic needs. This was due to the **degradation** of their immediate environment as well as the introduction of commercial farming, which replaced the growing of household food crops. But international trade controlled the price of the exports from these small-scale farmers and a reasonable and just income could not be guaranteed. I came to understand that when the environment is destroyed, plundered or mismanaged, we undermine our quality of life and that of future generations.

degradation:
decline in conditions

[1] **sustainable development:** construction or development of an area that can be maintained over a period of time without damaging the environment.
[2] **biodiversity:** the number and variety of organisms found within a specified geographic region.

2. ◀ **REREAD** Reread lines 15–21. What main idea is Maathai making in these lines?

She is explaining that her environmental work, promotion of democracy, and defense of human rights is the work of many people who seek to promote peace worldwide.

3. **READ** ▶ As you read lines 22–44, continue to cite evidence.
• Circle the statement Maathai makes about the ways in which the Nobel Peace Prize can benefit Africans.
• Underline text describing the link between environment, democracy, and peace.

4. **READ** ▶ As you read lines 45–66, continue to cite text evidence.
• Circle text describing what Maathai witnessed as a young girl growing up in Kenya.
• Underline text describing her reasons for starting the Green Belt Movement.
• Underline text describing a realization Maathai comes to.

5. ◀ **REREAD** Reread lines 55–66. What problems did the women Maathai worked with face?

They were running out of natural resources to provide their basic needs.

2. **READ AND CITE TEXT EVIDENCE**

B ASK STUDENTS to cite specific evidence from the text that supports Maathai's main idea. *Maathai's main idea is that, although she is the recipient of the Peace Prize, a global group of people have acted together in order to protect the environment, promote democracy and peace, and defend human rights, carrying out her work. Students should cite evidence from lines 15–19.*

3. **READ AND CITE TEXT EVIDENCE**

C ASK STUDENTS to infer the reason for the Nobel Committee's linkage of the environment, democracy, and peace in awarding the Peace Prize to Maathai. *Students should recognize that Maathai has linked the environment, democracy, and peace in her work for the past 30 years (lines 43–44), so the Nobel Committee is paying tribute to her work and making the world aware of the inextricable connection among the three ideas. Students should cite evidence from lines 39–44.*

4. **READ AND CITE TEXT EVIDENCE**

D ASK STUDENTS to consider how Maathai's founding of the Green Belt Movement was partly done in response to her wanting to help rural Kenyan women. *As a child, Maathai saw the damage caused by deforestation and later saw how Kenyan women lacked basic needs, including firewood. Students should cite lines 48–50 and 52–54.*

5. **REREAD AND CITE TEXT EVIDENCE**

E ASK STUDENTS why the women were especially aware of problems. *They were responsible for tilling the land and feeding their families, so they were the first to notice environmental damage (lines 55–58).*

Critical Vocabulary: degradation (line 60) Have students explain *degradation* as Maathai uses it here.

F **G** Tree planting became a natural choice to address some of the initial basic needs identified by women. Also, tree planting is simple, attainable and guarantees quick, successful results within a reasonable amount time. This sustains interest and commitment.

So, together, we have planted over 30 million trees that provide fuel, food, shelter, and income to support their children's education and household needs. The activity also creates employment and improves soils and watersheds. Through their involvement, women gain some degree of power over their lives, especially their social and economic position and relevance in the family. This work continues.

H Initially, the work was difficult because historically our people have been persuaded to believe that because they are poor, they lack not only capital, but also knowledge and skills to address their challenges. Instead they are conditioned to believe that solutions to their problems must come from 'outside.' Further, women did not realize that meeting their needs depended on their environment being healthy and well managed. They were also unaware

6. **READ ▶** As you read lines 67–76, underline the reasons why tree planting "became a natural choice."

7. **◀ REREAD** Reread lines 67–76. In your own words, explain Matthai's solution to the environmental destruction in her native Kenya. What other needs does her solution meet?

Her solution is to plant trees to reforest Kenya and to satisfy some of the basic needs identified by the rural Kenyan women, including the need for a clean environment, employment, and independence.

78

---

that a degraded environment leads to a scramble for scarce resources and may culminate in poverty and even conflict. They were also unaware of the injustices of international economic arrangements.

I In order to assist communities to understand these linkages, we developed a citizen education program, during which people identify their problems, the causes and possible solutions. They then make connections between their own personal actions and the problems they witness in the environment and in society. They learn that our world is confronted with a litany of woes: corruption, violence against women and children, disruption and breakdown of families, and disintegration of cultures and communities. They also identify the abuse of drugs and chemical substances, especially among young people. There are also devastating diseases that are defying cures or occurring in epidemic proportions. Of particular concern are HIV/AIDS, malaria and diseases associated with malnutrition.

On the environment front, they are exposed to many human activities that are devastating to the environment and societies. These include widespread destruction of ecosystems,[3] especially through deforestation,[4] climatic instability, and contamination in the soils and waters that all contribute to excruciating poverty.

[3] **ecosystem:** all the living things that share and interact in an environment.
[4] **deforestation:** the cutting down of trees in a large area.

8. **READ ▶** As you read lines 77–109, continue to cite text evidence.
- Circle the problem presented.
- Underline the solution Maathai proposes.
- In the margin, explain the problem and solution described in these lines.

9. **◀ REREAD** Reread lines 86–96. Do you think it's important that people "make connections between their own personal actions and the problems they witness?" Explain.

Making connections between personal actions and resulting problems makes people more responsible for their own behavior. By showing how large problems are started by personal decisions, one can start to solve a problem at the source.

Problem: Kenyans believed their problems are solved by others; women did not realize their needs depend on a healthy environment.

Solution: She formed an education program to help Kenyans identify and solve their own problems.

79

---

6. **READ AND CITE TEXT EVIDENCE**

F **ASK STUDENTS** why Maathai thought that tree planting would be a good choice to help solve some of the problems identified by the rural women of Kenya. *Students should cite evidence from lines 67–70, recognizing that Maathai supports her statement that tree planting was "a natural choice" to meet the women's basic needs by explaining that it was easy to do and achievable, netting successful results in a fairly short time.*

7. **REREAD AND CITE TEXT EVIDENCE**

G **ASK STUDENTS** to cite evidence from the text supporting the idea that Maathai's solution to environmental destruction also helped rural Kenyan women. *Students should cite specific evidence from lines 67–69 and 71–76.*

8. **READ AND CITE TEXT EVIDENCE**

H **ASK STUDENTS** to explain the problem and solution Maathai outlines in lines 77–109. *Maathai explains the problem— Kenyans believe that because they are poor, their problems must be solved from "outside"; Kenyan women did not realize that their basic needs depended on a healthy environment (lines 77–82). Her solution was to form a citizen education program to help people identify and solve their own problems (lines 86–90, 97–101, 102–105, and 107–109).*

9. **REREAD AND CITE TEXT EVIDENCE**

I **ASK STUDENTS** to cite evidence to support their response. *Students should cite evidence from lines 88–90, 92–93, and 95–96 to support the idea that connecting problems to personal actions is important.*

> ❝*Therefore, the tree became a symbol for the democratic struggle in Kenya.*❞

inertia:
a state of little activity or interest

In the process, the participants discover that they must be part of the solutions. They realize their hidden potential and are empowered to overcome **inertia** and take action. They come to recognize that they are the primary custodians and beneficiaries of the environment that sustains them.

Entire communities also come to understand that while it is necessary to hold their governments accountable, it is equally important that in their own relationships with each other, they exemplify the leadership values they wish to see in their own leaders, namely justice, integrity and trust.

110 Although initially the Green Belt Movement's tree planting activities did not address issues of democracy and peace, it soon became clear that responsible governance of the environment was impossible without democratic space. Therefore, the tree became a symbol for the democratic struggle in Kenya. Citizens were mobilised to challenge widespread abuses of power, corruption and environmental mismanagement. In Nairobi 's Uhuru Park, at Freedom Corner, and in many parts of the country, trees of peace were planted to demand the release of prisoners of conscience and a peaceful transition to democracy.

Through the Green Belt Movement, thousands of ordinary citizens were 120 mobilized and empowered to take action and effect change. They learned to overcome fear and a sense of helplessness and moved to defend democratic rights.

In time, the tree also became a symbol for peace and conflict resolution, especially during ethnic conflicts in Kenya when the Green Belt Movement used peace trees to reconcile disputing communities. During the ongoing re-writing of the Kenyan constitution, similar trees of peace were planted in many parts of the country to promote a culture of peace. Using trees as a

symbol of peace is in keeping with a widespread African tradition. For example, the elders of the Kikuyu carried a staff from the *thigi* tree that, when 130 placed between two disputing sides, caused them to stop fighting and seek reconciliation. Many communities in Africa have these traditions.

Such practises are part of an extensive cultural heritage, which contributes both to the conservation of habitats and to cultures of peace. With the destruction of these cultures and the introduction of new values, local biodiversity is no longer valued or protected and as a result, it is quickly degraded and disappears. For this reason, The Green Belt Movement explores the concept of cultural biodiversity, especially with respect to indigenous seeds and medicinal plants.

As we progressively understood the causes of environmental degradation, 140 we saw the need for good governance. Indeed, the state of any country's environment is a reflection of the kind of governance in place, and without good governance there can be no peace. Many countries, which have poor governance systems, are also likely to have conflicts and poor laws protecting the environment.

In 2002, the courage, resilience, patience and commitment of members of the Green Belt Movement, other civil society organizations, and the Kenyan public culminated in the peaceful transition to a democratic government and laid the foundation for a more stable society.

They are linked in that each needs the other—a healthy environment needs democracy, and without good governance there can be no peace.

---

10. **READ ►** As you read lines 110–148, continue to cite text evidence.

- Underline details that continue to develop the connection between the environment, democracy, and peace.
- In the margin, explain the connection among these ideas.

11. **◄ REREAD** Reread lines 110–148. Analyze the sequence of events that led from the tree planting of the Green Belt Movement to Kenya's transition to a stable, democratic society. How does the symbolic "tree of peace" connect these events?

At first, the tree became a symbol for the democratic struggle in Kenya. Through the Green Belt Movement, citizens were mobilized to affect change and defend democratic rights. In time, the tree became a symbol of peace and conflict resolution among disputing groups. With the destruction of these cultural conflicts, Kenya transformed itself into a democracy and a stable society.

---

10. **READ AND CITE TEXT EVIDENCE**

🟢 **ASK STUDENTS** to cite evidence to explain how the environment, democracy, and peace are connected. *Students should cite evidence from lines 110–113, 119–122, and 139–143.*

Critical Vocabulary: inertia (line 104) Have students share their definition of *inertia* and use it in a sentence.

FOR ELL STUDENTS Point out that the English word *democracy* (line 111) is derived from the Greek *demos*, meaning "people." Ask why this English word comes from the Greek word for *people*. *Students should see that a democracy is a government by the people and that Greece was the birthplace of democracy.*

11. **REREAD AND CITE TEXT EVIDENCE**

🟢 **ASK STUDENTS** why the Green Belt Movement began to change from simply improving the environment to pursuing democracy. *The people of the movement realized that they could not take care of the environment without good governance (lines 140–141).*

This water tank in Kenya was filled the night before, but is now below the level of the spigot. It will not be filled for another week.

Excellencies, friends, ladies and gentlemen,

150 It is 30 years since we started this work. Activities that devastate the environment and societies continue unabated. Today we are faced with a challenge that calls for a shift in our thinking, so that humanity stops threatening its life-support system. We are called to assist the Earth to heal her wounds and in the process heal our own—indeed, to embrace the whole creation in all its diversity, beauty and wonder. This will happen if we see the need to revive our sense of belonging to a larger family of life, with which we have shared our evolutionary process.

In the course of history, there comes a time when humanity is called to shift to a new level of **consciousness**, to reach a higher moral ground. A time 160 when we have to shed our fear and give hope to each other.

That time is now.

The Norwegian Nobel Committee has challenged the world to broaden the understanding of peace: there can be no peace without equitable development; and there can be no development without sustainable management of the environment in a democratic and peaceful space. This shift is an idea whose time has come.

I call on leaders, especially from Africa, to expand democratic space and build fair and just societies that allow the creativity and energy of their citizens to flourish.

consciousness:
being aware

---

170 Those of us who have been privileged to receive education, skills, and experiences and even power must be role models for the next generation of leadership. In this regard, I would also like to appeal for the freedom of my fellow laureate Aung San Suu Kyi[5] so that she can continue her work for peace and democracy for the people of Burma and the world at large.

Culture plays a central role in the political, economic and social life of communities. Indeed, culture may be the missing link in the development of Africa. Culture is dynamic and evolves over time, consciously discarding retrogressive traditions, like female genital mutilation (FGM), and embracing aspects that are good and useful.

180 Africans, especially, should re-discover positive aspects of their culture. In accepting them, they would give themselves a sense of belonging, identity and self-confidence.

Ladies and Gentlemen,

There is also need to galvanize civil society and grassroots movements to catalyse change. I call upon governments to recognize the role of these social movements in building a critical mass of responsible citizens, who help maintain checks and balances in society. On their part, civil society should embrace not only their rights but also their responsibilities.

Further, industry and global institutions must appreciate that ensuring 190 economic justice, equity and ecological integrity are of greater value than profits at any cost.

The extreme global inequities and prevailing consumption patterns continue at the expense of the environment and peaceful co-existence. The choice is ours.

I would like to call on young people to commit themselves to activities that contribute toward achieving their long-term dreams. They have the energy and creativity to shape a sustainable future. To the young people I say, you are a gift to your communities and indeed the world. You are our hope and our future.

The holistic approach to development, as exemplified by the Green Belt 200 Movement, could be embraced and replicated in more parts of Africa and beyond. It is for this reason that I have established the Wangari Maathai Foundation to ensure the continuation and expansion of these activities. Although a lot has been achieved, much remains to be done.

Excellencies, ladies and gentlemen,

As I conclude I reflect on my childhood experience when I would visit a stream next to our home to fetch water for my mother. I would drink water

---

[5] **Aung San Suu Kyi:** Burmese political leader who had been under house arrest for 15 years for espousing human rights; she was awarded the Nobel Peace Prize in 1991 and was freed in 2010.

She calls upon grassroots movements and governments to affect change, industry to ensure economic fairness and environmental integrity, and consumers to change their patterns to protect the environment.

12. **READ** ▶ Read lines 149–216. In the margin, explain what Matthai asks of her audience (lines 170–198). Continue to cite text evidence.

---

12. READ AND CITE TEXT EVIDENCE

🅛 **ASK STUDENTS** to explain the challenges Maathai describes in lines 150–160. *Students should explain that Maathai describes challenges such as the devastation of the environment and consequently our own well-being. She cites the challenge of having to shift our thinking to one in which we acknowledge "belonging to a larger family of life" (line 156).*

Critical Vocabulary: consciousness (line 159) Have students share their definitions of *consciousness*. Ask how the word fits into Maathai's discussion of how we must shift our thinking. *She thinks we must gain a new awareness of the environment to save it.*

WHEN STUDENTS STRUGGLE . . . To help students analyze the ideas Maathai is presenting, ask them to reread lines 170–198. Invite them to work with a small group to discuss how the specific ideas of this section interact and are developed over the course of the text.

FOR ELL STUDENTS A phrasal verb, a verb that is followed by a preposition that gives the verb another meaning, may be difficult for ELL students to comprehend. Make sure that students understand the actual meaning of *call on* (line 195), *pick up* (line 208), and *give back* (line 215). *Students should be able to understand from the context that* call on *means "to ask someone in a formal way to do something,"* pick up *means "to gather," and* give back *means "to return."* Ask students to use each of these phrasal verbs in several sentences.

CLOSE READ
Notes

She uses this story to show how we've changed the environment and to set a goal for the future.

straight from the stream. Playing among the arrowroot leaves I tried in vain to pick up the strands of frogs' eggs, believing they were beads. But every time I put my little fingers under them they would break. Later, I saw thousands of
210 tadpoles: black, energetic and wriggling through the clear water against the background of the brown earth. This is the world I inherited from my parents.

Today, over 50 years later, the stream has dried up, women walk long distances for water, which is not always clean, and children will never know what they have lost. The challenge is to restore the home of the tadpoles and give back to our children a world of beauty and wonder.

Thank you very much.

13. **◀ REREAD** Reread lines 205–216. Explain in the margin why Maathai ends with this story of her childhood.

SHORT RESPONSE

Cite Text Evidence Analyze Maathai's ideas that explain how the environment, democracy, and peace interact and are interconnected. Review your reading notes to trace the development of these ideas over the course of the speech, and **cite text evidence** in your response.

Maathai introduces this set of ideas by stating that in presenting this year's Peace Prize to her, the Nobel Committee has placed the issue of the environment and its linkage to democracy and peace before the world. She moves on to say that although the Green Belt Movement's tree planting did not address the issues of democracy and peace, it became clear to her that responsible governance of the environment could not be achieved without a democratic and peaceful space. She ends with the Nobel Committee's idea that "there can be no peace without equitable development; and there can be no development without sustainable management of the environment in a democratic and peaceful space."

84

---

13. REREAD AND CITE TEXT EVIDENCE

Ⓜ **ASK STUDENTS** how Maathai uses the story about the tadpoles to exemplify the changes in the environment. *She explains that when she was young, the water nearby was clean and the world was full of wonders. Now the stream has dried up and there are no tadpoles; even water that is a long way from home might not be clean. Her goal is to make the water clear again.*

SHORT RESPONSE

Cite Text Evidence Students should:

- explain how the environment, democracy, and peace are interrelated in Maathai's speech.
- cite specific evidence to trace the development of these ideas over the course of the text.

TO CHALLENGE STUDENTS . . .

For more context about Wangari Maathai, who died in 2011, have students conduct print or online research to find out about her legacy and the current activities of the Green Belt Movement.

ASK STUDENTS to work in small groups to find out more about the Green Belt Movement. Have groups report to the class on what they discover.

- What role is the movement taking politically? *It's trying to ensure peaceful political transitions in Kenya and helping those in danger from unrest. It encourages the people in Kenya to look beyond ethnic differences and to see one another as fellow Kenyans.*

- How is the Green Belt Movement active in the environment? *The movement helps women in rural areas establish nurseries, halt erosion, and harvest rainwater. It runs seminars to mobilize support for environmental protection and to influence national and international policies relating to forests and climate change.*

DIG DEEPER

With the class, return to Question 11, Reread. Have students engage in a group discussion to analyze the sequence of events that led from the tree planting of the Green Belt Movement to Kenya's becoming a democracy, explaining how the events interact and are developed over the course of the text.

ASK STUDENTS whether they were satisfied with the outcome of their small-group discussions. Have each group share its analysis of the sequence of events, stating the interactions and connections, including the role that the "tree of peace" played.

- Guide students to tell what evidence they cited from the text to support their ideas. Ask whether there were any disagreements among the group members and how these conflicts were resolved.

- Encourage groups to explain how they decided whether or not they had found sufficient textual evidence to connect the events and show how they were developed over the course of the text.

- After students have shared the results of the group discussion, ask if another group shared any ideas they wish they had considered.

ASK STUDENTS to return to their Short Response answer to revise it based on the class discussion.

CLOSE READING NOTES

Hatred

*my*SmartPlanner — Create lesson plans and access resources online.

Poem by Wisława Szymborska

Why This Text?

To understand and enjoy literature, students must analyze a text's language and determine its meaning. This lesson explores the use of personification, repetition, and parallelism in poetry, and has students analyze the meanings they convey.

Key Learning Objective: The student will be able to determine the figurative meanings of words and phrases as they are used to personify an idea.

Common Core Standards

RL 1 Cite textual evidence.

RL 2 Determine themes.

RL 4 Determine the meaning of words and phrases, including figurative meanings.

RL 6 Analyze a case in which grasping point of view requires distinguishing what is directly stated from what is really meant.

W 3d Use precise words and phrases, telling details, and sensory language.

L 3 Apply knowledge of language to understand how language functions in different contexts, to make effective choices for meaning or style.

L 5a Interpret figures of speech in context and analyze their role in the text.

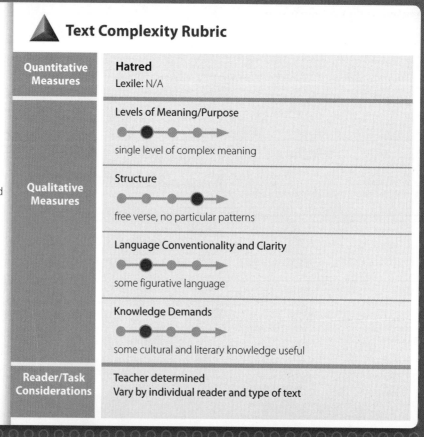

Text Complexity Rubric

Quantitative Measures

Hatred
Lexile: N/A

Qualitative Measures

Levels of Meaning/Purpose

single level of complex meaning

Structure

free verse, no particular patterns

Language Conventionality and Clarity

some figurative language

Knowledge Demands

some cultural and literary knowledge useful

Reader/Task Considerations

Teacher determined
Vary by individual reader and type of text

Background Have students read the information on Wisława Szymborska (vēs-wä´vä shĭm-bôr´skə). Point out that she lived through deeply turbulent times in Poland. The German invasion and devastation wrought by World War II was followed by Soviet domination and martial law. While Szymborska's poetry is pensive and given to examining her own thoughts and feelings, it also reflects what was going on around her. For this reason, Szymborska was a celebrity in Poland, and her poetry has been translated into more than twelve languages.

AS YOU READ Direct students to use the As You Read note to focus their reading.

Determine Figurative Meanings: Personification

COMMON CORE RL 4, L 5a

(LINES 1–11)

Explain that **personification** is figurative language in which human traits are given to nonhuman things.

A **CITE TEXT EVIDENCE** Ask students to reread lines 1–11 and explain what the author is comparing hatred to. *(a human-like monster with enormous strength and stamina)* Have them cite specific words and phrases, specifically verbs, that help create this picture of hatred as a flesh-and-blood being. *("keeps itself in shape," "vaults," "pounces," "gives birth")*

Analyze Language: Repetition and Parallelism (LINES 12–17)

COMMON CORE L 3

Explain that **repetition** is using a word or phrase more than once for emphasis. **Parallelism** is using the same grammatical structure to show that two or more phrases have equal importance. Poets use both devices to emphasize ideas and to create rhythm.

B **ASK STUDENTS** to reread lines 12–17 and to identify the use of repetition and parallelism. *(repetition: "one . . . or another," "whatever"; parallelism: "one religion or another . . . one fatherland or another")* Then ask what meaning this use of repetition and parallelism conveys. *(Hatred does not need a particular religion or nation; it can align itself with any faith or country and still be successful. The repetition of words and grammatical structures to express these ideas underscores hatred's persistence.)*

Wisława Szymborska (1923–2012) *was born in Poland and remained there throughout her life. She lived modestly, supporting herself with a full-time job at a literary magazine. Though her body of work includes only about 400 poems, it was remarkable enough to be recognized with a Nobel Prize in 1996. In her Nobel lecture, she compared poets to scientists because, just as scientists need to question what they know through rigorous experimentation, poets need to question what they know through writing. Though her poetry is sometimes seen as political, she considered her work to be more prosaic, dealing with ordinary people and life.*

Hatred

Poem by Wisława Szymborska

AS YOU READ Pay attention to the details that characterize hatred. Write down any questions you generate during reading.

> **A** See how efficient it still is,
> how it keeps itself in shape—
> our century's hatred.
> How easily it vaults the tallest obstacles.
> 5 How rapidly it pounces, tracks us down.
>
> It's not like other feelings.
> At once both older and younger.
> It gives birth itself to the reasons
> that give it life.
> 10 When it sleeps, it's never eternal rest.
> And sleeplessness won't sap its strength; it feeds it.
>
> One religion or another—
> whatever gets it ready, in position.
> One fatherland or another—
> 15 whatever helps it get a running start. **B**
> Justice also works well at the outset
> until hate gets its own momentum going.

Image Credits: (t) ©Filip Miller/AP; (b) ©Northfoto/Shutterstock

Hatred **395**

SCAFFOLDING FOR ELL STUDENTS

Vocabulary: Idioms Read aloud the first stanza of the poem (lines 1–5) as students follow along in the text. Focus students' attention on the phrase in line 2, "keeps itself in shape."

- Explain that the phrase is an **idiom,** a group of words that has a meaning different from the meaning of the individual words.
- Point out that *keep oneself in shape* means "stay fit and healthy."
- Explain that if students cannot use context clues to determine an idiom's meaning, they can usually find it in a dictionary.

ASK STUDENTS to use context clues or a dictionary to determine the meanings of "gives birth" in line 8, "get a running start" in line 15, and "has just what it takes" in line 28.

Analyze Language: Repetition and Parallelism

COMMON CORE RL 4, RL 6, L 3

(LINES 18–33)

Explain that repetition and parallelism can affect meaning and **tone**—the author's attitude toward the subject—and that tone can be determined by noting word choice and topic. Point out examples of tone: condescending, hostile, sympathetic, irreverent.

C CITE TEXT EVIDENCE Have students reread lines 18–33 to identify examples of repetition and parallelism. *(Repetition—"hatred" in line 18, "ever" in lines 26, 27, "all" in lines 30, 31, 32; Parallelism— short question with repetition of "ever" in lines 25–28, question fragment beginning with "all" in lines 31–33)* Discuss how repetition and parallelism affect the lines' meaning and tone. *(They give the sense that there is a wealth of evidence for the supremacy of hatred; these are but a few examples of many. The devices create a tone of admiration for hatred, although readers are meant to understand that the tone is ironic and the speaker is actually lamenting hatred's strength.)*

Determine Figurative Meanings: Personification

COMMON CORE RL 4, L 5a

(LINES 41–52)

Explain that personification is most often used fleetingly to convey a single image. However, Szymborska uses personification throughout her poem to draw a complete picture of hatred.

D ASK STUDENTS to reread lines 41–52 and to explain how the lines complete the image the poet creates of hatred. Ask them specifically to look at the images she evokes in the lines. *(The reference to the executioner and the sniper help complete the image of hatred as deadly and cruel. The last two lines note the persistence of hatred.)*

COLLABORATIVE DISCUSSION Have pairs discuss the details that create an image of hatred. Then have students share their insights with the class.

ASK STUDENTS to share any questions they generated in the course of reading and discussing the selection.

Hatred. Hatred.
Its face twisted in a grimace
20 of erotic ecstasy.

C Oh these other feelings,
listless weaklings.
Since when does brotherhood
draw crowds?
25 Has compassion
ever finished first?
Does doubt ever really rouse the rabble?
Only hatred has just what it takes.

Gifted, diligent, hard-working.
30 Need we mention all the songs it has composed?
All the pages it has added to our history books?
All the human carpets it has spread
over countless city squares and football fields?

Let's face it:
35 it knows how to make beauty.
The splendid fire-glow in midnight skies.
Magnificent bursting bombs in rosy dawns.
You can't deny the inspiring pathos of ruins
and a certain bawdy humor to be found
40 in the sturdy column jutting from their midst.

D Hatred is a master of contrast—
between explosions and dead quiet,
red blood and white snow.
Above all, it never tires
45 of its leitmotif—the impeccable executioner
towering over its soiled victim.
It's always ready for new challenges.
If it has to wait awhile, it will.
They say it's blind. Blind?
50 It has a sniper's keen sight
and gazes unflinchingly at the future
as only it can.

COLLABORATIVE DISCUSSION What impression of hatred does the poet create? With a partner, discuss the details that create a vivid image of hatred. Cite specific textual details from the poem to support your ideas.

APPLYING ACADEMIC VOCABULARY

drama	trigger

As you discuss the poem, incorporate the Collection 4 academic vocabulary words *drama* and *trigger*. Ask students to notice how Szymborska uses personification to **dramatize** the consequences of hatred. How do repetition and parallelism contribute to this drama? In what way does the use of personification **trigger** an emotional response in readers?

Determine Figurative Meanings: Personification

 COMMON CORE RL 4, L 5a

Personification is a figure of speech in which human qualities are given to objects, animals, ideas, or emotions. By imagining the non-human subject as human, the writer can express insights and abstractions in a concrete way that readers in turn can visualize and connect to their own realm of experience.

To convey her insights into the nature of hatred, Szymborska personifies the powerful emotion. She develops her message by commenting on hatred's actions, habits, accomplishments, and other attributes as if it were human. By the end of the poem, a detailed picture of hatred has been drawn; readers can almost see it standing before them: "Gifted, diligent, hard-working."

Analyzing the Text

 COMMON CORE RL 1, RL 4, RL 6, L 5a, W 3d

Cite Text Evidence   Support your responses with evidence from the selection.

1. **Analyze** What image of hatred is created by the personification in lines 1–5 and 12–20? What words contribute to this image?

2. **Synthesize** Explain the ideas about hatred conveyed through the apparent contradictions, or paradoxes, in lines 6–11.

3. **Compare** How does the poet use personification in lines 21–28 to contrast hatred with compassion, brotherhood, and doubt?

4. **Analyze** How would you describe the poem's tone? Cite evidence to support your response.

5. **Draw Conclusions** The poet locates phrases that seem to portray hatred positively—such as "it knows how to make beauty" (line 35)—near details that show how hatred triggers destruction. What message about hatred is the poet conveying through this juxtaposition?

PERFORMANCE TASK

Writing Activity: Comparison Why is personification an effective literary device?

- Choose three stanzas of "Hatred." Rewrite them, conveying the ideas without the use of personification.

- In a small group, read your rewritten version. Together, discuss how the absence of personification alters the poem's meaning and impact.

- Present your group's conclusions to the class.

PERFORMANCE TASK

COMMON CORE W 3d

Writing Activity: Comparison Have students work independently to rewrite the three stanzas. Suggest that they review the stanzas they have chosen and take notes on the meaning the author conveys with the use of personification. When students have completed their stanzas, have them read them aloud in a small group and then compare them to the original. Ask them to discuss how personification allows the author to convey meaning that is hard to convey by other means. Ask groups to present their conclusions to the class.

PRACTICE & APPLY

Determine Figurative Meanings: Personification

 COMMON CORE RL 4, L 5a

You may want to discuss these additional points about personification with your class:

Personification is used in everyday language. To say "That's an angry bruise" or "The place was hopping" is to use personification.

Using personification consistently throughout the poem, rather than a string of unrelated metaphors and similes, allows Symborska to build a single, imposing image in the reader's mind. As a result, the reader forms a mental picture of hatred that is vivid and enduring.

Analyzing the Text

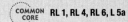 COMMON CORE RL 1, RL 4, RL 6, L 5a

1. *These two stanzas portray hatred as a vigorous athlete. It "vaults," "it pounces," it gets off to "a running start," and "gets its own momentum going."*

2. *The paradoxes are that hatred is older and younger than other feelings, that it gives birth to what gives it life, and that sleeplessness feeds it. Through these paradoxes, the poet is saying that hatred has always been around, yet it starts anew each day; that it generates a cycle, since actions that manifest hatred lead to more hatred; that "sleeplessness" or the prevalence of hatred also breeds more, "feeding it" by making it stronger.*

3. *Lines 21–28 personify compassion, brotherhood, and doubt as "listless weaklings." They lack the magnetism of hatred. They cannot compete.*

4. *The poem conveys a tone of irony; what is implied by the words used in the descriptions is the opposite of the poem's true meaning. Hatred is described as "efficient," "Gifted, diligent, hard-working," and "always ready for new challenges." These phrases suggest admiration, but the poet is actually expressing a sense of sadness or hopelessness in the face of hatred's enduring strength.*

5. *The poet is saying that hatred is attractive. It appears powerful and strong, which is why it draws so many followers. But, if one looks carefully at hatred, it creates nothing but devastation, sorrow, and more hatred.*

Language and Style: Repetition and Parallelism

COMMON CORE W 3d, L 3

Take students through the examples of repetition and parallelism and make sure they understand what each technique is. Point out the last example and explain that parallelism and repetition are often used together to add rhythm and emphasis. Then point out that there are several more examples of repetition and parallelism in the poem. Explain that these devices are also used in speeches and in narrative writing for the same purposes as in poetry, to create rhythm and emphasis.

Possible answers:

Students' poems should incorporate repetition, parallelism, and personification to accurately depict specific qualities of an emotion that they have selected.

Assess It!

Online Selection Test
- Download an editable ExamView bank.
- Assign and manage this test online.

Language and Style: Repetition and Parallelism

 COMMON CORE L 3

In poetry, the techniques of repetition and parallelism affect both sound and sense. They draw attention to key words or phrases, and they can contribute to the rhythm and tone of a poem.

Notice how the poet uses **repetition**, the repeating of key words and phrases, in "Hatred":

> **Need we mention all the songs it has composed?**
> **All the pages it has added to our history books?**
> **All the human carpets it has spread . . .**

The repetition of "all" directs readers' attention to the thought contained in each line. The meaning of the word itself emphasizes hatred's far-reaching impact.

Parallelism, using similar grammatical constructions to express ideas that are related or equal in importance, appears in these lines from "Hatred":

> **Hatred is a master of contrast—**
> **between explosions and dead quiet,**
> **red blood and white snow.**

The repeated grammatical construction of two nouns and modifiers joined by the conjunction *and* draws attention to the contrasts; in doing so, the poet shows how hatred multiplies its violent effects. She could have written the lines in this way:

> **Hatred is a master of contrast—**
> **between explosions and dead quiet,**
> **with red blood on white snow.**

The change in structure makes the last line less dramatic and shifts the rhythm, deemphasizing the last image.

Parallelism and repetition can be used together to add drama and tension to lines.

> **How easily it vaults the tallest obstacles.**
> **How rapidly it pounces, tracks us down.**

The repetition of *how* along with the same grammatical construction at the beginning of each line adds almost a physical punch to the lines, emphasizing the athleticism of hatred.

Practice and Apply Write a brief poem in the style of Szymborska, personifying an emotion such as happiness or nervousness. Include examples of both repetition and parallelism in your poem. Exchange your work with a partner and share feedback on each other's use of personification, repetition, and parallelism.

WHEN STUDENTS STRUGGLE . . .

Draw a web diagram on the board. Work with students to write their personification poems by having them choose an emotion and then imagine that emotion as a person. Model how they might use the web diagram by writing "fear" in the center. Ask them what fear looks, smells, and sounds like in human terms. Elicit responses such as "cloaked in black, sour smelling, hoarse voice." Write each example in the diagram. Then explain that you will use the descriptions in the diagram to create an image of fear for your poem.

ASK STUDENTS to complete their own web diagrams and to use these to write their personification poem. Remind them to use parallelism and repetition in their poems.

INTERACTIVE WHITEBOARD LESSON

Analyze Impact of Word Choice: Tone

COMMON CORE
RL 4

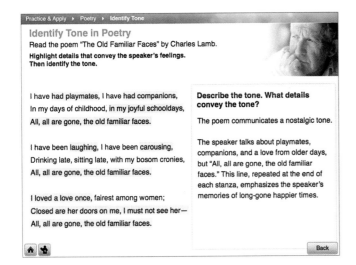

TEACH

Explain to students that **tone** in literature refers to an author's attitude toward the subject or audience. Point out that in spoken language, the speaker's voice conveys tone. But in written language, we cannot rely on angry shouts to determine if a tone is angry or on intonations to show humor. Instead, we must rely on the words, phrases, and images an author uses to describe the subject. Explain that tone in literature, just like tone of voice in speech, is an important part of meaning. Explain that readers determine tone by analyzing the following:

- an author's word choices, including descriptive words and action verbs
- figurative language and the images it creates for readers
- the poem's subject matter in relation to the author's word choice and imagery

PRACTICE AND APPLY

Display lines 34–40 of "Hatred" on the board or on a device. Have volunteers point out descriptive words and phrases that stand out in the stanza. *("beauty," "splendid fire-glow," "Magnificent," "rosy," "inspiring," "bawdy humor," "sturdy column")* Then ask students what images are created. *(beautiful glowing skies, smoke spiraling upward)* Ask students to determine the tone by thinking about whether the words and images used to describe hatred are at odds with the concept of hatred. *(The tone is ironic because the positive language and beautiful images are the opposite of what would normally be associated with hatred.)*

INTERACTIVE WHITEBOARD LESSON

Determine Theme

COMMON CORE
RL 2

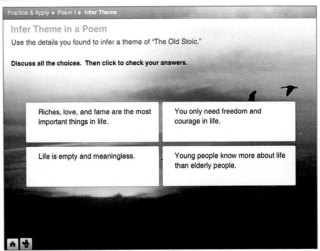

TEACH

Explain that a poem's **theme** or themes is/are its deeper meaning, the enduring message about life or humanity that the poet wants to convey to readers. Figuring out a poem's themes is different from determining what the poem is generally about. Unlike the topic of a poem, which is stated in a few words, a theme is stated as a sentence. Tell students that to determine themes, they should ask themselves the following questions:

- What is the poem mostly about?
- What is the tone of the poem?
- What are some powerful or recurring images in the poem?
- What do you know about the poet and his or her background?

COLLABORATIVE DISCUSSION

Display the questions above on the board or on a device. Have students work in groups of four to determine a central theme of the poem. Each group member should focus on a different question: What the poem is mostly about? *(the strength and stamina of hatred)* What is the tone of the poem? *(The tone of the poem is ironic.)* What images from the poem stand out? *(Possible answers: the image of hatred vaulting over obstacles and tracking us down, the image of bombs aglow in night skies and ruined cities)* How might the poet's background have influenced her message? *(Possible answer: The poet is from Poland and lived there during the Nazi occupation and World War II. She likely witnessed a lot of death and destruction.)* Have students as a group decide on a statement of theme, and present their responses to the class. *(Possible answers: Hatred is powerful and enduring. Hatred can fool us.)*

Writing: Use Precise Words and Phrases

COMMON CORE

W 3d

TEACH

Tell students that precise words and vivid imagery helps readers see, hear, smell, taste, and touch what they read. Explain that sensory language and exact words and phrases allow the reader to make a connection to the literature, to enter the poet's or writer's world.

- Demonstrate the point by reading lines 34–40, rewritten to exclude personification and vivid imagery: "Listen / hatred can produce pretty sights, too / with fires burning at night / and bombs blowing up in the morning / destroyed buildings can even make you feel sad / and it's sort of funny / when one tower remains standing while everything else is destroyed"

- Ask students if they could picture what the author was talking about. Then read lines 34–40 as the author wrote them. Ask them if they could better picture the scene now, and have them identify particular words that helped create vivid images.

- Explain that to use precise words and phrases, telling details, and sensory language to convey a vivid picture in writing, writers must eliminate unnecessary words and phrases and concentrate on strong action verbs and precise adjectives and adverbs. Point out that a thesaurus is a useful tool in finding just the right word to describe a setting or character.

PRACTICE AND APPLY

Provide students with a short paragraph: *The steamship sailed in the morning. There was a lot of fog. It was hard to see, and passengers felt nervous about the trip.* Ask students to add details, precise words and phrases, and vivid imagery to rewrite the paragraph so that readers can see, hear, smell, taste, and touch the scene that they describe. Have students share their writing in small groups and discuss the words and imagery that make the writing effective.

Determine Figurative Meanings: Personification

COMMON CORE

RL 4, L 5a

RETEACH

Review the definition of **personification**: a kind of figurative language in which human traits and actions are attributed to animals, objects, and ideas to create a vivid picture. Tell students that to demonstrate personification, you will describe a frosty morning in two different ways.

- Read the following description: *The temperature dropped in the early hours of the morning, and frost formed on tree branches and grass. It even glistened on mailboxes.*

- Then read the description with personification: *The frost waited until just before first light, creeping into the valley, touching each branch, each blade of grass, each mailbox, leaving its signature on everything it passed.*

- Ask students to list the words and phrases that contribute to personification in the second paragraph. *("waited," "creeping," "touching," "leaving its signature on everything it passed")* Then ask how personification helped them "see" the scene you described. *(Personification provides readers with a unique way to view frost. Giving it human attributes captures readers' attention.)*

 LEVEL UP TUTORIALS Assign the following *Level Up* tutorial: **Figurative Language**

CLOSE READING APPLICATION

Students can apply the skill to a book or magazine article. Ask them to look for instances of personification and to identify how the device helps the writer create a certain image for the reader.

COLLECTION **4**
PERFORMANCE TASK A

Interactive Lessons

If you need help with...
• **Writing an Informative Text**
• **Writing as a Process**

Write an Analytical Essay

This collection features individuals who are caught in cycles of violence. Look back at the anchor text *Hamlet* and the other texts you have read in the collection. How does violence affect people's ability to control their fates? Synthesize your ideas by writing an analytical essay.

COMMON CORE

W 2a–f Write informative/explanatory texts.
W 4 Produce clear and coherent writing.
W 5 Develop and strengthen writing.
W 9a–b Draw evidence from literary or informational texts.

An effective analytical essay

- clearly states a controlling idea about the relationship between violence and fate as it is portrayed in *Hamlet* and at least one other selection
- immediately engages the reader with an interesting observation, quotation, or detail from one of the selections
- organizes central ideas in a logically structured body that develops the controlling idea
- includes relevant textual evidence to illustrate central ideas
- uses transitions to create a cohesion between sections of the text and among ideas
- has a concluding section that follows logically from the body

> **PLAN**

Analyze the Texts Review *Hamlet* and one other text in this collection. Pay attention to the cause-effect relationships between violence and fate in each text.

myNotebook

Use the annotation tools in your eBook to find evidence to support your analysis. Save each piece of evidence to your notebook.

- Make notes about specific acts of violence mentioned in *Hamlet* and one other text in this collection.
- Consider how violence affects the characters' or people's ability to control their fates.
- Compare and contrast Shakespeare's portrayal of violence in *Hamlet* with that of one other writer. Note similarities and differences in the two writers' views about violence's effect on the ability to control one's fate.
- List details, examples, and quotations that support your conclusions.

WRITE AN ANALYTICAL ESSAY

COMMON CORE W 2a–7, W 4, W 5, W 9a–b

Introduce students to the Performance Task by reading the introductory paragraph with them and reviewing the criteria for an effective analytical essay. Point out that they can use the question in the prompt—*How does violence affect people's ability to control their fates?*—to focus their work. Suggest that they write it down and keep it prominently displayed as they develop their essays.

PLAN

ANALYZE THE TEXTS

View It!

Professional Development Podcast:

Performance Task

As students review the collection texts and decide which selection to feature alongside *Hamlet,* tell them to consider which one creates the most interesting pairing with the play. For example, they might choose a text that reaches a different conclusion on the effects of violence, or one that takes a very different path to reach the same conclusion.

PERFORMANCE TASK A

PLAN

GET ORGANIZED

Emphasize that a strong, clear controlling idea is essential to writing a coherent essay. The controlling idea, or thesis statement, should answer the question *How does violence affect people's ability to control their fates?*

PRODUCE

DRAFT YOUR ESSAY

Remind students that this stage of the writing process is about transferring their ideas from outline form into sentences and paragraphs. Encourage them not to get bogged down in trying to write perfect prose; they'll have time to polish their writing later. However, one thing they should be strict about is using quotation marks around text taken directly from the literature. This will help them avoid confusion later.

Get Organized Organize your details and evidence in an outline.

- Write your controlling idea about the causal relationship between violence and fate as portrayed in the texts. This will be the main idea of your essay.

- Search for an interesting quotation or detail from one of the texts to engage readers in your introduction.

- Decide what organizational pattern you will use for your essay. For example, you might present your central ideas about violence point by point, referring to the texts as you develop each point. Or, you could present your central ideas with regard to *Hamlet* first, followed by a discussion of your other chosen text, and then synthesize your ideas about the two texts at the end.

- Use your organizational pattern to arrange into a logical order the textual evidence you have gathered in support of your central ideas.

- Write down some ideas for your conclusion that reflect your own perspective on violence and fate, including textual or personal evidence that supports your ideas.

ACADEMIC VOCABULARY

As you develop your ideas about violence and fate, be sure to use these words.

> drama
> integrity
> mediate
> restrain
> trigger

PRODUCE

Draft Your Essay Write a draft of your essay, following your outline.

- Introduce your controlling idea. Be as explicit and clear as possible so that readers will immediately understand your point of view on the topic. Include and explain the significance of an attention-grabbing detail or quotation from one of the selections.

- Present your details, quotations, and examples from the selections in logically ordered paragraphs. Each paragraph should have a central idea with evidence to support it. Explain how each piece of evidence supports the central idea.

- Use transitions to link sections of the text and to clarify the relationships among your ideas.

- Write a satisfying conclusion that summarizes your analysis and synthesizes your central ideas.

As you draft your analytical essay, remember that this kind of writing requires formal language and a respectful tone. Essays that analyze texts are expected to be appropriate for an academic context.

my **WriteSmart**

Write your rough draft in *my*WriteSmart. Focus on getting your ideas down, rather than on perfecting your choice of language.

REVISE

IMPROVE YOUR DRAFT

Encourage peer reviewers to use the criteria in the chart on page 402 to pinpoint areas in their classmates' drafts that need improvement. Have them read the descriptions in each row of the chart to see which ones best fit each essay. Then they can tell the essay's author which parts need the most revision.

PRESENT

EXCHANGE ESSAYS

Other options for sharing students' essays include
- creating a display in the school library
- hosting another class for a reading of the completed essays, to be followed by an open discussion of the issues raised

REVISE

Improve Your Draft Revise your draft to make sure it is clear, coherent, and engaging. Refer to the chart on the next page to review the characteristics of a well-written analytical essay. Ask yourself these questions as you revise:

my **WriteSmart**

Have your partner or a group of peers review your draft in *my*WriteSmart. Ask your reviewers to note any evidence that does not support the controlling idea.

- Does my introduction present my controlling idea clearly? Will my readers want to continue reading?

- Are the titles and authors of the selections accurately identified in my introduction?

- Do my central ideas develop in a logical order? Are transitions smooth and coherent?

- Have I provided sufficient and relevant textual evidence to support my central ideas?

- Have I maintained a formal style of English appropriate for an analytical essay? Does my choice of words convey a knowledgeable and confident tone, or attitude, toward the topic?

- Have I used precise language and various types of sentence structures? Have I incorporated this collection's five Academic Vocabulary words in my essay?

- Have I provided a satisfying summary of my ideas in the conclusion?

PRESENT

Exchange Essays When your final draft is completed, exchange essays with a partner. Read your partner's essay and provide feedback. Reread the criteria for an effective analytical essay and ask yourself these questions:

- Which aspects of my partner's essay are particularly strong?

- Are any sections of the essay confusing? How could they be clarified?

Publish Online If your school has a website where you can post your writing, work with your classmates to publish your collection of essays online. First, review your own essay and look for places to add links to online sources that readers may find helpful, such as a video clip from a theatrical production or film version of *Hamlet*. Then, as a group, create a front page that introduces the collection and invites readers to explore the individual essays. You might also consider setting up a blog to allow readers to comment on the essays.

PERFORMANCE TASK A

ORGANIZATION

Have students look at the chart to evaluate their level of performance in the Organization category. Ask them to evaluate how well they organized central ideas and supporting evidence and used transitions to show logical connections between ideas. Have students choose one area of the essay that needs improvement and come up with a strategy to do so.

COLLECTION 4 **TASK A**
ANALYTICAL ESSAY

	Ideas and Evidence	Organization	Language
ADVANCED	• An eloquent introduction includes the titles and authors of the selections; the controlling idea presents a unique perspective on the topic as it relates to the texts. • Specific, relevant details support the central ideas. • A satisfying concluding section synthesizes the ideas and summarizes the analysis.	• Central ideas and supporting evidence are organized effectively and logically throughout the essay. • Varied transitions successfully show the relationships between ideas.	• The analysis has an appropriately formal style and a knowledgeable, objective tone. • Language is precise and captures the writer's thoughts with originality. • Sentence beginnings, lengths, and structures vary and have a rhythmic flow. • Spelling, capitalization, and punctuation are correct. • Grammar and usage are correct.
COMPETENT	• The introduction identifies the titles and authors of the selections but could be more engaging; the controlling idea adequately sets up the analysis. • One or two central ideas need more support. • The concluding section synthesizes most of the ideas and summarizes most of the analysis.	• The organization of central ideas and supporting evidence is confusing in a few places. • A few more transitions are needed to clarify the relationships between ideas.	• The style becomes informal in a few places, and the tone does not always communicate confidence. • Most language is precise. • Sentence beginnings, lengths, and structures vary somewhat. • Several spelling, capitalization, and punctuation mistakes occur. • Some grammatical and usage errors are repeated in the essay.
LIMITED	• The introduction identifies the titles and the authors of the selections; the controlling idea only hints at the main idea of the analysis. • Details support some central ideas but are often too general. • The concluding section gives an incomplete summary of the analysis and merely restates the controlling idea.	• Most central ideas are organized logically, but many supporting details are out of place. • More transitions are needed throughout the essay to connect ideas.	• The style is informal in many places, and the tone reflects a superficial understanding of the selections. • Language is repetitive or vague at times. • Sentence structures barely vary, and some fragments or run-on sentences are present. • Spelling, capitalization, and punctuation are often incorrect but do not make reading the essay difficult. • Grammar and usage are incorrect in many places, but the writer's ideas are still clear.
EMERGING	• The appropriate elements of an introduction are missing. • Details and evidence are irrelevant or missing. • The analysis lacks a concluding section.	• A logical organization is not used; ideas are presented randomly. • Transitions are not used, making the essay difficult to understand.	• The style and tone are inappropriate. • Language is inaccurate, repetitive, and vague. • Repetitive sentence structure, fragments, and run-on sentences make the writing monotonous and difficult to follow. • Spelling, capitalization, and punctuation are incorrect throughout. • Many grammatical and usage errors change the meaning of the writer's ideas.

Write an Argument

This collection focuses on revenge and the possibilities for reconciliation. In the anchor text "Blocking the Transmission of Violence," you learned about the violence interrupters' mission to act as mediators and prevent acts of revenge. Do you think revenge is always misguided, or is it justified in some cases? Synthesize your ideas about the anchor text and others in the collection by writing an argument for your position on revenge.

COMMON CORE

W 1a–e Write arguments.
W 4 Produce clear and coherent writing.
W 5 Develop and strengthen writing.
W 9a–b Draw evidence from literary or informational texts.

An effective argument

- states a clear claim on whether revenge is always misguided or whether it is sometimes justified
- develops the claim with valid reasons and relevant evidence from "Blocking the Transmission of Violence" and other texts from the collection
- anticipates counterclaims and addresses them with well-supported counterarguments
- establishes clear, logical relationships among claims, counterclaims, reasons, and evidence
- includes a logically structured body, including transitions
- has a satisfying conclusion that effectively summarizes the claim
- maintains a formal tone through the use of standard English

PLAN

Analyze the Texts Reread "Blocking the Transmission of Violence" and take notes about how revenge is viewed by the CeaseFire organization as well as victims of violence like Torres. Do they believe that revenge is always misguided, or do they think that it is justified in some cases? What reasons do they give? Pay attention to specific details, and gather evidence from the text. Then choose at least one other text from this collection and review it, making notes on the ideas it conveys about revenge and reconciliation.

myNotebook

Use the annotation tools in your eBook to find evidence to support your argument. Save each piece of evidence to your notebook.

WRITE AN ARGUMENT

COMMON CORE W 1a–e, W4, W 5, W 9a–b

Introduce the Performance Task by reading the introductory paragraph with students and reviewing the criteria for an effective argument. Make sure students understand that their claim should express their own viewpoint about revenge, not one of the selection authors'. They will use evidence from the texts to support their own position on the issue, or perhaps to provide a counterclaim that they will refute.

PLAN

ANALYZE THE TEXTS

Suggest that students review any notes they made while reading the selections, as well as their answers to the "Analyzing the Text" questions for each selection. As they review the texts, remind them to stay focused on the question *Is revenge always misguided, or is it justified in some cases?*

Professional Development Podcast:
Performance Task

PLAN

DEVELOP COUNTERARGUMENTS

Point out that students can use the mini-debate to work on the tone of their argument as well as the content. Emphasize that they should treat any counterclaims presented by their partner with seriousness and respect. They should acknowledge the logic behind each counterclaim but also refute it convincingly with strong reasons and evidence.

Make a Claim Based on the ideas conveyed in the anchor text and your other chosen text(s), write a claim that clearly and concisely states your position on revenge. Remember that you will have to provide sufficient evidence from the texts to convince your audience of your position.

Build Your Argument Create a graphic organizer that clearly outlines the reasons and evidence that support your claim.

- Begin with your claim stating your position on revenge.
- Outline several reasons that support your claim.
- Provide textual evidence including details, examples, and quotations to support each reason.

Develop Counterarguments In an argument you will also need to anticipate counterclaims, or claims that oppose your own, and develop counterarguments to refute them. Having a mini-debate with a partner can help you address opposing claims and develop your counterarguments.

- Make note of potential counterclaims. Add these notes to your graphic organizer, along with your counterarguments.
- Use your graphic organizer to present your position to your partner. State your claim and give two or three reasons to support your claim.
- Allow your partner to respond with an additional counterclaim. Listen carefully to your partner, and be prepared to modify your argument to respond to new ideas.
- Make a concluding statement that summarizes your argument.

When you are finished, discuss the debate with your partner. Ask your partner for feedback on how you can improve your argument. Talk about the reasoning and evidence used to support your claim. Take notes about your partner's counterclaims and how you can best refute them.

Get Organized Organize your ideas in an outline. Be sure to integrate any new information gathered from your mini-debate. Do you have sufficient reasons and evidence to support your claim? Can you effectively anticipate counterclaims? Are you able to respond with strong counterarguments?

ACADEMIC VOCABULARY

As you build your argument about revenge, be sure to use these words.

drama
integrity
mediate
restrain
trigger

Draft Your Essay
Write a draft of your essay, following your outline.

- Introduce your claim in a memorable way that will grab the attention of your readers.
- Present your reasons and evidence in logically ordered paragraphs.
- Explain how the evidence from the texts supports your ideas about revenge.
- Acknowledge counterclaims and defend your own claim with counterarguments.
- Include transitions to connect your reasons and evidence to your claim.
- Use formal language and a respectful tone appropriate for an academic context.
- Write a conclusion that summarizes your position.

*my*WriteSmart

Write your rough draft in *my*WriteSmart. Focus on getting your ideas down, rather than on perfecting your choice of language.

Improve Your Draft
Refer to the chart on the following page to review the characteristics of an effective argument. Ask yourself these questions as you revise:

- Does my introduction sound strong, confident, and persuasive?
- Have I provided sound reasoning and enough evidence to support my claim and defend it against counterclaims?
- Is my essay cohesive? Do I need additional transitions to make connections clear?
- Have I used a formal style of English and an objective tone?
- Does my conclusion follow logically from the body of my essay and provide an effective summary of my argument?

*my*WriteSmart

Have your partner or a group of peers review your draft in *my*WriteSmart. Ask your reviewers to note any reasons that do not support the claim or that lack sufficient evidence.

Exchange Essays
When your final draft is completed, exchange essays with a new partner. Read your partner's essay and provide feedback. Be sure to point out aspects of the essay that are particularly strong, as well as areas that could be improved.

PERFORMANCE TASK B

PRODUCE

DRAFT YOUR ESSAY

Remind students that the purpose of an argument is to persuade. As they write, they should imagine that they are speaking directly to their audience and trying to convince readers to accept their position on revenge. Emphasize that the drafting stage is a time to let their ideas flow; they will focus on revising the details of their writing later.

REVISE

IMPROVE YOUR DRAFT

Suggest that students read their drafts aloud to a partner. The partner should point out places where ideas are confusing or where the relevance of certain evidence is unclear.

PRESENT

EXCHANGE ESSAYS

Students may use their essays as the basis for a class discussion or debate on the topic of revenge. Invite each student to state his or her claim, supporting it with one strong reason and a piece of text evidence. Then open the floor to debate, allowing students to share more of their reasons and evidence as the discussion unfolds. Track different claims, along with accompanying reasons and evidence, on the board as the discussion progresses.

PERFORMANCE TASK B

IDEAS AND EVIDENCE

Have students look at the chart to evaluate their level of performance in the Ideas and Evidence category. Have them assess how well they anticipated and responded to counterclaims. Have students list any counterclaims they might have overlooked and come up with a few sentences to refute each one.

COLLECTION 4 TASK B
ARGUMENT

	Ideas and Evidence	Organization	Language
ADVANCED	• The introduction is memorable and persuasive; the claim clearly states a position on a substantive topic. • Valid reasons and relevant evidence from the texts convincingly support the writer's claim. • Counterclaims are anticipated and effectively addressed with counterarguments. • The concluding section effectively summarizes the claim.	• The reasons and textual evidence are organized consistently and logically throughout the argument. • Varied transitions logically connect reasons and textual evidence to the writer's claim.	• The writing reflects a formal style and an objective, or controlled, tone. • Sentence beginnings, lengths, and structures vary and have a rhythmic flow. • Spelling, capitalization, and punctuation are correct. • Grammar and usage are correct.
COMPETENT	• The introduction could do more to capture the reader's attention; the claim states a position on an issue. • Most reasons and evidence from the texts support the writer's claim, but they could be more convincing. • Counterclaims are anticipated, but the counterarguments need to be developed more. • The concluding section restates the claim.	• The organization of reasons and textual evidence is confusing in a few places. • A few more transitions are needed to connect reasons and textual evidence to the writer's claim.	• The style is informal in a few places, and the tone is defensive at times. • Sentence beginnings, lengths, and structures vary somewhat. • Several spelling and capitalization mistakes occur, and punctuation is inconsistent. • Some grammatical and usage errors are repeated in the argument.
LIMITED	• The introduction is ordinary; the claim identifies an issue, but the writer's position is not clearly stated. • The reasons and evidence from the texts are not always logical or relevant. • Counterclaims are anticipated but not addressed logically. • The concluding section includes an incomplete summary of the claim.	• The organization of reasons and textual evidence is logical in some places, but it often doesn't follow a pattern. • Many more transitions are needed to connect reasons and textual evidence to the writer's position.	• The style becomes informal in many places, and the tone is often dismissive of other viewpoints. • Sentence structures barely vary, and some fragments or run-on sentences are present. • Spelling, capitalization, and punctuation are often incorrect but do not make reading the argument difficult. • Grammar and usage are incorrect in many places, but the writer's ideas are still clear.
EMERGING	• The introduction is missing. • Significant supporting reasons and evidence from the texts are missing. • Counterclaims are neither anticipated nor addressed. • The concluding section is missing.	• An organizational strategy is not used; reasons and textual evidence are presented randomly. • Transitions are not used, making the argument difficult to understand.	• The style is inappropriate, and the tone is disrespectful. • Repetitive sentence structure, fragments, and run-on sentences make the writing monotonous and hard to follow. • Spelling and capitalization are often incorrect, and punctuation is missing. • Many grammatical and usage errors change the meaning of the writer's ideas.

Image Credits: ©Christoph Jorda/Corbis

Taking Risks

"It is only by risking our persons from one hour to another that we live at all."

CONNECTING WORD AND IMAGE

ASK STUDENTS to discuss how the collection opener image and the collection quotation work together to create a connection.

PERFORMANCE TASK PREVIEW

Point out to students that they will complete a performance task at the end of the collection. The performance task will require them to further analyze the selections in the collection and to synthesize ideas about these analyses. They will present their findings in a variety of products.

ACADEMIC VOCABULARY

View It!

Professional Development Podcast:

Academic Vocabulary

Students can acquire facility with the academic vocabulary words through frequent, repeated exposure as they analyze and discuss the selections in the collection. Academic vocabulary can be used in the following instructional contexts. This will enable students to incorporate the academic vocabulary words into their working vocabulary.

- Collaborative Discussion at the end of each selection
- Analyzing the Text questions for each selection
- Selection-level Performance Task
- Vocabulary instruction (for Critical Vocabulary and/or for Vocabulary Strategy)
- Language and Style
- End-of-collection Performance Task for all selections in the collection

ASK STUDENTS to review the Academic Vocabulary word list for this collection. You may wish to pronounce each word aloud, so students hear the correct pronunciation. Then discuss the definitions and the related forms for each word. Remind students that they will encounter these five academic vocabulary words throughout the collection.

Taking Risks

From mythical heroes to contemporary scientists, the individuals shown in this collection face the choice of taking a big risk.

hmhfyi.com

COLLECTION

PERFORMANCE TASK Preview

At the end of this collection, you will have the opportunity to complete a task:

- Present a speech on the importance of taking risks in life, citing examples from texts in the collection.

ACADEMIC VOCABULARY

Study the words and their definitions in the chart below. You will use these words as you discuss and write about the texts in this collection.

Word	Definition	Related Forms
assurance (ə-shŏŏr´əns) *n.*	a guarantee or pledge	assure, assured
collapse (kə-lăps´) *v.*	to break down or fall apart suddenly and cease to function	collapsed, collapsible
conceive (kən-sēv´) *v.*	to understand or form in the mind; to devise	conceivable, conceivably
devote (dĭ-vōt´) *v.*	to give one's entire energy or attention to something or someone	devoted, devotee, devotion
vision (vĭzh´ən) *n.*	ability to see; insight	visionary

USING COLLECTIONS YOUR WAY

Use the following information, along with the charts on the following pages, to help you decide how you want to introduce the collection. Based on your teaching style, your students' interests, or your instructional goals, you may want to structure this collection in various ways. You may choose different entry points each time you teach the collection.

"I love teaching traditional literature."

This epic poem stems from the great oral tradition in England. The tale draws readers into the world of the hero Beowulf, his battle against the monster Grendel, and his triumphant success.

Beowulf

Epic Poem by The Beowulf Poet   translated by Burton Raffel

Background The epic poem Beowulf grew from a rich oral tradition. In large wooden halls similar to the one described in the poem, poet-singers entertained groups of Anglo-Saxon warriors with tales celebrating great heroes. Sometime between the seventh and ninth centuries, a poet unified the accounts of the hero Beowulf, composing the Anglo-Saxon epic that survives today.

The Angles and the Saxons, as well as other Germanic tribes, came to England from northern Europe starting in the mid-fifth century. Their culture became the basis for English culture, and their languages fused into Old English, the Anglo-Saxon language. They struggled to survive the challenges of nature and frequent wars against new invaders. Anglo-Saxons lived communally for protection; devoted to their lord, they reserved their greatest loyalty for him and their kin. They believed in wyrd, or fate, rather than in an afterlife, but they hoped that acquiring fame and treasure through acts of valor would give them a kind of immortality. For this reason, poets were highly valued: their poems passed down the history of the Anglo-Saxons, taught their values, and ensured that great warriors would be remembered even after their society collapsed.

By the time the epic Beowulf was written down by a monk in the beginning of the eleventh century, the Anglo-Saxons had converted to Christianity. Thus, in the final version of the poem, Christian references are mingled with the original pagan beliefs. The poem is translated here from Old English; the characteristics of oral poetry remain, however, helping readers to hear the splendor of the epic.

AS YOU READ Pay attention to how the poet sustains suspense during each of Beowulf's battles. Write down any questions you generate during reading.

Beowulf **409**

Background The Challenger shuttle explosion marked the nation's first tragedy during a flight to space. The disaster, which occurred on January 28, 1986, killed the entire crew just moments after takeoff, including Christa McAuliffe, a high-school teacher who had been selected to pioneer NASA's Teacher in Space program. On the morning of the launch, students in schools across the country gathered to watch the event on live television. That evening, President Ronald Reagan addressed the nation.

Explosion of the Space Shuttle Challenger:
Address to the Nation

Speech by Ronald Reagan

AS YOU READ Pay attention to Reagan's comments about the Challenger crew. Write down questions you generate during reading.

Ladies and gentlemen, I'd planned to speak to you tonight to report on the state of the Union, but the events of earlier today have led me to change those plans. Today is a day for mourning and remembering. Nancy and I are pained to the core by the tragedy of the shuttle Challenger. We know we share this pain with all of the people of our country. This is truly a national loss.

Nineteen years ago, almost to the day, we lost three astronauts in a terrible accident on the ground.[1] But we've never lost an astronaut in flight; we've never had a tragedy like this. And perhaps we've forgotten the courage it took for the crew of the shuttle; but they, the Challenger Seven, were aware of the dangers, but overcame them and did their jobs brilliantly. We mourn seven heroes: Michael Smith, Dick Scobee, Judith Resnik, Ronald McNair, Ellison Onizuka, Gregory Jarvis, and Christa McAuliffe. We mourn their loss as a nation together.

For the families of the seven, we cannot bear, as you do, the full impact of this tragedy. But we feel the loss, and we're thinking

[1] **Nineteen years . . . ground:** In 1967, the crew of Apollo 1 died when a fire broke out while it was on the launch pad.

Explosion of the Space Shuttle Challenger **429**

"I like to connect literature to history."

The explosion of the *Challenger* in January of 1986 shook the nation, in particular because teacher Christa McAuliffe was on board. **President Ronald Reagan** addressed the nation in this speech on the day of the disaster.

Anthony Doerr has won many awards for his short stories, including four O. Henry prizes and Britain's Sunday Times EFG Short Story Award for "The Deep." In an interview with the journal Fugue, he explained that it is vital not to become used to life's wonder but to keep trying to see what is special about the world. He also described his desire to shake up structure and language so that readers are struck anew by some element in life or nature. He currently lives in Boise, Idaho, and writes for the Boston Globe and the New York Times when not at work on his fiction.

The Deep

Short Story by Anthony Doerr

AS YOU READ Pay attention to details the author adds to develop Tom's character throughout the story. Write down any questions you generate during reading.

Tom is born in 1914 in Detroit, a quarter mile from International Salt. His father is offstage, unaccounted for. His mother operates a six-room, underinsulated boardinghouse populated with locked doors, behind which drowse the grim possessions of itinerant salt workers: coats the color of mice, tattered mucking boots, aquatints[1] of undressed women, their breasts faded orange. Every six months a miner is fired or drafted or dies and is replaced by another, so that very early in his life Tom comes to see how the world continually drains itself of young men, leaving behind only objects—empty tobacco pouches, bladeless jack-knives, salt-caked trousers—mute, incapable of memory.

Tom is four when he starts fainting. He'll be rounding a corner, breathing hard, and the lights will go out. Mother will carry him indoors, set him on the armchair, and send someone for the doctor.

itinerant (ī-tĭn´ər-ənt) adj. migrant, or travelling from site to site.

[1] **aquatints:** prints that resemble watercolor paintings.

The Deep **433**

"I stress the importance of language and style."

In this short story, author **Anthony Doerr** creates a carefully structured text with expressive language to explore the idea that a life can be beautiful, even if that life is constrained by ill health and circumstance.

| *my*SmartPlanner | eBook | *my*Notebook | *my* WriteSmart | fyi hmhfyi.com |

Collection 5 Lessons	Media	Teach and Practice
Student Edition | eBook	▶ Video Links HISTORY A&E	**Close Reading and Evidence Tracking**

Close Reading and Evidence Tracking

Collection 5 Lessons	Media	Close Read Screencasts	Strategies for Annotation
ANCHOR TEXT — **Epic Poem by The Beowulf Poet, translated by Burton Raffel from** *Beowulf*	▶ **Video HISTORY** *The Battle of Beowulf and Grendl* ◀ **Audio** from *Beowulf*	**Close Read Screencasts** • Modeled Discussion 1 (lines 15–29) • Modeled Discussion 2 (lines 191–206) • Close Read application pdf (lines 531–544)	**Strategies for Annotation** • Analyze Language • Analyze Language: Old English Poetry
CLOSE READER — **Epic Poem by The Beowulf Poet, translated by Burton Raffel from** *Beowulf*	◀ **Audio** from *Beowulf*		
Speech by Ronald Reagan Explosion of the Space Shuttle *Challenger*: **Address to the Nation**	▶ **Video HISTORY** *America The Story of Us: The* Challenger *and the End of the Space Race* ◀ **Audio** Explosion of the Space Shuttle *Challenger*: Address to the Nation		**Strategies for Annotation** • Delineate and Evaluate an Argument
Short Story by Anthony Doerr "The Deep"	◀ **Audio** "The Deep"		**Strategies for Annotation** • Determine Themes • Analyze Story Elements: Setting • Language and Style: Tone
CLOSE READER — **Short Story by Mark Braizitis "Blackheart"**	◀ **Audio** "Blackheart"		
Science Article by Michael Specter "The Mosquito Solution"	◀ **Audio** "The Mosquito Solution"		**Strategies for Annotation** • Summarize the Text • Scientific Terms
CLOSE READER — **Science Writing by Paloma Reyes "Are Genetically Modified Foods Scary?"**	◀ **Audio** "Are Genetically Modified Foods Scary?"		
Collection 5 Performance Task: Present a Speech	fyi hmhfyi.com **hmhfyi.com**	**Interactive Lessons** **A** Writing as a Process **A** Using Textual Evidence **A** Giving a Presentation	

For Systematic Coverage of Writing and Speaking & Listening Standards	Interactive Lessons Writing a Narrative Producing and Publishing with Technology	Lesson Assessments Writing a Narrative Producing and Publishing with Technology

Assess		Extend	Reteach
Performance Task	**Online Assessment**	**Teacher eBook**	**Teacher eBook**
Writing Activity: Comparison	Selection Test	**Analyze Story Elements: Setting >** **Interactive Lessons >** Role of Setting	**Analyze Story Elements:** **Characteristics of an Epic > Level Up** **Tutorial >** Universal and Recurring Themes
Speaking Activity: Discussion	Selection Test	**Determine Connotative Meanings >** **Interactive Lessons >** Denotative and Connotative Meanings	**Delineate and Evaluate an Argument >** **Level Up Tutorial >** Evidence
Speaking Activity: Discussion	Selection Test	**Determine Figurative Meanings**	**Analyze Story Elements: Setting > Level Up** **Tutorial >** Setting: Effect on Plot
Writing Activity: Argument	Selection Test	**Interactive Whiteboard Lessons >** Analyze and Evaluate Structure	**Summarizing the Text > Level Up Tutorial >** Summarizing
Present a Speech	Collection Test		

Collection 5 Lessons	Key Learning Objective	Performance Task
ANCHOR TEXT **Epic Poem by The Beowulf Poet, translated by Burton Raffel from *Beowulf,* p. 409A**	**The student will be able to…** analyze characteristics of epic and oral poetry	Writing Activity: Comparison
Speech by Ronald Reagan **Lexile 780L** **"Explosion of the Space Shuttle *Challenger:* Address to the Nation," p. 429A**	**The student will be able to…** determine the author's purpose and delineate and evaluate an argument	Speaking Activity: Discussion
Short Story by Anthony Doerr **Lexile 860L** **"The Deep" p. 433A**	**The student will be able to…** determine themes in a story and analyze the role of setting	Speaking Activity: Discussion
Science Article by Michael Specter **Lexile 1130L** **"The Mosquito Solution" p. 453A**	**The student will be able to…** support inferences and draw conclusions from a scientific article	Writing Activity: Argument

Collection 5 Performance Task:
A Present a Speech

Vocabulary Strategy	Language and Style	Student Instructional Support	CLOSE READER Selection
Homophones	Mood	**Scaffolding for ELL Students:** • Vocabulary: Multiple-Meaning Words • Language: Sentence Structure • Language: Punctuation Cues • Language: Alliteration • Language: Verb Tense • Language: Homophones **When Students Struggle:** • Compare and Contrast • Cause and Effect • Story Structure • Read with Expression **To Challenge Students:** Research the Sutton Hoo Excavations • Discuss Characterization • Analyze Symbolism	Epic Poem by The Beowulf Poet, translated by Burton Raffel from *Beowulf,* p. 428b
		Scaffolding for ELL Students: • Vocabulary: Roots	
Analyze Nuance in Word Meanings	Tone	**Scaffolding for ELL Students:** • Language: Verb Tenses • Language: Conversational English Patterns • Vocabulary: Phrasal Verbs • Vocabulary: Cognates • Comprehension Support **When Students Struggle:** • Sequence • Fluent Reading • Key Ideas and Events **To Challenge Students:** • Analyze References to Time • Analyze the Story's Ending	Short Story by Mark Braizitis "Blackheart," p. 452b **Lexile 1420L**
Scientific Terms		**Scaffolding for ELL Students:** • Analyze Language • Analyze Cause and Effect • Analyze Phrasal Verbs • Analyze Language • Language: Pronoun Referents **When Students Struggle:** • Summarizing • Compare and Contrast • Context Clues • Drawing Conclusions **To Challenge Students:** • Examine Figurative Language • Evaluate an Argument	Science Writing by Paloma Reyes "Are Genetically Modified Foods Scary?" p. 470b **Lexile 1420L**

Beowulf

*my*SmartPlanner   Create lesson plans and access resources online.

Epic Poem by The Beowulf Poet   Translated by Burton Raffel

Why This Text?

Beowulf is a cornerstone of English literature, sweeping readers into the raw heroism of the Anglo-Saxon age. In this lesson, students explore the elements that distinguish the epic genre and make *Beowulf* a tale to tell aloud.

Key Learning Objective: The student will be able to analyze characteristics of an epic and oral poetry.

For practice and application:

Close Reader selection
from "Beowulf"
Epic Poem by The Beowulf Poet

COMMON CORE   Common Core Standards

RL 1 Cite textual evidence.
RL 2 Determine two or more themes.
RL 3 Analyze the impact of the author's choice of how to relate elements of a story.
RL 4 Determine the meaning of words and phrases as they are used in a text.
W 2 Write informative/explanatory texts.
L 3 Apply knowledge of language to understand how language functions in different contexts.
L 4a Use context as a clue to the meaning of a word or phrase.

▲ Text Complexity Rubric

Quantitative Measures	**Beowulf** Lexile: N/A
Qualitative Measures	**Levels of Meaning/Purpose** multiple levels of meaning (multiple themes)
	Structure complex structures, such as sonnets, villanelles, etc.
	Language Conventionality and Clarity complex and varied sentence structure
	Knowledge Demands increased amount of cultural and literary knowledge useful
Reader/Task Considerations	Teacher determined Vary by individual reader and type of text

CLOSE READ

For more context and historical background, students can view the video "The Battle of Beowulf and Grendl" in their eBooks.

Background Have students read the background on *Beowulf*. Then explain that although the poem was composed in England during the Anglo-Saxon age, it is set in sixth-century Scandinavia. Tell students that Beowulf, the hero of the epic, is a Geat, a person from what is now Sweden. He travels to Denmark to help the Danes, who are being terrorized by the monster Grendel. Then, having won fame, he returns home and becomes the king of the Geats, succeeding his uncle.

Explain that there is only one historical copy of *Beowulf* in existence. Scholars believe that it dates from the eleventh century. Several individual owners, in turn, had the manuscript in their collections; in 1702, it was given to the nation of Great Britain. Although a fire broke out in 1731 where the manuscript was being stored, it escaped relatively unscathed, but time and handling led to its deterioration. To preserve it, it was placed in frames in 1845. The manuscript now is part of the British Library's collection.

AS YOU READ Direct students to use the As You Read note to focus their reading.

Beowulf

Epic Poem by The Beowulf Poet   translated by Burton Raffel

Background *The epic poem* Beowulf *grew from a rich oral tradition. In large wooden halls similar to the one described in the poem, poet-singers entertained groups of Anglo-Saxon warriors with tales celebrating great heroes. Sometime between the seventh and ninth centuries, a poet unified the accounts of the hero Beowulf, composing the Anglo-Saxon epic that survives today.*

The Angles and the Saxons, as well as other Germanic tribes, came to England from northern Europe starting in the mid-fifth century. Their culture became the basis for English culture, and their languages fused into Old English, the Anglo-Saxon language. They struggled to survive the challenges of nature and frequent wars against new invaders. Anglo-Saxons lived communally for protection; devoted to their lord, they reserved their greatest loyalty for him and their kin. They believed in wyrd, *or fate, rather than in an afterlife, but they hoped that acquiring fame and treasure through acts of valor would give them a kind of immortality. For this reason, poets were highly valued: their poems passed down the history of the Anglo-Saxons, taught their values, and ensured that great warriors would be remembered even after their society collapsed.*

By the time the epic Beowulf *was written down by a monk in the beginning of the eleventh century, the Anglo-Saxons had converted to Christianity. Thus, in the final version of the poem, Christian references are mingled with the original pagan beliefs. The poem is translated here from Old English; the characteristics of oral poetry remain, however, helping readers to hear the splendor of the epic.*

AS YOU READ Pay attention to how the poet sustains suspense during each of Beowulf's battles. Write down any questions you generate during reading.

Close Read Screencasts   **View It!**

Modeled Discussions

Have students click the *Close Read* icons in their eBooks to access two screencasts in which readers discuss and annotate the following key passages:

- the introduction of the conflict (lines 15–29)
- the explanation of the connection between the Geats and Danes (lines 191–206)

As a class, view and discuss at least one of these videos. Then have students pair up to do an independent close read of an additional passage—Beowulf's final victory (lines 531–544).

Analyze Characteristics of an Epic (LINES 1–29)

COMMON CORE RL 1, RL 3

Point out that the setting, conflict, and characters are introduced near the beginning of the epic. As students read the first lines, have them note what they learn about these elements, directly and indirectly.

 CITE TEXT EVIDENCE Have students explain the contrast that is developed between Herot, home of the Danes, and Grendel's home. Ask them how the Biblical allusions extend this contrast. *(Grendel lives in darkness and in pain. He is associated with Cain, the first murderer. Herot is filled with music celebrating light, life, and joy. It is associated with the story of creation.)* Have students discuss what the hall and Grendel represent, based on their descriptions here. *(Herot represents life, light, peace, community, and goodness. Grendel represents the power of evil, darkness, and destruction.)* What conflict is foreshadowed through this contrast? *(Grendel will try to destroy the hall and what it represents.)*

Analyze Old English Poetry (LINES 33–37)

COMMON CORE RL 1, RL 4

Explain to students that one of the devices used in the oral tradition is **alliteration,** the repetition of the initial consonant sound in a line of poetry.

B **CITE TEXT EVIDENCE** Ask students to reread lines 33–37. What sound is alliterated throughout these lines? How does this sound create an image of the action? *(The s sound is alliterated in "sprawled in sleep, suspecting" and "slipped," "silence," "snatched," "smashed." The repetition of this soft sound emphasizes the unexpectedness of the attack and Grendel's ability to carry it out sneakily and in silence.)*

GRENDEL

Hrothgar (hrôth´gär´), *king of the Danes, has built a wonderful mead hall called Herot* (hĕr´ət), *where his subjects congregate and make merry. As this selection opens, a fierce and powerful monster named Grendel prepares to invade the mead hall.*

      A powerful monster, living down
In the darkness, growled in pain, impatient
As day after day the music rang
Loud in that hall, the harp's rejoicing
5 Call and the poet's clear songs, sung
Of the ancient beginnings of us all, recalling
The Almighty making the earth, shaping
These beautiful plains marked off by oceans,
Then proudly setting the sun and moon
10 To glow across the land and light it;
The corners of the earth were made lovely with trees
And leaves, made quick with life, with each
Of the nations who now move on its face. And then
As now warriors sang of their pleasure:
15 So Hrothgar's men lived happy in his hall
Till the monster stirred, that demon, that fiend,
Grendel, who haunted the moors, the wild
Marshes, and made his home in a hell
Not hell but earth. He was spawned in that slime,
20 Conceived by a pair of those monsters born
Of Cain, murderous creatures banished
By God, punished forever for the crime
Of Abel's death. The Almighty drove
Those demons out, and their exile was bitter,
25 Shut away from men; they split
Into a thousand forms of evil—spirits
And fiends, goblins, monsters, giants,
A brood forever opposing the Lord's
Will, and again and again defeated.

30   Then, when darkness had dropped, Grendel
Went up to Herot, wondering what the warriors
Would do in that hall when their drinking was done.
He found them sprawled in sleep, suspecting
Nothing, their dreams undisturbed. The monster's
35 Thoughts were as quick as his greed or his claws:
He slipped through the door and there in the silence
Snatched up thirty men, smashed them
Unknowing in their beds and ran out with their bodies,

17 moors (mŏŏrz): broad, open regions with patches of bog.

19 spawned: given birth to.

21 Cain: the eldest son of Adam and Eve. According to the Bible (Genesis 4), he murdered his younger brother, Abel.

WHEN STUDENTS STRUGGLE . . .

To help students understand the significance of this first stanza, draw a two-column chart with the headings "Grendel" and "Herot."

- Read aloud lines 1–2, 16–23. Ask students what they learn about Grendel. Encourage them to use phrases from the text. Write their responses in the appropriate column on the chart.

- Repeat the process for "Herot," reading aloud lines that specifically describe it. Write the words and phrases that students volunteer on the board.

ASK STUDENTS what idea is brought out by the words and phrases under each heading. *(Possible answer: Herot is a place of happiness, light, and goodness. Grendel is evil and dark.)* Explain that in the poem, those are the qualities that each represents or stands for.

The blood dripping behind him, back
40 To his lair, delighted with his night's slaughter.
    At daybreak, with the sun's first light, they saw
How well he had worked, and in that gray morning
Broke their long feast with tears and laments
For the dead. Hrothgar, their lord, sat joyless
45 In Herot, a mighty prince mourning
The fate of his lost friends and companions,
Knowing by its tracks that some demon had torn
His followers apart. He wept, fearing
The beginning might not be the end. And that night
50 Grendel came again, so set
On murder that no crime could ever be enough,
No savage assault quench his lust
For evil. Then each warrior tried
To escape him, searched for rest in different
55 Beds, as far from Herot as they could find,
Seeing how Grendel hunted when they slept.
Distance was safety; the only survivors
Were those who fled him. Hate had triumphed.
    So Grendel ruled, fought with the righteous,
60 One against many, and won; so Herot
Stood empty, and stayed deserted for years,
Twelve winters of grief for Hrothgar, king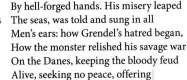
Of the Danes, sorrow heaped at his door
By hell-forged hands. His misery leaped
65 The seas, was told and sung in all
Men's ears: how Grendel's hatred began,
How the monster relished his savage war
On the Danes, keeping the bloody feud
Alive, seeking no peace, offering
70 No truce, accepting no settlement, no price
In gold or land, and paying the living
For one crime only with another. No one
Waited for reparation from his plundering claws:
That shadow of death hunted in the darkness,
75 Stalked Hrothgar's warriors, old
And young, lying in waiting, hidden
In mist, invisibly following them from the edge
Of the marsh, always there, unseen.
    So mankind's enemy continued his crimes,
80 Killing as often as he could, coming
Alone, bloodthirsty and horrible. Though he lived
In Herot, when the night hid him, he never
Dared to touch king Hrothgar's glorious
Throne, protected by God—God,
85 Whose love Grendel could not know. But Hrothgar's

73 reparation: something done to make amends for loss or suffering. In Germanic society, someone who killed another person was generally expected to make a payment to the victim's family as a way of restoring peace.

84 The reference to God shows the influence of Christianity on the Beowulf Poet.

Beowulf **411**

TEACH

CLOSE READ

Analyze Characteristics of an Epic (LINES 41–73 and 61–69)
COMMON CORE RL 1, RL 3

Tell students that community lay at the heart of Anglo-Saxon society. Have them note the effect of Grendel's actions on both Hrothgar, the Danes' leader, and on their hall.

C CITE TEXT EVIDENCE Have students identify the tone of lines 44–49. What details and words help to convey the attitude of the poet? *(The tone is somber and fearful. This is communicated through the words that indicate sorrow, such as "joyless," "a mighty prince mourning," and "wept" and the line that expresses Hrothgar's fear that "the beginning might not be the end.")* Have students discuss what happens to Hrothgar's hall. Why does the poet say "hate had triumphed"? *(The unity of the Danes is shattered since the only safety is in fleeing. Evil has undermined the bonds of community by entering into their hall.)*

Explain that, as in any good story, the poet grips the attention of the listeners by developing the conflict and the suspense.

D CITE TEXT EVIDENCE Ask students to identify the details that add to their understanding of the threat that Grendel poses. *(Grendel terrorizes the hall for twelve years. Hrothgar's misery becomes known far and wide. It "leaped the seas.")* Ask students what Grendel's unwillingness to accept gold or land to settle the feud means for the Danes. *(It suggests that there is no way to end this conflict.)*

Analyze Old English Poetry (LINES 74–78)
COMMON CORE RL 4

Tell students that another characteristic of oral poetry is the use of kennings. **Kennings** are compound words or phrases used to both name and describe an object or person or place.

E ASK STUDENTS to explain what the kenning "shadow of death" contributes to the characterization of Grendel. *(He is hard to see and harder to battle. Like the death that he brings, he is always present, a threat that awaits them every night.)*

Beowulf **411**

SCAFFOLDING FOR ELL STUDENTS

Vocabulary: Multiple-Meaning Words Remind students that many English words have multiple meanings, depending upon the context in which they appear. Point out the word "stirred" in line 16 on page 410. Explain that although it can mean "mixed with a circular motion," in this context, it means "became active."

ASK STUDENTS to work in pairs to look up each of the following words in a dictionary to determine the meaning that best fits the context of the poem: *back* (line 39), *broke* (line 43), *set* (line 50), *rest* (line 54). After reviewing their definitions, ask volunteers to identify any other words from pages 410–411 that they don't know. Working as a group, use context clues to define them.

CLOSE READ

Analyze Characteristics of an Epic (LINES 109–124; 116–129)

COMMON CORE RL 1, RL 3

Explain that the central character of an epic is a hero, a character who epitomizes the heroic ideal of a society. The hero incorporates the traits most admired by the culture.

F CITE TEXT EVIDENCE Have students identify details that tell them about Beowulf. What conclusions about the traits most valued by the Anglo-Saxons can be drawn from this description? *(He is "greater/And stronger than anyone anywhere else in this world." He is also loved by the Geats and quick to take action to help someone else. These details show that Anglo-Saxons prized courage, physical strength, and selflessness.)*

Remind students that the Anglo-Saxons believed that fate controlled one's life. Explain that the manner in which a warrior responded to his fate, however, determined how he was remembered.

G ASK STUDENTS why "none of the wise ones regretted his going." *(Beowulf's community understands that because he is a hero, it is his duty to fight evil and help others. By doing so, he will acquire fame and immortality.)*

CRITICAL VOCABULARY

affliction: Grendel's constant attacks on the Danes cause them great suffering.

ASK STUDENTS how the Danes try to end their affliction. *(They turn back to the "old stone gods" making "heathen vows" in the hope of enlisting the devil's help to fight the evil of Grendel.)*

Heart was bent. The best and most noble
Of his council debated remedies, sat
In secret sessions, talking of terror
And wondering what the bravest of warriors could do.
90   And sometimes they sacrificed to the old stone gods,
Made heathen vows, hoping for Hell's
Support, the Devil's guidance in driving
Their **affliction** off. That was their way,
And the heathen's only hope, Hell
95   Always in their hearts, knowing neither God
Nor His passing as He walks through our world, the Lord
Of Heaven and earth; their ears could not hear
His praise nor know His glory. Let them
Beware, those who are thrust into danger,
100 Clutched at by trouble, yet can carry no solace
In their hearts, cannot hope to be better! Hail
To those who will rise to God, drop off
Their dead bodies and seek our Father's peace!

BEOWULF

So the living sorrow of Healfdane's son
105 Simmered, bitter and fresh, and no wisdom
Or strength could break it: that agony hung
On king and people alike, harsh
And unending, violent and cruel, and evil.
In his far-off home Beowulf, Higlac's
110 Follower and the strongest of the Geats—greater
And stronger than anyone anywhere in this world—
Heard how Grendel filled nights with horror
And quickly commanded a boat fitted out,
Proclaiming that he'd go to that famous king,
115 Would sail across the sea to Hrothgar,
Now when help was needed. None
Of the wise ones regretted his going, much
As he was loved by the Geats: the omens were good,
And they urged the adventure on. So Beowulf
120 Chose the mightiest men he could find,
The bravest and best of the Geats, fourteen
In all, and led them down to their boat;
He knew the sea, would point the prow
Straight to that distant Danish shore. . . .

*Beowulf and his men sail over the sea to the land of the Danes to offer
help to Hrothgar. They are escorted by a Danish guard to Herot, where
Wulfgar, one of Hrothgar's soldiers, tells the king of their arrival.
Hrothgar is ready to welcome the young prince and his men.*

91 heathen (hē´thən): pagan; non-Christian. Though the Beowulf Poet was a Christian, he recognized that the characters in the poem lived before the Germanic tribes were converted to Christianity, when they still worshiped "the old stone gods."

affliction (ə-flĭk´shən) *n.* something that causes suffering or pain.

104 Healfdane's son: Hrothgar.

109–110 Higlac's follower: a warrior loyal to Higlac (hĭg´lăk´), king of the Geats (and Beowulf's uncle).

SCAFFOLDING FOR ELL STUDENTS

Language: Sentence Structure Help students grasp the poem's complex sentence structure. Remind them to find the subject and verb and then identify phrases that tell more about the subject and verb. Project lines 109–116. Have volunteers mark the text:

- Circle the subject of the sentence. *(Beowulf)*
- Highlight in blue all the phrases that relate to the subject. *(In his far-off home, Higlac's follower . . . world)* Then underline the compound verb. *(heard/commanded)*
- Highlight in yellow all the phrases related to the verb. *(how Grendel . . ., Proclaiming that he'd . . . was needed)*

ASK STUDENTS to summarize what Beowulf is going to do and why.

125 　　　　Then Wulfgar went to the door and addressed
The waiting seafarers with soldier's words:
　　　"My lord, the great king of the Danes, commands me
To tell you that he knows of your noble birth
And that having come to him from over the open
130 Sea you have come bravely and are welcome.
Now go to him as you are, in your armor and helmets,
But leave your battle-shields here, and your spears,
Let them lie waiting for the promises your words
May make."
　　　　　　　Beowulf arose, with his men
135 Around him, ordering a few to remain
With their weapons, leading the others quickly
Along under Herot's steep roof into Hrothgar's
Presence. Standing on that prince's own hearth,
Helmeted, the silvery metal of his mail shirt
140 Gleaming with a smith's high art, he greeted
The Danes' great lord:
　　　　　　　"Hail, Hrothgar!
Higlac is my cousin and my king; the days
Of my youth have been filled with glory. Now Grendel's
Name has echoed in our land: sailors
145 Have brought us stories of Herot, the best
Of all mead-halls, deserted and useless when the moon
Hangs in skies the sun had lit,
Light and life fleeing together.
My people have said, the wisest, most knowing
150 And best of them, that my duty was to go to the Danes'
Great king. They have seen my strength for themselves,
Have watched me rise from the darkness of war,

139 mail shirt:
flexible body armor
made of metal links
or overlapping metal
scales.

140 smith's high art:
the skilled craft of a
blacksmith (a person
who fashions objects
from iron).

142 cousin: here,
a general term for
a relative. Beowulf
is actually Higlac's
nephew.

Beowulf **413**

CLOSE READ

Support Inferences
 RL 1

(LINES 127–133)

Remind students that they can use the text details to make **inferences,** or logical assumptions, about what is not directly stated.

🅗 **ASK STUDENTS** why Wulfgar requests that the Geats leave their weapons outside the hall. *(The Danes have been weakened by Grendel's assaults for twelve years. Although Beowulf says he has come to help them, he might also be there to take advantage of their vulnerability.)*

Analyze Characteristics of an Epic (LINES 134–159)
 RL 3

Explain that the Danes have never met Beowulf. Ask students to think about the impression created by the Danes' first sight of him and by his words.

🅘 **ASK STUDENTS** to explain what Beowulf, seen in "the silvery metal of his mail shirt/Gleaming with a smith's high art," represents to the Danes. *(Beowulf shines in contrast to the dark menace he has come to fight. He is a sign of hope, symbolized by his glittering chain mail.)* Have students examine what he says to Hrothgar about himself and his past deeds. Ask them why he appears to boast about his accomplishments. *(He wants to inspire Hrothgar with confidence that he is up to the challenge of defeating Grendel. He must establish his credentials.)*

APPLYING ACADEMIC VOCABULARY

assurance	vision

As you discuss *Beowulf,* incorporate the Collection 5 academic vocabulary words *assurance* and *vision.* Ask students to explain how Beowulf provides Hrothgar with **assurance** that he is capable of ridding the Danes of Grendel. Have them analyze the Anglo-Saxon **vision** of a hero based on what Beowulf says and does.

Image Credits: ©David Lomax/Alamy

Analyze Characteristics of an Epic (LINES 160–175)

 COMMON CORE RL 1, RL 3

Tell students that an epic reflects the historical context from which it originated. From this passage, we can infer ideas about the sociopolitical conditions of the Anglo-Saxon.

Ⓙ CITE TEXT EVIDENCE Have students explain Beowulf's reasoning behind the method he will use to fight Grendel. What does this reveal about the relationship between warrior and leader? *(Beowulf will fight him with his bare hands because his lord Higlac will think more highly of him if he doesn't hide behind a shield. This shows that the warriors revered their leaders and valued their good opinion.)* Ask students to identify details that reveal Beowulf's attitude toward Hrothgar. Why does he feel this way? *(Beowulf asks Hrothgar if he will grant him "a single request"—that he not refuse him the favor of purging "all evil from this hall." This shows Beowulf's respect for Hrothgar, suggesting that even leaders of other communities were held in high regard.)*

CRITICAL VOCABULARY

purge: Beowulf wants to defeat Grendel and, in so doing, cleanse the hall of the evil that has tainted it.

ASK STUDENTS to explain the consequences for the Danes if Beowulf is able to purge the hall of Grendel's presence. *(The warriors will return. The community of the Danes will grow strong again.)*

Dripping with my enemies' blood. I drove
Five great giants into chains, chased
155 All of that race from the earth. I swam
In the blackness of night, hunting monsters
Out of the ocean, and killing them one
By one; death was my errand and the fate
They had earned. Now Grendel and I are called
160 Together, and I've come. Grant me, then,
Lord and protector of this noble place,
A single request! I have come so far,
Oh shelterer of warriors and your people's loved friend,
That this one favor you should not refuse me—
165 That I, alone and with the help of my men,
May **purge** all evil from this hall. I have heard,
Too, that the monster's scorn of men
Is so great that he needs no weapons and fears none.
Nor will I. My lord Higlac
170 Might think less of me if I let my sword
Go where my feet were afraid to, if I hid
Behind some broad linden shield: my hands
Alone shall fight for me, struggle for life
Against the monster. God must decide
175 Who will be given to death's cold grip.
Grendel's plan, I think, will be
What it has been before, to invade this hall
And gorge his belly with our bodies. If he can,
If he can. And I think, if my time will have come,
180 There'll be nothing to mourn over, no corpse to prepare
For its grave: Grendel will carry our bloody
Flesh to the moors, crunch on our bones
And smear torn scraps of our skin on the walls
Of his den. No, I expect no Danes
185 Will fret about sewing our shrouds, if he wins.
And if death does take me, send the hammered
Mail of my armor to Higlac, return
The inheritance I had from Hrethel, and he
From Wayland. Fate will unwind as it must!"

190   Hrothgar replied, protector of the Danes:
      "Beowulf, you've come to us in friendship, and because
Of the reception your father found at our court.
Edgetho had begun a bitter feud,
Killing Hathlaf, a Wulfing warrior:
195 Your father's countrymen were afraid of war,
If he returned to his home, and they turned him away.
Then he traveled across the curving waves
To the land of the Danes. I was new to the throne,

purge
(pûrj) *v.* to eliminate or wash away.

172 linden shield: a shield made from the wood of a linden tree.

172–174 Beowulf insists on fighting Grendel without weapons.

185 shrouds: cloths in which dead bodies are wrapped.

188 Hrethel (hrĕth´əl): a former king of the Geats—Higlac's father and Beowulf's grandfather.

189 Wayland: a famous blacksmith and magician.

193 Edgetho (ĕj´thō): Beowulf's father

194 Wulfing: a member of another Germanic tribe.

WHEN STUDENTS STRUGGLE . . .

To help them understand the relationships between the ideas in the first part of Hrothgar's speech, suggest that students use a cause-and-effect chain similar to the one shown. Have them work with a partner to reread lines 190–207, noting the consequences of Edgetho's action and what Hrothgar did in return.

ASK STUDENTS to compare their cause-and-effect chains. Then ask them why Hrothgar tells this story to Beowulf. *(to show the bond of friendship between their two peoples; to show that since Hrothgar once did a favor for Beowulf's father, it is fitting that Beowulf travel across the seas to help Hrothgar)*

Then, a young man ruling this wide
200 Kingdom and its golden city: Hergar,
My older brother, a far better man
Than I, had died and dying made me,
Second among Healfdane's sons, first
In this nation. I bought the end of Edgetho's
205 Quarrel, sent ancient treasures through the ocean's
Furrows to the Wulfings; your father swore
He'd keep that peace. My tongue grows heavy,
And my heart, when I try to tell you what Grendel
Has brought us, the damage he's done, here
210 In this hall. You see for yourself how much smaller
Our ranks have become, and can guess what we've lost
To his terror. Surely the Lord Almighty
Could stop his madness, smother his lust!
How many times have my men, glowing
215 With courage drawn from too many cups
Of ale, sworn to stay after dark
And stem that horror with a sweep of their swords.
And then, in the morning, this mead-hall glittering
With new light would be drenched with blood, the benches
220 Stained red, the floors, all wet from that fiend's
Savage assault—and my soldiers would be fewer
Still, death taking more and more.
But to table, Beowulf, a banquet in your honor:
Let us toast your victories, and talk of the future."
225   Then Hrothgar's men gave places to the Geats,
Yielded benches to the brave visitors
And led them to the feast. The keeper of the mead
Came carrying out the carved flasks,
And poured that bright sweetness. A poet
230 Sang, from time to time, in a clear
Pure voice. Danes and visiting Geats
Celebrated as one, drank and rejoiced. . . .

THE BATTLE WITH GRENDEL

*After the banquet, Hrothgar and his followers leave Herot, and Beowulf
and his warriors remain to spend the night. Beowulf reiterates his intent
to fight Grendel without a sword and, while his followers sleep, lies
waiting, eager for Grendel to appear.*

        Out from the marsh, from the foot of misty
Hills and bogs, bearing God's hatred,
235 Grendel came, hoping to kill
Anyone he could trap on this trip to high Herot.
He moved quickly through the cloudy night,

Beowulf **415**

CLOSE READ

Analyze Characteristics of an Epic (LINES 214–224)
COMMON CORE RL 3

Point out that in this part of the epic, Hrothgar responds to Beowulf's long speech with one of his own. Tell students that these long speeches are a characteristic of an epic. Often they include important ideas about values, behaviors, traditions, and beliefs of the culture and were used as a way to pass this information down from generation to generation.

 ASK STUDENTS to explain how Hrothgar's speech reflects the importance of courage and community. (*He praises the efforts that many of his men made in trying to fight Grendel. He calls Beowulf to the banquet, which offers an opportunity for the community to come together.*)

Analyze Old English Poetry (LINES 233–240)
COMMON CORE RL 4

Explain that because the old epics were often sung to the accompaniment of a harp, strong rhythm is a prominent feature. Tell students that in *Beowulf*, the lines have four stresses, which are often divided by a pause, or **caesura**.

ASK STUDENTS to reread lines 233 to 240. Have them note the punctuation that indicates the caesura in some of the lines. (*comma*) Then ask them how the rhythm created by those pauses reinforces the action described in the lines. (*The caesuras add suspense and increase the ominous mood. They convey the idea that nothing can stop Grendel.*)

Cause:	Effect/Cause:	Effect/Cause:	Effect/Cause:	Effect/Cause:	Effect:
Edgetho kills Hathlaf, a Wulfing warrior.	Edgetho's action starts a feud.	The Geats send Edgetho away to avoid war.	Edgetho asks Hrothgar for help.	Hrothgar sends treasure to settle the feud.	The Danes and Geats form bonds of friendship.

CLOSE READ

Analyze Old English Poetry (LINES 233–261)

COMMON CORE RL 1, RL 4

Point out how the poet uses imagery and foreshadowing in lines 241–261 to increase suspense.

Ⓜ CITE TEXT EVIDENCE Ask students what details reinforce the idea of Grendel as a force of evil. *(He is described as being "forever joyless," "snarling and fierce," with eyes that "gleamed in the darkness and burned with a gruesome light." His mind was "hot with the thought of food.")* Have students discuss how this view of Grendel increases suspense. Then ask them to identify foreshadowing in this passage and to explain why the poet includes it. *(Line 241 says that Grendel had never "found Herot defended so firmly, his reception/So harsh." Lines 257–259 state that fate "intended Grendel to gnaw the broken bones of his last human supper." By pointing ahead to Grendel's defeat, the poet reassures the audience that the outcome of this visit to Herot will be different and heightens their interest in finding out how Beowulf defeats him.)*

Support Inferences

COMMON CORE RL 1

(LINES 262–272)

Remind students that they can use what they know about a character and situation to infer motives.

Ⓝ ASK STUDENTS why Beowulf allows one of his followers to be taken by Grendel before he attacks him. *(Beowulf may want to lull Grendel into a false sense of complacency so that he can catch him off guard. He may be waiting for the right moment. The fact that Beowulf does this for a reason is supported by his success in overcoming challenges in the past.)*

Up from his swampland, sliding silently
Toward that gold-shining hall. He had visited Hrothgar's
240 Home before, knew the way—
But never, before nor after that night,
Found Herot defended so firmly, his reception
So harsh. He journeyed, forever joyless,
Straight to the door, then snapped it open,
245 Tore its iron fasteners with a touch
And rushed angrily over the threshold.
He strode quickly across the inlaid
Floor, snarling and fierce: his eyes
Gleamed in the darkness, burned with a gruesome
250 Light. Then he stopped, seeing the hall
Crowded with sleeping warriors, stuffed
With rows of young soldiers resting together.
And his heart laughed, he relished the sight,
Intended to tear the life from those bodies
255 By morning; the monster's mind was hot
With the thought of food and the feasting his belly
Would soon know. But fate, that night, intended
Grendel to gnaw the broken bones
Of his last human supper. Human
260 Eyes were watching his evil steps,
Waiting to see his swift hard claws.
Grendel snatched at the first Geat
He came to, ripped him apart, cut
His body to bits with powerful jaws,
265 Drank the blood from his veins and bolted
Him down, hands and feet; death
And Grendel's great teeth came together,
Snapping life shut. Then he stepped to another
Still body, clutched at Beowulf with his claws,
270 Grasped at a strong-hearted wakeful sleeper
—And was instantly seized himself, claws
Bent back as Beowulf leaned up on one arm.
        That shepherd of evil, guardian of crime,
Knew at once that nowhere on earth
275 Had he met a man whose hands were harder;
His mind was flooded with fear—but nothing
Could take his talons and himself from that tight
Hard grip. Grendel's one thought was to run
From Beowulf, flee back to his marsh and hide there:
280 This was a different Herot than the hall he had emptied.
But Higlac's follower remembered his final
Boast and, standing erect, stopped
The monster's flight, fastened those claws
In his fists till they cracked, clutched Grendel

246 threshold: the strip of wood or stone at the bottom of a doorway.

416 Collection 5

SCAFFOLDING FOR ELL STUDENTS

Language: Punctuation Cues Explain that in *Beowulf* the dash is used to signal a change or interruption in the action of the narrative. Project lines 239–278 on the board.

- Highlight the dash in line 240. Point out to students that the dash interrupts the narrative to foreshadow the trouble that Grendel will find when he arrives at Herot.
- Highlight the two remaining dashes in lines 271 and 276.

ASK STUDENTS to work in pairs to explain the change or contrast signaled by each mark of punctuation. *(line 271: the action reverses as Grendel becomes the victim; line 276: the action is interrupted to foreshadow the hopelessness of Grendel's situation)*

285 Closer. The **infamous** killer fought
For his freedom, wanting no flesh but retreat,
Desiring nothing but escape; his claws
Had been caught, he was trapped. That trip to Herot
Was a miserable journey for the writhing monster!
290   The high hall rang, its roof boards swayed,
And Danes shook with terror. Down
The aisles the battle swept, angry
And wild. Herot trembled, wonderfully
Built to withstand the blows, the struggling
295 Great bodies beating at its beautiful walls;
Shaped and fastened with iron, inside
And out, artfully worked, the building
Stood firm. Its benches rattled, fell
To the floor, gold-covered boards grating
300 As Grendel and Beowulf battled across them.
Hrothgar's wise men had fashioned Herot
To stand forever; only fire,
They had planned, could shatter what such skill had put
Together, swallow in hot flames such splendor
305 Of ivory and iron and wood. Suddenly
The sounds changed, the Danes started
In new terror, cowering in their beds as the terrible
Screams of the Almighty's enemy sang
In the darkness, the horrible shrieks of pain
310 And defeat, the tears torn out of Grendel's
Taut throat, hell's captive caught in the arms
Of him who of all the men on earth
Was the strongest.

        That mighty protector of men
315 Meant to hold the monster till its life
Leaped out, knowing the fiend was no use
To anyone in Denmark. All of Beowulf's
Band had jumped from their beds, ancestral
Swords raised and ready, determined
320 To protect their prince if they could. Their courage
Was great but all wasted: they could hack at Grendel
From every side, trying to open
A path for his evil soul, but their points
Could not hurt him, the sharpest and hardest iron
325 Could not scratch at his skin, for that sin-stained demon
Had bewitched all men's weapons, laid spells
That blunted every mortal man's blade.
And yet his time had come, his days
Were over, his death near; down
330 To hell he would go, swept groaning and helpless

infamous
(ĭn′fə-məs) *adj.*
having a bad
reputation.

taut
(tôt) *adj.* tense or
tightly flexed.

Beowulf **417**

TO CHALLENGE STUDENTS...

Research the Sutton Hoo Excavations Seeking buried treasure? Explain that for years, scholars remained skeptical about the description of the hall and the beautifully crafted treasures mentioned in *Beowulf*, believing that they were the product of an overactive poetic imagination. Tell students that the 1939 discovery of an Anglo-Saxon burial site changed such impressions completely.

Have students work in small groups to research the Sutton Hoo excavations. Suggest that each group explore a different facet of the topic: for example, the discovery, the archaeological techniques involved, the treasures unearthed, the historical information learned from the site, and its current status. Have groups share their information in the form of an oral report or a media presentation.

CLOSE READ

Support Inferences COMMON CORE RL 1
(LINES 290–305)

Remind students that although a particular segment of the text might focus on the action or a character, readers can also learn about other elements, such as setting, at the same time.

CITE TEXT EVIDENCE Ask students to explain what the setting details in this passage reveal about Anglo-Saxon civilization. *(Herot's walls are "shaped and fastened with iron," "artfully worked." It has gold-covered boards on the ceiling, and it is built to withstand all threats except fire. These details reveal the Anglo-Saxons to be skillful builders and craftsmen with a love of beauty.)*

Analyze Characteristics of an Epic COMMON CORE RL 3 (LINES 314–327)

Tell students that the epic hero typically confronts enemies who have supernatural qualities that make them particularly difficult to defeat.

ASK STUDENTS to explain why Grendel is such a formidable opponent. *(He cannot be harmed by weapons.)* Have them discuss the significance of the inability of Beowulf's men to help him. *(In order to claim the victory as his own, Beowulf must vanquish Grendel by himself.)*

CRITICAL VOCABULARY

infamous: Ironically, the instinct to destroy that led to Grendel's horrifying reputation diminished once he was in the grip of Beowulf.

ASK STUDENTS what instinct drives the infamous Grendel once Beowulf has hold of him. *(All Grendel wants is to survive by escaping.)*

taut: As Grendel throws his head back in agony, his screams rip through his tightened throat muscles.

ASK STUDENTS to explain how Beowulf's taut grip causes Grendel's agony. *(Beowulf is cracking Grendel's claws in his bare hands, determined not to let him escape.)*

TEACH

CLOSE READ

Determine Themes

COMMON CORE RL 1, RL 2

(LINES 332–359)

Remind students that symbols are objects or events that stand for something other than themselves. Explain that poets may incorporate symbolism into their works to convey deeper meaning.

Q CITE TEXT EVIDENCE Have students identify the evidence that supports the idea that the fight between Grendel and Beowulf is symbolic of the struggle between good and evil. *(Beowulf is aligned with the force of Almighty God in line 334, which overpowers the devilish Grendel, "the afflictor of men.")* How does the symbolism of Beowulf's gesture in lines 356–359 reveal a theme resulting from this conflict? *(Beowulf hangs Grendel's arm from the rafters. Since the arm can be seen as symbol of defeated evil, and Herot can be seen as a symbol of good, the gesture illustrates the triumph of good over evil.)*

Analyze Old English Poetry (LINES 370–375)

COMMON CORE RL 1, RL 4

Direct students to read this passage and to note the way in which Grendel's death is described.

R CITE TEXT EVIDENCE Ask students how the alliteration and imagery affect the impact of this part of the poem. *(The repetition of the b and d sounds emphasizes Grendel's bloody death and descent into darkness. The s sound is alliterated to draw attention to the description of the water, "steaming" and "swirling surf." The descriptive images of "bloody, steaming and boiling," "horrible pounding waves," and "murky darkness" create a feeling of Grendel's evil being drawn back into its source.)*

To the waiting hands of still worse fiends.
Now he discovered—once the afflictor
Of men, tormentor of their days—what it meant
To feud with Almighty God: Grendel
335 Saw that his strength was deserting him, his claws
Bound fast, Higlac's brave follower tearing at
His hands. The monster's hatred rose higher,
But his power had gone. He twisted in pain,
And the bleeding sinews deep in his shoulder
340 Snapped, muscle and bone split
And broke. The battle was over, Beowulf
Had been granted new glory: Grendel escaped,
But wounded as he was could flee to his den,
His miserable hole at the bottom of the marsh,
345 Only to die, to wait for the end
Of all his days. And after that bloody
Combat the Danes laughed with delight.
He who had come to them from across the sea,
Bold and strong-minded, had driven affliction
350 Off, purged Herot clean. He was happy,
Now, with that night's fierce work; the Danes
Had been served as he'd boasted he'd serve them; Beowulf,
A prince of the Geats, had killed Grendel,
Ended the grief, the sorrow, the suffering
355 Forced on Hrothgar's helpless people
By a bloodthirsty fiend. No Dane doubted
The victory, for the proof, hanging high
From the rafters where Beowulf had hung it, was the monster's
Arm, claw and shoulder and all.

360   And then, in the morning, crowds surrounded
Herot, warriors coming to that hall
From faraway lands, princes and leaders
Of men hurrying to behold the monster's
Great staggering tracks. They gaped with no sense
365 Of sorrow, felt no regret for his suffering,
Went tracing his bloody footprints, his beaten
And lonely flight, to the edge of the lake
Where he'd dragged his corpselike way, doomed
And already weary of his vanishing life.
370 The water was bloody, steaming and boiling
In horrible pounding waves, heat
Sucked from his magic veins; but the swirling
Surf had covered his death, hidden
Deep in murky darkness his miserable
375 End, as hell opened to receive him.

338 sinews (sĭn´yōōz): the tendons that connect muscles to bones.

SCAFFOLDING FOR ELL STUDENTS

Language: Alliteration Explain that because many epics were sung aloud, the sound of the words was as important as their meaning. Remind students that alliteration is the repetition of the same consonant sound at the beginning of words. Read aloud lines 338–341. Ask volunteers to repeat the words that are alliterated in these lines. *(bleeding, bone, broke; sinews, snapped, split)* Discuss with the class how the repetition of these sounds draws attention to the severity of Grendel's injuries.

ASK STUDENTS to work in pairs to identify the alliteration in lines 360–375. Have them read their examples aloud and discuss what feeling is expressed through the repetition of the sound.

Then old and young rejoiced, turned back
From that happy **pilgrimage**, mounted their hard-hooved
Horses, high-spirited stallions, and rode them
Slowly toward Herot again, retelling
380 Beowulf's bravery as they jogged along.
And over and over they swore that nowhere
On earth or under the spreading sky
Or between the seas, neither south nor north,
Was there a warrior worthier to rule over men.
385 (But no one meant Beowulf's praise to belittle
Hrothgar, their kind and gracious king!)
    And sometimes, when the path ran straight and clear,
They would let their horses race, red
And brown and pale yellow backs streaming
390 Down the road. And sometimes a proud old soldier
Who had heard songs of the ancient heroes
And could sing them all through, story after story,
Would weave a net of words for Beowulf's
Victory, tying the knot of his verses
395 Smoothly, swiftly, into place with a poet's
Quick skill, singing his new song aloud
While he shaped it, and the old songs as well. . . .

pilgrimage

(pĭl´grə-mĭj) *n.* a
journey to a historical
or religious site.

GRENDEL'S MOTHER

Although one monster has died, another still lives. From her lair in a
cold and murky lake, where she has been brooding over her loss,
Grendel's mother emerges, bent on revenge.

    So she reached Herot,
Where the Danes slept as though already dead;
Her visit ended their good fortune, reversed
400 The bright vane of their luck. No female, no matter

400 vane: a device
that turns to show
the direction the
wind is blowing—
here associated
metaphorically with
luck, which is as
changeable as the wind.

Beowulf **419**

TO CHALLENGE STUDENTS . . .

Discuss Characterization Are you guilty of stereotyping? Do you think Beowulf,
Hrothgar, and Grendel are "types" in the sense that they are either all good or all
bad? Or does the poet portray them as characters with more than one dimension?
Ask students to address these questions in small groups. Have them consider the
following points to help them answer the questions:

- What is the tone of the poet towards each character?
- What kennings and other descriptive words are used to develop an image of
  the character? What kinds of details reveal the traits of each character? What is
  the character's function?

Have students share their conclusions with the class.

CLOSE READ

Analyze Characteristics of an Epic (LINES 376–380)

COMMON CORE RL 3

(S) ASK STUDENTS how this passage relates to the
Anglo-Saxon view of immortality. *(Through killing*
Grendel, Beowulf has achieved fame, which will help
him to be remembered after his death.)

Analyze Old English Poetry (LINES 387–397)

COMMON CORE RL 4

Remind students that on one level, the epic can be
read as a thrilling narrative about a larger-than-life
hero. It can also be studied as a chronicle of life in the
historical period.

(T) ASK STUDENTS how this scene reflects the
techniques used by Anglo-Saxon poets. *(Anglo-Saxon*
poets would take the stories of heroes and, using
alliteration, kennings, and rhythm, "weave a net of
words" that they would sing to commemorate new as
well as old tales of courage.)

> **CRITICAL VOCABULARY**
>
> **pilgrimage:** As the news of Beowulf's victory
> over Grendel spreads, many people travel to see
> the site of this historic event.
>
> **ASK STUDENTS** to explain why the term *pilgrimage*
> is appropriate for those traveling to the site of
> Grendel's disappearance. *(Beowulf's victory*
> *demonstrates good overcoming evil, or the devil.*
> *Therefore, the site of this battle can be seen as*
> *a holy place.)*

Analyze Characteristics of an Epic (LINES 400–424)

 COMMON CORE RL 1, RL 3

Explain that an epic hero undergoes several trials to show that he truly deserves to be called a hero. Have students read these lines to discover Beowulf's next challenge.

Ⓤ CITE TEXT EVIDENCE Have students identify the details and techniques the poet uses to convey the brutality of Grendel's mother's attack. *(The strong verbs such as "smashing," "slashing," and "stabbing," the adjectives such as "bloody" and "gleaming," the kennings "hammer-forged" and "boar-headed," as well as the alliterative words all show the violence of this encounter.)* Have students discuss the significance of her actions. What do they foreshadow about future events? *(In revenge, she carries off a single Dane, Hrothgar's best friend, as well as Grendel's arm. These actions foreshadow that Beowulf will have to defeat Grendel's mother, this new source of evil, and that it will not be easy to do.)*

Determine Themes

COMMON CORE RL 1, RL 2

(LINES 425–445)

Remind students that the elements of a narrative poem, such as details of setting as well as character and plot, are often used to communicate deeper meaning.

Ⓥ CITE TEXT EVIDENCE Ask students to identify the descriptive images that link Grendel's mother's home to the concepts of death and darkness. *(The mist "steams like black clouds." The trees have "snakelike roots" that help keep the water dark. The lake "burns like a torch." The lake appears to be bottomless. Animals would rather die than jump into the water. The waves are "black.")* What does this lake symbolize? *(It symbolizes the underworld, or hell.)*

How fierce, could have come with a man's strength,
Fought with the power and courage men fight with,
Smashing their shining swords, their bloody,
Hammer-forged blades onto boar-headed helmets,
405   Slashing and stabbing with the sharpest of points.
The soldiers raised their shields and drew
Those gleaming swords, swung them above
The piled-up benches, leaving their mail shirts
And their helmets where they'd lain when the terror took hold of
    them.
410   To save her life she moved still faster,
Took a single victim and fled from the hall,
Running to the moors, discovered, but her supper
Assured, sheltered in her dripping claws.
She'd taken Hrothgar's closest friend,
415   The man he most loved of all men on earth;
She'd killed a glorious soldier, cut
A noble life short. No Geat could have stopped her:
Beowulf and his band had been given better
Beds; sleep had come to them in a different
420   Hall. Then all Herot burst into shouts:
She had carried off Grendel's claw. Sorrow
Had returned to Denmark. They'd traded deaths,
Danes and monsters, and no one had won,
Both had lost! . . .

Devastated by the loss of his friend, Hrothgar sends for Beowulf and recounts what Grendel's mother has done. Then Hrothgar describes the dark lake where Grendel's mother has dwelt with her son.

425   They live in secret places, windy
Cliffs, wolf-dens where water pours
From the rocks, then runs underground, where mist
Steams like black clouds, and the groves of trees
Growing out over their lake are all covered
430   With frozen spray, and wind down snakelike
Roots that reach as far as the water
And help keep it dark. At night that lake
Burns like a torch. No one knows its bottom,
No wisdom reaches such depths. A deer,
435   Hunted through the woods by packs of hounds,
A stag with great horns, though driven through the forest
From faraway places, prefers to die
On those shores, refuses to save its life
In that water. It isn't far, nor is it
440   A pleasant spot! When the wind stirs
And storms, waves splash toward the sky,

404 boar-headed helmets: Germanic warriors often wore helmets bearing the images of wild pigs or other fierce creatures in the hope that the images would increase their ferocity and protect them against their enemies.

420 Collection 5

WHEN STUDENTS STRUGGLE . . .

Remind students that identifying the way in which text is organized can help them better understand its meaning. Explain that lines 397–449 follow a problem-solution structure.

- Have students work in small groups to summarize the problem in lines 397–443. *(Grendel's mother attacks the Danes, killing Hrothgar's best friend.)*

- Ask groups to look at lines 443–449 to identify the solution. *(Beowulf must seek her out and kill her.)*

ASK STUDENTS to explain what will make this battle challenging for Beowulf. *(Grendel's mother lives at the bottom of a burning lake.)*

As dark as the air, as black as the rain
That the heavens weep. Our only help,
Again, lies with you. Grendel's mother

445 Is hidden in her terrible home, in a place
You've not seen. Seek it, if you dare! Save us,
Once more, and again twisted gold,
Heaped-up ancient treasure, will reward you
For the battle you win!". . .

THE BATTLE WITH GRENDEL'S MOTHER

*Beowulf accepts Hrothgar's challenge, and the king and his men
accompany the hero to the dreadful lair of Grendel's mother. Fearlessly,
Beowulf prepares to battle the terrible creature.*

450   He leaped into the lake, would not wait for anyone's
Answer; the heaving water covered him
Over. For hours he sank through the waves;
At last he saw the mud of the bottom.
And all at once the greedy she-wolf

455 Who'd ruled those waters for half a hundred
Years discovered him, saw that a creature
From above had come to explore the bottom
Of her wet world. She welcomed him in her claws,
Clutched at him savagely but could not harm him,

460 Tried to work her fingers through the tight
Ring-woven mail on his breast, but tore
And scratched in vain. Then she carried him, armor
And sword and all, to her home; he struggled
To free his weapon, and failed. The fight

465 Brought other monsters swimming to see
Her catch, a host of sea beasts who beat at
His mail shirt, stabbing with tusks and teeth
As they followed along. Then he realized, suddenly,
That she'd brought him into someone's battle-hall,

470 And there the water's heat could not hurt him,
Nor anything in the lake attack him through
The building's high-arching roof. A brilliant
Light burned all around him, the lake
Itself like a fiery flame.
                    Then he saw

475 The mighty water witch, and swung his sword,
His ring-marked blade, straight at her head;
The iron sang its fierce song,
Sang Beowulf's strength. But her guest

447–449 Germanic warriors placed great importance on amassing treasure as a way of acquiring fame and temporarily defeating fate.

476 His ring-marked blade: For the battle with Grendel's mother, Beowulf has been given an heirloom sword with an intricately etched blade.

Beowulf **421**

CLOSE READ

Analyze Characteristics of an Epic (LINES 450–473)

COMMON CORE RL 3

Point out that epics include detailed descriptions of the hero's battles.

W **ASK STUDENTS** to reread this passage, noting where the battle takes place. Have them discuss how Grendel's mother inadvertently gives Beowulf an advantage. *(By taking him into her hall, she unwittingly protects him from the other sea creatures that are attacking him.)*

WHEN STUDENTS STRUGGLE . . .

Tell students that when they read the account of the battle between Beowulf and Grendel's mother, they can use their voices to convey excitement and suspense to their listeners.

- Have students listen as you model how to read lines 450–475 with appropriate expression and attention to punctuation cues.
- Have students form pairs. Have one partner read the passage aloud and the other listen to evaluate how well the reader conveys the mood of this scene.
- Then have partners exchange roles for a second reading.

ASK STUDENTS to choose two or three lines to demonstrate their dramatic-reading proficiency to the class.

Analyze Characteristics of an Epic (LINES 485–523; 513–523)

COMMON CORE **RL 1, RL 3**

Tell students a performance of *Beowulf* would be sung over several nights. Therefore, the poet planned to develop and maintain the suspense in each new part.

X **CITE TEXT EVIDENCE** Ask students to explain how this battle differs from Beowulf's encounter with Grendel. (*This battle shows him suffering several disadvantages. His sword and helmet are both useless; Grendel's mother overpowers him and throws him to the floor [line 500]. He is saved from death only by his mail shirt [line 504].*) Then ask students to discuss the significance of the similarity between the two battles. (*In order to be a true hero, Beowulf fights both battles alone.*)

Remind students to note details that develop the image of the hero as an extraordinary individual.

Y **ASK STUDENTS** to discuss the significance of Beowulf's ability to wield the sword. (*He is shown to have extraordinary strength because he can pull it from its sheath and use it to behead Grendel's mother even though the sword is "so massive that no ordinary man could lift/Its carved and decorated length."*)

Discovered that no sword could slice her evil
480 Skin, that Hrunting could not hurt her, was useless
Now when he needed it. They wrestled, she ripped
And tore and clawed at him, bit holes in his helmet,
And that too failed him; for the first time in years
Of being worn to war it would earn no glory;
485 It was the last time anyone would wear it. But Beowulf
Longed only for fame, leaped back
Into battle. He tossed his sword aside,
Angry; the steel-edged blade lay where
He'd dropped it. If weapons were useless he'd use
490 His hands, the strength in his fingers. So fame
Comes to the men who mean to win it
And care about nothing else! He raised
His arms and seized her by the shoulder; anger
Doubled his strength, he threw her to the floor.
495 She fell, Grendel's fierce mother, and the Geats'
Proud prince was ready to leap on her. But she rose
At once and repaid him with her clutching claws,
Wildly tearing at him. He was weary, that best
And strongest of soldiers; his feet stumbled
500 And in an instant she had him down, held helpless.
Squatting with her weight on his stomach, she drew
A dagger, brown with dried blood, and prepared
To avenge her only son. But he was stretched
On his back, and her stabbing blade was blunted
505 By the woven mail shirt he wore on his chest.
The hammered links held; the point
Could not touch him. He'd have traveled to the bottom of the earth,
Edgetho's son, and died there, if that shining
Woven metal had not helped—and Holy
510 God, who sent him victory, gave judgment
For truth and right, Ruler of the Heavens,
Once Beowulf was back on his feet and fighting.

Then he saw, hanging on the wall, a heavy
Sword, hammered by giants, strong
515 And blessed with their magic, the best of all weapons
But so massive that no ordinary man could lift
Its carved and decorated length. He drew it
From its scabbard, broke the chain on its hilt,
And then, savage, now, angry
520 And desperate, lifted it high over his head
And struck with all the strength he had left,
Caught her in the neck and cut it through,
Broke bones and all. Her body fell
To the floor, lifeless, the sword was wet

480 Hrunting (hrŭn′tĭng): the name of Beowulf's sword. (Germanic warriors' swords were possessions of such value that they were often given names.)

Strategies for Annotation

✏️ 🖥 **Annotate it!**

Analyze Language

COMMON CORE **RL 4**

Have students use their eBook annotation tools to examine the language that the poet uses to describe the battle in lines 485–505.

- Highlight powerful verbs in green.
- Highlight sensory language in yellow.
- Underline examples of alliteration.
- Review your annotations. On a note, explain what the poet's language helps you to see, hear, and feel.

She fell, Grendel's fierce mother, and the Geats'

Proud prince was ready to leap on her. But she rose

At once and repaid him with her clutching claws,

Wildly tearing at him. He was weary, that best

And strongest of soldiers; his feet stumbled

And in an instant she had him down, held helpless.

525 With her blood, and Beowulf rejoiced at the sight.
    The brilliant light shone, suddenly,
As though burning in that hall, and as bright as Heaven's
Own candle, lit in the sky. He looked
At her home, then following along the wall
530 Went walking, his hands tight on the sword,
His heart still angry. He was hunting another
Dead monster, and took his weapon with him
For final revenge against Grendel's vicious
Attacks, his nighttime raids, over
535 And over, coming to Herot when Hrothgar's
Men slept, killing them in their beds,
Eating some on the spot, fifteen
Or more, and running to his **loathsome** moor
With another such sickening meal waiting
540 In his pouch. But Beowulf repaid him for those visits,
Found him lying dead in his corner,
Armless, exactly as that fierce fighter
Had sent him out from Herot, then struck off
His head with a single swift blow. The body
545 Jerked for the last time, then lay still.
    The wise old warriors who surrounded Hrothgar,
Like him staring into the monsters' lake,
Saw the waves surging and blood
Spurting through. They spoke about Beowulf,
550 All the graybeards, whispered together
And said that hope was gone, that the hero
Had lost fame and his life at once, and would never
Return to the living, come back as triumphant
As he had left; almost all agreed that Grendel's
555 Mighty mother, the she-wolf, had killed him.
The sun slid over past noon, went further
Down. The Danes gave up, left
The lake and went home, Hrothgar with them.
The Geats stayed, sat sadly, watching,
560 Imagining they saw their lord but not believing
They would ever see him again.
                —Then the sword
Melted, blood-soaked, dripping down
Like water, disappearing like ice when the world's
Eternal Lord loosens invisible
565 Fetters and unwinds icicles and frost
As only He can, He who rules
Time and seasons, He who is truly
God. The monsters' hall was full of
Rich treasures, but all that Beowulf took
570 Was Grendel's head and the hilt of the giants'

loathsome
(lōth´səm) *adj.*
hateful or repulsive.

550 graybeards: old men.

Beowulf **423**

TO CHALLENGE STUDENTS . . .

Analyze Symbolism Are you afraid of the dark? Ask students to imagine a world without electric light. Discuss how intense the darkness would be, especially during long winter nights, and how threatening that darkness would appear. Point out that images of dark and light appear throughout this poem as symbols of what the Anglo-Saxons feared and welcomed.

ASK STUDENTS to write a paragraph or two in which they analyze this symbolism, tracing the instances in which the contrasts are mentioned. Ask them to present their analyses in small groups before holding a class discussion.

Determine Themes

 COMMON CORE RL 1, RL 2

(LINES 526–545)

Ask students to consider the events' metaphorical meaning to interpret the poet's central message.

Z **CITE TEXT EVIDENCE** Have students identify images of light and connect them with Beowulf's victory. *(The "brilliant light" suggests he has overcome darkness and triumphed over evil.)* Ask: What does Beowulf cutting off Grendel's head symbolize? *(Beowulf wants to show his supremacy over the monster to eliminate all doubt, and to reassure the Danes they are safe. The source of evil has been destroyed.)*

Analyze Characteristics of an Epic (LINES 545–563; 546–568)

 COMMON CORE RL 3

A2 **ASK STUDENTS** what lines 546–568 reveal about Anglo-Saxon values. *(The value of fame is shown in the old men's comments that Beowulf lost life and fame in his defeat at the hands of Grendel's mother. The value of loyalty is shown in the vigil kept by the Geats, who refuse to believe that Beowulf won't return to them.)*

Explain that epic poets often use narrative techniques, such as shifts in time or setting, to increase the effectiveness of the story.

B2 **ASK STUDENTS** to identify and explain the shifts in this passage. What is the intended effect of these shifts on the audience? *(The poet uses shifts in setting to heighten the drama. In lines 545–546, the audience is taken from the bottom of the lake to the surface, where the Danes and Geats anxiously await, fearing the worst when they see the surging waves and blood. Then the action returns to the depths where the sword is melting and Beowulf is completing his task [line 562]. These shifts intensify the audience's eagerness to have the Danes and Geats learn of the battle's outcome.)*

> **CRITICAL VOCABULARY**

loathsome: Beowulf shows his disgust with Grendel, who preyed upon the Danes in their hall and also took many back to his repulsive lair.

ASK STUDENTS what image of Grendel's moor is evoked by calling it loathsome. *(It suggests bones scattered and remnants of decaying flesh heaped up.)*

CLOSE READ

Determine Themes RL 2

(LINES 574–578)

Remind students that universal themes are those that appear again and again in works of art throughout a civilizations' history.

C2 ASK STUDENTS to explain the transformation of the lake. What has Beowulf metaphorically restored? Explain. *(Beowulf has restored order to nature. He has restored light to darkness. This reinforces the theme of good triumphing over evil.)*

Analyze Characteristics of an Epic RL 1, RL 3

(LINES 587–605)

D2 CITE TEXT EVIDENCE Have students identify details in these final lines that reinforce the idea that Beowulf is superior to all others. *(It takes four men to carry Grendel's skull back to Herot; Beowulf is able to hold it by the hair to show Hrothgar.)*

COLLABORATIVE DISCUSSION Have students review the poem to identify the poet's suspense-building techniques. Have them share their conclusions with the class as a whole. Accept all reasonable responses.

ASK STUDENTS to share any questions they generated in the course of reading and discussing the selection.

Jeweled sword; the rest of that ring-marked
Blade had dissolved in Grendel's steaming
Blood, boiling even after his death.
And then the battle's only survivor
575 Swam up and away from those silent corpses;
The water was calm and clean, the whole
Huge lake peaceful once the demons who'd lived in it
Were dead.
        Then that noble protector of all seamen
Swam to land, rejoicing in the heavy
580 Burdens he was bringing with him. He
And all his glorious band of Geats
Thanked God that their leader had come back unharmed;
They left the lake together. The Geats
Carried Beowulf's helmet, and his mail shirt.
585 Behind them the water slowly thickened
As the monsters' blood came seeping up.
They walked quickly, happily, across
Roads all of them remembered, left
The lake and the cliffs alongside it, brave men
590 Staggering under the weight of Grendel's skull,
Too heavy for fewer than four of them to handle—
Two on each side of the spear jammed through it—
Yet proud of their ugly load and determined
That the Danes, seated in Herot, should see it.
595 Soon, fourteen Geats arrived
At the hall, bold and warlike, and with Beowulf,
Their lord and leader, they walked on the mead-hall
Green. Then the Geats' brave prince entered
Herot, covered with glory for the daring
600 Battles he had fought; he sought Hrothgar
To salute him and show Grendel's head.
He carried that terrible trophy by the hair,
Brought it straight to where the Danes sat,
Drinking, the queen among them. It was a weird
605 And wonderful sight, and the warriors stared. . . .

578 that noble protector of all seamen: Beowulf, who will be buried in a tower that will serve as a navigational aid to sailors.

604 queen: Welthow, wife of Hrothgar.

COLLABORATIVE DISCUSSION How does the poet keep readers on the edge of their seats? With a partner, discuss the ways in which the poet builds suspense. Cite specific textual evidence from the poem to support your ideas.

SCAFFOLDING FOR ELL STUDENTS

Language: Verb Tense Explain that while the poem is narrated primarily in past tense, some actions were completed further back in time. The poet uses the past perfect tense to indicate which past events occurred first. Project lines 572–575 on the board. Invite volunteers to mark them up.

- Underline verbs in the past tense.
- Highlight verbs in the past perfect tense.

Then read aloud line 577 and explain that "who'd lived" contains the past perfect verb "had lived", which indicates that demons once inhabited the lake before their death. Have students find other examples of the past perfect tense. As a class, discuss what each verb indicates about the sequence of action.

> Blade had dissolved in Grendel's steaming
>
> Blood, boiling even after his death.
>
> And then the battle's only survivor
>
> Swam up and away from those silent corpses;

Analyze Story Elements: Characteristics of an Epic

COMMON CORE RL 3

An **epic** is a long narrative poem that celebrates a hero's deeds. Traditional epics, such as *Beowulf*, began as oral poems and were retold by poets over many generations before they were finally written down. Epic poems share certain conventions and characteristics:

- The hero is a person of noble birth or high position who performs great deeds of strength and courage.
- The hero battles supernatural creatures and may undergo dangerous journeys in order to fulfill a quest.
- The hero's character traits reflect the ideals of the culture.
- The story conveys universal themes—themes found in the literature of all time periods and cultures—such as the importance of honor and the conflict between good and evil.
- The style features formal diction (word choice and syntax) and a serious tone (expression of the writer's attitude toward a subject).
- The dialogue often includes long speeches by major characters.

Analyze Language: Old English Poetry

COMMON CORE RL 4

Anglo-Saxon poets used techniques that made their verse easier to chant. This chart describes important techniques found in *Beowulf*:

Technique	Example
Alliteration is the repetition of consonant sounds at the beginning of words. This device helps unify the lines.	The **h**igh **h**all **r**ang, its **r**oof boards swayed,
The poem's strong **rhythm** is created by four stresses, or beats, in each line.	Grendel came, hoping to kill
A **caesura** is a pause that divides the line, with each part having two stresses. Usually, at least one stressed syllable in the first part alliterates with a stressed syllable in in the second part.	He took what he wanted, // all the treasures
Kennings are metaphorical compound words or phrases substituted for simple nouns.	The kennings "Higlac's follower" and "protector of men" are used in place of the name "Beowulf."

Beowulf **425**

TEACH

CLOSE READ

Analyze Story Elements: Characteristics of an Epic

COMMON CORE RL 3

Review the conventions of an epic with students. Then organize the class into six groups and assign each of them one of the bulleted characteristics. Ask students to find the passages in the poem that correspond to or illustrate that characteristic. Have representatives from the groups present their findings.

Analyze Language: Old English Poetry

COMMON CORE RL 4

Make sure students understand the terms that appear in the chart. Then ask them to work with a partner to create their own kennings and alliterative phrases to summarize the action in an assigned section of the poem. Have students read their summaries aloud and have listening students identify the techniques.

Strategies for Annotation · *Annotate it!*

Analyze Language: Old English Poetry

COMMON CORE RL 4

Have students use their eBook annotation tools to examine the techniques used by the Beowulf poet.

- Highlight in yellow examples of kennings.
- Highlight in pink alliterative words.
- Underline words that contain stressed syllables.
- Discuss: How did these techniques help the poet to remember the lines and sing the poem meaningfully?

So mankind's enemy continued his crimes,

Killing as often as he could, coming

Alone, bloodthirsty and horrible. Though he lived

In Herot, when the night hid him, he never

Dared to touch king Hrothgar's glorious

PRACTICE & APPLY

Analyzing the Text 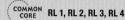 COMMON CORE RL 1, RL 2, RL 3, RL 4

Possible answers:

1. *These references align Hrothgar with good and Grendel with evil, and by extension, align the monarchy with heaven and its enemies with "hell." They also foreshadow the outcome of the conflict and hint at a possible theme.*

2. *These lines explain Beowulf's lineage and his identity; they also present his credentials, showing why he is qualified to take on Grendel. His words in these lines inspire the Danes with confidence. His exploits in the water foreshadow his battle with Grendel's mother, which also takes place in the water. He is shown to be physically strong, fearless, and motivated by loyalty.*

3. *In lines 1–2, the alliteration of the p and d develops an atmosphere of dread or evil. The alliteration of the h and t in lines 207–210 slows down the lines, helping to convey a tone of weariness and despair. In lines 293–300, the repetition of the b adds an intense, powerful sound that echoes the blows exchanged and the impact of the bodies against the walls of the hall.*

4. *Lines 179–189 reveal the Anglo-Saxon acceptance of fate. "Fate will unwind as it must." Beowulf matter-of-factly states that there will be nothing left of his body if Grendel defeats him; he asks that his chain mail be sent back to his lord to be passed to another warrior. Lines 204–207 suggest that debts are honored and repaid in Anglo-Saxon culture. Hrothgar helped Beowulf's father; now Beowulf helps him. Lines 380–385 show that fame is acquired through his acts of heroism. They also emphasize the importance of loyalty to one's lord. The Danes never waver in their regard for Hrothgar. Lines 446–449 indicate a belief that bravery and duty warrant material reward.*

5. *Beowulf descends "For hours"; "other monsters" join the fight; the water even in the depths is fiery and hot. These details equate Grendel's mother's lair with hell. The fact that Beowulf returns from this place implies that he has overcome death, the last great obstacle for a hero.*

6. *The battles illustrate the conflict between good and evil as well as life and death. Beowulf's victories show that good will overcome evil.*

7. *Grendel is described as having "hell-forged hands," being a "shepherd of evil" and a "guardian of crime" as well as "hell's captive." His mother is called a "she-wolf." These kennings show the poet's view that both are monstrous and subhuman.*

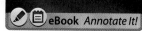 eBook *Annotate It!*

Analyzing the Text  COMMON CORE RL 1, RL 2, RL 3, RL 4, W 2

Cite Text Evidence   Support your responses with evidence from the selection.

1. **Draw Conclusions** Reread lines 15–29 and 81–85, which show the influence of Christianity on the epic. What is the purpose of referring to Hrothgar and Grendel in terms of their relationship to God?

2. **Analyze** How does Beowulf's speech in lines 141–175 contribute to his characterization?

3. **Analyze** Reread the following passages. How does the poet's use of alliteration influence the mood or tone of each passage?

   - "A powerful monster, living . . . growled in pain" (lines 1–2)
   - "My tongue grows heavy . . . In this hall." (lines 207–210)
   - "Herot trembled . . . across them." (lines 293–300)

4. **Analyze** Explain what is revealed in the following passages about Anglo-Saxon values and beliefs.

   - "And I think, if my time will have come . . . as it must!" (lines 179–189)
   - "I bought the end of Edgetho's . . . keep that peace." (lines 204–207)
   - "And over and over they swore . . . gracious king!)" (lines 380–385)
   - "Seek it, if you dare! . . . battle you win!" (lines 446–449)

5. **Draw Conclusions** Identify details about setting in lines 450–474. Why might the poet have chosen to provide such a detailed description of the setting of Beowulf's battle with Grendel's mother? How does this description influence the reader's impression of the battle?

6. **Analyze** What universal themes are conveyed by the descriptions of battles between Beowulf and Grendel and between Beowulf and Grendel's mother?

7. **Analyze** Identify kennings associated with Grendel and Grendel's mother. How do these phrases convey the poet's attitude toward the characters?

PERFORMANCE TASK

Writing Activity: Comparison How do heroes reveal the traits prized most highly by a culture?

- Identify Beowulf's qualities and what they reveal about the Anglo-Saxon culture.

- Choose a fictional hero from contemporary American culture. Explain what this character's traits reveal about values of modern society.

- Compare the values of Anglo-Saxons and modern Americans in a well-organized essay.

Assign this performance task.

PERFORMANCE TASK   COMMON CORE W 2

Writing Activity: Comparison Have students cite quotations from the poem to support their analysis of Beowulf's character and reflection of an Anglo-Saxon society's ideals. As a class, discuss the contemporary concept of heroism and brainstorm heroic traits. Invite students to name contemporary fictional heroes who possess such traits. Once students have chosen a fictional hero to compare to Beowulf, suggest they use a Venn diagram to organize their ideas.

Critical Vocabulary

affliction	purge	infamous
taut	pilgrimage	loathsome

Practice and Apply Explain whether the words in each pair are synonyms, antonyms, or unrelated.

1. pilgrimage/restoration
2. loathsome/appealing
3. taut/slack

4. affliction/burden
5. infamous/honorable
6. purge/expel

Vocabulary Strategy: Homophones

When listening to poetry read aloud, the audience has to be able to recognize **homophones.** These are words that have the same pronunciation but different spellings and meanings. Listeners can use context clues to figure out which word is intended. For example, the Vocabulary word *taut* is a homophone found in line 311: "the tears torn out of Grendel's/Taut throat." Although *taut* is pronounced in exactly the same way as the past tense of *teach*, the position of the word in the sentence indicates that it is an adjective, not a verb, and other context clues help to define the word as "stretched tight."

Practice and Apply Complete each of these sentences with the correct choice from the homophones in parentheses. Define the word you choose.

1. The sun (shown, shone) brightly, lighting up the (guilt, gilt) on the walls of Hrothgar's hall.

2. Beowulf tells Hrothgar how he swam the (straight, strait) killing monsters in the blackness of the night.

3. When the weeping was over, the hall was silent with the (wait, weight) of the Danes' (mourning, morning).

4. The (pain, pane) from his injury was too much for Grendel to (bare, bear)

5. Each (birth, berth) in the hall held a vigilant Geat, alert to Grendel's approach.

6. The arrival of Grendel's mother turned the (vein, vane, vain) of the Danes' luck back in the other direction.

7. The (foul/fowl) mist over the lake hinted at the danger that (weighted, waited) beneath.

8. A talented (bard, barred) sang about Beowulf's miraculous (feet, feat) of courage.

PRACTICE & APPLY

Critical Vocabulary

Answers:

1. *unrelated*
2. *antonyms*
3. *antonyms*
4. *synonyms*
5. *antonyms*
6. *synonyms*

Vocabulary Strategy: Homophones

Answers:

1. *shone; gilt*
2. *strait*
3. *weight; mourning*
4. *pain; bear*
5. *berth*
6. *vane*
7. *foul; waited*
8. *bard; feat*

Students' definitions of each word will vary.

SCAFFOLDING FOR ELL STUDENTS

Vocabulary: Homophones Write the sentences from the activity on the board. Explain to students that context clues can help them determine which word is correct.

- Read aloud the first sentence. Circle the words *brightly, lighting,* and *on the walls.*
- Then read the dictionary entries for each of the two pairs of words. Work with students to use context clues to identify the correct word.

ASK STUDENTS to work in pairs to identify the context clues in the sentences before they look up words in a dictionary. Review and discuss their answers as a class.

Language and Style: Mood

To help students understand the impact of language on the mood of a text, write these sentences on the board:

They live in cliffs and dens near waterfalls. There is mist, and the trees have long roots that extend into the water.

As a class, compare the feeling the sentences on the board create with the mood conveyed by the original text of the poem.

Possible answers:

Students should apply their knowledge of language to create original passages that reflect their understanding of mood. Passages should also indicate an accurate interpretation of the mood in their selected text.

Assess It!

Online Selection Test

- Download an editable ExamView bank.
- Assign and manage this test online.

Language and Style: Mood

Mood is the feeling or atmosphere that a writer creates for the reader. Poets may use imagery, figurative language, and word choices to create this atmosphere.

In lines 425–449, the Beowulf poet describes the lake in which Grendel's mother lives. Read this passage from the poem:

> They live in secret places, windy
> Cliffs, wolf-dens where water pours
> From the rocks, then runs underground, where mist
> Steams like black clouds, and the groves of trees
> Growing out over their lake are all covered
> With frozen spray, and wind down snakelike
> Roots that reach as far as the water
> And help to keep it dark. At night that lake
> Burns like a torch. . . .
> . . . When the wind stirs
> And storms, waves splash toward the sky,
> As dark as the air, as black as the rain
> That the heavens weep. . . .

Notice these literary devices used by the poet:

- imagery ("windy cliffs," "water pours from the rocks," "frozen spray")
- similes ("mist steams like black clouds," "snakelike roots," "that lake burns like a torch," "waves . . . as dark as the air, as black as the rain")
- personification ("the rain that the heavens weep")
- words with sinister connotations ("secret," "black," "dark")

These devices create an ominous, foreboding mood. This mood helps to develop the impression of Grendel's mother as the epitome of evil and darkness. The mood adds to the suspense as readers wonder whether Beowulf will make it back out of such a horrifying place alive. It also foreshadows the magnitude of the conflict that is about to occur.

Practice and Apply Complete these activities independently.

1. Choose a passage from the poem that conveys a distinct mood—for example, lines 15–40, 233–268, or 474–505. Identify the mood of the passage you've chosen and the words and phrases that help to create this mood.

2. Using the words and phrases you identified, write an original passage that creates a similar mood.

3. Read your passage aloud to a partner. Have your partner identify the mood and evaluate your success in conveying it.

Analyze Story Elements: Setting

COMMON CORE

RL 3

TEACH

Review the definition of **setting** with students. Remind them that it typically refers to the physical location and time frame in which a narrative takes place.

Next, explain that the settings of epics that originate from an oral tradition also include elements related to the civilization that produced them.

- **Historical context:** As poets passed down the story, they would interweave current sociopolitical conditions into the tale, thus making it more relevant to their audience.
- **Cultural context:** Epics reflect the beliefs, traditions, and values of the society from which they originate, providing an insight into the time period and the cultural influences upon the characters.

PRACTICE AND APPLY

Ask students what they know about the physical location and time period in which the action of *Beowulf* occurs. *(Beowulf is set in sixth-century Scandinavia.)* Have them explain how these elements of the setting affect the action of the poem. *(This region remains dark for much of the year. Beowulf battles against the forces of darkness, represented by Grendel and his mother. He brings light back to the world of the Danes, protecting them against the threats, both known and unknown, that stalked them from the darkness.)*

Have students discuss the political, social, and cultural contexts of the poem. How do they influence the narrative? *(These contexts shape the conflict and the characters' response. The Danes and Geats live in communities, represented by their halls. They are loyal to their leaders in good times and bad, as shown by the continued respect the Danes show Hrothgar. Grendel and his mother dare to violate the hall and disrupt the community, creating a conflict that demands resolution. The evil is vanquished by a warrior who embodies all of the traits most revered in a culture that constantly fought invaders and other dangers—courage and loyalty. The hero, Beowulf, reestablishes the order necessary for the group to survive and prosper.)*

 INTERACTIVE WHITEBOARD LESSON If students need further instruction, use this *Interactive Whiteboard Lesson*: **Role of Setting.**

Analyze Story Elements: Characteristics of an Epic

COMMON CORE

RL 3

RETEACH

Review the major epic conventions. Discuss the function of the original epic as a method of teaching younger generations not only the history of the group, but also its important traditions, beliefs, and values. Point out that although epics are not as intrinsic to today's society, they still appear in the forms of contemporary literature and films.

Have students identify contemporary epics, such as the *Star Wars* or *Harry Potter* series, or a film that reinterprets an ancient epic, such as *Troy*. Group students according to their familiarity with the choice. Then ask them to analyze the epic characteristics of their film or literary work, citing as many specific examples as possible.

Have groups present their analyses. Then, as a class, compare the themes expressed in *Beowulf* with those conveyed by the contemporary films or texts. Discuss the universality of those themes and what they might reveal about the human condition, both in Anglo-Saxon times and now.

 LEVEL UP TUTORIALS Assign the following *Level Up* tutorial: **Universal and Recurring Themes.**

CLOSE READING APPLICATION

Have students locate or provide them with information about one of the ancient Greek heroes, such as Theseus, Perseus, or Odysseus. Have them identify ways in which the hero epitomizes the same heroic traits as Beowulf.

from Beowulf

Epic Poem by the Beowulf Poet, translated by Burton Raffel

Why This Text

Though *Beowulf* is well over a thousand years old, its hero depicts individual will and courage in ways that can still inspire readers. The narrative includes motifs that remain popular in films and fantasy novels: swords, a dragon, a lone hero. With the help of the close-reading questions, students will analyze the elements that mark this work as an epic poem. This close reading will lead students to an understanding of how the poem's hero embodies traits that reflect his society's ideals.

Background Have students read the background about the epic poem *Beowulf*. Explain that many cultures valued individual bravery. In Germanic societies such as England and Scandinavia, a high value was often placed on personal honor expressed as fame earned by great deeds. The style of *Beowulf* typifies eighth-century English poetry. It uses alliteration rather than rhyme. It also uses kennings—metaphorical compound words or phrases substituted for single nouns, such as "the Geats' ring-giver" in place of Beowulf's name.

AS YOU READ Remind students that this portion of the poem shows Beowulf at the end of his life. What do we learn about his present and past actions that show that he is a true epic hero?

Common Core Support

- cite strong and thorough textual evidence
- determine a theme and analyze its development
- analyze story elements and the characteristics of an epic
- analyze the impact of specific word choices

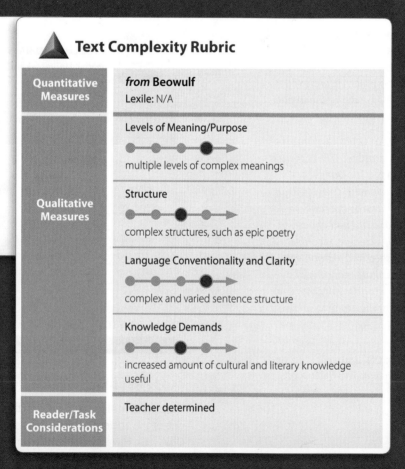

Text Complexity Rubric

Quantitative Measures

from Beowulf
Lexile: N/A

Qualitative Measures

Levels of Meaning/Purpose

multiple levels of complex meanings

Structure

complex structures, such as epic poetry

Language Conventionality and Clarity

complex and varied sentence structure

Knowledge Demands

increased amount of cultural and literary knowledge useful

Reader/Task Considerations

Teacher determined

Strategies for CLOSE READING

Analyze Story Elements: Characteristics of an Epic

Students should read the three sections all the way through. Close-reading questions at the bottom of the pages will help them understand how Beowulf and Wiglaf reflect the values of their society and the characteristics of an epic narrative poem. As they read, students should jot down comments or questions about the text in the margins.

WHEN STUDENTS STRUGGLE . . .

To help students understand characteristics of an epic hero, have them work in small groups to fill out a chart like the one shown below.

CITE TEXT EVIDENCE For practice in analyzing the main characters, ask students to identify what is revealed about the characters and their values from each text example in the chart.

Text from the Poem	What It Shows
"I've never known fear . . . But I will fight again, seek fame still..." (Beowulf's Last Battle, lines 1–4)	Beowulf is fearless and remains eager to seek personal glory even in old age.
"The Geats' great prince stood firm . . . waiting in his shining armor." (Beowulf's Last Battle, lines 55–58)	Beowulf is not afraid to face single combat with a dragon.
"Have The brave geats build me a tomb . . . and remember my name . . . " (The Death of Beowulf, lines 207–212)	Beowulf wants his name and the memory of his deeds to outlive him.

Background *The name of the English poet who created Beowulf is lost to history. The narrative probably originated on the European continent around the sixth century. Versions were carried to England by emigrating Germanic tribespeople and were passed down orally. Sometime in the eighth century, the story was probably shaped by a single unknown writer into the form in which it is known today. Beowulf is a powerful warrior of the Geats, a people from what is now Sweden. He is known for his bravery and his almost superhuman strength. In his youth, he killed a vicious monster known as Grendel and later his equally terrifying mother.*

from Beowulf

Epic Poem by The Beowulf Poet   translated by Burton Raffel

1. **READD** As you read lines 1–27, begin to collect and cite text evidence.
   - Underline courageous deeds Beowulf has done and what he promises to do.
   - In the margin, explain what you can infer about Beowulf (lines 1–6 and lines 20–27).

Beowulf's Last Battle

Beowulf is now king of the Geats and has ruled in peace and prosperity for fifty years. One day, a fire-breathing dragon begins terrorizing the Geats. Beowulf, now an old man, takes on the challenge of fighting it. He goes to the dragon's den with a hand-picked group of warriors.

    And Beowulf uttered his final boast:[1]
    "I've never known fear, as a youth I fought
In endless battles. I am old, now,
But I will fight again, seek fame still,
5 If the dragon hiding in his tower dares
To face me."

> Beowulf is fearless and likes the glory of fame.

[1] **boast:** a ritualized statement that is both a recitation of prior deeds and a vow to meet an approaching challenge.

87

---

1. **READ AND CITE TEXT EVIDENCE** The ritual boast was an important part of Beowulf's society. It wasn't looked upon as conceit in the way that bragging is seen in modern society. For one thing, a boast (*bēot* in Anglo-Saxon) wasn't empty. Warriors risked their lives to live up to their promises.

A ASK STUDENTS to read lines 1–25. Who is the source of evidence of what Beowulf has done and what he intends to do? What do we learn about his past from this passage? *Beowulf himself provides all the details about his deeds and how he will fight the dragon. We learn that he fought Grendel with his bare hands but that he will use a sword and shield against the dragon.*

CLOSE READ
Notes

Then he said farewell to his followers,
Each in his turn, for the last time:
　　　"I'd use no sword, no weapon, if this beast
Could be killed without it, crushed to death
10　Like Grendel, gripped in my hands and torn
Limb from limb. But his breath will be burning
Hot, poison will pour from his tongue.
I feel no shame, with shield and sword
And armor, against this monster: when he comes to me
15　I mean to stand, not run from his shooting
Flames, stand till fate decides
Which of us wins. My heart is firm,
My hands calm: I need no hot
Words. Wait for me close by, my friends.
20　　　We shall see, soon, who will survive
This bloody battle, stand when the fighting
Is done. No one else could do
What I mean to, here, no man but me
Could hope to defeat this monster. No one
25　Could try. And this dragon's treasure, his gold
And everything hidden in that tower, will be mine
Or war will sweep me to a bitter death!"
　　　Then Beowulf rose, still brave, still strong,
And with his shield at his side, and a mail shirt on his breast,

Beowulf is confident of his prowess, but aware that he may not win the fight.

2. **REREAD** Reread lines 1–6. When Beowulf talks about himself, which traits is he is proudest of? Support your answer with explicit textual evidence.

He values bravery ("I've never known fear"), the willingness to fight a dangerous adversary ("But I will fight again.../ If the dragon... dares / To face me"), and attaining personal glory ("seek fame still").

3. **READ** As you read lines 28–81, continue to cite textual evidence.

• Underline text that describes the setting.
• Circle text that shows the turning point in the battle.
• In the margin, explain how the details of the setting create tension (lines 36–55).

88

30　Strode calmly, confidently, toward the tower, under
The rocky cliffs: no coward could have walked there!
And then he who'd endured dozens of desperate
Battles, who'd stood boldly while swords and shields
Clashed, the best of kings, saw
35　Huge stone arches and felt the heat
Of the dragon's breath, flooding down
Through the hidden entrance, too hot for anyone
To stand, a streaming current of fire
And smoke that blocked all passage. And the Geats'
40　Lord and leader, angry, lowered
His sword and roared out a battle cry,
A call so loud and clear that it reached through
The **hoary** rock, hung in the dragon's
Ear. The beast rose, angry,
45　Knowing a man had come—and then nothing
But war could have followed. Its breath came first,
A steaming cloud pouring from the stone,
Then the earth itself shook. Beowulf
Swung his shield into place, held it
50　In front of him, facing the entrance. The dragon
Coiled and uncoiled, its heart urging it
Into battle. Beowulf's ancient sword
Was waiting, unsheathed, his sharp and gleaming
Blade. The beast came closer; both of them
55　Were ready, each set on slaughter. The Geats'
Great prince stood firm, unmoving, prepared
Behind his high shield, waiting in his shining
Armor. The monster came quickly toward him,
Pouring out fire and smoke, hurrying
60　To its fate. Flames beat at the iron
Shield, and for a time it held, protected

hoary:

gray with age

The descriptions of the heat and smoke create tension because they emphasize the power and size of the dragon and the difficulty of the task before Beowulf.

CLOSE READ
Notes

4. **REREAD** Reread lines 45–58. How does the poet show that the dragon is similar to Beowulf? What are those similarities? Support your answer with explicit textual evidence.

The poet shows us the dragon is ready: "Knowing a man had come." Like Beowulf, the dragon's heart urges it into battle. Both Beowulf and the dragon are "set on slaughter."

89

2. **REREAD AND CITE TEXT EVIDENCE**

B **ASK STUDENTS** to reread lines 1–25. In what way does Beowulf show the traits of an epic hero so far? *An epic hero usually shows individual bravery and is known for great deeds. Beowulf tells of his battle with Grendel using only his bare hands, and he says that he has "never known fear."*

3. **READ AND CITE TEXT EVIDENCE**

C **ASK STUDENTS** to look at lines 54–81. What are the main events in the battle so far? What major setback occurs? *The dragon advances toward Beowulf. Beowulf has held up his iron shield, but the dragon's fiery breath melts the shield. Beowulf strikes the dragon with his sword. The blade breaks, although it does pierce the dragon's skin. The dragon thrashes in pain and spews fire. Beowulf, without defense, is in danger of being killed.*

4. **REREAD AND CITE TEXT EVIDENCE**

D **ASK STUDENTS** to reread lines 39–60. What words does the poet use to describe the emotions of Beowulf and which to describe the dragon? *The word* angry *is used for both (line 40, line 44). In line 51, the dragon's heart is "urging it into battle." In line 55, both are "set on slaughter."*

Critical Vocabulary: hoary (line 43) Ask students to share their definitions of *hoary*. Point out that this word originally was used to describe a person whose hair is gray with age.

FOR ELL STUDENTS Clarify that *strode* (line 30) is the past tense of *stride*, meaning "to walk with long steps." Ask students to think of other verbs where the past tense is formed by changing the vowel rather than adding the suffix *-ed*.

Beowulf as he'd planned; then it began to melt,
And for the first time in his life that famous prince
Fought with fate against him, with glory
65   Denied him. He knew it, but he raised his sword
And struck at the dragon's scaly hide.
The ancient blade broke, bit into
The monster's skin, drew blood, but cracked
And failed him before it went deep enough, helped him
70   Less than he needed. The dragon leaped
With pain, thrashed and beat at him, spouting
Murderous flames, spreading them everywhere.
And the Geats' ring-giver² did not boast of glorious
Victories in other wars: his weapon
75   Had failed him, deserted him, now when he needed it
Most, that excellent sword. Edgetho's³
Famous son stared at death,
Unwilling to leave this world, to exchange it
For a dwelling in some distant place—a journey
80   Into darkness that all men must make, as death
Ends their few brief hours on earth.
         Quickly, the dragon came at him, encouraged
As Beowulf fell back; its breath flared,
And he suffered, wrapped around in swirling
85   Flames—a king, before, but now
A beaten warrior. None of his comrades
Came to him, helped him, his brave and noble
(E) Followers; they ran for their lives, fled
Deep in a wood. And only one of them
90   Remained, stood there, miserable, remembering,
As a good man must, what kinship should mean.
      His name was Wiglaf, he was Wexstan's son
And a good soldier; his family had been Swedish,
Once. Watching Beowulf, he could see

> ² **ring-giver:** king, lord; When someone swore allegiance to a Germanic lord in return for
> protection, the lord typically bestowed a ring on the follower to symbolize the bond.
> ³ **Edgetho:** Beowulf's father.

The narrator calls Beowulf's followers "brave and noble" as nearly all of them run for their lives.

(F) 95   How his king was suffering, burning. Remembering
Everything his lord and cousin had given him,
Armor and gold and the great estates
Wexstan's family enjoyed, Wiglaf's
Mind was made up; he raised his yellow
100   Shield and drew his sword. . . .
         And Wiglaf, his heart heavy, uttered
The kind of words his comrades deserved:
      "I remember how we sat in the mead-hall, drinking
And boasting of how brave we'd be when Beowulf
105   Needed us, he who gave us these swords
And armor: all of us swore to repay him,
When the time came, kindness for kindness
—With our lives, if he needed them. He allowed us to join him,
Chose us from all his great army, thinking
110   Our boasting words had some weight, believing
Our promises, trusting our swords. He took us
For soldiers, for men. He meant to kill
This monster himself, our mighty king,
Fight this battle alone and unaided,
115   As in the days when his strength and daring dazzled
Men's eyes. But those days are over and gone
And now our lord must lean on younger
Arms. And we must go to him, while angry
Flames burn at his flesh, help
120   Our glorious king! By almighty God,
I'd rather burn myself than see
Flames swirling around my lord.
And who are we to carry home
Our shields before we've slain his enemy
125   And ours, to run back to our homes with Beowulf
So hard-pressed here? I swear that nothing
He ever did deserved an end
Like this, dying miserably and alone,
Butchered by this savage beast: we swore
130   That these swords and armor were each for us all!" . . .

---

5.   **READ ▶**   As you read lines 82–130, continue to cite textual evidence.

• Underline text explaining what Wiglaf and his comrades promised in the past
and what Wiglaf wants them to do now.
• In the margin, explain the irony of narrator's words in lines 82–91.

6.   **◀ REREAD AND DISCUSS**   Reread lines 92–130. In a small group, discuss
the details Wiglaf gives that depict Beowulf as an honorable king. How does
Wiglaf show his own honor?

90

91

---

5.   **READ AND CITE TEXT EVIDENCE**   An important value in
Beowulf's society was the generosity of a king to his people.

(E)   **ASK STUDENTS**   to look at lines 89–111. What do Wiglaf's
unspoken thoughts reveal about obligations that a king and his
people have to one another? What do you learn about those
obligations from Wiglaf's speech to the other men? *Wiglaf thinks
of Beowulf's generosity to him and his family: "Armor and gold and
the great estates…" His speech reminds the men that Beowulf gave
them their swords and armor, and that they "swore to repay him"
and boasted how brave they would be "when Beowulf needed us."*

6.   **REREAD AND CITE TEXT EVIDENCE**

(F)   **ASK STUDENTS**   to reread lines 89–130. What do we learn
about Wiglaf's actions? *We learn that Wiglaf decides to stay and
raises his shield and draws his sword. He also demands that the other
men go with him to Beowulf now that he is under attack by the
dragon and can't defeat it alone.*

FOR ELL STUDENTS   Clarify that in line 100, *drew* does not mean
"made a drawing" but instead means "pulled out." Ask students to
think of other words that, like *draw*, can have two very different
meanings.

CLOSE READ
Notes

7. **READ ▶** As you read lines 131–189, continue to collect and cite textual evidence.

- Underline text that shows Beowulf's awareness of his approaching death and how he faces it.
- In the margin, explain why Beowulf's statement in lines 137–140 is important for the Geats.

The Death of Beowulf

Wiglaf joins Beowulf, who again attacks the dragon single-handedly; but the remnant of Beowulf's sword shatters, and the monster wounds him in the neck. Wiglaf then strikes the dragon, and he and Beowulf together finally succeed in killing the beast. Their triumph is short-lived, however, because Beowulf's wound proves to be mortal.

livid:
discolored from being bruised

Without a son, Beowulf does not have an heir to become king of the Geats on his death.

Beowulf spoke, in spite of the swollen,
G **Livid** wound, knowing he'd unwound
His string of days on earth, seen
As much as God would grant him; all worldly
135   Pleasure was gone, as life would go,
Soon:
    "I'd leave my armor to my son,
Now, if God had given me an heir,
A child born of my body, his life
H Created from mine. I've worn this crown
140   For fifty winters: no neighboring people
Have tried to threaten the Geats, sent soldiers
Against us or talked of terror. My days
Have gone by as fate willed, waiting
For its word to be spoken, ruling as well
145   As I knew how, swearing no unholy oaths,
Seeking no lying wars. I can leave
This life happy; I can die, here,
Knowing the Lord of all life has never
Watched me wash my sword in blood
150   Born of my own family. Belovèd
Wiglaf, go, quickly, find
The dragon's treasure: we've taken its life,
But its gold is ours, too. Hurry,

Bring me ancient silver, precious
155   Jewels, shining armor and gems,
Before I die. Death will be softer,
Leaving life and this people I've ruled
So long, if I look at this last of all prizes."
    Then Wexstan's son went in, as quickly
160   As he could, did as the dying Beowulf
Asked, entered the inner darkness
Of the tower, went with his mail shirt and his sword.
Flushed with victory he groped his way,
A brave young warrior, and suddenly saw
165   Piles of gleaming gold, precious
Gems, scattered on the floor, cups
And bracelets, rusty old helmets, beautifully
Made but rotting with no hands to rub
And polish them. They lay where the dragon left them;
170   It had flown in the darkness, once, before fighting
Its final battle. (So gold can easily
Triumph, defeat the strongest of men,
No matter how deep it is hidden!) And he saw,
Hanging high above, a golden
175   Banner, woven by the best of weavers
And beautiful. And over everything he saw
A strange light, shining everywhere,
On walls and floor and treasure. Nothing
Moved, no other monsters appeared;
180   He took what he wanted, all the treasures
That pleased his eye, heavy plates

8. **◀ REREAD** Reread lines 139–150. How does Beowulf summarize his 50-year reign? What ideals are reflected in his speech? Support your answer with explicit textual evidence.

Beowulf is facing certain death and thinking about what he has done with his life as a king ("ruling as well / As I knew how," protecting the Geats) and as a man (he has never killed anyone "Born of my own family"). His speech reveals his ideals about peace, justice, family loyalty, and honor.

92

93

---

7. **READ AND CITE TEXT EVIDENCE**

G **ASK STUDENTS** to look at lines 131–158. What does the narrator reveal about Beowulf's thoughts? Which of Beowulf's spoken words echo his unspoken thoughts? *Beowulf knows that he had "unwound his string of days on earth" (lines 132–133) and that "life would go, soon" (line 135). He speaks of not having an heir (lines 136–139), and he asks Wiglaf to go quickly to bring him some of the dragon's treasure, so he can see it "before I die" (line 156). He refers to the treasure as "the last of all prizes" (line 158).*

Critical Vocabulary: livid (line 132) Ask students to share their definitions of *livid*. Explain that *livid* also means "furiously angry." Which definition works better here?

8. **REREAD AND CITE TEXT EVIDENCE**

H **ASK STUDENTS** what honorable actions Beowulf claims for himself in these lines. *Here, Beowulf talks about protecting the Geats by fighting against neighboring people. He has sought "no lying wars." He has never killed a kinsman.*

CLOSE READ Notes

And golden cups and the glorious banner,
Loaded his arms with all they could hold.
Beowulf's dagger, his iron blade,
185 Had finished the fire-spitting terror
That once protected tower and treasures
Alike; the gray-bearded lord of the Geats
Had ended those flying, burning raids
Forever.
    Then Wiglaf went back, <u>anxious</u>
190 <u>To return while Beowulf was alive, to bring him
Treasure they'd won together. He ran,
Hoping his wounded king, weak
And dying, had not left the world too soon.</u>
Then he brought their treasure to Beowulf, and found
195 His famous king bloody, gasping
For breath. But Wiglaf sprinkled water
Over his lord, until the words
Deep in his breast broke through and were heard.
Beholding the treasure he spoke, haltingly:
200   "For this, this gold, these jewels, I thank
Our Father in Heaven, Ruler of the Earth—
For all of this, that His grace has given me,
Allowed me to bring to my people while breath
Still came to my lips. I sold my life
205 For this treasure, and I sold it well. Take
What I leave, Wiglaf, lead my people,
Help them; my time is gone. Have
The brave Geats build me a tomb,
When the funeral flames have burned me, and build it
210 Here, at the water's edge, high
On this spit of land, so sailors can see
This tower, and remember my name, and call it
Beowulf's tower, and boats in the darkness
And mist, crossing the sea, will know it."

Achieving lasting fame for one's deeds is very important to the Geats.

9. READ ▶ As you read lines 190–226, continue to cite textual evidence.
- Underline text that shows Wiglaf's feelings toward Beowulf.
- Circle text explaining who Beowulf chooses as a successor.
- In the margin, explain how lines 210–218 demonstrate a value important to the Geats.

94

215 Then that brave king gave the golden
Necklace from around his throat to Wiglaf,
Gave him his gold-covered helmet, and his rings,
And his mail shirt, and ordered him to use them well:
   "You're the last of all our far-flung family.
220 Fate has swept our race away,
Taken warriors in their strength and led them
To the death that was waiting. And now I follow them."
   The old man's mouth was silent, spoke
No more, had said as much as it could;
225 He would sleep in the fire, soon. His soul
Left his flesh, flew to glory. . . .
   And when the battle was over Beowulf's followers
Came out of the wood, cowards and traitors,
Knowing the dragon was dead. Afraid,
230 While it spit its fires, to fight in their lord's
Defense, to throw their **javelins** and spears,
They came like shamefaced jackals, their shields
In their hands, to the place where the prince lay dead,
And waited for Wiglaf to speak. He was sitting
235 Near Beowulf's body, wearily sprinkling
Water in the dead man's face, trying
To stir him. He could not. No one could have kept

javelins: light spears used as weapons

10. ◀ REREAD Reread lines 215–222. What happens in these lines? Why is it important that we have seen Wiglaf's courage in battle as well as his loyalty to Beowulf?

Before he dies, Beowful chooses Wiglaf to lead the Geats after his death. It's important that we know Wiglaf is brave and loyal, because the Geats value courage and loyalty.

11. READ ▶ As you read lines 227–265, continue to cite text evidence.
- Underline examples of kennings (metaphorical compound words substituted for a single noun) that stand for Beowulf's name.
- In the margin, explain how Wiglaf grows into his position as the new leader (lines 245–257).

95

---

9. READ AND CITE TEXT EVIDENCE

I ASK STUDENTS to read lines 1–6 on page 87 and then read lines 207–214. What early statement of Beowulf's is reflected in this last wish? *In Beowulf's words before the battle, he says that though he is old, he will "seek fame still." His wish for the Geats to build him a tomb that can be seen from far off shows that he wants fame that lasts after his death.*

FOR ELL STUDENTS Have a volunteer explain how context clues help convey the meaning of *gasping* (line 195). Have students work together to come up with a good definition.

10. REREAD AND CITE TEXT EVIDENCE

J ASK STUDENTS what they already know about Wiglaf's behavior. *He alone stays to help Beowulf; he tries to get the other warriors to stay also.*

11. READ AND CITE TEXT EVIDENCE

K ASK STUDENTS to look at lines 246–257. What does Wiglaf say in his first speech after Beowulf's death? *He decrees a punishment for the cowardly warriors who ran away.*

Critical Vocabulary: javelins (line 231) Ask students to share their definitions of *javelins*. Ask what other weapons and battle gear are named in the poem. *swords, shields, spears, armor*

CLOSE READ Notes

Life in their lord's body, or turned
Aside the Lord's will: world
240 And men and all move as He orders,
And always have, and always will.
        Then Wiglaf turned and angrily told them
What men without courage must hear.
Wexstan's brave son stared at the traitors,
245 His heart sorrowful, and said what he had to:
"I say what anyone who speaks the truth
Must say. . . .
        Too few of his warriors remembered
To come, when our lord faced death, alone.
250 And now the giving of swords, of golden
Rings and rich estates, is over,
Ended for you and everyone who shares
Your blood: when the brave Geats hear
How you bolted and ran none of your race
255 Will have anything left but their lives. And death
Would be better for them all, and for you, than the kind
Of life you can lead, branded with disgrace!". . .
        Then the warriors rose,
Walked slowly down from the cliff, stared
260 At those wonderful sights, stood weeping as they saw
Beowulf dead on the sand, their bold
Ring-giver resting in his last bed;
He'd reached the end of his days, their mighty
War-king, the great lord of the Geats,
265 Gone to a glorious death. . . .

Wiglaf is the one who scolds the men and tells them what will happen to them and their families.

12. **‹ REREAD** Reread lines 245–260. How does this passage demonstrate the importance of loyalty and bravery for the Geats?

Bravery and loyalty is so important to the Geats that the men's cowardice and abandonment of Beowulf will result in the loss of riches and lands for them and even their kin. All Geats will consider these men shamed and will not let them keep their possessions ("none of your race / Will have anything left but their lives").

96

13. **READ ▶** As you read lines 266–292, continue to collect and cite textual evidence.

- Underline text describing how the Geats mourned for Beowulf.
- In the margin, explain what the use of the word *beloved* reveals about the relationship between a leader and his people in the time of the Geats.

Mourning Beowulf

After Beowulf dies, the Geats fulfill his wish to build a tower as his tomb. The tower and the warriors' actions after building it serve to broadcast Beowulf's legacy not just to the Geats themselves but to others beyond the lands where Beowulf ruled.

Then the Geats built the tower, as Beowulf
Had asked, strong and tall, so sailors
Could find it from far and wide; working
For ten long days they made his monument,
270 Sealed his ashes in walls as straight
And high as wise and willing hands
Could raise them. And the riches he and Wiglaf
Had won from the dragon, rings, necklaces,
Ancient, hammered armor—all
275 The treasures they'd taken were left there, too,
Silver and jewels buried in the sandy
Ground, back in the earth, again
And forever hidden and useless to men.
And then twelve of the bravest Geats
280 Rode their horses around the tower,
Telling their sorrow, telling stories
Of their dead king and his greatness, his glory,
Praising him for heroic deeds, for a life
As noble as his name. So should all men
285 Raise up words for their lords, warm
With love, when their shield and protector leaves
His body behind, sends his soul
On high. And so Beowulf's followers
Rode, mourning their belovèd leader,
290 Crying that no better king had ever
Lived, no prince so mild, no man
So open to his people, so deserving of praise.

The leader had a personal relationship with his people, not a distant one.

97

12. **REREAD AND CITE TEXT EVIDENCE**

L **ASK STUDENTS** who the source of lands and riches for the Geats is. What might the king have the right to do to anyone who falls out of favor or violates laws or traditions? *The king is the giver of lands and riches, including at least some armor and swords. (Note that some swords are passed down through families.) Presumably the king can also take such gifts away.*

FOR ELL STUDENTS Clarify that *bolted* is used in line 254 to mean "to move very suddenly from one place." Ask students to supply another meaning for *bolt* and identify whether the word is being used as a noun or a verb in the meaning they suggest.

13. **READ AND CITE TEXT EVIDENCE**

M **ASK STUDENTS** in what way the Geats' actions reflect Beowulf's wishes. How do they reflect the values of the society? *As Beowulf wishes, the Geats build a tower that can be seen "far and wide" as a lasting monument to him. They also mourn him by riding around the tower and telling about his deeds and his noble life. This shows that the Geats value bravery and leadership and that they also value fame and glory that lasts even after death.*

FOR ELL STUDENTS Point out that the accent on *belovèd* in line 289 is a rare use of an accent mark in English. Here, it shows that the last syllable is pronounced separately, but generally an accent is used for that function only in poetry.

CLOSE READ Notes

14. **◀ REREAD** Reread lines 282–286. Notice the alliteration in the phrases "words for their lords" and "warm with love." How would you describe the tone of these lines? Cite another example of alliteration in your response.

The alliteration helps accentuate the reverential feeling the Geats had for Beowulf as well as help accentuate the values they found important such as "his greatness, his glory" and "a life / As noble as his name."

SHORT RESPONSE

Cite Text Evidence What traits make Beowulf an epic hero? Support your answer by **citing explicit textual evidence**.

Beowulf is a man of noble rank who has ruled as king for fifty years. He speaks of his virtues as a king as he is dying, and his mourners call him their "shield and protector." As king he is generous to his followers, as Wiglaf points out in detail. Beowulf is brave in battle. He also has seemingly superhuman strength as shown in his battle with the dragon. In his "final boast" before fighting the dragon, he speaks of having killed Grendel without any weapons. Beowulf also seeks fame and glory, which is reflected in his dying wish for a tower to be built on his tomb. Beowulf also says that he has lived with honor and lived for peace.

98

TO CHALLENGE STUDENTS . . .

Students can watch the video *Battle of Beowulf and Grendel* in their eBooks to learn more about the background to the battle.

ASK STUDENTS what they learn about Grendel in the video. *He is descended from Cain, the Bible's first murderer.* Why might Christianity play a role in an epic poem about heroes and monsters? *Anglo-Saxon society when* Beowulf *was written was a Christian society. The religion was part of everyday existence, so an epic story might be adapted to match the closely held beliefs of the day.*

DIG DEEPER

With the class, return to Question 6, Reread and Discuss, on page 91. Have students share their responses.

ASK STUDENTS to cite text evidence leading to their conclusions about how Beowulf and Wiglaf each show honor.

- Have students reread lines 82–130. What example of dishonorable behavior is shown here? How is that behavior evaluated, and by whom? *The other warriors "ran for their lives" instead of helping Beowulf. Wiglaf scolded them by citing Beowulf's generosity to them and their promises to him.*

- Have students look back at the passage. How does the behavior of the other warriors show by contrast the honorable actions of Beowulf and Wiglaf? *Beowulf honored his obligations by being generous to the warriors, but they ran away instead of honoring their obligations to him. Wiglaf shows honor by staying with Beowulf, in contrast to his cowardly comrades.*

ASK STUDENTS to continue their discussion and re-examine their views now that they have read the entire selection.

14. REREAD AND CITE TEXT EVIDENCE

ASK STUDENTS to look at lines 279–292. What examples of alliteration praise Beowulf's character and behavior? *"his greatness, his glory," "a life as noble as his name," "no prince so mild, no man so open to his people."*

SHORT RESPONSE

Cite Text Evidence Students' responses should include text evidence that supports their positions. They should:

- provide details showing Beowulf's position in the society.
- identify ways in which his behavior shows heroic traits.
- analyze what he says about himself before and after the battle.
- explain what others, including Wiglaf and Beowulf's mourners, say about him.

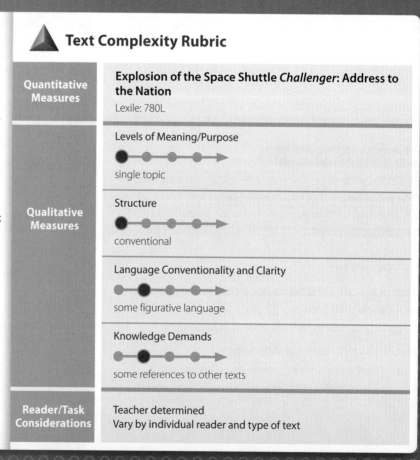

*my*SmartPlanner Create lesson plans and access resources online.

Explosion of the Space Shuttle *Challenger*: Address to the Nation

Speech by Ronald Reagan

Why This Text?

Students encounter arguments in many contexts, including personal conversations and discussions of current events in a variety of media and text sources. This lesson explores the function of persuasive techniques in developing arguments and shows how the author of this speech uses them to soothe and inspire a grieving population.

Key Learning Objective: The student will be able to determine the author's purpose and delineate and evaluate an argument.

 COMMON CORE **Common Core Standards**

RI 1 Cite textual evidence.
RI 4 Determine connotative meanings.
RI 6 Determine an author's purpose.
RI 8 Delineate and evaluate an argument and specific claims.
SL 1c Propel conversations by posing and responding to questions.
SL 2 Integrate information presented in diverse formats and media; evaluate the credibility and accuracy of each source.
SL 3 Evaluate a speaker's reasoning and evidence; assess premises, links, word choice, points of emphasis, and tone.

▲ Text Complexity Rubric

Quantitative Measures	**Explosion of the Space Shuttle *Challenger*: Address to the Nation** Lexile: 780L
Qualitative Measures	Levels of Meaning/Purpose single topic
	Structure conventional
	Language Conventionality and Clarity some figurative language
	Knowledge Demands some references to other texts
Reader/Task Considerations	Teacher determined Vary by individual reader and type of text

TEACH

CLOSE READ

For more context and historical background, students can view the video "America, The Story of Us: The *Challenger* and the End of the Space Race" in their eBooks

Background Have students read the background information about the *Challenger* explosion. Tell students that the explosion occurred on the shuttle's tenth mission. Seventeen years later, on February 1, 2003, another shuttle tragedy occurred: the *Columbia* broke apart during reentry, killing all seven astronauts aboard. In spite of these tragic events, NASA's fleet of five shuttles completed 135 missions between 1981 and 2011, when the shuttle program came to an end. (In addition to *Challenger* and *Columbia*, the fleet included *Discovery*, *Atlantis*, and *Endeavour*.) The shuttles played an important part in building the International Space Station, as well maintaining the Hubble Space Telescope.

AS YOU READ Direct students to use the As You Read suggestion to focus their reading.

Determine Author's Purpose (LINES 1–6)

COMMON CORE RI 1, RI 6

Tell students that an author's **purpose** is the reason for writing the work—what he or she hopes to achieve. An author may have one or more purposes, such as to inform, to persuade, to express opinions, or to influence an audience's emotions. Explain that an author of a speech can use one or more persuasive techniques to achieve his or her goals: **emotional appeals, appeals to loyalty,** and **appeals by association.**

Ⓐ CITE TEXT EVIDENCE Ask students to identify Reagan's general purpose or purposes for giving this speech. What persuasive technique does he use in lines 4–6? Cite specific evidence to support your answer. *(His purpose is to commiserate with his audience's emotions. He uses the technique of emotional appeals. When he says "Nancy and I are pained to the core [line 4] and "we share this pain" [line 5], he is showing that they are grieving with all Americans.)* If necessary, point out that "Nancy" (line 4) refers to the president's wife.

Background *The* Challenger *shuttle explosion marked the nation's first tragedy during a flight to space. The disaster, which occurred on January 28, 1986, killed the entire crew just moments after takeoff, including Christa McAuliffe, a high-school teacher who had been selected to pioneer NASA's Teacher in Space program. On the morning of the launch, students in schools across the country gathered to watch the event on live television. That evening, President Ronald Reagan addressed the nation.*

Explosion of the Space Shuttle *Challenger*:
Address to the Nation

Speech by Ronald Reagan

AS YOU READ Pay attention to Reagan's comments about the *Challenger* crew. Write down questions you generate during reading.

> Ladies and gentlemen, I'd planned to speak to you tonight to report on the state of the Union, but the events of earlier today have led me to change those plans. Today is a day for mourning and remembering. Ⓐ
>
> Nancy and I are pained to the core by the tragedy of the shuttle *Challenger*. We know we share this pain with all of the people of our country. This is truly a national loss.
>
> Nineteen years ago, almost to the day, we lost three astronauts in a terrible accident on the ground.[1] But we've never lost an astronaut in flight; we've never had a tragedy like this. And perhaps we've forgotten
> 10 the courage it took for the crew of the shuttle; but they, the Challenger Seven, were aware of the dangers, but overcame them and did their jobs brilliantly. We mourn seven heroes: Michael Smith, Dick Scobee, Judith Resnik, Ronald McNair, Ellison Onizuka, Gregory Jarvis, and Christa McAuliffe. We mourn their loss as a nation together.
>
> For the families of the seven, we cannot bear, as you do, the full impact of this tragedy. But we feel the loss, and we're thinking

[1] **Nineteen years . . . ground:** In 1967, the crew of Apollo 1 died when a fire broke out while it was on the launch pad.

SCAFFOLDING FOR ELL STUDENTS

Vocabulary: Roots Tell students that many English words have Greek or Latin roots. Explain that these roots have fixed meanings, and that learning these meanings can help them define many unfamiliar words.

Point out the word *astronaut* in line 7. Tell students that *astro* is the Greek root for "star." The second part of the word, *naut*, is the Greek root for "ship," and *nautēs* means "sailor." Elicit the literal meaning for *astronaut*: "star sailor." Ask students what other words they can think of, either in English or perhaps in their native language, that use these roots (i.e., *astronomy, nautical*).

ASK STUDENTS to determine the roots of *civilians* (line 41) and *decades* (line 46). Have pairs identify the meanings of the roots in a dictionary and then define the words.

Determine Author's Purpose (LINES 35–37)

 COMMON CORE RI 1, RI 6

Explain that readers often have to infer an author's purpose or purposes by analyzing the author's choice of words and details.

B **CITE TEXT EVIDENCE** What persuasive technique is Reagan using when he says, "We don't hide our space program. We don't keep secrets and cover things up. We do it all up front and in public. That's the way freedom is . . ." (lines 35–37)? What word suggests that he is using this technique and helps you infer Reagan's purpose in this passage? *(The technique is appeal to loyalty—patriotism. The word is we.)* What are Reagan's purposes in making this statement? *(His purposes are to persuade and to influence an audience's emotions.)*

Delineate and Evaluate an Argument (LINES 39–42)

COMMON CORE RI 8

Tell students that a **premise** is an assertion or statement on which additional affirmations or denials are based. It supports an author's **claim,** or position.

C **ASK STUDENTS** to identify the premise in the paragraph that begins on line 39? *(The first sentence in the paragraph affirms that the space program will continue.)*

COLLABORATIVE DISCUSSION Have students work in pairs to evaluate Reagan's response and to express and defend their opinions about its effectiveness. They should support their opinions with reasons and evidence used in the speech.

ASK STUDENTS to share any questions they generated in the course of reading and discussing the selection.

---

about you so very much. Your loved ones were daring and brave, and they had that special grace, that special spirit that says, "Give me a challenge and I'll meet it with joy." They had a hunger to explore the
20 universe and discover its truths. They wished to serve, and they did. They served all of us.

We've grown used to wonders in this century. It's hard to dazzle us. But for 25 years the United States space program has been doing just that. We've grown used to the idea of space, and perhaps we forget that we've only just begun. We're still pioneers. They, the members of the *Challenger* crew, were pioneers.

And I want to say something to the schoolchildren of America who were watching the live coverage of the shuttle's takeoff. I know it is hard to understand, but sometimes painful things like this happen.
30 It's all part of the process of exploration and discovery. It's all part of taking a chance and expanding man's horizons. The future doesn't belong to the fainthearted; it belongs to the brave. The *Challenger* crew was pulling us into the future, and we'll continue to follow them.

B I've always had great faith in and respect for our space program, and what happened today does nothing to diminish it. We don't hide our space program. We don't keep secrets and cover things up. We do it all up front and in public. That's the way freedom is, and we wouldn't change it for a minute.

C We'll continue our quest in space. There will be more shuttle
40 flights and more shuttle crews and, yes, more volunteers, more civilians, more teachers in space. Nothing ends here; our hopes and our journeys continue.

I want to add that I wish I could talk to every man and woman who works for NASA or who worked on this mission and tell them: "Your dedication and professionalism have moved and impressed us for decades. And we know of your anguish. We share it."

There's a coincidence today. On this day 390 years ago, the great explorer Sir Francis Drake died aboard ship off the coast of Panama. In his lifetime the great frontiers were the oceans, and an historian
50 later said, "He lived by the sea, died on it, and was buried in it." Well, today we can say of the *Challenger* crew: Their dedication was, like Drake's, complete.

The crew of the space shuttle *Challenger* honored us by the manner in which they lived their lives. We will never forget them, nor the last time we saw them, this morning, as they prepared for their journey and waved goodbye and "slipped the surly bonds of earth" to "touch the face of God."[2]

---

[2] **"slipped . . . God":** references to the first and last lines of "High Flight," a poem by John G. Magee, Jr.

COLLABORATIVE DISCUSSION With a partner, discuss whether you think Reagan responded effectively to the tragic deaths of the crew members.

APPLYING ACADEMIC VOCABULARY

assurance	vision

As you discuss the speech, incorporate the following Collection 5 academic vocabulary words: *assurance* and *vision*. Have students discuss what kind of **assurance** Reagan is offering to his audience. Would they (the students) have felt assured by his words? As students evaluate the effectiveness of Reagan's argument, ask them to describe his **vision** for the future of the space program.

Delineate and Evaluate an Argument

 COMMON CORE RI 8

President Reagan's response to the tragedy of the *Challenger* explosion includes an argument about the space program. Think about these questions to delineate and evaluate his argument.

- **Claim:** Is Reagan's claim, or position, about the space program credible and supported by logical reasoning and evidence?
- **Reasoning:** Upon what premises—statements affirming or denying something—is President Reagan's argument based? Does he make any logical errors in presenting his conclusions? For example, does he make any generalizations that are too broad?
- **Evidence:** Are the facts, examples, and other details included in the speech valid, authoritative, relevant, and sufficient? Is President Reagan able to support his vision of the future with evidence?

The answers to these questions will help you outline President Reagan's argument and look critically at the flow of ideas. Examining the relationships between ideas will help you evaluate the strength of his argument.

Determine Author's Purpose

 COMMON CORE RI 6

The author of a speech writes for one or more **purposes**, which may include to inform, to persuade, to express opinions, or to influence an audience's emotions. The reader often has to infer the author's purpose. As you identify and analyze the purposes of Reagan's speech, consider how he uses these persuasive techniques to help achieve them and add power to his message.

Persuasive Techniques	Examples
Emotional appeals sway an audience by focusing on strong feelings.	President Reagan identifies with Americans' grief by using phrases such as "painful things like this happen" and "we know of your anguish."
Appeals to loyalty rely on people's affiliation with a particular group.	President Reagan's use of the pronouns *us* and *we* appeals to Americans' sense of patriotism.
Appeals by association connect a cause with another widely accepted idea.	President Reagan compares the space program to the exploration of other frontiers.

CLOSE READ

Delineate and Evaluate an Argument

 COMMON CORE RI 8

Help students understand the terms. Point out that the core of Reagan's argument is embedded in a larger speech. Have students identify the introduction to the argument *(lines 1–21)*, and then ask them to characterize the introduction. *(In the introduction, Reagan uses the words "nation," "national," and "service" and also makes a reference to the Apollo I tragedy to reinforce the idea that the astronauts' loss is a loss to the country as well as to the space program.)* Ask how this is an effective introduction to the argument. *(The audience is already "with" Reagan when he begins the argument.)*

Determine Author's Purpose

 COMMON CORE RI 6

Review the terms *emotional appeals, appeals to loyalty,* and *appeals by association,* and have students examine the examples in the chart. Then ask them to brainstorm additional examples of these persuasive techniques they might encounter in other speeches and argumentative texts. Have students explain how identifying persuasive techniques helps them infer the author's purpose.

Strategies for Annotation  *Annotate it!*

Delineate and Evaluate an Argument

COMMON CORE RI 1, RI 8

Encourage students to use their eBook annotation tools to do the following:

- Highlight in yellow a premise in Reagan's argument.
- Highlight in blue evidence that supports the premise.
- On a note, state if Reagan has made any logical errors or generalizations that are too broad.

is hard to understand, but sometimes painful things like this happen. It's all part of the process of exploration and discovery. It's all part of taking a chance and expanding man's horizons. The future doesn't belong to the fainthearted; it belongs to the brave. The *Challenger* crew was pulling us into the future, and we'll continue to follow them.

PRACTICE & APPLY

Analyzing the Text COMMON CORE RI 6, RI 8

Possible answers:

1. In lines 25–26, Reagan first refers to the future when he says, "we forget that we've only just begun. We're still pioneers." He goes on to predict future expansion and further successes in lines 31–42.

2. He says that despite the space program's ability to instill awe and wonder, it is still in its infancy, relating to his claim that its most significant achievements still lie ahead.

3. Reagan directly addresses the victims' families, students who viewed live televised coverage of the disaster, and NASA personnel. His reassurances add to the emotional appeal of his message. He emphasizes that, although the tragedy has affected Americans differently, all are mourning.

4. Reagan suggests that all Americans value liberty (lines 38–39). He also appeals to their values of bravery and service to the nation (lines 17–22 and 30–33), hard work, and dedication (line 45–46).

5. According to Reagan, Drake and the seven astronauts were all dedicated explorers of the great frontiers of their times, the former on the sea and the latter in space. Some students may believe that Reagan makes a valid comparison. Others may point out that Drake was primarily engaged in acts of piracy and violence, and that he also participated in the African slave trade; the Challenger crew's purposes were peaceful.

6. Reagan's purposes are to console a grieving nation and to deflect criticism of the space program. He contributes to these purposes by framing his speech as an ode to fallen heroes (lines 9–12). He places the astronauts within the context of history and traditional values, arguing that the proper way to honor their patriotism and self-sacrifice is to continue in their cause.

7. Beyond references to the Apollo 1 fire and Drake's death at sea (from dysentery), Reagan offers little evidence to validate his claim that "painful things" represent a necessary part of "expanding man's horizons." He does not offer any facts or statistics to show that accidental deaths cannot be avoided.

8. Reagan uses the quote, which originally expressed the joyous exhilaration that aviators feel, to figuratively describe death. It is an effective conclusion because it provides an emotional release, evokes the audience's religious beliefs, and conveys an image of the victims passing peacefully into a pleasant afterlife.

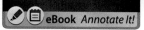 eBook *Annotate It!*

Analyzing the Text COMMON CORE RI 6, RI 8, SL 1c, SL 2, SL 3

Cite Text Evidence   Support your responses with evidence from the selection.

1. **Identify** What is Reagan's claim about the future of the space program?

2. **Identify** What premise about the space program does Reagan express in lines 22–26? How does this premise relate to his claim?

3. **Analyze** What specific groups of people does Reagan directly address in his speech? How do the assurances he makes to them impact his message?

4. **Interpret** What values does President Reagan suggest all Americans share in his appeals to their sense of patriotism?

5. **Analyze** According to Reagan, how are the *Challenger* astronauts similar to Sir Francis Drake? Is this a valid comparison? Explain why or why not.

6. **Analyze** Identify two purposes of Reagan's speech. How do the style and content of the speech contribute to his purposes?

7. **Evaluate** Is Reagan's statement that tragedies like the *Challenger* explosion are "all part of the process of exploration and discovery" valid? What types of evidence does Reagan provide to support this idea? What types of evidence does he not address?

8. **Critique** John G. Magee, Jr., died a few months after writing the poem "High Flight," which expresses his feelings about being a World War II pilot. Is Reagan's quote from the poem an effective way to end his speech? Explain your response.

PERFORMANCE TASK

Speaking Activity: Discussion President Reagan postponed his State of the Union address to deliver his speech on the *Challenger* explosion on television. Watch a video of the speech and then evaluate it in a small group discussion.

1. As you watch the speech, note how Reagan's tone of voice, facial expressions, and eye contact help support his message.

2. Discuss the power and effectiveness of Reagan's speech. Pose and respond to questions that probe Reagan's use of reasoning and evidence. Assess the premises on which his claim is based, his links among ideas, word choice, points of emphasis, and tone.

3. Take notes during the discussion and then write a brief summary of the group's conclusions.

Assign this performance task.

PERFORMANCE TASK COMMON CORE SL 1c, SL 2, SL 3

Speaking Activity: Discussion Have students reread the speech before viewing the video. Suggest that they note cues such as facial expressions, hand and head gestures, set design, and camera movement. Have groups discuss how these elements contribute to the tone and message. Students should cite text evidence and clear reasons to support their ideas about the speech's effectiveness. Have group members summarize their discussions for the class.

Determine Connotative Meanings

COMMON CORE

RI 4

TEACH

Remind students about the persuasive technique of making emotional appeals. Such appeals use language in a specific way in order to elicit certain feelings in an audience.

Explain that one way a writer can create an emotional appeal is by using words with strong connotations—positive or negative—that support their purpose. Identifying such words can help readers identify and evaluate a writer's purpose.

Explain the difference between connotation and denotation. A **connotation** is a shade of associated meaning of a word; a **denotation** is the literal, dictionary definition of a word.

As an example, point out the word *quest* on page 430, line 39. The denotation of the word is "a search." The connotation of the word, however, is positive and inspirational: "a noble journey that requires a hero to overcome many obstacles." Point out that the connotative meaning of the word reinforces Reagan's description of the astronauts as heroes and pioneers.

PRACTICE AND APPLY

Have students work individually or in pairs to complete the WordSharp Interactive Vocabulary Tutorial: **Denotative and Connotative Meanings.**

When they have completed the tutorial, have students find two to three more words in the speech that have strong connotations—positive or negative—and identify their effects.

Delineate and Evaluate an Argument

COMMON CORE

RI 8

RETEACH

Remind students that evaluating an argument involves judging whether the evidence used to support the claim is:

- **sufficient:** One or two pieces of evidence might not be enough to support an argument.
- **relevant:** Evidence may not apply nor closely connect to the argument.
- **credible:** Evidence might come from an unreliable source.

LEVEL UP TUTORIALS Assign the following *Level Up* tutorial: **Evidence.**

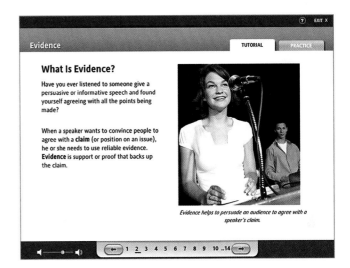

When students complete the tutorial, ask them to list evidence in the speech that supports Reagan's argument. Then have them determine whether the evidence is sufficient and whether each piece is relevant and credible.

CLOSE READING APPLICATION

Students can apply the skill to another speech or argument. Have them work independently to identify the claim, to determine the reasoning, and to evaluate the evidence.

The Deep

Short Story by Anthony Doerr

Why This Text?

To fully appreciate life, students must learn to empathize with people who live in very different circumstances and to recognize the common themes that connect the lives of all people. In this story, they will meet a fragile young man surviving in Depression-era Detroit whose surprising perspective on life is a lesson to us all.

▶ View It!

Professional Development Podcast:
Text-Dependent Analysis

Key Learning Objective: The student will be able to determine themes in a story and analyze the role of setting.

For practice and application:

Close Reader selection
"Blackheart"
Short Story by Mark Braizitis

⦿ COMMON CORE Common Core Standards

RL 1 Cite textual evidence to support analysis.

RL 2 Determine two or more themes and analyze their development, including how they interact and build on one another.

RL 3 Analyze the author's choices regarding how to develop elements of a story.

RL 4 Determine the meaning of words and phrases, including figurative meanings.

RL 5 Analyze an author's choices concerning how to structure specific parts of a text.

SL 1a Participate effectively in a range of collaborative discussions.

L 3 Apply knowledge of language to make effective choices for meaning or style.

L 5b Analyze nuances in the meaning of words with similar denotations.

▲ Text Complexity Rubric

Quantitative Measures	**The Deep** Lexile: 860L
Qualitative Measures	Levels of Meaning/Purpose ●—●—●—●—● ➝ multiple levels of meaning (multiple themes)
	Structure ●—●—●—●—● ➝ some unconventional story structure elements
	Language Conventionality and Clarity ●—●—●—●—● ➝ more complex descriptions
	Knowledge Demands ●—●—●—●—● ➝ some cultural and literary knowledge useful
Reader/Task Considerations	Teacher determined Vary by individual reader and type of text

CLOSE READ

Anthony Doerr Have students read the information about Anthony Doerr (dôr). Tell them that he writes a regular review of science-related books for the *Boston Globe*. His fascination with the natural world is apparent in "The Deep." Doerr believes in writing to explore subjects he does not yet know about but finds intriguing, and he spends a great deal of time doing research for his stories and novels.

AS YOU READ Direct students to use the As You Read note to focus their reading.

Analyze Story Elements: Setting (LINES 1–11)

 COMMON CORE RL 3

Remind students that **setting** is the time and place in which a story happens. However, setting is more than just a date and a spot on a map. It includes all the physical, social, political, and economic details one might notice about a specific city or town at a particular moment in history.

Ⓐ CITE TEXT EVIDENCE Have students reread the first paragraph and identify details the author uses to describe the precise setting into which Tom is born. *(The basic facts are "1914 in Detroit, a quarter mile from International Salt." Details that allow readers to imagine the setting are the "underinsulated boardinghouse" and the "grim possessions" of the salt workers who live there: "coats the color of mice," "salt-caked trousers," and so on. The fact that one worker is replaced by another every six months suggests the economic context of Tom's life.)*

CRITICAL VOCABULARY

itinerant: The salt workers who live in the boardinghouse do not stay long because they move from one job to another.

ASK STUDENTS how living in the boardinghouse with itinerant workers would lead Tom to conclude that "the world continually drains itself of young men." *(Because the men regularly move on to other jobs while Tom stays in one place, the men are continually disappearing or being drained from his life.)*

Anthony Doerr *has won many awards for his short stories, including four O. Henry prizes and Britain's Sunday Times EFG Short Story Award for "The Deep." In an interview with the journal* Fugue, *he explained that it is vital not to become used to life's wonder but to keep trying to see what is special about the world. He also described his desire to shake up structure and language so that readers are struck anew by some element in life or nature. He currently lives in Boise, Idaho, and writes for the* Boston Globe *and the* New York Times *when not at work on his fiction.*

The Deep

Short Story by Anthony Doerr

AS YOU READ Pay attention to details the author adds to develop Tom's character throughout the story. Write down any questions you generate during reading.

Ⓐ TOM IS BORN in 1914 in Detroit, a quarter mile from International Salt. His father is offstage, unaccounted for. His mother operates a six-room, underinsulated boardinghouse populated with locked doors, behind which drowse the grim possessions of **itinerant** salt workers: coats the color of mice, tattered mucking boots, aquatints[1] of undressed women, their breasts faded orange. Every six months a miner is fired or drafted or dies and is replaced by another, so that very early in his life Tom comes to see how the world continually drains itself of young men, leaving behind only objects—empty tobacco pouches, bladeless jack-knives, salt-caked trousers—mute, incapable of memory.

Tom is four when he starts fainting. He'll be rounding a corner, breathing hard, and the lights will go out. Mother will carry him indoors, set him on the armchair, and send someone for the doctor.

itinerant
(ī-tĭn′ər-ənt) *adj.*
migrant, or travelling from site to site.

10

---

[1] **aquatints:** prints that resemble watercolor paintings.

SCAFFOLDING FOR ELL STUDENTS

Language: Verb Tenses Have students read the first sentence in the story. Ask them to identify the tense of the verb *is*. *(present)* Explain that while many stories are written in the past tense, this author has chosen to write in the present tense, even though the story is set in the past. This technique makes readers feel as if they are experiencing story events as they happen.

Next, have students read lines 12–18 and identify verbs in the future tense. Explain that in lines 12–14, the future tense is used to indicate events that happen repeatedly. In line 16, the doctor uses the future tense in the more common way, to refer to the work Tom's heart will do in the future.

TEACH

CLOSE READ

Determine Themes

(LINES 15–23)

Remind students that a **theme** is a message about life conveyed through a literary work. A complex story usually has multiple themes that interact and develop as the story unfolds. Explain that a story's main conflict and the way characters respond to it often suggest themes.

 CITE TEXT EVIDENCE Ask students to reread lines 15–23. What major conflict is introduced in this passage? How does Tom's mother respond to the problem? *(The conflict is that Tom has a serious health problem, a "hole in the heart." The doctor predicts he will not live past his eighteenth birthday. Tom's mother responds by trying to protect him from anything that might excite or startle him—"no bright lights, no loud noises.")*

Support Inferences

(LINES 24–34)

Point out that the story's third-person narrator can tell readers what Tom is thinking, but readers must infer what Tom is feeling.

 ASK STUDENTS to review lines 24–34. What does Tom think about as he watches Mr. Weems leave for work? What can you infer about his feelings? *(Tom imagines what it would be like to ride the elevator down into the salt mine. Although the mine is not a glamorous place, Tom imagines it as a "city beneath the city" with "glittering rooms" and "vast arcades." He figures that if he only lives to be sixteen he will never get to see such interesting places. Readers can infer that he is fascinated by the world beyond his reach—all the places he can't visit or see for himself.)*

CRITICAL VOCABULARY

sporadic: Tom thinks the elevator shaft is quite dark because there are only a few lights placed in random spots along the way.

ASK STUDENTS whether they think Tom's fainting spells are sporadic, and why. *(They are probably sporadic because they happen only when he gets overly excited.)*

Atrial septal defect. Hole in the heart. The doctor says blood sloshes from the left side to the right side. His heart will have to do three times the work. Life span of sixteen. Eighteen if he's lucky. Best if he doesn't get excited.

Mother trains her voice into a whisper. *Here you go, there you*
20 *are, sweet little Tomcat.* She smothers the windows with curtains. She moves Tom's cot into an upstairs closet—no bright lights, no loud noises. Mornings she serves him a glass of buttermilk, then points him to the brooms or steel wool. *Go slow,* she'll say. He scrubs the coal stove, sweeps the marble stoop. Every so often he peers up from his work and watches the face of the oldest boarder, Mr. Weems, as he troops downstairs, a fifty-year-old man hooded against the cold, off to descend in an elevator a thousand feet underground. Tom imagines his descent, **sporadic** and dim lights passing and receding, cables rattling, a half dozen other miners squeezed into the cage beside him, each
30 thinking his own thoughts, sinking down into that city beneath the city, where mules stand waiting and oil lamps burn in the walls and glittering rooms of salt recede into vast arcades beyond the farthest reaches of the light.

Sixteen, thinks Tom. *Eighteen if I'm lucky.*

School is a three-room shed aswarm with the offspring of salt workers, coal workers, ironworkers. Irish kids, Polish kids, Armenian kids. *Don't run, don't fight,* whispers Mother. *No games.* For Tom the schoolyard seems a thousand acres of sizzling pandemonium. His first day, he lasts an hour. Mother finds him beneath a tablecloth with his
40 fist in his mouth. *Shhh,* she says, and crawls under there with him and wraps her arms around his like ropes.

He seesaws in and out of the early grades. By the time he's ten, he's in remedial everything. *I'm trying,* he mumbles, but letters spin off pages and hang themselves in the branches outside. *Dunce,* the other boys declare, and to Tom that seems about right.

Tom sweeps, scrubs, scours the stoop with pumice one square inch at a time. *Slow as molasses in January,* says Mr. Weems, but he winks at Tom when he says it.

Every day, all day, the salt finds its way in. It encrusts washbasins,
50 settles on the rims of baseboards. It spills out of the boarders, too: from ears, boots, handkerchiefs. Furrows of glitter gather in the bedsheets; a daily lesson in insidiousness.

Start at the center, then scrub out to the edges. Linens on Thursdays. Toilets on Fridays.

He's twelve when Ms. Fredericks asks the children to give reports. Ruby Hornaday goes sixth. Ruby has flames for hair, Christmas for a birthday, and a drunk for a daddy. She's one of two girls to make it to fourth grade.

She reads from notes in controlled terror. *If you think the lake is*
60 *big you should see the sea. It's three-quarters of Earth. And that's just*

sporadic
(spə-răd´ĭk) *adj.*
occasional; occurring at random intervals.

SCAFFOLDING FOR ELL STUDENTS

Language: Conversational English Patterns Explain that the author uses italic type to indicate dialogue as in lines 19–20. In dialogue and other passages, the characters and narrator sometimes use informal words typical of spoken English.

- Lines 15–18: The sentences "Hole in the heart" (which means the same as "Atrial septal defect") and "Life span of sixteen. Eighteen if he's lucky. Best if he doesn't get excited" leave out words. Help students complete the sentences. *(He has a hole in his heart. He'll have a life span of sixteen years. He might live to be eighteen if he's lucky. It's best if he doesn't get excited.)*

- Lines 19–20: "Here you go" and "there you are" are idiomatic expressions that can mean "It's OK" or "I'm taking care of you."

the surface. Someone throws a pencil. The creases in Ruby's forehead deepen. *Land animals live on ground or in trees rats and worms and gulls and such. But sea animals they live everywhere they live in the waves and they live in mid water and they live in canyons six and a half miles down.*

She passes around a thick, red book. Inside are blocks of text and full-color photographic plates that make Tom's heart boom in his ears. A blizzard of green fish. A kingdom of purple corals. Five orange starfish cemented to a rock.

70   Ruby says, *Detroit used to have palm trees and corals and seashells. Detroit used to be a sea three miles deep.*

Ms. Fredericks says, *Ruby, where did you get that book?* but by then Tom is hardly breathing. See-through flowers with poison tentacles and fields of clams and pink monsters with kingdoms of whirling needles on their backs. He tries to say, *Are these real?* but quicksilver bubbles rise from his mouth and float up to the ceiling. When he goes over, the desk goes over with him.

The doctor says it's best if Tom stays out of school. *Keep indoors,* the doctor says. *If you get excited, think of something blue.* Mother lets him
80   come downstairs for meals and chores only. Otherwise he's to stay in his closet. *We have to be more careful, Tomcat,* she whispers, and sets her palm on his forehead.

Tom spends long hours on the floor beside his cot, assembling and reassembling the same jigsaw puzzle: a Swiss village. Five hundred pieces, nine of them missing. Sometimes Mr. Weems sits and reads to Tom from adventure novels. They're blasting a new vein down in the mines and little cascades of plaster sift from the ceiling. In the lulls between Mr. Weems's words, Tom can feel explosions **reverberate** up through a thousand feet of rock and shake the fragile pump in his
90   chest.

He misses school. He misses the sky. He misses everything. When Mr. Weems is in the mine and Mother is downstairs, Tom often slips to the end of the hall and lifts aside the curtains and presses his forehead to the glass. Children run the snowy lanes and lights glow in the foundry windows and train cars trundle beneath elevated conduits. First-shift miners emerge from the mouth of the hauling elevator in groups of six and bring out cigarette cases from their overalls and strike matches and spill like little salt-dusted insects out into the night, while the darker figures of the second-shift miners stamp their feet in
100   the cold, waiting outside the cages for their turn in the pit.

In dreams he sees waving sea fans and milling schools of grouper and underwater shafts of light. He sees Ruby Hornaday push open the door of his closet. She's wearing a copper diving helmet; she leans over his cot and puts the window of her helmet an inch from his face.

He wakes with a shock and heat pooled in his groin. He thinks, *Blue, blue, blue.*

reverberate
(rĭ-vûr′bə-rāt′) *v.* to vibrate or resonate.

The Deep   **435**

Determine Themes COMMON CORE RL 2

(LINES 66–77)

Tell students that characters' behaviors and reactions can point to themes.

D **ASK STUDENTS** to reread lines 66–77. Does Tom's reaction to the book seem extreme? What does his reaction reveal about him? (*Tom reacts very strongly to the photographs in the book. He sees not just colorful sea creatures but "A blizzard of green fish. A kingdom of purple corals." After a moment, he faints and topples over. His reaction shows that he is sensitive to life's beauty and wonder, and that he longs to know about the world beyond his boardinghouse.*)

Analyze Story Elements: COMMON CORE RL 3
Symbol (LINES 91–100)

Remind students that a **symbol** is an object, event, place, or action that has a meaning beyond itself.

E **ASK STUDENTS** to reread lines 91–100 and also to recall the first mention of the curtains in line 20. What might the curtains symbolize for Tom? (*They symbolize the fear of death that separates Tom from the rest of the world. His mother "smothers the windows with curtains" to protect him from bright sunlight that might cause him too much excitement. When he "lifts aside the curtains and presses his forehead to the glass" to watch other people going about their lives, he imagines what his life would be like if he did not have to protect his weak heart.*)

> **CRITICAL VOCABULARY**
>
> **reverberate:** Explosions deep underground are echoed in the shaking of Tom's house and heart.
>
> **ASK STUDENTS** why the blasting in the salt mines reverberates in Tom's house. (*The salt mines are very near, and the explosions are powerful, so the ground under the house transmits the vibrations of the blasts.*)

APPLYING ACADEMIC VOCABULARY

collapse	conceive

As you discuss the story, incorporate the Collection 5 academic vocabulary words *collapse* and *conceive*. Ask students what causes Tom to **collapse** as he looks at the book about sea animals. As you discuss Tom's perspective on life at this point in the story, ask students whether he can **conceive** of living a normal life beyond the walls of the boardinghouse.

Analyze Story Elements: Character (LINES 111–125)

Tell students that authors use dialogue to create a unique voice for each character and reveal the character's traits.

F **CITE TEXT EVIDENCE** Ask student to reread lines 111–125, paying attention to the words spoken by Ruby and Mr. Weems. What does each character's manner of speaking reveal about his or her personality? *(Ruby's statements are direct and almost abrupt: "Seemed like you were interested in water creatures." "You're not going to faint again, are you?" "Keep 'em if you want." She is confident in herself. Mr. Weems often speaks in similes, or colorful comparisons, such as "she's damp as a church." His style of speaking suggests an imaginative view of the world and also a sense of humor.)*

Determine Figurative Meanings (LINES 115–116)

Remind students that **figurative language** is the use of words to mean something beyond their literal definitions. Mr. Weems's similes are one example, as when he calls Tom "slow as molasses in January" (line 47).

G **ASK STUDENTS** to reread the sentence in lines 115–116. What is the meaning of this figurative language? What does it reveal about Tom? *(When Tom opens the door and sees Ruby standing there with a jar of tadpoles, he is overwhelmed. He feels as if "the whole sky is rushing . . . into his mouth" because Ruby represents all the excitement that life has to offer. She has brought the world to his doorstep. This figurative language underscores the fact that Tom is eager to experience more of life than his mother, in her concern for his health, is allowing him to do.)*

One drizzly Saturday when Tom is thirteen, the bell rings. He's scrubbing behind the stove, Mother is changing linens upstairs, and Mr. Weems is in the armchair reading the newspaper. When Tom
110 opens the door, Ruby Hornaday is standing on the stoop in the rain.

Hello. Tom blinks a dozen times. Raindrops set a thousand intersecting circles upon the puddles in the road. Ruby holds up a jar: six black tadpoles squirm in an inch of water.

Seemed like you were interested in water creatures.

Tom tries to answer, but the whole sky is rushing through the **G** open door into his mouth.

You're not going to faint again, are you?

Mr. Weems stumps into the foyer. *Jesus, boy, she's damp as a church, you got to invite a lady in.*
120 Ruby stands on the tiles and drips. Mr. Weems grins. Tom mumbles, *My heart.*

Ruby holds up the jar. *Keep 'em if you want. They'll be frogs before long.* Drops shine in her eyelashes. Rain glues her shirt to her clavicles. *Well, that's something,* says Mr. Weems. He nudges Tom in the back. *Ain't it, Tom?*

Tom is opening his mouth. He's saying, *Maybe I could—*when Mother comes down the stairs in her big, black shoes. *Trouble,* hisses Mr. Weems. Heat crashes over Tom like a wave.

Mother dumps the tadpoles in a ditch. Her face says she's
130 composing herself but her eyes say she's going to wipe all this away.

436 Collection 5

WHEN STUDENTS STRUGGLE . . .

Explain that the passing of time is important in this story. When Tom is four years old, his doctor predicts that he will not live past eighteen years of age. Point out that the author allows readers to keep track of time by telling either the year or Tom's age when important events happen. Suggest that they begin a chart like the one shown to create a timeline of key events in Tom's life. Discuss which future dates or ages will be especially crucial in the context of the story. *(1929 is the year of the stock market crash that began the Great Depression. When Tom reaches age 16, he will be the age when his doctor predicted he would likely die.)*

Mr. Weems leans over the dominoes and whispers, *Mother's as hard as a cobblestone, but we'll crack her, Tom, you wait.*

Tom whispers, *Ruby Hornaday,* into the space above his cot. *Ruby Hornaday. Ruby Hornaday.* A strange and uncontainable joy inflates dangerously in his chest.

Mr. Weems has long conversations with Mother in the kitchen. Tom overhears scraps: *Boy needs to move his legs. Boy should get some air.*

Mother's voice is a whip. *He's sick.*

He's alive! What're you saving him for? How much time he got left?

140 Mother consents to let Tom retrieve coal from the depot and tinned goods from the commissary. Tuesdays he'll be allowed to walk to the butcher's in Dearborn. *Careful, Tomcat, don't hurry.*

Tom moves through the colony that first Tuesday with something close to rapture in his veins. Down the long gravel lanes, past pit cottages and surface mountains of blue and white salt, the warehouses like dark cathedrals, the hauling machines like demonic armatures.[2] All around him the monumental industry of Detroit pounds and clangs. The boy tells himself he is a treasure hunter, a hero from one of Mr. Weems's adventure stories, a knight on important errands, a spy

150 behind enemy lines. He keeps his hands in his pockets and his head down and his gait slow, but his soul charges ahead, sparking through the gloom.

In May of that year, 1929, fourteen-year-old Tom is walking along the lane thinking spring happens beneath the snow, beyond the walls—spring happens in the dark while you dream—when Ruby Hornaday steps out of the weeds. She has a shriveled rubber hose coiled over her shoulder and a swim mask in one hand and a tire pump in the other. *Need your help.* Tom's pulse soars.

I got to go to the butcher's.

160 *Your choice.* Ruby turns to go. But really there's no choice at all.

She leads him west, away from the mine, through mounds of rusting machines. They hop a fence, cross a field gone to seed, and walk a quarter mile through pitch pines to a marsh where cattle egrets stand in the cattails like white flowers.

In my mouth, she says, and starts picking up rocks. *Out my nose. You pump, Tom. You understand?* In the green water two feet down Tom can make out the dim shapes of fish gliding through weedy enclaves.

Ruby pitches the far end of the hose into the water. With waxed

170 cord she binds the other end to the pump. Then she fills her pockets with rocks. She wades out, looks back, says, *You pump,* and puts the hose into her mouth. The swim mask goes over her eyes; her face goes into the water.

---

² **armatures:** metal frames upon which sculptures are formed.

The Deep **437**

Year	Tom's Age	Events
1914		*Tom is born.*
1918	4	*Tom starts fainting.*
1924	10	*Tom is "in remedial everything" in school.*
1926	12	*Ruby gives her report on sea animals. The doctor says Tom should stay out of school.*
1927	13	*Ruby brings Tom tadpoles.*

Determine Themes COMMON CORE RL 2

(LINES 136–152)

Remind students that conflicts in a story can provide clues to themes.

Ⓗ ASK STUDENTS what conflict arises between Mother and Mr. Weems. How is the conflict resolved, and how does this resolution affect Tom? *(Mother and Mr. Weems argue over whether Tom should be allowed to go outdoors for exercise and fresh air. Mr. Weems prevails, and Tom is overjoyed as he walks through the city doing errands. It seems that this new freedom will be good for him.)*

Analyze Story Elements: Character (LINES 153–173) COMMON CORE RL 3

Point out that for a story to be effective, the relationships between characters must seem believable to readers.

Ⓘ ASK STUDENTS whether they find it believable that Ruby would seek out Tom. What do these two characters have in common? *(Students may say that although Ruby and Tom are different in many ways, they share an avid interest in life. They are both adventurous, as shown by Ruby's idea of going diving in the marsh and by Tom's decision to help her.)*

Analyze Story Elements: Irony (LINES 165–173) COMMON CORE RL 3

Tell students that **situational irony** is a contrast between what is expected and what actually happens.

Ⓙ ASK STUDENTS to explain what is ironic about Tom's pumping air through the hose while Ruby dives in the marsh. *(Tom's own "pump," his heart, is very weak and is expected to lead to an early death. Now he is called upon to be the pump that will sustain Ruby's life as she dives to the bottom of the marsh. It is surprising and ironic that she would select him to perform this role.)*

Determine Themes

COMMON CORE RL 2

(LINES 178–200)

Tell students that dramatic scenes often lead characters or readers to a new insight about life.

 CITE TEXT EVIDENCE Have students reread lines 178–200. What does Tom realize at the end of this scene? What details about the events at the marsh lead him to this realization? *(Tom states his realization in lines 199–200: "Everything . . . follows a path worn by those who have gone before." In other words, life is a cycle, and each individual takes part in the cycle and then disappears. He has come to this realization after initially feeling panicked as the pumping strained his heart [lines 178–180]. When Ruby emerges from the water and declares the experience "absolutely incredible," Tom is dazzled. Even though he coughs up blood on his way home, he feels that the risk has been worth it because the experience was so exhilarating.)*

Analyze Story Elements: Setting (LINES 201–211)

COMMON CORE RL 3

Point out that different settings within a story can represent ideas, feelings, or themes.

 ASK STUDENTS what the places described in lines 201–211 mean to Tom. *(The places he explores with Ruby represent life and adventure. He loves the beauty of the wild places and the powerful industry of the foundry.)*

The marsh closes over Ruby's back, and the hose trends away from the bank. Tom begins to pump. The sky slides along over-head. Loops of garden hose float under the light out there, shifting now and then. Occasional bubbles rise, moving gradually farther out.

One minute, two minutes. Tom pumps. His heart does its fragile work. He should not be here. He should not be here while this skinny, spellbinding girl drowns herself in a marsh. If that's what she's doing. One of Mr. Weems's similes comes back to him from some dingy corner of memory: *You're trembling like a needle to the pole.*

After four or five minutes underwater, Ruby comes up. A neon mat of algae clings to her hair, and her bare feet are great boots of mud. She pushes through the cattails. Strings of saliva hang off her chin. Her lips are blue. Tom feels dizzy. The sky turns to liquid.

Incredible, pants Ruby. *Absolutely incredible.* She holds up her wet, rock-filled trousers with both hands, and looks at Tom through the wavy lens of her swim mask. His blood storms through its lightless tunnels.

He has to trot to make the butcher's by noon. It is the first time Tom can remember permitting himself to run, and his legs feel like glass and his breath like quicksand. At the end of the lane, a hundred yards from home, he stops and pants with the basket of meat in his arms and spits a pat of blood into the dandelions. Sweat soaks his shirt. Dragonflies dart and hover. Swallows inscribe letters across the sky. The lane seems to ripple and fold and straighten itself out again.

Just a hundred yards more. He forces his heart to settle. *Everything*, Tom thinks, *follows a path worn by those who have gone before: egrets, clouds, tadpoles. Everything.*

The following Tuesday Ruby meets him at the end of the lane. And the Tuesday after that. They hop the fence, cross the field; she leads him places he's never dreamed existed. Places where the structures of the saltworks become white mirages on the horizon. Places where sunlight washes through groves of maples and makes the ground quiver with leaf-shadow. They peer into a foundry where shirtless men in masks pour molten iron from one vat into another; they climb a tailings pile where a lone sapling grows like a single hand thrust up from the underworld. Tom knows he's risking everything, but how can he stop? How can he say no? To say no to Ruby Hornaday would be to say no to the world.

Some Tuesdays Ruby brings along her red book, with its images of corals and jellies and underwater men breathing from hoses. She tells him that when she grows up she'll go to parties where hostesses row guests offshore and everyone puts on special helmets and goes for strolls along the sea bottom. She tells him she'll be a diver who sinks herself a half mile into the sea in a steel ball with one window. In the basement of the ocean she'll find a world of lights: schools of fish glittering green, whole galaxies wheeling through the black.

Strategies for Annotation ✏️ 🖥 *Annotate it!*

Determine Themes

COMMON CORE RL 2

Encourage students to use their eBook annotation tools to track details that suggest the various themes in the story.

- Using a different color for each theme, highlight details that point to the theme. Focus on key events, dialogue, and vivid descriptions.
- Underline sentences that come close to stating themes.
- On notes, state the themes in your own words and explain how they interact and build on each other.

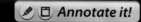

Everything, Tom thinks, *follows a path worn by those who have gone before: egrets, clouds, tadpoles. Everything.*

The following Tuesday Ruby meets him at the end of the lane. And the Tuesday after that. They hop the fence, cross the field; she leads him places he's never dreamed existed. Places where the structures of the

220   *In the ocean*, says Ruby, *the rocks are alive and half the plants are animals.*

They hold hands; they chew Indian gum. She stuffs his mind full of kelp forests and seascapes and dolphins. *When I grow up*, thinks Tom. *When I grow up . . .*

Four more times Ruby walks around beneath the surface of a River Rouge marsh while Tom stands on the bank working the pump. Four more times he watches her rise back out like a fever. *Amphibian.* She laughs. *It means two lives.*

Then Tom runs to the butcher's and runs home, and his heart
230 races, and spots spread like inkblots in front of his eyes. *Blue, blue blue.* But how does he know the blue he sees is the right color? Sometimes in the afternoons, when he stands up from his chores, his vision slides away in violet streaks and is a long while returning. Other colors spiral through his mind's eye, too: the glowing white of the salt tunnels, the red of Ruby's book, the orange of her hair—he imagines her all grown up, standing on the bow of a ship, and feels a core of lemon yellow light flaring brighter and brighter within him. It spills from the slats between his ribs, from between his teeth, from the pupils of his eyes. He thinks: *It is so much! So much!*

240 *So now you're fifteen. And the doctor says sixteen?*

Eighteen if I'm lucky.

Ruby turns her book over and over in her hands. *What's it like? To know you won't get all the years you should?*

I don't feel so shortchanged when I'm with you, he says, but his voice breaks at *short-* and the sentence falls apart.

They kiss only that one time. It is clumsy. He shuts his eyes and leans in, but something shifts and Ruby is not where he expects her to be. Their teeth clash. When he opens his eyes, she is looking off to her left, smiling slightly, smelling of mud, and the thousand tiny blonde
250 hairs on her upper lip catch the light.

The second-to-last time Tom and Ruby are together, on the last Tuesday of October, 1929, everything is strange. The hose leaks, Ruby is upset, a curtain has fallen somehow between them.

Go back, Ruby says. *It's probably noon already. You'll be late.* But she sounds as if she's talking to him through a tunnel. Freckles flow and bloom across her face. The light goes out of the marsh.

On the long path through the pitch pines it begins to rain. Tom makes it to the butcher's and back home with the basket and the ground veal, yet when he opens the door to Mother's parlor the
260 curtains seem to blow inward. The chairs seem to leave their places and come scraping toward him.

The daylight thins to a pair of beams, waving back and forth. Mr. Weems passes in front of his eyes, but Tom hears no footsteps, no voices: only an internal rushing and the wet metronome of his

The Deep   **439**

Analyze Story Elements: Symbol (LINES 229–239)
COMMON CORE RL 3, RL 4

Explain that the details an author includes can serve more than one purpose. For example, they might create **imagery** that appeals to readers' senses while also serving as symbols.

Ⓜ CITE TEXT EVIDENCE Ask students to describe the effect of the color imagery in lines 229–239. What do the various colors represent? *(The colors in this passage help readers see what Tom sees in "his mind's eye." Blue represents calmness and safety as he tries to protect his heart from overexcitement. The "glowing white," red, and orange represent life and adventure. The "core of lemon yellow light flaring brighter and brighter within him" symbolizes his love of life and his appreciation for all the beauty he sees.)* Point out to students that yellow, orange, and red are considered warm colors, while green, blue, and violet are cool colors. Why did the author choose yellow for the flame inside Tom's chest? *(Warmth is associated with life, while coldness suggests death.)*

Analyze Story Elements: Setting (LINES 251–252)
COMMON CORE RL 3

Remind students that the historical context is an important aspect of the story's setting.

Ⓝ ASK STUDENTS to explain the significance of "the last Tuesday of October, 1929." What changes occurred on this day in history? *(It is the date of the stock market crash that marked the beginning of the Great Depression, a time of great economic hardship across the nation and the world.)*

TO CHALLENGE STUDENTS . . .

Analyze References to Time How does Anthony Doerr make readers hear the clock ticking throughout this story? Point out the reference in line 264 to a metronome, a device used to sound a steady beat for a practicing musician. Tell students this is just one of many details that suggest the passage of time in the story. Challenge students to identify other such details, either singular or recurring. Have them share their findings in pairs or small groups and discuss the effect that these details have on readers. *(Details include references to Tom's age, to months and years, to Tuesdays [lines 201–202, 252, 478], and to the beating of Tom's heart. These references create tension because they remind readers that Tom is not expected to live long. They also suggest a theme about appreciating every moment of life.)*

Support Inferences   RL 1

(LINES 251–278)

Point out that this story is rich in figurative language, and that readers must often make inferences to understand what is happening.

Ⓞ CITE TEXT EVIDENCE Ask students to use text details to infer what happens to Tom. *(Tom senses "a curtain" between himself and Ruby. His distress at her coldness causes an immediate reaction; he feels "as if she's talking to him through a tunnel." By the time he gets home, he's "staring through a thick, foggy window." He loses consciousness and imagines he is in the salt mine watching "flowing signals of light in all directions.")*

Analyze Story Elements: RL 3
Setting (LINES 279–292)

Point out that when Tom wakes up, the world has changed. Remind students that the setting of a story, as well as any changes in the setting, can have a great impact on characters and plot.

Ⓟ ASK STUDENTS to summarize how the world has changed. What is the effect on Tom? *(The Great Depression has begun. Many people are losing jobs as businesses close. Food prices have soared. Boarders are moving out. Tom no longer goes outside because there are no errands to run. He is depressed and misses Ruby.)*

Support Inferences   RL 1

(LINES 293–294)

Tell students that when they encounter a statement that does not make sense, they should look for context clues to help them infer meaning.

Ⓠ CITE TEXT EVIDENCE Ask students to explain why, as Mr. Weems says, "No one is leaving addresses." *(The economic crisis has caused many people to lose their jobs: "The Ford plant is shedding men; the foundry shuts down" [line 281]. Men are leaving the boardinghouse because they can't afford to pay their rent, but they also have nowhere else to go. Since they are homeless, they do not have new addresses.)*

---

exhalations. Suddenly he's staring through a thick, foggy window into a world of immense pressure. Mother's face disappears and reappears. Her lips say, *Haven't I given enough? Lord God, haven't I tried?* Then she's gone.

In something deeper than a dream Tom walks the salt roads a
270   thousand feet beneath the house. At first it's all darkness, but after what might be a minute or a day or a year, he sees little flashes of green light out there in distant galleries, hundreds of feet away. Each flash initiates a chain reaction of further flashes beyond it, so that if he turns in a slow circle he can perceive great flowing signals of light in all directions, tunnels of green arcing out into the blackness—each flash glowing for only a moment before fading, but in that moment repeating everything that came before, everything that will come next. Like days, like hours, like heartbeats.

Ⓟ He wakes to a deflated world. The newspapers are full of suicides; the
280   price of gas has tripled. The miners whisper that the saltworks is in trouble. The Ford plant is shedding men; the foundry shuts down.

Quart milk bottles sell for a dollar apiece. There's no butter, hardly any meat. Most nights Mother serves only cabbage and soda bread. Salt.

No more trips to the butcher or the depot or the commissary. No more outside. He waits for Ruby to come to the door.

By November, Mother's boarders are vanishing. Mr. Beeson goes first, then Mr. Fackler. Still, Ruby doesn't come. Her face doesn't appear among the faces Tom watches from the upstairs window. Each
290   morning he clambers out of his closet and carries his traitorous heart down to the kitchen like an egg. Images of Ruby climb the undersides of his eyelids, and he rubs them away.

No addresses, mumbles Mr. Weems. *The world is swallowing people like candy, boy. No one is leaving addresses.*

Mr. Hanson goes next, then Mr. Heathcock. By April the salt-works is operating only two days a week, and Mr. Weems, Mother, and Tom are alone at supper.

Sixteen. Eighteen if he's lucky. Tom moves his few things into one of the empty boarders' rooms on the first floor, and Mother doesn't
300   say a word. He thinks of Ruby Hornaday: her pale blue eyes, her loose flames of hair. *Is she out there in the city, somewhere, right now? Or is she three thousand miles away?* Then he puts his questions aside.

Mother catches a fever in 1931. It eats her from the inside. She still puts on her high-waisted dresses, ties on her apron. She still cooks every meal and presses Mr. Weems's suit every Sunday. But within a month she has become somebody else, an empty demon in Mother's clothes—perfectly upright at the table, eyes smoldering, nothing on her plate.

She has a way of putting her hand on Tom's forehead while he
works. Tom will be hauling coal or mending a pipe or sweeping the
310   parlor, the sun glowing behind the curtains, and Mother will appear
from nowhere and put her icy palm over his eyebrows, and he'll close
his eyes and feel his heart tear just a little more.

Amphibian. It means two lives.

Mr. Weems is let go. He puts on his suit, packs up his dominoes,
and leaves an address downtown.

I thought no one was leaving addresses.

You're true as a map, Tom. True as the magnet to the iron. And
tears spill from the old miner's eyes.

One blue, icy morning not long after that, for the first time in
320   Tom's memory, Mother is not at the stove when he enters the kitchen.
He finds her upstairs sitting on her bed, fully dressed in her coat and
shoes and with her rosary clutched to her chest. The room is spotless,
the house wadded with silence.

Now remember, payments are due on the fifteenth. Her voice is ash.
*The flashing on the roof needs replacing. There's ninety-one dollars in
the dresser.*

Mother, Tom says.

Shhh, Tomcat, she hisses. *Don't get yourself worked up.*

Tom manages two more payments. Then the saltworks closes and the
330   bank comes for the house. He walks in a daze through blowing sleet
to the end of the lane and turns right and staggers over the dry weeds
awhile till he finds the old path and walks beneath the creaking pitch
pines to Ruby's marsh. Ice has interlocked in the shallows, but the
water in the center is dark as molten pewter.

He stands there a long time. Into the gathering darkness he says,
I'm still here, but where are you? His blood sloshes to and fro, and snow
gathers in his eyelashes, and three ducks come spiraling out of the
night and land silently on the water.

The next morning he walks past the padlocked gate of
340   International Salt with fourteen dollars in his pocket. He rides the
trackless trolley downtown for a nickel and gets off on Washington

The Deep   **441**

SCAFFOLDING FOR ELL STUDENTS

Vocabulary: Phrasal Verbs Remind students that a **phrasal verb** is a
verb joined with another word, such as a preposition, to take on a new
meaning. The meaning of a phrasal verb often cannot be determined from
the meanings of the individual words. Work with students to define these
examples, using context clues when possible:

- *let go* (line 314): "released from a job"
- *worked up* (line 328): "upset or excited"
- *comes for* (line 330): "takes ownership of"
- *moving in* (line 353): "coming to live in a place"

CLOSE READ

Determine Figurative Meanings (LINE 317)

Students are already aware that Mr. Weems often
speaks in similes. Draw their attention to the ones he
uses in line 317.

R   **ASK STUDENTS** to interpret the meaning of
these similes. What is the literal meaning of each
statement? What is the figurative meaning as it
applies to Tom? *("True as a map" means reliable; a map
provides objective information that shows people where
things are. "True as the magnet to the iron" has a similar
meaning. A magnet always attracts iron, in accordance
with its nature. Mr. Weems means that Tom has an
honest and reliable nature.)*

Support Inferences

(LINES 319–330)

Point out that sometimes authors leave out details
about an event and allow readers to infer what has
happened. This can help keep the story moving along
at a brisk pace, and it also keeps readers actively
engaged in the text. For this technique to be effective,
the author must provide a few telling details for
readers to interpret.

S   **CITE TEXT EVIDENCE** Ask students to reread
lines 319–330. What happens to Tom's mother? What
clues in the text allow readers to make this inference?
*(Tom's mother dies. Readers know from lines 303–307
that she has been ill with a fever. In lines 319–322, Tom
is surprised to find her in "sitting on her bed" instead of
making breakfast. She is "fully dressed in her coat and
shoes and with her rosary clutched to her chest," an
indication that she has been praying and also that she
has dressed herself as for a casket and burial. In lines
324–326, she tells Tom about paying bills and repairing
the roof—things he will need to take care of when she
is gone. Then, in line 329, the narrator says that "Tom
manages two more payments." This implies that his
mother is gone and he has taken over management of
the house.)*

Determine Themes

 COMMON CORE RL 2

(LINES 361–376)

Remind students that clues to a story's themes can be found in dialogue as well as in statements made by the narrator.

T **CITE TEXT EVIDENCE** What theme emerges from this passage? Cite details that suggest an insight about the nature of life. (*This passage develops the theme that life is a continuous cycle of birth and death. Tom had this insight after his first trip to the marsh with Ruby [lines 199–200]. Now it is reinforced by the observation of Mr. Weems's grandniece: "World goes to Hades, but babies still get born." The narrator further develops the idea by describing Tom's job at the hospital: "In the delivery room there's always new blood on the tiles to replace the old blood Tom has just mopped away." Both details suggest that life is an unstoppable force that is constantly renewing itself.*)

Analyze Story Elements: Recurring Images

 COMMON CORE RL 3

(LINES 377–381)

Explain that when students notice **recurring images**—images that are repeated throughout a story—they should ask themselves what the author is trying to emphasize through this repetition. Recurring images help tie the parts of a story together into a meaningful whole.

U **ASK STUDENTS** why the hospital feels to Tom as if it is underwater. What is significant about these images of the sea? (*These images recall Ruby's red book of sea creatures and everything that Ruby has meant to Tom, especially their marsh adventures, where Ruby becomes something of an underwater creature. Readers understand that Ruby is still important to him. They are also reminded that Tom is destined to see Ruby once more [line 251].*)

Boulevard. Between the buildings the sun comes up the color of steel, and Tom raises his face to it but feels no warmth at all. He passes catatonic drunks squatting on upturned crates, motionless as statues, and storefront after storefront of empty windows. In a diner a goitrous[3] waitress brings him a cup of coffee with little shining disks of fat floating on top.

350　The streets are filled with faces, dull and wan, lean and hungry; none belongs to Ruby. He drinks a second cup of coffee and eats a plate of eggs and toast, and then another. A woman emerges from a doorway and flings a pan out onto the sidewalk, and the wash water flashes in the light a moment before falling. In an alley a mule lies on its side, asleep or dead. Eventually the waitress says, *You moving in?* and Tom goes out. He walks slowly toward the address he's copied and recopied onto a sheet of Mother's writing paper. Frozen furrows of plowed snow are shored up against the buildings, and the little golden windows high above seem miles away.

　It's a boardinghouse. Mr. Weems is at a lopsided table playing dominoes by himself. He looks up, says, *Holy ghosts sure as gravity,*
360　and spills his tea.

 By a miracle Mr. Weems has a grandniece who manages the owl shift in the maternity ward at City General. Maternity is on the fourth floor. In the elevator Tom cannot tell if he is ascending or descending. The niece looks him up and down and checks his eyes and chest for fever and hires him on the spot. *World goes to Hades, but babies still get born,* she says, and issues him white coveralls.

　Rainy nights are the busiest. Full moons and holidays are tied for second. God forbid a rainy holiday with a full moon. Ten hours a night, six nights a week, Tom roves the halls with carts of laundry,
370　taking soiled blankets down to the cellar, bringing clean blankets up. He brings up meals, brings down trays.

　Doctors walk the rows of beds injecting expectant mothers with morphine and something called scopolamine that makes them forget. Sometimes there are screams. Sometimes Tom's heart pounds for no reason he can identify. In the delivery rooms there's always new blood on the tiles to replace the old blood Tom has just mopped away.

　The halls are bright at every hour, but out the windows the darkness presses very close, and in the leanest hours of those nights Tom gets a sensation like the hospital is deep underwater, the floor
380　rocking gently, the lights of neighboring buildings like glimmering schools of fish, the pressure of the sea all around.

　He turns eighteen, nineteen. All the listless figures he sees: children humped around the hospital entrance, their eyes vacant with hunger;

---

[3] **goitrous** (goi′trəs): having a swelled area, usually in the neck and caused by an enlarged thyroid gland.

WHEN STUDENTS STRUGGLE . . .

Tell students that the language of this story often has a rhythm that echoes the beating of a human heart. They can appreciate this aspect of the text by reading it aloud.

ASK STUDENTS to form pairs to practice fluent reading.

- Have students read lines 361–381 silently.
- Next, one partner should read lines 361–371 aloud, and then the other partner should read lines 372–381. Students should pay attention to how their partner uses pacing and emphasis to create rhythm and convey the meaning of the text.
- Have students switch sections and read the passage aloud again.

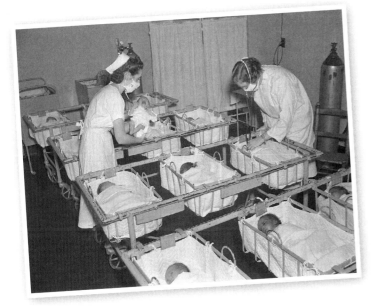

farmers pouring into the parks; families sleeping without cover—
people for whom nothing left on earth could be surprising. There
are so many of them, as if somewhere out in the countryside great
factories pump out thousands of new men every minute, as if the
ones shuffling down the sidewalks are but fractions of the immense
multitudes behind them.

390　　　And yet is there not goodness, too? Are people not helping one
another in these ruined places? Tom splits his wages with Mr. Weems.
He brings home discarded newspapers and wrestles his way through
the words on the funny pages. He turns twenty, and Mr. Weems bakes
a mushy pound cake full of eggshells and sets twenty matches in it,
and Tom blows them all out.

　　　He faints at work: once in the elevator, twice in the big, pulsing
laundry room in the basement. Mostly he's able to hide it. But one
night he faints in the hall outside the waiting room, and a nurse
named Fran hauls him into a closet. *Can't let them see you like that*, she
400　says, and he washes back into himself.

　　　Fran's face is brown, lived-in. She sits him on a chair in the corner
and wipes his forehead. The air is warm, steamy; it smells like soap.
For a moment he feels like throwing his arms around her neck and
telling her everything.

　　　The closet is more than a closet. On one wall is a two-basin sink;
heat lamps are bolted to the undersides of the cabinets. Set in the
opposite wall are two little doors.

The Deep　**443**

Image Credits: ©Bettmann/Corbis

CLOSE READ

Determine Themes　　　COMMON CORE　RL 3, RL 2

(LINES 382–404)

Tell students that elements of a story's setting may support its themes. In this story, the Great Depression provides the context in which Tom grows up and learns about life.

Ⓥ CITE TEXT EVIDENCE What theme is conveyed in this passage? Identify specific details that bring out this theme, including some about the Depression-era setting. *(This passage conveys the theme that although life can be very difficult, people often help each other. Tom sees great suffering around him—many children and adults are homeless and hungry, living on the streets [lines 382–385]. At the same time, he sees kindness and generosity. Mr. Weems has become like a father to him, and Tom shares with Mr. Weems the income from his job at the hospital [lines 391–395]. At work, Fran helps Tom hide the fact that he has fainting spells so that he will not lose his job [lines 396–404].)*

SCAFFOLDING FOR ELL STUDENTS

Vocabulary: Cognates This story contains challenging vocabulary, but Spanish speakers may recognize some cognates. Tell them that these cognates can serve as context clues for figuring out the meanings of the phrases or sentences in which the words appear. Discuss the following examples with students: (line 344): *catatonic/catatónico*; (line 362): *maternity/maternidad*; (line 363): *ascending/ascendente*, (line 363): *descending/descendente*; (line 383): *vacant/vacío*, (line 388): *fractions/fracciones*; (line 388): *immense/inmenso*; (line 389) *multitudes/multitud*.

CLOSE READ

Determine Themes

COMMON CORE RL 2

(LINES 408–429)

Point out to students that when a detail or a scene reminds them of something that happened earlier in the story, the author may be reinforcing an important idea or theme.

W CITE TEXT EVIDENCE Ask students to identify the earlier scene that is echoed in lines 408–429. What does this suggest about Tom's feelings as he watches Fran tend to the newborn babies? What theme does it suggest? *(Fran's way of speaking to the babies—"Why here you are, there you go," and so on—recalls what Tom's mother said to him right after they learned of his heart condition [lines 19–20]. This suggests that Tom identifies with the babies' fragility and helplessness. Like the babies, he has needed help from others to survive. This scene reinforces the theme that while life is hard, people get through it by helping each other.)*

Analyze Structure: Climax (LINES 436–441)

COMMON CORE RL 5

Remind students that the plot of a story builds toward a **climax,** a turning point when it becomes clear how the main conflict will be resolved.

X CITE TEXT EVIDENCE What clues in lines 436–441 suggest that the climax of the story is near? *(The story's main conflict revolves around Tom's fragile health; his doctor's statement that he would not live past age 18 has created tension throughout the story. Now, "Tom is twenty-one and fainting three times a week." He has outlived the doctor's prediction by three years, but his health is deteriorating. Another source of tension has been the description of Tom's previous meeting with Ruby as the "second-to-last time" [line 251]. Readers have been waiting to see how their last meeting would come about, and now Tom has finally spotted her in the hospital [lines 436–438]. These clues all suggest that the story is reaching its climax.)*

> ❝ Is there not goodness, too? Are people not helping one another in these ruined places? ❞

Tom returns to the chair in the corner of this room whenever he starts to feel dizzy. Three, four, occasionally ten times a night, he
410 watches a nurse carry an utterly newborn baby through the little door on the left and deposit it on the counter in front of Fran.

She plucks off little knit caps and unwraps blankets. Their bodies are scarlet or imperial purple; they have tiny, bright red fingers, no eyebrows, no kneecaps, no expression except a constant, bewildered wince. Her voice is a whisper: *Why here you are, there you go, okay now, baby, just lift you here.* Their wrists are the circumference of Tom's pinkie.

Fran takes a new washcloth from a stack, dips it in warm water, and wipes every inch of the creature—ears, scrotum, armpits,
420 eyelids—washing away bits of placenta,[4] dried blood, all the milky fluids that accompanied it into this world. Meanwhile the child stares up at her with blank, memorizing eyes, peering into the newness of all things. Knowing what? Only light and dark, only mother, only fluid.

Fran dries the baby and splays her fingers beneath its head and tugs its hat back on. She whispers, *Here you are, see what a good girl you are, down you go,* and with one free hand lays out two new, crisp blankets, and binds the baby—wrap, wrap, turn—and sets her in a rolling bassinet for Tom to wheel into the nursery, where she'll wait with the others beneath the lights like loaves of bread.

430 In a magazine Tom finds a color photograph of a three-hundred-year-old skeleton of a bowhead whale, stranded on a coastal plain in some place called Finland and covered with moss. He tears it out, studies it in the lamplight. *See,* he murmurs to Mr. Weems, *how the flowers closest to it are brightest? See how the closest leaves are the darkest green?*

Tom is twenty-one and fainting three times a week when he sees, among the drugged, dazed mothers in their rows of beds, the

---

[4] **placenta:** an organ connecting the mother and unborn fetus that provides nutrients and removes waste.

444 Collection 5

WHEN STUDENTS STRUGGLE...

As students read the end of the story, give them the following questions to focus their attention on key ideas and events. Then have them meet with partners to discuss and confirm their interpretations.

- What is the significance of the fact that "Tom is twenty-one and fainting three times a week"? (line 436)
- Why does Tom send Ruby the photo of the whale skeleton?
- Why does Tom suggest the aquarium as a place to meet?
- Why does Tom feel "absolutely lucky"? (line 560)
- What is the meaning of the "trapdoor" that Tom imagines opening under his feet in lines 563–564?

unmistakable face of Ruby Hornaday. Flaming orange hair, freckles
sprayed across her cheeks, hands folded in her lap, and a thin gold
440 wedding ring on her finger. The material of the ward ripples. Tom
leans on the handle of his cart to keep from falling.

Blue, he thinks. *Blue, blue, blue.*

He retreats to the chair in the corner of the washing room and
tries to suppress his heart. *Any minute*, he thinks, *her baby could come
through the door.*

Two hours later, he pushes his cart into the postdelivery room, and
Ruby is gone. Tom's shift ends; he rides the elevator down. Outside,
and icy January rain settles lightly on the city. The street-lights glow
yellow. The early morning avenues are empty except for the occasional
450 automobile, passing with a damp sigh. Tom steadies a hand against the
bricks and closes his eyes.

A police officer helps him home. Tom lies on his stomach in his
rented bed all that day and recopies the letter until little suns burst
behind his eyes. *Deer Ruby, I saw you in the hospital and I saw your
baby to. His eyes are viry prety. Fran sez later they will probly get blue.
Mother is gone and I am lonely as the arctic see.*

That night at the hospital Fran finds the address. Tom includes the
photo of the whale skeleton from the magazine and sticks on an extra
stamp for luck. He thinks: *See how the flowers closest to it are brightest.*
460 *See how the closest leaves are the darkest green.*

He sleeps, pays his rent, walks the thirty-one blocks to work,
and checks the mail each day. And each day winter pales and spring
strengthens and Tom loses a little bit of hope.

One morning over breakfast, Mr. Weems looks to him with
concern and says, *You ain't even here, Tom. You got one foot across the
river. You got to pull back to our side.*

But three weeks later, it comes. *Dear Tom, I liked hearing from
you. It hasn't been ten years but it feels like a thousand. I'm married,
you probably guessed that. The baby is Arthur. Maybe his eyes will turn
470 blue. They just might.*

A bald president is on the stamp. The paper smells like paper,
nothing more. Tom runs a finger beneath every word, sounding it out.
Making sure he hasn't missed anything.

*I know your married and I dont want anything but happyness for you
but maybe I can see you one time? We could meet at the acquareyem. If
you dont rite back thats okay I no why.*

Two more weeks. *Dear Tom, I don't want anything but happiness
for you, too. How about next Tuesday? I'll bring the baby, okay?*

The next Tuesday, the first one in May, Tom leaves the hospital after
480 his shift. His vision wavers at the edges, and he hears Mother's voice:
Be careful, Tomcat. It's not worth the risk. He walks slowly to the end

The Deep **445**

CLOSE READ

Analyze Story Elements: Character (LINES 452–473)

COMMON CORE RL 3

Tell students that a few well-chosen details can reveal
many aspects of a character in a brief passage.

Y CITE TEXT EVIDENCE What do the details in lines
452–473 reveal about Tom's background, personality,
and feelings? *(The misspelled words in his letter reflect
the fact that he was a poor student and did not finish
school. The simile at the end of the first letter, "I am
lonely as the arctic see," reveals both his loneliness and
his poetic imagination. The way he "recopies the letter
until little suns burst behind his eyes," trying to get the
words just right, and the way he hopes Ruby will see
the same beauty that he does in the photo of the whale
skeleton show how important it is for him to reconnect
with Ruby. When he does not hear back from her right
away, he grows weaker [lines 461–466]. His response to
her letter when it finally arrives, poring over every word
and "making sure he hasn't missed anything," reinforces
the idea that his relationship with Ruby is a matter of life
and death for him.)*

Analyze Story Elements: Symbol (LINES 479–495)

COMMON CORE RL 3, RL 4

Remind students that the details used to create
sensory images can also serve as symbols.

Z CITE TEXT EVIDENCE Ask students to find
examples of color imagery in lines 479–495. What do
these colors symbolize in Tom's imagination? *(The
colors mentioned in this passage are mostly shades
of yellow: "a golden dawn" [line 483], "a huge present
wrapped in yellow ribbon" [lines 484–485], "The sunlight
hits the dew and sets the lawns aflame" [lines 486–487],
"a yellow kite" [line 495]. This imagery recalls the "core of
lemon yellow light" that Tom imagined flaming within
him after his first trip to the marsh with Ruby [lines
236–239]. The color represents joy and a love of life.)*

SCAFFOLDING FOR ELL STUDENTS

Comprehension Support Point out that Tom's letters in lines 454–456 and
lines 474–476 contain many misspelled words. Suggest that students work in
pairs and read the letters aloud to figure out what words Tom intends, since he is
spelling by sound.

Language: Irregular Plurals Remind students that English contains many
irregular plural forms. Have them use their eBook annotation tools to highlight
the following plural nouns: *squid* (line 521), *octopi* (line 522), *cowfish* (line 522),
vertebrae (line 544). On notes, have them record the singular form of each noun,
consulting a dictionary as needed. Point out that there are alternate plural forms
for all of these words: *squids, octopuses, cowfishes, vertebras*.

CLOSE READ

Support Inferences

COMMON CORE RL 1, RL 3

(LINES 511–515)

Tell students that when they make inferences, they may need to draw upon text evidence from much earlier in the story. Ruby has been absent from Tom's life for about six years, so readers must recall what they know about her from when she and Tom were younger to understand some of her behavior now.

A2 **CITE TEXT EVIDENCE** Why does Ruby say nothing to Tom's comment? Cite evidence from earlier in the story to support your inference about her thoughts and feelings at this moment. *(Tom says to Ruby, "I thought maybe you went to sea." He remembers the passionate dreams she expressed in lines 213–221, when she discussed her plans to become a deep-sea diver. She may feel embarrassed by his reference to those dreams, either because she knows they were not realistic or because she is disappointed she was not able to pursue them.)*

CRITICAL VOCABULARY

translucent: Light shines through the bodies of the squid that Tom and Ruby see at the aquarium.

ASK STUDENTS whether it would be possible to see small details about a fish swimming on the other side of the translucent squid. Why? *(No. A squid's body is only semitransparent, meaning that some light shines through, but objects on the other side of the animal would appear blurry.)*

iridescent: The tiles on the ceiling of the aquarium produce a rainbow of colors.

ASK STUDENTS why the iridescent tiles on the ceiling "throw wavering patterns of light across the floor." *(The light wavers because the tiles produce different colors as light hits them from different angles.)*

---

of the block and catches the first trolley to Belle Isle, where he steps off into a golden dawn.

There are few cars about, all parked, one a Ford with a huge present wrapped in yellow ribbon on the backseat. An old man with a crumpled face rakes the gravel paths. The sunlight hits the dew and sets the lawns aflame.

The face of the aquarium is Gothic and wrapped in vines. Tom finds a bench outside and waits for his pulse to steady. The reticulated[5]
490   glass roofs of the flower conservatory reflect a passing cloud. Eventually a man in overalls opens the gate, and Tom buys two tickets, then thinks about the baby and buys a third. He returns to the bench with the three tickets in his trembling fingers.

By eleven the sky is filled with a platinum haze and the island is busy. Men on bicycles crackle along the paths. A girl flies a yellow kite.
Tom?

Ruby Hornaday materializes before him—shoulders erect, hair newly short, pushing a chrome-and-canvas baby buggy. He stands quickly, and the park bleeds away and then restores itself.
500   *Sorry I'm late*, she says.

She's dignified, slim. Two quick strokes for eyebrows, the same narrow nose. No makeup. No jewelry. Those pale blue eyes and that hair.

She cocks her head slightly. *Look at you. All grown up.*
I have tickets, he says.
How's Mr. Weems?
Oh, he's made of salt, he'll live forever.

They start down the path between the rows of benches and the shining trees. Occasionally she takes his arm to steady him, though
510   her touch only disorients him more.

A2   *I thought maybe you were far away*, he says. *I thought maybe you went to sea.*

Ruby doesn't say anything. She parks the buggy and lifts the baby to her chest—he's wrapped in a blue afghan—and then they're through the turnstile.

The aquarium is dim and damp and lined on both sides with glass-fronted tanks. Ferns hang from the ceiling, and little boys lean across the brass railings and press their noses to the glass. *I think he likes it*, Ruby says. *Don't you, baby?* The boy's eyes are wide open. Fish
520   swim slow ellipses through the water.

They see **translucent** squid with corkscrew tails, sparkling pink octopi like floating lanterns, cowfish in blue and violet and gold. **Iridescent** green tiles gleam on the domed ceiling and throw wavering patterns of light across the floor.

In a circular pool at the very center of the building, dark shapes race back and forth in coordination. *Jacks*, Ruby murmurs. *Aren't they?*

translucent
(trăns-lōō′sənt) *adj.*
semitransparent.

iridescent
(ĭr′ĭ-dĕs′ənt) *adj.*
having colors that change when seen from different angles.

---

[5] **reticulated:** having lines with a net-like pattern.

APPLYING ACADEMIC VOCABULARY

assurance	devote	vision

As you discuss the end of the story, incorporate the Collection 5 academic vocabulary words *assurance, devote,* and *vision*. Discuss why Tom **devotes** so much energy to writing his first letter to Ruby and waiting for a reply (lines 452–463). In the final scene, discuss what Tom's **vision** of the trapdoor means, and why he is able to give Ruby his **assurance** that he'll be "okay."

Tom blinks.

You're pale, she says.

Tom shakes his head.

530   She helps him back out into the daylight, beneath the sky and the trees. The baby lies in the buggy sucking his lips, and Ruby guides Tom to a bench.

Cars and trucks and even a limousine pass slowly along the white bridge, high over the river. The city glitters in the distance.

Thank you, says Tom.

For what?

For this.

How old are you now, Tom?

Twenty-one. Same as you. A breeze stirs the trees, and the leaves
540   vibrate with light. Everything is radiant.

World goes to Hades, but babies still get born, whispers Tom.

Ruby peers into the buggy and adjusts something, and for a moment the back of her neck shows between her hair and collar. The sight of those two knobs of vertebrae, sheathed in her delicate skin, fills Tom with a longing that cracks the lawns open. For a moment it seems Ruby is being slowly dragged away from him, as if he were a swimmer caught in a rip, and with every stroke the back of her neck recedes farther into the distance. Then she sits back, and the park heels over, and he can feel the bench become solid beneath him once more.

Determine Themes

COMMON CORE   RL 2

(LINES 528–541)

Remind students that repeated images or words are often meant to emphasize an important idea or theme in a story.

B2   ASK STUDENTS to explain why Tom says at this moment, "World goes to Hades, but babies still get born." *(He is repeating what Mr. Weems's grandniece said to him when she hired him [lines 365–366]. At this moment, his poor health is reminding him of his own mortality. At the same time, it is a beautiful, sunny day, and both Ruby's baby and the constant stream of vehicles over the bridge remind him that life goes on. This scene reinforces the theme that life is an endless cycle of birth and death.)*

Determine Themes RL 2

(LINES 550–560)

Tell students that sometimes a theme of a story is expressed through something a character learns after struggling with a conflict.

C2 **ASK STUDENTS** to summarize in their own words the theme that Tom expresses in this dialogue with Ruby. *(Possible answer: Life goes on, even as individuals pass into it and out of it, and the secret to happiness is to appreciate the chance to take part in life.)*

Determine Figurative Meanings (LINES 563–564) RL 4

Remind students that the author often uses figurative language to describe Tom's perspective on life.

D2 **ASK STUDENTS** to interpret the reference to a "trapdoor" under Tom's feet. *(The trapdoor and the blackness on the other side of it represent death. This metaphor suggests that Tom knows he does not have long to live. He has expended the last of his strength to meet Ruby one more time, and he is happy with his decision.)*

COLLABORATIVE DISCUSSION Have students form pairs to discuss the question and locate evidence in the text for their conclusions about Tom. Then invite pairs to share their ideas in a class discussion. Accept all reasonable responses.

ASK STUDENTS to share any questions they generated in the course of reading and discussing the selection.

---

550 *I used to think,* Tom says, *that I had to be careful with how much I lived. As if life was a pocketful of coins. You only got so much and you didn't want to spend it all in one place.*

Ruby looks at him. Her eyelashes whisk up and down.

But now I know life is the one thing in the world that never runs out. I might run out of mine, and you might run out of yours, but the world will never run out of life. And we're all very lucky to be part of something like that.

She holds his gaze. *Some deserve more luck than they've gotten.*

Tom shakes his head. He closes his eyes. *I've been lucky, too. I've* **560** *been absolutely lucky.*

The baby begins to fuss, a whine building to a cry, and Ruby says, *Hungry.*

A trapdoor opens in the gravel between Tom's feet, black as a keyhole, and he glances down.

You'll be okay?

I'll be okay.

Good-bye, Tom. She touches his forearm once, and then she goes, pushing the buggy through the crowds. He watches her disappear in pieces, first her legs, then her hips, then her shoulders, and finally the **570** back of her bright head.

And then Tom sits, hands in his lap, alive for one more day.

COLLABORATIVE DISCUSSION How would you describe Tom? With a partner, discuss how his relationships and life experiences help you understand the kind of person he is. Cite specific textual evidence from the story to support your ideas.

TO CHALLENGE STUDENTS...

Analyze the Story's Ending What exactly happens at the end of this story? Does Tom live only "one more day"? Does it matter? Have students consider these questions independently before sharing their ideas in small groups. Remind them to support their conclusions with text evidence and also to draw upon their understanding of the story's major themes.

Determine Themes

COMMON CORE RL 2

The **theme** of a short story is a message or central idea it conveys about life or human nature, particularly through the development of plot and character. It is not necessarily the subject of the story, though it does often revolve around a particular conflict in the plot. Themes are generally implied rather than directly stated. In a complex story such as "The Deep," there may be more than one theme, and the themes may interact and build on one another as the story develops.

By analyzing story elements, readers can get clues about theme in "The Deep." Ask yourself these questions:

- Does the story's title suggest a theme?
- What is the central conflict in the story? Is it resolved?
- What is revealed about Tom through his reaction to the conflict?
- Does Tom change over the course of the story? If so, what message does the change convey to readers?
- How do the actions of the other characters in the story, and their interactions with Tom, hint at a theme?

Analyze Story Elements: Setting

COMMON CORE RL 3

Authors make critical choices about the **setting** of their stories, deciding not only when and where the action will take place but also how important a role the setting will play. In "The Deep," the setting has a significant effect on the mood, the characters, and the conflict. It also contributes to the development of themes. The setting of "The Deep" involves the physical place and a specific time period, as well as the economic conditions that resulted from the historical era known as the Great Depression.

This chart shows how the setting of a story can affect readers' perceptions of characters as the story develops.

Setting	Effect
Detroit, near the salt mines: • underinsulated boardinghouse • "the salt finds its way in" • the salt "encrusts washbasins . . . spills out of the boarders" • the miners "spill like little salt-dusted insects out into the night"	The boardinghouse's location near the salt mines and the pervasiveness of this gritty salt create a gray, grim mood. The characters, and the lives they live, are drab and comfortless. Salt is a preservative, though food preserved with salt lacks the vitality of fresh food. This idea mirror's the dull routine of Tom's life, designed to keep him alive without really living.

The Deep   **449**

TEACH

CLOSE READ

Determine Themes

COMMON CORE RL 2

Review the instructions with students and clarify any questions they may have about theme. Point out that a theme is usually stated in a sentence rather than a word or phrase. Invite students to share their preliminary ideas about each of the bulleted questions, based on their first reading of the story. Focus on the second bullet and ask what message an author may be trying to convey if a central conflict is not resolved. *(The message may be that some conflicts in life cannot be resolved, and people must find ways to deal with that reality.)* Then, as students reread the selection, encourage them to look for specific details in the text that support their ideas about themes.

Analyze Story Elements: Setting

COMMON CORE RL 3

Review the instructions and the example in the chart. Make sure students know enough about the Great Depression to recognize references to it in the story—for example, that "Black Tuesday" in October 1929 marked its beginning, when the stock market crashed and people lost their investments and savings. Years of very high unemployment followed as businesses closed and people could not find work. Ask students what kinds of themes could be developed in this context. *(themes about loss and hardship, and how people survive these situations)*

Strategies for Annotation   ✎ ▣ Annotate it!

Analyze Story Elements: Setting

COMMON CORE RL 3

Share these strategies for guided or independent analysis:

- Highlight in yellow details about the urban, industrial setting of Detroit.
- Highlight in green details about the setting of the marsh. *(lines 331–334)*
- Highlight in blue details that reflect the economic situation of the Great Depression.
- On notes, write your thoughts about how the setting of the story affects characters, plot, and themes.

rides the trackless trolley downtown for a nickel and gets off on Washington Boulevard. Between the buildings the sun comes up the color of steel, and Tom raises his face to it but feels no warmth at all. He passes catatonic drunks squatting on upturned crates, motionless as statues, and storefront after storefront of empty windows. In a diner a

PRACTICE & APPLY

Analyzing the Text 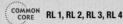 RL 1, RL 2, RL 3, RL 4

Possible answers:

1. *Mr. Weems believes that Tom should be allowed to experience life. He says to Tom's mother, "He's alive! What're you saving him for?" He encourages Tom's friendship with Ruby and keeps Tom anchored in the world of the living. Tom's mother, by contrast, restricts his life. She wants to protect him from dying. Both characters act out of love.*

2. *Examples of figurative language include "Ruby has flames for hair" (line 56), "Heat crashes over Tom like a wave" (line 128), and "her bare feet are great boots of mud" (line 184). The vivid language in these scenes reveals Tom's adoration of Ruby and her vitality.*

3. *Ruby is suddenly distant; "a curtain has fallen somehow between them." The marsh is no longer full of light—excitement and joy—if Tom cannot enjoy it with Ruby. Now it is simply a swamp.*

4. *Tom's mother is deprived of her meager livelihood as boarders lose their jobs and move out. Food becomes scarce. Mr. Weems moves out and Tom's mother falls ill. Finally, he loses the house and must move to the city. Once there, Tom makes the best of the situation. The Depression setting with all its hardships reveals his resiliency and optimism.*

5. *The marsh represents life with all of its risks and rewards, and freedom from the constant worry over Tom's health. The hospital represents the cycle of life, because "World goes to Hades, but babies still get born." The whale skeleton represents Tom's ability to find beauty even in mortality and death: "See how the flowers closest to it are brightest."*

6. *Possible themes include the following: Life is a constant cycle of birth and death, destruction and renewal; Being alive requires taking risks; Life is hard, but people can help each other get through it; Appreciate beauty and love wherever you find it. All of these are lessons that Tom learns over the course of the story as he copes with his fragile health. His relationships with Mr. Weems, Ruby, and Fran help him feel "lucky" by the end of the story (lines 559–560).*

7. *Tom's problem with his heart condition is not solved, but he has resolved his conflict. He used to think "life was a pocketful of coins. You only got so much and you didn't want to spend it all in one place." But he now knows that "life is the one thing in the world that never runs out." His new vision teaches that life is to be lived, not hoarded. Accept all reasonable responses as to whether this resolution is effective.*

 eBook *Annotate It!*

Analyzing the Text  RL 1, RL 2, RL 3, RL 4, SL 1a

Cite Text Evidence   Support your responses with evidence from the selection.

1. **Compare** How does the way Tom is treated by Mr. Weems differ from the way he is treated by his mother? What motivates their attitudes toward his health?

2. **Cite Evidence** Identify examples of metaphors and similes that the author uses to describe Tom's interactions with Ruby. How does this figurative language help reveal Tom's thoughts and feelings about her?

3. **Interpret** Reread lines 251–256. What does the author convey with the statement, "The light goes out of the marsh"?

4. **Cause/Effect** The story is set during the Great Depression. In what ways does this historical event affect Tom's life? How does the author use these changes to develop his character?

5. **Analyze**   A **symbol** is a person, place, or thing that stands for something beyond itself. What do the following places and things symbolize for Tom?

   - the marsh
   - the hospital
   - the whale skeleton

6. **Synthesize** Identify two themes in the story. Explain how these themes interact and build on each other.

7. **Evaluate** Throughout the story, Tom struggles with the fear that he will die young. How does Tom resolve this conflict at the end of the story? Do you find this resolution effective? Explain.

PERFORMANCE TASK

Speaking Activity: Discussion What is the significance of the story's title?

- Review the story, jotting down ideas about what you see as the significance of the title as well as specific references to water or "the deep."

- Meet in a small group and share ideas about the meaning of the title, including

how it relates to a possible theme. Does it have more than one meaning in the story?

- Summarize the important ideas from your discussion, and present them to the class.

Assign this performance task.

PERFORMANCE TASK  SL 1a

Speaking Activity: Discussion Have students work independently to gather evidence from the story in preparation for the discussion. In their summaries, students should present valid insights about the significance of the title. They should connect the title to ideas about water, the hospital, Ruby, and Tom's final realization at the aquarium.

Critical Vocabulary

 COMMON CORE L 5b

itinerant	sporadic	reverberate
translucent	iridescent	

Practice and Apply Explain which of the two situations best fits each Critical Vocabulary word's meaning.

itinerant	(a) a door-to-door salesperson	(b) a store owner
sporadic	(a) a bell that tolls every hour	(b) a bell that rings when there is a fire
reverberate	(a) shouting in a canyon	(b) shouting down the street
translucent	(a) a window with frosted glass	(b) a window with closed shutters
iridescent	(a) an oil slick on a road	(b) a muddy puddle on a sidewalk

Vocabulary Strategy: Analyze Nuances in Word Meanings

Writers choose words carefully, deciding which ones to use based on shades of difference, or **nuances,** in their meaning. For example, the Critical Vocabulary word *translucent* and the word *transparent* have a similar **denotation,** or literal meaning, but there are subtle differences between them that affect the mood of the story. As used in "The Deep," *translucent* means something that transmits light but that can't be completely seen through. *Transparent* refers to something that transmits light and that can be seen through. Read this sentence from the story: "They see translucent squid with corkscrew tails. . . ." The word *transparent* would not be accurate, nor would it evoke the same image that the word *translucent* does.

Practice and Apply Complete these activities with a partner.

1. The words in each pair are similar in meaning but not exactly identical. Look up the definition of each word in a dictionary, or use the meaning in the text to define the Critical Vocabulary word in each pair.

   - itinerant/migrant
   - iridescent/colorful
   - sporadic/periodic
   - fragile/feeble

2. Explain the nuance in meaning between the words in each pair.

3. Choose one of the pairs and write a sentence for each word that illustrates its exact meaning. Share your sentences with the class.

Critical Vocabulary

 COMMON CORE L 5b

Answers:

itinerant: *(a) a door-to-door salesperson*

sporadic: *(b) a bell that rings when there is a fire*

reverberate: *(a) shouting in a canyon*

translucent: *(a) a window with frosted glass*

iridescent: *(a) an oil slick on a road*

Vocabulary Strategy: Analyze Nuance in Word Meanings

Possible answers:

Itinerant *has to do with moving for the sake of a job or duty.* ***Migrant*** *means moving from one region to another but not necessarily for a reason such as work; it may be moving just for the sake of it.*

Iridescent *is colorful in a shimmery, brilliant way.* ***Colorful*** *does not include that same idea of shimmery or brilliant.*

Sporadic *means occurring at irregular intervals.* ***Periodic*** *is occurring at regular intervals.*

Fragile *means easily broken.* ***Feeble*** *means weak or ineffective.*

PRACTICE & APPLY

Language and Style: Tone L 3

Review the instructions with students. Have volunteers read aloud the two passages, and then discuss the differences between them, especially in the rhythm of the prose. Ask students to identify specific words and phrases in the first passage that illustrate the author's use of powerful words and figurative language. *(The phrase "rapture in his veins," the image of the "mountains of blue and white salt," and the similes used to describe the warehouses and the hauling machines exemplify passages in the story that describe times when Tom feels most alive.)*

Answers:

Students' narratives should convey a recognizable tone. They should also show understanding of the relationship between diction, syntax, and tone.

Language and Style: Tone L 3

In a work of fiction, the author creates a narrative **tone**. That is, the author chooses words and arranges them in a way that conveys the narrator's attitude toward the characters and events.

In "The Deep," the author intersperses lush, flowing descriptions with ideas expressed in a terse, or abrupt, syntax. These two passages from the text illustrate the differing styles:

> Tom moves through the colony that first Tuesday with something close to rapture in his veins. Down the long gravel lanes, past pit cottages and surface mountains of blue and white salt, the warehouses like dark cathedrals, the hauling machines like demonic armatures.

> Quart milk bottles sell for a dollar apiece. There's no butter, hardly any meat. Most nights Mother serves only cabbage and soda bread. Salt.

The first passage describes Tom's internal world, the world experienced through his newly awakened senses. The narrator's tone, created by powerful words, figurative language, and the melodious rhythm of the prose, might be described as reverential or sensitive. The second passage describes the physical world that Tom inhabits, with all of its limitations. The abrupt, disjointed sentences and humdrum vocabulary suggest the harshness of this existence. The narrator's tone here is matter-of-fact and unsentimental.

Practice and Apply A writer may show any number of attitudes toward a subject, such as formal, casual, serious, lighthearted, sarcastic, or mournful. Complete these activities to show your understanding of tone.

1. Choose an actual incident from your life as the basis for a brief narrative.

2. Before writing, think about the tone you want to convey. After writing, replace and rearrange words to better reflect your desired tone.

3. Read your narrative to a partner and discuss whether or not you effectively communicated your tone.

Strategies for Annotation 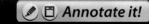 Annotate it!

Language and Style: Tone L 3

Have students locate additional passages that convey a strong tone regarding some aspect of Tom's life, such as lines 35–41 and lines 201–211. Encourage them to use their eBook annotation tools to do the following:

- Highlight in pink words and phrases that create vivid images, including words that describe colors.
- Underline figurative language.
- Use notes to identify passages in which the language and syntax reflect the harsher realities of Tom's life.

The following Tuesday Ruby meets him at the end of the lane. And the Tuesday after that. They hop the fence, cross the field; she leads him places he's never dreamed existed. Places where the structures of the saltworks become white mirages on the horizon. Places where sunlight washes through groves of maples and makes the ground quiver with leaf-shadow. They peer into a foundry where shirtless men in masks

Determine Figurative Meanings

COMMON CORE

RL 4

TEACH

"The Deep" is loaded with figurative language on every page. Define three major types of figures of speech—**metaphor, simile,** and **personification**—and discuss examples from the story. Emphasize how each example conveys meaning and mood by describing something in a fresh, imaginative way.

- **Metaphor** A metaphor compares two things that would normally appear to have nothing in common. Examples include "Mother's voice is a whip" (line 138) and "In the basement of the ocean she'll find a world of lights" (lines 217–218).

- **Simile** Like a metaphor, a simile compares two unlike things, but it uses the word *like* or *as*. Examples include "First-shift miners . . . spill like little salt-dusted insects out into the night" (lines 96–98) and "Mother's as hard as a cobblestone, but we'll crack her" (lines 131–132).

- **Personification** Personification gives human traits to a non-human entity. Examples include "Swallows inscribe letters across the sky" (lines 196–197) and "The world is swallowing people like candy" (lines 293–294).

Challenge students to explain how this sentence includes all three figures of speech: "Each morning he clambers out of his closet and carries his traitorous heart down to the kitchen like an egg" (lines 289–291). *("Carries" is metaphorical because Tom does not literally have his heart in his hands; "traitorous" personifies his heart as being capable of either loyalty or treachery; "like an egg" is a simile that describes the fragility of his heart.)*

PRACTICE AND APPLY

Have students apply their understanding of figurative language by completing one of the following activities:

- Find a paragraph in "The Deep" that does not use figurative language and rewrite it to include metaphor, simile, and/or personification. Be sure that your figures of speech reflect the mood of the scene described in the original passage.

- Write a descriptive paragraph about a place that is familiar to you. Think about the mood this place evokes. Use figurative language to describe the place and the way it makes you feel.

Analyze Story Elements: Setting

COMMON CORE

RL 3

RETEACH

Review the definition of **setting** as where and when a story occurs, as well as the social, political, and economic factors affecting a community at a particular time in history. Remind students that setting has an effect on other elements of a story.

- Setting can affect the plot by creating conflicts for the characters or making certain conflicts plausible. In "The Deep," the Great Depression's economic hardships create problems for Tom when boarders move out of the boardinghouse and he cannot afford to keep up the place.

- Setting can affect characters by shaping their response to problems. In "The Deep," Tom does not have the option of trying to locate Ruby by using an Internet search engine. He must wait until he happens to see her again in the hospital and then ask Fran to get him Ruby's mailing address.

LEVEL UP TUTORIALS Assign the following *Level Up* tutorial: **Setting: Effect on Plot.**

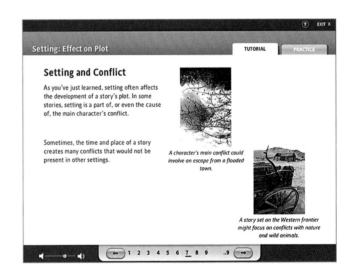

CLOSE READING APPLICATION

Have students apply their understanding of setting to other fiction selections they have read. Create Jigsaw groups and assign each student (or pair of students) one selection. Have them answer these questions and share their responses with the group: What is the setting? How does it affect the central conflict in the story? How does it affect the characters? Could the story have taken place in a different setting? Why or why not?

Blackheart

Short Story by Mark Brazaitis

Why This Text

"Blackheart" is a story with layers of meaning: On the one hand, it's a story in which a lonely young girl neglected by her parents seeks out danger, possibly as a form of retribution; on the other hand, it is a cautionary tale about what can go wrong when somone makes a "special connection" with a dangerous animal. Students may have difficulty recognizing these multiple themes—especially because they are not stated explicitly. With the help of the close-reading questions, students will analyze the central ideas in the story and how they interact and develop together.

Background Have students read the background information about the author. Explain that while living in Guatemala, Brazaitis became fluent in Spanish and developed a working knowledge of the local Maya language, Pokomchi. Operating in a language besides his native English helped him to appreciate the importance of using precise words. ("Saying 'thing' all the time wasn't going to help me get toilet paper at the local store.") Similarly, living with people from another culture forced him to work harder to understand them, a skill that he uses to this day to create realistic fictional characters.

AS YOU READ Ask students to pay attention to the way the author uses story elements such as setting to convey the story's theme.

Common Core Support

- cite strong and thorough textual evidence
- determine two or more themes and analyze their development
- analyze the impact of word choice on meaning and tone

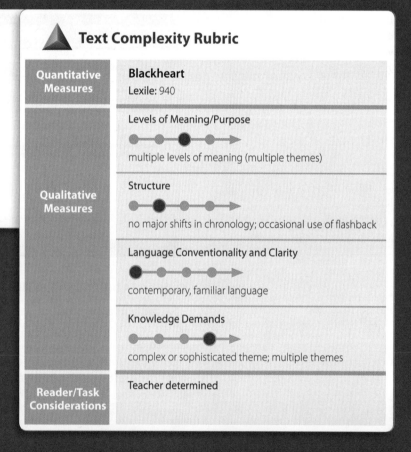

Text Complexity Rubric

Quantitative Measures	**Blackheart** Lexile: 940
Qualitative Measures	Levels of Meaning/Purpose — multiple levels of meaning (multiple themes)
	Structure — no major shifts in chronology; occasional use of flashback
	Language Conventionality and Clarity — contemporary, familiar language
	Knowledge Demands — complex or sophisticated theme; multiple themes
Reader/Task Considerations	Teacher determined

Strategies for CLOSE READING

Determine Themes

Students should read this story carefully all the way through. Close-reading questions at the bottom of the page will help them use details in the text to determine the story's theme. As they read, students should jot down comments or questions about the text in the margins.

WHEN STUDENTS STRUGGLE . . .

To help students determine themes in "Blackheart," have them work in small groups to fill out a chart like the one shown below.

CITE TEXT EVIDENCE For practice in using details in the text to make inferences about the theme, have students analyze each of the following examples from the story.

Detail	What It Reveals
". . . most days, her mother and Ed drive off into the Uco valley . . ." (lines 22–23)	Emily is left behind while her mother explores with Ed.
"Emily leaves her schoolwork and wanders around the vineyard singing songs she knows and songs she makes up." (lines 23–24)	The songs comfort her; they keep her company.
"The dictionary became a game between them, a game to see who could find the right word, who could speak it well enough so the other person understood." (lines 61–63)	Emily values the trouble Daniel takes to communicate with her, as no one else seems to have the time.
"'It's only me, Boy,' she says. If he could speak in a language she understood, she wonders if he would tease her like a brother would." (lines 149–150)	The only "friends" Emily develops are with animals she names and talks to.
"'You scared me, Boy. Maybe you wanted to? In fun, I mean. Like a brother would?'" (lines 179–180)	Emily imagines her relationship with the owl is like one she might have with a brother.

Background Mark Brazaitis *was born in Cleveland, Ohio, in 1966. He is the author of five books, including* The Incurables: Stories. *Brazaitis has said, ". . . the place I learned to write was Guatemala, where I was a Peace Corps Volunteer from 1990 to 1993. To step out of one's culture and one's language is to see oneself and one's country and everything one has ever believed in in fresh and even startling ways."*

Blackheart

Short Story by Mark Brazaitis

CLOSE READ
Notes

1. **READ ▶** As you read lines 1–32, begin to collect and cite text evidence.

- Circle text describing the setting.
- Underline things Emily's mother tells her.
- In the margin, explain why Emily could not stay with her father (lines 5–15) and why she is in Argentina (lines 16–32).

The moon is full, the sky cloudless. It is summer in Argentina—"All your friends in Ohio are shivering in the snow," her mother told her the other day—but the nights are cool. She walks across the garden's lawn toward the door on the other end. It is the door to the vineyard. Black Heart is behind it.

Her mother and Ed are eating dinner in Mendoza. It is late, but dinner always starts late in Argentina. The restaurants open at eight at night. Emily has eaten dinner at a restaurant in Argentina only once, and she fell asleep (A) before dessert. Waking her, her mother said, "You'll never be mistaken for an Argentine." Ed had said the same in relation to her red hair and blue-green
10 eyes, inherited from her father. Emily wanted to stay with her father in Sherman instead of coming here, but he has a new girlfriend and Emily's presence, he said, would be inconvenient now. There was a time between her parents' separation and divorce when her father wanted her to spend all her time with him. Her mother said this was only because he wanted to look good in the eyes of the divorce judge. After the divorce, he became busy.

So did her mother, who met Ed in an adventure writing class he'd taught in Cleveland. Older than her mother by sixteen years, he has a balloon belly and

Her dad becomes too busy with his new girlfriend after his divorce.

1. **READ AND CITE TEXT EVIDENCE** Emily's mother and step-father agree that she will "never be mistaken for an Argentine."

(A) ASK STUDENTS to cite evidence showing how Emily's appearance and behavior might give her away. *She falls asleep before dessert; she has red hair and blue-green eyes.*

Her mother's friend Ed has taken them to Argentina, where he can write about food and wine.

Maria might feel bad for Emily because she is always left alone.

waddles rather than walks. He is a travel writer, a food writer, a wine writer. He has rented this house outside of Mendoza so he can write about Mendoza's foods and wines. Her mother is supposed to be home-schooling her—Emily's fifth-grade teacher gave her mother a packet to cover January and February, the months they would be gone—but most days, her mother and Ed drive off into the Uco valley, and Emily leaves her schoolwork and wanders around the vineyard singing songs she knows and songs she makes up. Beyond the last row of grapevines, there is an elevated spot a grass altar where she likes to lie on her back and stare at the Andes Mountains, off to the west snow-capped and shimmering like a picture in a storybook. Sometimes Maria, the wife of the man who looks after the property, finds her and asks if she's all right. Maria's Spanish is only a little better than Emily's. Maria and her husband, Daniel, who live in the two-room cottage next to the house where she is staying, are from Bolivia. Her mother says their first language is . . . Emily can't remember. It starts with a q, like question.

Daniel is in charge of keeping the robbers and the killers and the rapists out of the vineyard and out of the garden and out of the house. One night, she overheard her mother and Ed discussing what happened to a Canadian woman who owns a hotel in Mendoza. When her mother discovered her hiding behind the kitchen door, she said, "You don't have to worry, sweetheart. We have Daniel and the dogs."

Their house sits in the north end of the garden, and the garden is surrounded by a black iron fence topped with barbed wire. On three sides of the black fence, separated from it by a ten-foot-wide corridor, is a chain-link fence, also topped with barbed wire. On the fourth side of the garden, on the south end, is the vineyard, which is surrounded by only a five-foot-tall wooden picket fence without barbed wire. Before Daniel goes to bed, he releases three bullmastiffs into the corridors between the black fence and the chain-link fence. Into the vineyard Daniel sends a fourth dog, some combination of pit bull, Rottweiler, German shepherd, and wolf, an animal as cruel and vicious as any animal on earth, or so Daniel told her. Daniel has given several names to

2. **◀ REREAD** Reread lines 10–32. In the margin, explain why you think Maria asks Emily if she's "all right."

3. **READ ▶** As you read lines 33–69, continue to cite textual evidence.
- Underline text describing Black Heart.
- In the margin, make an inference about why Emily is so interested in the dogs (lines 49–57).

this dog in his language, but in Spanish he calls him Black Heart. Black Heart was the topic of her mother's sternest lecture: *At night, don't ever open the door to the vineyard. Black Heart is on guard, and he's trained to kill whomever he finds.* "Even me?" *Anyone. Please, darling.* "Why would he kill me?" *Please. Never open the door.*

When they arrived in Argentina, Ed thought she should be curious about wine and empanadas and tango dancing. But Emily was curious about the guard dogs. How old were they? Were the three bullmastiffs brothers? Had the three bullmastiffs ever met Black Heart? Had Black Heart ever killed anyone?

Ed didn't know anything about them. "Ask Daniel," he said. So Emily did, in her bad Spanish. The next time they saw each other, Daniel pulled a tattered paperback Spanish-English dictionary from his back pocket. The print was so small even Emily had trouble reading it. The dictionary became a game between them, a game to see who could find the right word, who could speak it well enough so the other person understood. Daniel is only an inch or two taller than her five feet (she is the tallest girl in her class), and he has the blackest, straightest hair she's ever seen. His nose is large, and his nostrils seem, in proportion, even larger. Her mother and Ed call him Evo, because he supposedly looks like the president of Bolivia. Saturday is his night off. Sometimes on Saturday nights he stays home with Maria and sometimes he meets up with his Bolivian friends in Mendoza.

Often when Daniel returns late at night, she hears him singing, and this reminds her of her father, who loves to sing. Daniel's voice is light and sweet; her father's is low like a rumble or a growl. When her parents were married, the three of them would go camping every summer in southern Ohio, and every night around the fire, her mother would play her guitar and her father would

Coming from Ohio, Emily never had the need for guard dogs. Now they fascinate her, maybe more so because they are off-limits.

4. **◀ REREAD** Reread lines 58–69. How does Emily forge a relationship with Daniel and his dogs? What might this relationship have to do with the theme of the story?

Emily wants to talk to Daniel about his dogs. He gives her a Spanish-English dictionary which they use to understand each other. The theme might have to do with relationships and communication.

5. **READ ▶** As you read lines 70–117, continue to cite textual evidence.
- Underline text that mentions Emily's father.
- Make notes in the margin about the appearance and behavior of Black Heart.

2. **REREAD AND CITE TEXT EVIDENCE** Explain that in lines 22–27 we learn that "most days her mother and Ed drive off into the Uco valley," leaving Emily to do her schoolwork.

B **ASK STUDENTS** to draw inferences: How do students think their behavior affects Emily? *Students may suggest: It makes her feel left out, sad, lonely.* How does she spend the time while they're away? *She wanders around the vineyard singing, she lies on the grass and stares at the mountains.*

3. **READ AND CITE TEXT EVIDENCE** Point out that Ed was surprised by Emily's interest in the dogs.

C **ASK STUDENTS** to tell what Ed had expected her to be curious about. *He had expected her to be curious about wine and empanadas and tango dancing.* Have students make an inference about what this says about Ed and Emily's relationship. *He really doesn't know her.*

4. **REREAD AND CITE TEXT EVIDENCE**

D **ASK STUDENTS** to explain the "game" Emily and Daniel share. *Since they don't speak the same language, they struggle to communicate. The dictionary game helps them "talk" to one another.*

5. **READ AND CITE TEXT EVIDENCE** In lines 70–72, Daniel reminds Emily of her father.

E **ASK STUDENTS** to cite evidence showing how Daniel and Emily's father are alike and how they are different. *They both love to sing; Daniel's voice is "light and sweet" while her father's is "like a rumble or a growl."*

enchanting:

*magical;
casting a spell*

sing, his voice booming above the crackling flames. On the last couple of trips, Emily sang with him. Although her voice was as thin as air, it was beautiful, her father said, beautiful and **enchanting**. "You could sing a fish out of the water," he said. "You could sing a dog away from a bone."

F

80   In the week before she left for Argentina, Emily called her father every day, always when she thought his girlfriend wouldn't be with him. Even when she wasn't, their conversations were short. One time Emily called him and his girlfriend interrupted to ask him, "What do you think of this ring?" The last time she spoke to him, he was at a party and there was music in the background. "Remember this song?" he said, and she sang to show him she did. But she realized he had been speaking to someone else. Embarrassed, she hung up. The next day, she was on a plane to Argentina.

Emily hears a sound in the bougainvillea that covers the black iron fence on her left. Her heart springs into her throat. But it is only the stray tiger cat who visits some nights. Daniel calls him Romeo because he supposedly

90   fathered all the recent litters in the neighborhood. He paws his way from the top of the fence, **cascades** down the purple flowers, and tumbles onto the grass. He is the thinnest cat she has ever seen, but her mother assured her he isn't starving.

cascades:

*tumbles down
rapidly, like
water*

Romeo rubs himself against her leg, and she crouches down to pet him. His fur is like none she has touched before. It is thick and prickly like she imagines a groundhog's would be. "Do you know what I'm doing tonight?" she asks Romeo. "I'm going to visit Black Heart." He looks up at her, responding to her voice. "Don't worry. He's my friend. I've been visiting him in his cage. I sing to him." She pretends he says something. "He's not my boyfriend! He's a dog!"

100   She laughs and shakes her head.

In her first week in Argentina, after they had become friends, Daniel brought her to see the dogs in their cages, located in the corridor between the

---

6. **◄REREAD** Reread lines 70–86. Describe how Emily's relationship with her father has changed. Support your answer with explicit textual evidence.

*Emily and her parents used to go camping together. Her father
enjoyed hearing her voice. After the divorce, "their conversations
were short" and he doesn't even hear her singing over the phone.*

---

two fences at the front of the property. They were like cages at the zoo, except they were no taller than her chest. The three bullmastiffs, who shared a cage, barked at her, but when Daniel scolded them, they whimpered like doves. When they reached Black Heart's cage, he attacked the bars, barking like no dog she'd ever known, like some creature from mythology. Surprised and frightened, she backpedaled and tripped. Daniel alternately spoke sympathetically to her and harshly to Black Heart. From where she'd fallen, she

110   gazed, trembling, at Black Heart, who never ceased barking. She wondered how strong the bars of his cage were. She imagined them snapping and Black Heart pouncing on her and enclosing her neck in his mouth.

Black Heart looked less like a dog and more like a mammal from the period after the dinosaurs died. He was husky and broad-shouldered like a gorilla and his square face and dark, marble eyes seemed bison-like. He had scars everywhere—on his forehead, on his chest, in several places on his back—and she wondered what violent encounter each scar represented.

Thereafter whenever Daniel fed the dogs she accompanied him—except when her mother was around. Her mother didn't want her near the dogs. "They

120   are not your friends," she said. "Okay, Emily? Okay?"

When she was with Daniel, she stood by his side, so close she could smell him. He wore cologne, but this didn't disguise his other smells, which she thought her mother would find repulsive but which she grew used to and found reassuring. As soon as Daniel fed the three bullmastiffs, which he did by sliding their bowls into a space on the bottom of their cage, they stopped being interested in anything but the food. But Black Heart wouldn't eat his food until Daniel and Emily retreated behind the garden wall. If they craned their heads around the wall to stare at Black Heart, he would start barking like he smelled blood. To watch him eat, Daniel taped a hand-held mirror to a long stick and

G

130   held it at such an angle that they could gaze into it and see him. He ate the brown nuggets with slow pleasure. She remembered the last time she ate dinner with her father, how he picked at the rotisserie chicken, finishing everything on the bones.

When Daniel lets Black Heart into the vineyard every night, he carries a bullwhip. The whip looks like a snake—*una culebra*—and Black Heart is scared

---

7. **READ▶** As you read lines 118–172, continue to cite textual evidence.
    - Make notes in the margin about Emily's relationship with Black Heart.
    - Underline the reference to Emily's father.
    - Circle the sentence that describes the danger Black Heart might present.

*Black Heart
is like a
creature from
mythology.*

*Black Heart
never stops
barking.*

*Black Heart
is husky
and covered
with scars.*

*Emily goes
with Daniel to
feed the dogs.*

*Emily watches
while Black
Heart eats.*

---

6. **REREAD AND CITE TEXT EVIDENCE** Explain that in the week before she left for Argentina, Emily felt estranged from her father.

    F **ASK STUDENTS** to describe the phone conversations Emily has with her father. *Emily would call him when she thought his girlfriend wasn't around; even so, he would appear distracted.*

    Critical Vocabulary: enchanting (line 77) Have students explain the meaning of *enchanting*. Ask them to identify singers they have heard whose voices they would describe as "enchanting."

    Critical Vocabulary: cascades (line 91) Have students explain the meaning of *cascades*. Point out that the cat in the story "cascades down the purple flowers." What if he jumped down instead? Describe the difference. *Students may say that cascading is gentler and more fluid; jumping is abrupt, jerky.*

7. **READ AND CITE TEXT EVIDENCE** Explain that the way Black Heart eats reminds Emily of her father (lines 130–133).

    G **ASK STUDENTS** to describe the dog's eating habits. *He won't eat while Daniel and Emily watch. He ate the "brown nuggets with slow pleasure" and he finishes everything on the bones.*

CLOSE READ Notes

Emily brings Black Heart food.

subsequent:
following

Emily sings to Black Heart.

enunciate:
speak or pronounce clearly

of nothing in the world except the whip. Even so, he growls at it as if to say, Keep your distance or I will attack you. A week ago, as she leaned out of her open bedroom window, she saw Daniel leading Black Heart into the vineyard. Under his breath, he said, "One night he won't be afraid of the whip." And then

140　what?" He looked up at her, surprised to see her. She smiled like she did when she didn't understand his Spanish.

"All right, Romeo," she says, "you be good. Be good to all your girlfriends." He darts off to the other side of the garden and disappears beneath the weeping willow tree, which in the night looks like a hunched giant with a thousand thin arms. She resumes her walk toward the door, but is stopped by a sound of "Who? Who? Who?" It is Boy, the white-faced owl, in his nook in the palm tree twenty feet above her. She always thought of owls as old, but this owl looks like a teenager—thus the name she gave him.

"It's only me, Boy," she says. If he could speak in a language she

150　understood, she wonders if he would tease her like a brother would. Or would he say something like the man at the mall said to her cousin, who is fourteen but, with her European haircut, looks twenty?

"I'm going to visit Black Heart," she tells the owl. "It's all right. You'll see." Some days when Daniel is out in the vineyard and Maria is at the market in Luján de Cuyo and her mother and Ed are napping under the thin-bladed ceiling fan in their bedroom or sampling wines in Chacras de Coria, she visits Black Heart in his cage. She used to bring him pieces of steak and chicken she slipped into her palm at dinner and saved in a paper bag beneath her bed. The first time, she tossed the pieces of meat between the bars of his cage and

160　retreated behind the fence so he could eat them in private. When, on **subsequent** visits, she lingered, he snarled, growled, and barked at her but eventually, between his hostile sounds, devoured her offering.

 One day, she sang to him after giving him his meat, and his vicious sounds ceased. Even with his gigantic, square head and his razor-blade teeth and his terrible scars, he looked familiar and approachable, like a misunderstood monster. The song she'd sung was one she'd heard often on Maria's radio. She didn't understand all of the Spanish words, but she could **enunciate** them clearly, and Black Heart cocked his head as if to hear better. As soon as she stopped, his face again became strange and hideous, and his barking shocked

170　her ears until she fled, terrified.

The next day, she returned with only her voice. As long as she sang, he was silent, docile, calm. Content, even. Perhaps even happy.

Boy flutters his white and brown wings and swoops down toward her, his mouth open, his talons spread and pointed like daggers. As she ducks and

104

---

covers her eyes, she feels the wind from his wings fill her hair. She shivers from fear and a strange pleasure before she hears a squeal, high-pitched and hopeless. She turns to see Boy pluck a mouse from the grass and retreat with his feast to the palm tree.

"You scared me, Boy. Maybe you wanted to? In fun, I mean. Like a brother

180　would?"

The day she touched Black Heart, the air was a white mist. She couldn't see her feet. But she knew the path to his cage as if it were illuminated. When she stood before it, she couldn't see him; she could only hear his terrible bark. When she sang, his barking stopped instantly, as if she'd cast a spell. Piercing the bars of his cage, she held out her hand to him, palm open. She felt his mouth engulf it. She felt his teeth touch her skin. She thought he was going to bite down. But his mouth held steady. Carefully, she slipped her left hand into the cage so she could stroke his head and neck and back. His fur was like the leather of her father's jacket.

190　A moment later, she felt his tongue sweep the underside of her fingers and his teeth nibble, soft as a kiss, her fingertips. She felt her heart fly. She felt adored. For hours afterward, she didn't wash either hand.

During her last visit before tonight, as she sang a song she'd invented about a girl and a dog and the iron between them, he looked at her with what she swore was a plea. *I want to know you without bars between us.*

She uses her singing to control the dog.

She puts her hands into the cage.

8. **◀ REREAD** Reread lines 163–172. How does Emily's singing affect Black Heart? What might singing have to do with the theme of the story?

Emily's singing seems to soothe and calm Black Heart. She doesn't even need to bring him food to make him stop barking, she just sings. Singing represents power and communication in the story—where it once connected her to her father, now it connects her to Black Heart.

9. **READ ▶** As you read lines 173–209, continue to cite textual evidence.

- Underline text describing Emily's reactions to Boy and Black Heart.
- Circle the words that Emily imagines Black Heart speaks.
- In the margin, explain how Emily is testing the limits of her power.

105

Critical Vocabulary: subsequent (line 161) Have students explain the meaning of *subsequent*. How was Emily's first visit with Black Heart different from subsequent visits? Have students use the word *subsequent* in the answer. *Students may say that at first she tossed him his food, whereas on subsequent visits she lingered.*

Critical Vocabulary: enunciate (line 167) Have students explain the meaning of *enunciate*. Why is proper enunciation important? *How you enunciate has a direct bearing on how you communicate.*

FOR ELL STUDENTS Students will have guessed from context clues that the weeping willow (lines 143–144) is a kind of tree. They will need to know that to understand the image that follows ("a hunched giant with a thousand thin arms") (lines 144–145). Spanish-speaking students will know exactly what kind of tree it is if you point out the word *weeping*. (In Spanish the name of the tree is a literal translation of the English name, *sauce llorón*.)

8. **REREAD AND CITE TEXT EVIDENCE** Point out that Emily's singing has a strange effect on the dog.

H **ASK STUDENTS** to describe the way Black Heart's behavior changes when she stops singing (lines 168–170). *When she starts singing, his vicious sounds cease, he looks familiar and approachable, he cocks his head; when she stops singing, he resumes barking and his face becomes hideous again.*

9. **READ AND CITE TEXT EVIDENCE**

I **ASK STUDENTS** what details in this section have an "otherworldly" quality. *The dog's barking stops "as if she'd cast a spell" (line 184); "the air was a white mist" (line 181); the fact that she couldn't see her feet but knew the way to the dog's cage (lines 181–182).*

J Ten feet from the door separating her and Black Heart, she stops. She can sense his presence. She hears a growl so soft it might be a purr. If she moves any closer, he will erupt and wake Maria, asleep in her tiny house. If this happens, her plan will come to nothing, and she will never again have the chance to visit 200 him. Ed and her mother will keep her with them, even if they'd rather not. Besides, their time in Argentina is coming to an end.

Another week, and they will be heading home.

She sings, softly at first, a sound like small waves hitting sand. He stops growling. She reaches the door. There are three deadbolt locks, the highest an inch beyond her reach. But she jumps and slaps it open. In jumping, her singing stops, and Black Heart growls. She slaps the second lock open, her singing coming jagged, and Black Heart continues to growl, his voice climbing in register the way it does before he attacks the bars of his cage. She tries to make her singing calm, but this is difficult because of her pounding heart.

K 210 She has one deadbolt left to open before she can turn the doorknob and release him into the garden. She gives herself a moment to doubt. The wisest part of her says she should go back to the house, go to bed. But her hand, which she can barely feel as her heart thunders, acts otherwise. It snaps the deadbolt to the side.

Stop, she tells herself. Think. If Black Heart were to attack her, Maria could do nothing. Daniel is in Mendoza with his friends. He might come home in five minutes. He might come home in three hours. And Ed and her mother? Even if they were to come, what could they do?

Emily opens the locks to Black Heart's cage.

---

10. ◀ **REREAD** Reread lines 196–202. What is Emily's plan? Why is her relationship with Black Heart important to her? Support your answer with explicit textual evidence.

Emily wants to be with Black Heart outside his cage. She wants to believe that only she can soothe his "killer" ways.

11. **READ** ▶ As you read lines 210–264, continue to cite textual evidence.
- Underline text that describes Emily's excitement and fear.
- Circle verbs and verb phrases that show that Black Heart's movements.

These reservations register the way the deepest fear does, like fingers 220 squeezing her heart, but they cannot overcome her desire. She pulls open the door. Boy cries as if he's been wounded, leaps from his cave in the palm tree, and flies over her, his wings filling her hair with a warning wind.

Too late. Black Heart is at her side, so close she can feel heat coming from him. She thinks, I'm going to die. At the same time, **exhilaration** fills her. She feels like she owns the night. She turns, singing, and walks to the middle of the garden. Black Heart circles her, a slow loop on the grass, his eyes never leaving her. He might be dancing with her. Or he might be a lion circling its prey.

The moon blazes above her, and she feels powerful and magical and adored. Every so often, she touches Black Heart's back, at once smooth and 230 rough. I can sing all night. But after a minute or five or ten—she has no watch, the night tells no time—her exhilaration fades into worry. She doesn't know how long she can stand here and sing. Perhaps she can make her way back to the house, open the door, slip in. It is only fifty feet from where she's standing. But when she steps toward it, Black Heart quickly moves in front of her and issues a clear, low sound, less a growl than a warning a human might give.

When Black Heart is at the farthest point in his circle away from the house, she again moves toward it. Again, he moves swiftly to block her. This time, his warning is louder and more insistent. She backs up to her original spot. She hears nothing but her voice against the inside of her ears and the swish of Black 240 Heart moving in the grass. My God, she thinks, I'll have to sing all night.

She wonders if she should run toward the house. She wonders if she should shout Maria's name. But she fears—she knows—that if she broke off her song even for a second, Black Heart would attack her, devour her.

As she sings, she prays Daniel will come home. She prays Ed and her mother will become bored at the dinner and will drive the car into the middle of the garden to save her. She prays Maria will step outside and Black Heart will charge her, and this will give her the chance to flee. But the night radiates with brilliant indifference and fatigue weighs on her like something living, something growing. Her song has lost words.

250 When they find me, they won't know he loved me. They'll think I was a stupid girl who thought she could play with a mean dog.

She feels her eyes flutter from fatigue; she feels herself stagger. As in a dream, she feels Black Heart at her side, his head butting her thigh, insistent and strong. He prods her toward the vineyard's open door. A moment later, she is surrounded by grapes, silver-blue in the moonlight. Her **arid** mouth craves their delicious juice, but Black Heart jabs her and she keeps moving. She hears Maria calling her. She hears Ed's car limp up the gravel drive. She even hears, or thinks she hears, Daniel, or perhaps it's her father, singing in the distance.

exhilaration:
excitement, joy, liveliness

arid:
dry, like a desert

---

10. **REREAD AND CITE TEXT EVIDENCE** Point out that if Emily's plan fails, "Ed and her mother will keep her with them, even if they'd rather not."

J **ASK STUDENTS** what Emily is afraid will happen to foil her plans. *She is afraid that if she moves any closer, Black Heart will wake Maria and she will tell her mother and stepfather what she was doing.*

11. **READ AND CITE TEXT EVIDENCE** Point out that in lines 210–264, the author creates a sense of excitement and fear.

K **ASK STUDENTS** to cite passages from the text that create suspense or fear. *Students may mention the short, punchy sentences the author uses; for example: "Stop, she tells herself. Think. If Black Heart were to attack her, Maria could do nothing. Daniel is in Mendoza with his friends. He might come home in five minutes. He might come home in three hours" (lines 215–217).*

Critical Vocabulary: exhilaration (line 224) Have students explain the meaning of *exhilaration*. What would they describe as exhilarating? *Students may suggest riding on a roller coaster; skiing; flying in a plane; swimming in the ocean.*

Critical Vocabulary: arid (line 255) Have students share definitions of *arid*.

FOR ELL STUDENTS Explain that *limp up* (line 257) means "to proceed with difficulty." Ask a volunteer what the sentence "She hears Ed's car limp up the gravel drive" means.

CLOSE READ
Notes

The sounds fade. She wants to scream, but, so deep in the vineyard, she
260 knows no one would hear her.

I'll find my way back, she vows, but stumbles, collapses. On her back on the
grass altar, she sees, as if on a different planet, the snow-capped Andes. She
discovers that, remarkably, she is still singing in a voice charged with emotion.
I'm safe. But—no—it is Black Heart, mouth at her ear, who is singing.

12. **◀ REREAD** Reread lines 250–264. What do you think happens to Emily at
the end of the story? Support your answer with explicit textual evidence.

Possible response: Black Heart leads Emily out of the vineyard and
kills her at the end of the story. She "stumbles, collapses" and Black
Heart is "trained to kill whomever he finds."

SHORT RESPONSE

Cite Text Evidence Identify the central theme of the story. What is the
author saying about relationships? Review your reading notes, and be sure to
cite text evidence in your response.

The theme of the story is about the loss of communication that
leads to failed relationships. Emily is left alone, with little
communication from either of her parents. She forges relationships
with the local animals and focuses on Black Heart who responds to
her singing. Emily longs for closeness and she mistakenly decides to
get closer to Black Heart, even though she knows in her heart she is
being foolish. Sometimes those who are supposed to be the closest to
us succeed only in making us feel more alone.

108

TO CHALLENGE STUDENTS . . .

Tell students that in this story the author depicts a particularly
vicious guard dog that is "some combination of pit bull,
Rottweiler, German shepherd, and wolf." Tell students that vicious
dogs are usually trained by humans intent on using them for their
own purposes.

ASK STUDENTS to work with a partner or small group to
research the subject of guard dogs. Have them address questions
such as the following:

* What techniques are used to train guard dogs and dogs
   meant to attack? How long does this training take? At what
   age does training start? How does is it differ from the way
   most pets are trained?

* Which breeds make the best guard dogs? What qualities do
   guard dogs need? Are dogs specially bred to be guard dogs?

* Is training a dog to be a guard dog cruel to the dog? How
   does the animal rights community feel about the training of
   guard dogs?

* Should there be restrictions on the use and training of guard
   dogs? What evidence do we have of guard dogs running
   amuck, attacking people indiscriminately—even attacking
   household members?

12. REREAD AND CITE TEXT EVIDENCE Have students note the
words *I'm safe* in line 264.

L ASK STUDENTS to reread the line in context. Why would
she say this? Does she really think she is safe? *Students may say
she is living in a fantasy world and believes her singing will protect
her from Black Heart.*

SHORT RESPONSE

Cite Text Evidence Students' responses should include text
evidence that supports their positions. They should:

* analyze the story's central theme.
* identify details that support that theme.
* determine how the story's ending supports the story's message.

DIG DEEPER

1. With the class, return to Question 2, Reread. Have students share their responses.

ASK STUDENTS to think about Emily's behavior and why Maria is concerned about her.

- Is Emily "all right" in this section of text? *Students may say that she seems confused, lonely, and depressed.* What does she lack? *She lacks friends, parental attention; she lacks the familiar objects of home.*

- What about Emily's behavior suggests she wants to be anywhere but where she is? *She wanders around singing made-up songs; she lies on an altar and stares at the mountains that shimmer "like a picture in a storybook."*

2. With the class, return to Question 8, Reread. Have students share their responses.

ASK STUDENTS to think about the way the author describes Black Heart calming down when Emily sings to him.

- Remind students about what happened in lines 76–79. What was Emily's father's reaction to her singing voice? *He paid attention to her; he complimented her on her "enchanting" voice. He made her feel like she had the power to do anything; i.e., she could "sing a dog away from a bone."* How did Emily feel as a result of this attention? *She felt adored; she felt special.*

- Why does Emily now believe that singing gives her power over the dog? *She has taken her father's words literally; she thinks her voice is enchanting and that she has special powers.* How does she view her relationship with Black Heart? *She believes that she alone knows how to communicate with him.*

- How does Black Heart take the place of Emily's father? *Emily sings to Black Heart instead of her father; he adores her the way her father used to; they have a special connection like she once had with her father.*

ASK STUDENTS to return to their Short Response answer and revise it based on the class discussion.

CLOSE READING NOTES

The Mosquito Solution

*my*SmartPlanner — Create lesson plans and access resources online.

Science Article by Michael Specter

Why This Text?

In the media and in conversations, students may encounter a wide variety of opinions regarding genetic engineering or genetically modified foods. This article, by award-winning science journalist Michael Specter, explores a program testing the use of genetic modification to combat a deadly tropical disease.

Key Learning Objective: The student will be able to support inferences and draw conclusions from a scientific article.

For additional practice:

Close Reader selection
"Are Genetically Modified Foods Scary?"
Science Writing by Paloma Reyes

COMMON CORE · Common Core Standards

RI 1 Cite textual evidence to support inferences.
RI 2 Provide an objective summary of the text.
RI 3 Analyze ideas and events.
RI 4 Determine the meaning of words and phrases.
RI 5 Analyze and evaluate structure.
RI 6 Determine author's purpose in a text.
W 1 Write arguments to support claims.
L 6 Use domain-specific words and phrases accurately.

▲ Text Complexity Rubric

Quantitative Measures	**The Mosquito Solution** Lexile: 1130L
Qualitative Measures	**Levels of Meaning/Purpose** more than one purpose; implied, easily identified from context
	Structure organization of main ideas and details complex but mostly explicit; may exhibit disciplinary traits
	Language Conventionality and Clarity increased unfamiliar, academic, or domain–specific words
	Knowledge Demands somewhat complex science concepts
Reader/Task Considerations	Teacher determined Vary by individual reader and type of text

Michael Specter Have students read the information about the author. Tell them that Specter has been a journalist since 1985, working as the national science reporter at the *Washington Post* and as a foreign correspondent for the *New York Times* before becoming a staff reporter at the *New Yorker* in 1998. He has earned numerous awards for his science journalism. Explain that this article appeared in the *New Yorker* in July 2012.

AS YOU READ Direct students to use the As You Read directions to focus their reading.

Summarize the Text

COMMON CORE **RI 2**

(Subhead, LINES 1–9)

Explain that **summarizing** requires readers to identify the **central ideas,** or main points, in a piece of writing and that headings and subheadings can provide clues to what an author considers the central ideas of the piece.

A **ASK STUDENTS** to reread the question that serves as the subheading of this article and explain why Specter might have chosen to begin the article in this way. *(He wanted to pose a question that he intended to answer in the article. It also serves as a provocative way to draw readers into the article.)* Call on a volunteer to explain the meaning of the phrase "genetic modification." *(using technology to change the genes in a living organism)* Then ask students how the question might be related to the title and what kind of information they expect to find in the article. *(The question suggests that genetic modification might be the solution referred to in the title; there might be information about the particular tropical disease and the particular type of genetic modification that is being used to try to eliminate the disease.)*

Then explain that a **summary** is a brief restatement of a passage that includes only the central idea and the most important supporting details.

B **ASK STUDENTS** to reread lines 1–9 and summarize the paragraph in one sentence. *(The* Aedes aegypti *mosquito can breed anywhere that there is a small amount of water.)* Invite students to discuss how this passage might be related to the subhead. *(It suggests that the tropical disease in question is caused by a particular mosquito and that the author is going to talk about genetic modification to that mosquito.)*

Michael Specter *has written for the* Washington Post *and the* New York Times; *currently he is a staff writer for the* New Yorker. *He often covers topics related to science, technology, and public health. Specter has received awards for articles on the AIDS epidemic in Africa and for his war reporting. His 2009 book* Denialism *reflects his growing concern over opposition to science by various groups and individuals, which he believes could have disastrous consequences for the planet.*

The Mosquito Solution

Science Article by Michael Specter

Image Credits: (b) ©James Gathany/Center For Disease Control; (t) ©Courtesy of Michael Specter

AS YOU READ Pay attention to the clues that tell you how the author feels about "the mosquito solution." Write down any questions you generate during reading.

Can genetic modification eliminate a deadly tropical disease?

Few people, unless they travel with an electron microscope,[1] would ever notice the egg of an *Aedes aegypti* mosquito. But the insects follow us nearly everywhere we go. *Aedes* can breed in a teaspoon of water, and their eggs have been found in tin cans, beer bottles, barrels, jugs, flower vases, cups, tanks, tubs, storm drains, cisterns, cesspools, catch basins, and fishponds. They mate in the dew of spider lilies, ape plants, guava trees, palm fronds, in the holes of rocks formed from lava, and in coral reefs. More than any other place, perhaps, *Aedes aegypti* thrive in the moist, hidden gullies of used automobile tires.

---

[1] **electron microscope:** an instrument that uses beams of electrons rather than light to magnify tiny objects.

The Mosquito Solution **453**

SCAFFOLDING FOR ELL STUDENTS

Analyze Language Guide students to identify and understand words associated with key concepts in the article.

- Ask students to reread lines 1–9 and identify words associated with the mosquitoes' eggs. *(breed, mate)*
- Then ask them to identify words associated with water. *(dew, moist)*

ASK STUDENTS what all the items listed in lines 4–9 ("tin cans, beer bottles . . . . automobile tires.") have in common? How are they related to mosquitoes' eggs? *(They are all places where water collects and places where mosquitoes lay their eggs.)*

CLOSE READ

Support Inferences: Draw Conclusions (LINES 10–24)

 COMMON CORE **RI 1**

Explain that a **conclusion** is a statement based on evidence, experience, and reasoning. **Evidence** can include facts, examples, and expert opinions.

C CITE TEXT EVIDENCE Ask students to reread lines 10–24 and identify the conclusion and evidence that Specter presents in the paragraph. *(Conclusion: "Aedes are among the deadliest creatures on earth" [lines 11–12]; Evidence: The mosquito transmits the yellow-fever virus, which killed millions before there was a vaccine [lines 12–16] and also carries the dengue virus, which infects "at least fifty million people a year," including "more than half a million people [who] become seriously ill from the disease." [lines 16–21])*

Analyze Language (LINES 29–51)

 COMMON CORE **RI 4, L 6**

Explain that Specter uses domain-specific vocabulary to explain Oxitec's work at Moscamed.

D CITE TEXT EVIDENCE Have students reread lines 29–52 to identify technical words that explain what Oxitec is doing at Moscamed. *("modify the genetic structure of the male Aedes mosquito" [line 30]; "transforming it into a mutant" [line 31]; "Oxitec's engineered mosquito" [line 38]; "entomological assembly line" [lines 41–42]; "eggs fertilized by those genetically modified males" [line 47])*

CRITICAL VOCABULARY

fetid: Specter describes the laboratory at Moscamed as being damp and bad-smelling.

ASK STUDENTS why a laboratory that breeds mosquitoes might be described as fetid. *(Mosquitoes breed in damp conditions and that might create an unpleasant odor in the laboratory.)*

entomological: Specter says Moscamed has been transformed into an insect-making assembly line.

ASK STUDENTS why Specter describes Moscamed as an "entomological assembly line." *(It has become a place where genetically modified mosquitoes are produced in large quantities.)*

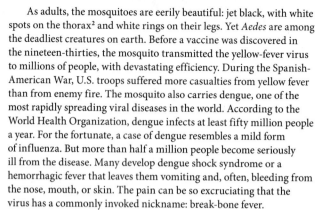

10 As adults, the mosquitoes are eerily beautiful: jet black, with white spots on the thorax[2] and white rings on their legs. Yet *Aedes* are among the deadliest creatures on earth. Before a vaccine was discovered in the nineteen-thirties, the mosquito transmitted the yellow-fever virus to millions of people, with devastating efficiency. During the Spanish-American War, U.S. troops suffered more casualties from yellow fever than from enemy fire. The mosquito also carries dengue, one of the most rapidly spreading viral diseases in the world. According to the World Health Organization, dengue infects at least fifty million people a year. For the fortunate, a case of dengue resembles a mild form

20 of influenza. But more than half a million people become seriously ill from the disease. Many develop dengue shock syndrome or a hemorrhagic fever that leaves them vomiting and, often, bleeding from the nose, mouth, or skin. The pain can be so excruciating that the virus has a commonly invoked nickname: break-bone fever.

There is no vaccine or cure for dengue, or even a useful treatment. The only way to fight the disease has been to poison the insects that carry it. That means bathing yards, roads, and public parks in a fog of insecticide. Now there is another approach, promising but experimental: a British biotechnology company called Oxitec has

30 developed a method to modify the genetic structure of the male *Aedes* mosquito, essentially transforming it into a mutant capable of destroying its own species. A few weeks ago, I found myself standing in a dank, **fetid** laboratory at Moscamed, an insect-research facility in the Brazilian city of Juazeiro, which has one of the highest dengue rates in the world. A plastic container about the size of an espresso cup sat on a bench in front of me, and it was filled with what looked like black tapioca: a granular, glutinous[3] mass containing a million eggs from Oxitec's engineered mosquito. Together, the eggs weighed ten grams, about the same as a couple of nickels.

40 Oxitec, which is short for Oxford Insect Technologies, has essentially transformed Moscamed into an **entomological** assembly line. In one tightly controlled, intensely humid space, mosquitoes are hatched, nurtured, fed a combination of goat's blood and fish food, then bred. Afterward, lab technicians destroy the females they have created and release the males to pursue their only real purpose in life: to find females in the wild and mate with them. Eggs fertilized by those genetically modified males will hatch normally, but soon after, and well before the new mosquitoes can fly, the fatal genes will prevail, killing them all. The goal is both simple and audacious: to overwhelm

50 the native population of *Aedes aegypti* and wipe them out, along with the diseases they carry.

The engineered mosquitoes, known officially as OX513A, lead a brief but privileged life. The entire process, from creation to

fetid
(fĕt´ĭd) *adj.* having an unpleasant odor; bad-smelling.

entomological
(ĕn´tə-mə-lŏj´ĭ-kəl) *adj.* related to the study of insects.

---

[2] **thorax:** the part of a body between the head and abdomen.
[3] **glutinous:** thick and sticky, like glue.

APPLYING ACADEMIC VOCABULARY

assurance	vision

As you discuss the selection, incorporate the following Collection 5 academic vocabulary words: *assurance* and *vision*. Ask students to explain the **vision** that scientists have for the eradication of dengue. Discuss why Specter may appreciate Oxitec's work as a solution to the health crisis posed by dengue, but also recognize the need for **assurances** that there won't be problematic consequences.

destruction, takes less than two weeks. The eggs, oval spheres no longer than a millimetre, are milky white when laid. Within a couple of hours they harden, forming a protective cuticle and turning shiny and black. Looking around the lab, I saw long white sheets lining the shelves; each sheet was covered in tens of thousands of pin-sized dots and resembled some sort of computer code. The eggs can survive that 60 way for a year; after four days, however, they are plunged into jam jars filled with water at twenty-seven degrees Celsius—a temperature that enables the eggs to hatch in less than an hour.

"These mosquitoes are relatively easy to breed and cost almost nothing to transport," Andrew McKemey, Oxitec's chief field officer, said as he led me around the lab. McKemey, a lanky man who was dressed in a green madras shirt and khaki cargo pants, spends much of his time in Brazil, teaching local scientists how to manufacture the company's prize product. The lab churns out about four million mutant eggs a week, and will soon increase production to ten million. 70 "That's a start," McKemey said. "In theory, we can build hundreds of millions of mosquitoes in this place."

The field trial, which began a year ago, is a collaboration between Moscamed, Oxitec, and the University of São Paulo. Preliminary results have been impressive: the group recently collected a sample of eggs in two neighborhoods where the engineered mosquitoes had been released, and found that eighty-five per cent of them were genetically modified. With a large enough number of those eggs, the *Aedes* population would fall, and so would the incidence of dengue. "This is not a **panacea**," Giovanini Coelho, who coördinates the Brazilian 80 Ministry of Health's National Program for Control of Dengue, told me. "I am not saying this alone will solve the problem or that there are no risks. There are always risks—that's why we start with small studies in geographically isolated neighborhoods. But people are dying here, and this mosquito is resistant to many insecticides. We really do need something better than what we have."

In Juazeiro, where few families remain unaffected by dengue, the Moscamed team and its mosquitoes are treated with reverence. The researchers drive around in white vans that have pictures of mosquitoes and the word *transgenico*[4] painted on the side. They try 90 to visit every house in areas where they release mosquitoes, to explain that OX513A "are friendly bugs that protect you against dengue" and that, because the scientists are targeting *Aedes aegypti* where they live, under sofas and in back yards, the engineered mosquitoes can kill their brethren without harming any other plant or animal.

It's an elegant approach to a health crisis that threatens much of the world, but it will take more than biological success to make it work. That's because OX513A is not like other mosquitoes. In fact, it's like nothing else on earth—a winged creature, made by man, then released

panacea
(păn′ə-sē′ə) *n.* a cure or solution for all problems.

---
[4] *transgenico* (trăns-jĕn′ĭ-kô): a Spanish term meaning "genetically modified."

SCAFFOLDING FOR ELL STUDENTS

Analyze Cause and Effect Define **cause** as an event that directly results in another event or action. An **effect** is the direct or logical outcome or result of an event or action. Explain that causes and effects may be linked in a chain of events and signaled by words such as *because* or *as a result*. Students will need to infer the cause and effect by figuring out how two events are related. Read aloud lines 72–78 and ask students to identify the first cause *("engineered mosquitoes had been released")* and the first effect *("eighty five percent of them [eggs] were genetically modified")*. Then ask students to identify the chain of cause and effect. *(A large number of such eggs would cause the* Aedes *population to fall and there would be less dengue.)*

Support Inferences: Draw Conclusions (LINES 72–85)

COMMON CORE RI 1, RI 2

Tell students that they may have to make **inferences,** or logical assumptions, based on evidence the author states to determine main ideas and draw conclusions.

E ASK STUDENTS to reread lines 72–85 to infer the paragraph's central idea. *(Early evidence from a field trial of OX513A indicates that the process has a good chance of reducing dengue outbreaks.)* Discuss how Specter presents the evidence and what conclusions he wants readers to draw. *(He states that the results are "preliminary" but "impressive" and supports the assertion with data. By quoting Coelho, he sets a tone of cautious optimism and leads readers to conclude that, for Brazilians, genetically modified mosquitos may be a viable solution.)*

Analyze Language

COMMON CORE RI 4, L 6

(LINES 86–94)

Explain that scientists use technical language to describe their work and often need to find ways to make that work understandable to people who are not scientists.

F CITE TEXT EVIDENCE Ask students to reread lines 86–94 and identify examples of technical and nontechnical language used to communicate with the people of Juazeiro. *(The words* transgenico, Aedes aegypti, *and* engineered mosquitoes *are technical terms. Calling the mosquitoes "'friendly bugs that protect you against dengue'" and explaining that scientists are looking for them "under sofas and in back yards" and that these mosquitoes will not harm "any other plant or animal" are more understandable terms.)*

CRITICAL VOCABULARY

panacea: A Brazilian health minister admits that Oxitec's solution will not take care of all the problems associated with dengue.

ASK STUDENTS to explain why Brazilian officials acknowledge Oxitec's solution will not be a panacea for dengue. *(They understand it will not solve all the problems or eradicate the disease.)*

Summarize the Text COMMON CORE RI 2

(LINES 99–107)

Explain that it is important to notice when an author introduces a new idea and to consider how it relates to the central ideas previously presented.

G **ASK STUDENTS** to reread lines 99–107 and summarize the paragraph in one sentence. *(Many people are concerned about the risks associated with genetically modified animals because of unknown consequences.)* Discuss why Specter might have chosen to introduce this idea at this point in the article. *(He wants to balance the optimism about OX513A with a statement of people's worst fears about such experiments.)*

Support Inferences: Draw Conclusions (LINES 122–132) COMMON CORE RI 1

Explain that a key to drawing conclusions is evaluating new evidence as it is presented and judging whether it supports previous inferences or calls them into question.

H **ASK STUDENTS** to reread lines 122–132 and explain how the evidence presented in this paragraph relates to earlier evidence Specter has presented. *(Specter enumerates additional mosquito-borne illnesses and introduces the idea that "viruses and parasites borne by mosquitoes evolve rapidly to resist pesticides and drugs." [lines 130–131])* Then ask students to draw a conclusion about why Specter might have chosen to introduce this evidence at this point in the article. *(This evidence argues against those who have concerns about the risks associated with genetically modified mosquitoes [lines 99–107] by presenting the real risks associated with not eradicating the Aedes aegypti. By saying that older insecticides are no longer effective, Specter implies that genetic modification might be the best, if not the only, solution.)*

 into the wild. Despite the experiment's scientific promise, many people
100 regard the tiny insect as a harbinger of a world where animals are built by nameless scientists, nurtured in beakers, then set loose—with consequences, no matter how noble the intention, that are impossible to anticipate or control. "This mosquito is Dr. Frankenstein's monster, plain and simple," Helen Wallace, the executive director of the British environmental organization GeneWatch, said. "To open a box and let these man-made creatures fly free is a risk with dangers we haven't even begun to contemplate."

There are more than three thousand species of mosquito, but the vast majority take no interest in us; they feed mostly on rotting fruit
110 and other sources of sugar. Only a few hundred species, including *Aedes aegypti*, need blood to survive. (The males never bite, but without a blood meal the females would be unable to nourish their eggs.) Mosquito mating habits can be brutal. "In the most successful encounters, the pair may become so tightly locked together that the male has some difficulty escaping in the end," the late Harvard entomologist Andrew Spielman wrote in his 2001 book, "Mosquito: The Story of Man's Deadliest Foe." "An unfortunate few males manage to get away only by leaving their sex organs behind." Yet Spielman also noted that the briefest exchanges can be highly productive: "A single
120 minute or so of passion allows her to produce all the fertile eggs she will ever lay."

There has never been a more effective killing machine. Researchers estimate that mosquitoes have been responsible for half the deaths in human history. Malaria accounts for much of the mortality, but mosquitoes also transmit scores of other potentially fatal infections, including yellow fever, dengue fever, chikungunya, lymphatic filariasis, Rift Valley fever, West Nile fever, and several types of encephalitis. Despite our technical sophistication, mosquitoes pose a greater risk to a larger number of people today than ever before. Like
130 most other pathogens, the viruses and parasites borne by mosquitoes evolve rapidly to resist pesticides and drugs. Many insecticides once used against *Aedes aegypti* are now considered worthless.

Aedes aegypti is an invasive species in the Americas. It most likely arrived on slave boats from Africa in the seventeenth century, along with the yellow fever it carried. The mosquitoes bred easily in the casks that provided drinking water on sailing ships. During the eighteenth century, a severe yellow-fever epidemic swept through New England and Philadelphia, as well as other American port cities; it took another century to discover that mosquitoes were the bearers of
140 the disease.

Traditional mosquito control all but eradicated *Aedes aegypti* (and the diseases it carries) from the United States fifty years ago. But globalization has been good to mosquitoes, particularly species like *Aedes aegypti*, which travel easily and can lie dormant in containers for months. In recent years, the mosquito and dengue have returned

WHEN STUDENTS STRUGGLE . . .

Encourage students to approach the task of summarizing the text in small steps.

- Have students read the selection in pairs.
- Tell them to take turns reading aloud each paragraph of the selection. At the end of the paragraph, the reading partner asks the listening partner to state the central idea of the paragraph and identify the most important supporting details.
- Have students record their ideas in a chart like the one shown.
- When they have completed the selection, have them review their chart and look for ideas that are repeated and most strongly supported to determine the central ideas of the selection and write an objective summary of the text.

to Texas, Hawaii, and Florida. The disease has also been transmitted for the first time in France and Croatia. "We have dragged mosquitoes around the world in billions of used tires," Paul Reiter told me. Reiter, a professor of medical entomology at the Pasteur Institute, in Paris, is
150 one of the world's experts on the natural history of mosquito-borne diseases. Before moving to France, he spent more than two decades in the Dengue Branch of the Centers for Disease Control, devoting a surprising amount of his time to studying tires. He found that they are ideal incubators for mosquitoes: tires absorb heat, trap rainwater, and nurture bacteria in the puddles they create. The exponential growth of dengue fever—the number of cases reported to the World Health Organization has increased thirtyfold since 1965—can, at least in part, be attributed to the enormous increase in tire exports.

Aedes aegypti don't fly far or live long; a major traveller would
160 move a few hundred yards and, on average, survive as an adult for ten days. But it is a particularly wily insect. Most mosquitoes are noisy enough to wake a sleeping man and slow enough that one bite is all they'll get before escaping or being crushed with an angry swat. *Aedes aegypti* feed during the day and strike in silence; they mostly stay low to the ground, preferring to bite people in the ankles or legs. The mosquito is highly sensitive to motion—as you move, it will, too, often stabbing its victim several times during each feeding, depositing pathogens with every bite and, in turn, increasing its chances of picking up dengue from infected people to pass along to others.
170 (Unlike most mosquitoes, which can lay hundreds of eggs in a single raft the size of a grain of rice, *Aedes aegypti* usually deposits its eggs in multiple locations, thereby raising the odds that some will survive.)

Dengue has always been considered a tropical illness. But its mode of transport, the mosquito, rarely lives more than a hundred yards from the vector's principal source of sustenance—us—and as our demographics have changed so have those of the mosquito. *Aedes aegypti* has adapted to the city with great dexterity. Even the most effective modern larvicides often miss the mosquito's well-hidden urban breeding grounds. "Dengue is a terrible disease, just terrible,"
180 Reiter said. "Its danger is impossible to exaggerate. And none of the methods used right now for dengue control are working. None."

It is not easy for an egg to become an OX513A. Most were originally modified in Oxitec's laboratories, in the English countryside not far from Oxford, where scientists, working with glass needles so small they can be seen only under a powerful microscope, insert two genes into eggs no bigger than a grain of salt. One gene carries instructions to manufacture far too much of a protein required to maintain healthy new cells; the results are lethal. Scientists keep the gene at bay, and the mosquitoes alive, by placing the antibiotic
190 tetracycline in the insects' food. The drug latches on to the protein and acts as a switch that can turn it on or off. As long as tetracycline is present, the mosquitoes live and reproduce normally and can be

CLOSE READ

Support Inferences: Draw Conclusions (LINES 159–172)

Explain that authors present details to support their central ideas. Analyzing the details provides the evidence that is then combined with readers' experience and/or prior knowledge which allows them to make inferences and draw conclusions.

Ⓘ ASK STUDENTS to reread lines 159–172 and describe the types of details that Specter presents about the *Aedes aegypti*. (*He describes how the* Aedes *is different from other mosquitoes—being quiet, biting legs and ankles multiple times during the day, and laying eggs in multiple locations.*) **Then ask:** What is the purpose of presenting these details? (*These details provide additional evidence about why the* Aedes *is so dangerous and needs to be eradicated.*)

Analyze Language (LINES 173–176)

Remind students that Specter uses **specialized vocabulary** or words with specific scientific meanings in this article. Context clues can help readers determine the meaning of such terms.

Ⓙ ASK STUDENTS to reread lines 173–176 and explain the meaning of the term *vector*. Then have them identify the context clues that helped them infer the meaning. (*Vector refers to the mosquito that carries dengue; "its [dengue] mode of transport, the mosquito . . . the vector's principal source of sustenance—us . . ."*)

Central Idea	Key Details
Mosquitoes are responsible for half of human deaths throughout history.	Mosquitoes transmit large numbers of diseases; pesticides and drugs lose effectiveness
Dengue has returned to the U. S. and other areas because of globalization.	Tires are ideal breeding ground for Aedes; increase in tire exports a key factor in increase in dengue

Support Inferences: Draw Conclusions (LINES 198–209)

 COMMON CORE RI 1

Explain that readers must ground their inferences in the evidence that is directly stated by the author and then add their own knowledge and experience to arrive at valid logical assumptions.

K **ASK STUDENTS** to reread lines 198–209 and infer why the scientists include the marker gene in the mosquitoes. *(They need to be able to see if their modification has been successful and to track the results when engineered mosquitoes are released into the environment.)* Then ask them why "the process succeeds only when the genes work their way into the critical germ cells the eggs need to reproduce." (lines 203–205) *(The purpose of the process is to reduce the number of mosquitoes by creating mutant males that can mate in the wild and produce mutant eggs that will all die off.)*

Summarize the Text (LINES 232–242)

COMMON CORE RI 2

Explain that authors sometimes state the central idea of a paragraph in a **topic sentence,** which is often the first or last sentence of a paragraph. To determine whether a sentence is a topic sentence, see if the details in the paragraph support the idea in that sentence.

L **CITE TEXT EVIDENCE** Ask students to reread lines 232–242 and indicate whether there is a topic sentence in the paragraph. *(First sentence: "The Oxitec mosquito grew out of a pest-control method called sterile insect technique, or SIT, which has been used for decades.").* Then ask them to cite details that show how the topic is developed. *(Billions of insects sterilized by radiation have been released in the wild and are then unable to reproduce. This process eradicated the screw worm but is hard to replicate on small insects like mosquitoes.)*

bred for generations. Once they are released from the lab, however, the antidote is gone; the lethal gene goes unchecked. Within days the males, along with any eggs they help to create, will perish. In fact, Oxitec has already modified all the *Aedes aegypti* eggs the world may ever need.

 200 The other gene is a fluorescent marker—the molecular version of a branding iron—that helps distinguish normal mosquitoes from modified ones. The naked eye sees nothing, but under the microscope the larvae give off a rich red glow, like a soft neon sign. Most of the altered eggs will die. Others will fail to incorporate the new genes into their DNA; these are useless, because the process succeeds only when the genes work their way into the critical germ cells the eggs need to reproduce. The task is difficult and tedious: the technicians can go through thousands of eggs to hit on just one that will pass the new genes to the next generation of mosquitoes. But once a sufficient number of eggs have been correctly modified they can, after many generations, produce millions of mutant mosquitoes.

210 OX513A are raised in the relative splendor of the laboratory. After they hatch, they are moved from petri dishes to plastic tanks the size of a home aquarium. Males are fed sugar; females, first lured by the smell of human sweat, feed on goat's blood obtained weekly from a nearby abattoir. "Thank God for that place," McKemey said with a laugh. "You can't make mosquitoes without blood." He stood in the close quarters of the rearing room as all around him eggs were morphing into larvae, hatching in the type of long trays bakers use to store loaves of bread. Across the room, in transparent, water-filled pails covered with cheesecloth, thousands of larvae, known to biologists as 220 wrigglers, were frantically trying to work themselves out of their cases and emerge as pupae, the final stage before becoming an adult.

Adolescent mosquitoes have enormous heads and prominent eyes; under the microscope they look like sea horses or miniature versions of E.T.[5] While the mosquitoes are still sheathed in their cases, their transparent wings are pinned behind their bodies. By this point, the mosquito has begun breathing through its syphon, a curling, segmented tube that pokes above the surface of the water like a snorkel. When the moment is right, the pupae inhale, expand their abdomens, burst their cases, and emerge head first as adults. "It's 230 thrilling to see," McKemey said, as we watched the young mosquitoes take their first tentative flights. "I never tire of it."

 The Oxitec mosquito grew out of a pest-control method called sterile insect technique, or SIT, which has been used for decades. Billions of insects, all sterilized by intense bursts of radiation, have been reared in laboratories like Moscamed and released to mate in the wild. In 1982, SIT, which prevents the organism from reproducing,

---

[5] **E.T.:** Extraterrestrial, referring to the central character in the movie of that name.

SCAFFOLDING FOR ELL STUDENTS

Analyze Phrasal Verbs Explain that a **phrasal verb** is a verb and another word that function together as one verb. Point out "the larvae give off a rich red glow" in line 201. Explain that *give* and *off* are words with multiple meanings and that *off* can be an adjective, an adverb, or a preposition. The two words together form a phrasal verb that means "to emit or send forth."

ASK STUDENTS to use context clues to define these phrasal verbs in the selection: *work into* (line 157), *work out* (lines 220, 251), *bump into* (line 246), *turn off* (line 270), *spun off* (line 272), *set off* (line 284), *ran into* (line 359), *come at* (line 423), *kill off* (line 430), and *wipe out* (line 437).

A mosquito larva shown through an electron microscope

successfully eradicated the screw-worm—a parasite that attacks the flesh of warm-blooded animals—from North America. But radiation is difficult to use properly on insects as small as mosquitoes.
240 Administer too little and they remain virile; zap them too powerfully and the insects are left so weak that they are unfit to compete for mates.

In the early nineties, Oxitec's chief scientist, Luke Alphey, was investigating the developmental genetics of *Drosophila*, the common fruit fly. One day, Alphey, now a visiting professor of zoology at Oxford, bumped into a colleague who was talking about sterile insect technique. Alphey, who knew little about the field, began to think about how to supplant radiation with the practices of modern molecular biology. Alphey is reserved, with a mop of brown hair and
250 pensive eyes; one can practically see his brain in motion as he works out a scientific problem. His goal was not exactly to sterilize the males but to alter their genes so that any **progeny** would die. If he could do that without using radiation, he reasoned, the insects should be fit to compete sexually for wild females.

Alphey faced several scientific hurdles. He would have to engineer only males. (Female mosquitoes bite, so genetically modified females could, in theory, pass novel proteins to humans, with unknown consequences.) "I was trying to think of ways around the radiation issue," he said. "I wondered, What if the engineered lethal system
260 could be sex-specific? It turns out that, with *Aedes aegypti*, females are

progeny
(prŏj´ə-nē) *n.*
offspring or
descendants.

The Mosquito Solution **459**

CLOSE READ

Support Inferences: Draw Conclusions (LINES 243–254) COMMON CORE RI 1

Explain that Specter sometimes presents conclusions drawn by the people he is writing about. Readers must then evaluate whether there is sufficient evidence and valid reasoning to support those conclusions.

M **ASK STUDENTS** to reread lines 243–254 and trace the reasoning that Luke Alphey followed to reach his conclusion about adapting SIT-like results to smaller insects. *(Alphey reasoned that he might use an approach from molecular biology instead of radiation so that the offspring of treated insects would die off. He reasoned that if such insects weren't sterile from radiation they could mate successfully in the wild.)* Do they believe the evidence presented supports Alphey's conclusion? By including this information, does Specter strengthen or weaken his argument? *(Accept any valid answer that is supported by details from the text.)*

CRITICAL VOCABULARY

progeny: Luke Alphey wanted to alter an insect's genes so that its offspring would not survive.

ASK STUDENTS why using a method other than sterilization would allow genetically modified insects to produce progeny. *(Insects that have not been sterilized are able to mate and produce offspring.)*

TO CHALLENGE STUDENTS . . .

Examine Figurative Language Why might a science writer use figurative language like a poet or novelist does? Invite students to explore this question by rereading the selection individually and looking for examples of similes, metaphors, or other types of figurative language and comparisons. Encourage them to notice where Specter uses this language and identify places where additional figurative language might have been useful.

Have students bring their examples to a small group discussion and discuss Specter's reasons for using this language.

Summarize the Text

COMMON CORE RI 2

(LINES 272–292)

Explain that following the development of ideas over several paragraphs allows readers to understand the central ideas an author is communicating and create an objective summary of the text.

 ASK STUDENTS to reread lines 272–292 and summarize the process that Oxitec followed to bring its OX513A program to market. *(Oxitec presented its ideas at conferences and gained financial support. Then it ran a series of field trials in the Cayman Islands, Malaysia, and Brazil to see how well the process worked in the wild. These smaller tests were preparation for doing tests in the United States.)*

Support Inferences: Draw Conclusions (LINES 280–285)

COMMON CORE RI 1

Explain that readers often need to make inferences about the meaning of certain words and phrases to make broader inferences about a paragraph's meaning and draw conclusions.

 ASK STUDENTS to reread lines 280–285 and interpret what a "test of feasibility" does and doesn't do. *(Such a test only determines whether the process works outside the lab, that is, whether the mutant males are able to mate and produce mutant eggs leading to a decrease in the mosquito population. It doesn't determine whether that decrease actually leads to a decrease in dengue or how the engineered mosquitoes affect the environment of the place.)* Invite students to reread the question that opened the article and discuss how it is related to this passage. *(The question directly relates to the feasibility ["can"] of using genetic modification to eliminate dengue {"a deadly tropical disease"].)* Then ask what is meant by "a cascade of events that nobody would be able to control." *(A series of events that are set off by the presence of the engineered mosquitoes in the environment and that cannot be reversed once it is set in motion. Specter once again refers to the concern about the possible unknown and unintended consequences of this experiment.)*

---

considerably larger than the males. That was a lucky break, because it means you can easily separate them on the basis of their size."

Once released, the males would have to live long enough to impregnate females, and they would need to be healthy enough to compete with wild males for the right to do so. "You want the insect to breed successfully in the lab but to be dependent on an antidote that will no longer be available in nature," Alphey said. "It was difficult to know how to do that." But chance again intervened: he happened to attend a seminar at which researchers described using tetracycline as a

270 switch to turn off a gene. "The molecule prevents the deadly gene from working," Alphey said. "It was a perfect solution."

In 2002, Oxitec was spun off as a company apart from the university. Alphey began to speak at tropical-disease meetings and in dengue-infested countries; he also gathered support from private investors and public-health philanthropies, including the Gates Foundation and the Wellcome Trust. In 2010, the company ran a series of field trials in the Cayman Islands, releasing 3.3 million genetically altered mosquitoes on sixteen hectares[6] of land. OX513A became the first engineered mosquito set free on the planet.

280 The number of wild *Aedes aegypti* mosquitoes in the area fell by eighty per cent in two months. It was only a test of feasibility; no one knew how it might affect the local ecology or whether it would actually reduce the incidence of dengue. Environmental activists feared that the release of engineered insects could set off a cascade of events that nobody would be able to control.

"They don't know how it will function in the real environment," Silvia Ribeiro, the director in Latin America for an environmental organization called the ETC Group, said. "And once they release it they can't take it back." In 2010, Oxitec began a smaller trial in

290 Malaysia. But the Brazilian experiment has been the biggest test so far, and it has laid the groundwork for Oxitec's battle over entry into the world's most significant market: the United States.

In 2009, Key West, Florida, suffered its first dengue outbreak in seventy-three years. There were fewer than thirty confirmed cases—a trifling number compared with the millions who are infected each year in South America, Africa, and Asia. There are just twenty thousand full-time residents in Key West, but, with more than two million visitors each year, the town is highly dependent on tourists. I was there during spring break, which is not the best time to visit

300 unless you have a particular interest in keggers, tequila, or Eagles cover bands.

"They feed this town," a woman who runs a cigar stand told me as we watched scores of sunburned students work their way down Truman Street and head toward Jimmy Buffett's bar, Margaritaville,

---

[6] **hectares:** metric units of area measurement, with one hectare equivalent to 10,000 square meters.

WHEN STUDENTS STRUGGLE...

To help students keep track of people and organizations on both sides of this issue have them work in pairs to fill out a chart like the one shown. Encourage them to refer to the chart as they read to see if a particular person or group has been previously mentioned. If so, they should add information as they encounter it. Explain that their purpose is to understand how each person relates to the central ideas of the article.

You may wish to use a modified Jigsaw approach by assigning groups of students to track particular individuals or organizations, assigning some to track supporters and some to track opponents. Students could then summarize what they know about the people and organizations they are tracking to other groups in order to gain a complete understanding of the information presented in the article.

> ## "Environmental activists feared that the release of engineered insects could set off a cascade of events."

ground zero for the aggressively laid-back Key West life style. "Sometimes it's a little gross out there," she said. "But take the tourists away and we are just a bunch of taco stands, bars, and beach bums."

Even a small dengue outbreak in Key West would send a troubling message. After 2009, the Florida Keys Mosquito Control District
310 added ten inspectors to join the battle against *Aedes aegypti*. In 2010, there were twice as many cases. "Clearly, we have the potential for serious dengue outbreaks," Michael S. Doyle told me. Doyle, an entomologist, is the district's executive director. He moved to Key West in 2011, after spending five years at the Centers for Disease Control. "Part of our problem is the image of dengue," he said. "A couple of hundred cases here could be devastating to the tourist economy.

"Think about it," he continued. "Somebody in Milwaukee is cruising through Web sites and asks his wife, 'Where should we go on
320 vacation, honey, Key West or some place in the Caribbean?' And the wife says, 'Hey, didn't I hear something about dengue in Key West?'" We were sitting in a café not far from Ernest Hemingway's house, the city's most heavily visited tourist site. Like many public buildings, the café has open windows and no screens; mosquitoes danced in the air beside us. "We live with open doors and windows," Doyle said. "And they live with us. We are an ideal host."

Doyle is a soft-spoken man with rimless eyeglasses and a neatly trimmed mustache. He pointed out that, when it comes to contracting dengue, the way people live is as important as where they live: from
330 1980 to 1999, Texas reported sixty-four cases of dengue along the Rio Grande, whereas there were more than sixty thousand cases in the Mexican states just across the river. "The population of *Aedes aegypti* was actually larger in Texas," he said. But Texans have screens on their windows (and keep the windows closed), drive air-conditioned cars, and spend little time outdoors.

Doyle wanted to lower the risk of a dengue outbreak in Key West, but the district was already spending more than a million dollars

The Mosquito Solution **461**

Support OX513A	Oppose OX513A
Andrew McKemey, Oxitec chief field officer Moscamed	Helen Wallace, Gene Watch
Giovanini Coelho, Brazilian health minister People of Juazeiro, Brazil	Silvia Ribeiro, ETC Group
Paul Reiter, entomologist at Pasteur Institute	Chris O'Brien, resident of Key West Friends of the Earth
Luke Alphey, Oxitec chief scientist	
Michael Doyle, Florida Keys Mosquito Control District	

CLOSE READ

Summarize the Text

(LINES 306–326)

Explain that it is important to analyze the types of details an author presents to support his central ideas.

P CITE TEXT EVIDENCE Ask students to reread lines 306–326 and identify the central idea and supporting details that Specter presents in the passage. *(Central idea: "Even a small dengue outbreak in Key West would send a troubling message." [lines 308–309]; Details: importance of tourism to Key West [lines 306–307] and how the "image of dengue" would harm that economy [lines 315–321], presented in quotations from two different people in Key West, a small business owner and an entomologist.)* Discuss why Specter might have chosen these two different people to quote. *(He wanted to show that concern about dengue and its impact on tourism is a broad concern and that it is not just scientific experts who are concerned about the possible problem.)*

Support Inferences: Draw Conclusions (LINES 327–335)

Explain that when writers want readers to draw certain conclusions, they must present evidence that is relevant, or related in a meaningful way, to their central idea. The concept of relevance also helps readers to understand why authors present certain evidence at certain places in a piece of writing.

Q ASK STUDENTS to reread lines 327–335 and discuss how this paragraph is relevant to the situation in Key West as outlined in previous paragraphs. *(Specter presents evidence to show that lifestyle is an important factor in the severity of dengue outbreaks. People in Key West live more like the people in Mexico (where outbreaks are large) with "open windows and no screens . . . open doors and windows" [lines 324–326] than the people in Texas (where outbreaks are small) who "have screens . . . (and keep the windows closed), drive air-conditioned cars, and spend little time outdoors." [lines 333–335])*

Summarize the Text

COMMON CORE RI 2

(LINES 341–358)

Explain that authors often link central ideas by repeating key words and phrases to show how ideas may be related. Such clues can help readers when they are summarizing a text.

 CITE TEXT EVIDENCE Ask students to reread lines 341–358 and identify an aspect of the Oxitec work that is mentioned by supporters and opponents. *(Doyle says other approaches to dealing with controlling the Aedes mosquito are "more environmentally challenging" than the Oxitec approach. [lines 342–343]; opponents were concerned about the effects of "releasing and testing genetically modified (manmade) mosquitoes on . . . the environment." [lines 354–357])* Discuss why Specter might have chosen to link these ideas. *(He wants to show that even though opponents are concerned about the environmental effects of Oxitec's process, scientists actually see it as less environmentally damaging than the traditional approaches, namely using insecticides.)*

Support Inferences: Draw Conclusions (LINES 370–383)

COMMON CORE RI 1

Explain that Specter drew his own conclusions as he learned more about Oxitec's project, but he does not always explicitly reveal his reasoning process.

 ASK STUDENTS to reread lines 370–383 and infer why Specter concluded that the protesters "had been briefed by the Friends of the Earth." *(He bases his conclusions on the statements made by the protesters, quoting Chris O'Brien specifically. He is likely familiar with language that reflects Friends of the Earth's talking points rather than O'Brien's natural way of speaking. For example, information about the enzymes in female mosquitoes and the effects of their bites on humans and the concern about the food chain, suggest that it came from someone who had studied the issue and taken a position on it. Compare these sentences with O'Brien's previous statements in line 365–369 that reflect a more personal belief about the possible risk of dengue fever.)*

a year on insecticide, and he was loath to dump more chemicals in people's yards. Then a colleague attended a meeting of the American
340 Society for Tropical Medicine and Hygiene and told him about OX513A. "I remember thinking that if this actually worked we would win in every possible way," he said. "Other approaches are more costly and more environmentally challenging. The data looked solid, and certainly we need to think differently about mosquito control than we have in the past."

In March, Doyle invited Luke Alphey, Oxitec's founder, and Hadyn Parry, its chief executive, to explain their approach at a town meeting. It would be the first in a series of hearings intended to explore the possibility of testing the mosquitoes in one relatively
350 isolated Key West neighborhood. "I don't really know what to expect," Alphey told me early on the day of the meeting. "But I hope the people of Key West understand that they have been lucky. Because they are living in a sea of dengue."

Opponents mobilized within hours of receiving notice of the meeting. Boldly colored flyers, stating that the mosquito-control board was "planning on releasing and testing genetically modified (man-made) mosquitoes on you, your family and the environment," were pasted onto half the city's walls.

Before the meeting, I ran into Chris O'Brien, an artfully
360 dishevelled woman with shoulder-length hair and searching blue eyes. She was dressed in the peaches and pinks one associates with southern Florida. She was also wearing combat boots. O'Brien is a "conch," a term that describes people who are born, raised, and spend their lives in Key West. Her children and grandchildren are conchs, too.

"People live with mosquitoes here," she said. "We always have. We have had no dengue for two years and maybe, at most, we will have a few cases. It's not a huge deal. Certainly not big enough to bring in an unnatural insect about which we know so little. You are in much more danger of being hit by a car."
370 It is impossible to predict the likelihood of a dengue outbreak based on the number of past infections. All it takes is the presence of the mosquito and the virus. Key West has plenty of the former; the rest is a matter of aggressive pest control—and chance. Once infectious mosquitoes start biting humans, an epidemic can erupt within weeks, as the virus moves from vector to host and back again. O'Brien, like many of her fellow-protesters, had been briefed by the Friends of the Earth about the concept of introducing man-made creatures into the local environment. "How do we know the females won't breed and bite people?" she asked. "They would have enzymes in their bodies that
380 don't exist in real life. What would happen if they bit us? Getting rid of dengue would be wonderful, of course, but what would happen if we did succeed and these mosquitoes simply vanished from the earth? Isn't there a food chain to worry about?"

APPLYING ACADEMIC VOCABULARY

devote	conceive

As you discuss the selection, incorporate the following Collection 5 academic vocabulary words: *devote* and *conceive*. Discuss with students how Specter **devotes** part of his article to evidence that reveals the perspectives of supporters and opponents of Oxitec's work. Ask whether students think different groups are open to one another's ideas or whether these groups can't **conceive** the possible validity of ideas different from their own.

Those are reasonable concerns. But ecologists are quick to note that *Aedes aegypti* have been in America for only two hundred years or so; that's not enough time for a species to make an evolutionary impact. Many biologists argue that if *Aedes aegypti*, or, indeed, all mosquitoes, were to disappear, the world wouldn't miss them, and other insects would quickly fill their ecological niche—if they have one. "More than most other living things, the mosquito is a self-serving creature," Andrew Spielman has written. "She doesn't aerate the soil, like ants and worms. She is not an important pollinator of plants, like the bee. She does not even serve as an essential food item for some other animal. She has no 'purpose' other than to perpetuate her species. That the mosquito plagues human beings is really, to her, incidental. She is simply surviving and reproducing."

Not everyone agrees with Spielman's assessment. "Genetic modification leads to both intended and unintended effects," Ricarda Steinbrecher, of EcoNexus, a not-for-profit, public-interest research organization based in England, says. In a lengthy letter to government regulators in Malaysia, she stressed that there could be **ancillary** impacts "if the mosquitoes are eliminated altogether." For instance, what would happen to those fish, frogs, other insects, and arthropods that feed on larval or adult mosquitoes? "What if their interactions with other organisms in the environment change?" she wrote. "There is also the question of what will fill the gap or occupy the niche should the target mosquitoes have been eliminated. Will other pests increase in number? Will targeted diseases be able to switch vectors? Will these vectors be easier or more difficult to control?"

It would be irresponsible to deploy transgenic insects widely without adequate answers to those questions, but most have been addressed in environmental-impact statements and by independent research. If the results were put to the vote of biologists, the overwhelming response would be: the potential benefits far outweigh the risks. There are no birds, fish, or other insects that depend solely on *Aedes aegypti*. It doesn't pollinate flowers or regulate the growth of plants. It is not what entomologists call a "keystone" species in the United States.

"It is frankly difficult to see a downside," Daniel Strickman, the national program leader in veterinary and medical entomology at the Agricultural Research Service, told me. "My job is to try and prevent human disease by modifying behavior and killing mosquitoes. So I come at it from that perspective. I am biased against mosquitoes. And *Aedes aegypti* cause immense damage. Raging epidemics of dengue would affect our economy badly. Go back to the days of yellow fever in this country and it had real demographic consequences. Whole towns died. Life expectancies in certain areas were reduced." Strickman added, "I look at this new approach and there is nothing greener. It's targeted at one species. If the sole question is what will happen if we kill off this single species of mosquito, it doesn't seem like a close call."

ancillary
(ăn′sə-lĕr′ē) *adj.*
additional and related.

The Mosquito Solution   **463**

CLOSE READ

Summarize the Text   COMMON CORE RI 2
(LINES 384–430)

Explain that authors may include details and examples to support central ideas, but a summary should include only key details. Tell students that restating the details and examples in a brief, general way helps to see what they have in common.

T ASK STUDENTS to reread lines 384–430 and restate Specter's central idea in one sentence. *(Opponents have raised reasonable questions but most scientists have already answered them and support Oxitec's approach.)* Then discuss how Specter supports this idea. *(He cites evidence from a number of scientific experts, namely "ecologists" [line 384], Andrew Spielman [lines 390–396], "environmental-impact statements and by independent research . . . biologists" [lines 412–413], and Daniel Strickman [lines 419–430].)*

Determine Author's Purpose (LINES 410–415)   COMMON CORE RI 6

Tell students that authors generally write to inform, persuade, entertain, or express ideas or feelings.

U ASK STUDENTS to reread lines 410–415 and infer Specter's purpose in writing this article. Ask them to give reasons for their answer. *(His purpose is to persuade readers that it would be a good idea to test Oxitec's solution in the United States. This passage reflects an explicit argument. Here he anticipates an objection and presents a counterargument to refute it.)*

CRITICAL VOCABULARY

ancillary: Some environmentalists are concerned that there could be additional effects related to Oxitec's plan to use genetic modification to eliminate the *Aedes* mosquito.

ASK STUDENTS to identify some possible ancillary effects of eliminating the *Aedes* mosquito. *(Animals that feed on the mosquito might interact with other organisms differently if that food source is gone. Other pests might increase; the dengue virus might move to another insect and it might be more difficult to control that vector.)*

SCAFFOLDING FOR ELL STUDENTS

Analyze Language Explain that Specter sometimes uses conversational language rather than formal language to describe the issue of dengue fever and the mosquitoes that cause it. Sometimes he quotes other people who use such language. Have students reread lines 302–369 in pairs and use context clues to help them figure out the meaning of these phrases in order to understand central ideas.

- "ground zero for the aggressively laid-back Key West life style" (line 305)
- "cruising through Web sites" (line 319)
- "dump more chemicals in people's yards" (lines 338–339)
- "living in a sea of dengue" (line 353)
- "It's not a huge deal." (line 367)

Summarize the Text $\overset{\text{COMMON}}{\text{CORE}}$ RI 2

(LINES 440–454)

Encourage students to notice how Specter continues to explore both sides of the issue of using genetic modification to try to eliminate dengue.

V **ASK STUDENTS** to reread lines 440–454 and briefly restate the two different positions presented in the passage. *(Environmentalists are concerned about the possible harm to humans if genetically modified females are released in the wild. Reiter and other scientists say there seems to be nothing harmful to humans in the modified mosquitoes, and that there is no way for substances to be transmitted to humans through a bite.)*

Support Inferences: Draw $\overset{\text{COMMON}}{\text{CORE}}$ RI 1
Conclusions (LINES 455–462)

Point out that Specter presents conclusions without making all of the evidence that supports those conclusions explicit. In making inferences about the evidence, students need to draw on all the previously presented evidence as well as on their own knowledge and experience.

W **ASK STUDENTS** to reread lines 455–462 and infer why Specter says "The biggest question raised by the creation of OX513A is who will regulate it and how." *(Without clarity about how OX513A will be regulated, it will be impossible for Oxitec to know what it needs to do to win approval for tests of OX513A in the United States. Questions about the details of the experiment and its effects are less important than the question of regulation.)*

Mark Q. Benedict agrees. Benedict, an entomologist at the University of Perugia, has researched genetically modified insects for years and written about them extensively. "There are unanswered questions and there always will be," he said. "But there are also unanswered questions about the effect of insecticides on children, and we use them every day to try and kill the very same mosquitoes. It's important to remember: we're already trying to wipe this species out, and for good reason. The risk involved in eliminating them is very, very small. The risk in letting them multiply is enormous."

440 Environmentalists have expressed concern about what might happen if some of the modified females survived and, while biting people, injected them with an engineered protein. Oxitec separates males from females, but, with so many mosquitoes, a few genetically modified females inevitably slip by—Oxitec puts the number at about one in three thousand. "This is a nightmare scenario, and we don't have any published data that answers this question," Eric Hoffman, a food-and-technology policy campaigner for Friends of the Earth, told me. Hoffman has assiduously followed the Oxitec experiments. Reiter says that none of the protein introduced into transgenic

450 mosquitoes enters its salivary glands—which means it couldn't spread to the humans it bites. In addition, he has recognized nothing in the genetic structure of the modified mosquitoes that could cause humans harm. But he and others are eager to see papers published, by groups unconnected to Oxitec, that confirm those conclusions.

The biggest question raised by the creation of OX513A is who will regulate it and how. In Brazil, a single government body—the National Technical Commission on Biosafety—oversees the approval of all genetically modified organisms. In the United States, however, the regulatory structure is far more complex. It's not clear whether

460 engineered mosquitoes will be regarded as animals, under the jurisdiction of the Department of Agriculture, or as drugs, governed by the Food and Drug Administration.

> ❝ We're already trying
> to wipe this species out,
> and for good reason. ❞

WHEN STUDENTS STRUGGLE . . .

Help students understand the differences in terminology used by Oxitec and its opponents. Direct students to lines 466–479. Ask them to reread this passage and summarize their understanding of the reasons why Eric Hoffman of Friends of the Earth is concerned about Oxitec's statements and what Oxitec's response is. Encourage students to read the whole passage through without trying to figure out the meaning of every technical term to see if they can get the central idea from context clues. *(Hoffman thinks the use of the term "sterile" is somewhat misleading and that Oxitec is trying to avoid using the term "genetically modified." Oxitec does use the term "genetically modified" and says it is just trying to communicate a complex scientific idea with a term (sterile) that is the closest they can find to describe the effects of their experiment.)*

"I would be so eager to have a clear regulatory situation in the United States," Alphey told me, his frustration at the process barely held in check. "We do not want to move forward unless one is properly in place." To the consternation of many, Oxitec recently applied to the F.D.A. for approval of its mosquito. "We are concerned that Oxitec has been less than forthcoming in their statements to the public," Hoffman told me. "They are saying that these mosquitoes are sterile,

470 but they are not sterile, since they impregnate females. They are genetically modified, and the public needs to know that." Oxitec does call its mosquitoes sterile, but has not denied that they are genetically modified; almost all their literature says as much. "There is no layman's term for 'passes on an autocidal gene that kills offspring,'" Alphey said. "'Sterile' is the closest common term. OX513A is sterile in very much the same sense as radiation-sterilized insects are sterile." Hoffman stops short of calling Alphey's message deceptive, but he certainly doesn't agree. "This country just doesn't have the law or regulations necessary to move this project forward right now," he said.

480 In Key West, the Oxitec scientists, along with Doyle and his team from the mosquito-control district, faced a packed room at the Harvey Government Center. It was a warm, sunny day, and many in the crowd had left work early to be there. Doyle explained how a small experiment might proceed; Oxitec made its case; then the floor was opened to the public. The meeting quickly became emotional and, at times, rancorous. Oxitec—a small company that had emerged from a zoology department—was portrayed as an international conglomerate willing to "play God" and endanger an American paradise. The insects were referred to as "robo-Franken mosquitoes." More than a

490 dozen people rose to speak; none defended the project or noted that, if successful, it would reduce a health threat and ease the county's heavy reliance on insecticides. Overwhelmingly, the people with whom I spoke said they assumed that this decision had already been made; the meeting was taken up with accusations of lies and secrecy. But nothing had been decided. Every question asked, at the meeting or later, in writing, was forwarded to state regulators for their consideration.

"It breaks my heart to think that you guys have the nerve to come here and do this to our community," one woman said. "Anything genetically modified should not be touched. I have a feeling that"—

500 she pointed to Doyle and his colleagues on the dais— "your minds are made up. I know it. I can just sense it. I feel the vibe." She concluded to thunderous applause. Another speaker, Rick Worth, was even more direct. "I, for one, don't care about your scientific crap," he said. "I don't care about money you spend. You are not going to cram something down my throat that I don't want. I am no guinea pig."

One afternoon before leaving Brazil, I found myself inching along the rutted dirt roads of a neighborhood called Itaberaba, with Aldo Malavasi, the highly animated director of Moscamed. Itaberaba is only a few miles from the center of Juazeiro, and, as we drove, loudspeakers

---

TO CHALLENGE STUDENTS ...

Evaluate an Argument Are Oxitec and its opponents in Key West fighting fair? Ask students to reread the arguments made by Oxitec and by its opponents in Key West and evaluate the logic and reasoning used by each side. Encourage them to notice the types of evidence, language, and appeals used by both sides and to identify any logical fallacies.

Then have students meet in small groups to discuss the arguments made by each side. Encourage them to explore why "the meeting quickly became emotional, and at times, rancorous." (lines 485–486)

CLOSE READ

Analyze Language RI 4
(LINES 466–478)

Point out that certain words used to describe Oxitec's work can have very strong **connotations**, or emotional shades of meaning.

Ⓧ CITE TEXT EVIDENCE Ask students to reread lines 466–478 and identify terms that seem to have strong connotations and explain why the terms are a source of contention between Oxitec and its opponents. *(The term "genetically modified" has strong negative connotations according to Hoffman and he thinks Oxitec should use that term more clearly rather than the term "sterile," which he suggests has a more neutral connotation. Oxitec does use the term "genetically modified" in its literature but also uses the term "sterile" because the company says it is the term that best describes the outcome of the process and it's a term that people easily understand.)* Then invite students to evaluate each side's position on this use of language. (Some may agree with Hoffman that "sterile" is not completely accurate; others may say that Hoffman and others are playing on people's concerns about genetic modification rather than fully looking at the scientific evidence.)*

Support Inferences: Draw Conclusions RI 1
(LINES 480–505)

Remind students to combine their own knowledge and experience with the evidence directly stated in the selection to make inferences and draw conclusions.

Ⓨ ASK STUDENTS to reread lines 480–505 and explain why the people who attended the meeting in Key West seemed to have so much mistrust of Oxitec and its scientific supporters. *(Key West is a small community and people feared that outsiders were going to force something on them that they didn't understand. People seemed to have preconceptions about corporations, science, and genetic modification that were not necessarily accurate for this particular situation.)*

CLOSE READ

Support Inferences: Draw Conclusions (LINES 521–548)

 COMMON CORE **RI 1**

Tell students that Specter presents many examples as evidence to support more general ideas. Explain that he presents examples from different places to allow readers to find areas of similarity and difference between them.

Z **CITE TEXT EVIDENCE** Ask students to reread lines 521–548 and identify an attitude that the people of Bahia and the people in Western countries have in common. *(People are suspicious of genetically modified food in both instances: "'You tell people you are messing with soybeans and corn and they get suspicious.'" [lines 527–528]; "Many people, particularly in the rich Western world, object to modified food . . ." [lines 538–539]).* Next, ask them to identify an attitude that is different. *(People in Bahia understand "the value of the modified mosquito" [line 525–526] more easily than people in richer countries [lines 530–537 and 541–548]).* Then ask them what Specter means when he says "such complaints are almost never heard against the same scientific process when it is used to make insulin or heart medicine." (lines 539–541) *(People in Western countries don't object to genetic modification to make medicine for diabetes and heart disease. They may not even realize that it's the same process because the term "genetically modified" is probably not on the label of the medicines.)* Finally, invite them to draw conclusions about why there are more objections to Oxitec's program in the United States than in Brazil. *(People in the United States have little experience with dengue, so they are more concerned about potential problems arising from using genetically modified mosquitoes than they are about the effects of the disease.)*

CRITICAL VOCABULARY

benign: Paul Reiter thinks that Oxitec's approach is less harmful to the environment than other approaches.

ASK STUDENTS what Paul Reiter means when he says that Oxitec's approach is "more environmentally benign." *(Reiter thinks the engineered mosquitoes will cause less harm to the environment than other approaches, such as using insecticide.)*

---

510 on the front of the car announced our arrival. "We are here to talk about the transgenic mosquito project," the speakers said. "We are here to explain this program to you and answer your questions." Malavasi, a large and charismatic man, said, "There is only one way to get people on your side: talk to them. This is a new technology. It is scary. But it also carries tremendous possibilities. People are not stupid. You just have to tell them all of that. Lay it out so they can decide." Moscamed has spoken to nearly everyone living in the affected areas. When a team leaves a house, they etch the outlines of a mosquito on the doorframe, so that colleagues will know which houses still need to be

520 visited.

Z   Bahia is one of Brazil's most important fruit-growing regions. We passed warehouses full of guavas, mangoes, limes, pineapples, and papayas. The scent of rotted fruit filled the humid air. People live in small, brightly painted cottages in these towns, and it seemed that at least one member of every family had had dengue. It isn't as hard to explain to them the value of a modified mosquito as it is of, say, modified corn. "You tell people you are messing with soybeans or corn and they get suspicious," Malavasi said. "This is different. They have suffered."

530   When it comes to genetic engineering, acceptance clearly depends on the product. Opponents often invoke a one-sided interpretation of the "precautionary principle," which argues against introducing activities into the environment that, in theory, could cause harm to human health. The sentiment is difficult to dispute, but so is the fact that dengue fever strikes tens of millions of people every year, that the threat is growing, and that there is no treatment or cure. The worry about theoretical risks tends to overwhelm any discussion of possible benefits. Many people, particularly in the rich Western world, object to modified food, but such complaints are almost never aired against

540 the same scientific process when it is used to make insulin or heart medicine. "Sometimes I despair of these issues," Paul Reiter, who has advised Oxitec, told me. "The objections so rarely have anything to do with the science or the safety of the research. It is an opposition driven by fear. I understand that, but this technology has been used in a different form for years." He was referring to sterile insect technique. "The Oxitec approach is safer and more environmentally **benign**," Reiter said. "If the phrase 'genetically modified' was not attached, I don't think people would even mind."

    Malavasi shrugged when I brought up the opposition. "I know

550 this sounds like science fiction," he said. "And I am not naïve. But to get rid of the virus, we have to get rid of the mosquitoes. And, at least in this small experiment, it's working." He noted that the name of the program, the Projeto *Aedes* Transgenico—the Transgenic *Aedes* Project—was not accidental. "We put the word 'transgenic' right in the name of the program for everyone to see," he said. "We hide nothing."

benign
(bĭ-nīn´) *adj.*
harmless.

SCAFFOLDING FOR ELL STUDENTS

Language: Pronouns Referents Explain that a **pronoun** is used in place of a noun or another pronoun. Most pronouns clearly refer to a word or group of words, called the **antecedent**. Sometimes the pronouns *it, this, that, which,* or *such* refer to a general idea rather than a particular antecedent, and this usage can make meaning unclear. Listeners and readers need to use context clues to determine the meaning.

Read aloud the quotation from Malavasi (lines 512–516) and call on volunteers to restate each instance of a pronoun to clarify what is said. For example, "This is a new technology" might be restated as "Genetic modification of mosquitoes is a new technology." Encourage students to use a similar process when they encounter other general references as they read the selection.

We had stopped at a random spot on an unmarked road. The heat was oppressive as we emerged from the car; a small stream burbled by the roadside. "We are in mosquito heaven," Malavasi said. As he spoke, a team from Moscamed began unloading several casserole-size Tupperware containers from the back of their van. The containers had white plastic lids, and one by one they were flipped open, releasing thousands of male mosquitoes. Each time a top was removed, scores of the tiny insects would alight, briefly, on the researchers' bodies— not to bite but to orient themselves. It was the first time they had experienced freedom. For a moment, they seemed reluctant to fly away. Then, almost as a unit, they would lift off and, after hovering for a few seconds in the moist afternoon air, form a kind of flying carpet, and set off to fulfill their destiny.

COLLABORATIVE DISCUSSION Does the author believe that OX513A should be used to combat dengue? What does he think about its opponents? With a partner, discuss the details in the article that help you understand the author's perspective on his subject.

CLOSE READ

Support Inferences: Draw Conclusions (LINES 556–568) COMMON CORE RI 1

Remind students to combine their own knowledge and experience with the evidence directly stated in the selection to make inferences and draw conclusions.

A2 ASK STUDENTS to reread lines 556–568 and infer why Specter might have chosen to end his article with this paragraph. (*He wanted to show that people in Brazil, where there are huge numbers of the* Aedes *mosquito and where dengue is common, are going ahead with the Oxitec program. He describes a peaceful scene to reinforce the idea that the project does not pose a threat to humans. He reminds readers that male mosquitoes don't bite and refers to "their destiny," which is to destroy their species.*)

COLLABORATIVE DISCUSSION Encourage students to draw their own conclusions about Specter's beliefs and identify evidence to support their conclusions before they meet to discuss the questions with their partners. Then have them share their conclusions with the class as a whole. Accept all reasonable responses.

ASK STUDENTS to share any questions they generated in the course of reading and discussing the selection.

WHEN STUDENTS STRUGGLE...

Help students find evidence to support a conclusion. You may use a graphic organizer to show students the relationships between information in the text.

Ask: Should genetic modification be used to eliminate dengue?

- Call on volunteers to answer the question. Write any reasonable conclusion on the board or in a chart.
- Allow students time to reread the selection to find facts and details to support the conclusion. List suggested facts and details on the board.
- Ask students to evaluate each piece of evidence to see if it leads to the conclusion.

TEACH

CLOSE READ

Summarize the Text

Call on volunteers to read aloud the first two paragraphs in the selection and summarize them in one or two sentences. (The Aedes aegypti mosquito reproduces quite easily in a wide variety of natural and man-made habitats.)

Then have students reread lines 182–209 of the selection and compare the original with the summary to see how the two are related. (Producing a genetically modified egg that will allow the male mosquito to reproduce in the wild is very difficult.)

Support Inferences: Draw Conclusions

Tell students that drawing conclusions requires that they apply correct reasoning to the evidence—facts and details—combined with their own relevant knowledge and experience.

- Tell them to read carefully to understand the ideas, examples, and facts the author presents.
- In reading Specter's article, they should be aware of their own prior knowledge and opinions about genetic modification and see how the information presented by the author relates to them.
- Suggest that they ask questions of the material as they read to see what inferences they make.

Summarize the Text

When readers **summarize**, they identify the central ideas and most important details in a text and retell them in their own words. Summarizing a long, fact-filled article such as "The Mosquito Solution" enables readers to remember key points and better understand how they relate to one another.

"The Mosquito Solution" discusses numerous facts about the *Aedes aegypti* mosquito and Oxitec's approach to neutralizing the threat it poses to humans. The article also describes the strenuous opposition that researchers have encountered as they try to persuade communities to test their genetically modified pest. Ideas about these topics are developed over the course of the article.

To make sure that you understand all the important ideas in the article, summarize each major section or passage in one or two sentences. For example, these sentences summarize lines 182–209: "OX513A mosquitoes are genetically altered by the insertion of two genes. One gene leads to the destruction of the mosquito and its eggs after it has mated; the other tells scientists whether the egg has been modified." Notice that in this summary, only the essential details have been included, and the summary shows how they are related.

Support Inferences: Draw Conclusions

In his article, Specter provides extensive information on a complex and controversial issue. Readers can use evidence from the text and their own knowledge to make **inferences**, or logical assumptions, about things that are not directly stated in the text. For example, readers might infer from statements and actions by some people opposed to the release of OX513A that they made up their minds before listening to any scientific arguments.

Inferences can be the basis for **conclusions**, or more general statements about a text. The following chart shows a conclusion that is based on evidence in lines 173–181 and on an inference about this evidence.

Evidence	Inference	Conclusion
Aedes aegypti have adapted to city habitats. Pesticides cannot eradicate them in urban areas. They are carriers of dengue.	Populated areas could be at high risk of a dengue epidemic.	If traditional methods cannot offer assurance that such a dangerous pest can be controlled, then alternative approaches should be tried.

Strategies for Annotation  Annotate it!

Summarize the Text

Share these strategies for guided or independent analysis:

- Highlight in yellow any topic sentences that state the central idea of a paragraph.
- Underline the most important details that support the central idea of a paragraph.
- If the central idea of a paragraph is not stated in a topic sentence, infer it and write it on a note.

The Oxitec mosquito grew out of a pest-control method called <u>sterile insect technique</u>, or SIT, which has been used for decades. <u>Billions of insects</u>, all <u>sterilized</u> by intense bursts of <u>radiation</u>, have been reared in laboratories like Moscamed and released to mate in the wild. In 1982, <u>SIT</u>, which <u>prevents the organism from reproducing</u>, successfully <u>eradicated the screw worm</u>—a parasite

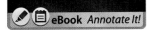

Analyzing the Text

COMMON CORE RI 1, RI 2, RI 3, W 1

Cite Text Evidence   Support your responses with evidence from the selection.

1. **Summarize** Write a brief summary of the information that explains why the *Aedes aegypti* mosquito poses such a danger to humans.

2. **Interpret** Why does the author call OX513A "an elegant approach" to the health crisis?

3. **Summarize** Reread lines 243–279, and summarize how the OX513A mosquito was developed. Why might the author have chosen to include such a detailed explanation of this process?

4. **Compare** How do the reactions of the Juazeiro residents to the use of OX513A mosquitoes compare with the reactions of the Key West residents? What might account for the differences in the reactions of the two populations?

5. **Evaluate** Why do groups such as Friends of the Earth and EcoNexus devote time to voicing their concerns about OX513A? Does this article provide sufficient evidence to support or refute their concerns? Explain.

6. **Draw Conclusions** Has Oxitec done enough to reassure the residents of Key West that it would be safe to release OX513A into their community? Identify the evidence and inferences you used to draw this conclusion.

7. **Draw Conclusions** How does the regulation of genetically modified organisms in Brazil differ from the regulation of them in the United States? Which system do you consider preferable? Explain the basis for this conclusion.

PERFORMANCE TASK

Writing Activity: Argument Is OX513A a safe solution to the problem of the *Aedes aegypti* mosquito? Write a brief argument expressing your conclusion.

- State your claim.
- Develop reasons and draw evidence from the text in support of them.
- Anticipate and refute a counterclaim—for example, address the use of pesticides.
- Present your conclusion.

Make sure to organize your support logically, and include statistics and examples as necessary.

Assign this performance task.

PERFORMANCE TASK

COMMON CORE W 1

Writing Activity: Argument Begin by dividing the class into small groups and having members state and explain their opinions about OX513A. Encourage discussion between students with differing opinions, possibly by reorganizing the class into groups or pairs of students with opposing views. Have students take notes on ideas to apply when writing their arguments and counterclaims, which should be supported by reason and textual evidence.

PRACTICE & APPLY

Analyzing the Text

COMMON CORE RI 1, RI 2, RI 3

Possible answers:

1. *Aedes aegypti transmits dengue fever to humans, a disease without a treatment or cure. The mosquito lays eggs in many places, increasing the odds that its offspring will survive. It is resistant to many pesticides. It is also silent and can bite a person many times without being noticed, thus depositing more pathogens into the blood and making it more likely to pass dengue from infected people to others.*

2. *OX513A is elegant because it targets only mosquitoes, it is easy to transport and implement, and it can be used wherever Aedes aegypti mosquitoes appear.*

3. *Lines 243–279 trace the development of OX513A over two decades. Alphey first considered sterilizing the male mosquito using molecular biology, because radiation would not work. Then he adjusted his goal to make sure that male mosquitoes would avoid passing on novel proteins to humans. He wanted the males to breed before they died, passing on a lethal gene that would kill their offspring. These details underscore the painstaking process of developing this engineered mosquito and how much thought went into making sure it would be safe but effective*

4. *The residents of Juazeiro generally favor the plan, probably because they see dengue fever as a serious problem that affects all of them (line 86). Because Key West residents rarely contract the disease (line 254), they are significantly resistant to introducing OX513A (line 354).*

5. *They are concerned that releasing a genetically engineered species into the environment could affect the food chain and adversely affect other species. They also worry about the unknown consequences of genetically engineered female mosquitoes biting a human. Though the concerns are valid, scientists have considered them. The author offers sufficient evidence to refute most of the concerns, but not sufficient to persuade opponents.*

6. *Although it conducted a public hearing (line 346) and gained the support of the local Mosquito Control District (line 309), noted entomologists, and some ecologists, Oxitec must conduct greater educational outreach to gain acceptance from the general public.*

7. *Brazil has a clear regulatory process through a single agency; the United States follows a complex, often confusing process that makes approval nearly impossible (lines 455–479). Student preferences will vary with individual opinions.*

PRACTICE & APPLY

Critical Vocabulary

Possible answers:

1. *Tires hold heat, collect water, and encourage the growth of bacteria, all of which create a perfect habitat for mosquitoes and other insects.*

2. *The offspring die before they can fly.*

3. *Related concerns, such as worries about OX513A's environmental impact, prevent it from being embraced as the perfect solution to the problem.*

Vocabulary Strategy: Scientific Terms

Possible answers:

hemorrhagic fever: *a disease that leads to bleeding and high fever;* **insecticide:** *a poisonous substance used to kill insects;* **biotechnology:** *the use of biological substances or organisms to perform a practical function;* **mutant:** *having undergone a process that changed or altered a characteristic or element;* **pathogen:** *something that causes disease;* **parasite:** *an organism that lives off another organism;* **larvae:** *wingless and wormlike insects in the stage of metamorphosis between egg and pupa;* **pupae:** *insects in the last stage before becoming an adult; they are encased in a cocoon;* **syphon:** *a protruding tube that allows the mosquito to breathe under water as it emerges from its case*

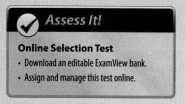

Assess It!

Online Selection Test
- Download an editable ExamView bank.
- Assign and manage this test online.

Critical Vocabulary

fetid	entomological	panacea
progeny	ancillary	benign

Practice and Apply Use a complete sentence to answer each question and demonstrate that you understand the meaning of each Critical Vocabulary word.

1. Why are the *fetid* conditions within tires an *entomological* paradise?

2. In what way are the *progeny* of OX513A rendered *benign* in terms of their threat to humans?

3. What *ancillary* issues prevent OX513A from being called a *panacea* for the problem of mosquitoes?

Vocabulary Strategy: Scientific Terms

In order to convey his information accurately, the author of "The Mosquito Solution" relies on **scientific terms** related to his topic, such as the Critical Vocabulary words *entomological* and *progeny*. These words have specialized meanings in the context of his article; to replace them with more familiar terms would decrease the precision of his writing. Readers can define scientific terms by following a series of steps:

- Read footnotes or other explanations within the text.
- Use the context of the article, as well as the passage and sentence, to determine meaning.
- Identify familiar word parts, such as roots or affixes, and use their meanings to help define the word.
- Consult a print or digital dictionary. Refer to a specialized dictionary as needed.

Practice and Apply With a partner, complete these activities.

1. Locate these terms in the text: *hemorrhagic fever* (line 22), *insecticide* (line 28), *biotechnology* (line 29), *mutant* (line 31), *pathogens* (line 130), *parasites* (line 130), *larvae* (line 201), *pupae* (line 221), *syphon* (line 226).

2. Use context clues, word parts, or a dictionary to define each of them.

Strategies for Annotation  **Annotate it!**

Scientific Terms

Have students locate the sentences containing the terms *hemorrhagic fever, insecticide, biotechnology, mutant, pathogen, parasites, larvae, pupae,* and *syphon* in the selection. Encourage them to use their eBook annotation tools to do the following:

- Highlight each assigned word.
- Reread the surrounding sentences, looking for clues to the word's meaning. Underline any clues you find.
- Review your annotations and try to infer the word's meaning.

> of influenza. But more than half a million people become seriously ill from the disease. Many develop dengue shock syndrome or a hemorrhagic fever that leaves them vomiting and, often, bleeding from the nose, mouth, or skin. The pain can be so excruciating that the virus has a commonly invoked nickname:

INTERACTIVE WHITEBOARD LESSON
Analyze and Evaluate Structure

COMMON CORE
RI 5

Learn the Skill ▸ Recognizing Text Structures

Recognizing Text Structures
Click to explore different text structures.

Main Idea & Details
Chronological Order
Sequence or How-To
Cause-and-Effect
Comparison-Contrast
Classification
Problem-Solution
Order of Importance
Multiple Structures

Main Idea & Supporting Details

With this pattern, a writer will introduce a **main or central idea** (the most important one) at the beginning of the text or paragraph and then support that idea with details, such as facts, statistics, or examples.

Main Idea
Working part-time while in high school has many advantages.

Detail	Detail	Detail
Teaches time management	Teaches responsibility	Improves decision-making skills

TEACH

Review the types of text structure and the characteristics of each so that students can recognize them. Then present these steps for analyzing text structure.

- **Step 1: Identify the Topic and Purpose** Remind students that an author's purpose, or reason for writing, may be to inform, persuade, express ideas or feelings, or entertain.
- **Step 2: Locate Signal Words** Explain that certain words signal different types of text structure by showing how ideas are related.
- **Step 3: Track the Ideas** Suggest that using a graphic organizer will help students make sure that they understand the central ideas in the piece of writing.
- **Step 4: Evaluate Text Structure** Explain that the text structure should be effective in helping readers follow the author's ideas.

COLLABORATIVE DISCUSSION

Have students work individually to apply the sentence frames presented on Screen 10 in the activity to "The Mosquito Solution" and then share their responses with a partner. Remind them that an author may use multiple structures in a single piece of writing. Encourage them to discuss how understanding more about structure helped them better understand the author's ideas.

Summarizing the Text

COMMON CORE
RI 2

RETEACH

Review that summaries are retellings of a story's main idea in one's own words. Share these summaries of a familiar tale.

- A wicked queen orders a hunter to kill her lovely stepdaughter, Snow White. He tricks the queen; Snow White takes refuge with seven dwarfs in the woods. The queen finds the girl and feeds her a poisonous apple. A prince falls in love with Snow White in her glass-topped coffin. As he moves the coffin, the apple dislodges from her throat. Snow White wakes up. The two marry. The queen is punished.
- A queen is jealous of her stepdaughter because a magic mirror says the girl is more beautiful. The hunter brings back the heart of a deer as proof that the girl is dead. There are seven dwarfs who have different names. The mirror tells the queen that the girl is alive. Later, Snow White marries a prince and the queen is punished.

ASK STUDENTS to explain which summary is better. *(The first is a better summary because it recounts the most important ideas from the story. The second focuses on minor details and omits key ideas.)*

LEVEL UP TUTORIALS Assign the following *Level Up* tutorial: **Summarizing.**

(?) EXIT X

Summarizing | TUTORIAL | PRACTICE

What Is a Summary?

When you tell people about a movie you just saw or a book you've just read, you are probably giving them a **summary**.

When you summarize a text, you briefly retell the main ideas or key events using your own words.

Let me tell you about this great movie I saw!

◄ ●── ◄) | 1 **2** 3 4 5 6 7 8 9 10 ..14 ➡

CLOSE READING APPLICATION

Have students apply the skill to a current magazine or newspaper article or a passage from a textbook to determine the central idea and most important supporting details in the piece.

Are Genetically Modified Foods Scary?

Science Writing by Palome Reyes

Why This Text

Students often have difficulty with science texts that examine the pros and cons of new scientific discoveries. This science article is such a text. With the help of the close-reading questions, students will summarize the scientific information as well as the arguments for and against the use of genetically modified foods. The results of their close reading will help students develop a thorough understanding of genetically modified foods and the arguments for and against their use.

Background Have students read the background information describing the ways farmers throughout history have tried to increase agricultural production. Tell students that this article examines the pros and cons of genetically modified foods, foods that could potentially increase agricultural production throughout the world.

AS YOU READ Tell students to pay close attention to the main idea in each paragraph.

Common Core Support

- cite strong and thorough textual evidence
- provide an objective summary of a text
- support inferences drawn from the text

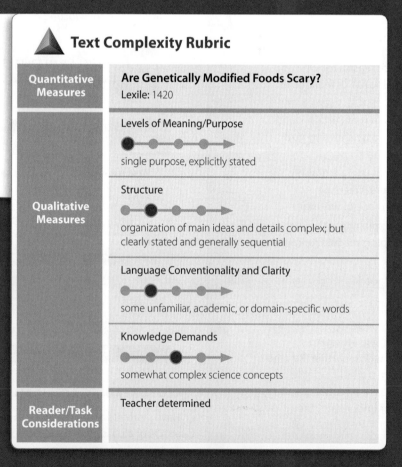

Text Complexity Rubric

Quantitative Measures	**Are Genetically Modified Foods Scary?** Lexile: 1420
Qualitative Measures	Levels of Meaning/Purpose single purpose, explicitly stated
	Structure organization of main ideas and details complex; but clearly stated and generally sequential
	Language Conventionality and Clarity some unfamiliar, academic, or domain-specific words
	Knowledge Demands somewhat complex science concepts
Reader/Task Considerations	Teacher determined

Summarize the Text

Students should read the article carefully, thinking about the major points the author is trying to make. Close-reading questions will help students collect and cite text evidence to support their summaries of the author's main ideas. As they read, students should write notes or questions in the margin.

WHEN STUDENTS STRUGGLE . . .

To help students summarize, have them work in small groups to fill out a chart like the one shown below.

CITE TEXT EVIDENCE For practice summarizing, ask students to summarize the text evidence shown below.

Text Evidence	Summary
"Recent advances . . . saved Hawaii's papaya industry." (lines 11–17)	Genetically modified foods could have prevented the "Great Hunger."
"Proponents of GM foods counter . . . from these foods." (lines 44–49)	People who support GM foods argue that no one has become sick from eating them.

Background *Ever since the first farmers began to plant and harvest grains more than 10,000 years ago, humans have been looking for ways to increase agricultural production. Over the centuries and across the globe, farmers have developed tools and techniques to boost yields, such as irrigation, crop rotation, fertilizers and pesticides. Today's agricultural innovations are more effective than ever—but also more controversial.*

Are Genetically Modified Foods Scary?

Science Writing by Palome Reyes

CLOSE READ
Notes

1. **READ ▶** As you read lines 1–28, begin to collect and cite text evidence.
   - Underline the effects of the potato blight.
   - Circle the claim that is made about preventing "The Great Hunger."
   - Underline desired traits of genetically modified food in lines 18–28.

Ireland, between the years 1845 and 1852, experienced a seven-year siege of mass starvation, disease, and emigration known today as "The Great Hunger." During this time, approximately one million people starved to death and another two million fled for their lives, emigrating to England, America, Australia, New Zealand, Canada, and other countries. The immediate cause of the famine was a potato blight, a disease that ravaged potato crops throughout Europe. The impact was most severe in Ireland because one-third of the population was dependent on the potato crop for survival. Political, social, and economic factors only **exacerbated** the horrendous results of the potato blight
10   in Ireland.

exacerbated:
made worse

109

---

1. **READ AND CITE TEXT EVIDENCE** Remind students that they have underlined phrases that describe the effects of the "Great Hunger" in Ireland.

   Ⓐ ASK STUDENTS to cite evidence from lines 1–10 to summarize the effects of the "Great Hunger." *Possible response: One million people starved to death; two million fled for their lives.*

   Critical Vocabulary: exacerbated (line 9) Have students share their definitions of *exacerbated*. Then ask students to think of a time when their behavior exacerbated an already bad situation. *Answers will vary. Possible response: When my brothers were arguing, I joined in and made things worse.*

CLOSE READ Notes

virulent:
highly infective and harmful

Recent advances in the field of genetically modified (GM) food could have prevented the "Great Hunger" by introducing potatoes resistant to the disease that destroyed Ireland's potato crop. In the 1990s, Hawaii's papaya industry was facing disaster because of the **virulent** papaya ring spot virus. In this case, a genetically modified papaya *did* save the day. Developed and used since 1999, this genetically modified papaya, which resists the virus, has saved Hawaii's papaya industry.

B The term "genetically modified food" refers to crop plants created for
20 human and animal consumption that use the latest molecular biology techniques to enhance desired traits, such as resistance to disease and herbicides or increased nutritional content. Traditionally this enhancement would have been done through plant breeding. But, breeding is time consuming and often not very accurate. Genetic engineering—actually isolating and inserting genes with the desirable trait into plants—can create plants with the desired trait very rapidly and with great accuracy. For example, plant geneticists can isolate a gene for pest resistance and insert that gene into another plant. The plant created as a result of the inserted genes will have the desired trait of being resistant to pests.

C As exciting as the promise of GM foods may seem, some people are raising
30 questions about the safety and long-term effects of such foods. Although most

2. ◀ **REREAD** Reread lines 18–28. Summarize the information in these lines to create a one-sentence definition of genetically modified food.

Genetically modified food is food from crop plants that have been genetically altered in order to boost desired traits.

3. **READ** ▶ As you read lines 29–57, continue to cite textual evidence

- Underline text that explains doubts about GM food.
- Circle information that is presented as fact.
- In the margin, list one possible advantage of GM foods.

scientists **concur** that no harmful effects have yet been associated with consuming GM crops, the anti-GM-food people resist the idea of big agricultural and biotech companies (the forces spearheading production of GM foods) trying to control what goes into the food we eat. These opponents contend that genetic breeding is radically different from what human beings have previously done, and that, as a result, we are now consuming products that have never before been considered food. There is no way of predicting what long-term effects these plants may have on the human beings and animals that consume them. Neither is there any way of predicting what effect these
40 foods might have on other plants or on the environment in general. A widely publicized study published in the fall of 2012 only added fuel to the controversy when it noted that rats fed a lifetime diet of GM corn developed tumors, whereas those fed a non-GM diet did not.

Proponents of GM foods counter that GM plants, with their built-in protections against disease, pests, herbicides, cold, drought, and floods will help increase food production worldwide and thereby stem the tide of worldwide hunger. Furthermore, they argue that, although Americans have been eating GM food for years, no one has been able to cite a single case of someone actually getting sick from these foods.

CLOSE READ Notes

concur:
agree

GM foods may help solve the problem of world hunger.

---

2. **REREAD AND CITE TEXT EVIDENCE**

B **ASK STUDENTS** to find phrases in lines 18–28 that describe genetically modified foods. *Possible response: "crop plants," "enhance desired traits," "resistance to disease," "increased nutritional content."*

3. **READ AND CITE TEXT EVIDENCE**

C **ASK STUDENTS** to summarize the facts about genetically modified foods stated in lines 29–57. *Possible response: The majority of scientific research indicates that genetically modified foods pose no threat to consumers.*

Critical Vocabulary: virulent (line 14) Have students share their definition of *virulent*. Then have them think of a disease from the past that was especially virulent. *Possible responses: smallpox, influenza, polio, bubonic plague.*

Critical Vocabulary: concur (line 31) Have students think of a time when they concurred with another person's argument or point of view. *Answers will vary. Possible response: When my friend suggested that we should research the invasion of Normandy for our history project, I agreed and thought it was a great idea.* Then have students share their definition of *concur*.

FOR ELL STUDENTS Encourage students to analyze the meaning of the compound word *spearheading* (line 33). Have a volunteer identify the two base words and their meanings. Then have another volunteer infer the meaning of the complete word. *to be the leader in an activity*

CLOSE READ
Notes

D 50   It is difficult to ignore the fact that the majority of scientific research thus far indicates that GM foods pose no threat to consumers. On the other hand, eating is something that we all do every day. Should the choice about what we put into our mouths be left up to us or to businesses with financial interests in GM products? The GM opponents argue that the choice should be ours and that, at the very least, GM crops should be labeled. In this way consumers would know what they are eating and could, therefore, choose to take the risk or not.

4. ◀ **REREAD AND DISCUSS** Reread lines 50–57. With a small group, discuss the idea of labeling GM food. Do you think this is a good option to please both GM opponents and supporters? Explain.

SHORT RESPONSE

Cite Text Evidence   Summarize the article in the lines below. First, identify the central idea and its most important details, and then retell them in your own words. Review your reading notes, and be sure to **cite text evidence** from the article in your response.

Genetically modified foods can help prevent disastrous effects to crops, increasing food production and easing world hunger. GM foods can be engineered quickly to have "resistance to disease" and "to pests." They can also have "increased nutritional content." The positive aspects of GM foods seem compelling. However, some opponents of GM foods point out that the long-term effects—on people and on the environment—are not known. They point out that people should be able to make the choice of what they eat by having GM foods labeled. Supporters of GM foods point out that nobody has any examples of people getting sick from them.

112

---

4. REREAD AND CITE TEXT EVIDENCE

D **ASK STUDENTS** to assign a reporter for each group to present specific text evidence to support opinions about the labeling of genetically modified foods.

SHORT RESPONSE

Cite Text Evidence   Students' responses will vary, but they should cite evidence from the text to support their answers. They should:

- summarize the central idea of the article.
- identify the most important details in the article.
- retell the central idea and important details in their own words.

TO CHALLENGE STUDENTS . . .

To extend students' understanding of this article, have them research current debates on genetically modified foods.

ASK STUDENTS to research at least three articles on the subject to prepare to debate for or against genetically modified foods. Some areas that students might direct their research toward include:

- the extent and causes of poverty and worldwide hunger.
- what GM foods could offer poor countries where hunger is a persistent problem.
- hazards or drawbacks of GM foods.
- how food production can be increased for poor countries.
- social and political implications of the production of GM foods, especially in poorer countries.

After students have completed their research, have them form two groups: students in favor of GM foods, and students against GM foods. In preparation for the debate, have each group discuss the points it will present. Then act as moderator of the debate.

DIG DEEPER

With the class, return to Question 4, Reread and Discuss. Have students share and discuss their answers.

ASK STUDENTS to note how their responses are alike and how they are different.

- Have students discuss the pros and cons of labeling genetically modified foods.
- Have students discuss the current labeling of foods in supermarkets. What kinds of information are included in food labels? Is the labeling helpful? Do you or your parents pay attention to the labels? Why or why not?
- How strongly do you feel that consumers have a right to know what they are eating?
- What are some of the disadvantages of labeling genetically modified foods?

ASK STUDENTS to return to their responses to Question 4 and revise them based on their discussion.

PERFORMANCE TASK

Interactive Lessons

If you need help . . .
- **Writing as a Process**
- **Using Textual Evidence**
- **Giving a Presentation**

Present a Speech

COMMON CORE

W 9a–b Draw evidence from literary or informational texts.

SL 4 Present information, findings, and supporting evidence.

This collection explores the idea of taking risks. Look back at the anchor text, *Beowulf*, and at the other texts in the collection. Consider the risks described in each selection. Why do the characters and people decide to take these risks? What do they learn from their risk-taking experiences? Synthesize your ideas by preparing and presenting a speech on the importance of taking risks in life.

An effective speech

- introduces a clear and logical controlling idea about taking risks
- has a logically structured body, including transitions
- provides evidence from *Beowulf* and one other text that illustrates the controlling idea
- has a satisfying conclusion that follows logically from the body of the speech
- demonstrates appropriate and clear use of language
- engages the audience with appropriate emphasis, volume, and gestures
- maintains a formal tone through the use of standard English

PLAN

*my*Notebook

Use the annotation tools in your eBook to find evidence that supports your ideas about taking risks. Save each piece of evidence to your notebook.

Gather Evidence Review and analyze the texts in this collection.

- Reread *Beowulf*, identifying and taking notes on the risks Beowulf takes. Consider the poet's vision regarding why Beowulf took certain risks and what he learned from them.
- Choose one other text from the collection, also identifying and analyzing the risks that the characters or people in that text take.
- As you review the texts, note specific details, examples, and quotations that you could use in your speech to support your ideas about risk taking.

Once you have reviewed the texts, write a clear statement that summarizes your thoughts about the importance of taking risks in life. This will be the controlling idea of your speech, which you will need to support with sufficient textual evidence.

PERFORMANCE TASK

PRESENT A SPEECH

COMMON CORE **W 9a–b, SL 4**

Introduce students to the Performance Task by reading the introductory paragraph with them and reviewing the criteria for an effective speech. Point out the two equally important parts of this task: writing the speech and delivering it to an audience.

PLAN

GATHER EVIDENCE

▶ **View It!**

Professional Development Podcast:

Performance Task

Suggest that students write a draft version of their controlling idea after they finish reviewing *Beowulf*. This statement can guide their review of the other collection texts and help them decide which selection best complements *Beowulf* for the purposes of their speech. Then they can refine their controlling idea to better fit the evidence from both texts.

PERFORMANCE TASK

PLAN

GET ORGANIZED

Discuss with students some of the ways a speaker can engage his or her audience at the beginning of a speech. Ideas include asking an intriguing question, telling a brief story (for example, relating a scene from *Beowulf*), or connecting the topic of risk to audience members' lives.

PRODUCE

WRITE YOUR SPEECH

Emphasize that this stage of the writing process is about getting ideas down in rough form. Suggest that students pause occasionally to read aloud what they have written. This will help them determine whether their ideas will make sense to listeners. It will also help them gauge the tone of their writing, which should be formal but also engaging. Encourage students to continually review their written speech as they write and to make revisions to improve content and organization.

REVISE

PRACTICE YOUR SPEECH

Suggest that students make a copy of their speech with double-spaced text large enough to be read easily at arm's length. They need to be able to see the text and their annotations at a glance so that they can maintain good eye contact with the audience.

Remind peer reviewers to give feedback on both the content and the delivery of their partner's speech. Encourage them to focus on a few key points that need the most improvement.

Get Organized Create an outline to organize your central ideas, details, and evidence. Devoting plenty of time to this organizational stage will make writing your speech easier.

- Write your controlling idea at the top of your outline. Consider how you will engage your audience at the beginning of your speech.
- List the central ideas that support your controlling idea about risk taking.
- For each central idea, cite evidence from *Beowulf* and your other chosen text that support it.
- Jot down some ideas for a final statement that will leave your audience with something to think about at the end of your speech.

ACADEMIC VOCABULARY

As you share your ideas about taking risks, be sure to incorporate these words.

assurance
collapse
conceive
devote
vision

PRODUCE

Write Your Speech Draft a logically organized speech, following your outline. Keep your purpose and audience in mind as you write. Remember to include

- an introduction that immediately grabs the interest of your audience
- a logically ordered body, including transitions between the main sections of your speech
- details, quotations, and examples from the texts to support your ideas
- language and structures appropriate for a speech
- a variety of grammatical structures that will keep your audience engaged and interested in your speech
- a conclusion that leaves your audience with a lasting impression

myWriteSmart

Write your rough draft in *my*WriteSmart. Focus on getting your ideas down, rather than perfecting your choice of language.

REVISE

Practice Your Speech When you deliver your speech to your classmates, you will need to make it come alive with appropriate expression, volume, and gestures. Read over your draft and mark places in the text where you might want to emphasize a word, insert a pause, or use gestures to convey meaning or emotion. Then practice your speech with a partner. Remember to speak loudly enough for everyone to hear you, to vary your pitch and tone, and to maintain eye contact with your partner. When listening to your partner's speech, ask yourself these questions:

- Is the introduction memorable? Does my partner present a clear and concise controlling idea?
- Is there sufficient textual evidence to support my partner's ideas?

myWriteSmart

Have your partner or a group of peers review your draft in *my*WriteSmart. Ask your reviewers to note any evidence that does not support the controlling idea.

- Can I follow the reasoning, organization, and development of the speech? Are there any sections of the speech where the logic collapses?
- Does the conclusion reiterate the main points of the speech and end with a thought-provoking statement?
- Does my partner use appropriate tone, emphasis, and gestures?
- Can I hear my partner clearly? Does he or she need to speak louder?
- How is my partner's pace? Does he or she need to slow down or speed up in certain sections or throughout the speech?

Evaluate and Revise After you and your partner have presented your speeches, give each other feedback. Use the chart on the next page to evaluate the substance and style of your partner's speech as well as your own. Mention what your partner did particularly well and what he or she could have done better. Then revise your draft based on your partner's feedback, the chart, and your own observations of your speech.

PRESENT

Deliver Your Speech Present your speech to the whole class. The audience should listen, take notes, and be prepared to respond to your speech.

- Introduce yourself and briefly state the topic of your speech.
- Speak clearly at an appropriate volume and pace.
- Maintain an appropriate and formal tone throughout your speech.
- At the end of your speech, invite your audience to ask questions or make comments.
- Find out which aspects of your speech were particularly strong and ask how your speech could be improved.
- Thank your audience for their time and attention.

PRESENT

DELIVER YOUR SPEECH

If possible, give students the option of videotaping their speeches. They can review the video footage later to evaluate their performance. Students might also turn video or audio recordings into podcasts to be posted on the school's website.

PERFORMANCE TASK

SPEECH

Have students look at the chart to evaluate their level of performance in each of the three main categories. Then have them examine how well their speech meets the characteristics of the highest level of proficiency and list some things they could do during the drafting and composition of their next speech to strengthen their claim and make a compelling presentation to the audience.

COLLECTION 5 TASK
SPEECH

	Ideas and Evidence	Organization	Language
ADVANCED	• The introduction is intriguing and informative; the controlling idea clearly identifies a compelling topic. • The topic is strongly developed with relevant facts, concrete details, interesting quotations, and examples from the texts. • The concluding section capably follows from and supports the ideas presented.	• The organization is effective and logical throughout the speech. • Transitions are well crafted and successfully connect related ideas.	• The speech reflects a formal style and an objective, knowledgeable tone. • Language is vivid and precise. • Sentence beginnings, lengths, and structures vary and have a rhythmic flow. • Grammar and usage are correct.
COMPETENT	• The introduction could do more to attract the audience's curiosity; the controlling idea identifies a topic. • One or two key points could use additional support in the form of relevant facts, concrete details, quotations, and examples from the texts. • The concluding section mostly follows from and supports the ideas presented.	• The organization is confusing in a few places. • A few more transitions are needed to connect related ideas.	• The style is inconsistent in a few places, and the tone is subjective at times. • Vague language is used in a few places. • Sentence beginnings, lengths, and structures vary somewhat. • Some grammatical and usage errors are repeated in the speech.
LIMITED	• The introduction provides some information about a topic but does not include a controlling idea. • Most key points need additional support in the form of relevant facts, concrete details, quotations, and examples from the texts. • The concluding section is confusing and does not follow from the ideas presented.	• The organization is confusing in some places and often doesn't follow a pattern. • More transitions are needed throughout to connect related ideas.	• The style is too informal; the tone conveys subjectivity and a lack of understanding of the topic. • Vague, general language is used in many places. • Sentence structures barely vary, and some fragments or run-on sentences are present. • Grammar and usage are incorrect in many places, but the speaker's ideas are still clear.
EMERGING	• The appropriate elements of an introduction are missing. • Facts, details, quotations, and examples from the texts are missing. • The speech lacks an identifiable concluding section.	• A logical organization is not used; information is presented randomly. • Transitions are not used, making the speech difficult to follow.	• The style and tone are inappropriate for the speech. • Language is too vague or general to convey the information. • Repetitive sentence structure, fragments, and run-on sentences make the speech monotonous and difficult to follow. • Many grammatical and usage errors change the meaning of the speaker's ideas.

Finding Ourselves in Nature

" How often I've wanted to escape to a wilderness where a human hand has not been in everything. "

CONNECTING WORD AND IMAGE

ASK STUDENTS to discuss how the collection opener image and the collection quotation work together to create a connection.

PERFORMANCE TASK PREVIEW

Point out to students that they will complete a performance task at the end of the collection. The performance task will require them to further analyze the selections in the collection and to synthesize ideas about these analyses. They will present their findings in a variety of products.

ACADEMIC VOCABULARY

View It!

Professional Development Podcast:

Academic Vocabulary

Students can acquire facility with the academic vocabulary words through frequent, repeated exposure as they analyze and discuss the selections in the collection. Academic vocabulary can be used in the following instructional contexts. This will enable students to incorporate the academic vocabulary words into their working vocabulary.

- Collaborative Discussion at the end of each selection
- Analyzing the Text questions for each selection
- Selection-level Performance Task
- Vocabulary instruction (for Critical Vocabulary and/or for Vocabulary Strategy)
- Language and Style
- End-of-collection Performance Task for all selections in the collection

ASK STUDENTS to review the Academic Vocabulary word list for this collection. You may wish to pronounce each word aloud, so students hear the correct pronunciation. Then discuss the definitions and the related forms for each word. Remind students that they will encounter these five academic vocabulary words throughout the collection.

COLLECTION **6**

Finding Ourselves in Nature

hmhfyi.com

This collection reveals personal insights gained through encounters with the natural world.

COLLECTION
PERFORMANCE TASK Preview

At the end of this collection, you will have the opportunity to complete a task:

- Write a personal narrative in which you describe and reflect on a memorable encounter with nature. Compare your experience with those portrayed in "Living Like Weasels" and another selection in the collection.

ACADEMIC VOCABULARY

Study the words and their definitions in the chart below. You will use these words as you discuss and write about the texts in this collection.

Word	Definition	Related Forms
encounter (ĕn-koun´tər) *n.*	an unplanned or unexpected meeting	counter, encounter (v.)
intensity (ĭn-tĕn´sĭ-tē) *n.*	high degree or concentration; power or force	intense, intensify, Intensive
restore (rĭ-stôr´) *v.*	to bring back to original condition; to renew; to revive	restoration, restorative
theme (thēm) *n.*	an idea that is implied or that recurs in a work; a message conveyed in a literary work	thematic
visualize (vĭzh´ŏŏ ə-līz´) *v.*	to form a mental image of something or someone	envision, revision, vision, visual

476

USING COLLECTIONS YOUR WAY

Use the following information, along with the charts on the following pages, to help you decide how you want to introduce the collection. Based on your teaching style, your students' interests, or your instructional goals, you may want to structure this collection in various ways. You may choose different entry points each time you teach the collection.

"I love to concentrate on contemporary literature."

This essay by **Annie Dillard** discusses human nature through the lens of living "without bias or motive" as an animal such as a weasel might. Readers are invited to consider how to live a meaningful life given the challenges of modern life.

Annie Dillard (b. 1945) *was born and raised in Pittsburgh. Her parents encouraged her to explore intellectual and creative interests and to reject conformity. Dillard has written in many different genres; her books range widely in subject matter, though she is best known for writing about nature. Pilgrim at Tinker Creek, her 1974 nonfiction narrative about the fields, creeks, and woods near Roanoke, Virginia, won the Pulitzer Prize and has been compared to Thoreau's Walden.*

Living Like Weasels

Essay by Annie Dillard

AS YOU READ Pay attention to the details that help you understand Dillard's attitude toward nature. Write down any questions you generate during reading.

A WEASEL IS WILD. Who knows what he thinks? He sleeps in his underground den, his tail draped over his nose. Sometimes he lives in his den for two days without leaving. Outside, he stalks rabbits, mice, muskrats, and birds, killing more bodies than he can eat warm, and often dragging the carcasses home. Obedient to instinct, he bites his prey at the neck, either splitting the jugular vein at the throat or crunching the brain at the base of the skull, and he does not let go. One naturalist refused to kill a weasel who was socketed into his hand deeply as a rattlesnake. The man could in no way pry the tiny weasel off, and he had to walk half a mile to water, the weasel dangling from his palm, and soak him off like a stubborn label.

And once, says Ernest Thompson Seton[1]—once, a man shot an eagle out of the sky. He examined the eagle and found the dry skull of a weasel fixed by the jaws to his throat. The supposition is that the eagle had pounced on the weasel and the weasel swiveled and bit as

supposition
(sŭp′ə-zĭsh′ən) *n.* something thought to be the case; an assumed truth or hypothesis.

[1] Ernest Thompson Seton: (1860–1946) author, artist, and naturalist known for his portrayals of wildlife.

Living Like Weasels **477**

Background *Dan Horgan grew up on a farm in California. He loved the outdoors and created his first garden at age nine, planting tulips and rimming the edge with rocks. When he came home from serving in the Vietnam War, Horgan needed to restore his inner balance. He did so by designing landscapes that incorporated both rocks and plants. Then, in the 1990s, he was galvanized by the work of artist Andy Goldsworthy to focus on creating art just with rocks. His art pieces are built and left in the environments that inspired them, keeping Horgan close to the nature that he loves.*

MEDIA ANALYSIS

Being Here: The Art of Dan Horgan

Documentary directed by Russ Spencer

AS YOU VIEW Pay attention to the methods the filmmaker uses to reveal Horgan's personality and attitude toward his art.

COLLABORATIVE DISCUSSION What is your impression of Horgan? With a partner, discuss how the filmmaker uses his craft to convey important aspects of the artist's character.

Being Here: The Art of Dan Horgan **491**

"I like to use a digital product as a starting point."

The art of **Dan Horgan** is presented through this documentary film. Viewers are given the opportunity to see his art and learn more about his artistic philosophy. In particular, the connection between nature and art is highlighted.

"I want to challenge my students to the utmost."

This short story by **Rick Bass** uses figurative language and imagery to describe natural settings that are both realistic and fantastic. The frame story pulls readers into the tension of a survival situation and leaves them with a sense of wonder about people and nature.

Rick Bass (b. 1958) *grew up in Texas, where he became interested in nature at an early age. He studied geology at Utah State University and worked as a petroleum geologist for several years. During his lunch hours he started writing short stories. Since then, he has written and edited over 25 books, both fiction and nonfiction, and has received many literary awards. His passion for nature is reflected in his environmental activism as well as his writing. He moved to Montana in 1987 and is involved in efforts to protect areas such as the Glacier National Park.*

The Hermit's Story

Short Story by Rick Bass

AS YOU READ Think about whether Ann's story is credible or not. Write down any questions you generate during reading.

A n ice storm, following seven days of snow; the vast fields and drifts of snow turning to sheets of glazed ice that shine and shimmer blue in the moonlight, as if the color is being fabricated not by the bending and absorption of light but by some chemical reaction within the glossy ice; as if the source of all blueness lies somewhere up here in the north—the core of it beneath one of those frozen fields; as if blue is a thing that emerges, in some parts of the world, from the soil itself, after the sun goes down.

Blue creeping up fissures and cracks from depths of several hundred feet; blue working its way up through the gleaming ribs of Ann's buried dogs; blue trailing like smoke from the dogs' empty eye sockets and nostrils—blue rising like smoke from chimneys until it reaches the surface and spreads laterally and becomes entombed, or trapped—but still alive, and smoky—within those moonstruck fields of ice.

Blue like a scent trapped in the ice, waiting for some soft release, some thawing, so that it can continue spreading.

fabricate
(făb′rĭ-kāt′) *v.* to construct or make.

The Hermit's Story **501**

*my*SmartPlanner | eBook | *my*Notebook | *my*WriteSmart | fyi hmhfyi.com

Collection 6 Lessons	Media	Teach and Practice
Student Edition | eBook	▶ **Video Links** HISTORY A+E	**Close Reading and Evidence Tracking**
ANCHOR TEXT Essay by Annie Dillard **"Living Like Weasels"**	🔊 **Audio** "Living Like Weasels"	**Close Read Screencasts** • Modeled Discussion 1 (lines 14–23) • Close Read application pdf (lines 116–122) **Strategies for Annotation** • Analyze Style
CLOSE READER Memoir by Louise Erdrich **Local Deer**	🔊 **Audio** "Local Deer"	
Poem by Elinor Wylie **"Wild Peaches"** Poem by William Carlos Williams **"Spring and All"**	🔊 **Audio** "Wild Peaches" **Audio** "Spring and All"	**Strategies for Annotation** • Demonstrate Knowledge of Foundational Works
CLOSE READER Poetry by William Carlos Williams and Jennifer Chang **"Pastorals"**	🔊 **Audio** "Pastorals"	
Documentary Directed by by Russ Spencer **"Being Here: The Art of Dan Horgan"**	🔊 **Audio** "Being Here: The Art of Dan Horgan"	
Essay by Linda Hogan **"Dwellings"**	🔊 **Audio** "Dwellings"	**Strategies for Annotation** • Comprehend Cultural Context
CLOSE READER Essay by Baron Wormser **"Trees"**	🔊 **Audio** "Trees"	
Short Story by Rick Bass **"The Hermit's Story"**	🔊 **Audio** "The Hermit's Story"	**Strategies for Annotation** • Analyze Story Elements: Character • Analyze Structure: Frame Story
Collection 6 Performance Task: Write a Personal Narrative	fyi hmhfyi.com **hmhfyi.com**	**Interactive Lessons** **A** Writing a Narrative **A** Writing as a Process

	For Systematic Coverage of Writing and Speaking & Listening Standards	**Interactive Lessons** Writing Informative Texts Giving a Presentation	**Lesson Assessments** Writing Informative Texts Giving a Presentation

Assess		**Extend**	**Reteach**
Performance Task	**Online Assessment**	**Teacher eBook**	**Teacher eBook**
Writing Activity: Essay	Selection Test	**Analyze Ideas and Events**	**Analyze Word Choice: Tone > Level Up Tutorial >** Tone
Writing Activity: Opinion	Selection Test	**Analyze Word Choice**	**Analyze Structure> Level Up Tutorial >** Elements of Poetry
Media Activity: Art Analysis	Selection Test	**Determine Central Ideas**	**Integrate and Evaluate Information> Level Up Tutorial >** Synthesizing Information
Writing Activity: Comparison	Selection Test	**Analyze Key Terms**	**Support Inferences > Level Up Tutorial >** Inferences
Speaking Activity: Discussion	Selection Test	**Making Inferences > Interactive Whiteboard Lesson >** Making Inferences **Figurative Language and Imagery> Interactive Whiteboard Lesson >** Figurative Language and Imagery **Determine Theme > Level Up Tutorial >** Theme	**Analyze Structure: Frame Story**
Write a Personal Narrative	Collection Test		

Collection 6 Lessons	Key Learning Objective	Performance Task
ANCHOR TEXT **Essay by Annie Dillard** **"Living Like Weasels," p. 477A** **Lexile 1040L**	**The student will be able to…** discuss the impact of word choice, syntax, other stylistic traits, and figurative language on the author's ability to achieve her purpose	Writing Activity: Essay
Poem by Elinor Wylie **"Wild Peaches," p. 485A** **Poem by William Carlos Williams** **"Spring and All," p. 485A**	**The student will…** demonstrate knowledge of foundational works of American literature, in part by analyzing their structural forms	Writing Activity: Opinion
Documentary Directed by Russ Spencer **"Being Here: The Art of Dan Horgan," p. 491A**	**The student will be able to…** integrate and evaluate information presented in film footage and an audio track	Media Activity: Art Analysis
Essay by Linda Hogan **"Dwellings," p. 493A** **Lexile 1070L**	**The student will be able to…** make inferences about the author's ideas, supporting them with evidence from the text, and identify the effect of the author's cultural context	Writing Activity: Comparison
Short Story by Rick Bass **"The Hermit's Story," p. 501A** **Lexile 1500L**	**The student will be able to…** determine themes in a short story and analyze a frame structure that presents two related stories	Speaking Activity: Discussion
		Collection 6 Performance Task: Write a Personal Narrative

Vocabulary Strategy	Language and Style	Student Instructional Support	CLOSE READER Selection
Domain-Specific Words	Use Precise Details	**Scaffolding for ELL Students:** Organizational Patterns: Time Sequence **When Students Struggle:** Unconventional Syntax **To Challenge Students:** Explore Point of View	Memoir by Louise Erdrich "Local Deer," p. 484b **Lexile 900L**
		Scaffolding for ELL Students: Vocabulary Support **When Students Struggle:** Imagery **To Challenge Students:** Research a Foundational Work	Poetry by William Carlos Williams and Jennifer Chang "Pastorals," p. 490b
		Scaffolding for ELL Students: Culture: Comprehension Support	
	Appositives and Appositive Phrases	**Scaffolding for ELL Students:** • Vocabulary: Context Clues • Comprehension: Organizational Patterns **When Students Struggle:** Cause and Effect **To Challenge Students:** Synthesize Ideas	Essay by Baron Wormser "Trees," p. 500b **Lexile 990L**
		Scaffolding for ELL Students: • Fluency: Read Aloud • Language: Author's Style • Vocabulary: Specialized Terms • Language: Punctuation **When Students Struggle:** • Point of View • Context Clues **To Challenge Students:** • Trace References to Dreams • Compare Perspectives on Animals	
Consult a Thesaurus			

ANCHOR TEXT EXEMPLAR

*my*SmartPlanner Create lesson plans and access resources online.

Living Like Weasels

Essay by Annie Dillard

Why This Text?

Well-written essays may employ a wide variety of literary techniques to make the language memorable and emphasize key points. This lesson explores the impact of Dillard's word choice, syntax, and other stylistic traits such as her use of figurative language.

Key Learning Objective: The student will be able to analyze and discuss the impact of word choice, syntax, and other stylistic traits such as figurative language on the author's ability to achieve her purpose.

For additional practice:

Close Reader selection
"Local Deer"
Memoir by Louise Erdrich

COMMON CORE Common Core Standards

RI 1 Cite textual evidence to support inferences.
RI 2 Determine central ideas of a text.
RI 3 Analyze a complex set of ideas or events.
RI 4 Determine figurative meanings.
RI 6 Determine an author's point of view.
W 3a Write narratives to engage and orient the reader.
W 3e Write a conclusion that reflects on what is experienced.
L 3 Understand how language functions in different contexts.
L 5a Demonstrate understanding of figures of speech.
L 6 Acquire and use domain-specific words and phrases.

▲ Text Complexity Rubric

Quantitative Measures	**Living Like Weasels** Lexile: 1040L
Qualitative Measures	**Levels of Meaning/Purpose**  more than one purpose; implied, but easy to infer
	Structure organization of main ideas and details complex but mostly explicit; may exhibit disciplinary traits
	Language Conventionality and Clarity figurative, less accessible language
	Knowledge Demands somewhat complex science concepts
Reader/Task Considerations	Teacher determined Vary by individual reader and type of text

Annie Dillard Have students read the information about the author. Tell them that this essay came from the collection of essays, *Teaching a Stone to Talk*, published in 1982. Some critics have compared Dillard's work to that of Henry David Thoreau, who found inspiration and meaning through observations of the natural world around Walden Pond in the 1840s. (A selection from Thoreau's *Civil Disobedience* appears in Collection 3.) In this encounter, Dillard is inspired to compare human nature with the instinctive and unconsidered actions of a wild animal.

AS YOU READ Direct students to use the As You Read note to focus their reading. Remind them to write down any questions they generate during reading.

Analyze Style (LINES 1–7)　COMMON CORE　RI 6

Explain that writers may use a variety of types of sentences and differing arrangements of words within sentences to make the writing memorable and focus the reader's attention on certain images and ideas. This use of **syntax** is part of what defines a writer's **style**.

 ASK STUDENTS to reread lines 1–7 and describe the varied syntax and its effects. *(The paragraph begins with a short, simple sentence. Sentences 2–7 gradually become longer and more complex. This style helps grab the reader's attention and then focus the reader on Dillard's detailed description.)*

CRITICAL VOCABULARY

supposition: Dillard explains the assumed cause of the weasel skull at the eagle's throat.

ASK STUDENTS to explain why the explanation for what happened between the eagle and the weasel must be a supposition. *(Since no one witnessed the events, the details could only be inferred from the remaining evidence.)*

Annie Dillard (b. 1945) *was born and raised in Pittsburgh. Her parents encouraged her to explore intellectual and creative interests and to reject conformity. Dillard has written in many different genres; her books range widely in subject matter, though she is best known for writing about nature. Pilgrim at Tinker Creek, her 1974 nonfiction narrative about the fields, creeks, and woods near Roanoke, Virginia, won the Pulitzer Prize and has been compared to Thoreau's Walden.*

Living Like Weasels

Essay by Annie Dillard

AS YOU READ Pay attention to the details that help you understand Dillard's attitude toward nature. Write down any questions you generate during reading.

A WEASEL IS WILD. Who knows what he thinks? He sleeps in his underground den, his tail draped over his nose. Sometimes he lives in his den for two days without leaving. Outside, he stalks rabbits, mice, muskrats, and birds, killing more bodies than he can eat warm, and often dragging the carcasses home. Obedient to instinct, he bites his prey at the neck, either splitting the jugular vein at the throat or crunching the brain at the base of the skull, and he does not let go. One naturalist refused to kill a weasel who was socketed into his hand deeply as a rattlesnake. The man could in no way pry the tiny weasel off, and he had to walk half a mile to water, the weasel dangling from his palm, and soak him off like a stubborn label.

10　　And once, says Ernest Thompson Seton[1]—once, a man shot an eagle out of the sky. He examined the eagle and found the dry skull of a weasel fixed by the jaws to his throat. The **supposition** is that the eagle had pounced on the weasel and the weasel swiveled and bit as

supposition
(sŭp´ə-zĭsh´ən) *n.* something thought to be the case; an assumed truth or hypothesis.

---

[1] **Ernest Thompson Seton:** (1860–1946) author, artist, and naturalist known for his portrayals of wildlife.

Image Credits: (b) ©Moodboard/Corbis; (t) ©Richard Howard/Time & Life Pictures/Getty Images

---

Close Read Screencasts　 ▶ View It!

Modeled Discussions

Have students click the *Close Read* icons in their eBooks to access a screencast in which readers discuss and annotate the following key passage:

- Dillard describes the tenacious qualities of the weasel and her reason for thinking about them (lines 14–23).

As a class, view and discuss the video. Then have students pair up to do an independent close read of an additional passage—Dillard ponders living with the weasel in its den (lines 116–122).

Analyze Style

COMMON CORE **RI 6**

(LINES 19–21; 32–49)

Explain that a writer's style may include the use of sound devices such as **alliteration** (repeating consonant sounds at the beginning of words) and **consonance** (repeating consonants within words).

B CITE TEXT EVIDENCE Have students reread lines 19–21. Have them identify Dillard's use of alliteration and consonance and describe their effect on the text's overall meaning. (*The words* breast, bending, beak, beautiful, *and* bones *are instances of alliteration, while* airborne *uses the same sound within the word as an example of consonance. The use of these sound devices helps emphasize the eagle's predatory nature and create a memorable image for the reader.*)

Another stylistic technique Dillard uses is **juxtaposition**—placing two contrasting images near each other to highlight the contrast between them.

C CITE TEXT EVIDENCE Have students reread lines 32–49 to identify instances of juxtaposition and explain how the images suggest a contrast between broader ideas. (*lines 32–35: water lilies as both floor and ceiling; line 38: a muskrat hole/a beer can; lines 40–41: motorcycle tracks/turtle nests; lines 48–49: shallow water/a deep sky; The examples show a contrast between the ways in which various species interact with nature. These juxtapositions highlight contrasts Dillard observes in the natural world and a contrast between the natural world and encroaching civilization.*)

CRITICAL VOCABULARY

talons: Dillard suggests what might have happened between the eagle and the weasel. **ASK STUDENTS** to explain why the eagle's talons may have helped it survive its encounter with the weasel. (*Because it had sharp talons, the eagle may have been able to kill the weasel.*)

inexplicably: Dillard describes her chance encounter with the weasel. **ASK STUDENTS** to explain why this encounter is described as inexplicable. (*Dillard turned her head to encounter the weasel because a bird suddenly caught her eye. Because it was an unscripted moment that depended on split-second timing, there is no simple explanation of why it happened, and so it is inexplicable.*)

---

instinct taught him, tooth to neck, and nearly won. I would like to have seen that eagle from the air a few weeks or months before he was shot: was the whole weasel still attached to his feathered throat, a fur pendant? Or did the eagle eat what he could reach, gutting the living

B 20 weasel with his **talons** before his breast, bending his beak, cleaning the beautiful airborne bones?

talon
(tăl´ən) *n.* the claw of a predator bird.

I have been reading about weasels because I saw one last week. I startled a weasel who startled me, and we exchanged a long glance.

Twenty minutes from my house, through the woods by the quarry and across the highway, is Hollins Pond, a remarkable piece of shallowness, where I like to go at sunset and sit on a tree trunk. Hollins Pond is also called Murray's Pond; it covers two acres of bottomland near Tinker Creek with six inches of water and six thousand lily pads. In winter, brown-and-white steers stand in the

30 middle of it, merely dampening their hooves; from the distant shore they look like miracle itself, complete with miracle's nonchalance. Now, in summer, the steers are gone. The water lilies have blossomed and spread to a green horizontal plane that is terra firma to plodding blackbirds, and tremulous ceiling to black leeches, crayfish, and carp.

This is, mind you, suburbia. It is a five-minute walk in three directions to rows of houses, though none is visible here. There's a 55 mph highway at one end of the pond, and a nesting pair of wood ducks at the other. Under every bush is a muskrat hole or a beer can. The far end is an alternating series of fields and woods, fields and woods,

C 40 threaded everywhere with motorcycle tracks—in whose bare clay wild turtles lay eggs.

So. I had crossed the highway, stepped over two low barbed-wire fences, and traced the motorcycle path in all gratitude through the wild rose and poison ivy of the pond's shoreline up into high grassy fields. Then I cut down through the woods to the mossy fallen tree where I sit. This tree is excellent. It makes a dry, upholstered bench at the upper, marshy end of the pond, a plush jetty raised from the thorny shore between a shallow blue body of water and a deep blue body of sky.

50 The sun had just set. I was relaxed on the tree trunk, ensconced in the lap of lichen, watching the lily pads at my feet tremble and part dreamily over the thrusting path of a carp. A yellow bird appeared to my right and flew behind me. It caught my eye; I swiveled around— and the next instant, **inexplicably**, I was looking down at a weasel, who was looking up at me.

inexplicably
(ĭn-ĕk´splĭ-kə-blē) *adv.* in a way that is hard or impossible to explain.

Weasel! I'd never seen one wild before. He was ten inches long, thin as a curve, a muscled ribbon, brown as fruitwood, soft-furred, alert. His face was fierce, small and pointed as a lizard's; he would have made a good arrowhead. There was just a dot of chin, maybe two

60 brown hairs' worth, and then the pure white fur began that spread

SCAFFOLDING FOR ELL STUDENTS

Organizational Patterns: Time Sequence Note that although the essay includes observations and reflections on the actions of wild animals and humans, there is also a portion that describes a factual encounter. Help students follow this presentation by focusing on the following sections and guiding them to identify the sequence of events.

- Lines 42–49: Dillard crosses the highway to get to the pond and sits down on a fallen tree.

- Lines 50–55: Dillard notices a bird and turns her head to find a weasel staring at her.

- Lines 56–66: Dillard describes what she sees and the weasel's reaction.

- Lines 67–76: Dillard describes the intensity of what she feels and the weasel's ultimate action—he disappears.

down his underside. He had two black eyes I didn't see, any more than you see a window.

The weasel was stunned into stillness as he was emerging from beneath an enormous shaggy wild rose bush four feet away. I was stunned into stillness twisted backward on the tree trunk. Our eyes locked, and someone threw away the key.

D 70 Our look was as if two lovers, or deadly enemies, met unexpectedly on an overgrown path when each had been thinking of something else: a clearing blow to the gut. It was also a bright blow to the brain, or a sudden beating of brains, with all the charge and intimate grate of rubbed balloons. It emptied our lungs. It felled the forest, moved the fields, and drained the pond; the world dismantled and tumbled into that black hole of eyes. If you and I looked at each other that way, our skulls would split and drop to our shoulders. But we don't. We keep our skulls. So.

He disappeared. This was only last week, and already I don't remember what shattered the enchantment. I think I blinked, I think I retrieved my brain from the weasel's brain, and tried to memorize what I was seeing, and the weasel felt the yank of separation, the 80 careening splashdown into real life and the urgent current of instinct. He vanished under the wild rose. I waited motionless, my mind suddenly full of data and my spirit with pleadings, but he didn't return.

E Please do not tell me about "approach-avoidance conflicts."[2] I tell you I've been in that weasel's brain for sixty seconds, and he was in mine. Brains are private places, muttering through unique and secret tapes—but the weasel and I both plugged into another tape simultaneously, for a sweet and shocking time. Can I help it if it was a blank?

90 What goes on in his brain the rest of the time? What does a weasel think about? He won't say. His journal is tracks in clay, a spray of feathers, mouse blood and bone: uncollected, unconnected, loose-leaf, and blown.

I would like to learn, or remember, how to live. I come to Hollins Pond not so much to learn how to live as, frankly, to forget about it. That is, I don't think I can learn from a wild animal how to live in particular—shall I suck warm blood, hold my tail high, walk with my footprints precisely over the prints of my hands?—but I might learn something of mindlessness, something of the purity of living in the 100 physical senses and the dignity of living without bias or motive. The weasel lives in necessity and we live in choice, hating necessity and dying at the last **ignobly** in its talons. I would like to live as I should, as the weasel lives as he should. And I suspect that for me the way is like

ignobly
(ĭg-nō′blē) *adv.*
dishonorably.

---

[2] **approach-avoidance conflicts:** a state of psychological conflict or indecision that occurs when an individual is faced with a situation that has both positive and negative characteristics.

Living Like Weasels **479**

CLOSE READ

Determine Figurative Meanings: Hyperbole

 COMMON CORE RI 4, L 5a

(LINES 67–75)

Explain that **hyperbole** is an intentional exaggeration that writers use for emphasis or effect.

D **CITE TEXT EVIDENCE** Have students reread lines 67–75. They should identify examples of hyperbole and describe the overall effect. *(line 67: "lovers, or deadly enemies"; lines 71–73: "emptied our lungs," "felled the forest," "moved the fields," "drained the pond," "world dismantled"; lines 73–74: "skulls would split." This use of hyperbole emphasizes that, for Dillard, staring at the weasel for only an instant was a momentous, highly-charged exchange.)*

Analyze Style (LINES 84–93)

 COMMON CORE RI 6

Point out that writers often use **rhetorical questions** that are meant to require contemplation rather than an answer.

E **CITE TEXT EVIDENCE** Have students reread lines 84–93. Ask them to identify the rhetorical questions and describe their effect. *(Lines 88–89 "Can I help it . . . ?"; lines 90–91 "What goes on . . . ?" and "What does . . . ?"; Dillard uses these questions to emphasize that the weasel does not think as human beings do and that the only communication the weasel provides are the physical signs of the weasel's actions—"tracks," "feathers," "blood and bone.")*

CRITICAL VOCABULARY

ignobly: Dillard describes choices that people make for their lives as dishonorable.

ASK STUDENTS why Dillard thinks people act ignobly. *(Unlike the weasel, people make choices. They hate that necessity makes choosing impossible, and the ultimate necessity is death, which takes choice and the chance to act nobly away from them.)*

WHEN STUDENTS STRUGGLE . . .

Explain that Annie Dillard uses unconventional syntax to create a dramatic effect and help readers focus on particular images or ideas.

ASK STUDENTS to read the following sentences and discuss how the unconventional syntax helps emphasize an idea or image.

- Line 35: "This is, mind you, suburbia." *(This reminds readers that the natural scene Dillard describes exists within a densely settled area.)*
- Lines 42–44: "I had crossed. . . grassy fields." *(This emphasizes how the motorcycle tracks help her navigate through the thorns and poison ivy.)*
- Lines 96–100: "That is. . . or motive." *(This emphasizes animal behaviors that are not reasonable or possible for humans.)*

Analyze Style (LINES 123–129) RI 6

Another part of a writer's style is **tone**. Some writers prefer to use an informal tone, as if the writer and reader are carrying on a casual conversation.

F **ASK STUDENTS** to reread lines 123–129 and describe Dillard's tone in this paragraph and throughout the essay. *(She addresses readers directly and informally in line 123. Her tone suggests a familiarity between people who might find themselves in the same situation: people living in ways that are not true to their "calling.")*

Point out that Dillard also uses alliteration and consonance in lines 123–129.

G **CITE TEXT EVIDENCE** Have students identify the use of alliteration and consonance and explain the ideas these sound devices help emphasize. *(Alliteration: stalk, certain, skilled, supple, spot [lines 125–126]; plug, pulse [line 126]; Consonance: calling, skilled, locate [lines 125–126; The devices help emphasize how people can learn from animals.)*

COLLABORATIVE DISCUSSION Have students form pairs to discuss the reasons Dillard goes to Hollins Pond and the role of nature in her life. Students may note that Dillard goes to Hollins Pond to connect with nature and to contemplate a mindless, pure way of life. Students should refer to specific lines and/or paragraphs to support their ideas.

ASK STUDENTS to share any questions they generated in the course of reading and discussing the selection.

---

the weasel's: open to time and death painlessly, noticing everything, remembering nothing, choosing the given with a fierce and pointed will.

I missed my chance. I should have gone for the throat. I should have lunged for that streak of white under the weasel's chin and held on, held on through mud and into the wild rose, held on for a
110 dearer life. We could live under the wild rose wild as weasels, mute and uncomprehending. I could very calmly go wild. I could live two days in the den, curled, leaning on mouse fur, sniffing bird bones, blinking, licking, breathing musk, my hair tangled in the roots of grasses. Down is a good place to go, where the mind is single. Down is out, out of your ever-loving mind and back to your careless senses. I remember muteness as a prolonged and giddy fast, where every moment is a feast of utterance received. Time and events are merely poured, unremarked, and ingested directly, like blood pulsed into my gut through a jugular vein. Could two live that way? Could two live
120 under the wild rose, and explore by the pond, so that the smooth mind of each is as everywhere present to the other, and as received and as unchallenged, as falling snow?

We could, you know. We can live any way we want. People take vows of poverty, chastity, and obedience—even of silence—by choice. The thing is to stalk your calling in a certain skilled and supple way, to locate the most tender and live spot and plug into that pulse. This is yielding, not fighting. A weasel doesn't "attack" anything; a weasel lives as he's meant to, yielding at every moment to the perfect freedom of single necessity.

130 I think it would be well, and proper, and obedient, and pure, to grasp your one necessity and not let it go, to dangle from it limp wherever it takes you. Then even death, where you're going no matter how you live, cannot you part. Seize it and let it seize you up aloft even, till your eyes burn out and drop; let your musky flesh fall off in shreds, and let your very bones unhinge and scatter, loosened over fields, over fields and woods, lightly, thoughtless, from any height at all, from as high as eagles.

COLLABORATIVE DISCUSSION Why does Dillard go to Hollins Pond? With a partner, discuss the role that nature plays in the author's life. Cite specific evidence from the essay to support your ideas.

APPLYING ACADEMIC VOCABULARY

visualize	intensity	encounter

As you discuss the text and Dillard's techniques, incorporate the Collection 6 academic vocabulary words *visualize, intensity,* and *encounter.* Ask students to suggest ways that Dillards's language helps them **visualize** the **intensity** of the **encounter** between Dillard and the weasel. Ask them if they have ever had a similar encounter with a wild animal.

Analyze Style

Annie Dillard's style—her unique and beautiful way of communicating ideas—makes readers feel as if they are experiencing the events that she writes about and the emotions that she is feeling. To analyze how she achieves this immediacy, note the elements of her style described in the chart:

Stylistic Elements
Word Choice Dillard carefully chooses words with connotations, or shades of meaning, to evoke a particular emotional response in the reader. For example, she describes herself as being "ensconced in the lap of lichen." The word *ensconced* suggests a cozy security; this suggestion is reinforced by her choice of the word *lap*.
Alliteration Particularly in significant passages, Dillard repeats consonant sounds at the beginning of words to add emphasis and draw attention to ideas.
Syntax Dillard often writes long sentences to clarify connections between ideas and create a smooth, flowing rhythm in her prose. Periodically she disrupts this rhythm with short sentences that convey a sense of surprise or wonder.
Tone Through her choice of words and phrases, Dillard achieves a conversational tone that establishes an intimacy with her readers. For example, she opens her essay by saying "A weasel is wild. Who knows what he thinks?" These simple sentences give the impression that she is speaking directly to her audience.

Determine Figurative Meanings

COMMON CORE RI 4, L 5a

Another important element of Dillard's style is **figurative language**, language that communicates ideas beyond the literal meanings of the words. She uses both **metaphors** (which compare two things directly) and **similes** (which compare things using the word *like* or *as*) to suggest ideas that create an impression in readers' minds. Consider this sentence from her essay:

> The water lilies have blossomed and spread to a green horizontal plane that is terra firma to plodding blackbirds, and tremulous ceiling to black leeches, crayfish, and carp.

In this passage, Dillard compares the water lilies in the pond to "terra firma"—solid ground—for blackbirds and to a flimsy, trembling ceiling to those creatures that live below it. Her metaphors help readers visualize the mass of water lilies that carpet the surface of the pond, as well as the teeming life both below and above the water.

TEACH

CLOSE READ

Analyze Style
COMMON CORE RI 6

Work with students to identify other examples of the author's style, such as the following. Discuss how the examples contribute to the power of the text.

- **Word Choice:** *"Our eyes locked, and someone threw away the key."* (lines 65–66); This choice of words emphasizes that it was impossible for Dillard or the weasel to look away.
- **Alliteration:** *"bright blow to the brain, or a sudden beating of brains"* (lines 69–70); This helps the reader feel the excitement of the encounter.
- **Syntax:** *"This tree is excellent. It makes . . . "* (lines 46–49); The varied sentence lengths encourage the reader to pause for observation just as Dillard observes her surroundings.
- **Tone:** *"I have been reading about . . ."* (line 22); Dillard's conversational tone helps create familiarity between her and the reader.

Determine Figurative Meanings
COMMON CORE RI 4, L 5a

Have students classify the following examples as a simile or a metaphor and explain each comparison:

- "soak him off like a stubborn label" (line 11): *(simile; The adherence of the weasel is compared to a stuck label.)*
- "was the whole weasel . . . a fur pendant?" (lines 18–19): *(metaphor; The weasel is compared to a necklace around the eagle's throat.)*

Strategies for Annotation   ✎ 🗐 *Annotate it!*

Analyze Style
COMMON CORE RI 4

Share these strategies for guided or independent analysis:

- Highlight in yellow word choices that provoke an emotional response.
- Underline instances of alliteration or consonance.
- Highlight in blue distinctive syntax.
- Highlight in green examples of Dillard's conversational tone.

> Please do not tell me about "approach-avoidance conflicts."[2] I tell you I've been in that weasel's brain for sixty seconds, and he was in mine. Brains are private places, muttering through unique and secret tapes—but the weasel and I both plugged into another tape simultaneously, for a sweet and shocking time. Can I help it if it was a blank?

PRACTICE & APPLY

Analyzing the Text COMMON CORE RI 1, RI 2, RI 3, RI 4, RI 6, L 5a

Possible answers:

1. *The weasel is tenacious. This idea is expressed through the descriptions of one clinging to the naturalist's hand and of the eagle with a weasel skull stuck to its throat. Words and phrases that help develop this idea include "crunching," "socketed," "like a stubborn label," "fixed by the jaws," and "swiveled."*

2. *Dillard's purpose is to portray a meaningful encounter with a creature and share the lesson learned from it. Lines 24–29 provide a context for the encounter and suggest through the juxtaposition of images that humans living in proximity to nature must remain open and sensitive to it.*

3. *She uses metaphors and similes to describe the weasel as "thin as a curve," "a muscled ribbon," and "brown as fruitwood." She compares its face to a lizard's and "a good arrowhead." His eyes are like windows. Her descriptions create a vivid impression of an energetic, vital being that is impossible to overlook or ignore.*

4. *Strong verbs ("stunned," "locked," "dismantled," and "tumbled") convey the power of the encounter and contribute to the tone of awe and shock. Alliteration ("bright blow to the brain" and "beating of brains") emphasizes the excitement. Varying sentence lengths creates an unexpected, jolting syntax that reflects the encounter with the weasel.*

5. *She says that weasels live mindlessly, by instinct, in the present, while humans are trapped by consciousness. Humans live in choice; weasels live in necessity. Dillard shows her admiration for and envy of the weasel in such phrases as "purity of living in the physical senses," "dignity of living," "open to time and death painlessly," and "fierce and pointed will."*

6. *Simile: "as received and as unchallenged, as falling snow." Metaphor: "every moment is a feast of utterance." "I should have gone for the throat" is an implicit metaphor; "go for the throat" represents being a weasel. These figures of speech make abstract ideas more tangible. Dillard expresses how directly she could live as a weasel.*

7. *She means that a weasel lives in harmony with its nature, its instinct. Instinct dictates what the weasel will do; the weasel has no choice in the matter.*

8. *The first two paragraphs develop the idea of the weasel's tenacious hold on whatever it seizes. The last two paragraphs express the author's desire to live that way, fixing on one reality, releasing all that is superfluous, in order to soar and reach new heights, just like the weasel affixed to an eagle.*

 eBook *Annotate It!*

Analyzing the Text COMMON CORE RI 1, RI 2, RI 3, RI 4, RI 6, L 5a, W 3a, W 3e

Cite Text Evidence   Support your responses with evidence from the selection.

1. **Infer** What idea about the weasel is communicated in the first two paragraphs of the essay? Identify words and phrases that develop this idea.

2. **Analyze** In lines 24–49, Dillard juxtaposes images of nature with evidence of human habitation. Explain how these lines relate to her overall purpose.

3. **Analyze** What does Dillard compare the weasel to in lines 56–62? What impression of the weasel is evoked by this figurative language?

4. **Cite Evidence** How does Dillard convey the intensity of her encounter with the weasel in lines 63–75? Consider how these stylistic elements contribute to the effectiveness of this passage:

   - word choice
   - tone
   - use of alliteration
   - syntax

5. **Analyze** What contrast between humans and the weasel does Dillard make in lines 94–106? How does she feel about these differences? Explain.

6. **Draw Conclusions** Identify the similes and metaphors in lines 107–122. Think about what Dillard is describing in this paragraph. What function does this figurative language fulfill?

7. **Interpret** What does Dillard mean in lines 127–128 when she writes, "A weasel doesn't 'attack' anything; a weasel lives as he's meant to"?

8. **Connect** Explain how Dillard unifies her essay by connecting the ideas in the first two paragraphs to those in her last two paragraphs. What central idea do these paragraphs develop?

PERFORMANCE TASK

Writing Activity: Essay In her essay, Dillard's observation of the weasel leads her to reflect on her own life. Write your own personal essay, following these steps.

- Write about a memorable event in your life.
- Explain how this event led to an insight about your own life or about the human condition.
- Organize your ideas into a unified essay.

Assign this performance task.

PERFORMANCE TASK COMMON CORE W 3a, W 3e

Writing Activity: Essay Explore possible topics in a whole-class prewriting discussion. Ask volunteers to suggest memorable events or encounters. Then, through questions and student comments, elicit ideas about ways in which each personal experience might be emblematic of a general truth. Explain that essays should progress from the personal to the universal, and that students should include specific details to help the reader understand the insights they gained from their experiences.

Critical Vocabulary

supposition   talon   inexplicably   ignobly

Practice and Apply Create a semantic map for each Critical Vocabulary word. Follow the example given here, which is for a word that appears in line 31 of the essay. Use a dictionary or thesaurus as needed.

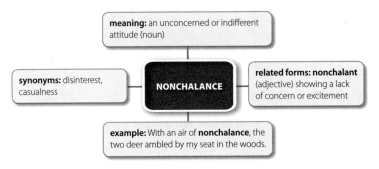

meaning: an unconcerned or indifferent attitude (noun)

synonyms: disinterest, casualness

NONCHALANCE

related forms: nonchalant (adjective) showing a lack of concern or excitement

example: With an air of **nonchalance**, the two deer ambled by my seat in the woods.

Vocabulary Strategy: Domain-Specific Words

As she writes about nature, Dillard uses **domain-specific words**—vocabulary associated with a specific field of study. Such words allow her to be more precise and concise in her writing. Domain-specific words also help broaden readers' knowledge of nature. The Critical Vocabulary word *talons* in line 20 is an example of a domain-specific word.

Another domain-specific word, *carcasses*, occurs in line 5. To determine the meaning of this word, readers can follow these steps:

- Read the sentence in which the word *carcasses* appears and the adjacent sentences. Identify possible context clues, such as "killing" and "bodies."
- Identify the root of the word to see if you recognize it. Then look for any prefix or suffix that might indicate the word's part of speech, number, or tense. The suffix –es indicates that *carcasses* is a plural noun.
- Use a dictionary to confirm meaning. *Carcass* is defined as "a dead body, especially one killed for food."

Practice and Apply Work in a small group to complete these activities.

1. Identify additional domain-specific words that appear in the essay.

2. Write a definition for each word using context clues or a dictionary.

3. Share your words and definitions with the class. Together, write sample sentences for each domain-specific word.

PRACTICE & APPLY

Critical Vocabulary

COMMON CORE L 6

Answers:

supposition

meaning: something assumed to be true (*n.*)
related words: suppose, supposing
synonyms: assumption, premise

talon

meaning: the claw of a bird of prey (*n.*)
related words: talus
synonyms: claw

inexplicably

meaning: being impossible to explain (*adv.*)
related words: inexplicable, inexplicability, explicable, explicate, explain
synonyms: unaccountably, unfathomably, mysteriously

ignobly

meaning: in a manner that lacks qualities of high moral character (*adv.*)
related words: noble, ignominious
synonyms: dishonorably, shamefully, meanly

Example sentences will vary.

Vocabulary Strategy: Domain-Specific Words

Students should identify and adequately define some or all of the following words: *den, instinct, prey, jugular vein, musk.* Sample sentences will vary.

TO CHALLENGE STUDENTS . . .

Explore Point of View What *does* a weasel think about? Dillard poses this question as a central part of her essay. Discuss her answer. (*A weasel does not think as humans do, but simply acts according to instinct.*)

Challenge students to take the opposite view and write a short description of the encounter between Dillard and the weasel from the weasel's point of view. Have students use the information about weasels in the essay as background and imagine the weasel's thoughts when confronted by a human being in an area near the weasel's den. Students may even mimic Dillard's considerations of nature by having the weasel share thoughts about humans.

When writing is complete, ask volunteers to share their work with the class.

Language and Style: Use Precise Details

Review the examples in the chart and make sure students understand how each one adds to the power of the writing.

Answers:

Students' revisions should demonstrate their ability to include precise details and should improve the clarity and effectiveness of their personal essays.

Assess It!

Online Selection Test
- Download an editable ExamView bank.
- Assign and manage this test online.

Language and Style: Use Precise Details

One characteristic of Dillard's style is her use of **precise details**. These details make it less likely that readers will overlook or misinterpret her meaning. Read the following passage from her essay:

> It is a five-minute walk in three directions to rows of houses, though none is visible here. There's a 55 mph highway at one end of the pond, and a nesting pair of wood ducks at the other. Under every bush is a muskrat hole or a beer can.

In these sentences, Dillard uses concrete words and phrases, such as "nesting pair of wood ducks," "muskrat hole," and "beer can." These phrases create vivid and specific pictures in readers' minds. She also uses measurements—"five-minute walk" and "55 mph highway"—to make her description more specific.

Contrast the effectiveness of her writing with this version of the passage:

> There are houses around the pond, but they can't be seen. There's a highway at one end of the pond and some ducks at the other. There are bushes with holes and trash under them.

Notice how vague and dull this description is. Concrete words have been replaced with imprecise adjectives and nouns, such as "some" and "trash." Not only are these words open to interpretation, the sharp contrast between nature and civilization set up in the first passage is lost.

The chart shows some ways to make writing more precise.

Method	Example
Use appositives or prepositional phrases to provide additional description or clarity to explanations.	"Was the whole weasel still attached to his feathered throat, a fur pendant?" "It covers two acres of bottomland near Tinker Creek with six inches of water and six thousand lily pads."
Include specific adjectives, adverbs, nouns, and verbs.	"In winter, brown-and-white steers stand in the middle of it, merely dampening their hooves." "He was ten inches long, thin as a curve, a muscled ribbon, brown as fruitwood, soft-furred, alert."

Practice and Apply Revise your personal essay from the Performance Task, following these guidelines.

1. Replace vague adjectives, adverbs, nouns, or verbs with concrete and specific words. Original: I fell a long distance. Revision: I plummeted 15 feet.

2. Add prepositional phrases or appositives that more precisely define, explain, or describe. Revision: From the cliff's edge, I plummeted 15 feet, splashing into a sparkling glacial lake.

Analyze Ideas and Events

COMMON CORE

RI 3

TEACH

Tell students that an essay such as "Living Like Weasels" presents a series of complex ideas that may not seem related at first. The writer's job is to connect ideas in a way readers can follow, leading to new insights. Dillard's overall message— people might be happier if they lived more like weasels—is one that, on the face of it, seems a bit preposterous. But through her skillful observations and writing, Dillard presents a case that living more like weasels *in certain ways* might let people live more honorably and more true to a "calling."

One way to connect ideas is through an **analogy** or comparison in which one set of events is presented as similar to another set of events. An analogy may involve just a single reference, or it can be extended throughout a piece of writing to involve several different aspects of the idea. Dillard uses an extended analogy to suggest that people should live more like weasels.

PRACTICE AND APPLY

Explain that the weasel's behavior in its encounter with the eagle serves as an extended analogy throughout the essay. Direct students to the following lines and discuss how they relate to the analogy and what meaning Dillard is communicating through the analogy.

- Lines 12–21 *(The weasel reacted instinctively to the attack and never released its hold on the eagle, even after it died. Dillard is highlighting the importance of tenacity in the weasel's character.)*

- Lines 100–102 *(The weasel is a creature of instinct, doing what it must. People live by choice, hating that in the end, like the weasel, death—or necessity—will claim them anyway.)*

- Lines 107–110 *(Dillard suggests that she should live like the weasel, that by "going for the throat," she could live by the pure purpose she sees in the weasel.)*

- Lines 130–137 *(Dillard suggests that people should seize whatever their "necessity" is in life and let it take them wherever it might, even if it kills them, like the eagle's flight did to the weasel at its throat.)*

Analyze Word Choice: Tone

COMMON CORE

RI 4

RETEACH

LEVEL UP TUTORIALS Assign the following *Level Up* tutorial: **Tone**

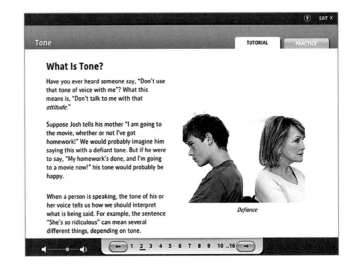

Review the term *tone*. In a work of nonfiction, **tone** is the writer's attitude and approach towards ideas and readers. Explain that a writer's tone may be very formal, as if he or she is teaching a lesson to a group of young students, or more informal, as if the writer is speaking with a friend.

- Have students reread Dillard's description of Hollins Pond in lines 24–34.

- Ask: Would you describe Dillard's tone in this paragraph as formal or informal? *(informal)* Why? *(She is telling a simple story as she might to a friend, describing a favorite place.)*

- Ask: How would you describe Dillard's attitude towards Hollins Pond? *(She obviously loves it and has observed it very carefully in many seasons.)*

- Ask: Why is this type of tone moving and convincing? *(The reader feels as if Dillard is a friend who has stories to share and who shares her love of nature easily with others.)*

CLOSE READING APPLICATION

Students can apply the skill to another essay or nonfiction work they have read. Have them select a passage that strongly conveys the writer's tone and then identify words or phrases that convey the tone. Students may share their analyses in pairs or small groups.

Local Deer

Essay by Louise Erdrich

Why This Text

Although "Local Deer" is an essay, its beauty lies in its prose style and the way the author communicates subtleties of behavior through the use of figurative language, word connotation, syntax, and sentence style. Students may have difficulty finding big ideas in what is essentially an account of what the author sees outside her house while her baby is napping and she is trying to write. With the help of the close-reading questions, students will see how the author uses her powers of language and observation to give us a glimpse of her world.

Background Tell students that most of what Louise Erdrich writes—poems, novels, stories, and essays—is set in a place she knows firsthand. One novel is set on a highway outside of Fargo, North Dakota; another is set on an Ojibwa reservation. The essay they are about to read reflects Erdrich's observations of her backyard in New Hampshire. Of all Erdrich's considerable talents, one of the most significant is her ability to evoke a sense of place.

AS YOU READ Ask students to pay attention to the way the author uses figurative language, word choice, and tone to convey her observations and draw attention to her ideas.

Common Core Support

- cite strong and thorough textual evidence
- analyze the author's use of figurative language over the course of a text
- determine an author's point of view in a text
- analyze how style and content contribute to a text

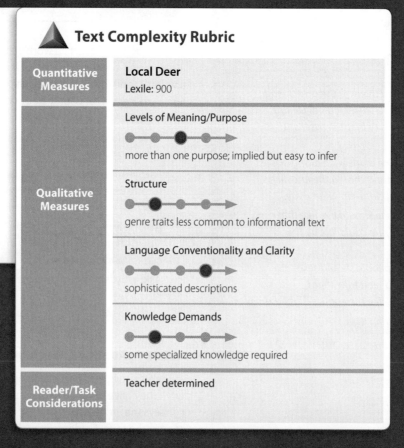

Text Complexity Rubric

Quantitative Measures	**Local Deer** Lexile: 900
Qualitative Measures	**Levels of Meaning/Purpose** more than one purpose; implied but easy to infer
	Structure genre traits less common to informational text
	Language Conventionality and Clarity sophisticated descriptions
	Knowledge Demands some specialized knowledge required
Reader/Task Considerations	Teacher determined

Strategies for CLOSE READING

Analyze Style

Students should read this essay carefully all the way through. Close-reading questions at the bottom of the page will help them analyze the author's style. As they read, students should jot down comments or questions about the text in the margins.

WHEN STUDENTS STRUGGLE . . .

To help students recognize and interpret elements of the author's style, have them work in small groups to fill out a chart like the one shown below.

CITE TEXT EVIDENCE For practice in recognizing how the author uses language and sentence style to convey meaning, have them analyze the effect of each of the following examples from the text.

Example from the Text	Effect
"No matter how hard I stomp they continue to loll and dig and play. They knock into the underground gas furnace, and love the big noise." (lines 7–9)	The author depicts the woodchucks as playful children.
"I'm thinking of a sentence, businesslike, a thing I can write down, when I look up from my woodchuck. A young buck deer is watching me." (lines 18–20)	The short, set-off sentence signals that something unexpected has happened.
". . . he looks straight at me, the apple round and whole in his teeth, like the apple in the mouth of a suckling pig." (lines 39–40)	The buck looks like a roasted pig; he's assessing his situation before he eats the apple.
". . . she is watching me, her eyes deep-water mussels, endless and grave, purple-black." (lines 51–52)	The language used to describe the doe gives her a sense of solemnity and gravitas.

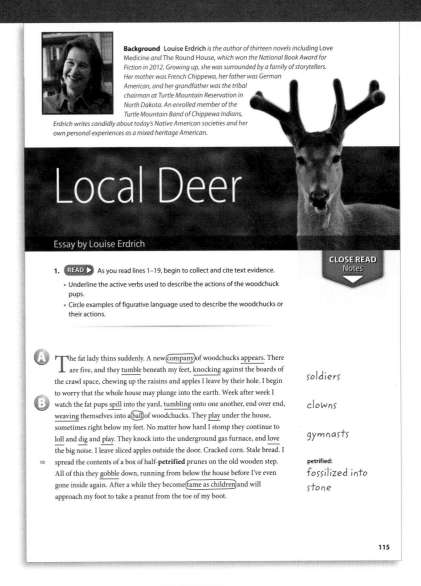

Background Louise Erdrich *is the author of thirteen novels including* Love Medicine *and* The Round House, *which won the National Book Award for Fiction in 2012. Growing up, she was surrounded by a family of storytellers. Her mother was French Chippewa, her father was German American, and her grandfather was the tribal chairman at Turtle Mountain Reservation in North Dakota. An enrolled member of the Turtle Mountain Band of Chippewa Indians, Erdrich writes candidly about today's Native American societies and her own personal experiences as a mixed heritage American.*

Local Deer

Essay by Louise Erdrich

CLOSE READ
Notes

1. **READ ▷** As you read lines 1–19, begin to collect and cite text evidence.

- Underline the active verbs used to describe the actions of the woodchuck pups.
- Circle examples of figurative language used to describe the woodchucks or their actions.

The fat lady thins suddenly. A new company of woodchucks appears. There are five, and they tumble beneath my feet, knocking against the boards of the crawl space, chewing up the raisins and apples I leave by their hole. I begin to worry that the whole house may plunge into the earth. Week after week I watch the fat pups spill into the yard, tumbling onto one another, end over end, weaving themselves into a ball of woodchucks. They play under the house, sometimes right below my feet. No matter how hard I stomp they continue to loll and dig and play. They knock into the underground gas furnace, and love the big noise. I leave sliced apples outside the door. Cracked corn. Stale bread. I

10 spread the contents of a box of half-**petrified** prunes on the old wooden step. All of this they gobble down, running from below the house before I've even gone inside again. After a while they become tame as children and will approach my foot to take a peanut from the toe of my boot.

soldiers

clowns

gymnasts

petrified:
fossilized into
stone

115

1. **READ AND CITE TEXT EVIDENCE** In lines 1–19 the author worries that because of the woodchucks the whole house may "plunge into the earth."

Ⓐ ASK STUDENTS to name things the woodchucks do. *They gobble up the food she leaves for them; they spill into the yard and tumble around; they loll and dig and play; they knock against the boards of the crawlspace and into the underground furnace; they make a racket.*

Critical Vocabulary: petrified (line 10) Have students explain the meaning of *petrified*. What kind of prune is "half-petrified"? *Students may say an old, dried-out one.*

So here I sit, with a peanut on my foot, as though I'm not a writer, as though I've got nothing to do but watch these careful nuisances steal toward me one muscle at a time. I should be working because our baby is asleep, but I am too busy training woodchucks. It is late summer now, the air filled with a round clarity. I'm thinking of a sentence, businesslike, a thing I can write down, when I look up from my woodchuck.

20   A young buck deer is watching me.

I've never seen one here before, although they leave their tracks, two split moons, at the edge of the field and far from the road. I've fixed No Hunting signs into the sides of the trees. I've watched. I've waited the way my father taught me to wait for deer. But New Hampshire's deer herd is about half the size of Vermont's and they are nowhere near the nuisance they are in the northeastern suburbs. Simple politics. I live in a section of the state where for the price of a license a hunter can shoot any deer, doe, or fawn. Vermont has more restrictive laws, it also has a bigger winter kill-off. Deer eat rare plants as well as boring shrubs, so I know they're a mixed blessing. It is our human fault

30   that they're now pests in many areas. At any rate, the deer I see are an unusual presence in my hunted-down stretch of the Northeast.

2. ◀ **REREAD** As you reread lines 1–13, list in the margin the different images the descriptions of the woodchucks bring to mind. How does the author use figurative language to present a detailed picture of these animals? Support your answer with explicit textual evidence.

The figurative language conjures up images of the woodchucks as soldiers, clowns, gymnasts, and children. Phrases like "the fat pups spill into the yard, tumbling onto one another, end over end, weaving themselves into a ball of woodchucks" emphasize their childlike fascinating behavior.

3. **READ** ▶ As you read lines 20–57, continue to cite textual evidence.
- Underline all the references to looking, seeing, watching, visibility, and invisibility.
- Circle short sentences that interrupt the author's descriptions.
- In the margin, make notes about the attitude and behavior of the young buck.

> He is the bronze of dead pine needles and his eyes are black rimmed in black, still and large.

The young buck stands fifteen feet away, under the old apple tree someone planted here a hundred years ago. His antlers are small, still cased in velvet.[1] He is the bronze of dead pine needles and his eyes are black rimmed in black, still and large. His neck is limber and strong. When a car passes, he freezes, but he does not move. I don't move either. He watches me carefully and then with nervous care he reaches down and picks up a hard, green apple. His head jerks up and he looks straight at me, the apple round and whole in his teeth, like the apple in the mouth of a suckling pig.

40   The apple begins to vanish. His tongue extends and pushes the whole thing back into his throat. I am alarmed, suddenly, as when one of my children bites off a piece of something too large to swallow. I mentally review the Heimlich maneuver.[2] But the apple vanishes. He reaches down for another. And then, through the wide screen door, he hears the baby shake her rattle. She has awakened and she **brandishes** her toy at the buck. He takes one step backward, and stands in an attitude of absolute alertness, testing the noise. The rattle spins again. He turns. He walks carefully into the trees.

Deer return until the apples are gone, a doe with the young buck. She is the same shade of russet,[3] her wide-set ears flickering and nervous, all air and

50   grace. I look up and she is watching me, her eyes deep-water mussels, endless and grave, purple-black. She moves from the brush. Her tail is long, a dog's tail, curved and sinuous, tipped with black. She sweeps it back and forth as she browses. I grow used to them and soon I find that the deer are there, always

[1] **velvet:** a soft, fuzzy layer of skin that covers a male deer's antlers while they are growing.
[2] **Heimlich maneuver:** first aid technique to dislodge an obstruction from the throat of a person who is choking.
[3] **russet:** reddish brown in color.

The deer is cautious, but not skittish.

It acts carefully and nervously.

It does not run, but leaves deliberately.

brandishes:
waves as if in a threat or warning

2. **REREAD AND CITE TEXT EVIDENCE** Point out that in lines 1–13 the woodchucks are depicted as playful children or as a company of circus tumblers.

B **ASK STUDENTS** to cite text showing how the author's use of imagery helps you to visualize the woodchucks at play. What mental pictures does she create? *Students may suggest: they "spill into the yard, tumbling onto one another, end over end"; they "loll and dig and play"; they "love the big noise" (lines 5, 8–9).*

3. **READ AND CITE TEXT EVIDENCE** Point out that the author notices the young buck in line 20.

C **ASK STUDENTS** to look at the sentence "A young buck deer is watching me." How does the author use sentence style to signal that something important is happening? *She makes this sentence stand out; it's shorter than the others and on its own line.* What new tone is set? *Students may suggest a tone of excitement, suspense, drama.*

Critical Vocabulary: brandishes (line 45) Have students explain the meaning of *brandishes*. Why is the idea of "brandishing" a toy humorous? *Usually we talk about brandishing a sword or other weapon.*

FOR ELL STUDENTS Point out to students that the verb *to freeze* has more than one meaning. It can mean "to become ice," "to make or become very cold," or "to stop in fright." Ask students to tell which meaning is correct in this context. *"to stop in fright"*

CLOSE READ
Notes

there, in the shadows and the shapes of other things. Invisible and obvious, gray as talc and calm as sand, the deer divide themselves from the spars[4] and bones of trees. They make themselves whole suddenly. I am not looking, and then I am looking into their eyes.

[4] **spars:** thick, strong poles, such as those used for a mast in a ship.

4. ◀ **REREAD** As you reread 48–57, note the author's description of the doe. How does her word choice affect your vision of the animal?

Erdrich's tone is reverential. Her detailed descriptions and figurative language ("her eyes deep-water mussels, endless and grave") give the creature a magical, almost mythical aura.

SHORT RESPONSE

Cite Text Evidence In what way does the author's style help you understand her attitude towards the animals in her yard? Analyze Erdrich's style, including her use of figurative language. Review your reading notes, and be sure to **cite text evidence** in your response.

The careful, detailed, and complex language the author uses to describe the deer is an indication of her appreciation for their beauty, complexity, and spiritual presence. The author includes elegant descriptions of the deer's eyes that emphasize the fact that the author is as much observed as observer. By using phrases such as "the deer divide themselves from the spars" and "they make themselves whole suddenly" the author indicates that the deer control whether or not they will be seen. The deer appear almost magical, not there and everywhere, "invisible and obvious."

118

---

4. **REREAD AND CITE TEXT EVIDENCE** Have students compare the author's tone when describing the doe with her tone when describing the woodchucks (lines 1–13).

   Ⓓ **ASK STUDENTS** to note the tone of the lines describing the doe. What words would they use to describe this change of tone in lines 48–58? *The woodchucks are described as playful, energetic, boisterous, wild, uncontrolled, childlike; the doe is described as quiet, still, deep, self-contained, noble, remote.*

SHORT RESPONSE

Cite Text Evidence Students should support their ideas with text evidence. They should:

- explain how the author's use of figurative language effects meaning.
- explain how the author's choice of words reflects her attitude toward her subject.
- recognize and interpret symbolism.

TO CHALLENGE STUDENTS . . .

Tell students that Louise Erdrich has always drawn on her Ojibwa (or Chippewa) roots for inspiration. Her stories are based on the experiences of her family, her observations about life, and the rich oral tradition of Ojibwa storytelling handed down to her from her mother and grandparents. Explain that the Ojibwa, who live in the Great Lakes region of the U.S. and Canada, are among the largest of the Native American nations north of Mexico. Students can gain insight into Louise Erdrich's writings by researching the history and background of the Ojibwa people.

ASK STUDENTS to find out more about the Ojibwa. Groups can research and share information on:

- the history, location, and background of the Ojibwa.
- traditional Ojibwa storytelling.
- the oral language of the Ojibwa people, specifically the English words borrowed from the Ojibwa language.
- how Ojibwa cultural traditions and customs have changed over time.
- the close connection between the Ojibwa way of life and the natural world.
- the role of religion and mysticism in Ojibwa culture.

DIG DEEPER

With the class, return to Question 4, Reread. Have students share their responses.

ASK STUDENTS to think about the words the author uses to describe the doe. How does style and word choice add meaning to the text?

- Have students note the author's observations of the doe in lines 48–58. What words does she use? *Students may suggest "invisible and obvious", "gray as talc and calm as sand", "in the shadows and shapes of other things."*
- What do these words suggest about the deer? *Students may say that the deer is aloof, detached, neutral, inscrutable, superior.*
- In line 51 the author notes that the deer is watching her. What does this behavior suggest about the deer? *Students may say it suggests that the deer is curious, but wary of humans.*

ASK STUDENTS to return to their Short Response answer and revise it based on the class discussion.

Wild Peaches

Spring and All

Poem by Elinor Wylie

Poem by William Carlos Williams

Why These Texts?

Both poems in this lesson take inspiration from the pastoral tradition but experiment with new themes and forms. By analyzing ways in which the poems build on but also depart from the tradition to create uniquely American forms, students will understand how literary movements constantly expand our ways of viewing the world.

Key Learning Objective: The student will demonstrate knowledge of foundational works of American literature, in part by analyzing their structural forms.

For practice and application:

Close Reader selection
"Pastorals"
Poetry by William Carlos Williams and Jennifer Chang

COMMON CORE Common Core Standards

RL 2 Determine themes and analyze their development.

RL 4 Analyze the impact of specific word choices on meaning and tone.

RL 5 Analyze how an author's choices concerning how to structure a text contribute to its meaning as well as its aesthetic impact.

RL 9 Demonstrate knowledge of early-twentieth-century foundational works of American literature, including how two texts from the same period treat similar topics.

W 9a Draw evidence from literary texts to support analysis; demonstrate knowledge of foundational works of American literature.

▲ Text Complexity Rubric

	Wild Peaches	Spring and All
Quantitative Measures	Lexile: N/A	Lexile: N/A
Qualitative Measures	Levels of Meaning/Purpose — single level of complex meaning	Levels of Meaning/Purpose — multiple levels of meaning (multiple themes)
	Structure — regular stanzas with some liberties taken	Structure — free verse, no particular patterns
	Language Conventionality and Clarity — figurative, less accessible language	Language Conventionality and Clarity — more complex sentence structure
	Knowledge Demands — some cultural and literary knowledge useful	Knowledge Demands — some cultural and literary knowledge useful
Reader/Task Considerations	Teacher determined Vary by individual reader and type of text	Teacher determined Vary by individual reader and type of text

TEACH

CLOSE READ

Background Have students read the background information. Explain that the Imagist movement in poetry was an outgrowth of modernism. Ezra Pound officially started the movement in 1912 when he identified its elements in a poem by Hilda Doolittle, known as H.D. In reaction against the flowery, abstract language of Romantic poetry, the Imagist poets sought to remove all unnecessary words and let a poem's rhythm flow from the phrasing, rather than manipulating the phrasing to fit a prescribed meter. Students will find a good example of the Imagist style in Williams's "Spring and All."

Elinor Wylie After students have read the information about the author, explain that Wylie, born Elinor Morton Hoyt, had a privileged but difficult childhood that included the suicide of one of her brothers. Her health was delicate, and she suffered from migraine headaches. After leaving her first husband for a married man, Horace Wylie, she was ostracized from polite society. Despite these difficulties, she eventually made friends in literary circles in New York, where she worked as an editor for several magazines as well as wrote her own poetry and novels. While preparing her collection *Angels and Earthly Creatures* for publication, she died suddenly of a stroke at age 43.

William Carlos Williams Elaborate on the author information by telling students that Williams sought to write in the language of ordinary Americans. He was of mixed ancestry—his father English and his mother Spanish, French, Dutch, and Jewish—and he felt that the United States was the only country he could possibly call home. In his career as a doctor, Williams made many house calls and saw the people in his community through all stages of life. Whenever a poetic phrase came to his mind, he would grab a prescription form or any available scrap of paper to jot it down. Such images from real life in Rutherford, New Jersey, formed the basis of his uniquely American poetry and prose.

AS YOU READ Direct students to use the As You Read note to focus their reading.

Background *In the early 20th century, American poetry was heavily influenced by the literary movement known as modernism. Poets such as Ezra Pound, T. S. Eliot, and William Carlos Williams experimented with literary form, rarely using regular meter or rhyme schemes. They also avoided moral commentary, preferring to let images speak for themselves, which often made their poems difficult to interpret. Yet some famous poets of the period, including Robert Frost and Elinor Wylie, continued to use traditional forms and expressed their ideas more directly.*

Wild Peaches | Spring and All

Poem by Elinor Wylie | Poem by William Carlos Williams

Elinor Wylie (1885–1928) *led a life marked by scandal and personal tragedy, yet her poetry is restrained and traditional in form. She published her first volume anonymously in 1912. Her second volume,* Nets to Catch the Wind, *published in 1921, is considered by many critics to contain her best poems, including the widely anthologized "Velvet Shoes" and the poem in this lesson, "Wild Peaches." Her work was well received by critics and readers during her lifetime; she went on to write three more volumes of poetry as well as four novels. After Wylie's death, her poetry fell out of fashion, but since the 1980s it has experienced a revival of interest.*

William Carlos Williams (1883–1963) *lived an outwardly conventional life as a full-time medical doctor in the city of his birth, Rutherford, New Jersey, yet his poetry was highly innovative. Inspired by his friendship with Ezra Pound, Williams developed a poetic style that was direct, vigorous, and unfettered by previous poetic conventions of form. His volume* Spring and All *contains not only this selection but some of his most famous poems, including the important "The Red Wheelbarrow." Modestly acclaimed in his lifetime, Williams is now recognized for significantly influencing several new schools of poetry, including the Beat movement.*

AS YOU READ Notice how each poet uses imagery to help readers visualize nature. Write down any questions you generate during reading.

TO CHALLENGE STUDENTS . . .

Research a Foundational Work What's so important about a red wheelbarrow? Ask students to locate the text of William Carlos Williams's poem "The Red Wheelbarrow" and research its place in the Imagist movement and in the broader history of American poetry. Have students discuss their findings and prepare a short presentation to the rest of the class that includes a reading of the poem and an explanation of its significance. They might present their information in the form of a dialogue between someone who's read the poem for the first time and doesn't see its value and another person who explains it.

Demonstrate Knowledge of Foundational Works

 COMMON CORE RL 9

(LINES 1–14)

Explain that a **pastoral** is a poem that celebrates the beauty of nature and the joys of a simple life in the country, often with a romantic partner.

 CITE TEXT EVIDENCE Ask students to identify words and phrases in Part 1 that present idealized images of nature, romance, and a simple life. *("We'll live among wild peach trees" and "You'll wear a coonskin cap, and I a gown/Homespun" suggest romantic bliss in a rural setting. "The autumn amber-hued, sunny and hot, / Tasting of cider and of scuppernong" and "The squirrels in their silver fur" create appealing images of nature.)* Which lines hint at a different attitude toward the situation? *(The last two lines in each stanza have a different tone. Lines 7–8 refer to lotus-eaters lost in oblivion and to drowning. Lines 13–14 describe the speaker's lover shooting squirrels out of the trees.)*

Analyze Structure

 COMMON CORE RL 5

(LINES 15–28)

Remind students that **traditional poetry** has certain predictable features. There is a **rhyme scheme,** or a regular pattern of rhyming words at the ends of lines. The length of the lines and the number of lines in each stanza also follow a regular pattern.

 ASK STUDENTS how they can tell from Part 2 that this poem has a traditional form. *(Part 2 follows the same pattern as Part 1. The first stanza has eight lines with a rhyme scheme of abbaabba. The second stanza has six lines with a rhyme scheme of cdceed. All lines are roughly the same length, with the same number of syllables.)*

Wild Peaches
by Elinor Wylie

1

When the world turns completely upside down
You say we'll emigrate to the Eastern Shore[1]
Aboard a river-boat from Baltimore;
We'll live among wild peach trees, miles from town,
5 You'll wear a coonskin cap, and I a gown
Homespun, dyed butternut's dark gold colour.
Lost, like your lotus-eating ancestor,[2]
We'll swim in milk and honey till we drown.

The winter will be short, the summer long,
10 The autumn amber-hued, sunny and hot,
Tasting of cider and of scuppernong;[3]
All seasons sweet, but autumn best of all.
The squirrels in their silver fur will fall
Like falling leaves, like fruit, before your shot.

2

15 The autumn frosts will lie upon the grass
Like bloom[4] on grapes of purple-brown and gold.
The misted early mornings will be cold;
The little puddles will be roofed with glass.
The sun, which burns from copper into brass,
20 Melts these at noon, and makes the boys unfold
Their knitted mufflers; full as they can hold,
Fat pockets dribble chestnuts as they pass.

Peaches grow wild, and pigs can live in clover;
A barrel of salted herrings lasts a year;
25 The spring begins before the winter's over.
By February you may find the skins
Of garter snakes and water moccasins[5]
Dwindled and harsh, dead-white and cloudy-clear.

---

[1] **Eastern Shore:** land on the east side of the Chesapeake Bay, part of the Delmarva Peninsula.

[2] **lotus-eating ancestor:** an allusion to the *Odyssey*, in which Odysseus encounters a lotus-eating society whose diet makes people forget their cares and become lazy.

[3] **scuppernong:** a type of grape native to the southeastern United States.

[4] **bloom:** a white, powdery coating that can form on the surface of fruits.

[5] **water moccasins:** thick-bodied, venomous snakes, also called cottonmouths.

486 Collection 6

SCAFFOLDING FOR ELL STUDENTS

Vocabulary Support Pair students with fluent partners to read the poem aloud and discuss challenging vocabulary. Make sure they understand the idiomatic expressions *milk and honey* in line 8 (abundance, plenty), *live in clover* in line 23 (live well), and *go begging* in line 33 (be left over or unwanted). Suggest that they make a chart or glossary of terms in categories such as clothing, animals, colors, and fruit. (Examples: clothing: *coonskin cap, gown, knitted mufflers;* animals: *squirrels, pigs, garter snakes, water moccasins, blackbird, partridge, quail, canvasback;* colors: *gold, amber-hued, silver, purple-brown, copper, brass, dead-white, blue, red, sombre-bloomed, black, bronze, pearly monotones, slate, milky, snowy gray;* fruit: *peaches, grapes, chestnuts, strawberries, plums, cherries, persimmons)*

3

When April pours the colours of a shell
30 Upon the hills, when every little creek
Is shot with silver from the Chesapeake
In shoals new-minted by the ocean swell,
When strawberries go begging, and the sleek
Blue plums lie open to the blackbird's beak,
35 We shall live well—we shall live very well.

The months between the cherries and the peaches
Are brimming cornucopias which spill
Fruits red and purple, sombre-bloomed and black;
Then, down rich fields and frosty river beaches
40 We'll trample bright persimmons, while you kill
Bronze partridge, speckled quail, and canvasback.[6]

4

Down to the Puritan marrow of my bones
There's something in this richness that I hate.
I love the look, austere, immaculate,
45 Of landscapes drawn in pearly monotones.
There's something in my very blood that owns
Bare hills, cold silver on a sky of slate,
A thread of water, churned to milky spate[7]
Streaming through slanted pastures fenced with stones.

50 I love those skies, thin blue or snowy gray,
Those fields sparse-planted, rendering meagre sheaves;
That spring, briefer than apple-blossom's breath,
Summer, so much too beautiful to stay,
Swift autumn, like a bonfire of leaves,
55 And sleepy winter, like the sleep of death.

---

[6] **canvasback:** a type of diving duck.
[7] **spate:** rising or flowing water.

Wild Peaches   **487**

Analyze Structure
COMMON CORE RL 5

(LINES 29–41)

Point out that poets may include a break in a traditional poem's form to create an effect.

C **CITE TEXT EVIDENCE** Ask how the form of Part 3 differs from Parts 1 and 2. *(The first stanza has seven lines with a break in the rhyme scheme for the missing line.)* Why might the poet have done this? *(The break suggests imperfections in the land of "milk and honey.")*

Demonstrate Knowledge of Foundational Works
COMMON CORE RL 9

(LINES 36–41)

Remind students that a pastoral poem traditionally paints an ideal picture of life in a rural setting.

D **CITE TEXT EVIDENCE** Have students identify words in lines 36–41 that create a jarring contrast to the images of beauty and abundance. *(*sombre-bloomed and black *and the words* trample *and* kill *clash with the positive images and optimistic mood.)*

Determine Themes
COMMON CORE RL 2

(LINES 42–55)

Remind students that poets use structure and language to convey **themes,** or insights about life.

E **ASK STUDENTS** to summarize the speaker's attitude about life on the Eastern Shore as expressed in Part 4. What theme does it convey? *(The speaker finds "something in this richness that I hate" preferring a more "austere" landscape. The theme is that there is a false quality to a life that is too rich and easy because it denies hardship and death.)* How does the poem's structure contribute to the theme? *(Parts 1–3 have positive images of the lush landscape and luxurious life, but each stanza hints at the speaker's struggles with darker thoughts. The last part expresses his disdain for the pastoral ideal and suggests a gradual awakening to the truth. People learn as they age that romantic ideals have little value because they ignore life's realities.)*

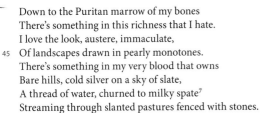

APPLYING ACADEMIC VOCABULARY

intensity	themes	visualize

As you discuss the poems, incorporate the Collection 6 academic vocabulary words *intensity, themes,* and *visualize.* In each poem, ask students to identify specific words and phrases that help them **visualize** the landscapes described. Discuss the **themes** expressed in the poems, and compare the **intensity** of feeling conveyed through the style and language of each poem.

Demonstrate Knowledge of Foundational Works COMMON CORE RL 9

(LINES 1–8)

Tell students that the images of nature in a traditional pastoral poem emphasize beauty and fertility.

 CITE TEXT EVIDENCE How do the images in lines 1–8 depart from the pastoral tradition? Cite specific words and phrases and the feelings they evoke. *(The poet begins by alluding to disease—with "the contagious hospital." The images are realistic rather than idealized. There are "blue / mottled clouds driven from the / northeast" by "a cold wind"—harsh, austere images. The speaker describes a landscape in very early spring, when the "muddy fields" are still "brown with dried weeds," instead of describing a later time with more evidence of budding life. A poet trying to paint an idealized picture would also have omitted the "patches of standing water," which sound stagnant and unattractive.)*

Analyze Structure COMMON CORE RL 5

(LINES 9–23)

Remind students that traditional forms of poetry feature regular patterns of rhyme, meter, and stanza length.

 ASK STUDENTS to describe the ways in which Williams departs from traditional form. *(There is no pattern of rhyming words at the ends of lines. The stanzas vary in length because the poet uses however many lines he requires to express an idea or image in each one. Several stanzas end in dashes, and the sentences are not strictly grammatical.)*

COLLABORATIVE DISCUSSION Have students pair up to discuss the question. Then have them share their conclusions with the class as a whole. *(Students may describe Wylie's description as extravagant with hints at disillusionment, while Williams is spare but precise. Wylie's images of nature in the first three parts are sensuous and rich. Williams creates an unflinchingly realistic landscape.)*

ASK STUDENTS to share any questions they generated in the course of reading and discussing the selections.

Spring and All
by William Carlos Williams

By the road to the contagious hospital[8]
under the surge of the blue
mottled clouds driven from the
northeast—a cold wind. Beyond, the
5   waste of broad, muddy fields
brown with dried weeds, standing and fallen

patches of standing water
the scattering of tall trees

All along the road the reddish
10   purplish, forked, upstanding, twiggy
stuff of bushes and small trees
with dead, brown leaves under them
leafless vines—

Lifeless in appearance, sluggish
15   dazed spring approaches—

They enter the new world naked,
cold, uncertain of all
save that they enter. All about them
the cold, familiar wind—

20   Now the grass, tomorrow
the stiff curl of wildcarrot leaf

One by one objects are defined—
It quickens: clarity, outline of leaf

But now the stark dignity of
25   entrance—Still, the profound change
has come upon them: rooted, they
grip down and begin to awaken

---

[8] **contagious hospital:** a medical facility for people with infectious diseases.

COLLABORATIVE DISCUSSION What adjectives would you apply to each poet's descriptive style? With a partner, compare your impressions of the landscape created by the imagery in each poem. Cite specific evidence from the poems to support your ideas.

WHEN STUDENTS STRUGGLE . . .

Tell students that Williams's poem is not entirely grammatical; there are many incomplete sentences intended to create an image but not to present a wholly formed thought. Readers are expected to piece together the fragmentary images into a complete picture. Use a whiteboard to display the poem, and work with students to divide it into meaningful sections of text. Discuss how Williams sometimes uses stanza breaks in place of end punctuation to signal where one image or idea ends and the next begins. *(Possible sections are lines 1–4 [through "a cold wind"], lines 4–8, lines 9–13, lines 14–15, lines 16–23, and lines 24–27.)*

ASK STUDENTS what the pronoun "They" in line 16 refers to. *(the "grass" and "wildcarrot leaf" in the next stanza)*

Demonstrate Knowledge of Foundational Works RL 9

For many centuries, poets who wrote about landscapes often followed the conventions of **pastoral** literature, which presents idealized scenes of nature populated with innocent shepherds and nymphs. Pastoral poems have a regular meter and rhyme, and they feature highly artificial language. The popularity of this genre faded in the 18th century, but echoes of it live on even today. Some modern poets have played off the tradition by alluding to pastoral themes, such as the carefree existence of country folk and the contrast between rural and urban life. Others have responded by rejecting any idealization of nature.

Both Wylie and Williams describe scenes of nature in their poems. To compare their depictions of landscape, examine the following elements:

- the types of images that appear in each poem, and the way in which these images are presented to allow the reader to visualize the landscape
- how each poet's word choices contribute to the speaker's tone
- the theme conveyed by each poem

Analyze Structure RL 5

Though both poems share a focus on nature, Wylie and Williams chose very different ways of presenting their ideas. "Wild Peaches" has a **traditional form**, with a regular pattern of rhyme and meter and mostly regular grouping of lines. "Spring and All" is an example of **organic form** because its free verse does not follow any fixed rules.

"Wild Peaches"	"Spring and All"
Wylie predominantly uses **iambic pentameter,** a pattern of alternating unstressed and stressed syllables in ten-syllable lines.	Williams's free verse does not have a regular meter or pattern of end rhyme.
Parts 1, 2, and 4 are **sonnets,** fourteen-line poems that have a regular pattern of end rhyme.	He uses **enjambment,** the continuation of a phrase or clause over a line break.
Wylie end-stops many of her lines, using semicolons, commas, or periods.	Williams uses dashes at the end of several of his lines. The two periods in the poem occur within lines, not at the end of lines.

Consider how the authors' choices affect the meaning and aesthetic impact of their poems.

Demonstrate Knowledge of Foundational Works RL 9

Review the instruction with students. Then show them an example of a pastoral landscape painting. Ask them to identify aspects of the painting that place it in the pastoral genre, such as lush vegetation, people living a simple but happy life, and so on. Point out that these are the kinds of details a traditional pastoral poem would include.

Ask students what words might describe the tone of a pastoral poem toward nature. *(enthralled, awed, grateful)* Discuss how a poet might express a different tone, such as distaste. *(by choosing details that show unappealing aspects of nature)*

Analyze Structure RL 5

Review the information in the chart and discuss how the details illustrate the differences between traditional and organic form. Point out that Wylie's sonnets could be classified as Petrarchan sonnets because each is divided into an octave (eight lines) and a sestet (six lines). Read aloud several lines to illustrate the rhythm of iambic pentameter. Ask students to describe the aesthetic impact of this traditional form. *(The sound devices of rhyme and rhythm create a musical effect.)* What aesthetic effect might an organic form have? *(Some readers may find a freer, more natural use of language more pleasing.)*

Strategies for Annotation  Annotate it!

Demonstrate Knowledge of Foundational Works RL 9

Share these strategies for guided or independent analysis:

- Highlight in green words and phrases that create images of nature you would expect to find in a traditional pastoral.
- Highlight in blue words and phrases that create contrasting images and feelings.
- On notes, describe the tone conveyed by each set of words and by the contrast between them.

The months between the cherries and the peaches

Are brimming cornucopias which spill

Fruits red and purple, sombre-bloomed and black;

Then, down rich fields and frosty river beaches

We'll trample bright persimmons, while you kill

Bronze partridge, speckled quail, and canvasback.

> Contrast between "trample" and "bright persimmons" creates ambivalent or ironic tone.

PRACTICE & APPLY

Analyzing the Text 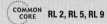 RL 2, RL 5, RL 9

Possible answers:

1. Examples include "autumn amber-hued... / Tasting of cider" [lines 10–11] and "When April pours the colours of a shell / Upon the hills" [lines 29–30]. These details set up an expectation of an ideal and happy existence.

2. The speaker views with distaste the abundance and lushness described in the first three parts. Instead of riotous warmth and spilled fruits, she prefers austerity and coldness: "I love the look, austere, immaculate, / Of landscapes drawn in pearly monotones" [lines 44-45].

3. These words remind that nothing lasts. The most beautiful of seasons is transient; a life of plenty is not permanent. The poet might also mean that a life of the senses is destructive to those who indulge in it. These ideas overturn the pastoral ideal that nature can nurture a utopian life.

4. Wylie uses content and structure to contrast between luxuriance and austerity. The poem is a "brimming cornucopia" of imagery. But her structure is restrained with its precise meter and rhyme scheme. She focuses readers' attention on the individual lines enabling them to absorb ideas more clearly than they could with a looser structure.

5. Williams uses parallel prepositional phrases to draw the reader into the scene: "By the road," "under the surge," and "Beyond." After line 6, he inserts a stanza break, followed by the first of four couplets, each of which focuses the reader's eye on a part of the scene. Repetitions drive home the stark images: "cold wind" [lines 4 and 19]; "brown" [lines 6 and 12]; a third instance of "cold" [line 17].

6. The images of winter are barren and cheerless, not the idealized setting of a pastoral poem. But spring returns, bringing with it life that "quickens." This theme of rebirth and renewal is connected to the pastoral tradition, but here rebirth is tested by cold, inhospitable elements.

7. The speaker's objective tone in "Spring and All" clarifies his or her role as that of detached observer. The speaker in "Wild Peaches" is a participant in the poem whose ambivalence toward nature brings out the theme.

8. "Spring and All" begins with images of the barrenness of winter and lack of life. Yet the poem celebrates hard-won renewal. "Wild Peaches" begins by celebrating the bounty of nature, yet the poet reminds us that everything dies.

Assess It!

Analyzing the Text  COMMON CORE RL 2, RL 5, RL 9, W 9a

Cite Text Evidence   Support your responses with evidence from the selections.

1. **Cite Evidence** Identify details that Wylie uses to idealize the Eastern shore landscape in parts 1–3 of the poem. What expectation do these details create for readers?

2. **Analyze** What conflict does Wylie introduce with the lines "Down to the Puritan marrow of my bones / There's something in this richness that I hate"? How do the lines in the stanza develop this conflict?

3. **Draw Conclusions** What do the words "briefer," "too beautiful to stay," and "sleep of death" in the last stanza of Wylie's poem suggest about nature's bounty and a life of plenty and ease? Do these ideas support or overturn the conventions of pastoral poetry? Explain.

4. **Evaluate** How does Wylie use the structure of "Wild Peaches" to help develop the poem's ideas? Would an organic form have been as effective? Why or why not.

5. **Analyze** Although William Carlos Williams rejected traditional verse forms, he still believed that it was important to use poetic devices to distinguish verse from prose. What poetic devices does he use in "Spring and All"? How do these devices draw attention to significant images in the poem?

6. **Draw Conclusions** What theme does "Spring and All" convey about nature? Discuss how this theme relates to the conventions of pastoral poetry.

7. **Compare** Compare the tones of "Wild Peaches" and "Spring and All." How does the tone of each poem reflect the role of the speaker?

8. **Evaluate** Both poems end with a shift in thought or a reversal of expectations. Discuss the shift or reversal in each poem, and explain whether you think it provides an effective conclusion.

PERFORMANCE TASK

Writing Activity: Opinion Which poem speaks to you on a more personal level? Why?

- Choose your favorite of the two poems. Identify reasons that you prefer it, including ideas related to content, style, and form. Incorporate details from the poem to support your reasons.

- Consider why the other poem does not appeal to you in the same way. Identify specific reasons.

- Organize your ideas logically and present them in a brief written analysis.

Assign this performance task.

PERFORMANCE TASK   COMMON CORE W 9a

Writing Activity: Opinion As students gather evidence and begin to draft their essays, encourage them to use precise literary terms such as *pastoral, traditional form, organic form, rhyme, meter, enjambment,* and *imagery.* Students' essays should include thoughtful reasons and support that shows their understanding of both poems.

Analyze Word Choice

COMMON CORE
RL 4

TEACH

Point out that one of the central characteristics of traditional pastoral literature is the **tone,** or attitude, it expresses toward nature, love, and life in a rural setting. This tone is generally celebratory, since the subjects are portrayed in an idealized or romanticized way. As in all forms of writing, authors of pastorals achieve their tone through the deliberate choice of words and details.

Review the poets' choice of words in these passages and discuss the tone created in each case:

- "Wild Peaches," lines 42–49 (*The speaker's tone toward the landscape is explicitly stated in lines 44–45: "I love the look . . . / Of landscapes drawn in pearly monotones." Some of the descriptive words Wylie chooses underscore the cold beauty she admires: "immaculate," "pearly," "cold silver." Knowing the speaker's attitude infuses other words that could be neutral or negative with a sense of beauty: "austere," "Bare hills," "churned to milky spate."*)

- "Spring and All," lines 16–27 (*Williams's speaker does not state his or her attitude directly; it must be inferred from subtle word choices. Earlier stanzas describe a landscape that appears mostly dead. Here, however, signs of life are beginning to emerge. Words and phrases such as "clarity," "stark dignity," "profound," and "rooted, they/grip down and begin to awaken" suggest admiration and respect for the forces of life that reawaken each spring. The new plants "enter the new world naked, / cold, uncertain of all," and yet they persevere.*)

PRACTICE AND APPLY

Have students locate a painting or photograph of a landscape that they find intriguing. The landscape might be appealing, repugnant, or something in between. Ask them to write a short poem that conveys their attitude toward the landscape through carefully chosen words, details, and images. They may write in free verse or a traditional form. Then have students exchange poems with a partner. Partners should analyze each other's poems and identify the tone. Have them discuss whether each poem is successful in conveying the intended tone and which words and phrases are most effective.

Analyze Structure

COMMON CORE
RL 5

RETEACH

Review the terms *traditional poetry* and *organic poetry.* Remind students of these features of a traditional poem:

- It has a regular pattern of end rhyme. The first four lines of "Wild Peaches" end with the words *down, Shore, Baltimore,* and *town,* creating a **rhyme scheme** of *abba.*

- It has a regular **meter** created by a pattern of stressed syllables. A common meter in English is **iambic pentameter:** each line has five units (feet) made up of an unstressed syllable and a stressed syllable.

- Each stanza has a predictable number of lines, although the poet may break the pattern. In "Wild Peaches," the stanzas generally alternate between eight and six lines.

An organic poem, also called **free verse,** often has none of these features. The rhythm is more like everyday speech, and the length of lines and stanzas is determined by the ideas the poet wants to express. "Spring and All" is an organic poem.

LEVEL UP TUTORIALS Assign the following *Level Up* tutorial: **Elements of Poetry**

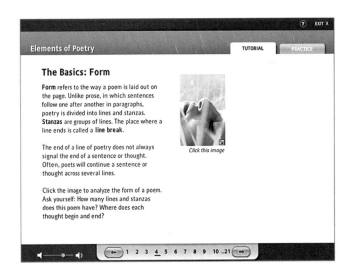

CLOSE READING APPLICATION

Have students locate two poems, one traditional and the other organic. Working independently or in pairs, ask them to compare and contrast the structure of the poems, including rhyme scheme, meter, and stanza length. Also have them evaluate how the form of each poem reflects the poet's message.

Pastorals

Pastoral

by William Carlos Williams

Pastoral

by Jennifer Chang

Why These Texts

Certain poems allude to, or "play off," poetic conventions of the past. These poems by William Carlos Williams and Jennifer Chang are such poems, both alluding to the centuries-old convention of pastoral poetry. Readers of poetry may be unaware of the conventions that a poet incorporates into his or her poem, and this can diminish readers' understanding of such poems. Recognizing how poets incorporate older conventions can make reading their poems more interesting.

Background Have students read the background information about the conventions of pastoral poetry as well as the biographical information about the two poets, William Carlos Williams and Jennifer Chang. Tell students that having an understanding of the conventions of pastoral poetry of the past will help them appreciate the more contemporary take on the convention displayed here by Williams and Chang.

AS YOU READ Tell students to pay close attention to how the two poems treat the idealized view of country life, rustic characters, and details from the natural world.

Common Core Support

- cite strong and thorough textual evidence
- analyze how an author's choices concerning structure contribute to meaning and aesthetic impact

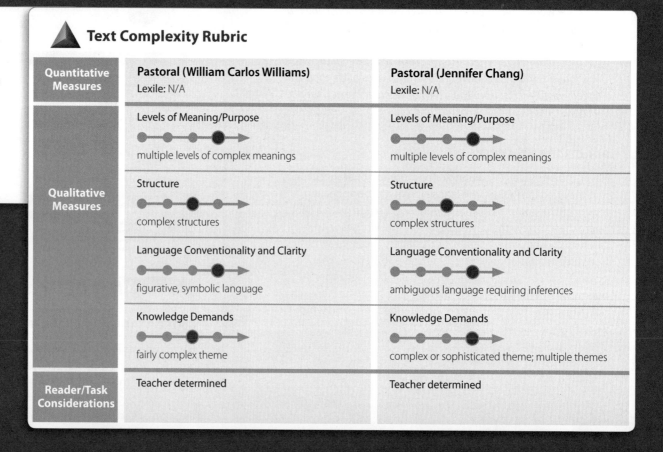

Text Complexity Rubric

	Pastoral (William Carlos Williams) Lexile: N/A	Pastoral (Jennifer Chang) Lexile: N/A
Quantitative Measures		
Qualitative Measures	Levels of Meaning/Purpose multiple levels of complex meanings	Levels of Meaning/Purpose multiple levels of complex meanings
	Structure complex structures	Structure complex structures
	Language Conventionality and Clarity figurative, symbolic language	Language Conventionality and Clarity ambiguous language requiring inferences
	Knowledge Demands fairly complex theme	Knowledge Demands complex or sophisticated theme; multiple themes
Reader/Task Considerations	Teacher determined	Teacher determined

Strategies for CLOSE READING

Analyze Structure

Students should read both poems carefully, noting how the two poets present their ideas about the natural world, including the use of free verse and the repetition of words. Close-reading questions will help students cite text evidence that will help them analyze the structure of each poem. Students should jot down in the margin their responses to the Read questions.

WHEN STUDENTS STRUGGLE . . .

To help students recognize and analyze the structure of each poem, have them work in small groups to fill out a chart like the one shown below.

CITE TEXT EVIDENCE For practice analyzing the structure of poetry, ask students to cite evidence, or lack thereof, from each poem to support their responses to each category in the chart below.

"Pastoral" by William Carlos Williams	"Pastoral" by Jennifer Chang
Poetic Form: free verse	Poetic Form: free verse
Rhyme: no	Rhyme: no
Repeated Words: none	Repeated Words: Something; hyphenated "noise" words

Background *Pastoral poetry—a tradition stretching back to the ancient Greeks—presents an idealized vision of simple country life, describing bucolic landscapes, shepherds and their flocks, and the glory of nature. Even after its popularity faded in the eighteenth century, poets continued to refer to the pastoral style and ideas—contrasting rural and urban settings, and lamenting the loss of a simpler and truer connection between humankind and the natural world.*

Pastorals

Pastoral . . . . William Carlos Williams
Pastoral . . . . Jennifer Chang

William Carlos Williams *(1883–1963), one of the most influential poets of the twentieth century, lived most of his life in Rutherford, New Jersey. He was both a doctor and a writer, keeping up a medical practice and becoming a prolific and successful poet, playwright, essayist, and novelist. Williams advocated "the local," taking his subject matter from the lives and circumstances of ordinary people. "Pastoral" is one of several poems he wrote with the same name.*

Jennifer Chang *was also born in New Jersey. "Pastoral" is from her first book of poems,* The History of Anonymity, *published in 2008. Her poetry has appeared in many prestigious publications, including* Poetry, The New Republic, The Kenyon Review, *and* The Nation. *Her lyrical poems often connect the natural world with the emotional world of the self. Chang also co-chairs the advisory board of Kundiman, an organization dedicated to the support and promotion of Asian American poetry.*

119

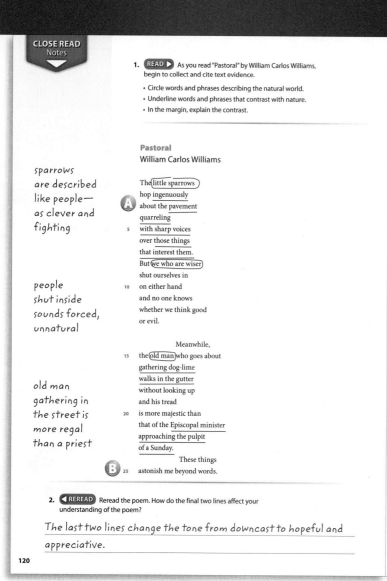

CLOSE READ Notes

1. **READ ▶** As you read "Pastoral" by William Carlos Williams, begin to collect and cite text evidence.

- Circle words and phrases describing the natural world.
- Underline words and phrases that contrast with nature.
- In the margin, explain the contrast.

Pastoral
William Carlos Williams

sparrows are described like people— as clever and fighting

The little sparrows
hop ingenuously
about the pavement
quarreling
5 with sharp voices
over those things
that interest them.
But we who are wiser
shut ourselves in
10 on either hand
and no one knows
whether we think good
or evil.

people shut inside sounds forced, unnatural

Meanwhile,
15 the old man who goes about
gathering dog-lime
walks in the gutter
without looking up
and his tread
20 is more majestic than
that of the Episcopal minister
approaching the pulpit
of a Sunday.
These things
25 astonish me beyond words.

old man gathering in the street is more regal than a priest

2. **◀ REREAD** Reread the poem. How do the final two lines affect your understanding of the poem?

The last two lines change the tone from downcast to hopeful and appreciative.

120

CLOSE READ Notes

3. **READ ▶** As you read "Pastoral" by Jennifer Chang, continue to cite text evidence.

- Circle each use of the word *something*.
- Underline text that describes something wrong or unnatural.
- In the margin, note when the author contradicts herself.

Pastoral
Jennifer Chang

Something in the field is
working away. Root-noise.
Twig-noise. Plant
of weak chlorophyll, no
5 name for it. Something
in the field has mastered
distance by living too close
to fences. Yellow fruit, has it
pit or seeds? Stalk of wither. Grass-
10 noise fighting weed-noise. Dirt
and chant. Something in the
field. Coreopsis.[1] I did not mean
to say that. Yellow petal, has it
wither-gift? Has it gorgeous
15 rash? Leaf-loss and worried
sprout, its bursting art. Something in the. Field fallowed and
cicada. I did not mean to
say. Has it roar and bloom?
20 Has it road and follow? A thistle
prick, fraught burrs, such
easy attachment. Stem-
and stamen-noise. Can I lime-
flower? Can I chamomile?[2]
25 Something in the field cannot.

she doesn't know what is in the field

does the fruit have pits or seeds?

she misspeaks

she misspeaks again

she seems to misuse words

[1] **coreopsis:** a plant of the daisy family, with bright yellow flowers.
[2] **chamomile:** an herb also of the daisy family, with small, aromatic white flowers often used to make an herbal tea.

121

---

1. **READ AND CITE TEXT EVIDENCE** Remind students that one of the conventions of pastoral poetry of the past was to include details about nature and the setting.

Ⓐ **ASK STUDENTS** to identify the detail from lines 1–7 that most differs from an idealized natural pastoral world. *pavement; there would not have been paved roads or sidewalks in the fields hundreds of years ago.*

2. **REREAD AND CITE TEXT EVIDENCE** Remind students that the tone of a poem can change quickly and that they must read it carefully to understand these changes in tone.

Ⓑ **ASK STUDENTS** to identify the words in the last two lines that change the tone of the poem. *astonish, beyond words*

FOR ELL STUDENTS Point out that *ingenuously* is an adverb formed from the adjective *ingenuous*; Spanish speakers will recognize the cognate *ingenuo*, and understand that *ingenuously* means "in a frank or straightforward manner."

3. **READ AND CITE TEXT EVIDENCE** You may wish to point out the pronunciation of the word *coreopsis*, noting that the accent is on the third syllable.

Ⓒ **ASK STUDENTS** to explain what they think the speaker thinks the word *something* means in the poem. *Possible response: The speaker does not seem to know exactly what the word* something *means. It seems to refer to some abstract quality, or essence, associated with the field.*

CLOSE READ
Notes

4. ◀ **REREAD** As you reread the poem, note the poet's use of sentence fragments, hyphenated words, non-traditional syntax, and sudden line breaks. How does this chaotic structure affect your experience as a reader?

The jumbled and hectic mix in the presentation make the reading experience halting, tense, and confusing. The author's word choices and structure create a tone of struggle and bewilderment which conflicts with the pastoral ideals of natural simplicity and beauty.

SHORT RESPONSE

Cite Text Evidence Compare how the two poems entitled "Pastoral"—published almost 100 years apart—play on the traditional pastoral form which presents idealized scenes of nature. What is each poem saying about the relationship between humankind and nature? Be sure to **cite text evidence** in your response.

Williams modernizes the pastoral by setting it in a city where the sparrows "hop ingeniously . . . quarreling." The speaker seems more touched by the old man than anything specific in nature. Williams's poem finds the ordinary and the everyday beautiful. Chang's poem focuses on images of nature, but presents the speaker as unsure and even confused. The speaker seems to relate to the struggles in nature, the "working away" of "something in the field" and the conflicting ideas of beauty and danger in terms like "gorgeous rash" and "roar and bloom."

122

TO CHALLENGE STUDENTS . . .

Students might be interested to learn that Williams wrote several other poems titled "Pastoral." Encourage students to research (in libraries and online) and compare these similarly titled poems, noting their structures and poetic features.

ASK STUDENTS to create a brief class presentation exploring the poems. Have students:

- read aloud or present for the class the poems they have chosen.
- describe the poetic structure of the different poems.
- identify any conventions used in the poems.

Have students discuss what interests them most about the poems. Encourage them to also discuss what they like or dislike about the poems.

DIG DEEPER

With the class, return to Question 2, Reread, on page 120. Have students share and discuss their responses.

ASK STUDENTS to identify details throughout the poem that help create its tone.

- Have students identify details that establish the rather dismal or "downcast" tone of much of the poem. *lines 9–13: "shut ourselves in, no one knows/whether we think good/or evil"; lines 15–19: "old man, gathering dog-lime, in the gutter, without looking up."*
- Have students describe the change in tone that occurs at the end of the Williams poem. *The speaker's claim that all of the "downcast" details astonish him is surprising and changes the tone to one of amazement at human activity.*

ASK STUDENTS to return to their response to Question 2 and revise it based on their discussion.

---

4. **REREAD AND CITE TEXT EVIDENCE** Help students identify examples of "chaotic structure" in the poem.

Ⓓ **ASK STUDENTS** to point out examples of sentence fragments, hyphenated words, and non-traditional syntax in lines 1–5 of the poem. *Sentence fragments/hyphenated words: "Root-noise, Twig-noise"; Non-traditional syntax: "Plant of weak chlorophyll, no name for it."*

SHORT RESPONSE

Cite Text Evidence Students' responses will vary, but they should cite evidence from the text to support their answers. Students should:

- identify details from each poem that use the traditions of pastoral poetry.
- explain what each poem says about the relationship between humans and the natural world.
- cite specific evidence from the text to support their ideas.

*my*SmartPlanner — Create lesson plans and access resources online.

Being Here: The Art of Dan Horgan

Documentary directed by Russ Spencer

Why This Text?

Students regularly encounter documentary films in the theater, online, or in broadcast media. This lesson explores a documentary about environmental artist Dan Horgan that uses video footage, music, and commentary to present information.

Key Learning Objective: The student will be able to integrate and evaluate information presented in film footage and an audio track.

COMMON CORE — Common Core Standards

RI 2 Determine two or more central ideas of a text and provide an objective summary.

RI 7 Integrate and evaluate information presented in different media.

SL 5 Make strategic use of digital media in presentations.

▲ Text Complexity Rubric

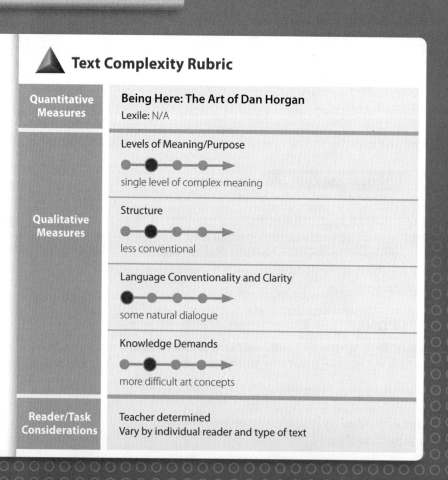

Quantitative Measures

Being Here: The Art of Dan Horgan
Lexile: N/A

Qualitative Measures

Levels of Meaning/Purpose
single level of complex meaning

Structure
less conventional

Language Conventionality and Clarity
some natural dialogue

Knowledge Demands
more difficult art concepts

Reader/Task Considerations

Teacher determined
Vary by individual reader and type of text

TEACH

CLOSE READ

Background Dan Horgan's boyhood home at the base of the Sierra foothills inspired his love of nature and of tulips, his favorite flower. The Sierra foothills is an area between Yosemite and Kings Canyon National Parks with grasslands, foothills, and forests. Dan Horgan's love of nature sustained him when he returned from Vietnam after being drafted into the Marine Corps in 1964. His work is inspired by and includes natural elements such as rocks, shells, sand, straw, and pinecones.

AS YOU VIEW Instruct students to use the As You View note to focus their viewing. Remind them to write down any questions they generate as they view the selection.

Integrate and Evaluate Information

COMMON CORE RI 7

Tell students that this documentary contains moving images, spoken commentary by the subject of the video, and music. Students need to integrate, or bring together, these visual and audio elements to evaluate the filmmaker's meaning and purpose. Students will need to make **inferences,** or logical assumptions based on details in the documentary and their own knowledge and experience, to reach their conclusions.

 ASK STUDENTS how the filmmaker helps the viewer consider Horgan's comments about his art—for example, the piece created using the students at the school. *(The filmmaker uses the background music to string together images of pieces. This pause in the artist's narration gives the viewer several moments to think about what the artist has said and consider how it relates to the art he has created.)* Ask students to explain why the filmmaker has the artist talk about pieces created in different locations. *(The filmmaker wants to show viewers the breadth of Horgan's work. Without the film, many viewers would not have the opportunity to see or understand these works of art. The artist's explanation helps viewers understand his perspective, but the film also allows viewers time to bring their own perspectives to the works of art.)*

COLLABORATIVE DISCUSSION Before students work with their partners, lead a class discussion about how the craft of the filmmaker and the addition of the soundtrack help convey information about the artist. Ask students to comment on what they know about the artist's character due to the interaction of the background music and the gentle motion of the film shots.

Background *Dan Horgan grew up on a farm in California. He loved the outdoors and created his first garden at age nine, planting tulips and rimming the edge with rocks. When he came home from serving in the Vietnam War, Horgan needed to restore his inner balance. He did so by designing landscapes that incorporated both rocks and plants. Then, in the 1990s, he was galvanized by the work of artist Andy Goldsworthy to focus on creating art just with rocks. His art pieces are built and left in the environments that inspired them, keeping Horgan close to the nature that he loves.*

MEDIA ANALYSIS

Being Here: The Art of Dan Horgan

Documentary directed by Russ Spencer

AS YOU VIEW Pay attention to the methods the filmmaker uses to reveal Horgan's personality and attitude toward his art.

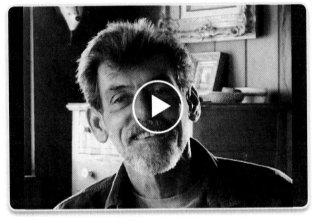

Image Credits: ©Bison Films

COLLABORATIVE DISCUSSION What is your impression of Horgan? With a partner, discuss how the filmmaker uses his craft to convey important aspects of the artist's character.

Being Here: The Art of Dan Horgan **491**

SCAFFOLDING FOR ELL STUDENTS

Culture: Comprehension Support Have students work in pairs with native English speakers to view the film and identify things they would like to know more about. Have pairs research or define terms and answer questions about ideas such as the following:

- "Andy Goldsworthy:" What similarities are there between Dan Horgan's work and the work of Andy Goldsworthy, an artist who inspired Horgan? *(Both work with natural materials that they find, and they create art pieces that they leave behind at the sites where they find the materials.)*

- "oblique light:" Why might oblique light be important to Dan Horgan's sand pieces? *(Oblique light, or light from an angle, highlights the sand pieces and creates shadows that define the image.)*

Integrate and Evaluate Information

 COMMON CORE RI 7

Help students integrate and evaluate visual information from the film by reviewing terms such as *tilt, pan, zoom in, zoom out, widen out, camera angle, close up,* and *aerial view.* Challenge students to think about how the filmmaker views the subject and brings his vision of the art to the viewer.

Analyzing the Media

 COMMON CORE RI 7

Possible answers:

1. *The camera is continually in motion when filming the art. It tilts and pans across the sculptures and their settings, then zooms in or widens out. This motion brings the sculptures to life. The cinematographer uses multiple camera angles from which to view the same piece. The audience can see details in the close-ups and the physical context of the art in wide shots. Aerial views reveal the way in which a piece integrates into the landscape.*

2. *In his creative process Horgan sees himself as a partner with nature. He works primarily with rocks, although he will, at times, employ other materials that he finds at a site. He sees rocks as the "bones of the planet." He explains that the environment inspires him to create certain shapes in his art. For example, the Navajo Sentinel mirrors forms in the landscape. Horgan builds in the wilderness because he feels no need to take his work away with him. He explains that he "sets his art free," and the liberating process of creating it sets him free as well.*

3. *Spencer's purpose is to show how Horgan's art is a natural outgrowth of his personality and beliefs. His work is integral to his nature; it is organic. The filmmaker accomplishes this purpose by having Horgan discuss his creative process as his works of art appear on film. This approach merges artist and art, allowing viewers to understand exactly how ideas become tangible and why they must take a certain form. The background music also contributes: it echoes the feelings of the art and draws the audience's attention to particular pieces.*

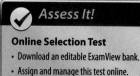

Assess It!

Online Selection Test
- Download an editable ExamView bank.
- Assign and manage this test online.

Integrate and Evaluate Information

 COMMON CORE RI 7

A documentary is a nonfiction film that provides information about a social, political, or historical subject. In this film about artist Dan Horgan, the filmmaker provides footage of Horgan and his works as well as an audio track with background music and the artist's commentary on his process. To evaluate how these different media build the audience's understanding of the subject, consider what these features contribute to the film:

Visual	Sound
• the movement of the camera • the variety of camera angles used • the synchronization of the commentary with the images • the appearance of the artist at the beginning and at the close of this segment	• the sound of the artist's own voice talking about the creative process • the content of the artist's commentary • the choice of background music

Analyzing the Media

 COMMON CORE RI 7, SL 5

Cite Text Evidence   Support your responses with evidence from the selection.

1. **Analyze** What camera techniques are used to film Horgan's art, such as the *Navajo Sentinel?* Explain how these techniques influence the audience's perception of the art.

2. **Cite Evidence** How do Horgan's insights about his creative process help viewers understand the choice of materials, location, form, and themes of his work? Cite specific comments that relate to these ideas in your response.

3. **Evaluate** Explain how the different media used by the filmmaker all work together to help achieve the purpose of this documentary.

PERFORMANCE TASK

Media Activity: Art Analysis Complete these activities independently.

- Review the clip, identifying two or three of Horgan's works that provoke a reaction in you.

- Create speaking notes that explain what you see, feel, and think about the form, materials, location, and meaning of each work. Draw from what you have learned about Horgan's art in the video.

- Present your critique to the class, pausing the film at each work of art that you have chosen.

- Invite classmates to share their ideas about the work as well.

Assign this performance task.

PERFORMANCE TASK

 COMMON CORE SL 5

Media Activity: Art Analysis After students select the works that most appeal to them, ask them to write down a few initial impressions and interpretations for each one. Then have pairs identify their selections, share their notes, and ask questions about each partner's ideas. Students' presentations of their analyses should demonstrate a grasp of Horgan's artistic principles and his ability to apply them to specific works of art.

Determine Central Ideas

COMMON CORE

RI 2

TEACH

Explain to students that the **central ideas** of a documentary are the most important points conveyed in the film. Sometimes the central ideas are stated or shown specifically, but more often, the central ideas need to be **inferred,** or deduced, from specific images or soundtrack details. Remind students to keep notes while viewing a documentary to understand the development of the central ideas over the course of the film. Have students use these strategies.

- Identify the topic or subject of each part of the documentary, which can usually be stated in one or two words. Point out that *Being Here: The Art of Dan Horgan* can be separated by the works of art presented.

- If the images or soundtrack don't give explicit information about the topic, infer the main ideas from the details presented.

- Listen for information that Dan Horgan gives in his narration about the main idea or message of his work.

- Consider how the topic of each section relates to the title of the documentary.

PRACTICE AND APPLY

Organize students into small groups. Have each group discuss these questions:

- What does the title of the documentary suggest about the central ideas of the documentary? *(The central ideas will be connected to art and to Dan Horgan.)*

- How does the filmmaker's use of camera angles, lighting, and soundtrack support the central ideas? *(The filmmaker uses camera angles to highlight each artwork. The use of natural lighting emphasizes the idea that this art is an extension of the environment, an idea that is reinforced by the artist describing his work.)*

- What central ideas is the filmmaker trying to convey? *(Possible answer: Creating art or viewing art is a way to maintain a balance in life. Art is an extension of "being here," or staying aware of the artistry available in each moment and environment.)*

Have groups write an objective summary of their answers. Then have them use their summaries to discuss how the central ideas have influenced the way they view their environment and the possibilities for artistic expression.

Integrate and Evaluate Information

COMMON CORE

RI 7

RETEACH

Review with students that there are several sources of information and ideas in *Being Here: The Art of Dan Horgan:* the video footage that Russ Spencer has shot, the soundtrack of Dan Horgan discussing his work, and the music used in the background. Tell students that to integrate these sources of information and evaluate how successful the filmmaker has been in answering his audience's questions about the topic, they should consider the following:

- Why are Dan Horgan's descriptions of his thought process and ideas for each work of art important?

- How would you describe the camera angles used in the film? Why might the filmmaker have chosen to shoot the pieces of art from different angles?

- What mood does the music in the film convey? How does it help the audience understand the art and the artist?

- How do the images, words, and music interact in the documentary to answer questions about Horgan's work?

 LEVEL UP TUTORIALS Assign the following *Level Up* tutorial: **Synthesizing Information**

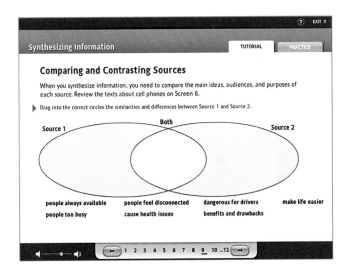

CLOSE READING APPLICATION

Have students choose a topic about which they have questions and then find one or more documentaries about that subject online. Tell students to synthesize the information they learn about their topic in a paragraph.

Dwellings

Essay by Linda Hogan

Why This Text?

Well-written essays may state connections between ideas directly, or imply them and rely on readers to make the connections. At the same time, a writer's cultural background and beliefs may strongly affect the content and message of the essay. This lesson explores both the explicit and implied connections between the natural world and people and the impact of a writer's cultural experiences.

Key Learning Objective: The student will be able to make inferences about the author's ideas, supporting them with evidence from the text, and identify the effect of the author's cultural context.

For practice and application:

Close Reader selection
"Trees"
Essay by Baron Wormser

COMMON CORE   Common Core Standards

RI 1   Cite textual evidence to support inferences.
RI 2   Determine the central ideas of a text.
RI 3   Analyze a set of complex ideas or events.
RI 4   Determine figurative meanings.
RI 6   Analyze an author's style.
RI 10 Comprehend literary nonfiction.
W 2   Write informative/explanatory texts to convey complex ideas.
L 3   Understand how language functions in different contexts.

▲ Text Complexity Rubric

Quantitative Measures	**Dwellings** Lexile: 1070L
Qualitative Measures	**Levels of Meaning/Purpose**  more than one purpose; implied but easy to infer
	Structure  organization of main ideas and details complex but mostly explicit; may exhibit disciplinary traits
	Language Conventionality and Clarity clear, direct language
	Knowledge Demands some specialized knowledge required
Reader/Task Considerations	Teacher determined Vary by individual reader and type of text

TEACH

CLOSE READ

Linda Hogan Have students read the information about the author. Tell them that this essay is the title essay from a book of essays subtitled *A Spiritual History of the Living World*. Explain that in her writing Hogan combines Native American spiritual beliefs with knowledge of modern science and history. Discuss or explain the meaning of the phrase "ecologically sound, indigenous environmental practices" as it is used in the background material *(practices that do not harm the balance of nature in the long run and that have been practiced by people native to an area).*

AS YOU READ Direct students to use the As You Read note to focus their reading.

Support Inferences COMMON CORE RI 1

(LINES 1–13)

Point out that authors try to share ideas with readers. Sometimes they state these ideas explicitly but, at other times, readers must make inferences to understand them. Review that inferences are logical assumptions that readers can make by combining text evidence with their own prior knowledge and experience.

Ⓐ CITE TEXT EVIDENCE Ask students to examine lines 1–13 to determine Hogan's relationship with nature. What does she share explicitly? What must readers infer? *(Possible answer: She is a close observer of nature who respects and admires the natural world. She states this explicitly in lines 4–7 by suggesting the eroded wall of earth is "something wonderful" and represents something as "intricate and well made" as human-made things. Readers can infer from "This hill is a place that could be the starry skies of night . . ." that Hogan feels there is a connection between the environment's smaller and larger elements.)*

Analyze Key Terms (LINE 13) COMMON CORE RI 4

In order to develop an idea or theme, an author may use a certain word or phrase in a unique way, or in a way that expands upon the literal meaning of the word or phrase.

Ⓑ ASK STUDENTS to define the phrase "dwelling places" in line 13, using a dictionary if necessary. Ask them how using this term to describe bee tunnels affects the reader's view of the bees. *(a home, abode, most often used in reference to humans; the phrase suggests the bees and their work is important and worthy of notice)*

Linda Hogan *has received many awards for her writing. Much of her work focuses on environmental themes, often from a Native American perspective. She especially wants to help people understand the importance of ecologically sound, indigenous environmental practices. Hogan says she had no idea that writing would become her profession. In her private journals, she found herself focusing on nature and realized that she could convey her ideas to a wider audience by making them public. She is currently the Writer in Residence for the Chickasaw Nation.*

Dwellings

Essay by Linda Hogan

AS YOU READ Consider what you learn about the author from the details in this essay. Write down any questions you generate during reading.

Ⓐ Not far from where I live is a hill that was cut into by the moving water of a creek. Eroded this way, all that's left of it is a broken wall of earth that contains old roots and pebbles woven together and exposed. Seen from a distance, it is only a rise of raw earth. But up close it is something wonderful, a small cliff dwelling that looks almost as intricate and well made as those the Anasazi[1] left behind when they vanished mysteriously centuries ago. This hill is a place that could be the starry skies of night turned inward into the thousand round holes where solitary bees have lived and died. It is a hill of tunneling rooms.
10 At the mouths of some of the excavations, half-circles of clay beetle out like awnings shading a doorway. It is earth that was turned to clay in the mouths of the bees and spit out as they mined deeper into their Ⓑ dwelling places.

This place where the bees reside is at an angle safe from rain. It faces the southern sun. It is a warm and intelligent architecture

---

[1] **Anasazi** (ä´nə-sä´zē): an ancient Native American culture of the American Southwest.

Dwellings **493**

SCAFFOLDING FOR ELL STUDENTS

Vocabulary: Context Clues Explain that many words in English have multiple meanings. Some words can have analogous—related—meanings while other words have no connection between the different meanings. Remind students to use context clues to understand how a multiple-meaning word is used. Have pairs use context clues to define these words as they are used in the text and confirm the definitions in a dictionary.

- Line 3 "wall" *(a dividing structure on land or in a building, anything resembling a wall)*
- Line 3 "woven" *(constructed of fabric, anything intertwined)*
- Line 4 "rise" *(verb: to increase in altitude, noun: a small hill)*
- Line 4 "raw" *(uncooked, untouched or worked upon)*
- Line 10 "beetle" *(jut out, protrude)*

Support Inferences

 COMMON CORE RI 1

(LINES 14–30)

Point out that authors may not state ideas explicitly. Instead, an author's choice of words allow readers to make inferences about the author's ideas or values.

C **ASK STUDENTS** why the author includes this flashback to the time that the bees were alive. What do lines 24–30 reveal about her and her thoughts about life? *(They show Hogan's deep reverence for all life, past and present. She uses words associated with human activity ["they are following an invisible map"] to describe the bees. This and humanized references to the abandoned dwelling ["intelligent architecture," "catacombs"] reveal her admiration for their lives—comparable to our admiration for ancient civilizations—and express her sadness for their fate.)*

Comprehend Cultural Context (LINES 31–50)

COMMON CORE RI 2, RI 10

Explain that a writer's background or cultural influences can affect his or her writing.

D **ASK STUDENTS** to reread line 31–50, identify the similarities between the "dwelling places," and explain how Hogan's Native American background may have influenced these descriptions. *(The dwelling places are in harmony with nature. Since for Hogan writing from a Native American perspective includes sharing "ecologically sound" practices, it makes sense that her preferences about how to live are in harmony with nature.)*

Analyze Key Terms

 COMMON CORE RI 4

(LINES 32–46)

As a writer repeats the use of a key term, its meaning can expand and change.

E **ASK STUDENTS** how Hogan has expanded the meaning of "dwelling places" in lines 32–46. What can be inferred from her descriptions? *("dwelling places" now includes actual places [Manitou] and imaginary homes ["vapor cave," line 45]. The reader can infer that a dwelling place is a safe, warm, almost embryonic place.)*

of memory, learned by whatever memory lives in the blood. Many of the holes still contain the gold husks of dead bees, their faces dry and gone, their flat eyes gazing out from death's land toward the other uninhabited half of the hill that is across the creek from these catacombs.

20

The first time I found the residence of the bees, it was dusty summer. The sun was hot, and land was the dry color of rust. Now and then a car rumbled along the dirt road and dust rose up behind it before settling back down on older dust. In the silence, the bees made a soft droning hum. They were alive then, and working the hill, going out and returning with pollen, in and out through the holes, back and forth between daylight and the cooler, darker regions of inner earth. They were flying an invisible map through air, a map charted by landmarks, the slant of light, and a circling story they told one another about the direction of food held inside the center of yellow flowers.

30

Sitting in the hot sun, watching the small bees fly in and out around the hill, hearing the summer birds, the light breeze, I felt right in the world. I belonged there. I thought of my own dwelling places, those real and those imagined. Once I lived in a town called Manitou, which means "Great Spirit," and where hot mineral springwater gurgled beneath the streets and rose up into open wells. I felt safe there. With the underground movement of water and heat a constant reminder of other life, of what lives beneath us, it seemed to be the center of the world.

40

A few years after that, I wanted silence. My daydreams were full of places I longed to be, shelters and solitudes. I wanted a room apart from others, a hidden cabin to rest in. I wanted to be in a redwood forest with trees so tall the owls called out in the daytime. I daydreamed of living in a vapor cave a few hours away from here. Underground, warm, and moist, I thought it would be the perfect world for staying out of cold winter, for escaping the noise of living.

And how often I've wanted to escape to a wilderness where a human hand has not been in everything. But those were only dreams of peace, of comfort, of a nest inside stone or woods, a sanctuary where a dream or life wouldn't be invaded.

50

Years ago, in the next canyon west of here, there was a man who followed one of those dreams and moved into a cave that could only be reached by climbing down a rope. For years he lived there in comfort, like a troglodite.[2] The inner weather was stable, never too hot, too cold, too wet, or too dry. But then he felt lonely. His utopia needed a woman. He went to town until he found a wife. For a while after the marriage, his wife climbed down the rope along with him, but before long she didn't want the mice scurrying about in the cave, or the untidy bats that wanted to hang from stones of the ceiling. So they built a door.

---

[2] **troglodite:** a mythical or prehistoric cave dweller.

WHEN STUDENTS STRUGGLE . . .

After reading lines 31–46, discuss how an experience can trigger a feeling you connect with a memory—for example, how visiting a playground might remind you of you of how you felt when you were in elementary school. Explain that this kind of cause-effect pattern shapes this passage in Hogan's essay. Have pairs complete a cause-effect diagram like the one below to answer these questions: How do the bees buzzing underground make Hogan feel? What remembered feelings does this trigger?

| Hogan observes the bees buzzing in the earth. | Hogan "felt right in the world," as if she "belonged there." | Hogan felt safe in Manitou, where the hot springs burbled underground. |
| | | Hogan daydreamed about solitude and shelter. |

60 Because of the closed entryway, the temperature changed. They had to put in heat. Then the inner moisture of earth warped the door, so they had to have air-conditioning, and after that the earth wanted to go about life in its own way and it didn't give in to the people.

In other days and places, people paid more attention to the strong-headed will of earth. Once homes were built of wood that had been felled from a single region in a forest. That way, it was thought, the house would hold together more harmoniously, and the family of walls would not fall or lend themselves to the unhappiness or arguments of the inhabitants.

70 An Italian immigrant to Chicago, Aldo Piacenzi, built birdhouses that were dwellings of harmony and peace. They were the incredible spired shapes of cathedrals in Italy. They housed not only the birds, but also his memories, his own past. He painted them the watery blue of his Mediterranean, the wild rose of flowers in a summer field. Inside them was straw and the droppings of lives that layed eggs, fledglings who grew there. What places to inhabit, the bright and sunny birdhouses in dreary alleyways of the city.

One beautiful afternoon, cool and moist, with the kind of yellow light that falls on earth in these arid regions, I waited for barn swallows
80 to return from their daily work of food gathering. Inside the tunnel where they live, hundreds of swallows had mixed their saliva with mud and clay, much like the solitary bees, and formed nests that were perfect as a potter's bowl. At five in the evening, they returned all at once, a dark, flying shadow. Despite their enormous numbers and the crowding together of nests, they didn't pause for even a moment before entering the nests, nor did they crowd one another. Instantly they vanished into the nests. The tunnel went silent. It held no outward signs of life.

But I knew they were there, filled with the fire of living. And what
90 a marriage of elements was in those nests. Not only mud's earth and water, the fire of sun and dry air, but even the elements contained one another. The bodies of prophets and crazy men were broken down in that soil.

I've noticed often how when a house is abandoned, it begins to sag. Without a tenant, it has no need to go on. If it were a person, we'd say it is depressed or lonely. The roof settles in, the paint cracks, the walls and floorboards warp and slope downward in their own natural ways, telling us that life must stay in everything as the world whirls and tilts and moves through boundless space.

100 One summer day, cleaning up after long-eared owls where I work at a rehabilitation facility for birds of prey, I was raking the gravel floor of a flight cage. Down on the ground, something looked like it was moving. I bent over to look into the pile of bones and pellets I'd

Dwellings **495**

APPLYING ACADEMIC VOCABULARY

intensity	visualize

As you discuss the text and Hogan's relationship to the content of the essay, incorporate the Collection 6 academic vocabulary words *intensity* and *visualize*. Ask students to cite ways that Hogan describes the **intensity** of her relationship to nature and to various types of dwellings. Ask them how Hogan's ability to **visualize** and describe both real and imagined dwellings helps the reader understand her ideas about the connection that exists or should exist between all living things and the earth.

Comprehend Cultural Context (LINES 64–93)

 COMMON CORE RI 10

Explain that cultural values can shape an author's perspective. Through the anecdotes she chooses to relate, Hogan expresses her own values.

F CITE TEXT EVIDENCE How is the dwelling described in this paragraph different from the other specific examples that Hogan describes? *(Unlike the other dwellings Hogan describes, these birdhouses are built by a particular person in an urban setting.)* What connects Piacenzi's birdhouses to the other dwellings described in lines 64–93? *(Each of the dwellings represents a memory—the memory of a forest in the house's lumber, the cultural memory reflected in the birdhouses' design, and the elemental memory of the swallow's nests.)* What value does this commonality reflect for the author? *(The value of connectedness, with the past or the earth or both.)*

Determine Figurative Meanings: Personification

COMMON CORE RI 4, RI 6

(LINES 64–69; 94–99)

Writers often use figurative language to make a particular point, or create a memorable image. In these passages, Hogan uses **personification,** a figure of speech where human qualities are given to an object, animal, or idea.

G ASK STUDENTS where personification occurs in lines 64–69. *(The earth has a "strong-headed . . . will" [lines 64–65]; the walls of a house are a "family" [line 68].)* Where does it occur in lines 94–99? *(A tenantless house has "no need to go on" [line 95].)* How does Hogan's use of personification serve her purpose for writing? *(By giving the earth and dwellings human qualities, Hogan emphasizes the interconnectedness of all things, one of the themes running through her essay.)*

Support Inferences

COMMON CORE RI 1

(LINES 104–118)

Point out that a reader must often use details from a text to infer and make connections about the author's ideas. In this essay, the author uses personal observations of the natural world to convey ideas about life and death.

 CITE TEXT EVIDENCE What does Hogan mean when she states in lines 117–118 that "Death and life feed each other"? Explain with evidence from lines 104–118. (*Hogan suggests that both life and death are necessary and complementary parts of the natural world and that one is not possible without the other. Her description of the small mice being bitten in lines 108–111 shows that the mice are dying so that the ants can live. They are being "bitten out of life." The author intervenes to save the mice from the pain, but then says that the ants "were drowning in the water." She acknowledges that death and life are dependent on each other in the phrase, "I was trading one life for another..." in lines 114–115. This implies that in the natural world life is not possible without some death.*)

Comprehend Cultural Context

COMMON CORE RI 10

(LINES 133–142)

Point out that Hogan's Native American background colors the lens through which she views the world. From this perspective, the actions of the Zia and the tourists who visit the pueblo take on similar features.

 ASK STUDENTS to reread lines 133–142 and summarize the differences in how Zia's inhabitants and the tourists treat ancient, broken pottery. (*The Zia, a Native American people, leave the shards of pottery where they lie so they can be "smoothed back to earth"; but the tourists, "younger nations ... who have come to inhabit this land," want pieces of this pottery for themselves.*) In Hogan's view, how are the motivations of the native Zia and the non-native tourists similar? (*The Zia believe the potshards are "fragments of ... earlier lives" that must be returned to the earth as a part of the natural relationship between humans and the earth. The tourists see the potshards as "a lifeline to an unknown land" that will "help them remember that they live in the old nest of the earth."*)

 just raked together. There, close to the ground, were two fetal mice. They were new to the planet, pink and hairless. They were so tenderly young. Their faces had swollen blue-veined eyes. They were nestled in a mound of feathers, soft as velvet, each one curled up smaller than an infant's ear, listening to the first sounds of earth. But the ants were biting them. They turned in agony, unable to pull away, not yet
110 having the arms or legs to move, but feeling, twisting away from, the pain of the bites. I was horrified to see them bitten out of life that way. I dipped them in water, as if to take away the sting, and let the ants fall in the bucket. Then I held the tiny mice in the palm of my hand. Some of the ants were drowning in the water. I was trading one life for another, exchanging the lives of ants for those of mice, but I hated their suffering, and hated even more that they had not yet grown to a life, and already they inhabited the miserable world of pain. Death and life feed each other. I know that.

Inside these rooms where birds are healed, there are other lives
120 besides those of mice. There are fine gray globes the wasps have woven together, the white cocoons of spiders in a corner, the downward tunneling anthills. All these dwellings are inside one small walled space, but I think most about the mice. Sometimes the downy nests fall out of the walls where their mothers have placed them out of the way of their enemies. When one of the nests falls, they are so well made and soft, woven mostly from the chest feathers of birds. Sometimes the leg of a small quail holds the nest together like a slender cornerstone with dry, bent claws. The mice have adapted to life in the presence of their enemies, adapted to living in the thin wall between beak and
130 beak, claw and claw. They move their nests often, as if a new rafter or wall will protect them from the inevitable fate of all our returns home to the deeper, wider nest of earth that houses us all.

 One August at Zia Pueblo[3] during the corn dance I noticed tourists picking up shards of all the old pottery that had been made and broken there. The residents of Zia know not to take the bowls and pots left behind by the older ones. They know that the fragments of those earlier lives need to be smoothed back to earth, but younger nations, travelers from continents across the world who have come to inhabit this land, have little of their own to grow on. The pieces of earth that
140 were formed into bowls, even on their way home to dust, provide the new people a lifeline to an unknown land, help them remember that they live in the old nest of earth.

 It was in early February, during the mating season of the great horned owls. It was dusk, and I hiked up the back of a mountain to where I'd heard the owls a year before. I wanted to hear them again, the voices so tender, so deep, like a memory of comfort. I was halfway up the trail when I found a soft, round nest. It had fallen from one of the

---

[3] **Zia Pueblo:** a small community in central New Mexico.

TO CHALLENGE STUDENTS ...

Synthesize Ideas Are imagined dwelling places real? Why or why not? Guide students in a discussion of the meaning of the phrase *dwelling places*. Point out that in line 33 Hogan speaks of thinking about her own dwelling places and then goes on to describe some of them in lines 33–50. Discuss how Hogan expresses a symbolic meaning of the phrase that goes beyond a physical place.

Challenge students to write a paragraph about their own *dwelling places* using stylistic features of word choice, syntax, and figurative language similar to Hogan's. Stress that whether the place is real or imagined, students should use concrete details to describe physical attributes as Hogan does in lines 41–44. They should also describe the dwellings' abstract qualities, as Hogan does in lines 46–48.

bare-branched trees. It was a delicate nest, woven together of feathers, sage, and strands of wild grass. Holding it in my hand in the rosy
150 twilight, I noticed that a blue thread was entwined with the other gatherings there. I pulled at the thread a little, and then I recognized it. It was a thread from one of my skirts. It was blue cotton. It was the unmistakable color and shape of a pattern I knew. I liked it, that a thread of my life was in an abandoned nest, one that had held eggs and new life. I took the nest home. At home, I held it to the light and looked more closely. There, to my surprise, nestled into the gray-green sage, was a gnarl of black hair. It was also unmistakable. It was my daughter's hair, cleaned from a brush and picked up out in the sun beneath the maple tree, or the pit cherry where birds eat from the
160 overladen, fertile branches until only the seeds remain on the trees.

I didn't know what kind of nest it was, or who had lived there. It didn't matter. I thought of the remnants of our lives carried up the hill that way and turned into shelter. That night, resting inside the walls of our home, the world outside weighed so heavily against the thin wood of the house. The sloped roof was the only thing between us and the universe. Everything outside of our wooden boundaries seemed so large. Filled with night's citizens, it all came alive. The world opened in the thickets of the dark. The wild grapes would soon ripen on the vines. The burrowing ones were emerging. Horned owls sat in
170 treetops. Mice scurried here and there. Skunks, fox, the slow and holy porcupine, all were passing by this way. The young of the solitary bees were feeding on pollen in the dark. The whole world was a nest on its humble tilt, in the maze of the universe, holding us.

COLLABORATIVE DISCUSSION With a partner, discuss how the ideas and thoughts included in this essay create a portrait of the author. Cite specific evidence from the text to support your ideas.

Dwellings **497**

CLOSE READ

Support Inferences

 COMMON CORE RI 1

(LINES 143–163)

Remind students to consider their own prior knowledge and experiences as they think about details that Hogan provides to help convey ideas to her readers.

CITE TEXT EVIDENCE What ideas about the relationship between human culture and the natural world does Hogan express through the details in lines 143–163? *(Hogan suggests that there is an essential connection between the natural world and that of humans illustrated by her mention of the thread in the nest in lines 151–153 and the hair from her daughter's head in lines 156–158.)* How does Hogan clarify her ideas in lines 153–155? *(Hogan makes the connection more explicit in lines 153–155 by establishing that "the thread of my life was in an abandoned nest, one that held eggs and new life" and in lines 162–163 by considering "the remnants of our lives" being turned into shelter.)*

COLLABORATIVE DISCUSSION Have students form pairs to discuss what they have learned about the author. They should note her excitement and wonder at the workings of the natural world, her respect for all of the animals she describes, and her observations on the importance of living in harmony with nature. They should also note specific instances where her Native American heritage and beliefs are expressed clearly and forcefully. Students should refer to specific lines and/or paragraphs to support their views.

ASK STUDENTS to share any questions they generated in the course of reading and discussing the selection.

SCAFFOLDING FOR ELL STUDENTS

Comprehension: Organizational Patterns Point out that in the last paragraph, the writer uses an organizational pattern called *enumeration* to describe the night world outside her house. In using this pattern, the writer draws together the threads of various ideas she developed throughout the essay. Read the passage aloud starting at line 167, and ask students to raise their hands when they recognize something in Hogan's enumeration, or list, that she referred to earlier. Have students work in mixed language-ability jigsaw groups to discuss the effect of Hogan's list in lines 167–174. Ask them: Is the night world oppressive as it weighs on the house, comforting, or something else? Have each group share their ideas with the class.

TEACH

CLOSE READ

Support Inferences

COMMON CORE RI 1

Note that while inferences *must* be supported by textual evidence, prior knowledge can also help readers make inferences. Ask students for examples of prior knowledge or experience that some readers might have had that reinforce this inference. *(Students may suggest that readers may have had an experience or know about others' experiences where humans did not live in harmony with nature and when nature "didn't give in to the people." Examples might include houses built on cliffs or too near the ocean that were destroyed in natural disasters.)*

Comprehend Literary Nonfiction: Cultural Context
COMMON CORE RI 10

Review the concept that the cultural context of an author affects the author's thoughts and ideas. Review and discuss an example for each bullet.

- Topic *(dwellings—every living creature has one)*
- Descriptions of nature *(author's descriptions of animals and their dwellings, from the humans' to the lowliest creatures, are treated with equal dignity)*
- Direct statements of theme *(students might cite lines 64–65, 172–173)*
- Author's actions *(studying bees, actions with mice)*
- Details *(actions of bees, swallows, other nest builders)*
- Reflections *(lines 139–143, among others)*

Support Inferences

COMMON CORE RI 1

Inferences are logical assumptions that readers make by combining evidence from the text with their own prior knowledge and experience. Inferences are important in reading because authors may not be explicit about the connections they want you to make. In this reflective essay, the author develops ideas from personal observations of the natural world and human interactions with nature. Hogan states some of her ideas explicitly; others must be inferred by readers from the details in the text.

Consider this passage, in which the author describes the experience of a man who created a dwelling in nature:

> For years he lived there in comfort, like a troglodite. The inner weather was stable, never too hot, too cold, too wet, or too dry. . . . but before long she [his wife] didn't want the mice scurrying about in the cave, or the untidy bats that wanted to hang from stones of the ceiling. So they built a door. Because of the closed entryway, the temperature changed. They had to put in heat. Then the inner moisture of earth warped the door, so they had to have air-conditioning, and after that the earth wanted to go about life in its own way and it didn't give in to the people.

These details show that when the man accepted what nature provided, conditions were perfect. When he added his own "improvements," he upset the balance of nature and suffered the consequences; he had to compensate for more and more deficiencies. From this account, readers can infer the author's message—that humans would be happier if they could find a way to live in greater harmony with nature.

Comprehend Literary Nonfiction: Cultural Context

COMMON CORE RI 10

The **cultural context** of a work refers to the traditions, beliefs, and values that influenced its creation. As a Native American, Hogan's perspective is shaped by the key beliefs and values of her culture. These include an acute awareness of the connection between all living things; the realization that humans are restored when they live in harmony with their environment; a deep respect for other species of animal and plant life; and the belief that humans have a responsibility to care for nature.

To analyze the impact of the author's cultural context on "Dwellings," readers can look for the way those values are revealed in these aspects of the essay:

- the choice of topic
- the author's description of elements of nature
- the author's direct statements of theme
- the author's actions
- the kinds of details the author notices
- the author's reflections on what she observes

Strategies for Annotation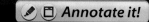

Comprehend Literary Nonfiction: Cultural Context

COMMON CORE RI 10

Share these strategies for guided or independent analysis:

- Highlight in yellow paragraphs or lines which indicate a unique cultural context.
- On a note, explain how the text reflects the author's particular cultural perspectives about the natural world.

In other days and places, people paid more attention to the strong-headed will of earth. Once homes were built of wood that had been felled from a single region in a forest. That way, it was thought, the house would hold together more harmoniously, and the family of walls would not fall or lend themselves to the unhappiness or arguments of the inhabitants.

> The author refers to the earth as having a will of its own. The author reveals her own perspective, not just that of the people of older days.

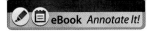  **eBook** *Annotate It!*

Analyzing the Text

Cite Text Evidence   Support your responses with evidence from the selection.

1. **Infer** Note the details that Hogan uses in lines 14–39 to describe the community of bees. What is the tone of this description? What might the bees represent for the author to make her have this attitude?

2. **Analyze** Explain why the author felt "safe" in Manitou. How might her perceptions of this place reflect her Native American beliefs?

3. **Compare** What characteristics do the dwellings in lines 64–77 have in common? Are these characteristics viewed positively or negatively by the author?

4. **Analyze** In lines 82–83, the author says that swallows form "nests that were perfect as a potter's bowl." Explain the literal meaning of this simile as well as what it implies.

5. **Cite Evidence** Cite evidence that reveals the author's belief in the interconnectedness of all things.

6. **Analyze** What does the author's work at the wildlife facility reveal about the relationship between her values and her life?

7. **Synthesize** Based on the author's descriptions of various dwellings she has encountered, what would be her idea of an ideal dwelling?

8. **Draw Conclusions** In the last sentence of the essay, the author states, "The whole world was a nest on its humble tilt, in the maze of the universe, holding us." What does this statement suggest about her overall purpose in writing this essay?

PERFORMANCE TASK

Writing Activity: Comparison Do Annie Dillard and Linda Hogan share the same view of nature?

- Review Hogan's essay and Dillard's "Living Like Weasels" (also in this collection). Identify each author's perspective and the details that reveal that view of nature.

- Include direct quotations as well as original analysis of each author's work. Organize your ideas logically and in a way that shows the comparison clearly.

- Be sure to follow the conventions of standard written English.

Assign this performance task.

PERFORMANCE TASK

Writing Activity: Comparison Divide the class into pairs (or triads), assigning half to Dillard and half to Hogan. Ask partners to review their author's essay and prepare a brief "statement of belief" about her view of nature, based on examples from the text. Next, combine pairs that have focused on different authors and have them discuss similarities and differences. Individual students should produce written comparisons that accurately reflect both essayists' views of nature and cite specific, relevant details.

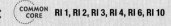

PRACTICE & APPLY

Analyzing the Text

Possible answers:

1. *Hogan adopts a peaceful, pastoral tone that reflects her fondness of the bees. The site of their hives is "a warm and intelligent architecture of memory." The phrases describing their activity depict bees as purposeful and deliberate: "soft droning hum," "working the hill," "in and out," "back and forth," "flying an invisible map through air . . . yellow flowers." Hogan "felt right in the world." To her, bees represent the symmetry, intelligence, and beauty of nature.*

2. *As a Native American dedicated to "ecologically sound, indigenous environmental practices" (according to the background notes), Hogan views the earth as a source of physical, and perhaps spiritual, life. Its proximity to "the underground movement of water and heat" made Manitou, or "Great Spirit," feel like the "center of the world" and instilled in her a sense of security.*

3. *The homes of indigenous wood and the birdhouses both connect to a region, to a sense of place. They retain the memories of those places, put there by their creator or by the material from which they are made. The author approves of dwellings with such connections. She sees them as harmonious and conducive to peaceful living.*

4. *Like pottery, the smooth nests are made of moist clay; their shapes accommodate the swallows precisely. The simile implies level of "craftsmanship" among the swallows comparable to that of a skilled potter.*

5. *The concept of interconnectivity pervades the essay. The swallows use mud that incorporates earth, water, sun, dry air, and the "bodies of prophets and crazy men broken down in that soil." Shards of old pottery form "lifelines to an unknown land," connecting the young and the old. A bird's nest attests to this connection: woven tightly within the nest the author finds a thread from her skirt and wisps of her daughter's hair, "remnants of our lives . . . turned into shelter."*

6. *The author lives according to her values. She believes that humans have a responsibility to other creatures. At work she helps both birds of prey and baby mice.*

7. *The author's ideal dwelling would have the following characteristics: its location would "feel right," with a sense of life around it; it would comprise materials native to its surroundings; it would exude a spirit of harmony and peace; it would protect and harbor; it would bear reminders of what its inhabitants consider important.*

8. *The earth is like a nest prepared to shelter and protect all living creatures.*

Language and Style: Appositives and Appositive Phrases

Review the examples in the text and the chart and make sure students understand how appositives and appositive phrases can improve the flow of the writing and provide either essential or nonessential information.

Sample answers:

1. *The hummingbird, a colorful, hovering creature, prefers nectar . . .*

2. *The car, a blue sedan, raised a cloud of dust . . .*

3. *She worked to rehabilitate eagles, large birds of prey.*

4. *Her home, a tiny log cabin, was built . . .*

5. *The enthusiastic hiker she met was botanist Ed Reyes.*

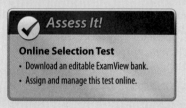

Assess It!

Online Selection Test
- Download an editable ExamView bank.
- Assign and manage this test online.

Language and Style: Appositives and Appositive Phrases

Writers may provide additional information about a noun or pronoun in a sentence by using **appositives** and **appositive phrases**. An appositive is a noun or pronoun that identifies or renames another noun or pronoun. An appositive phrase includes an appositive and its modifiers.

Read this sentence from the essay:

An Italian immigrant to Chicago, Aldo Piacenzi, built birdhouses that were dwellings of harmony and peace.

The author could have expressed the same ideas this way:

Aldo Piacenzi was an Italian immigrant to Chicago. He built birdhouses that were dwellings of harmony and peace.

In the original text, the appositive ("Aldo Piacenzi") clarifies who the Italian immigrant is. Though the second version is correct, the original sentence flows more naturally and is more concise.

The chart shows the two types of appositives and appositive phrases.

Appositive/Appositive Phrase	Example
Essential: Provides information that is necessary to identify the preceding noun or pronoun. It is not set off by commas, and the meaning of the sentence would be altered by deleting it.	Hogan's book *Mean Spirits* was nominated for a Pulitzer Prize. (The title *Mean Spirits* is an appositive for the word *book*. Without it, readers would not know which of Hogan's books was nominated.)
Nonessential: Adds extra information to a noun or pronoun that is already clearly identified. It is set off by commas. If it were deleted, the meaning of the sentence would still be clear.	Hogan, an active public speaker, has given talks on environmental issues. (The appositive phrase *an active public speaker* adds more information but is not required for the sentence to make sense.)

Practice and Apply Add an appositive or an appositive phrase to the italicized noun or pronoun in each of these sentences. Share your sentences with a partner. Discuss how the appositive or appositive phrase affects the meaning of each sentence.

1. The *hummingbird* prefers the nectar from red flowers.

2. The *car* raised a cloud of dust as it sped along the dirt road.

3. She worked to rehabilitate *eagles*.

4. Her *home* was built on the edge of a redwood forest.

5. The enthusiastic hiker she met was a *botonist*.

Analyze Key Terms

COMMON CORE

RI 4

TEACH

Tell students that in an essay like "Dwellings," writers may use a particular word or phrase repeatedly throughout the text. In some cases, the writer chooses the word or phrase to become a symbol that extends beyond the literal meaning or may define it in a special way unique to the writer's thinking or the text.

Review the side column notes related to the key term *dwelling places* in the text and note how Hogan expands the meaning beyond the common literal sense of a home mainly for humans to include the homes of animals and imagined places which are described only conceptually and are realistically impractical.

PRACTICE AND APPLY

Explain that another key term used by Hogan many times throughout the text is *nest*. Discuss the traditional definition of *nest* as a home for a bird or small animal. Note that the word can also be used to describe a human location that is comfortable and safe. Direct students to the following lines and discuss the usage of the term in each instance and whether it complies with a traditional definition or is a unique one created by Hogan.

- Line 49 *(unique use indicating a comfortable human place in unconventional locations such as "stone or woods")*
- Lines 80–90 *(conventional use, birds' homes)*
- Lines 123–130 *(conventional use, homes of mice)*
- Line 132 *(unique use, a grave)*
- Line 142 *(unique use, the earth becomes a nest or a home for all humans which "new people" need)*
- Lines 147–161 *(conventional use, bird's home)*
- Line 172 *(unique use, the whole world as a nest, suggesting that it is the appropriate and comfortable place for the entire natural and human world)*

Support Inferences

COMMON CORE

RI 1

RETEACH

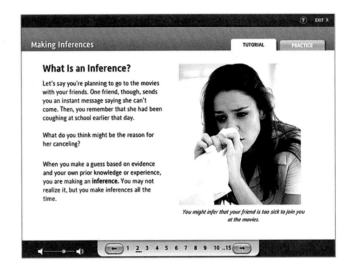

LEVEL UP TUTORIALS Assign the following *Level Up* tutorial: Making **Inferences**

Review the idea that an inference must involve some text evidence and may involve a reader's prior knowledge and experience. Ask students to provide text evidence for the following inferences from the text and discuss them as necessary.

- Hogan loves and respects nature. *(Lines 1–13, 78–88, 119–132)*
- Hogan believes people should live in harmony with nature. *(Lines 51–69)*
- Hogan believes human civilization and the natural world are closely connected. *(Lines 65–69, 143–173)*

CLOSE READING APPLICATION

Students can apply the skill to another essay or nonfiction work they have read. Have them select a passage that they can use to make an inference about the writer's beliefs and then identify sentences or clauses that support their inference.

Trees

Essay by Baron Wormser

Why This Text

Although "Trees" is an essay, the author has a poet's sensibility, and poets dwell in the realm of the suggestive. While some of the ideas in this essay are explicit, others must be inferred from the details in the text. The author uses his personal experience and close observations of nature to reveal universal truths about nature and life. With the help of the close-reading questions, students will combine textual evidence with their own prior knowledge and experience to make logical assumptions about the essay's deeper meaning.

Background Have students read the background and information about Baron Wormser. Explain that for Wormser and his family, living off-the-grid meant living without electricity or running water, growing their own food, and reading by kerosene lamp. While part of the "back to the land" movement of the 1970s, the Wormsers' choice of habitat was not mere protest: they had simply built their house too far from the road and could not afford to bring in power lines. Over the years, however, the family settled into a life of quiet observation and reflection.

AS YOU READ Ask students to pay attention to the way the author uses sensory details, imagery, language, and analogy to convey his point of view.

COMMON CORE Common Core Support

- cite complete and thorough textual evidence

- support inferences with details from the text and prior knowledge

- analyze the effectiveness of the structure the author uses

- examine how the author's point of view changes during the course of the essay

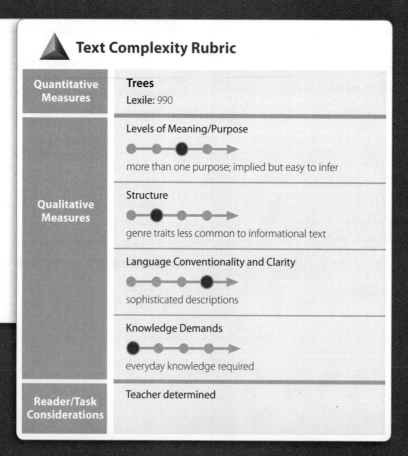

Text Complexity Rubric

Quantitative Measures	Trees Lexile: 990
Qualitative Measures	**Levels of Meaning/Purpose** more than one purpose; implied but easy to infer
	Structure genre traits less common to informational text
	Language Conventionality and Clarity sophisticated descriptions
	Knowledge Demands everyday knowledge required
Reader/Task Considerations	Teacher determined

Strategies for CLOSE READING

Support Inferences

Students should read this essay carefully all the way through. Close-reading questions at the bottom of the page will help them make inferences about the essay's deeper meaning. As they read, students should jot down comments or questions about the text in the margins.

WHEN STUDENTS STRUGGLE . . .

To help students make inferences about the essay's central idea, have them work in small groups to fill out a chart like the one shown below.

CITE TEXT EVIDENCE For practice recognizing the author's use of sensory details and word choice to convey meaning, have students paraphrase each of the following examples from the essay.

Example from the Essay	Paraphrase
"What man leaves behind is happenstance. The cutters might trust indomitable nature; they might trust cooperative, university-based science; or they might be indifferent." (lines 18–20)	The woodcutters are simply making a living; if they happen to do "good" it is unintended; whatever happens as a result of their behavior is of no interest to them.
"We were fortunate. . . . I could pick each tree I was going to fell according to how healthy (or unhealthy) the tree was and whether I should thin that one to allow others to grow. I could fell the tree so it would do the least damage to others." (lines 34–38)	Since we didn't have to cut trees to make a living, we had the luxury of cutting only those trees we wanted to cut.
"Anything that didn't honor the dollar equation was recreation." (lines 45–46)	Some people thought that unless you were cutting trees for profit you were a free spirit.

Background Baron Wormser *is a widely-acclaimed American poet born in Baltimore, Maryland, in 1948. From 1975 to 1998, he lived "off the grid" with his wife and children on 48 acres of pristine woodland in Mercer, Maine, earning a living as a librarian and creative writing teacher. He wrote a book about the experience called* The Road Washes Out in Spring *from which this excerpt is taken. In 2000, he was appointed Poet Laureate of Maine. Since 2002, Wormser has been conducting poetry writing workshops with students and teachers in schools and universities throughout Maine.*

Trees

Essay by Baron Wormser

CLOSE READ
Notes

1. **READ ▶** As you read lines 1–20, begin to cite textual evidence.

- Underline text describing what the author did to build his dream house.
- Circle text describing the results of these actions.
- In the margin, make notes about what the author values (lines 12–20).

Our house was quite literally in the woods. I cut down poplars, a few spavined[1] apple trees, some white pines, and a number of tall, thin, red maples to create an adequate opening to situate the house and let the sun in over the tree tops. The apple trees must have been the remnant of a little orchard that had been planted near where the farmhouse once stood. The others had grown up randomly as the site of what once was a farm became woods. We used a compass to **orient** the house to the south. This was not a development lot that had to have its house squarely facing the street. The sun that came up over the trees could be seen from our bedroom window. We

10 could follow it across the front of the house throughout the day. On a frigid but sunny winter day, the south windows **suffused** a gentle warmth.

orient:
position

suffuse:
to spread over

[1] **spavined:** damaged, deteriorated, or ruined.

123

1. **READ AND CITE TEXT EVIDENCE** In lines 12–20 the author describes the pine trees behind his house.

A ASK STUDENTS how the author feels about these trees. *He "reveres" them.* What makes them special? *They are old.*

Critical Vocabulary: orient (line 7) Have students compare their definitions of *orient*. Ask them how sailors of the past would orient their ships. *They used the position of the stars.*

Critical Vocabulary: suffuse (line 11) Have students compare their definitions of *suffuse*. Ask them what it would mean if the sky were suffused with pink and orange. *Those colors would be spread through the sky; it would probably be sunrise or sunset.*

The author values the old, large pine trees.

indomitable:
impossible to defeat

The author describes the felled trees as if they were war casualties.

venerate:
honor; admire

(A) (B) In front of and in back of the house stood a number of very straight pines that were fifty to sixty years old. We revered them, though we knew any city person strolling in a park—a domain where aesthetics trumped board feet—would see larger and older trees. In rural Maine lumbering is always an issue; one sees very few, really old trees in the endless woods because those woods are being cut time and time again. The works of man, the industry that drives each economic day, are what the Maine woods call to mind. What man leaves behind is happenstance. The cutters might trust **indomitable** nature; they might trust cooperative, university-based science; or they might be indifferent.

(C) When I first began to roam the backcountry where we lived, I was routinely appalled when I encountered tracts that had been lumbered recently. Limbs and sections of trunks that were unusable were strewn everywhere. Young trees had been toppled and left eventually to collapse under snow. Splintered trees whose tops had been sheared off when other trees fell on them stood like big, ragged toothpicks. Huge ruts from the skidders that moved the logs were everywhere. Piles of brush sat like so much unwanted debris. It looked like a war had occurred, a war against the trees. Of course, woodcutting isn't an issue of beautification. It's an issue of humankind making a buck off some trees that the rest of humankind needs for paper and lumber. The whole notion of trees as something to regard and **venerate** would have seemed bizarre to the men with the chainsaws and trucks. The trees were there for people to use. Such is the way of workaday humanity.

We were fortunate. For us, the trees were not part of any crucial, economic equation. When I cut trees for the firewood that kept us warm and that heated our water, I could pick each tree I was going to fell according to how healthy (or unhealthy) the tree was and whether I should thin that one to allow others to grow. I could fell the tree so it would do the least damage to others. I could use virtually the entire tree because I sawed up the limbs for our cook stove. I could arrange the brush on the ground so that it would compact reasonably quickly. You had to take a careful look to notice that a tree had been felled.

(D) Although we heated our house with the trees I cut on our land and although we had no backup heat whatsoever, more than one woodcutter told me that, despite my exertions, I was doing little more in the woods than playing. I could understand. Anything that didn't honor the dollar equation was recreation. Caleb cut trees, sold them for pulp, and used the money to pay for oil heat. He informed me he was "way ahead" by doing this. When I asked him, "Ahead of what?" he only snorted. He had endured a lifetime of starting fires in wood stoves, getting up in the middle of winter nights to put in more wood, then waking in the morning to the cold misery of ashes. I could have it. I was off in my labor-intensive poetic Oz.

I had to confess that I was quite happy in my Oz of trees. At any time I could walk a few steps and literally be in the woods. In the heat of summer, I had the shade, the coolness, and the ever-changing play of the sifted light. The

2. ◀ **REREAD** Reread lines 12–20. Make an inference about the author's feelings about lumbering. Cite evidence from the text.

The author says he "revered" the old trees and explains how rare it is to see them in the woods. You can infer that he might not like lumbering, because it cuts down these old specimens.

3. **READ** ▶ As you read lines 21–51, continue to cite textual evidence.
- Underline details that explain why trees are cut down.
- In the margin, note how the author describes recently lumbered tracts (lines 23–28).
- Circle text that describes the author's initial reaction toward lumbering.

4. ◀ **REREAD** Reread lines 42–51. What does Caleb mean when he says he "was way ahead?" Support your answer with explicit textual evidence.

Caleb is now heating his house with oil rather than wood—he'd had enough of "getting up in the middle of winter nights to put in more wood, then waking in the morning to the cold misery of ashes."

5. **READ** ▶ As you read lines 52–90, continue to cite textual evidence.
- Underline text the author uses instead of "trees."
- Circle the sensory language the author uses to describe the trees.

2. REREAD AND CITE TEXT EVIDENCE

(B) **ASK STUDENTS** to cite evidence from lines 12–17 describing how lumberers have changed Maine. *There are fewer old trees: "one sees very few, really old trees." The lumberers have cut them down: "those woods are being cut time and time again."*

3. READ AND CITE TEXT EVIDENCE

(C) **ASK STUDENTS** to cite text that helps you to visualize the scene in lines 21–51. *Limbs were strewn everywhere; toppled trees had been left to collapse; trees looked like big, ragged toothpicks.*

Critical Vocabulary: indomitable (line 19) Tell students that some individuals are described as having an *indomitable* spirit. What does this mean? *It means that the person is uncrushable.*

Critical Vocabulary: venerate (line 31) Have students explain the meaning of *venerate*. Who do they most venerate? *Students may name celebrities, sports figures, musicians, and so on.*

4. REREAD AND CITE TEXT EVIDENCE
In lines 42–51 the author describes how Caleb's views and lifestyle differ from his own.

(D) **ASK STUDENTS** to use text evidence to explain how Caleb makes a living. *He cuts down trees, sells them for pulp, and uses the money to pay for oil heat.*

5. READ AND CITE TEXT EVIDENCE

(E) **ASK STUDENTS** to name the different kinds of trees the author talks about. *He mentions white pines, poplars, sugar maples, white birches, yellow birches, and gray birches.* What can students infer from the way he describes the trees? *Students may infer that he is a close observer of trees and knows them well; he sees them with a poet's eye; he sees beauty in each and every tree.*

FOR ELL STUDENTS Encourage students to explain how context clues helped them understand the meaning of the noun *lumbering* in line 15. *"cutting down trees"*

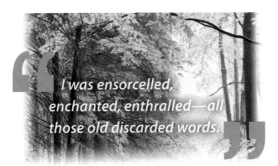

> I was ensorcelled,
> enchanted, enthralled—all
> those old discarded words.

analogies to a cathedral were not far-fetched. In the heights of the trees there
was audible mystery—pewees and tanagers[2] I heard but rarely saw. I marveled
at the relentless yearning toward the sun, how the maples made their way amid
a canopy of pines. In winter I watched the bare forms gesturing like still
dancers. I listened to the spry clatter of branches in a strong wind. They
60 sounded like little bones. In all seasons, the waver and dapple of shadow
sighed. When I examined a stump, I saw in the growth rings the shapes of
years, some bunched, some even, some **protuberant**. I was ensorcelled,
enchanted, enthralled—all those old discarded words.

(E)   Part of living with the trees lay in considering their ways. Each type of tree
was deeply singular. There were the trademark white pines that a friend once
likened to huge stalks of celery on account of how their tops waved in a wind.
There were the smooth-trunked beeches that held onto their parchment-like
leaves throughout the winter and rattled dryly. There were the poplars (or
"popple" in the local designation) that were "trash" trees, their loosely fibrous
70 wood considered not good for much of anything. Their diminutive leaves were
attuned to every breeze and shimmered with audible movement. In a stiff wind
they seemed almost frenetic. There were the deeply furrowed sugar maples
along the road to our house that had been tapped to make maple syrup and
now were dying as their huge limbs rotted and fell. There were the white
birches, with their peeling, papery strips of bark, yellow birches that were not a
bright yellow, but a silvery yellow, and gray birches that sometimes were bent
almost to the ground from the winter's snow.

    And there were the elms left over from the nineteenth century when
farmers had planted whips—slender, unbranched shoots of American elm—to
(F) 80 domesticate and beautify the homestead. It was sad to see them—massive

[2] **pewees and tanagers:** two types of perching birds.

protuberant:
sticking out

126

---

torsos that the seasons were breaking down bit by bit. The wood was gnarled
and almost impossible to split. Occasionally, we came upon them in the middle
of what seemed like nowhere but wasn't—once a farmhouse had stood there.
Sentinels, the elms had died on their watch. Nearby, weathered clapboards soft
with decay lay on the ground along with the usual array of rusty pots, pans,
and broken crockery. We stared up at the dead trees and down at the shards of
lives. The massive leafless stillness spoke to the wretched indifference of time.
Their ruined dignity warned the **encroaching** woods that the arboreal world
was a mere wink. Even the most stolid matter was corruptible. They were
90 sculptures of loss.
(G)   When I looked at one of my familiars, such as the pine in back of our
house that had grown up in a gigantic U-shape, two fifty-foot limbs rising from
the trunk at around thirty feet, I considered the hazards of growth. Some
(H) impediment had caused this curious formation. The awkward tree kept
growing as I kept on living. Habit had a sort of genius, yet it might take shapes
that made the eye wince. I thought of the terrible ability of living creatures to
adapt, to get along, to say the current regime is okay when the current regime is
not okay. Eventually a windstorm would wreck those two unnatural limbs that
had become trunks. The tree would have lived a reasonably long life, however.
100 Like many people under many regimes, it had managed. Its awkwardness had
not been ruinous; its inconvenience was silent.

    The bark was surprisingly delicate, and the pitch was sticky. The fragrance
was that thick, turpentine sweetness that is pine. I didn't have a problem
understanding how people had once worshipped trees. Perhaps, as pantheists[3]

[3] **pantheists:** people who believe that God is identical with the universe.

encroaching:
invading,
trespassing

*It's important
to adapt,
because even
"unnatural"
change is
natural.*

6. ◀ **REREAD** Reread lines 78–90. Make an inference about what the author
means when he describes the trees as "sculptures of loss?"

*The trees remaining where there had once been a farmhouse grow in
contrast to the decay from the house. The "indifference of time"
creates "sculptures of loss" as the trees grow despite the
disappearance of the house's inhabitants.*

7. **READ** ▶ As you read lines 91–108, continue to cite textual evidence.

• Underline details that describe the unusual pine in the back of the house.
• In the margin, explain what the trees teach the author about adaptation.

127

Critical Vocabulary: protuberant (line 62) Have students
explain the meaning of *protuberant*. Which desert animal
has a protuberance on its back? *Students may say a camel; the
protuberance is its hump.*

FOR ELL STUDENTS Clarify the meaning of the idiom
far-fetched (line 55). Tell students that while the literal meaning is
something that is brought from far away, in this idiom it means
"improbable, not likely to happen or be true."

6. **REREAD AND CITE TEXT EVIDENCE**

(F) ASK STUDENTS to cite a reference to broken sculpture in
lines 80–81. *Students may cite the phrase "massive torsos . . .
breaking down bit by bit."* What happens to sculptures that also
happens to trees? *They break down, bit by bit.*

7. **READ AND CITE TEXT EVIDENCE**   In lines 91–101, the author
predicts that the disfigured tree will adapt and change.

(G) ASK STUDENTS what the author thinks will happen to the
tree with the passage of time. How will it change? *The author
predicts that a windstorm "would wreck those unnatural limbs that
had become trunks," but the tree would keep on growing and have a
"reasonably long life."*

Critical Vocabulary: encroaching (line 88) Have students
explain the meaning of *encroaching*. How do they feel when
someone encroaches on their territory? *Students may suggest
they feel crowded, suffocated, threatened, jealous, possessive.*

CLOSE READ
Notes

felt, God spoke through the trees. It seemed a pretty thought but an unnecessary one. I wasn't inclined to look further or deeper than what I saw and smelled and heard. If my senses were stupid and childlike, so be it. These great, leafy delusions were vulnerable, yet **stalwart**.

stalwart:
strong, brave

8. **◄ REREAD** Reread lines 91–101. Why does the author call the ability to adapt "terrible?" Cite evidence from the text.

Although the ability of living things to adapt to change is part of the
natural order of things, it sometimes comes in the form of
disfigurement ("might take shapes that made the eye wince").

SHORT RESPONSE

Cite Text Evidence In what way has Wormser's view of the natural world changed over the years? Make inferences about the author's point of view, **citing text evidence** in your response.

Wormser romanticized the woods, and built his house "literally in the
woods." At first, he he was "routinely appalled" by the butchered
tree limbs everywhere. But over time he began to realize the
"terrible ability of living creatures to adapt." He saw that the trees
would survive one onslaught after another, just as people did. He was
able to look at a tree that had been disfigured ("some impediment
had caused this curious formation") and see it as part of the natural
order of things. He realized that trees kept growing and changing, no
matter what. They didn't need to be deified, revered, or
sentimentalized—or even kept in their pristine state. They did not
have to have a "deeper meaning"; they were strong enough to stand
on their own.

128

---

8. **REREAD AND CITE TEXT EVIDENCE** In lines 95–96, the author makes the following comment about adaptation: "Habit had a sort of genius, yet it might take shapes that made the eye wince."

Ⓗ ASK STUDENTS to paraphrase this statement. *Students may say that even physical deformity is part of the natural order of things.*

Critical Vocabulary: stalwart (line 108) Have students explain the meaning of *stalwart*. What does the author describe as "vulnerable, yet stalwart"? *He describes trees this way.*

SHORT RESPONSE

Cite Text Evidence Students should:

• infer the author's point of view about the natural world.

• examine the author's use of sensory details to describe the physical world.

• draw conclusions about changes in the author's attitude.

TO CHALLENGE STUDENTS . . .

For more context about logging in Maine, have students research its history and modern alternative techniques such as Low Impact Forestry (LIF).

ASK STUDENTS to research the history of traditional industrial logging in Maine as well as the less-invasive techniques that are increasing in popularity. They should find photographs and exhibits as well as videos that explain logging in Maine.

• Have students report on some of the tools used by loggers in the past. *Some vintage tools include steam haulers, chainsaws, logging sleds, and tractors.*

• Have students report on the goal of Low Impact Forestry, and how it differs from industrial logging. *The goal of LIF is to maintain a healthy and diverse indigenous forest environment while extracting high quality wood. It is sometimes called "sustainable forestry" or "ecoforestry" because it leaves behind a functional forest that maintains the forest's great diversity of wildlife and plants. In much industrial logging, all the trees in an area are cut down, even if new saplings are planted immediately afterwards.*

DIG DEEPER

1. With the class, return to Question 4, Reread. Have students share their responses.

ASK STUDENTS to think about the different points of view represented by the author, Caleb, and the woodcutters.

- According to the author, more than one woodcutter had told him he was doing "little more in the woods than playing." What kinds of things was the author doing that prompted this criticism? *He heated the house with trees he cut from his land; he had no backup heater; he didn't make money from cutting down his trees.*

- Caleb thinks that selling wood for pulp is "way ahead" of using it for heating. What does Caleb do when the author asks "Ahead of what?" *He snorts derisively.* What is his problem with using the wood for heating? *It doesn't bring in any money; it doesn't "honor the dollar equation."*

- The author suggests that Caleb thinks he lives a "labor-intensive poetic Oz." Why would Caleb think that? *Students may say Caleb believes the author is living in a dream-world, albeit a labor-intensive one.*

2. With the class, return to Question 8, Reread. Have students share their responses.

ASK STUDENTS to review the author's ideas about adaptation in lines 91–101. Draw their attention to the following text: "I thought of the terrible ability of living creatures to adapt, to get along, to say the current regime is okay when the current regime is not okay" (lines 96–98).

- The author's use of the phrase "current regime" signals a shift in focus. What kind of adaptation is he talking about now? *He is widening the discussion to include political systems as well as systems that occur in nature.*

- What point is he making about society's "terrible" ability to adapt? *He is saying that things might look bad now but they will self-correct—it's all part of a never-ending process of change.*

ASK STUDENTS to return to their Short Response answer and revise it based on the class discussion.

CLOSE READING NOTES

*my*SmartPlanner — Create lesson plans and access resources online.

The Hermit's Story

Short Story by Rick Bass

Why This Text?

As readers and as writers, students should be aware of the many choices that are available for structuring a work of fiction and the advantages afforded by each one. In this lesson, students read a frame story and consider how two related narratives interact to convey themes about the power of nature and the relationship of humans to larger forces.

Key Learning Objective: The student will be able to determine themes in a short story and analyze a frame structure that presents two related stories.

Common Core Standards

RL 1 Cite textual evidence to support inferences.
RL 2 Determine themes of a text.
RL 3 Analyze the impact of the author's choices regarding how to develop elements of a story.
RL 4 Analyze the impact of specific word choice on meaning and tone.
RL 5 Analyze an author's choices concerning how to structure a text.
RL 10 Read and comprehend literature, including stories.
SL 1a Participate effectively in collaborative discussions.
L 4c Consult reference materials (thesauruses).
L 5a Interpret figures of speech in context and analyze their role in the text.
L 5b Analyze nuances in the meaning of words with similar denotations.

▲ Text Complexity Rubric

Quantitative Measures

The Hermit's Story
Lexile: 1500L

Qualitative Measures

Levels of Meaning/Purpose
multiple levels of meaning (multiple themes)

Structure
some unconventional story structure elements

Language Conventionality and Clarity
complex and varied sentence structure

Knowledge Demands
fairly complex theme

Reader/Task Considerations
Teacher determined
Vary by individual reader and type of text

Rick Bass Have students read the information about the author. Tell them that in the 1990s, Bass did organizing and publicity work to try to preserve the Yaak Valley in Montana, where he lived at the time. He advocated replacing clear-cut logging practices, which he believed endangered the environment, with smaller-scale, sustainable practices. His book *The Lost Grizzlies: A Search for Survivors in the Wilderness of Colorado* (1997) tells some of the stories related to Bass's work with others to convince the government that grizzly bears were not extinct there, since he had seen one up close. Bass later edited *The Roadless Yaak* (2002), a collection of essays that argue for the preservation of the valley's wild acres. Bass has a deep and enduring relationship with nature, as evidenced in the title work from his 2002 fiction collection *The Hermit's Story*.

AS YOU READ Direct students to use the As You Read note to focus their reading.

Analyze Language (LINES 9–15) **COMMON CORE** **RL 4**

Explain that in this story Bass uses a great deal of figurative language and imagery, or sensory details, to create vivid descriptions and to establish a **tone**—the narrator's attitude toward what is described.

Ⓐ **CITE TEXT EVIDENCE** Direct students to reread lines 9–15 and explain how the images and figurative language help establish the narrator's view of nature. *(The narrator describes a pervasive blueness rising from a source deep within the earth, "blue rising like smoke" through the buried dogs' "gleaming ribs" and "empty eye sockets and nostrils," finally ending up "trapped—but still alive" under the winter landscape. This imagery and figurative language give the impression that nature is a powerful life force that is indifferent to the life and death of individual animals, and by extension, humans.)*

fabricated: The narrator imagines the blueness of the ice as being created by the ice itself.

ASK STUDENTS to explain the distinction between light being reflected to appear blue and blue light being fabricated by the ice. *(The idea of blue light being fabricated by the ice is fanciful; it is a figurative description that emphasizes the intensity and apparent depth of the color. In fact, the structure of the ice's surface reflects light in a way that makes it appear blue.)*

Rick Bass (b. 1958) *grew up in Texas, where he became interested in nature at an early age. He studied geology at Utah State University and worked as a petroleum geologist for several years. During his lunch hours he started writing short stories. Since then, he has written and edited over 25 books, both fiction and nonfiction, and has received many literary awards. His passion for nature is reflected in his environmental activism as well as his writing. He moved to Montana in 1987 and is involved in efforts to protect areas such as the Glacier National Park.*

The Hermit's Story

Short Story by Rick Bass

AS YOU READ Think about whether Ann's story is credible or not. Write down any questions you generate during reading.

An ice storm, following seven days of snow; the vast fields and drifts of snow turning to sheets of glazed ice that shine and shimmer blue in the moonlight, as if the color is being **fabricated** not by the bending and absorption of light but by some chemical reaction within the glossy ice; as if the source of all blueness lies somewhere up here in the north—the core of it beneath one of those frozen fields; as if blue is a thing that emerges, in some parts of the world, from the soil itself, after the sun goes down.

10   Blue creeping up fissures and cracks from depths of several hundred feet; blue working its way up through the gleaming ribs of Ann's buried dogs; blue trailing like smoke from the dogs' empty eye sockets and nostrils—blue rising like smoke from chimneys until it reaches the surface and spreads laterally and becomes entombed, or trapped—but still alive, and smoky—within those moonstruck fields of ice.

Blue like a scent trapped in the ice, waiting for some soft release, some thawing, so that it can continue spreading.

fabricate (făb′rĭ-kāt′) *v.* to construct or make.

SCAFFOLDING FOR ELL STUDENTS

Fluency: Read Aloud Explain that Bass uses the first three paragraphs to describe the landscape after an ice storm. Point out that each paragraph consists of a single sentence, although none of these is a grammatically complete sentence with a subject and a verb. Read lines 1–17 aloud, using appropriate phrasing guided by the punctuation. Clarify any vocabulary that students do not understand. Then have pairs of students read the passage aloud with one student reading the first paragraph and the other reading the second two, then switching paragraphs to read it aloud again. Discuss the tone that is established through the imagery, figurative language, and the use of long sentences. *(Bass uses vivid imagery and figurative language to describe an almost surreal scene consisting of blue light, snow, and ice. The tone establishes the idea that nature is a mysterious and beautiful force as well as a harsh one containing buried bones and skulls.)*

Determine Theme

COMMON CORE RL 2

(LINES 18–34)

Remind students that a **theme** consists of a writer's underlying message conveyed through the elements of a story. When a writer returns to an idea repeatedly, it is probably a way of developing a theme.

 CITE TEXT EVIDENCE Ask students to reread lines 18–34. What main idea is expressed through the narrator's description of this Thanksgiving Day? Cite details that convey this idea. *(The main idea is that people can live in harmony with nature if they choose to do so. Line 19 explains that the storm has "knocked out all power down in town," and line 28 describes power lines "dragged down by the clutches of ice." Lines 30–34 confirm that the narrator and his neighbors always live without power, and that through their preparation they feel "snug and cozy." Because they are not wholly dependent on the trappings of civilization, they are able to enjoy the snowstorm rather than suffer from it.)*

Analyze Structure: Frame Story

COMMON CORE RL 5

(LINES 48–53)

Explain that a **frame story** is a structure in which a story is told within the frame of another story. Usually, events at the beginning and end of the story serve as the frame or context for another "story within the story." This second story is often told by one of the characters in the frame story.

 ASK STUDENTS to reread lines 48–53 and explain how this transition serves to frame the story of Ann's experiences in Canada with Gray Owl. *(The four characters in the frame story have just finished their Thanksgiving dinner when "Ann has a story for us." The sentence "It was twenty years ago, she says—her last good job" signals the beginning of Ann's voice, although the narrator paraphrases her words rather than quoting her directly. Ann's story is told in the past tense; the next paragraph begins, "She worked the dogs all summer. . . .")*

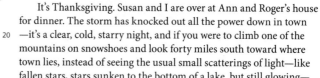

It's Thanksgiving. Susan and I are over at Ann and Roger's house for dinner. The storm has knocked out all the power down in town —it's a clear, cold, starry night, and if you were to climb one of the mountains on snowshoes and look forty miles south toward where town lies, instead of seeing the usual small scatterings of light—like fallen stars, stars sunken to the bottom of a lake, but still glowing— you would see nothing but darkness—a bowl of silence and darkness in balance for once with the mountains up here, rather than opposing or complementing our darkness, our peace.

As it is, we do not climb up on snowshoes to look down at the dark town—the power lines dragged down by the clutches of ice—but can tell instead just by the way there is no faint glow over the mountains to the south that the power is out: that this Thanksgiving, life for those in town is the same as it always is for us in the mountains, and it is a good feeling, a familial one, coming on the holiday as it does—though doubtless too the townspeople are feeling less snug and cozy about it than we are.

We've got our lanterns and candles burning. A fire's going in the stove, as it will all winter long and into the spring. Ann's dogs are asleep in their straw nests, breathing in that same blue light that is being exhaled from the skeletons of their ancestors just beneath and all around them. There is the faint, good smell of cold-storage meat—slabs and slabs of it—coming from down in the basement, and we have just finished off an entire chocolate pie and three bottles of wine. Roger, who does not know how to read, is examining the empty bottles, trying to read some of the words on the labels. He recognizes the words *the* and *in* and *USA*. It may be that he will never learn to read—that he will be unable to — but we are in no rush, and—unlike his power lifting—he has all of his life in which to accomplish this. I for one believe that he will learn it.

Ann has a story for us. It's about one of the few clients she's ever had, a fellow named Gray Owl, up in Canada, who owned half a dozen speckled German shorthaired pointers and who hired Ann to train them all at once. It was twenty years ago, she says—her last good job.

She worked the dogs all summer and into the autumn, and finally had them ready for field trials. She took them back up to Gray Owl—way up in Saskatchewan—driving all day and night in her old truck, which was old even then, with dogs piled up on top of each other, sleeping and snoring: dogs on her lap, dogs on the seat, dogs on the floorboard. How strange it is to think that most of us can count on one hand the number of people we know who are doing what they most want to do for a living. They invariably have about them a kind of wildness and calmness both, possessing somewhat the grace of animals that are fitted intricately and polished into this world. An academic such as myself might refer to it as a kind of biological confidence. Certainly I think another word for it could be *peace*.

WHEN STUDENTS STRUGGLE . . .

Direct students to lines 22–26, in which the narrator describes what the town probably looks like when all the power is out. Be sure that students understand the term *complementing* in line 26. *(It means completing or making whole.)* Ask students to identify what two things are being discussed *(the town and the mountains)* and what they might symbolize *(the world of human civilization and the natural world)*. Discuss how lines 24–26 establish the narrator's view of the town in relationship to nature. *(He is ambivalent, believing that the human world sometimes opposes the natural world but also may complement it.)* Ask students if they think this view will be further developed in the story. *(Yes, it will probably be developed as part of the story's theme.)*

Ann was taking the dogs up there to show Gray Owl how to work them: how to take advantage of their newly found talents. She could be a sculptor or some other kind of artist, in that she speaks of her work as if the dogs are rough blocks of stone whose internal form exists already and is waiting only to be chiseled free and then released by her, beautiful, into the world.

70 Basically, in six months the dogs had been transformed from gangling, bouncing puppies into six raging geniuses, and she needed to show their owner how to control them, or rather, how to work with them. Which characteristics to nurture, which ones to discourage. With all dogs, Ann said, there was a tendency, upon their leaving her **tutelage**—unlike a work of art set in stone or paint—for a kind of chitinous[1] encrustation to set in, a sort of oxidation, upon the dogs leaving her hands and being returned to someone less knowledgeable and passionate, less committed than she. It was as if there were a tendency in the world for the dogs' greatness to disappear back into

80 the stone.

So she went up there to give both the dogs and Gray Owl a check-out session. She drove with the heater on and the window down; the cold Canadian air was invigorating, cleaner, farther north. She could smell the scent of the fir and spruce, and the damp alder and cottonwood leaves beneath the many feet of snow. We laughed at her when she said it, but she told us that up in Canada she could taste the fish in the streams as she drove alongside creeks and rivers.

She listened to the only radio station she could pick up as she drove, but it was a good one. She got to Gray Owl's around midnight.

90 He had a little guest cabin but had not heated it for her, uncertain as to the day of her arrival, so she and the six dogs slept together on a cold mattress beneath mounds of elk hides: their last night together. She had brought a box of quail with which to work the dogs, and she built a small fire in the stove and set the box of quail next to it.

The quail muttered and cheeped all night and the stove popped and hissed and Ann and the dogs slept for twelve hours straight, as if submerged in another time, or as if everyone else in the world were submerged in time—encased in stone—and as if she and the dogs were pioneers, or survivors of some kind: upright and exploring the present,

100 alive in the world, free of that strange chitin.

She spent a week up there, showing Gray Owl how his dogs worked. She said he scarcely recognized them afield, and that it took a few days just for him to get over his amazement. They worked the dogs both individually and, as Gray Owl came to understand and appreciate what Ann had crafted, in groups. They traveled across snowy hills on snowshoes, the sky the color of snow, so that often it was like moving through a dream, and except for the rasp of the snowshoes beneath

---

[1] **chitinous** (kīt´n-əs): like a hard, biological substance found in the shells or exoskeletons of certain creatures.

tutelage
(to͞ot´l-ĭj) n. instructional authority.

SCAFFOLDING FOR ELL STUDENTS

Language: Author's Style Explain that a common feature of Bass's writing style is the use of parallel phrases or clauses to create layers of description. For example, in line 23, the phrase *fallen stars* is followed by a comma and the phrase *stars sunken to the bottom of a lake, but still glowing*. Both phrases describe the same thing, but the second phrase adds more detail to the description. Point out lines 71–73, which offer four ways to complete the grammatical structure *"she needed to show their owner . . ."* (how to control them, how to work with them, which characteristics to nurture, which characteristics to discourage). Discuss additional examples in lines 64–65, lines 75–76, and lines 96–100, and tell students to watch for similar constructions throughout the story.

CLOSE READ

Determine Theme
COMMON CORE RL 2

(LINES 57–63)

Tell students that the characters in a story—their qualities and their behaviors—often provide clues to themes the author wants to communicate.

D **ASK STUDENTS** to reread lines 57–63. What kind of person is Ann? Does the narrator's tone suggest a more universal idea about people? Explain. (*The narrator says that people like Ann, who are "doing what they most want to do for a living," have both "wildness and calmness" about them. He summarizes the way they fit into the world as "peace," a word with very positive connotations. The narrator's admiration for Ann and others like her suggests a more universal idea: People are happy and at peace when they are doing what they love.*)

Analyze Language
COMMON CORE RL 4

(LINES 64–80)

Explain that an **extended metaphor** is a figure of speech that compares one thing to another without using *like* or *as* and that continues the comparison over several sentences, paragraphs, or pages.

E **CITE TEXT EVIDENCE** Ask students to reread lines 64–80. Have them identify the metaphor and specific lines in which the narrator extends the metaphor. (*The narrator compares Ann to a sculptor and the dogs to blocks of stone in lines 65–69. In lines 78–80, the narrator continues the metaphor by suggesting that the dogs may "disappear back into the stone."*)

> **CRITICAL VOCABULARY**
>
> **tutelage**: The dogs that Ann trains often lose their skills once they are no longer under her authority as a teacher.
>
> **ASK STUDENTS** to describe why Ann's relationship with the dogs is described as tutelage, while the owner's relationship with the dogs is not. (*Ann has trained the dogs carefully, and they respect her authority. The owner does not know which of the dogs' "characteristics to nurture, which ones to discourage" and will not be able to control them.*)

Determine Theme

COMMON CORE **RL 2**

(LINES 125–144)

Note that Ann's story is interspersed with the narrator's reflections on it. These reflections often provide clues to themes.

 ASK STUDENTS to reread lines 125–144. Which part of this passage tells the narrator's thoughts about Ann's story? What larger idea or theme do these reflections hint at? *(The first paragraph tells Ann's story. In lines 138–141, the narrator reflects on the events she has described before returning to another detail from her story—the fact that snow is obscuring their tracks very quickly. The narrator's observation that Ann and Gray Owl's tracks might seem random if viewed from above, even though they actually reflect "the purpose, the focus that was burning hot in both their and their dogs' hearts" suggests the idea that other people's paths in life may be mysterious to us, but we should not presume to judge whether they make sense.)*

---

them, and the pull of gravity, they might have believed they had ascended into some sky-place where all the world was snow.

110   They worked into the wind—north—whenever they could. Ann would carry birds in a pouch over her shoulder—much as a woman might carry a purse—and from time to time would fling a startled bird out into that dreary, icy snowscape—and the quail would fly off with great haste, a dark feathered buzz bomb disappearing quickly into the teeth of cold, and then Gray Owl and Ann and the dog, or dogs, would go find it, following it by scent only, as always.

Snot icicles would be hanging from the dogs' nostrils. They would always find the bird. The dog, or dogs, would point it, at which point Gray Owl or Ann would step forward and flush it—the beleaguered

120   bird would leap into the sky again—and then once more they would push on after it, pursuing that bird toward the horizon as if driving it with a whip. Whenever the bird wheeled and flew downwind, they'd quarter away from it, then get a mile or so downwind from it and push it back north.

 When the quail finally became too exhausted to fly, Ann would pick it up from beneath the dogs' noses as they held point staunchly, put the tired bird in her game bag and replace it with a fresh one, and off they'd go again. They carried their lunch in Gray Owl's day pack, as well as emergency supplies—a tent and some dry clothes—in case

130   they should become lost, and around noon each day (they could rarely see the sun, only an eternal ice-white haze, so that they relied instead only on their rhythms within) they would stop and make a pot of tea on the sputtering little gas stove. Sometimes one or two of the quail would die from exposure, and they would cook that on the stove and eat it out there in the tundra, tossing the feathers up into the wind as if to launch one more flight and feeding the head, guts, and feet to the dogs.

Perhaps seen from above their tracks would have seemed aimless and wandering rather than with the purpose, the focus that was

140   burning hot in both their and the dogs' hearts—perhaps someone viewing the tracks could have discerned the pattern, or perhaps not—but it did not matter, for their tracks—the patterns, direction, and tracing of them—were obscured by the drifting snow, sometimes within minutes after they were laid down.

Toward the end of the week, Ann said, they were finally running all six dogs at once, like a herd of silent wild horses through all that snow, and as she would be going home the next day, there was no need to conserve any of the birds she had brought, and she was turning them loose several at a time: birds flying in all directions; the dogs, as

150   ever, tracking them to the ends of the earth.

It was almost a whiteout that last day, and it was hard to keep track of all the dogs. Ann was sweating from the exertion as well as the tension of trying to keep an eye on, and evaluate, each dog—the sweat was freezing on her in places, so that it was as if she were developing

---

SCAFFOLDING FOR ELL STUDENTS

Vocabulary: Specialized Terms Explain that Ann has trained the dogs for hunting. In a real hunting situation, the dogs' owner would shoot a bird dead and the dogs would run ahead to find it and point at it until the hunter arrived. In the "field trials" that Ann conducts, Ann releases live birds (quail) and has the dogs track them down. Have students use this background and context clues to define these hunting terms:

- *flush* (line 119), "scare a bird so that it flies into the air"
- *held point* (line 126), "stayed still while pointing to the bird"
- *tracking* (line 150), "finding by scent"
- *retrieve* (line 168), "bring back to the hunter"
- *whoaed* (line 212), "gave the command to stay"

> 66 They might have **believed** they had ascended into some **sky-place** where all the world was **snow**. 99

an ice skin. She jokingly told Gray Owl that next time she was going to try to find a client who lived in Arizona, or even South America. Gray Owl smiled and then told her that they were lost, but no matter, the storm would clear in a day or two.

160 They knew it was getting near dusk—there was a faint dulling to the sheer whiteness, a kind of increasing heaviness in the air, a new density to the faint light around them—and the dogs slipped in and out of sight, working just at the edges of their vision.

The temperature was dropping as the north wind increased—"No question about which way south is; we'll turn around and walk south for three hours, and if we don't find a road, we'll make camp," Gray Owl said—and now the dogs were coming back with frozen quail held gingerly in their mouths, for once the birds were dead, they were allowed to retrieve them, though the dogs must have been puzzled that there had been no shots. Ann said she fired a few rounds of the

170 cap pistol into the air to make the dogs think she had hit those birds. Surely they believed she was a goddess.

They turned and headed south—Ann with a bag of frozen birds over her shoulder, and the dogs, knowing that the hunt was over now, all around them, once again like a team of horses in harness, though wild and prancy.

After an hour of increasing discomfort—Ann's and Gray Owl's hands and feet numb, and ice beginning to form on the dogs' paws, so that the dogs were having to high-step—they came in day's last light to the edge of a wide clearing: a terrain that was remarkable and soothing for its lack of hills. It was a frozen lake, which meant—said Gray

180 Owl—they had drifted west (or perhaps east) by as much as ten miles.

Ann said that Gray Owl looked tired and old and guilty, as would any host who had caused his guest some unasked-for inconvenience. They knelt down and began massaging the dogs' paws and then lit the little stove and held each dog's foot, one at a time, over the tiny blue flame to help it thaw out.

Gray Owl walked out to the edge of the lake ice and kicked at it with his foot, hoping to find fresh water beneath for the dogs; if they ate too much snow, especially after working so hard, they'd get violent

The Hermit's Story **505**

CLOSE READ

Determine Theme

 RL 2

(LINES 151–158; 176–186)

Explain that the narrator continues to develop a theme related to nature in these lines.

G CITE TEXT EVIDENCE Direct students to reread lines 151–158. Ask them to identify Bass's attitude toward nature as expressed by the narrator's words, and lines that support their answer. *(The narrator emphasizes the power of nature, the vulnerability of humans in the face of it, and its unpredictable nature. In lines 151–153, he notes that the storm makes the humans almost blind in a "whiteout." In lines 153–155 he notes that it is so cold that Ann is almost developing an "ice skin." In lines 157–158, he describes nature's power and its unpredictability by noting Ann and Gray Owl are "lost" and that the storm may end "in a day or two.")*

Note that as the plot develops, the relationship between the characters and nature becomes even more clear.

H CITE TEXT EVIDENCE Direct students to reread lines 176–186. Ask them to identify lines in which Bass's attitude toward nature is further developed. *(The narrator emphasizes the power of nature by describing the discomfort suffered by Ann, Gray Owl, and the dogs [lines 176–178]; the way the storm takes away much of Gray Owl's strength [line 182]; and the fact that they need to help the dogs keep their paws from freezing [lines 184–186].)*

APPLYING ACADEMIC VOCABULARY

intensity	visualize

As you discuss the figurative language and imagery used by the author, incorporate the Collection 6 academic vocabulary words *intensity* and *visualize*. Ask students to identify figurative language and imagery that Bass uses to help readers **visualize** the **intensity** of the storm that traps Ann and Gray Owl.

Analyze Story Elements: Character (LINES 196–209)

 COMMON CORE RL 3

Explain that characters can be revealed through self-observation or the observation of others.

 CITE TEXT EVIDENCE Ask students to reread lines 196–209. What details in this passage show an interesting new side of Ann's character? *(The narrator has portrayed Ann as calm and unworried through the stress of the storm, and she remains extremely practical rather than emotional when Gray Owl disappears into the lake. She is "sorry for Gray Owl . . . and worried for his dogs" in case they decide to follow him into the lake. However, she must "be perfectly honest" and admit that her main concern is her own survival. She needs the supplies in Gray Owl's pack. So, she immediately begins to formulate a plan "to get that day pack off of the drowned man and set up the wet tent in the blizzard.")*

190 diarrhea and might then become too weak to continue home the next day, or the next, or whenever the storm quit.

Ann said she could barely see Gray Owl's outline through the swirling snow, even though he was less than twenty yards away. He kicked once at the sheet of ice, the vast plate of it, with his heel, then disappeared below the ice.

Ann wanted to believe that she had blinked and lost sight of him, or that a gust of snow had swept past and hidden him, but it had been too fast, too total: she knew that the lake had swallowed him. She was sorry for Gray Owl, she said, and worried for his dogs—afraid they

200 would try to follow his scent down into the icy lake, and be lost as well—but what she was most upset about, she said—to be perfectly honest—was that Gray Owl had been wearing the little day pack with the tent and emergency rations. She had it in her mind to try to save Gray Owl, and to try to keep the dogs from going through the ice, but if he drowned, she was going to have to figure out how to try to get that day pack off of the drowned man and set up the wet tent in the blizzard on the snowy prairie and then crawl inside and survive. She would have to go into the water naked, so that when she came back out—if she came back out—she would have dry clothes to put on.

210 The dogs came galloping up, seeming as large as deer or elk in that dim landscape, against which there was nothing else to give them perspective, and Ann whoaed them right at the lake's edge, where they stopped immediately, as if they had suddenly been cast with a sheet of ice.

Strategies for Annotation   ✎ 🖿 *Annotate it!*

Analyze Story Elements: Character

 COMMON CORE RL 3

Share these strategies for guided or independent analysis:

- Highlight in blue passages that tell what the narrator thinks about Ann.
- Highlight in pink passages in which Ann reveals insights about herself.
- On notes, write what you learn about Ann.

too fast, too total: she knew that the lake had swallowed him. She was sorry for Gray Owl, she said, and worried for his dogs—afraid they would try to follow his scent down into the icy lake, and be lost as well—but what she was most upset about, she said—to be perfectly honest—was that Gray Owl had been wearing the little day pack with the tent and emergency rations. She had it in her mind to try to save

Ann's main concern is for her own survival.

Ann knew they would stay there forever, or until she released them, and it troubled her to think that if she drowned, they too would die—that they would stand there motionless, as she had commanded them, for as long as they could, until at some point—days later, perhaps—they would lie down, trembling with exhaustion—they
220   might lick at some snow, for moisture—but that then the snows would cover them, and still they would remain there, chins resting on their front paws, staring straight ahead and unseeing into the storm, wondering where the scent of her had gone.

Ann eased out onto the ice. She followed the tracks until she came to the jagged hole in the ice through which Gray Owl had plunged. She was almost half again lighter than he, but she could feel the ice crackling beneath her own feet. It sounded different too, in a way she could not place—it did not have the squeaky, percussive resonance of the lake-ice back home—and she wondered if Canadian ice froze
230   differently or just sounded different.

She got down on all fours and crept closer to the hole. It was right at dusk. She peered down into the hole and dimly saw Gray Owl standing down there, waving his arms at her. He did not appear to be swimming. Slowly, she took one glove off and eased her bare hand down into the hole. She could find no water, and **tentatively**, she reached deeper.

Gray Owl's hand found hers and he pulled her down in. Ice broke as she fell, but he caught her in his arms. She could smell the wood smoke in his jacket from the alder he burned in his cabin. There was
240   no water at all, and it was warm beneath the ice.

"This happens a lot more than people realize," he said. "It's not really a phenomenon; it's just what happens. A cold snap comes in October, freezes a skin of ice over the lake—it's got to be a shallow one, almost a marsh. Then a snowfall comes, insulating the ice. The lake drains in fall and winter—percolates down through the soil"— he stamped the spongy ground beneath them—"but the ice up top remains. And nobody ever knows any differently. People look out at the surface and think, *Aha, a frozen lake.*" Gray Owl laughed.

"Did you know it would be like this?" Ann asked.
250   "No," he said. "I was looking for water. I just got lucky."

Ann walked back to shore beneath the ice to fetch her stove and to release the dogs from their whoa command. The dry lake was only about eight feet deep, but it grew shallow quickly closer to shore, so that Ann had to crouch to keep from bumping her head on the overhead ice, and then crawl; and then there was only space to wriggle, and to emerge she had to break the ice above her by bumping and then battering it with her head and elbows, like the struggles of some embryonic hatchling; and when she stood up, waist-deep amid sparkling shards of ice—it was nighttime now—the dogs barked
260   ferociously at her, but remained where she had ordered them to stay, and she was surprised at how far off course she was when she climbed

tentatively
(tĕn′tə-tĭv-lē) *adv.* with uncertainty; cautiously.

Determine Theme

 RL 2

(LINES 215–223; 231–250)

Explain that revealing a character's thoughts can be an important way to develop a theme.

J **ASK STUDENTS** to reread lines 215–223. What aspect of nature is highlighted through Ann's thoughts? *(Nature is characterized in these lines as indifferent to the lives or deaths of individuals. Ann calmly accepts the fact that she may drown. The image of the snow covering the dogs as they die shows that nature will continue to run its course regardless of the consequences for dogs or humans.)*

Note that an unexpected plot development helps emphasize another aspect of nature in lines 231–250.

K **CITE TEXT EVIDENCE** Direct students to reread this passage. Ask them to describe an aspect of nature that is emphasized in these lines, citing specific text evidence. *(This unexpected turn of events highlights the fact that nature is not only very powerful, but also unpredictable. The lack of water under the ice is "just what happens," according to Gray Owl, and it allows people to "look out at the surface" and make an incorrect judgment. Gray Owl himself did not expect to find the dry land under the ice; he merely "got lucky." This suggests that nature's unpredictability can lead to wonderful surprises as well as to disaster.)*

CRITICAL VOCABULARY

tentatively: Ann reaches cautiously under the ice.

ASK STUDENTS why Ann acts tentatively as she puts her hand through the hole in the ice. *(She is exploring a new and strange situation, since Gray Owl is standing at the bottom of the lake waving at her, and she expects her hand to be engulfed in frigid water at any moment.)*

Analyze Language

RL 4

(LINES 281–286)

Note that the world beneath the ice is unlike anything Ann had ever experienced, and she provides many details to help her listeners experience it as she did during those first moments. Bass uses imagery appealing to different senses to bring this subterranean world to life.

Ⓛ **ASK STUDENTS** to reread lines 281–286 and explain how Ann, through the narrator, describes the air beneath the ice. What is the tone of this passage? How does this description add to the development of the story? (*Even the most common thing people take for granted—the air—is different under the ice because of its unique taste, odor and density. The tone of wonder or amazement gives readers the sense that they are about to experience an unusual adventure.*)

out; she had traveled only twenty feet, but already the dogs were twice that far away from her. She knew humans had a poorly evolved, almost nonexistent sense of direction, but this error—over such a short distance—shocked her. It was as if there were in us a thing—an impulse, a catalyst—that denies our ever going straight to another thing. Like dogs working left and right into the wind, she thought, before converging on the scent.

270 Except that the dogs would not get lost, while she could easily imagine herself and Gray Owl getting lost beneath the lake, walking in circles forever, unable to find even the simplest of things: the shore.

She gathered the stove and dogs. She was tempted to try to go back in the way she had come out—it seemed so easy—but considered the consequences of getting lost in the other direction, and instead followed her original tracks out to where Gray Owl had first dropped through the ice. It was true night now, and the blizzard was still blowing hard, plastering snow and ice around her face like a mask. The dogs did not want to go down into the hole, so she lowered them to Gray Owl and then climbed gratefully back down into the warmth

280 herself.

The air was a thing of its own—recognizable as air, and breathable, as such, but with a taste and odor, an essence, unlike any other air they'd ever breathed. It had a different density to it, so that smaller, shallower breaths were required; there was very much the feeling that if they breathed in too much of the strange, dense air, they would drown.

They wanted to explore the lake, and were thirsty, but it felt like a victory simply to be warm—or rather, not cold—and they were so exhausted that instead they made pallets out of the dead marsh grass

290 that rustled around their ankles, and they slept curled up on the tiniest of hammocks, to keep from getting damp in the pockets and puddles of dampness that still lingered here and there.

All eight of them slept as if in a nest, heads and arms draped across other ribs and hips, and it was, said Ann, the best and deepest sleep she'd ever had—the sleep of hounds, the sleep of childhood—and how long they slept, she never knew, for she wasn't sure, later, how much of their subsequent time they spent wandering beneath the lake, and then up on the prairie, homeward again—but when they awoke, it was still night, or night once more, and clearing, with bright stars

300 visible through the porthole, their point of embarkation; and even from beneath the ice, in certain places where, for whatever reasons—temperature, oxygen content, wind scour—the ice was clear rather than glazed, they could see the spangling of stars, though more dimly; and strangely, rather than seeming to distance them from the stars, this phenomenon seemed to pull them closer, as if they were up in the stars, traveling the Milky Way, or as if the stars were embedded in the ice.

SCAFFOLDING FOR ELL STUDENTS

Language: Punctuation Note that Bass uses **dashes** in his writing, often creating informal grammatical structures. Explain that dashes can replace commas, semicolons, colons, and parentheses to indicate emphasis, an interruption, or a clarifying detail. Discuss the use of dashes in the following lines, including what other punctuation could have been used and what each dash signifies.

- Lines 264–265 (*commas could be used; emphasis*)
- Line 273 (*parentheses; clarifying detail*)
- Line 298 (*semicolon; emphasis*)
- Line 308 (*parentheses; clarifying detail*)
- Line 339 (*commas; an interruption common in speech patterns*)

It was very cold outside—up above—and there was a steady stream, a current like a river, of the night's colder, heavier air plunging
310 down through their porthole, as if trying to fill the empty lake with that frozen air—but there was also the hot muck of the earth's massive respirations breathing out warmth and being trapped and protected beneath that ice, so that there were warm currents doing battle with the lone cold current.

The result was that it was breezy down there, and the dogs' noses twitched in their sleep as the images brought by these scents painted themselves across their sleeping brains in the language we call dreams but which, for the dogs, and perhaps for us, was reality: the scent of an owl *real*, not a dream; the scent of bear, cattail, willow, loon, *real*, even
320 though they were sleeping, and even though those things were not visible, only over the next horizon.

The ice was contracting, groaning and cracking and squeaking up tighter, shrinking beneath the great cold—a concussive, grinding sound, as if giants were walking across the ice above—and it was this sound that had awakened them. They snuggled in warmer among the rattly dried yellowing grasses and listened to the tremendous clashings, as if they were safe beneath the sea and were watching waves of starlight sweeping across their hiding place; or as if they were in some place, some position, where they could watch mountains being
330 born.

After a while the moon came up and washed out the stars. The light was blue and silver and seemed, Ann said, to be like a living thing. It filled the sheet of ice just above their heads with a shimmering cobalt light, which again rippled as if the ice were moving, rather than the earth itself, with the moon tracking it—and like deer drawn by gravity getting up in the night to feed for an hour or so before settling back in, Gray Owl and Ann and the dogs rose from their nests of straw and began to travel.

"You didn't—you know—*engage?*" Susan asks: a little
340 mischievously, and a little proprietary, perhaps.

Ann shakes her head. "It was too cold," she says. I sneak a glance at Roger but cannot read his expression. Is he in love with her? Does she own his heart?

"But you would have, if it hadn't been so cold, right?" Susan asks, and Ann shrugs.

"He was an old man—in his fifties—and the dogs were around. But yeah, there was something about it that made me think of . . . those things," she says, careful and precise as ever.

"I would have done it anyway," Susan says. "Even if it was cold,
350 and even if he was a hundred."

"We walked a long way," Ann says, eager to change the subject. "The air was damp down there, and whenever we'd get chilled, we'd stop and make a little fire out of a bundle of dry cattails." There were little pockets and puddles of swamp gas pooled here and there, she

TO CHALLENGE STUDENTS . . .

Trace References to Dreams How much of Ann's story is real, and how much is from the world of dreams? Have students review the story and identify references to sleep and dreams. Have them conclude whether this is an intentional **motif,** or recurring idea, that Bass uses to develop a theme. Students should discuss their ideas in pairs or small groups before sharing their insights with the class. *(References to sleep and dreams occur in lines 95–100, 105–109, 293–299, 315–321, 428–433, 454–467, and 487–491. Students might also note references to being lost in lines 156–158, 269–271, and 369. The motif of being lost in a dream world—and having it seem more vivid and satisfying than one's waking life—may suggest the importance of connecting with a more primal existence underlying the one offered by civilization.)*

CLOSE READ

Determine Theme

COMMON CORE **RL 2**

(LINES 331–338)

Explain that descriptions of a story's setting can reveal the narrator's tone and also hint at themes the author wants to communicate.

M ASK STUDENTS to reread lines 331–338. What is the tone in this passage? How does this description of the setting help develop a theme about nature? *(Ann describes a scene of extraordinary beauty that includes the moon and its light filtering through the ice, which seems like a moving, active entity. The tone is one of wonder and admiration. The description suggests the theme that nature is powerful, unpredictable, and beautiful, all at the same time.)*

Analyze Structure:
Frame Story (LINES 339–351)

COMMON CORE **RL 5**

Explain that while the frame story is mostly developed at the beginning and end of the story, the author may occasionally interrupt the inner story with events that happen in the frame.

N ASK STUDENTS to reread lines 339–351 and suggest why Bass may have chosen to interrupt the inner story at this time and in this way. *(Bass may want to emphasize that the characters in the frame story believe Ann's fantastical tale, since Susan is asking for additional details about it. He may want to give the reader a break from the surreal world Ann describes and note that the same character, Ann, inhabits both the surreal world under the ice and the current world established at the dinner party. Susan's question about whether Ann's wanted to "engage" sexually with Gray Owl also grounds the magical world in common, worldly thoughts and urges.)*

Analyze Structure: Frame Story (LINES 378–386)

 COMMON CORE RL 5

Explain that when reading a frame story, it's important to consider whose thoughts are being expressed in any given passage and which story they belong to. In this selection, the distinction is often subtle because the narrator is telling the frame story and also paraphrasing Ann's story, referring to Ann in the third person in both cases.

ⓞ ASK STUDENTS to reread lines 378–386. Is this paragraph part of the inner story or the frame story? Explain. *(The narrator is most likely expressing his own thoughts as a part of the frame story. The paragraphs before and after this one advance the narrative of Ann's story, while this paragraph pauses to reflect on what is happening in that narrative. Accept all reasonable responses if some students argue this passage gives Ann's reflections on her own story.)*

CRITICAL VOCABULARY

subterranean: Ann and Gray Owl wander through the world beneath the surface of the ice.

ASK STUDENTS to explain why both the blue and the orange light are described as subterranean. *(The orange light comes from the torches and fires lit beneath the frozen surface of the lake. The blue light comes from the moon but has entered the world below the lake through "rents in the ice" [line 367] and would appear from above to be coming from beneath the surface.)*

---

said, and sometimes a spark from the cattails would ignite one of those, and all around these little pockets of gas would light up like when you toss gas on a fire—these little explosions of brilliance, like flashbulbs, marsh pockets igniting like falling dominoes, or like children playing hopscotch—until a large-enough flash-pocket was 360 reached—sometimes thirty or forty yards away from them, by this point—that the puff of flame would blow a chimney-hole through the ice, venting the other pockets, and the fires would crackle out, the scent of grass smoke sweet in their lungs, and they could feel gusts of warmth from the little flickering fires, and currents of the colder, heavier air sliding down through the new vent-holes and pooling around their ankles. The moonlight would strafe down through those rents in the ice, and shards of moon-ice would be glittering and spinning like diamond-motes in those newly vented columns of moonlight; and they pushed on, still lost, but so alive.

370   The mini-explosions were fun, but they frightened the dogs, and so Ann and Gray Owl lit twisted bundles of cattails and used them for torches to light their way, rather than building warming fires, though occasionally they would still pass through a pocket of methane and a stray ember would fall from their torches, and the whole chain of fire and light would begin again, culminating once more with a vent-hole being blown open and shards of glittering ice tumbling down into their lair . . .

ⓞ 380   What would it have looked like, seen from above—the orange blurrings of their wandering trail beneath the ice; and what would the sheet of lake-ice itself have looked like that night—throbbing with the ice-bound, **subterranean** blue and orange light of moon and fire? But again, there was no one to view the spectacle: only the travelers themselves, and they had no perspective, no vantage or loft from which to view or judge themselves. They were simply pushing on from one fire to the next, carrying their tiny torches. The beauty in front of them was enough.

They knew they were getting near a shore—the southern shore, they hoped, as they followed the glazed moon's lure above—when the dogs began to encounter shore birds that had somehow found

subterranean
(sŭb´tə-rā´nē-ən) *adj.*
underground.

"They pushed on, still lost, but so alive."

WHEN STUDENTS STRUGGLE . . .

Encourage students to use context clues or a dictionary to define these terms. Discuss how they are central to the narrator's descriptions.

- *rents, shards* (line 367) *("tears in a surface"; "sharp splinters like broken glass")*
- *motes* (line 368) *("small particles of dust")*
- *vantage* (line 383) *("place from which to get a broad view")*
- *fissures and rifts* (line 390) *("cracks and breaks in a surface")*
- *immolate* (line 401) *("set on fire")*
- *cobalt* (line 405) *("a very deep shade of blue")*
- *translucent* (line 407) *("allowing light to shine through")*

their way beneath the ice through small fissures and rifts and were taking refuge in the cattails. Small winter birds—juncos, nuthatches, chickadees—skittered away from the smoky approach of their torches; only a few late-migrating (or winter-trapped) snipe held tight and steadfast, and the dogs began to race ahead of Gray Owl and Ann, working these familiar scents—blue and silver ghost-shadows of dog-muscle weaving ahead through slants of moonlight.

The dogs emitted the odor of adrenaline when they worked, Ann said—a scent like damp fresh-cut green hay—and with nowhere to vent, the odor was dense and thick around them, so that Ann wondered if it too might be flammable, like the methane—if in the dogs' passions they might literally immolate themselves.

They followed the dogs closely with their torches. The ceiling was low—about eight feet, as if in a regular room—so that the tips of their torches' flames seared the ice above them, leaving a drip behind them and transforming the milky, almost opaque cobalt and orange ice behind them, wherever they passed, into wandering ribbons of clear ice, translucent to the sky—a script of flame, or buried flame, ice-bound flame—and they hurried to keep up with the dogs.

Now the dogs had the snipe surrounded, as Ann told it, and one by one the dogs went on point, each dog freezing as it pointed to the birds' hiding places, and it was the strangest scene yet, Ann said, seeming surely underwater; and Gray Owl moved in to flush the birds, which launched themselves with vigor against the roof of the ice above, fluttering like bats; but the snipe were too small, not powerful enough to break through those frozen four inches of water (though they could fly four thousand miles to South America each year and then back to Canada six months later—is freedom a lateral component, or a vertical one?), and as Gray Owl kicked at the clumps of frost-bent cattails where the snipe were hiding and they burst into flight, only to hit their heads on the ice above them, they came tumbling back down, raining limp and unconscious back to their soft grassy nests.

The dogs began retrieving them, carrying them gingerly, delicately—not preferring the taste of snipe, which ate only earth-worms—and Ann and Gray Owl gathered the tiny birds from the dogs, placed them in their pockets, and continued on to the shore, chasing that moon, the ceiling lowering to six feet, then four, then to a crawlspace, and after they had bashed their way out (with elbows, fists, and forearms) and stepped back out into the frigid air, they tucked the still-unconscious snipe into little crooks in branches, up against the trunks of trees and off the ground, out of harm's way, and passed on, south—as if late in their own migration—while the snipe rested, warm and terrified and heart-fluttering, but saved, for now, against the trunks of those trees.

Long after Ann and Gray Owl and the pack of dogs had passed through, the birds would awaken, their bright dark eyes luminous in the moonlight, and the first sight they would see would be the

CLOSE READ

Determine Theme

COMMON CORE · RL 2

(LINES 409–433)

Explain that an author may develop a theme by introducing situations or characters that are parallel to others in the story.

P ASK STUDENTS to reread lines 409–421. In what ways is the situation of the snipe similar to that of Ann and Gray Owl? How do these similarities reinforce a theme about nature? *(The snipe are trapped by the ice in the same way that Ann and Gray Owl are trapped by the storm. The snipe are too small to free themselves, and their panic puts them in danger. If Ann and Gray Owl took panicked actions, they would be injured or killed just as the snipe are. These similarities reinforce the idea that individuals are often at the mercy of nature.)*

Point out that sometimes a contrast between two situations may serve to reinforce a theme.

Q ASK STUDENTS to reread lines 422–433. How does Ann and Gray Owl's behavior with the snipe contrast with their actions with the quail used to train the dogs? *(Ann and Gray Owl take great pains to save the snipe by carrying them from underneath the lake to nestle them in tree branches so they can survive. The quail, on the other hand, are simply used to train the dogs until they die of exhaustion; then they are eaten and disposed of.)* How does this contrast help reinforce one of the author's themes about nature? *(Human behavior is unpredictable, like the forces of nature. Just as Ann and Gray Owl may choose to kill some birds and rescue others, nature may take the form of a deadly storm or a warm, dry lakebed protected under a roof of ice.)*

TEACH

CLOSE READ

Determine Theme

COMMON CORE RL 2

(LINES 454–480)

Point out that the author explores the situation of the snipe at some length. The discussion of the snipe reinforces themes about human life.

R **CITE TEXT EVIDENCE** Ask students to reread lines 454–467. Have them cite details that show how the snipe's situation sheds light on that of the story's human characters. *(The narrator imagines that the snipe will think that "a thing like grace had passed through while they slept . . . and rewarded them for their faith and endurance." The idea of grace is one that people use to explain the mysterious way in which good things may happen in the midst of life's greatest difficulties. Ann and Gray Owl's rescue of the birds is similar to the way in which the frozen lake rescued them from the storm. Like the birds' experience, it may later seem to them like "one of winter's dreams.")*

Point out another passage in which the narrator interrupts to express his own thoughts on an aspect of Ann's story.

S **ASK STUDENTS** to reread lines 468–480 and explain the connection the narrator makes between the snipe's belief in spring and his political beliefs. *(The narrator says the belief in spring is like "green fire" in people's hearts. This fire is a kind of grace that will allow the country to survive because enough people still believe in the spiritual values that lie beneath the surface appearance of things.)*

CRITICAL VOCABULARY

insipid: The narrator rejects dull ideas that reflect only the surface of things.

ASK STUDENTS to explain why both the "long snowy winter" and some people's belief in the "surface of things" are both described as insipid. *(The winter removes color and energy with its blankets of snow and ice. When people see only the surface of things, they miss out on the vital energy—the "green fire"—that inspires the richest and most exciting experiences in life.)*

frozen marsh before them, with its chain of still-steaming vent-holes stretching back across all the way to the other shore. Perhaps these were birds that had been unable to migrate owing to injuries, or some genetic absence. Perhaps they had tried to migrate in the past but had found either their winter habitat destroyed or the path down there so fragmented and fraught with danger that it made more sense—to these few birds—to ignore the tuggings of the stars and seasons and instead to try to carve out new lives, new ways of being, even in such a stark and severe landscape: or rather, in a stark and severe period—knowing that lushness and bounty were still retained within that landscape. That it was only a phase; that better days would come. That in fact (the snipe knowing these things with their blood, ten-million-years-in-the-world), the austere times were the very thing, the very imbalance, that would summon the resurrection of that frozen richness within the soil—if indeed that richness, that magic, that hope, did still exist beneath the ice and snow. Spring would come like its own green fire, if only the injured ones could hold on.

R And what would the snipe think or remember, upon reawakening and finding themselves still in that desolate position, desolate place and time, but still alive, and with hope?

Would it seem to them that a thing like grace had passed through, as they slept—that a slender winding river of it had passed through and rewarded them for their faith and endurance?

Believing, stubbornly, that that green land beneath them would blossom once more. Maybe not soon; but again.

If the snipe survived, they would be among the first to see it. Perhaps they believed that the pack of dogs, and Gray Owl's and Ann's advancing torches, had only been one of winter's dreams. Even with the proof—the scribings—of grace's passage before them—the vent-holes still steaming—perhaps they believed it was only one of winter's dreams.

S It would be curious to tally how many times any or all of us reject, or fail to observe, moments of grace. Another way in which I think Susan and I differ from most of the anarchists and militia members up here is that we believe there is still green fire in the hearts of our citizens, beneath this long snowy winter—beneath the chitin of the **insipid**. That there is still something beneath the surface: that our souls and spirits are still of more worth, more value, than the glassine, latticed ice-structures visible only now at the surface of things. We still believe there's something down there beneath us, as a country. Not that we're better than other countries, by any means, but that we're luckier. That ribbons of grace are still passing through and around us—even now, and for whatever reasons, certainly unbeknownst to us, and certainly undeserved, unearned.

insipid (ĭn-sĭp′ĭd) *adj.* dull; lacking color or zest.

T Gray Owl, Ann, and the dogs headed south for half a day until they reached the snow-scoured road on which they'd parked. The road

APPLYING ACADEMIC VOCABULARY

encounter	restore

As you discuss the end of the story, incorporate the Collection 6 academic vocabulary words *encounter* and *restore*. Point out Ann and Gray Owl's decision to **restore** the snipe to safe places in trees, and discuss how the author uses this scene to introduce a discussion of grace. Ask students how the narrator thinks Ann's **encounter** with the strange and beautiful frozen lake affects her life twenty years later.

looked different, Ann said, buried beneath snowdrifts, and they didn't
know whether to turn east or west. The dogs chose west, and so Gray
Owl and Ann followed them. Two hours later they were back at their
truck, and that night they were back at Gray Owl's cabin; by the next
night Ann was home again. She says that even now she still sometimes
has dreams about being beneath the ice—about living beneath the
ice—and that it seems to her as if she was down there for much longer
490 than a day and a night; that instead she might have been gone for
years.

It was twenty years ago, when it happened. Gray Owl has since
died, and all those dogs are dead now too. She is the only one who still
carries—in the flesh, at any rate—the memory of that passage.

Ann would never discuss such a thing, but I suspect that it, that
one day and night, helped give her a model for what things were like
for her dogs when they were hunting and when they went on point:
how the world must have appeared to them when they were in that
trance, that blue zone, where the odors of things wrote their images
500 across the dogs' hot brainpans. A zone where sight, and the appearance
of things—surfaces—disappeared, and where instead their essence—
the heat molecules of scent—was revealed, illuminated, circumscribed,
possessed.

I suspect that she holds that knowledge—the memory of that
one day and night—especially since she is now the sole possessor—
as tightly, and securely, as one might clench some bright small gem
in one's fist: not a gem given to one by some favored or beloved
individual but, even more valuable, some gem found while out on
a walk—perhaps by happenstance, or perhaps by some unavoidable
510 rhythm of fate—and hence containing great magic, great strength.

Such is the nature of the kinds of people living, scattered here and
there, in this valley.

COLLABORATIVE DISCUSSION Do you believe that the events in Ann's story
could happen? With a partner, discuss the details in the text that support
your view of whether the occurrence is or is not real. Cite specific evidence
from the story to support your ideas.

The Hermit's Story **513**

CLOSE READ

Analyze Structure: Frame Story (LINES 481–503)

 COMMON CORE RL 5

Explain that a frame-story structure usually ends with
the conclusion of the inner story and a return to the
frame narrative.

T CITE TEXT EVIDENCE Direct students to reread
lines 481–503. Ask them to identify where the
transition from the inner story to the frame story
occurs. *(The transition occurs in line 495, when the
narrator says, "Ann would never discuss such a thing, but
I suspect...." Clearly this is no longer Ann telling her own
story.)* How does the return to the narrator's own voice
give perspective on the inner story? *(The narrator
provides his interpretation of what Ann's experience
might have meant to her. In the process, he reinforces
the theme about looking past the surface of things and
seeking the essence of life.)*

COLLABORATIVE DISCUSSION Have partners
discuss the believability of Ann's story. Students
might conclude that the dry lakebed below the ice is
believable due to the abundant and exquisitely detailed
descriptions Ann gives. Other details, such as the nature
of the job that brought her to Canada and the fact that
it was the "last good job she had," also add a certain air
of credibility to the story. Finally, her dinner companions
believe her story, so readers may be inclined to as well.

ASK STUDENTS to share any questions they generated
in the course of reading and discussing the selection.

TO CHALLENGE STUDENTS...

Compare Perspectives on Animals Do Rick Bass and Annie Dillard think about
animals in the same way? Ask students to review the descriptions of animals in "The
Hermit's Story," including the dogs and the birds under the lake. What attributes does
the narrator give them? How does this compare with Dillard's characterization of
weasels in "Living Like Weasels" (also in this collection)? Challenge students to write a
few paragraphs that answer these questions. Ask volunteers to share their work with
the class and respond to any questions from other students. *(In "The Hermit's Story,"
the narrator gives animals the ability to think like humans in lines 171, 315–321, and
440–467. In "Living Like Weasels," students may refer to lines 1–7, 90–93, and 100–106, in
which Dillard talks about the instincts that drive weasel behavior.)*

TEACH

Determine Theme **RL 2, RL 10**

Remind students that determining one or more themes is not a task with single, definitive answers. Critical readers may disagree about the importance of a theme or describe a theme using different words and emphasis. Note that determining a theme is a process that often takes place over a full reading of a text and by considering the text through a second or third reading. Explain that the bulleted questions are particular to this text, but that similar questions can be used for all texts to help determine theme.

Analyze Structure: Frame Story **RL 5**

Encourage students to answer each of the questions in the chart. Discuss their answers.

- **Point of View** *(The narrator is able to reflect and comment on Ann's story in a way that Ann cannot.)*
- **Parallels in Setting** *(Both settings reinforce the power of nature and the need for humans to adapt to it.)*
- **Interruptions of Inner Story by Frame Story Characters** *(These help to make the inner story a bit more believable and remind readers that the same character, Ann, takes part in both the frame story and the inner story.)*

Determine Theme **RL 2, RL 10**

The **theme** of a story is an underlying message about life or human experience that the author wants to share with readers. This message is implied by the author as the story unfolds. A story may have more than one theme. In "The Hermit's Story," the characters' interaction with nature is key to understanding and appreciating the story's theme. For instance, think about how nature is presented as mysterious and unpredictable. Look for repeating patterns and symbols. See if you identify with any of the characters or with a particular event that is recounted in the story.

Asking and answering questions such as these will help you draw accurate conclusions about this story's theme or themes:

- What is the setting of the story Ann tells, and how does it create conflict for the characters?
- How do the characters' actions, as well as the setting itself, resolve the conflict?
- How does narrator feel about the events in the story? What words and phrases convey his attitude?
- How does the outer story influence the way readers understand Ann's story?
- Is it significant that the events Ann recounts occurred two decades earlier?

Analyze Structure: Frame Story **RL 5**

A **frame story** is a narrative structure in which one or more stories are told within a story. Typically, the opening and closing of the story constitute the frame, and another story is told within that frame. Chaucer's *The Canterbury Tales* and the Arabic classic *One Thousand and One Nights* are well-known frame stories. This literary device can help make a story more believable by grounding a fantastical narrative in an ordinary experience—in the case of "The Hermit's Story," a dinner party. Authors might also choose this structure because the ideas in the frame can contribute to readers' understanding of the inner story; because it creates new meaning for the work as a whole; or simply because it enhances the story's aesthetic impact.

The frame story in "The Hermit's Story" introduces a setting and characters and provides a context for the inner story. To analyze the significance of the frame story structure, readers should note these elements:

> **Point of View** The first-person narrator of the frame story *retells* Ann's story instead of having Ann tell it directly. Think about why the author chooses to do this.
>
> **Parallels in Setting** The settings of the two stories are similar. In what way might these parallels contribute to the theme of the overall story?
>
> **Interruptions of Inner Story by Frame Story Characters** At one point, the guests break into Ann's story to have a conversation; later in Ann's story, the narrator comments on what she has said. Think about the purpose of these interruptions.

Strategies for Annotation 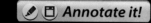 **Annotate it!**

Analyze Structure: Frame Story **RL 5**

Share these strategies for guided or independent analysis:

- Highlight sentences that mark a transition between the frame story and inner story, or vice versa.
- Highlight in yellow the first or last sentence related to the frame story.
- Highlight in green the first or last sentence related to the inner story.

> . . . I for one believe that he will learn it.
>
> Ann has a story for us. It's about one of the few clients she's ever had, a fellow named Gray Owl, up in Canada, who owned half a dozen speckled German shorthaired pointers and who hired Ann to train them all at once. It was twenty years ago, she says—her last good job.

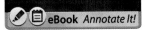

Analyzing the Text

COMMON CORE RL 1, RL 2, RL 3, RL 4, RL 5, SL 1a

Cite Text Evidence   Support your responses with evidence from the selection.

1. **Connect** Which details in the frame are similar to details in Anne's description of her story's setting? What do these details suggest about nature?

2. **Interpret** The narrator uses the word *grace* in line 60 and lines 434–461. What idea does he suggest through the use of this word?

3. **Cite Evidence** Which sensory details does Bass include to highlight the unusual nature of Ann's experience under the ice?

4. **Infer** What is Ann's perspective on her experience? Which words and phrases indicate this attitude?

5. **Analyze** What theme is conveyed by Ann's conflict with nature and by the resolution of this conflict?

6. **Interpret** Reread lines 495–512. What lasting effect does Ann's experience under the ice have on her? Why does the narrator find it to be significant?

7. **Evaluate** Does narrating Ann's story within the frame of a dinner party make it more believable? Identify specific details from the text to support your response.

8. **Critique** Why might the author have chosen to call his story "The Hermit's Story"? Is this an effective and appropriate title? Explain why or why not?

PERFORMANCE TASK

Speaking Activity: Discussion Some critics have suggested that Bass views nature as mystical—having a spiritual significance. Do you agree?

- Identify and jot down details that describe nature in the story. Use them to draw your own conclusion about Bass's view.

- In a small group, share your conclusion and support for it. Reach a consensus, or analyze reasons for conflicting views.

- Summarize important ideas generated by the discussion.

- Present your summary of the discussion to the class.

The Hermit's Story   **515**

Assign this performance task.

PERFORMANCE TASK

 COMMON CORE SL 1a

Speaking Activity: Discussion Remind students that certain words carry both denotative and connotative meanings. Suggest that as they review the text, students look for words that carry mystical or otherworldly connotations. Summaries should include the key points of the group's discussion, which should address and hopefully resolve the question of Bass's view of nature.

PRACTICE & APPLY

Analyzing the Text

COMMON CORE RL 1, RL 2, RL 3, RL 4, RL 5

Possible answers:

1. *The effects of an ice storm permeate the frame setting: vast drifts of snow crusted over by glazed ice, frozen fields, and blue light "creeping up fissures and cracks." In Ann's story, the snowscape offers an "eternal ice-white haze," and snow obscures tracks within minutes. The light "seemed, Ann said, to be like a living thing." The details present nature as a living, powerful character with stark yet ethereal qualities.*

2. *In line 60, grace reflects animals' (and some people's) elegance and poise within the environment, while lines 434–461 evoke its meaning as a beneficent spiritual force. The narrator is suggesting that living in harmony with nature is a spiritual experience.*

3. *Sensory details include the smell of the dense air, redolent with scents "of bear, cattail, willow, loon," and other organic substances; the feelings of warmth and of cold air "sliding down through . . . vent-holes"; the sights of light from "strange shards of moon-ice," orange methane bursts, torchlight, and "blue and silver ghost-shadows"; and the sounds of "mini-explosions" creaking ice, and splinters of "ice tumbling down."*

4. *Ann remains calm, without fear or concern. She seems entranced by the beauty of the surreal landscape. Indicative phrases include "explosions of brilliance," "the scent of grass smoke sweet in their lungs," "gusts of warmth," "glittering and spinning like diamond-motes," and "still lost, but so alive."*

5. *The conflict and resolution stress the theme that during "stark and severe" periods, one must remain aware of life's inherent "lushness and bounty," and maintain a belief that "better days would come" (lines 440–447).*

6. *Anne retains knowledge of an essential level of awareness that transcends our normal perceptions. The narrator considers her experience precious—a "bright small gem . . . containing great magic."*

7. *The frame story makes Ann's adventure more believable. Within the context of a mundane after-dinner conversation (and with frequent narrative interjections of "Ann said"), her wild tale becomes a realistic anecdote that her dinner mates matter-of-factly accept, and this helps the reader believe it, too.*

8. *The hermit of the title, Gray Owl, is not a central character, but it is "his" story because through his discovery and guidance, Ann has a life-altering experience and an amazing tale to tell.*

PRACTICE & APPLY

Critical Vocabulary

COMMON CORE L 4c, L 5b

Answers:

1. it included many fascinating details.

2. they seemed impossible to have actually occurred.

3. they were protected from the harsh weather above the surface.

4. they were not sure it could support their weight.

5. they were untrained and undisciplined.

Vocabulary Strategy: Consult a Thesaurus

Answers:

1. coaching

2. uncertainly

3. devised

4. trite

5. underground

 Assess It!

Online Selection Test
- Download an editable ExamView bank.
- Assign and manage this test online.

Critical Vocabulary

COMMON CORE L 4c, L 5b

fabricate	tutelage	tentatively
subterranean	insipid	

Practice and Apply Complete each sentence in a way that shows comprehension of the Critical Vocabulary word.

1. The story she told was far from *insipid* because . . .

2. The guests wondered if she *fabricated* the events because . . .

3. The animals were safe in their *subterranean* world because . . .

4. They stepped out onto the ice *tentatively* because . . .

5. Her *tutelage* of the dogs was necessary because . . .

Vocabulary Strategy: Consult a Thesaurus

A **thesaurus,** or a dictionary of synonyms (words that share a similar meaning), can be used to expand your vocabulary and make better word choices in your own writing. A print thesaurus might be organized alphabetically or by subject with an alphabetical index; an online thesaurus allows the user to search for synonyms of a word.

When choosing a synonym, it is important to remember that not all word choices will precisely match the intended meaning of the original word. There are usually subtle distinctions, or nuances, that make some words more suitable alternatives. For example, *eminent* and *notorious* are both valid synonyms of the word *famous*, but *eminent* has a positive connotation and *notorious* a negative one. It is important to choose synonyms that create the right impact when you write.

Practice and Apply With a partner, use a thesaurus to replace each Critical Vocabulary word with a synonym that best fits the word's meaning as it is used in the sentence. Consult a dictionary to confirm your choices.

1. He required extra *tutelage* in order to be the kicker for the team.

2. The child approached the dogs *tentatively*.

3. The two *fabricated* a plan that would get them home safely.

4. She would be a good speaker if her insights were less *insipid*.

5. The group shunned publicity, preferring to stay *subterranean*.

INTERACTIVE WHITEBOARD LESSON
Making Inferences

COMMON CORE

RL 1

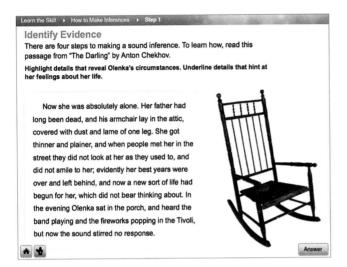

Learn the Skill ▸ How to Make Inferences ▸ Step 1

Identify Evidence

There are four steps to making a sound inference. To learn how, read this passage from "The Darling" by Anton Chekhov.

Highlight details that reveal Olenka's circumstances. Underline details that hint at her feelings about her life.

Now she was absolutely alone. Her father had long been dead, and his armchair lay in the attic, covered with dust and lame of one leg. She got thinner and plainer, and when people met her in the street they did not look at her as they used to, and did not smile to her; evidently her best years were over and left behind, and now a new sort of life had begun for her, which did not bear thinking about. In the evening Olenka sat in the porch, and heard the band playing and the fireworks popping in the Tivoli, but now the sound stirred no response.

Answer

TEACH

Before asking students to begin work on the Performance Task, review the steps involved in making inferences:

- **Step 1: Identify Evidence** Note that "The Hermit's Story" is filled with evocative details. Ask students to identify some that may indicate Bass's attitude toward nature and may indicate a mystical or spiritual nature or the lack of it. *(Possible support for a mystical nature is in lines 1–17, 322–330, 447–453, 457–467, 478–480, 487–491; possible support for non-mystical, random nature is in lines 241–250.)*

- **Step 2: Use Knowledge and Experience** Students may consider any extraordinary experiences they have had or heard about involving encounters with nature to assess whether Bass shows any of the same types of attitudes.

- **Step 3: Make an Inference** Students need to combine the textual evidence with their own prior knowledge to make an inference.

COLLABORATIVE DISCUSSION

Have students work in pairs to prepare for the Performance Task activities. They can compare notes and conclusions and discuss similarities and differences in their opinions before participating in the larger group.

INTERACTIVE WHITEBOARD LESSON
Figurative Language and Imagery

COMMON CORE

RL 4, L 5a

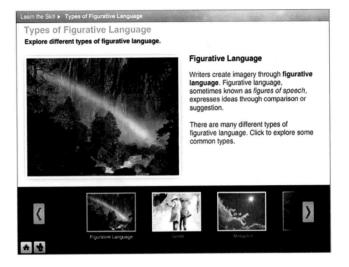

Learn the Skill ▸ Types of Figurative Language

Types of Figurative Language

Explore different types of figurative language.

Figurative Language

Writers create imagery through **figurative language**. Figurative language, sometimes known as *figures of speech*, expresses ideas through comparison or suggestion.

There are many different types of figurative language. Click to explore some common types.

Figurative Language   Simile   Metaphor

TEACH

Discuss the basic types of figurative language covered in the Interactive Whiteboard Lesson:

- **Similes** compare two unlike things using *like* or *as*.
- **Metaphors** compare two unlike things without using *like* or *as* and simply stating that one thing is another.
- **Personification** gives a nonhuman object human qualities.

PRACTICE AND APPLY

Direct students to the following examples and ask them to identify the type of figurative language used, the things being compared or described, and how it adds to the power of the writing.

- Line 16 *(simile in which the color blue is like a smell; enhances the sensory image of the landscape)*
- Lines 22–23 *(simile in which lights of the town are like stars; connects nature with human effects of artificial light)*
- Lines 70–71 *(personification in which the dogs become "geniuses"; enhances the idea of the power of Ann's work)*
- Lines 113–114 *(metaphor in which quail are "buzz bombs"; enhances the image of the quail's speed and energy)*

Determine Theme

COMMON CORE

RL 2

RETEACH

 LEVEL UP TUTORIALS Assign the following *Level Up* tutorial: **Theme**

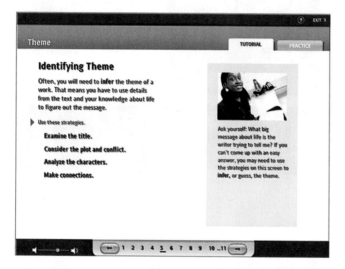

Review the terms *topic* and *theme*. Discuss the idea that if a class were assigned to write a fictional narrative on a particular topic, such as modern warfare or contemporary music, the themes expressed by various students could be wildly different. For example, one narrative on modern warfare might suggest that it is more humane and civilized than traditional warfare, while another might suggest that new technology makes modern warfare much more cruel and impersonal than it was previously.

CLOSE READING APPLICATION

Students can apply the skill to another text, movie, or television performance. They can begin by identifying the basic topic and then they can determine the writer's message about the topic. They should be able to identify specific lines of text or characters' words or actions that support their opinions.

Analyze Structure: Frame Story

COMMON CORE

RL 5

RETEACH

Review the definitions related to a frame-story structure, also known as a story-within-a-story structure:

- The **frame story** is the story told at the beginning and end of the piece. It establishes the setting in which another story is told. The characters in the frame story are often telling or listening to the second story.
- The **inner story** is the second story, which is usually told by one of the characters from the frame story. In some cases, the inner story is not directly identified as being told by a character, but a transition hints at the change.

Explain that an author may choose to use a frame story to tell two different stories in one piece of writing and make connections between them. Other authors choose the frame story as a way of making comments about or assessments of the inner story. In other cases, the author may use the inner story as a plot device to advance the action of the frame story.

CLOSE READING APPLICATION

Students can apply the skill by selecting another story in which the frame-story structure is used. If they are not familiar with another story using this structure, you may refer them to the following:

- *Hamlet*, Act III, Scene 2 (in Collection 4), in which Hamlet manages to present a play within a play in order to mimic what he believes are the King's actions
- The popular movie *The Wizard of Oz* starring Judy Garland, in which the frame story involves a young girl caught in a tornado and the inner story tells the fabulous story of the girl and her dog in the land of Oz

Students should identify both the frame story and the inner story and the ways in which this structure enhances the story.

COLLECTION 6
PERFORMANCE TASK

Interactive Lessons

If you need help with...
• **Writing a Narrative**
• **Writing as a Process**

Write a Personal Narrative

This collection explores people's interactions with nature. Review the experiences described in the anchor text, "Living Like Weasels," and in the other selections. What insights about the natural world did you gain from them? Which selections did you find particularly thought-provoking? Write a personal narrative in which you describe and reflect on your own experience in nature while comparing it with those portrayed in "Living Like Weasels" and at least one other selection in the collection.

COMMON CORE

W 3a–e Write narratives.
W 4 Produce clear and coherent writing.
W 5 Develop and strengthen writing.
W 9a–b Draw evidence from literary or informational texts.

An effective personal narrative

- introduces an experience or encounter the writer had with the natural world
- establishes a first-person point of view in the unique voice of the writer
- engages readers by vividly describing people, places, and events
- describes a clear and logical sequence of events with the effective use of transitions
- uses descriptive details and realistic dialogue to re-create the writer's experience
- makes meaningful comparisons with "Living Like Weasels" and another selection
- concludes by summarizing the encounter with nature and by offering a final reflection on the experience

PLAN ....

Find Inspiration Review the collection to find inspiration for your personal narrative.

- Reread "Living Like Weasels" and take notes about any new perspectives or understanding about the natural world that you gain from the text. What aspects of Dillard's experience with nature do you find especially thought-provoking?
- Review the remaining selections, noting important ideas about nature conveyed by each writer or artist.
- Jot down any ideas or insights inspired by the selections that you want to communicate in your personal narrative. How do these ideas or insights relate to your own experiences with nature?

*my***Notebook**

Use the annotation tools in your eBook to find interesting ideas and details about nature. Save each example to your notebook.

PERFORMANCE TASK

WRITE A PERSONAL NARRATIVE

COMMON CORE W 3a–e, W 4, W 5, W 9a–b

Introduce students to the Performance Task by reading the introductory paragraph with them and reviewing the criteria for an effective personal narrative. Clarify that a personal narrative tells the story of a real experience the writer had. The overall structure is a chronological description of events. However, the narrative details are interspersed with the writer's reflections—including, in this case, comparisons with "Living Like Weasels" and one other text.

PLAN

FIND INSPIRATION

View It!

Professional Development Podcast:
Performance Task

As students note ideas and insights about nature in "Living Like Weasels," suggest that they also pay attention to how Dillard weaves together narrative details and her reflections on them. How does she begin her essay? At what point does the narrative begin? How does she build on the events in the narrative to make larger points about nature and human life? Students may choose a different structure for their own essay, but they can get some ideas from Dillard's model.

PLAN

GET ORGANIZED

If students have trouble recalling details, tell them they may incorporate details they recall from similar experiences. For example, they can add details of setting drawn from more than one episode in the same location.

Point out that while students' narratives will mostly follow chronological order, they may choose to relate some events out of order. For example, it might be effective to describe an event from the middle or end of the experience in their introduction and then circle back to tell the story from the beginning.

Brainstorm Write down some ideas for your narrative. What experience(s) with the natural world have you had that resulted in a new understanding of nature? Which selections, including "Living Like Weasels," can you easily compare and contrast with your own experience? Once you have chosen another selection, create a semantic map to generate ideas for your narrative. Include themes, people, setting, and events. Remember that your personal narrative is a nonfiction account and should

- describe an experience with nature such as a hike, a camping trip, a walk in the park, a day at the beach, or a picnic
- convey your reflections about this experience, including an insight you gained from it
- make comparisons with "Living Like Weasels" and one other selection

Get Organized Organize your notes, using an outline or a graphic organizer.

- Decide on the structure of your narrative and create an outline or use a story map to reflect your ideas. Look back at the narrative texts in this collection to help you. Ask yourself these questions about each one:
  - How does the story begin? What techniques are used to engage the audience?
  - How does the writer develop the narrative? What is the sequence of events? How are the main ideas organized?
  - How does the writer use setting, people or characters, conflict, and events to reveal a theme about experiencing the natural world?
  - How does the narrative end? Is there a final observation or reflection on nature?
- Flesh out your narrative with descriptive details. Visualize the places and people in your narrative, and write down details about them. Be sure to include qualities and characteristics that make them unique.
- Record some ideas for revealing the insight you gained from this experience.

ACADEMIC VOCABULARY

As you draft your personal narrative, be sure to use these words.

encounter
intensity
restore
theme
visualize

Draft Your Narrative Write a draft of your narrative, following your notes, outline, and/or graphic organizers.

my WriteSmart

Write your rough draft in *my*WriteSmart. Focus on getting your ideas down rather than on perfecting your choice of language.

- Begin by introducing your readers to the setting, people, and experience that will be central to the narrative.

- Describe a chronological sequence of events.

- Write from the first-person point of view, and allow your own unique voice to shine through.

- Use sensory language and descriptive details to make the setting, people, and events realistic for your readers.

- Provide a powerful conclusion. A personal narrative should end with reflections on the events and experiences that have been described.

REVISE

Improve Your Draft Exchange drafts with a partner. When reading your partner's draft, ask yourself the questions shown here. Then use the chart on the following page and feedback from your partner to revise your own draft.

my WriteSmart

Have your partner or a group of peers review your draft in *my*WriteSmart. Ask your reviewers to note any evidence that does not support your comparison.

- Is the narrative told from the first-person point of view?

- Are the events, setting, and people fully developed? Is the dialogue realistic?

- How could your partner make the narrative more interesting for readers? Suggest additional sensory language or descriptive details that could be used.

- Does the narrative move along at a good pace? What might your partner do to speed up the action in sections that feel too slow? Are there any places where your partner should add more descriptive details to slow readers down and give them time to reflect?

- Is the sequence of events clear? Are ideas presented in a logical way? Could more transitions help clarify the narrative?

- Does your partner's reflection successfully reveal the insight he or she gained from the experience?

PRESENT

Share Your Narrative When your final draft is completed, read your narrative to a small group. Use your voice and gestures to present a lively reading of the narrative. Be prepared to answer questions or respond to comments from your group members.

Collection Performance Task **519**

PERFORMANCE TASK

PRODUCE

DRAFT YOUR NARRATIVE

Emphasize that a personal narrative should convey the authentic voice of the writer. Suggest that, as they write, students imagine they are relating their experience to a friend. Their tone should be engaging and approachable while also appropriate for an academic essay. Remind students that their essay must not only narrate events but also compare their experience to those described in two collection texts.

REVISE

IMPROVE YOUR DRAFT

Suggest that peer reviewers read their partner's essay at least twice. During the first reading, they should look at the big picture. Does the narrative have a beginning, a middle, and an end? Does it relate to two selection texts? During the second reading, they can give feedback to help the writer make sentence-level improvements. Remind them to give positive feedback about parts of the essay that are done well.

PRESENT

SHARE YOUR NARRATIVE

If possible, allow students to record their readings. They might publish their essays on the school website and include a link to the recording as an added feature. Another option is for students to build multimedia presentations around their essays, incorporating visuals, sound, and text.

PERFORMANCE TASK

LANGUAGE

Have students look at the chart to evaluate their level of performance in the Language category. Ask them to trade narratives with a partner and take turns reading each essay aloud. Have partners discuss their use of sensory language and note places for improvement. Students can then revise their narratives with their partner's suggestions in mind.

COLLECTION 6 TASK
PERSONAL NARRATIVE

	Ideas and Evidence	Organization	Language
ADVANCED	• The introduction creates a vivid impression, clearly establishes the setting, and identifies the experience. • The narrative provides informative background to help explain events. • Descriptive details, realistic dialogue, and reflection dramatically re-create the experience. • The conclusion powerfully summarizes the importance of the experience and offers an insightful observation.	• The organization is effective; ideas are arranged logically and events are organized chronologically. • The pace is effective. • Well-chosen transitions clearly connect ideas and show the sequence of events.	• A consistent, first-person point of view creates a unique voice. • Sensory language is used creatively to describe people, places, and events in vivid ways. • Sentence beginnings, lengths, and structures vary and have a rhythmic flow. • Spelling, capitalization, and punctuation are correct. • Grammar and usage are correct.
COMPETENT	• The introduction identifies the experience but could do more to present the setting and engage readers. • Helpful background is needed to explain some events. • More descriptive details, dialogue, and reflection are needed to re-create the experience. • The conclusion summarizes most of the writer's ideas and feelings about the experience.	• The organization of ideas is generally logical; the sequence of events is confusing in a few places. • At times, the pace is too slow or too fast. • A few more transitions are needed to explain the sequence of events.	• The point of view shifts from the first person in a few places. • More sensory language is needed to describe people, places, and events. • Sentence beginnings, lengths, and structures vary somewhat. • Several spelling, capitalization, and punctuation mistakes occur. • Some grammatical and usage errors are repeated in the narrative.
LIMITED	• The introduction is mundane; it mentions an experience and hints at the setting. • More background is needed throughout the narrative. • A few descriptive details create lively scenes, but most details are commonplace; dialogue and reflection are lacking. • The conclusion lacks any reflection on the importance of the experience.	• The organization of ideas often doesn't follow a pattern; the sequence of events is sometimes confusing. • The pace is somewhat choppy and distracting to the reader. • More transitions are needed throughout to clarify the sequence of events.	• The narrative frequently shifts from the first-person point of view. • The narrative lacks sensory language in many key parts. • Sentence structures barely vary, and some fragments or run-on sentences are present. • Spelling, capitalization, and punctuation are often incorrect but do not cause confusion. • Grammar and usage are incorrect in many places.
EMERGING	• The introduction does not focus on an experience or establish a setting. • Necessary background is missing. • Details, dialogue, and reflection are irrelevant or missing. • The narrative lacks a conclusion.	• The narrative is not organized; information and details are presented randomly. • The pace is ineffective. • Transitions are not used, making the narrative difficult to understand.	• The narrative lacks a consistent point of view. • Sensory language is not used. • Repetitive sentence structure, fragments, and run-on sentences make the writing hard to follow. • Spelling, capitalization, and punctuation are mostly incorrect. • Many grammatical and usage errors change the meaning of the writer's ideas.

TEACHER NOTE:
The page numbers to the left indicate pages in the Student Edition. Except for the two entries below, the page numbers in the Student Edition and the Teacher's Edition correspond.

Writing Arguments

COMMON CORE W 1a–e

Many of the Performance Tasks in this book ask you to craft an argument in which you support your ideas with text evidence. Any argument you write should include the following sections and characteristics.

Introduction

Clearly state your **claim**—the point your argument makes. As needed, provide context or background information to help readers understand your position, possibly citing expert opinions to establish the knowledge base for your claim. Note the most common opposing views as a way to distinguish and clarify your ideas. From the very beginning, make it clear for readers why your claim is strong; consider providing an overview of your reasons or a quotation that emphasizes your view in your introduction.

EXAMPLES

Vague claim: Social media is good for learning.	**Precise, knowledgeable claim:** According to a leading digital news source, teachers across the nation find that social media helps students make gains in education.
Opposing views presented without reference to writer's claim: Teachers complain that students can't pay attention anymore.	**Writer's claim distinguished from opposing view:** While one recent study said teachers blame social media for students' diminishing attention spans, the study also showed that today's connected students are more self-sufficient learners.
Confusing relationship of ideas: A Portland, Oregon, teacher piloted a social media site in her own classroom. Grades will increase and absenteeism will decrease school-wide.	**Logical relationship of ideas:** If the recent experience of a program piloted in Portland, Oregon, is any indication, social media sites around each school subject area will cause grades and attendance to improve within a year.

Development of Claims

The body of your argument must provide logical reasons for your claim and thoroughly support those reasons with relevant evidence. A **reason** tells why your claim is valid; **evidence** provides specific examples that illustrate a reason. In developing your claim you should also refute **counterclaims,** or opposing views, with reasons and evidence. To demonstrate that you have thoroughly considered your view, provide a well-rounded look at both the strengths and limitations of your claim and opposing claims. Consider how much your audience may already know about your topic to avoid boring or confusing them. Consider, too, your audience's values; by failing to recognize their biases, you may miss the mark entirely.

EXAMPLES

Claim lacking reasons: Teachers should use social media.	**Claim developed by reasons:** Social media is a big part of most students' lives, and it's not going away; it makes sense to use social media to advance educational goals.
Omission of limitations: If educators ignore social media, they are totally disconnected from students' reality.	**Fair discussion of limitations:** Of course, other digital tools, like search engines and educational websites, also engage students and play a significant role in their education.
Inattention to audience's knowledge: Most adults probably don't understand that social media is where young people get together online.	**Awareness of audience's knowledge:** If you're one of the nearly 50% of adults in the U.S. that use social media, you already understand its potential for enhancing communication.

continued

Ignorance of audience's bias: Teachers don't understand that sitting in a classroom is boring; we can't wait to check our phones!	Recognition of audience's bias: If teachers feel they must compete with social media for students' attention, it makes sense to engage them through that media.

Links Among Ideas

Even the strongest reasons and evidence will fail to sway readers if it is unclear how the reasons relate to the central claim of an argument. Use transitional words and phrases, and also clauses and even entire sentences, as a bridge between ideas you have already discussed and ideas you are introducing. By demonstrating control over your language and syntax through the skilled use of transitional expressions, you'll enhance your credibility as a writer. Virginia Tufte's *Artful Sentences* is a well-known guide to syntax.

EXAMPLES

Transitional word linking reason to claim: Even students who are uncomfortable speaking up in class will interact with teachers and other students through a virtual community; **therefore,** social media allows more students to become engaged in the learning process.

Transitional phrase linking reason and evidence: Social media can help students feel better about themselves. **According to one study,** about half the students who labeled themselves as "shy" said that social media helped them feel more confident and outgoing.

Transitional clause linking claim and counterclaim: With social media's omnipresence in the world outside of school, it makes no sense for classrooms to be utterly disconnected. **But valid concerns create obstacles to the widespread use of social media in schools:** educators worry about the safety and privacy issues surrounding its use.

Appropriate Style and Tone

An effective argument is most often written in a direct and formal style. The style and tone you choose in an argument should not be an afterthought—the way you express your argument can either drive home your ideas or detract from them. Even as you argue in favor of your viewpoint, take care to remain objective in tone; avoid using loaded language when discussing opposing claims.

EXAMPLES

Informal style, inattention to conventions: Social media in schools makes sense—just get it done!	Formal style: Because in-school social media offers so many educational as well as emotional benefits, it is logical for our school to create or adopt a social media site.
Biased tone: Nervous Nellies need to Google *social media safe for schools* and stop wringing their hands.	Objective tone: While its detractors have valid safety and privacy concerns, social media specifically designed for school settings already exists and is easy to adopt.

Conclusion

Your conclusion may range from a sentence to a full paragraph, but it must wrap up your argument in a satisfying way; a conclusion that sounds tacked-on helps your argument no more than providing no conclusion at all. A strong conclusion is a logical extension of the argument you have presented. It carries forth your ideas through an inference, question, quotation, or challenge.

EXAMPLES

Inference: The migration to social media in the classroom will require a leap by administrators and teachers.

Quotation: To paraphrase Marshall MacLuhan, The (social) medium is the message.

Question: Students have gotten the message; have educators?

Challenge: If so, they need to do more than nod to social media through Twitter feeds; they need to adopt and implement fully functional, school-wide social media tools.

Writing Informative Texts

Most of the Performance Tasks in this book ask you to write informational or explanatory texts in which you present a topic and examine it thoughtfully, through a well-organized analysis of relevant content. Any informative or explanatory text that you create should include the following parts and features.

Introduction

Develop a strong **thesis statement.** That is, clearly state your **topic** and the **organizational framework** through which you will develop a unified composition, in which each new idea logically flows from and extends the one before it. For example, you might state that your text will compare ideas, examine causes and effects, or analyze a single text or a group of texts.

EXAMPLE

Topic: Shakespeare's *Hamlet*
Sample Thesis Statements
Compare-contrast analysis: Hamlet and his foil Laertes represent two different views of revenge—Laertes being unequivocal about the need to repay bloodshed with bloodshed, and Hamlet perseverating about the futility of vengeance.
Cause-effect analysis: Hamlet's hesitancy to undertake revenge inadvertently causes the deaths of many characters in the play.
Evaluation: Hamlet's "To be or not to be" soliloquy is often interpreted as a contemplation of suicide; however, this interpretation is not borne out by the hero's actions throughout the play.

Clarifying the organizational framework up front will help you organize the body of your essay, suggesting **headings** you can use to guide your readers or graphics that might illustrate the text. Most important, it can help you identify any ideas that you may need to clarify. For example, if you are analyzing the cause and effect of the deaths in *Hamlet*, you may use the following framework:

Initial cause: Hamlet hesitates to heed the will of father's ghost.

▼

He pretends madness while investigating his uncle's guilt.

▼

Polonius spies on Hamlet due to his strange behavior.

▼

Hamlet accidentally kills Polonius.

▼

Ophelia, distraught at her father's murder by her beloved, kills herself, etc.

Development of the Topic

In the body of your text, flesh out the organizational framework you established in your introduction with strong supporting paragraphs. Include only the most significant evidence relevant to your topic. If you are using outside sources, don't rely on a single source, and make sure the sources you do use are reputable and current. The table below illustrates types of support you might use to develop different types of topics. It also shows how transitions link text sections, create cohesion, and clarify the relationships among ideas.

Types of Support in Explanatory/ Informative Texts (in italics)	Uses of Transitions in Explanatory/ Informative Texts
Fact: *While Hamlet could not have known that his elaborate ruse to "catch the conscience of the king" would ultimately result in a pile of dead bodies, it certainly seemed unnecessary. After all, there were three other witnesses to the ghost.*	The entire transitional sentence introduces a fact supporting Hamlet's excessive hesitancy.
Concrete details: Hamlet doesn't truly understand the inevitability of death until he holds it in his hands, contemplating *the skull of Yorick,* the jester to whom he was close as a child.	A transitional clause explains the significance of a concrete detail in a literary evaluation.
Textual evidence: Unlike Hamlet, who barely seems to know where to direct his angst, Laertes' rage after Ophelia's death is immediate and visceral: *"O, treble woe / Fall ten times treble on that cursèd head / Whose wicked deed thy most ingenious sense / Deprived of thee!"*	The phrase *Unlike Hamlet* signals the use of a quotation from Act V, Scene 1, to support comparison between Hamlet and Laertes.

You can't always include all of the information you'd like to in a short essay, but you can plan to point readers directly to useful **multimedia links** either in the body of or at the end of your essay.

Style and Tone

Use formal English to establish your credibility as a source of information. To project authority, use the language of the domain, or field, that you are writing about. However, be sure to define unfamiliar terms and avoid jargon. Provide extended definitions when your audience is likely to have limited knowledge of the topic. Using quotations from reputable sources can also give your text authority; be sure to credit the source of quoted material. In general, keep the tone neutral, avoiding slangy or biased expressions. However, don't shy away from figurative language: Well-placed metaphors, similes, and analogies can convey a complex idea more succinctly than a paragraph of strictly objective language.

Informal, biased language:	Formal style, neutral tone, with figurative language to express complex ideas:
Who knows why we do what we do, but still, it's no accident that Hamlet was so spineless.	Assigning causation to the actions of literary characters may seem as pointless as a playing a game of "What if?" with history. Shakespeare made the characters do what they do to forward the plot. However, ample evidence suggests that Shakespeare intended to highlight the consequences of Hamlet's equivocating nature.

Conclusion

Wrap up your essay with a concluding statement or section that sums up or extends the information in your essay.

EXAMPLES

Articulate implications: Though Shakespeare makes all of the play's character's pay dearly for Hamlet's hesitation, he was not condemning his lack of certitude. Instead, he was making a broader statement about turmoil we all face when confronted with a moral dilemma.

Emphasize significance: If "To be, or not to be" is not a question about suicide but about fear of death, Hamlet's change of heart in Act V makes much more sense. He never contemplated taking his own life to avoid dealing with unpleasant reality; his struggle was always with whether he should risk his life in the first place.

Writing Narratives

COMMON CORE W 3a-e

When you compose a fictional tale or a factual account of something that happened to you, you are writing in the narrative mode. That means telling a story with a beginning, a climax, and a conclusion. Though there are important differences between fictional and nonfiction narratives, you use similar processes to develop them.

Identify a Significant Problem or Situation, or Make an Observation

For a nonfiction narrative, dig into your memory bank for a significant problem you dealt with or an important observation you've made about life. For fiction, try to invent a problem or situation that can unfold in interesting ways.

EXAMPLES

Observation (nonfiction)	Grandparents are often the best people to turn to when you're feeling isolated or ashamed.
Situation (fiction)	Marissa's parents didn't understand what she meant by "gap year." They thought she wanted to work in retail rather than go to college.

Establish a Point of View

Decide who will tell your story. If you are writing a reflective essay about an important experience or person in your own life, you will be the narrator of the events you relate. If you are writing a work of fiction, you can choose to create a first-person narrator or tell the story from the third-person point of view. In that case, the narrator can focus on one character or reveal the thoughts and feelings of all the characters. The examples below show the differences between a first- and third-person narrator.

First-person narrator (nonfiction)	When I smashed the rear end of my mother's car in the library parking lot, she just shook her head in utter disbelief; then she extended her hand, silently demanding the key back. I would never drive that car again, her look told me.

Third-person narrator (fiction)	She felt her stomach tighten as her parents stared at her blankly. She realized this would be a difficult conversation.

Gather Details

To make real or imaginary experiences come alive, you will need to use techniques such as description and dialogue. The questions in the left column in the chart can help you imagine or recall details that will flesh out your narrative. You don't have to respond in full sentences, but try to capture the sights, sounds, and feelings that bring your narrative to life.

Who, What, When, Where?	Narrative Techniques
People: Who are the people or characters involved in the experience? What did they look like? What did they do or say?	**Description:** My mother's lips pursed, eyes burning; my grandfather's wrinkled fingers holding the newspaper as he sits in his chair. **Dialogue:** "Did I ever tell you about the time your mother totaled my sedan?" Grampa asked.
Experience: What led up to or caused the event? What is the main event in the experience? What happened as a result of the event?	**Description:** I didn't have to go to the library to do homework; I was hoping to see a girl I had a crush on. She wasn't even there. The only thing that got crushed was my mother's bumper. Why are the parking spaces so small? For ruining the bumper on her new car, it seemed I had lost driving privileges indefinitely.

continued

Who, What, When, Where?	Narrative Techniques
Places: When and where did the events take place? What were the sights, sounds, and smells of this place?	**Description:** It happened during my junior year. I had just gotten my license, and I was just getting used to the independence it brought me. Other than the surprisingly strong jarring my body felt when I hit the other car, and the loud crunch, I also remember the smell of beef stew that was simmering in the house when I got home.

Sequence Events

Before you begin writing, list the key events of the experience or story in chronological, or time, order. Place a star next to the point of highest tension—for example, the point at which a key decision determines the outcome of events. In fiction, this point is called the climax, but a gripping nonfiction narrative will also have a climactic event.

To build suspense—the uncertainly a reader feels about what will happen next—you'll want to think about the pacing or rhythm of your narrative. Consider disrupting the chronological order of events by beginning at the end, then starting over. Or interrupt the forward progression or flow of events with a flashback, which takes the reader to an earlier point in the narrative. Another way to build suspense is with multiple plot lines.

Use Vivid Language

As you revise, make an effort to use vivid language. Use precise words and phrases to describe feelings and action. Use telling details to show, rather than directly state, what a character is like. Use sensory language that lets readers see, feel, hear, smell, and taste what you or your characters experienced. Overall, select language that conveys a consistent tone throughout your narrative.

First Draft	Revision
I heard a crash and felt a thump.	The unpleasant sound of metal hitting metal—hard—hit my ears as my head snapped back against the headrest. [sensory details]
My mother glared at me, and my grandfather just sat there.	While my mother stood in mute judgment, my peripheral vision caught my grandfather's head peaking around the newspaper, which was quivering in his hands. Was he suppressing laughter? [telling details]
I was angry and embarrassed.	As I lay on my bed, replaying the accident in my mind, I castigated myself for being so careless, and for having lost my driving privileges in the dubious pursuit of a girl who probably didn't even know my name. [precise words and phrases]

Conclusion

At the conclusion of the narrative, you or your narrator will reflect on the meaning of the events. The conclusion should follow logically from the climactic moment of the narrative. The narrator of a personal narrative usually reflects on the significance of the experience—the lessons learned or the legacy left. A fictional narrative will end with the resolution of the conflict described over the course of the story.

EXAMPLE

The next day, Grampa took me out to drive—in *his* car.

"I like what it says on that rearview mirror," Grampa said.

"'Objects in the mirror are closer than they appear'?"

"Old age is like looking into the rearview mirror. It gives you a broader perspective. When your mom totaled my car, I was just as angry with her as she is with you. But now I can see that I was more scared than angry. And what you need isn't to have the keys taken away—well, not for long, anyway—but to practice driving. So buckle up. And check your mirrors."

PRACTICE AND APPLY

Remind students to write legibly as they develop their lists of key events.

Conducting Research

COMMON CORE W 2a-f, W 7, W 8, L 3a

The Performance Tasks in this book will require you to complete research projects related to the texts you've read in the collections. Whether the topic is stated in a Performance Task or is one you generate, the following information will guide you through your research project.

Focus Your Research and Formulate a Question

Some topics for a research project can be effectively covered in three pages; others require an entire book for a thorough treatment. Begin by developing a topic that is neither too narrow nor too broad for the time frame of the assignment. Also check your school and local libraries and databases to help you determine how to choose your topic. If there's too little information, you'll need to broaden your focus; if there's too much, you'll need to limit it.

With a topic in hand, formulate a research question; it will keep you on track as you conduct your research. A good research question cannot be answered in a single word and should be open-ended. It should require investigation. You can also develop related research questions to explore your topic in more depth.

EXAMPLES

Possible topics about George Orwell	• How do Orwell's writings reflect the concerns of the day—too broad? • How is Big Brother like Stalin—too narrow? • What ideas or events inspired Orwell to write *1984*?
Research question	• How was Orwell's own world like the world he presents in *1984*?
Related questions	• What threats to personal freedom existed in Britain after World War II? • What was occurring the Soviet Union at that time? • Why do people compare Big Brother to Stalin?

Locate and Evaluate Sources

To find answers to your research question, you'll need to investigate primary and secondary sources, whether in print or digital formats. **Primary sources** contain original, firsthand information, such as diaries, autobiographies, interviews, speeches, and eyewitness accounts. **Secondary sources** provide other people's versions of primary sources in encyclopedias, newspaper and magazine articles, biographies, and documentaries.

Your search for sources begins at the library and on the World Wide Web. Use **advanced search features** to help you find things quickly. Add a minus sign (-) before a word that should not appear in your results. Use an asterisk (*) in place of unknown words. List the name of and location of each possible source, adding comments about its potential usefulness. Assessing, or evaluating, your sources in an important step in the research process. Your goal is to use sources that are credible, or reliable and trustworthy, and that are appropriate to your task, purpose, and audience.

Criteria for Assessing Sources	
Relevance: It covers the target aspect of my topic and helps me achieve my purpose for writing.	• How will the source be useful in answering my research question?
Accuracy: It includes information that can be verified by more than one authoritative source.	• Is the information up-to-date? Are the facts accurate? How can I verify them? • What qualifies the author to write about this topic? Is he or she an authority?

continued

Criteria for Assessing Sources	
Objectivity: It presents multiple viewpoints on the topic.	• What, if any, biases can I detect? Does the writer favor one view of the topic?
Coverage: It covers the topic at a level appropriate for my grade level and audience.	• Is the treatment of the material too juvenile for my audience? Is it too advanced?

Incorporating and Citing Source Material

When you draft your research project, you'll need to include material from your sources. This material can be **direct quotations, summaries,** or **paraphrases** of the original source material. Two well-known **style manuals** provide information on how to cite a range of print and digital sources: the *MLA Handbook for Writers of Research Papers* (published by the Modern Language Association) and Kate L. Turabian's *A Manual for Writers* (published by The University of Chicago Press). Both style manuals provide a wealth of information about conducting, formatting, drafting, and presenting your research, including guidelines for citing sources within the text (called parenthetical citations) and preparing the list of Works Cited, as well as correct use of the mechanics of writing. Your teacher will indicate which style manual you should use. The following examples use the format in the *MLA Handbook.*

EXAMPLES

Direct quotation
[The writer is citing an analysis by literary critic Isaac Deutcher.]

Orwell was satirizing the English and not the Soviets when he created a party that didn't try to "indoctrinate the working class" (35).

Summary
[The writer is summarizing a passage from a study of the Cold War.]

Many Europeans (especially the French) respected the Communists not only for helping to win World War II but also for resisting the Nazis (24–25).

Paraphrase
[The writer is para-phrasing, or stating in his own words, the same passage summarized above. Since paraphrases include more details from the original passage, they are longer than the summaries.]

Many people respected the Soviet Union's Red Army, which had fought mightily against the Nazis and had been largely responsible for their defeat.... French people linked the Communists with their own brave resistance fighters in France (24–25).

As you write, it's important not too rely too heavily on any one source but to synthesize information from a variety of sources. Furthermore, any material from sources must be completely documented, or you will commit **plagiarism,** the unauthorized use of someone else's words or ideas. Plagiarism is not honest. As you take notes for your research project, be sure to keep complete information about your sources so that you can cite them correctly in the body of your paper. This applies to all sources, whether print or digital. Having complete information will also enable you to prepare the list of Works Cited. The list of Works Cited, which concludes your research project, provides author, title, and publication information for both print and digital sources. The following section shows the *MLA Handbook's* citation formats for a variety of sources.

PRACTICE AND APPLY
Remind students to write legibly as they take notes.

MLA Citation Guidelines

You may be able to find free websites that help you create citations for research papers. While these sites may save time, you should always check your citations carefully before you turn in your paper. The MLA (Modern Language Association) has developed guidelines for documenting research. You can follow these examples to create the Works Cited list for your research paper.

Books

One author

Orwell, George. *1984 and Related Readings*. 1949. Evanston: McDougal, 1998. Print.

Two authors or editors

Isaacs, Jeremy, and Taylor Downing. *Cold War: An Illustrated History, 1945–1991*. Boston: Little, 1998. Print.

Three authors or editors

Randolph, Carolyn, Catherine Coleman, and Thomas Mullens. *The Soviet Union During the Stalin Years*. Dallas: Strom, 2008. Print.

Four or more authors or editors

List only the first author followed by the abbreviation et al., *which means "and others."*

Reed, Nahid, et al. *Orwell the Satirist*. Milwaukee: Steuben, 2008. Print.

Parts of Books

An introduction, a preface, a foreword, or an afterword written by someone other than the author or authors of a work

Symons, Julian. Introduction. *Nineteen Eighty-Four*. By George Orwell. New York: Knopf, 1992. ix–xiii. Print.

A poem, a short story, an essay, or a chapter in a collection of works

Pritchett, V.S. "1984." *Twentieth Century Interpretations of 1984*. Ed. Samuel Hynes. Englewood Cliffs: Prentice, 1971. 20–23. Print.

A poem, a short story, an essay, or a chapter in an anthology of works by several authors

Orwell, George. "Shooting an Elephant." *The Great English and American Essays*. Ed. Edmund Fuller. New York: Avon, 1964. Print.

A novel or play in a collection

Orwell, George. *Animal Farm*. The Penguin Complete Novels of George Orwell. Harmondsworth, Eng.: Penguin, 1983. Print.

Magazines, Newspapers, and Encyclopedias

An article in a newspaper

Vincent, Anne-Marie. "In the Land of Big Brother: Six Decades Later." *Fairview Press* 7 July 2008: B12. Print.

An article in a newspaper accessed from a database

Schorer, Mark. "An Indignant and Prophetic Novel." *New York Times* 12 June 1949: BR1. *ProQuest Historical Newspapers*. Web. 9 Apr. 2010.

An article in a magazine or journal

Mayers, Oswald J. "The Road to 1984: George Orwell, the life that shaped the vision." *Library Journal* 15 Nov. 1986: 68. Print.

An article in an encyclopedia

Fisher, Christopher T. "Cold War." *Encyclopedia of Espionage, Intelligence, and Security*.

Eds. K. Lee Lerner and Brenda Wilmoth Lerner. 3 vols. Detroit: Gale, 2004.

Miscellaneous Nonprint Sources

An interview

Delibes, Taisha. Personal interview. 19 Mar. 2011.

A video recording or film

Nineteen Eighty-Four. Dir. Michael Radford. Perf. John Hurt, Richard Burton, Suzanna Hamilton, and Cyril Cusack. 1984. MGM, 2003. DVD.

A sound recording

Fears, J. Rufus. "George Orwell, *1984*." *Books That Have Made History: Books That Can Change Your Life*. Part 2 of 3. Chantilly, VA: Teaching Company, 2005. CD.

Electronic Publications

A document from an Internet site

Author or compiler	Title or description of document	Title of Internet site
Bixby, Ilana.	"George Orwell's London."	*George Orwell: Lone Crusader.*

Site sponsor	Date of Internet site	Medium of Publication	Date of access
Orwell Institute.	Jan. 2008.	Web.	9 Apr. 2010.

An Online Book or E-Book

Bloom, Harold. *George Orwell's Nineteen Eighty-Four*. New York: Chelsea, 1996. *Netlibrary*.

A CD-ROM

"Stalin, Joseph." *Britannica Student Encyclopedia*. 2004 ed. Chicago: Encyclopædia Britannica, 2004. CD-ROM.

Participating in Collaborative Discussions

Often, class activities, including the Performance Tasks in this book, will require you to work collaboratively with classmates. Whether your group will analyze a work of literature or try to solve a community problem, use the following guidelines to ensure a productive discussion.

Prepare for the Discussion

A productive discussion is one in which all the participants bring useful information and ideas to share. If your group will discuss a short story the class read, first re-read and annotate a copy of the story. Your annotations will help you quickly locate evidence to support your points. Participants in a discussion about an important issue should first research the issue and bring notes or information sources that will help guide the group. If you disagree with a point made by another group member, your case will be stronger if you back it up with specific evidence from your sources.

EXAMPLES

> **Disagreeing without evidence:** Our school should not have done away with vocational training. Not everyone wants to go to college.

> **Providing evidence for disagreement:** Not everyone wants to go to college, and I have proof: I'm one of them. I want to be an electrician, and four-year colleges don't prepare electricians.

Set Ground Rules

Your group's rules will depend on what you are expected to accomplish. A discussion of a poem's theme will be unlikely to produce a consensus; however, a discussion aimed at developing a solution to a problem should result in one strong proposal arrived at with the participation of all group members. Answer the following questions to set ground rules that fit your group's purpose:

- What will this group produce? A range of ideas, a single decision, a plan of action, or something else?
- How much time is available? How much of that time should be allotted to each part of our discussion (presenting ideas, summarizing or voting on final ideas, creating a product such as a written analysis or speech)?
- What roles need to be assigned within the group? Do we need a leader, a note-taker, a timekeeper, or other specific roles?
- What is the best way to synthesize our group's ideas? Should we take a vote, list group members as "for" or "against" in a chart, or use some other method to reach consensus or sum up the results of the discussion?

Move the Discussion Forward

Everyone in the group should be actively involved in synthesizing ideas. To make sure this happens, ask questions that draw out ideas, especially from less-talkative members. If an idea or statement is confusing, try to paraphrase it, or ask the speaker to explain more about it. If you disagree with a statement, say so politely and explain in detail why you disagree.

SAMPLE DISCUSSION

Effective Behavior	How It Works
Support others' contributions. Tyra states that she believes the ultimate goal of a high school education is to enable students to go to college. She mentions how important it has been in her family that she will be the first to go to college, and the same is true of several of her friends' families. Virgil listens attentively to Tyra. He has just come from a meeting with the school's guidance counselor. He is interested in options for developing a fulfilling career by learning a trade.	Tyra shares her opinion, supporting it with evidence. Virgil disagrees with Tyra but still listens carefully. He avoids making faces or rolling his eyes while Tyra presents her views.
State your own views thoughtfully. When Tyra finishes speaking, Virgil restates her points to make sure he understands her perspective. He comments, "I understand Tyra's position because in my family it is also important to succeed. But college training doesn't prepare everyone for his or her idea of a successful career. People who want to learn a trade, like plumbing or auto mechanics, won't get the training they need in a traditional four-year college. How can high school help prepare students with these ambitions?"	Virgil verifies that he understands Tyra's point. Then, he offers another viewpoint, supporting it with an example. As Virgil did, Tyra listens carefully and respectfully as he explains his perspective.

Respond to Ideas

In a diverse group, everyone may have a different perspective on the topic of discussion, and that's a good thing. Consider what everyone has to say, and don't resist changing your view if other group members provide convincing evidence for theirs. If, instead, you feel more strongly than ever about your view, don't hesitate to say so, and provide relevant reasons. Before wrapping up the discussion, try to synthesize the claims made on both sides.

That means pulling sometimes contradictory ideas together to arrive at a new understanding.

SAMPLE DISCUSSION

Effective Behavior	How It Works
Synthesize various viewpoints to arrive at a new, alternative understanding. Andreas speaks next. First he summarizes Tyra's and Virgil's opposing views, then offers an alternative. "It may look like there is a contradiction here. Either high school spends its limited budget to prepare students for a four-year college, or it re-introduces vocational training at the expense of some parts of the college prep program. What if high school maintains its college-track emphasis but also develops an apprenticeship program with local employers who can teach vocational skills?"	By combining both arguments, Andreas creates an alternative view of the issue. This expands the discussion by allowing different viewpoints to co-exist.
Justify your views or consider new ones. Tyra considers what Andreas has said. She prepares to offer more evidence that preparing everyone for a college track is the most reasonable route, and extends her argument to respond to Virgil's point as well. Perhaps community colleges can open vocational classes to students who haven't earned their high school degrees yet. She decides to mention this when her turn comes up again. Andreas's point makes Virgil think, too. He makes a note to ask the group, "I think Andreas makes a good point. What other ways could the school provide early access to vocational training?" His question will also expand the discussion.	Tyra and Virgil consider Andreas's point. Andreas's alternative offers an opportunity to delve into the original question and expand their own arguments. Through the contributions of each participant, the discussion has led to a true collaboration about the topic.

Debating an Issue

COMMON CORE SL 1a-d, SL 3, SL 4

The selection and collection Performance Tasks in this text will direct you to engage in debates about issues relating to the selections you are reading. Use the guidelines that follow to have a productive and balanced argument about both sides of an issue.

The Structure of a Formal Debate

If you've ever tried to settle a disagreement with a friend or sibling, you've used persuasive techniques to engage in a debate—a discussion in which individuals or teams argue opposing sides of an issue. In a **formal debate**, two teams, each with three members, present their arguments on a given proposition or policy statement. One team argues for the proposition or statement and the other team argues against it. Each debater must consider the proposition closely and must research both sides of it. To argue convincingly either for or against a proposition, a debater must be familiar with both sides of the issue.

Plan the Debate

The purpose of a debate is to allow participants and audience members to consider both sides of an issue. Use these planning suggestions to hold a balanced and productive debate:

- **Identify Debate Teams** Form groups of six members based on the issue that the Performance Tasks involves. Three members of the team will argue for the affirmative side of the issue—that is, they support the issue. The other three members will argue for the negative side of the issue—that is, they will not support the issue.
- **Appoint a Moderator** The moderator plays a neutral role in the debate, promoting a civil discussion and keeping everyone on task. The moderator begins by introducing the topic of the debate and then recognizes speakers, alternating between affirmative and negative.
- **Assign Debate Roles** One team member introduces the team's claim and with supporting reasons and evidence. Another team member exchanges questions with a member of the opposing team to clarify and challenge reasoning. The last member presents a strong closing argument.

Prepare Briefs and Rebuttals

A **brief** is an outline of the debate, accounting for the evidence and arguments of both sides of the **proposition** (topic). Debaters also prepare a **rebuttal**, a follow-up speech to support their arguments and counter the opposition's. Propositions are usually one of four types:

- **Proposition of fact**—Debaters determine whether a statement is true or false. An example is "Social media is changing society for the better."
- **Proposition of value**—Debators determine the value of a person, place, or thing. An example is "Every individual has a moral obligation to help people in need."
- **Proposition of problem**—Debators determine whether a problem exists and whether it requires action.
- **Proposition of policy**—Debators determine the action that will be taken. An example is "The federal government should invest more money to develop alternative energy sources."

Use the following steps to prepare a brief:

- **Gather Information** Consult a variety of primary and secondary sources to gather the most reliable, up- to-date information about the proposition.
- **Identify Key Ideas** Sort out the important points and arrange them in order of importance.
- **List Arguments For and Against Each Key Idea** Look for strong arguments that support your side of the proposition, and also note those that support your opponents' side.
- **Support Your Arguments** Find facts, quotations, expert opinions, and examples that support your arguments and counter your opponents' arguments.
- **Write the Brief** Begin your brief with a statement of the proposition. Then list the

arguments and evidence that support both sides of the proposition.

The rebuttal is the opportunity to rebuild your case. Use the following steps to build a strong rebuttal:

- Listen to your opponents respectfully. Note the points you wish to overturn.
- Defend what the opposition has challenged.
- Cite weaknesses in their arguments, such as points they overlooked.
- Present counterarguments and supporting evidence.
- Offer your summary arguments. Restate and solidify your stance.

Hold the Debate

A well-run debate can be a vehicle for expressing your opinions in an assertive but respectful manner. Participating in a debate challenges you to synthesize comments made on both sides of an issue, pose probing questions, clarify ideas, and appreciate divergent perspectives.

FORMAL DEBATE FORMAT

Speaker	Role	Time
Affirmative Speaker 1	Present the claim and supporting evidence for the affirmative ("pro") side of the argument.	5 minutes
Negative Speaker 1	Ask probing questions that will prompt the other team to address flaws in the argument.	3 minutes
Affirmative Speaker 2	Respond to the questions posed by the opposing team and counter any concerns.	3 minutes
Negative Speaker 2	Present the claim and supporting evidence for the negative ("con") side of the argument.	5 minutes
Affirmative Speaker 3	Summarize the claim and evidence for the affirmative side and explain why your reasoning is more valid.	3 minutes
Negative Speaker 3	Summarize the claim and evidence for the negative side and explain why your reasoning is more valid.	3 minutes

Evaluate the Debate

Use the following guidelines to evaluate a team in a debate:

- What was the proposition, or premise, being debated? Was each team's stance with respect to the topic— whether affirmative or negative—clear?
- How effectively did the team present reasons and evidence, including evidence from the texts, to support the proposition? Were the links among ideas clear?
- Did the team avoid fallacious, or flawed, reasoning? Did the team avoid disguising exaggerated or distorted evidence with persuasive rhetoric? In general, was the team's word choice appropriate?
- How effectively did the team rebut, or respond to, arguments made by the opposing team?
- Did the speakers maintain eye contact and speak at an appropriate rate and volume?
- Did the speakers observe proper debate etiquette—that is, did they follow the moderator's instructions, stay within their allotted time limits, and treat their opponents respectfully? Did they use verbal techniques of emphasis and tone to highlight their argument rather than to ridicule their opponent?

PRACTICE AND APPLY

Possible answers:
Students should create a chart like the one on page R16. The chart should include details similar to the ones below. Remind students to write legibly as they complete their chart.
claim: Soda should not be banned from schools.
reasons: There is not enough hard evidence to prove soda causes obesity.
evidence: A Georgetown University study found no link between obesity and soda consumption. The surgeon general states that lack of physical activity is a factor in obesity.
counterargument: Advocates of the ban say that soda has no nutritional value and its high sugar content contributes to obesity. However, there are no studies to support this.

Reading Arguments

An argument expresses a position on an issue or problem and supports it with reasons and evidence. Being able to analyze and evaluate arguments will help you distinguish between claims you should accept and those you should not.

Analyzing an Argument

A sound argument should appeal strictly to reason. However, arguments are often used in texts that also contain other types of persuasive devices. An argument includes the following:

- A **claim** is the writer's position on an issue or problem.
- **Support** is any material that serves to prove a claim. In an argument, support usually consists of reasons and evidence.
- **Reasons** are declarations made to justify an action, decision, or belief—for example, "You should sleep on a good mattress in order to avoid spinal problems."
- **Evidence** consists of the specific references, quotations, facts, examples, and opinions that support a claim. Evidence may also consist of statistics, reports of personal experience, or the views of experts.
- A **counterargument** is an argument made to oppose another argument. A good argument anticipates the opposition's objections and provides counterarguments to disprove or answer them.

Claim	Winston Churchill's contribution to victory in World War II was significant.

Reason	Churchill's strong leadership and persuasive rhetoric raised the morale of British citizens and soldiers.

Evidence	British citizens and soldiers never let London fall to the Germans, and British soldiers played a key role in the defeat of Germany.

Counter-argument	His ideas seemed impractical and he was unpopular with much of England, but he succeeded in leading Britain to victory.

Practice and Apply

Use a chart like the one shown to identify the claim, reasons, evidence, and counterargument in the following article.

Should Soft Drinks Be Banned from Schools?

A new substance has joined the list of those banned on school grounds: soft drinks. As the number of obese teenagers rises, there is a growing movement to limit the products of empty calories that are available in school vending machines. Los Angeles has banned the sale of soft drinks on the district's high school and elementary campuses. Other districts are debating whether to implement similar policies. Activists who favor the soda ban say schools must make a choice between student health and vending machine revenues.

Advocates of banning sodas point out that a typical can of soda has at least 10 teaspoons of sugar. Its 140 calories contain no vitamins, minerals, fiber, or other nutritional value. Poor eating habits contribute to teenage obesity. Dr. Jonathan E. Fielding, director of public health for Los Angeles County, describes obesity as a fast-growing, chronic disease that is "entirely preventable."

However, not everyone agrees that carbonated soft drinks are a hazard to students' health. A Georgetown University study found no link between obesity and the soda consumption of 12- to 16-year-olds. Surgeon General David Satcher, while concerned about unhealthy eating habits, considers lack of physical activity another important cause of excess weight.

Some schools are responding to the problem by expanding instead of restricting students' choices. A pilot program that offered Metro Detroit students a choice of pop or flavored milk was so successful that the district installed 80 more milk machines. . . . Other schools offer students a selection of juice-based drinks. Stakes on both sides of the question are high: student health versus

continued

the $750 million that students put into school vending machines each year. The evidence currently available does not prove that the availability of soda pop in school vending machines causes obesity. Until that evidence is provided, I believe banning pop is an extreme solution. Instead, schools should keep both students and the budget healthy by offering both soft drinks and healthier alternatives.

Recognizing Persuasive Techniques

Persuasive texts typically rely on more than just the logical appeal of an argument to be convincing. They also rely on ethical and emotional appeals, as well as other **persuasive techniques**—devices that can sway you to adopt a position or take an action.

The chart shown here explains several of these techniques. Learn to recognize them, and you will be less likely to be influenced by them.

Persuasive Technique	Example
Appeals by Association	
Bandwagon appeal Suggests that a person should believe or do something because "everyone else" does	Don't be the last person on earth to use High Speed TurboWhip for your Internet needs.
Testimonial Relies on endorsements from well-known people or satisfied customers	Seven top chefs from Sonoma County recommend Fivar Cutlery— why not feature it at your next dinner party?
Snob appeal Taps into people's desire to be special or part of an elite group	Diamondshire Hotels provide luxurious accommodations in a premier setting.
Transfer Connnects a product, candidate, or cause with a positive emotion or idea	Volunteer with Elderly Help and go home happy— you've touched the life of someone special.
Appeal to loyalty Relies on people's affiliation with a particular group	Buy a bumper sticker from the Skooner Seahawks today and show your true team spirit!
Emotional Appeals	
Appeals to pity, fear, or vanity Use strong feelings, rather than facts, to persuade	Help! Bear Habitat needs refurbishing. Without your donation, polar bears at Cityside Zoo will die!
Word Choice	
Glittering generality Makes a generalization that includes a word or phrase with positive connotations, such as *freedom* or *action-packed,* to promote a product or idea.	Elect E. Willmington and preserve dignity and honor.

Practice and Apply

Identify the persuasive techniques used in the model.

Our city high schools are failing, and they need your help. Half of this city's freshmen drop out before their senior prom. Inner-city students need quality education and well-trained teachers. Your signature on our petition can make it happen and will show your loyalty to our city. Our petition demands re-evaluation of the city's fiscal priorities and a promise that more funds will be allocated for teachers next year. Sign our petition and you'll be in good company. Respected elected officials such as Alderman Donna Jones and County Clerk Tony Fitzharmon support this effort 100 percent. By signing, you will be on the frontline of a most important battle—the battle for the minds of our youth.

COMMON CORE RI 6

PRACTICE AND APPLY

Answers:
appeal to fear: "Our city high schools are failing, and they need your help."
appeal to loyalty: "show your loyalty to our city"
bandwagon: "Sign our petition and you'll be in good company. Respected elected officials such as Alderman Donna Jones and County Clerk Tony Fitzharmon . . ."
glittering generality: "By signing, you will be on the front line of a most important battle—the battle for the minds of our youth."

Analyzing Logic and Reasoning

When you evaluate the credibility of an argument, look closely at the writer's logic and reasoning. To do this, it is helpful to identify the type of reasoning the writer is using.

The Inductive Mode of Reasoning

When a writer leads from specific evidence to a general principle or generalization, that writer is using **inductive reasoning** to make **inferences,** or logical assumptions, and draw conclusions from them. Here is an example of inductive reasoning.

The Inductive Mode of Reasoning
Specific Facts
Fact 1 *Oliver Twist* is about the hard life of a young orphan boy.
Fact 2 *Great Expectations* is about a poor young man who is given money to become a gentleman.
Fact 3 *David Copperfield* is about a young man's growth into adulthood.
Generalization
One of Charles Dickens's main themes is that of a young person maturing into adulthood, often under challenging circumstances.

Strategies for Determining the Soundness of Inductive Arguments

Ask yourself the following questions to evaluate an inductive argument:

- **Is the evidence valid and does it provide sufficient support for the conclusion?** Inaccurate facts lead to inaccurate conclusions. Make sure all facts are accurate.
- **Does the conclusion follow logically from the evidence?** Make sure the writer has used sound reasons—those that can be proved—as a basis for the conclusion and has avoided logical fallacies, such as circular reasoning.
- **Is the evidence drawn from a large enough sample?** Even though there are only three facts listed above, the sample is large enough to support the claim. By qualifying the generalization with words such as *sometimes*, *some*, or *many*, the writer indicates that the generalization is limited to a specific group.

The Deductive Mode of Reasoning

When a writer arrives at a conclusion by applying a general principle to a specific situation, the writer is using **deductive reasoning** to make inferences and draw conclusions. Here's an example.

Practices that harm others should be outlawed.	General principle or premise
▼	
Secondhand smoke has been proven to harm others.	Specific situation
▼	
Cigarette smoking in public should be outlawed.	Specific conclusion

Strategies for Determining the Soundness of Deductive Arguments

Ask yourself the following questions to evaluate a deductive argument:

- **Is the general principle stated, or is it implied?** Note that writers often use deductive reasoning in an argument without stating the general principle. They assume readers will understand the principle. You need to identify the writer's implicit assumptions.
- **Is the general principle sound?** Don't assume the general principle is sound. Ask yourself whether it is really true based on the evidence.
- **Is the conclusion valid?** To be valid, a conclusion in a deductive argument must follow logically from the general principle and the specific situation.

The following chart shows two conclusions drawn from the same general principle.

General Principle: All members of the soccer fan club wore red yesterday to support their team.	
Accurate Deduction	**Inaccurate Deduction**
Aida is a member of the soccer fan club; therefore, Aida wore red yesterday.	Clyde wore red yesterday; therefore Clyde is a member of the soccer fan club.

The inference that Clyde must be a member of the soccer fan club because he wore red lead to an inaccurate conclusion; Clyde may have chosen red for another reason.

Practice and Apply

Identify the mode of reasoning used in this passage. Determine whether the argument is sound and valid.

Some literary critics believe that numerous works attributed to William Shakespeare may actually have been written by other authors of the time. Edward de Vere was the 17th earl of Oxford and a contemporary of William Shakespeare's. He was a nobleman in Queen Elizabeth I's court, highly educated and very well traveled. Although de Vere was a writer in his early years, no literary manuscripts exist from later in his life. He seemed to have mysteriously stopped writing. Sir Francis Bacon, also a contemporary of Shakespeare's, wrote prolifically throughout his life. Experts note that his correspondences, memoirs,

continued

and notebooks express "coincidences" and parallels with the life of the Bard.

Another writer close to Shakespeare was poet and dramatist Christopher Marlowe. He was allegedly stabbed to death in a bar fight in 1593, but many believe his death was faked and that he lived a long and secret life as a spy for the queen.

All of these three men had the occasion and the talent to have written a number of plays using the nom de plume of William Shakespeare. Therefore, Shakespeare was not the sole author of the works that bear his name.

 COMMON CORE **RI 5**

PRACTICE AND APPLY
Possible answer:
Inductive reasoning is used to argue that Shakespeare did not write all of the works that have been attributed to him. The argument is not sound and valid because the conclusion does not follow logically from the evidence.

Identifying Faulty Reasoning

Sometimes an argument at first appears to make sense, but as you take a closer look at the reasoning, you can see it isn't valid because it is based on a fallacy. A **fallacy** is an error in logic based on inaccurate inferences or invalid assumptions. Learn to recognize these common fallacies.

Type of Fallacy	Definition	Example
Circular reasoning	Supporting a statement by simply repeating it in different words	That restaurant is popular because more people **go there than to any other restaurant in town.**
Either/or fallacy	A statement that suggests that there are only two choices available in a situation that really offers more than two options	**Either** you come pick me up **or** I will be stranded here forever.
Oversimplification	An explanation of a complex situation or problem as if it were much simpler than it is	If you make the manager laugh during the interview, **you will get the job.**
Overgeneralization	A generalization that is too broad. You can often recognize overgeneralizations by the use of words such as *all, everyone, every time, anything, no one,* and *none.*	**No one ever** wants to wear a bicycle helmet.

PRACTICE AND APPLY

Answers:

name-calling: "Those people are dreamy-eyed do-gooders."

non sequitur: "Of course you can build on wetlands. Like my father said before me—hard work pays off and you get what you want."

circular reasoning: "We are now competing internationally, so we need to expand in order to be competitive globally."

oversimplification: "If we expand runways, it will solve all our city's problems."

continued

Stereotyping	A dangerous type of overgeneralization. Stereotypes are broad statements about people on the basis of their gender, ethnicity, race, or political, social, professional, or religious group.	**People from big cities** are unfriendly.
Attacking the person or name-calling	An attempt to discredit an idea by attacking the person or group associated with it. Candidates often engage in name-calling during political campaigns.	The mayor's new program was developed by a **fool.**
Evading the issue	Refuting an objection with arguments and evidence that do not address its central point	Yes, I broke the window, **but then I mowed the lawn—doesn't the lawn look nice?**
Non sequitur	A conclusion that does not follow logically from the "proof" offered to support it. A non sequitur is sometimes used to win an argument by diverting the reader's attention to proof that can't be challenged.	I'm against building the new stadium **because I've lived in this town my whole life.**
False cause	The mistake of assuming that because one event occurred after another event, the first event caused the second one to occur	My brother sang in the shower this morning, **so when he auditioned for the spring musical this afternoon, he got the lead role.**
False analogy	A comparison that doesn't hold up because of a critical difference between the two subjects	If you are unable to understand T. S. Eliot, **you probably won't understand modernism.**
Hasty generalization	A conclusion drawn from too little evidence or from evidence that is biased	My job interview did not go well. **I'll never get a job.**

Practice and Apply

Look for examples of faulty reasoning in the following argument. Identify each one and explain why you identified it as such.

Let's address the proposed expansion of our airport. Opponents claim that the land west of the airport is wetlands, and that we can't build on wetlands. Those people are dreamy-eyed do-gooders. Of course you can build on wetlands. Like my father said before me—hard work pays off and you get what you want. We are now competing internationally, so we need to expand in order to be competitive globally. If we expand runways, it will solve all our city's problems.

Evaluating Persuasive Texts

Learning how to evaluate the credibility of persuasive texts by identifing bias will help you become more selective when doing research and also help you improve your own reasoning and arguing skills. **Bias** is an inclination for or against a particular opinion or viewpoint. A writer may reveal a strongly positive or negative opinion on an issue by presenting only one way of looking at it or by heavily weighting the evidence on one side of the argument. Additionally, the presence of either of the following is often a sign of bias:

Loaded language consists of words with strongly positive or negative connotations that are intended to influence a reader's attitude.

EXAMPLE

A vote for our candidate is a vote to secure your financial future, to ensure safe streets for your children, and to guarantee prosperity for people of all ages. (Secure future, safe for children, and guarantee prosperity are phrases of loaded language with positive connotations.)

Propaganda is any form of communication that is so distorted that it conveys false or misleading information. Many logical fallacies, such as name-calling, the either/or fallacy, and false causes, are often used in propaganda. The following example shows an oversimplification. The writer uses one fact to support a particular point of view but does not reveal another fact that does not support that viewpoint.

EXAMPLE

Since that new restaurant opened on our block, it is impossible to find a parking place on the street. (The writer does not include the fact that two new apartment buildings recently opened, adding to the demand for street parking.)

Strategies for Evaluating Evidence

It is important to have a set of standards by which you can evaluate persuasive texts. Use the questions below to help you critically assess facts and opinions that are presented as evidence.

- **Are the facts presented verifiable?** Facts can be proved by eyewitness accounts, authoritative sources such as encyclopedias and almanacs, experts, or research.
- **Are the claims presented credible?** Any opinions offered should be supported by facts, research, eyewitness accounts, or the opinions of experts on the topic.
- **Is the evidence thorough?** Thorough evidence leaves no reasonable questions unanswered. If a choice is offered, background for making the choice should be provided. If taking a side is called for, all sides of the issue should be presented.
- **Is the evidence biased?** Be alert to evidence that contains loaded language and other signs of bias.
- **Is the evidence authoritative?** The people, groups, or organizations that provided the evidence should have credentials that verify their credibility.
- **Is it important that the evidence be current?** Where timeliness is crucial, as in the areas of medicine and technology, the evidence should reflect the latest developments in the areas.

Practice and Apply

Read the argument below. Identify the facts, opinions, and elements of bias.

It is time to end the logging industry's destruction of the world's oldest and largest rain forests. Despite protests from environmentalists and conservationists, nature-hating, big-money interests still pay millions to have pristine forests mowed down, just to make roads! This is so their toxic, diesel-pumping logging trucks can haul cut-up pieces of the world's most precious woodlands to the mills. The worst part is that taxpayers fund the whole process—to the tune of $60 million a year. I don't know about you, but I'm going to make sure my hard-earned money isn't contributing to the destruction of the planet.

COMMON CORE · RI 5

PRACTICE AND APPLY

Answers:
facts: the logging industry cuts down trees in the world's largest and oldest rain forests to make roads; environmentalists and conservationists have protested this process; taxpayers pay $60 million a year to fund the logging industry's activities
opinions: the logging industry must stop cutting down trees; taxpayers should not fund this process
elements of bias: "nature-hating, big-money interests" are cutting down "pristine forests;" they use "toxic, diesel-pumping" trucks to haul pieces of "precious woodlands" to the mills

PRACTICE AND APPLY

Answers:

Most students will answer that the editorial uses an ineffective argument in its attempt to make an important point about the city's future.

either/or fallacy: "We must face facts: either we submit a bid to host the games, or our city will never grow."

unsupported opinion; loaded language: "Families citywide would be ecstatic to think that talented, famous people from all over the world would be invited to their lovely communities."

non sequitur: "There's no doubt families would open up their homes to guests from overseas, because they want our city to be considered the friendliest in the United States."

name-calling: "These antagonists have simply been too lazy to do proper research."

hasty generalization: "Two other U.S. cities that have hosted the games profited immensely, which means our city could put millions of dollars toward education after the games."

emotional appeal: "You wouldn't want to deprive your child of the chance to see Olympic athletes in action, would you?"

stereotyping: "If the mayor decides not to put in a bid for our city, he'll be just like every other politician, always making wrong choices."

Strategies for Evaluating an Argument

Make sure that all or most of the following statements are true:

- The argument presents a claim or thesis.
- In a deductive argument, the claim is connected to its support by a **general principle,** or assumption, that most readers would readily agree with. Valid general principle: *It is the job of a corporation to provide adequate health benefits to full-time employees.* Invalid general principle: *It is the job of a corporation to ensure its employees are healthy and physically fit.*
- The reasons make sense.
- The reasons are presented in a logical and effective order.
- The claim and all reasons are adequately supported by sound, credible evidence.
- The evidence is adequate, accurate, and appropriate.
- The logic is sound. There are no instances of faulty reasoning.
- The argument adequately anticipates and addresses reader concerns and counterclaims with counterarguments.

Practice and Apply

Use the preceding criteria to evaluate the strength of the following editorial.

This city should submit a bid to host the summer Olympics. The building and development to plan such an event would take years, but it would also create jobs, lower unemployment, and boost the city's economy. We must face facts: either we submit a bid to host the games, or our city will never grow.

Families citywide would be ecstatic to think that talented, famous people from all over the world would be invited to their lovely communities. There's no doubt families would open up their homes to guests from overseas, because they want our city to be considered the friendliest in the United States.

Some people claim that being a host city is not as important as building new schools, so surplus money should go toward education. These antagonists have simply been too lazy to do proper research. Two other U.S. cities that have hosted the games profited immensely, which means our city could put millions of dollars toward education after the games. You wouldn't want to deprive your child the chance to see Olympic athletes in action, would you?

We can't afford not to make the bid—and we can't afford not to win it! If the mayor decides not to put in a bid for our city, he'll be just like every other politician, always making wrong choices. So, write a letter to your alderman today, encouraging a vote for the summer games. Our city will be better for it.

Grammar

COMMON CORE L 1, L2, L 2a, L 3a, L 4a, L4b

Writing that has a lot of mistakes can confuse or even annoy a reader. A business letter with a punctuation error might lead to a miscommunication and delay a reply. A sentence fragment might lower your grade on an essay. Paying attention to grammar, punctuation, and capitalization rules can make your writing clearer and easier to read.

Quick Reference: Parts of Speech

Part of Speech	Function	Examples
Noun	names a person, a place, a thing, an idea, a quality, or an action	
common	serves as a general name, or a name common to an entire group	king, monster, ship, ocean
proper	names a specific, one-of-a-kind person, place, or thing	Chaucer, London, Thames River
singular	refers to a single person, place, thing, or idea	woman, river, leaf, flame
plural	refers to more than one person, place, thing, or idea	women, rivers, leaves, flames
concrete	names something that can be perceived by the senses	rose, church, bell, sky
abstract	names something that cannot be perceived by the senses	contentment, honor, faith, trust
compound	expresses a single idea through a combination of two or more words	sunshine, middle class, mother-in-law
collective	refers to a group of people or things	crop, crew, family
possessive	shows who or what owns something	Burns's, mice's, nature's, fields'
Pronoun	takes the place of a noun or another pronoun	
personal	refers to the person making a statement, the person(s) being addressed, or the person(s) or thing(s) the statement is about	I, me, my, mine, we, us, our, ours, you, your, yours, she, he, it, her, him, hers, his, its, they, them, their, theirs
reflexive	follows a verb or preposition and refers to a preceding noun or pronoun	myself, yourself, herself, himself, itself, ourselves, yourselves, themselves
intensive	emphasizes a noun or another pronoun	(same as reflexives)

continued

Part of Speech	Function	Examples
demonstrative	points to one or more specific persons or things	this, that, these, those
interrogative	signals a question	who, whom, whose, which, what
indefinite	refers to one or more persons or things not specifically mentioned	both, all, most, many, anyone, everybody, several, none, some
relative	introduces an adjective clause by relating it to a word in the clause	who, whom, whose, which, that
Verb	expresses an action, a condition, or a state of being	
action	tells what the subject does or did, physically or mentally	run, reaches, listened, consider, decides, dreamed
linking	connects the subject to something that identifies or describes it	am, is, are, was, were, sound, taste, appear, feel, become, remain, seem
auxiliary	precedes the main verb in a verb phrase	be, have, do, can, could, will, would, may, might
transitive	directs the action toward someone or something; always has an object	The wind **snapped** the young tree in half.
intransitive	does not direct the action toward someone or something; does not have an object	The young tree **snapped.**
Adjective	modifies a noun or pronoun	**frightened** man, **two** epics, **enough** time
Adverb	modifies a verb, an adjective, or another adverb	walked **out, really** funny, **far** away
Preposition	relates one word to another word	at, by, for, from, in, of, on, to, with
Conjunction	joins words or word groups	
coordinating	joins words or word groups used the same way	and, but, or, for, so, yet, nor
correlative	used as a pair to join words or word groups used the same way	both . . . and, either . . . or, neither . . . nor
subordinating	introduces a clause that cannot stand by itself as a complete sentence	although, after, as, before, because, when, if, unless
Interjection	expresses emotion	whew, yikes, uh-oh

Quick Reference: The Sentence and Its Parts

The diagrams that follow will give you a brief review of the essentials of a sentence and some of its parts.

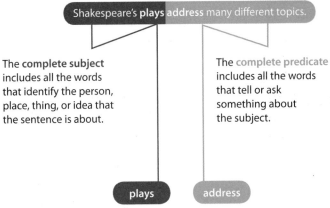

Shakespeare's plays address many different topics.

The **complete subject** includes all the words that identify the person, place, thing, or idea that the sentence is about.

The **complete predicate** includes all the words that tell or ask something about the subject.

plays

address

The **simple subject** tells exactly whom or what the sentence is about. It may be one word or a group of words, but it does not include modifiers.

The **simple predicate** tells what the subject does or is. It may be one word or several, but it does not include modifiers.

Every word in a sentence is part of a complete subject or a complete predicate.

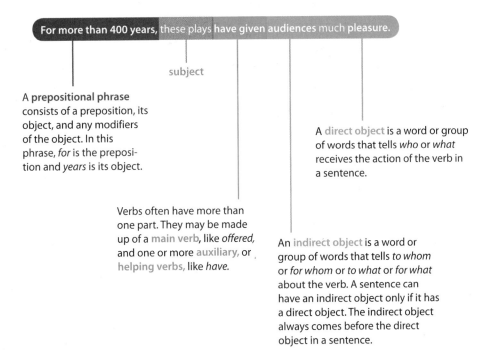

For more than 400 years, these plays **have given audiences** much **pleasure.**

subject

A **prepositional phrase** consists of a preposition, its object, and any modifiers of the object. In this phrase, *for* is the preposition and *years* is its object.

A **direct object** is a word or group of words that tells *who* or *what* receives the action of the verb in a sentence.

Verbs often have more than one part. They may be made up of a **main verb**, like *offered,* and one or more **auxiliary,** or **helping verbs,** like *have.*

An **indirect object** is a word or group of words that tells *to whom* or *for whom* or *to what* or *for what* about the verb. A sentence can have an indirect object only if it has a direct object. The indirect object always comes before the direct object in a sentence.

Quick Reference: Punctuation

Mark	Function	Examples
End Marks period, question mark, exclamation point	end a sentence	The games begin today. Who is your favorite contestant? What a play Jamie made!
period	follows an initial or abbreviation **Exception:** postal abbreviations of states	Prof. Ted Bakerman, D. H. Lawrence, Houghton Mifflin Co., P.M., A.D., oz., ft., Blvd., St. NE (Nebraska), NV (Nevada)

period	follows a number or letter in an outline	I. Volcanoes
		  A. Central-vent
		    1. Shield

Comma	separates parts of a compound sentence	I have never disliked poetry, but now I really love it.
	separates items in a series	She is brave, loyal, and kind.
	separates adjectives of equal rank that modify the same noun	The slow, easy route is best.
	sets off a term of address	O wind, if winter comes . . . Come to the front, children.
	sets off a parenthetical expression	Hard workers, as you know, don't quit. I'm not a quitter, believe me.
	sets off an introductory word, phrase, or dependent clause	Yes, I forgot my key. At the beginning of the day, I feel fresh. While she was out, I was here. Having finished my chores, I went out.
	sets off a nonessential phrase or clause	Ed Pawn, the captain of the chess team, won. Ed Pawn, who is the captain, won. The two leading runners, sprinting toward the finish line, finished in a tie.
	sets off parts of dates and addresses	Send it by August 18, 2010, to Cherry Jubilee, Inc., 21 Vernona St., Oakland, Minnesota.
	follows the salutation and closing of a letter	Dear Jim, Sincerely yours,
	separates words to avoid confusion	By noon, time had run out. What the minister does, does matter. While cooking, Jim burned his hand.

Part of Speech	Function	Examples
Semicolon	separates items in a series if one or more items contain commas	We invited my sister, Jan; her friend, Don; my uncle Jack; and Mary Dodd.
	separates parts of a compound sentence that are not joined by a coordinating conjunction	The small books are on the top shelves; the large books are below. I dusted the books; however, I didn't wipe the shelves.
	separates parts of a compound sentence when the parts contain commas	After I ran out of money, I called my parents; but only my sister was home, unfortunately.
Colon	introduces a list	Those we wrote were the following: Dana, John, and Will.
	introduces a long quotation	Mary Wollstonecraft wrote: "It appears to me necessary to dwell on these obvious truths, because females have been insulted. . . ."
	follows the salutation of a business letter	Dear Ms. Williams: Dear Senator Wiley:
	separates certain numbers	1:28 P.M., Genesis 2:5
Dash	indicates an abrupt break in thought	I was thinking of my mother—who is arriving tomorrow—just as you walked in.
Parentheses	enclose less important material	Throughout her life (though some might think otherwise), she worked hard. The temperature on this July day (would you believe it?) is 65 degrees!
Hyphen	joins parts of a compound adjective before a noun	She lives in a first-floor apartment.
	joins parts of a compound with *all-, ex-, self-,* or *-elect*	The president-elect is a well-respected woman.
	joins parts of a compound number (to ninety-nine)	Today, I turn twenty-one.
	joins parts of a fraction	My cup is one-third full.
	joins a prefix to a word beginning with a capital letter	The post-Victorian era was marked by great technological advancements.
	indicates that a word is divided at the end of a line	Yeats knew Lady Gregory, an influential Irish gentlewoman.

continued

Part of Speech	Function	Examples
Apostrophe	used with *s* to form the possessive of a noun or an indefinite pronoun	my friend's book, my friends' books, anyone's guess, somebody else's problem
	replaces one or more omitted letters in a contraction or numbers in a date	don't (omitted *o*), he'd (omitted *woul*), the class of '99 (omitted *19*)
	used with *s* to form the plural of a letter	I had two A's on my report card.
Quotation Marks	set off a speaker's exact words	Sara said, "I'm finally ready." "I'm ready," Sara said, "finally." Did Sara say, "I'm ready"? Sara said, "I'm ready!"
	set off the title of a story, an article, a short poem, an essay, a song, or a chapter	So far, we've read Swift's essay "A Modest Proposal," Eliot's poem "Preludes," and Joyce's short story "Araby."
Ellipses	replace material omitted from a quotation	"Candide listened attentively . . . for he thought Miss Cunegund excessively handsome. . . ."
Italics	indicate the title of a book, a play, a magazine, a long poem, an opera, a film, or a TV series, or the names of ships, trains, and spacecraft	*The Canterbury Tales, The Tragedy of Macbeth, Rolling Stone, Beowulf, Aida, Shakespeare in Love, The Office, Titanic*

Quick Reference: Capitalization

Category	Examples
People and Titles	
Names and initials of people	Samuel Johnson, E. M. Forster
Titles used before or in place of names	Professor Holmes, Senator Long
Deities and members of religious groups	Jesus, Allah, Buddha, Zeus, Baptists, Roman Catholics
Names of ethnic and national groups	Hispanics, Jews, African Americans
Geographical Names	
Cities, states, countries, continents	New York, Maine, Haiti, Africa
Regions, bodies of water, mountains	the South, Lake Erie, Mount Katahdin
Geographic features, parks	Continental Divide, Everglades, Yellowstone
Streets and roads, planets	55 East Ninety-fifth Street, Maple Lane, Venus, Jupiter
Organizations, Events, Etc.	
Companies, organizations, teams	General Motors, Lions Club, Utah Jazz
Buildings, bridges, monuments	the Alamo, Golden Gate Bridge, Lincoln Memorial
Documents, awards	the Constitution, World Cup
Special named events	Super Bowl, World Series
Government bodies, historical periods and events	the Supreme Court, U.S. Senate, Harlem Renaissance, World War II
Days and months, holidays	Friday, May, Easter, Memorial Day
Specific cars, boats, trains, planes	Mustang, *Titanic, California Zephyr*
Proper Adjectives	
Adjectives formed from proper nouns	American League, French cooking, Dickensian period, Arctic waters
First Words and the Pronoun *I*	
First word in a sentence or quotation	This is it. He said, "Let's go."
First word of sentence in parentheses that is not within another sentence	The spelling rules are covered in another section. (Consult that section for more information.)
First words in the salutation and closing of a letter	Dear Madam, Very truly yours,
First word in each line of most poetry Personal pronoun *I*	Then am I A happy fly If I live Or if I die.
First word, last word, and all important words in a title	"A Vindication of the Rights of Woman," *Waiting for Godot*

1 Nouns

A **noun** is a word used to name a person, a place, a thing, an idea, a quality, or an action. Nouns can be classified in several ways.

1.1 COMMON NOUNS

Common nouns are general names, common to entire groups.

> EXAMPLES: *mountain, country, lake*

1.2 PROPER NOUNS

Proper nouns name specific, one-of-a-kind things.

Common	Proper
mountain, country, lake	Mt. Everest, Italy, Lake Michigan

1.3 SINGULAR AND PLURAL NOUNS

A noun may take a singular or a plural form, depending on whether it names a single person, place, thing, or idea or more than one. Make sure you use appropriate spellings when forming plurals.

Singular	Plural
church, lily, wife	churches, lilies, wives

1.4 COMPOUND AND COLLECTIVE NOUNS

Compound nouns are formed from two or more words but express a single idea. They are written as single words, as separate words, or with hyphens. Use a dictionary to check the correct spelling of a compound noun.

> EXAMPLES: *sunshine, middle class, mother-in-law*

Collective nouns are singular nouns that refer to groups of people or things.

> EXAMPLES: *army, flock, class, species*

1.5 POSSESSIVE NOUNS

A **possessive noun** shows who or what owns something.

> EXAMPLES: *Conrad's, jury's, children's*

2 Pronouns

A **pronoun** is a word that is used in place of a noun or another pronoun. The word or word group to which the pronoun refers is called its **antecedent.**

2.1 PERSONAL PRONOUNS

Personal pronouns change their form to express person, number, gender, and case. The forms of these pronouns are shown in the following chart.

	Nominative	Objective	Possessive
Singular			
First Person	I	me	my, mine
Second Person	you	you	your, yours
Third Person	she, he, it	her, him, it	her, hers, his, its
Plural			
First Person	we	us	our, ours
Second Person	you	you	your, yours
Third Person	they	them	their, theirs

2.2 AGREEMENT WITH ANTECEDENT

Pronouns should agree with their antecedents in number, gender, and person.

If an antecedent is singular, use a singular pronoun.

> EXAMPLE: *Gulliver reaches Lilliput after his ship breaks apart.*

If an antecedent is plural, use a plural pronoun.

> EXAMPLES: *The **Lilliputians** shoot their arrows into Gulliver. Gulliver cuts the **flies** into pieces as they fly through the air.*

The gender of a pronoun must be the same as the gender of its antecedent.

EXAMPLES: *The king enjoys spending his time with Gulliver. The queen places Gulliver in her hand.*

The person of the pronoun must be the same as the person of its antecedent. As the chart in Section 2.1 shows, a pronoun can be in first-, second-, or third-person form.

EXAMPLE: *They invite Gulliver into their home.*

Practice and Apply

Rewrite each sentence so that the underlined pronoun agrees with its antecedent.

1. The readers of *Gulliver's Travels* love the book as an adventure story, but <u>you</u> like the humor too.
2. In the book, Gulliver travels to strange lands that <u>she</u> never could have imagined.
3. You would be surprised, too, to find <u>their</u> arms and legs suddenly tied down.
4. At first, the Lilliputians fear for <u>its</u> lives.

2.3 PRONOUN CASE

Personal pronouns change form to show how they function in sentences. Different functions are shown by different cases. The three cases are **nominative, objective,** and **possessive.** For examples of these pronouns, see the chart in Section 2.1.

A **nominative pronoun** is used as a subject or a predicate nominative in a sentence.

An **objective pronoun** is used as a direct object, an indirect object, or the object of a preposition.

SUBJECT   OBJECT   OBJECT OF PREPOSITION
He explained it to me.

A **possessive pronoun** shows ownership. The pronouns **mine, yours, hers, his, its, ours,** and **theirs** can be used in place of nouns.

EXAMPLE: *These letters are yours.*

The pronouns **my, your, her, his, its, our,** and **their** are used before nouns.

EXAMPLE: *These are your letters.*

WATCH OUT! Many spelling errors can be avoided if you watch out for *its* and *their.* Don't confuse the possessive pronoun *its* with the contraction *it's,* meaning "it is" or "it has." The homonyms *they're* (a contraction of *they are*) and *there* ("in that place") are often mistakenly used for *their.*

TIP To decide which pronoun to use in a comparison, such as "He tells better tales than (I or me)," fill in the missing word(s): *He tells better tales than I tell.*

Practice and Apply

Replace the underlined words in each sentence with an appropriate pronoun and identify the pronoun as a nominative, objective, or possessive pronoun.

1. <u>Percy Bysshe Shelley</u> was a romantic poet.
2. <u>Percy Bysshe Shelley's</u> friend Lord Byron was also a well-known poet.
3. The writer Mary Wollstonecraft Shelley was <u>Shelley's</u> wife.
4. Mary's novel *Frankenstein* has entertained <u>readers</u> for nearly 200 years.
5. Many film versions of <u>Frankenstein</u> exist.

2.4 REFLEXIVE AND INTENSIVE PRONOUNS

These pronouns are formed by adding *-self* or *-selves* to certain personal pronouns. Their forms are the same, and they differ only in how they are used.

A **reflexive pronoun** follows a verb or a preposition and reflects back on an earlier noun or pronoun.

EXAMPLES: *He threw himself forward. Danielle mailed herself the package.*

Intensive pronouns intensify or emphasize the nouns or pronouns to which they refer.

EXAMPLES: *The queen herself would have been amused.*
I saw it myself.

PRACTICE AND APPLY

Remind students to write legibly as they compose their responses to the Practice and Apply activities.

Answers:
1. *The readers of Gulliver's Travels love the book as an adventure story, but they like the humor, too.*
2. *In the book, Gulliver travels to strange lands that he never could have imagined.*
3. *You would be surprised, too, to find your arms and legs suddenly tied down.*
4. *At first, the Lilliputians fear for their lives.*

PRACTICE AND APPLY

Answers:
1. *He was a romantic poet. (nominative)*
2. *His friend Lord Byron was also a well-known poet. (possessive)*
3. *The writer Mary Wollstonecraft Shelley was his wife. (possessive)*
4. *Mary's novel Frankenstein has entertained them for nearly 200 years. (objective)*
5. *Many film versions of it exist. (objective)*

WATCH OUT! Avoid using *hisself* or *theirselves.* Standard English does not include these forms.

> NONSTANDARD: *He had painted hisself into a corner.*

> STANDARD: *He had painted himself into a corner.*

2.5 DEMONSTRATIVE PRONOUNS

Demonstrative pronouns point out things and persons near and far.

	Singular	Plural
Near	this	these
Far	that	those

2.6 INDEFINITE PRONOUNS

Indefinite pronouns do not refer to specific persons or things and usually have no antecedents. The chart shows some commonly used indefinite pronouns.

Singular	Plural	Singular or Plural	
another	both	all	none
anybody	few	any	some
no one	many	more	most
neither	several		

TIP Indefinite pronouns that end in *one, body,* or *thing* are always singular.

> INCORRECT: *Anyone who wants their research report can pick it up later today.*

> CORRECT: *Anyone who wants his or her research report can pick it up later today.*

If the indefinite pronoun might refer to either a male or a female, *his* or *her* may be used to refer to it, or the sentence may be rewritten.

> EXAMPLES: *Everybody wants his or her report back. All the students want their reports back.*

2.7 INTERROGATIVE PRONOUNS

An **interrogative pronoun** is used to ask a question. The interrogative pronouns are *who, whom, whose, which,* and *what.*

> EXAMPLES: *Who is going to the store? What time are we leaving?*

TIP *Who* is used as a subject, *whom* as an object. To find out which pronoun you need to use in a question, change the question to a statement.

> QUESTION: *(Who/Whom) did you meet there?*

> STATEMENT: *You met (?) there.*

Since the verb has a subject (**you**), the needed word must be the object form, **whom.**

> EXAMPLE: *Whom did you meet there?*

WATCH OUT! A special problem arises when you use an interrupter, such as *do you think,* within a question.

> EXAMPLE: *(Who/Whom) do you believe is the more influential musician?*

If you eliminate the interrupter, it is clear that the word you need is *who.*

2.8 RELATIVE PRONOUNS

Relative pronouns relate, or connect, dependent (or subordinate) clauses to the words they modify in sentences. The relative pronouns are *that, what, whatever, which, whichever, who, whoever, whom, whomever,* and *whose.*

Sometimes short sentences with related ideas can be combined by using a relative pronoun.

> SHORT SENTENCE: *William Blake was underappreciated by his contemporaries.*

> RELATED SENTENCE: *William Blake was both an artist and a poet.*

> COMBINED SENTENCE: *William Blake, who was both an artist and a poet, was underappreciated by his contemporaries.*

Practice and Apply

Choose the appropriate interrogative or relative pronoun from the words in parentheses.

1. William Blake wrote *Songs of Innocence,* (who, which) was a collection of poems.
2. (Who, Whom) or what was the inspiration for these poems?
3. Blake based the poems on street ballads and rhymes (that, what) children sang.
4. Blake was a visionary (whom, who) was ahead of his time.

2.9 PRONOUN REFERENCE PROBLEMS

The referent of a pronoun should always be clear.

An **indefinite reference** occurs when the pronoun *it, you,* or *they* does not clearly refer to a specific antecedent.

UNCLEAR: *When making bread, they must not overknead the dough.*

CLEAR: *When making bread, a baker must not overknead the dough.*

A **general reference** occurs when the pronoun *it, this, that, which,* or *such* is used to refer to a general idea rather than a specific antecedent.

UNCLEAR: *Jamie practices piano every day. This has made her an accomplished musician.*

CLEAR: *Jamie practices piano every day. Practicing has made her an accomplished musician.*

Ambiguous means "having more than one possible meaning." An **ambiguous reference** occurs when a pronoun could refer to two or more antecedents.

UNCLEAR: *Sarah talked to Beth while she folded laundry.*

CLEAR: *While Sarah folded laundry, she talked to Beth.*

Practice and Apply

Rewrite the following sentences to correct indefinite, ambiguous, and general pronoun references.

1. In "The Wife of Bath's Tale," it tells about a knight who is sent on a quest to find out what women most desire.
2. The knight is given the choice of either accepting the quest or being put to death. This makes him sorrowful.
3. An old woman provides the knight with the correct answer. This saves his life.
4. The queen agrees to the old woman's request that she marry the knight as a reward.

3 Verbs

A **verb** is a word that expresses an action, a condition, or a state of being.

3.1 ACTION VERBS

Action verbs express mental or physical activity.

EXAMPLES: *I walked to the store.*

3.2 LINKING VERBS

Linking verbs join subjects with words or phrases that rename or describe them.

EXAMPLES: *You are my friend.*

3.3 PRINCIPAL PARTS

Action and linking verbs typically have four principal parts, which are used to form verb tenses. The principal parts are the **present,** the **present participle,** the **past,** and the **past participle.**

Action verbs and some linking verbs also fall into two categories: regular and irregular. A **regular verb** is a verb that forms its past and past participle by adding *-ed* or *-d* to the present form.

COMMON CORE L 1

PRACTICE AND APPLY

Answers:
1. *which*
2. *Who*
3. *that*
4. *who*

COMMON CORE L 1

PRACTICE AND APPLY

Possible answers:
1. *"The Wife of Bath's Tale" is about a knight who is sent on a quest to find out what women most desire.*
2. *The knight is given the choice of either accepting the quest or being put to death. This choice makes him sorrowful.*
3. *An old woman provides the knight with the correct answer. This answer saves his life.*
4. *The queen agrees to the old woman's request that the old woman marry the knight as a reward.*

Present	Present Participle	Past	Past Participle
shift	(is) shifting	shifted	(has) shifted
hope	(is) hoping	hoped	(has) hoped
stop	(is) stopping	stopped	(has) stopped
marry	(is) marrying	married	(has) married

An **irregular verb** is a verb that forms its past and past participle in some other way than by adding -ed or -d to the present form.

Present	Present Participle	Past	Past Participle
bring	(is) bringing	brought	(has) brought
swim	(is) swimming	swam	(has) swum
steal	(is) stealing	stole	(has) stolen
grow	(is) growing	grew	(has) grown

3.4 VERB TENSE

The **tense** of a verb indicates the time of the action or state of being. An action or state of being can occur in the present, the past, or the future. There are six tenses, each expressing a different range of time.

The **present tense** expresses an action or state that is happening at the present time, occurs regularly, or is constant or generally true. Use the present part.

NOW: *That ballad sounds great.*

REGULAR: *I read every day.*

GENERAL: *The sun rises in the east.*

The **past tense** expresses an action that began and ended in the past. Use the past part.

EXAMPLE: *The storyteller finished his tale.*

The **future tense** expresses an action or state that will occur. Use **shall** or **will** with the present part.

EXAMPLE: *They will attend the next festival.*

The **present perfect tense** expresses an action or state that (1) was completed at an indefinite time in the past or (2) began in the past and continues into the present. Use *have* or *has* with the past participle.

EXAMPLE: *Poetry has inspired readers throughout the ages.*

The **past perfect tense** expresses an action in the past that came before another action in the past. Use *had* with the past participle.

EXAMPLE: *The messenger had traveled for days before he delivered his knight's response.*

The **future perfect tense** expresses an action in the future that will be completed before another action in the future. Use *shall have* or *will have* with the past participle.

EXAMPLE: *They will have finished the novel before seeing the movie version of the tale.*

TIP The past-tense form of an irregular verb is not paired with an auxiliary verb, but the past-perfect-tense form of an irregular verb is always paired with an auxiliary verb.

INCORRECT: *I have went to that restaurant before.*

INCORRECT: *I gone to that restaurant before.*

CORRECT: *I have gone to that restaurant before.*

3.5 PROGRESSIVE FORMS

The progressive forms of the six tenses show ongoing actions. Use forms of *be* with the present participles of verbs.

PRESENT PROGRESSIVE: *She is rehearsing her lines.*

PAST PROGRESSIVE: *She was rehearsing her lines.*

FUTURE PROGRESSIVE: *She will be rehearsing her lines.*

PRESENT PERFECT PROGRESSIVE: *She has been rehearsing her lines.*

PAST PERFECT PROGRESSIVE: *She had been rehearsing her lines.*

FUTURE PERFECT PROGRESSIVE: *She will have been rehearsing her lines.*

WATCH OUT! Do not shift from tense to tense needlessly. Watch out for these special cases:

- In most compound sentences and in sentences with compound predicates, keep the tenses the same.
  INCORRECT: *We work hard, and they paid us well.*
  CORRECT: *We work hard, and they pay us well.*

- If one past action happened before another, indicate this with a shift in tense.
  INCORRECT: *They wished they started earlier.*
  CORRECT: *They wished they had started earlier.*

Practice and Apply

Identify the tense of the verb(s) in each of the following sentences. If you find an unnecessary tense shift, correct it.

1. The tales of King Arthur and his knights were popular in the Middle Ages, and they continue to be popular today.
2. Gawain, Arthur's nephew, bravely accepts the Green Knight's challenge and will agree to the pact proposed by the Green Knight.
3. After Gawain cuts off the Green Knight's head, the Green Knight remained alive.
4. Gawain meets the Green Knight again, just as the Green Knight had instructed him to do the year before.
5. This time Gawain receives the blow of the Green Knight's ax, but he did not die.

3.6 ACTIVE AND PASSIVE VOICE

The voice of a verb tells whether its subject performs or receives the action expressed by the verb. When the subject performs the action, the verb is in the **active voice.** When the subject is the receiver of the action, the verb is in the **passive voice.**

Compare these two sentences:

ACTIVE: *Gawain and the Green Knight make a pact with each other.*

PASSIVE: *A pact is made between Gawain and the Green Knight.*

To form the passive voice, use a form of **be** with the past participle of the verb.

WATCH OUT! Use the passive voice sparingly. It can make writing awkward and less direct.

AWKWARD: *A meeting between the two knights is arranged.*

BETTER: *The two knights arrange a meeting.*

There are occasions when you will choose to use the passive voice because

- You want to emphasize the receiver: *The king was shot.*
- The doer is unknown: *My books were stolen.*
- The doer is unimportant: *French is spoken here.*

Practice and Apply

For the four items below, identify the boldfaced verb phrase as active or passive.

1. King Arthur **was confronted** by the Green Knight.
2. The Green Knight **had been searching** for someone brave enough to meet his challenge.
3. Gawain **did** not **want** King Arthur to subject himself to the challenge.
4. The Green Knight **was struck** by the ax.

 L1

PRACTICE AND APPLY
Answers:

1. *were (past), continue (present)*
2. *accepts (present), will agree (future)*
   Correction to verb tense: Change will agree *to* agrees.
3. *cuts (present), remained (past)*
   Correction to verb tense: Change remained *to* remains.
4. *meets (present), had instructed (past perfect)*
5. *receives (present), did not die (past)*
   Correction to verb tense: Change did not die *to* does not die.

COMMON CORE **L1**

PRACTICE AND APPLY
Answers:

1. *passive*
2. *active*
3. *active*
4. *passive*

4 Modifiers

Modifiers are words or groups of words that change or limit the meanings of other words. Adjectives and adverbs are common modifiers.

4.1 ADJECTIVES

Adjectives modify nouns and pronouns by telling which one, what kind, how many, or how much.

WHICH ONE: *this, that, these, those*

EXAMPLE: *That girl used to live in my neighborhood.*

WHAT KIND: *large, unique, anxious, moldy*

EXAMPLE: *I bought a unique lamp at the yard sale.*

HOW MANY: *ten, many, several, every, each*

EXAMPLE: *I wake up at the same time every day.*

HOW MUCH: *more, less, little, barely*

EXAMPLE: *We bought more food than we could possibly eat.*

4.2 PREDICATE ADJECTIVES

Most adjectives come before the nouns they modify, as in the previous examples. A **predicate adjective,** however, follows a linking verb and describes the subject.

EXAMPLE: *My friends are very intelligent.*

Be especially careful to use adjectives (not adverbs) after such linking verbs as **look, feel, grow, taste,** and **smell.**

EXAMPLE: *The weather grows cold.*

4.3 ADVERBS

Adverbs modify verbs, adjectives, and other adverbs by telling where, when, how, or to what extent.

WHERE: *The children played outside.*

WHEN: *The author spoke yesterday.*

HOW: *We walked slowly behind the leader.*

TO WHAT EXTENT: *He worked very hard.*

Adverbs may occur in many places in sentences, both before and after the words they modify.

EXAMPLES: *Suddenly the wind shifted.*
The wind suddenly shifted.
The wind shifted suddenly.

4.4 ADJECTIVE OR ADVERB?

Many adverbs are formed by adding -*ly* to adjectives.

EXAMPLES: *sweet, sweetly; gentle, gently*

However, -*ly* added to a noun will usually yield an adjective.

EXAMPLES: *friend, friendly; woman, womanly*

4.5 COMPARISON OF MODIFIERS

Modifiers can be used to compare two or more things. The form of a modifier shows the degree of comparison. Both adjectives and adverbs have three forms: the **positive,** the **comparative,** and the **superlative.**

The **positive form** is used to describe individual things, groups, or actions.

EXAMPLES: *Jonathan Swift was a great satirist.*
He had a savage wit.

The **comparative form** is used to compare two things, groups, or actions.

EXAMPLES: *I think Jonathan Swift was a greater satirist than Voltaire.*
Swift had a more savage wit.

The **superlative form** is used to compare more than two things, groups, or actions.

EXAMPLES: *I think Jonathan Swift was the greatest satirist who ever lived.*
Swift had the most savage wit of any writer.

4.6 REGULAR COMPARISONS

Most one-syllable and some two-syllable adjectives and adverbs have comparatives and superlatives formed by adding -*er* and -*est*. All three-syllable and most two syllable modifiers have comparatives and superlatives formed with *more* and *most*.

Modifier	Comparative	Superlative
tall	taller	tallest
kind	kinder	kindest
droopy	droopier	droopiest
expensive	more expensive	most expensive
wasteful	more wasteful	most wasteful

WATCH OUT! Note that spelling changes must sometimes be made to form the comparatives and superlatives of modifiers.

EXAMPLES: *friendly, friendlier* (Change *y* to *i* and add the ending.)
sad, sadder (Double the final consonant and add the ending.)

4.7 IRREGULAR COMPARISONS

Some commonly used modifiers have irregular comparative and superlative forms. They are listed in the following chart.

Modifier	Comparative	Superlative
good	better	best
bad	worse	worst
far	farther *or* further	farthest *or* futhest
little	less *or* lesser	least
many	more	most
well	better	best
much	more	most

4.8 PROBLEMS WITH MODIFIERS

Study the tips that follow to avoid common mistakes:

Farther and **Further** Use *farther* for distances; use *further* for everything else.

Double Comparisons Make a comparison by using *-er/-est* or by using more/most. Using *-er* with *more* or using *-est* with *most* is incorrect.

INCORRECT: *I like her more better than she likes me.*

CORRECT: *I like her better than she likes me.*

Illogical Comparisons An illogical or confusing comparison results when two unrelated things are compared or when something is compared with itself. The word *other* or the word *else* should be used in a comparison of an individual member to the rest of a group.

ILLOGICAL: *I think the orchid is more beautiful than any flower.* (implies that the orchid isn't a flower)

LOGICAL: *I think the orchid is more beautiful than any other flower.* (identifies that the orchid is a flower)

Bad vs. **Badly** *Bad,* always an adjective, is used before a noun or after a linking verb. *Badly,* always an adverb, never modifies a noun. Be sure to use the right form after a linking verb.

INCORRECT: *Ed felt badly after his team lost.*

CORRECT: *Ed felt bad after his team lost.*

Good vs. **Well** *Good* is always an adjective. It is used before a noun or after a linking verb. *Well* is often an adverb meaning "expertly" or "properly." *Well* can also be used as an adjective after a linking verb when it means "in good health."

INCORRECT: *Helen writes very good.*

CORRECT: *Helen writes very well.*

CORRECT: *Yesterday I felt bad; today I feel well.*

Double Negatives If you add a negative word to a sentence that is already negative, the result will be an error known as a double negative. When using *not* or *-n't* with a verb, use *any-* words, such as *anybody* or *anything,* rather than *no-* words, such as *nobody* or *nothing,* later in the sentence.

INCORRECT: *I don't have no money.*

CORRECT: *I don't have any money.*

PRACTICE AND APPLY
Answers:
1. *most favorite*
2. *was*
3. *gravest*
4. *bad*
5. *anything*
6. *well*
7. *stronger*
8. *anything*
9. *bad*
10. *noblest*

Using *hardly, barely,* or *scarcely* after a negative word is also incorrect.

> **INCORRECT:** *They couldn't barely see two feet ahead.*

> **CORRECT:** *They could barely see two feet ahead.*

Misplaced Modifiers Sometimes a modifier is placed so far away from the word it modifies that the intended meaning of the sentence is unclear. Prepositional phrases and participial phrases are often misplaced. Place modifiers as close as possible to the words they modify.

> **MISPLACED:** *The ranger explained how to find ducks in her office.* (The ducks were not in the ranger's office.)

> **CLEARER:** *In her office, the ranger explained how to find ducks.*

Dangling Modifiers Sometimes a modifier doesn't appear to modify any word in a sentence. Most dangling modifiers are participial phrases or infinitive phrases.

> **DANGLING:** *Coming home with groceries, our parrot said, "Hello!"*

> **CLEARER:** *Coming home with groceries, we heard our parrot say, "Hello!"*

Practice and Apply

Choose the correct word or words from each pair in parentheses.
1. Sir Launcelot was King Arthur's (most favorite, favoritest) knight.
2. Launcelot, however, (wasn't, was) hardly loyal to Arthur.
3. He made the (most gravest, gravest) mistake when he fell in love with Gwynevere, the king's wife.
4. King Arthur felt (bad, badly) about their friendship coming to an end, but what could he do?
5. Launcelot tried to make peace with the king, but Sir Gawain, the king's nephew, didn't want (nothing, anything) to do with Launcelot.
6. Gawain challenged Launcelot to a battle, and Gawain initially fought very (good, well).

continued

7. After three hours of battle, however, Launcelot became the (stronger, more strong) of the two men.
8. Though Gawain was injured in the battle, he wouldn't let (anything, nothing) stop him from fighting Launcelot again.
9. Launcelot felt (badly, bad) about having to fight Gawain once more, but he knew he had to do it.
10. Once again, Launcelot spared Gawain's life, proving himself to be the (nobler, noblest) of all knights.

5 Prepositions, Conjunctions, and Interjections

5.1 PREPOSITIONS

A preposition is a word used to show the relationship between a noun or a pronoun and another word in the sentence.

Commonly Used Prepositions			
above	down	near	through
at	for	of	to
before	from	on	up
below	in	out	with
by	into	over	without

A preposition is always followed by a word or group of words that serves as its object. The preposition, its object, and modifiers of the object are called the **prepositional phrase.** In each example below, the prepositional phrase is highlighted and the object of the preposition is in boldface type.

> **EXAMPLES:** *The future of the entire kingdom is uncertain.*
> *We searched through the deepest woods.*

Prepositional phrases may be used as adjectives or as adverbs. The phrase in the first example is used as an adjective modifying the noun *future.* In the second example, the phrase is used as an adverb modifying the verb *searched.*

WATCH OUT! Prepositional phrases must be as close as possible to the word they modify.

> MISPLACED: *We have clothes for leisurewear of many colors.*

> CLEARER: *We have clothes of many colors for leisurewear.*

5.2 CONJUNCTIONS

A conjunction is a word used to connect words, phrases, or sentences. There are three kinds of conjunctions: **coordinating conjunctions, correlative conjunctions,** and **subordinating conjunctions.**

Coordinating conjunctions connect words or word groups that have the same function in a sentence. Such conjunctions include *and, but, or, for, so, yet,* and *nor.*

Coordinating conjunctions can join nouns, pronouns, verbs, adjectives, adverbs, prepositional phrases, and clauses in a sentence.

These examples show coordinating conjunctions joining words of the same function:

> EXAMPLES: *I have many friends but few enemies.* (two noun objects)
> *We ran out the door and into the street.* (two prepositional phrases)
> *They are pleasant yet seem aloof.* (two predicates)
> *We have to go now, or we will be late.* (two clauses)

Correlative conjunctions are similar to coordinating conjunctions. However, correlative conjunctions are always used in pairs.

Correlative Conjunctions		
both . . . and	neither . . . nor	whether . . . or
either . . . or	not only . . . but also	

Subordinating conjunctions introduce subordinate clauses—clauses that cannot stand by themselves as complete sentences. The subordinating conjunction shows how the subordinate clause relates to the rest of the sentence. The relationships include time, manner, place, cause, comparison, condition, and purpose.

Subordinating Conjunctions	
Time	after, as, as long as, as soon as, before, since, until, when, whenever, while
Manner	as, as if
Place	where, wherever
Cause	because, since
Comparison	as, as much as, than
Condition	although, as long as, even if, even though, if, provided that, though, unless, while
Purpose	in order that, so that, that

In the example below, the boldface word is the conjunction, and the highlighted words form a subordinate clause:

> EXAMPLE: ***Though** Grendel is a loathsome beast, Beowulf does not fear him.*

Beowulf does not fear him is an independent clause because it can stand alone as a complete sentence. *Though Grendel is a loathsome beast* cannot stand alone as a complete sentence; it is a subordinate clause.

Conjunctive adverbs are used to connect clauses that can stand by themselves as sentences. Conjunctive adverbs include *also, besides, finally, however, moreover, nevertheless, otherwise,* and *then.*

> EXAMPLE: *She loved the fall; however, she also enjoyed winter.*

5.3 INTERJECTIONS

Interjections are words used to show strong emotion, such as *wow* and *cool.* Often followed by an exclamation point, they have no grammatical relationship to any other part of a sentence.

Grammar   **R39**

EXAMPLE: *Beowulf seizes Grendel, grasping the monster in his fists. Unbelievable!*

6 The Sentence and Its Parts

A **sentence** is a group of words used to express a complete thought. A complete sentence has a subject and a predicate.

6.1 KINDS OF SENTENCES

There are four basic types of sentences.

Types	Definition	Example
Declarative	states a fact, a wish, an intent, or a feeling	I just finished reading *Macbeth*.
Interrogative	asks a question	Have you ever read it?
Imperative	gives a command or direction	You must read it sometime.
Exclamatory	expresses strong feeling or excitement	It's so compelling!

6.2 COMPOUND SUBJECTS AND PREDICATES

A compound subject consists of two or more subjects that share the same verb. They are typically joined by the coordinating conjunction *and* or *or*.

EXAMPLE: *The knight and his horse rode into the forest.*

A compound predicate consists of two or more predicates that share the same subject. They too are typically joined by a coordinating conjunction, usually *and, but,* or *or.*

EXAMPLE: *Sir Gawain beheaded the Green Knight but did not kill him.*

6.3 COMPLEMENTS

A **complement** is a word or group of words that completes the meaning of the sentence. Some sentences contain only a subject and a verb. Most sentences, however, require additional words placed after the verb to complete the meaning of the sentence. There are three kinds of complements: direct objects, indirect objects, and subject complements.

Direct objects are words or word groups that receive the action of action verbs. A direct object answers the question *what* or *whom.*

EXAMPLES: *The students asked many questions.* (Asked what?)
The teacher quickly answered the students. (Answered whom?)

Indirect objects tell to whom or what or for whom or what the actions of verbs are performed. Indirect objects come before direct objects. In the examples that follow, the indirect objects are highlighted.

EXAMPLES: *My sister usually gave her friends good advice.* (Gave to whom?)
Her brother sent the store a heavy package. (Sent to what?)

Subject complements come after linking verbs and identify or describe the subjects. A subject complement that names or identifies a subject is called a **predicate nominative.** Predicate nominatives include **predicate nouns** and **predicate pronouns.**

EXAMPLES: *My friends are very hard workers.*
The best writer in the class is she.

A subject complement that describes a subject is called a **predicate adjective.**

EXAMPLE: *The pianist appeared very energetic.*

7 Phrases

A **phrase** is a group of related words that does not contain a subject and a predicate but functions in a sentence as a single part of speech.

7.1 PREPOSITIONAL PHRASES

A **prepositional phrase** is a phrase that consists of a preposition, its object, and any modifiers of the object. Prepositional phrases that modify nouns or pronouns are called **adjective phrases.** Prepositional phrases that modify verbs, adjectives, or adverbs are **adverb phrases.**

> ADJECTIVE PHRASE: *The central character of the story is a villain.*

> ADVERB PHRASE: *He reveals his nature in the first scene.*

7.2 APPOSITIVES AND APPOSITIVE PHRASES

An **appositive** is a noun or pronoun that identifies or renames another noun or pronoun. An **appositive phrase** includes an appositive and modifiers of it.

An appositive can be either **essential** or **nonessential.** An **essential appositive** provides information that is needed to identify what is referred to by the preceding noun or pronoun.

> EXAMPLE: *The poet Percy Bysshe Shelley frequently used nature as the subject of his poems.*

A **nonessential appositive** adds extra information about a noun or pronoun whose meaning is already clear. Nonessential appositives and appositive phrases are set off with commas.

> EXAMPLE: *The skylark, a bird noted for its melodious song, is the subject of one of Shelley's poems.*

8 Verbals and Verbal Phrases

A **verbal** is a verb form that is used as a noun, an adjective, or an adverb. A **verbal phrase** consists of a verbal along with its modifiers and complements. There are three kinds of verbals: **infinitives, participles,** and **gerunds.**

8.1 INFINITIVES AND INFINITIVE PHRASES

An **infinitive** is a verb form that usually begins with to and functions as a noun, an adjective, or an adverb. An **infinitive phrase** consists of an infinitive plus its modifiers and complements. The examples that follow show several uses of infinitive phrases.

> NOUN: *To travel the world is my long-term plan.* (subject)
> *I'm trying to find a solution.* (direct object)
> *Her greatest wish was to return to her native country.* (predicate nominative)

> ADJECTIVE: *We supported his goal to become a pilot.* (adjective modifying goal)

> ADVERB: *To prepare for the marathon, Julie maintained a strict exercise regimen.* (adverb modifying maintained)

Because infinitives usually begin with *to,* it is usually easy to recognize them. However, sometimes *to* may be omitted.

> EXAMPLE: *Should you dare [to] speak these forbidden words, a curse will fall upon you.*

8.2 PARTICIPLES AND PARTICIPIAL PHRASES

A **participle** is a verb form that functions as an adjective. Like adjectives, participles modify nouns and pronouns. Most participles are present-participle forms, ending in -*ing,* or past-participle forms ending in -*ed* or -*en.* In the examples that follow, the participles are highlighted:

> MODIFYING A NOUN: *The crying baby needed a nap.*

> MODIFYING A PRONOUN: *Scared, she decided not to walk home alone.*

Participial phrases are participles with all their modifiers and complements.

> MODIFYING A NOUN: *The light streaming in through the window woke up the boy.*

> MODIFYING A PRONOUN: *Walking across the field, she thought she saw a fox.*

PRACTICE AND APPLY

Answers:

1. *gerund phrase*
2. *appositive phrase*
3. *participial phrase*
4. *infinitive phrase*
5. *gerund phrase*

8.3 DANGLING AND MISPLACED PARTICIPLES

A participle or participial phrase should be placed as close as possible to the word that it modifies. Otherwise the meaning of the sentence may not be clear.

> MISPLACED: *The boys were looking for squirrels searching the trees.*
>
> CLEARER: *The boys searching the trees were looking for squirrels.*

A participle or participial phrase that does not clearly modify anything in a sentence is called a **dangling participle.** A dangling participle causes confusion because it appears to modify a word that it cannot sensibly modify. Correct a dangling participle by providing a word for the participle to modify.

> DANGLING: *Running like the wind, my hat fell off.* (The hat wasn't running.)
>
> CLEARER: *Running like the wind, I lost my hat.*

8.4 GERUNDS AND GERUND PHRASES

A **gerund** is a verb form ending in *-ing* that functions as a noun. Gerunds may perform any function nouns perform.

> SUBJECT: *Running is my favorite pastime.*
>
> DIRECT OBJECT: *I truly love running.*
>
> INDIRECT OBJECT: *You should give running a try.*
>
> SUBJECT COMPLEMENT: *My deepest passion is running.*
>
> OBJECT OF PREPOSITION: *Her love of running keeps her strong.*

Gerund phrases are gerunds with all their modifiers and complements.

> SUBJECT: *Wishing on a star never got me far.*
>
> OBJECT OF PREPOSITION: *I will finish before leaving the office.*
>
> APPOSITIVE: *Her avocation, flying airplanes, finally led to full-time employment.*

Identify the underlined phrases as appositive phrases, infinitive phrases, participial phrases, or gerund phrases.

1. In D. H. Lawrence's story "The Rocking-Horse Winner," the protagonist becomes obsessed with <u>betting on horses.</u>
2. The protagonist, <u>a young boy,</u> starts to win a lot of money from the races.
3. <u>Feeling unbeatable,</u> the boy continues to bet more and more money.
4. He wants <u>to win as much as possible</u> but makes himself sick in the process.
5. After the boy dies of his illness, the mother discovers that <u>having a lot of money</u> isn't so important after all.

9 Clauses

A **clause** is a group of words that contains a subject and a verb. There are two kinds of clauses: independent clauses and subordinate clauses.

9.1 INDEPENDENT AND SUBORDINATE CLAUSES

An **independent clause** can stand alone as a sentence, as the word **independent** suggests.

> INDEPENDENT CLAUSE: *T. S. Eliot wrote a poem called "The Naming of Cats."*

A sentence may contain more than one independent clause.

> EXAMPLE: *T. S. Eliot wrote a poem called "The Naming of Cats," and he also wrote a poem called "The Hollow Men."*

In the preceding example, the coordinating conjunction *and* joins two independent clauses.

A **subordinate clause** cannot stand alone as a sentence. It is subordinate to, or dependent on, an independent clause.

> EXAMPLE: *Although Eliot was born in America, he later moved to England.*

The highlighted clause cannot stand by itself; it must be joined with an independent clause to form a complete sentence.

9.2 ADJECTIVE CLAUSES

An **adjective clause** is a subordinate clause used as an adjective. It usually follows the noun or pronoun it modifies. Adjective clauses are typically introduced by the relative pronoun *who, whom, whose, which,* or *that.*

> EXAMPLES: *"The Naming of Cats" is the poem that I like best.*
> *The poem, which is very humorous, discusses the difficulty of naming cats.*
> *I think the people who enjoy the poem most are cat lovers.*

An adjective clause can be either essential or nonessential. An **essential adjective clause** provides information that is necessary to identify the preceding noun or pronoun.

> EXAMPLE: *Eliot was a poet who wrote about many different topics.*

A **nonessential adjective clause** adds additional information about a noun or pronoun whose meaning is already clear. Nonessential clauses are set off with commas.

> EXAMPLE: *Eliot, who was always fond of Lewis Carroll, decided to try his hand at humor.*

TIP The relative pronouns **whom, which,** and **that** may sometimes be omitted when they are objects in adjective clauses.

> EXAMPLE: *The names [that] I like best are Augustus and Demeter.*

9.3 ADVERB CLAUSES

An **adverb clause** is a subordinate clause that is used to modify a verb, an adjective, or an adverb. It is introduced by a subordinating conjunction. Adverb clauses typically occur at the beginning or end of sentences.

> MODIFYING A VERB: *When we need you, we will call.*

> MODIFYING AN ADVERB: *I'll stay here where there is shelter from the rain.*

> MODIFYING AN ADJECTIVE: *Roman felt as good as he had ever felt.*

9.4 NOUN CLAUSES

A **noun clause** is a subordinate clause that is used as a noun. A noun clause may be used as a subject, a direct object, an indirect object, a predicate nominative, or the object of a preposition. Noun clauses are introduced either by pronouns, such as *that, what, who, whoever, which,* and *whose,* or by subordinating conjunctions, such as *how, when, where, why,* and *whether.*

TIP Because the same words may introduce adjective and noun clauses, you need to consider how a clause functions within its sentence. To determine if a clause is a noun clause, try substituting *something* or *someone* for the clause. If you can do it, it is probably a noun clause.

> EXAMPLES: *I asked her when I should leave.* ("I asked her *something*." The clause is a noun clause, direct object of the verb *asked*.)
> *Whoever decides to go can get a ride with me.* ("*Someone* can get a ride with me." The clause is a noun clause, functioning as the subject of the sentence.)

10 The Structure of Sentences

When classified by their structure, there are four kinds of sentences: simple, compound, complex, and compound-complex.

10.1 SIMPLE SENTENCES

A **simple sentence** is a sentence that has one independent clause and no subordinate clauses. Various parts of simple sentences may be compound, and simple sentences may contain grammatical structures such as appositive and verbal phrases.

> EXAMPLES: *William Blake, a rare talent, wrote poetry and created art.* (an appositive phrase and a compound predicate)
> *Inspired by both the human and the divine, Blake wanted to share his unique vision with the world.* (a participial phrase and an infinitive phrase)

Grammar   **R43**

10.2 COMPOUND SENTENCES

A **compound sentence** consists of two or more independent clauses. The clauses in compound sentences are joined with commas and coordinating conjunctions (*and, but, or, nor, yet, for, so*) or with semicolons. Like simple sentences, compound sentences do not contain any subordinate clauses.

> **EXAMPLES:** *I like to exercise, but it can be difficult to find the time. I went to the store first; then I went to the bank.*

WATCH OUT! Do not confuse compound sentences with simple sentences that have compound parts.

> **EXAMPLE:** *He vacuumed the floor and shook out the rugs.* (Here *and* joins parts of a compound predicate, not a compound sentence.)

10.3 COMPLEX SENTENCES

A **complex sentence** consists of one independent clause and one or more subordinate clauses. Each subordinate clause can be used as a noun or as a modifier. If it is used as a modifier, a subordinate clause usually modifies a word in the independent clause, and the independent clause can stand alone. However, when a subordinate clause is a noun clause, it is a part of the independent clause; the two cannot be separated.

> **MODIFIER:** *As soon as I am finished with this, I will move on to the next project.*
> **NOUN CLAUSE:** *We're going to the park with whoever else wants to come along.* (The noun clause is the object of the preposition *with* and cannot be separated from the rest of the sentence.)

10.4 COMPOUND-COMPLEX SENTENCES

A **compound-complex sentence** contains two or more independent clauses and one or more subordinate clauses. Compound-complex sentences are, simply, both compound and complex. If you start with a compound sentence, all you need to do to form a compound-complex sentence is add a subordinate clause.

> **COMPOUND:** *We're going to the baseball game, and then we're going to get some ice cream.*
> **COMPOUND-COMPLEX:** *We're going to the baseball game that begins at six o'clock, and then we're going to get some ice cream.*

10.5 PARALLEL STRUCTURE

When you write sentences, make sure that coordinate parts are equivalent, or **parallel,** in structure.

> **NOT PARALLEL:** *I am going to hike and swimming.* (To *hike* is an infinitive; *swimming* is a gerund.)
> **PARALLEL:** *I am going hiking and swimming.* (*Hiking* and *swimming* are both gerunds.)
> **NOT PARALLEL:** *I like steak and to eat potatoes.* (*Steak* is a noun; *to eat potatoes* is a phrase.)
> **PARALLEL:** *I like steak and potatoes.* (*Steak* and *potatoes* are both nouns.)

11 Writing Complete Sentences

Remember, a sentence is a group of words that expresses a complete thought. In formal writing, try to avoid both sentence fragments and run-on sentences.

11.1 CORRECTING FRAGMENTS

A **sentence fragment** is a group of words that is only part of a sentence. It does not express a complete thought and may be confusing to a reader or listener. A sentence fragment may be lacking a subject, a predicate, or both.

> **FRAGMENT:** *Went for a boat ride.* (no subject)
> **CORRECTED:** *We went for a boat ride.*
> **FRAGMENT:** *People of all ages.* (no predicate)
> **CORRECTED:** *People of all ages tried to water ski.*

FRAGMENT: *After the boat ride.* (neither subject nor predicate)

CORRECTED: *We dried off by the fire after the boat ride.*

In your writing, fragments may be a result of haste or incorrect punctuation. Sometimes fixing a fragment will be a matter of attaching it to a preceding or following sentence.

FRAGMENT: *We saw the two girls. Waiting for the bus to arrive.*

CORRECTED: *We saw the two girls waiting for the bus to arrive.*

11.2 CORRECTING RUN-ON SENTENCES

A **run-on sentence** is made up of two or more sentences written as though they were one. Some run-ons have no punctuation within them. Others may have only commas where conjunctions or stronger punctuation marks are necessary. Use your judgment in correcting run-on sentences, as you have choices. You can make a run-on two sentences if the thoughts are not closely connected. If the thoughts are closely related, you can keep the run-on as one sentence by adding a semicolon or a conjunction.

RUN-ON: *We found a place for the picnic by a small pond it was three miles from the village.*

MAKE TWO SENTENCES: *We found a place for the picnic by a small pond. It was three miles from the village.*

RUN-ON: *We found a place for the picnic by a small pond it was perfect.*

USE A SEMICOLON: *We found a place for the picnic by a small pond; it was perfect.*

ADD A CONJUNCTION: *We found a place for the picnic by a small pond, and it was perfect.*

WATCH OUT! When you form compound sentences, make sure you use appropriate punctuation: a comma before a coordinating conjunction, a semicolon when there is no coordinating conjunction. A very common mistake is to use a comma alone instead of a comma and a conjunction. This error is called a **comma splice.**

INCORRECT: *He finished the apprenticeship, he left the village.*

CORRECT: *He finished the apprenticeship, and he left the village.*

Practice and Apply

Rewrite the following paragraph, correcting all fragments and run-ons.

The Book of Margery Kempe details the tremendous difficulties that Kempe experiences. After the birth of her first child. She sees demons and fears for her own life, her keepers restrain her so that she cannot do harm to herself. She says that one day she is visited by Jesus. And that, afterwards, she becomes calm and rational again. After this transformative experience, Kempe goes on to become a preacher. And a religious visionary.

12 Subject-Verb Agreement

The subject and verb in a clause must agree in number. Agreement means that if the subject is singular, the verb is also singular, and if the subject is plural, the verb is also plural.

12.1 BASIC AGREEMENT

Fortunately, agreement between subjects and verbs in English is simple. Most verbs show the difference between singular and plural only in the third person of the present tense. In the present tense, the third-person singular form ends in *-s.*

 COMMON CORE L1

PRACTICE AND APPLY
Possible answer:
The Book of Margery Kempe *details the tremendous difficulties that Kempe experiences after the birth of her first child. She sees demons and fears for her own life. Her keepers restrain her so that she cannot do harm to herself. She says that one day she is visited by Jesus and that, afterwards, she becomes calm and rational again. After this transformative experience, Kempe goes on to become a preacher and a religious visionary.*

Grammar **R45**

Present-Tense Verb Forms	
Singular	**Plural**
I eat	we eat
you eat	you eat
she, he, it eats	they eat

12.2 AGREEMENT WITH *BE*

The verb *be* presents special problems in agreement, because this verb does not follow the usual verb patterns.

Forms of *Be*			
Present Tense		**Past Tense**	
Singular	**Plural**	**Singular**	**Plural**
I am	we are	I was	we were
you are	you are	you were	you were
she, he, it is	they are	she, he, it was	they were

12.3 WORDS BETWEEN SUBJECT AND VERB

A verb agrees only with its subject. When words come between a subject and a verb, ignore them when considering proper agreement. Identify the subject and make sure the verb agrees with it.

> EXAMPLES: *Several items in the storage unit need to be thrown out.*
> *Many of the puppies in the litter are smaller than others.*

12.4 AGREEMENT WITH COMPOUND SUBJECTS

Use plural verbs with most compound subjects joined by the word *and*.

> EXAMPLE: *My mother and her sisters call each other every Sunday.*

To confirm that you need a plural verb, you could substitute the plural pronoun *they* for *my mother and her sisters*.

If a compound subject is thought of as a unit, use a singular verb. Test this by substituting the singular pronoun *it*.

> EXAMPLE: *Liver and onions [it] is Robert's least favorite dish.*

Use a singular verb with a compound subject that is preceded by *each, every,* or *many a*.

> EXAMPLE: *Every man, woman, and child is being ordered off the ship.*

When the parts of a compound subject are joined by *or, nor,* or the correlative conjunctions *either . . . or* or *neither . . . nor*, make the verb agree with the noun or pronoun nearest the verb.

> EXAMPLES: *Cheddar or Swiss is my favorite cheese.*
> *Either my brother or my sisters are coming to pick me up.*
> *Neither I nor my two friends were here at the time of the accident.*

12.5 PERSONAL PRONOUNS AS SUBJECTS

When using a personal pronoun as a subject, make sure to match it with the correct form of the verb *be*. (See the chart in Section 12.2.) Note especially that the pronoun *you* takes the forms *are* and *were*, regardless of whether it is singular or plural.

WATCH OUT! *You is* and *you was* are nonstandard forms and should be avoided in writing and speaking. *We was* and *they was* are also forms to be avoided.

> INCORRECT: *You is facing the wrong direction.*

> CORRECT: *You are facing the wrong direction.*

> INCORRECT: *We was telling ghost stories.*

> CORRECT: *We were telling ghost stories.*

12.6 INDEFINITE PRONOUNS AS SUBJECTS

Some indefinite pronouns are always singular; some are always plural.

Singular Indefinite Pronouns		
another	everybody	no one
anybody	everyone	nothing

continued

anyone	everything	one
anything	much	somebody

Singular Indefinite Pronouns		
each	neither	someone
either	nobody	something

EXAMPLES: *Each of the writers was given an award.*
Somebody in the room upstairs is sleeping.

Plural Indefinite Pronouns			
both	few	many	several

EXAMPLES: *Many of the books in our library are not in circulation.*
Few have been returned recently.

Still other indefinite pronouns may be either singular or plural.

Singular or Plural Indefinite Pronouns		
all	more	none
any	most	some

The number of the indefinite pronoun *any* or *none* often depends on the intended meaning.

EXAMPLES: *Any of these topics has potential for a good article.* (any one topic)
Any of these topics have potential for good articles. (all of the many topics)

The indefinite pronouns *all, some, more, most,* and *none* are singular when they refer to quantities or parts of things. They are plural when they refer to numbers of individual things. Context will usually give a clue.

EXAMPLES: *All of the flour is gone.* (referring to a quantity)
All of the flowers are gone. (referring to individual items)

12.7 INVERTED SENTENCES

Problems in agreement often occur in inverted sentences beginning with *here*

or *there;* in questions beginning with *how, when, why, where,* or *what;* and in inverted sentences beginning with phrases. Identify the subject—wherever it is—before deciding on the verb.

EXAMPLES: *There clearly are far too many cooks in this kitchen.*
What is the correct ingredient for this stew?
Far from the embroiled cooks stands the master chef.

Practice and Apply

Locate the subject of each clause in the sentences below. Then choose the correct verb.

1. The work *A History of the English Church and People* (contain, contains) important historical information.
2. Few books (is, are) as valuable for researching early British history.
3. Many stories in the book (discuss, discusses) the spread of Christianity in England.
4. During the fifth century, both the pagan faith and the Christian faith (were, was) present in Britain.
5. Each of King Edwin's counselors (was, were) in agreement that the king should convert to Christianity.
6. Neither the counselors nor the king (were, was) convinced that he should continue to follow the pagan faith.
7. In the end, none of the pagan temples and altars (was, were) left standing.

12.8 SENTENCES WITH PREDICATE NOMINATIVES

When a predicate nominative serves as a complement in a sentence, use a verb that agrees with the subject, not the complement.

EXAMPLES: *The poems of John Keats are one component of this book.* (The subject is the plural noun *poems,* not *component,* and it takes the plural verb *are.*)
One component of this book is the poems of John Keats. (The subject is the singular noun *component,* and it takes the singular verb *is.*)

 COMMON CORE L1

PRACTICE AND APPLY
Answers:
1. *work; contains*
2. *books; are*
3. *stories; discuss*
4. *both; were*
5. *Each; was*
6. *Neither; was*
7. *none; were*

12.9 *DON'T* AND *DOESN'T* AS AUXILIARY VERBS

The auxiliary verb *doesn't* is used with singular subjects and with the personal pronouns *she, he,* and *it.* The auxiliary verb *don't* is used with plural subjects and with the personal pronouns *I, we, you,* and *they.*

SINGULAR: *He doesn't have time to wait any longer.*
Doesn't Emily know where to meet us?

PLURAL: *We don't think we can make it to the party.*
The campers don't have enough wood to build a fire.

12.10 COLLECTIVE NOUNS AS SUBJECTS

Collective nouns are singular nouns that name groups of persons or things. *Family,* for example, is the collective name of a group of individuals. A collective noun takes a singular verb when the group acts as a single unit. It takes a plural verb when the members of the group act separately.

EXAMPLES: *Her family is moving to another state.* (The family as a whole is moving.)
Her family are carrying furniture out to the truck. (The individual members are carrying furniture.)

12.11 RELATIVE PRONOUNS AS SUBJECTS

When the relative pronoun *who, which,* or *that* is used as a subject in an adjective clause, the verb in the clause must agree in number with the antecedent of the pronoun.

SINGULAR: *The scent that wafts through the air is jasmine.*

The antecedent of the relative pronoun *that* is the singular *scent;* therefore, *that* is singular and must take the singular verb *wafts.*

PLURAL: *The muffins, which are an old family recipe, get eaten quickly.*

The antecedent of the relative pronoun *which* is the plural *muffins.* Therefore, *which* is plural, and it takes the plural verb *are.*

Vocabulary and Spelling

COMMON CORE L 1a, L 1b, L 2b, L 4, L 4a–c, L 5, L 6

The key to becoming an independent reader is to develop a toolkit of vocabulary strategies. By learning and practicing the strategies, you'll know what to do when you encounter unfamiliar words while reading. You'll also know how to refine the words you use for different situations—personal, school, and work.

Being a good speller is important when communicating your ideas in writing. Learning basic spelling rules and checking your spelling in a dictionary will help you spell words that you may not use frequently.

1 Using Context Clues

The context of a word is made up of the punctuation marks, words, sentences, and paragraphs that surround the word. A word's context can give you important clues about its meaning.

1.1 GENERAL CONTEXT

Sometimes you need to infer the meaning of an unfamiliar word by reading all the information in a passage.

Since he has received perfect scores on all of the tests, I'd say his forte is definitely history.

You can tell from the context that *forte* means "strength."

1.2 SPECIFIC CONTEXT CLUES

Sometimes writers help you understand the meanings of words by providing specific clues such as those shown in the chart.

Specific Context Clues		
Type of Clue	**Key Words/ Phrases**	**Example**
Definition or restatement of the meaning of the word	or, which is, that is, in other words, also known as, also called	During the last week of the *dog days*—**that hot period of summer from July to early September**—our town was hit by a hurricane.
Example following an unfamiliar word	such as, like, as if, for example, especially, including	The hurricane wreaked *havoc*, including **downed power lines, toppled trees, and flooded roads.**
Comparison with a more familiar word or concept	as, like, also, similar to, in the same way, likewise	The detective we hired was as *tenacious* **as a bulldog.**
Contrast with a familiar word or experience	unlike, but, however, although, on the other hand, on the contrary	The reporter was usually **focused,** but today he was *preoccupied.*
Synonym	An unfamiliar word is followed by a familiar word with a similar meaning	A reporter *impassively* relayed what happened in an equally **unemotional** account.

1.3 IDIOMS, SLANG, AND FIGURATIVE LANGUAGE

Use context clues to figure out the meanings of idioms, figurative language, and slang.

An **idiom** is an expression whose overall meaning is different from the meaning of the individual words.

> *With only seconds left before the bell, Alison made it to class by the skin of her teeth.* (*By the skin of her teeth* means "just in time.")

Figurative language is language that communicates meaning beyond the literal meaning of the words.

> *His heart was on the verge of love.* (*Verge* means "the point beyond which something is likely to occur.")

Slang is informal language composed of made-up words and ordinary words that are used to mean something different from their meanings in formal English.

> *We both thought the movie was really cool because of all the special effects.* (*Cool* means "excellent.")

2 Analyzing Word Structure

Many words can be broken into smaller parts, such as base words, roots, prefixes, and suffixes.

2.1 BASE WORDS

A **base word** is a word part that by itself is also a word. Other words or word parts can be added to base words to form new words.

2.2 ROOTS

A **root** is a word part that contains the core meaning of the word. Many English words contain roots that come from older languages such as Greek, Latin, Old English (Anglo-Saxon), and Norse. Knowing the meaning of a word's root can help you determine the word's meaning.

Root	Meaning	Example
log (Greek)	word; study	epilogue, ecology
card (Greek)	heart	cardiogram
stat (Greek)	standing	static
meter (Greek)	measure	thermometer
hydra / hydro (Greek)	water	hydraulics
cosm / cosmo (Greek)	world	cosmic
ped (Latin)	foot	pedestrian
pel / pul (Latin)	drive; thrust	repel, repulse
equ / equi (Latin)	equal	equitable

2.3 PREFIXES

A **prefix** is a word part attached to the beginning of a word. Most prefixes come from Greek, Latin, or Old English.

Prefix	Meaning	Example
di- / dia- (Greek)	through	disect
micro- (Greek)	small	microphone
a- (Anglo-Saxon)	in, on; away	asleep
quad- (Latin)	four	quadrangle
pro- (Latin)	forward	progress

2.4 SUFFIXES

A **suffix** is a word part that appears at the end of a root or base word to form a new word. Some suffixes do not change word meaning. These suffixes are

- added to nouns to change the number of persons or objects

- added to verbs to change the tense
- added to modifiers to change the degree of comparison

Suffix	Meaning	Example
-s, -es	to change the number of a noun	trunk + s = trunks
-d, -ed, -ing	to change verb tense	sprinkle + d = sprinkled
-er, -est	to change the degree of comparison in modifiers	cold + er = colder icy + est = iciest

Other suffixes can be added to a root or base to change the word's meaning. These suffixes can also determine a word's part of speech.

Suffix	Meaning	Example
-ence	state or condition of	independence
-ous	full of	furious
-ate	to make	activate
-ly, -ily	manner	quickly

Strategies for Understanding Unfamiliar Words

- Look for any prefixes or suffixes. Remove them to isolate the base word or the root.
- See if you recognize any elements—prefix, suffix, root, or base—of the word. You may be able to guess its meaning by analyzing one or two elements.
- Use the context in the sentence and the word parts to make a logical guess about the word's meaning.
- Consult a dictionary to see whether you are correct.

Practice and Apply

Make inferences about the meanings of the following words from the fields of science and math. Consider what you have learned in this section about Greek, Latin, and Old English (Anglo-Saxon) word parts.

cardiology	hydrometer
perimeter	pathology
diameter	microcosm
diagram	hydrostatic
cosmology	electrocardiogram
quadruped	propulsion

3 Understanding Word Origins

3.1 ETYMOLOGIES

Etymologies show the origin and historical development of a word. When you study a word's history and origin, you can find out when, where, and how the word came to be. Histories of language and dictionaries are valuable tools for exploring how forms and meanings of words have changed through time:

boy•cott (boi´kŏt´) *tr.v.* **-cott•ed, -cott•ing, -cotts** To abstain from or act together in abstaining from using, buying, or dealing with as an expression of protest or disfavor or as a means of coercion. See synonyms at **blackball**. *n.* The act or an instance of boycotting. [After Charles C. *Boycott* (1832–1897), English land agent in Ireland.]— boy´-cott´er *n.*

quo•rum (kwôr´əm, kwōr´-) *n.*, **1.** The minimal number of officers and members of a committee or organization, usually a majority, who must be present for valid transaction of business. **2.** A select group. [Middle English, quorum of justices of the peace, from Latin *quo̅rum*, of whom (from the wording of a commission naming certain persons as members of a body), genitive pl. of *qui̅*, who.]

COMMON CORE **L 4c**

PRACTICE AND APPLY

Note that students will need to look up some word parts in a dictionary to complete this activity. Remind students to write legibly as they compose their responses to the Practice and Apply activities.

Answers:

cardiology: the study of the heart; from the Greek card, "heart," and log, "study"

perimeter: the distance around something; from the Greek per, "around" and meter, "measure"

diameter: the measurement through the middle of something; from the Greek dia, "through," and meter, "measure"

diagram: an explanatory illustration; from the Greek dia, "through" and gram/graph, "write"

cosmology: the study of the universe; from the Greek cosmo, "world, universe," and log, "study"

quadruped: four-footed; from the Latin quad, "four," and ped, "foot"

Hydrometer: a device for analyzing liquids; from the Greek hydro, "water," and meter, "measure"

pathology: the study of disease; from the Greek pathos, "suffering, disease," and log, "study"

microcosm: a tiny ecosystem; from the Greek micro, "small," and cosmo, "world"

hydrostatic: having to do with water levels; from the Greek hydro, "water," and stat, "standing"

electrocardiogram: a printout showing electrical impulses from the heart; from the Greek elektron, "shining," card, "heart," and gram, "write"

propulsion: a means of pushing something forward; from the Latin pro, "forward," and pel/pul, "thrust"

COMMON CORE L 4c

PRACTICE AND APPLY

Answers:

appropriate: from Latin; ad ("to") + proprius ("one's own"); to make something one's own

carpetbagger: refers to unwelcome Northerners who carried light luggage called carpetbags when going to the South after the Civil War

caucus: from Greek kaukos ("drinking cup"); this term for a political gathering is named after the 18th-century Caucus Club, where members would socialize and talk politics

communism: from an Old French word meaning "to make common"; an economic system in which the whole community, rather than an individual, owns property

constitution: from Latin com ("together") + statuere ("to set"); the Constitution reflects what the Founders together set forth as our basis of government.

filibuster: from a Spanish word meaning "one who engages in unauthorized warfare;" in politics, a filibuster is a long speech intended to block a vote.

immigrate: from Latin in ("into") + migrare ("to move to a new location"); to move to a new country

impeach: from Latin in ("in") + pedica ("fetter"); to hinder an official by challenging or accusing of wrongdoing

pacifism: from Latin pacificare, "to make peaceful"; opposition to any military force

ratify: from Latin ratus ("to reckon") + facere ("to make"); to make a law official

referendum: from Latin referre, "to bear back"; taking a law back to the people for a vote

secession: from Latin secessio, "apart"; a state's act of placing itself apart from the country to which it previously belonged

tariff: from Arabic ta' rīf, "explanation"; a tariff is a list of taxes or fees, or the tax or fee itself.

veto: from Latin vetare, "to forbid"; a veto prevents a bill passed by Congress from becoming a law.

Practice and Apply

Trace the etymology of the words below, often used in the fields of history and political science.

appropriate	filibuster	referendum
carpetbagger	immigrate	secession
caucus	impeach	tariff
communism	pacifism	veto
constitution	ratify	

3.2 WORD FAMILIES

Words that have the same root make up a word family and have related meanings. The chart shows a common Greek and a common Latin root. Notice how the meanings of the example words are related to the meanings of their roots.

Latin Root	*gen:* "race, kind"
English Words	**generalize** to reduce to a general form, class, law
	generation a stage in the life cycle
	regenerate to form or create anew
	engender to bring into existence
	generic relating to a group or class

Greek Root	*log:* "speech, word, reason"
English Words	**apology** an expression of regret
	epilogue a short poem or speech
	monologue a long speech made by one person
	syllogism reasoning from the general to the specific
	logic a system of reasoning

3.3 WORDS FROM CLASSICAL MYTHOLOGY

The English language includes many words from classical mythology. You can use your knowledge of these myths to understand the origins and meanings of these words. For example, *herculean task* refers to the strongman Hercules. Thus, you can guess that **herculean task** means "a job that is large or difficult." The chart shows a few common words from mythology.

Greek	Roman	Norse
panic	cereal	Wednesday
atlas	mercurial	gun
adonis	Saturday	berserk
mentor	January	valkyrie

Practice and Apply

Look up the etymology of each word in the chart and locate the myth associated with it. Use the information from the myth to explain the origin and meaning of each word.

3.4 FOREIGN WORDS

The English language includes words from diverse languages, such as French, Dutch, Spanish, Italian, and Chinese. Many words stayed the way they were in their original language. Histories of the language trace how similar words become integrated into English.

French	Dutch	Spanish	Italian
entree	maelstrom	rodeo	pasta
nouveau riche	trek	salsa	opera
potpourri	cookie	bronco	vendetta
tête-à-tête	snoop	tornado	grotto

4 Understanding the English Language

The English language has a documented history of 1,400 years, but its earliest beginnings stretch back to the speakers of Proto-Indo-European who ranged from India to Europe. Proto-Indo-European gave rise to many languages, including English, Swedish, Hindi, Greek, Russian, Polish, Italian, French, Spanish, and German—now collectively referred to as Indo-European. Here's a brief overview of the development of English:

- **Proto-English:** Besides the Romans who spoke Latin, the early inhabitants of Britain were Britons and Celts. The Angles, Saxons, and Jutes—Germanic peoples—arrived around 449 A.D. Proto English incorporated Latin words as well as those drawn from the languages of the Britons, Celts, and the Germanic peoples.

- **Old English:** From about the mid-fifth century to the twelfth century, Old English, the language of the Anglo-Saxons, was the spoken language in Britain. Latin remained the language of writing and of the church, schools, and international relations. Old English would be unintelligible to the speaker of Modern English, given the differences in its grammar, spellings, and pronunciations. The most well-known work in Old English is the epic poem *Beowulf.*

- **Middle English:** After the Norman Conquest in 1066, the nobility spoke Anglo-Norman. Middle English, derived from Anglo-Norman, thrived from the late eleventh century to the late fifteenth century. It also underwent significant changes in grammar and vocabulary. The most famous writer of this period is Geoffrey Chaucer, whose *The Canterbury Tales* remains a staple of the English literature curriculum.

- **Early Modern English:** During the fifteenth century, the so-called "Great Vowel Shift" occurred—a major change in the pronunciation of English. Conventions of spelling were also being established during this time. With the spread of a London-based dialect and the standardization that results from printing, Early Modern English is recognizable to the speaker of Modern English. For example, William Shakespeare, the great English dramatist, wrote during the late phase of Early Modern English, The first edition of the *King James Bible* also was published during this time. Early Modern English lasted until about the seventeenth century.

- **Modern English:** Modern English emerged in the late seventeenth century and continues to the present day. Its development was spurred by Samuel Johnson's *Dictionary of the English Language,* published in 1755, which standardized spelling and usage. The significant characteristic of contemporary Modern English is its extensive vocabulary, which partly arises from technological and scientific developments, as well as from the worldwide variety of its speakers. As various communication devices are increasingly adopted, technology-specific language and vocabulary—such as that used in texting—further influence English. Thus, the development of English continues in the present day.

5 Synonyms and Antonyms

5.1 SYNONYMS

A **synonym** is a word with a meaning similar to that of another word. You can find synonyms in a thesaurus or a dictionary. In a dictionary, synonyms are often given as part of the definition of a word. The following word pairs are synonyms:

dry/arid   enthralled/fascinated
gaunt/thin

COMMON CORE **L 4c**

PRACTICE AND APPLY

Answers:

panic: Greek; in Greek mythology, Pan was the god of wild animals and nature. When people panic, they run wild with irrational fear.

atlas: Greek; in Greek mythology, Atlas is a Titan who is forced to hold up the world. An atlas, a book of maps, can be said to hold the world.

adonis: Greek; in Greek mythology, the goddess Aphrodite falls in love with a handsome young man named Adonis. An adonis is a handsome young man.

mentor: Greek; in the Odyssey, Mentor was Odysseus' wise and loyal advisor. A mentor acts as a teacher or experienced advisor.

cereal: Latin; in Roman mythology, Ceres was the goddess of agriculture. A cereal is a grain or a ready-to-eat food made from grain.

mercurial: Latin; in Roman mythology, Mercury was the swift-footed messenger god. Someone described as mercurial quickly and frequently changes moods and ideas.

Saturday: Latin; in Roman mythology, Saturn was an important god. The last day of the week was designated as Saturn's day.

January: Latin; in Roman mythology, Janus was the god of portals, beginnings, and endings. As the first month of the year, January would have been guarded by Janus.

Wednesday: Norse; the chief Norse god was Odin, or Woden. The weekday Wednesday is Woden's day.

gun: Norse; a powerful medieval military weapon was given the name of a Scandinavian woman, Gunnhildr. A shortened version of the name now applies to a particular class of powerful weapons, guns.

berserk: Norse; ferocious early Norse warriors were called berserkers. Someone who behaves in a frenzied, furious way is said to have gone berserk.

valkyrie: Norse; in Norse mythology, the Valkyries took the souls of heroes who died in battle to Valhalla the great hall of the chief god, Odin.

5.2 ANTONYMS

An **antonym** is a word with a meaning opposite that of another word. The following word pairs are antonyms:

friend/enemy   absurd/logical

courteous/rude   languid/energetic

6   Denotation and Connotation

6.1 DENOTATION

A word's dictionary meaning is called its **denotation.** For example, the denotation of the word *rascal* is "an unethical, dishonest person."

6.2 CONNOTATION

The images or feelings you connect to a word add a finer shade of meaning, called **connotation.** The connotation of a word goes beyond the word's basic dictionary definition. Writers use connotations of words to communicate positive or negative feelings.

Positive	Neutral	Negative
save	store	hoard
fragrance	smell	stench
display	show	flaunt

Make sure you understand the denotation and connotation of a word when you read it or use it in your writing.

7   Analogies

An **analogy** is a comparison between two things that are similar in some way but are otherwise dissimilar. Analogies are sometimes used in writing when unfamiliar subjects or ideas are explained in terms of familiar ones. Analogies often appear on tests as well, usually in a format like this:

TERRIER : DOG ::   A) rat : fish

                       B) kitten : cat

                       C) trout : fish

                       D) fish : trout

                       E) poodle : collie

Follow these steps to determine the correct answer:

- Read the part in capital letters as "**terrier** is to **dog** as . . ."
- Read the answer choices as "**rat** is to **fish**," "**kitten** is to **cat**," and so on.
- Ask yourself how the words **terrier** and **dog** are related. (A terrier is a type of dog.)
- Ask yourself which of the choices shows the same relationship. (A kitten is a kind of cat, but not in the same way that a terrier is a kind of dog. A kitten is a baby cat. A trout, however, is a type of fish in the sense that a terrier is a type of dog. Therefore, the answer is C.)

8   Homonyms and Homophones

8.1 HOMONYMS

Homonyms are words that have the same spelling and sound but have different origins and meanings.

I don't want to bore you with a story about how I had to bore through the living room wall.

Bore can mean "cause a person to lose interest," but an identically spelled word means "to drill a hole."

My dog likes to bark while it scratches the bark on the tree in the backyard.

Bark can refer to the sound made by a dog. However, another identically spelled word means "the outer covering of a tree." Each word has a different meaning and its own dictionary entry.

Sometimes only one of the meanings of two homonyms may be familiar to you. Use context clues to help you figure out the meaning of an unfamiliar word.

8.2 HOMOPHONES

Homophones are words that sound alike but have different meanings and spellings. The following homophones are frequently misused:

it's/its   they're/their/there

to/too/two   stationary/stationery

Many misused homophones are pronouns and contractions. Whenever you are unsure whether to write **your** or **you're** and **who's** or **whose,** ask yourself if you mean **you are** or **who is/has.** If you do, write the contraction. For other homophones, such as **scent** and **sent,** use the meaning of the word to help you decide which one to use.

9 Words with Multiple Meanings

Some words have acquired additional meanings over time that are based on the original meaning.

> EXAMPLES: *I was in a hurry so I jammed my clothes into the suitcase.*
> *Unfortunately, I jammed my finger in the process.*

These two uses of **jam** have different meanings, but both of them have the same origin. You will find all the meanings of **jam** listed in one entry in the dictionary.

10 Specialized Vocabulary

Specialized vocabulary includes technical vocabulary, domain-specific language, and jargon. Each term refers to the use of language specific to a particular field of study or work. Of these three terms, *jargon* has the strongest connotation, suggesting a kind of language that is difficult to understand or unintelligible to anyone not involved in that field of study or work.

Science, mathematics, history, and literature all have domain-specific vocabularies. For example, science includes words such as *photosynthesis* and *biome* which indicate specific scientific processes or concepts. In literature, words such as *foreshadowing, motif,* and *irony* enable you and others to use a common vocabulary to discuss and interpret literary works.

To figure out specialized terms, you can use context clues and reference sources, such as dictionaries on specific subjects, atlases, or manuals. Many of the resources you use in school include reference aids for that particular subject area. For example, this textbook includes a "Glossary of Literary and Informational Terms," as well as a "Glossary of Academic Vocabulary."

11 Preferred and Contested Usage

English is a constantly evolving language, and standard usage is affected by time and place. For example, Americans often use different words and phrases than the British. Within the United States itself, people speak and write differently than they did 200 years ago. English usage even varies depending on whether the setting is formal or informal. Some nonstandard usages are contested but may become accepted and standard over time. Consult references like *The American Heritage Dictionary of the English Language, Fifth Edition* and its website to determine whether a certain usage is acceptable. See the chart for examples of common usage problems and preferred and contested usages.

The English language continues to change, and technology plays a part in that. The increasing use of texting as a means of communications has created a contested language all its own. Terms like *great, in my opinion,* and *laughing out loud* have become a commonly used part of the vocabulary.

ain't	*Ain't* is nonstandard. Avoid *ain't* in formal speaking and in all writing other than dialogue.
all right	*All right* means "satisfactory," "unhurt," "safe," "correct," or, as a reply to a question or a preface to a remark, "yes." Although some dictionaries include *alright* as an optional spelling, it is contested and has not become standard usage.
can, may	*Can* expresses ability; *may* expresses possibility.
hopefully	Used as an adverb, as in the following sentence, the term is uncontested. EXAMPLE: We waited hopefully for the announcement of the election results last night. Some contest the use of *hopefully* as a disjunct, that is, as an adverb that expresses the speaker's comments on the content of a statement. EXAMPLE: Hopefully the candidate I like wins. Merriam–Webster's online dictionary says the second use is "entirely standard."
like, as if, as though	In formal situations, avoid using *like* for the conjunction *as if* or *as though* to introduce a subordinate clause. INFORMAL: I feel like I have the flu. FORMAL: I feel as if I have the flu.
literally, figuratively	*Literally* means "in a strict sense." It is sometimes used in non-literal situations for emphasis, when *figuratively* is the more appropriate term. This type of use is contested. UNCONTESTED: I literally baked five-dozen cupcakes. CONTESTED: He literally went nuts. Usage experts for *The American Heritage Dictionary* suggest that the term is acceptable when used as an intensive adverb.
off, off of	Do not use *off* or *off of* for *from*. NONSTANDARD: I got some good advice off that mechanic. STANDARD: I got some good advice from that mechanic.
some, somewhat	In formal situations, avoid using *some* to mean "to some extent." Use *somewhat*. INFORMAL: Tensions between the nations began to ease some. FORMAL: Tensions between the nations began to ease somewhat.
who, whom	*Who* is used as a subject or a predicate nominative. *Whom* is used as a direct object, an indirect object or an object of a preposition. However, in spoken English, most people use *who* instead of *whom* in all cases.

12 Using Reference Sources

12.1 DICTIONARIES

A **general dictionary** will tell you not only a word's definitions but also its pronunciation, its parts of speech, and its history and origin. A **specialized dictionary** focuses on terms related to a particular field of study or work. Use a dictionary to check the spelling of any word you are unsure of in your English class and other subjects as well.

12.2 THESAURI

A **thesaurus** (plural, thesauri) is a dictionary of synonyms. A thesaurus can be helpful when you find yourself using the same modifiers over and over again.

12.3 SYNONYM FINDERS

A **synonym finder** is often included in word-processing software. It enables you to highlight a word and be shown a display of its synonyms.

12.4 GLOSSARIES

A **glossary** is a list of specialized terms and their definitions. It is often found in the back of textbooks and sometimes includes pronunciations. In fact, this textbook has three glossaries: the **Glossary of Literary and Informational Terms, the Glossary of Academic Vocabulary,** and the **Glossary of Vocabulary.** Use these glossaries to help you understand how terms are used in this textbook.

13 Spelling Rules

Consult and employ the following English spelling rules as you write, achieving increasing accuracy.

13.1 WORDS ENDING IN A SILENT *E*

Before adding a suffix beginning with a vowel or *y* to a word ending in a silent *e,* drop the *e* (with some exceptions).

> amaze + -ing = amazing
>
> love + -able = lovable
>
> create + -ed = created
>
> nerve + -ous = nervous

Exceptions: *change + -able = changeable; courage + -ous = courageous.*

When adding a suffix beginning with a consonant to a word ending in a silent *e,* keep the *e* (with some exceptions).

> late + -ly = lately
>
> spite + -ful = spiteful
>
> noise + -less = noiseless
>
> state + -ment = statement

Exceptions: *truly, argument, ninth, wholly, awful,* and others.

When a suffix beginning with *a* or *o* is added to a word with a final silent *e,* the final *e* is usually retained if it is preceded by a soft *c* or a soft *g.*

> bridge + -able = bridgeable
>
> peace + -able = peaceable
>
> outrage + -ous = outrageous
>
> advantage + -ous = advantageous

When a suffix beginning with a vowel is added to words ending in *ee* or *oe,* the final silent *e* is retained.

> agree + -ing = agreeing
>
> free + -ing = freeing
>
> hoe + -ing = hoeing
>
> see + -ing = seeing

13.2 WORDS ENDING IN Y

Before adding most suffixes to a word that ends in **y** preceded by a consonant, change the **y** to **i.**

> **easy + -est = easiest**
>
> **crazy + -est = craziest**
>
> **silly + -ness = silliness**
>
> **marry + -age = marriage**

Exceptions: *dryness, shyness,* and *slyness.*

However, when you add **-ing,** the **y** does not change.

> **empty + -ed = emptied**   but
>
> **empty + -ing = emptying**

When adding a suffix to a word that ends in **y** preceded by a vowel, the **y** usually does not change.

> **play + -er = player**
>
> **employ + -ed = employed**
>
> **coy + -ness = coyness**
>
> **pay + -able = payable**

13.3 WORDS ENDING IN A CONSONANT

In one-syllable words that end in one consonant preceded by one short vowel, double the final consonant before adding a suffix beginning with a vowel, such as **-ed** or **-ing.**

> **dip + -ed = dipped**   **set + -ing = setting**
>
> **slim + -est = slimmest**   **fit + -er = fitter**

The rule does not apply to words of one syllable that end in a consonant preceded by two vowels.

> **feel + -ing = feeling**   **peel + -ed = peeled**
>
> **reap + -ed = reaped**   **loot + -ed = looted**

In words of more than one syllable, double the final consonant when (1) the word ends with one consonant preceded by one vowel and (2) the word is accented on the last syllable.

> **be•gin´   per•mit´   re•fer´**

In the following examples, note that in the new words formed with suffixes, the accent remains on the same syllable:

> **be•gin´ + -ing = be•gin´ning = beginning**
>
> **per•mit´ + -ed = per•mit´ted = permitted**

Exceptions: In some words with more than one syllable, though the accent remains on the same syllable when a suffix is added, the final consonant is nevertheless not doubled, as in the following examples:

> **tra´vel + -er = tra´vel•er = traveler**
>
> **mar´ket + -er = mar´ket•er = marketer**

In the following examples, the accent does not remain on the same syllable; thus, the final consonant is not doubled:

> **re•fer´ + -ence = ref´er•ence = reference**
>
> **con•fer´ + -ence = con´fer•ence = conference**

13.4 PREFIXES AND SUFFIXES

When adding a prefix to a word, do not change the spelling of the base word. When a prefix creates a double letter, keep both letters.

> **dis- + approve = disapprove**
>
> **re- + build = rebuild**
>
> **ir- + regular = irregular**
>
> **mis- + spell = misspell**
>
> **anti- + trust = antitrust**
>
> **il- + logical = illogical**

When adding **-ly** to a word ending in **l,** keep both **l's,** and when adding **-ness** to a word ending in **n,** keep both **n's.**

> **careful + -ly = carefully**
>
> **sudden + -ness = suddenness**
>
> **final + -ly = finally**
>
> **thin + -ness = thinness**

13.5 FORMING PLURAL NOUNS

To form the plural of most nouns, just add **-s.**

> **prizes   dreams   circles   stations**

For most singular nouns ending in **o,** add **-s.**

> **solos   halos   studios   photos   pianos**

For a few nouns ending in **o,** add **-es.**

> **heroes   tomatoes   potatoes   echoes**

When the singular noun ends in **s, sh, ch, x,** or **z,** add **-es.**

> **waitresses   brushes   ditches**
>
> **axes   buzzes**

When a singular noun ends in **y** with a consonant before it, change the **y** to **i** and add **-es.**

army—armies	**candy—candies**
baby—babies	**diary—diaries**
ferry—ferries	**conspiracy—conspiracies**

When a vowel (**a, e, i, o, u**) comes before the **y**, just add **-s.**

boy—boys	**way—ways**
array—arrays	**alloy—alloys**
weekday—weekdays	**jockey—jockeys**

For most nouns ending in **f** or **fe,** change the **f** to **v** and add **-es** or **-s.**

life—lives	**calf—calves**
knife—knives	**thief—thieves**
shelf—shelves	**loaf—loaves**

For some nouns ending in **f,** add **-s** to make the plural.

roofs   chiefs   reefs   beliefs

Some nouns have the same form for both singular and plural.

deer   sheep   moose   salmon   trout

For some nouns, the plural is formed in a special way.

man—men	**goose—geese**
ox—oxen	**woman—women**
mouse—mice	**child—children**

For a compound noun written as one word, form the plural by changing the last word in the compound to its plural form.

stepchild—stepchildren   firefly—fireflies

If a compound noun is written as a hyphenated word or as two separate words, change the most important word to the plural form.

brother-in-law—brothers-in-law

life jacket—life jackets

13.6 FORMING POSSESSIVES

If a noun is singular, add **'s.**

mother—my mother's car

Ross—Ross's desk

Exception: The **s** after the apostrophe is dropped after *Jesus', Moses',* and certain names in classical mythology

(*Hermes'*). These possessive forms can be pronounced easily.

If a noun is plural and ends with **s,** just add an apostrophe.

parents—my parents' car

the Santinis—the Santinis' house

If a noun is plural but does not end in **s,** add **'s.**

people—the people's choice

women—the women's coats

13.7 SPECIAL SPELLING PROBLEMS

Only one English word ends in **-sede: supersede.** Three words end in **-ceed: exceed, proceed,** and **succeed.** All other verbs ending in the sound "seed" are spelled with **-cede.**

concede   precede   recede   secede

In words with **ie** or **ei,** when the sound is long **e** (as in **she**), the word is spelled **ie** except after **c** (with some exceptions).

i before *e*	thief	relieve	field
	piece	grieve	pier
except after c	conceit	perceive	ceiling
	receive	receipt	

Exceptions: *either, neither, weird, leisure, seize.*

14 Commonly Confused Words

Words	Definition	Example
accept/except	The verb *accept* means "to receive or believe"; *except* is usually a preposition meaning "excluding."	**Except** for some of the more extraordinary events, I can **accept** that the *Odyssey* recounts a real journey.
advice/advise	*Advise* is a verb; *advice* is a noun naming that which an *adviser* gives.	I **advise** you to take that job. Whom should I ask for **advice?**
affect/effect	As a verb, *affect* means "to influence." *Effect* as a verb means "to cause." If you want a noun, you will almost always want *effect.*	Did Circe's wine **affect** Odysseus' mind? It did **effect** a change in Odysseus' men. In fact, it had an **effect** on everyone else who drank it.
all ready/ already	*All ready* is an adjective meaning "fully ready." *Already* is an adverb meaning "before or by this time."	He was **all ready** to go at noon. I have **already** seen that movie.
allusion/ illusion	An *allusion* is an indirect reference to something. An *illusion* is a false picture or idea.	There are many **allusions** to the works of Homer in English literature. The world's apparent flatness is an **illusion.**
among/ between	*Between* is used when you are speaking of only two things. *Among* is used for three or more.	**Between** *Hamlet* and *King Lear,* I prefer the latter. Emily Dickinson is **among** my favorite poets.
bring/take	*Bring* is used to denote motion toward a speaker or place. *Take* is used to denote motion away from such a person or place.	**Bring** the books over here, and I will **take** them to the library.
fewer/less	*Fewer* refers to the number of separate, countable units. *Less* refers to bulk quantity.	We have **less** literature and **fewer** selections in this year's curriculum.
leave/let	*Leave* means "to allow something to remain behind." *Let* means "to permit."	The librarian will **leave** some books on display but will not **let** us borrow any.
lie/lay	*Lie* means "to rest or recline." It does not take an object. *Lay* always takes an object.	Rover loves to **lie** in the sun. We always **lay** some bones next to him.
loose/lose	*Loose* (lo͞os) means "free, not restrained"; *lose* (lo͞oz) means "to misplace or fail to find."	Who turned the horses **loose?** I hope we won't **lose** any of them.
precede/ proceed	*Precede* means "to go or come before." Use *proceed* for other meanings.	Emily Dickinson's poetry **precedes** that of Alice Walker. You may **proceed** to the next section of the test.

continued

Words	Definition	Example
than/then	Use *than* in making comparisons; use *then* on all other occasions.	Who can say whether Amy Lowell is a better poet **than** Denise Levertov? I will read Lowell first, and **then** I will read Levertov.
their/there/they're	*Their* means "belonging to them." *There* means "in that place." *They're* is the contraction for "they are."	**There** is a movie playing at 9 P.M. **They're** going to see it with me. Sakara and Jessica drove away in **their** car after the movie.
two/too/to	*Two* is the number. *Too* is an adverb meaning "also" or "very." Use *to* before a verb or as a preposition.	Meg had **to** go **to** town, **too.** We had **too** much reading **to** do. **Two** chapters is **too** many.

Glossary of Literary and Informational Terms

Act An act is a major unit of action in a play, similar to a chapter in a book. Depending on their lengths, plays can have as many as five acts.

See also Drama; Scene.

Allegory An allegory is a work with two levels of meaning, a literal one and a symbolic one. In such a work, most of the characters, objects, settings, and events represent abstract qualities. Personification is often used in traditional allegories. As in a fable or parable, the purpose of an allegory may be to convey truths about life, to teach religious or moral lessons, or to criticize social institutions.

Alliteration Alliteration is the repetition of consonant sounds at the beginnings of words. Poets use alliteration to impart a musical quality to their poems, to create mood, to reinforce meaning, to emphasize particular words, and to unify lines or stanzas.

Allusion An allusion is an indirect reference to a person, place, event, or literary work with which the author believes the reader will be familiar.

Almanac *See* Reference Works.

Ambiguity Ambiguity is a technique in which a word, phrase, or event has more than one meaning or can be interpreted in more than one way. Some writers deliberately create this effect to give richness and depth of meaning.

Analogy An analogy is a point-by-point comparison between two things for the purpose of clarifying the less familiar of the two subjects.

Anapest *See* Meter.

Anecdote An anecdote is a brief story that focuses on a single episode or event in a person's life and that is used to illustrate a particular point.

Anglo-Saxon Poetry Anglo-Saxon poetry, which was written between the 7th and 12th centuries, is characterized by a strong rhythm, or cadence, that makes it easily chanted or sung. It was originally recited by **scops,** poet-singers who traveled from place to place. Lines of Anglo-Saxon poetry are unified through alliteration and through use of the same number of accented syllables in each line. Typically, a line is divided by a **caesura,** or pause, into two parts, with each part having two accented syllables. Usually, one or both of the accented syllables in the first part share a similar sound with an accented syllable in the second part.

Another characteristic of Anglo-Saxon poetry is the use of **kennings,** metaphorical compound words or phrases substituted for simple nouns. Kennings from *Beowulf* include "shepherd of evil" for Grendel, and "folk-king" for Beowulf.

Antagonist An antagonist is usually the principal character in opposition to the **protagonist,** or hero of a narrative or drama. The antagonist can also be a force of nature.

See also Character; Protagonist.

Antithesis Antithesis is a figure of speech in which sharply contrasting words, phrases, clauses, or sentences are juxtaposed to emphasize a point. In a true antithesis, both the ideas and the grammatical structures are balanced.

Aphorism An aphorism is a brief statement that expresses a general observation about life in a witty, pointed way incorporating **subtlety,** or careful distinctions. Unlike proverbs, which may stem from oral folk tradition, aphorisms originate with specific authors.

Appeals by Association Appeals by association imply that one will gain acceptance or prestige by taking the writer's position.

Appeal to Authority An appeal to authority calls upon experts or others who warrant respect.

Appeal to Reason See Logical Appeal.

Apostrophe Apostrophe is a figure of speech in which an object, an abstract quality, or an absent or imaginary person is addressed directly, as if present and able to understand.

Writers use apostrophe to express powerful emotions.

Archetype An archetype is a pattern in literature that is found in a variety of works from different cultures throughout the ages. An archetype can be a plot, a character, an image, or a setting. For example, the association of death and rebirth with winter and spring is an archetype common to many cultures.

Argument An argument is speech or writing that expresses a position on an issue or problem and supports it with reasons and evidence. An argument often takes into account other points of view, anticipating and answering objections that opponents of the position might raise.

See also Claim; Counterargument; Evidence; General Principle.

Aside In drama, an aside is a short speech directed to the audience, or another character, that is not heard by the other characters on stage.

See also Soliloquy.

Assonance Assonance is the repetition of a vowel sound in two or more stressed syllables that do not end with the same consonant. Poets use assonance to emphasize certain words, to impart a musical quality, to create a mood, or to unify a passage. An example of assonance is the repetition of the long e sound in the following sentence. Note that the repeated sounds are not always spelled the same.

> What I fear is that I will seem invisible,
> and all my tears will go unnoticed.

See also Alliteration; Consonance; Rhyme.

Assumption An assumption is an opinion or belief that is taken for granted. It can be about a specific situation, a person, or the world in general. Assumptions are often unstated.

See also General Principle.

Atmosphere *See* Mood.

Audience Audience is the person or persons who are intended to read or hear a piece of writing. The intended audience of a work determines its form, style, tone, and the details included.

Author's Message An author's message is the main idea or theme of a particular work.

See also Main Idea; Theme.

Author's Perspective An author's perspective is a unique combination of ideas, values, feelings, and beliefs that influences the way the writer looks at a topic. **Tone**, or attitude, often reveals an author's perspective.

See also Author's Purpose; Tone.

Author's Position An author's position is his or her opinion on an issue or topic.

See also Claim.

Author's Purpose A writer usually writes for one or more of these purposes: to inform, to entertain, to express himself or herself, or to persuade readers to believe or do something. For example, the purpose of a news report is to inform; the purpose of an editorial is to persuade the readers or audience to do or believe something.

Autobiographical Essay *See* Essay.

Autobiography An autobiography is a writer's account of his or her own life. Autobiographies often convey profound insights as writers recount past events from the perspective of greater understanding and distance. A formal autobiography involves a sustained, lengthy narrative of a person's history, but other autobiographical narratives may be less formal and briefer. Under the general category of autobiography fall such writings as diaries, journals, memoirs, and letters. Both formal and informal autobiographies provide revealing insights into the writer's character, attitudes, and motivations, as well as some understanding of the society in which the writer lived.

See also Diary; Memoir.

Ballad A ballad is a narrative poem that was originally intended to be sung. Traditional folk ballads, written by unknown authors and handed down orally, usually depict ordinary people in the midst of tragic events and adventures of love and bravery. They tend to begin abruptly, focus on a single incident, use dialogue and repetition, and suggest more than they actually state. They often contain supernatural elements.

Typically, a ballad consists of four-line stanzas, or quatrains, with the second and fourth lines of each stanza rhyming. Each stanza has a strong rhythmic pattern, usually with four stressed syllables in the first and third lines and three stressed syllables in the second and fourth lines. The rhyme scheme is usually *abcb* or *aabb.*

A **literary ballad** is a ballad with a single author. Modeled on the early English and Scottish folk ballads, literary ballads became popular during the romantic period.

See also Narrative Poem; Rhyme; Rhythm.

Bias Bias is an inclination toward a particular judgment on a topic or issue. A writer often reveals a strongly positive or strongly negative opinion by presenting only one way of looking at an issue or by heavily weighting the evidence. Words with intensely positive or negative connotations are often a signal of a writer's bias.

Bibliography A bibliography is a list of books and other materials related to the topic of a text. Bibliographies can be good sources of works for further study on a subject.

See also Works Consulted.

Biography A biography is a type of nonfiction in which a writer gives a factual account of someone else's life. Written in the third person, a biography may cover a person's entire life or focus on only an important part of it. Modern biography includes a popular form called **fictionalized biography,** in which writers use their imaginations to re-create past conversations and to elaborate on some incidents.

Blank Verse Blank verse is unrhymed poetry written in **iambic pentameter.** Because iambic pentameter resembles the natural rhythm of spoken English, it has been considered the most suitable meter for dramatic verse in English. Shakespeare's plays are written largely in blank verse. Blank verse has also been used frequently for long poems.

See also Iambic Pentameter; Meter; Rhythm.

Business Correspondence Business correspondence includes all written business communications, such as business letters, e-mails, and memos. Business correspondence is to the point, clear, courteous, and professional.

Caesura A caesura is a pause or a break in a line of poetry. Poets use a caesura to emphasize the word or phrase that precedes it or to vary the rhythmical effects.

See also Anglo-Saxon Poetry.

Cast of Characters The cast of characters is a list of all the characters in a play, usually in the order of appearance. This list is found at the beginning of a script.

Cause and Effect A **cause** is an event or action that directly results in another event or action. An **effect** is the direct or logical outcome of an event or action. Basic **cause-and- effect relationships** include a single cause with a single effect, one cause with multiple effects, multiple causes with a single effect, and a chain of causes and effects. The concept of cause and effect also provides a way of organizing a piece of writing. It helps a writer show the relationships between events or ideas.

Character Characters are the people, and sometimes animals or other beings, who take part in the action of a story or novel. Events center on the lives of one or more characters, referred to as **main characters.** The other characters, called **minor characters,** interact with the main characters and help move the story along.

Characters may also be classified as either static or dynamic. **Static characters** tend not to change much over the course of the story. They do not experience life-altering moments and seem to act the same, even though their situations may change. In contrast, **dynamic characters** evolve as individuals, learning from their experiences and growing emotionally.

See also Antagonist; Characterization; Foil; Motivation; Protagonist.

Characterization Characterization refers to the techniques that writers use to develop characters. There are four basic methods of characterization:

- A writer may use physical description.
- A character's nature may be revealed through his or her own speech, thoughts, feelings, or actions.

- The speech, thoughts, feelings, and actions of other characters can be used to develop a character.
- The narrator can make direct comments about the character's nature.

See also Character; Narrator.

Chorus In the theater of ancient Greece, the chorus was a group of actors who commented on the action of the play. Between scenes, the chorus sang and danced to musical accompaniment, giving insights into the message of the play. The chorus is often considered a kind of ideal spectator, representing the response of ordinary citizens to the tragic events that unfold. Certain dramatists have continued to employ this classical convention as a way of representing the views of the society being depicted.

See also Drama.

Chronological Order Chronological order is the arrangement of events in their order of occurrence. This type of organization is used both in fictional narratives and in historical writing, biography, and autobiography.

Claim In an argument, a claim is the writer's position on an issue or problem. Although an argument focuses on supporting one claim, a writer may make more than one claim in a work.

Clarify Clarifying is a reading strategy that helps a reader to understand or make clear what he or she is reading. Readers usually clarify by rereading, reading aloud, or discussing.

Classification Classification is a pattern of organization in which objects, ideas, or information is presented in groups, or classes, based on common characteristics.

Cliché A cliché is an overused expression. "Better late than never" and "hard as nails" are common examples. Good writers generally avoid clichés unless they are using them in dialogue to indicate something about characters' personalities.

Climax In a plot structure, the climax, or turning point, is the moment when the reader's interest and emotional intensity reach a peak. The climax usually occurs toward the end of

a story and often results in a change in the characters or a solution to the conflict.

See also Plot; Resolution.

Comedy A comedy is a dramatic work that is light and often humorous in tone, usually ending happily with a peaceful resolution of the main conflict. A comedy differs from a **farce** by having a more believable plot, more realistic characters, and less boisterous behavior.

See also Drama; Farce.

Comic Relief Comic relief consists of humorous scenes, incidents, or speeches that are included in a serious drama to provide a reduction in emotional intensity. Because it breaks the tension, comic relief allows an audience to prepare emotionally for events to come.

Compare and Contrast To compare and contrast is to identify similarities and differences in two or more subjects. Compare-and-contrast organization can be used to structure a piece of writing, serving as a framework for examining the similarities and differences in two or more subjects.

Complication A complication is an additional factor or problem introduced into the rising action of a story to make the conflict more difficult. In some cases, a plot complication presents a character with a moral dilemma or quandry that seems to make it harder or nearly impossible for a character to get what he or she wants.

Conceit *See* Extended Metaphor.

Conclusion A conclusion is a statement of belief based on evidence, experience, and reasoning. A **valid conclusion** is a conclusion that logically follows from the facts or statements upon which it is based. A **deductive conclusion** is one that follows from a particular generalization or premise. An **inductive conclusion** is a broad conclusion or generalization that is reached by arguing from specific facts and examples.

Conflict A conflict is a struggle between opposing forces that is the basis of a story's plot. An **external conflict** pits a character against nature, society, or another character. An **internal**

conflict is a conflict between opposing forces within a character.

See also Antagonist; Plot.

Connect Connecting is a reader's process of relating the content of a text to his or her own knowledge and experience.

Connotation Connotation is the emotional response evoked by a word, in contrast to its **denotation**, which is its literal meaning. *Kitten,* for example, is defined as "a young cat." However, the word also suggests, or connotes, images of softness, warmth, and playfulness.

Consonance Consonance is the repetition of consonant sounds within and at the ends of words, as in the following example:

> He ate most of the fruit in the kitchen yesterday.

See also Alliteration; Assonance.

Consumer Documents Consumer documents are printed materials that accompany products and services. They are intended for the buyers or users of the products or services and usually provide information about use, care, operation, or assembly. Some common consumer documents are applications, contracts, warranties, manuals, instructions, package inserts, labels, brochures, and schedules.

Context Clues When you encounter an unfamiliar word, you can often use context clues as aids for understanding. Context clues are the words and phrases surrounding the word that provide hints about the word's meaning.

Contradiction *See* Paradox

Controlling Idea *See* Thesis Statement.

Controlling Image *See* Extended Metaphor; Imagery.

Counterargument A counterargument is an argument made to oppose another argument. A good argument anticipates opposing viewpoints and provides counterarguments to refute (disprove) or answer them.

Counterclaim *See* Counterargument.

Couplet A couplet is a rhymed pair of lines. A simple couplet may be written in any rhythmic pattern.

A **heroic couplet** consists of two rhyming lines written in iambic pentameter. The term *heroic* comes from the fact that English poems having heroic themes and elevated style have often been written in iambic pentameter.

Creation Myth *See* Myth.

Credibility *Credibility* refers to the believability or trustworthiness of a source and the information it contains.

Critical Essay *See* Essay.

Critical Review A critical review is an evaluation or critique by a reviewer or critic. Different types of reviews include film reviews, book reviews, music reviews, and artshow reviews.

Dactyl *See* Meter.

Database A database is a collection of information that can be quickly and easily accessed and searched and from which information can be easily retrieved. It is frequently presented in an electronic format.

Debate A debate is an organized exchange of opinions on an issue. In academic settings, *debate* usually refers to a formal contest in which two opposing teams defend and attack a proposition.

See also Argument.

Deductive Reasoning Deductive reasoning is a way of thinking that begins with a generalization, presents a specific situation, and then advances with facts and evidence to a logical conclusion. The following passage has a deductive argument imbedded in it: "All students in the drama class must attend the play on Thursday. Since Ava is in the class, she had better show up." This deductive argument can be broken down as follows: generalization— all students in the drama class must attend the play on Thursday; specific situation—Ava is a student in the drama class; conclusion—Ava must attend the play.

Denotation *See* Connotation.

Dénouement *See* Plot.

Description Description is writing that helps a reader to picture scenes, events, and characters. It helps the reader understand exactly what someone or something is like. To create description, writers often use sensory images—words and phrases that enable the reader to see, hear, smell, taste, or feel the subject described—and figurative language. Effective description also relies on precise nouns, verbs, adjectives, and adverbs, as well as carefully selected details.

See also Diction; Figurative Language; Imagery.

Dialect Dialect is a particular variety of language spoken in one place by a distinct group of people. A dialect reflects the colloquialisms, grammatical constructions, distinctive vocabulary, and pronunciations that are typical of a region. At times writers use dialect to establish or emphasize settings, as well as to develop characters.

Dialogue Dialogue is conversation between two or more characters in either fiction or nonfiction. In drama, the story is told almost exclusively through dialogue, which moves the plot forward and reveals characters' motives.

See also Drama.

Diary A diary is a writer's personal day-to-day account of his or her experiences and impressions. Most diaries are private and not intended to be shared. Some, however, have been published because they are well written and provide useful perspectives on historical events or on the everyday life of particular eras.

Diction A writer's or speaker's choice of words is called diction. Diction includes both vocabulary (individual words) and syntax (the order or arrangement of words). Diction can be formal or informal, technical or common, abstract or concrete. In the following complex sentence, the diction is formal.

See also Connotation; Style.

Dictionary *See* Reference Works.

Drama Drama is literature in which plot and character are developed through dialogue and action; in other words, drama is literature in play form. It is performed on stage and radio and in films and television. Most plays are divided into acts, with each act having an emotional peak, or climax, of its own. The acts sometimes are divided into scenes; each scene is limited to a single time and place. Most contemporary plays have two or three acts, although some have only one act.

See also Act; Dialogue; Scene; Stage Directions.

Dramatic Irony *See* Irony.

Dramatic Monologue A dramatic monologue is a lyric poem in which a speaker addresses a silent or absent listener in a moment of high intensity or deep emotion, as if engaged in private conversation. The speaker proceeds without interruption or argument, and the effect on the reader is that of hearing just one side of a conversation. This technique allows the poet to focus on the feelings, personality, and motivations of the speaker.

See also Lyric Poetry; Soliloquy.

Draw Conclusions To draw a conclusion is to make a judgment or arrive at a belief based on evidence, experience, and reasoning.

Dynamic Character *See* Character.

Editorial An editorial is an opinion piece that usually appears on the editorial page of a newspaper or as part of a news broadcast. The editorial section of a newspaper presents opinions rather than objective news reports.

See also Op-Ed Piece.

Either/Or Fallacy An either/or fallacy is a statement that suggests that there are only two possible ways to view a situation or only two options to choose from. In other words, it is a statement that falsely frames a dilemma, giving the impression that no options exist but the two presented — for example, "Either we stop the construction of a new airport, or the surrounding suburbs will become ghost towns."

Elegy An elegy is an extended meditative poem in which the speaker reflects upon death—often in tribute to a person who has died recently—or on an equally serious subject. Most elegies are written in formal, dignified language and are serious in tone.

Elizabethan (Shakespearean) Sonnet
See Sonnet.

Emotional Appeals Emotional appeals are messages that evoke strong feelings—such as fear, pity, or vanity—in order to persuade instead of using facts and evidence to make a point. An **appeal to fear** is a message that taps into people's fear of losing their safety or security. An **appeal to pity** is a message that taps into people's sympathy and compassion for others to build support for an idea, a cause, or a proposed action. An **appeal to vanity** is a message that attempts to persuade by tapping into people's desire to feel good about themselves.

Encyclopedia *See* Reference Works.

End Rhyme *See* Rhyme.

English (Shakespearean) Sonnet
See Sonnet.

Epic Hero An epic hero is a larger-than-life figure who often embodies the ideals of a nation or race. Epic heroes take part in dangerous adventures and accomplish great deeds. Many undertake long, difficult journeys and display great courage and superhuman strength.

Epic Poem An epic is a long narrative poem on a serious subject presented in an elevated or formal style. An epic traces the adventures of a hero whose actions consist of courageous, even superhuman, deeds, which often represent the ideals and values of a nation or race. Epics typically address universal issues, such as good and evil, life and death, and sin and redemption. *Beowulf* is an enduring epic of the Anglo-Saxon period.

Epic Simile *See* Simile.

Epitaph An epitaph is an inscription on a tomb or monument to honor the memory of a deceased person. The term *epitaph* is also used to describe any verse commemorating someone who has died. Although a few humorous epitaphs have been composed, most are serious in tone.

Epithet An epithet is a brief phrase that points out traits associated with a particular person or thing.

Essay An essay is a brief work of nonfiction that offers an opinion on a subject. The purpose of an essay may be to express ideas and feelings, to analyze, to inform, to entertain, or to persuade. In a **persuasive essay,** a writer attempts to convince readers to adopt a particular opinion or to perform a certain action. Most persuasive essays present a series of facts, reasons, or examples in support of an opinion or proposal.

Essays can be formal or informal. A **formal essay** examines a topic in a thorough, serious, and highly organized manner. An **informal essay** presents an opinion on a subject, but not in a completely serious or formal tone. Characteristics of this type of essay include humor, a personal or confidential approach, a loose and sometimes rambling style, and often a surprising or unconventional topic. Mary Wollstonecraft's *A Vindication of the Rights of Woman* is a formal essay, meant to analyze and persuade.

A **personal essay** is a type of informal essay. Personal essays allow writers to express their viewpoints on subjects by reflecting on events or incidents in their own lives.

Ethical Appeals Ethical appeals establish a writer's credibility and trustworthiness with an audience. When a writer links a claim to a widely accepted value, for example, the writer not only gains moral support for that claim but also establishes a connection with readers.

Evaluate To evaluate is to examine something carefully and judge its value or worth. Evaluating is an important skill for gaining insight into what you read. A reader can evaluate the actions of a particular character, for example, or can form an opinion about the value of an entire work.

Evidence Evidence is the specific pieces of information that support a claim. Evidence can take the form of facts, quotations, examples, statistics, or personal experiences.

Exaggeration *See* Hyperbole.

Exemplum An exemplum is a short anecdote or story that helps illustrate a particular moral point. Developed in the Middle Ages, this form was widely used by Geoffrey Chaucer in *The Canterbury Tales.*

Exposition *See* Plot.

Expository Essay *See* Essay.

Extended Metaphor Like any metaphor, an extended metaphor is a comparison between two essentially unlike things that nevertheless have something in common. It does not contain the word *like* or *as.* In an extended metaphor, two things are compared at length and in various ways—perhaps throughout a stanza, a paragraph, or even an entire work.

Like an extended metaphor, a **conceit** parallels two essentially dissimilar things on several points. A conceit, though, is a more elaborate, formal, and ingenious comparison than the ordinary extended metaphor. Sometimes a conceit forms the framework of entire poem.

See also Figurative Language; Metaphor; Simile.

External Conflict *See* Conflict.

Fact versus Opinion A **fact** is a statement that can be proved or verified. An **opinion**, on the other hand, is a statement that cannot be proved because it expresses a person's beliefs, feelings, or thoughts.

See also Inference; Generalization.

Fallacy A fallacy is an error in reasoning. Typically, a fallacy is based on an incorrect inference or a misuse of evidence. Some common logical fallacies are **circular reasoning, either/or fallacy, oversimplification, overgeneralization,** and **stereotyping.**

See also Either/Or Fallacy; Logical Appeal; Overgeneralization

Falling Action *See* Plot.

Farce A farce is a type of exaggerated comedy that features an absurd plot, ridiculous situations, and humorous dialogue. The main purpose of a farce is to keep an audience laughing. The characters are usually **stereotypes,** or simplified examples of different traits or qualities. Comic devices typically used in farces include mistaken identity, deception, wordplay—such as puns and double meanings—and exaggeration.

See also Comedy; Stereotype.

Faulty Reasoning *See* Fallacy.

Feature Article A feature article is a main article in a newspaper or a cover story in a magazine. A feature article is focused more on entertaining than on informing. Features are lighter or more general than hard news and tend to be about human interest or lifestyles.

Fiction Fiction refers to works of prose that contain imaginary elements. Although fiction, like nonfiction, may be based on actual events and real people, it differs from nonfiction in that it is shaped primarily by the writer's imagination. The two major types of fiction are novels and short stories. The four basic elements of a work of fiction are **character, setting, plot,** and **theme.**

See also Novel; Short Story.

Figurative Language Figurative language is language that communicates ideas beyond the literal meaning of words. Figurative language can make descriptions and unfamiliar or difficult ideas easier to understand. Special types of figurative language, called **figures of speech,** include **simile, metaphor, personification, hyperbole,** and **apostrophe.**

Figures of Speech *See* Figurative Language.

First-Person Point of View *See* Point of View.

Flashback A flashback is a scene that interrupts the action of a narrative to describe events that took place at an earlier time. It provides background helpful in understanding a character's present situation.

Foil A foil is a character whose traits contrast with those of another character. A writer might use a minor character as a foil to emphasize the positive traits of the main character.

See also Character.

Folk Ballad *See* Ballad.

Folk Tale A folk tale is a short, simple story that is handed down, usually by word of mouth, from generation to generation. Folk tales include legends, fairy tales, myths, and fables. Folk tales often teach family obligations or societal values.

See also Legend; Myth.

Foot *See* Meter.

Foreshadowing Foreshadowing is a writer's use of hints or clues to indicate events that will occur later in a story. Foreshadowing creates suspense and at the same time prepares the reader for what is to come.

Form At its simplest, form refers to the physical arrangement of words in a poem—the length and placement of the lines, the grouping of lines into stanzas, and any graphical element that enhances the poem's meaning. The term can also refer to other kinds of patterning in poetry—anything from rhythm and other sound patterns to the design of a traditional poetic type, such as a sonnet or dramatic monologue.

See also Genre; Stanza.

Frame Story A frame story exists when a story is told within a narrative setting or frame—hence creating a story within a story.

> **Examples:** The collection of tales in Chaucer's *The Canterbury Tales,* including "The Wife of Bath's Tale," are set within a frame story. The frame is introduced in "The Prologue," in which 30 characters on a pilgrimage to Canterbury agree to tell stories to pass the time.

Free Verse Free verse is poetry that does not have regular patterns of rhyme and meter. The lines in free verse often flow more naturally than do rhymed, metrical lines and thus achieve a rhythm more like that of everyday human speech.

See also Meter; Rhyme.

Functional Documents *See* Consumer Documents; Workplace Documents.

Generalization A generalization is a broad statement about a class or category of people, ideas, or things, based on a study of only some of its members.

See also Overgeneralization.

General Principle In an argument, a general principle is an assumption that links the support to the claim. If one does not accept the general principle as a truth, then the support is inadequate because it is beside the point.

Genre Genre refers to the distinct types into which literary works can be grouped. The four main literary genres are fiction, poetry, nonfiction, and drama.

Gothic Literature Gothic literature is characterized by grotesque characters, bizarre situations, and violent events.

Government Publications Government publications are documents produced by government organizations. Pamphlets, brochures, and reports are just some of the many forms these publications may take. Government publications can be good resources for a wide variety of topics.

Graphic Aid A graphic aid is a visual tool that is printed, handwritten, or drawn. Charts, diagrams, graphs, photographs, and maps can all be graphic aids.

Graphic Organizer A graphic organizer is a visual illustration of a verbal statement that helps a reader understand a text. Charts, tables, webs, and diagrams can all be graphic organizers. Graphic organizers and graphic aids can look the same. However, graphic organizers and graphic aids do differ in how they are used. Graphic aids are the visual representations that people encounter when they read informational texts. Graphic organizers are visuals that people construct to help them understand texts or organize information.

Graphics *See* Form.

Haiku Haiku is a form of Japanese poetry in which 17 syllables are arranged in three lines of 5, 7, and 5 syllables. The rules of haiku are strict. In addition to the syllabic count, the poet must create a clear picture that will evoke a strong emotional response in the reader. Nature is a particularly important source of inspiration for Japanese haiku poets, and details from nature are often the subjects of their poems.

Hero A hero, or **protagonist,** is a central character in a work of fiction, drama, or epic poetry. A traditional hero possesses good qualities that enable him or her to triumph over an antagonist who is bad or evil in some way.

The term *tragic hero,* first used by the Greek philosopher Aristotle, refers to a central character in a drama who is dignified or noble. According to Aristotle, a tragic hero possesses a defect, or tragic flaw, that brings about or contributes to his or her downfall. This flaw may be poor judgment, pride, weakness, or an excess of an admirable quality. The tragic hero, Aristotle noted, recognizes his or her flaw and its consequences, but only after it is too late to change the course of events. The characters Macbeth and Hamlet in Shakespeare's tragedies are tragic heroes.

A **cultural hero** is a hero who represents the values of his or her culture. Such a hero ranks somewhere between ordinary human beings and the gods. The role of a cultural hero is to provide a noble image that will inspire and guide the actions of mortals. Beowulf is a cultural hero.

In more recent literature, heroes do not necessarily command the attention and admiration of an entire culture. They tend to be individuals whose actions and decisions reflect personal courage. The conflicts they face are not on an epic scale but instead involve moral dilemmas presented in the course of living. Such heroes are often in a struggle with established authority because their actions challenge accepted beliefs.

See also Epic; Protagonist; Tragedy.

Heroic Couplet *See* Couplet.

Historical Context The historical context of a literary work refers to the social conditions that inspired or influenced its creation. To understand and appreciate some works, the reader must relate them to events in history.

Historical Documents Historical documents are writings that have played a significant role in human events or are themselves records of such events. The Declaration of Independence, for example, is a historical document.

Historical Writing Historical writing is the systematic telling, often in narrative form, of the past of a nation or group of people. Historical writing generally has the following

characteristics: (1) it is concerned with real events; (2) it uses chronological order; and (3) it is usually an objective retelling of facts rather than a personal interpretation.

See also Primary Sources; Secondary Sources.

How-To Book A how-to book is a book that is written to explain how to do something— usually an activity, a sport, or a household project.

Humor In literature there are three basic types of humor, all of which may involve exaggeration or irony. **Humor of situation** is derived from the plot of a work. It usually involves exaggerated events or situational irony, which occurs when something happens that is different from what was expected. **Humor of character** is often based on exaggerated personalities or on characters who fail to recognize their own flaws, a form of dramatic irony. **Humor of language** may include sarcasm, exaggeration, puns, or verbal irony, which occurs when what is said is not what is meant.

See also Comedy; Farce; Irony.

Hyperbole Hyperbole is a figure of speech in which the truth is exaggerated for emphasis or for humorous effect.

See also Figurative Language; Understatement.

Iamb *See* Meter.

Iambic Pentameter Iambic pentameter is a metrical pattern of five feet, or units, each of which is made up of two syllables, the first unstressed and the second stressed. Iambic pentameter is the most common meter used in English poetry; it is the meter used in blank verse and in the sonnet.

See also Blank Verse; Meter; Sonnet.

Idiom An idiom is a common figure of speech whose meaning is different from the literal meaning of its words. For example, the phrase "raining cats and dogs" does not literally mean that cats and dogs are falling from the sky; the expression means "raining heavily."

Imagery The term *imagery* refers to words and phrases that create vivid sensory experiences for the reader. The majority of images are visual, but imagery may also appeal to the senses of smell, hearing, taste, and touch. In addition, images may re-create sensations of heat (thermal), movement (kinetic), or bodily tension (kinesthetic). Effective writers of both prose and poetry frequently use imagery that appeals to more than one sense simultaneously.

When an image describes one sensation in terms of another, the technique is called **synesthesia.**

A poet may use a **controlling image** to convey thoughts or feelings. A controlling image is a single image or comparison that extends throughout a literary work and shapes its meaning. A controlling image is sometimes an **extended metaphor.**

See also Description; Kinesthetic Imagery.

Implied Main Idea *See* Main Idea.

Index The index of a book is an alphabetized list of important topics and details covered in the book and the page numbers on which they can be found. An index can be used to quickly find specific information about a topic.

Inductive Reasoning Inductive reasoning is the process of logical reasoning from observations, examples, and facts to a general conclusion or principle.

Inference An inference is a logical assumption that is based on observed facts and one's own knowledge and experience.

Informal Essay *See* Essay.

Informational Text Informational text is a category of writing that includes exposition, argument, and functional documents. These texts normally provide factual, historical, or technical information. However, the term also covers texts that make logical or emotional arguments in defense of a position. Examples include biographies, journalism, essays, narrative histories, instruction manuals, and speeches.

Interior Monologue *See* Monologue; Stream of Consciousness.

Internal Conflict *See* Conflict.

Internal Rhyme *See* Rhyme.

Internet The Internet is a global, interconnected system of computer networks that allows for communication through e-mail, listservers, and the World Wide Web.

Interview An interview is a conversation conducted by a writer or reporter in which facts or statements are elicited from another person, recorded, and then broadcast or published.

Irony Irony is a contrast between expectation and reality. This incongruity often has the effect of surprising the reader or viewer. The techniques of irony include hyperbole, understatement, and sarcasm. Irony is often subtle and easily overlooked or misinterpreted.

There are three main types of irony. **Situational irony** occurs when a character or the reader expects one thing to happen but something else actually happens. **Verbal irony** occurs when a writer or character says one thing but means another. An example of verbal irony is the title of Jonathan Swift's essay "A Modest Proposal." The reader soon discovers that the narrator's proposal is outrageous rather than modest and unassuming. **Dramatic irony** occurs when the reader or viewer knows something that a character does not know.

Italian (Petrarchan) Sonnet *See* Sonnet.

Journal A journal is a periodical publication issued by a legal, medical, or other professional organization. Alternatively, the term may be used to refer to a diary or daily record.

See also Diary.

Kenning *See* Anglo-Saxon Poetry.

Kinesthetic Imagery Kinesthetic imagery re-creates the tension felt through muscles, tendons, or joints in the body.

See also Imagery.

Legend A legend is a story passed down orally from generation to generation and popularly believed to have a historical basis. While some legends may be based on real people or situations, most of the events are either greatly exaggerated or fictitious. Like myths, legends may incorporate supernatural elements and magical deeds. But legends differ from myths in that they claim to be stories about real human beings and are often set in a particular time and place.

Letters *Letters* refers to the written correspondence exchanged between acquaintances, friends, or family members. Most letters are private and not designed for publication. However, some are published and read by a wider audience because they are written by well-known public figures or provide important information about the period in which they were written.

Limited Point of View *See* Point of View.

Line The line is the core unit of a poem. In poetry, line length is an essential element of the poem's meaning and rhythm. There are a variety of terms to describe the way a line of poetry ends or is connected to the next line. Line breaks, where a line of poetry ends, may coincide with grammatical units. However, a line break may also occur in the middle of a grammatical or syntactical unit, creating a pause or emphasis. Poets use a variety of line breaks to play with meaning, thereby creating a wide range of effects.

Literary Ballad *See* Ballad.

Literary Criticism Literary criticism refers to writing that focuses on a literary work or a genre, describing some aspect of it, such as its origin, its characteristics, or its effects.

Literary Nonfiction Literary nonfiction is informational text that is recognized as being of artistic value or that is about literature. Autobiographies, biographies, essays, and eloquent speeches typically fall into this category.

Loaded Language Loaded language consists of words with strongly positive or negative connotations intended to influence a reader's or listener's attitude.

Logical Appeal A logical appeal relies on logic and facts, appealing to people's reasoning or intellect rather than to their values or emotions. Flawed logical appeals—that is, errors in reasoning—are considered logical fallacies.

See also Fallacy.

Logical Argument A logical argument is an argument in which the logical relationship between the support and the claim is sound.

Lyric A lyric is a short poem in which a single speaker expresses personal thoughts and feelings. Most poems other than dramatic and narrative poems are lyrics. In ancient Greece, lyrics were meant to be sung—the word *lyric* comes from the word *lyre,* the name of a musical instrument that was used to accompany songs. Modern lyrics are not usually intended for singing, but they are characterized by strong, melodic rhythms. Lyrics can be in a variety of forms and cover many subjects, from love and death to everyday experiences. They are marked by imagination and create for the reader a strong, unified impression.

See also Poetry.

Main Character *See* Character.

Main Idea A main idea is the central, controlling, or most important, idea about a topic that a writer or speaker conveys. It can be the central idea of an entire work or of just a paragraph. Often, the main idea of a paragraph is expressed in a topic sentence. However, a main idea may just be implied, or suggested, by details. A main idea and supporting details can serve as a basic pattern of organization in a piece of writing, with the central idea about a topic being supported by details.

Major Character *See* Character.

Make Inferences *See* Inference.

Maxim A maxim is a brief and memorable statement of general truth, one that often imparts guidance or advice.

Memoir A memoir is a form of autobiographical writing in which a person recalls significant events and people in his or her life. Most memoirs share the following characteristics: (1) they usually are structured as narratives told by the writers themselves, using the first-person point of view; (2) although some names may be changed to protect privacy, memoirs are true accounts of actual events; (3) although basically personal, memoirs may deal with newsworthy events having a significance beyond the confines of the writer's life; (4) unlike strictly historical accounts, memoirs often include the writers' feelings and opinions about historical events, giving the reader insight into the impact of history on people's lives.

See also Autobiography.

Metaphor A metaphor is a figure of speech that compares two things that have something in common. Unlike similes, metaphors do not use the words *like* or *as,* but make comparisons directly.

See also Extended Metaphor; Figurative Language; Simile.

Meter Meter is the repetition of a regular rhythmic unit in a line of poetry. Each unit, known as a **foot,** has one stressed syllable (indicated by a ´) and either one or two unstressed syllables (indicated by a ˘). The four basic types of metrical feet are the **iamb,** an unstressed syllable followed by a stressed syllable; the **trochee,** a stressed syllable followed by an unstressed syllable; the **anapest,** two unstressed syllables followed by a stressed syllable; and the **dactyl,** a stressed syllable followed by two unstressed syllables.

Two words are typically used to describe the meter of a line. The first word identifies the type of metrical foot— iambic, trochaic, anapestic, or dactylic—and the second word indicates the number of feet in a line: **monometer** (one foot); **dimeter** (two feet); **trimeter** (three feet); **tetrameter** (four feet); **pentameter** (five feet); **hexameter** (six feet); and so forth.

See also Free Verse; Iambic Pentameter; Rhythm; Scansion.

Minor Character *See* Character.

Mise-en-Scène *Mise-en-scène* is a term from the French that refers to the various physical aspects of a dramatic presentation, such as lighting, costumes, scenery, makeup, and props.

Modernism Modernism was a movement roughly spanning the time period between the two world wars, 1914–1945. Modernist writers departed from 19th century traditions, such as **realism,** preferring more flexible, experimental approaches emphasizing subjectivity and fragmentation, such as **stream-of-consciousness** and **free verse.** Modernist works often focus on the theme of the alienation of the individual.

Monitor Monitoring is the strategy of checking your comprehension as you are reading and modifying the strategies you are using to suit your needs. Monitoring may include some or all of the following strategies: **questioning, clarifying, visualizing, predicting, connecting, and rereading.**

Monologue In a drama, the speech of a character who is alone on stage, voicing his or her thoughts, is known as a monologue. In a short story or a poem, the direct presentation of a character's unspoken thoughts is called an **interior monologue.** An interior monologue may jump back and forth between past and present, displaying thoughts, memories, and impressions just as they might occur in a person's mind.

See also Stream of Consciousness; Dramatic Monologue.

Mood Mood is the feeling or atmosphere that a writer creates for the reader. The writer's use of connotation, imagery, figurative language, sound and rhythm, and descriptive details all contribute to the mood.

See also Connotation; Description; Diction; Figurative Language; Imagery; Style; Tone.

Motif A motif is a recurring word, phrase, image, object, idea, or action in a work of literature. Motifs function as unifying devices and often relate directly to one or more major themes.

Motivation Motivation is the stated or implied reason behind a character's behavior. The grounds for a character's actions may not be obvious, but they should be comprehensible and consistent, in keeping with the character as developed by the writer.

See also Character.

Myth A myth is a traditional story, passed down through generations, that explains why the world is the way it is. Myths are essentially religious because they present supernatural events and beings and articulate the values and beliefs of a cultural group.

Narrative A narrative is any type of writing that is primarily concerned with relating an event or a series of events. A narrative can be imaginary, as is a short story or novel, or factual, as is a newspaper account or a work of history. The word *narration* can be used interchangeably with *narrative,* which comes from the Latin word meaning "tell."

See also Fiction; Nonfiction; Novel; Plot; Short Story.

Narrative Poem A narrative poem is a poem that tells a story using elements of character, setting, and plot to develop a theme. Epics, such as *Beowulf* and the *Iliad,* are narrative poems, as are ballads.

See also Ballad.

Narrator The narrator of a story is the character or voice that relates the story's events to the reader.

Naturalism An extreme form of realism, naturalism in fiction involves the depiction of life objectively and precisely, without idealizing. However, the naturalist creates characters who are victims of environmental forces and internal drives beyond their comprehension and control. Naturalistic fiction conveys the belief that universal forces result in an indifference to human suffering.

See also Realism.

Neoclassicism *Neoclassicism* refers to the attitudes toward life and art that dominated English literature during the Restoration and the 18th century. Neoclassicists respected order, reason, and rules and viewed humans as limited and imperfect. To them, the intellect was more important than emotions, and society was more important than the individual. Imitating classical literature, neoclassical writers developed a style that was characterized by strict form, logic, symmetry, grace, good taste, restraint, clarity, and conciseness. Their works were meant not only to delight readers but also to instruct them in moral virtues and correct social behavior. Among the literary forms that flourished during the neoclassical period were the essay, the literary letter, and the epigram. The heroic couplet was the dominant verse form, and satire and parody prevailed in both prose and poetry.

See also Romanticism.

News Article A news article is a piece of writing that reports on a recent event. In newspapers, news articles are usually written in a concise manner to report the latest news, presenting the most important facts first and then more detailed information. In magazines, news articles are usually more elaborate than those in newspapers because they are written to provide both information and analysis. Also, news articles in magazines do not necessarily present the most important facts first.

Nonfiction Nonfiction, or informational text, is writing about real people, places, and events. Unlike fiction, nonfiction is largely concerned with factual information, although the writer shapes the information according to his or her purpose and viewpoint. Biography, autobiography, and newspaper articles are examples of nonfiction.

See also Autobiography; Biography; Diary; Essay; Letters; Memoir.

Novel A novel is an extended work of fiction. Like the short story, a novel is essentially the product of a writer's imagination. The most obvious difference between a novel and a short story is length. Because the novel is considerably longer, a novelist can develop a wider range of characters and a more complex plot.

Octave *See* Sonnet.

Ode An ode is a complex lyric poem that develops a serious and dignified theme. Odes appeal to both the imagination and the intellect, and many commemorate events or praise people or elements of nature.

Off Rhyme *See* Rhyme.

Omniscient Point of View *See* Point of View.

Onomatopoeia Onomatopoeia is the use of words whose sounds echo their meanings, such as *buzz, whisper, gargle,* and *murmur.* Onomatopoeia as a literary technique goes beyond the use of simple echoic words, however. Skilled writers, especially poets, choose words whose sounds in combination suggest meaning.

Op-Ed Piece An op-ed piece is an opinion piece that usually appears opposite ("op") the editorial page of a newspaper. Unlike editorials, op-ed pieces are written and submitted by named writers.

Oral Literature Oral literature is literature that is passed from one generation to another by performance or word of mouth. Folk tales, fables, myths, chants, and legends are part of the oral tradition of cultures throughout the world.

See also Folk Tale; Legend; Myth.

Organization *See* Pattern of Organization.

Overgeneralization An overgeneralization is a generalization that is too broad. You can often recognize overgeneralizations by the appearance of words and phrases such as *all, everyone, every time, any, anything, no one,* and *none.* Consider, for example, this statement: "None of the sanitation workers in our city really care about keeping the environment clean." In all probability, there are many exceptions. The writer can't possibly know the feelings of every sanitation worker in the city.

Overstatement *See* Understatement.

Overview An overview is a short summary of a story, a speech, or an essay. It orients the reader by providing a preview of the text to come.

Oxymoron *See* Paradox.

Parable A parable is a brief story that is meant to teach a lesson or illustrate a moral truth. A parable is more than a simple story, however. Each detail of the parable corresponds to some aspect of the problem or moral dilemma to which it is directed.

Paradox A paradox is a statement that seems to contradict, or oppose, itself but, in fact, reveals some element of truth. Paradox is found frequently in the poetry of the 16th and 17th centuries. A special kind of concise paradox is the **oxymoron**, which brings together two contradictory terms. Examples are "cruel kindness" and "brave fear."

Parallel Plot A parallel plot is a particular type of plot in which two stories of equal importance are told simultaneously. The story moves back and forth between the two plots.

Parallelism Parallelism is the use of similar grammatical constructions to express ideas that are related or equal in importance. The parallel elements may be words, phrases, sentences, or paragraphs.

See also Repetition.

Paraphrase Paraphrasing is the restating of information in one's own words.

See also Summarize.

Parody Parody is writing that imitates either the style or the subject matter of a literary work for the purpose of criticism, humorous effect, or flattering tribute.

Pattern of Organization A pattern of organization is a particular arrangement of ideas and information. Such a pattern may be used to organize an entire composition or a single paragraph within a longer work. The following are the most common patterns of organization: **cause-and-effect, chronological order, compare-and-contrast, classification, deductive, inductive, order of importance, problemsolution, sequential,** and **spatial.**

See also Cause and Effect; Chronological Order; Classification; Compare and Contrast; Problem-Solution Order; Sequential Order.

Periodical A periodical is a publication that is issued at regular intervals of more than one day. For example, a periodical may be a weekly, monthly, or quarterly journal or magazine. Newspapers and other daily publications generally are not classified as periodicals.

Persona *See* Speaker.

Personal Essay *See* Essay.

Personification Personification is a figure of speech in which human qualities are attributed to an object, animal, or idea. Writers use personification to communicate feelings and images in a concise, concrete way.

See also Figurative Language; Metaphor; Simile.

Persuasion Persuasion is the art of swaying others' feelings, beliefs, or actions. Persuasion normally appeals to both the intellect and the emotions of readers. **Persuasive techniques** are the methods used to influence others to adopt certain opinions or beliefs or to act in certain ways. Types of persuasive techniques include emotional appeals, ethical appeals, logical appeals, and loaded language. When used properly, persuasive techniques can add depth to writing that's meant to persuade. Persuasive techniques can, however, be misused to cloud factual information, disguise poor reasoning, or unfairly exploit people's emotions in order to shape their opinions.

See also Appeals by Association; Appeal to Authority; Emotional Appeals; Ethical Appeals; Loaded Language; Logical Appeal.

Persuasive Writing Persuasive writing is intended to convince a reader to adopt a particular opinion or to perform a certain action. Effective persuasion usually appeals to both the reason and the emotions of an audience.

Petrarchan Sonnet *See* Sonnet.

Plot The plot is the sequence of actions and events in a literary work. Generally, plots are built around a **conflict**—a problem or struggle between two or more opposing forces. Plots usually progress through stages: exposition, rising action, climax, and falling action.

The **exposition** provides important background information and introduces the setting, characters, and conflict. During the **rising action,** the conflict becomes more intense, and suspense builds as the main characters struggle to resolve their problem. The **climax** is the turning point in the plot when the outcome of the conflict becomes clear, usually resulting in a change in the characters or a solution to the conflict. After the climax, the **falling action** shows the effects of the climax. As the falling action begins, the suspense is over but the results of the decision or action that caused the climax are not yet fully worked out. The **resolution,** or **dénouement,** which often blends with the falling action, reveals the final outcome of events and ties up loose ends.

See also Climax; Complication; Conflict.

Poetry Poetry is language arranged in lines. Like other forms of literature, poetry attempts to re-create emotions and experiences. Poetry, however, is usually more condensed and suggestive than prose.

Poems often are divided into stanzas, or paragraph-like groups of lines. The stanzas in a poem may contain the same number of lines or may vary in length. Some poems have definite patterns of meter and rhyme. Others rely more on the sounds of words and less on fixed rhythms and rhyme schemes. The use of figurative language is also common in poetry.

The form and content of a poem combine to convey meaning. The way that a poem is arranged on the page, the impact of the images, the sounds of the words and phrases, and all the other details that make up a poem work together to help the reader grasp its central idea.

See also Form; Free Verse; Meter; Rhyme; Rhythm; Stanza.

Point of View Point of view refers to the narrative perspective from which events in a story or novel are narrated.

In the **first-person point of view,** the narrator is a character in the work who tells everything in his or her own words and uses the pronouns *I, me,* and *my.* In the **third-person point of view,** events are related by a voice outside the action, not by one of the characters. A third-person narrator uses pronouns like *he, she,* and *they.* In the **third-person omniscient point of view,** the narrator is an all-knowing, objective observer who stands outside the action and reports what different characters are thinking. In the **third-person limited point of view,** the narrator stands outside the action and focuses on one character's thoughts, observations, and feelings.

See also Narrator.

Predict Predicting is a reading strategy that involves using text clues to make a reasonable guess about what will happen next in a story.

Primary Sources Primary sources are accounts of events written by people who were directly involved in or witness to the events. Primary sources include materials such as diaries, letters, wills, and public documents. They also can include historical narratives in which the writer sets out to describe the specific experience of participating in or observing an event.

See also Secondary Sources; Sources.

Prior Knowledge Prior knowledge is the knowledge a reader already possesses about a topic. This information might come from personal experiences, expert accounts, books, films, or other sources.

Problem-Solution Order Problem-solution order is a pattern of organization in which a problem is stated and analyzed and then one or more solutions are proposed and examined. Writers use words and phrases such as *propose, conclude, reason for, problem, answer,* and *solution* to connect ideas and details when writing about problems and solutions.

Prologue A prologue is an introductory scene in a drama.

Prop Prop, an abbreviation of *property,* refers to a physical object that is used in a stage production.

Propaganda Propaganda is a form of communication that may use distorted, false, or misleading information. It usually refers to manipulative political discourse.

Prose Generally, *prose* refers to all forms of written or spoken expression that are not in verse. The term, therefore, may be used to describe very different forms of writing—short stories as well as essays, for example.

Protagonist The protagonist is the main character in a work of literature, who is involved in the central conflict of the story. Usually, the protagonist changes after the central conflict reaches a climax. He or she may be a hero and is usually the one with whom the audience tends to identify.

See also Antagonist; Character; Tragic Hero.

Psychological Fiction An offshoot of **realism,** psychological fiction focuses on the conflicts and motivations of its characters. In such literature, plot events are often less important than the inner workings of each character's mind. A technique closely associated with psychological fiction is **stream of consciousness,** which presents the random flow of a character's thoughts. Though psychological fiction is often viewed as a 20th-century invention found in the writing of Virginia Woolf, James Joyce, and others, earlier

writers—such as George Eliot, Elizabeth Gaskell, and Thomas Hardy—can be said to employ this technique in varying degrees.

See also Realism.

Public Documents Public documents are documents that were written for the public to provide information that is of public interest or concern. They include government documents, speeches, signs, and rules and regulations.

See also Government Publications.

Purpose *See* Author's Purpose.

Quatrain A quatrain is a four-line stanza.

See also Poetry; Stanza.

Realism As a general term, *realism* refers to any effort to offer an accurate and detailed portrayal of actual life. Thus, critics talk about Shakespeare's realistic portrayals of his characters and praise the medieval poet Chaucer for his realistic descriptions of people from different social classes.

More specifically, realism refers to a literary method developed in the 19th century. The realists based their writing on careful observations of ordinary life, often focusing on the middle or lower classes. They attempted to present life objectively and honestly, without the sentimentality or idealism that had colored earlier literature. Typically, realists developed their settings in great detail in an effort to re-create a specific time and place for the reader. Elements of realism can be found in the novels of Jane Austen and Charles Dickens, but it is not fully developed until the fiction of George Eliot.

See also Naturalism.

Recurring Theme *See* Theme.

Reference Works General reference works are sources that contain facts and background information on a wide range of subjects. More specific reference works contain indepth information on a single subject. Most reference works are good sources of reliable information because they have been reviewed by experts. The following are some common reference works: **encyclopedias, dictionaries, thesauri, almanacs, atlases, chronologies, biographical dictionaries,** and **directories.**

Reflective Essay *See* Essay.

Refrain In poetry, a refrain is part of a stanza, consisting of one or more lines that are repeated regularly, sometimes with changes, often at the ends of succeeding stanzas.

Repetition Repetition is a technique in which a sound, word, phrase, or line is repeated for emphasis or unity. Repetition often helps to reinforce meaning and create an appealing rhythm. The term includes specific devices associated with both prose and poetry, such as **alliteration** and **parallelism.**

See also Alliteration; Parallelism; Sound Devices.

Resolution *See* Plot.

Review *See* Critical Review.

Rhetorical Devices *See* Analogy; Repetition; Rhetorical Questions

Rhetorical Questions Rhetorical questions are those that do not require a reply. Writers use them to suggest that their arguments make the answer obvious or self-evident.

Rhyme Words rhyme when the sounds of their accented vowels and all succeeding sounds are identical, as in *amuse* and *confuse.* For true rhyme, the consonants that precede the vowels must be different. Rhyme that occurs at the end of lines of poetry is called **end rhyme.** End rhymes that are not exact but approximate are called **off rhyme,** or **slant rhyme.** Rhyme that occurs within a single line is called **internal rhyme.**

Rhyme Scheme A rhyme scheme is the pattern of end rhyme in a poem. A rhyme scheme is charted by assigning a letter of the alphabet, beginning with *a,* to each line. Lines that rhyme are given the same letter.

See also Ballad; Couplet; Quatrain; Rhyme; Sonnet.

Rhythm Rhythm is a pattern of stressed and unstressed syllables in a line of poetry. Poets use rhythm to bring out the musical quality of language, to emphasize ideas, to create mood, to unify a work, and to heighten emotional response. Devices such as alliteration, rhyme, assonance, consonance, and parallelism often contribute to creating rhythm.

See also Anglo-Saxon Poetry; Ballad; Meter; Spenserian Stanza.

Rising Action *See* Plot.

Romance The romance has been a popular narrative form since the Middle Ages. Generally, the term refers to any imaginative adventure concerned with noble heroes, gallant love, a chivalric code of honor, daring deeds, and supernatural events. Romances usually have faraway settings, depict events unlike those of ordinary life, and idealize their heroes as well as the eras in which the heroes live. Medieval romances often are lighthearted in tone, consist of a number of episodes, and involve one or more characters in a quest.

Romanticism *Romanticism* refers to a literary movement that flourished in Britain and Europe throughout much of the 19th century. Romantic writers looked to nature for their inspiration, idealized the distant past, and celebrated the individual. In reaction against neoclassicism, their treatment of subjects was emotional rather than rational, imaginative rather than analytical. The romantic period in English literature is generally viewed as beginning with the publication of *Lyrical Ballads,* poems by William Wordsworth and Samuel Taylor Coleridge.

See also Neoclassicism.

Sarcasm Sarcasm, a type of **verbal irony,** refers to a critical remark expressed in a mocking fashion. In some cases, a statement is sarcastic because its literal meaning is the opposite of its actual meaning.

See also Irony.

Satire Satire is a literary technique in which ideas, customs, behaviors, or institutions are ridiculed for the purpose of improving society. Satire may be gently witty, mildly abrasive, or bitterly critical, and it often uses exaggeration to force readers to see something in a more critical light. Often, a satirist distances himself or herself from a subject by creating a fictional speaker—usually a calm and often naïve observer—who can address the topic without revealing the true emotions of the writer. Whether the object of a satiric work is an individual person or a group of people, the force of the satire will almost always cast light on foibles and failings that are universal to human experience.

There are two main types of satire, named for the Roman satirists Horace and Juvenal; they differ chiefly in tone. **Horatian satire** is playfully amusing and seeks to correct vice or foolishness with gentle laughter and sympathetic understanding. **Juvenalian satire** provokes a darker kind of laughter. It is biting and criticizes corruption or incompetence with scorn and outrage. Jonathan Swift's "A Modest Proposal" is an example of Juvenalian satire.

See also Irony.

Scanning Scanning is the process of searching through writing for a particular fact or piece of information. When you scan, your eyes sweep across a page, looking for key words that may lead you to the information you want.

Scansion The process of determining meter is known as scansion. When you scan a line of poetry, you mark its stressed (´) and unstressed (˘) syllables in order to identify the rhythm.

See also Meter.

Scene In drama, a scene is a subdivision of an act. Each scene usually establishes a different time or place.

See also Act; Drama.

Scenery Scenery is a painted backdrop or other structures used to create the setting for a play.

Screenplay A screenplay is a play written for film.

Script The text of a play, film, or broadcast is called a script.

Secondary Sources Accounts written by people who were not directly involved in or witnesses to an event are called secondary sources. A history textbook is an example of a secondary source.

See also Primary Sources; Sources.

Sensory Details Sensory details are words and phrases that appeal to the reader's senses of sight, hearing, touch, taste, and smell. For example, the sensory detail "a fine film of rain" appeals to the senses of sight and touch.

Sensory details stimulate the reader to create images in his or her mind.

See also Imagery.

Sequential Order A pattern of organization that shows the order in which events or actions occur is called sequential order. Writers typically use this pattern of organization to explain steps or stages in a process.

Sestet *See* Sonnet.

Setting The setting of a literary work refers to the time and place in which the action occurs. A story can be set in an imaginary place, such as an enchanted castle, or a real place, such as London or Hampton Court. The time can be the past, the present, or the future. In addition to time and place, setting can include the larger historical and cultural contexts that form the background for a narrative. Setting is one of the main elements in fiction and often plays an important role in what happens and why.

Setting a Purpose The process of establishing specific reasons for reading a text is called setting a purpose.

Shakespearean (English) Sonnet *See* Sonnet.

Short Story A short story is a work of fiction that centers on a single idea and can be read in one sitting. Generally, a short story has one main conflict that involves the characters, keeps the story moving, and stimulates readers' interest.

See also Fiction.

Sidebar A sidebar is additional information set in a box alongside or within a news or feature article. Popular magazines often make use of sidebar information.

Signal Words Signal words are words and phrases that indicate what is to come in a text. Readers can use signal words to discover a text's pattern of organization and to analyze the relationships among the ideas in the text.

Simile A simile is a figure of speech that compares two things that have something in common, using a word such as *like* or *as.* Both poets and prose writers use similes to intensify emotional response, stimulate vibrant images, provide imaginative delight, and concentrate the expression of ideas.

An **epic simile** is a long comparison that often continues for a number of lines. It does not always contain the word *like* or *as*.

See also Figurative Language; Metaphor.

Situational Irony *See* Irony.

Slant Rhyme *See* Rhyme.

Soliloquy A soliloquy is a speech in a dramatic work in which a character speaks his or her thoughts aloud. Usually the character is on the stage alone, not speaking to other characters and perhaps not even consciously addressing the audience. (If there are other characters on stage, they are ignored temporarily.) The purpose of a soliloquy is to reveal a character's inner thoughts, feelings, and plans to the audience. Soliloquies are characteristic of Elizabethan drama.

Sonnet A sonnet is a lyric poem of 14 lines, commonly written in **iambic pentameter.** For centuries the sonnet has been a popular form because it is long enough to permit development of a complex idea, yet short and structured enough to challenge any poet's skills. Sonnets written in English usually follow one of two forms.

The **Petrarchan,** or **Italian, sonnet,** introduced into English by Sir Thomas Wyatt, is named after Petrarch, the 14th century Italian poet. This type of sonnet consists of two parts, called the **octave** (the first eight lines) and the **sestet** (the last six lines). The usual rhyme scheme for the octave is *abbaabba.* The rhyme scheme for the sestet may be *cdecde, cdccdc,* or a similar variation. The octave generally presents a problem or raises a question, and the sestet resolves or comments on the problem.

The **Shakespearean,** or **English, sonnet** is sometimes called the **Elizabethan sonnet.** It consists of three quatrains, or four-line units, and a final couplet. The typical rhyme scheme is *abab cdcd efef gg.* In the English sonnet, the rhymed couplet at the end of the sonnet provides a final commentary on the subject developed in the three quatrains. Shakespeare's sonnets are the finest examples of this type of sonnet.

A variation of the Shakespearean sonnet is the **Spenserian sonnet,** which has the same structure but uses the interlocking rhyme scheme *abab bcbc cdcd ee.*

Some poets have written a series of related sonnets that have the same subject. These are called **sonnet sequences,** or **sonnet cycles.** Toward the end of the 16th century, writing sonnet sequences became fashionable, with a common subject being love for a beautiful but unattainable woman.

See also Iambic Pentameter; Lyric; Meter; Quatrain.

Sound Devices *See* Alliteration; Assonance; Consonance; Meter; Onomatopoeia; Repetition; Rhyme; Rhyme Scheme; Rhythm.

Sources A source is anything that supplies information. **Primary sources** are materials written or created by people who were present at events, either as participants or as observers. Letters, diaries, autobiographies, speeches, and photographs are primary sources. **Secondary sources** are records of events that were created sometime after the events occurred; the writers were not directly involved or were not present when the events took place. Encyclopedias, textbooks, biographies, most newspaper and magazine articles, and books and articles that interpret or review research are secondary sources.

Spatial Order Spatial order is a pattern of organization that highlights the physical positions or relationships of details or objects. This pattern of organization is typically found in descriptive writing. Writers use words and phrases such as *on the left, to the right, here, over there, above, below, beyond, nearby,* and *in the distance* to indicate the arrangement of details.

Speaker The speaker of a poem, like the narrator of a story, is the voice that talks to the reader. In some poems, the speaker can be identified with the poet. In other poems, the poet invents a fictional character, or a persona, to play the role of the speaker. *Persona* is a Latin word meaning "actor's mask."

Speech A speech is a talk or public address. The purpose of a speech may be to entertain, to explain, to persuade, to inspire, or any combination of these aims.

Stage Directions *See* Drama.

Stanza A stanza is a group of lines that form a unit in a poem. A stanza is usually characterized by a common pattern of meter, rhyme, and number of lines. During the 20th century, poets experimented more freely with stanza form than did earlier poets, sometimes writing poems without any stanza breaks.

Static Character *See* Character.

Stereotype A stereotype is an oversimplified image of a person, group, or institution. Sweeping generalizations about "all English people" or "every used-car dealer" are stereotypes. Simplified or stock characters in literature are often called stereotypes. Such characters do not usually demonstrate the complexities of real people.

Stereotyping Stereotyping is a dangerous type of overgeneralization. Stereotypes are broad statements made about people on the basis of their gender, ethnicity, race, or political, social, professional, or religious group.

Stream of Consciousness Stream of consciousness is a technique that was developed by modernist writers to present the flow of a character's seemingly unconnected thoughts, responses, and sensations. A character's stream of consciousness is often expressed as an interior monologue, which may reveal the inner experience of the character on many levels of consciousness.

See also Characterization; Modernism; Point of View; Psychological Fiction; Style.

Structure The structure of a literary work is the way in which it is put together—the arrangement of its parts. In poetry, structure refers to the arrangement of words and lines to produce a desired effect. A common structural unit in poetry is the stanza, of which there are numerous types. In prose, structure is the arrangement of larger units or parts of a selection. Paragraphs, for example, are a basic unit in prose, as are chapters in novels and acts in plays. The structure of a poem, short story, novel, play, or nonfiction selection usually emphasizes certain important aspects of content.

See also Form; Stanza.

Style Style is the distinctive way in which a work of literature is written. Style refers not so much to what is said but how it is said. Word choice, sentence length, tone, imagery, and use of dialogue all contribute to a writer's style. A group of writers might exemplify common stylistic characteristics, as, for example, in the case of the 17th-century metaphysical poets, who employed complex meanings and unconventional rhythms and figurative language to achieve dramatic effect.

Subtlety *See* Aphorism.

Summarize To summarize is to briefly retell, or encapsulate, the main ideas of a piece of writing in one's own words.

See also Paraphrase.

Supernatural Tale A supernatural tale is a story that goes beyond the bounds of reality, usually by involving supernatural elements—beings, powers, or events that are unexplainable by known forces or laws of nature.

In many supernatural tales, **foreshadowing**—hints or clues that point to later events—is used to encourage readers to anticipate the unthinkable. Sometimes readers are left wondering whether a supernatural event has really taken place or is the product of a character's imagination. In an effective supernatural tale, the writer manipulates readers' feelings of curiosity and fear to produce a mounting sense of excitement.

Support Support is any material that serves to prove a claim. In an argument, support typically consists of reasons and evidence. In persuasive texts and speeches, however, support may include appeals to the needs and values of the audience.

See also General Principle.

Supporting Detail *See* Main Idea.

Surprise Ending A surprise ending is an unexpected plot twist at the end of a story.

See also Irony.

Suspense Suspense is the excitement or tension that readers feel as they become involved in a story and eagerly await the outcome.

See also Plot.

Symbol A symbol is a person, place, or object that has a concrete meaning in itself and also stands for something beyond itself, such as an idea or feeling.

Synesthesia *See* Imagery.

Synthesize To synthesize information is to take individual pieces of information and combine them with other pieces of information and with prior knowledge or experience to gain a better understanding of a subject or to create a new product or idea.

Text Features Text features are design elements that indicate the organizational structure of a text and help make the key ideas and the supporting information understandable. Text features include headings, boldface type, italic type, bulleted or numbered lists, sidebars, and graphic aids such as charts, tables, timelines, illustrations, and photographs.

Theme A theme is an underlying message that a writer wants the reader to understand. It is a perception about life or human nature that the writer shares with the reader. In most cases, themes are not stated directly but must be inferred. In addition, there may be more than one theme in a work of literature.

Recurring themes are themes found in a variety of works. For example, authors from varying backgrounds might convey similar themes having to do with the importance of family values. **Universal themes** are themes that are found throughout the literature of all time periods.

Thesaurus *See* Reference Works.

Thesis Statement In an argument, a thesis statement, or controlling idea, is an expression of the claim that the writer or speaker is trying to support. In an essay, a thesis statement is an expression, in one or two sentences, of the main idea or purpose of the piece of writing.

Third-Person Point of View *See* Point of View.

Title The title of a literary work introduces readers to the piece and usually reveals something about its subject or theme. Although works are occasionally untitled or, in the case of some poems, merely identified by their first line, most literary works have been deliberately and carefully named. Some titles are straightforward, stating exactly what the reader can expect to discover in the work. Others hint at the subject and force the reader to search for interpretations.

Tone Tone is a writer's attitude toward his or her subject. A writer can communicate tone through diction, choice of details, and direct statements of his or her position. Unlike mood, which refers to the emotional response of the reader to a work, tone reflects the feelings of the writer. To identify the tone of a work of literature, you might find it helpful to read the work aloud, as if giving a dramatic reading before an audience. The emotions that you convey in an oral reading should give you hints as to the tone of the work.

> **Examples:** The tone of Jonathan Swift's "A Modest Proposal" is searingly ironic. In "The Prologue" from *The Canterbury Tales,* Chaucer's jovial tone accounts for much of the work's humor.

See also Connotation; Diction; Mood; Style.

Topic Sentence The topic sentence of a paragraph states the paragraph's main idea. All other sentences in the paragraph provide supporting details.

Tragedy A tragedy is a dramatic work that presents the downfall of a dignified character who is involved in historically, morally, or socially significant events. The main character, or **tragic hero,** has a **tragic flaw,** a quality that leads to his or her destruction. The events in a tragic plot are set in motion by a decision that is often an error in judgment caused by the tragic flaw. Succeeding events are linked in a cause-and-effect relationship and lead inevitably to a disastrous conclusion, usually death. Shakespeare's plays *Macbeth, Hamlet, Othello,* and *King Lear* are famous examples of tragedies.

Tragic Flaw *See* Hero; Tragedy.

Tragic Hero *See* Hero; Tragedy.

Traits *See* Character.

Transcript A transcript is a written record of words originally spoken aloud.

Trochee *See* Meter.

Turning Point *See* Climax.

Understatement Understatement is a technique of creating emphasis by saying less than is actually or literally true. It is the opposite of **overstatement,** a form of **hyperbole,** or exaggeration. One of the primary devices of **irony,** understatement can be used to develop a humorous effect, to create satire, or to achieve a restrained tone.

See also Hyperbole; Irony.

Universal Theme *See* Theme.

Verbal Irony *See* Irony.

Verisimilitude Verisimilitude refers to the appearance of truth and actuality.

Visualize Visualizing is the process of forming a mental picture based on written or spoken information.

Voice The term **voice** refers to a writer's unique use of language that allows a reader to "hear" a human personality in his or her writing. The elements of style that determine a writer's voice include sentence structure, diction, and tone. For example, some writers are noted for their reliance on short, simple sentences, while others make use of long, complicated ones. Certain writers use concrete words, such as *lake* or *cold,* which name things that you can see, hear, feel, taste, or smell. Others prefer abstract terms such as *memory,* which name things that cannot be perceived with the senses. A writer's tone also leaves its imprint on his or her personal voice. The term *voice* can be applied to the narrator of a selection, as well as to the writer.

See also Diction; Tone.

Website A website is a collection of "pages" on the World Wide Web that is usually devoted to one specific subject. Pages are linked together and are accessed by clicking hyperlinks or menus, which send the user from page to page within the site. Websites are created by companies, organizations, educational institutions, branches of the government, the military, and individuals.

Word Choice *See* Diction.

Wordplay Wordplay is the intentional use of more than one meaning of a word to express ambiguities, multiple interpretations, and irony.

Workplace Documents Workplace documents are materials that are produced or used within a work setting, usually to aid in the functioning of the workplace. They include job applications, office memos, training manuals, job descriptions, and sales reports.

Works Cited A list of works cited lists names of all the works a writer has referred to in his or her text. This list often includes not only books and articles but also nonprint sources.

Works Consulted A list of works consulted names all the works a writer consulted in order to create his or her text. It is not limited just to those works cited in the text.

See also Bibliography.

Using the Glossaries

The following glossaries list the Academic Vocabulary and Critical Vocabulary words found in this book in alphabetical order. Use these glossaries just as you would a dictionary—to determine the meanings, parts of speech, pronunciation, and syllabication of words. (Some technical, foreign, and more obscure words in this book are not listed here but are defined for you in the footnotes that accompany many of the selections.)

Many words in the English language have more than one meaning. These glossaries give the meanings that apply to the words as they are used in this book. Words closely related in form and meaning are listed together in one entry (for instance, **consumption** and **consume**), and the definition is given for the first form.

The following abbreviations are used to identify parts of speech of words:

adj. adjective   *adv.* adverb   *n.* noun   *v.* verb

Each word's pronunciation is given in parentheses. A guide to the pronunciation symbols appears in the Pronunciation Key below. The stress marks in the Pronunciation Key are used to indicate the force given to each syllable in a word. They can also help you determine where words are divided into syllables.

For more information about the words in the glossaries or for information about words not listed in them, consult a dictionary.

Pronunciation Key

Symbol	Examples	Symbol	Examples	Symbol	Examples
ă	pat	m	mum	v	valve
ā	pay	n	no, sudden	w	with
ä	father	ng	thing	y	yes
âr	care	ŏ	pot	z	zebra, xylem
b	bib	ō	toe	zh	vision, pleasure, garage
ch	church	ô	caught, paw		
d	deed, milled	oi	noise	ə	about, item, edible, gallop, circus
ĕ	pet	ŏŏ	took		
ē	bee	ōō	boot	ər	butter
f	fife, phase, rough	ou	out		
g	gag	p	pop		
h	hit	r	roar	**Sounds in Foreign Words**	
hw	which	s	sauce	KH	*German* ich, ach; *Scottish* loch
ĭ	pit	sh	ship, dash	N	*French,* bon fin
ī	pie, by	t	tight, stopped	œ	*French* feu, œuf; *German* schön
îr	pier	th	thin		
j	judge	*th*	this	ü	*French* tu; *German* über
k	kick, cat, pique	ŭ	cut		
l	lid, needle*	ûr	urge, term, firm, word, heard		

* In English the consonants *l* and *n* often constitute complete syllables by themselves.

Stress Marks

The relevant emphasis with which the syllables of a word or phrase are spoken, called stress, is indicated in three different ways. The strongest, or primary, stress is marked with a bold mark (´). An intermediate, or secondary, level of stress is marked with a similar but lighter mark (´). The weakest stress is unmarked. Words of one syllable show no stress mark.

Glossary of Academic Vocabulary

accumulate (ə-kyoom′yə-lāt′) *v.* to gather or pile up.

appreciation (ə-prē′shē-ā′shən) *n.* recognition of the quality, significance, or value of someone or something.

assurance (ə-shoor′əns) *n.* a guarantee or pledge.

bias (bī′əs) *n.* predisposition toward; preference for one thing over another.

collapse (kə-lăps′) *v.* to break down or fall apart suddenly and cease to function.

complementary (kŏm′plə-měn′tə-rē) *adj.* completing; forming a whole.

conceive (kən-sēv′) *v.* to understand or form in the mind; to devise.

conform (kən-form′) *v.* to be similar to or match something or someone; to act or be in accord or agreement.

controversy (kŏn′trə-vûr′sē) *n.* public disagreement, argument.

convince (kən-vĭns′) *n.* persuade or lead to agreement by means of argument.

devote (dĭ-vōt′) *v.* to give one's entire energy or attention to something or someone.

drama (drä′mə) *n.* a prose or verse composition that is intended to be acted out.

encounter (ĕn-koun′tər) *n.* an unplanned or unexpected meeting.

ethics (ĕth′ĭks) *n.* rules of conduct or set of principles.

exploit (ĭk-sploit′) *v.* to take advantage of; to use for selfish or unethical purposes.

inclinations (ĭn′klə-nā′shəns) *n.* leanings toward; propensities for.

integrity (ĭn-tĕg′rĭ-tē) *n.* quality of being ethically or morally upright.

intensity (ĭn-tĕn′sĭ-tē) *n.* high degree or concentration; power or force.

mediate (mē′dē-āt′) *v.* to settle differences between two individuals or groups.

persistence (pər-sĭs′təns) *n.* the act or quality of holding firmly to a purpose or task in spite of obstacles.

predominance (prĭ-dŏm′ə-nəns) *n.* superiority in control, force, or influence.

radical (răd′ĭ-kəl) *adj.* extreme; desirous of change in established institutions or practices.

reinforce (rē′ĭn-fors) *v.* to strengthen; to give more force to.

restore (rĭ-stôr′) *v.* to bring back to original condition; to renew; to revive.

restrain (rĭ-strān′) *v.* to hold back or control.

tension (tĕn′shən) *n.* mental strain or excitement.

theme (thēm) *n.* an idea that is implied or that recurs in a work; a message conveyed in a literary work.

trigger (trĭg′ər) *v.* to set off a chain of events.

vision (vĭzh′ən) *n.* ability to see; insight.

visualize (vĭzhōōə-līz′) *v.* to form a mental image of something or someone.

Glossary of Critical Vocabulary

abrogate (ăb′rə-gāt′) *v.* to revoke or nullify.

acrid (ăk′rĭd) *adj.* strongly unpleasant in smell or taste.

adamant (ăd′ə-mənt) *adj.* inflexible and insistent, unchanging.

admonition (ăd′mə-nĭsh′ən) *n.* critical advice.

affiliation (ə-fĭl′ē-ā′shən) *n.* association with.

affliction (ə-flĭk′shən) *n.* something that causes suffering or pain.

ancillary (ăn′sə-lĕr′ē) *adj.* additional and related.

anomaly (ə-nŏm′ə-lē) *n.* peculiarity; an unusual example.

apparition (ăp′ə-rĭsh′ən) *n.* an unexpected, unexplained vision; a ghostly image of a person.

bellicose (bĕl′ĭ-kōs′) *adj.* aggressively inclined to fight.

benign (bĭ-nīn′) *adj.* harmless.

bequeath (bĭ-kwēth′) *v.* to pass on to heirs.

calamity (kə-lăm′ĭ-tē) *n.* a disaster or catastrophe.

cognitive (kŏg′nĭ-tĭv) *adj.* related to knowledge or understanding.

cohort (kō′hôrt′) *n.* a companion or associate.

collateral (kə-lăt′ər-əl) *adj.* additional, accompanying.

congenial (kən-jēn′yəl) *adj.* agreeable, sympathetic.

counterintuitive (koun′tər-ĭn-tōō′ĭ-tĭv) *adj.* contrary to what one expects.

degenerate (dĭ-jĕn′ə-rāt′) *v.* to decline in quality.

desultory (dĕs′əl-tôr′ē) *adj.* lacking a fixed plan.

discredit (dĭs-krĕd′ĭt) *v.* to damage the reputation of.

dissimulation (dĭ-sĭm′yə-lā′shən) *n.* deceit or pretense.

double entendre (dŭb′əl än-tän′drə) *n.* an expression having a double meaning.

emulation (ĕm′yə-lā′shən) *n.* competitive imitation.

engender (ĕn-jĕn′dər) *v.* to bring into existence.

enmity (ĕn′mĭ-tē) *n.* hatred or hostility towards an enemy.

entail (ĕn-tāl′) *v.* involve as a consequence.

entomological (ĕn′tə-mə-lŏj′ĭ-kəl) *adj.* related to the study of insects.

eviscerate (ĭ-vĭs′ə-rāt′) *v.* to remove the necessary or important parts of.

extortionist (ĭk-stôr′shən-ĭst) *n.* one who obtains something by force or threat.

extricate (ĕk′strĭ-kāt′) *v.* to free from difficulty.

fabricate (făb′rĭ-kāt′) *v.* to construct or make.

facile (făs′əl) *adj.* easy to make or understand.

fetid (fĕt′ĭd) *adj.* having an unpleasant odor; bad-smelling.

genre (zhän′rə) *n.* a category within an art form, based on style or subject.

hierarchy (hī′ə-rär′kē) *n.* a ranking of status within a group.

hypocrite (hĭp′ə-krĭt′) *n.* one who professes good qualities but does not demonstrate or possess them.

ignobly (ĭg-nō′blē) *adv.* dishonorably.

implicit (ĭm-plĭs′ĭt) *adj.* understood but not directly stated.

indigenous (ĭn-dĭj′ə-nəs) *adj.* native to a land.

inducement (ĭn-dōōs′mənt) *n.* an incentive or stimulus.

inexplicably (ĭn-ĕk′splĭ-kə-blē) *adv.* in a way that is hard or impossible to explain.

infamous (ĭn′fə-məs) *adj.* having a bad reputation.

innate (ĭ-nāt´) *adj.* possessed at birth.

insipid (ĭn-sĭp´ĭd) *adj.* dull; lacking color or zest.

insurgency (ĭn-sûr´jən-sē) *n.* rebellion or revolt.

inviolate (ĭn-vī´ə-lĭt) *adj.* secure against change or violation.

iridescent (ĭr´ĭ-dĕs´ənt) *adj.* having colors that change when seen from different angles.

itinerant (ī-tĭn´ər-ənt) *adj.* migrant, or travelling from site to site.

loathsome (lōth´səm) *adj.* hateful or repulsive.

malleable (măl´ē-ə-bəl) *adj.* able to be shaped or molded.

marginal (mär´jə-nəl) *adj.* just meeting a very low standard of success.

motley (mŏt´lē) *adj.* unusually varied or mixed.

naïveté (nī´ēv-tā´) *n.* lack of knowledge or experience.

panacea (păn´ə-sē´ə) *n.* a cure or solution for all problems.

paraphernalia (păr´ə-fər-nāl´yə) *n.* necessary equipment or utensils.

pilgrimage (pĭl´grə-mĭj) *n.* a journey to a historical or religious site.

preamble (prē´ăm´bəl) *n.* an introductory statement.

prodigious (prə-dĭj´əs) *adj.* remarkably great; huge.

progeny (prŏj´ə-nē) *n.* offspring or descendants.

pugnacious (pŭg-nā´shəs) *adj.* belligerent, inclined to quarrel.

purge (pûrj) *v.* to eliminate or wash away.

rampant (răm´pənt) *adj.* growing wildly without restraint or limit.

rebuke (rĭ-byōōk´) *v.* to reprimand or scold.

recalcitrant (rĭ-kăl´sĭ-trənt) *adj.* uncooperative and resistant of authority.

reparations (rĕp´ə-rā´shəns) *n.* compensation or payment from a nation for damage or injury during a war.

resolution (rĕz´ə-lōō´shən) *n.* determination.

retribution (rĕt´rə-byōō´shən) *n.* appropriate punishment or revenge.

reverberate (rĭ-vûr´bə-rāt´) *v.* to vibrate or resonate.

rudiment (rōō´də-mənt) *n.* basic principle or aspect.

ruminate (rōō´mə-nāt´) *v.* to consider or think about carefully; contemplate.

savvy (săv´ē) *adj.* shrewd, confidently clever.

scalloped (skŏl´əpt) *adj.* having a wavy edge, border, or design.

scrupulous (skrōō´pyə-ləs) *adj.* honorable; moral.

signify (sĭg´nə-fī´) *v.* to have meaning or importance.

solace (sŏl´ĭs) *v.* give comfort or relief to.

sovereignty (sŏv´ər-ĭn-tē) *n.* independent rule or authority.

sporadic (spə-răd´ĭk) *adj.* occasional; occurring at random intervals.

stoic (stō´ĭk) *adj.* enduring difficulty without expressing emotion or complaint.

subterranean (sŭb´tə-rā´nē-ən) *adj.* underground.

supposition (sŭp´ə-zĭsh´ən) *n.* something thought to be the case; an assumed truth or hypothesis.

susceptibility (sə-sĕp´tə-bĭl´ĭ-tē) *n.* vulnerability or the likeliness to be affected.

talon (tăl´ən) *n.* the claw of a predator bird.

taut (tôt) *adj.* tense or tightly flexed.

tentatively (tĕn´tə-tĭv-lē) *adv.* with uncertainty; cautiously.

translucent (trăns-lōō´sənt) *adj.* semitransparent.

tutelage (to͞ot´l-ĭj) *n.* instructional authority.

tyranny (tĭr´ə-nē) *n.* oppressive rule by an absolute power.

ubiquity (yo͞o-bĭk´wĭ-tē) *n.* constant presence or prevalence.

unmitigated (ŭn-mĭt´ĭ-gā´tĭd) *adj.* complete and undiminishing.

vindication (vĭn´dĭ-kā´shən) *n.* justification.

virtue (vûr´cho͞o) *n.* purity or virginity.

Index of Skills

Key:

Teacher's Edition page numbers and subject entries are printed in **boldface** type.

Subject entries and page references that apply to both the Student Edition and the Teacher's Edition appear in lightface type.

There is no content from the Close Reader in this index.

external, 60, R65
internal, 60
in tragedy, 233
conjunctions, R24, R39
coordinating, 122, 185, R24, R39
correlative, R24, R39
subordinating, 122, R24, R39
conjunctive adverbs, R39
connect, R66
connotations, 41, 43, **140a, 152, 154, 155, 162, 163,** 165, 197, 220, 428, **432a, 465,** R54, R66
consonance, 112, **478,** R66
consumer documents, R66
context clues, **4, 47, 140a, 200, 211, 493,** R66
antonyms, 17
determining word meaning using, 17, 139, 176, 211
restatement, 17
synonyms, 17
types of, R49
using, R49–R50
context, cultural, 498
context guide activity, 210
context, historical, **152,** 209
contractions, 254, 369
contrast, 113, R49
controlling idea. *See* thesis statement
controlling image, R72
conversational English patterns, 434
coordinating conjunctions, 122, 185, R24, R39
correlative conjunctions, R24, R39
counter, **115**
counterarguments, 27, **114, 116, 117,** 119, 120, **122a, 212a,** R16, R66
couplets, R66
credibility, R5, R66
credible sources, R8–R9
criteria
for compare-contrast essay, 71
for debates, 67
for group discussions, 145, 221
for informative essay, 141
for personal narrative, 517
for satire, 225
for speeches, 471
critical review, R66
Critical Vocabulary, 4, 5, 6, 10, 14, 17, **21, 22, 23,** 29, **33, 35,** 45, **78, 79, 82, 85,** 87, 91, **98, 100, 101, 102, 103,** 107, **113, 114, 115, 116, 117,** 121, **132, 134,** 139, **151, 152, 154, 155, 159, 162, 163,** 167, **170, 172,** 176, **188, 189, 193,** 197, **200, 201, 202, 203,** 206, 211, **361, 362, 364, 365,** 368, **379, 380, 382, 383, 385, 386, 390,** 393, **412, 414, 417, 419, 423,** 427, **433, 434, 435, 446,** 451, **454, 455, 459, 463, 466,** 470, **477, 478, 479,** 483, **501, 503, 507, 512,** 516. *See also* Glossary of Critical Vocabulary
critiques, 28, 64, 90, 138, 184, 216, 360, 367, 392, 432, 515
cultural context, **494, 495, 496,** 498
cultural hero, R71
cultural references, 340

cultural setting, 105

D
dangling participles, R42
dashes, 46, **272,** R27
database, R66
debates, 67–70, 138, R14–R15, R66
affirmative side in, R14, R15
building arguments for, 68
elements of effective, 67
evaluating, R15
format for, R15
holding, 69, R15
moderators, R14
negative side in, R14, R15
Performance Task Evaluation Chart, 70
planning, 67–68, R14
practicing for, 69
preparing briefs and rebuttals for, R14–R15
propositions in, R14
roles in, R14
structure of formal, R14
teams for, R14
declarative sentences, R40
deductive conclusion, R65
deductive reasoning, R18–R19, R66
definition, as context clue, R49
demonstrative pronouns, R24, R32
denotations, 197, 451, R54, R66
dénouement, R77
description
narrative technique of, R6–R7, R67
writing activity, 106
details
analyzing, 15
concrete, R5
gathering, R6–R7
precise, 484
to support central idea, 137
to support inferences, 105
determining
author's point of view, 137
author's purpose, 431
central ideas, 15, 137, 366
connotative meanings, 165
figurative meanings, 111, **327, 347, 395, 396,** 397, **398b, 436, 441, 448, 452a,** 481
theme, **398a,** 449, 514, **516b**
dialect, **48, 49,** 62, R67
dialogue, 64, 233, R67
diary, 16, R67
diction, 43, R67. *See also* word choice
dictionaries, 107, 176, R57
direct objects, R25, R40
direct quotations, 394, R9
discussions. *See also* Collaborative Discussion
collaborative, **66a,** R12–R13
group, 145–148, 221–224
speaking activity, 61, 283, 377, 392, 432, 450, 515
documentary films, 491–492
documents
consumer, R66
foundational, 174, 175, 186

historical, R71
doesn't, R48
domain-specific words, 91, 368, 483
don't, R48
double comparison, R37
double negatives, R37–R38
drafts
of compare-contrast essay, 72
of essays, 72, 142
of informative essay, 142
of personal narrative, 519
revising, 73, 143, 227, 519
of satires, 226
writing, 72, 142, 226, 519
drama, **50,** R67
acts, 233
analyzing, 60, 61
casting, 66
comedies, 231
conflict in, 60, 354
dialect in, 62
dialogue in, 64, 233
elements of, **48, 49, 50, 51, 52, 53, 54, 55, 56, 57, 58, 59,** 60, **62a, 66b, 265, 275, 291,** 354, **356a, 360a**
Hamlet, 236–353
Ile, 47–59
inferences about, 61
interpretations of, **63,** 64, **65,** 66, **66b,** 359, **360a**
media versions of, 63–66, 357–360
mood, 61
production images, 65
Renaissance, 231
scenes, 233, R80
Shakespearean, 231–234
stage directions, 233
staging, 66
symbols in, 60
tragedy, R83
verse drama, 233
dramatic conventions, in Shakespeare, 233–234
dramatic irony, 234, 283, **307,** R72
dramatic monologue, R767
dynamic characters, R64

E
Early Modern English, R53
eBook, 127, 166, 175, 184, 196, 210, 216, 220, 262, 283, 310, 332, 355, 469, 482, 490, 499, 515
editorials, R67
either/or fallacy, R19, R67
electronic publications, citing, R11
elegy, R67
Elizabethan theater, 231
ellipses, R28
elliptical language, 236, 273
ELL students. *See* Scaffolding for ELL Students
emotional appeals, **171,** 174, **429,** 431, R17, R68
encyclopedia articles, citing, R11
end rhyme, R79
English language
Early Modern English, R53

Middle English, R53
Modern English, R53
Old English, R53
preferred and contested usage, R56
proto-English, R53
understanding, R53
English sonnets, R81
enjambment, 489
epic heroes, 425, R68
epic poems, R68
analyzing, 425, 426
Beowulf, 409–424
characteristics of, **410, 411, 412, 413, 414, 415, 417, 419, 420, 421, 422, 423, 424,** 425, **428a**
mood in, 428
epitaph, R68
epithet, R68
essays, R68
analytical, 399–402
citing, R10
compare-contrast, 71–74
conclusion, R5
drafts of, 72, 142, 400
examples, 3–14, 131–136, 169–173, 187–194, 477–480, 493–497
formal, R68
informal, R68
informative, 141–144, R4–R5
personal, 137, R68
persuasive, R68
photo, 213–216
presenting, 143, 401
revising, 73, 143, 401
writing, 71–74, 141–144, 399–402
writing activity, 482
essential adjective clauses, R43
essential appositives, 500, R41
ethical appeals, **171,** 174, R68
etymologies, 45, R51–R52
evading the issue, R20
evaluating, R68
arguments, 27, 28, **30a,** 165, **168a, 180,** 183, **186a, 212a,** 367, 431, **432a, 465,** R22
author's purpose, 175
debates, R15
evidence, R21
film, 492
group discussions, 147
information, 15, **18a,** 130, **130a,** 216, **216a, 492a**
news articles, 127
poetry, 90, 111, 490
point of view, 377
speeches, 166, 473
stories, 450, 515
structure, 212a, 470a
style, 138
text, 44, 469
events
analyzing, 129, 195, **198a, 385, 386, 388, 389, 390,** 391, **484a**
sequencing, **378a,** R7
evidence, R68
analyzing, **177**
authoritative, 27

homophones in, 427
iambic pentameter, 233, 489, R71, R81
imagery in, 220
interpreting, 111
lines, R73
modern, 485–488
mood in, 428
narrative, 77–88, R75
Old English, 425, R62
oral reading of, 111
organic form, 489
parallelism in, 398
pastoral, 489
quatrain, R78
refrain, R79
repetition in, 398
rhyme, R79
rhythm, 425, R79
scansion, R80
sonnets, 489, R81
sound devices in, 112
speaker in, R81
stanza, R82
structure of, 489
tone in, 111, 220
traditional form, 489
writing activity, 220
point of view, **92a, 358,** R80
analyzing, **55, 337, 343, 344, 345, 346,**
349, 369, 372, 373, 374, 376
of author, 137, 198a, 206, 209, 212a
changing, 326
comparing, 42
considering, 252
determining author's, 137
establishing, R6
evaluating, 377
explicit, 198a
exploring, 483
first-person, 44, R77
in frame story, 514
implicit, 198a
information to support, 66b
shifting, 376
third-person, R77
policy statements, R14
political arguments, 113–120
possessive nouns, R23, R30, R59
possessive pronouns, R31
possessives, 320
precede/proceed, R60
precise details, 484
predicate
adjectives, R36
complete, R25
compound, R40
nominative, R40, R57
nouns, R40
pronouns, R40
predicting, R77
prefixes, 29, **162, 177,** R50, R59
identifying, 244
with multiple meanings, 29
premises, 183, **430,** 431
prepositional phrases, 484, R25, R38–R39,
R41
prepositions, R24, R38–R39

presentations, **66b**
of essays, 143
oral, 120
present participle, R33–R34
present perfect progressive tense, R35
present perfect tense, R34
present principal part, R33–R34
present progressive tense, R34
present tense, R374
primary sources, R8, R77, R81
print cues, 93, 361
prior knowledge, **186a,** R78
problems, **212a,** R6
problem-solution organization, 391, R81
proceed/precede, R60
production images, 65
prologue, R78
pronouns, R23, R30
antecedent agreement, R30–R31
cases, R31
demonstrative, R24, R32
indefinite, R24, R29, R46–R47
intensive, R23, R32
interrogative, R24, R32
nominative, R31
objective, R31
personal, R23, R30, R46
possessive, R31
predicate, R40
reference problems, R36
referents, 157, 238, 466
reflexive, R26, R34–R33
relative, R24, R32–R33, R43, R48
pronunciation key, R85
propaganda, R21, R78
proper nouns, R23, R30
propositions, R14
protagonists, R70, R78
proto-English, R53
psychological fiction, R78
public documents, R78
punctuation
apostrophes, **316,** R27–R28
colons, **93, 163,** R27
commas, **93,** R26
dashes, 46, **416, 508,** R27
of direct quotations, 394
ellipses, R28
exclamation points, R26
fluent reading and, 172
hyphens, R27
parentheses, R27
periods, **163,** R26
question marks, R26
quick reference, R26–R28
quotation marks, **163,** R28
semicolons, R27
puns, 262
purpose
determining author's, **130a, 140a,** 155,
193, 216a, 394a, 431
evaluating, 174

questions
research, R8
rhetorical, 119, 166, R79
and subject-verb agreement, 18
quotation marks, R28
quotations, **264**
colons before, R27
direct, 394, R9
indirect, 394

R

reading aloud, 342, 501
reading arguments, R16–R22
realism, 62, R74, R78
reasoning, **177, 212a**
in arguments, 431
circular, R19
deductive, R18–R19, R66
errors in, 27, 183
evaluating, in arguments, 183
faulty, R21–R23
inductive, 165, R18, R72
to support arguments, 366
to support claims, 27, R2
rebuttals, in debates, R14–R15
recurring images, 442
recurring themes, **428a,** R83
reference sources, R78
bibliographies, R64
dictionaries, 107, 176, R57
glossaries, R57
for preferred and contested usage, R56
synonym finders, R57
thesaurus, 516, R57
using, R57
reflexive pronouns, R23, R31–R32
refrain, R79
regular verbs, R33–R34
relative pronouns, R24, R32–R33, R41, R48
relevant evidence, 432a
Renaissance drama, 231
repetition, **168a,** 174, **218, 220a, 395, 396,**
398, R79
research, **417, 485**
conducting, R8–R9
focus of, R8
formulating question for, R8
research questions, R8
research reports, 184
resolution, R80. *See also* falling action
restatement, as context clue, 17
reteaching. *See* Extend and Reteach
reviews, 20, 166
reviews, writing activity, 20, 166
rhetorical devices, **113, 116, 118,** 119, 120,
166, **168a.** *See also* literary devices
rhetorical features, 170
rhetorical questions, 119, 166, R79
rhyme, R79
rhyme scheme, **486,** R79
rhythm, 425, R82
rising action, R79
role play activity, 186
romance, R79
roots, 393, **429,** R50
rough drafts. *See* drafts
run-on sentences, R45

S

sarcasm, R79
satire, 207, 208, 343, 344, 345, 346, R79–R80
draft of, 226
elements of effective, 225–228
example, 199–208
Horatian, R80
Juvenalian, R80
literary devices for, 209, 210
organization, 226
Performance Task Evaluation Chart, 228
planning, 225–226
point of view and, **201, 202, 205, 206,**
209, 212a
revising, 227
in Shakespearean drama, 355
writing, 225–228
Scaffolding for ELL Students, 4, 13, 19, 21,
25, 32, 34, 36, 37, 47, 49, 52, 56, 63, 78,
86, 93, 97, 100, 101, 109, 113, 115, 123,
126, 132, 152, 157, 162, 163, 169, 172,
177, 187, 189, 192, 200, 208, 211, 213,
217, 233, 236, 238, 240, 244, 248, 254,
264, 268, 272, 273, 277, 278, 286, 288,
294, 307, 316, 320, 328, 335, 342, 357,
361, 363, 369, 371, 380, 385, 389, 393,
395, 411, 412, 416, 418, 424, 427, 429,
433, 434, 441, 443, 445, 453, 455, 458,
463, 466, 478, 486, 491, 493, 497, 501,
503, 504, 508
scanning, R80
scansion, R80
scenery, R80
scenes, in play, 233, R80
science articles, 21–26, 453–467
scientific terms, 470
secondary sources, R8, R80, R81
semantic maps, 167, 483
sensory details, R80
sensory language, **38, 108a,** R7
sentence fragments, 140, R44–R45
sentences
combining, 185
complements, R40
complete, writing, R44–R47
complex, R44
compound, 185, R44
compound-complex, R44
compound subjects and predicates, R40
declarative, R40
exclamatory, R40
imperative, R40
interrogative, R40
inverted, 18, 92, R47
length of, 140
parallel structure, R47
parts of, R25, R40
with predicate nominative, R50
run-on, R45
simple, R43
structure of, R43–R44
subject-verb agreement, R45–R48
syntax, 28, 43, 140, 378, 481
topic, R83
types of, R40
sentence structure
conjunctions in, 122

207, 234, 252, 257, 259, 271, 279, 287, 295, 301, 306, 317, 326, 340, 352, 365, 374, 387, 417, 419, 423, 439, 448, 459, 465, 483, 485, 495, 509, 513

tone, 452, R83
  analyzing, 111, 155, 175, 217, 484a, 490a
  of argument, R3
  biased, R3, R5
  comparing, 186
  formal, R3
  informal, R3
  for informative essay, R4
  narrator's, 89, 210, 452
  objective, R3, R5
  and style, 481
  and word choice, 43, 46a, 220, 220a, 296, 398a
  of writer, 480
topic
  developing, R4–R5
  introducing, R5
  research, R8
  of work, 15
topic sentences, 458, R83
traditional form, 489
traditional poetry, 486
tragedy, R83. See also drama
  catharsis, 232
  characteristics of, 232–233
  Greek origins of, 232
  plot of, 233
  Shakespearean, 231–233
  theme of, 233
tragic flaw, 232, 233, R83
tragic heroes, 231, 233, R71, R83
transitions, 97, R3, R5
transitive verbs, R24
trimeter, R74
trochee, R74
Tufte, Virginia, R3
Turabian, Kate L., R9
two/too/to, R61

U

understatement, 209, R84
universal themes, 428a, R83
usage, 91
usage, preferred and contested, R56

V

valid conclusion, R65
valid reasons, to support claims, R15
vanity, appeals to, R17, R68
varying syntax, 370, 378
verbal irony, 55, 209, 310, R72
verbal phrases, R41–R42
verbals, R41–R42
verbs, 268, R24, R33
  action, R24, R33
  active, 212
  active voice, 212, R32
  auxiliary, R24, R25, R48
  forms of, 248
  gerunds, 198, R42
  helping, R25
  imperative mood, 168
  indicative mood, 168

intransitive, R24
irregular, R34
linking, R24, R33
main, R25
mood of, 168
participles, R47
passive, 212
passive voice, 212, R35
phrasal, 34, 389, 441, 458
principal parts, R33–R34
progressive forms, R34–R35
regular, R33–R34
subject-verb agreement, 18, R45–R48
tenses, 37, 208, 424, 433, R33–R35
transitive, R24
usage of, 56
verse drama, 233
video
  analyzing, 129
  citing, R11
  interviews in, 129
  news, 128, 130
  visualizing, R84
View It!, 2, 3, 67, 76, 141, 145, 150, 221, 225, 230, 237, 263, 284, 311, 333, 397, 399, 403, 408, 409, 471, 476, 477, 517
visuals, analysis of, 216a
vivid language, R7
vocabulary
  Academic Vocabulary, 2, 67, 71, 76, 142, 146, 150, 221, 226, 230, 408, 472, 476
  Applying Academic Vocabulary, 5, 10, 22, 35, 38, 51, 53, 79, 94, 104, 114, 124, 129, 134, 153, 160, 178, 182, 188, 201, 204, 214, 218, 243, 281, 289, 298, 314, 322, 339, 348, 358, 362, 370, 384, 388, 396, 413, 430, 435, 446, 454, 462, 480, 487, 495, 505, 512
  commonly confused words, R60–R61
  Critical Vocabulary, 4, 5, 6, 10, 14, 17, 21, 22, 23, 29, 33, 35, 45, 78, 79, 82, 85, 87, 91, 98, 100, 101, 102, 103, 107, 113, 114, 115, 116, 117, 121, 132, 134, 139, 151, 152, 154, 155, 159, 162, 163, 167, 170, 172, 176, 188, 189, 193, 197, 200, 201, 202, 203, 206, 211, 361, 362, 364, 365, 368, 379, 380, 382, 383, 385, 386, 390, 393, 412, 414, 417, 419, 423, 427, 433, 434, 435, 446, 451, 454, 455, 459, 463, 466, 470, 477, 478, 479, 483, 501, 503, 507, 512, 516
  specialized, R55
  strategies for understanding, 176, R49–R61
  supporting, 192, 486
Vocabulary Strategy
  clarifying precise meaning, 176
  connotations, 197
  consulting a dictionary, 107
  context clues, 17, 139, 211, R49–R50
  denotations, 197
  domain-specific words, 368, 483
  etymology, 45
  homophones, 427
  Latin roots, 393

multiple meanings, 121
nuances in word meanings, 451
prefixes with multiple meanings, 29
scientific terms, 470
suffixes, 167
thesaurus, consulting a, 516
voice, R84
  active, 212
  passive, 212

W

website, R84
When Students Struggle, 8, 14, 23, 26, 33, 39, 48, 54, 58, 65, 80, 84, 88, 95, 96, 110, 116, 118, 125, 128, 133, 135, 154, 158, 161, 171, 173, 179, 190, 202, 205, 212, 215, 219, 232, 235, 239, 245, 246, 250, 255, 260, 266, 274, 282, 293, 297, 302, 304, 308, 313, 315, 324, 330, 336, 345, 351, 359, 364, 372, 382, 386, 390, 398, 410, 414, 420, 421, 436, 442, 444, 456, 460, 464, 467, 479, 488, 494, 502, 510
who/whom, R56
Why This Text?, 3A, 19A, 21A, 31A, 47A, 63A, 77A, 93A, 109A, 113A, 123A, 131A, 151A, 169A, 187A, 199A, 213A, 217A, 231A, 357A, 361A, 369A, 395A, 397A, 409A, 429A, 433A, 453A, 477A, 485A, 491A, 493A, 501A
word choice
  analyzing, 12, 31, 33, 35, 36, 38, 40, 41, 42, 43, 220
  and mood, 428
  and style, 481
  synonyms, 516
  and tone, 220
word families, R52
word meanings
  clarifying precise, 176
  connotations, 165, 197
  denotations, 197, 451
  determining, from context clues, 17, 139, 176, 211
  figurative, 111, 397, 481
  nuances in, 451
word origins, R51–R52
wordplay, 336, R84
workplace documents, R84
works cited, R9, R10, R84
works consulted, R84
writer's purpose, 429
writer's style, 477. See also Language and Style; style
writing
  analytical essays, 399–402
  arguments, 403–406, R2–R3
  compare-contrast essays, 71–74
  complete sentences, R44–R45
  drafts, 72, 142, 226, 519
  essays, 71–74, 141–144, 399–402
  informative essays, 141–144
  informative texts, R4–R5
  narratives, R6–R7
  personal narratives, 517–520
  satire, 225–228
  sensory details in, 108a

speeches, 472
writing activity
  analysis, 262
  argument, 367, 469
  character analysis, 90
  comparison, 397, 426, 499
  context guide, 210
  critique, 64
  description, 106
  diary, 16
  essay, 482
  journal entry, 332
  letter, 44, 175
  opinion, 490
  paragraph, 28
  poem, 220
  reviews, 20, 166

Index of Titles and Authors

Key:

Authors and titles that appear in the Student Edition are in lightface type.
Authors and titles that appear in the Close Reader are in **boldface** type.
Names of authors who appear in both the Student Edition and the Close Reader are lightface. For these authors, Student Edition page references are lightface and Close Reader page references are **boldface**.

Student Edition Acknowledgments

The American Heritage Dictionary of the English Language, Fifth Edition. Text copyright © 2011 by Houghton Mifflin Harcourt. Adapted and reprinted by permission from *The American Heritage Dictionary of the English Language, Fifth Edition.*

Excerpts from *Beowulf* translated by Burton Raffel. Text copyright © 1963 by Burton Raffel. Text copyright renewed © 1991 by Burton Raffel. Reprinted by permission of Penguin Group (USA), Inc. and Lippincott Massie McQuilkin on behalf of the author.

Excerpt from "Blocking the Transmissions of Violence" by Alex Kotlowitz from *The New York Times Magazine,* May 4, 2008. Text copyright © 2008. Reprinted by permission of PARS International on behalf of the New York Times.

Excerpts from *The Canterbury Tales* by Geoffrey Chaucer, translated by Nevill Coghill. Text copyright © 1951, 1958, 1960, 1975, 1977 by Nevill Coghill. Reprinted by permission of Penguin Group UK and Curtis Brown Group, Ltd., London on behalf of the Estate of Nevill Coghill.

"The Clan of One-Breasted Women" from *Refuge: An Unnatural History of Family and Place* by Terry Tempest Williams. Text copyright © 1991 by Terry Tempest Williams. Reprinted by permission of Vintage Books, a division of Random House, Inc.

Adapted from "The Deep" from *Memory Wall* by Anthony Doerr. First published in *Zoetrope.* Text copyright © 2010 by Anthony Doerr. Reprinted by permission of International Creative Management, Inc., on behalf of the author.

"Dwellings" from *Dwellings: A Spiritual History of the Living World* by Linda Hogan. Text copyright © 1995 by Linda Hogan. Reprinted by permission of W. W. Norton & Company, Inc.

Excerpt from "Hamlet's Dull Revenge" by René Girard from *Stanford Literature Review 1,* Fall 1984. Text copyright © 1984 by René Girard. Reprinted by permission of René Girard.

"Hatred" from *View with a Grain of Sand* by Wislawa Szymborska, translated by Stanislaw Barariczak and Clare Cavanagh. Text copyright © 1993 by Wislawa Szymborska. Reprinted by permission of Houghton Mifflin Harcourt.

"The Hermit's Story" by Rick Bass from *The Paris Review.* Text copyright © 1998 by Rick Bass. Reprinted by permission of the Rick Bass.

"Imagine the Angels of Bread" from *Imagine the Angels of Bread* by Martín Espada. Text copyright © 1996 by Martín Espada. Reprinted by permission of W. W. Norton & Company, Inc.

"In a Scattered Protest, Saudi Women Take the Wheel" by Neil MacFarquhar and Dina Salah Amer from *The New York Times,* June 17, 2011. Text copyright © 2011 by the New York Times. Reprinted by permission of PARS International on behalf of the New York Times.

Excerpt from "Interview of Martín Espada" by Bill Moyers at martinespada.net. Text copyright © 2007 by Martín Espada. Reprinted by permission of Martín Espada.

"Living Like Weasels" from *Teaching a Stone to Talk* by Annie Dillard. Text copyright © 1982 by Annie Dillard. Reprinted by permission of HarperCollins Publishers and Russell & Volkening on behalf of the author.

"Mallam Sile" from *The Prophet of Zongo Street* by Mohammed Naseehu Ali. Text copyright © 2005 by Mohammed Naseehu Ali. Reprinted by permission of HarperCollins Publishers.

"Marita's Bargain" from *Outliers* by Malcolm Gladwell. Text copyright © 2008 by Malcolm Gladwell. Reprinted by permission of Little, Brown and Company. All rights reserved.

"The Men We Carry in Our Minds" from *The Paradise of Bombs* by Scott Russell Sanders. First published in *Mildweed Chronicle.* Text copyright © 1984 by Scott Russell Sanders. Reprinted by permission of Scott Russell Sanders.

"The Mosquito Solution" by Michael Specter from *The New Yorker,* July 9 and 16, 2012. Text copyright © 2012 by Michael Specter. Reprinted by permission of Michael Specter.

"My Father's Sadness" from *Monsoon History* by Shirley Geok-Lin Lim. Text copyright © 1994 by Shirley Geok-Lin Lim. Reprinted by permission of Shirley Geok-Lin Lim.

"The Secret to Raising Smart Kids" from *Scientific American,* November 28, 2007. Text copyright © 2007 by Scientific American. Reprinted by permission of Scientific American.

Excerpt from "Speech on the Vietnam War, New York City, April 4, 1967" by Martin Luther King, Jr. Text copyright © 2000 by the Heirs to the Estate of Martin Luther King, Jr. Reprinted by permission of Writers House LLC on behalf of the Estate of Martin Luther King, Jr.

"Spring and All" from *The Collected Poems: Volume I, 1909–1939* by William Carlos Williams. Text copyright © 1938 by New Directions Publishing Corp. Reprinted by permission of New Directions Publishing Corp. and Carcanet Press Ltd.

"Tell Them Not to Kill Me!" from *The Burning Plain and Other Stories* by Juan Rulfo, translated by George D. Schade. Text copyright © 1967 by Fondo de Cultura Económica, Mexico. Translation copyright © 1967 by George D. Schade. Text copyright renewed © 1996 by George D. Schade. Reprinted by permission of the University of Texas Press and Agencia Literaria Carmen Balcells S.A. on behalf of the author.

Excerpt from "Terry Tempest Williams" biography at nationalbook.org. Text copyright © Terry Tempest Williams. Reprinted by permission of Terry Tempest Williams.

Excerpts from *Third World America* by Alison Wright. Text copyright © 2009 by Alison Wright. Adapted and reprinted by permission of Alison Wright.

"A Walk to the Jetty" from *Annie John* by Jamaica Kincaid. Text copyright © 1983, 1984, 1985 by Jamaica Kincaid. Reprinted by permission of Farrar, Straus and Giroux, LLC.

Close Reader Acknowledgments

Excerpt from *Beowulf,* translated by Burton Raffel. Text copyright © 1963, renewed © 1991 by Burton Raffel. Reprinted by permission of Dutton Signet, a division of Penguin Group (USA) Inc. and Russell & Volkening as agents for the author.

"Blackheart" by Mark Brazaitis from *Witness,* Vol. XXV No. 2, www.witness. blackmountaininstitute.org. Text copyright © Summer 2012 by Mark Brazaitis. Reprinted by permission of Black Mountain Institute at University of Nevada, Las Vegas.

Excerpts from *The Canterbury Tales* by Geoffrey Chaucer, translated by Nevill Coghill. Text copyright © 1952 by Nevill Coghill. Reprinted by permission of Curtis Brown Group Ltd.

"The Clan of One-Breasted Women" from *Refuge: An Unnatural History of Family and Place* by Terry Tempest Williams. Text copyright © 1991 by Terry Tempest Williams. Reprinted by permission of Vintage Books, a division of Random House, Inc.

"Elsewhere" from *The Arkansas Testament* by Derek Walcott. Text copyright © 1987 by Derek Walcott. Reprinted by permission of Farrar Straus and Giroux LLC and Faber and Faber Ltd.

Excerpt from *How Children Succeed: Grit, Curiosity, and the Hidden Power of Character* (Retitled: "Kewauna's Ambition") by Paul Tough. Text copyright © 2012 by Paul Tough. Reprinted by permission of Houghton Mifflin Harcourt.

Excerpt from "Interview of Martín Espada" by Bill Moyers at martinespada.net. Text copyright © 2007 by Martín Espada. Reprinted by permission of Martín Espada.

"Local Deer" from *The Blue Jay's Dance: A Birth Year* by Louise Erdrich. Text copyright © 1995 by Louise Erdrich. Reprinted by permission of HarperCollins Publishers.

"Next Term, We'll Mash You" from *Pack of Cards and Other Stories* by Penelope Lively. Text copyright © 1978 by Penelope Lively. Reprinted by permission of Grove Atlantic, Inc.

"Nobel Lecture," (Retitled: "Nobel Peace Prize Lecture") by Wangari Maathai from www.nobelprize.org. December 10, 2004. Text copyright © Pressens Bild AB 2004, SE-112. Reprinted by permission of The Nobel Foundation.

"Pastoral" from *The Collected Poems of William Carlos Williams, Vol. I* by William Carlos Williams. Text copyright © 1986 by A. Walton Litz and Christopher MacGowan. Reprinted by permission of New Directions Publishing Corporation.

"Pastoral" from *The History of Anonymity* by Jennifer Chang. Copyright © 2008 by Jennifer Chang. Reprinted by permission of University of Georgia Press.

Excerpt from *Pink Think: Becoming a Woman in Many Uneasy Lessons* (Retitled: "Pink Think") by Lynn Peril. Text copyright © 2002 by Lynn Peril. Reprinted by permission of W.W. Norton & Company, Inc.

"A Right to Choose a Single-Sex Education" by Kay Bailey Hutchison and Barbara Mikulski from *The Wall Street Journal,* October 16, 2012, www.wsj.com. Text copyright © 2012 by The Wall Street Journal. Reprinted by permission of Dow Jones and Company.

Excerpt from *The Road Washes Out in Spring* (Retitled: "Trees") by Baron Wormser. Text copyright © 2006 by Baron Wormser. Reprinted by permission of University Press of New England.

"Who Speaks for the 1%," by Joel Stein from *Time* Magazine, October 31, 2011, www. timemagazine.com. Text copyright © 2011 by Time, Inc. Reprinted with permission of Time, Inc.